The Cambridge Encyclopedia of **Human Evolution**

MAN IS BVT A WORM

The Cambridge Encyclopedia of

Human Evolution

Edited by **Steve Jones**, **Robert Martin** and **David Pilbeam**

Executive editor **Sarah Bunney**

Foreword by **Richard Dawkins**

CAMBRIDGE
UNIVERSITY PRESS

Published by the Press Syndicate of the University of Cambridge
The Pitt Building, Trumpington Street, Cambridge CB2 1RP
40 West 20th Street, New York, NY 10011-4211, USA
10 Stamford Road, Oakleigh, Victoria 3166, Australia

First published 1992
Reprinted 1994
First paperback edition 1994

Printed in Great Britain at the University Press, Cambridge
Typeset & originated by Wyvern Typesetting Ltd, Bristol

A catalogue record for this book is available from the British Library

Library of Congress cataloguing in publication data
The Cambridge encyclopedia of human evolution
edited by Steve Jones, Robert Martin, and David Pilbeam:
foreword by Richard Dawkins.
     p.   cm.
Includes index.
ISBN 0 521 32370 3
1. Human evolution — Encyclopedias.
I. Jones, Steve, 1944– .
II. Martin, R. D. (Robert D.), 1942– .
III. Pilbeam, David R.
GN281.C345 1992
579.2–dc20 92–18037 CIP
ISBN 0 521 32370 3 hardback
ISBN 0 521 46786 1 paperback

A CAMBRIDGE REFERENCE BOOK

Editor: Peter Richards
Designers: Dale Tomlinson, Andrew Shoolbred
Illustrators: Joanna Cameron, Alison Marshall,
Anne-Elise Martin, Priscilla Barrett, Swanston Graphics
Picture research: Callie Kendall
Index: Jean Macqueen

Half-title: Charles Darwin caricatured in *Punch* magazine, 1881.
Frontispiece: Computer-generated composite of human
and chimpanzee faces.
Endpapers: Handaxes and cleavers about 700 000 years old from
Olduvai Gorge, Tanzania.

Contents

Part Ten
Human populations, past and present
387

Reference tables

Maps

Contributors

Dr Leslie C. Aiello
University College London

Professor R. McNeill Alexander
University of Leeds

Dr Peter Andrews
Natural History Museum, London

Dr Marian Annett
University of Leicester

Dr Paul G. Bahn
Hull

Professor Paul T. Baker
Pennsylvania State University

Dr Anna K. Behrensmeyer
National Museum of Natural History,
Washington DC

Professor Lewis R. Binford
Southern Methodist University

Dr Francis H. Brown
University of Utah

Sarah Bunney
London

Dr Matt Cartmill
Duke University

Dr David J. Chivers
University of Cambridge

Dr Juliet Clutton-Brock
Natural History Museum, London

Dr Richard Dawkins
University of Oxford

Professor Michael H. Day
Natural History Museum, London

Dr Terrence W. Deacon
Harvard University

Dr Christopher Dean
University College London

Dr Joy D.A. Delhanty
University College London

Professor Eric Delson
Lehman College, City University of
New York and
American Museum of Natural
History, New York

Dr Alan F. Dixson
University of Cambridge

Dr Andrew Dobson
Princeton University

Dr Robin Dunbar
University College London

Professor John G. Fleagle
State University of New York, Stony Brook

Dr Robert Foley
University of Cambridge

Dr Adrian E. Friday
University of Cambridge

Professor Philip D. Gingerich
University of Michigan

Dr Kenneth E. Glander
Duke University

Professor Morris Goodman
Wayne State University

Dr John A.J. Gowlett
University of Liverpool

Professor David R. Harris
Institute of Archaeology,
University College London

Dr Paul H. Harvey
University of Oxford

Professor Frank Hole
Yale University

Professor William W. Howells
Harvard University

Barbara Isaac
Harvard University

Dr Steve Jones
University College London

Dr Jay Kelley
University of Illinois, Chicago

Jonathan Kingdon
University of Oxford

Dr John Landers
All Souls College, Oxford

Dr Phyllis C. Lee
University of Cambridge

Dr D. Iwan Lewis-Jones
University of Liverpool

Dr Philip Lieberman
Brown University

Dr Virginia Luling
Survival International, London

Dr Georgina Mace
Zoological Society of London

Dr Jonathan Marks
Yale University

Professor Robert Martin
Universität Zurich-Irchel

Professor Alan S. McNeilly
University of Edinburgh

Dr Richard S. Meindl
Kent State University

Dr Russell A. Mittermeier
Conservation International,
Washington DC

Professor David Pilbeam
Harvard University

Dr Richard Potts
Smithsonian Institution,
Washington DC

Dr Andrew F. Read
University of Edinburgh

Professor Alison F. Richard
Yale University

Dr Neil Roberts
Loughborough University of
Technology

Dr Alfred L. Rosenberger
National Zoological Park,
Washington DC

Dr Shahin Rouhani
Sharif University, Tehran

Dr Vincent Sarich
University of California, Berkeley

Dr E.S. Savage-Rumbaugh
Emory University

Dr Brian T. Shea
Northwestern University, Chicago

Professor Charles G. Sibley
Santa Rosa, California

Professor Elwyn Simons
Duke University

Eleanor J. Sterling
Yale University

Dr Christopher B. Stringer
Natural History Museum, London

Dr Robert W. Sussman
Washington University, St Louis

Professor James M. Tanner
Institute of Child Health,
University of London

Professor Erik Trinkaus
University of New Mexico and
Université de Bordeaux I

Dr Angela K. Turner
University of Sussex

Professor Nicholaas J. van der Merwe
Harvard University

Professor Friedrich Vogel
Ruprecht-Karls-Universität,
Heidelberg

Dr David Whitehouse
University College London

Dr Peter J. Whybrow
Natural History Museum, London

Professor Bernard A. Wood
University of Liverpool

Dr Stephen Young
Aberystwyth, Wales

Dr Elke Zimmermann
German Primate Center, Göttingen

Foreword

The hauntingly wistful portrait on the cover of this Encyclopedia is of a creature that has never existed and probably never will. It is a computed intermediate between a human and a chimpanzee face, and is perhaps what a hybrid between the two species might look like – in the unlikely event that it could ever be bred. It reminds us of two near-contradictory truths. We are extremely close cousins of other species. And yet we have grown light years away from them.

We can dramatise our closeness to chimpanzees by imagining a 'hands across Africa' chain of ancestors. You stand on the beach on the east coast of Africa, the mother continent, at the Equator, latitude zero. You hold the hand of your mother. She holds the hand of her mother, your grandmother. Your grandmother holds her mother's hand, and so on back through the generations. The chain of ancestors wends its way up the beach and across the savanna along the Equator. How far would the chain go before we met the common ancestor of ourselves and chimpanzees? The answer is a surprisingly short distance. According to reliable molecular evidence, our common ancestor with chimpanzees lived only about 5 million years ago, say 250 000 generations. Allowing 1 metre for each hand-holding ancestor, the chain back to our common ancestor is only 250 kilometres long. We have hardly penetrated Africa at all; we are still on the coastal strip and have barely begun to climb towards the continental plateau.

Not only are we very close to chimpanzees, we are far closer to chimpanzees and gorillas than they are to other apes such as orang-utans and gibbons. If there is some category – 'apes' – to which chimpanzees and orangs both belong, we must count ourselves in it too. We are apes. More, we are African apes, for we are in a category that includes chimpanzees and gorillas but excludes orangs and gibbons. There is even some evidence that we are closer to the two species of chimpanzees than they are to gorillas, which is why Jared Diamond has called our species 'the third chimpanzee'.

But looked at another way, the brief 250-kilometre trip becomes the longest journey in the world. So much changes as we walk back from the interior to the coast, past those 250 000 ancestors. Somewhere along the way they lose most of their body hair and rise to fully erect walking. They develop tools and technology, language and culture, history and epic poetry. And that is why we need not just a book of human evolution but an encyclopedia.

And *what* an Encyclopedia this is! From archaeology to zoology, genetics to linguistics, it encompasses the full range. Moreover, you can read it confident that you are getting the authoritative, well-informed and up-to-date view of qualified experts. This applies not only to the team of editors (who are also responsible for many of the articles), but to the other authors who have been brought in to write on particular topics. And the editors have somehow succeeded in encouraging a readably uniform style. It is a book for browsing, for looking things up, but also, unlike most encyclopedias, for reading from cover to cover.

It may be helpful if I take just one vignette to stand for many, an epitome of the Encyclopedia's up-to-dateness, authority and clarity. Extravagant publicity has been lavished on the so-called 'African Eve'. Mitochondrial DNA is inherited only down the female line, and it evolves at a high and measurable rate. Evidence has been presented that all mitochondrial DNA in non-African women originates from a single common ancestor living in Africa between 50 000 and half a million years ago. This would suggest that our ancestry went through a 'bottleneck', a single, individual woman who lived in Africa within the last few hundred thousand years. This hypothetical woman has been given the all-too-catchy name of Eve.

I have been surprised at the number of people that have asked me whether the alleged evidence of 'bottlenecking' supported the Biblical account of the origin of humanity! It is hard to blame these questioners when one reads some accounts of the 'Eve' story by people who should know better.

As it happens, very recent evidence now calls into question the story of African Eve, and this Encyclopedia is right up to date. But I want to concentrate on a more important point, one that is also clearly made in the Encyclopedia and one that remains true regardless of the new evidence. This is that 'any Eve can never be more than a statistical artefact' (p. 321). To put it another way, it is statistically certain that there is not just one 'Eve' but many, scattered back through our history, and many 'Adams' too. Although it takes me beyond the usual brief of a Foreword, I'd like to explain this further.

Each of us has two parents, four grandparents, eight great grandparents, sixteen great great grandparents, and so on. Except that, if you think about it, it can't really go on being 'and so on'. If it were, the number of my ancestors alive half a million years ago would be a ridiculously large number with more than 1000 noughts! What have we done wrong in our calculation? We've forgotten that an individual can be an ancestor in more than one way. One's mate is always one's (usually distant) cousin, many times over. Go back sufficiently far in history, and the following statement must be true. If an individual from remote antiquity has any descendants alive today, we are all her descendants. If I am not descended from a particular remotely ancient individual, then neither are you, and neither is anyone.

You can prove this to yourself by the following piece of simple reasoning. Go back a ridiculously long way, say to a fish-like ancestor 400 million years ago. It must be true of an individual fish that either you are descended from her or you are not. If you are, it is obvious that I am too. If you are not, I am not. Survey this population of Devonian fishes, and the individuals would divide up into those from whom all modern humans are descended, and those from whom no modern humans are descended. There are no intermediates.

Let's invent the term 'focal ancestor' for any individual that is ancestral to all living humans. It is clear that there is no focal ancestor alive today. From the argument of the previous paragraph it is also clear that, if you go sufficiently far back into the past, you are bound to find a focal ancestor. Somewhere between these two extremes must be the most recent focal ancestor. There is room for us to wonder when and where the most recent focal ancestor lived.

So, as far as the *existence* of an 'Eve' is concerned (as opposed to where she lived and how long ago), the mitochondrial evidence tells us nothing that we couldn't have worked out from an armchair. There must have been lots of individuals that were focal ancestors of any given group of humans. There is no reason to suspect a true bottleneck in the sense of a very small population: 'Eve', wherever and whenever she lived, was very likely surrounded by multitudes of friends and relations.

There are two points that I should like to add to this Encyclopedia's own treatment. First, contrary to many articles on 'African Eve', the mitochondrial method is very unlikely to find the most *recent* focal ancestor. It finds ancestors only down the female-female-female line. There are millions more ways of being an ancestor than purely down the female line, and correspondingly millions more candidates for being a focal ancestor. Think of it this way. You have eight great grandparents, but only one purely maternal great grandparent. You have 32 great great great grandparents, but still only one purely maternal great great great grandparent. In this generation, there are 31 other ancestors. In any one generation, it is *possible* that the female-line-only ancestor is a focal ancestor. But since, in that generation, there are so many more non-female-line-only ancestors, it is far more likely that one of these is a focal ancestor. Therefore, whoever the most recent mitochondrial focal ancestor may have been, and whether she lived in Africa or not, she is highly unlikely to be the most recent of all focal ancestors. She is almost certainly far more ancient than the most recent focal ancestor.

My second point is that the most recent focal ancestor was, anyway, probably an Adam. Harems of females are more likely than harems of males. Therefore if anybody fails to reproduce, it is most likely to be a male. And if anybody has a disproportionate share of descendants, it, too, is likely to be a male. So, in any one generation, if anybody is the ancestor of a large number of descendants, that ancestor is probably a male. And this goes for our most recent focal ancestor.

This Encyclopedia's pithy statement that 'any Eve can never be more than a statistical artefact' hits the nail on the head. I have taken it as just one example of many nails smartly struck by the editors and authors of this admirable volume. I recommend the whole collection with enthusiasm. If you were allowed to take only one book to a desert island (the Bible and Shakespeare being already provided), this Encyclopedia would be a serious candidate.

Richard Dawkins

What makes us human?

Humans are fascinated by humanity. We see ourselves, for good or for ill, at the centre of the evolutionary stage: abundant, occupying every corner of the planet, with an impact on the environment that grows as our ecological appetite becomes more voracious.

A visitor from another galaxy might have a different perspective. True, there are many of us in many places, but there is only one species of modern human – we score much lower than rodents, for example, if species number is a measure of evolutionary success. Our species, or, as some would have it, our subspecies – *Homo sapiens sapiens* – is young, little more than 100 000 years old, whereas the typical mammalian species has lasted for a million of the past 65 million years. If our extragalactic friend were a regular visitor, coming every 100 000 years, human success would seem a very recent thing; on the last visit there would have been little hint of what to expect in the world today.

The study of human evolution is not a single science. Instead, it is a broad question, which requires the application of many sciences. To reconstruct the evolution of any group – and not just humans – we need to integrate genetics, morphology, physiology and behaviour. Hence the eclectic nature of this encyclopedia. For example, to infer the diet of our extinct relative *Paranthropus* it is necessary to study not only the dietary habits but also the chemical composition and surface wear of the teeth of many living primates and other mammals to build up an understanding of the relationship between chemistry, wear and diet. This broad, comparative approach is much used by evolutionary biologists.

Not only do we find ourselves fascinating, but most of us assume the inevitability of our existence. Take the theme of the film *Planet of the Apes*: if something happens to humans to remove them from the evolutionary stage, then other apes will become human because that is what evolution is striving for. Evolutionary biologists, in contrast, do not see the origin of any species as inevitable. Rather, they see it involving a long series of events, each depending on the other, and each unpredictable and unique.

To understand human evolution we need to know what makes us human. Only then do we have an agenda for studying the past. There are many ways in which we differ from other species, some trivial and some important. For the most part we can only guess at what our remote progenitor, the last common ancestor of human and ape, looked like. We can, however, say with some confidence that most human features did not evolve in one step, nor together as one package. What is more, the functions of various features have changed; fingers now playing Bach fugues did not evolve to do so.

The Taung child skull found by Raymond Dart in 1924.

Any list of human attributes is bound to depend on who makes it. Most evolutionary biologists would focus on bipedalism – two-footed walking and running – as a critical human development. Other attributes, such as beards, are less popular. One of my favourite personal views of the uniqueness of humanity is that of an early Stuart doctor:

> Man is of a far different structure in his guts from ravenous creatures such as dogs, wolves etc. who, minding only their belly, have their guts descending almost straight down from their ventricle or stomach to the fundament: whereas in this noble microcosm man, there are in these intestinal parts many anfractuous circumvolutions, windings and turnings, whereby, longer retention of his food being procured, he might so much the better attend upon sublime speculations, and profitable employments in Church and Commonwealth.*

What follows are some thoughts on the nature and history of what makes us human in a few behavioural, physiological, anatomical and genetic features.

Population size and distribution

Humans are by far the commonest primates; there are around 5400 million of us, found all over the earth's surface. The human species can tolerate such a range because each of us carries a tropical microenvironment in the form of clothes and dwellings. The common ancestor of humans and apes was a tropical creature, and members of the human family did not spread out of the tropics and subtropics until about a million years ago. Even 12 000 years ago, the size of the human population was low, with a world population of only around 10 million.

Genetic structure

Humanity has a higher ratio of genetic variation within local populations than among them; we are a geographically uniform species. Were all human populations except for one to disappear, about three-quarters of the total human genetic diversity would be preserved. (The exact figure would depend on which group was the chance survivor; native Americans would show a lower level of variation, some Africans a higher.) The average genetic difference at the molecular level between two randomly chosen humans from the same place is considerably less than that between two chimpanzees, probably because humanity is a much younger species than its close relative. All human populations today probably derive from an ancestral group living only about 100 000 years ago, rather than a million or more years ago.

Humans are medium-sized mammals, with modest differences in size between the sexes and some degree of geographical variation in the shape of the skull and body, body size, hair form and distribution, and so on. The differences between groups in such characters may exceed that in characters controlled by single genes. We do not know how long it has taken to produce today's differences in body features, but to judge from those bones and teeth that leave a record it seems that most of them have evolved within the past 20 000 years, long after the first appearance of modern humans.

Skin

The skin of humans differs from that of apes in having a special type of sweat gland. Each of us has more than a million of these glands all over our bodies. Our hair cover, too, is reduced. Populations of possibly ancient origin in Africa are pigmented and, although most other populations are lighter, they retain the ability to become tanned. Some of these features are adaptations to the heat stress generated by walking and running in a hot climate. Early human ancestors

*James Hart, *Diet of the Diseased*, p. 36 (1633).

(hominids) in Africa were probably pigmented and hairless, and sweated profusely. Black skin colour does not itself protect against high temperature, as black objects heat up more in the sun than do light objects. Dark skin in the tropics is more plausibly explained by the balance of vitamin D synthesised by the action of ultraviolet light, preventing the synthesis of too much. Dark-skinned infants in high latitudes may be unable to synthesise sufficient vitamin D, and this could explain reduced pigmentation in high-latitude populations. Many such adaptations probably evolved in parallel with the increased activity made possible by bipedal running.

Feeding

Humans eat almost any plant or animal food and we have done so for much of our history. Several aspects of our diet have changed with time. Nearly all human populations now depend on agriculture, but this is a recent development. Only 15 000 years ago all of humanity hunted animals, fished and gathered plants. The modern pattern of planned and co-operative food collecting, involving the transport, storage, preparation and sharing of food, had appeared by about 40 000 years ago. Before 200 000 years ago we know almost nothing about how hominids obtained food. The amount of meat in the diet was probably less – and did not include sea fish – and was collected by scavenging as much as hunting; and food was not much shared. Before 2.5 million years, the diet was similar to that of predominantly vegetarian apes.

But human feeding also depends on the use of tools, and has done for more than 2 million years. The elaboration of tools throughout prehistory reflects an increase in skill and a diversification of the means of staying alive. Our ancestors' chewing teeth were once more thickly enamelled than our own, implying a diet of tough foods of low quality. As more meat was eaten and food preparation improved, teeth became smaller. Our guts also are adapted to a varied diet: we have relatively simple stomachs and small large intestines like other mammals with much meat in their diet.

Posture

Humans have many skeletal, muscular and physiological adaptations for bipedal walking and running. As our hands are not involved in locomotion we can simultaneously carry and handle things. This is important in gathering food, and some of these features evolved before hominids took up hunting. There is no fossil record of the first hominids and we do not know what the earliest bipeds were like or what produced them. Before the first species of Homo appeared some 2 or more million years ago, the australopithecines were bipeds (albeit with an anatomy different from Homo's). It is possible that they could walk but not run, and were probably active climbers.

Life history

Humans differ from chimpanzees in their reproductive behaviour and physiology. The receptivity of women varies less through the reproductive cycle, and there are many unique features of human family structure. However, in other ways reproduction of humans and chimpanzees does not differ greatly. The age of sexual maturity is delayed in humans, from 9 to 12 or more years, and we live longer (up to 80 or more rather than 40 to 50 years). Although the interval between births is a little less in human hunters and gatherers than in apes, females of the two groups stop having offspring at about the same age, around 40; many human females therefore have an unusual, long, post-reproductive phase in their lives. Because the brain is relatively undeveloped, a newborn human infant is more helpless than a chimpanzee baby, particularly during the first year of life, and depends on its parents for food, transport and comfort for a longer period.

It is not easy tracking the history of these patterns of maturation, but it does seem that hominids at the australopithecine stage were ape-like in their rate of development. Post-australopithecines (*Homo*) showed a progressive approach to the modern human condition, but it was not reached until the past few tens of thousands of years.

Social organisation

Humans have uniquely complex social organisation, involving marriage and extensive societal networks. Marriage is a relationship with important reproductive and economic functions (once referred to, in a memorable typographical error, as paid – rather than pair – bonding). The relationship can be between one man and one woman (monogamy), one man and several wives (polygyny) or one woman and several husbands (polyandry). All marriages may be dissolved.

Families may be closely linked through formal kinship relations. As we can identify and label these, family structure (including the care of children and their acquisition of social skills) may become complex, with variable degrees of child care by parents or relatives. Kinship networks usually extend throughout any population speaking the same language, although such 'tribal' clusters vary greatly in size and density. Language groups of hunter-gatherers may cover more territory than those of agriculturalists, but there are far fewer people involved. Families occupy a particular place, be it a camp or a palace, for long periods. Individuals may leave the home base for a time, but usually return – a striking contrast to the way that other primates occupy space. Archaeology can tell us little more than that the human use of space was established only in the past few tens of thousands of years.

Social behaviour

The most obviously human of our characteristics is the range and complexity of our behaviour. This has led to the appearance of nations, states and empires. Much social behaviour depends on language, the quintessential human attribute. Speech is a reflection of unique adaptations of the brain that make possible the symbolic structuring of our world and the extraordinary impact that we have upon it.

Our brain is at least three times as large as that of an ape with the same body size. Although much remains unknown about the way in which it is adapted for language, several brain areas involved in speech production and perception are greatly expanded, so that the increase in human brain size was probably linked to selection for changes in vocal communication.

Language allows us to use symbols, and symbolic thinking is now so pervasive that we are generally unaware of its use. Language also permits the planning needed for complex subsistence and the rules governing kinship, alliance and marriage. It makes possible sharing, exploitation and the delay of reward or punishment; the structuring of relationships; propaganda; art; the division of labour; warfare; and the aggregation and socialisation of masses of people. Its most essential feature is that it allows human behaviour to be governed by the complex and subtle rules that together make up human culture.

Humans have an internal world that maps and expands the world outside, and a consciousness of self, of death and even the possibility of transcending death.

To what extent do other primates approach us in this? It is hard to compare the intelligence or behaviour of different species. It was long assumed that there is a huge behavioural chasm between humans and animals. Thirty years of work on primates have changed that view. We now know that higher primates – and some other mammals – have complex behaviours that are learned, differ among populations, and can be transmitted from one generation to the next. Even if these patterns of behaviour are not in themselves cultural, all their attributes are needed for the evolution of culture.

Monkeys cannot learn anything that we would call language. They are astute interpreters of each other's behaviour, but there is little indication that they can assess underlying motives. On the other hand, some patterns of ape behaviour, while not cultural or linguistic in the human sense, do enable us to suggest plausible ways in which selection could shape them towards the human condition. Chimpanzees can be taught simple language-like skills and can relate objects symbolically to goals, needs and intentions. They can organise 'words' – gestures, plastic chips or responses to computer keys – into simple grammatical constructs and can commmunicate with and manipulate the behaviour of each other. Chimpanzees can see themselves as objects, and hence have a sense of self-awareness. They are intellectually and emotionally complex and competent creatures. The complexity of their behaviour is still far from understood, but on a behaviour scale chimpanzees are closer to humans than are monkeys and give us a glimpse of what our earliest hominid ancestors might have been like.

Exactly how behaviour changed from australopithecines to modern humans is not clear. Unequivocal evidence for modern patterns of behaviour does not appear in the fossil record until some 40 000 years ago, well after the emergence of early modern humans. The course of behavioural change must be reconstructed as carefully as that of morphological change. The function of many of our structural features changes through time, and a character shaped by selection towards one end often plays a different role later. This is very likely to be true in a system as complex as the human mind. Language and culture make possible an enormous range of behaviours: but only a few of them are likely to have been directly favoured by natural selection originally.

What of the future? The contingent and uncertain pattern of evolution makes it impossible to say very much. As nearly all past species have become extinct, this fate is possible even for ourselves. Despite the relative brevity of our sojourn here, we shall at least leave an archaeological record. I have always found Alexander Pope's words apposite and rather comforting:

Created half to rise and half to fall;
Great Lord of all things, yet prey to all;
Sole judge of truth, in endless error hurled;
The Glory, jest and riddle of the world!

David Pilbeam

Part One

Patterns of primate evolution

Thomas Huxley, who earned the title of 'Darwin's bulldog' by championing the theory of evolution during its early stages, himself made a major contribution to studies of primate evolution with his book *Man's Place in Nature* (1864). This title neatly expresses his insight that the human species is a part of the natural world, and is subject to the same evolutionary processes and principles. Although the Swedish naturalist Carl von Linné (Linnaeus) had included human beings in the order Primates a hundred years earlier, it remained for Darwin and Huxley to develop the idea of human evolution.

Huxley concentrated on the anatomical evidence for an evolutionary relationship between human beings and other primates. His main aim was to show that there is no sharp division between humans and the rest of the animal world. Nowadays, however, the idea of 'man's place in nature' has acquired an added depth and significance.

In evolutionary terms, we now know a great deal more about living primates and their evolutionary relationships than did Darwin and Huxley. This knowledge has been greatly strengthened in the last few decades by the explosive expansion of information about the basic genetic material, DNA, and about the biochemical basis for evolutionary change (**1.1**). Studies at the biochemical level have confirmed Huxley's original conclusion that there is no sharp division between humans and other primates. Indeed, the evidence from molecular biology has led to the surprising conclusion that the degree of relationship between us and our closest zoological relatives – the African great apes – is as close or closer than indicated by a comparison of anatomical features. The striking anatomical specialisations associated with expansion of the brain, remodelling of the jaw apparatus and adaptations for walking on two legs during human evolution are not matched by equivalent differences at the molecular level – the difference between a human and a chimpanzee is only slightly less than that between a chimpanzee and a gorilla.

Now that we have confirmation from biochemical evidence of our place in the natural world, we can pursue the reconstruction of our evolutionary origins with greater confidence. The comparative study of living primates (**1.3**) must clearly play a central part in this understanding, not least because studies at the molecular level are confined to living species. There are some 200 species of living primates, mostly confined to tropical and subtropical forests (**1.4**), and comparisons of these provide the foundation for a proper understanding of human evolution.

Studies of primate evolution also benefit from increased attention to the methods used to infer patterns of genealogical (phylogenetic) relationships

Computer-generated image
of a haemoglobin molecule.

(**1.2**). There is fruitful interaction between the more traditional studies of form (morphology) and biochemistry. Information from molecular biology is easy to quantify and this has led to developments in the computerised building of evolutionary trees. Zoologists concerned with anatomical features have established basic principles that are essential for the inference of phylogenetic relationships. The development of techniques for determining the branching-points of a phylogenetic tree (cladistics) has led to a more objective analysis of the way the features, or characters, of an organism change. This approach has transformed our thinking in evolutionary biology, but it has been less successful when applied to classification.

Although there are occasional disagreements between molecular biologists and morphologists, their conclusions about primate evolution generally agree quite closely. Both confirm the theories of primate evolution that date back to Darwin and Huxley, and support the anatomical approach to the inference of phylogenetic relationships. This is crucial, as the fossil evidence depends essentially on anatomical comparisons.

The idea of 'man's place in nature' has also been developed to encompass behaviour and ecology. Studies of the patterns of primate evolution now include the natural environments inhabited by primates. Field studies play an increasing part in adding to the picture, but much remains to be done. Attention has been concentrated on Old World monkeys and apes and many New World monkey and prosimian species are still poorly studied. The natural environment provides the context within which selection operates and behavioural change is often the precursor to morphological change.

The need for field studies and an understanding of primate evolution has never been greater. Our place in nature is now a question of disruption, rather than harmony. Unbridled exploitation of the environment has led to a situation where many species are threatened with extinction (**1.4**). Primates, as forest-living creatures, are particularly vulnerable. It is ironic that although several new primate species have been discovered in recent years these will be among the first to become extinct because they are rare. Efforts are now under way to reverse the decline of natural populations of primates. For this to succeed, we must apply our knowledge of the evolutionary biology of primates, from genetics to ecology. Within the overall framework of primate conservation, captive breeding of endangered primate species has a valuable supporting part to play: this may be the only source of supply for the study of some primates in the future.

The nature of evolution

Life began about 3000 million years ago, probably just once. The earliest organisms were short stretches of nucleic acid floating in a chemical sea. Since then, tens – perhaps hundreds – of millions of different species of animals and plants have appeared on earth. Most are extinct, but many millions are alive today. Where did they all come from?

One view is that every living being has a distinct and independent origin by special creation. Another is that most organisms evolved from simple life-forms but that humans are unique, as they are the Deity's representatives on earth. These views are simple and consistent and should not be dismissed only because many people think otherwise. However, most biologists believe that all creatures are interrelated and descend from a common ancestor. The most effective proponent of this idea was Charles Darwin. His theory of evolution, set out in 1859 in *The Origin of Species*, is now so widely accepted that it is in danger of becoming an orthodoxy. Most of this book accepts the fact of human evolution; an acceptance now so complete that we forget that in its day it represented a complete reversal of our view of our place in nature. Automatic acceptance of one fundamental fact is not a basis for any scientific argument. Why do nearly all scientists believe that evolution has occurred and that we are its products?

Darwin as a young man with his son William.

Darwin's argument of 'descent with modification' is simple. It has four main parts:

- Organisms differ from each other in ways that are inherited – there is *variation*
- More are born than can survive – a *struggle for existence*
- Certain inherited variants increase the chances of their carriers surviving and reproducing – *natural selection*
- Selection leads to the accumulation of favoured variants, which over a long period produce new forms of life – the *origin of species*

Darwin described *The Origin of Species* as 'one long argument'. He used many kinds of evidence to support it: from domesticated creatures, from variation in nature, from embryology, from comparative anatomy and 'relict organs' (such as the wings of flightless birds), from plant and animal distribution, and from fossils. Much of modern biology is a reaffirmation of his work. This Encyclopedia is no exception. None of the evidence in *The Origin* came from humans. However, we can now reconstruct every step of Darwin's argument using information from ourselves and our relatives. Indeed, some of the best evidence for the fact of evolution now comes from the human lineage. Just how true this is can be seen by imagining *The Origin* as Darwin might have written it had he known what we do about human biology.

His book starts with two chapters on variation, in domestic animals and in the wild. Perhaps the most consistent message to emerge from human genetics is that variation is universal: every individual is unique. Diversity is everywhere, whether we look at the surfaces of cells, where the science of immunology depends on the existence of inherited variation; at the proteins, which are their building blocks; at the chromosomes, the microscopically visible units of inheritance; or at the structure of genes themselves. One estimate is that there are 3 million variable sites in the genetic message that goes to make up each one of us.

Darwin then points out that more animals are born than can possibly survive. This has always been true of humans: both ancient and modern populations have had to struggle with starvation and disease. Only occasionally, when there is a cultural breakthrough, such as the origin of tools, language, agriculture or medicine, have we been able to win a skirmish in the struggle for existence and show our potential for population growth.

The centre of Darwin's argument is that the chances of survival are influenced by the genetic constitution of those involved. Much of modern anthropology – and even medicine – proves the truth of this statement. People with genes for different body build or skin colour differ in their ability to cope with climate, which is why Inuit (Eskimos) are short, squat and quite fair-skinned and many Africans are long-limbed with black skins. Genetic differences also alter susceptibility to disease, and people with different genes are more or less likely to die from particular illnesses. Although infectious disease has largely been controlled, genetic differences are still important as many children die from inborn defects. Each of us probably carries single copies of three different genes that would kill us if two copies were present, so that there are still many opportunities for natural selection.

Continued selection leads to evolutionary progress and to the appearance of new forms of life. This is best seen in the fossil record. The fossil history of humans and our relatives is not a particularly good one, and Darwin's description is still valid: 'A history of the world, imperfectly kept. Of this history we possess the last volume alone . . . Of this volume, only here and there a chapter has been preserved; and of each page only here and there a few lines'. However, enough exists to show how modern humans have emerged from primitive ancestors, appearing in modern form only 130 000 to 100 000 years ago.

The theory of evolution tells us that we are all living fossils; that we all preserve within ourselves the genes of our ancestors. Darwin himself used comparative anatomy to support his views, and he makes great play with the structural differences that underly the apparent similarities of creatures such as birds and bats as clues to common ancestry. One of the triumphs of molecular biology has been to uncover thousands of other cues of relatedness hidden in our genes. We share many of these with other primates; for example, humans and chimpanzees have blood groups, proteins and great stretches of DNA in common. The only illustration in *The Origin* is an evolutionary tree of relatedness based on shared body structures. The new comparative anatomy based on molecules makes it possible to draw accurate trees for humans and our relatives.

If one assumes that the differences between evolving lineages accumulate at a constant rate then the fossil record can be used to calibrate a 'molecular clock' of genetic distance between living species. There is now good agreement between the fossil and the molecular evidence of our antecedents, and about when the lines leading to modern humans, chimpanzees and gorillas began to separate.

Other parts of Darwin's evidence are abundantly supported by our new understanding of human biology. He emphasised the importance of small and isolated populations, such as those of finches on the Galápagos Islands, in evolution. We are ourselves ideal for studying random genetic change in small populations, as in many places there are historical records of population size. Such isolates – tribal groups in earlier times or modern peoples isolated by geography or cultural barriers – can quickly accumulate genetic differences and diverge from their ancestors. Our

escape from Africa may have involved a population bottleneck still manifest in a reduction in the genetic diversity of non-Africans compared to Africans. Again, evidence from our own species confirms and extends Darwin's arguments.

To emphasise the importance of evolution in understanding our place in nature I will use the evolution of one molecule – haemoglobin – as an illustration of how the structure, function and patterns of relatedness of different animals or separate human populations make sense only in the context of shared descent and of natural selection.

The haemoglobin molecule

The earliest life existed in a world without oxygen. However, nearly all modern animals and plants use oxygen from the air. Many possess specialised molecules to transfer it from the outside world to the tissues. In humans, this molecule is haemoglobin, the most widely studied of all our body constituents. It is made up of two pairs of protein chains, the alpha (α) and beta (β) globins in adults, and an iron-containing portion known as haem. The proteins themselves consist of chains of amino acids. Each amino acid is a nitrogen-containing molecule, usually bearing an electrical charge. The amino acid sequence and the structure of the DNA that underlies it is known for many species. This allows us to place human haemoglobin into an evolutionary context. The picture that emerges is close to that painted by Darwin to explain the evolution of morphological characters. However, there are also some surprises, particularly as regards DNA.

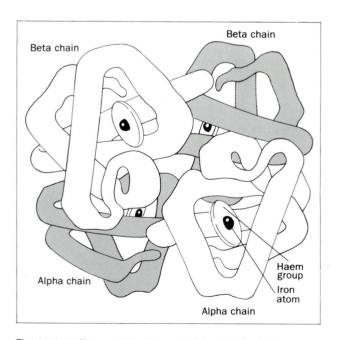

The structure of haemoglobin. Haemoglobin is a protein with four subunits (two α polypeptides and two β polypeptides). Each subunit contains a haem group with an iron atom.

Haemoglobin picks up oxygen in the lungs and loses it where oxygen is needed. This involves changes in shape, which partly result from haemoglobin's simultaneous role in transporting carbon dioxide from the tissues back to the lungs. The balance between gain and loss of oxygen in different species is beautifully adapted to the environment. For example, crocodiles spend a long time underwater, and their haemoglobin is very efficient at retaining oxygen. The haemoglobin of bony fish can pump almost pure oxygen into the swimbladder. Even mammals living at high altitudes have parallel adaptations in haemoglobin; for example, the haemoglobin of llamas is more effective at carrying oxygen than is that of their lowland relatives. All this is evidence for natural selection.

Such evidence also emerges from the patterns of haemoglobin use during development. Darwin was impressed by the parallels between the changes that take place from egg to adult and those that characterise the evolution of life

1. THE STRUCTURE OF DNA

The DNA molecule and the mushroom cloud are the icons of the twentieth century: twin images of life and death. Yet early genetics scarcely concerned itself with the physical nature of the gene. Not until the 1930s was a 'transforming principle', which could be extracted from one bacterium and used to alter the inherited characteristics of another, isolated. This molecule, deoxyribose nucleic acid or DNA, consists of a double helix made up of nucleic acid bases and deoxyribose sugars twisted around each other. The twin strands are complementary; each can act as a template to make a matching copy of itself and generate a message which is translated into the protein products of genes.

The building blocks of DNA are simple; four *nucleotides*, each consisting of a pentose sugar called deoxyribose (with five carbon atoms) attached to a phosphate and to a flat nitrogenous molecule, or *base*, with one ring (a pyrimidine) or two rings (a purine). The nucleotides are joined into a chain with thousands of links by the attachment of the phosphate element of one to part of the sugar molecule of the next. There are four different bases: adenine, guanine, cytosine and thymine. Their ratios differ from one species to the next, but the amount of adenine (A) is always the same as that of thymine (T), and that of guanine (G) the same as cytosine (C), a finding that was the key to understanding how DNA works.

From 1951, James D. Watson and Francis Crick studied the scattering patterns of X-rays passing through DNA. They proposed that the molecule consists of two polynucleotide strands, each coiled in a helix (which is normally right-handed), with the two chains held together by weak hydrogen bonds – base A pairing with T and G with C.

It was soon found that certain enzymes – *DNA polymerases* – can quickly generate a matching chain of bases from a single strand of DNA, so that DNA possesses the central attribute of life: the ability to make a copy of itself or *replicate*.

By labelling one of the two complementary chains with a heavy isotope of nitrogen and tracing the passage of the labelled molecules down the generations it became clear that DNA replication was 'semiconservative'; a single chain remains intact for many generations, producing daughter copies of its own sequence. This allows genetic information to be retained as succeeding copies are made. The information is held in the order of the four bases along the chain as the *genetic code* (see Box 2).

Inevitably, the beautiful clarity of this picture has become clouded as we have learned more about DNA. For example, in some viruses DNA is but a single strand, and in others the genetic information is carried in ribonucleic acid (*RNA*), which also consists of only a single strand, but this time a chain of ribonucleotide subunits containing the sugar ribose instead of deoxyribose, and with the nucleotide uracil instead of the thymine in DNA. Occasionally, DNA reverses its twist so that it is a left-handed rather than a right-handed spiral, and in mitochondria – cell organelles – it is a closed circle.

The double helix of DNA is extensively coiled around a protein scaffolding, itself arranged in a supercoiled state. However, the original insights about DNA gained in the medieval period of molecular biology – the 1950s – have been abundantly confirmed and remain the basis of the whole of modern genetics. *Steve Jones*

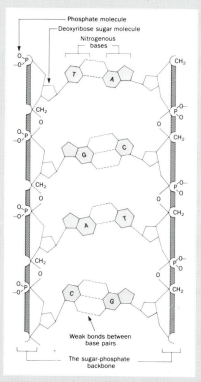

The chemical structure of a DNA molecule. A short segment of DNA showing the sugar and phosphate backbone of each strand, together with the four different classes of DNA bases: adenine, guanine, cytosine and thymine. The complementary pairing of A with T and G with C is what holds the strands together and acts as the basis for DNA replication, the ability of the molecule to make copies of itself.

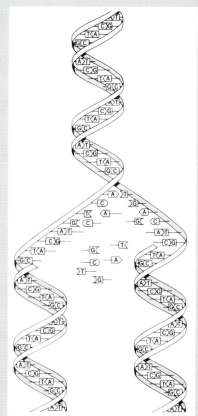

Replication of DNA, showing how the molecule unwinds and, by pairing of the complementary bases with each other, makes two identical copies of the original DNA sequence.

2. THE GENETIC CODE

DNA carries the information needed to synthesise all 50 000 or so proteins in our bodies. The code is contained in the order of nucleotide bases, many thousands of which go to make up a single gene. The genetic complement, or *genome*, of humans contains some 3 billion (3×10^9) of these bases in different combinations.

That DNA contains all the instructions for maintaining life was shown when it became possible to make proteins such as haemoglobin in the test tube, simply by adding the raw materials to an appropriate length of nucleic acid obtained from a living cell or synthesised chemically.

Each base 'letter' in the 'word' that goes to make up a gene can, as we have seen, exist in four different states (A, G, C or T; see Box 1). As there are about 20 different amino acids – the building blocks of proteins – and only four DNA bases, each amino acid must be coded for by more than one base; in fact, three are involved.

The first clue about the nature of the code came from an alternative type of nucleic acid, RNA, which has the base uracil (U) instead of thymine (T) in its nucleotides. When supplied with a mixture of amino acids, artificial strings of 'U' bases (UUUUU . . .) produce large amounts of a protein chain made up of only one amino acid, phenylalanine.

Artificial genes containing two constituents – for example, A and C – can incorporate 6 of the 20 or so amino acids into a synthetic protein, suggesting that a message containing two different letters is enough to code for some but not all proteins.

A three-letter code based on the four different bases in DNA gives 64 combinations, more than the number of amino acids. However, an ingenious genetic experiment on bacteria showed that the code is indeed a three-letter one, each amino acid being determined by a triplet of letters, read from one end. The blocks of three bases are called *codons*.

Certain chemicals cause *mutations* – inherited changes in the structure of genes – by inserting extra bases into the DNA chain. If one or two bases are inserted into a length of DNA, then the message further along the DNA becomes garbled, and produces no protein. However, if three bases are inserted, the message is restored and a protein is generated.

Using a simple analogy, if the correct message is 'THE CAT ATE THE RAT', insertion of a single base might give a meaningless 'THE RCA TAT ETH ERA T'. Three inserts, however, could produce 'THE RED CAT ATE THE RAT', which is meaningful, or perhaps 'THE RDT CAT ATE THE RAT', which almost makes sense. We

now know the genetic code for every amino acid.

Some of the codons have other functions. In RNA, for example, UGA, UAA and UAG are *stop* codons: just like the full stop in a sentence they mark the point where the synthesis of a particular protein should end. One codon, AUG, codes for the amino acid methionine, which is the first unit in all newly synthesised proteins and hence acts as a *start* point.

In addition, the code is *degenerate* as some amino acids are coded for by more than one codon. For example, CGU, CGC, CGA and CGG all code for arginine. Degeneracy always involves the last letter in the triplet code, which seems to be less important than are the first two.

Changes or mistakes in copying codons lead to mutations. If a codon producing a new amino acid is formed – for example, UGC cysteine (Cys) to UGG tryptophan (Trp) – the protein may still function. However, if the mutation is to a stop codon, such as UGA, then the growing amino acid chain will be cut off – a *nonsense mutation*. Conversely, if a stop codon mutates, an abnormally long protein emerges because of the failure of chain termination, such as the 'Constant Spring' mutation of human haemoglobin, which has 172 amino acids rather than the normal 141.

The code is almost universal, with the same codons producing the same amino acids in creatures as different as bacteria and humans. This suggests that it originated a very long time ago. Surprisingly enough, some of the details of the code in the DNA of the mitochondrion, which has its own set of genes, differ from the general rule. For example, UGA is not a stop signal in mitochondrial DNA, but codes for an amino acid. Perhaps this is a clue to a distant evolutionary past, in which mitochondria were free-living organisms before their incorporation into the ancestors of today's human cells.

Steve Jones

		Second position				
		U	C	A	G	
U		UUU] Phe UUC] UUA] Leu UUG]	UCU] UCC] Ser UCA] UCG]	UAU] Tyr UAC] UAA Stop UAG Stop	UGU] Cys UGC] UGA Stop UGG Trp	U C A G
C		CUU] CUC] Leu CUA] CUG]	CCU] CCC] Pro CCA] CCG]	CAU] His CAC] CAA] Gln CAG]	CGU] CGC] Arg CGA] CGG]	U C A G
A		AUU] AUC] Ile AUA] AUG Met	ACU] ACC] Thr ACA] ACG]	AAU] Asn AAC] AAA] Lys AAG]	AGU] Ser AGC] AGA] Arg AGG]	U C A G
G		GUU] GUC] Val GUA] GUG]	GCU] GCC] Ala GCA] GCG]	GAU] Asp GAC] GAA] Glu GAG]	GGU] GGC] Gly GGA] GGG]	U C A G

(First position — left; Third position — right)

The genetic code. The groups of three capital letters are the codons. U, A, G and C (in messenger RNA) are the four bases uracil, adenine, guanine and cytosine. The amino acids are phenylalanine (Phe), leucine (Leu), isoleucine (Ile), methionine (Met), valine (Val), serine (Ser), proline (Pro), threonine (Thr), alanine (Ala), tyrosine (Tyr), histidine (His), glutamine (Gln), asparagine (Asn), lysine (Lys), aspartic acid (Asp), glutamic acid (Glu), cysteine (Cys), tryptophan (Trp), arginine (Arg) and glycine (Gly).

from single-celled aquatic animals to complex creatures able to live on land. Such parallels exist in haemoglobin. Early embryos switch on a gene for a haemoglobin that is very effective at extracting oxygen from their mother's blood; later embryos have a haemoglobin with rather less oxygen affinity, and adults have one suited to the easy availability of oxygen in the air. Each molecule is adapted to the environment in which it must function.

How did these adaptations arise? The basic mechanisms are those proposed by Darwin: variation and natural selection. Changes in oxygen affinity need involve only a few structural changes. An alteration in the electrical charge of an amino acid at one critical point in the molecule can greatly alter its shape and hence its ability to bind oxygen. Carp and human haemoglobins, for example, differ in

about 140 amino acid sites, but just one of these is largely responsible for their differences in function. The differences in function between embryonic, fetal and adult haemoglobins in humans also involve changes in their amino acids. These are much greater than between the adult haemoglobins of ourselves and other primates, suggesting that embryonic and adult haemoglobins diverged long ago, even before mammals appeared on earth.

The new methods of molecular biology (see Boxes 1–3) mean that we can establish the actual orders of the letters in the DNA alphabet that underlie the functioning haemoglobin molecule. The results raise new questions about evolution. Genes for the adult α and β chains of haemoglobin each turn out to be members of a different *gene family*: a group of functionally related DNA sequences close to

3. TRANSLATING THE GENETIC MESSAGE

The genetic code is a language, a set of instructions as to how to construct a living creature. Like all languages, its message needs to be translated. The mechanism is surprisingly cumbersome and lacks the beautiful simplicity of the genetic code, perhaps because it evolved in a piecemeal fashion as life progressed from simple replicating molecules floating in a chemical sea to the complex organisms of today.

Cellular machinery is all based on proteins – long chains of amino acids folded into complex shapes. The 20 major amino acids that make up all the proteins in our bodies are each coded for by a DNA triplet (Box 2). Several steps are involved in the flow of information from DNA to protein. As proteins are largely synthesised outside the nucleus an intermediary molecule, ribonucleic acid (RNA), carries the message from nucleus to cytoplasm. It has several forms and, unlike DNA, is usually a single – rather than a paired – strand.

The 'central dogma' of how genes work, first set forth by Francis Crick, is that DNA makes RNA makes protein. The first step is known as *transcription*. An appropriate section of the DNA message is copied into a length of *messenger RNA* (mRNA), which passes from nucleus to cytoplasm. Transcription involves a specific set of enzymes, the RNA polymerases. Only one of the two strands of DNA is copied into mRNA, and, just like the English language, the DNA message can be read only from one end, the so-called 5′ end.

RNA polymerases recognise a short stretch of DNA, the *promoter* of the gene, which tells the enzyme where to start copying the genetic message. Different promoters are more or less efficient in initiating mRNA synthesis, and this is one way in which the rate of production of proteins is controlled. But how particular genes are switched on when needed – *gene regulation* – is still far from fully understood.

Simultaneously, the appropriate amino acids floating in the cell become attached to other RNA molecules, the *transfer RNAs* (tRNAs). Each tRNA contains only about 75 nucleotides. Each has a specific code that allows it to recognise and become attached to a particular amino acid, and a further section that attaches it to the template provided by the mRNA. Transfer RNAs have a clover-leaf or hairpin shape.

Most of the cell's RNA exists in a third form, *ribosomal RNA* (rRNA). The ribosomes are the site of protein synthesis. They consist of two subunits, each containing rRNA and a variety of ribosomal proteins. Very often ribosomes are found in strings, or polyribosomes, linked together by a length of mRNA. This is the key to protein synthesis. Amino acids with their tRNA adaptor are picked up by rRNA and assembled into chains, in which their order – and hence the shape of the resulting protein – is determined by the code in the mRNA. Each mRNA molecule has several ribosomes attached to it, so that protein production can proceed rapidly.   *Steve Jones*

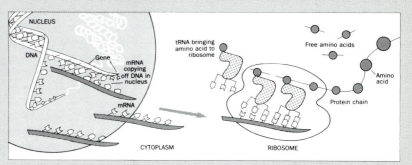

How proteins are synthesised, using the information coded in the order of DNA bases. The system involves co-operation between DNA and RNA — ribose nucleic acid, whose structure is rather similar to that of DNA but which uses ribose rather than deoxyribose sugars and has a slightly different genetic code.

each other on the chromosome. The α-globin family is on chromosome 16 whereas the β-globin family is on chromosome 11. Each consists of sections of 30 000 to 50 000 DNA bases coding for a total of eight functional and specialised globin molecules. This probably reflects a history of duplication and divergence: an ancestral globin-like gene in early vertebrates doubled up to produce a copy lying next to the original. The new copy was free to accumulate changes by mutation, and to adapt to the new functions demanded by a changing world. This happened several times. Exactly how duplication happens is not known, but it illustrates once again how genes with a common ancestry can diverge and adapt under natural selection.

In both the α- and the β-globin cluster, there are lengths of DNA that have a general similarity to that of the working globin genes, but produce no protein. These are the *pseudogenes* – rusting hulks of functional genes, which have accumulated so many errors by mutation that they can no longer produce a protein. There is a pleasing parallel here with one of Darwin's arguments in *The Origin*.

Darwin pointed out that many animals have 'relict organs'. For example, beetles on windy islands have small atrophied wings and embryonic blue whales have teeth that are soon lost. The existence of these rudimentary characters is itself evidence of evolution. Once selection is relaxed, errors can accumulate by mutation, and the organ loses its function. Exactly the same has happened to pseudogenes.

Much of the structure of haemoglobin fits well with the Darwinian mechanism of evolution, albeit with some unexpected twists. However, there are some aspects of its constitution that are harder to explain. For example, in the globin gene clusters most of the DNA seems to do nothing. Each working globin gene is separated from its neighbour by great stretches of DNA that produce no protein at all. Perhaps some of it is 'selfish DNA' that reproduces in its own interests, almost as a molecular parasite, and confers no advantage on its carriers. Another surprise is that even within functioning parts of the gene there are lengths of DNA, termed *introns*, which do not participate in making protein. Again, we do not understand the evolutionary role of these, although they might be relics of a distant time when short segments of DNA that produced rudimentary proteins joined together to produce the complex genes we see today.

Human haemoglobins and natural selection

The structure of the globin genes gives us an insight into their evolutionary history; one not very different from that first gained by Darwin. The comparative anatomy of these genes can in itself tell us little about the mechanism of evolution. We can, however, get some clues as to how evolution actually happened by seeing it at work on the haemoglobins of the peoples of the modern world.

Most of us share the same amino acid sequence in our globin chains. However, nearly 500 variants have been found, many of them confined to a few families. They have probably arisen fairly recently by *mutation*, the accidental change of one DNA message into another. Some are harmful and will soon disappear because of natural selection; for example, those that reduce the stability of the molecule and cause anaemia. In contrast, selection favours others and increases the ability of their carriers to survive and reproduce.

Much of this selection has to do with resistance to malaria. This disease became a problem only when populations became dense enough to allow it to spread. It is due to a single-celled protozoan parasite, *Plasmodium*, which is transmitted by blood-feeding mosquitoes. The parasite multiplies in the liver and blood stream, and can be fatal. Humans have evolved several ways of dealing with it. One haemoglobin variant, haemoglobin S (Hb^S) or 'sickle-cell' haemoglobin (which involves a single amino acid change in the sixth position of the β chain), is common only in malarious regions. Those with two copies of this gene suffer from sickle-cell anaemia. Their haemoglobin crystallises into long strands when oxygen levels are low, causing the red blood cells to distort to a crescent or sickle shape. These collapsed cells block capillaries and produce a variety of dangerous symptoms from anaemia to heart failure. Sufferers often die young.

Why, then, is the gene so common? The answer lies in the advantage gained by heterozygotes – those with one copy of a normal and one of the abnormal haemoglobin gene. Such people are resistant to malaria, perhaps because the partial collapse of their haemoglobin molecules kills the parasites. Selection hence acts to retain the sickle-cell gene: those with two doses are in danger from anaemia and those with normal haemoglobin from malaria, but those with both forms survive. A similar mechanism is at work elsewhere. For example, Hb^C, Hb^D and Hb^E, each of which arise from distinct single amino acid changes in the β chain, are common in Africa, in India and in the Far East; all these regions are malarious areas. Just as the haemoglobins of crocodiles and llamas have evolved adaptations to their environment, human populations faced with a selective challenge have produced new forms of the gene.

A clue as to how pseudogenes evolve also comes from the pattern of amino acid changes in modern haemoglobins. Inherited variants are much less common in the more important parts of the molecule – those sections that bind on to oxygen, to the haem or to the other amino acid chains. Only in the segments that link the working parts of the globin does natural selection allow mutations to accumulate: these sections are hence more variable than are those with a narrowly defined function. In pseudogenes, a mutation at some crucial point seems to have switched them off in the distant past and the long absence of any function has allowed more and more changes to accumulate.

Other changes in the sequence of the haemoglobin of living humans also give a clue as to how the globin gene family may have evolved. Sometimes, lengths of two or three amino acids in the haemoglobin molecule are duplicated. A few people even have a whole extra copy of an α chain, perhaps because of an error in copying that section of chromosome during the formation of a sperm or egg. Others have sections of chain missing, or one globin chain fused to another. An understanding of the mechanisms of

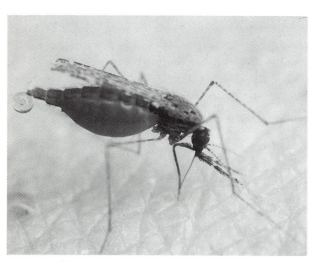

Malarial mosquito (*Anopheles balabacensis*) feeding on blood from a human arm.

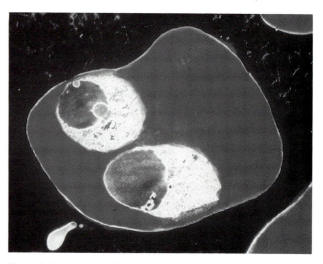

Transmission electron micrograph of a red blood cell attacked by two malaria parasites.

these changes may give us an insight into how the ancestral global genes duplicated and diverged long ago. Further clues may come from those families in which a form of haemoglobin normally found only in the fetus persists until adulthood. Just as Darwin said, studies of the present can offer us the key to the past.

Humanity has spread across the world from its home in Africa, and the geographic patterns of today's globins retain a memory of these migrations. Some are quite recent, and are recorded in history. For example, the sickle-cell gene is found in North America, whence it was brought by African slaves. Sometimes the evidence of migrations is preserved only in the genes. Studies of DNA in the β-globin gene family in Africa show that there are two separate lineages for the sickle-cell mutation. Although all those with Hb^s have an identical change in the amino acid chain, this mutation is associated with a different set of changes in DNA in different parts of Africa; so that it probably happened twice. What was once a single identifying letter – the S form of haemoglobin – is now surrounded by other inherited clues, which tells us that there are two distinct 'families' involved. One lives in West Africa, with a few members as far north as Morocco, and the other in West Central Africa, with branches to the east. This pattern tells us that the

4. EVOLUTION, CREATION AND CONTROVERSY

Evolution – unlike, say, chemistry – still attracts the odd. Chemistry itself went through an eccentric phase of transmutation of base metals into gold, of alchemy, and so on, but was cured of this long ago. Indeed, many of the bizarre views of early chemists played an important part in the development of the subject. The same cannot be said of the various theories of human origins that reject evolution.

There is a kind of invincible ignorance among anti-evolutionists that bores – when it does not exasperate – those seriously interested in the subject. However, creationism is still a serious threat to knowledge in many parts of the world, with more than 40 per cent of Americans in a recent survey denying that humans evolved from lower animals, and with continuing attempts by creationists to force their prejudice onto children by tampering with school textbooks. For this reason alone it deserves a mention in this encyclopedia.

Before Darwin, there seemed little reason to doubt the biblical account of creation. Indeed, the word 'prehistoric' was not invented until the middle of the nineteenth century. Before then, the whole of history was thought to be recorded in the Bible, and in 1650 the Irish Archbishop James Ussher worked out from the ages of the prophets recorded in the Old Testament that humans were created in precisely 4004 BC.

Within a hundred years or so, however, fossils were causing a real problem for those who held this view. Some saw them as survivors of the biblical Flood, and one optimist even pointed out that some fossilised creatures appeared to have been standing on tiptoe when they died, presumably to escape the rising waters. Others felt that fossils had been inserted into rocks by the Devil to tempt the unwary, or even by God to deceive geologists. When the first human fossil, Neanderthal Man, was discovered in 1856, it was dismissed by a German anatomist as a Cossack who had died in the retreat from Moscow. Fortunately, other scientists realised its antiquity.

The Origin of Species, published in 1859, was sensational because it destroyed these views. As Thomas Henry Huxley remarked, it was seen as a 'decidedly dangerous book by old ladies of both sexes'.

Darwin's evidence for evolution is compelling. It draws together many different sorts of evidence – from agriculture, the distribution of animals and plants, fossils, comparative anatomy and behaviour, embryology, and much else. His 'one long argument' is so convincing that it was soon accepted by nearly all biologists and most members of the public.

Creationists continue to deny the fact of evolution, and particularly human evolution. In so doing, they deliberately ignore most of biology since Darwin.

In 1925 in Tennessee, a part-time schoolteacher, John Scopes, was put on trial for breaking a state law forbidding the teaching of evolution; he had indeed broken the law, and was found guilty of so doing. The trial generated so much publicity, however, that the creationist cause was widely discredited and the Tennessee law fell into disuse (although it was not repealed until 1967). In court, the creationists could produce no scientific evidence for their views and were reduced to phrases such as 'we are interested in the Rock of Ages, not the Ages of Rocks'.

For some time, it seemed that such foolish challenges to evolution were things of the past. Unfortunately, this was not so. The Institute for Creation Research was set up in the USA in 1972. It uses the Bible as a textbook for the so-called science of creationism, and its proponents have used considerable guile in arguing that as both creationism and evolution are no more than theories they should be given equal prominence in biology classes.

Various pieces of 'evidence' have been used to bolster the creationists' cause. For example, some dinosaur footprints are accompanied by shallow natural depressions that they claim to be the prints of human feet – so that the dates set forth by conventional evolution are wrong. Legislation to block the teaching of Dawrwinism was passed in Arkansas in the 1970s, using the argument that creationism deserved the same treatment in schools as did evolution. The law was defined as unconstitutional in 1985, on the grounds that it was an attempt to teach religion in a state school. However, creationists have continued their efforts, and it seems that the proportion of Americans who believe their propaganda is on the increase.

Darwin did not have nearly as much evidence about our own ancestry as he did about the evolution of other creatures. *The Origin* scarcely mentions human evolution. Indeed, when Darwin was formulating his theories for the book he knew of no human fossils. Since his time, this balance has changed completely: we know more about some aspects of human evolution than about the evolution of any other animal.

All the lines of evidence that Darwin mustered in *The Origin* turn out to apply to our own species. We are highly variable in ways that are inherited; there has usually been a struggle for existence in human history, with population limited by resources; and the chance of surviving and passing on our genes is affected by inherited differences in susceptibility to disease and to other causes of death.

There is also a mass of evidence from comparative anatomy of our close relationship to other living primates. Perhaps most striking of all, the new knowledge about genes provided by molecular biology shows that we are closer to the great apes than even the most enthusiastic evolutionist had guessed. Finally, and crucially, we now have fossils dated by the new methods of geology that link living humans to extinct ancestors.

Creationists continue to play on the credibility of those who will listen, and will no doubt continue to force their views onto children who lack the information needed to refute them. Perhaps this encyclopedia will help to convince its readers that, although there is disagreement about the details of how it took place, the evidence for the fact of human evolution is overwhelming.   *Steve Jones*

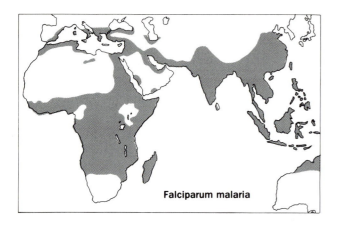

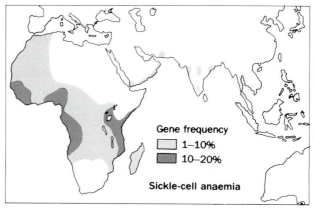

Gene frequency
- 1–10%
- 10–20%

Sickle-cell anaemia

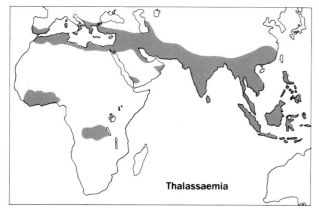

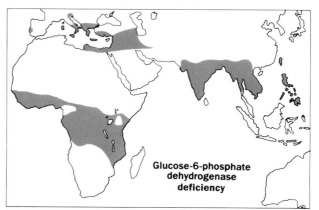

Glucose-6-phosphate dehydrogenase deficiency

The distribution of malaria and some of the genes that protect against the disease. Sickle-cell anaemia is just one amino-acid change in the haemoglobin molecule, β-thalassaemia the loss of a whole section. Glucose-6-phosphate dehydrogenase deficiency involves a completely different enzyme. There are several other genetic mechanisms for protection against malaria, including blood groups, enzymes and various haemoglobin changes. Natural selection seems to use whatever mutation makes available.

Moroccan sickle-cell gene probably came with migrants from the West, and the Kenyan copy from the other lineage.

Variation in the order of bases in the DNA around the globin genes also gives an insight into movements in the very distant past. Recent surveys of β globins show that Africa has a group of DNA sequence changes in this part of the genome which is quite distinct from those in the rest of the world. This might be a relict of the escape of modern humans from their ancestral continent. Fossil evidence suggests that fully modern *Homo sapiens* first appeared in Africa perhaps 130 000 years ago, and did not leave until about 100 000 years ago.

Once the escape had been made, humans spread rapidly over the globe, finally reaching the Americas in the past 20 000 years. The shift in pattern from the African ancestors might be the modern reflection of an ancient population bottleneck. Populations founded by a few migrants – such as the Afrikaners who came from Holland to South Africa – share a few genes as they are descended from a few founders. An episode of reduced numbers has caused the descendant population to shift away from its ancestor. Statistical trickery makes it possible to estimate how small the bottleneck was by comparing the new with the original population. In the case of the world's globin patterns, one estimate is that the band of emigrants from Africa was less than a hundred people. This effect is analogous to that uncovered by Darwin when he noticed that animals and plants on small islands – which were each probably founded by a few immigrants – produce some of the best evidence for evolution. Once again, many of the findings of molecular biology fit neatly into the intellectual framework built by Darwin. This is perhaps the most satisfying aspect of modern evolutionary biology, and one on which the rest of this encyclopedia is based.

Steve Jones

See also 'Evolution of early humans' (p. 241), Parts 7 and 8 (pp. 253–321) and 'People and disease' (p. 411)

Classification and evolutionary relationships

Once biologists had accepted the Darwinian notion that living organisms are derived from common ancestors by a continuing process of evolutionary change, they turned to reconstructing evolutionary trees. The primates have attracted particular attention, being the zoological group

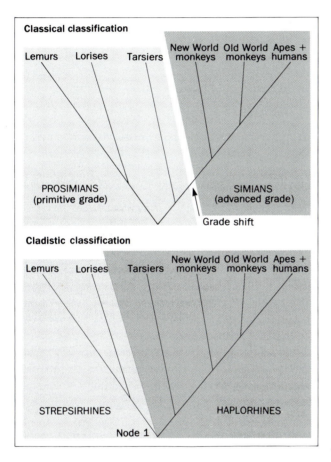

Classical classification

Lemurs Lorises Tarsiers New World monkeys Old World monkeys Apes + humans

PROSIMIANS (primitive grade) SIMIANS (advanced grade)

Grade shift

Cladistic classification

Lemurs Lorises Tarsiers New World monkeys Old World monkeys Apes + humans

STREPSIRHINES HAPLORHINES

Node 1

An outline phylogenetic tree for the six natural groups of living primates, showing alternative approaches to classification. In a classical classification, of the type recommended here, divisions are based on the grade of organisation. Groups that have retained a relatively high proportion of primitive features are allocated to a lower grade, while groups characterised by advanced features are allocated to a higher grade. Members of an advanced grade share specific novel features that define a 'grade shift'. Lemurs, lorises and tarsiers have generally retained many primitive features and are therefore allocated to the suborder Prosimii (literally 'before the monkeys'). Monkeys, apes and humans share several advanced features that are lacking in prosimians (e.g. in the skull, dentition, brain and reproductive apparatus) and are allocated to the suborder Anthropoidea. This classification has the advantage that all early fossil forms, which are necessarily primitive, are allocated to the Prosimii.

In a cladistic classification, by contrast, divisions are directly based on the sequence of branching within the tree. Individual groups are therefore clades rather than grades. The initial division in this tree separates lemurs and lorises from tarsiers, monkeys, apes and humans and so the order Primates is subdivided into the two suborders Strepsirhini and Haplorhini. One disadvantage of this classification is the requirement that very early fossil forms, which are often fragmentary, should ideally be separated into strepsirhines and haplorhines.

to which human beings belong. The basic biological unit is the species and the construction of an evolutionary tree requires a preliminary clustering of the species in the group being studied. Anybody interested in the evolutionary biology of primates must therefore face two fundamental issues. The first is *classification* – allocating species to groups and giving them individually distinctive names or a *nomenclature*. The second task is inferring the *pattern of relationships* within and among living and extinct members of those groups.

From the beginning, the question of classification became so closely linked to that of the reconstruction of evolutionary relationships that biologists often consider the two together as if they were virtually inseparable. As a result, there is considerable confusion over the correct terms to be used for reconstructing the genealogy, or *phylogeny*, of any group, such as the primates. As we shall see, what some biologists call 'classification' should more correctly be termed 'phylogenetic reconstruction'.

A good way of avoiding confusion is to use the term *taxonomy* for the study of classification. This term was well defined by the American palaeontologist George Gaylord Simpson as 'the theoretical study of classification, including its bases, procedures and rules'. The term *taxon* (plural: *taxa*) is widely used to refer to a set of species at any level in a classification, and much of taxonomy is concerned with the practical definition of such taxa. Often, however, biologists wrongly imply that the reconstruction of phylogenetic relationships is simply a part of taxonomy.

Another term, *systematics*, is also prone to misinterpretation, because the word is sometimes used exclusively for the inference of phylogenetic relationships but is sometimes taken to include classification as well. Simpson defined systematics very broadly as 'the scientific study of the kinds and diversity of organisms and all relationships among them'. He thus specifically included the topic of classification in his definition. There is hence no widely recognised term that refers exclusively to the inference of the patterns of phylogenetic relationships between organisms. However, *phylogenetic reconstruction* is as good as any and this will be used here.

Classification and phylogenetic reconstruction

It is important at the outset to be clear about the distinction between classification and phylogenetic reconstruction; the two are complementary fields of study with a relatively small area of overlap. Classifications must, above all, serve the practical function of allowing scientists to organise material so that they can communicate easily with each other. A classification provides a set of names for shorthand reference to biologically meaningful groups of species. As for any language, if biologists keep on changing the classification, effective communication collapses. It is therefore essential for any biological classification to have stability. In sharp contrast, hypothetical reconstructions of phylogenetic relationships between species must always be open to change, as new evidence accumulates and as new methods of analysis are applied.

Most biologists accept that a classification should in some way reflect likely evolutionary relationships among the taxa included. This, however, is not recognised by members of the school of *numerical taxonomy*. Numerical taxonomists feel that a quantitative assessment of overall similarity between organisms, without any evolutionary implications, can provide an adequate basis for classification. At the other end of the spectrum, the *cladistic* school of classification founded in the 1950s by Willi Hennig favours a direct matching between classifications and inferred phylogenetic trees. Sequences of branching-points (*nodes*) in a tree are taken as the basis for grouping species in a hierarchical scheme. In such a scheme, taxonomic groups represent *clades* rather than *grades*.

Should any classification be too closely matched to a phylogenetic tree, however, there is a clash between the need for stable taxonomic categories and that for progressive refinement of phylogenetic reconstructions. Indeed, as no two authors ever agree in detail on the primate phylogenetic tree, cladistic philosophy in its pure form implies that every author should use a uniquely personal classification. For this and other reasons, the *classical* school of evolutionary classification advocated by Simpson and by Ernst Mayr and others is to be preferred. This employs the concept of *grade of organisation* to distinguish taxa with well-defined specialisations from others that have remained relatively primitive. The great advantage of such a classification is that it can, within limits, be made compatible with a variety of interpretations of phylogenetic relationships without directly reflecting inferred branching-points. It then becomes possible to modify interpretations of phylogenetic relationships without necessarily having to change the classification.

Species: the unit of classification

The basic unit of biological classification, the *species*, may be simply defined as a group of actually or potentially interbreeding natural populations that is reproductively isolated from other such groups. Although there are some difficulties with the practical application of this definition – notably, with the identification of extinct species in the fossil record – recognition of individual species is usually relatively straightforward. Smaller taxonomic units, such as the *subspecies*, may be identified in cases where full reproductive isolation does not seem to have evolved, but taxonomy is primarily concerned with the recognition of species and their organisation into a hierarchy of higher taxa:

Class
  Subclass
    Order
      Infraorder
        Superfamily
          Family
            Subfamily
              Tribe
                Subtribe
                  Genus
                    Species

In contrast to the species, higher taxa from the genus upwards have essentially arbitrary definitions, which depend on the taxonomist's assessment of overall degrees of difference.

The procedure of naming species and higher taxonomic categories is governed by the *International Rules of Zoological Nomenclature*. The most important rule is that any species must bear two names – the first (with a capital letter) indicating the *genus* (plural: *genera*), the second (with a small letter) indicating the species. Accordingly, the scientific name for the human species is *Homo sapiens*. Although there may be several species in a given genus and a particular specific name may be used in different genera, the combination of the two names is unique. In print, it is standard practice to use a different typeface (usually italics) for generic and specific names.

Another important rule governs the endings of the names of certain higher taxa; for example, names of tribes end in '-ini', subfamily names end in '-inae' and family names end in '-idae'. The endings of names for taxonomic groups above the family level are not governed in this way.

Striped possum   Aye-aye

A marsupial and a primate, both active at night, have developed special adaptations for feeding on wood-boring insect larvae. The striped possum (*Dactylopsila*) and the aye-aye (*Daubentonia*) have rodent-like teeth for gnawing wood and one finger on each hand serves as a probe to extract the grubs. These special features developed independently (a case of convergent evolution) because different digits have been modified as probes – the middle finger in the aye-aye and the fourth finger in the possum.

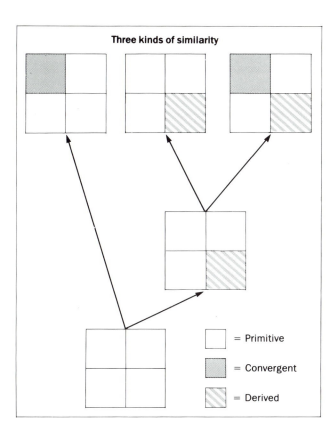

Three kinds of similarity

= Primitive

= Convergent

= Derived

As a general rule, organisms that share many similarities are likely to be closely related; but there are numerous exceptions. The inference of phylogenetic relationships in fact requires a basic distinction between three kinds of similarity. It is first necessary to distinguish between convergent similarities, which have been developed independently, and homologous similarities, which are based on inheritance from a common ancestor. Homologous similarities must then be divided into primitive features that were present in the initial common ancestor of the group concerned and derived features that were developed in a later ancestor within the tree. Only shared derived similarities indicate the pattern of relationships within the tree.

Common names derived from formal taxonomic names are always written with a small letter; for instance, the formal name of the order Primates (the taxonomic unit in which humans, apes, monkeys, lemurs, lorises and tarsiers are grouped) yields the common name 'primate' and the human family name Hominidae gives us the common name 'hominid'.

Primate classification

It is widely recognised that living primates fall into six natural groups, and these are reflected in one way or another in most current classifications: (1) the lemurs of Madagascar; (2) the lorises and bushbabies; (3) the tarsiers; (4) the New World monkeys; (5) the Old World monkeys; and (6) the apes and humans. Opinions differ about the relationships between these groups of living species and about their affinities with various fossil groups, a problem that is discussed in greater detail in Part 6. Nevertheless, the basic division of living primates into six natural groups provides a useful starting-point for the reconstruction

of their relationships and shows how classification and phylogenetic reconstruction can interact.

Evolutionary trees

Phylogenetic reconstruction is mainly concerned with the inference of ancestral relationships between species and hence with constructing trees that indicate the positions and relative timing of the main branching-points or nodes. Such a hypothetical tree is an essential foundation for considering other aspects of evolutionary biology. A diagram of inferred phylogenetic relationship is commonly referred to as a *cladogram*, as it identifies clusters of phylogenetically related species in clades. In principle, a *phylogenetic tree* may incorporate more information than just the positions of nodes indicated by a cladogram. It may, for example, indicate grade distinctions or differential rates of evolution. In practice, however, the term 'phylogenetic tree' is used in a very general way to refer to any diagram, including a cladogram, that illustrates inferred patterns of relationships.

Phylogenetic relationships are inferred on the basis of patterns of similarities shared between species. Although only morphological characters were considered initially, it has now become common to use behavioural, physiological, chromosomal and biochemical features to make such inferences. It might be thought that the degree of phylogenetic relationship should be indicated in some simple way by the numbers of similarities between pairs of species. However, there are two reasons why this is not always so and why straightforward numerical analysis is unlikely to yield reliable phylogenetic trees or lead to classifications compatible with probable phylogenetic relationships.

Convergent, primitive and derived characters
In the first place, two species may develop similar features independently, either by chance or because of adaptation to meet a similar functional requirement. For example, among primates the rare aye-aye (*Daubentonia madagascariensis*) has developed very large, continuously growing incisor teeth for breaking into hard fruits and gnawing wood to get at wood-boring grubs. However, this adaptation has undoubtedly occurred quite separately from the same feature in rodents. Such *convergent* similarities do not indicate ancestral relationships. We must instead seek *homologous* similarities between species – that is, those based on characters inherited from a common ancestor – before reconstructing their relationships. Even then, a second problem remains.

For any group of species, there is an initial common ancestor with a particular set of features. Retention by later members of the group of any of these *primitive* features, although they are indeed homologous, does not provide any information on subsequent patterns of branching within the phylogenetic tree. For instance, both tree

CLASSIFICATION OF PRIMATES

The classification of the order Primates shown here is close to that originally proposed by George Gaylord Simpson in his influential classification of mammals (1945). A few modifications have been made – for example, by Elwyn Simons (1972) and Robert Martin (1990) – but Simpson's basic framework is still clearly recognisable.

The classification is a classical one; it is based on the concept of grade or general level of organisation. This kind of classification is relatively stable because it is compatible with a variety of different phylogenetic trees and need not reflect any particular interpretation of evolutionary relationships. Many other classifications of primates have been proposed, mainly to emphasise hypotheses about phylogeny based on cladistic principles, but none has so far achieved widespread adoption.

For example, some authorities suggest that there is little, if any, connection between Plesiadapiformes (archaic primates) and other primates (primates of modern aspect or euprimates). There has thus been an increasing tendency to separate these two main groups more clearly. One solution is to raise the Plesiadapiformes to the rank of a separate suborder, placing the group on a par with Prosimii and Anthropoidea. A more extreme solution is a classification with a primary division between Plesiadapiformes and Euprimates. The most radical solution of all would be to exclude the Plesiadapiformes from the primates altogether.

The division between the two main groups Prosimii (prosimians) and Anthropoidea (simians or anthropoids) in the classification shown here is based on the notion that prosimians are generally more primitive than simians. This view has the advantage that all early fossil primates can be classified as prosimians (it can be difficult to determine the relationships between such early forms and modern prosimians, especially when only fragmentary fossils are available).

There is, however, considerable evidence suggesting that modern tarsiers are more closely related to simians than to other prosimians. Many authorities thus favour an alternative division between the suborder Strepsirhini (lemurs and lorises) and the suborder Haplorhini (tarsiers and simians). However, the degree of relationship between fossil tarsier-like primates in the family Omomyidae and modern tarsiers is still not certain, so that the place of the fossil forms in such a scheme remains unclear.

The early Tertiary lemur-like primates (superfamily Adapoidea) are usually included in the Lemuriformes, because they resemble modern lemurs in some features. There is, however, an increasing trend to create a separate infraorder Adapiformes to emphasise the distinctiveness of the fossil forms and to raise the subfamilies Adapinae and Notharctinae to family level (Adapidae and Notharctidae) to emphasise the separation between them.

A major problem arises with the classification of modern lemurs (superfamily Lemuroidea) and modern members of the loris group (superfamily Lorisoidea), because several workers have found morphological affinities between the Cheirogaleidae (mouse and dwarf lemurs) and the Lorisidae. The Cheirogaleidae and the Lorisidae are hence often classified together in the superfamily Lorisoidea.

A specific phylogenetic relationship between Cheirogaleidae and Lorisidae is, however, based solely on the interpretation of certain features of the skull and receives no support from studies of chromosomes, proteins or DNA.

With a grade-based classification, in which lemurs are regarded as generally more primitive than lorises, it is not necessary to shift the Cheirogaleidae into the Lorisoidea. Some now raise the two subfamilies Lorisinae and Galaginae to family level (Lorisidae and Galagidae); such shifts in taxonomic rank are largely a matter of taste.

The classification of the New World monkeys (infraorder Platyrrhini, superfamily Ceboidea) has been subject to much upheaval in recent years as evolutionary relationships within this group of primates are still far from clear. There exist quite different conclusions about the phylogenetic tree of the New World monkeys and the basic principles of cladistic classification applied by many necessarily lead to markedly different classifications. These are discussed in Chapter 6.2. A grade-based classification is not prone to such fluctuation. This is once again an example of the advantage such a classical scheme has over more modern cladistic approaches.

The classification of Goeldi's monkey, *Callimico goeldii* (subfamily Callimiconinae) is particularly open to alternative approaches because this species is morphologically intermediate between other New World monkeys of the family Cebidae and the marmosets and tamarins (family Callitrichidae).

It has long been uncertain whether Goeldi's monkey is more closely related to cebids or to callitrichids, although most now favour a relationship to marmosets and tamarins. *Callimico* has been placed in the Cebidae (as in the classification shown here), in the Callitrichidae and in a family of its own (Callimiconidae).

In a grade-based classification, it is still possible to classify *Callimico* with the Cebidae, as it lacks some obvious specialisations of the marmosets and tamarins – for example, complete loss of the third molar tooth. This solution has been followed here. In cladistic classifications, however, it is now usual to classify *Callimico* with marmosets and tamarins in the Callitrichidae.

A more radical revision of the New World monkeys is proposed in Chapter 6.2. Alfred Rosenberger believes that the larger New World monkeys (here placed in the family Cebidae) do not form a cohesive group and that some of them, such as squirrel monkeys, are more closely related to *Callimico* and to marmosets and tamarins.

The classification of the Old World monkeys (infraorder Catarrhini, superfamily Cercopithecoidea) is relatively straightforward, as they form a well-characterised group with a fairly clear division between two subfamilies: leaf monkeys with a complex stomach (Colobinae) and monkeys with cheek pouches (Cercopithecinae).

With respect to the apes (superfamily Hominoidea), there has been controversy over the extinct family Oreopithecidae, which is linked by some with the Old World monkeys and by others with the apes. Because there is now good evidence that *Oreopithecus* is related to the apes, and because Old World monkeys are well defined by a dental specialisation called bilophodonty lacking in *Oreopithecus*, it seems appropriate to include the Oreopithecidae within the Hominoidea.

There is also confusion over the distinction between the families Pongidae and Hominidae within the Hominoidea. Originally, all great apes (orang-utans, gorillas and chimpanzees) were classified in the family Pongidae and the family Hominidae was reserved for humans and their direct fossil relatives. Because it is now widely accepted that the African apes (gorillas and chimpanzees) are more closely related to humans than are orang-utans, there have been numerous attempts to reflect this in new classifications.

One solution (shown left) is to place orang-utans in the Pongidae and to combine African apes and humans in the Hominidae. An unfortunate outcome of such a scheme is that the term 'hominid' may now mean 'African apes and humans' instead of just humans and their direct ancestors.

Robert Martin

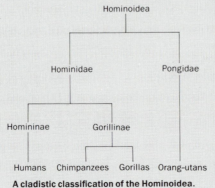

A cladistic classification of the Hominoidea.

SUBORDER	INFRAORDER	SUPERFAMILY	FAMILY	SUBFAMILY
PROSIMII (prosimians)	PLESIADAPIFORMES (archaic primates)		Plesiadapidae	
			Paromomyidae	
			Carpolestidae	
			Picrodontidae	
			Microsyopidae	
			Saxonellidae	
	LEMURIFORMES (lemuriforms)	ADAPOIDEA	Adapidae (lemur-like primates)	Adapinae
				Notharctinae
		LEMUROIDEA (lemurs)	Cheirogaleidae (mouse and dwarf lemurs)	
			Lemuridae	Lemurinae (true lemurs)
				Lepilemurinae (sportive lemurs)
			Indridae (indri group)	
			Daubentoniidae (aye-aye)	
			Megaladapidae	
	LORISIFORMES (lorisiforms)	LORISOIDEA (loris group)	Lorisidae	Lorisinae (lorises)
				Galaginae (bushbabies)
	TARSIIFORMES (tarsiers)	TARSIOIDEA	Omomyidae (tarsier-like primates)	Omomyinae
				Microchoerinae
				Anaptomorphinae
			Tarsiidae (tarsiers)	
ANTHROPOIDEA (simians or anthropoids)	PLATYRRHINI (New World simians)	CEBOIDEA (New World monkeys)	Cebidae (true monkeys)	Cebinae (capuchins, etc.)
				Aotinae (owl monkeys, etc.)
				Atelinae (spider monkeys, etc.)
				Alouattinae (howler monkeys)
				Pitheciinae (sakis, etc.)
				Cebupithecinae
				Callimiconinae (Goeldi's monkey)
			Callitrichidae (marmosets and tamarins)	
	CATARRHINI (Old World simians)	CERCOPITHECOIDEA (Old World monkeys)	Cercopithecidae	Parapithecinae
				Victoriapithecinae
				Cercopithecinae (check-pouched monkeys)
				Colobinae (leaf monkeys)
		HOMINOIDEA (apes and humans)	Oreopithecidae	
			Hylobatidae (gibbons)	Pliopithecinae
				Hylobatinae
			Pongidae (great apes)	Dryopithecinae
				Ponginae
			Hominidae (hominids)	Australopithecinae
				Homininae

Extinct groups

A classification of the order Primates.

shrews and primates possess a caecum (a blind pouch of the digestive tract at the junction of the small and large intestines). However, this does not indicate any special relationship between these two groups, as the ancestral placental mammals that preceded them probably already had this structure. A phylogenetic tree must hence be based on shared *derived* homologous features, each of which developed in an intermediate ancestor later in the tree and has been retained in a specific group of descendants. We must thus make a triple distinction between convergent, primitive and derived similarities in reconstructing the phylogenetic relationships of any group of organisms.

Such a triple distinction is exceedingly difficult to achieve in practice. In the first place, there is a problem of circularity: if convergence is defined as the independent development of similar features, its recognition then requires that the ancestral condition should already be known. Yet reliable reconstruction of ancestral features requires some means of separating convergent from homologous similarities. In practice, it is often possible to identify convergence in complex characters because the similarity is incomplete, merely being enough to ensure functional equivalence. For example, although there is a superficial similarity between the wings of birds and the wings of bats, because both have developed to meet the needs of flight, there are many differences of detail. But with many convergent characters, especially those of a relatively simple nature – for example, parallel replacement of one amino acid in a protein by another in two species – the similarity may be complete. In such cases, recognition of convergence must be a result of phylogenetic reconstruction rather than a step in analysis.

Distinction of primitive from derived homology is also problematical, in this case because of uncertainties about just what was the primitive condition of a character for a given group of organisms. Here, we must have some independent means of recognising the initial ancestral (primitive) condition for the distinction to be made.

Rates of evolution

The need to distinguish between primitive and derived similarities arises largely because of differential rates of evolution. If evolutionary rates were constant, then the degree of phylogenetic relationship between taxa would be simply proportional to the numbers of shared homologous features, whether primitive or derived. However, because rates of evolution often differ greatly between species, a phylogenetic connection between a rapidly diverging species and a more slowly evolving one may be obscured.

Because of the need to reconstruct phylogenetic trees without prior knowledge of ancestral conditions, general rules of thumb must be used to infer the primitive condition for a given character. None of these rules is absolutely reliable and all of them must be applied to as many species and to as many characters as possible to obtain satisfactory

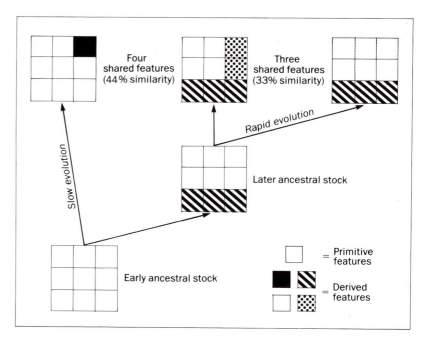

Once convergent similarities have been excluded, it might be expected that the relative frequencies of the remaining homologous similarities should indicate phylogenetic relationships without the need to distinguish between primitive and derived features. This is not the case, however, because of the confounding effect of different rates of evolution. Slowly evolving forms will retain a relatively large number of primitive features and will resemble one another for this reason, whereas rapid evolution will reduce similarities between closely related forms. In this example, a form that has evolved at moderate speed (top middle) shares more homologous features with a slowly evolving form (top left) than with its rapidly evolving relative (top right). It is necessary to identify the derived features developed in the intermediate ancestor to show that the form that has evolved at moderate speed is in fact more closely related to the rapidly evolving form.

results. Given several alternative states of a character, the primitive condition may be inferred as follows:

- One condition may be logically more primitive than another: for example, small brains are probably more primitive than large brains
- Embryonic development often provides indications of the primitive condition: for example, the bony element bearing the eardrum, the ectotympanic, is ring-shaped during early development in all primates, although in the adults of most species it is secondarily modified, sometimes forming a long tube; hence, the ring-shaped ectotympanic of adult lemurs is likely to be primitive
- A large selection of early fossil species with the same geological age is likely to have more primitive characters than a similar selection of fossil species dating from more recent times: for example, early mammals generally have more teeth than do recent mammals, indicating a general trend towards reduction in the numbers of teeth; hence, in any group the species with the maximum number of teeth is likely to be the most primitive
- A character that is very widespread within a group is

often more primitive than a rare one: for example, all non-human primates have a grasping big toe whereas humans do not; possession of a grasping big toe is probably primitive for primates

- The *sister-group principle* states that if there are some alternative states of a character within one group, the character state (if there is only one) found in the next most closely related group of species is the primitive condition: for example, among New World monkeys the marmosets and tamarins have only two molar teeth in each jaw whereas the other forms have three molars; in Old World monkeys, apes and humans three molar teeth are typically present in each jaw, so possession of three molars is the primitive condition

As the rules are no more than guidelines, it must always be remembered that any phylogenetic tree is based on inference and cannot be taken as a definitive statement. There are known exceptions to all of these guidelines, so they must be used with caution.

When several hypothetical phylogenetic trees have been constructed for a group such as the Primates, it is possible to test them in various ways. Many biologists claim that the *principle of parsimony* is the most reliable criterion for doing this, the optimal tree being that requiring the least evolutionary change. But there are problems with parsimony: there is marked variation in rates of evolution and Nature is not necessarily parsimonious. For this reason, it is best to use as many different kinds of data as possible and construct a series of phylogenetic trees for any group of species. If this is done, it should eventually be possible to assess compatibility between the trees based on different data sets to select a consensus tree.

The best criterion for assessing the reliability of any phylogenetic tree for primates must be its capacity to absorb new fossil finds without major changes and to explain features such the changing pattern of primate distribution in the light of new information on the movements of the continents. After many years of controversy, broad agreement about evolutionary relations among primates may now not be far away.

Robert Martin

See also 'Non-human primates' (p. 24), 'The fossil history of primates' (p. 199), 'Evolution of New World monkeys' (p. 209), 'Evolution of Old World monkeys' (p. 217) and 'Evolution of apes' (p. 223)

Non-human primates

When Linnaeus set up a group including lemurs, monkeys, apes and humans in his 1758 classification of the mammals, he chose to name it the *Primates*, a medieval Latin word meaning 'chieftains'. No doubt he had human beings in mind when he gave the group this name. Apart from the human species, there is nothing particularly chieftainly about the order Primates; it is one of the smaller and less successful mammalian orders, comparable in diversity and number of species to the single family of squirrels (Sciuridae).

The primates derive not only their name but also most of their scientific interest from the fact that people are primates. Biologists since Darwin have studied them with an eye to their relationship to human beings, and have focused on those that could be taken as representing successive stages in human evolution. From the 1920s until the 1970s, most students of primate evolution saw the group as governed by a series of evolutionary trends that culminated in the human species, *Homo sapiens*. Primate groups that did not exhibit the approved tendencies towards big brains, reduced ability to smell (olfaction), increased manual dexterity, upright posture and comparable human characteristics were regarded as aberrant or backward deviants from the mainstream.

This approach is now largely discredited. It may be illuminating to see human beings as atypical primates, but it is not very instructive to regard other primates as a mere preface to humanity. A better insight into primate evolution can be gained through comparing primates not with humans but with other animals that have become adapted to similar ways of life.

Adaptations for life in trees

Nearly all the approximately 230 species of living primates spend most of their time in trees in tropical and subtropical forests. The worldwide shrinkage of such forests during the past 30 million years has probably been one of the factors that has limited the order's evolutionary success; and the modern destruction of tropical forest, driven by human greed and desperation, may result in the extermination of most primates in nature during the next century.

Many of the features that distinguish primates from other placental mammals can be interpreted as adaptations to living in trees. The most striking of these are in the anatomy of the hands and feet. The great (big) toe of all non-human primates is opposed to the other four, and is set off from them by a broad cleft used for grasping tree branches. The thumb is offset from the four fingers in many primate hands (including our own). The pads of the palms and soles,

which in typical non-primate mammals form protuberant fatty cushions like those seen in dogs or cats, are in primates more or less fused into a broad, soft contact surface covered with fingerprint ridges (dermatoglyphics). The claws of the great toes – and generally those of the other digits of the hands and feet as well – are modified (from the primitive gouge-like shape retained in a dog or a rat) into flattened shields overlying enlarged, sensitive toetips and fingertips.

Various non-primate animals also have grasping feet. The hind feet of opossums and other primitive marsupials are particularly like those of primates; they have clawless, widely divergent great toes and are used for grasping and hanging from branches. South American tree porcupines, climbing mice, chameleons and various other animals with grasping hind feet have similar arboreal habits. The comparison suggests that this feature is indeed an arboreal adaptation, and that the last common ancestor of the living primates, like most of its descendants, must have been a tree-dwelling creature.

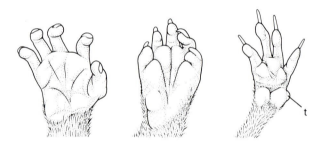

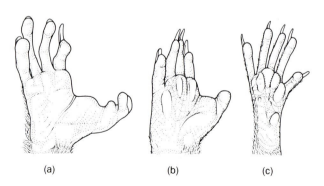

Right hands (top row) and right feet (bottom row) of three arboreal mammals. (a) A representative primate – the thick-tailed bushbaby (*Otolemur crassicaudatus*). The thumb and first (great) toe are opposed to the other digits, the digits bear flattened nails (except for the grooming claw on the second toe), and the broad, soft palm and sole are covered with fingerprint ridges (dermatoglyphics). (b) The North American opossum (*Didelphis marsupialis*). The first toe is opposed to the others, but the thumb is not divergent, and all digits except the first toe are tipped with sharp pointed claws. (c) The Carolina grey squirrel (*Sciurus carolinensis*). All digits are roughly parallel and bear claws – except the thumb (t), which is greatly reduced and used only in holding food between the two hands.

The arboreal theory of primate evolution

This inference seems so clear that early twentieth-century students of primate evolution attempted to extend it to other distinctive primate features. Most of these involve the eyes and the sense of vision. Compared with other, more typical or primitive mammals, primates have enlarged eyes and associated visual parts of the brain. Their eyes lie close together and point in the same direction, and each is enclosed in a bony ring or cup that forms a complete orbit (eye socket). In contrast, the smelling (olfactory) apparatus is strikingly reduced in monkeys, apes and humans.

In the past, most primate biologists linked these specialisations to arboreality; they felt confident that vision must be vastly more important than smell to an animal that lives in trees. A tree-dweller, it was argued, cannot simply snuffle along following scent trails in its search for food and mates; it must find its way to both by using its eyes and brain to spy out likely paths through a tangled network of branches. It was believed that, because such an animal must occasionally jump across gaps, it needs stereoscopic depth perception to gauge distances by looking before it leaps. Thus, the traditional explanation goes, natural selection favours changes that leave the eyes set close together, pointing in the same direction. This change exposes the eyes to injury from the side and demands their protection by bony orbital rings.

Arboreality has also been invoked to account for other primate traits. The opening out of the claws into flattened nails has been interpreted as a device for making the toetips and fingertips more pliant in clinging to the bark of trees. Enlargement of the brain, which is characteristic of most living primates, supposedly reflects the greater demands that the tricky and dangerous arboreal environment makes on an animal's wits. A corollary of all these changes is the gradual replacement of the snout by the eye and hand as organs of investigation and manipulation – a trend culminating in the human hand, which is exclusively tactile and manipulatory and has lost all function in locomotion.

This 'arboreal theory' of primate evolution is persuasive and elegant, and dominated biology textbooks for many years. Its fatal flaw is that it does not stand up to the test of comparative functional anatomy. Most arboreal mammals look nothing like primates. Squirrels are successful arboreal types and outnumber primates in most of the world's forests; yet they have sideways-facing eyes, large snouts, and non-opposable digits tipped with sharp claws. Claws, which allow an animal to cling to large vertical supports, are retained by almost all non-primate tree-dwellers, including those with grasping feet. Indeed, some arboreal primates – the aye-aye (*Daubentonia madagascariensis*), Goeldi's monkey (*Callimico goeldii*) and marmosets and tamarins – have redeveloped claw-like structures from ancestral nails.

Although bringing the eyes together at the front of the head does increase the arc of stereoscopic vision, it diminishes its value for a leaping animal by reducing the distance over which stereoscopic depth perception can operate. No arboreal mammals other than primates have conspicuously smaller organs of smell or larger brains than their less-arboreal relatives. Squirrels are not less keen-scented than rats; koalas are not brainier than wombats; kinkajous are not more dextrous than raccoons. Thus, the 'arboreal theory' does not apply in most of those non-primate instances where it ought to succeed.

The visual-predation theory of primate evolution

No new theory of primate adaptations and evolution has emerged from the ruins of the arboreal theory. Some distinctive primate peculiarities probably do not represent adaptations to any particular way of life, but are just alternative solutions to common mammalian problems. The best example of this is the bony enclosure of the middle-ear space (see p. 26). In primates, this space is enclosed chiefly by an outgrowth of the same bone (the petrosal) that houses the inner-ear apparatus , whereas in most other placental mammals a separate entotympanic bone forms the floor of the middle-ear space. An enclosure of some sort is adaptively advantageous, but any bone will do the job.

Other traits common to living primates, however, do hint at an ancestral adaptation to arboreal life, which may be recognisable today among some primates and tree-dwelling non-primates. Among birds and mammals, close-set eyes that point in the same direction are typical of owls, cats and other predators that rely on vision in hunting, especially those that hunt by night. The most plausible explanation of these features in living primates is that their last common ancestor was a small, big-eyed, nocturnal creature that prowled through trees and bushes on the lookout for insects as some small primates do today. Modern chameleons and certain marsupials, some of which even

Heads of loris, squirrel and cat. Note the close-set eyes of the primate and cat, and the sideways-facing eyes of the squirrel. Close-set eyes that point in the same direction are typical of predators that rely on vision in hunting, especially those that hunt by night. A plausible explanation of this and other features of living primates is that their last common ancestor was a small, big-eyed nocturnal, insect-eating creature.

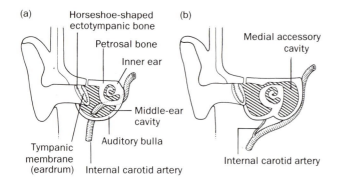

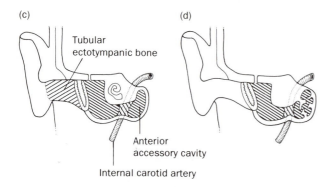

Diagrammatic cross-sections through the right ears of four primates: (a) lemur; (b) loris; (c) tarsier; and (d) New World monkey.

resemble primates in having reduced claws, have a similar way of life.

In the primate fossil record, the conspicuous adaptations characteristic of living primates first appear in lemur-like (adapid) and tarsier-like (omomyid) prosimians of the early part of the Eocene epoch, some 50 million years ago. The earliest representatives of these primates are small animals with teeth resembling those of modern insect-eating (insectivorous) primates. This gives further support to the 'visual predation' theory of modern primate origins.

The major groups of primates

Fossil and living forms in the order Primates can be divided into two groups: the archaic primates (Plesiadapiformes) and the modern primates (Euprimates). Plesiadapiforms became extinct in the Eocene. They lacked most of the characteristic primate specialisations of the head, hands and feet, and it has recently been suggested that at least some members of this group were more closely related to colugos or 'flying lemurs' (order Dermoptera) than to modern primates.

As can be seen in the outline primate classification in Chapter 1.2 (p. 21), the living primates comprise two major groups: the suborder Prosimii containing the prosimians (lemurs, lorises, galagos and tarsiers) and the suborder Anthropoidea containing the 'higher primates' or simians (monkeys, apes and humans). An alternative grouping links the tarsiers with the simians, or anthropoids, in the sub-

order Haplorhini; the lemurs, lorises and galagos are then grouped in the suborder Strepsirhini.

Lemurs, lorises and galagos

The strepsirhine primates are distinguished chiefly by primitive traits. The left and right halves of their lower jaws are separated by a joint in the chin region (as is the case in most mammals). Their olfactory apparatus is well developed and retains such standard features as multiple, branching ethmoturbinals (the bony scrolls inside the snout that carry the olfactory nerve endings), large olfactory bulbs of the brain, and a moist nose like a dog's.

With few exceptions, strepsirhines have smaller brains than do living simians of similar size. Strepsirhine retinas lack the fovea (a small retinal area, characteristic of anthropoids, which is used for extremely detailed vision), and most of them have a reflecting layer (the *tapetum lucidum*) that produces eyeshine like a cat's when the animals are caught in a beam of light at night. These retinal traits suggest that primitive strepsirhines were nocturnal.

The few non-primitive traits that unite the living strepsirhines are adaptations for grooming. The second toe of all strepsirhines bears not a nail but a claw, used for scratching in a doglike fashion; and the lower front teeth of all but one species, the aye-aye, are modified to form a comb used for grooming the fur and for feeding.

Malagasy lemurs

Most living strepsirhine primates are confined to Madagascar, where they have undergone a modest evolutionary radiation in the absence of higher primates (or, indeed, most other mammals). Until human beings came to Madagascar around 2000 years ago, the island's primate fauna included several large and curiously specialised strepsirhines that can be described as imitation tree sloths, baboons, giant koalas, and so on. The surviving primates of Madagascar are collectively known as lemurs, and are usually grouped into four families.

The family Lemuridae is typified by the true lemurs (*Lemur*) and the variegated lemurs (*Varecia*). These long-snouted plant-eaters (herbivores), looking something like monkeys with the heads of foxes, are a familiar sight in zoos.

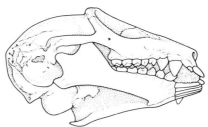

Skull of the fork-marked lemur (*Phaner furcifer*), showing the well-developed toothcomb in the lower jaw. The comb, which is used for grooming the fur, consists of two incisors and one canine on each side. The structure is present in all living lorises and in most lemurs.

Mongoose lemur (*Lemur mongoz*).

Verreaux's sifaka (*Propithecus verreauxi*).

Aye-aye (*Daubentonia madagascariensis*).

Lesser or Senegal bushbaby (*Galago senegalensis*).

The family Indridae, which contains the indri (*Indri*), the avahi (*Avahi*) and the sifakas (*Propithecus*), are specialised leaf-eaters (folivores) with long hindlimbs that propel them in spectacular leaps through the treetops. Indrids use their chisel-like toothcombs in browsing and in peeling bark from trees. Like most leaf-eating primates, they have long, capacious guts and are finicky and delicate animals that do not adapt easily to captivity.

The family Daubentoniidae contains a single living species, the exceedingly rare aye-aye. Perhaps the most bizarre of living primates, it sports rodent-like gnawing incisors instead of a toothcomb and has a long, very slender third finger on each hand. The aye-aye feeds on wood-boring grubs, using its gnawing teeth to open the grubs' tunnels and its thin middle fingers to probe the tunnels and spear their occupants. This lemur thus fills the ecological niche of

woodpeckers, which are not found in Madagascar.

The remaining five genera of Madagascar's primates make up the family Cheirogaleidae, the mouse and dwarf lemurs. These small, nocturnal animals feed on fruit, insects and plant gums. Their only conspicuous specialisation is the use of the tail as a site for fat storage in the mouse lemurs (*Microcebus*) and dwarf lemurs (*Cheirogaleus*); when obese, these animals look like large mice towing fur-covered sausages. The chief interest of the mouse and dwarf lemurs is in their anatomical similarities to the galagos and lorises (subfamilies Galaginae and Lorisinae) of mainland Africa and Asia.

Galagos and lorises

Galagos or bushbabies (subfamily Galaginae) are restricted to Africa. The smallest forms resemble the smaller cheirogaleids in appearance and habits; the largest, the greater bushbabies (*Otolemur*), are the size of a house cat. All are nocturnal, with large, delicate ears that can fold up like venetian blinds. The ankle bones of galagos are elongated; their hindlimbs look a bit like rabbit legs ending in monkey hands. In galagos, as in rabbits, this elongation of the foot is an adaptation for hopping, and some of the smaller galagos leap acrobatically through trees.

The other group of continental strepsirhines, the subfamily Lorisinae, have gone to the opposite extreme. Lorises are exaggeratedly cautious, slow-moving animals with vice-like hands and feet, which never give up their grasp on one support without securing a firm grip on the next. A loris walking along a branch suggests a small, short-tailed lemur seen in slow motion. Lorises are active at night in the humid tropical forests of Africa and Asia, where they feed on fruit and insects.

The continental strepsirhines have toothcombs and grooming claws like those of Madagascar's lemurs, but they differ in details of ear anatomy. The middle ear of primates (see p. 26) is complex and plays an important part in classification. In the primates of Madagascar, the air-filled middle-ear space is a large, simple chamber that extends sideways below the eardrum. The internal carotid artery (one of the main channels through which blood reaches the brain) runs forwards across the roof of this chamber to enter the braincase. In lorises and galagos, the middle-ear cavity does not extend sideways below the eardrum, and the internal carotid is a thread-like vestige. The job of supplying blood to the brain is taken over by another artery that does not traverse the middle ear. The mouse and dwarf lemurs of Madagascar also have a loris-like arterial arrangement, and some have speculated that they may represent the ancestral stock from which the strepsirhines of continental Africa and Asia evolved. However, molecular evidence suggests that the galago–loris group has no closer ties to cheirogaleids than to the other lemurs.

Tarsiers

Tarsius, the single living representative of the family Tarsiidae, is a puzzling intermediate between strepsirhines and anthropoids. Tarsiers differ from lemurs and resemble anthropoids in their lack of a wet, dog-like snout and in their reduced olfactory apparatus. For these reasons, they are often classified with simians in the suborder Haplorhini. Although tarsiers do not have the enlarged brains and fused lower jaws characteristic of living simians and are therefore classified separately (with other prosimians), they resemble simians in many other anatomical details.

In its embryological development, the fertilised tarsier ovum sinks into the lining of the mother's uterus and becomes surrounded with lakes of maternal blood. In this, it is similar to people, apes and monkeys, but not to lemurs, lorises and galagos, whose developing embryos are walled off from direct contact with the mother's bloodstream. Like the internal carotid artery of anthropoids, that of tarsiers is partly enclosed by an air-filled outpocketing from the front of the middle-ear cavity. Although the eyes of tarsiers are very much enlarged – each eyeball is roughly the size of the brain – they display some simian characteristics. Their retinas have a tiny fovea and lack the tapetum lucidum; and a bony wall, the *postorbital septum* (otherwise found only in simians), is interposed between the eye and the chewing muscles that lie behind it, as it is in our own skulls.

Tarsiers are in the size range of hamsters or kittens. They live in secondary growth in the forests of Borneo, Sumatra, Sulawesi and the Philippines, where they leap about at night in search of animal prey. They prefer to rest on and move among plant stems, trunks and other vertical sup-

Slender loris (*Loris tardigradus*).

Borneo tarsier (*Tarsius bancanus*).

ports, rather than on horizontal branches. Like galagos, tarsiers have elongated ankle bones, from which they take their name (Latin *tarsus* = ankle). Their upright posture and their long hindlimbs give these primates a vaguely human appearance. A similar habit endows the indrids and some of the galagos with a comparable human allure.

Simian primates

The simian primates are divided into two major groups: the platyrrhines (broad-nosed monkeys) of tropical America and the catarrhines (narrow-nosed monkeys and apes) of the Old World. Living catarrhines differ from platyrrhines in features of the teeth and ears. However, the oldest known fossil simians of the Old World resemble the American monkeys in these and other respects.

New World monkeys

The New World monkeys (platyrrhines) are a diverse group, and the evolutionary relationships among them are hard to discern. Some genera can be grouped into fairly distinct clusters of closely related forms, and it is customary to recognise two families: Callitrichidae (marmosets and tamarins) and Cebidae (the remaining New World monkeys).

Marmosets and tamarins · The most distinctive of these groups comprises the marmosets (*Callithrix* and *Cebuella*) and tamarins (*Leontopithecus* and *Saguinus*). These little monkeys are usually regarded as a separate family, the Callitrichidae, but some authorities group them in a subfamily (Callitrichinae) within the family Cebidae. They are notable for their small body size (as little as 100 grams in the pygmy marmoset, *Cebuella*), their relatively small brains, and the sharp, squirrel-like claws on all their digits except the great toe. Their reproductive habits are also distinctive: twins are normally born and the newborn offspring are carried around by their father and their older siblings when their mother is not nursing them.

A large part of the callitrichid diet often consists of gums scraped from the surface of trees, and the small size and claws of marmosets and tamarins may be feeding specialisations. The loss of the third molar teeth and the reproductive peculiarities of callitrichids may also be associated with their small size and distinctive diet. Despite their claws, callitrichids are adept in the trees, and can do all the things that claws were once thought to interfere with, such as leaping and stalking insects among the slender branches of shrubs. This leaves primatologists with no convincing explanation for the loss of claws in the ancestors of euprimates.

Goeldi's monkey (*Callimico goeldii*) occupies a special place among New World monkeys. It resembles marmosets and tamarins in its small body size and the possession of claws, but resembles other New World monkeys in retaining the full set of molar teeth and in having only a single offspring. For this reason, it has sometimes been classified in the family Callitrichidae, sometimes in the Cebidae and sometimes in its own family, Callimiconidae.

Young Goeldi's monkey (*Callimico goeldii*).

Black-handed spider monkey (*Ateles geoffroyi*).

Red howler monkeys (*Alouatta seniculus*).

Night or owl monkey (*Aotus trivirgatus*).

Red uakari (*Cacajao rubicundus*).

Howler monkeys (*Alouatta*) have prehensile tails like those of the atelines and are sometimes classified with them, although they are often placed in their own sub-family Alouattinae. They are more quadrupedal than spider and woolly monkeys and rarely hang from branches. Howler monkeys (named for the sonorous bellowing noises they make with their enlarged voiceboxes) and the rare ateline, the muriqui or woolly spider monkey (*Brachyteles arachnoides*), are the most leaf-eating (folivorous) of the New World monkeys, but they still feed extensively on fruit; none of the platyrrhines is as specialised for eating leaves as are the indrids or some of the Old World monkeys.

Spider and woolly monkeys · Another distinct cluster of three genera, the spider and woolly monkeys (subfamily Atelinae), lies at the opposite extreme of the spectrum of New World monkey adaptations. Atelines are large animals (up to 15 kilograms) with specialised, elongated limbs and long, prehensile tails, which they use in clambering and swinging through the trees, often hanging suspended from branches. The most familiar atelines are the spider monkeys (*Ateles*), in which the tail serves almost as a fifth limb in locomotion and manipulation. The tip of the ateline tail even looks like a fingertip, and is covered with finger-print ridges.

Capuchins, squirrel monkeys, sakis and owl monkeys · The remaining platyrrhine genera are medium-sized quad-rupedal monkeys without any striking specialisations of the limbs. Capuchins (*Cebus*) have a prehensile tail, but it is not as specialised as that of spider, woolly or howler monkeys and has probably evolved independently. Some authorities group capuchins with squirrel monkeys (*Saimiri*) in the sub-family Cebinae, whereas others prefer to place squirrrel monkeys in their own subfamily, Saimiriinae. The sakis (*Pithecia* and *Chiropotes*) and uakaris (*Cacajao*) have distinctive front teeth and are usually set aside in the subfamily Pithe-ciinae; the owl monkey, *Aotus* (subfamily Aotinae), is the only nocturnal simian. Its enlarged eyes are reminiscent of those of *Tarsius*, and their structure suggests that both these nocturnal haplorhines are descended from ancestors that were active during the day.

Old World simians

The living anthropoids of the Old World (catarrhines) can be divided into two clear groups: the tailed, quadrupedal monkeys (cercopithecoids) and the tail-less, arm-swinging apes (hominoids). Human beings are classed with the latter. Apart from the human lineage, the hominoids have not proved to be a very successful group and have been largely replaced by cercopithecoids in Africa and Asia during the past 10 million years.

Old World monkeys · From the neck down, Old World (cercopithecoid) monkeys are less specialised than hominoids. Their chief peculiarity is a pair of calloused buttock-like skin pads, or *ischial callosities*, which support their weight when they sit. The important cercopithecoid specialisations, which may account for their success, lie in their feeding apparatus. Compared with hominoids, cercopithecoids have molars with higher and more pointed cusps, connected by sharp shearing crests. The front lower premolar of cercopithecoids has evolved into an elongated blade that acts as a whetstone, against which the dagger-like upper canine is honed to a keen cutting edge. These adaptations make cercopithecoids effective leaf-eaters and fearsome antagonists in a fight.

The living cercopithecoids are usually divided into two subfamilies – Cercopithecinae (guenons, macaques, mangabeys and baboons) and Colobinae (leaf monkeys) – on the basis of differing feeding adaptations. Colobines are specialised folivores that have evolved stomachs with multiple subdivisions rather like those of a cow. These store leafy forage for decomposition and digestion by bacteria. Like other folivorous mammals, colobines do not digest leaves as such, but rather live off the by-products of the bacterial colonies in their internal compost heaps. Colobines have long, slender hands and feet and their thumbs are small or vestigial. These and other features of the colobine skeleton are paralleled among monkeys and apes that habitually use their hands as hooks in swinging from overhead branches; but colobines seldom do this, and the value of such specialisations to them is unclear.

Cercopithecines lack the colobines' specialised stomachs, and most are principally fruit-eaters (frugivores). Like some rodents, they have cheek pouches. Food items crammed into the pouches while foraging can be extracted and eaten at leisure and in safety. Although all cercopithecines seek safety and shelter in trees, many spend most of their time on the ground. Perhaps the most familiar of the terrestrial cercopithecines are the baboons (*Papio* and *Theropithecus*). These large, long-snouted monkeys are common in the plains and savannas of eastern and southern Africa, where they roam in herds of 50 or more searching for a wide variety of foods – from seeds and grass rhizomes to baby antelope. The forest baboons or drills (*Papio* or *Mandrillus*) of West Africa are famous for the brilliantly coloured faces and behinds of adult males.

In addition to the baboon group, Africa boasts a considerable variety of smaller cercopithecines. Most of these are predominantly tree-dwelling animals in the genus *Cercopithecus*, whose 20-odd species chiefly inhabit tropical forests. Vervets (*Cercopithecus aethiops*) and patas monkeys (*Erythrocebus patas*) are related East African forms with more terrestrial habits. The only cercopithecines found outside Africa are the macaques (*Macaca*), a successful, predominantly Asian, genus that include arboreal and terrestrial types in over a dozen species found as far west as North Africa, as far north as Japan, and east into Indonesia as far as Sulawesi.

The terrestrial habits of many cercopithecines are evident in their vertebral column and limb bones, which approach the forms seen in typical non-primate quadrupeds – for example, a narrow thorax, with a reduced ability to spread the arms and hence a reorientation of shoulder blades and shoulder joints. These changes are particularly noticeable in patas monkeys, which have become fleet, rather greyhound-like terrestrial runners. The terrestrial habits of baboons and macaques are reflected in their relatively short fingers, which, together with their strong and fully opposable thumbs, give the hands a strikingly human appearance.

Apes and humans · Exactly the opposite tendencies are seen in the non-human hominoids, or apes (as distinct from monkeys). There are two groups of apes: the gibbons (family Hylobatidae) and the great apes (chimpanzees, gorillas and orang-utans; family Pongidae). All have elongated arms and fingers and they differ from catarrhine monkeys and resemble human beings in having a wide

Japanese macaques (*Macaca fuscata*).

Young orang-utan (*Pongo pygmaeus*).

Chimpanzee (*Pan troglodytes*).

thorax, reduction of the length of the spine between rib-cage and pelvis, and extremely flexible shoulders, elbows and wrists.

The value of these peculiarities is evident when we watch a gibbon (*Hylobates*) moving through the trees. The animal does not walk on branches on all fours as a macaque does, but swings along underneath them hand over hand. To do this, it needs to be able to rotate its hand through a full 180°, from a pronated (palm down) to a supinated (palm up) position, and to reach out as far as possible directly side-ways. The broad back and the mobile forelimb joints all increase the range of these movements. The shortened lower back aids in keeping the dangling pelvis and hind-limb under control. The tail, no longer needed in balancing on branches, is reduced to a vestige.

All these features of gibbons are found in the larger hominoids as well. However, although human beings and the great apes can swing along gibbon-fashion underneath branches, they do not do so as frequently or as freely. We ourselves are terrestrial bipeds who rarely climb trees as adults, and our short, baboon-like fingers and relatively puny arms are a handicap in arm-swinging.

Orang-utans (*Pongo*) spend virtually all their time in trees, where they do hang and swing below branches; but they are so big and heavy (up to 90 kilograms for males) that they have to be much more cautious than gibbons, and they make far more use of their hindlimbs to support their weight in clambering through the trees. Gorillas (*Gorilla*), with adult males weighing almost 200 kilograms, simply cannot function safely as arboreal animals and spend most of their waking hours feeding on foliage on or near the ground. Chimpanzees (*Pan*) are more gibbon-like in their activity than are the other large hominoids, but even they do not habitually fling themselves through space like trapeze artists, as do gibbons.

The hands of chimpanzees and gorillas show both ter-restrial and arboreal specialisations: although they have long, hooked fingers like those of a gibbon or an orang-utan, they fold them into their palms when on the ground and walk on the backs of their knuckles, which sport thick weight-bearing pads covered with friction ridges.

The peculiar postcranial anatomy of the large hominoids has vividly been interpreted by some biologists as a legacy from a more acrobatic, arm-swinging common ancestor that resembled a modern gibbon. But, here again, compara-tive evidence suggests a different conclusion. The most ape-like limb anatomy among the other living primates is seen in animals that seldom (atelines) or never (lorises) launch themselves into free flight between supports. Among other orders of mammals, only the exceedingly non-acrobatic tree sloths show any striking parallels to hominoids in the structure of the skeleton. This indicates that ape-like traits can evolve as a device for *avoiding* acro-batics. Large arboreal animals cannot leap with impunity across gaps between branches. In order to be able to move prudently and cautiously to a support ahead, while retain-ing a grip on the support behind, such animals might be expected to develop an ape-like elongation and flexibility of the limbs, as well as an ape-like habit of hanging beneath supports (instead of balancing precariously on top). It may hence be that descent from a large arboreal ancestor accounts for the anatomical peculiarities shared by the great apes and humans.

Matt Cartmill

See also 'Classification of primates' (p. 20), 'Conservation of primates' (p. 33), 'Jaws and teeth' (p. 56), 'Diets and guts' (p. 60), 'Primate locomotion and posture' (p. 75), 'Primate reproduction' (p. 86), 'The fossil history of primates' (p. 199), 'Evolution of New World monkeys' (p. 209) and 'Evolution of Old World monkeys' (p. 217)

Conservation of primates

Today, the world's primates – some 236 species – are divided fairly evenly between the island of Madagascar (30 species) and three southern continents: mainland Africa (around 63 species), Asia (63 species), and South and Central America (80 species). Almost all of them live in the tropical and subtropical regions of these continents. Only a few macaques (e.g. the Japanese macaque, *Macaca fuscata*) and leaf-monkeys (e.g. the Hanuman langur, *Presbytis entellus* and snub-nosed langurs, *Rhinopithecus* spp.) live in the temperate zone.

The primate order is notable for its diversity, with 14 different families. The other exclusively or largely tropical mammalian orders – for example, the Dermoptera ('flying lemurs' or colugos), the Tubulidentata (aardvarks) and the Pholidota (pangolins) – contain only one to three families apiece. Primates are also characterised by a dependence on tropical forests. Of the species living in the tropics, 90 per cent are restricted to forest habitats, mainly rain forest.

Primates are not restricted to tropical rain forests because of an intrinsic inability to adapt to other environments. Some African species, such as baboons (*Papio* spp.), the vervet monkey (*Cercopithecus aethiops*), the patas monkey (*Erythrocebus patas*) and the common chimpanzee (*Pan troglo-*

dytes), live in open or lightly wooded savanna. However, none of the living primates in the New World and Asia is adapted to savannas, possibly because of competition with other creatures such as hoofed mammals (ungulates) and rodents. Madagascar had some savanna, or savanna woodland, species, but these are now extinct.

Much of the diversity of primates is at risk, with many species now existing as small and declining populations. More than half of all primate species are in jeopardy and one in five may not last into the next century if conservation measures are not undertaken at once (Box 1). The three major threats to primate populations today are destruction of forest habitats, hunting and live capture for trade.

Habitat destruction

Tropical forests are being cut down at a rate of approximately 12 to 22 million hectares per year. Habitat destruction occurs most notably through shifting slash-and-burn agriculture, through the removal of trees for charcoal and firewood, through industrial logging and mining, and through hydroelectric projects. Species that have been profoundly affected by destruction of their habitats include the muriqui (*Brachyteles arachnoides*) of the Atlantic forests of eastern Brazil, the mountain gorilla (*Gorilla gorilla beringei*) of Rwanda, Uganda and Zaire, and the lion-tailed macaque (*Macaca silenus*) of southern India.

Wild populations of the muriqui in Brazil are now only between 400 and 500 individuals, thus making it one of the most endangered primate species in the world. The remaining habitat of this monkey is at risk from fire destroying isolated reserves and from squatters moving into protected areas. The animal itself is still shot by poachers.

The 400 or so mountain gorillas left in the world are confined to a small area at the junction between Rwanda, Uganda and Zaire and are separated into two populations by a barrier of cultivated land. Over one-third of the area originally set aside to conserve the mountain gorilla has since been converted to farmland and the pressure to convert more land will continue as long as human population growth in the region remains at an annual rate of 3 to 4 per cent. However, international conservation organisations have been working with the three governments concerned to counteract this pressure and the problems of poaching. Populations of mountain gorillas may now be beginning to increase in response to these efforts, and some conservationists think that this species is faring better than most other highly endangered primates.

Wild populations of lion-tailed macaques are currently between 400 and 4000 individuals, making this one of the

1. SOME ENDANGERED PRIMATES

Species	Range
PROSIMIAS	
Allocebus trichotis (hairy-eared dwarf lemur)	Tiny portion of rain forest in northeastern Madagascar
Daubentonia madagascariensis (aye-aye)	Restricted areas of rain forest, eastern coast of Madagascar
Hapalemur aureus (golden bamboo lemur) and *H. simus* (greater bamboo lemur)	Restricted areas of rain forest, southeastern Madagascar
Propithecus diadema perrieri (Perrier's sifaka)	Tiny area in northeastern Madagascar
SIMIANS	
Brachyteles arachnoides (muriqui)	Restricted areas of remnant forests of southeastern Brazil, from Espirito Santo to São Paulo states
Colobus badius gordonorum (red colobus)	Uzungwa Mountains and Magombera Forest Reserve, Tanzania
Gorilla gorilla beringei (mountain gorilla)	Virunga Volcanoes of Zaire, Rwanda and Uganda; Bwindi Forest, Uganda
Leontopithecus chrysomelas (golden-headed lion tamarin), *L. chrysopygus* (golden-rumped lion tamarin), *L. rosalia* (golden lion tamarin) and *L. caissara* (black-faced lion tamarin)	Lowland forest of southeastern Brazil
Rhinopithecus roxellanae (golden snub-nosed monkey)	Mountains of western and central China
Rhinopithecus avunculus (Tonkin snub-nosed monkey)	North Vietnam
Simias concolor (simakobu)	Mentawai Islands off Sumatra, Indonesia

Two endangered primates: (above) the muriqui of the Atlantic Forest, Brazil, and (below) the golden bamboo lemur of southeastern Madagascar.

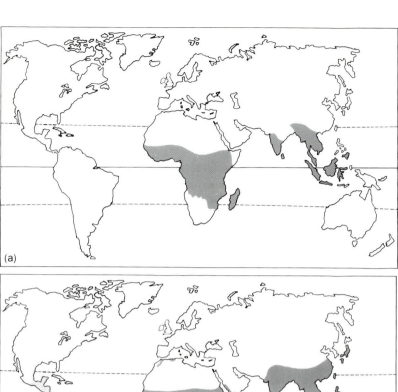

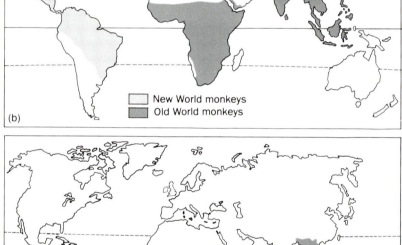

New World monkeys
Old World monkeys

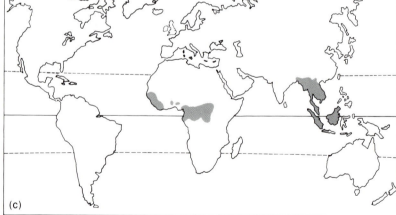

Distribution of the major groups of modern primates: (a) prosimians; (b) Old and New World monkeys; (c) apes.

most endangered primates in Asia. Its habitat has been destroyed by invading human settlements and by the conversion of forests to tree plantations, producing areas that lion-tailed macaques can neither feed in nor traverse to find other populations isolated by cultivation. Tree felling to make clearings, road construction, cultivation, firewood removal and proposed hydroelectric projects all threaten the remaining lion-tailed macaques with extinction.

Hunting

Although habitat destruction is the major threat to primate populations, hunting is a serious factor as well. Human predation of primates involves hunting them for food or because they are agricultural pests and using them as bait to trap other animals. Primates are also killed for their body parts for use as ornaments or medicinal purposes. Hunting

The black-capped capuchin (*Cebus apella*) is hunted for food along the Brazil/Surinam border.

pressure is especially severe in Amazonia and in the Upper Guinean and Zaire Basin forests of West and Central Africa. Here, hunting for sale in the marketplace is usually a more serious factor than subsistence hunting.

Species particularly threatened by hunting for food are spider monkeys (*Ateles* spp.) and woolly monkeys (*Lagothrix* spp.) of Amazonia, and the drill (*Papio (Mandrillus) leucophaeus*) of West Africa. Woolly monkeys and spider monkeys are the largest primates in Amazonia and in many places are much hunted for food. Many African primates, such as guenons (*Cercopithecus* spp.), mangabeys (*Cercocebus* spp.), and mandrills (*Papio (Mandrillus)* spp.), are also hunted, even though some of them are endangered.

In South and Central America, primates are used as bait to catch fish, turtles and large cats. The black-headed uakari (*Cacajao melanocephalus*), the mantled howler (*Alouatta palliata*) and the white-browed spider monkey (*Ateles belzebuth marginatus*) are all utilised in this way. Some species are also hunted for their skin, fur or other body parts for decorative or medicinal purposes. This is a less-pervasive threat than other kinds of primate hunting, but it can have a severe effect on rare or endangered species, such as the golden monkey (*Cercopithecus mitis kandti*) or the mountain gorilla, both found in the Virunga Volcanoes of Rwanda, Zaire and Uganda.

Hunting of primates as agricultural pests mainly affects the more adaptable and partly terrestrial primates such as baboons, vervets and macaques. Its effects on primate populations are poorly understood. However, major extermination programmes like those once carried out in Uganda and Sierra Leone, where up to 19 000 primates were killed each year, indicate that such hunting can be a major local cause of primate decline.

Live capture

The third major threat to primates – capture of live primates for local pet markets or for export to international markets – has decreased in recent years, but is still an important factor in the decline of populations. Large-scale use of primates in biomedical research started in the late nineteenth and early twentieth centuries, and, by the late 1950s and early 1960s, around 200 000 primates were being imported into the United States alone each year. This was estimated to be about one-half of the world's imports of primates at that time. Fortunately, the demand for wild-caught primates has decreased substantially in the past 25 years. For example, the United States imported 15 000 primates in 1984 and 13 790 in 1985.

Four factors have contributed to this decrease. First, export bans were introduced by many countries in the mid-1970s. Simultaneously, importing countries began implementing strict quarantine procedures, which made costs prohibitively high. In addition, demand for laboratory animals decreased as other methods of testing and production were developed. Finally, domestic and international legislation served to reduce both supply and demand. The Convention on International Trade in Endangered Species of Wild Fauna and Flora (CITES) has been particularly useful in terms of regulating the trade in primates.

Although this trade is now fairly well controlled, there is still illicit trading in, for example, chimpanzees, golden-headed lion tamarins (*Leontopithecus chrysomelas*), white-cheeked gibbons (*Hylobates concolor*) and orang-utans (*Pongo pygmaeus*). The golden-headed lion tamarin has been especi-

Captured baby orang-utans on display in Kalimantan, Indonesia.

2. STUDYING PRIMATES IN THE WILD

Primates are studied in the wild by researchers from several disciplines, notably anthropology, psychology and biology. The objectives of primate field studies vary widely. For instance, data from wild primates have been used to reconstruct the lifestyles of our ancestors, to shed light on 'human nature', to help explain how some tropical plants disperse their seeds or pollinate their flowers, and to help develop conservation plans for tropical forests. Diverse as the goals of these studies are, the methods used almost always have three features in common: observations are made over *long periods of time* on *individually identified animals* that have been *habituated to the presence of an observer*.

New techniques in field research have made possible studies of the relationship between primate behaviour and biology. In the early days, behaviour was simply described as it occurred. A notebook and pencil are still essential pieces of equipment, and the careful description of behaviour is as important now as it was 50 years ago. However, several ways of sampling behaviour systematically and quantitatively have been developed in the

past 30 years. For example, with scan sampling the behaviour of several individuals is recorded at predetermined intervals; with focal sampling, the behaviour of a single individual is recorded.

Each of these techniques has advantages and drawbacks, and decisions about which one to use depend on the kinds of questions the researcher hopes to answer as well as on working conditions.

In the past few years, the use of box traps, blowpipes and dart guns, in conjunction with new anaesthetics, has made it possible to capture animals safely. Collars containing radios have made it easier to find and follow certain species, particularly those active at night, and computer technology has speeded up the rate at which data can be recorded and stored.

The development of safe techniques for capturing animals is valuable because it helps to integrate the study of primate biology and behaviour: wild individuals held briefly in captivity can be weighed and measured, their age can be estimated from the condition of their teeth, blood samples can be taken, and even the rate at which

they use up energy (their basal metabolic rate) can be measured.

Information of this kind is making it possible to address a new range of issues. For instance, how does the social structure of a population influence its genetic structure, and how are the members of a social group related to one another genetically? Are socially high-ranking animals generally healthier or better nourished than low-ranking ones? What are the energetic costs of reproduction, and how do these costs affect the timing of reproduction and a mother's treatment of her young?

Safe capture methods also have important implications for conservation, because they facilitate the movement, or *translocation*, of primate populations threatened with extinction because of habitat destruction or because, living near human habitation, they become agricultural pests. Such populations – for example, the baboons at Gilgil in Kenya that took to raiding corn from fields next to their range – can often be moved successfully to more remote areas where their habitat is intact and they do not run the risk of being eliminated as pests.

A.F. Richard

ally affected by illegal trade in recent years. More than 700 orangs have been recorded in Taiwan. The international trade in primates is not as significant a threat as is habitat destruction, but it can be quite detrimental to particular species, especially if they are endangered or vulnerable, like the cotton-top tamarin (*Saquinus oedipus*) or chimpanzees. Capture of primates for the local pet trade does not by itself constitute a serious threat to most species. However, if a species is also affected by habitat destruction and hunting, the sale of animals as pets for local people can contribute significantly to the decline of the species. This has happened, for instance, to the woolly monkey (*Lagothrix lagotricha*) in Amazonia.

The effects of live capture of primates, either for export or for the local market, are made worse by traditional capture methods that involve shooting the mother (and sometimes other adults as well) to obtain infants. This method of capture and subsequent deaths during transport may mean that 5 to 10 primates die for every one entering the market.

Primate conservation

Conservationists are using various approaches in an attempt to reverse the decline in primate populations: field surveys to determine the status of poorly known primates,

conservation-oriented research on endangered species to provide the data on behaviour and ecology needed for long-term management. There is increasing protection of primate species in parks and reserves with important populations, but new protected areas need to be established. Captive breeding has a role as well (Box 3). This work is accompanied by local educational campaigns designed to increase public awareness of the importance of primates and their habitats, and by the training of local people in techniques of primate conservation. Such initiatives have led to an expansion of the worldwide network of primate conservationists, and a new emphasis on increased communication between field researchers and specialists in zoos and research institutions.

The fundamental objective of modern primate conservation is to encourage an awareness of its importance in tropical countries and to improve the local capacity to conserve primates and their habitats. In this way, today's conservationists hope to improve the chances of all primate species surviving into the twenty-first century and, with good fortune, much longer. The activities of *Homo sapiens*, the most successful of all primates, have caused most of the problems for non-human primates. Now, it is only with the positive involvement of humans that our closest relatives will be able to survive.

Russell A. Mittermeier
Eleanor J. Sterling

3. BREEDING PRIMATES IN CAPTIVITY

Conservation programmes depend on the protection of natural habitats through a well-designed system of reserves. However, it has become increasingly clear that the breeding of endangered species in captivity has a valuable supporting part to play within the general framework of conservation biology. Indeed, it is now widely accepted that conservation has become a question of overall management of species populations in the wild and in captivity.

Because of the drastic reduction and fragmentation of original habitat areas, the apparent distinction between natural and captive populations has become increasingly blurred. Human activities have taken their toll on environments everywhere and the difference between wild and captive primates is in many respects simply one of degree of interference. For example, the need for genetic monitoring and management of small residual populations in reserves is just as pressing as for captive stocks.

Breeding of endangered species in captivity – mainly in zoos, but also in other institutions – can contribute to conservation in at least four ways. First, by displaying rare species in a suitable context, zoos can increase public awareness of conservation issues. This is directly connected with the second task of education, especially through schools and universities. Third, scientific research based on captive animals can contribute directly to conservation programmes, notably by providing baseline information on reproductive patterns and genetic features. Last, but not least, captive-bred populations can provide an insurance policy against extinction in the wild and can release stocks for specific reintroduction programmes. Good zoos, such as that maintained by the Jersey Wildlife Preservation Trust in the Channel Islands (UK), are specifically devoted to endangered species and to promoting international conservation efforts.

The capacity of any individual zoo is strictly limited, the average area being only 20 hectares, and co-operation between zoos to establish viable populations of selected species is therefore crucial. Even so, given that the total area covered by world zoos is about 12 000 hectares, careful choice of species for captive-breeding programmes remains essential.

About a third of the roughly 230 modern primate species are already listed in the *Red Data Book* published by the International Union for the Conservation of Nature (IUCN). Of these, according to a recent survey, 45 are currently held in world zoos. Only 22 species, however, are represented by total captive populations of at least 30 individuals.

Successful breeding programmes (those with birth rates exceeding death rates)

currently exist for only 15 of these: the fat-tailed dwarf lemur (*Cheirogaleus medius*), the red-fronted lemur (*Lemur fulvus rufus*), the cotton-top tamarin (*Saguinus oedipus*), the golden lion tamarin (*Leontopithecus rosalia*), Goeldi's monkey (*Callimico goeldii*), the black-handed spider monkey (*Ateles geoffroyi*), the black spider monkey (*A. paniscus*), the lion-tailed macaque (*Macaca silenus*), the Barbary macaque (*M. sylvanus*), the white-cheeked gibbon (*Hylobates concolor*), the orang-utan (*Pongo pygmaeus*), the pygmy chimpanzee or bonobo (*Pan paniscus*), the common chimpanzee (*P. troglodytes*) and the gorilla (*Gorilla gorilla*).

Missing from this list, however, are several of the most endangered primate species – for example, the indri (*Indri indri*), the aye-aye (*Daubentonia madagascariensis*), the muriqui or woolly spider monkey (*Brachyteles arachnoides*) and the golden snub-nosed monkey (*Rhinopithecus roxellanae*). So much needs to be done.

Leading zoos already co-operate closely by exchanging animals for breeding, by maintaining studbooks for individual species and by promoting research. They also contribute to central computer data bases, including ISIS (International Species Inventory System) and ARKS (Animal Records Keeping System), and co-operate closely with the Captive Breeding Group of IUCN.

Reintroductions of captive-bred primates to the wild have as yet been few, although the need for such initiatives will doubtless increase as the pressures on dwindling wild populations become more acute. The prime example of a well-planned introduction programme so far is that developed for the golden lion tamarin in Brazil.

The current captive population of more than 500 individuals (95 per cent bred in

captivity) of this species is about twice the size of the estimated wild population. In collaboration with the Rio de Janeiro Primate Center, a programme of progressive release of captive-bred tamarins in the Poço das Antas Reserve in Rio de Janeiro State has been under way since 1984. Sixteen zoos worldwide, including the National Zoological Park (Washington, DC), the Los Angeles Zoo, the Brookfield Zoo (Chicago), the Frankfurt Zoo (Germany), the Skansen Aquarium (Sweden) and the Jersey Zoo (UK), have contributed animals to the release programme.

Reintroduction of the captive-bred tamarins has been conducted within a carefully designed framework that has included behavioural and ecological investigation of the natural tamarins in the reserve, genetic monitoring of the captive population, follow-up of the released animals, and provision of an effective local education programme.

The survival rate of the first animals released was low, but refinement of the procedure to include special training of tamarins before and after release has led to improved results. By the end of 1990, the release of 61 captive-bred tamarins into the Poço das Antas Reserve had increased the population by 46, although the breeding of captive-bred animals after release had not quite balanced losses from predation and disease.

Publicity surrounding the release of the golden lion tamarins has generated numerous beneficial spin-offs, including the participation of local landowners in a scheme to increase the area of forest available for the total population. However, it has cost about US$22 000 for every tamarin added to the natural population. Properly planned reintroduction programmes for primates are thus major undertakings requiring a substantial investment of resources.   *Robert Martin*

The lion tamarin island at Jersey Zoo.

Part Two

The life of primates

Most modern primates live in tropical or subtropical forests and have many adaptations for life in trees. Such arboreal behaviour probably reflects the lifestyle of a common ancestor that lived towards the end of the Cretaceous period, at least 70 million years ago. Only a few species today — notably some Old World simian primates, including humans — have become ground-dwellers. Terrestrial behaviour is a secondary development in primate evolution and seems to be associated with sexual dimorphism (differences in body size between males and females) in Old World simians (**2.3**).

All living primates, except humans, have the big toe opposed to the other four, which allows the foot to act like a pincer. This is doubtless related to an original adaptation for grasping tree branches. The fact that our big toe cannot grasp shows that secondary adaptation for terrestrial life is at a greater extreme in humans than in any other primate. As humans have a highly specialised pattern of locomotion — striding bipedalism (**2.8** and **2.9**) — this is hardly surprising. Humans have various other special adaptations as well, such as sweating (**2.2**).

All living primates have relatively large, forward-facing eyes associated with developments in the brain for three-dimensional vision (**3.1**). This is obviously useful for active movement in trees, whether by arm-swinging, leaping, or running along branches (**2.8**). The emphasis on vision among primates has long been recognised and led to the 'arboreal theory' of primate evolution. This has been criticised on the grounds that other arboreal mammals such as squirrels do not have close-set eyes or opposable digits. A modified version, the 'arboreal predation theory', was therefore proposed. According to this, ancestral primates were adapted for preying on insects, which they hunted at night using their large, forward-facing eyes (**1.3**).

Ancestral primates may, however, have been adapted for foraging among lianas and in the outermost parts of trees, occupying the 'fine-branch niche', where a grasping foot would have been useful. Unlike most other mammals, primates usually have flat nails instead of claws on their fingers and toes. The switch from claws to nails is probably an adaptation for gripping narrow supports, as on thicker branches the grappling action of claws is more effective. Primates have a relatively primitive skeleton with little sign of the loss or fusion of elements that is common among terrestrial mammals. The key adaptation in the origin of modern primates may not have been a shift from the ground to the trees but rather a shift within trees out into the fine branches.

Living primates range in average weight from about 60 grams to about 120 kilograms and this accounts for many of the differences among species

A male chimpanzee eating figs, Gombe National Park, Tanzania.

(**2.1**). Small-bodied species need food with a high energy yield. Most primates consume at least some fruit but a general trend is recognisable: small species typically have a diet of arthropods and fruits (or other carbohydrate-containing plant products, such as gums), medium-sized species a fruit-dominated diet and large species eat a significant proportion of leaves (**2.5**). There are some exceptions to this trend. For example, small species can tolerate a low-energy diet if they have a low metabolic rate and large species may eat high-energy food if enough is available.

Primates are usually very selective in their choice of plant food because many plant parts, especially leaves, are protected by toxins (**2.6**). Unripe fruits may also contain toxins, which is why primates are so choosey about picking only the ripest fruits. The use of fire by ancient humans may have served to detoxify plant foods (**2.7**).

The diversity of primate diets is matched by diversity in primate teeth. One dental feature is shared by all living primates: the number of incisors has been reduced to a maximum of two in each tooth row and these teeth are arranged transversely instead of in a longitudinal row, as in primitive mammals (**2.4**). This reflects the fact that primates do not need to grasp with their teeth; food is seized with the hands instead.

In non-human primates, the hand cannot grasp as well as the foot, but all primates use their hands for holding things. The prehensile capacity of the hand is best developed in terrestrial primates, particularly humans. Humans show a curious reversal of the condition found in tree-dwelling primates: the grasping function of the foot has been suppressed whereas the fine control of the hand grip has increased to the point where tools can be made and used.

Many aspects of reproduction, such as the feedback system of sex hormones (**2.11**), show a common pattern in all mammals. Primates have one distinctive reproductive characteristic: they breed slowly (**2.10**, **2.12** and **2.13**). They produce few offspring in a given period, emphasising quality rather than quantity. Some primates produce two or three infants but most have only one at a time, and development is always relatively slow. Sexual maturity is achieved rather late, gestation periods are quite long and intervals between births are also usually extended. All these factors combine to make primates among the slowest breeders, relative to body size, among mammals. To put it another way, primates invest only a small proportion of their daily resources in reproduction. This may reflect their evolution in tropical rain forests where selection favours slow breeding (**2.12**).

Even though primates invest a rather small proportion of resources in reproduction, they devote great care to their infants. Infants are usually carried by a parent — usually the mother but sometimes the father — for a long time after birth. When an infant is clinging to the parent's fur, its grasping big toe has yet another use.

Body size and energy requirements

Primates have a wide range of body weights. The largest primate, the gorilla, has an average weight of 117 kilograms, over 1800 times heavier than the two smallest primates – Demidoff's dwarf bushbaby (*Galago demidovii*, 65 grams) and the lesser mouse lemur (*Microcebus murinus*, 66 grams). If we consider the two suborders of the Primates separately, the simians (monkeys, apes and humans) show a range of body size almost as great as that of the primates as a whole – from 117 kilograms for the gorilla to 72 grams for the pygmy marmoset (*Cebuella pygmaea*). By contrast, the largest of the living prosimians (lemurs, lorises and tarsiers), the indri (*Indri indri*), has a weight of around 6 kilograms; it is 92 times the size of the smallest prosimians (the dwarf bushbaby and the lesser mouse lemur).

Underlying these figures is a close relationship between body weight and lifestyle. For example, all nocturnal primates, with the exception of the aberrant aye-aye (*Daubentonia madagascariensis*) of Madagascar, weigh less than 1 kilogram. Insectivorous primates weigh less than 250 grams whereas largely folivorous (leaf-eating) species are typically much larger. In addition, few large-bodied primates live mainly in trees; nearly all primates in excess of 10 kilograms spend most of their time on the ground.

Many of the relationships between body weight and lifestyle are best understood in the context of a broader relationship between mammalian body weight and energy requirements. This relationship, known as *Kleiber's law*, is described by the equation

$$BMR = kW_B^{0.75}$$

where BMR is the basal metabolic rate (the rate at which energy obtained from food is used by a resting animal in its thermoneutral zone – where it does not need to use extra energy either for warming or for cooling itself), k is a constant and W_B is body weight. Because the exponent (0.75) is less than 1, Kleiber's law indicates that, although larger mammals obviously require more energy, smaller mammals have higher basal metabolic rates per unit body weight.

Size and diet

This relationship has a direct effect on the dietary habits of primates and hence on their time of activity. The higher metabolic rate per unit body weight in smaller-bodied animals means that they need more energy-rich food than larger animals with lower metabolic requirements per unit body weight. Small primates (below around 250 grams) all have a diet of insects and fruits or gums rich in carbohydrates. Efficient folivory is typically confined to larger primates at least 5 kilograms in weight. This is because

leaves are relatively low-energy foods – they have high levels of fibre and cellulose and they also often contain toxic compounds. Without special adaptations, smaller animals cannot sustain themselves on leaves because they cannot process enough leaves to extract the energy needed to support their relatively high metabolic rates. Not only are their guts too small but the time taken by food to pass through is too short. Larger-bodied primates cannot sustain themselves on insects because they cannot find enough in a day (or night) to support their higher total metabolic requirements.

The need for high-energy food might put smaller-bodied primates in direct competition with forest birds, but such competition is avoided by the nocturnal lifestyle of most small-bodied primates (and other forest mammals). Birds need to fly, and as a result have to be relatively small. Only primates weighing more than about 1 kilogram (such as most simians) can avoid direct competition for food with birds and can become diurnal. The evolution of the simians therefore probably involved both an increase in body size and a transition from a night-time to a day-time lifestyle.

A larger body does not necessarily demand a low-energy diet, but it does give the animal the opportunity of subsisting on such a diet. For any weight, there is considerable variation in basal metabolic rates around the value predicted by Kleiber's law. This variation in BMR can be correlated with either the diet or the lifestyle (arboreal or terrestrial) of the animal. Most folivorous mammals have a

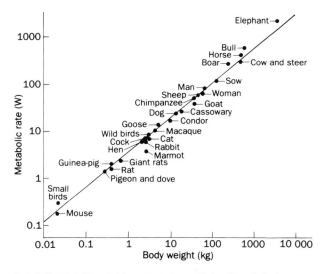

Metabolic rates (in watts) for mammals and birds, when plotted against body mass on logarithmic coordinates, tend to fall along a straight line. As predicted by the Kleiber equation (see text), smaller mammals have higher basal metabolic rates per unit body weight than do larger mammals. The metabolic rate for the average adult human is as expected for his or her body weight.

1. SCALING

When comparing different species of primate the *scaling effects* of body size need to be taken into account. For any feature, such as the size of the brain, it is obvious that there will be a progressive increase as body size increases. If we wish to recognise any adaptations of individual species, we might restrict comparisons to species of the same body size. The problem is that this greatly limits the number of comparisons that can be made.

Another approach is to estimate the effect of body size and 'remove' this factor so that specialised adaptations become recognisable. If we compare a small-bodied arboreal species with a large-bodied terrestrial species, how can we separate the effect of the difference in body size from differences caused by life in the trees rather than life on the ground?

A feature that we wish to study may increase in direct proportion to body size (*isometry*). We can then take a ratio of that feature to body size to eliminate the size effect. Isometric scaling is the exception rather than the rule in primate biology and examples are few. The size of the lungs or the heart shows direct proportional scaling to body size as does the volume of blood circulating in the body; this represents a standard proportion of body weight — about 10 per cent.

The weight of the skeleton also scales isometrically to body weight and typically accounts for about 7 per cent of total body weight in primates. In this respect, primates differ from typical terrestrial mammals, whose skeletons represent only 6 per cent of body weight. The relative increase in primates is because they have longer limbs than other mammals, doubtless because they are adapted for life in trees.

In most cases, however, scaling to body size is non-linear (*allometric*). In other words, the proportional relationship between a given character and body size

changes progressively with increasing body size.

One of the most striking examples of allometry is the size of the eye. In primate species of different body sizes there is a general tendency for the volume of the eye to increase as body size increases, but with the eye representing an ever-decreasing proportion of total body volume. For this reason, a simple ratio between eye size and body size will not remove the effect of body size. This makes comparisons difficult.

For instance, a nocturnal primate of a given body size typically has larger eyes than does a diurnal primate of the same size. However, allometric scaling means that the ratio of eye size to body size will be the same in large-bodied nocturnal primates as in small-bodied diurnal primates. So, if we do not remove the non-linear scaling influence of body size, primates with very different adaptations cannot be distinguished.

The scaling effects that apply to most features of the primate body can be taken into account by applying the allometric formula

$$Y = kX^{\alpha}$$

(where X is body size, Y is the size of the feature of interest, k is the allometric coefficient and α is the allometric exponent).

This formula can be converted to a linear relationship by changing it into a logarithmic form:

$$\log Y = \alpha \log X + \log k$$

It is then relatively simple to determine a straight line which provides a convenient description of the general trend for Y to increase with body size (X); see p. 41.

Having determined a best-fit line for a double logarithmic plot of, for example, brain size against body size, the scaling effects of body size can be separated from

the special adaptations of individual species. The best-fit line represents the general scaling trend and the 'expected' size of the brain for any given species can be taken as its size — as indicated by the line — for the body weight of that species.

The special adaptations of individual species are indicated by positive (upward) or negative (downward) deviations from the line. In comparison to other primates, for example, humans stand out with a far larger brain size than expected for their body size. The vertical distance of any point from the line (its *residual value*) gives a measure of the special adaptation concerned.

An *index* or *quotient value* for each species can be calculated by dividing the actual value of a dimension by its expected value. This gives a ratio that is now freed from the effect of body size, and is the basis for calculating *encephalisation quotients* (EQs) for relative brain size. Compared with the general scaling trend for placental mammals, humans have a brain size about five times larger than expected for their body size (EQ = 5). The same procedure can be applied to many different biological features — for example, in calculating the relative length of the gestation period.

In these examples, allometric scaling is considered only in the context of comparisons between species (*interspecific scaling*). The points on the graph are average values for body size and for the size of a particular feature, such as the brain, across adults of a species.

Scaling can also be used for studying relationships within species (*intraspecific scaling*). Non-linear scaling is commonly found in the growth of features during an individual's development (*ontogenetic scaling*) and when adults of different body sizes are compared.

Allometric relationships can also be used as a basis for prediction. One of the best examples of this is given by the estimation of body size for fossil species, which is essential if they are to be included in quantitative comparisons on the same footing as are living species.

For example, a best-fit line can be determined for the relationship between a dental dimension (such as the length of a given cheek tooth) and body size in living primates and that relationship can then be used to estimate body size from tooth size for fossils. These estimates of body size can then be used, for example, to investigate the scaling of brain to body size in fossil primates. Encephalisation quotients for fossil primates calculated in this way show that the relative size of the brain has increased in all lineages during primate evolution.

Robert Martin

Slender loris   Cotton-top tamarin   Aye-aye   Black-capped capuchin

Nocturnal primates generally have larger eyes than diurnal primates — if body weight is held constant. For example, among small primates the nocturnal slender loris (*Loris tardigradus*; weight *c.* 300 g) clearly has larger eyes than the diurnal cotton-top tamarin (*Saguinus oedipus*; weight *c.* 400 g). Similarly, among medium-sized primates the nocturnal aye-aye (*Daubentonia madagascariensis*; weight *c.* 3 kg) has larger eyes than the diurnal black-capped capuchin (*Cebus apella*; weight *c.* 3 kg). Relative to the size of the face, however, the medium-sized aye-aye has eyes no larger than those of the small tamarin. This is because the size of the eye increases at a slower rate than does the overall size of the body. Other things being equal, therefore, the ratio between eye size and body size must decrease with increasing body size. For this reason, the scaling effect of body size must be taken into account when comparing species of different body sizes. Only then does it become clear that — relative to its body size — the aye-aye does have larger eyes than the cotton-top tamarin.

See also 'Primate brains and senses' (p. 109)

low BMR relative to body size and the degree of BMR depression is related to the proportion of leaves in the diet. Folivorous primates should have lower basal metabolic rates than primates with other diets. Arboreal species have a muscle mass that makes up a smaller proportion of the total body mass of the animal than is the case for terrestrial species, and low basal metabolic rates are associated with a muscle mass less than a third of body mass. The slow lorises (*Nycticebus*) and the potto (*Perodicticus potto*) are examples of prosimian primates that do not eat leaves, but have relatively low metabolic rates and muscles masses for their body sizes.

A relatively low BMR (as in the potto) is also correlated with a poor ability to regulate body temperature and a reduced *metabolic scope* (the ratio between the maximal rate of metabolism that can be sustained and the basal rate). It is also most probably associated with a constraint on mobility and a relatively small brain. This last association is particularly strong in the Old World monkeys, where the highly folivorous colobines (leaf monkeys) have relatively smaller brains than do the primarily fruit-eating cercopithecines, such as guenons and vervets.

Size and reproduction

Low metabolic rates are associated with a decrease in reproductive potential and the main advantage of a high metabolic rate may well be an increase in the potential for reproduction. In placental mammals as a whole, species with a high metabolic rate have a shorter gestation time, an increase in the rate of postnatal growth and an increase in the number of young born. All of these factors increase the potential for rapid population growth. Not enough is known of primate metabolism and reproduction to test the applicability of this relationship. However, it is true that pottos and slow lorises, which have extremely low metabolic rates, have the longest gestation lengths, relative to their body weights, of the 70 primate species for which information is available.

The slow loris (*Nycticebus coucang*) has an exceptionally low basal metabolic rate for its body size.

Size and locomotion

Body weight and the efficiency of terrestrial locomotion are also closely related. Small animals need relatively more oxygen per unit speed than larger animals. Studies of terrestrial mammals in general give the relationship

$$M_{run} = 0.533\ W_B^{-0.316}$$

between the energy consumed in locomotion M_{run} (measured in millilitres of oxygen consumed per metre covered per kilogram of body weight) and body weight (W_B). The negative exponent (-0.316) indicates that larger animals are more efficient at terrestrial locomotion than are smaller ones.

Humans, as well as other primates, fit this general mammalian relationship, suggesting that there was no energetic disadvantage in the change to bipedalism during human evolution. In fact, at walking speeds human bipedalism is significantly more efficient than ape quadrupedalism.

Although larger primates are energetically more efficient than smaller ones in terrestrial locomotion, it does not necessarily follow that they are more efficient in arboreal locomotion. The reason for this is that arboreal locomotion

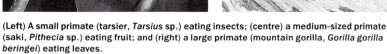

(Left) A small primate (tarsier, *Tarsius* sp.) eating insects; (centre) a medium-sized primate (saki, *Pithecia* sp.) eating fruit; and (right) a large primate (mountain gorilla, *Gorilla gorilla beringei*) eating leaves.

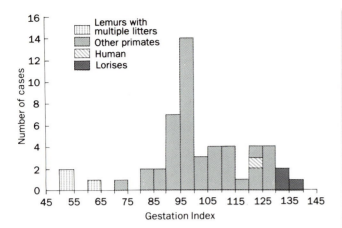

A low metabolic rate is associated with slow development of the fetus. Primates with a low metabolic rate will therefore tend to produce relatively small offspring, unless the gestation period is extended. Comparisons must, of course, take the mother's body size into account.

The length of the gestation period can be corrected for the effects of body size by taking the residual values (the distances above or below the best-fit line) for the scaling relationship between gestation and maternal body size. The residual value can be expressed as a percentage relative to the 'expected value' for the maternal body size of a species. This percentage value – the *gestation index* – will be 100 per cent for a species lying on the line, greater than 100 per cent for one above the line and less than 100 per cent for one below the line.

This histogram shows the distribution of gestation periods in primates after appropriate adjustment. Although humans have the longest gestation period of any living primate in absolute terms, correction for the effects of body size shows that slow-climbing lorises – the slender loris (*Loris tardigradus*), slow lorises (*Nycticebus*) and the potto (*Perodicticus potto*) – in fact have the longest gestation periods in relative terms. These prosimians have low basal metabolic rates, so their long pregnancies (about 35% longer than expected) may compensate for the limitation this sets on the pace of fetal growth. The shortest gestation periods, relative to maternal body size, are in the fast-breeding lemurs with multiple litters, such as dwarf lemurs (*Cheirogaleus*), mouse lemurs (*Microcebus*) and the ruffed or variegated lemur (*Varecia variegata*). These primates have gestation periods about 50 per cent shorter than expected.

involves movement not only in a horizontal plane but also a vertical one. The amount of energy required per unit body mass to move vertically is independent of size: it is about the same in both small and large animals.

Because the energetic cost of horizontal locomotion per unit body mass is much greater in smaller than in larger animals, the amount of energy required by a small animal to climb a particular distance is relatively small compared to the energy needed to move horizontally. In larger animals, climbing can be two to three times more costly in energy terms than horizontal locomotion, a relationship that may explain why arboreality is largely confined to smaller primates. The obvious exception to this pattern is the arboreal orang-utan – the largest arboreal mammal with an approximate average body weight of 55 kilograms. It is, however, both highly specialised in its anatomy and fairly lethargic, climbing slowly and deliberately.

Such physical correlates of size and weight provide limits to the lifestyle available to individual primate species and are therefore fundamental to any understanding of primate evolution.

L.C. Aiello

2. HUMAN BODY SIZE AND ENERGY

In relation to other primates, humans have relatively large bodies. Based on a sample of 149 human populations from around the world, the average human weight is 57 kilograms (male average, 61 kilograms; female average, 53 kilograms). Among the heaviest people are European males, with average weights as high as 80 kilograms, while among the lightest are females from African and Australian pygmoid populations with average weights as low as 37 kilograms.

In relation to stature, the heaviest human groups weigh as much as 136 per cent of their expected weight for stature and include native American females from North and South America. The lightest people in relation to stature are the Nilotic males from the Sudan, who weigh on average only 75 per cent of their expected weight for stature.

Much of this variation in body size in humans is related to the conditions in which people live and particularly to heat and cold tolerance. For example, body weight in humans generally increases with decreasing mean annual temperature.

In hot climates, humans are small in size (both short in stature and light in weight) or have low body weights for their statures. Both of these conditions increase the surface area of the body in relation to body volume and thereby maximise the area over which the heat generated in the core of the body can be dissipated.

Conversely, in cold climates humans will tend to be large in body size with generous layers of subcutaneous fat. The fat layer acts as insulation and the large body size decreases the surface area of the body in relation to the core volume, thereby reducing the area over which heat generated in the core can be dissipated. How much these relationships are genetically determined and how much environmentally determined is still a matter of debate.

Other factors are also important in determining human body size. One of these is nutritional status. It is well known that periods of malnutrition will arrest the growth of children. If the malnutrition is severe or long-lasting the child's stature, weight and skinfold thickness (a measure of body fat) will be affected. Such children will also be developmentally backward.

These factors and associated problems, such as parasite load, chronic disease, even psychological disturbance, result in adults who are smaller than might otherwise be expected.

It has also been suggested that chronic obesity in certain populations – in, for example, native Americans – results at least in part from the relatively recent adoption of a Western diet by peoples who may be genetically adapted to a dietary intake lower in sugars and carbohydrates.

Variations in human body size are also directly related to differences in energy needs. On average, up to 70 per cent of a person's daily enery requirement is determined by basal metabolism. The remainder is fixed primarily by physical activity and also by *thermogenesis* (for example, temperature regulation, digestion and hormonal changes).

Because basal metabolic rate (BMR) increases with body weight, a large-bodied person typically has higher total metabolic requirements than a smaller-bodied person. Furthermore, physical tasks that require movement of the body, such as walking, also need more energy in a large-bodied than in a smaller-bodied person. The specific relationship between body size and energetics is, however, also dependent on such factors as age, sex, reproductive status, general health, geographical area of origin and level of physical activity.

The relationship between BMR and age is particularly interesting. Adult humans, on average, have the expected BMR for their body weight predicted by the Kleiber equation for the relationship between BMR and weight in all mammals (BMR = $kW_B^{0.75}$; see p. 41). However, the Kleiber predictions do not apply to a newborn baby, which has an unusually low BMR for its body weight.

Because a baby has been part of its mother during its 9-month gestation, at birth it has a metabolic rate consistent with the mother's larger body size. However, within the first 36 hours of life its BMR increases to the rate consistent with its own small body size, as predicted by Kleiber.

During the first year of life, the infant's BMR increases in direct proportion to body weight and much more rapidly than predicted by Kleiber. This increase is associated with the unusually high metabolic demands of rapid growth, particularly with the fast growth of the brain. At this early age the metabolic demands of the brain account for more than 50 per cent of the total BMR of the baby. This is because the brain is an unusually expensive metabolic tissue and in an infant makes up a much larger percentage of total body weight (14 per cent) than in an adult (2.0–2.7 per cent).

See also 'Diets and guts' (p. 60), 'Selecting and processing food' (p. 65), 'Human locomotion' (p. 80), 'Primate reproduction' (p. 86), 'Life-history patterns' (p. 95) and 'Primate brains and senses' (p. 109)

Energetic cost (in kilocalories*) of various activities in an average man and woman

Activity	Energy cost (kcal/min)	Average man Hours/day	Energy expenditure (kcal)
Lying still	1.1	8	528
Sitting	1.5	6	540
Standing	2.5	6	900
Walking	3.0	2	360
Other (e.g. heavy work)	4.5	2	540
Total		24	2868

Activity	Energy cost (kcal/min)	Average woman Hours/day	Energy expenditure (kcal)
Lying still	1.0	8	480
Sitting	1.1	6	396
Standing	1.5	6	540
Walking	2.5	2	300
Other (e.g. heavy work)	3.0	2	360
Total		24	2076

*1 kilocalorie = 4.1868 kilojoules.

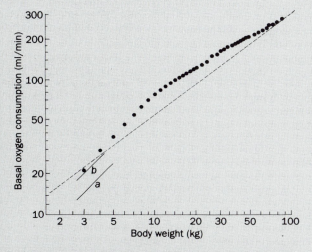

Basal metabolic rate (BMR) in humans is related to body weight from birth to adult life. At birth, a baby's BMR is much lower than would be expected for its body weight (line a). Within 18 to 30 hours, its BMR (line b) increases to the level predicted by the 'mouse to elephant' line of Kleiber (see p. 41). During the first year of life, BMR increases much more rapidly in relation to body weight than predicted, and after the first year it increases more slowly (curve ●).

After the first year of life, the growth of the brain slows considerably and the ratio of brain weight to body weight decreases to its adult values. During this part of the growth period the relationship between BMR and body weight closely parallels the relationship between the weight of the metabolically expensive body organs (brain plus heart, liver and kidneys) and overall body weight.

Energy requirements in adult humans are exceedingly variable. In the same population undertaking the same activities, requirements can vary as much as two-fold. However, irrespective of this variation, there are certain consistencies that characterise human energetics.

Of particular interest is the fact that among adult humans BMR scales to body weight to the 0.5 power rather than to the 0.75 power predicted by Kleiber. This means that within human populations – that is, intraspecifically – BMR does not rise with increasing body weight at the same rate as it does between mammalian species, or interspecifically.

Moreover, BMR in humans is more closely related to lean body weight (without the weight of the body fat) than it is to total body weight. This explains why obese people often have a lower BMR per unit total body weight than do less obese people. It also explains why on average females, who have a larger percentage of body fat than males, also have a lower BMR per unit total body weight.

There is no difference between males and females, or between most obese and normal people, in their basal metabolic rates per unit lean body weight. However, females generally have increased energy requirements during pregnancy and while they are breastfeeding. Both of these activities are metabolically very expensive and Western women are usually advised to increase their energy intake by about 200 to 300 kilocalories during pregnancy and lactation. Against this, recent studies suggest that in some populations of women pregnancy may pose little or no additional metabolic burden and, for Gambian women at least, it may actually confer an energy advantage.

Human populations living in tropical climates usually have lower BMRs than populations in more northerly or southerly latitudes, but the reason for this is not clear. It is also the case that immigrants to hotter climates usually develop lower BMRs than they had before immigration; however, this effect is variable and more common in people of European origin.

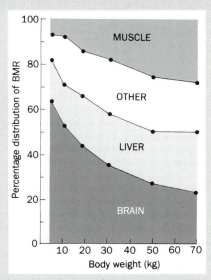

The brain, liver and muscle are metabolically expensive body organs in the human body, especially during childhood.

Another interesting example of population variation is found in Australian Aborigines, who have the ability to tolerate cold temperatures without elevating their metabolic rates above the basal level to the same degree that would be necessary in others.

Inevitably, there are regular changes in adult energy requirements and energy usage during periods of food shortage or famine. One of the first changes to occur is a marked decline in physical activity to reduce the level of energy expenditure over and above that required by basal metabolism.

As the food shortage continues there is a reduction in body fat, muscle mass and weight of the metabolically expensive organs. Because body weight is considerably reduced, the BMR is also reduced. However it is important to note that this is an absolute reduction – in relation to unit lean body weight, the BMR is normal. With return to a normal diet, both body weight and BMR increase to their previous levels and there is a rapid return to normal activity.   L.C. Aiello

See also 'Human adaptations to the physical environment' (p. 46), 'Human locomotion' (p. 80), 'Primate brains and senses' (p. 109)

Human adaptations to the physical environment

During human evolution, people have settled in all the climatic zones of the world. They have had to adjust to very different environments – to extremes of temperature, of solar radiation, of humidity and of seasonal fluctuations in climate, and even to atmospheric pressure less than half that at sea level. Considering that our precursors were confined to the tropics or subtropics and, for the early forms at least, to wooded or open savannas, this global spread involved some remarkable adaptations. Still more remarkable is the fact that modern human populations still belong to a single, fully interfertile species.

Early European explorers and settlers often found it very difficult to survive in new parts of the world and believed that the native people they met possessed special inherited characteristics that accounted for their survival. However, many of them later discovered that if they adopted the clothing, housing, food and behaviour of the indigenous inhabitants their chances of survival were greatly enhanced – a reflection of the basic mechanism that allows humans to survive in a variety of environments. In a new environment, humans have the ability to invent and transmit ways of recreating part of the physical environment lived in by our ancestors. For example, although the Inuit (Eskimos) live in the Arctic, their combination of clothing, habitation and behaviour make the air temperature next to any individual's body generally comparable to that in the tropics. The principal exception occurs in the hands and feet, as even the best-insulated gloves and boots cannot prevent severe cooling under arctic winter conditions unless the individual is constantly active.

Despite human ingenuity in recreating a tropical environment, artificial microenvironments are seldom perfect replicas of our ancestral habitat. Until recently, no one could reproduce the year-round ultraviolet levels of tropical savannas, the sea-level atmospheric pressures in high mountains, or the low levels of air moisture in savannas. For populations to cope with new and challenging habitats there must be an interaction between their genetic structure and their physiological response to allow them to survive a variety of environmental stresses. Both natural selection and physiological plasticity contribute to our ability to cope with environmental stress, and their interaction is so close that it is meaningless to attempt to disentangle the two mechanisms. The science of human adaptability involves the study of such adjustments, which may involve variability in disease susceptibility, food preference and social system. Specifically biological responses to the physical environment are the subject of this chapter.

Anatomy and climate

An association between human physical characteristics and the environment was first noticed in ancient Greece. People from the interior of Africa were discovered to have dark skins and it was assumed that this difference was caused by the intensity of the tropical sun. Despite these early observations on humans, associations between climate and morphology were first measured in other animals. In 1847, the Swedish anatomist C. Bergmann formulated a rule that 'within a polytypic warm-blooded species, the body size of the subspecies usually increases with the decreasing mean temperature of its habitat'. In 1877, another rule was formulated by J.A. Allen: 'In warm-blooded species, the relative size of exposed portions of the body decreases with the decrease of mean temperature.'

Body size

These rules were not applied to humans until the middle of the twentieth century, when large surveys showed that there was a strong association between human body size and average annual temperature. Bergmann's and Allen's rules can hence be applied to the human species. However, the cause of such relationships is still debated.

Climate affects disease patterns and food availability. Some of the associations may arise from stunting of growth in modern tropical populations, an explanation that excludes genetic differences between populations as a cause of differences in size and shape. Adequate diet and the control of infectious disease have indeed led to an increase in adult height and weight in some populations. However, there is no evidence that human populations from different parts of the world would be nearly identical in size if given the same food and exposure to disease. Furthermore, diet and disease do not affect body proportions in adults. If population differences are indeed genetic, then they probably reflect the action of natural selection.

Differences in food, survival behaviour and disease arising from climatic differences may each have contributed to selection on size and shape. Climate also has an important direct effect: in all warmblooded species (mammals and birds), large-bodied animals with short extremities tolerate cold climates better because heat loss is reduced in relation to energy production and the storage of heat. In addition, in humans and other species that use sweat for cooling, a high ratio of skin surface to body mass is advantageous in heat regulation if sufficient water is available.

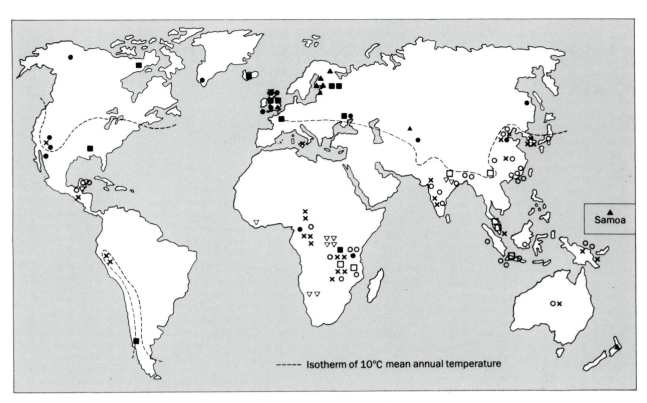

People living in cold areas of the world characteristically have a heavier build than those in warmer areas, as this distribution map shows (the weights are averages for indigenous males). Some Polynesian populations are an exception. They live in a hot and humid environment yet have the heaviest body weights of any population in the world. Key: ▲, very high (69.5 kg and above); ■, high (64.5–69.4 kg); ●, fairly high (59.5–64.4 kg); ×, medium (54.5–59.4 kg); ○, fairly low (49.5–54.4 kg); □, low (44.5–49.4 kg); ▽, very low (44.4 kg and below).

There are some more specific associations of morphology with climate. Broad, short noses tend to be characteristic of hot tropical environments, while long thin noses are found in cold climates. The amount of water vapour in the air is the climatic factor most strongly associated with nose shape, possibly because long thin noses aid in moisturising dry air before it reaches the lungs.

Skin colour

Skin colour is the best understood of all the associations between external characteristics and climate. Many factors contribute to individual differences in this character, but the most important is the amount of the black and brown pigment called *melanin* in the dermal layer. Melanin levels are primarily under genetic control, and differences in skin colour between populations may largely be attributed to three to five allelic pairs of genes. Exposure to ultraviolet light will increase the amount of melanin in the skin of all populations, and, for unknown reasons, suntanning appears to increase skin melanin by about the same degree in all groups. We do not notice this in dark-skinned individuals, because there is only a small absolute change in light reflectance.

As the Greeks suspected, there is a close relationship

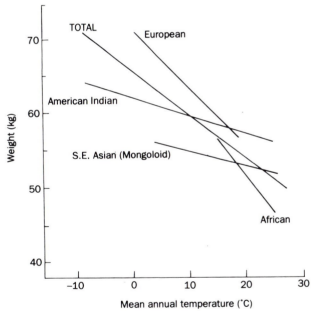

Relationship between body weight and average annual temperature for four major population groups (figures are for males).

between skin colour and solar radiation throughout the world. Some populations, such as the American Indians and the Mongoloid peoples in Asia, do not show much geographic variation in relation to radiation intensity. In contrast, the relationship is so close in European populations that skin colour is lightest in people from the Baltic, which has the cloudiest weather in Europe.

The most convincing selective mechanism is associated with the capacity of melanin to block ultraviolet light. Light-

SWEATING – THE HUMAN RESPONSE TO HEAT

Many mammals sweat, but the human system is the most effective, for at least three reasons.

First, thermal sweat is produced by *eccrine glands* that pour on to the skin a watery solution with virtually no fats or protein and very little salt. Most other mammals that cool by sweating depend mainly on *apocrine glands*, which produce solutions rich in fats, proteins and salt. These evaporate more slowly, reducing the rate of heat loss. In people, apocrine glands are limited to such areas as the face and hands.

Second, human skin is covered by more than 1.5 million sweat glands, which produce copious amounts of sweat over the whole body. The number of active glands does not vary significantly among human populations; any differences appear to be the result of acclimatisation rather than genetics.

Third, our lack of body hair also ensures that sweat provides very efficient cooling as it evaporates from the heated skin.

The efficiency of the human cooling system incurs one significant liability: the need for a large intake of water. A man weighing 90 kilograms can sweat over 2 litres of water in an hour of normal walking on a hot day in the desert. Active young men will normally lose over 8 litres of water during a day when the desert temperature at midday is above 40 °C. Although we can still function with modest dehydration, water loss must be replaced daily or mental derangement and death quickly follow.

Throughout evolution, human populations in hot savannas must have stayed relatively close to water until they were able to domesticate animals to carry their water supply – and that was only in the past few thousand years. The efficient cooling provided by sweating may have been a significant factor in allowing people to run long distances because the high

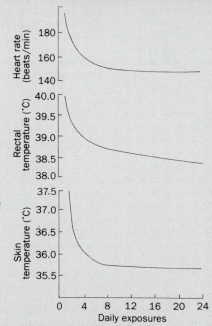

All humans can acclimatise to heat stress, as shown in this experiment. When men walk a treadmill (300 kcal per m² per hour) for 60 to 90 minutes daily in a temperature of 40 °C and relative humidity 23 per cent, their pulse rate falls, and their body and skin temperatures fall.

levels of heat produced through running provide a subtantial heat load.

Although sweating is an efficient cooling mechanism in dry heat, it becomes decreasingly so as the moisture in the air rises. The most stressful hot climates in the world are probably those of the shores of the Red Sea and Arabian Gulf, where moderately hot air temperatures in summer are accompanied by unusually high vapour pressures. In very deep mines, where the air is saturated with water and the

temperature is 35 °C, work must be limited to periods of 30 minutes followed by intervals of body cooling to avoid the risk of heat stroke.

The decreased effectiveness of sweating in tropical forests and other hot, wet environments suggests that novel forms of selection may have operated in such places. There is reduced evaporation and the basic need is to dissipate metabolic heat into an environment whose temperature is lower than that of the body.

In principle, a small body will improve heat tolerance because the surface area for heat loss in relation to the heat-producing mass of the body is relatively large. Long extremities will also be advantageous, as these increase conductive and radiative cooling. The extremely small size of Pygmies in the tropical forests of Africa and Southeast Asia may have arisen through such selection – although there is as yet no experimental proof of this.

When young men from hot and cold climates are first exposed to a heat load, there are substantial differences in their heat tolerance. However, if these individuals then work in the heat for 7 to 10 days the difference between them almost disappears, because heat acclimatisation is a universal human capability.

During acclimatisation, sweat rates rise and the sweat becomes less salty; under a given heat and work load, body temperature also rises less and strain on the cardiovascular system decreases. Heat acclimatisation is closely attuned to heat load and will recur with increased heat load or disappear over a few months if the heat stress is removed.

Why we have such a reversible adaptive response is not known, but such responses are common to many animals and to a number of environmental stresses.

P. T. Baker

skinned individuals may suffer from skin damage in very sunny areas and often develop potentially lethal skin cancers if exposed to ultraviolet rays for long periods. Shorter exposures can lead to possibly serious skin damage and infection in spite of tanning. As is discussed in Chapter 7.6, dense layers of melanin in the skin can be disadvantageous in places with low ultraviolet radiation because they inhibit the synthesis of vitamin D, which takes place when ultraviolet radiation penetrates the skin. Deficiency in this vitamin can lead to poor ossification of bone and permanent skeletal deformation or rickets.

The case of skin melanin shows how difficult it is to identify the details of human adaptive responses to climate. It is no doubt true that in other, more obscure adaptations, the mechanisms that allowed people to become established in all parts of the world have been at least as complex as this.

Heat tolerance

As most early human evolution was in the tropics or subtropics and our fossil ancestors occupied semi-arid environments, it is not surprising that modern humans are well adapted to rather hot and dry conditions. Although camels exceed our abilities, humans are one of the few mammals that can stay moderately active during the day in the hottest regions of the world. This ability results primarily from an efficient *sweating* mechanism (see Box).

Humans are genetically well adapted to hot, dry conditions and, with the possible exception of a decrease in body size in tropical forests, there is no evidence of differing genetic adaptations to heat in different populations. In spite of this, most groups have developed behavioural specialisations that reduce exposure to uncomfortable heat.

Cold tolerance

Although early human populations were established in quite cold climates long before the evolutionary appearance of *Homo sapiens*, modern humans have a very low tolerance of cold. Because we lack insulation such as fur and hair, nude exposure to still air temperatures as high as 26 °C causes constriction of blood vessels in the skin. At around 20 °C, increased heat production, manifest as shivering, begins, and at 5 °C inactive young adults may suffer such a reduction in brain temperature that they become unconscious in a few hours.

Most non-human primates have relatively poor cold tolerance but some bear cold better than humans do. For example, colonies of Japanese macaques (*Macaca fuscata*) successfully inhabit the cold wintry environments of central Japan. In contrast, without the culture that produced clothing and fire and without access to some kind of shelter, our predecessors were limited to places where it never became colder than about 10 °C.

Subcutaneous fat, which is more uniformly distributed in infants than in adults, has a low thermal conductivity and reduces loss of central body heat to the skin in cold conditions. The extent of cold protection provided by this layer of fat is directly related to its thickness, so that temperatures that cause violent shivering and a drop in core temperatures in thin individuals may cause only mild skin discomfort in those who are fat. Fat is particularly beneficial in cold water, because neither fur nor clothing provides significant insulation in these conditions. It is not surprising that all successful swimmers of the English Channel have heavy fat layers and that many of them are women (who tend to have markedly more fat than men do).

Because the skin is the primary agent of heat loss and body mass is the main agent of heat production, a small skin area in relation to body mass improves tolerance to cold.

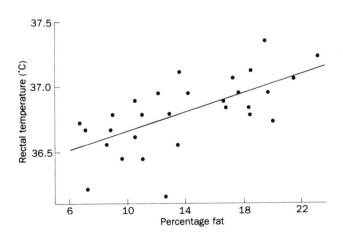

The amount a person is protected from the cold depends on the thickness of the layer of fat under the skin. This graph shows what happens to the body temperature of young men exposed nude to an air temperature of 15 °C for 2 hours. Temperatures that cause violent shivering and a drop in core body temperature in thin individuals may cause only slight skin discomfort in those who are fat.

Our relatively large adult size, therefore, aids cold tolerance, but it also follows that infants and young children require more protection against cold.

Although humans have the ability to acclimatise to heat, there is no evidence that short-term exposure to cold improves cold tolerance. Intermittent exposure for several months to conditions that produce shivering may reduce the intensity of this muscular response, but this does not reduce heat loss. Although most people suffer less discomfort from cold after long-term exposure, this appears to be a product of psychological habituation rather than a significant change in cold tolerance. The most important adaptations that allowed humans to inhabit temperate zones were the cultural adjustments that led to the creation of an artificial microenvironment like that of the tropics. Nevertheless, there are real population differences in the physiological responses of individuals to cold stress on hands and feet.

Adaptations to cold

If an adult immerses a finger in freezing water, there is an immediate stoppage of blood flow to the affected part. Among Europeans the subsequent response varies. For some, finger temperature will quickly drop to near water temperature and stay there. For others, it will drop to near water temperature but then rise and fall in short cycles; still others have a finger temperature that stays substantially above 0 °C and shows little cycling. These differences are associated with the degree and timing of the *constriction* of arteries to the hand.

Similar responses occur when the whole hand or foot is exposed to cold. A continuous constriction of the blood vessels might appear to be highly adaptive, as it keeps heat loss to a minimum. However, when temperatures are below freezing, the affected part would freeze without heat from the general circulation. Even in temperatures above freezing, a few days of cold-induced vasoconstriction will kill the skin cells. The most adaptive response for each individual depends on the length and severity of exposure to cold.

There are also real differences among populations exposed to cooling of this kind. Men of African black origin have a much lower average finger temperature in iced water than do European men and show less temperature cycling. Europeans in their turn have a less effective response than do the Inuit and highland Peruvian American Indians. During cold nights in central Australia, the blood vessels of the Aborigines constrict so that blood flow into the arms and legs is reduced to an extent sufficient to decrease total heat loss from the body significantly. This means that, while sleeping in conditions cold enough to raise the metabolic heat production of Europeans by 15 per cent, Australian Aborigines remain at basal metabolic levels. Their extreme vasoconstriction allows skin temperature to fall to 2.5 °C lower than that of Europeans, so reducing heat loss.

An Inuit waiting immobile for a seal to rise at its breathing hole would soon get frostbite if his fingers and toes were not rewarmed by heat from his general circulation. Although the fur clothing provides excellent insulation when dry, it must be removed daily and cleared of sweat-formed ice crystals.

The relative importance of acclimatisation and genetics in the responses of different populations to finger cooling is not yet known. An increase in vasodilation occurs after a month or two of exposure of the hands to cold, and studies of North Atlantic fishermen suggest that cold exposure over many years may enhance this response. Even so, the fishermen's response is not as great as that of the Inuit, and North Americans of European and West African heritage have different responses even though they have spent their lives in similar microclimates.

Whatever the genetic basis of population differences in the response of limbs to cold, they are climatically adaptive. Vasoconstriction in central Australian Aborigines (and perhaps in other tropical savanna groups) allows them to exploit a savanna with cold nights without the need for clothing, housing or extra food. For the Inuit in a bitterly cold environment, clothing and housing give an adequate body core temperature, but even mittens and boots cannot prevent frostbite unless the vasoconstrictive response is relaxed to allow the central body heat to rewarm fingers and toes.

Altitude tolerance

Several changes in the physical environment occur with increasing altitude. Average air temperature and water vapour decline in a nearly linear fashion. Radiation increases, and, perhaps most important, atmospheric pressure declines. Within the altitudinal range of human habitation, the decline in pressure is nearly linear and the proportions of nitrogen and oxygen in the air remain constant. At 5000 metres, atmospheric pressure is only half that at sea level, so that each breath fills the lungs with only half as many oxygen atoms.

Some lowlanders can stay conscious for a few hours at altitudes just above 8000 metres, but a rapid ascent to only 5000 metres produces mental distress and even loss of consciousness for many people. Professional mountaineers find that a few days at intermediate altitudes improve their performance, but a stay of several months above 5000 metres leads to a rapid decline in fitness. Although some permanent human settlements in the tropics reach this height, attempts to establish yet higher permanent settlements have failed, even when the residents have normally lived above 4000 metres.

Although the decline in air pressure is linear with altitude, its physiological influence is not. At 1000 metres, there is no discernible effect. By 1500 metres, the major effect is a slight diminution in the birth weight of infants born to mothers who spent their pregnancy at that altitude. At 2500 metres, there is a reduction in athletic performance among newcomers, infants are even smaller at birth, and more of them have defects in their blood circulation that prevent full oxygenation of the blood. For lowlanders disembarking at the 4000-metre-high airport at La Paz, Bolivia, the effects of altitude are soon apparent. Most develop rapid heartbeats, shortness of breath, a headache

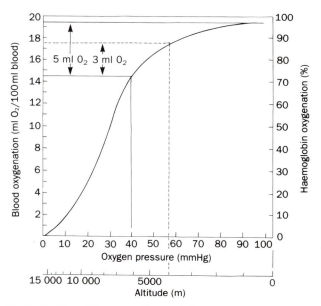

The oxygen dissociation curve of haemoglobin, showing the amounts of oxygen that our blood can carry at different oxygen pressures. At an altitude of 2000 metres, the haemoglobin can carry 96 per cent of the oxygen that it can at sea level; at 4000 metres, the figure drops to about 88 per cent. Thus, an extra gain in height of 2000 metres reduces the oxygen level in the blood by twice as much as the initial 2000 metres above sea level.

and possibly faintness. A hearty meal usually produces severe nausea. Vigorous excise may have more serious consequences, because the combination of such a low atmospheric pressure and heavy exercise can cause an accumulation of fluid in the lungs or increase fluid pressure inside the skull.

The non-linear effects of altitude arise from the non-linear oxygen-binding ability of the haemoglobin in our blood. At an altitude of 2000 metres, haemoglobin can carry 96 per cent of the oxygen that it can at sea level. However, at 4000 metres it can carry only about 88 per cent of sea-level values: an additional 2000-metre gain in height hence reduces the oxygen level in the blood by twice as much as the initial 2000 metres. At very high altitudes, there is a greatly increased breathing rate. This certainly helps to raise the oxygen level in the lungs, but also reduces blood carbon dioxide and leads to headaches, faintness and irregular breathing.

For the high-altitude visitor, the acute symptoms usually disappear within a few days, because of an acclimatisation that produces better regulation of breathing. The newcomer to 4000 metres may then feel perfectly adjusted to altitude but physiological tests show that he or she has lost some 20 to 30 per cent of the maximal work capacity at sea level because of a reduced ability to deliver oxygen to the muscles. This loss of aerobic capacity persists for at least a year or two at high altitudes but is immediately reversed upon return to sea level.

With continuing residence at high altitude, the number of red blood cells rises for several months. This was once thought to be an adaptation because it increases the oxygen-carrying capacity of the blood, even though it slows blood circulation. However, research now suggests that the red-cell count may be primarily an indication of the amount of altitude stress an individual experiences: there is no evidence that this rise in the red-cell count increases aerobic capacity.

Adaptations to high altitude

High-altitude American Indians in the Andean mountains show many of the same altitude effects as lowlanders. Mothers produce smaller infants at high than at low altitudes, and, even with comparable nutrition and care, children grow more slowly during infancy and adolescence. Despite these similarities, adults show a much higher aerobic capacity than do even long-term migrants from the lowlands. This difference arises mainly from the greater efficiency in extracting oxygen from the air shown by the highlanders. Maximal aerobic capacity of the highlanders does not increase when they descend to low altitude.

It is not known what produces this high oxygen-extractive ability. Perhaps the unusually large chest and lungs of these highland American Indians help, but comparable efficiencies are found in the Sherpas of Nepal, who do not

Quechua Indians planting potatoes on the Andean Altiplano, 4000 metres (13 000 ft) above sea level. They and other native highlanders extract oxygen from the air more efficiently than lowlanders.

have unusually large chests. There may be a genetic element in the highlander's ability, as such individuals who grow up at sea level lose only half as much oxygen-extracting ability at high altitude compared with native lowlanders. However, physiological flexibility is also involved: adults brought to high altitudes during early childhood (but not those who moved during adolescence) have an oxygen-extractive capability close to that of the native highlanders. There is hence a long-term or developmental acclimatisation to low oxygen tensions.

Microenvironments – the clue to human adaptability

Without doubt, the major adaptations enabling human populations to live in such a variety of physical environments is the creation of microenvironments that approximate to the conditions in which we evolved. This replication is, however, imperfect. Furthermore, although human populations have great potential for acclimatisation, natural selection has also produced variations in skin colour, body size, nose shape and other traits that improve our ability to function in particular environments. Selection has also resulted in differences in physiology, such as peripheral vasoconstriction and oxygen extraction, which improve survival in harsh environments such as the Arctic and the Andes. In short, natural selection, physiological plasticity and the evolution of culture have combined to render the human species uniquely able to adapt to a great diversity of physical environments.   P.T. Baker

See also 'Natural selection in humans' (p. 284)

Differences between the sexes

Charles Darwin was one of the first to consider the distribution of *sexual dimorphism* (physical differences between the males and females of a species) in animals and its significance, especially to humans. In most animals, the sexes differ not only in characters directly linked to reproduction (the *primary sexual characters*), but in others also – the *secondary sexual characters*, which are diagnostic of each sex. In primates, secondary sexual characters range from those closely involved in the process of mating or reproduction, such as the female sexual swellings of some macaques (*Macaca*), to others that have little apparent functional significance, such as the mane of the male Hamadryas baboon (*Papio hamadryas*) and the striking facial coloration of the male mandrill (*Papio* (or *Mandrillus*) *sphinx*).

It is not only the nature of the sexually dimorphic characters that varies between species. Even between closely related species, there are variations in the extent of sexual dimorphism. Sometimes, the sexes are virtually indistinguishable, but in other cases the differences are so striking that males and females might be thought different species. It was this bewildering variety that led Darwin to consider the evolutionary forces involved. He suggested that agents distinct from natural selection operate on secondary sexual characters, by 'sexual selection'. The distinction between natural and sexual selection, and assessment of their relative importance, has been a central concern in the study of sexual dimorphism.

Sexual selection and natural selection

Darwin coined the term *sexual selection* for selection that operates solely on characters giving some members of one sex a reproductive advantage over others of the same sex. He suggested that ornaments arise because males with them have a reproductive advantage, and not because of the value of these characters in increasing survival. Sexual selection may lead to sexual dimorphism; but not all sexual dimorphism is the result of sexual selection. Accessory sex organs, such as the mammary glands of female mammals and other characters involved in parental care, are the result of natural selection, as are other features that result directly from differences in habits between the sexes. Two types of character may evolve by sexual selection: those directly involved in competition between males for access to females, and male ornaments that influence female choice.

Sexual selection and natural selection may grade into one another, especially in the case of display characters. These may help males and females to find each other, or to synchronise their activities, and are hence a product of natural selection. Once established, however, they may be enhanced by sexual selection, possibly beyond the point at which they are favoured by natural selection. Various characters, not generally seen as secondary sexual characters, can be influenced by competition between members of one sex. For example, relative size of the testes in primates is associated with the degree of direct competition among males for females. In the same way, many characters related to fighting ability are selected for in males, although they would not be classified as secondary sexual characters.

In interpreting sexually dimorphic characters, it is therefore useful to consider them in terms of the different selection pressures operating on males and females, rather than to try and distinguish between the products of sexual and natural selection.

Sexual dimorphism in primates

Several characteristics (apart from the primary sex organs) differ between the sexes in primates. They include the following:

(Above) Very dimorphic male and female olive baboons (*Papio anubis*) contrasted with (right) hardly dimorphic male and female white-handed gibbons (*Hylobates lar*).

- Body weight and muscular development, and dimensions such as head, body and tail length
- Coat (pelage) coloration and skin markings, especially on the face
- Particular anatomical features such as the bulbous nose of the male proboscis monkey (*Nasalis larvatus*), or the cheek flanges of the male orang-utan (*Pongo pygmaeus*)
- Age-related, seasonal or periodic morphological changes directly associated with reproduction, such as changes in the skin colour of the male scrotum, or sexual swelling and coloration associated with the female ovarian cycle

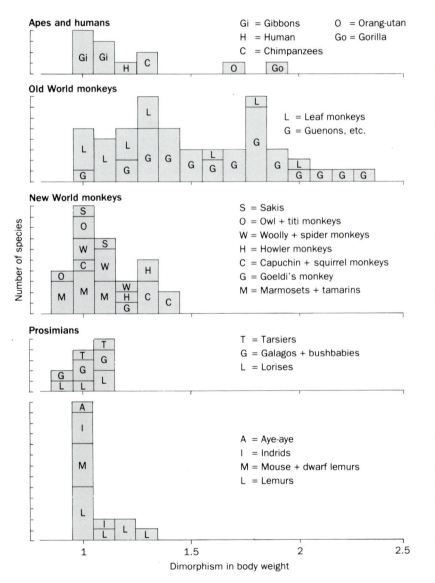

Dimorphism in body size (male weight/female weight) varies widely among the primate groups. It is generally slight in prosimians, and is not marked in New World monkeys – with the exception of howlers and capuchins. Among tamarins, some females are in fact slightly larger than males. Old World monkeys show the most extreme sexual dimorphism, especially cercopithecines (guenons and their relatives). Humans, although much less dimorphic in size than gorillas and orang-utans, have other dimorphic characters, such as the distribution of hair and metabolic rate.

The occurrence of such dimorphic characters varies widely among the major primate groups. Dimorphism in body size is generally slight in prosimians (lemurs, lorises and tarsiers), in which, apart from occasional colour differences, the sexes are usually quite similar. In New World monkeys, the most extreme dimorphism in body size occurs in howler monkeys (*Alouatta*); males may weigh up to 35 per cent more than females. Males are slightly larger than females in most other species, although the differences are slight in marmosets and tamarins; in tamarins (*Saguinus*), most females are in fact slightly larger than males. There is colour dimorphism in some species of spider monkeys (*Ateles*) and in some capuchins (*Cebus*), but sexual dimorphism is generally not pronounced among New World monkeys.

In contrast, the most extreme forms of sexual dimorphism are seen in Old World monkeys and apes. In several genera of Old World monkeys – for example, mandrills, baboons (*Papio*), the patas monkey (*Erythrocebus patas*) and the proboscis monkey – males weigh almost twice as much as females. Canine teeth in males are often large and well developed, especially in gelada baboons (*Theropithecus gelada*) and macaques.

There are other striking characters, such as shoulder capes and manes, in male Hamadryas baboons and in gelada baboons, together with extreme examples of facial and body patterning and coloration. Complex colour changes and swellings also occur in the anal and genital regions of females in association with the ovarian cycle (see p. 91). However, some groups of Old World monkeys, especially most leaf monkeys (colobines), do not usually display such extreme dimorphism, and males and females are in general rather similar in size and coloration.

The extent of sexual dimorphism is highly variable among apes. Some species of gibbons (*Hylobates*) have colour dimorphism, but males and females in all cases are very similar in body weight. Male gorillas and orang-utans weigh almost twice as much as females and have distinctive anatomical characteristics – for example, the crests in the skulls of the gorilla and the cheek flanges of the orang-utan. In humans, there is relatively slight dimorphism in size, but there are other dimorphic characters, such as the distribution of body hair, the voice and longevity.

Theories of sexual dimorphism

Various hypotheses have been proposed to account for sexual dimorphism. They have been tested by examining dimorphism in species classified into different ecological or social categories. Comparative studies of this kind have concentrated on three groups of dimorphic characters: (1) the size and structure of weaponry and ornaments; (2) size dimorphism of teeth (especially the canines); and (3) body size dimorphism.

Weaponry and ornaments

If the elaborate skin coloration and ornaments of male Old World monkeys are a result of female choice, they should be especially developed in the more *polygynous* species (those with a higher ratio of females to males in breeding groups). These characters are, indeed, found in a restricted group of Old World monkeys, all of which are polygynous, are terrestrial and live in large groups. Because of the restricted geographical distribution of these species, it is not easy to test for an association with particular ecological or social patterns. Across the primates as a whole, however, it is clear that an absence of sexual dimorphism is commonly associated with *monogamy* (having one mate only, usually for the animals' lifetime), whereas its presence is generally correlated with polygyny.

In other mammals, it is possible to test for the association of particular dimorphic characters with intersexual or intrasexual selection. For example, in many deer, antlers are used in competitions among males for possession of harems. Across species, antler size increases with body size. Even when the effects of body size are removed, antler size is related to the size of the breeding group, and, by implication, to the intensity of intrasexual competition. Intersexual selection is harder to demonstrate. In birds, at least, females have been shown to select mates. If the tails of male African long-tailed widowbirds are artificially shortened, males with longer tails are more successful in attracting females to nest on their territories than are those with the shortest tails. On the other hand, tail length has little effect on direct competition among males.

Tooth size

In a variety of primate species, males have strikingly larger canines than females. Is this because larger canines allow males to fight more successfully over females, or because they are used in defence against predators and help males to protect the family group? If fighting for mates is important, then canine size should be related to the extent of competition among males and should be greatest in species that form harems and least in monogamous species. A role in antipredator defence would mean that males of terrestrial species that move in large groups should have the largest canines.

Because dimorphism in canine teeth is also related to dimorphism in body size (species that are more dimorphic in body size are also more so in tooth size), these predictions must be tested using measures of tooth size that are independent of the size of the body. When this is done, monogamous species are found to have less dimorphic teeth than polygynous ones. There is a relationship between the degree of polygyny and relative size of male canines, but this is complicated by difficulties in finding a measure that accurately reflects intermale competition. Terrestrial species have greater dimorphism in canine size, independent of both body weight and breeding system.

It appears, therefore, that both intrasexual selection and defence against predators are significant in the evolution of canine tooth dimorphism.

Body size

Body size dimorphism varies from primates in which males weigh more than twice as much as females to those in which females are slightly larger than males. If body size influences male competition, then sexual selection should produce larger males, to a degree dependent on the intensity of intermale competition. The latter can be estimated from the *socionomic sex ratio* (the ratio of adult males and females in a group) and it is indeed related to size dimorphism among primates. However, the overall relationship is determined largely by the monogamous species, which are generally monomorphic, and it is weak if these are excluded. This may be because socionomic sex ratio does not much reflect intermale competition in primates, or because other factors such as body size, terrestriality and phylogeny obscure any relationship that may exist.

Larger primates tend to be more dimorphic. More polygynous species also tend to be large, but the relationship between size and dimorphism persists when the effects of polygyny are held constant. It seems likely that this association may result from a common influence exerted by another variable, but no convincing explanation has yet emerged.

Body size dimorphism is generally considered to result from selection on increased male size. However, differences in ecological preference could lead to a progressive divergence in the body sizes of the sexes, or could lead to selection for reduced body size in females. Males and females may compete for food, and, especially in monogamous territorial species, a pair might exploit their territory more efficiently if they occupied slightly different ecological niches. In monogamous birds, such niche divergence explains much diversity in body size and beak shape, but

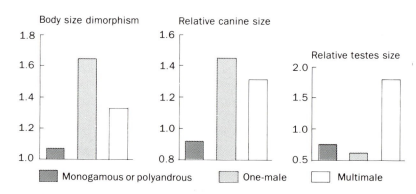

Primate species living in monogamous or polyandrous social groups (one female with one or more males) can be distinguished from species living in polygynous social groups (several females with one or more males) by their dimorphism in body size (male weight/female weight) and relative canine size (male canine length/female canine length). Polygynous species that form large multimale groups have relatively larger testes than do those that live in one-male groups.

this may be less true for primates. For example, although niche divergence predicts that the sexes might differ, it does not explain why males are almost always the larger sex. Niche divergence would be particularly expected to lead to dimorphism in monogamous and territorial species, but these are the least dimorphic of all. Although niche divergence may not be a general explanation, however, it may apply to some closely related species.

The costs of pregnancy and lactation are borne only by females and will increase any differences in energy budgets between males and females occupying different niches. Selection on body size may differ in the two sexes. In addition, smaller species carry relatively larger babies, and the load imposed on females makes it more difficult for arboreal species to climb trees. Differences in relative brain size suggest that in some species dimorphism results from a decrease in female size rather than an increase in the size of males.

Phylogeny also confuses the interpretation of sexual dimorphism in body size. Closely related species tend to have similar morphology and to live in similar ways, and, because they are descended from a common ancestor, do not supply independent pieces of information. Comparisons of genera or of families suggest that much of the variation in the degree of body size dimorphism among species is accounted for by phylogeny, with body size itself as a second important factor. The breeding system and pressure from predators seem to have a relatively minor influence. Clearly, tests of adaptive explanations of sexual dimorphism must be clearly constructed.

Sexual dimorphism in humans

Humans are sexually dimorphic in size and strength (males are larger and more muscular), in physiology (males have higher metabolic rates), in hair distribution and in life history (males have higher juvenile mortality, attain sexual maturity later and die younger). Darwin postulated that differences in size and strength between men and women are, as in other primates, a product of sexual selection. Many discussions of human sexual dimorphism are preoccupied with separating genetical from environmental influences in dimorphic traits. However, the two are always closely intertwined. For example, genetically based hormonal differences must have implications for patterns of growth and development, which will generate disparities in mortality, susceptibility to certain diseases, strength and other physical distinctions, and some behavioural disparities. However, cultural influences are so strong in human societies that they will nearly always disguise any broad patterns of human sexual dimorphism.   *Georgina Mace*

See also 'Mating and parental care' (p. 150)

Jaws and teeth

The jaws and teeth of animals act as a food processor. In some, they simply trap prey; in others, they have become more specialised and must slice, cut or grind the food as well as grasp it. Mammals can extract energy efficiently from food and can keep their body temperature constant. Their teeth and jaws are the most complex found in the jawed vertebrates.

Mammals, including primates, are unique in that they can chew food on one side of the jaw and can apply maximal force on this side only. Other jawed vertebrates simply chew on both sides of the jaw at once. The jaws of prosimian primates (lemurs, lorises and tarsiers) are made up of left and right parts joined in the middle, or at the *mandibular symphysis*, by strong ligaments. Simian primates (monkeys and apes) have mandibular symphyses that fuse together early in life such that the lower jaw, or *mandible*, acts as a single rigid bone during chewing. This means that muscles acting on both sides of the face can apply force to teeth in contact, or *occluding*, on one side of the jaw. The relative bite force acting on food in simians is thus greatly increased. These changes in jaw morphology are accompanied by changes in tooth shape from the simple puncturing and crushing teeth of insectivorous prosimians to the powerful grinders of modern humans and their fossil hominid ancestors.

Dental formulae

Primitive mammals had three incisors, one canine, four premolars and three molars in each quadrant of the mouth. In living prosimians, this number is reduced to a maximum of two incisors, one canine, three premolars and three molars. This can be represented as the *dental formula*, which is I2/2; C1/1; P 3/3; M3/3 for most prosimians. Among New World monkeys, this formula is unchanged in the Cebidae. Marmosets and tamarins (Callitrichidae) are an exception: they have lost another molar tooth to give them the formula I2/2; C1/1; P3/3; M2/2. Secondary reduction in body size

may have led to shortening of the row of back teeth by loss of a molar (rather than a premolar). The upper molar teeth of marmosets and tamarins are also reduced to three large *cusps* (raised points on the crown) rather than the four typical of other simians.

Old World monkeys, apes and hominids (modern and fossil) all have two incisors, one canine, two premolars and three molars in each quadrant of the jaws (I2/2; C1/1; P2/2; M3/3). There has been a reduction by one incisor and two premolars from the primitive mammalian dental pattern. The premolars nearest the canine have probably disappeared in sequence, so that the premolars in monkeys, apes and hominids are usually called P3 and P4, reflecting the loss of the first two.

Deciduous teeth

Because mammals are so small when they are young and grow so rapidly, they have a set of *deciduous* or *milk teeth* that erupt quickly after birth while the permanent teeth are growing within the jaws. Teeth that directly replace deciduous teeth from below are known as *successional teeth*. All the permanent incisors, canines and premolars are successional. The permanent molars grow in the jaws behind the deciduous dentition as space becomes available. Apes and humans (hominoids) have two deciduous incisors, one deciduous canine and two deciduous premolars (sometimes called milk molars). In primates with three or four premolars, there are an equal number of deciduous premolars.

Permanent teeth

Incisors

The incisors of prosimians have evolved from simple conical teeth; in some, lower incisors form toothcombs. In the aye-aye (*Daubentonia madagascariensis*), the incisors even grow continually throughout life, as they do in rodents. In simians, incisors are blade-like or shovel-shaped (*spatulate*) and are used to cut, pare, peel or strip foodstuffs. There is an evolutionary trend through the Old World monkeys, apes and hominids to reduce the relative size of the incisors so that those of modern humans are quite small in comparison to ape or monkey incisors. Their role in food preparation may have been largely supplanted by the human hand.

Canines

Canine teeth are important in primate social life and tend to be large in monkeys and apes. They are often bigger in

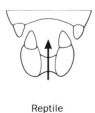
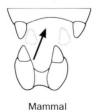

Reptile   Mammal

The relation of lower and upper teeth in reptiles and mammals. Reptiles bite vertically and their teeth do not meet. In contrast, a mammal bite has a transverse component so that the teeth come into contact or occlude.

males than in females and can be used in threats to subordinate members of a group. Modern humans have relatively small canines with very little sexual dimorphism; baring our teeth at foes or other animals has no effect, and we do most of our tooth baring when we laugh.

In monkeys and apes, the upper canine occludes with the lower first premolar, which is a *sectorial* tooth with its front surface long and blade-like for shearing. Together, the lower premolar and the upper and lower canines fit together to form a complex that can *hone* or sharpen.

Premolars

Sectorial premolar teeth are typical of apes and monkeys and distinguish them from humans. Some of the earliest hominids, such as *Australopithecus afarensis* dated between 3 and 4 million years old, have lower first premolars that quite closely resemble a sectorial premolar. In all the later fossil hominids, and in modern humans, the first premolar is a *bicuspid* tooth, with two cusps on the biting surface.

All the remaining premolars in monkeys, apes and hominids are bicuspid. Some early fossil hominids were adapted to eating tough and fibrous plant foods (such as

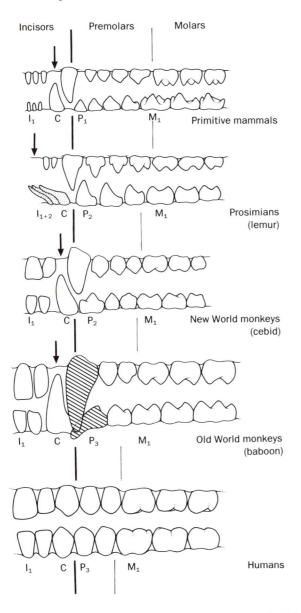

The teeth of a primitive mammal and the special features of the main primate groups. There is a progressive reduction in the number of incisors and premolars but the occlusal relationships remain constant. The proportions of each part of the dentition differ (shown by the distance between the vertical lines through the centre of the upper canine and the contact point between the last upper premolar and the first upper molar). A gap or diastema (arrowed) between the upper lateral incisor and the upper canine for the occlusion of the lower canine is present in all but prosimians (represented here by lemurs), in which the lower canine is incorporated into the comb (stippled). Lemurs and lorises have a median diastema (arrowed). The molar series reduces in size from front to back in all the groups except Old World monkeys and apes (represented here by baboons). The honing complex formed by the upper canine and lower sectorial first premolar is hatched in the baboon.

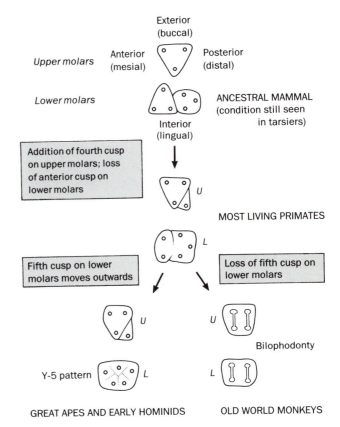

The molar teeth of ancestral placental mammals had a basically triangular pattern. The upper molars were simple triangles with only three main cusps. The lower molars were similarly shaped with three main cusps, but the distal side (towards the back of the jaw) also had a small heel or talon bearing two or three extra cusps. This basic pattern is still recognisable in modern tarsiers. In other living primates, however, there has been a trend to add a fourth cusp on the inside of the rear end of the upper molar and to lose the leading cusp on the main triangle of the lower molar, leaving only four or five cusps. This arrangement has been developed in various ways. The most striking change is found in Old World simians. Both upper and lower molars of Old World monkeys have four cusps linked in pairs by transverse ridges (bilophodonty). By contrast, the lower molars of great apes have five well-developed cusps and the rearmost of these has migrated outwards. The valleys between the five cusps – three on the outside and two on the inside – form an easily recognisable letter Y and the lower molars of great apes are hence said to have a Y-5 pattern.

certain fruits and tubers) and had premolars with expanded biting surfaces, or even extra cusps. These *molarised premolars* resemble molar teeth. Fossil hominids such as *Australopithecus africanus*, *Paranthropus* (or *Australopithecus*) *robustus* and *Paranthropus* (or *Australopithecus*) *boisei* have bigger premolar teeth than do *Australopithecus afarensis* or later fossil hominids in the genus *Homo*. There have been many changes in the transition from ape-like premolar to a typical hominid premolar and the shape of this tooth gives valuable taxonomic information.

Molars

The number of molars in primates (except for marmosets and tamarins) has remained constant. However, their morphology has changed greatly. Monkeys almost always have four-cusped molar teeth. In Old World monkeys, the cusps are joined in pairs across the tooth surface to form two ridges or *lophs*, one at the front and one at the back. These *bilophodont* teeth are especially well developed in the leaf-eating colobines and cut up food as the upper and lower teeth slice past each other.

The molar teeth of apes and hominids are less specialised and resemble the cusped teeth of some prosimians. The molars in the upper jaw typically have four cusps, whereas the lower molars have five. The pattern of grooves between the lower cusps forms a Y-shaped fissure that lies across the tooth from side to side (this is not typical of gibbons). The cusps on the molar teeth of gorillas are very tall but those of orang-utans are more rounded.

Diet has been important in the evolution of molar cusps among hominoids. Fossil hominids either have massive molars with greatly expanded biting surfaces for processing lots of low-grade food, such as seeds or hard fruits, or re-duced molars – as in early *Homo*, which shifted its diet to include quantities of meat.

Evolution of hominid teeth

The bigger the molar and premolar teeth in hominids, the bigger and more robust the jaws. The bending and torsional stresses in the mandible that result from the pull of the chewing muscles have to be resisted and the cross-section of the mandible and its symphysis is enlarged in concert with the back teeth in some fossil hominids. This is especially so in the 'robust' australopithecines; the smaller, more 'gracile' hominids such as *Homo habilis*, *Australopithecus africanus* and *Australopithecus afarensis* – in which the back teeth are less massive – have more lightly built jaws.

The fossil hominid with the largest back teeth (*Paranthropus boisei*, nicknamed 'Nutcracker Man') has the smallest incisors and canines and the fossil hominid with the smallest back teeth (*Australopithecus afarensis*) has the largest incisors and canines. This reflects the evolutionary shift from the general form of ape teeth to that of hominids, but may also suggest that some fossil hominids relied less on their front teeth than on their hands to prepare food. The need for large canines might have lessened because social groups were smaller and more manageable or because the evolution of language made it easier to communicate emotions without using the teeth.

Clues from enamel

The fine structure of tooth tissue, especially of *enamel*, tells us a lot about human evolution. Teeth are made up of a core of mineralised tissue called *dentine*, which is covered with a

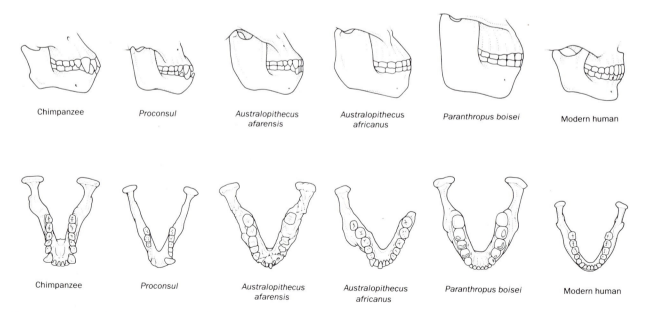

Chimpanzee   Proconsul   *Australopithecus afarensis*   *Australopithecus africanus*   *Paranthropus boisei*   Modern human

Chimpanzee   Proconsul   *Australopithecus afarensis*   *Australopithecus africanus*   *Paranthropus boisei*   Modern human

During human evolution the height of the mandible and the length of the jaws have changed, resulting in hominids with less-protruding jaws and taller faces. The form of the tooth row, or dental arcade, has also changed from a U-shaped or straightsided to a rounded or parabolic form. The dental arch of *Australopithecus afarensis* is more ape-like than that of *Australopithecus africanus* and *Paranthropus boisei*.

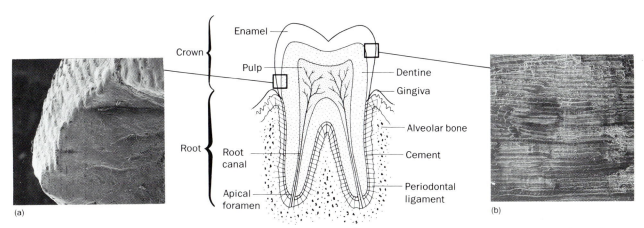

The microanatomy of teeth. At high magnification (b) enamel can be seen to be composed of many rods and prisms that run from the junction between the enamel and dentine to the tooth surface. Lower power (a) reveals coarser incremental lines that run across the prisms at near-weekly intervals and crop out at the surface of the tooth as perikymata (alternating ridges and troughs). These can be counted in some fossil hominid teeth and used to calibrate developmental events, such as the time of the emergence of the first permanent molar.

thin layer of enamel over the *crown* and an extremely thin layer of *cementum* over the *root*. In the centre of the tooth is a *pulp chamber* full of blood vessels and nerves.

Enamel is the hardest biological substance known. The teeth of gorillas and chimpanzees have a thinner layer than those of fossil hominids, modern humans, orang-utans or even fossil apes such as *Sivapithecus*. Although tough food might favour the evolution of thick enamel, body size and the time that teeth have to function over a lifetime may also have some affect. The thin enamel of the African apes might expose an edge of enamel and dentine on the cusps early, so that the teeth can cut foliage more efficiently, rather like the lophs of Old World monkey teeth.

The enamel layer in orang-utans is only slightly thicker than in gorillas and chimpanzees, but it does not wear away as rapidly. In modern apes at least, there is thus a less than straightforward relationship between the rate of tooth wear and thick enamel. The back teeth of the robust australopithecines *Paranthropus robustus* and *P. boisei* have the thickest enamel of any primate, being massively expanded in the heavy jaws. In hominids and modern humans, thick enamel probably evolved to combat the effects of a tough diet.

Enamel preserves growth lines and it is possible to make thin sections of teeth and time the formation of a tooth crown. This method has been used in fossil hominids to calibrate other events, such as the time of emergence of the first permanent molar tooth. This is at 6 years in modern humans and at 3.5 years in great apes. In several young fossil hominids – for example, the juvenile fossil hominid from Taung in southern Africa – it seems to have erupted at about 3 to 4 years. Early fossil hominids might therefore have had patterns of growth and development similar to those of modern great apes. This is also suggested from the size of their brains and their body size.

Modern humans have shorter jaws and smaller teeth than apes. Our teeth lie in small rounded *dental arcades* whereas those of apes are aligned in a U-shaped pattern with long, straight sides. Most congenital abnormalities in the number and form of human teeth also occur in apes, albeit at different frequencies. In gorillas, for example, it is common to find extra molar teeth (usually four but sometimes five molars in a quadrant). This pattern occurs rarely in modern humans. In contrast, it is unusual to find the third molars missing in great apes but quite common to do so in modern humans. Even two early fossil hominids (Omo 75/14A from Ethiopia and Lantian from China), both *Homo erectus*, have congenitally missing third molars.

The last tooth in a series is particularly susceptible to variation in morphology and number. In humans, the upper lateral incisor is commonly peg-shaped or missing altogether. The lower second premolar (P_4) is quite commonly missing beneath the second deciduous molar, and it is also common to find supernumerary (extra) teeth both in the incisor region and the premolar region.

The last molar to erupt – the *wisdom tooth* – is often absent in modern humans, reflecting, perhaps, a shortening of the dental arcade. It is not clear why this should be so. Perhaps the differences in number and form of human teeth compared to ape teeth reflect the relationship between tooth size and space available in the jaws. In some modern human populations, there is plenty of room in the jaws and the frequency of missing teeth might be expected to be low, whereas in others teeth are crowded in the jaws and more of them might be predicted to be congenitally absent. There is no clear pattern of variability in modern humans – there are high and low frequencies among African, European and Far Eastern populations. An understanding of just why these trends have taken place demands a lot more work.   *Christopher Dean*

See also 'Non-human primates' (p. 24), 'Evolution of New World monkeys' (p. 209), 'Evolution of Old World monkeys' (p. 217), 'Evolution of apes' (p. 223), 'Evolution of australopithecines' (p. 231), 'The hominid way of life' (p. 325)

Diets and guts

In their natural habitats, our primate relatives select foods to obtain nutrients of three main types – lipids, carbohydrates and proteins. Food selection is also influenced by the need for minerals, vitamins and some essential amino acids. In most plants, however, there are protective compounds, such as inhibitors of digestion (e.g. tannins) and toxins (e.g. cyanides), that are potentially harmful to the herbivores that eat them. Food selection is thus a compromise between maximising the intake of nutrients and minimising the ingestion of plant protective compounds.

Primates are essentially fruit-eaters (*frugivores*), with guts showing proportions intermediate between the dominating small intestines of meat-eaters (*faunivores*) and the much enlarged stomach or caecum and colon of leaf-eaters (*folivores*). This gives a unique dietary flexibility, so that smaller primates supplement fruit with animal matter, and larger species have some folivorous adaptations. All show considerable variation in diet throughout the year, especially in areas with marked seasonality.

Nutrients in the natural diets of primates occur in three main forms:

- Animal matter (mostly insects and other arthropods but occasionally small vertebrates), which provides protein, lipids and essential amino acids
- Fruits and seeds, which provide non-structural carbohydrates and lipids. These reproductive plant parts may have mechanical or chemical defences to protect them from being eaten
- Leaves and flowers, which contain many structural carbohydrates, such as cellulose. Structural carbohydrates can be broken down only by bacteria living in the gut in a co-operative or *symbiotic* relationship. Leaves tend to have high concentrations of digestive inhibitors (and sometimes of toxins) but are usually rich in protein. Some flowers produce nectar

The most abundant potential foods – leaves – are the least digestible. Mostly, only large mammals, such as ungulates (cattle, antelope, horses and related forms), have guts sufficiently capacious to be able to digest large quantities of this food resource. Other mammals, such as carnivores (dogs and cats), insectivores (shrews and moles) and cetaceans (dolphins and whales), have adapted to exploiting the more nourishing, but rarer and mobile, animal foods. Among mammals, only primates have exploited the resources of intermediate availability – fruits. The success of primates relates to a relative lack of specialisation, and it is instructive therefore to compare gastrointestinal adaptations of primates with those of other, more specialist feeders – the folivores and faunivores.

Some primates, such as many nocturnal prosimians, have retained links with their insectivorous ancestry by remaining small and faunivorous. Fruit-eating seems to be the key to the evolution of monkeys and apes. Some species that have become (or have stayed) small, still use animal matter as a key dietary component (e.g. the smaller New World monkeys). Others have become larger and their guts have become adapted to varying degrees to digesting a significant intake of leaves (e.g. the Old World colobine monkeys, the howler monkeys of the New World and the gorilla among great apes). Because, for anatomical and physiological reasons, no mammal can exploit large amounts of both animal matter and leaves, the widely used term 'omnivore' is singularly inappropriate, even for primates. Humans might reasonably be called omnivores, however, as a result of food processing and cookery.

Diets of wild primates

It is easiest to obtain information on the diets of wild primates in terms of the amount of time spent feeding on each type of food. However, it is the actual amount of any food ingested that is central to metabolism and to functional anatomy. Although we are best informed about feeding times, we know enough about the amounts of individual items (from studies of langurs, macaques, gibbons and gorillas), to make corrections to simple measures of feeding time. Such measures tend to overestimate the intake of leaves and animal matter by weight, and to underestimate fruit intake (fruit tends to be eaten faster).

Diets can be represented in the form of a triangular diagram, with 100 per cent faunivory, 100 per cent frugivory and 100 per cent folivory at the three corners. Such diagrams represent annual averages and hence encompass considerable month-to-month variation, especially important for primates. As the main spectrum of variation among primates is from faunivory to folivory, a simpler and useful dietary index ranges from 100 per cent faunivory to 100 per cent folivory, but there are few primates close to these regimes. Exclusive frugivory is practically impossible, because certain essential amino acids and other nutrients are found only in leaves or in animal matter.

Tigers, foxes and pangolins occur at or near 100 per cent faunivory, whereas horses, sheep and rabbits lie at or near 100 per cent folivory. Most primates range between these poles, between 55 and 80 per cent frugivory. Two members of the loris group, the angwantibo (*Arctocebus calabarensis*) and the slender loris (*Loris tardigradus*), as well as tarsiers (*Tarsius*) are examples of predominant faunivores. Most primates are frugivores, supplementing their diets with animal matter or leaves to varying degrees. The gorilla (*Gorilla gorilla*) is a folivore, whereas sportive lemurs (*Lepilemur*), howler monkeys (*Alouatta*), and colobus monkeys (*Colobus*) and the related langurs (*Presbytis*) are folivore–frugivores, eating virtually no animal matter. There are no primate species much below the centre of the triangular diagram, where one might find true omnivores. Because of cooking and food processing, humans can be described as the only omnivores, but we shall see that their gut dimensions are those of a faunivore.

Prosimians

Prosimian primates have diverged in isolation in Madagascar to span the dietary spectrum. Some species, such as Coquerel's mouse lemur (*Microcebus coquereli*), remain faunivorous; others, such as dwarf lemurs (*Cheirogaleus*) and the ring-tailed lemur (*Lemur catta*), are frugivorous. Sportive lemurs and the indri (*Indri*) are folivorous, with sifakas (*Propithecus*) intermediate. These differences relate to the different habitats in which the Malagasy lemurs live, from the forests of the wet east and north to the more open habitats of the dry south and west of the island. Even on the African mainland, the larger species of bushbaby (*Otolemur*) and the related potto (*Perodicticus potto*) are frugivorous.

New World monkeys

New World monkeys, confined as they are to forests, show marked variation both in body size and in ecological niche.

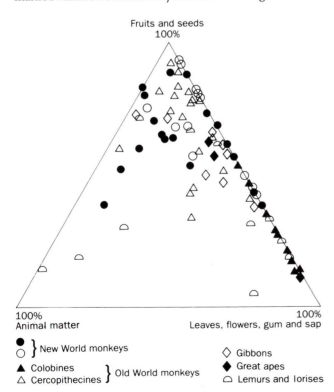

Fruits and seeds
100%

100%
Animal matter

100%
Leaves, flowers, gum and sap

● ○ } New World monkeys

▲ Colobines
△ Cercopithecines } Old World monkeys

◇ Gibbons
◆ Great apes
⌂ Lemurs and lorises

Diets can be represented in the form of a triangular diagram, with 100 per cent faunivory, 100 per cent folivory and 100 per cent frugivory at the three corners. Here, the average diets of 80 primates are shown with fauni-frugivores to the left and foli-frugivores to the right; prosimian species are particularly variable in their diets.

The small marmosets and tamarins, such as *Callithrix* and *Saguinus*, are frugivores, although they may eat animal matter, gums and sap as supplements (see Box). The smaller cebid monkeys, the owl monkey (*Aotus trivirgatus*), titi monkeys (*Callicebus*), squirrel monkeys (*Saimiri*) and capuchin monkeys (*Cebus*) are even more frugivorous, although animal matter is still a significant component of the diet. The medium-sized uakaris and sakis (*Cacajao*, *Chiropotes* and *Pithecia*) are seed-eaters (rather than eaters of fruit pulp), with leaves as the main supplement. The largest cebid monkeys are either pulp-eating frugivores (spider and woolly monkeys: *Ateles*, *Brachyteles*, *Lagothrix*) or pulp-eating frugivore–folivores (howler monkeys).

Old World monkeys

Old World monkeys are less variable in body size than New World monkeys, so their diets are generally also less variable. However, the specialised leaf-eating monkeys of the subfamily Colobinae are a special case. They are relatively large for arboreal primates and are distinctive for their extreme folivory. African colobines (e.g. *Colobus*) tend to eat more leaves than Asian species (e.g. *Presbytis*), which eat more seeds. This special feature of Asiatic colobines reflects both competition between closely related species and the fact that leaves in forest growing on poorer soils tend to have better chemical defences. The fruits eaten by langurs are generally dry and unripe. Seed-eating by colobines is most common in the smaller species, which have relatively greater metabolic needs.

Cercopithecine monkeys (guenons and their relatives) eat mainly sweet, succulent fruit, although species of *Cercopithecus* are divided into those that eat roughly comparable amounts of fruit and leaves (frugivore–folivores), and those that are 75 to 85 per cent folivorous. Most cercopithecine monkeys eat significant amounts of animal matter (10 to 25 per cent). Mangabeys (*Cercocebus*) eat fruit, supplemented with some leaves and a few animals. The smallest species, the talapoin (*Miopithecus talapoin*), has the highest intake of animal matter (about 35 per cent) in addition to its staple diet of fruit. The more terrestrial African baboons (*Papio*) and Asian macaques (*Macaca*) consume 70 to 80 per cent of their diets as fruit. Baboons also eat foliage (including herbs, grasses and roots) as a major supplement, and both baboons and macaques eat significant amounts of animal matter, including small vertebrates. Cercopithecines seem to be quite opportunistic so long as they achieve a long-term balance in the intake of primary nutrients.

Apes

Apes are similar to cercopithecine monkeys, in that they typically consume ripe fruit. The larger they are, the greater the intake of leaves – for example, the siamang (*Hylobates syndactylus*) among the lesser apes and the gorilla among the great apes. Apes must eat young leaves and ripe fruit, however, as they lack the ability of monkeys to counteract the digestion inhibitors in older leaves and unripe fruit. The mainly terrestrial chimpanzees (*Pan*) are less frugivorous than the arboreal orang-utan (*Pongo pygmaeus*) and spend much time foraging for animal matter, including mammals.

Form of the mammalian gut

The guts of faunivores are dominated by the small intestine – the main compartment in the gut for absorption. By contrast, the stomach (foregut) of faunivores is simple, the colon (hindgut) is short, and the caecum is commonly vestigial or absent. Folivores require a much-expanded compartment for the bacterial fermentation of the cellulose cell walls in leaves. In functional terms, this is most simply achieved by lengthening and widening the caecum and the first part of the colon (the terminal part of the primitive midgut loop). Such is the case in horses and rabbits, and to a lesser extent in leaf-eating primates, such as sportive lemurs and howler monkeys.

Deficiencies in digestion in the smaller mammalian herbivores are such that they must reingest the faeces produced from the first passage of food through the gut. More efficient is the stomach of ruminants (deer, antelope, cattle, sheep and goats) with its many pouches or sacs. Some authorities have related the evolution of this type of *sacculated stomach* to the spread of luxuriant grasslands in the Miocene epoch, since 20 million years ago. Development of the complex stomach has been paralleled in some other mammals, including colobine monkeys. Hence, the evolution of the sacculated stomach is now equated by some with an initial focus on seed-eating; the adaptations were subsequently used for leaf-eating. All small folivores, including ruminants, are selective feeders, suporting the idea that larger ruminants may have passed through such a selective phase.

Expanding a sac rather than a tube, however, presents problems in the provision of an adequate absorptive area with increasing volume. The surface area of a cylinder increases proportionately with volume, while that of a sphere lags increasingly behind. For this reason, complex stomachs have developed compartments, folds and papillae, with constraints on the maximum size they can reach. The passage rate of digestion can be altered much more easily through tubes than sacs, which is important for fluctuating food quality.

The guts of frugivores are intermediate in size and proportions between those of faunivores and folivores. The frugivore's stomach and, particularly, the large intestine are larger than in faunivores, reflecting the requirements for digesting fruit, along with a supplement of young foliage in the larger species.

Effects of body size

Making dietary comparisons between primate species is impeded if the scaling effects of differing body size are

A colobine monkey, the dusky langur (*Presbytis obscurus*) from Malaysia, eating leaves. It has an expanded, sacculated stomach and enlarged caecum and colon for fermentation of cellulose by bacteria.

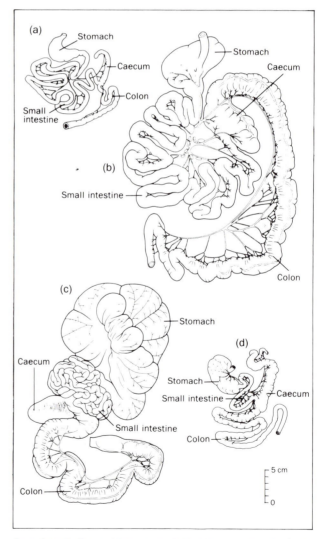

Gastrointestinal tracts (stomach, small intestine, caecum and colon) of (a) a faunivore: angwangtibo (*Arctocebus*); (b) a frugivore: macaque (*Macaca*); (c) and (d) folivores: langur (*Presbytis*) and sportive lemur (*Lepilemur*). The trend is for relative decrease in size of the small intestine and relative increase in stomach and/or caecum and colon.

PRIMATE GUM-EATERS

Most primates eat at least some fruit, with insects or leaves making up the rest of their food. However, a few exploit another source of carbohydrates – substances that seep from the trunks and branches of many trees and shrubs (plant *exudates*). Many exudates – such as resins from conifers, the acidic derivatives of phenol or terpine – are unpalatable. But some plants, particularly trees in the family Mimosaceae, produce edible gums.

Gums consist mainly of polymerised pentose sugars but also contain varying amounts of protein and trace minerals. A well-known example of some commerical importance is gum arabic, which is collected from *Acacia senegal*. Some prosimians and small New World monkeys called marmosets are specialised gum-feeders, or *gummivores*.

Gums and resins are usually produced in response to injury, such as that resulting from penetration of bark by wood-boring insects. In acacia trees, for example, it is common to find tunnels beneath the bark drilled by beetle or moth larvae. Exit holes are made when the insects leave their retreats. Plant exudates are thus an 'emergency plug' to seal such wounds. Animals that feed on gums hence exploit the natural defence mechanism of certain plants.

Numerous mammals include gums in their diets. Specialised gummivores are, however, relatively rare because the polymerised sugars in gums are difficult to digest and seem to require the enzymatic

activities of symbiotic bacteria. For this reason, mammalian gummivores typically have an enlarged caecum to house a population of bacteria.

Feeding on gum is quite widespread among primates – as might be expected from their generally arboreal habits – but there are only a few specialised gummivores. Among them are two

A fork-marked lemur (*Phaner furcifer*) feeding on gum exuding from a tree trunk.

nocturnal prosimians, the fork-marked lemur (*Phaner furcifer*) and the needle-clawed bushbaby (*Euoticus elegantulus*).

In both these prosimians, gums are a major part of the diet and the caecum, with its population of bacteria, is greatly enlarged. Night-time travel is largely governed by the need to visit a succession of gum-producing trees. Both species have

a striking modification of the nails so that they can cling to broad trunks and branches while feeding on gum; the nails bear sharp points at their tips, the 'needle claws' referred to in the common name of the bushbaby species.

Lemurs and lorises use the tooth-comb at the front of the lower jaw as a scoop to collect soft gum. The structure is, however, too fragile to make holes in the bark of trees to stimulate gum production. It is hence possible that its evolution was connected with the exploitation of naturally occurring gum-licks by the common ancestor of lemurs and lorises.

Among diurnal simian primates, marmosets also show specialisations in connection with gum-feeding. The incisors and canines in the lower jaw are of equal length, forming a tough scoop. Using this, marmosets can make holes in bark and thus reach plant sap as well as gum. Like gum-feeding prosimians, marmosets have an enlarged caecum.

Some tamarins also feed on gums but they have to rely on naturally occurring gum-licks as they lack the dental specialisations of marmosets – the canines are longer than the incisors and the lower front teeth do not form a scoop.

Marmosets and tamarins are also unusual in having claw-like appendages rather than nails on most digits. This may be a secondary adaptation that enables these small monkeys to cling to tree trunks while harvesting gum.

Robert Martin

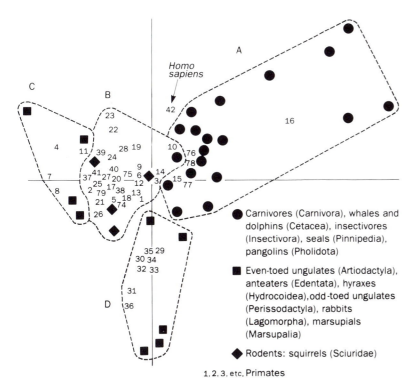

Homo sapiens

A

C

B

D

Carnivores (Carnivora), whales and dolphins (Cetacea), insectivores (Insectivora), seals (Pinnipedia), pangolins (Pholidota)

Even-toed ungulates (Artiodactyla), anteaters (Edentata), hyraxes (Hydrocoidea), odd-toed ungulates (Perissodactyla), rabbits (Lagomorpha), marsupials (Marsupialia)

Rodents: squirrels (Sciuridae)

1, 2, 3, etc. Primates

Multidimensional plot of indices for surface areas of stomach, small intestine and caecum + colon for 80 primates and other mammals: A, faunivores spreading to upper right, with 'insectivores' and cetaceans more extreme than 'carnivores'; B, frugivores, with most primates in the 'central' cluster; C, midgut-fermenting folivores, with primates near to the frugivore cluster and the horse most extreme; D, foregut-fermenting folivores, with ruminants more extreme than colobine monkeys.

Primates are numbered: 1, *Arctocebus calabarensis*; 2, *Avahi laniger*; 3, *Cheirogaleus major*; 4, *Euoticus elegantulus*; 5, *Galago alleni*; 6, *G. demidovii*; 7, *Lepilemur mustelinus*; 8, *L. leucopus*; 9, *Loris tardigradus*; 10, *Microcebus murinus*; 11, *Perodicticus potto*; 12, *Saguinus geoffroyi*; 13, *Aotus trivirgatus*; 14, *Ateles belzebuth*; 15, *Saimiri oerstedii*; 16, *Cebus capucinus*; 17, *Alouatta palliata*; 18, *Lagothrix lagotricha*; 19, *Miopithecus talapoin*; 20, *Cercopithecus cephus*; 21, *C. neglectus*; 22, *C. nictitans*; 23, *Cercocebus albigena*; 24, *Macaca sylvanus*; 25, *M. sinica*; 26, *M. fascicularis*; 27, *Papio (Mandrillus) sphinx*; 28, *Erythrocebus patas*; 29, *Colobus polykomos*; 30, *Presbytis entellus*; 31, *P. cristata*; 32, *P. obscura*; 33, *P. melalophos*; 34, *P. rubicunda*; 35, *Nasalis larvatus*; 36, *Pygathrix nemaeus*; 37, *Hylobates pileatus*; 38, *H. syndactylus*; 39, *Pongo pygmaeus*; 40, *Pan troglodytes*; 41, *Gorilla gorilla*; 42, *Homo sapiens*; 43, *Cacajao calvus*; 44, *C. melancephalus*; 45, *Cebus apella*; 46, *Saimiri sciureus*; 47, *S. vanzolinii*; 48, *Alouatta seniculus*.

neglected. Volumes of the stomach and the large intestine (in relation to fermentation) and the areas of the small intestine (in relation to absorption) must hence be examined in relation to body size. Overall, the volumes of potential fermenting chambers increase in direct proportion to body size, whereas the areas of the main absorbing region scale according to the three-quarters power of body size. This indicates that the surface area of the small intestine scales in the same way as basal metabolic rate (Kleiber's law); see p. 41.

Quantitative analysis shows the extent to which the size of each part of the gut is larger or smaller than expected. A multidimensional plot combining such information for stomach, intestine, caecum and colon confirms the more marked specialisations of exclusive meat-eaters – for example, carnivores and insectivores (upper right of the figure, p. 63) – and of exclusive leaf-eaters – for example, artiodactyls (ruminants), perissodactyls and rodents (enlarged stomachs: lower part of the figure; enlarged caecum/colon: upper left).

Most primates occupy a central position in this diagram, providing a frugivore cluster, but some species occur in the three specialist branches away from this cluster. Seed-eaters are at the base of the caeco-colic-fermenting branch, indicating similar digestive problems to processing young leaves; gum-eaters are further into this cluster. Humans are on the inner edge of the faunivore cluster, showing the distinctive adaptations of their guts for meat-eating, or for some other rapidly digested foods, in contrast to the frugivorous apes (and monkeys). Colobine monkeys lie in the cluster containing folivorous species with enlarged stomachs.

These analyses show that it is essential to remove the effects of body size to understand the relationship between structure and function in the mammalian gastrointestinal tract. We still need to study more species and to clarify the anatomical requirements for the digestion of seeds, nectar, gums and saps, and different components of the structural parts of plants. In addition, knowledge of food passage times is crucial for more detailed interpretation of dietary and digestive patterns. However, it is already clear that the direct functional adaptation of the gastrointestinal tract of each species emerges as a more important factor in determining the patterns of primate guts than does phylogenetic affinity.

D.J. Chivers

See also 'Body size and energy requirements' (p. 41), 'Selecting and processing food' (p. 65) and 'Human diet and subsistence' (p. 69)

Selecting and processing food

Most primates, including humans, obtain some part of their food from plants. Only tarsiers (*Tarsius* spp.) are absolutely carnivorous. Meat generally presents few problems for primate digestive tracts. However, plant foods call for adaptive changes in behaviour and anatomy to allow this widely available, but chemically complex, energy source to be used. Special mechanisms have evolved to deal with the poisonous secondary compounds in many plant parts. Every part of a plant may be eaten by primates, but leaves make up the bulk of vegetable matter consumed by many species.

Plants vary widely in their chemical composition. The main components are complex structural carbohydrates (cellulose and hemicellulose) and related polymers (lignins). These are the most abundant potential source of energy, but primates (and other mammals) cannot utilise them directly because they lack the enzymes required for their digestion. To make use of this abundant resource, primates and other mammals have evolved a co-operative or *symbiotic* relationship with micro-organisms such as bacteria and single-celled organisms called protozoans that live in the gut and provide the enzymes needed to digest the cellulose.

Digestion of cellulose

Microbial fermentation occurs either in the enlarged foregut (stomach) or in the caecum. Among non-human primates, there is known to be foregut fermentation in langurs (*Presbytis*) and colobus monkeys (*Colobus*), and caecal fermentation in howler monkeys (*Alouatta*). Foregut fermenters have large stomachs with many pouch-like parts or sacs, whereas caecal fermenters have simple stomachs but a large, divided caecum.

The products of fermentation in both foregut and caecal fermenters are volatile fatty acids, carbon dioxide, methane and microbial cells. The gases (carbon dioxide and methane) are waste products, while the energy-rich fatty acids and microbial cells are used by the host. In mammals with caecal fermentation, food is digested in the stomach before microbial fermentation takes place. This means that the simple structural carbohydrates (from fruit and nectar) are digested and absorbed in the stomach and small intestine before the complex carbohydrates are acted on in the caecum by the gut's microbial inhabitants.

Fermentation in the caecum may have an advantage over fermentation in the foregut because plant toxins are not broken down (they remain biologically inactive) until after the food and any toxins it contains have passed through the small intestine with its highly absorptive walls. This means

that the breakdown of toxins is carried out primarily by the micro-organisms in the caecum and not by the host's liver, which could get damaged as a result. Also, because the large intestine (colon) is less absorptive, there is less chance of the by-products of the toxins being taken up by the body. Of course, this may also mean that absorption of nutrients is reduced. Gorillas and the sportive lemur (*Lepilemur*), which are both caecal fermenters, ingest their own faeces in the wild so that there is a second passage of food material, this time newly detoxified, through the intestine.

The long intestine of some herbivores delays the passage of food through it but may increase the efficiency of the gut micro-organisms. In primates, the time taken for food passage is positively correlated with body size; in other words, the larger the primate the slower the rate of passage. Although large primates need absolutely more food, metabolic costs per unit body weight decrease as body size increases. Thus, small primates have relatively higher energetic costs per unit body weight and must select high-quality food because they do not have the space in their gut to process large amounts of low-quality food. Large primates do not have this problem.

How primates deal with toxic chemicals

Plant parts are more than convenient packets of nutrients waiting to be unwrapped by micro-organisms in the digestive tracts of primates. Plants can and do defend themselves from hungry primates by using chemical defences, based on secondary compounds. These evolved as a defence against insects. In turn, insects evolved methods of handling the new plant chemicals and thus were able to maintain their association with their plants: an evolutionary 'arms race'. The fact that some plant secondary chemicals are also toxic, and serve as a deterrent to primates (which evolved much later than insects), is incidental but is nevertheless of value to the plant that contains them.

Plant-eating primates must deal with these rapidly evolving chemicals, which range from compounds that reduce digestibility (e.g. protein-binding tannins and enzymes) to toxins (e.g. alkaloids, cyanogenic glycosides and non-protein amino acids). Both physiology and behaviour are involved in helping primates to deal with the secondary compounds of plants.

Mammals use two main methods to detoxify such compounds. They can be degraded by microsomal enzymes in the liver and kidneys or by the gut micro-organisms. Indeed, the need to detoxify the secondary compounds of plants may have led to the evolution of foregut fermentation in the first place. For example, the micro-organisms

FOOD IN A PRIMATE'S LIFE

In order to survive and reproduce, a primate must find enough to eat and yet avoid being eaten itself. Much is now known about primate diets, especially about how primates select food items and how different species living in the same forest divide up its resources. Less clear, but equally important, is the link between the spatial and temporal distribution of the food available and the social organisation of primates.

The diets of most primates are made up predominantly of plant parts. Some species also eat insects and a few, particularly macaques and baboons, occasionally prey on nestling birds, lizards, or even the odd frog or crab. Baboons and chimpanzees hunt mammals as well, but meat is not a major item in their diet. Only the little tarsiers of Southeast Asia have never been seen to eat plants: they feed exclusively on insects and other small animals.

Why does a primate select particular kinds of food in preference to others? Body size and specialisations of the teeth and gut strongly influence choices. Large-bodied primates, for instance, need bulky and abundant foods to meet their energy, protein and other nutritional needs. Leaves, a major source of protein, figure importantly in their diet, and fleshy fruits provide energy in the form of fruit sugar. Leaves are difficult to process, and leaf-eating primates have teeth specialised for shearing and grinding leaf blades, and guts specialised for digesting them. In contrast, small-bodied primates tend to seek out insects, which constitute a high-quality, though sparse, source of protein, and they supplement their diet with energy-rich fruit or gums.

In the early days of field reseach, primates were considered wasteful, clumsy feeders because they frequently drop food, particularly fruit, from the trees in which they are feeding. Subsequent work has shown that in fact they are highly selective, and the fruit raining down has been discarded as either unripe or too ripe. The nutritional qualities of fruit and leaves vary from one plant species to another, and from one season to another, and primates use taste, vision and smell to choose amongst them. For example, almost all leaf-eating primates have a strong preference for immature leaves, which tend to be higher in protein and lower in fibre and poisons than mature ones.

The discovery of poisonous compounds in some leaves has encouraged research on primate–plant relationships from the plants' point of view, and a whole array of defensive strategies used by plants against herbivores, including primates, has now been uncovered. Some plants use primates to disperse their seeds: they produce fleshy fruits that attract primates, but the seeds pass unharmed through the digestive tract of many of these fruit-eaters, and are then deposited in faeces, often far from the parent tree.

The dietary choices of primates are influenced by their own attributes and those of the plants and animals potentially available as food. It has been suggested that competition for food between primate species living in the same forest may also help determine diet, by preventing one species from eating food that is important in the diet of another. The role of competition in establishing and maintaining ecological differences among primates (*niche separation*) is still unclear, but niche separation itself has been found wherever it has been sought: from South American rainforest communities contain-

Capped langurs (*Presbytis pileata*) on a fruit tree in Assam, India.

ing 11 primate species, through African communities with as many as 15, to Malaysian communities of 6. No two primate species use the forest in identical ways.

A primate's diet affects many aspects of its life. Primates with leafy diets tend to be less active than those preferring fruit, moving shorter distances each day and occupying a smaller home range. Determining the ways in which the ecology of a primate species influences its social organisation is a particularly challenging problem.

We know that insect-eating primates tend to be solitary or to live in small social groups, probably because it is easier to hunt insects alone, and that fruit-eating primates often live in social groups that fragment and rejoin, depending on the size of fruiting patches. But many factors influence social organisation and it is difficult to evaluate their relative influence.

For instance, in order to survive, a primate must not only find food but also avoid predators. Species (e.g. savanna baboons) living where predators are abundant usually live in larger social groups than their relatives occupying a forest environment: the old maxim of 'safety in numbers' contains some real truth. Against this, large group size presents a potential disadvantage for its members, because competition for food is likely to be greater than in a small group.

A final complicating factor in attempts to sort out the relationship between primate ecology and social organisation is the possibility that ecological influences affect males and females differently. For example, it has been suggested that female chimpanzees distribute themselves primarily in relation to the distribution of food, but that males distribute themselves primarily in relation to females.

In sum, it is clear that food plays a much larger part in the life of a primate than merely providing the means for staying alive and healthy. Less clear is precisely how diet is linked to other spheres of a primate's life.   *A.F. Richard*

in the stomach of the Hanuman langur (*Presbytis entellus*) may protect this primate from the large amounts of alkaloids in the fruit of the clearing nut (*Strychnos potatorum*).

Very little is known about the biochemical pathways used by non-human primates to detoxify plant chemicals. Comparative studies of drug metabolism in primates suggest that non-human primates metabolise drugs much as humans do. The relative importance of enzymes and gut micro-organisms in detoxifying foreign substances is unknown for most plant secondary compounds. No single species of primate can possibly have all the mechanisms needed to handle every kind of plant poison. They must also depend on behaviour to cope with the toxic chemicals produced by plants.

Selective feeding

A primate can either become a specialist and feed on only one or very few food species, or it can become a generalist and feed on a wide variety of plants. Extreme specialists, such as the marsupial koala bear, which feeds only on the leaves of the eucalyptus (and in some cases favours only one eucalyptus species, *Eucalytpus viminalis*), have to deal with only one or a few secondary compounds. However, because they feed on only a few plant species they could be

Most primates do not specialise on one or two plants but selectively feed on a variety of species. Here (above), a red-fronted lemur (*Lemur fulvus rufus*) is feeding on leaf buds of red maple (*Acer rubrum*) and (right) a mantled howler monkey (*Alouatta palliata*) is choosing new leaves of fig (*Ficus*). In this way, generalist feeders avoid plant parts containing toxic chemicals at certain times of the year and get a balanced diet.

in serious trouble should these become scarce. Generalists, on the other hand, are faced with a wide variety of chemicals and they cannot maintain detoxification systems for all of them. Therefore, they reduce the total number of chemicals or the amount of any one that they must process by selecting plants or plant parts that contain few chemicals or by ingesting small amounts of many foods. This varied diet provides generalists with a balanced intake of nutrients and protects them against a shortage of any one food.

Most primates are generalists, so most of the herbivorous species do not specialise on one or a few plants but selectively feed on a variety of species. For example, mantled howlers (*Alouatta palliata*) in Costa Rica and on Barro Colorado Island, Panama, prefer new leaves, fruits and flowers to mature leaves and thus avoid material containing certain secondary compounds. Black colobus monkeys (*Colobus satanas*) in Cameroon avoid the mature leaves of all common tree species and the new leaves of most of them, while feeding selectively on relatively rare tree species or on colonising plant species. The mature leaves of the common Cameroonian trees contain very high concentrations of toxic phenolic compounds. Black-and-white colobus monkeys (*Colobus guereza*) and vervets (*Cercopithecus aethiops*) are now known to behave in a similar way. Mountain gorillas (*Gorilla gorilla beringei*) on Mt Visoke, Rwanda, do not even sample balsam (*Impatiens*), one of the most common plants in their home ranges.

Medicinal uses of plants

Consumption of plants with known medicinal properties have been observed in chacma and Hamadryas baboons (*Papio ursinus* and *P. hamadryas*) and in common chimpanzees (*Pan troglodytes*). The leaves and berries of *Balanites aegyptiaca*

could be eaten by the baboons as a protection against schistosomiasis. A female chimpanzee in the Mahale Mountains, Tanzania, has been seen chewing and then sucking the juice of bitter leaf (*Vernonia amygdalina*). She appeared ill with an influenza-like sickness from which she gradually recovered after swallowing the astringent juice of a bitter leaf. Bitter leaf is used by people throughout Africa for parasites and gastrointestinal disorders. Given this ethnomedicinal use of plants by humans, it is not unreasonable to assume a similar use by other primates.

Plant poisons and human evolution

Humans also rely on plants for a considerable amount of their food. The secondary compounds of plants have major implications for our ancestors and for ourselves.

Our early hominid ancestors, who were primarily planteaters and did not have the benefits of fire, were faced with the same problems as those faced by non-human primates. It has even been suggested that the numbers of early humans were limited by food availability because of plant toxins. Before the use of fire for cooking, which may have come relatively late in human evolution, early humans were exposed to the full impact of plant secondary compounds. These ingested secondary compounds may have had important effects on general fitness and even on the age of reproduction. For example, some species of yams (*Dioscorea*) contain diosgenin, which is widely used in birth-control drugs. Initially, such effects were probably unsuspected, but with increasing awareness our ancestors could have chosen specific effects by ingesting certain foods. The modern Aguaruna Jívaro of Peru regularly use natural plant products as contraceptives, suppressors of menstruation, abortifacients, aphrodisiacs and reproductive enhancers.

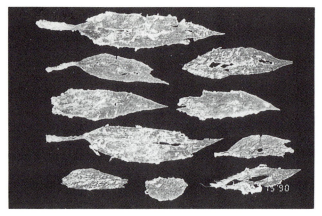

Chimpanzees and baboons – and probably other primates as well – eat plants with known medicinal properties. Chimpanzees, for example, make special foraging trips at dawn to eat young leaves of *Aspilia plurisetta* (left), a member of the sunflower family and a popular African herbal remedy. The leaves contain a potent antibiotic, which is also effective against parasitic worms. Normally, a chimpanzee stuffs leaves into its mouth as fast as it can pull them off the branches, and chews them quickly before swallowing them. It adopts quite a different method for *Aspilia* leaves. It chooses each bristly leaf carefully and then rolls it around its mouth slowly before swallowing it whole. Chimpanzees select and eat the leaves of *Commelina*, another herb with pharmacological properties, in a similar way. The leaves pass through the chimpanzee's gut undigested and appear in the dung whole, presumably having released medicinal chemicals on the way (above).

Some plant secondary compounds, such as caffeine, nicotine, quinine and tannin, are actively sought by humans. Carbonated water with quinine in it is mixed with gin and imbibed. The quality of tea and wine is determined in part by the amount of tannin present. The drinking of tea and wine has been linked to oesophageal cancer, but if milk is added to tea it binds the tannin and prevents its harmful effects. No similar protection is known for wine.

Special ways of treating or preparing many of the foods used by modern humans are required because of plant secondary compounds. For example, clay is often eaten with acorns to absorb tannin and manioc (*Manihot*) must be soaked because it contains cyanogenic glucosides that can cause nerve disorders. Even the common potato (*Solanum tuberosum*) contains the toxic α-solanine and α-chaconine as well as coumarin and must be cooked to make it safe to eat. However, cooking is no guarantee that the toxins have been destroyed or that processed foods are safe. The tubers of parsnips (*Pastinaca sativa*) contain toxic psoralens that are not destroyed in cooking, though these are not in dangerous quantities. Similarly, even though they are processed, coffee, chocolate and tobacco still contain the potentially poisonous caffeine and nicotine, yet we ingest them daily.

Cyanide, morphine and cocaine are all plant secondary compounds that affect humans. Most cyanide poisonings are accidental, but many people are exposed daily to low concentrations of cyanogenic compounds in foods such as nuts. Humans can detoxify fairly large amounts of such compounds, but chronic intake may cause damage to the nervous system. Morphine and cocaine can have positive effects on humans when used as medicines or negative ones when abused. And any food eaten to excess can be poisonous – for example, vitamin A found in liver and in carrots. There is a possible example of this in the human evolutionary record of 1.7 million years ago. Pathological changes in a *Homo erectus* skeleton (KNM-ER 1808) found at Koobi Fora in Kenya are consistent with chronic hyper-vitaminosis A that could have been caused by the individual eating the livers of carnivores or honeybee broods, both of which contain large amounts of vitamin A.

The impact of plant poisons on our evolutionary past remains unknown, but modern humans continue to suffer in the battle with such compounds. An understanding of how our close relatives have dealt with this problem may assist our own survival.
Kenneth E. Glander

See also 'Body size and energy requirements' (p. 41), 'Diets and guts' (p. 60) and 'Human diet and subsistence' (p. 69)

Human diet and subsistence

Modern human societies eat a bewildering array of foods prepared in myriad different ways. National and regional cuisines are very diverse but these culturally regulated eating patterns tend to obscure the biological similarities that underlie them.

Nutrients for health and growth

All humans have two basic needs for food: to supply energy for body processes and physical activity; and to build the protein and mineral components of the body. Both needs vary with age, activity and environment, as well as from individual to individual. All human diets must – if they are to maintain health and promote growth – include five types of nutrient: proteins, carbohydrates, lipids (mainly fats and oils), minerals (including trace elements) and vitamins. Each fulfills a distinct nutritional role, although their body-building and body-maintaining functions interact in complex ways.

Proteins (which can be derived from animals or plants) provide the amino acids needed for building and repairing tissue. Some are synthesised internally, but there are nine essential amino acids that have to be ingested. Balanced or *high-quality proteins* contain amino acids in the proportions required for the human body and are obtained from meat, milk, fish and eggs. Unbalanced or *low-quality proteins* lack one or more of the essential amino acids and are generally derived from plants.

Our muscles function as stores of protein that can be converted into energy when carbohydrate and fat supplies are inadequate, a process that gives rise to the protein-energy malnutrition (PEM) widespread in parts of the tropical world today. Traditional diets lacking high-quality proteins and based largely on plants – such as the tropical American combination of maize, beans, squash and chili pepper – often blend grains and vegetables with complementary amino acid patterns. When such foods are eaten together they can fulfil our requirements for amino acids and, provided enough is consumed, provide a dietary equivalent to protein derived from animals.

Carbohydrates, which mainly come from plants, are converted into glucose in the body and are the main source of energy. The most abundant carbohydrates in modern diets are (1) starch from grains, roots and tubers; (2) sucrose from sugar cane, beet, etc.; and (3) lactose from milk and milk products. In many tropical and some temperate regions, this last item is a very minor source of carbohydrate (and fats), partly because many people are unable to digest lactose.

Lipids, mainly in the form of animal and plant-derived fats and oils, are our most concentrated sources of food energy, and they also carry the fat-soluble vitamins (A, D, E and K) and certain essential fatty acids. Unlike proteins, lipids can be stored in the body; when the intake of proteins, carbohydrates or lipids exceeds energy requirements the excess is deposited as fat in adipose tissue, where it is available to be mobilised later to make up any energy deficit.

Minerals and vitamins are required in much smaller amounts than proteins, carbohydrates and lipids, but at least 14 minerals and 12 vitamins are essential for human growth and health. They are derived from a wide range of plant and animal foods and enter into complex reactions with other nutrients. Unfortunately, they are particularly subject to losses during food-processing.

Most of the minerals that we need occur commonly in foods and are seldom deficient in the diet, but calcium and phosphorus, which are the main constituents of the skeleton, are sometimes in short supply. They are obtained from such plants as beans, peas and nuts, as well as from animal foods, especially milk. Iron is required for the daily synthesis of haemoglobin, which is necessary for oxygen transport. A lack of sufficient iron causes anaemia; an excess can be harmful. Meat is the richest source of iron; and it is also obtained from eggs, nuts, seeds and some leafy vegetables.

Vitamins are organic substances needed in very small amounts to promote particular metabolic reactions. They occur in many different plants and animals, but the lack of certain vitamins is associated with specific diseases. For example, beri-beri is caused by a lack of thiamine in diets based on refined cereals (e.g. polished rice) and lacking

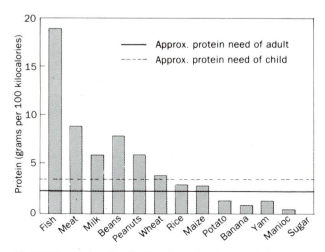

The protein: calorie ratios of various foods. The approximate dietary requirement of protein, in grams per 100 kilocalories of food consumed, for adults and children are shown.

Manioc or cassava (left) needs special processing to make it safe to eat. A Yanomami woman (above) grates soaked tubers.

in meat, and pellagra is associated with largely meatless, maize-based diets.

Toxins

Human health may be affected by toxic substances that occur naturally in foods, especially plant secondary compounds that inhibit the digestion of nutrients or even act as direct poisons. For instance, oxalates in such vegetables as spinach and rhubarb can inhibit calcium absorption, and the cyanogenic glycosides present in certain staple tropical crops such as manioc (cassava) and lima beans can be fatal if not removed during processing. Techniques of detoxification were developed by many agricultural and non-agricultural (hunter-gatherer) peoples in the past, especially in the tropics. They represent an important technological breakthrough, of unknown antiquity, in the evolution of human diet.

Are humans meat-eaters or plant-eaters?

Because the nutrients necessary for life occur in so many food resources distributed throughout the world, our species is endowed with enormous adaptive potential. Modern humans, *Homo sapiens*, emerged as flexible, broad-spectrum feeders or *diversivores* within the past 100 000 years or so. They subsequently spread through all the continents (except Antarctica), and occupied all terrestrial habitats from equatorial rain forest to arctic tundra, in most of which they became ecologically dominant.

In the quest for food, humans intervene in all levels of the food chain. They occupy central positions in food webs, behaving as primary, secondary and tertiary consumers of green plants, of plant-eating and meat-eating animals, and even of decomposers such as fungi. Therefore, like our primate relatives, we are generalist feeders. And, like most primates, we are also highly selective, and usually eat only a small proportion of the diverse food resources available.

Arguments often arise as to whether humans are 'naturally' more faunivorous or herbivorous. This question has little meaning if the whole species is considered, but the balance between meat-eating and plant-eating does vary considerably from population to population, for both environmental and cultural reasons. Meat usually constitutes a very small proportion of the total intake of food, except in high latitudes where plants are scarce and there has been physiological adaptation to diets high in animal fats and proteins (as among the Inuit in the Arctic).

Historical records of 58 hunting, gathering and fishing societies show that hunting was the dominant mode of subsistence only at latitudes greater than 60°. In the cool- to cold-temperate latitudes between 40° and 59°, fishing was dominant among non-agricultural groups, and throughout the warm-temperate, subtropical and tropical parts of the world, between 40° and the Equator, gathering (mainly of plant foods) was the dominant mode of subsistence.

Although hunting was rarely the primary source of food, it made a remarkably consistent contribution to the diet of hunter-gatherer-fisher societies: with only one exception, all such societies derived at least a fifth of their diet from hunting mammals, and, in general, about a third of total food came from this source.

Whether such studies of recent societies can provide an insight into the diet of early humans is debatable. They do, however, accord with the ecological expectation that plant foods, and relatively immobile animal foods such as shell-

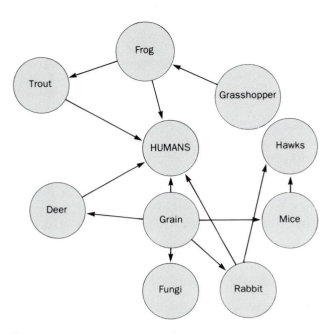

Humans at the centre of a simplified food web.

fish, will constitute the basic daily food supply of non-agricultural peoples. Such foods are spatially and temporally more predictable, as well as more easily procurable, than are game animals. The only exceptions to this pattern involve groups occupying habitats such as tundra, with few plant foods and abundant animal resources (e.g. caribou).

Among agricultural societies, which depend mainly on domesticated crop plants, animals contribute still less to the average diet. Most agriculturalists depend on staple grain or root crops to provide most of their energy. These are supplemented by other crops and sometimes by animal foods. However, one agricultural system – *mixed grain and livestock farming* – incorporates domesticated ungulates (e.g. cattle, sheep, goats and horses) as consumers of crop surpluses and wastes and as providers of meat, milk, hides, horn, hair, wool, transport, traction and fertiliser. This system is associated with grain production in temperate Europe, where it has proved ecologically and nutritionally well adapted to sustaining dense human populations over long periods without a decline in soil fertility. A variant form of mixed grain and livestock farming evolved in South America, in the high-altitude and temperate central Andes. Even here, however, the contribution of animal foods, including meat, milk, cheese and eggs, to the caloric intake of most of the farming population is low, although this system does produce a much greater dietary supply of animal fats and proteins than other systems of agriculture.

Food preferences and avoidances

An ecological view of human nutrition must include the cultural values that societies place on particular foods. Food preferences and avoidances are widespread and operate differentially on people of different sex, age and class. Sexual division of labour in food-connected activities is usual, and in all human groups there are individuals or classes that are exempt from direct participation in the quest for and preparation of food.

In most hunting and gathering societies, women are almost exclusively responsible for gathering and men for hunting. By contrast, among subsistence agriculturalists (for whom hunting is usually a minor activity), agricultural tasks tend to be divided between men and women according to the physical demands of, and status associated with, different activities.

Preferential access to, and prohibitions against, particular foods also vary between individuals, classes and societies. Many hunter-gatherers limit women's access to meat, and prohibitions against the eating of particular foods by individuals, including pregnant women, or by low-status groups within the population, are characteristic of many village farming communities. Culturally regulated food avoidances also operate at the level of whole societies. They apply almost exclusively to animal foods and include the Hindu avoidance of beef, the Moslem and Jewish avoidance of pork, and the Christian avoidance of dog flesh.

The diet of hunter-gatherers

Direct evidence of the diet of early hominids, in the form of food remains, is at present so meagre or equivocal that most research relies on inference. Information comes from:

- Hominid skeletal evidence, especially teeth
- Animal bones and stone tools in archaeological sites
- Dietary studies of other primates
- Analogy with the behaviour of modern hunter-gatherers

There is much controversy over the relative importance of animal and plant foods in early hominid diets, and over the question of whether early hominids obtained meat on the

Aboriginal father and son digging for wild yams in coastal thicket, eastern Cape York Peninsula, Australia.

African savannas primarily by hunting or by scavenging. There is even a possibility that some of the African sites assumed to represent early hominid occupations are actually bone assemblages attributable to the activities of non-human predators and scavengers.

Nothing conclusive can yet be said about the diets of the earliest hominids. Nevertheless, by (possibly unjustified) analogy with modern hunter-gatherers and with non-human terrestrial primates, it may be argued that plant foods (including roots, tubers and seeds) probably contributed much more to the diet than did the flesh of savanna herbivores.

By 2 million years ago, hominids were almost certainly diversivores, feeding in woodland, grassland and aquatic ecosystems in the tropical and subtropical seasonal environments of Africa. By 1 million years ago they had spread widely within the Old World tropics. After the appearance of anatomically modern humans, the process of colonisation continued until, by about 12000 years ago, hunter-gatherers had occupied all the habitable continents.

During this dispersal, the human population adapted to many new habitats and added many new terrestrial and aquatic foods to the dietary repertoire. Adaptation involved the development of novel techniques for capturing and processing food, such as stone-tipped spears, the bow and arrow, fishing devices, grinding stones and methods of detoxifying plant foods, although not enough archaeological evidence is yet available to establish the chronology of such innovations.

Fire

The control and, later, the making of fire was the most important of these innovations. Fire-drives to hunt game, and burning of vegetation to promote new growth to attract grazing and browsing herbivores and to improve the production of certain nuts and other seeds, improved the efficiency of hunting and gathering. Control of fire led to cooking and had a direct and profound effect on human diet by expanding the range of foods available. By roasting and parching, and, later, when pottery and other containers became available, by boiling, steaming and frying, inedible or indigestible foods could be made palatable. Cooking improves the digestibility of some nutrients, particularly starch, although it also leads to some nutrient loss, especially of vitamins and amino acids. It can also eliminate certain toxins.

Cooking is practised by all known hunter-gatherers. Remains of hearths and of charred animal bones have been found at sites occupied by hominids between 400000 and 300000 years ago in Europe and Asia (e.g. Terra Amata in southern France, Vértesszöllös in Hungary and Zhoukoudian (formerly Choukoutien) in northern China), suggesting that by then *Homo erectus* could obtain and control fire, and use it for roasting. Hearths are not common in the archaeological record, however, until about 40000

years ago, after the appearance of modern humans in western Eurasia. By then, the ability to make fire had definitely been acquired.

The colonisation of temperate and cold regions, particularly during the last ice age between 100000 and 10000 years ago, was helped by fire, and led to a greater dependence on terrestrial and aquatic animal foods at the expense of plants. An increased dependence on the resources of the sea is indicated by the appearance of coastal shell middens. Making and carrying fire was essential to the occupation of areas near the ice sheets. Perhaps then, for the first time, fire began to be used to dry and smoke meat and fish, and to preserve other foods to help overcome seasonal shortages.

The transition to agriculture

By around 12000 years ago at the end of the Pleistocene epoch, a worldwide rise in sea level brought coastlines close to their present position. By then, human populations dependent on wild plant and animal foods were established in most parts of the world. Population figures from modern hunter-gatherer-fisher groups suggest that densities of three to six persons per kilometre of coast or river bank could easily have been maintained. In such habitats, seasonal fluctuations in food availability are less extreme than in drier areas, and human populations could readily occupy favoured settlement sites all year. However, prolonged occupation of the same river valley or strip of coast is likely to have led to population growth, which would in turn have intensified pressure on food supplies.

Studies of modern hunter-gatherers show that there is a correlation between population density and the specialised use of particular foods. Examples include the systematic exploitation (in some cases even involving the

Prehistoric coastal midden under excavation, Torres Strait Islands, Australia. Mollusc shells and the bones of fish, marine turtles and dugongs have accumulated in layers to form the midden.

Australian Aborigines increase the productivity of cycad plants by firing, as here in a eucalyptus wood in the Atherton Tableland, North Queensland. The plants soon regenerate and fruit.

sowing) of wild grasses and other herbaceous plants for their seeds, and the replanting of wild yams and other tubers to ensure continuity of supply. Hunter-gatherers sometimes extend the range of plant and animal resources by transferring them to new habitats, and increase productivity by burning and even by irrigation – for example, the burning of savanna woodlands by Australian Aborigines to increase the production of cycad fruits, and the irrigation of wild stands of grasses and tuberous plants by Paiute Indians in western North America. They also have various methods of processing plants and animals to increase food output and to improve storage – for example, grinding, grating, cooking, drying, smoking and salting.

Many of these methods of resource manipulation by hunter-gatherers approximate closely to domestication and agriculture, and they diminish the contrast between 'hunter-gatherers' and 'agriculturalists'. The transition to agriculture can be seen as a threshold on a gradient of increasing interaction of humans with plants and animals that may have been scarcely perceptible at the time, yet which involved a gradual increase in input of human energy into food production.

Cultivation was an important energy threshold because of the effort required for clearance of vegetation and tillage before sowing or planting domesticated crops (those in which the reproductive system of the plant has been so altered by human intervention that it can no longer survive in the wild). Crop cultivation marked the beginning of agriculture, and, because it involves year-round effort in a more restricted area than hunting and gathering, it is probable that the threshold into agriculture was crossed only by populations that were already sedentary.

There is little archaeological evidence for the actual initiation of cultivation and domestication, despite many attempts to unearth such remains, particularly in Southwest

Asia and Mexico. Plant and animal residues that show characteristics of domestication (such as the non-shattering seed heads of cereals) are commonly recovered from excavations, but transitional forms between the wild and domestic types are almost never found. This may be partly because of inadequate excavation techniques, but it may also imply that in some organisms the selection of domesticated forms took place so rapidly – perhaps within a few decades – that they cannot be detected archaeologically. Recent experimental work on the selection of features of domestication in cereals supports this view.

The diet of early farmers

Archaeological evidence indicates that plants and animals were domesticated in parts of all the inhabited continents, except Australia, between 12000 and 6000 years ago, but little is yet known about how long it took for agriculture to become dominant in these areas, and to spread to others. Nevertheless, some ecological and dietary trends can be discerned.

Foremost among these is a reduction in the diversity of foods. Increasing populations of agriculturalists came to depend on a less-varied repertoire of plants and animals than had their less-numerous hunter-gatherer predecessors. For example, in the pre-agricultural levels at the archaeological site of Tell Abu Hureyra in Syria, there are traces of over 150 species of plants that yield edible seeds or fruits, compared with a very small range of domesticated cereals and pulses in the succeeding agricultural levels.

The prehistoric transition from hunting and gathering to agriculture represents a shift of the human population towards a greater dependence on primary producers, particularly seed-, root- and tuber-bearing plants. This increased the proportion of carbohydrates in the diet, not

Stone grinding equipment for cereal processing at the Neolithic site of Beidha, Jordan.

only by increasing the amount of starch-rich food eaten but also because the domestication process itself selected for plants with larger caloric yields. For example, the grains of domesticated cereals such as wheat, maize and rice contain more carbohydrate and relatively less protein than those of wild grasses. The greater carbohydrate intake of early agricultural populations compared with hunter-gatherers led to nutritional imbalance and to protein- and vitamin-deficiency diseases, the effects of which are still manifest in their skeletal remains.

This relative reduction in the availability of protein and lipids in early agricultural diets was mitigated where herd animals were domesticated. As sheep, goats, cattle, horses, asses and camels were integrated into agricultural production in western Asia, Europe and northern Africa, milk and milk products made a growing contribution to human diets. All these domesticated animals have been milked in historical times, but it is not known when this practice began. There is pictorial evidence of milking in Egypt and Mesopotamia in the late fourth millennium BC, over 3000 years after the appearance of domesticated cereals, pulses, sheep, goats and cattle; but milking may well have been practised considerably earlier.

Milking, as a source of animal fats, may have helped to increase the human population of those regions in later prehistoric and early historic times, because low levels of dietary fat are associated with late menstruation and the suppression of ovulation during lactation. Indeed, the increasing consumption of milk fat – together with the availability of cereal gruels suitable for infant feeding – may have been partly responsible for the increased population in Mesopotamia and Egypt and the appearance of cities.

Mixed grain and livestock farming emerged in western Asia and spread through Europe in prehistoric times, giving rise eventually to specialised cereal and dairy farming. An equivalent integrated system did not develop in the central Andes, where llama and alpaca were domesticated, despite the presence of seed crops (such as quinoa, maize and beans); nor were the animals milked. Early Andean agricultural populations obtained most of their carbohydrate, protein and fat from vegetable foods and thus resembled other agricultural populations who lacked domesticated herd animals, such as those in Mexico and Central America, the South American lowlands, western Africa and Ethiopia. In northern China and southeastern Asia, where grain farming based on millets and rice developed early, domesticated livestock were incorporated into agricultural production, chiefly as draught animals. Some of them were introduced from western Asia and others, such as the water buffalo, were domesticated locally.

By the beginning of historical times, distinct agroecosystems had evolved in all these regions and had spread so extensively (except in Australia) that hunter-gatherers no longer occupied most of the world's land area. Each agroecosystem incorporated a particular mix of crops, but all included grains, pulses and other herbaceous seed crops, as well as root crops, shrubs and trees. The relative importance of these types of crop varied from place to place, and each region had a distinct set of domesticated species. However, each assemblage gave a sufficiently diverse range of carbohydrates, proteins, lipids, minerals and vitamins to provide a balanced diet.

Thus, most of the human population came to depend for sustenance on a narrower spectrum of plants and animals than during the many preceding millennia of hunting and gathering. Nevertheless, early agroecosystems were more biotically diverse and more nutritionally self-sufficient than the specialised systems of production that have now replaced them in all but the remotest recesses of the world.

D.R. Harris

See also 'Diets and guts' (p. 60), 'Selecting and processing food' (p. 65), 'The hominid way of life' (p. 325), 'Reconstructing prehistoric diet' (p. 369), 'Origins of agriculture' (p. 373), 'Domestication of animals' (p. 380), 'Reconstructing ancient populations' (p. 402)

Primate locomotion and posture

Primates have an extraordinary diversity of ways of moving about. Some species run along branches, some along the ground. Some swing by their arms whereas others leap from tree to tree. Some species walk with their hands flat on the ground, others walk on the tips of their fingers, and still others walk on their knuckles. Finally, there is just one primate, the human species, that moves in an upright posture on two legs. Each of these different ways of moving enables a species to exploit a particular aspect of its environment, and each requires particular anatomical adaptations in muscles and bones.

Primate locomotory behaviour can be divided into five general categories:

- *Arboreal quadrupedalism*: walking and running on all fours along branches
- *Terrestrial quadrupedalism*: moving on all fours on the ground. A variation of this is *knuckle-walking*, in which the animal uses its knuckles for support

- *Leaping*: moving between tree trunks and branches by rapid extension of the hindlimbs
- *Suspension*: hanging below arboreal supports
- *Bipedalism*: walking and running on two limbs

Arboreal quadrupedalism

This is the most common type of locomotion among both prosimian and simian primates. It was probably used by the earliest primates and many other, more specialised locomotory behaviours seem to have evolved from it. Among primates that move in this way are the dwarf bushbaby (*Galago demidovii*), slow-climbing lorises such as the potto (*Perodicticus potto*), and many monkeys – for example, the squirrel monkeys (*Saimiri*) of the New World.

The quadrupedal gaits of primates are different from those of most other mammals in several ways. For example, primate hindlimbs provide a larger proportion of the propulsive force than in other mammals. Primates also tend to use more erratic, lopsided gaits than other mammals, perhaps because twigs and branches are irregular and unsteady.

The skeletal proportions of arboreal quadrupeds and the anatomy of muscles and bones reflect the greatest problem faced by animals with this type of locomotion: maintaining balance when moving from branch to branch. They usually have grasping hands and feet, and their forelimbs and hindlimbs are similar in length and relatively short, so that the centre of gravity is close to the branch. Many arboreal quadrupeds, such as the arboreal guenons (*Cercopithecus*), have a long tail, which is used for balancing.

Terrestrial quadrupedalism

Although most primates are primarily arboreal, a few regularly walk and run across the ground. This type of locomotion is particularly common among Old World monkeys, such as baboons (*Papio*). Like arboreal quadrupeds, these primates have forelimbs and hindlimbs that are similar in length. However, because the ground is flat and stable, they have much shorter fingers and toes, and their longer limbs allow longer strides when running. The tails of many terrestrial quadrupeds, such as the pig-tailed macaque (*Macaca nemestrina*), are also shorter than those of their arboreal relatives.

The African apes (chimpanzees and gorillas) belong to a special category of quadrupedal primates that rest their hands on the knuckles rather than on the palms or fingers. Knuckle-walking enables them to walk quadrupedally

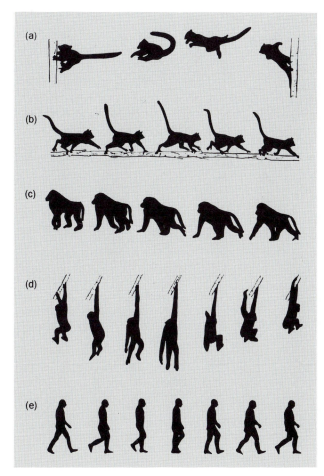

The five main types of primate locomotion: (a) vertical clinging and leaping; (b) arboreal quadrupedalism; (c) terrestrial quadrupedalism; (d) brachiation; (e) bipedalism.

on the ground while retaining long curved fingers for climbing.

Leaping

In leaping from branch to branch, propulsion is largely from extension of the hindlimbs and the back; the fore-limbs are used mainly on landing. This type of locomotion is characteristic of various lemurs, such as members of the indri family, and is also typical of most bushbabies and of tarsiers. Leapers have relatively long hindlimbs and long, flexible backs, particularly in the lower (lumbar) region. Small leapers, such as bushbabies and tarsiers, also have elongated ankles. Because leapers are arboreal, they have long hands and feet.

Suspension

This category of locomotion includes many different pat-terns, such as the *brachiation* of gibbons (*Hylobates*), in which

the animals swing by their arms, and *climbing and bridging*, in which both arms and legs are used for support. Large New World monkeys such as spider monkeys (*Ateles*) often use the latter type of locomotion. In all forms of suspensory locomotion, the limbs function more in tension than in compression, because the weight of the primate is below the support. A large primate can hence move among small supports, at angles that it could not otherwise manage, by spreading its weight among many slender supports. Suspensory primates have long hindlimbs, very long fore-limbs and flexible joints. They have long, slender hands and feet for grasping supports of different size. Their trunk is usually short and stiff (as a long flexible trunk might become dangerously twisted and bent) and many have lost the tail, which is no longer needed for balance.

Bipedalism

Humans are the only bipedal primates. The structural prob-lems involved in balancing and moving our body atop two

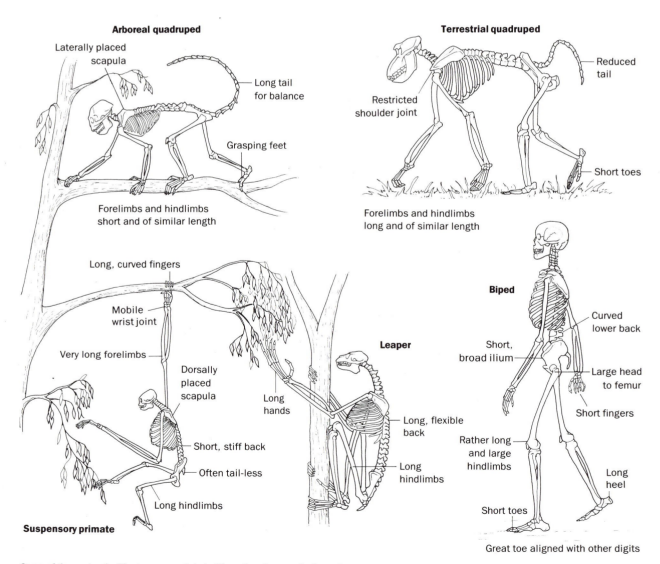

Some of the anatomical features associated with each main type of primate locomotion.

limbs have led to many distinctive features of muscles and bones. Our hindlimbs are long, providing a relatively long stride; and our foot lacks the grasping abilities of all other living primates. It has become a stiff propulsive lever with a long heel and short toes, and with the hallux (great toe) aligned with the other digits.

Movement and anatomy

From field studies we can learn the movements of each species and the ecological context in they are used, but to understand the function of a particular muscle we must rely on electrical recordings or *electromyography*. Films show patterns of limb movements during locomotion, moving x-ray pictures the movements that take place at each joint, and studies of bone strain the forces acting on a bone. Measurements of oxygen consumption during locomotion show the energetic cost of different types of movement.

Understanding how anatomy is related to movement is complicated by the fact that most primates can move in many ways. Most leap at some times and run quadrupedally at others, and many occasionally suspend themselves from branches. Anatomy hence reflects a series of compromises and an ability to do many things. Nevertheless, differences in the frequencies with which primate species use different types of locomotion are reflected in muscles and bones. For example, two closely related species of langur (*Presbytis*) from Malaysia show differences in muscular and skeletal anatomy that are associated with the fact that one leaps about 20 per cent more frequently than the other.

Posture and anatomy

The way a species sits, stands or hangs during feeding also influences its anatomy. For example, a siamang's ability to hang by its arms and legs may be more important in enabling it to feed from small branches than as a means of moving from one place to another. Likewise, the structure of a marmoset's hands is influenced by the need to hold and process food as well as to grasp a support when moving.

We can relate many details of primate anatomy to differences in locomotion and posture and can use such information to reconstruct the behaviour of species known only from fossils. However, we scarcely understand why some species leap, others are arboreal quadrupeds, some swing by their arms, and one is a biped.

What influences locomotion?

Many factors seem to influence a species' pattern of movement. One is body size. Among arboreal primates, smaller species are more likely to be leapers because they cannot reach across the gaps between branches and trees. Larger primates are more likely to be suspensory because it is

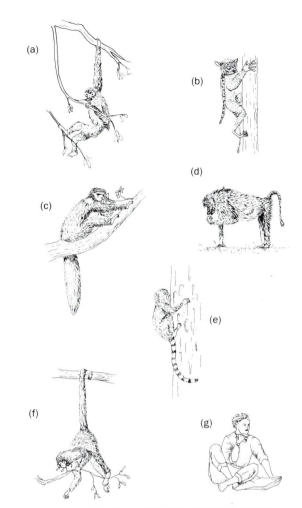

Feeding postures of (a) gibbon, (b) tarsier, (c) colobus monkey, (d) baboon, (e) pygmy marmoset, (f) spider monkey and (g) human.

easier to support their weight below many small supports rather than above a single branch. For the same reason, larger primates are often terrestrial.

The locomotor habits of a primate are also influenced by its environment. Primates that live in open woodland, such as some chimpanzees and macaques, must be able to move across the ground between trees. There are no horizontal branches available to species such as the gentle lemurs (*Hapalemur*) living in bamboo forest, and they must be able to leap between vertical supports. There are also differences in the availability of supports in different parts of a tropical rain forest.

Primates that feed and move in forest understorey made up largely of vertical trunks and vines are often leapers. The quadrupedal and suspensory species mainly occupy the more continuous middle canopy. An ability to move effectively in different forests or different levels of the canopy may enable a species to exploit foods inaccessible to others.

The evolution of bipedalism

Reconstructing the ecological factors that led to bipedalism is a fascinating and controversial issue in the study of

WALKING ON TWO LEGS

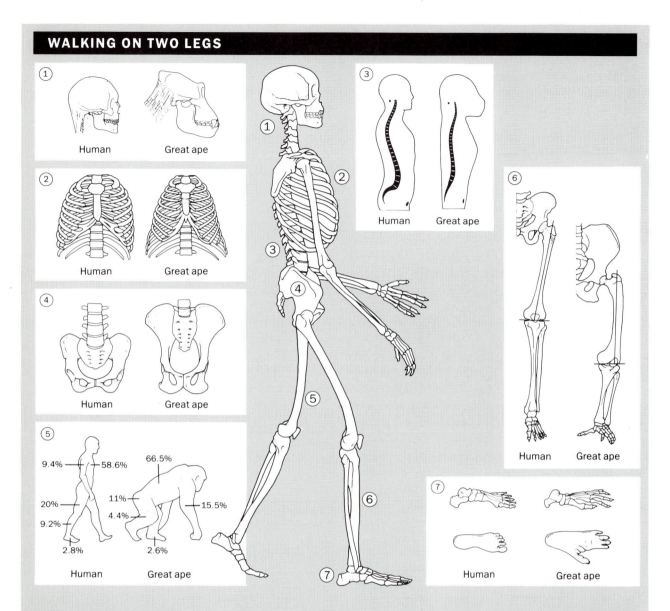

① Human   Great ape

② Human   Great ape

③ Human   Great ape

④ Human   Great ape

⑤ 9.4% — 58.6%   66.5%
20%   11% — 15.5%
9.2%   4.4%
2.8%   2.6%
Human   Great ape

⑥ Human   Great ape

⑦ Human   Great ape

Humans have acquired some unique skeletal adaptations for taking their weight on the hind legs and for balancing on one leg only as each stride is taken. The resulting changes in the skeleton can be seen from head to toe.

The head is balanced on the backbone or vertebral column, and the *foramen magnum*, through which the brain connects with the spinal cord, is shifted forwards beneath the skull (**1**). Because the head is more or less balanced on the backbone, there is no need for powerful neck muscles to keep it in position. The area for muscle attachment on the underside of the back end of the skull (*nuchal region*) is thus very small and only small spines are needed for muscle attachment on the neck vertebrae.

Because humans no longer use their arms for locomotion, the ribcage has become barrel-shaped (**2**). In great apes, it is shaped like an inverted funnel. The vertebral column has also been modified by the development of a forward curvature in the neck and lower back regions (**3**). These

two extra curves, added to the backward curvature in the middle of the backbone (a basic mammalian feature), give the backbone an undulating profile and it acts like a spring.

Modifications to the hips have resulted in a lower and broader pelvis (**4**). These changes have reduced the distance between the *sacroiliac joint*, linking the backbone to the pelvis, and the hip joint. The iliac blades of the pelvis, as seen from above, have taken on an S-profile in association with the complete remodelling of the hip musculature.

In contrast to apes, human legs are longer than the arms and represent a far greater proportion of the body weight, lowering the body's centre of gravity (**5**).

The arrangement of the human knee joint also differs. The thigh bone (femur) is angled outwards from the knee, rather than standing upright as in great apes (**6**). This *carrying angle* ensures that the knee is brought well under the body and closer to the line of action of body weight.

Humans – but not great apes – can extend the leg fully during bipedal striding, so that the femur and lower leg bones (tibia and fibula) form a straight line. Special adaptations of the knee prevent overextension of the leg when it swings forwards.

The most obvious adaptation of the human foot for bipedalism is that, uniquely among living primates, the big toe (hallux) is not opposed to the other toes, so the foot can no longer grasp (**7**). During walking, the big toe represents the last point of contact with the ground before the leg is swung forwards and it has become elongated and aligned with the other toes.

A human footprint therefore has several distinctive features, which include a curving pattern of weight transmission from the heel to the big toe. The foot itself has also been modified, especially through the development of transverse and longitudinal arches, which help to absorb shocks.

Robert Martin

1 Carrying

1a Weapons and tools

1b Vegetable foods, water, and infants

2 Travelling between food trees

3 Feeding from bushes

4 Feeding on grass seeds

5 Provisioning family

Some theories of the origin of bipedal locomotion.

human origins. There are many theories of the emergence of this unique pattern of locomotion. Some argue that bipedalism evolved in conjunction with the use of stone tools. This is not supported by the fossil record, which indicates that human ancestors were bipedal well before they made such artefacts. Others suggest that the evolution of bipedalism is associated with freeing the hands for transporting food and water from distant foraging sites to off-spring and other family members, so that bipedalism is related to individual reproductive success. Bipedalism, particularly when combined with the loss of body hair, also presents special problems for carrying young infants.

The evolution of bipedalism has also been linked with the need to forage in open woodland with widely scattered food resources. Bipedal walking seems to be an energetically efficient way for a large primate to travel long distances over flat country.

We do not yet know which of these theories best reflects the early stages of human locomotor evolution, although we can be certain that it was associated with the ecological adaptations of early hominids. Recent evidence suggests that early hominids climbed trees – perhaps for protection at night-time and to escape from day-time predators. The skeleton of *Australopithecus afarensis* ('Lucy') from Hadar in Ethiopia (see p. 237) has relatively long arms and curved fingers and toes, which suggest this behaviour.

Quite apart from these indications of climbing abilities, it is clear that the adaptations for bipedal locomotion in *Australopithecus afarensis* were not equivalent to those in modern humans. Indeed, in several features, 'Lucy' is closer to the common ancestor of great apes and humans. This hominid also had some of its own specialisations in, for example, the form of the pelvis. The modern pattern of bipedal locomotion hence has a long and complex evolutionary history.

John G. Fleagle

See also 'Non-human primates' (p. 24), 'Human locomotion' (p. 80), 'Evolution of apes' (p. 223), 'Evolution of australopithecines' (p. 231)

Human locomotion

People stand and walk on two legs, but almost all other mammals stand and walk on four. Mammals that do stand on two feet use postures quite different from ours. Kangaroos and a few other mammals hop on their hind legs, but their hopping is quite unlike our walking and running. Two-legged (*bipedal*) gaits more like human ones are sometimes used by apes and a few monkeys. Chimpanzees usually travel on the ground by knuckle-walking – walking on all fours with fingers bent, resting the knuckles rather than the palms of the hands on the ground. However, in long grass or when carrying loads chimpanzees often stand up on their hindlegs and walk bipedally. Captive gibbons walk bipedally on the ground, but wild ones seldom leave the trees. Some monkeys occasionally walk bipedally, especially when carrying food.

Apes and monkeys seem to be pre-adapted to bipedalism because, even when walking quadrupedally, they carry an unusually large proportion – about 60 per cent – of their weight on their hindlegs. By contrast, typical mammals such as dogs and horses carry only 40 per cent of their weight on their hindlegs.

Posture

The human bipedal posture is distinctly different from postures of other primates. We stand erect with our backs vertical and our legs straight, but our primate relatives stand with sloping backs and bent legs. Our upright, bipedal stance has consequences for our backs, our pelvic girdles, our legs and our feet. These will be considered in turn.

Most of the weight of the human trunk is in front of the backbone, so it tends to bend the vertebral column forwards. This is counteracted in two ways: by tension in the muscles that straighten the back and by pressure in the body cavity caused by the abdominal muscles. The load on any vertebra is the weight of the parts of the body above it, plus the tension of the back muscles, minus the vertical force due to abdominal pressure.

It might be thought that the vertebrae of the lower part of the back (the *lumbar* vertebrae) would have to be stronger than those of quadrupeds to support the weight of the body. This does not seem to be true: body weight is small compared with the forces that the muscles can exert on the vertebrae, and when a man bends over to lift a load equal to his own weight the compressive force on his lumbar vertebrae may reach 12 times his body weight.

When an animal stands, its feet must be under its centre of mass. The centre of mass of standing humans is between (and a little above) the hip joints. That of a chimpanzee, standing bipedally with its trunk leaning forwards, is well in

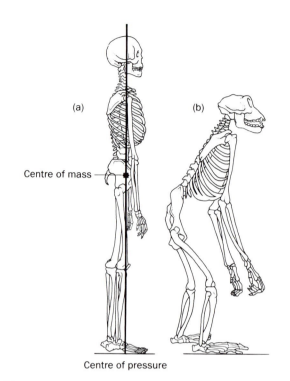

A human and a chimpanzee standing bipedally. Body weight acts vertically through the centre of mass, which is between the hip joints in humans but in front of them in standing apes.

front of the hip joint. Consequently, a person must stand with the feet under the hips (as seen in side view) but a chimpanzee must keep its feet forwards of the hips. This, and the chimpanzee's bent knees, requires the femur (thigh bone) to slope forwards from the vertebral column, as it does also in quadrupedal mammals. In contrast, the femur of a standing person, seen in side view, is more or less parallel to the backbone. Both in people and in chimpanzees, the femur swings forwards and backwards during walking, with a mean position that is close to the standing position.

This presents a problem for the arrangement of human thigh muscles. The most important of the muscles that swing the femur back, in apes and quadrupedal mammals generally, are the hamstring muscles. These run from the posterior end of the pelvic girdle to the knee. If the back and femur of a chimpanzee were rotated to vertical positions, the pelvic attachment of the hamstrings would be close to the femur. The hamstrings would then have a very small lever action about the hip and would not be well placed to swing the femur further back for the end of a walking step.

This difficulty has been overcome by evolution of the distinctive human pelvic girdle, and by modification of the gluteus maximus muscle (the flesh of the buttocks).

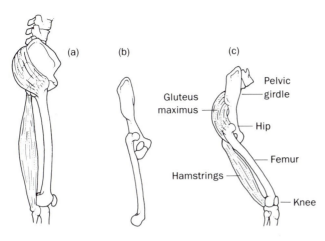

The upper part of the leg skeleton with the gluteus maximus and hamstring muscles in (a) a human standing, (b) a chimpanzee standing like a human and (c) a chimpanzee standing bipedally. Because we stand differently from apes, we need a different-shaped pelvic girdle.

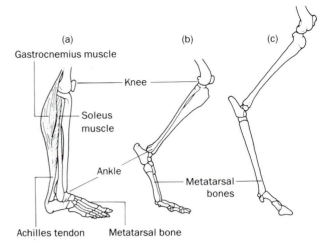

The skeletons of (a) a plantigrade foot of a human (with the whole sole on the ground), (b) the digitigrade foot of a dog (with just the toes on the ground) and (c) the unguligrade foot of a deer (with only the hoof on the ground). Some muscles are also shown.

Remodelling of the pelvic girdle during human evolution has moved the upper attachment of the hamstrings so that it is behind the hip joint, even when standing.

The change in angle of the femur relative to the vertebral column has made the hamstrings less able to swing the leg back but it has also made the gluteus maximus more able to do so. In quadrupedal mammals and apes, this muscle is principally an abductor of the hip – it tends to swing the leg out to the side. In humans, it is principally an extensor, helping the hamstrings to swing the leg back, and is much enlarged.

When humans stand with their feet close together, the knees are closer together than the hips. This posture is strikingly knock-kneed, and contrasts with the standing posture of apes. It is made possible by the peculiar shape of the lower end of the femur that is involved in the knee joint.

It would be difficult for us to balance on very small feet, because it would be hard always to keep the centre of mass of the body over them. This may be why the soles of our feet are so large in comparison, for example, with those of deer. However, bipedal ostriches put a smaller area of foot on the ground than we do, and have no obvious problems of balance.

Mammals stand and walk in three different ways. Humans are *plantigrade*, placing the heel as well as the toes on the ground; dogs are *digitigrade*, putting only their toes on the ground; and cattle and deer are *unguligrade*, standing on hooves that have evolved from their ancestors' claws. Hoofed mammals have very long metatarsal bones, so that the foot (from heel to toe) is very long, but the heel is far from the ground and the area on the ground is small. Our plantigrade stance ensures that a large area of the foot is on the ground, thus making it easy for us to balance on two feet, or even on one. Monkeys and apes also set their hind-feet down in plantigrade fashion, but their feet are much more hand-like than ours, and are adapted for grasping.

The arch of the foot is a human peculiarity. When we stand barefoot on a flat, rigid surface, the heel and the ball of the foot rest on the ground, but the arch between is raised. In contrast, the whole length of the chimpanzee's foot rests on the ground.

People need remarkably little muscle activity to stand in a relaxed posture. This has been demonstrated by the technique of *electromyography*, in which electrodes are used to detect the electrical activity that occurs in a muscle when it is exerting a force. Much information about muscles that lie close to the surface of the body has been obtained from electrodes fastened to the skin, but fine wire electrodes pushed through hypodermic needles into muscles have also been used. In relaxed standing, the soleus muscle in the calf of the leg is active, but the muscles of the thigh show very little activity unless we sway backwards or forwards. Thigh muscles become active when we stand with our knees bent, and are active in apes when they are standing bipedally.

To understand this, we need to know where the force acts on the sole of the foot. It is, of course, distributed over a substantial area, but can be considered as acting at a point (the centre of pressure), just as the weight of the body can be considered as acting at the centre of mass. The centre of pressure of the foot can be located by having the subject stand on a force-sensitive platform set into the floor. Electrical outputs from the platform give the size and direction of any force acting on it, and also the position of the centre of pressure. Force-platform observations show that we can move the centre of pressure around. It moves forwards as we stand on our toes and back as we rest on our heels. However, its normal position in relaxed standing is slightly less than halfway along the foot, from heel to toe. This is well in front of the ankle, so the soleus muscle has to be active to maintain the position of the ankle and stop us from falling forwards.

A vertical line drawn upwards through the centre of pressure, in a relaxed standing posture, passes through or close to the *patella* (kneecap), and so slightly in front of the axis of the knee joint (see p. 80) Therefore, our weight tends tends to extend the knee further. However, the knee is already extended so far that any further extension would be resisted by the ligaments and other tissues that limit its movement. It could be extended a little further, but only if sufficent force were applied. Thus the ligaments and other tissues are enough, or almost enough, to maintain the position of the knee, and little or no muscle activity is needed. Bending the knee, both in people and in standing apes, puts it in front of the centre of pressure, so that muscle action is needed to prevent further bending. When we stand with the trunk erect, the upper parts of the body are almost balanced on the hip joints, so that little activity is needed in the muscles.

It seems natural to conclude from these observations that human standing is remarkably economical of energy. However, direct experimental evidence gives a different impression. The rates of oxygen consumption of humans and other animals can be measured by collecting and analysing the air they breathe out. The rate is higher when standing than when lying down, indicating that there is increased energy consumption. However, the increase when standing (per unit body mass) is greater for people than for sheep and cattle. Unfortunately, no information is available for apes.

Walking

People walk to travel slowly and run to go faster. Although these two gaits differ from each other in many ways, it is convenient to choose one to distinguish between them. The *duty factor* is the fraction of total time for which each foot is on the ground. In walking, the duty factor is greater than 0.5: each foot is on the ground for more than half the time,

so there are times when both are on the ground simultaneously. In running, the duty factor is less than 0.5 and there are times when both feet are off the ground simultaneously. Normal ranges of duty factors are 0.55 to 0.70 for walking and 0.25 to 0.40 for running. Lower values apply at higher speeds.

In a walking step, each leg remains fairly straight while its foot is on the ground. At stages 1 and 5 (see below), the legs slope and the head and trunk are relatively low. At stage 3, the supporting leg is vertical and the head and trunk are high. Thus the walker's gravitational *potential energy* (PE) is low at stages 1 and 5 and high at stage 3.

Walking over force platforms shows that while each foot is on the ground, it exerts a force more or less in line with the leg. (If it acted in any other direction, the hip muscles would have to exert larger forces, and would use more energy.) The force acts downwards and forwards on the ground at stage 2, decelerating the walker. Thus travel is fastest and *kinetic energy* (KE) is at a maximum at stages 1 and 5, but slowest and with minimum KE at stage 3.

Notice that kinetic energy is highest when potential energy is lowest, and vice versa. This makes walking very economical. While walking, energy is needed to develop tension in the muscles and to do the work necessary to make the muscles shorten while exerting tension. Work must be done by the muscles whenever the total energy increases. This work is lost again when the total decreases: it is degraded to heat by muscles that extend while exerting tension and act as brakes. The advantage of having potential and kinetic energy fluctuate out of phase with each other is that energy is shuttled back and forth between the two (as in a swinging pendulum). The total energy remains fairly constant, so little work is needed in each stride.

Remember that the centre of mass of the body is lowest at stages 1 and 5. At these stages, therefore, it must have an upward acceleration and total vertical force (exerted by both feet) must exceed body weight. The body is highest

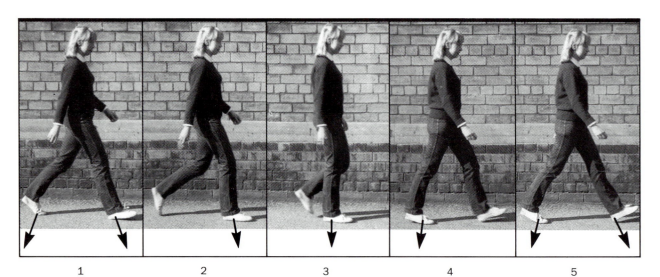

Stages in a walking stride. The arrows show the direction of the forces on the ground.

and has a downward acceleration at stage 3, so the vertical force then must be less than body weight. This pattern of force can be obtained by having each foot exert two peaks of force – the first with the heel and the second with the ball of the foot on the ground – with a trough between.

Mammals such as dogs and horses walk on their toes and do not have the heel-and-toe action of human walking. They nevertheless exert two-peaked forces with their feet. The walk of a quadruped is like that of two bipeds walking one behind the other, and is economical of energy for the same reason.

The faster a person walks, the bigger the vertical accelerations that are needed and the deeper the trough between the two force peaks must be. The energy-saving style of walking becomes impossible at very high speeds because the vertical force would then have to become negative.

Consider a simple model of walking, with a person keeping each leg absolutely straight while the foot is on the ground. The trunk moves forwards in a series of arcs of circles of radius l, which is the same as leg length. If the speed of walking is v, then the trunk has downward acceleration v^2/l as it passes over the supporting foot. (It is a standard result in mechanics that a body moving with speed v round a circle of radius l has acceleration v^2/l towards the centre.)

Because negative ground forces are impossible, v^2/l cannot exceed the gravitational acceleration g. Thus walking speed cannot exceed $(gl)^{\frac{1}{2}}$, which is 3 metres per second (m/s) for a man of leg length 0.9 metres. Men change from walking to running at about 2.5 m/s, only a little below the speed suggested by the simple theory. Children, with shorter legs (smaller l), change at lower speeds.

The speed limit for walking can be raised above 4 m/s by athletes using the racing walk. The pelvis is tilted as the trunk passes over the supporting foot, so the trunk is not raised as high as in normal walking, and vertical accelerations are reduced. This style of walking is expensive of energy because the balance between fluctuations in potential energy and kinetic energy is disturbed.

Running

In running, the duty factor is less than 0.5. The periods when both feet are off the ground are, in effect, leaps, in which the body rises and then falls. Thus the body is highest

(a)
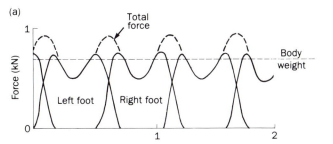

(b)
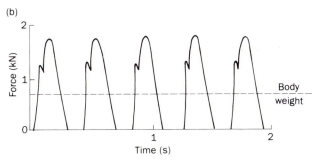

Forces exerted on the ground by a man (a) walking and (b) running. They were measured by means of an instrumental panel set into the floor.

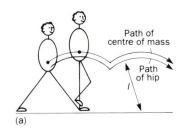
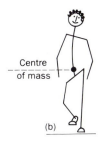

A simple model of walking, with a person keeping each leg absolutely straight while the foot is on the ground (a). The trunk moves forwards in a series of arcs of circles of radius l, which is the same as leg length. In (b), an athlete is performing the racing walk. In this style of walking, vertical movements of the centre of mass are reduced by tilting the pelvis.

Stages in a running stride. The arrows show the direction of forces on the ground.

ENERGY FOR WALKING AND RUNNING

It is advantageous to use as little energy as possible for locomotion. How much is needed for walking or running cannot easily be measured directly, but it can be calculated from the oxygen used in respiration. Oxygen consumption is measured by fitting a face mask, from which the air a person breathes out is sucked through a tube into gas analysis equipment. The experiment is most conveniently done by asking a person to run on a moving conveyor belt, so that he or she remains stationary relative to the apparatus.

Measurements of the rate of oxygen consumption can be plotted against speed for people walking and running (see graphs below). The faster we go, the more we use food energy. Notice that the graph for running is not simply a continuation of the graph for walking. The two graphs cross each other. Below this crossover speed, walking is more economical than running. Above it, the converse is true.

Similar measurements can be made with animals, such as ponies. In this case, there are three gaits instead of two, but the same principle applies as for people. Each gait is most economical in the range of speeds at which it is used.

For different mammals, it is nearly true that the rate of energy consumption (power, P) is related to speed (v) by the equation

$$P = P_0 + Cv$$

where P_0 is the power used when stationary, and C is the energy used in travelling a unit distance, over and above what would be used if standing still.

In birds and mammals, C is related to body weight. Deviations from the general relationship – the line in the diagram on the right – show that some species are unusually economical for their size, whereas others are unusually extravagant of energy. For example, a penguin, which waddles in an ungainly way, uses proportionately twice as much energy for travelling overland as a graceful gazelle.

There is no clear difference beween bipeds and quadrupeds. Ponies and ostriches of equal body weight use about the same power, for running at equal speeds. Chimpanzees use about the same power for walking only on their hindlegs as they do for walking on all fours. The point for humans is a little above the line, showing that running is a little more costly for us than for typical mammals of equal

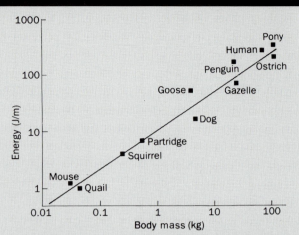

The energy (C) birds and mammals need to walk or run a unit distance, over and above what they would use when standing still, plotted against body mass. Deviations from the general relationships – the line in the diagram – show that some animals (e.g. dogs) are unusually economical for their size whereas others (e.g. penguins) are unusually extravagant of energy. The line is based on 62 points, only a few of which are shown here. This type of experiment shows that locomotion for us is a little more costly than for typical mammals of the same body mass.

body weight. Human walking (not included in the diagram) is less costly.

Not only are we rather uneconomical runners, we are also rather slow. Maximum speeds of human athletes are about 10 m/s for races of 200 metres, 7 m/s for the 2000 metres and 6 m/s for the 20 000 metres. In contrast, horse races of 1600 metres (1 mile) and under are usually won at 15 to 17 m/s. Greyhound races of about 500 metres are usually won at 15 to 16 m/s.

There is little reliable information about maximum speeds of wild animals and many published speeds seem to be grossly exaggerated. However, antelopes of various species, ranging in mass from 20 to 500 kilograms, have been filmed galloping at 12 to 14 m/s. Compared with the performance of those animals, that of humans is unimpressive.

R. McNeill Alexander

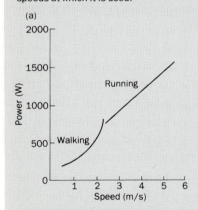

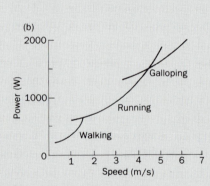

Power (rate of oxygen consumption) plotted against speed for (a) humans walking and running and (b) ponies walking, trotting and galloping. The graphs show that each gait is most economical in the range of speeds at which it is used.

at stages 1 and 5 and lowest at stage 3. As in walking, the foot exerts a decelerating force at stage 2 and an accelerating force at stage 4. Both kinetic energy and potential energy are highest at stages 1 and 5, and lowest at stage 3. Plainly, the pendulum principle that saves energy in walking does not operate in running. Instead, energy is saved by the principle of the bouncing ball; as it is converted back and forth between kinetic energy and potential energy on the one hand, and elastic strain energy on the other.

The trunk is lowest at stage 3 of the stride, and must then have a large upward acceleration. This is when the force on the ground is largest (see figure on p. 83). The supporting leg is somewhat bent, and its extensor muscles and tendons are taut. These muscles and tendons work as springs: they stretch during stage 3, storing elastic strain energy, and recoil elastically at stage 4.

The tendons are much more important as springs than are the muscles. This is most easily seen in hoofed mammals such as horses and deer, which have very long tendons attached to short-fibred muscles in the lower leg and foot, but it also seems to be true of humans. Tendon is a remarkably good elastic material, in that 93 per cent of the work done stretching it is returned in the elastic recoil. It can stretch by only 8 per cent of its length before breaking, so long tendons are needed to make effective springs. Observations on horses and calculations for some other mammals indicate that tendons are seldom stretched by more than 5 per cent in running.

The most important spring in the human leg is probably the Achilles tendon, which connects the calf muscles (gastrocnemius and soleus) to the heel (see p. 81). The tendons and ligaments of the arch of the foot are also springs. In hoofed mammals, the part of the foot that corresponds to the human sole is very long, and does not rest on the ground. The tendons in it are the most important springs of hoofed mammals, which are much more highly adapted than humans for saving energy by tendon elasticity.

In one respect, human running resembles the running of dogs, horses and other medium-sized to large mammals, while the running of other primates is peculiar. This concerns the lengths of our strides. *Stride length* is the distance between successive footprints of the same foot. It depends on speed: the faster we go, the longer the strides we take. It also depends on size: at corresponding speeds, large animals (or people) take longer strides than small ones.

Physics tells us that speeds can be regarded as corresponding if they are proportional to the square root of leg length. The legs of a giraffe are about nine times as long as the legs of a cat, so any speed for the giraffe is equivalent to the square foot of nine (i.e. three) times the corresponding speed for the cat. For example, 3 m/s for a giraffe is equivalent to 1 m/s for a cat. When giraffes and cats run at these corresponding speeds, they can be expected to use the same gait and to take strides in proportion to their leg lengths.

Predictions like this work very well for mammals of the size of cats and upwards, but not for comparisons between them and small mammals such as rats, which run on strongly bent legs. People take strides of about the length that would be expected from measurements on typical mammals such as cats, dogs and horses. Other primates, however, take strides of one and a half to two times the predicted length. This has been demonstrated for bushbabies, monkeys and chimpanzees, both for quadrupedal and for bipedal running. Like some other aspects of locomotion, it has not yet been explained.   *R.McNeill Alexander*

See also 'Primate locomotion and posture' (p. 75)

Primate reproduction

The reproductive features of primates are useful both for distinguishing the group from other mammals and for recognising major subdivisions within the order itself. Primates as a group are characterised by small litters of well-developed offspring and by long life-phases relative to body size – an extended period of suckling, late attainment of sexual maturity, relatively long gestation and extended lifespan. The combined effect of these features is that all primates show a slow pace of reproduction associated with a long-term investment in individual offspring: in other words, quality rather than quantity. This slow *reproductive turnover* means that *maternal investment* of resources per unit time is low. Although several other groups of mammals also have a slow reproductive turnover, primates are unique with respect to the special emphasis on the allocation of resources to brain development.

Within the primate order, there is a major difference between strepsirhines (lemurs and lorises) and haplorhines (tarsiers, monkeys, apes and humans) in the form of the placenta and the relative size of the newborn infant. In both respects, humans correspond to the pattern typical of haplorhine primates, but they are unusual in that the central nervous system continues to grow in a 'fetal' fashion for the first year after birth, with the result that human infants are particularly dependent on parental care.

Because primates typically have small litters, females have only a small number of teats (*mammae*). Although several small-bodied species (mouse lemurs, dwarf lemurs, some bushbabies, and marmosets and tamarins) have litters of two or even three offspring, most primates have only a single infant at each birth. Prosimian primates (lemurs, lorises and tarsiers) may have up to three pairs of teats, but simians (monkeys, apes and humans) have only one pair.

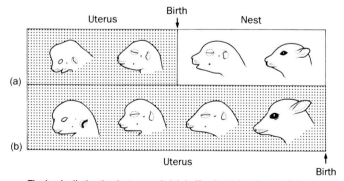

The basic distinction between altricial offspring (a) and precocial offspring (b). Altricial offspring are born after a relatively short gestation period (stippling) and their eyes and ears are still sealed at birth. They typically develop for some time in a nest before emerging into the outside world. Precocial offspring are born after a relatively long gestation period, and their eyes and ears are open at birth or soon afterwards; the 'nest phase' of altricial neonates is thus part of uterine development in precocial mammals.

State of development at birth

A small litter size and a long gestation period are linked to the relatively advanced condition of primate offspring at birth. Among placental mammals, there is quite a sharp division between species that produce large litters of relatively small and poorly developed (*altricial*) offspring and those that produce small litters of large and well-developed (*precocial*) offspring.

Altricial offspring are born after a relatively short gestation period; they are virtually naked at birth and their eyes and ears are sealed by membranes. This probably represents an adaptation for life in the nest, as such offspring typically spend some time in one before emerging into the outside world. By contrast, precocial offspring are born after a relatively long gestation period, the neonate usually has a well-developed coat of hair and the eyes and ears open by birth or very soon afterwards. The altricial strategy is probably primitive. In precocial mammals, the eyes and ears are sealed during development in the uterus and then re-open at about the time of birth, suggesting that precocial mammals are derived from an altricial ancestor.

The type of offspring is strongly associated with taxonomic group in mammals. True insectivores (Insectivora), tree-shrews (Scandentia), carnivores (Carnivora), mouse-like rodents (Myomorpha) and squirrel-like rodents (Sciuromorpha) nearly all have short gestation periods and altricial offspring. In addition to primates, even-toed hoofed mammals (Artiodactyla), odd-toed hoofed mammals (Perissodactyla), elephants (Proboscidea), hyraxes (Hyracoidea), dolphins and whales (Cetacea), porcupine-like rodents (Hystricomorpha) and elephant-shrews (Macroscelidea) generally have long gestation periods and produce precocial offspring.

Altricial mammals breed far more rapidly than precocial mammals. Slow reproduction is a feature that primates share with several other groups of precocial mammals. However, primates differ from these groups in their pace of fetal development. Once the effects of body size have been taken into account, fetal growth rates in primates are slower overall than in other precocial mammals, for all parts of the body except the brain. Hence, at any given total body weight, the brain of a primate fetus will be almost twice as large as that of a non-primate fetus, a difference that is still clearly observable in the newborn. Primates are unique in this respect.

Although human infants are relatively helpless for the first year of postnatal life, they are not genuinely altricial. The human gestation period is relatively long and the infant quite large (relative to maternal body size) at birth, at which stage the eyes and ears are open. There is a coat of hair, the *lanugo*, over the body of the fetus during late pregnancy, but this hair is normally shed just before birth. In all of these ways, humans fit the precocial rather than the altricial pattern.

The special dependence of the human infant on parental care is a by-product of the large size of the adult human brain. Because the mother's pelvis limits the maximum size of the neonate's head, a relatively large proportion of brain growth must take place after birth. The typically fetal pattern of relatively rapid brain growth in relation to body size continues for a year after birth – a specialisation unique to humans. Considered in terms of brain development, human gestation is really 21 months long, with 9 months in the uterus followed by 12 months in the mother's care. The human neonate is sometimes described as 'secondarily altricial', but in stark contrast to genuinely altricial mammals humans have a low reproductive potential relative to body size.

The female reproductive cycle

Altricial and precocial mammals have different female reproductive cycles, another contrast that is linked to the higher reproductive capacity of altricials. In all mammals, the egg (oocyte) develops in a follicle within the ovary and *ovulation* occurs when the ripe egg is released into the oviduct. The residue of the follicle in the ovary may then be converted into a 'yellow body' (*corpus luteum*), which secretes hormones to maintain the early stages of pregnancy.

In most altricial mammals, ovulation occurs only if mating has taken place (*induced ovulation*) and a corpus luteum then forms automatically. In some altricial mammals, however, ovulation will occur without mating, but mating is then required for the residue of the follicle to be converted to a corpus luteum (*induced luteinisation*). In all altricial mammals, however, there is the same end effect – no corpus luteum forms without mating and the female is soon ready to ovulate again. In other words, in altricial mammals such as tree-shrews oestrous cycles are short, as they represent little more than a sequence of follicular growth periods. In precocial mammals, by contrast, ovulation and formation of a corpus luteum both typically take place whether or not mating occurs (*spontaneous ovulation*). In precocial mammals such as primates, therefore, each oestrous cycle contains both follicular and luteal phases and is correspondingly lengthy.

Form of the uterus

The fertilised egg (*zygote*) develops to form a *blastocyst* that implants on the internal wall of the uterus. The form of the uterus differs significantly between prosimians and simians: in prosimians, there are two separate uterine

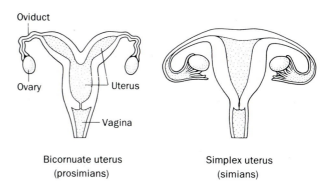

Simplified diagrams of the adult female reproductive system in (a) prosimian primates and (b) simian primates. In both, paired ovaries shed their eggs into paired oviducts, where fertilisation takes place. Prosimians (tarsiers, lemurs and lorises) have two uterine chambers (bicornuate uterus) whereas simians (monkeys, apes and humans) have a single uterine chamber (simplex uterus).

chambers (a *bicornuate uterus*), whereas in simians there is a single chamber (a *simplex uterus*). The bicornuate uterus is primitive for placental mammals in general and is also a feature of tree-shrews. Tarsiers share this primitive mammalian feature with lemurs and lorises. The single-chambered condition is very rare among mammals and is probably a specialisation that took place in the ancestral stock of the simian primates.

The fusion of the original two uterine horns to form a single-chambered uterus was probably associated with reduction of the litter size to a single offspring, especially as living simians also have only one pair of teats. Although marmosets and tamarins usually produce twins, this seems to be a secondary condition associated with their marked reduction in body size (dwarfism) and consequent increased reproductive potential. They have a simplex uterus and a single pair of teats and the development of the twins is very unusual in that there is a shared placental circulation.

The placenta and embryonic membranes

There are major differences in the form of the placenta and embryonic membranes between the two main groups of primates. These differences separate strepsirhines from haplorhines and provided the first indication of a specific phylogenetic link between tarsiers and simians. The primary distinction is in the form of the placenta and depends on the degree of invasion of the uterine wall by the outer layer of the blastocyst or *trophoblast*.

In strepsirhine primates, the placenta scarcely invades the maternal tissue and is termed *epitheliochorial*, because the outer membrane of the embryo (chorion) remains in contact with the intact layer of uterine epithelium. In haplorhine primates, by contrast, the placenta is very invasive; the chorion is directly bathed by maternal blood, because of the breakdown of the uterine epithelium and of the walls of the maternal capillaries supplying the placenta. Because of its invasive nature, the *haemochorial* placenta of haplorhines

POSTURE AND CHILDBIRTH

Humans have larger brains relative to body size than any other primate. This special characteristic and bipedalism have affected the size and shape of our pelvis and the mechanism of giving birth.

The primate pelvis is a complete bony ring made up of two hip bones that articulate together at the front and several fused vertebrae (the *sacrum*) at the back. The propulsive power of the legs in climbing, walking or running acts on the backbone directly through the hip joints, which are reinforced. Another function of the pelvis, apart from giving support to the abdominal organs, is to allow a full-term fetus to be delivered.

In human evolution, a compromise has been reached between efficient upright posture and bipedal locomotion and the size of the birth canal in relation to its ability to transmit the fetus. The anatomical differences between the human male and female pelvises that result from this conflict of functions, because of the childbirth needs of the female, led to less-efficient bipedalism in the female – as shown today by the differences between male and female Olympic running and jumping records.

When, at least 4 million years ago, human ancestors changed from moving on all fours to using two legs only, the backbone became vertical. Some of this change in position was achieved by the development of concavities in the neck and lower back. These curves allow us to balance our weight efficiently over our feet when we move bipedally.

The other angular change involved the pelvis. This changed shape, and the sacrum and the back of the hip bones rotated backwards to produce a different orientation in relation to the legs and backbone compared to that in apes. In male hominids, these changes to the pelvis improved the efficiency of bipedal locomotion. But bipedal females had the complication of having to give birth to a fetus with a large head.

One of the evolutionary trends in the human lineage is an increase in the size of the adult brain. This is apparent in the uterus and the result, coupled with a longer gestation than apes, means that humans may have problems at childbirth.

Quadrupedal apes, which are free of the restrictions on the size and shape of the pelvic ring imposed by the anatomical

needs of bipedalism, can pass a baby ape through the birth canal without problems. The baby's head enters, passes through and leaves the female ape's pelvis in a single front-to-back orientation. By contrast, a human baby must enter transversely, rotate through 90 degrees in mid-cavity and exit front-to-back – a manoeuvre calling for some effort on the part of the mother and which may need help from midwives and doctors.

Little is known about the pelvis of early hominids, but two australopithecine pelvises are known sufficiently to allow reconstructions. One is the pelvis of 'Lucy' (AL 288-1), the 3-million-year-old female *Australopithecus afarensis* from Hadar, Ethiopia (see p. 237); the other (Sts 14), from Sterkfontein, South Africa, is of much the same age.

Both pelvises probably belonged to individuals who were bipedal, although there is some debate about how well adapted they were for this locomotion. The pelvis of australopithecines of this date was wider in transverse diameter and narrower from front to back (and thus more oval) than is a modern human pelvis. As a result, these early hominids may have given birth in a different way from either modern humans or apes.

An australopithecine baby may have had to enter and leave the birth canal

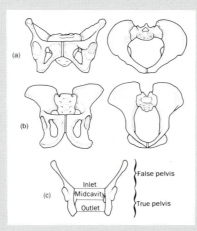

A human pelvis (a) and a chimpanzee pelvis (b) from the anterior (ventral) and the superior (cranial) views. The levels of the pelvic inlet, midcavity and outlet in the human pelvis are shown in (c).

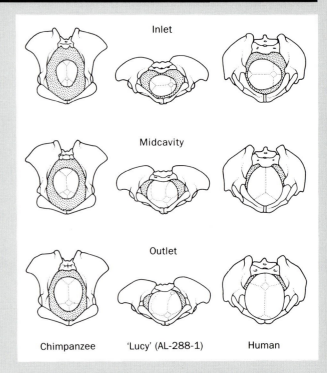

Chimpanzee   'Lucy' (AL-288-1)   Human

The mechanism of birth has competed with bipedality in shaping the modern human pelvis. The birth process is shown here in a chimpanzee, 'Lucy' (*Australopithecus afarensis*) and a human. The pelvis and fetus are shown from the inferior view. The dotted lines on the fetal cranium represent the sutures of the cranial vault; the diamond shape is the anterior fontanelle; the stippling represents the muscular wall of the birth canal. The head of the australopithecine baby is shown passing through the birth canal turned sideways and then tilted. But it could have rotated as does the head of a human modern infant.

transversely. Alternatively, it could have entered transversely, or obliquely, and then rotated in the birth canal as does a modern human infant.

The first view implies that the australopithecine pelvis was fully adapted for bipedal locomotion but that the head of the full-term fetus had not increased in size at this stage in evolution; the second that increased brain size already affected the birth mechanism 3 million years ago.

M.H. Day

See also 'Primate locomotion and posture' (p. 75), 'The human brain' (p. 115) and 'Evolution of australopithecines' (p. 231)

is localised and discoid in shape, whereas the non-invasive epitheliochorial placenta of strepsirhines is diffuse.

The epitheliochorial type of placenta is often thought to be primitive and the haemochorial type advanced. According to this view, lemurs and lorises retain the primitive mammalian placenta and only the haplorhines have become specialised. However, it is also possible that

ancestral placental mammals had an intermediate, semi-invasive type of placenta in which the uterine epithelium was broken down but the walls of the maternal capillaries remained intact: this is termed an *endotheliochorial* placenta as blood vessel walls are formed from endothelium. Such placentas exist in a variety of modern mammals, such as tree-shrews and carnivores.

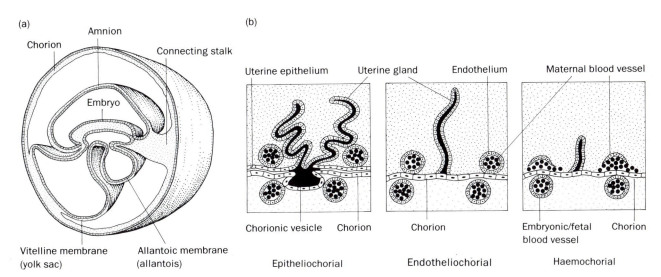

(a) The embryonic or fetal membranes in a typical placental mammal. (b) Three types of placenta. Embryonic or fetal tissues (light stippling) and maternal tissues (heavy stippling) are typically separated by the chorion, which forms a barrier to diffusion between maternal and embryonic/fetal blood vessels (seen in section). Uterine glands, which produce uterine milk, are best developed in species with the epitheliochorial type of placenta, in which special areas of the chorion (e.g. chorionic vesicles) are related to grouped outlets of such glands.

If the endotheliochorial type of placenta is indeed primitive, it follows that in primate evolution there has been divergence, with invasiveness reduced in strepsirhines and increased in haplorhines. The specialised nature of the epitheliochorial placenta is indicated by the fact that mammals with this kind of placentation typically have the advanced precocial type of offspring rather than the primitive altricial type. Furthermore, dolphins, which have exceptionally large brains relative to their body size, have an epitheliochorial placenta. lt is also significant that the lesser mouse lemur (*Microcebus murinus*) has an endotheliochorial zone within its epitheliochorial placenta – perhaps a primitive retention from an ancestral primate that still possessed an endotheliochorial placenta.

Strepsirhine and haplorhine primates differ also in the part played by two other embryonic membranes – the *yolk-sac* and the *allantois* – during pregnancy. In most mammals, blood vessels associated with these membranes constitute the circulatory system linking the embryo or fetus to the placenta, and the yolk-sac vessels usually develop before those of the allantois. This condition is characteristic of strepsirhine primates. In haplorhines, however, the yolk-sac is typically suppressed and the circulatory system of the placenta depends only on the allantois, which does not

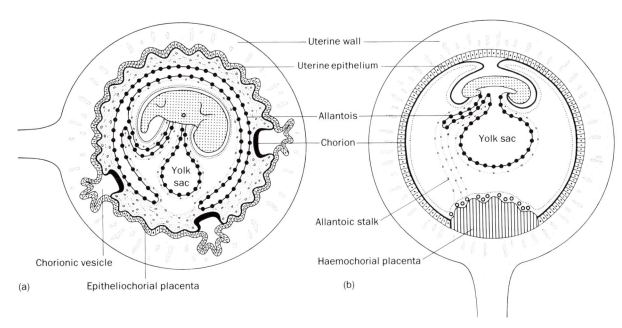

The fetal membranes and placentation in (a) strepsirhine primates (lemurs and lorises) and (b) haplorhine primates (tarsiers, monkeys, apes and humans). Notice the diffuse epitheliochorial form of placentation in the strepsirhine, associated with the development of chorionic vessels, and the contrasting discoidal form of placentation in the haplorhine. In haplorhines, the vessels of the yolk sac are not involved in placentation and the allantois develops only as a vestigial, stalk-like structure.

develop as a proper sac (as in the original mammalian condition) but is reduced to a stalk bearing blood vessels.

The placentation of strepsirhine primates is hence fundamentally different from that of haplorhines. The apparently derived features of placentation shared by tarsiers and simians provide convincing evidence of a specific phylogenetic relationship between them.

Size at birth

Another difference between strepsirhine and haplorhine primates is in the relationship between the weight of the neonate and that of the mother. For any given size of the mother, a haplorhine primate produces a neonate about three times larger than a strepsirhine neonate. This is not simply the result of differences in gestation periods, as there is no clear separation between the two groups in the relationship between gestation length and body weight.

Strepsirhine primates may produce smaller neonates because of the non-invasive nature of their epitheliochorial placenta, which is sometimes seen as 'less efficient'. However, the largest neonates, relative to maternal body weight, are those of ungulates (hoofed mammals) and of dolphins, which have epitheliochorial placentas. The non-invasive epitheliochorial placenta is hence not 'inefficient' in other mammals and we do not yet know why strepsirhine neonates are smaller than haplorhine neonates. The difference may reflect a fundamental contrast in reproductive strategies between strepsirhines and haplorhines, with the former favouring maternal investment in postnatal growth and the latter favouring investment in fetal growth. Whatever the explanation, it is clear that there is a sharp division between strepsirhine and haplorhine primates with respect to both placentation and the relative size of the neonate.

Robert Martin

See also 'Body size and energy requirements' (p. 41), 'Hormones and sexual behaviour' (p. 91), 'Life-history patterns' (p. 95) and 'Fertility control: past, present and future' (p. 425)

Hormones and sexual behaviour

Hormones secreted by the gonads (ovaries and testes) and the adrenal glands have important effects on sexual behaviour in many primates. However, environment and experience also influence sexual activity, so that relationships between hormones and behaviour are variable and complex, and especially difficult to demonstrate in humans.

A hormone can influence sexual interactions in many ways, either by a direct action on the brain or by peripheral effects on the genitalia and secondary sexual characteristics. For example, female primates may attempt to initiate sexual interactions with males by using *proceptive* displays, such as sexual presentations and special facial expressions. Proceptivity should be distinguished from a female's sexual *receptivity* or willingness to allow the male to copulate. Sexual *attractiveness* must also be considered, because in some primates ovarian hormones alter genital cues, such as odours or sexually attractive sexual skin swellings that stimulate the male's copulatory behaviour.

Copulation

Patterns of copulation show considerable variation among primates. A common pattern is for ejaculation to occur during a single, brief insertion of the penis (*intromission*) with pelvic thrusting, as, for example, in the owl monkey (*Aotus trivirgatus*), marmosets (*Callithrix*), the talapoin (*Miopithecus talapoin*) and chimpanzees (*Pan*). By contrast, multiple intromissions are required to achieve ejaculation in rhesus and Japanese macaques (*Macaca mulatta* and *M. fuscata*). In a few primates, such as some bushbabies (*Galago*), there is prolonged copulation, involving a genital 'lock'. Males may initiate most copulations as, for example, in the orang-utan (*Pongo pygmaeus*), chimpanzees and the bonnet macaque (*Macaca radiata*). However, female proceptivity plays an important part in the sexual behaviour of many monkeys, such as capuchins (*Cebus*), the muriqui (*Brachyteles arachnoides*) and rhesus macaques; in the gorilla (*Gorilla gorilla*), most copulations are initiated by females.

The frequency of sexual activity also varies with the mating system. Thus, many primates that live in multimale social groups – such as most baboons (*Papio*), macaques, the red colobus monkey (*Colobus badius*) and chimpanzees – usually copulate more often, have relatively larger testes, and frequently show more complex mating patterns than those living in monogamous family groups, such as titi monkeys (*Callicebus*), owl monkeys and gibbons (*Hylobates*).

Sexual patterns are used in social communication as well as for copulatory purposes. Members of the same, as well as the opposite, sex may 'present' to each other, embrace, inspect the genitalia, or mount and make thrusting movements. Hence the term *sociosexual behaviour* is often used to describe such interactions in macaques, baboons, chimpanzees and many other primates.

Seasons of sexual activity

Apes are not seasonal breeders, but some monkeys and most prosimians show seasonal changes in mating behaviour. In ring-tailed lemurs (*Lemur catta*), for instance, mating typically occurs during a two-week period in April or May in Madagascar, and individual females are usually sexually receptive for only about a day at this time. Research on captive ringtails has shown that, as in other lemurs, changes in daylength (*photoperiod*) trigger both the onset of activity of the gonads and sexual behaviour. In male squirrel monkeys (*Saimiri*), there is an increase in sperm production (*spermatogenesis*) and secretion of the steroid hormone testosterone during the annual mating season. Individuals also increase in bulk around the shoulders and chest (the 'fatted male condition'); females apparently prefer to approach males that are in such breeding fettle.

Rhesus macaques also show annual cycles in the activity of the testes and in sexual behaviour. When female rhesus macaques are treated with oestradiol (one of the ovarian steroid hormones) in the non-mating season, males show a premature onset of testicular activity and sexual behaviour. Hence, social and sexual cues may co-ordinate seasonal cycles of sexual activity. Some monkeys that breed seasonally live near the Equator, such as talapoins, so it

The female chacma baboon (*Papio ursinus*) on the right is showing her pink 'sexual skin', which is swollen to its greatest extent around the time of ovulation. She engages the seated male in eye contact and swivels her hindquarters towards him as a sexual presentation. Here, proceptive behavioural patterns and sexually attractive visual stimuli are combined in a complex fashion. The female's attractiveness and proceptivity are greatest around the time of ovulation although she is receptive (able to receive the male) throughout the menstrual cycle.

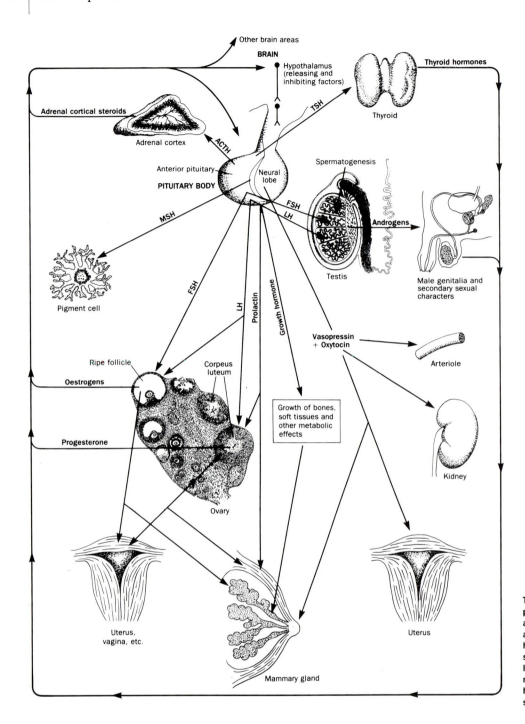

The main actions of the pituitary, gonadal and adrenal hormones. ACTH, adrenocorticotrophic hormone; FSH, follicle-stimulating hormone; LH, luteinising hormone; MSH, melanocyte-stimulating hormone; TSH, thyroid-stimulating hormone.

seems unlikely that changes in daylength provide a major cue to sexual behaviour. Other factors such as rainfall and vegetational changes are probably involved, with 'fine tuning' achieved by means of cues between the members of the social group.

Ovarian rhythms

The rhythmic changes in sexual behaviour that take place during ovarian cycles in many primates are subtle and difficult to demonstrate in human females. Alterations in female proceptivity, receptivity and attractiveness can all contribute to cycles of sexual activity. Among prosimians,

such as lemurs and bushbabies, females typically have periods of sexual receptivity or *oestrus* only during the fertile phase of the cycle. Removing the ovaries (*ovariectomy*) of a bushbaby makes the female sexually unreceptive, as is the case in rodents, carnivores and many other mammals.

Among most monkeys and apes there is less restriction of mating to the time of ovulation, although sexual interactions tend to increase at this time and to decrease during the luteal phase following ovulation. Although interactions decrease after ovariectomy in many monkeys and in chimpanzees, mating is not necessarily abolished, and copulation may even continue, as, for example, in the stump-tailed macaque (*Macaca arctoides*) and marmoset (*Callithrix jacchus*).

A reduction in sexual activity is not therefore necessarily caused by loss of receptivity, as it may result from a loss of female attractiveness or a reduction in proceptive behaviour. A minute dose of oestradiol applied to the vagina of an ovariectomised female rhesus macaque restores her attractiveness and stimulates the male to mount. But a dose of the hormone progesterone depresses her attractiveness. Oestradiol stimulates proceptivity in an ovariectomised female marmoset, whereas progesterone inhibits such displays.

The ovaries secrete other steroid hormones, including androgens such as testosterone, with peak levels during the ovulatory phase of the cycle. However, there is little evidence that proceptivity or receptivity changes as a result of mid-cycle increases in testosterone secretion. The adrenal glands secrete androgens, including androstenedione, and this is converted to testosterone in the bloodstream.

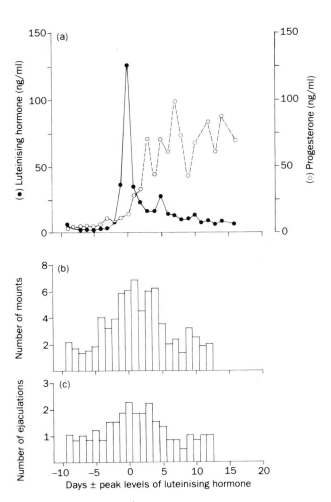

The rhythmic changes in sexual behaviour that take place during ovarian cycles in many primates are subtle and difficult to demonstrate in human females, but can be shown in many non-human primates as, for example, family groups of marmosets (*Callithrix jacchus*). In females (a), levels of luteinising hormone peak just before ovulation (day 0) and those of progesterone increase subsequently in the luteal phase of the cycle and in early pregnancy. As the histograms show, mounts (b) by males and ejaculations (c) are more frequent around the time of ovulation although sexual activity is not restricted to this period.

Adrenal androgens may influence sexual activity in rhesus macaques and in women, but in other species (stumptailed macaque and common marmoset) removal of the glands has no effect on the female's sexual behaviour.

Testicular hormones

Androgens, which are secreted by the testes during fetal development, influence the central nervous mechanisms that control some sexually distinctive behavioural patterns. If pregnant rhesus macaques are treated with a synthetic androgen (testosterone propionate), the female offspring are born as *pseudohermaphrodites*, with masculinised external genitalia. When young, such monkeys initiate more play, and show more rough-and-tumble play patterns and more sociosexual mounting than normal females. However, when pseudohermaphrodites become adult they display proceptive and receptive behaviour, despite their masculinised genitalia.

Thus, although these monkeys show some masculinisation of behaviour, they are apparently not defeminised as adults and show normal feminine sexual orientation; they are like humans in this respect. These findings contrast with those in non-primates such as rodents or dogs, in which early exposure to androgen greatly masculinises and defeminises adult sexual response.

The adrenal glands of humans can be congenitally overactive and this condition (adrenogenital syndrome) provides a natural parallel to animal experiments. The developing fetus is exposed to abnormally high levels of androgens, secreted by the adrenal cortex. Female infants born with adrenal overdevelopment (hyperplasia) have an enlarged clitoris, which may need surgical correction. As they develop, these girls often become athletic and 'tomboyish', although in adulthood menstrual cycles and sexual orientation are quite normal.

Early experience can have pronounced effects on later

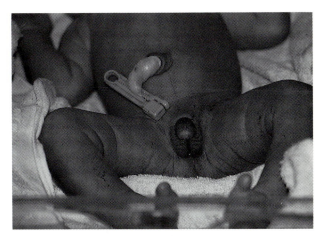

The adrenal glands of humans can be congenitally hyperactive – a condition called adrenogenital syndrome. Female infants born with this syndrome have an enlarged clitoris, which may need surgical correction.

sexual behaviour in many primates. If infant rhesus macaques are raised in isolation for 6 to 12 months after birth, their patterns of adult social, sexual and parental behaviour become grossly abnormal. They tend to be extremely aggressive and often mistreat their offspring. In humans, problems of sexual development can often be related to endocrine abnormalities or to social factors, such as mistaken gender assignment. Boys with the inherited X-linked condition known as *testicular feminisation syndrome* have an insensitivity of the peripheral organs to androgens, and, because their external genitalia look feminine, are often raised as girls. Despite being genetically male, such individuals often have a feminine gender identity when adult.

Boys with Imperato-McGinley syndrome, a rare condition first described in Dominica, have incomplete growth of the external genitalia caused by an enzyme deficiency during fetal life and a consequent lack of conversion of testosterone to dihydrotestosterone (the androgen responsible for development of the genital tissues). The abnormal external genitalia of these babies result in their being raised as girls. At puberty, an increase in testosterone results in growth of the penis and scrotum, descent of the testes and development of a masculine appearance.

It has been claimed that such individuals alter their psychosexual orientation to behave as males once past puberty. However, care must be taken when interpreting these findings. Their parents are aware that these infants are unusual and refer to them by special names, such as *guevodoces* ('penis-at-twelves'). It is unlikely that parents rear guevodoces in exactly the same way as they do girls, so that changes in behaviour at puberty may not represent a genuine reversal of gender identity from feminine to masculine. Indeed, more recent studies of boys with Imperato-McGinley syndrome in New Guinea confirm that social factors play an important part in the psychosexual development of such individuals.

Attempts to account for the development of human homosexual behaviour entirely on the basis of prenatal hormonal abnormalities are not convincing. Homosexuality refers not to the use of specific behavioural patterns during sexual interactions, but to an erotic preference for a member of the same sex. Thus, although prenatally androgenised female rhesus macaques often mount other group members, this is not equivalent to human lesbianism. Male monkeys very rarely prefer other males as partners for copulation when attractive females are available. We therefore need to know much more about the development of the mechanisms that control sexual recognition and attractiveness in primates if we are to understand how a homosexual orientation arises.

mates, including men. After castration (loss or removal of both testes), there is a gradual decline in sexual behaviour because of the lack of androgens. The severity of the effect varies between individual males. Sexual behaviour returns to normal if hypogonadal men (those with small testes) or castrated monkeys are treated with synthetic androgens.

Androgens have many peripheral effects on male primates. For example, in the human male, they include growth of the penis and accessory sexual organs during puberty, increased muscular development, deepening of the voice, and growth of the beard and pubic hair. These peripheral changes may influence a male primate's behaviour as well as the reactions of other members of the same species towards him.

In many vertebrates, testosterone is converted to oestrogen in the brain by a process called *aromatisation* and this can be important in the control of sexual behaviour (in, for example, the rat, sheep or red deer stag). In primate brains, testosterone is also aromatised to oestrogen, but there is no evidence that this affects sexual behaviour. In rhesus macaques, dihydrotestosterone (which is not aromatised to oestrogen in the brain) can nonetheless activate sexual behaviour in castrated males. The importance of aromatisation varies considerably between species in other mammals and there have been few comparative studies of primates.

Testosterone accumulates in particular parts of the primate brain, such as the hypothalamus, amygdala, stria terminalis and hippocampus. Many of the same regions also accumulate oestrogen. Damage to brain areas that bind testosterone or oestrogens have a variety of effects on male sexual behaviour. Destruction of the anterior hypothalamus or preoptic area causes a prompt and dramatic decrease in mounting (although some sexual interest may persist after such damage in rats, dogs, rhesus macaques and marmosets). Destruction of the anterior hypothalamus in female monkeys (common marmosets) also affects sexual behaviour but here the main change is a decrease in proceptivity whereas sexual receptivity is often unaffected.

Clinical evidence also suggests that the hypothalamus plays a critical part in the co-ordination of sexual arousal and copulatory behaviour in humans. Yet we still know relatively little about how gonadal hormones influence the human brain to affect sexual behaviour. Most experimentation is this field has involved rodent and bird species rather than primates. There is little doubt that further studies of hormone–brain–behaviour interrelationships in monkeys will also illuminate the fundamental problems of human sexual physiology.   A.F. Dixson

Development of the adult male

Testicular hormones, and especially testosterone, play a major part in maintaining sexual behaviour in male pri-

See also 'Primate brains and senses' (p. 109), 'Mating and parental care' (p. 150) and 'Smell as a signal' (p. 157)

Life-history patterns

If a female lesser mouse lemur and a female gorilla were born at the same time, and we assume equal reproductive success of males and females, the mouse lemur could leave 10 million descendants before the gorilla became sexually mature. This astonishing difference arises because of the differences in life-history patterns between the two species. The mouse lemur (*Microcebus murinus*) can reproduce within a year of birth, can produce two litters a year, and each litter may have up to three offspring. In comparison, the gorilla does not breed until it is about 10 years old, and even then it can produce but a single young every 4 or 5 years.

Mouse lemurs weigh less than 100 grams and gorillas more than 100 kilograms. Body size is generally a good predictor of lifestyle. In this respect, it is useful to compare the life-history patterns of primates with those of other mammals. Among mammals, the lengths of different life-history periods tend to increase with body size whereas litter sizes decrease. Larger species have longer gestation lengths, later ages at weaning and reproduction, longer lifespans, and smaller litters.

Body size, however, is not the whole story. When animals of the same size from different mammalian orders are compared, they can have different life-history patterns. For example, primates live slowly. In comparison with other mammals, they have long gestation periods, long lifespans, and they mature late. These differences are asso-

A mouse lemur, the smallest living primate, and a gorilla, the largest living primate. Differences in body size account for a large part of the variation in primate life-history patterns. Even when body size is held constant, however, species may differ because of adaptation to particular habitats.

ciated with the state of development of the young at birth. Slower-developing mammals, such as primates, produce young whose eyes are open at birth, and are said to be *precocial*, in contrast to the *altricial* young of mammals that develop more rapidly. It therefore follows that precocial mammals, such as primates, have relatively longer gestation periods than altricial mammals, such as carnivores.

Primates also have relatively large brains for their bodies. Perhaps the size of the brain rather than that of the whole body is evolutionarily tied to life-history variation. For example, the brain might be a controlling organ that enables primates to have relatively long lives and, as brain tissue is slow to grow, the development of the brain might dictate a slow development. This type of explanation is particularly appealing when we consider the human species, the slowest developing and longest-lived primate of all, which is noted for its massive brain. Indeed, if our gestation length was any longer, the neonatal brain could not be delivered through the birth canal.

Size

Whatever the functional connections, the timing of life-history events is highly correlated with size, be it the size of the whole body or of an organ such as the brain. Although primates develop relatively slowly and live for a relatively long time, the scaling factors that link size to timing events are similar to those found in other animals. Life-history events tend to vary, so that timings are *allometrically* scaled to body size in different ways, following the formula $Y = kX^{\alpha}$

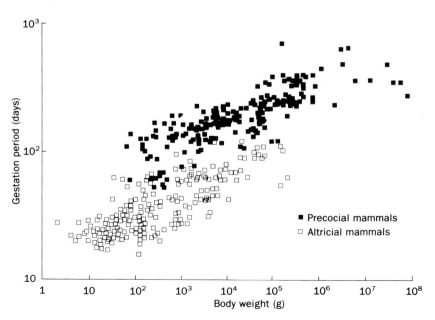

Logarithmic plot of gestation period against maternal body weight for 394 species of placental mammals. Precocial mammals, such as primates, usually have a much longer gestation period than altricial mammals; there is a four-fold difference overall.

95

(where Y is the life-history variable, X is body weight, α is the allometric exponent and k is the allometric coefficient).

For individual life-history periods, the value k tends to be large for primates, whereas α is similar to the values found among other mammals. The exponent α lies in the range 0.1 to 0.6 for most measures of life-history timing. For example, gestation length scales to body size with $\alpha = 0.13$, while for age at maturity $\alpha = 0.49$. When α is less than one, a doubling of body size does not lead to a proportionate increase in timing. For example, a female gorilla is more than a thousand times heavier than a female mouse lemur, but their gestation lengths differ only by a factor of about four (256 compared with 62 days).

The pace of life

Some primates tend to develop more slowly than others, even after a correction has been made for the effects of body size. One interesting but unexplained finding about such relative measures of life-history variation among primates is that species with short gestation lengths do not compensate by having late ages at weaning. Instead, it seems that the whole pace of life is slowed down or speeded up. For example, lemurs tend to be fast developers: in relation to their adult body (or brain) sizes, they have short gestation lengths (and consequently give birth to small young), early ages at weaning and maturity, and

RATES OF BREEDING

The effects of natural selection on breeding patterns of tropical species differ from those affecting species living at higher latitudes. In addition, small-bodied species usually breed faster than those with large bodies. These patterns reflect differences in optimal patterns of breeding, which underlie the idea of r- and K-selection, introduced by Robert MacArthur and Edward Wilson in 1967.

Population growth usually follows an S-shaped or sigmoid curve. When numbers are low, there are few limits on growth and the population expands in an accelerating, geometric fashion. The rate of expansion is then primarily determined by its intrinsic rate of population increase (r). For mammals, this depends on gestation period, litter size, interbirth interval, age at sexual maturity and lifespan.

Once numbers of individuals in the population have increased beyond a certain level, however, limiting factors such as food availability and predation limit population growth, and this decelerates. Eventually, population size stabilises at carrying capacity (K), when breeding is approximately balanced by food availability and predation.

In practice, of course, a population that has reached carrying capacity fluctuates for various reasons, but its level can remain roughly constant over time as long as the environment stays stable.

If there is a reduction in population because of seasonal reduction in food resources or through climatic differences between years, limits on breeding will be removed as soon as conditions improve. Some populations can hence fluctuate, with phases of geometric increase, periods of population stability and phases of population decline. Selection should favour a high breeding potential for such species, living as they do in variable and unpredictable environments. Their intrinsic rate of population increase is high and they are r-selected.

For species living in relatively stable environments, selection might favour a low reproductive output combined with

relatively high investment in individual offspring ('quality rather than quantity'). Their intrinsic rate of population increase is then kept at a low level by the constraints of living under competitive conditions close to carrying capacity: they are K-selected.

There is a wide spectrum, from extremely r-selected to extremely K-selected species, and all statements are relative. For example, mammals generally breed far less rapidly than insects and are therefore relatively K-selected. However, there are also marked differences between rapid breeders and slow breeders among mammals.

This model of r- and K-selection can explain why some tropical species breed more slowly. Higher latitudes generally show more extensive seasonal fluctuations in temperature and rainfall than the tropics, and differences from year to year also tend to be more pronounced. Temperate species should hence be relatively r-selected.

The model can also account for the association between body size and breeding pattern. Large mammals may be more likely to reach the carrying capacity of a given environment, especially as dietary specialisation tends to increase with body size. Large species may also be less vulnerable to environmental fluctuation and less affected by predation, so drastic population decline is less likely.

Because body size has such a strong influence, scaling effects must be taken into account when comparing the breeding patterns of different species. Regardless of environmental factors, it is only to be expected that gorillas should breed far more slowly than mouse lemurs.

Detailed field information is needed to determine values of r and K for natural populations but short cuts can help. One approach is to determine the *maximum* value for the intrinsic rate of population increase (r_{max}) in captivity. On this basis, primates have – relative to body size – a lower reproductive potential than other mammals and are therefore K-selected.

This may indicate that from the outset primates have been adapted for tropical forests, which are relatively stable environments. Most living and fossil primates are indeed associated with tropical or subtropical forests.

Relative to body size, humans have a very low value for r_{max} – even in comparison to other primates. This suggests that selection has favoured a low breeding potential during human evolution. Any model of human evolution should take this into account.

Differences in breeding potential also exist among primate species. Primates, of course, obey the general rule that large species breed more slowly than small ones, but differences are also apparent when the effects of body size have been removed. One study showed that, as expected, r_{max} is relatively higher for primate species living in variable environments, such as savanna woodland, than for those living in more stable habitats, such as tropical rain forest.

However, some species living in tropical rain forest show unexpectedly high values for r_{max} – for example, the variegated lemur (*Varecia variegata*), which has the highest value of r_{max} relative to body size of any primate. Such exceptions may simply show that special factors – for example, heavy predation – affect certain species, but they also suggest that the concept of r- and K-selection alone is not sufficient to explain patterns of breeding.

The rate of breeding might, for example, be influenced by age-specific patterns of mortality. High mortality among juveniles in fluctuating environments may favour adaptation of the adults to spreading their breeding over a long period of time, and high mortality among adults may favour rapid breeding.

Such a 'bet-hedging' model might explain the low reproductive output in primates because of relatively heavy mortality affecting young individuals. However, there is little information to test this idea, for primate breeding ecology is still a neglected field.   *Robert Martin*

An elderly man, Luzon Island, Philippines. Humans live much longer than other primates.

short lifespans. In contrast, tarsiers are slow developers with long gestation lengths, large neonates, late weaning and maturity, and long lives.

Many of these differences in pace of life are associated with habitat, as species living in tropical rain forest typically live more extended lives (relative to body size) than do those living in savanna or secondary forest. For example, Allen's bushbaby (*Galago alleni*) in the West African rain forest has single births and breeds relatively slowly compared with the lesser bushbaby (*G. moholi*) in wooded savanna regions of southern Africa, which has twin births and two breeding seasons a year. Humans have extended life histories even in comparison with other primates. The human lifespan is the longest both absolutely and relatively.

Why should these particular habitats be associated with different paces of life? One explanation is that tropical rain forests provide more stable habitats where natural selection favours the channelling of resources into the production of competitive young, which are slow to develop. In contrast, secondary forest and savanna may be unstable environments in which there are periods of plenty (when there is selection for rapid production of young) interspersed with population crashes. Following the notation used in mathematical models that describe the theory of population dynamics, species that put more resources into the production of offspring with high competitive ability are said to be more K-selected than the r-selected species that invest in rapid reproduction (see Box).

The differences in life history mentioned above are those remaining after the effects of size have been removed. Size itself, as we have already been seen, is a very strong correlate of life-history variation. In many ways, this correlation between size and life history is not surprising because large-bodied species will inevitably take longer to grow to adult size. This means that ecological correlates of size will usually be good predictors of life history. For example, large primates (such as gorillas) tend to be terrestrial, diurnal and leaf-eaters. Those same species will also have long gestation lengths, slow postnatal development and long lives. Furthermore, they will also have large brains and low metabolic rates.

Under such circumstances, with many factors varying in the same ways, it is very difficult to identify the targets of natural selection. Although we have some clues, the full adaptive significance of species differences in life-history variation among primates has yet to be understood.

Paul H. Harvey

See also 'Body size and energy requirements' (p. 41) and 'Primate reproduction' (p. 86)

Human growth and development

Primates generally have a slow reproductive turnover and drawn-out life histories. As part of this pattern, the pace of growth from birth to adulthood is retarded and in monkeys, apes and humans, at least, it is possible to recognise special features of the growth curve associated with the attainment of sexual maturity (puberty). These characteristics were once supposed to be unique to humans but other primates were later found to have them as well. The distinctive form of the human growth curve was first established in the eighteenth century. Sexual differences in the curve, originally denied, were confirmed in the 1880s, but the evolutionary significance of its shape only became clear after 1950.

The oldest published record of the growth of a child was made from 1759 to 1777 by Comte Philibert Gueneau de Montbeillard and is of his son; it was published by his friend Comte de Buffon in a supplement to the *Histoire Naturelle*. If we think of growth as a form of motion, then the upper curve in the figure below is one of distance travelled, and the lower curve is one of speed or *velocity*.

The velocity, or rate of growth, reflects the child's state at a particular time better than does actual height, which depends largely on how much the child has grown throughout life. The blood and tissue concentrations of those substances that change with age are thus more likely to accompany the velocity than the distance curve. In some circumstances, acceleration of growth rather than its velocity may reflect physiological events; the increase in secretion from the endocrine glands at adolescence, for example, is seen most clearly in an acceleration of growth.

The velocity of growth in height decreases from birth onwards, but this decrease is interrupted shortly before the end of the growth period. At this time, from 13 to 15 years of age in the boy in the figure, there is a marked acceleration of growth – the adolescent or pubertal *growth spurt*. A slight increase in velocity, the *mid-growth spurt*, may also occur between about 6 and 8 years, providing a second peak on the general velocity curve.

Prenatal growth

Although the velocity of growth in body length is greater at birth than at any later period, in fetal life the velocity is greater still. Its peak is reached at about the eighteenth week of postmenstrual age. (Age in the fetal period is usually reckoned from the first day of the last menstrual period – an average of 2 weeks prior to actual fertilisation – but is usually the only easily located landmark of pregnancy.)

Growth in fetal weight follows the same general pattern, except that the peak velocity is reached later, usually at the

thirty-fourth postmenstrual week. From about 36 weeks to birth at 40 weeks, the rate of growth slows down, perhaps because the space available in the uterus is becoming fully occupied. The growth of twins slows down earlier, when their combined weight is approximately the weight of a 36-week singleton fetus. Birth weight and birth size reflect the maternal environment more than the child's genotype and the slowing-down mechanism enables a genetically large child developing in the uterus of a small mother to be delivered successfully. Directly after birth, the growth rate increases again, particularly in genetically large children, and the rate of weight gain reaches its peak at the age of approximately 2 months.

The velocity of growth in length is not very great during the first 2 months of fetal life, the period of the embryo.

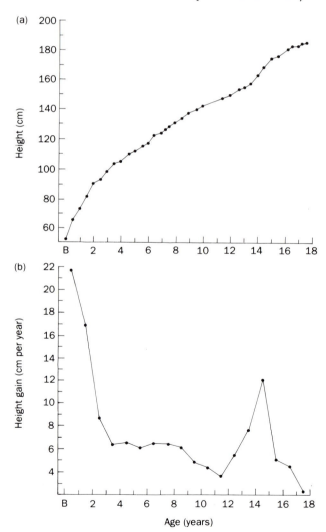

Growth in height of Comte de Montbeillard's son from birth (B) to 18 years, 1759–77: (a) the child's height attained at each age (distance curve); (b) increments in height from one age to the next (velocity curve).

During this period, there is *differentiation* ('regionalisation') of the originally homogeneous whole into regions such as the head and arms, and *histogenesis*, the differentiation of cells into specialised tissues such as muscle or nerve. At the same time, each region is moulded, by differential growth of cells or by cell migration, into a definite shape. This process, termed *morphogenesis*, continues up to adulthood, and, indeed, in some parts of the body into old age. But the major part of it is completed by the eighth postmenstrual week and by then the embryo has assumed a recognisably human appearance.

The high rate of growth of the fetus, compared with that of the child, is due largely to *cell multiplication*. The proportion of cells undergoing division becomes less as the fetus gets older, and few, if any, new muscle cells or nerve cells (apart from neuroglia, the cells surrounding the neurones themselves) appear after the sixth month of fetal life.

The muscle cells and nerve cells of the fetus differ in appearance from those of the child or adult. Both have very little cytoplasm around the nucleus. In fetal muscle, there is more intercellular substance and a much higher proportion of water than in mature muscle. The later fetal and postnatal growth of muscle consists of building up the

cytoplasm of the muscle cells; salts are incorporated and proteins formed. The cells become bigger, the intercellular substance largely disappears, and the concentration of water decreases.

This process continues quite actively up to about 3 years of age and slowly thereafter; at adolescence, it briefly speeds up again, particularly in boys, as more substances are incorporated into the fibres under the influence of androgenic and growth hormones. During the same period there is an increase in the amount of DNA, indicating that further nuclei are appearing. In the nervous system, cytoplasm is added, nucleoprotein bodies appear, and axons and dendrites grow. Thus, for most tissues, postnatal growth is a period of development and enlargement of existing cells, rather than the formation of new ones.

Postnatal growth

The dimensions of most bones and muscles and of organs such as the liver, spleen and kidneys follow approximately the same growth curve as that of height. However, certain other tissues – the brain and skull, the reproductive organs, the lymphoid tissue and the subcutaneous fat – have rather different curves. The size attained at successive ages is plotted as a percentage of the total size gain from birth to maturity. Height and most of the body measurements follow the 'general' curve. The external and internal reproductive organs follow a curve that is perhaps not very different in principle but is so in effect. Their growth before puberty is slow whereas their growth at adolescence is very rapid; they are less sensitive than the skeleton to one set of hormones and are more sensitive to another.

The brain, together with the skull, eyes and ears, develops earlier than any other part of the body, and has its own characteristic postnatal growth curve. At birth, it is already 25 per cent of its adult weight; at age 5 years, it is 90 per cent; and at age 10 years it is about 95 per cent of the adult weight. Thus, if the brain has any adolescent spurt at all, it is very small. The face follows a curve midway between that of the brain-covering portion of the skull and the remainder of the skeleton.

The lymphoid tissue – tonsils, adenoids, appendix, intestine and spleen – has quite another growth curve. Growth rate reaches its maximum before adolescence, and then, probably under the influence of the sex hormones, declines to its adult value.

The subcutaneous fat layer has a somewhat complicated growth curve. The width of this layer can be measured by ultrasound or by calipers applied to a fold of fat pinched up from the underlying muscle. Subcutaneous fat begins to be laid down in the fetus at about 34 weeks and increases from then until birth, and from birth until about 9 months (in the average child; the peak may be reached as early as 6 months in some and as late as a year or 15 months in others). From 9 months, the subcutaneous fat decreases, until age 6 to 8

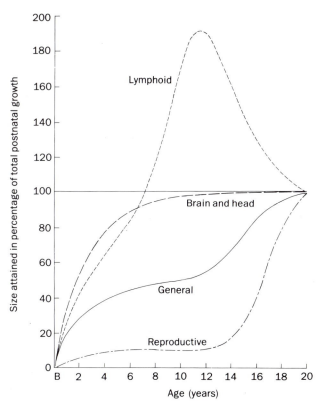

Growth curve of parts and tissues of the body, showing the four chief types. All the curves are of size attained, plotted as a percentage of total gain from birth (B) to maturity (20 years) so that size at age 20 years is 100 on the vertical scale. Lymphoid type: thymus, lymph nodes and intestinal lymph masses. Brain and head type: brain and its parts, membrane (dura), spinal cord, optic apparatus and head dimensions. General type: the body as a whole, external dimensions (except head), respiratory and digestive organs, kidneys, aortic and pulmonary trunks, musculature and blood volume. Reproductive type: testis, ovary, epididymis, prostate, seminal vesicles and Fallopian tubes.

1. EVOLUTION OF THE HUMAN GROWTH CURVE

The characteristic form of the human growth curve is shared by apes and monkeys. It is apparently distinctive to higher primates; neither rodents nor cattle have curves that resemble it.

The figure shows the weight velocity curves of mice, monkeys, apes and humans. In the mouse, there is little interval between weaning and puberty, and no visible adolescent spurt because there is no period of low rate of growth between birth and maturity. In rhesus macaques (*Macaca mulatta*), a considerable period intervenes between birth and the adolescent growth spurt; in chimpanzees, this interval is greater, and in humans it is greater still. The mechanism involves hormones.

During the latter part of fetal life and for a short time after birth in all three primates, gonadotrophin-releasing hormone is secreted by the cells of the arcuate nucleus in the brain. But at about 12 months after birth in humans and 6 months in rhesus macaques, the secretion stops and the nucleus becomes silent, or almost so. This period of silence has become progressively lengthened during primate evolution.

We do not yet understand the mechanism of this suppression. Some of the evolutionary reasons for the progressive lengthening of this period are easy to find: it allows learning — especially learning to co-operate in group or family life — to take place while the individual remains relatively docile and before he or she comes into sexual competition with adult males or females.

Differences in the velocity of growth of particular parts of the body produce many of the fetal, childhood and adult differences in morphology of different species or genera. Humans are distinct from apes in having longer legs relative to body or arms; and this comes about by our greater velocity of leg growth from early fetal life onwards.

Furthermore, the joint between the back of the head and the vertebral column is situated further forwards in humans than in monkeys and apes. At birth, however, this distinction is not present; all simians have the joints in about the same relative position. However, the postnatal growth of the head in monkeys and apes is greater in front of the occipital condyles (the rounded protuberances on the back of the skull) than behind them, and so the joint shifts backwards.

In humans, the growth rates of the pre- and post-condylar parts of the head are more nearly equal, and the position of the joint remains unchanged. Differential growth rates are very often the mechanism of morphological evolution in primates (see Box 2).

Rhesus macaques show an adolescent growth spurt similar to that in humans. It occurs at a similar degree of skeletal maturation and with a similar relationship to menarche. However, the limbs (at least the forelimbs) lengthen faster than the trunk, whereas the reverse is the case in humans.

James M. Tanner

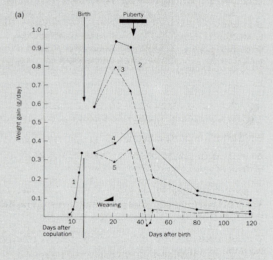

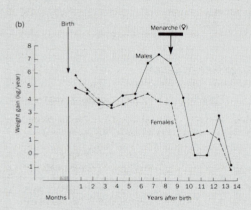

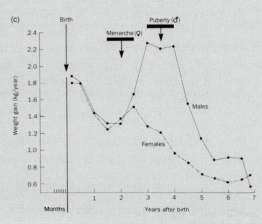

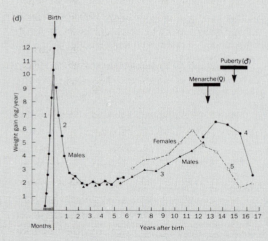

Weight gain in mice, monkeys, apes and humans. (a) Mouse: curve 1 = sexes combined; curves 2 and 3 = males and females, large strain; curves 4 and 5 = males and females, small strain. The mean age at onset of puberty (first oestrus), 37 days, is marked with an arrow; the range by horizontal bars. (b) Chimpanzee: males and females. Average age of menarche is 8.8 years (range 7.0–10.8 years). (c) Rhesus macaque. (d) Human: curve 1 = sexes combined; curves 2 = sexes combined; curves 3 and 4 = males; curve 5 = females.

years, when it again begins to increase. This increase occurs in both sexes and in both limb fat and body fat. At adolescence, however, the limb fat in boys decreases and is not regained until the age of about 20 years. In boys, the loss of trunk fat is much smaller. In girls, increase in limb fat slows down (but no loss occurs) and the trunk fat shows a steady rise.

Regulation of growth

Growth is highly regulated. If a child's growth is slowed down because of food shortage or lack of growth hormone, then when food or the hormone is again supplied growth resumes at a velocity greater than that appropriate for that age. The child is said to 'catch-up' in growth. When the child's height has reached the previous growth curve once more, growth slows down and continues along this curve. Growth therefore has a target-seeking character. The mechanism by which the young organism 'knows' how large it should be, and can compare this with how large it actually is, is entirely obscure.

The same regulatory mechanism normally comes into play for a year or 18 months after birth. In the case of twins, for example, the differences in length at birth between monozygotic (or 'identical') pairs are just as great as the differences between dizygotic ('fraternal') pairs. But in the ensuing months monozygotics grow to be increasingly alike, dizygotics increasingly different.

Adolescent growth

The adolescent growth spurt occurs in all children, although it varies in intensity and duration from one to another. The peak velocity of growth in height averages about 10 centimetres a year in boys, and slightly less than this in girls. In boys, the spurt takes place on average between 12.5 and 15.5 years of age, and in girls some 2 years earlier.

Girls are more advanced in maturity at all ages from birth onwards. The sex difference in height in adulthood is due mostly to the longer period of male growth. Of the 13 centimetres' difference, about 2 centimetres result from a difference in prepubertal growth, 7 centimetres from the later occurrence of the spurt in males and 4 centimetres from its greater intensity.

Practically all parts of the skeleton and muscles take part in the spurt, though not to an equal extent. Most of the spurt in height results from growth of the trunk rather than the legs. The muscles have the peak of their spurt about 3 months after the height peak, and the weight peak occurs a further 3 months later.

Many of the sex differences in adult body size and shape result from differential growth patterns at adolescence. In shoulder width, for example, males have a relatively much greater spurt than females, whereas in hip width the reverse

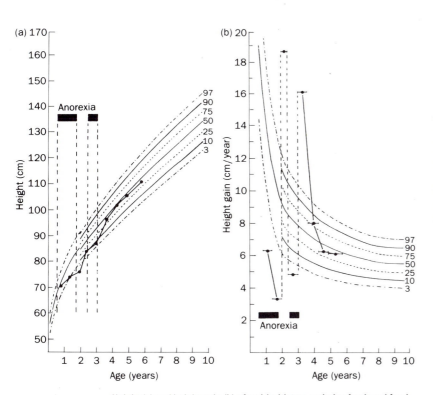

Height (a) and height gain (b) of a girl with two periods of reduced food intake (anorexia), each followed by catch-up growth: left, distance curve; right, velocity curve, together with the percentiles of a representative population.

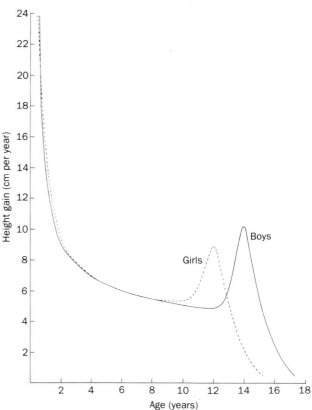

The adolescent growth spurt in boys and girls. In girls, the spurt takes place on average between 10½ and 13½ years; in boys, it comes about 2 years later.

is the case. However, not all sex differences arise in this way. The greater length of male legs relative to the trunk is a consequence of the longer prepubescent period of male growth, because the legs are growing faster than the trunk at this time. Other sex differences begin still earlier. The male forearm is longer, relative to the upper arm or the height, than the female's. This difference is already established at birth, and increases gradually throughout the whole growing period.

The adolescent spurt in skeletal and muscular dimensions is closely related to the rapid development of the reproductive system that takes place at this time. The acceleration in the growth of the penis, for example, begins on average at about age 12.5 years, but may occur as early as 10.5 years and sometimes as late as 14 years. Thus, there are a few boys who do not begin their spurts in height or penis development until those earliest to mature have completed theirs. At age 13 and 14, there is an enormous variability in development within any group of boys, who range prac-

tically all the way from complete maturity to pre-adolescence. The fact raises difficult social and educational problems and may itself contribute to the psychological maladjustments of adolescence.

In girls, as in boys, there is a large variation in the time at which the spurt begins, though the sequence of events is fairly constant. The appearance of the breast bud is usually the first sign of puberty, although the appearance of pubic hair may sometimes precede it. The uterus and vagina develop at the same time as the breast. The first menstrual period (*menarche*) almost invariable occurs after the peak of the height spurt has been passed, and does not usually mark the attainment of full reproductive function, as early menstrual cycles frequently occur without an ovum being shed. In one study, 75 per cent of cycles during the first 2 years after menarche were anovulatory, and even during the subsequent 2 years half the cycles did not produce an egg. Two years later the figure was down to 25 per cent.

Great changes in physiology coincide with the adolescent growth spurt. They are more marked in boys than in girls and confer on the male his greater strength and physical endurance. Before adolescence, boys are on average a little stronger than girls, but the difference is quite small. After adolescence, boys are much stronger, chiefly by virtue of having larger muscles; their muscles produce no more force per gram of tissue than do the muscles of girls. Boys have relatively larger hearts and lungs, more red blood cells and a greater capacity for carrying oxygen in the blood, and a greater ability to neutralise the chemical products of exercise. In short, males become at adolescence more adapted for the tasks of hunting, fighting and the manipulation of heavy objects – as was necessary in certain forms of food acquisition in our prehistoric past (and still is the case in some societies today).

These anatomical and physiological changes mean that the athletic ability of boys increases greatly at adolescence, and the popular notion that boys 'outgrow their strength' has little scientific support. The peak velocity of strength increase does occur a year or so later than the peak velocity of most skeletal measurements, so that there may be a short period when an adolescent, having completed his skeletal growth, still does not have the strength of a young adult of the same size and shape. However, this is a temporary phase; power, athletic skill and physical endurance all increase progressively and rapidly throughout adolescence.

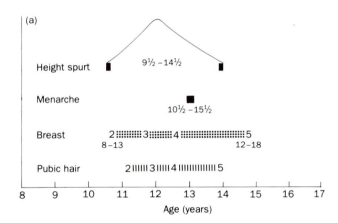

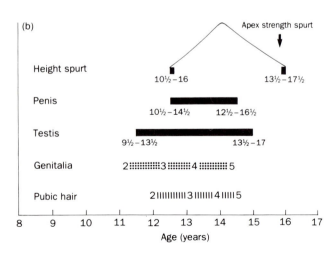

Sequence of events at adolescence in girls (a) and boys (b). An average child is represented; for example, the average girl enters breast stage (B2) just before the age of 11, as marked, B3 a year later, etc. The horizontal bars against penis and testis indicate the average age for the beginning of those aspects of maturation (left-hand end of bar) and completing them (right-hand end). The range of ages within which each event charted may begin and end is given by the figures placed below its start and finish; for example, the range for B2 is 8.0 to 13.0 years.

Tempo of growth

Though all the events of adolescence usually occur together and follow a uniform sequence, the age at which they happen varies greatly. From a file of photographs of normally developing boys aged exactly 14.0 years it is easy to select three examples that illustrate this. One boy in the photograph (right) is small, with childish muscles and no development of reproductive organs or body hair; he

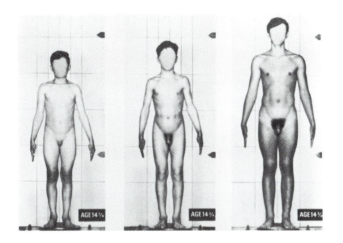

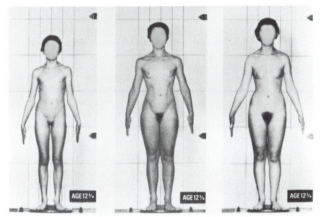

The age when adolescence events happen varies greatly, as these pictures show. In the upper row are three boys all aged 14¾ years. In the lower row are three girls all aged 12¾ years. At each age, the left-hand child is pre-adolescent and the right-hand child is approaching maturity.

could be mistaken for a 12-year-old. Another is practically a grown man, with broad shoulders, strong muscles, adult genitalia and a bass voice. The third boy is in a stage intermediate between these two. It is clearly wrong to consider all three as equally grown-up physically, or – because much behaviour at this age is conditioned by physical status – in their social relations. The statement that a boy is 14 years old is in most contexts hopelessly vague; everything depends, morphologically, physiologically and sociologically on whether he is pre-adolescent, mid-adolescent, or post-adolescent. The same is true of girls, albeit at a slightly earlier age.

These pictures illustrate differences in what is called the *tempo* of growth. Some children play through their childhood rapidly, with a tempo marked *allegro* (the analogy with music is quite exact); others go *andante*; still others, the late-maturers, progress *lento*. In normal children, tempo and final adult height are entirely unrelated: on average, the later maturers catch up to exactly the same height as the early maturers. But at the time when they are 15 centimetres smaller, much weaker and sexually less developed, they may find this hard to believe. Children with a slow tempo

have a difficult time at adolescence. Early maturers, particularly girls, are also at increased psychological risk. An understanding of differences in the tempo of growth is essential for teachers, parents and doctors.

Role of hormones

The endocrine glands are very important in the control of growth and development, and are one of the chief agents for translating the instructions of the genes into the reality of adult form, at the pace and with the result permitted by the environment.

Growth hormone, secreted by the pituitary gland, is, as its name implies, one of the most important. In its absence, males reach an adult height of only about 135 centimetres (4 ft 5 in), females only 125 centimetres (4 ft 1 in). It acts by causing the cells of the cartilage growth plates to produce an intermediary hormone called insulin-like growth factor I (IGF-I), which results in cell multiplication and growth. At adolescence, growth hormone and IGF-I both increase, and produce the growth spurt. These increases are dependent on the secretion of *sex hormones* (testosterone and oestrogen) from the testes and ovaries. It is the sex hormones, scarcely present in the blood of prepubertal children, that increase at puberty and cause the growth of the breasts, genitalia and pubic hair.

The growth and development of the testes and ovaries themselves is controlled by other hormones – *gonadotrophins* – from the pituitary gland. Both growth hormone and the gonadotrophins are in turn regulated by *releasing hormones* secreted by the nerve cells of the hypothalamus, a part of the brain near the pituitary gland. Between infancy and puberty the cells of the arcuate nucleus of the hypothalamus stop secreting gonatrophin-releasing hormone. The events of puberty are the direct result of the brain beginning once more to secrete the releaser. What turns this hormone off and what turns it on, is not known.

Other hormones such as thyroid hormone, insulin and the adrenal hormones are necessary for normal growth but their role is more that of producing conditions that permit growth rather than direct responsibility for growth.

Heredity and environment

Growth is the result of a continuous interaction of genes and environment. The plan of growth – both of ultimate size and of tempo – is laid down in the genes, but it is a long way from the possession of a certain set of genes to the acquisition of a particular height. All that is inherited is DNA; everything else is developed, and involves a continuous interaction with the environment. Thus the degree to which height, say, is genetically controlled can be specified only for particular environmental and social conditions, and not in an absolute way. In favourable environments, genetical control is fairly precise, as is shown by the growth of identical twins – even when separated – so long as both are in good environments. Identical twin sisters reach menarche an average of 2 months apart; non-identical sisters reach it on average 10 months apart.

Physique

Humans differ greatly in body size and shape. *Physique*, an appraisal of shape as distinct from size, has been classified in several ways, the most trenchant being W.H. Sheldon's *somatotyping*. In this system, everybody is regarded as a mixture of three components of physique, called endomorphy, mesomorphy and ectomorphy. Some people are high in the first component and low in the others; some high in the second and low in the others; and some about equal in all components. Somatotypes are assigned by examination of the body, or a photograph of it. They refer specifically to the morphogenotype, or underlying physique, and are

2. NEOTENY

For a hundred years, a process called *neoteny* ('holding on to youth') has been invoked by evolutionists. It involves a slowing in the rate of shape change to yield an adult morphology resembling the juvenile stages of an ancestor. Some amphibians, for example, rather than metamorphosing to the terrestrial adult state, attain maturity as aquatic larvae.

This idea has been applied to human evolution, with a suggestion that early humans arose from pygmy groups that had developed from even earlier forms as a result of neoteny.

Many differences between humans and non-human primates have been claimed to result from retardation of development and the persistence of ancestral fetal features. Our relative hairlessness, large brains, short faces, and structure of the hands and feet have all been claimed to be examples of human fetalised morphology. Even morphological variation among modern human groups – such as Asians compared to Africans – has been claimed to result from differential 'advancement' along a pathway of fetalisation, perhaps because of simple hormonal alterations.

Neoteny is just one example of the general evolutionary phenomenon of *heterochrony*, or morphological changes resulting from shifts in the rate and timing of ancestral patterns of development. From the beginning, neoteny has been a controversial idea, and few anthropologists now find it a convincing explanation for changes in the human lineage.

There are many supposedly neotenic features of *Homo sapiens*. They include the structure of the hand and foot, the lack of brow ridges, the flat face, the large brain and prominent nose – even long life, sense of humour, dance and song. However, this list disguises a variety of very different developmental processes.

For example, body proportions often change with size by allometry, and there may be great morphological changes from a simple truncation or extension of the interrelationships between size and shape. If length of the growth period is altered, the adult size in descendants may change. In true neoteny, the size and shape relationships of ancestors are dissociated so that adult descendants have a juvenile shape when they are the same size as an ancestral adult (see figure).

Changes in timing during development have undoubtedly been important in human evolution. However, it is much less clear that many human features form a complex arising from a simple change in the relationship between size and shape because of a slowing of shape change in development. For example, almost none of the morphological features associated with bipedal locomotion are related to neoteny. These pervade our muscles, skeletons and even guts, and bipedal locomotion was the most fundamental adaptation of early hominids, preceding even expansion of the brain.

Many human features ascribed to neoteny (particularly differences between sexes and populations) are simply allometric correlates of differences in body size. The gracile skeletons, narrow joints and relatively large brains of females in

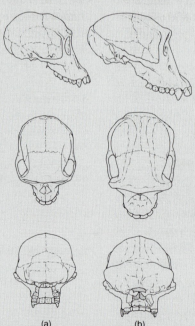

(a)   (b)

The skull and face of an adult pygmy chimpanzee (a) resemble those of a juvenile common chimpanzee, even though the two chimpanzees are comparable in body size and length of their growth periods. The skull of an adult common chimpanzee (b) is shown for comparison. This is an example of genuinely neotenic evolution.

comparison with males do not result from neoteny, but from common developmental pathways that reach differing overall size.

Humans have small faces tucked under large brains, vertical foreheads and a flexed skull base with a central foramen magnum. However, this resemblance between our skull form and that of juvenile apes is superficial. The modern adult human is produced by growth processes different from those of apes. Development of soft tissues, bones and the skull base are all specifically human specialisations, rather than retention of a juvenile form.

The evolution of speech resulted in many changes in the skull base and pharynx; and human infants resemble adult apes, rather than the converse predicted by neoteny. In addition, although we share relatively small and flat faces with the juveniles of non-human primates, this state is attained by patterns of bone resorption and deposition that are quite divergent in the two groups. We do resemble fetal apes in the relative size of our brain, but depart from them in terms of total brain size and shape: our enlarged brains may be produced by the retention of high fetal rates of brain growth, but it is scarcely fair to conclude that all lineages that have relatively large brains are neotenic.

The superficiality of the resemblance between adult humans and juvenile apes in skull form is emphasised by the genuinely neotenic evolution of skull form in the pygmy to the common chimpanzee. The two chimpanzees are comparable in body size and the duration of developmental periods, but adult pygmy chimpanzees have a juvenilised skull and face that result from a slowing of growth processes. Why this happened is not clear, but it may be related to the pygmy chimpanzee's reduced sexual dimorphism.

The persistent attraction of neoteny – and its fatal flaw – is its claim to provide a single explanation for the morphological, developmental and behavioural changes associated with the emergence of humankind. Our evolutionary history has been far too complex to yield to so simple a thesis.   *Brian T. Shea*

See also 'Scaling' (p. 42) and 'Human speech and language' (p. 134)

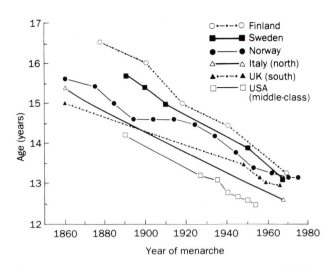

The trend towards faster growth is shown by the decline in the age of menarche in six Western countries, 1860–1980.

not changed by overeating or weight-training, though, of course, the appearance of the body is.

Variation among populations

There are enormous differences in the growth rates and ultimate size of children belonging to different populations of the world. Many of these differences are simply due to differences between rich and poor, urban and rural dwellers, children subject to periodic or chronic undernutrition and children deluged with the marketing propaganda of the giant food corporations. But even among children that are all well nourished and well circumstanced, there are some differences that depend on genetics. Far Eastern peoples, such as the Japanese, under good environmental circumstances, have puberty about a year earlier than western Europeans, and end up about 6 centimetres less tall. On the other hand, the growth in height of Americans of African origin is very similar to that of Americans of European origin.

As living conditions improve, the growth of children speeds up and adult height increases. The trend towards faster tempo is shown by the age of menarche. In the industrialised nations, these trends are now slowing up and in some cases have almost disappeared, at least in the children of the rich. Differences in growth between rich and poor are still present in practically all countries; only in Sweden and Norway have they been eliminated.

The environmental effect on growth means that the growth of children is one of the best monitors of the health of a population. Continuous surveillance of this is carried out in several countries, including the United Kingdom. Reduced growth rates readily identify disadvantaged sections of a population, and pinpoint the area where public health and governmental action is needed.

The study of growth thus has practical value in monitoring the health of individuals and surveying the living conditions of populations. Growth is also an easily measured and well-defined characteristic that has the potential to tell us a great deal about the past and present of our species.

James M. Tanner

See also 'Primate reproduction' (p. 86), 'Hormones and sexual behaviour' (p. 91) and 'The human brain' (p. 115)

Part Three

The brain and language

Compared with other primates humans stand out in three main respects: their skeleton is adapted for striding locomotion, they have modified teeth and jaws and, above all, they have very large brains. The unique behaviour of humans probably emerges from the increase in brain size during human evolution. However, it is not easy to identify features of the human brain that account for our behavioural distinctiveness. Our brain is unusually large, but its internal wiring shows only subtle differences from other mammals (**3.2**).

A simple measure of the degree of development of a brain is its overall size: bigger brains might simply be better. But it soon becomes obvious that absolute size says little about capability. The brain of an elephant, for example, is four times bigger than ours, but we are clearly ahead of elephants in terms of behavioural complexity.

If brain size is related to body size, larger bodies will need larger brains to control the basic functions. Thus, the effect of body size has to be considered (**3.1**). A simple ratio of brain size to body size might cancel out the scaling effect, but this does not work either. In the humble mouse lemur (*Microcebus murinus*), the brain represents 3 per cent of body weight whereas in humans it accounts for only 2 per cent. This is because, although brain size in mammals increases with increasing body size, the brain increases at a slower rate than does the body.

Other things being equal, a ratio of brain to body size will therefore decline with increasing body size. Among mammals, brain size scales to body size with a power function of about 0.75 and this non-linear relationship has to be taken into account in estimating the relative size of a brain. When this is done, it emerges that humans do have the largest brains, relative to body size, of all mammals. Most primates have larger brains than other mammals. This is only an average effect, however, and there is overlap when individual species are compared. For example, the relative brain size of sportive lemurs (*Lepilemur*) is below the average for mammals.

The brains of most simian primates (anthropoids) are relatively bigger than those of prosimians, but there is some overlap with some large-brained prosimians (such as the aye-aye, *Daubentonia madagascariensis*) and with other large-brained mammals, such as seals. Hence, it is not correct to claim that all primates have relatively bigger brains than all other mammals.

Another common claim is that apes have bigger brains than monkeys. This is correct only with respect to absolute brain size. When the scaling effect of body size is taken into account, apes are not distinct from monkeys in relative brain size. Indeed, the gorilla has a small brain, relative to body size, compared with monkeys. The highest value for relative brain size among non-

Fossilised casts of australopithecine brains from cave deposits in the Transvaal, South Africa.

human primates is found not in an ape but in the New World capuchin monkeys (*Cebus*). If we want to find a parallel to humans among non-human primates with respect to brain expansion in evolution, we should therefore look to capuchins rather than chimpanzees.

Compared with the average for simian primates, the human brain is three times bigger than expected. This represents a dramatic increase in just a few million years. Such a lively pace of increase in brain size is unique. In terms of the end result, however, humans are not as outstanding as is often thought.

Although the overall size of the brain relative to the body is only a crude measure of the development of the central nervous system, it can at least be studied in the fossil record. With well-preserved skulls, internal impressions of the braincase (endocasts) can be made. These give an estimate of brain size and can reveal interesting features of the external contours of the brains of extinct species (**3.2**).

Studies of endocasts in relation to body size reveal that there has been a tendency for brains to increase in size in all mammalian lineages and that differences among modern species have arisen because of differences in rates of brain expansion. It seems likely that larger brains are better. Why, then, have rates of expansion differed among mammals? Perhaps the metabolic costs of brain development and function can be carried only if a high-energy diet is available. Large brains are expensive — an adult human brain consumes 20 per cent of the body's energy. The imbalance is even greater early in life. The brain of a human newborn represents 10 per cent of body weight and consumes about 60 per cent of the baby's energy. In this respect, then, it really is appropriate to talk of 'feeding the brain'.

Instead of asking why particular species need large brains, perhaps we should ask how they can afford them. If enough energy is available to support a large brain it can be put to good use by almost any animal, although the functions developed may differ from species to species. When we apply this reasoning to human evolution, the intriguing possibility emerges that all three distinctive features of humans — the remodelled jaw apparatus, bipedalism and the large brain — are intimately connected. In mammals generally, locomotion is crucial in food collection, teeth and jaws in food processing; the energy obtained from food meets the high running costs of the brain.

In this light, the evolution of the human brain can be explained at two levels. At the first, the increase in size from australopithecines through to early modern *Homo* probably depended on a shift in feeding habits that led to increased energy turnover. At the second level, specific selection pressures must have led to changes in the internal wiring of the increasing mass of brain tissue, which allowed improvements in problem-solving, the origin of sophisticated toolmaking (**Part 9**) and, most important, the emergence of language and culture.

Comparative work on primates, especially great apes, has led to a better understanding of the origins of human speech and language. Once it was realised that it was pointless to try and teach apes to speak, as they lack the necessary apparatus (**3.5**), other approaches to language (such as signs instead of words and better analyses of primate vocalisations) enabled an effective exploration of language-like abilities in non-human primates and other mammals (**3.3**, **3.4** and **3.6**). There is still controversy over the use of the term 'language' for primates other than humans, but this may be a red herring. What is important is that new approaches to studies of the behaviour of non-human primates have revealed that, as with the structure of the brain, the gap between them and us is not as wide as was once thought.

Primate brains and senses

The brains of humans and other primates have many similarities and many human mental abilities have their roots in our primate heritage. In spite of great differences in size and shape, the brains of all primates share features that distinguish them from those of other mammals. Within the primate order itself, the most striking differences are between the brains of prosimians and simians (anthropoids). The brains of great apes and humans stand out as a group from those of the lesser apes (gibbons and siamangs) and the New and Old World monkeys, primarily because of their large size.

We cannot make detailed comparisons of neural circuitry and biochemistry for most primates. However, the brains of macaques, squirrel monkeys, owl monkeys and galagos have been intensively studied, and these represent New and Old World monkeys and prosimians. For other species we must rely on gross morphology and measurements of brain structures for clues.

Shape and structure

All primate brains have a distinct *temporal lobe*. This is separated from the *parietal* and *frontal* regions by a deep cleft, the *Sylvian fissure*, which includes within its depths a large island of *cortex*. This fissure is present to some degree even in the smallest and least-convoluted primate brains.

Within the temporal lobe are the auditory areas (on the dorsal surface), some *association* visual areas (on the ventral surface) and some *limbic* structures (the amygdala and hippocampus, on the medial surface), which are associated with emotion, attention and memory. Some neuroanatomists suggest that the expansion of visual or auditory areas in primates is responsible for the increase in size of the temporal lobe, but it might equally represent an incidental change in shape arising from some of the unique structural features of the primate braincase.

The shift to more upright posture in early primates led to a change in the position of the *foramen magnum* (the large opening at the base of the skull from which the spinal cord emerges). The exit of the *brainstem* and the position of the face (including optic and olfactory nerves) have converged and form almost a right angle in primates. This effectively pulls the cerebellum and brainstem beneath the cortex and draws the posterior end of the cortex beneath the frontal and parietal lobes to form the temporal lobe.

There is partial convergence of the eyes in prosimians. This is essentially complete in simian primates and is associated with a progressive reduction of the nose and organs of smell. The frontal lobes, which in other mammals extend between the orbits of the eyes, are also displaced upwards

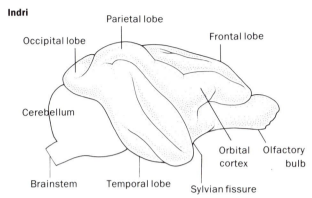

Indri

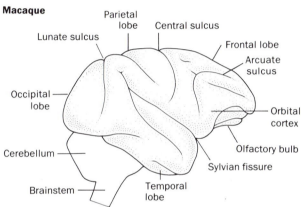

Macaque

Brains of a large prosimian (indri) and a typical monkey (macaque) seen from the side, showing some major surface landmarks. The macaque's brain is slightly larger. Each has an obvious temporal lobe and also a Sylvian fissure dividing the temporal lobe (below) from the parietal and frontal lobes (above). The Sylvian fissure hides an expanse of cortex termed the insula. The indri has a relatively larger olfactory bulb but the macaque has a central sulcus dividing the motor areas (ahead) from the somatic sensory cortex behind.

over the top of the orbits, and the tips of the temporal lobes shape themselves around the back of these structures.

Another feature that may play an important part in shaping the primate brain is the *claustrum*, a sheet-like, or planar, nuclear structure lying just beneath the insular cortex within the Sylvian fissure and overlying the large basal ganglia. This planar form of the claustrum is unique to primates and may also be significant in determining the pattern of folding of the Sylvian fissure. Some other large-brained creatures such as elephants and whales have a comparable 'pseudo-Sylvian' fissure caused by enlargement of the nasal sinus system, which compresses the brain from front to back and expands it temporally, but no planar claustrum or insula.

Surface features

There is considerable variability in the surface of primate brains, which arises from differences in the extent of folding of the cortex. What determines this variation has long been debated. The question is important to studies of extinct species because cortical folding is one of the few features visible in casts of the insides of fossil skulls (see p. 116).

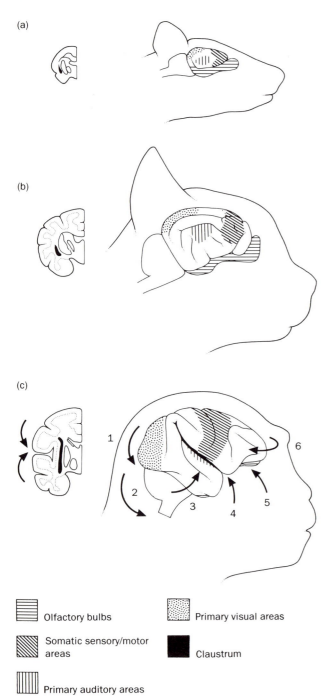

(a)

(b)

(c)

▤ Olfactory bulbs

▨ Somatic sensory/motor areas

▥ Primary auditory areas

▦ Primary visual areas

■ Claustrum

The brains of a rat (a), a cat (b) and a monkey (c), showing the relative placement of major sensory and motor specialised areas in each and the factors that contribute to the morphology of primate brains: (1) descent of the occipital lobe of the brain in response to (2) downward 'torsion' of the brain stem with respect to the forebrain, associated with the shift to a more upright posture; (3) an upward and outward 'compression' of the lower surface of the brain; (4) infolding of the Sylvian fissure and burying of the insular cortex to form the temporal lobe; (5) drastic reduction of the olfactory bulbs and formation of the orbital cortex because of the convergence of the eyes; and (6) expansion of the prefrontal cortex onto the lateral surface of the brain.

The degree of folding is related to brain size. However, the variations in patterns of folding are influenced by differences in cortical thickness and the positions of underlying structures and fibre tracts. Cortex in the depths of a fissure or *sulcus* may be thinner and have reduced deep cortical layers. Deep layers are the main source of nerves descending from the cortex, so that these sulcal regions may correspond to transitions between areas of cortex that project to distinct subcortical targets. The folds found most consistently in primate and other brains often occur near the boundaries between functional areas.

The sulcal patterning of monkey brains differs from that in other mammalian brains of corresponding size because of the predominance of vertical folds over those running front to back. Prosimian brains show an intermediate pattern. The *central sulcus* – a vertical sulcus that separates the motor cortex (ahead) from the tactile sensory cortex (behind) – is present in living simian but not prosimian brains. It first appears in the fossil primate *Aegyptopithecus*, an early simian from the early Oligocene of Egypt.

Size

There is a remarkable consistency in the scaling of brain to body size among mammals. Brain and body size in adults can be accurately predicted from body size by a simple power function: brain size is proportional to body size raised to a power that depends on the taxonomic group under consideration. For the entire class Mammalia, this is about three-quarters (0.75); for primates, estimates range from 0.66 to more than 0.80; and for prosimians or simians taken separately, the value falls to below 0.70. Depending on which baseline comparisons are used, assessments of the size of primate brains and their evolution may differ. After a century of investigation, the meaning of comparative brain size is still uncertain and controversial.

However, there is an agreement that the average primate has a larger brain for its body size than most non-primate mammals. This applies not only to adults, but to every stage in development. In the fetal stage, all primates (including humans) follow a common brain and body growth trajectory that parallels that of most other mammals, except that at every corresponding stage primates have about twice the proportion of brain to body.

We still do not understand the significance of the shift in primate brain to body proportions. It is often assumed that the relatively larger brain for body size of primates correlates with an increase in intelligence. The superior visual and manual skills of monkeys and apes, which makes them so well adapted to life in trees, could be attributed to their proportionately enlarged brains. However, other explanations for this shift in proportions are also plausible. The shift in brain to body proportions in fetal life is, in fact, a result of relatively reduced body growth and not increased rates of brain growth. Reduction of some other body parts

1. TESTING THE INTELLIGENCE OF APES

The cognitive capacities of apes have been studied since the early 1900s and apes have often been used as models for understanding the human mind. There are three essential questions: what can an ape learn, how does it learn and what does it know about what it learns?

Early experiments with chimpanzees tested performance and insight. They were given sticks and other objects that could be used to reach food. Animals with experience of playing with sticks performed better than did those confronted with novel situations, but many chimpanzees were able to solve complicated problems — such as making poles to reach suspended foods.

Later research tested the apes' ability to discriminate the relations between objects. Again, this found spontaneous problem-solving based on insight, suggesting that chimpanzees have a mental representation of objects that were not present but which could be used to solve a given task.

In the late 1960s and early 1970s, various studies examined the nature of chimpanzee consciousness. Could a chimpanzee recognise itself? Did it have a concept of 'self' in parallel with the ability to perceive 'self'?

Chimpanzees were presented with a mirror. First, they responded socially; the reflection was recognised as 'chimp-other'. After a time, they began to relate to the reflection as 'self'. The animals were then anaesthetised and a blob of red dye was placed on their forehead. When they woke and looked in the mirror, they used their reflection to groom off the red spot.

This result may sound trivial, but human infants under 18 months old seldom recognise themselves as individuals in a mirror. The chimpanzees seem to have formed an image of themselves from exposure to their reflection. When that image was altered, they perceived this and used their image to correct the fault. Chimpanzees without experience of mirrors could not use the reflection to remove the red dye.

Of all the apes tested for 'self' recognition, chimpanzees perform the best. Although orang-utans can learn to recognise themselves in a mirror, gorillas do not appear to discriminate 'self' from 'other' in mirror tests.

Another early series of tests of chimpanzee cognitive skills involved aspects of learning and its application within a social context. Chimpanzees were taken round their enclosure and shown boxes with hidden food. They were then returned to their social partners. The group was allowed into the enclosure and the leader would take all the others to the hidden foods, not using the original route but the most efficient and quickest path. Wild chimpanzee males call to others when they find large fruiting trees, providing information on where food is located. Individual knowledge hence appears to be shared in chimpanzee societies.

The chimpanzees in experiments showed a further fascinating response to hidden food. One male had the alternative of taking his companions to the food or to a snake in a food box. He chose the snake, the others fled and he ate the food alone. Chimpanzees may thus be capable of deceit and of predicting the responses of others, manipulating those responses to their own advantage.

The language experiments on the learning skills and cognitive abilities of chimpanzees and gorillas are described in Chapter 3.6. They show that chimpanzees form logical combinations of signs, can discriminate categories of words and objects and, with training, can understand numerical concepts (at least up to six). They can even communicate with each other using these new skills.

A female gorilla called Koko has in addition learned to communicate with signs and can express emotions, such as sadness and humour as well as making statements or requests. Chantek, a language-trained orang-utan, also forms spontaneous signs.

Work with chimpanzees trained to use lexigrams suggests that they can form abstract representations of the relations between objects, once they have been trained to use language. Language makes it possible for chimpanzees to realise this potential. The words, symbols, signs or computer keys are not the object; rather, they represent an object and thus allow reference to it at a distance in time and space, and the attribution of characteristics, such as colour, numbers or category.

Other tests, such as pulling strings to obtain foods, and discrimination tests where individuals need to detect associations and even reversals of associations, assess the ability to learn. All this shows that apes have the capacity to make inferences, to innovate, to attribute relations between objects and to form mental representations — all of which are aspects of intelligence. *P.C. Lee*

See also 'Language training of apes' (p. 138)

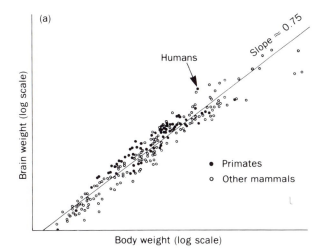

(a)

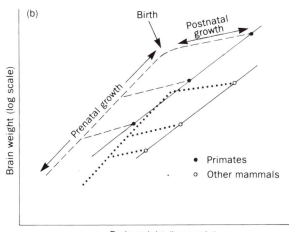

(b)

Brain and body size in primates compared with other placental mammals in adulthood and during growth. The relationships between brain and body are shown as logarithms and so appear as straight lines. (a) The scaling relationship of brain size and body size among primates and other mammals. (b) The trajectories of relative brain and body growth during development in primates (— — —) and more 'typical' mammals (· · ·). The brains of primates are about twice as large for a given body size as in most other mammals, and this distinction is to some extent still apparent in adults as primates have bigger brains than other mammals on average. During the prenatal phase of brain growth, both brain and body grow at about the same rate; during the postnatal phase, brain growth is essentially completed but body growth continues at high rates.

with respect to the brain might be an adaptation to climbing and suspensory locomotor behaviour.

Stereoscopic vision

Nearly complete convergence of the eyes and corresponding changes in the brain's visual structures are common to all primates. Their depth perception is improved as the overlap of the visual fields means that most parts of the visual field are viewed from two perspectives at once. Inputs to the brain from each eye are more evenly divided than in other mammals.

This has produced striking changes in the *superior colliculus*, an ancient visual area of the midbrain involved in orientation to visual stimuli. In nearly all other vertebrates information from the whole of each eye is represented in the colliculus on the opposite side. This is appropriate in species with eyes directed to each side, where the separate retinal fields correspond to the non-overlapping fields of view. In primates, however, this correspondence breaks down, and the connection pattern between the eyes and brain is altered so that half of each retina facing the opposite (contralateral) visual field is represented in each colliculus.

The superior colliculi are connected directly and indirectly to several cortical visual areas involved in the perception of movement and position, the control of eye movement, and the direction of visual attention. The reorganisation of the colliculus led to changes in these cortical areas as well. Such specialisations produce the excellent depth perception of primates and were probably present even in such early forms as *Tetonius* that lived during the early Eocene about 56 million years ago and had forward convergence of the eyes.

The parallel evolution of a high degree of visual convergence in owls, cats and some bats suggests that extensive visual overlap is particularly valuable to animals that navigate by sight at night. The ancestors of all primates were almost certainly nocturnal, arboreal, insect-eating creatures, as are many present-day prosimians. The retention of visual convergence in diurnal primates, even though it has disadvantages for predator defence, may reflect the difficulties of reversing this evolutionary change.

Colour vision

Another specialisation of some primates rare in other mammals is three-colour vision. The colour-blindness of many mammals is probably derived, because colour vision is common in birds, reptiles and even fish. It may reflect our ancestry as nocturnal predators. The secondary evolution of colour perception in monkeys and apes required specialisations of the retina and of the cerebral cortex.

Colour vision depends on three types of cone-shaped receptor cells within the retina. Because cones are only responsive to a narrow range of light frequencies they are

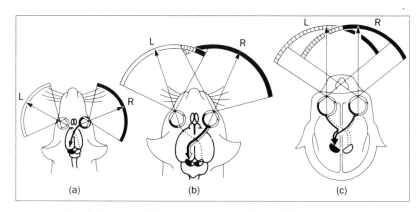

Reorganisation of visual projections to the superior colliculus of the brainstem in response to convergence of the eyes. Organisation of this system in (a) rat, (b) cat and (c) monkey brains shows the logic of the typical vertebrate pattern (e.g. rat) where laterally directed retinas send their total output to the opposite side of the brain. Because all sensory and motor systems are crossed in this way – that is, the right side of the brain receives input from and controls output to the left side of the body – the visual input is in register with other systems. The cat brain represents a compromise in which the old pattern of crossed connection is not entirely consistent with the slight degree of binocular overlap. The almost complete binocular overlap of primates would result in inappropriate mapping of half the visual field into the brain if the ancestral mammalian connection pattern was maintained. Instead, each retina sends only the appropriate half of its output to the opposite side and the other half to the same side of the brain.

less sensitive to light than are the other rod-shaped receptors of the retina, which are not so narrowly tuned. Monkey retinas have a dense concentration of cones in the *fovea* (the region of the retina focused on the centre of gaze) and a predominance of rods around the edges. Rods predominate in the whole retina of most other mammals and in nocturnal prosimians. Although colour vision requires receptor specialisation in the retina, colour is determined by analyses within the cerebral cortex. There is a distinct area of the monkey secondary visual cortex that is specialised for calculating the relative colour of objects.

The earliest true primate, such as the tarsier-like *Tetonius*, had relatively large eyes – a feature typical of nocturnal species. The living nocturnal prosimians have retained this trait as well as a light-sensitive, rod-filled retina. However, all but one simian (*Aotus*, the nocturnal owl monkey of South America) have smaller eyes and are capable of colour vision.

The 'rediscovery' of colour vision in primate evolution probably occurred at the same time as activity moved towards the day, perhaps to accompany a shift to feeding on fruits that advertise ripeness by changing colour. This signal of ripeness itself probably coevolved with the evolution of seed-foraging by birds, which also have well-developed colour vision. Many monkey species utilise bright colours for social communication. For example, some male guenons (*Cercopithecus*) have bright-blue underbellies and bright-red genitals, and male mandrills (*Papio* or *Mandrillus sphinx*) have bright red, white and blue skin on their faces. Although common among birds, such colourful signals are not found in other mammals.

2. SLEEP AND DREAMING

Primates, like other mammals, must spend a part of each day asleep, but the purpose of this periodic withdrawal from the world remains controversial. Sleep may be an opportunity for mental and physical recuperation, a time for routine maintenance or running repairs. It could also be a means of immobilising the body at times when activity would be unprofitable, expensive or dangerous. Both notions have a role in the understanding of sleep.

Intuition and experiment tell us that sleep is a restorative, but this on its own cannot account for the differences in the amount of sleep taken by various creatures. Humans are among the least somnolent of primates, taking a modest daily ration of about 8 hours. At the other extreme stands the owl or night monkey (*Aotus trivirgatus*), which is reported to spend 17 hours of each day asleep. Chimpanzees and various monkeys sleep for slightly longer than we do (around 10 hours), while the gorilla takes 12 hours.

Sleep, it seems, is an adaptable habit. Should circumstances make prolonged slumber desirable, then sleep may extend to fill the time available. If, on the other hand, there is a premium on wakefulness, sleep can be curtailed.

If animals are to rest in safety, long and short sleepers alike must choose their sleeping quarters with care. In the highlands of Ethiopia, geladas (*Theropithecus gelada*) resort to steep cliff faces at night. Forest species take

advantage of the security provided by trees, dividing up the available space. Baboons (*Papio*), for example, choose the low branches, whereas colobus monkeys and mangabeys (*Cercocebus*) resort to different sites in the crown.

Many monkeys sleep in the sitting position, balancing on small branches, which vibrate and arouse the sleeper if predators approach. Chimpanzees, gorillas and orang-utans construct elaborate arboreal nests for overnight accommodation. In captivity, they sleep supine, or on their sides, often pillowing the head on the arms in a distinctly human manner. They also tend to snore.

Sleep is an amalgam of two disparate elements: *REM sleep* (named after the rapid eye movements that accompany it) and *non-REM sleep*, which can itself be broken down into phases of different depth. Bouts of non-REM and REM sleep alternate through the night.

For sleeping humans and chimpanzees, episodes of REM sleep arrive every 90 minutes. In rhesus macaques and baboons, the cycle repeats every 40 minutes or so. People awoken from REM sleep usually report that they have been dreaming, but dreams occasionally accompany non-REM sleep as well. In adult humans, REM sleep accounts for a quarter of the night's quota of sleep; in 4-year-old chimpanzees it makes up about the same fraction.

REM sleep is the subject of many theories. Human neonates devote more than a half of their sleeping time to REM sleep – and fetuses take even more – so it may be essential for the growing brain. In adults, REM sleep could be a time for resolving mental conflicts or for sorting and consolidating memories. Alternatively, the dreams of REM sleep could simply be mental cinema, designed to keep us entertained as we sleep.

Do non-human primates dream? This question raises problems. Observers from Lucretius to Montaigne have noted the twitches and yelps of sleeping dogs and ascribed them to canine dreams. The faces of monkeys quiver in a similar fashion. Experiments on cats show that a part of the brain suppresses movements during REM sleep; when this region is damaged, sleeping cats cavort as if acting out their dreams. If cats dream, then there seems to be no reason to deny any primate admission to the land of dreams.

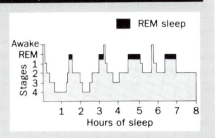

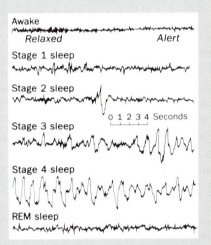

Human sleep can be divided into several different stages on the basis of electrical activity in the brain. Researchers detect this activity with the help of special electrodes on the scalp and record it in the form of an electroencephalogram, or EEG. The traces show the changes in the EEG through the various stages of sleep. Throughout the night, the stages succeed one another in an orderly fashion, with bouts of REM sleep (named after the rapid eye movements that accompany it) appearing every 90 minutes or so. As the sleep deepens from stages 1 to 4, the pulses of brain activity become slower and of larger amplitude.

Yet a nagging doubt remains. Although children enjoy much more REM sleep than adults, their dreams are surprisingly bare. Simple narratives begin to appear at around 5 years of age and become more complex with the passing years. If our capacity to dream grows as the mind develops, then the dreams of non-human primates may be very sketchy.

Stephen Young

'The Nightmare' by Henry Fuseli (1741–1825).

Central specialisation of vision

The primate visual cortices are the most complex visual-processing system ever evolved. Nearly half the cerebral cortex in macaques is directly involved in visual processing, and there are around two dozen cortical visual areas in its brain, each receiving different inputs and analysing different aspects of the visual world. Even within the same cortical areas there may be segregation of visual signals relating to different aspects of visual information. For example, colour and pattern may be processed independently of movement and depth in the primary visual cortex and each is relayed to separate cortical areas. The primary visual cortex of primates is also unique among mammals because of its high density of cells and the complexity of its cellular architecture.

Cortical areas on the lower surface of the temporal lobe are particularly important for visual learning. They are specialised for the analysis of visual form. Some cells within this region are selectively activated by the perception of hands and faces but are relatively unaffected by their orientation or distance. This probably reflects the importance of face-to-face communication and of co-ordination of hand and eye in monkeys. Even in humans, localised brain damage can specifically impair the ability to recognise faces.

Smell

The nasal cavity is reduced in primates because of the convergence of the eyes. With it many other organs of smell are also reduced in diurnal species. The sense of smell depends on receptors embedded in the mucous membranes of the nasal sinus and nerves that extend into the brain and contact the *olfactory bulbs*, two specialised extensions of the primitive cortex of the base of the brain. Both diurnal prosimians and simians have relatively smaller olfactory bulbs than other mammals of the same size. Apes, monkeys and tarsiers have a smaller olfactory system than lemurs and lorises, and have also lost the damp nasal skin (rhinarium) common to lemurs, lorises and other mammals. Humans have the most reduced olfactory apparatus of all primates; only dolphins and whales have more reduced olfaction.

Although the olfactory organs are reduced in many primates, the parts of the brain to which they connect have not become similarly diminished. The structures receiving smell information form part of the limbic system and are central in regulating emotional arousal. Arousal in primates is less responsive to smell and more responsive to other sensory inputs than in most other animals.

Touch and movement

Although the parts of the cortex and spinal tracts associated with touch and movement are well developed in most mammals, they are particularly striking in primates. This corresponds to primate specialisations – the hands for grasping and manipulation and the face for communicating by gestures. Damage to the *pyramidal tracts* – the bundle of fibres originating from cells in the motor cortex and ending on motor neurones of the spinal cord – produces far more serious and persistent impairment of locomotion, strength and fine-movement control in primates than in other species.

There are spatial maps of sensory surfaces and muscle systems in the cerebral cortex. In primates, the hand occupies a uniquely large part of these maps. Some South American monkeys have a prehensile tail. This has specialised musculature and a smooth, hairless pad at the tip rich in tactile sensors. Its representation in the sensory and motor cortex is much larger than in the corresponding area in other monkeys.

Although muscles of the mouth and throat are well represented in the primate motor cortex, the production of vocal sounds is not under skilled motor control. Vocalisation depends much more on the limbic cortex and numerous subcortical arousal systems, including the amygdala, the hypothalamus and the central grey area of the midbrain. Primate calls are in this way more similar to automatic and stereotypic human sounds such as laughter, sobbing and shrieks than to human speech.

Hearing

The auditory system of primates is no more or less specialised than is that of many other land-living mammals. There is some reduction of the external sound-focusing structures of the ear. In many mammals, including the nocturnal prosimians, both ears can be aimed towards a sound to amplify and locate it. In diurnal monkeys and apes, the external ears are small and comparatively immobile.

The areas of cortex specialised for auditory perception in primates are on the upper surface of the temporal lobe within the Sylvian fissure. In some species, processing of different classes of sounds is specialised to opposite sides of the brain. In monkeys, the perception of rapid sequences of sounds is handled better by the left side of the brain, and in Japanese macaques (*Macaca fuscata*) analyses of vocal calls between members of the species are carried out primarily in the left hemisphere. There is a parallel here with the lateralisation of language processes in the human brain.

Are ape brains special?

Their curiosity and ability to bond with humans has led to the view that great apes are more intelligent than monkeys. Although rates of learning in the two are similar only apes have been shown to learn by insight. Although the brains of orang-utans, chimpanzees and gorillas are larger than any monkey brain they are no larger than expected for those of monkeys of comparable body size, and in terms of their internal organisation there is no significant divergence from the basic monkey pattern. Nonetheless, the large size of ape brains may have led to the appearance of different functional capabilities.

Terrence W. Deacon

See also 'Non-human primates' (p. 24), 'The human brain' (p. 115), 'Vocal communication by non-human primates' (p. 124) and 'Facial patterns as signals and masks' (p. 161)

The human brain

The human brain is smaller than the brain of an elephant or whale, but is capable of intricate mental processes that no other brain can approach. The brain of a normal human adult ranges between 1000 and 2000 grams, with the average around 1330 grams. Brains of women are lighter and those of men heavier only because of differences in body size. The brain makes up about 2 per cent of body weight yet consumes as much as 20 per cent of metabolic energy at rest. It may contain as many as 10000 million neurones, each of which has thousands of synaptic connections with other neurones.

Our brain is the largest primate brain that has ever existed, both in absolute terms and with respect to body size. However, its structure is typical of that of other primates, with the same major cortical and subcortical structures, arranged in the same configurations and composed of neurones with the same cell architectures. Nevertheless, the human brain must be unique in anatomy and function because it controls such special human adaptations as symbolic communication, speech, tool production and culture.

There are numerous morphological differences between our brain and other brains, but it is not obvious which aspects of brain anatomy are central to human abilities and which are incidental. Three unique features of the human brain are visibly obvious: its large size with respect to the body; the asymmetry between left and right hemispheres; and the reduction of its olfactory apparatus. However, these features provide only hints about the fundamental differences between human and other primate brains.

We know far more about the functional uniqueness of the human brain than about its structural uniqueness. Theories to explain these extraordinary abilities include:

- Expansion of the brain to increase intelligence and memory, enabling humans to learn complicated skills such as toolmaking and language
- Addition of new brain structures to provide new functions such as specialised language abilities
- Reorganisation of the connections of existing brain structures to allow them to serve novel functions such as the analysis of grammar
- Changes in the relative sizes of different brain areas, expanding certain structures to augment particular abilities

The evidence for each of these will be reviewed in turn.

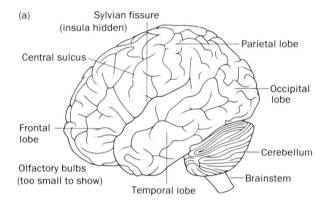

(a)
Sylvian fissure (insula hidden)
Central sulcus
Parietal lobe
Occipital lobe
Frontal lobe
Cerebellum
Olfactory bulbs (too small to show)
Brainstem
Temporal lobe

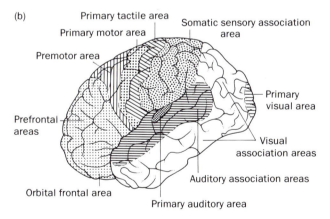

(b)
Primary tactile area
Somatic sensory association area
Primary motor area
Premotor area
Primary visual area
Prefrontal areas
Visual association areas
Auditory association areas
Orbital frontal area
Primary auditory area

The major morphological features of the human brain are visible on the surface of this side view (a). The Sylvian fissure dividing the temporal lobes (below) from the parietal and frontal lobes (above) hides a large expanse of the cortex called the insula. This is also present in other primates. In (b) some major functional divisions of the cerebral cortex are shown. The three major sensory and motor districts are each divided to show the primary and association areas that comprise them. The one primary area for each sensory or motor function is organised into a single topographic map of its external representation (e.g. maps of the retina, cochlea, body surface and muscles). Each major functional district also has several association areas that are often not organised as simple functional maps and whose functions are less well understood. Although it is impossible to determine the details of the map structure of the human cerebral cortex, information from studies on cell architecture and new imaging techniques, such as positron emission tomography (PET), suggest that cortical maps of humans resemble those found in other primates.

Brain size

The human brain is unusually large with respect to body size, although just why is a subject of debate. For two centuries, popular and scientific opinion assumed that intelligence is determined by brain size. As a result, studies of the brain have focused on this measure, at the expense of others. This idea has been grossly misused in the study of racial, sexual and individual differences. There is still no proof that bigger means smarter. In fact, there are several problems with this approach to comparisons of intelligence.

The volume of the brain or the number of neurones might seem to be an obvious measure of brain size. More neurones with more interconnections should be able to perform more complex calculations. However, this leads to the unlikely prediction that large ungulates are more intelligent than monkeys and that elephants and whales are more intelligent than ourselves. Comparisons of the size of the brain with respect to the body give more reasonable predictions of comparative intelligence, especially with regard to humans. Perhaps the body demands more of the brain to control its vegetative processes as body size increases.

Differences in intelligence among species might depend on how many 'extra neurones' are not committed to these essential bodily functions. The more extra neurones, the more intelligent. However, the smallest animals have brains larger and more densely packed with neurones with respect to body size than do humans. A simple ratio of brain to body size therefore fails to live up to common-sense expectations.

A more satisfying approach comes from the use of allometric corrections for the effect of body size. These take into account the differences in the rates of brain and body growth. Species whose values of brain for body size fall significantly above or below the average for mammals may have relatively more or fewer 'extra neurones': they differ in *encephalisation quotients*. On this measure, mammals are more encephalised than lizards and fish, primates and dolphins are more encephalised than other mammals, and humans are the most encephalised of all. This fits well with our feelings about the intelligence of these animals.

Any measure of human encephalisation must depend on the species chosen for comparison. In the context of simian primates, for example, the human brain is approximately three times larger than the value predicted for an 'average' monkey or ape with our body size.

Evolution of brain size

The timing of hominid brain expansion is fairly well established. The brains of australopithecine hominids fall within the range of modern great apes, with a mean weight of approximately 450 grams (assuming that 1 cubic centimetre of brain weighs 1 gram). It is not clear whether the slightly higher brain to body ratio of australopithecines is a significant departure from that of apes. Encephalisation probably first exceeded the ape range at least 2 million years ago, with the appearance of the first member of our genus, *Homo habilis*. The fossil KNM-ER 1470 from Koobi Fora in Kenya is a highly encephalised specimen of this group, with a brain weight of approximately 750 grams (Box 1).

By 1.5 million years ago the brains of *Homo erectus* weighed almost 1000 grams. Brain size continued to increase without a corresponding increase in body size until the appearance of the first *Homo sapiens* perhaps 400000 years

ago. Early *Homo sapiens* brains were as large as ours. The Neanderthals of Europe and the Middle East also had a modern brain size, and many have argued that Neanderthals should hence be included in *Homo sapiens*. Although there has been debate about the suitability of their vocal tracts for language, Neanderthals might have been comparable to modern humans in their mental abilities.

1. IMPRESSIONS OF ANCESTRAL BRAINS

The brain is enveloped by a fibrous membrane called the *dura mater*, which forms a protective barrier between the brain and the inner surface of the braincase. Nevertheless, many surface features of brains, including *gyri* and *sulci* (folds and valleys of the cerebral cortex) and major blood vessels encased in the dura mater, leave their impressions on the inside of the skull. Plaster or latex casts (endocranial casts or *endocasts*) of the insides of skulls – even of fossil skulls – can reveal these features. It is thus possible to discern the shape of the brain of an extinct species, even though the brain itself has long since perished.

Several factors complicate the collection and analysis of endocasts. As brains enlarge the cortical folding becomes tighter and the dura becomes thicker and less pliable. Cortical details are therefore much more difficult to see on ape and human endocasts than on smaller primate brains. Fossil crania usually require careful reconstruction and often suffer from missing parts, deformities or other damage. All this leaves considerable room for different interpretations of the same features. Even the identification of major features has been hotly debated.

Can endocasts tell us much about the internal organisation of ancestral human brains? Cortical folding patterns are ultimately determined by the processes of growth. Surface morphology and

underlying brain functions are not directly correlated in most cases, and we must be careful when drawing functional interpretations from endocasts.

One of the most contentious issues in endocast research is the position of the *lunate sulcus* in australopithecine brains. This sulcus is functionally significant because it seems to mark the border between the primary and secondary visual areas. It is assumed that a relatively posterior position of the lunate sulcus in australopithecine endocasts would show that the functional divisions of the brain changed towards a more human pattern. Debates about the accurate identification of its position therefore translate into claims about the advancement of mental abilities.

Hominid bipedal locomotion was an important contributor to brain morphology and probably affected this structure. The adoption of a more upright posture made the orientation of the brainstem more vertical than that of apes. It lowered the position of the cerebellum with respect to the occipital lobes (which filled in the vacated space) and moved some of the visual cortex on the lateral surface into the posterior midline. These changes would produce a more posterior position of the lunate sulcus in australopithecines and later hominids.

Another easily recognised surface feature that seems to be associated with boundaries between functionally distinct cortical areas is the *central sulcus*. The presence or absence of this structure distinguishes brains of monkeys from those of prosimians. A central sulcus visible on the endocast of the Oligocene anthropoid *Aegyptopithecus* hence suggests that this fossil represents one of the first monkeys. Because the central sulcus divides somatic from motor cortex in monkeys its first appearance in the fossil record may represent some underlying restructuring of these functional divisions.

The *Sylvian fissure* is the most noticeable of all surface landmarks. It

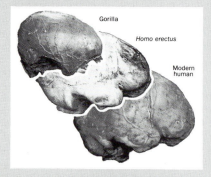

Gorilla
Homo erectus
Modern human

Endocasts from a gorilla, a fossil hominid (*Homo erectus*) and a modern human (all to the same scale). The *Homo erectus* endocast, from Asia (Zhoukoudian), is made of plaster; the human and gorilla endocasts are made of latex. The gross shape of the brain and a few major surface landmarks can be discerned in each. Blood vessels in the fibrous membrane called the dura mater are particularly well delimited. Notice how completely the dura mater has obscured the impressions made by the folds (gyri) and valleys (sulci) of the cerebral cortex. Even the large Sylvian fissure is difficult to delineate, except near the tip of the temporal lobe.

The large size of the human brain with respect to body is reflected in unique differences in the relative growth of these structures. All primate fetuses, including those of humans, follow a common brain and body growth curve (see p. 111), in which the brain is about 12 per cent of body size and both grow at about the same rate. In most primates, this pattern changes around the time of birth as brain growth slows but body growth continues. In human infants, this slowing of brain growth does not occur until more than a year after birth while body growth follows patterns similar to those of the great apes. As a result, the shape of the curve described by human brain and body growth differs from that of other primates (see next page).

Our brains grow as though they were in the body of a very large primate. This has consequences for human birth and infancy. A mother's body is incapable of sustaining this level of fetal growth and we give birth to babies only slightly larger than expected for our size but which are neurologically quite immature. The increased parental care required by the helplessness of our large-brained infants was probably important in the evolution of human social behaviour.

Increase in comparative brain size may not be the whole story of human brain evolution and may not be enough to explain unique human mental abilities. Comparative size of a brain may not be as important as its internal organisation.

demarcates the upper boundary of the temporal lobe and is lower and longer on the left side than on the right in most modern human brains. This is also seen in some endocasts of archaic members of the genus *Homo*. In modern humans, this is correlated with the larger size of Wernicke's language area on the left.

The similarity in some fossils initially suggested that these ancestors had a spoken language. But a simple association with language is challenged because corresponding asymmetries are found in some living ape and monkey brains. Nevertheless, cortical asymmetries in the fossil record may tell us something about the origins of more generalised functional asymmetries.

The sulcal markings associated with Broca's language area (see main text) have recently been demonstrated in *Homo habilis* and *H. erectus* endocasts. These folds do not appear on endocasts of australopithecine brains. Does this mean that Broca's area first appeared in the brains of early *Homo*? Yes, if we define it only in morphological terms. But if we are interested in the evolution of the language functions of Broca's area, the endocast evidence is less compelling for several reasons. There is variability in the presence and position of these sulci in human brains and some inconsistency in the correspondence of the landmarks with the locations of language functions. More importantly, an homologous area has been demonstrated in monkey brains, so the appearance of these gyri and sulci in fossils does not indicate the appearance of a totally new structure.

Finally, the increase in brain size between australopithecines and early *Homo* increased the number of folds in all parts of the cerebral cortex. These new folds may simply be an effect of this overall size increase rather than a specific change. These hominids may have been the first to use Broca's area for language, but endocasts alone are not enough to prove it.

Despite the many difficulties of interpretion, endocasts are our only record of the shape of ancient brains, and provide an invaluable source of information about brain evolution. Their value is mainly limited by our minimal understanding of how surface morphology correlates with brain functions.   *Terrence W. Deacon*

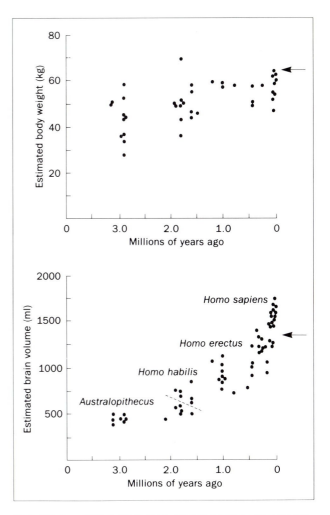

During human evolution, the brain has increased in size with respect to the body, especially during the past 2 million years when the stature of early humans hardly changed. Estimates of body size used for these diagrams were computed from long-bone lengths and are subject to error. Although individual points are not reliable, the trends are probably representative. The ranges of brain size in succeeding species overlap, suggesting no sudden transitions. Arrows indicate modern mean values.

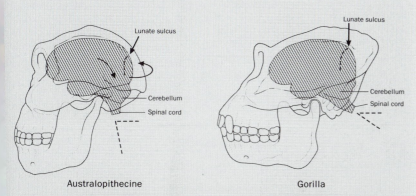

Australopithecine   Gorilla

The major morphological changes of the brain in an australopithecine compared with a modern ape (gorilla). Because of habitual upright posture the orientation of the head on the spinal cord is more vertical in australopithecines, shifting the orientation of the brainstem with respect to the rest of the brain. Secondary shape changes resulting from the lowering of this structure and particularly the cerebellum (the large rounded structure on the back of the brainstem) produce an infolding of some of the cortical surface on the back and base of the brain. Researchers argue about the position of the lunate sulcus in australopithecine endocasts and whether, as a result, this indicates that these fossil species had ape-like or human-like brains. The change in the base of the brain would tend to produce a more posterior sulcus position but this shape change would not in itself suggest any internal reorganisation different from ape brains.

Questions about the importance of size against organisation reflect the fundamental debate between those who argue that humans differ from other species only by virtue of possessing increased general intelligence and those claiming that human intelligence differs because we alone have unique and unprecedented special abilities – those underlying language.

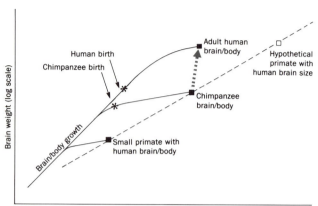

Growth curve for human brain and body compared with that for other primate species. The length of the human fetal phase (in which brain and body grow at the same rate) is extended but the postnatal phase (in which body growth continues at high rates but brain growth slows) is not longer in proportion. If the body grew at the primate rate in a manner appropriate to brain growth, adult humans would weigh 454 kilograms (1000 pounds) and stand nearly 3.1 metres (10 feet) tall (indicated by the point in the upper right of the figure). Small primates can have the same 2 per cent brain/body ratio as humans (indicated by the point in the lower left).

Comparing intelligence

Although we are used to comparing the intelligence of different people, the concept of an 'intelligence quotient' (IQ) may be simplistic, combining, as it does, too many dimensions of human mental variation. It may be impossible to compare accurately the intelligence of different species. Comparing intelligence may be analogous to comparing 'feeding' or 'movement': the locomotor adaptations of moles, bats, horses, monkeys and seals cannot be usefully compared on a single scale. Trying to calculate a single value for an animal's intelligence (with humans highest) is also unlikely to be fruitful. Just as different species' locomotor abilities are specialised, depending on where they live, so too must mental abilities be specialised with respect to the particular perceptual, motor and cognitive demands of their adaptations.

There are problems with allowing for differences in sensory perception, attention and motivation when the learning abilities of species are compared. Even simple learning tests using different cues (auditory or visual) or different motor responses give conflicting ranks of 'general intelligence' when applied to species that are differently specialised for these abilities. These tests must always confuse the effects of species specialisations with measures of general mental efficiency or capacity. It is even more difficult to control for the effect of language when comparing the intelligence of humans and other species.

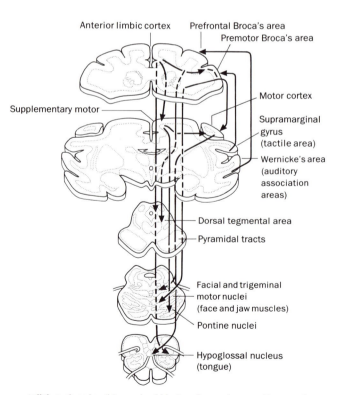

Descending neural pathways controlling vocalisation in primates (left) and those specific to human speech (right). Primate pathways originate from brain systems controlling emotional arousal, those for speech from cortical areas controlling skilled behaviour. The pathways of primate vocalisation are probably also involved in human 'innate calls', such as laughter and sobbing, and may play a part in speech intonation, and tone and rhythm. Although shown separately, these vocal control pathways work together in humans and converge on the same output nuclei for the larynx, tongue and facial muscles.

Individual differences in human intelligence as measured by intelligence testing are not comparable to the results obtained from comparisons of different species. Human IQ tests rely almost entirely on the use of language or the analysis of symbolic relationships, both of which cannot be tested in other species. The increase in efficiency provided by linguistic and symbolic encoding of information gives humans an unfair advantage, even in tests not directly dependent on language ability. It is a bit like comparing humans and bats on tasks based on echo-location. For this reason, many consider language abilities to be a 'special intelligence' of humans. Perhaps, when all such species-specific biases are taken into account, 'general intelligence' will be found to be less variable among species than once thought.

The assumption of an evolutionary stepladder or *scala naturae* of brain function is a relict of nineteenth-century reasoning. Few rankings of animal intelligence are actually based on tests of comparative intelligence, and most studies simply depend on comparative brain size as a measure of comparative intelligence. However, when specific learning abilities and encephalisation are compared this relation has not held. Comparative brain size confounds many hidden variables of brain structure and function into a single statistic. Some mental abilities may indeed be influenced by brain size, but these must be distinguished from the complicated growth relationships of brains and bodies. The fact that human brain size is exceptionally large for a primate of our body size requires explanation, but any comparison that ignores the underlying specialisations is unlikely to provide much insight.

Language

The most important specialisation of the human brain is its capacity for language. There is as yet no comprehensive theory of how language is produced. However, studies of disrupted language arising from brain disorders, electrophysiological and imaging studies of language processes,

and work on the anatomy and physiology of related structures in primate brains tell us much about the nature of language and primate vocalisations.

There are several ways to study the neural basis of vocal calls in primates. These include electrical stimulation or selective damage of brain structures and the tracing of their interconnections using labelled amino acids, proteins or dyes. Primate calls are controlled by neural circuits in the forebrain and midbrain that are also responsible for emotion and physiological arousal, but not by the motor cortex, even though this area can control the muscles of the larynx and mouth. Stimulation of the vocalisation areas in a monkey brain often also produces other signs of arousal – such as hair standing on end, display postures, facial gestures and even ejaculation.

Human speech uses a very different set of neural circuits. It depends on the region of motor cortex that controls the mouth, tongue and larynx and the areas in front of it. Repeated efforts to train primates to mimic even simple speech sounds have had little success. The unique skill involved in learning to speak suggests that this human facility may reflect some critical neurological difference. The ability to combine a large number of component sounds to form larger units, words and phrases, makes possible the syntactic complexity of speech. Common brain areas may be involved in speech production and grammatical processes because defects in grammar and speech production caused by brain damage often occur together.

Language areas in the brain

The areas of the brain specialised for language are in the region surrounding the Sylvian fissure of the left hemisphere (see diagram below). This also contains cortical centres for auditory perception, as well as for tactile perception and motor control of the face, mouth and larynx. *Broca's area* (immediately in front of the motor area) and *Wernicke's area* (immediately behind and to the side of the auditory area) are most directly involved in language. The

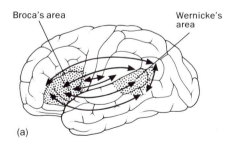
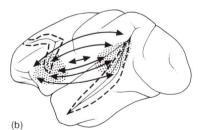
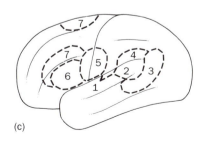

Language representation and circuitry in the cerebral cortex.
(a) A human brain with the neural connections involved in language arrowed; Broca's and Wernicke's language areas are indicated by stippling.
(b) Corresponding areas in the macaque brain (not to scale).
(c) Parts of the human brain where damage results in language disturbances: 1, central deafness; 2, phonemic errors in comprehension and speech (Wernicke's aphasia); 3, semantic disturbances (transcortical sensory aphasia); 4, difficulties of naming and repetition (conduction aphasia); 5, paralysis of the speech musculature (anarthria); 6, difficulty with articulation and grammar (Broca's aphasia); and 7, difficulty with initiating or sustaining speech (transcortical motor aphasia).

positions of these areas have been inferred from patients with brain damage that has caused different forms of *aphasia* (language loss or impairment).

Brain damage to the primary oral-motor area produces paralysis of the muscles of sound production. Damage to the adjacent Broca's area may produce problems in producing the complex sound sequences of words, without producing paralysis and may also disrupt grammar and syntax. Individuals with damage to Broca's area are often unable to use grammatical information, but can still understand the meanings of content words, such as nouns and verbs. Their speech is halting, laboured and telegraphic in style, and often lacks verb tenses or case markings.

Brain damage to the primary auditory area results in cortical deafness, but does not affect the comprehension of written material or disturb speech. Damage to the adjacent Wernicke's area does not produce deafness, but does disturb language comprehension in speech and reading. Wernicke's aphasics find it difficult to recognise familiar words and often misinterpret their meaning without realising. They can often speak fluently, but make many inappropriate substitutions of sounds or even whole words so that their speech can become unintelligible jargon.

Brain damage that includes both Broca's and Wernicke's areas results in global aphasia – an inability either to produce or to comprehend speech. It has been suggested that damage to the fibre tracts connecting Broca's and Wernicke's areas produces only an inability to repeat speech, or *conduction aphasia*. Recent studies attribute this more to damage to the tactile sensory cortex just above the Sylvian fissure and within the insula, as well as to auditory areas.

Anomia is an inability to name familiar objects. It may be associated with aphasia but it is also found alone. Anomia can be remarkably specific to certain word categories (such as fruit and vegetables), and usually does not exclude the patient's ability to discuss, in detail, the characteristics of the unnamable object in question (even from memory) or to produce a definition when given the appropriate word. The sites where brain damage results in anomia are the most diverse of all those leading to language disorder and usually overlap with, or are next to, the major language areas.

Transcortical aphasias are so-called because they were once thought to involve long projections from association areas of the cortex to areas controlling language. Transcortical – or 'semantic' – *sensory* aphasia involves confusions of word meaning without errors in the sounds of words. It is often associated with damage to parts of the brain near Wernicke's area. Transcortical *motor* asphasia leads to a reduction in spontaneous speech and a very simplified sentence structure. Damage to many different frontal structures (including the 'supplementary motor area', the prefrontal cortex near Broca's area and parts of the basal ganglia receiving prefrontal connections) may all produce it.

People with transcortical aphasias retain an ability to repeat what is heard and, in some cases, have a tendency to

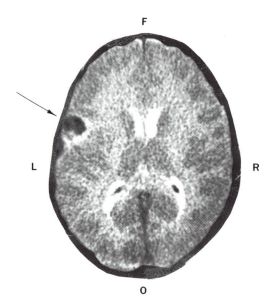

CAT scan (computed axial tomography) of the brain of a patient with damage (indicated by the arrow) that involves part of Broca's area and part of the motor area for controlling the face in the left hemisphere. This brain damage produced a severe disturbance of the patient's ability to speak; that is, Broca's aphasia (see text). The image is made by an x-ray technique and shows a horizontal cross-section through the head at a level just above the ears. Frontal pole (front), occipital pole (back), left and right hemispheres are indicated by corresponding letters.

repeat, to echo or to complete what has just been heard. Brain damage that affects both these areas (but not Broca's and Wernicke's language areas) can impair both semantic comprehension and speech initiation. In these cases, patients cannot communicate but may still retain the ability to complete common phrases or to learn to sing the words of songs (though they do not understand them).

New techniques have led to a broader view of human language areas. Electrical stimulation of the brains of neurosurgical patients in Broca's area, Wernicke's area and the inferior parietal cortex, as well as in many adjacent areas, shows that they are all important for language. It has also shown that different aspects of language functions – such as sequence of oral movements, phoneme identification, grammar, reading, naming and verbal short-term memory – are controlled by different subdivisions of these areas as well as by areas outside classic language areas.

Surprisingly enough, these studies show that the spatial distribution of language functions vary from one person's brain to another. Radioactive computer-imaging techniques, such as the mapping of cerebral blood flow and positron emission tomography (PET) scanning, further emphasise the complexity and distribution of language areas. We can now see how different language functions recruit many different brain systems. Most notably, they have shown the importance of prefrontal parts of the brain in front of Broca's area for speech comprehension and for generating word associations.

Asymmetric specialisation of the brain

One major language specialisation of the brain for language is the differential role of the two hemispheres. The cause of this 'lateralisation' is unknown. In about 90 per cent of all

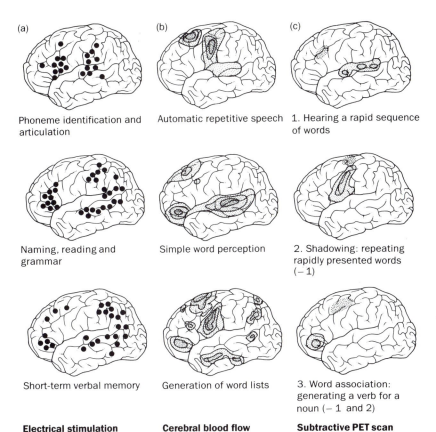

Phoneme identification and articulation

Automatic repetitive speech

1. Hearing a rapid sequence of words

Naming, reading and grammar

Simple word perception

2. Shadowing: repeating rapidly presented words (− 1)

Short-term verbal memory

Generation of word lists

3. Word association: generating a verb for a noun (− 1 and 2)

Electrical stimulation   **Cerebral blood flow**   **Subtractive PET scan**

Stylised presentations of brain activity in people during different types of information processing.
(a) The effects of electrical stimulation of the cortex in awake, locally anaesthetised patients undergoing brain surgery. The top figure shows stimulation sites that block the identification of simple speech sounds (phonemes) as well as disturb the ability to reproduce simple sequences of oral movements (although it does not block movement per se). The middle figure shows stimulation sites that make it difficult to name familiar objects, disturb reading ability and produce grammatical errors. The lower figure shows stimulation sites that disturb short-term memory for words.
(b) Changes of cerebral blood flow (presumed to indicate metabolic activity) made visible by inhaling radioactive gases during three types of language tasks. The top figure shows cerebral blood flow in such repetitive tasks as counting from 1 to 10 over and over or reciting the days of the week. The middle figure shows cerebral blood flow while attending to the sounds and meanings of spoken words. The bottom figure shows cerebral blood flow in a word association/production task, such as listing all the furniture in a room by memory.
(c) Effects of related language tasks on brain metabolism as imaged with positron emission tomography (PET) scans. To show the differences between language tasks, images were subtracted from one another by computer. The top figure shows the effect of passive attentive listening to rapidly presented words after subtracting the effects of alert attention (the control state). The middle figure shows the effects of repeating out loud the words being presented after subtracting the control and passive listening effects. The bottom figure shows the effects of producing a difficult word association (verb for a noun) to the presented words after subtracting all previous effects. The dotted areas in the upper and lower figures indicate activity in different parts of the cingulate cortex and the dotted area in the middle figure shows activity in the supplementary motor cortex.

people the left hemisphere is dominant in the production and analysis of language. This figure includes around 95 per cent of all right-handers and 70 per cent of all left-handers. The tendency for the dominant hand to accompany the representation of language in the left hemisphere suggests that handedness and language ability are linked. The evolution of stone-tool manufacture, handedness and lateralisation of language are probably interdependent (Box 2).

Manipulation and speech both depend on the skilled control of movements. Even skilled left-hand movements, although controlled by the right hemisphere, depend in right-handed people on input from the left hemisphere. However, specialisation of the left hemisphere and even lateralisation itself are not essential for language, because people with reversed dominance or no obvious dominance speak normally. Even those who have lost most of the left hemisphere in early childhood can develop a usable language.

The right hemisphere also has a role in language. It is important for the production and analysis of the 'prosodic' features of speech, such as rhythm, emphasis and intonation, and for non-verbal forms of expression, such as facial gestures. Its involvement in the conceptual analysis of language is manifest in patients with a damaged right hemisphere who have difficulty understanding metaphors, jokes and the context of stories. In patients who have had the neural connections between the hemispheres severed to prevent the spread of epilepsy the isolated right hemisphere is largely unable to comprehend or produce speech but often understands many words. The right hemisphere also plays a dominant part in the analysis of spatial relationships.

Not only humans have hemispheric specialisations. For example, the left hemisphere is specialised for song production in many birds, the left auditory cortex for call perception in Japanese macaques, and the right hemisphere for spatial processes such as maze running in rodents. Although no other primate shows such a clear preference for one hand over the other during manipulation, many primates do show differences in the use of left and right arms for locomotion and support.

Analysis of brain asymmetries suggests that such specialisations may be associated with differences in relative growth of the two sides. Broca's and Wernicke's areas are larger on the left in most brains. There are similar asymmetries of shape in other primate brains and hominid fossils (see Box 1). Human lateralisation of language may hence have developed from earlier forms of asymmetry.

Some lateral segregation of functions is present at birth. It develops considerably during childhood, and some lateralised function may shift. Lateralisation is a dynamic relationship that minimises competitive interference between similar functions on opposite sides. The lateralisation process may initially be biased to one side by subtle anatomical differences present even in the embryo.

2. THE BRAIN AND LEFT-HANDEDNESS

Human handedness has been attributed to the position of the heart or other internal organs, conditioning by nurses and to deviant personality, but it is now generally agreed that it is related to the function of the cerebral hemispheres.

About 90 per cent of humans depend on the left side of the brain for speech and about the same number use the right hand (controlled by the left side) for writing. Is this a direct connection or does it depend on some other variable?

Although the left hemisphere takes a major responsibility for speech, the right hemisphere has a main role in tasks where words are not helpful, such as recognising faces, understanding spatial relationships and responding to emotional cues.

The left brain may have a special facility for organising the sequences of fine movement required for speech and skilled hand control. Another theory is that the right hemisphere has become specialised for postural control while the left gets on with manipulations by the right hand. Humans, gorillas and chimpanzees all tend to carry infants on the left arm.

These theories, however, say nothing about left- and mixed-handers nor about those whose speech is controlled by the right brain or bilaterally.

Some suggest that the exceptions are 'abnormal'. The idea that left-handedness is caused by damage to the brain early in its development is unlikely but difficult to disprove conclusively. The problem is that early brain injuries do increase the probability of left-handedness (and mixed-handedness), so giving a higher proportion among the mentally handicapped. Surveys of abilities often find left-handers slightly poorer than the rest, presumably because of the presence of pathological cases. A recent variation of this theme implicates weakness of the immune system and the male sex hormone testosterone in left-handedness.

It seems unlikely that all human left-handers are pathological because left-handers are often exceptionally able and because left-handedness occurs naturally in up to half of our closest primate relatives. Some chimpanzees, gorillas and monkeys are strongly left-handed, but an equal number are strongly right-handed and many animals use either hand when reaching for food. They have strong hand preferences, therefore, but differ from humans in that none shows a species bias to one side. It is argued that actions requiring more skill than reaching might reveal species biases, but the issue is unresolved.

When people perform several skilled actions, some 60 to 70 per cent use the right hand consistently. What has to be explained is the relatively slight increase in bias to the right compared with our primate cousins. Dextral bias has probably been present since the early stages of human evolution. All human societies have some left-handers and this has been true since biblical times (Judges 20:16).

Left-handers have more left-handed children than do right-handers, in biological but not in adoptive families. The chances of a left-handed child are only slightly increased, however, and no more than half the children of two left-handed parents are left-handed: a recessive gene for left-handedness would predict 100 per cent. The right-shift (RS) theory suggests that there is a dominant gene increasing the probability of right-handedness and a recessive allele giving no bias to either side. The family distributions can then be explained by Mendelian principles.

Handedness in all species with hand and paw preferences, including humans, may result from chance differences between

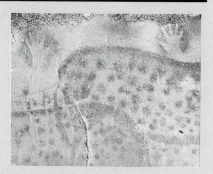

Images of right and left human hands at the Magdalenian cave site of Pech Merle in the Lot region of France.

the two sides of the body that arise during early growth. In most humans an additional factor gives a slight advantage to the left hemisphere over the right one. This is sufficient to displace the chance distribution in a dextral direction.

The link between brain specialisation and handedness could thus depend on a factor (the rs^+ allele) that gives the left hemisphere an advantage for speech and incidentally increases the chances of right-handedness. Those who do not carry the gene have equal chances of developing speech in either hemisphere, and perhaps both; they should be equally often left- and right-handed for skill, but cultural pressures to use the right hand would make more right- than left-handed.

These expectations were fulfilled in a study of a physical asymmetry of the brain. People with the typical pattern of left-sided speech were biased to one side. Those with atypical speech were evenly divided for bias to each side and 55 per cent were right-handed. Similarly, the children of two left-handed parents were about equally divided between the hands for skill, but were slightly more often right- than left-handed.

Why should a gene assisting speech evolve and then not spread throughout the population? Perhaps the gene carries disadvantages as well as advantages, because it works by handicapping the right hemisphere. The estimates of genotype proportions suggest that there might be advantages for those with one copy, in comparison with those with no copies and those with two copies.

Strong right-handers have weak left-hand skills and lower scores on several types of ability test. Children at both extremes of the distribution may have reading difficulties. The increased proportion of left-handers in groups of outstanding ability, whether in sport, mathematics or art, might simply be explained by the absence of strong right-handers.

Marian Annett

	Left better Left	L=R Mixed	Right better for skill Right for preference	
Human	4%	30%	66%	Human
Non-human	25%	50%	25%	Non-human

The right-shift theory is based on the idea that the difference between the hands in skill (Right–Left) and hand preference are related, as shown here. The left, mixed and right percentages in non-human species (mice, rats and chimpanzees) and in several samples of humans are shown. There is a normal distribution of R–L differences for measures of strength and of skill.

See also 'The hominid way of life' (p. 325)

Brain reorganisation

Are new brain functions always associated with new structures? The evolutionary novelty of human language might suggest that language areas were somehow added on to an otherwise complete primate brain, a view supported by the large size of the human brain. However, there are many reasons to reject such a simple 'additive' model. Similar criticisms apply to theories that involve extensive 'rewiring' of the evolving brain. The interdependence of neural systems and the difficulties of genetically specifying billions of new connections argue against wholesale reorganisation. Although the study of comparative brain structure is still in its infancy, much current evidence suggests that new structures and novel connections are not the basis for species differences in brain structure. Instead, systematic reorganisation, elaboration or reduction of existing structures or shifts in the proportions of existing connections are far more common.

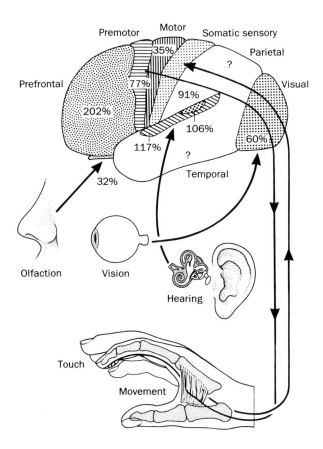

Deviation of the sizes of regions of the human cortex from predictions based on scaling of brain structures in other primates (expressed in percentage of the predicted size for a typical primate with a human-sized brain). Connections of different regions to peripheral organs are indicated. The prefrontal cortex does not connect directly with any peripheral system. Parts of the cortex specialised for peripheral functions seem to be constrained by the comparatively small size of their corresponding sense organs, whereas prefrontal cortex is not so constrained and 'inherits' space not taken up by peripheral functions.

The recruitment of existing brain structures and circuits for new mental tasks is nowhere more striking than in the evolution of human language. Language could not have been the result of the addition of a new structure because it is controlled not by any single structure of the brain but by a network of interdependent cortical areas, each contributing a particular function. Each of these structures has its counterpart in the brains of primates incapable of language. For example, recent studies of the primate counterparts of Broca's and Wernicke's areas show patterns of neural connections that correspond with those found in humans. Such studies can provide a much more detailed picture of human language circuitry than can information from humans themselves (which is limited to work on gross brain damage and imaging techniques). This information, together with studies of development and growth in humans and other primates, can provide new hints about these brain structures.

Evolution has 'recruited' for language purposes brain structures that performed other functions in non-human primates. In the process of recruitment they have become modified to meet different, and far more demanding, functional requirements. The sizes of different brain structures suggest that brain enlargement in human evolution was not uniform in all brain areas and followed trends different from brain expansion in other primates. For example, compared to the primate trends, the human prefrontal cortex is considerably larger than expected. Broca's area and the language areas in front of it are included in this expanded region. Although the basic organisation of human language areas has been borrowed from our ancestors, these language areas are many times larger than would be expected in a typical primate brain. Changes in the relative size of these areas has also changed their function by altering connections between structures.

Syntax and grammar present the brain with very demanding calculations. It is therefore not surprising that the preferential regions underlying these capabilities are among those that diverge furthest from the size predictions emerging from primate trends.

Changes in the brain give intriguing clues about the nature and uniqueness of human intelligence. They suggest that the human brain has been shaped by evolutionary processes that elaborated the capacities needed for language, and not just by a general demand for greater intelligence.

Terrence W. Deacon

See also 'Body size and energy requirements' (p. 41), 'Primate brains and senses' (p. 109), 'Vocal communication by non-human primates' (p. 124), 'Biological aspects of language' (p. 128), 'Human speech and language' (p. 134), 'Language training of apes' (p. 138), 'Evolution of australopithecines' (p. 231), 'Evolution of early humans' (p. 241) and 'Early human mental abilities' (p. 341)

Vocal communication by non-human primates

Vocal communication by non-human primates is of great interest when studying the biology of human speech and language. Real research in this area did not begin until the middle of this century, because, before then, vocalisations could be described only in terms of the subjective impressions of the human ear. In 1962, sound-analysing machines, or *sonagraphs*, became available and vocal signals recorded on tape could be displayed visually as *sonagrams*. These make it possible to characterise the acoustic patterns used by primates for social communication, and to compare them in shape and size.

We now know a lot about the physical structure of primate vocalisations, and the physiology and psychology of sound production and perception. A new understanding of the evolution of vocal communication, its development and neural basis is beginning to emerge.

Vocal repertoires

Non-human primates have developed a rich array of differentially structured sounds for communication. Groups of gelada baboons (*Theropithecus gelada*) kept outdoors under semi-natural conditions give calls of four different types and some mixed calls. Harmonic calls with frequency modulations and relative high energy in the lower frequency domain (category A) are exchanged during friendly contacts. Aspirated calls with harmonic and sometimes noisy elements (B) are uttered in agonistic encounters and threatening displays. Short noisy 'kecker' calls (C) are emitted by submissive animals when threatened, and, finally, scream calls (D) with broadband harmonic spectra, relatively high formants (the most intense frequency bands within a vocalisation) and rapid frequency modulations are given towards higher-ranking individuals during agonistic encounters. Animals emitting kecks and screams move away from the sound's target.

Mixed vocalisations combine the structural and behavioural characteristics of these four categories. In addition, different calls may be emitted in sequence. The information exchanged during such complex vocal episodes is difficult to assess, even when the group members, their life histories and the organisation of social bonds within the group are well known.

Even small prosimian primates, such as the tiny nocturnal mouse lemur (*Microcebus murinus*) of Madagascar, have a complex vocal repertoire. This species produces calls that may be noisy or harmonic, constant frequency or frequency modulated, and narrowband or broadband. Calls are given singly or in series with a particular structural grammar during social interactions with members of the same species. Their vocalisations cover a broad frequency band from a few hundred hertz up to near ultrasonic range (about 40 000 Hz).

The message conveyed by vocalisations may be inferred by the observation of the behaviour of the communicator, as well as through the response that a call may evoke from the recipient. Primate calls can encode information on species or population affiliation, sex, age and individual identity. They can also give more or less voluntarily controlled information about internal states or intentions (such as contact, aggression, defense or alarm), objects (such as food, predators or social companions) and social relationships, including dominance–subordinance relations. It is not easy to decide the relative contributions of intention, cognition and affect (or emotion) to non-human primate vocal signals, but this is not surprising because even in humans these components are difficult to separate.

Acoustic 'fingerprinting'

The complex acoustic pattern of the vocalisations of non-human primates can help to identify species that are other-

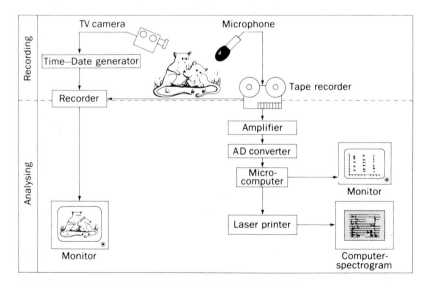

Schematic representation of the equipment used for recording and analysing primate vocal signals and their use. For studying the physical structure of a sound, tape recordings are digitised by an analog-digital converter, fitted into a microcomputer system and transformed using a Fast Fourier algorithm. Oscillograms (amplitude–time), sonograms (frequency–time) and power spectra (relative energy spectra) are calculated and displayed on the screen of a monitor or printed by a plotter or laser printer. These visual displays are then measured and used to characterise the physical structure of the vocalisations.

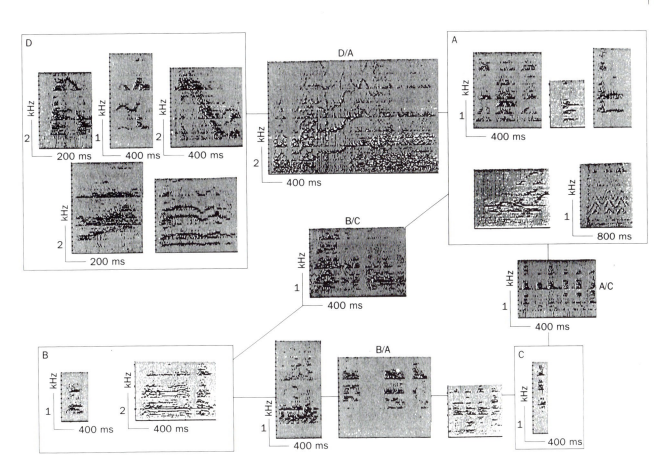

Computer spectrographs of the different vocal patterns of the gelada baboon (*Theropithecus gelada*). The calls are grouped into four categories : A, harmonic calls; B, aspirated aggressive and defensive calls; C, noisy kecker defensive calls; D, scream aggressive and defensive calls. Connecting lines = mixed calls.

wise difficult to distinguish. Such a taxonomic approach is becoming important in conservation or when the geographic range of a species must be recorded.

An illustration is provided by the nocturnal, very secretive prosimian group, the bushbabies or galagos. Similarities in coat colour, skull morphology and body size led to many uncertainties about the number of distinct populations within the three main groups of the dwarf, lesser and greater galagos. Comparison of vocalisations from homologous contexts for eight different bushbaby populations revealed large and consistent differences in the acoustic pattern of the 'loud' or 'advertisement call'. This call forms an essential part of the species-specific mate recognition system. It has a fairly distinct and stereotyped structure and is used over long distances for attracting mates, for enhancing the cohesion of social groups and for ensuring spacing between rivals. Each call is population specific and its acoustic pattern reveals a clear separation between two forms of greater galago (*Galago* (or *Otolemur*) *crassicaudatus* and *G. garnettii*) that had been included in a single species and three lesser galagos (*G. senegalensis*, *G. moholi* and *G. zanzibaricus*) that had also been lumped together. Certain calls can hence be used as an acoustic 'fingerprint' for discriminating taxa that have a very similar appearance.

These calls also give new insights into the phylogeny of bushbabies (see diagram on p. 126). The loud call of adults develops from the isolation call of infants, which is, in turn, structurally similar to the calls of a closely related group of prosimians, the lorises. Assuming that shared acoustic characteristics result from a common ancestry, it is possible to assess which species of galagos are most conservative and which are most derived from the ancestral form. A similar approach has been used to examine the relationships among different human languages.

Development of vocal communication

There was until recently little evidence for developmental variation in the vocal signals of non-human primates. Even sound deprivation or deafness during early development, which seriously affect the development of human speech and language, do not seem to alter the differentiation of the species-specific vocal repertoire. Recent research suggests that things are more complicated and that some non-human primates do show complex developmental patterns. Such studies challenge the uniqueness of language learning in humans.

Newborn rhesus macaques (*Macaca mulatta*) and Japanese macaques (*M. fuscata*) were cross-fostered between species in order to study the effects of auditory experience on vocal development. The pattern of vocalisation showed con-

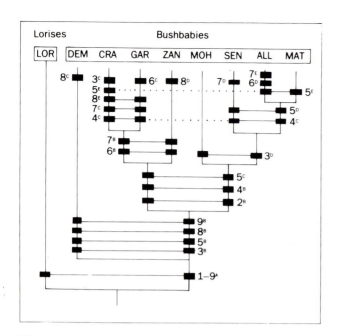

Character		Character state				
		A	B	C	D	E
2.	Frequency range	Broad	Narrow			
3.	Duration of call series	Very short	Short	Medium	Long	
4.	Call repetition rate	High	Medium	Slow		
5.	Call duration	Very short	Short	Medium	Long	Very long
6.	Frequency pattern	CF	FM	MFM	NCF	
7.	Fundamental frequency	Medium	Medium–high	Low–medium	Low	Medium +high
8.	Intonation	IR	1	2	3	4
9.	Sound intensity	Low	High			

Hypothetical phylogenetic relationships among bushbabies (subfamily Galaginae) based on shared acoustic characters (black blocks) of their loud calls. The subfamily Lorisinae was used for an outgroup comparison. Characters are symbolised by numbers: 1 = contact isolation calls of infant lorises and bushbabies, which display a similar acoustic pattern in both groups; this pattern is retained until adulthood in lorises but is transformed in bushbabies; the other characters are explained in the table.

Character states are designated by superscript letters. Bushbabies: DEM, *Galago demidovii* (Demidoff's or dwarf galago); CRA, *G. crassicaudatus* (large-eared greater galago); GAR, *G. garnettii* (Garnett's greater galago); ZAN, *G. zanzibaricus* (Zanzibar bushbaby); MOH, *G. moholi* (South African lesser bushbaby); SEN, *G.senegalensis* (Senegal bushbaby); ALL, *G. alleni* (Allen's bushbaby); MAT, *G. matschiei* (Matschie's galago). Lorises (LOR): *Nycticebus coucang* (slow loris); *N. pygmaeus* (pygmy slow loris); *Perodicticus potto* (potto). Abbreviations used in the table: CF, harmonic call with relatively uniform fundamental frequency from start to end; NCF, harmonic call similar to CF but with noisy components; FM, harmonic call with modulated fundamental frequency; MFM, harmonic call with multiple fundamental frequency.

sistent and reliable differences compared with that of monkeys reared with parents of their own species. Complex developmental trends also exist in prosimians. Young mouse lemurs and other highly vocal species, such as bushbabies, show striking contrasts in vocal pattern and usage compared with adults. During suckling, young mouse lemurs produce an array of different calls when interacting with their mother. This resembles to some degree the babbling of human infants.

There are five developmental categories in mouse lemurs, with calls similar or different in structure and usage to those of adults; similar in structure but different in usage; and specific to adults or young. Some calls change during development towards the adult pattern and lose plasticity. Hand-reared mouse lemurs seem to retain the high variability in vocal structure characteristic of youngsters even when they became sexually mature. Two explanations are possible for these findings. They may be caused either by maturation of the structures around the larynx and their motor control areas in the brain, or they may be triggered by social experience. A mixture of the two causes is also conceivable. Learning may be involved because hand-rearing experiments reveal differences in the nature or use of calls compared with normal social conditions.

Transmitting and receiving vocal signals

The supralaryngeal tract of non-human primates is quite different from that of humans. However, the cerebral organisation of vocal behaviour shows some striking similarities, so that non-human primates may be a useful partial model of the evolution of speech and language. The most detailed investigation has been on squirrel monkeys (*Saimiri sciureus*). Lesions and electrical stimulation of the brain show that the same subcortical areas of the brain are involved in the motor control of the production of certain sounds in this highly vocal primate species as in humans. On the other hand, only humans seem to elicit vocalisations on both sides of the cortex.

The general morphology and physiology of sound perception is also similar in non-human primates and humans. Vocalisations received by the ears are dispersed according to frequency along the cochlea in the inner ear. The main areas of the brain that process auditory signals are in the brainstem, the midbrain and the thalamus as well as the cortex. Lower brain areas code the relatively simple acoustic features, such as particular frequencies, intensities or interaural differences, whereas the higher areas – especially in the cortex – help to distinguish communicative from non-communicative sounds.

The main differences between human and non-human primates are in the structural and functional differentiation of the brain rather than in its gross anatomy and physiology. We still lack detailed knowledge of the neuronal mechanisms that allow monkeys, apes and humans to separate species-specific signals from meaningless noise and to distinguish among their own vocal signals.

'Categorical perception' is essential for the production and comprehension of language. In humans, this involves the division of fluent speech into segments using some physical features to set category boundaries and ignoring others. For most people, the left cerebral hemisphere is specialised for the perception of language (lateralisation of language perception). Consequently, humans recognise

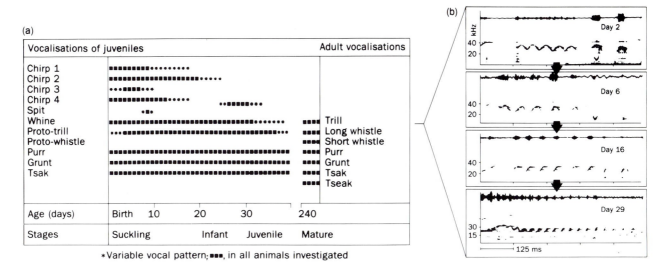

(a)

Vocalisations of juveniles					Adult vocalisations
Chirp 1					
Chirp 2					
Chirp 3					
Chirp 4					
Spit					
Whine					Trill
Proto-trill					Long whistle
Proto-whistle					Short whistle
Purr					Purr
Grunt					Grunt
Tsak					Tsak
					Tseak
Age (days)	Birth 10	20	30	240	
Stages	Suckling	Infant	Juvenile	Mature	

*Variable vocal pattern; ▪▪▪, in all animals investigated

Developmental changes in the vocalisations of the mouse lemur (*Microcebus murinus*). (a) The first appearance and disappearance of the different vocal patterns; (b) an example of the high variability in one distinct acoustic pattern – the proto-trill call in youngsters of different ages. Newborns show a fairly high fundamental frequency and a highly variable temporal pattern compared to adults. The stereotyped adult vocalisations appear around weaning.

speech signals better if they are presented to the right rather than the left ear. Recently, a similar phenomenon has been found in various non-human primates.

As an example, Japanese macaques produce an extensive repertoire of close-range contact (or 'coo') calls with slightly different acoustic structure in distinct social situations. Two of these calls – smooth early high (SEH) and smooth late high (SLH) coos – are tonal, frequency-modulated signals that vary greatly in length, fundamental frequency, presence of harmonics, modulation depth, and so on. In SEH calls, the frequency-modulated segment is in the first two-thirds of the call, whereas in the SLH calls it appears in the last third. Japanese macaques identify each one by focusing their attention on the timing of the frequency-modulated segment. They show a right-ear advantage in recognising species-specific signals, but no such

advantage when tested with non-communicative calls. This suggests that they do indeed have a left-hemisphere specialisation used for processing species-specific sounds.

Vocal communication in non-human primates hence gives new and unexpected insights into the biological basis of language in humans. Both seem to have developed gradually by means of natural selection rather than by the sudden development of a unique language 'organ' specific to humans. We need to learn a lot more about other primates before we have a real understanding of the use of sounds as signals.   *Elke Zimmermann*

See also 'Primate brains and senses' (p. 109), 'The human brain' (p. 115), 'Biological aspects of language' (p. 128) and 'Human speech and language' (p. 134)

Biological aspects of language

Language is an adaptation unique to humans, and yet the nature of its uniqueness and its biological basis are notoriously difficult to define. After centuries of speculation and research into the mystery there still remain many fundamental questions to answer. All languages have features that distinguish them from other languages; but can all languages be distinguished from non-linguistic communication in other animals? Does language have properties unique in the evolution of animal communication and cognition?

Three central features are fundamental to a definition of language: the duality of patterning of its basic units; the rule-governed combination of these into larger units; and language's unique form of reference and meaning. All three elements may be interdependent.

Duality of patterning refers to the fact that the basic sound units (distinctive features) of speech lack intrinsic meaning. This makes it possible for the speaker to combine them in innumerable possible orders to form words and other meaningful units (*morphemes*), such as plural endings and tense markings. The ability to create new meanings can be realised only if the building blocks do not themselves have innate and predetermined meanings. Although physiological constraints on speech and hearing limit the number of these phonetic building blocks and their combinations, the number of possible combinations available is huge.

Morphemes are combined into higher order units of meaning (phrases, sentences, arguments, stories) according to the rules of *syntax*. These conventions determine the assignment of logical relationships to the meaningful units making up a phrase or sentence. In turn, this controls how the meaning of each affects the interpretation of the others. Even totally novel combinations of morphemes can hence be assigned unambiguous new meanings as soon as they are heard. Syntax is also essential for interpreting the meaning of words as it removes ambiguity by picking out one of the many shades of meaning that a word might convey. This ability to generate new combinations among simple units gives almost unlimited possibilities for language to adapt to new contexts.

Symbolic reference is the most fundamental feature of language and requires the other two. It is also the least well understood. It has two related features: the independence or arbitrariness of the sign-vehicle (that is, lack of resemblance to, or necessary connection with, what is represented); and *semanticity* or *displacement of reference* (the ability to refer to things not immediately present and to things that do not exist except in some abstract sense). An explanation of this referential capacity is central to any comparison of language with other forms of communication.

Is there language-like communication in other species?

There are no non-human animal languages. However, some cases have some of the properties essential to language. Understanding these may help to clarify what we mean by 'language'.

Honeybees communicate about direction and distance to a nectar source by what has been called a 'dance language'. One component of this, a 'waggle dance', indicates the flight path with respect to the sun by the angle to vertical and distance by the number and intensity of waggle movements. Although innate and stereotyped, and with a fixed reference to the environment, this behaviour shows that even a simple nervous system is capable of referential (although not symbolic) communication.

The seasonal songs of the humpback whale (*Megaptera novaeangliae*) seem to be examples of learned vocal mimicry, duality of patterning and syntax-like combinatorial variety. Males have complex songs with many distinct vocal phrases produced in order and lasting up to 20 minutes. They are sung over and over again during the mating season. At any one time all singers in a population produce essentially the same song. However, through the breeding season and between seasons the song changes, with alterations in the sounds themselves, in phrase structures, and in combinations or repetitions of phrases. It is hence unlikely that sound elements or phrases have intrinsic meaning; they are certainly not innately predetermined.

The temporal changes of the songs' structure and mimicry of the same song by all singers during a season also argue against the existence of distinct referential morphemes. There are also no apparent categorical rules of substitution or recombination. Most changes in song structure involve gradual sound modifications, deletions and repetitions. The entire song is probably a mating display in which females can perceive the expression of an individual's strengths and weaknesses as a prospective mate. Change and mimicry of the songs may reflect competition or deception by males.

The alarm calls of vervet monkeys (*Cercopithecus aethiops*) convey information about objects and their spatial relationships. They have been compared to 'names' for predators. The different alarm calls each specify a distinct predator type, such as eagles, leopards and snakes. When alarm calls for eagles or for leopards are produced by a monkey or by a tape recorder all the others look in the appropriate direction (up or down) and behave in the appropriate way, climbing a tree to avoid a leopard, or down to avoid an eagle. Do these calls represent 'leopard' or 'eagle' in the same way that the word or name does?

Clues come from the inflexibility of this relationship. The basic sound structure of each call is fixed from birth and it is produced only in the context of actually perceiving a predator. Finally, the response to hearing an alarm call is the alertness, fear and escape behaviour expected on seeing the predator itself: vervets cannot comment about a leopard seen the other day.

These functional relationships are not arbitrary and they are not learned. But learning is important in other ways. Infants produce alarm calls in other frightening circumstances, and adults tend not to react to these as they would to adult calls. The young monkey must learn both when to call and how to distinguish infant from adult calls. Some monkeys might even use alarm calls in the absence of

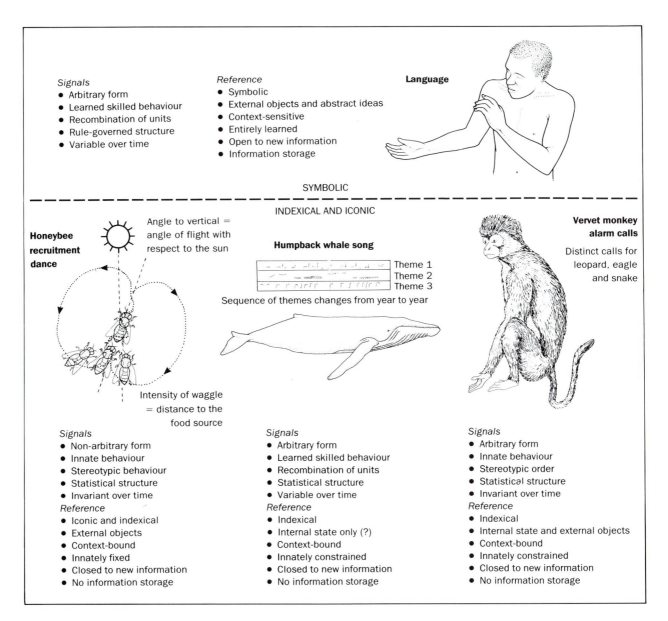

Signals
- Arbitrary form
- Learned skilled behaviour
- Recombination of units
- Rule-governed structure
- Variable over time

Reference
- Symbolic
- External objects and abstract ideas
- Context-sensitive
- Entirely learned
- Open to new information
- Information storage

Language

SYMBOLIC

INDEXICAL AND ICONIC

Honeybee recruitment dance

Angle to vertical = angle of flight with respect to the sun

Intensity of waggle = distance to the food source

Humpback whale song

Theme 1
Theme 2
Theme 3

Sequence of themes changes from year to year

Vervet monkey alarm calls

Distinct calls for leopard, eagle and snake

Signals
- Non-arbitrary form
- Innate behaviour
- Stereotypic behaviour
- Statistical structure
- Invariant over time

Reference
- Iconic and indexical
- External objects
- Context-bound
- Innately fixed
- Closed to new information
- No information storage

Signals
- Arbitrary form
- Learned skilled behaviour
- Recombination of units
- Statistical structure
- Variable over time

Reference
- Indexical
- Internal state only (?)
- Context-bound
- Innately constrained
- Closed to new information
- No information storage

Signals
- Arbitrary form
- Innate behaviour
- Stereotypic order
- Statistical structure
- Invariant over time

Reference
- Indexical
- Internal state and external objects
- Context-bound
- Innately constrained
- Closed to new information
- No information storage

Physical characteristics of signals and representational features of three relatively complex animal communication systems – the recuitment dance of the honeybee, the mating song of the humpback whale and alarm calls of the vervet monkey – compared with corresponding features of human language. Although these animal communication systems have many of the superficial structural characteristics of human languages, crucial differences divide language from non-language. This is indicated by the line dividing symbolic referential relationships from indexical and iconic referential relationships.

Iconic reference depends on the physical correspondence between the sign and object; for example, that between the vertical orientation of the bee dance and the flight path to the flower with respect to the sun. Indexical reference depends on temporal and spatial linkage of the sign and object; for example, the production of an alarm call, the arrival of a predator, and the elicitation of the appropriate state of arousal and defensive behaviours. Learned associations between stimuli and responses are also indexical.

Human language learning also depends on iconic and indexical representations, and language can be used for iconic and indexical purposes. However, our ability to create new meanings for words and to refer to abstract entities as well as to novel events and objects has no non-human counterparts. The syntactic structure of language also differs by being governed by abstract rules as opposed to stereotypic order or statistical combinations of elements. This, too, demonstrates the centrality of symbolic representation, because abstract rules cannot be represented without symbols.

predators to manipulate the behaviour of others. Learning does therefore play a part; not for acquiring the calls or for assigning meaning to them but only for determining when to use or when to trust them.

Alarm calls refer to their objects in the same way as does pointing. They usually occur in the same physical context as that to which they refer, and fail only by mistake or through deception. This makes it possible for calls to coevolve with their objects of reference. The mutually exclusive defence strategies against the different predators may account for the evolution of discrete alarm calls and their associations with a specific predator. An ambiguous call could lead to ineffective behaviour. This same evolutionary logic has also produced distinct alarm calls for predator types in several non-primate species.

Although names and words may also be used to indicate or point out objects, this is not a necessary feature of their symbolic reference. Their association with what they represent is conventional and not physical. Because of this, specific symbolic referential relationships are not subject to biological evolution and must always be learned. However, not all learned associations between a sign and what it represents are symbolic.

A simple conditioned association between a stimulus sign and some object is like an alarm call in its form of reference. It must always be learned with the sign and its object must always be present. The association will disappear when this relationship becomes consistently unreliable. The relationship between a call and its object or a conditioned stimulus and what it indicates does not depend on the 'meanings' of other calls or stimuli. However, the relationship between a word, its meaning and its reference is determined with respect to the meaning and reference of other words. This relationship requires an ability to relate words to others (something that would not make sense with animal calls) in order to interpret their meaning and reference correctly. This is the essence of syntax.

The difference between simple conditioned associations and symbolic associations and syntax is clarified by studies of the symbol-learning capabilities of apes. These have begun to provide clues about the origins and nature of human language.

Early attempts to teach American Sign Language (ASL) to apes suggested that these animals had remarkable and near-human language abilities. However, recent, more carefully analysed work has led to reassessment of these early claims. Although some symbolic reference and combinatorial abilities have been found in apes, sea mammals and possibly even parrots, each new demonstration brings up new questions about the adequacy of our definitions of these language features. In the end, they may tell us more about what we mean by language than about the abilities of other creatures.

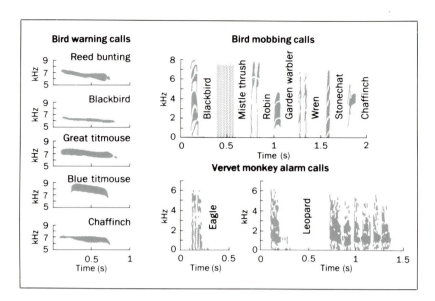

The alarm calls of birds and vervet monkeys specify a distinct type of predator. Warning and mobbing calls produced by different birds sound similar because of selection for the need to identify or obscure where the caller is. Mobbing calls are short, click-like calls with broad sound spectra and no clear pitch, whereas warning calls are longer, high-pitched, single-tone calls. Both distinguish predators and corresponding antipredator behaviours. Vervet alarm calls also distinguish predators (with slightly different patterns for snakes and baboons) but, like bird alarm calls, their sound spectra do not differ. This suggests that selection for differences in vervet alarm calls has not been influenced by a need for cryptic calls but only by predator hunting stategies and vervet defence behaviours. Referential differences in bird and monkey alarm calls are the result of 'disruptive' selection. The defence strategies for the different predators are mutually exclusive so that intermediate behaviours or calls that could be confusing will be selected against.

Language innateness and language acquisition

The extent to which the rules of grammar and syntax are built into the human brain has been investigated by looking at the acquisition of language by children. The similarity and order of acquisition of syntactical rules in different children and in different languages, their sharing of syntactical and referential errors, the rareness of grammatical correction by adults, and the speed with which children can acquire language even without organised training all favour the existence of innate biases in language learning, if not of innate rules. Childrens' errors are especially convincing. They show that the child is trying to apply a rule consistently, even despite knowledge of a correct but irregular usage – such as switching from 'went' to 'goed'.

Other evidence comes from the study of brain damage in children. During their first 5 years children have a remarkable ability to recover from language loss arising from brain damage. Even total removal of the left hemispheres in some children with cancer need not result in any long-term language impairment. After this early period, however, damage to the left hemisphere usually produces some permanent language loss. Studies of deprived and so-called 'feral' children not exposed to language in early childhood, and of those who acquire a second language at various ages

BRAIN MATURATION AND LANGUAGE ACQUISITION

Only a few parts of the brain — the deep spinal and brainstem connections (motor nerves, tactile sensory nerves, the optic nerve and the auditory nerve) — are mature at birth. Innate behaviours, such as crying and thumb-sucking, are probably controlled by the subcortical systems. Subcortical auditory pathways mature in the first few months, along with the inputs to the visual cortex, and social smiling and laughing in response to social interaction begin to develop during this period.

Visual abilities are the first to reach adult levels. The beginning of babbling probably depends on the maturation of cortical motor and subcortical auditory pathways, but maintains its somewhat random character because of the still-immature state of the motor and auditory systems. The maturation of pyramidal (cortical) motor systems and of inputs to the tactile cortex correspond with the appearance of simple word mimicry and skilled locomotor behaviours, such as walking.

The ability to create meaningful sentences and the acquisition of syntax do not begin until auditory cortical connections are well on the way to adult levels and do not reach a mature form until cortical association connections are approaching mature levels in mid-childhood.

The late maturation of the corpus callosum (the large bundle of nerve fibres linking the two cerebral hemispheres) parallels the progressive specialisation of the left hemisphere for language. Before the age of 5 years, damage to the left hemisphere can be partially compensated for by takeover of language functions by the right hemisphere.

The comparatively early maturation of the visual cortex compared with the auditory cortex might help explain why children of deaf signers copy their first hand signs at an earlier age than hearing children copy their first words. However, the mastery of syntax is not faster in signing children and suggests that this ability depends on relatively slow-maturing auditory and association connections.

Terrence W. Deacon

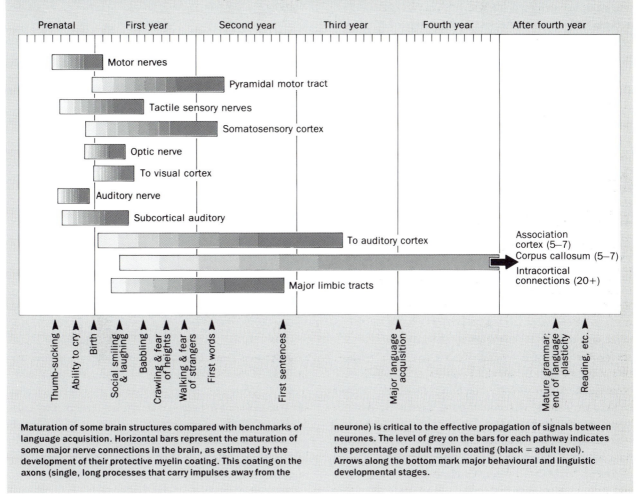

Maturation of some brain structures compared with benchmarks of language acquisition. Horizontal bars represent the maturation of some major nerve connections in the brain, as estimated by the development of their protective myelin coating. This coating on the axons (single, long processes that carry impulses away from the neurone) is critical to the effective propagation of signals between neurones. The level of grey on the bars for each pathway indicates the percentage of adult myelin coating (black = adult level). Arrows along the bottom mark major behavioural and linguistic developmental stages.

suggest that language learning is far less efficient after the first 4 or 5 years.

Comparative linguistics also suggests that there are innate predispositions for certain language structures. Various 'pidgin' and 'creole' languages have developed at the cultural interfaces between colonial and indigenous peoples. These recent and widely scattered languages may show structural features in common that they do not share with their parent languages. This could happen only if innate predispositions or other a priori contraints were more influential than environmental input.

However, there is mounting evidence that the 'language-learning environment' of young children is far more structured than once thought, and may partly account for the ease with which language is learned. Language is used from the very start and is not learned merely as a set of abstract

(a)
Child: Ball. Kick. Kick. Daddy kick.
Mother: That's right, you have to kick it, don't you.
Child: Mmm. Um. Um. Kick hard. Only kick hard.
  Our play that. On floor. Our play that on floor. Now.
  Our play that. On floor. Our play that on floor. No
  that. Now.
Mother: All right.
Child: Mummy, come on floor me.
Mother: Yes.
Child: You tip those out.
Mother: Mm. All right.
Child: That one broke.

(b)
Child: Hester be fast asleep, mummy.
Mother: She was tired.
Child: And why did her have two sweets, mummy?
Mother: Because you each had two, that's why.
  She had the same as you. Ooh dear, now what?
Child: Daddy didn't give me two in the end.
Mother: Yes, he did.
Child: He didn't.
Mother: He did.
Child: Look he given one to – two to Hester, and two
  to us.
Mother: Yes, that's right.
Child: Why did he give?
Mother: 'Cos there were six sweets. That's two each.

Speech of a 2-year-old (a) and a 3-year-old child (b). This 2-year-old's speech includes numerous repetitions of apparently stereotypic phrases, some of which were probably learned and repeated without being analysed. Most of these utterances also lack a full subject–predicate structure so that the agent, the action or the object of the utterance must be supplied in the behavioural context. However, the child is able to combine and recombine a few words into several phrases with different meanings. In contrast, the 3-year-old's speech shows sophisticated subject–predicate structure, recognition of the conventional difference between sentence types (e.g. questions and statements), and evidence of incorrect regularisations of verbs and pronouns (e.g. 'be fast asleep' and 'did her have') that could not have been copied, suggesting a beginning awareness of rules or conventions of usage.

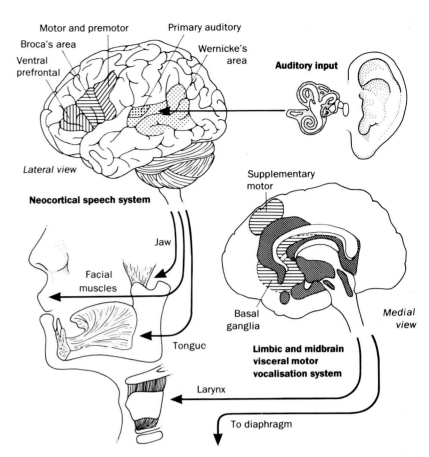

The parts of the brain responsible for vocal call production in monkeys and for speech in humans. The lateral (side) view shows the neocortical areas involved in language comprehension (stippled) and production (striped). The medial (midline) view shows the limbic and midbrain structures involved in the production of primate calls and human laughter and crying (grey) and some structures important to both speech and calls (striped). The neocortical speech system produces skilled movements of the face and mouth muscles whereas the subcortical call system produces automatic movements of the visceral muscles of the larynx and diaphragm. Limbic structures are also the source of emotional experience and expression. The functions of the call system are subordinated to the speech system in humans but can interfere with speech at times of intense emotion.

associations. It is used to request, to ask, to explain, to show or to interact, and all the child's attempts at speech have consequences that provide immediate feedback on their success or failure to communicate. Parent–child inter-actions embed language learning in a web of interactions, turn-taking, object exchange and games. These structure the contexts in which words are first used. The language of parents talking with young children is also exaggerated and simplified in ways that help to focus attention on its content.

The structure of grammar and syntax may in part derive from the general principles that underlie the guidance of all purposeful actions. Objects, agents and actions may also be the basis for syntactical categories. Such functional cate-gorisation of grammatical units into topic versus comment, figure versus ground, or bound versus free information, provides a framework for understanding language struc-ture, which is more general than the more abstract linguis-tic categories (such as subject, verb, object, adjective and pronoun). This kind of analysis is particularly useful when trying to compare languages that have different formal structures. Parallels between action and syntax might also explain why brain disorders that disrupt understanding of grammar may also disrupt speech production and why language and skilled manual behaviour are both specialised to the left side of the brain.

Language acquisition certainly depends on predisposi-tions. The search for an innate set of 'rules' is giving way to the investigation of environmental, behavioural, percep-tual and learning biases that form the 'scaffolding' of lan-guage construction.

Adaptations for language

The American linguist Noam Chomsky has proposed that a unique 'language organ' or 'language acquisition device'

(LAD) evolved within the human brain. Although there is no anatomical evidence for a new 'organ', it is clear that the control of language within the human brain is very different from the neural control of vocalisation in the brains of other primates.

Adaptation for language involved many subtle changes in the brain and peripheral systems controlling every aspect of its input, output, analysis and use. The diverse language adaptations help to reduce the complexity facing the learner and speaker. An increased volitional control of vocalisation and a reduced repertoire of stereotypic calls, together with a spontaneous impulse to vocalise (as reflected in infant babbling) and an urge and ability to mimic speech sounds during childhood supports the awesome task of learning thousands of words and practising combinations of them. In addition, there is a critical period during early childhood when language learning can produce profound and permanent brain changes that contribute to the unconscious ease with which we use language as adults. We also have an enlarged, more malleable vocal tract that increases the range of sounds that we can produce, together with a propensity to articulate in a perceptually distinctive way. Our ability to learn and analyse complex combinatorial relationships enhances our capacity for skilled oral movement sequences and our ability to manipulate grammatical information quickly. More generally, we have a social proclivity to develop interaction rituals that frame speech events.

Many constraints of motor behaviour, perceptual analysis and cognition have been inherited from our prelinguistic ancestry. These include the left-hemispheric specialisation for analysis of vocalisations, the perception of certain vocal sound differences, and the capacity for analysing and producing skilled sequential activities.

Origin of language

Why and when language arose, and what its early forms were like are still shrouded in mystery. Because language leaves no fossil record, all the evidence is circumstantial. Comparative linguistics was once used to estimate a date for a single common precursor for existing languages. Most theorists now turn to anatomical and archaeological information to suggest a date of origin for language.

Those who argue for a relatively recent origin correlate it with the appearance of anatomically modern humans with modern-sized brains and a fully descended vocal tract. The flowering of late Palaeolithic culture with its tools and artistic expression suggests a major advance in communication. Those in favour of an earlier origin point to the first appearance of stone tools and the beginning of brain enlargement in *Homo habilis* or early *Homo erectus* as a stimulus for language.

The timing of language origins has important implica-
tions for the nature of mind. If it appeared recently – in anatomically modern *Homo sapiens* – language was secondary to previous non-linguistic changes in the brain, possibly increased general intelligence, and there was not much time for it to influence the structure of the brain or vocal tract. If it appeared early in our evolution it probably passed through many different forms and had a major influence on the evolution of the brain and vocal tract. The multitude of language adaptations seamlessly integrated into human nature provide strong evidence for an ancient origin for language. Adaptations of early hominids to aid speech acquisition may still influence how we learn, use and understand language today.

Some authorities have suggested that the earliest languages were not spoken, but rather signed or sung. Darwin himself suggested that an early stage in language evolution might have depended on chants and ritual singing. Apes have limited voluntary control of vocalisation but good control of their hands, so the evolution of increased vocal skill and loss of innate calls may have been aided by manual gestures. Unlike deaf signed languages, however, early languages probably always included aspects of singing, ritual, speech and gesture. Gestures, changes in intonation and rhythm still help specify reference and organise speech interactions, but were likely more integral to the syntax and semantics of early languages.

Another view is that early languages were like the speech of young children, so that language learning recapitulates its evolution. This view is misleading: the speech of a child results from the use of an immature but language-specialised brain to try and understand a fully developed language suited to the adult user. Early hominids would have used adult brains to produce an adult language whose form was appropriate to that comparatively unspecialised brain. Like the speech of children, ancient hominid speech would inevitably be simpler than that of modern adults. But the reasons are quite different and any similarities would be superficial.

Why did language first evolve? In hindsight it is easy to justify as a useful means of communication, but the fact that it evolved only once gives us no comparative perspective. Hominid ancestors were the first to achieve the necessary mental conditions for language, but we do not know what these were. Given its enormous mental cost and early crudeness perhaps it was favoured only under one unique set of conditions. The predominant uses of language today are probably quite different from the critical uses that brought it into existence in the first place.

Terrence W. Deacon

See also 'The human brain' (p. 115), 'Vocal communication by non-human primates' (p. 124), 'Human speech and language' (p. 134) and 'Language training of apes' (p. 138)

Human speech and language

Our language involves innate and genetically transmitted anatomical and neural mechanisms. Some of these, particularly those related to speech, are found only in humans, and the same may be true of aspects of language, such as a complex syntax governed by rules and a complex word structure. Large gaps remain in our understanding of human language and speech but we think that these uniquely human anatomical and neural mechanisms evolved to enhance our ability to use language. In contrast, the ability to acquire and to use words in a simple way is present in non-human animals.

Johannes Müller demonstrated in 1848 that the production of human speech involves the modulation of acoustic energy by the airway above the larynx (the *supralaryngeal tract*). This acoustic energy is generated by the larynx or by turbulent airflow at a constriction in the airway. Until the 1960s, however, it was not realised that speech is itself an important component of the human ability to use language. Speech allows us to transmit phonetic 'segments' (which are approximated by the letters of the alphabet) at the remarkable rate of up to 25 per second. By contrast, it is impossible to identify non-speech information at rates greater than seven to nine items per second. A short sentence, such as this one, contains about 50 speech sounds. These phonetic segments can be uttered in 2 seconds. If this sentence were transmitted at the non-speech rate, it would take so long that a listener might well forget the beginning of the sentence before hearing its end.

The high transmission rate of human speech is thus an integral part of our linguistic ability, as it allows complex ideas to be transmitted within the constraints of short-term memory. Although sign language can also achieve a high rate of data transmission, the signer's hands cannot simultaneously be used for other tasks. Vocal language represents a continuation of the hominid evolutionary trend towards freeing the hands that followed from upright bipedal locomotion.

The high transmission rate of speech is achieved by the generation of *formant frequency patterns* and of rapid temporal and spectral cues by the unique human supralaryngeal airway and its control mechanisms. A pipe organ allows maximum acoustic energy through at certain frequencies. Formant frequencies are the 'peaks' of acoustic energy passing through the supralaryngeal airway. Both the pipe organ and the supralaryngeal tract thus act as 'filters', letting relatively more acoustic energy through at particular frequencies.

The sound energy for speech is generated at the larynx for 'phonated' vowels and consonants such as [m] and [v]. Turbulent noise generated at constrictions in the airway can also serve as a source of acoustic energy as, for example, in the production of such sounds as [t] or [s]. During phonation, the vocal cords of the larynx open and close rapidly at a rate that determines the *fundamental frequency* (F_0) of phonation. Higher-pitched voices have higher average fundamental frequencies. Average energy is present at the fundamental frequency and its *harmonics* – that is, at integral multiples of F_0 ($2F_0$, $3F_0$, $4F_0$, etc.).

When people sing they systematically vary the fundamental frequency of phonation. Many 'tone' languages such as Chinese also differentiate words using patterned variations in fundamental frequency. However, fundamental frequency is independent of the formant frequency pattern, which derives from the supralaryngeal vocal tract filtering the acoustic energy of the source; this energy is the fundamental frequency and its higher harmonics for phonation or the total energy spectrum of turbulent noise.

The formant frequencies are determined by the shape and length of the supralaryngeal airway. The process is not unlike that which occurs when we view a stained-glass window: the daylight that strikes the window is the source of energy, and the image that we view derives from the filtering properties of the stained glass acting on the source.

During the production of speech, we continually change the shape, and make small adjustments in the length of, the supralaryngeal airway, thereby generating a changing formant frequency pattern. The sounds of human speech hence differ in their formant frequency patterns, as well as in respect of timing and the acoustic source that is filtered.

The speech apparatus

The human supralaryngeal airway differs from that of any other adult mammal. In chimpanzees, for example, the

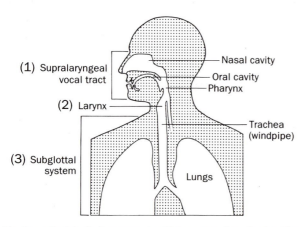

(1) Supralaryngeal vocal tract
(2) Larynx
(3) Subglottal system

Nasal cavity
Oral cavity
Pharynx
Trachea (windpipe)
Lungs

The three physiological components of human speech production. The subglottal system – the lungs and their associated muscles – provide the power for speech production.

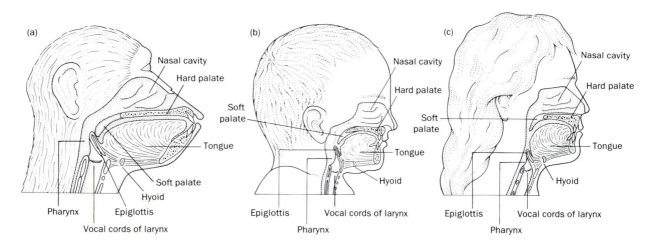

Diagrams of the heads of (a) adult chimpanzee, (b) infant and (c) adult human, showing the airway as it would appear if the heads were sectioned on their midline from back to front. Note that the chimpanzee's tongue forms the lower boundary of the mouth; the high position of the larynx allows it to lock into the nasal cavity during respiration. By contrast, more than half of the human tongue is below the mouth where it forms the front boundary of the pharynx; the right-angled bend in the human airway where the mouth cavity and pharynx meet, and the proportions of the human tongue, make it possible to produce vowels such as [i] and [u] as well as the velar consonants [g] and [k]. In contrast to the chimpanzee's supralaryngeal airway, the soft palate, or velum, can seal off the nasal cavity from the rest of the supralaryngeal airway during speech production. The vocal tract of a human infant resembles a chimpanzee's.

tongue is positioned entirely within the oral cavity and forms its lower margin. The position of the long, relatively thin tongue reflects the high position of the larynx. The larynx moves up into the nasopharynx during respiration, providing a pathway for air from the nose to the lungs that is isolated from any liquid that may be in the animal's mouth.

Until the age of 3 months, human infants have the same-shaped airway as non-human mammals and can breathe and drink at the same time. Liquid moves to either side of the raised larynx, which, like a raised periscope protruding through the oral cavity, connects the lungs with the nose. In adult humans, the larynx has lowered into the neck. The round tongue forms the forward margin of the pharynx as well as the lower margin of the oral cavity. Air, liquids and solid food all use a common pathway through the pharynx. Humans are hence more liable than any other land animals to choke when they eat, because food can fall into the larynx and obstruct the pathway into the lungs.

During development, the human palate moves backwards along the base of the skull, which is itself restructured in a unique fashion to achieve the human supralaryngeal airway. Human adults are less efficient at chewing because the roof of the mouth and the lower jaw have been reduced compared with non-human primates and archaic hominids. This reduced palate and mandible crowd our teeth and may lead to infection because of impaction – a potentially fatal condition before modern medicine.

These deficiencies in the mouth of an adult human are offset by the increased phonetic range of the supralaryngeal airway. The human vocal tract can seal off the air pathway that leads through the mouth from the nose, so yielding non-nasal sounds. This results in clearer, more readily identified formant frequency patterns. Nasalised speech is inherently subject to more errors in interpretation than is unnasalised speech – for example, 30–50 per cent error rates for nasal vowels as against 5 per cent for unnasalised vowels under similar conditions.

Moreover, the round human tongue moving in the space defined by the palate and spinal column can generate the formant frequency patterns that define vowels such as [i], [u] and [a] (the vowels of the words *meet*, *boo* and *mama*) and consonants such as [k] and [g]. These sounds and consonants, such as [b], [p], [d] and [t], have formant frequency patterns that make them better suited for vocal communication than other sounds. They are the most common sounds in different human languages and are acquired early on by children. The error rate for misidentification of the vowel [i] is particularly low. It can serve as an optimal cue for vocal-tract *normalisation* in the perception of speech, in which a listener compensates for the length of an individual speaker's supralaryngeal vocal tract.

Speech perception

Although the perception of human speech involves general auditory mechanisms that play a part in hearing other sounds, speech perception is a complex process that has been 'matched' to the supralaryngeal airway by means of natural selection. Specialised neural mechanisms operate at different stages in a 'speech mode' of perception, in which listeners seem to apply to speech different strategies to those for non-speech signals.

Human listeners first must 'extract' the formant and fundamental frequencies of speech signals. They can do this even when these signals have been degraded by telephone circuits or noise (computer systems designed to recognise speech cannot). We seem to extract the formant frequencies using an internal, neural knowledge of the filtering characteristics of our supralaryngeal airway. Human listeners use a process of vocal-tract normalisation in which they unconsciously estimate the probable length of the speaker's supralaryngeal airway to assign a particular formant frequency pattern to a particular speech sound.

The length of the human supralaryngeal airway differs greatly: the airway of a young child is only half the length of that in adults. Because of this variation there is overlap between the formant frequency patterns that convey different speech sounds. For example, although the formant frequencies of the word *bit* are always higher than those of *bet* spoken by the same speaker, the word *bit* spoken by a large adult male speaker can have the same formant frequency pattern as the word *bet* produced by a smaller individual. The longer supralaryngeal airway of the larger speaker produces formants of lower frequency for his *bit* than that of the smaller person, and his *bit* can match the smaller person's *bet*.

The different formant frequency patterns that signal the same sound can be extreme; those of 4-year-old children typically are twice as high as adults. However, human listeners are able to identify speech sounds correctly because they unconsciously *normalise*, by taking into account the probable length of a given speaker's supralaryngeal vocal tract. The vowel thus provides a selective advantage in the process of speech perception to hominids able to produce it.

When listening to speech, human beings also take advantage of acoustic cues and contextual constraints, such as rate and phonetic context. For example, different formant frequency patterns will signal the stop consonant [d] when it occurs before the vowel [i] versus [u]. These different formant frequency patterns result from the inherent constraints of the physiology of speech. In this case, the supralaryngeal tract must move from the shape that yields the sound to the different shapes that yield [i] and [u]; the formant frequency patterns reflect the two different transitions. Although the formant frequency pattern at the onset of the syllables [di] and [du] is quite different, we hear the 'same' sound [t] in the initial position for both syllables.

We identify such patterns and short-term spectral cues as discrete categories in a manner that suggests that we have a series of neural detectors tuned to respond to the particular acoustic signals produced by the organs of human speech. These detectors are analogous to the simpler ones that exist in other species, such as frogs and crickets, which can be identified using electrophysiology and behavioural techniques.

More than a century ago, the French surgeon Paul Broca identified the area of the human brain in which the programmes that control the production of human speech are stored or accessed. The articulatory manoeuvres that occur during speech are among our most complex. Children younger than 10 cannot attain adult standards, even for basic manoeuvres such as the lip positions that produce different vowels. Damage to the neural pathways that connect Broca's area to other parts of the brain result in faults in speech production. The damage need not even involve Broca's region itself. Patients with this defect cannot produce distinct speech sounds but they can move individual articulators, or use their tongue and lips to swallow food.

Great apes (which lack a functional equivalent of Broca's area and connecting pathways) cannot be taught to control their supralaryngeal airways to produce sounds in any way similar to those of human speech. Although the pongid airway is inherently unable to produce all of the sounds of human speech, it does have the mechanical potential to

EVOLUTION OF THE SPEECH APPARATUS

The counterpart of Broca's area in non-human primates may be the lateral precentral cortex, which is involved in the regulation of mouth and facial gestures used in communication. The elaboration of such gestures in consort with the evolution of the supralaryngeal airway may have promoted the evolution of Broca's area in humans.

The evolutionary matching of the human speech apparatus with a mechanism of speech perception is similar to the match between anatomy and sound perception in other species, such as crickets, frogs and monkeys. Human speech makes use of structures and neural mechanisms present in other species; the larynx is similar in all hominids, and rodents have the mechanisms needed to hear linguistic cues, such as the timing between phonation and lip opening that differentiates the sounds [b] and [p].

The structures and neural control mechanisms necessary for the production of the complex patterns of human speech seem to have evolved only in the past 1.6 million years or so. The comparative anatomy of living primates and of hominid fossils suggests that the evolution of the human supralaryngeal vocal tract probably started in early African populations of *Homo erectus* and was not completed until the appearance of fully modern humans.

The later, or classic, Neanderthals of Europe were the last to retain the ancient non-human supralaryngeal vocal tract. But predating the late Neanderthals, around 100 000 years ago, were other hominids — for example, those from the Israeli sites of Skhūl and Jebel Qafzeh — with human supralaryngeal airways. Because these hominids had other resemblances to modern humans they probably had the brain mechanisms necessary to produce human speech.

The existence of a modern form of supralaryngeal airway in a fossil hominid suggests that there were matching neural motor controls and perceptual mechanisms. The deficiencies of the human supralaryngeal airway for breathing and swallowing must be outweighed by the adaptive value of rapid speech. Speech may even have served as an isolating mechanism, hence promoting speciation in the evolution that led to anatomically modern *Homo sapiens*.

Philip Lieberman

See also 'Evolution of early humans' (p. 241)

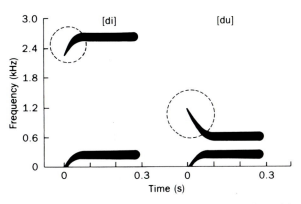

Schematised first and second formant frequencies as functions of time for the syllables [di] and [du] – the words *tea* and *too*. The first formant frequency pattern, F_1, is lowest, the second one, F_2, is above. Note that the circled F_2 transitions at the start of the syllable are quite different.

produce at least some of them. However, non-human primates lacking the brain mechanisms necessary for controlling the voluntary articulatory manoeuvres that underlie human speech are unable intentionally to produce even these sounds.

Syntax

There seems also to be a link between the neural mechanisms involved in speech motor control and those responsible for syntax. Victims of Broca's aphasia and Parkinson's disease, in which the brain mechanisms that regulate the motor control of speech are damaged, are often deficient in grammar and lose their command of the more complex aspects of syntax. In this, they resemble young children, who are unable to understand sentences that have a complex syntax. Chimpanzees have been taught to communicate by means of sign language, but they do not seem to use any complex syntax in communication.

Other complex motoric activity, such as that involved in toolmaking, may have been involved in the evolution of the brain mechanisms that are necessary for human speech and syntax. However, syntactic ability seems to be linked to speech production and probably reached its present level in comparatively recent times with the appearance of anatomically modern *Homo sapiens*. In contrast, the ability to use words may rest on neural mechanisms that are present in reduced form in other living species and that were elaborated quite early during hominid evolution.

Philip Lieberman

See also 'The human brain' (p. 115), 'Biological aspects of language' (p. 128), 'Language training of apes' (p. 138), and 'Evolution of early humans' (p. 241)

Language training of apes

Can apes learn to communicate with human beings? Scientists have been attempting to answer this question since the late 1960s when it was first reported that a young chimpanzee named Washoe in Reno, Nevada had been taught to produce hand signs similar to those used by deaf humans.

Washoe was reared much like a human child. People made signs to her throughout the day and she was given freedom to move about the caravan where she lived. She could even go outdoors to play. She was taught how to make different signs by teachers who moved her hands through the motions of each sign while showing her the object she was learning to 'name'. If she began to make a portion of the hand movement on her own she was quickly rewarded, either with food or with something appropriate to the sign. For example, if she was being taught the sign for 'tickle' her reward was a tickling game.

This training method was termed 'moulding' because it involved the physical placement of Washoe's hands. Little by little, Washoe became able to produce more and more signs on her own. As she grew older, she occasionally even learned to make new signs without moulding. Once Washoe had learned several signs she quickly began to link them together to produce strings of signs such as 'you me out'. Such sequences appeared to her teachers to be simple sentences.

Many biologists were sceptical of the claims made for Washoe. While they agreed that Washoe was able to produce different gestures, they doubted that such signs really served as names. Perhaps, to Washoe, the gestures were just tricks to be used to get the experimenter to give her things she wanted; even though Washoe knew how and when to make signs, she really did not know what words meant in the sense that people do.

The disagreement was more than a scholarly debate among scientists. Decades of previous work had demonstrated that many animals could learn to do complex things to obtain food, without understanding what they were doing. For example, pigeons had been taught to bat a ball back and forth in what looked liked a game of ping pong. There were also taught to peck keys with such words as 'Please', 'Thank you', 'Red' and 'Green' printed on them. They did this in a way that made it appear that they were communicating, but they were not; they had simply learned to peck each key when a special signal was given.

This type of learning is called *conditioned discrimination* learning, a term that simply means that an animal can learn to make one set of responses in one group of circumstances and another in different circumstances. Although some aspects of human language can be explained in this way, such as 'Hello', 'Goodbye', 'Please' and 'Thank you', most cannot. Human beings learn more than what to say when: they learn what words stand for.

If Washoe had simply signed 'drink' when someone held up a bottle of soda, there would be little reason to conclude that she was doing anything different from other animals. If, however, Washoe used the sign 'drink' to represent any liquid beverage, then she was doing something very different – something that everyone had previously thought only humans could do.

It was difficult to determine which of these possibilities characterised her behaviour, as the question of how to distinguish between the 'conditioned response' and a 'word' had not arisen. Before Washoe, the only organisms that used words were human beings, and to determine if a person knew what a word stood for was easy: one simply asked. This was impossible with Washoe, because her use of symbols was not advanced enough to allow her to comprehend complex questions. One- and two-year-old children are also unable to answer questions such as these. However, because children are able to answer such questions later on, the issue of determining how and when a child knows that words have meanings had not until then been seen as critical.

Teaching syntax

Several scientists attempted to solve this problem by focusing on sentences instead of words. Linguists argue that the essence of human language lies not in learning to use individual words, but rather in an ability to form a large number of word combinations that follow the same set of specific rules. These rules are seen as a genetic endowment unique to humans. If it could be shown that apes learn syntactical rules, then it must be true that they were using symbols to represent things, not just perform tricks.

Three psychologists in the 1970s each used a different method in an attempt to teach apes syntax. One group followed the method used with Washoe and began teaching another chimpanzee, Nim, sign language. Another opted for the use of plastic symbols with the chimpanzee Sarah. Still another used geometric symbols, linked to a computer keyboard, with a chimpanzee named Lana. Both Lana and Sarah were taught a simple syntax, which required them to fill in one blank at a time in a string of words. The number of blanks was slowly increased until the chimpanzee was forming a complete 'sentence'. Nim was asked to produce syntactically correct strings by making signs along with his teacher.

Without help from his teachers, Nim was unable to form sentences that displayed the kind of syntactical rules used

Lana uses her keyboard to type out the practice sentence 'You put piece of bread in machine?'. In response, a person would fill Lana's machine with bread. Lana could then request it by selecting the symbols for 'Please machine give piece of bread'. Lana thus had to learn to address her requests to people to fill the machine when it was empty and to the machine itself to obtain food when food was available.

by humans. Nim's sign usage could best be interpreted as a series of 'conditioned discriminations' similar to, albeit more complex than, behaviours seen in many less-intelligent animals. This work suggested that Nim, like circus animals but unlike human children, was using words only to obtain rewards.

However, the other attempts to teach sentences to apes arrived at a different conclusion, perhaps because a different training method was used. Both Sarah and Lana learned to fill in the blanks in sentences in ways that suggested they had learned the rules that govern simple sentence construction. Moreover, 6 per cent of Lana's sentences were 'novel' in that they differed from the ones that she had been taught. Many of these sentences, such as 'Please you move coke in cup into room', followed syntactical rules and were appropriate and meaningful communications. Other sentences followed the syntactical rules that Lana had learned, but did not make sense; for example, 'Question you give beancake shut-open'. Thus, apes appeared to be able to learn rules for sentence construction, but they did not generalise these rules in a way that suggested full comprehension of the words.

By 1980, Washoe had matured and given birth. At this time there was great interest in whether or not she would teach her offspring to sign. Unfortunately, her infant died. However, another infant was obtained and given to Washoe. This infant, Loulis, began to imitate many of the hand gestures that Washoe used, though the imitations were often quite imprecise. Washoe made few explicit attempts to mould Loulis's hands. Although Loulis began to make signs, it was not easy to determine why he was mak-

ing them or what, if anything, he meant. Loulis has not yet received any tests like those that were given to Washoe to determine if he can make the correct sign when shown an object. It is clear that he learned to imitate Washoe, but it is not clear that he learned what the signs meant.

The question of whether or not apes understand words caused many developmental psychologists to study earlier and earlier aspects of language acquisition in children. Their work gave, for the first time, a detailed insight into how children use words during the 'one-word' stage of language learning and showed that children usually learn to understand words before they begin to use them. At the same time, there was a new approach to the investigation of ape language. Instead of teaching names by pairing an object with its sign or symbol and rewarding correct responses, there was a new emphasis on the communicative aspect of symbols. For example, to teach a symbol such as 'key', a desirable item was locked in a box that was given to the chimpanzee. When the chimpanzee failed to open it, he was shown how to ask for and how to use a key. On other occasions, the chimpanzee was asked to retrieve a key for the teacher, so that she might open the box.

This new approach was first used with two chimpanzees named Sherman and Austin. It resulted in a clearer symbolic use of words than that found in animals trained by other methods. In addition, because these chimpanzees were taught comprehension skills, they were able to communicate with one another and not just with the experimenters. Sherman and Austin could use their symbols to tell each other things that could not be conveyed by simple glances or by pointing. For example, they could describe foods they had seen in another room, or the types of tools they needed to solve a problem. Although other apes had been reported to sign in each other's presence, there was no evidence that they were intentionally signing to each other or that they responded to each other's signs.

Most important, Sherman and Austin began to show an aspect of symbol usage that they had not been taught; they used symbols to say what they were going to do *before* they did it. Symbol use by other apes had not included descriptions of intended actions; rather, communications had been begun by a teacher, or limited to simple requests.

Sherman and Austin also began to use symbols to share information about objects that were not present and they passed a particularly demanding test, which required them to look at symbols and answer questions that could be answered only if they knew what each symbol represented. For example, they could look at printed lexigram symbols such as 'key', 'lever', 'stick', 'wrench', 'apple', 'banana', 'pineapple' and 'juice', and state whether each lexigram belonged to the class of 'food' words or 'tool' words. They could do this without ever being told whether these lexigram symbols should be classified as foods or tools. These findings were important, because they revealed that by using symbols an ape can describe what it is about to do.

How similar is ape language to human language?

Even though it was generally agreed that apes could do something far more complex than most other animals, there still remained much disagreement as to whether ape's symbols were identical to human symbols. This uncertainty arose for two reasons: apes did not acquire words in the same manner as children – that is, by observing others use them; and apes did not appear to use true syntactical rules to construct multiple-word utterances.

(Above) Sherman asks for a food he would like to have (cherries) while Austin watches; (centre) Austin selects some cherries for Sherman and will then have some also (Austin is smiling because he is happy that Sherman has chosen cherries); (below) they change places and Austin then uses the keyboard to tell Sherman the food he would like to eat next.

The first of these differences between ape and child has recently been challenged by a young pygmy chimpanzee or bonobo named Kanzi. Most previous studies had focused on common chimpanzees because pygmy chimpanzees are very rare (they are in great danger of having their habitat destroyed in the coming decade and have no protected parks).

In contrast to other apes, Kanzi learned symbols simply by observing human beings point to them while speaking to him. He did not need to have his arms placed in position, or to be rewarded for using a correct symbol. More important, he did not need to be taught to comprehend symbols or taught that symbols could be used for absent objects as well as those present. Kanzi spontaneously used symbols to announce his actions or intentions and, if his meaning was ambiguous, he often invented gestures to clarify it, as young children do.

Kanzi learned words by listening to speech. He first comprehended certain spoken words, then learned to read the lexigram symbols. This was possible because his caretakers pointed to these symbols as they spoke. For example, Kanzi learned 'strawberries' as he heard people mention the word when they ran across wild strawberries growing in the woods. He soon became able to lead people to strawberries whenever they asked him to do so. He similarly learned the spoken names of many other foods that grew outdoors, such as wild grapes, honeysuckle, privet berries, blackberries and mushrooms, and could take people to any of these foods upon spoken request.

Unlike previous apes reared as human children, Kanzi was reared in a semi-natural woodland. Although he could not produce speech, he understood much of what was said to him. He could appropriately carry out novel spoken requests such as 'Will you take some hamburger to Austin?', 'Can you show your new toy to Kelly?' and 'Would you give Panzee some of your melon?'. There appeared to be no limit to the number of sentences that Kanzi could understand as long as the words in the sentences were in his vocabulary.

During the first 3 or 4 years of his life, Kanzi's comprehension of spoken sentences was limited to things that he heard often. However, when he was 5 years old, he began to respond to novel sentences upon first hearing them. For example, the first time he heard someone talk about throwing a ball in the river, he suddenly turned and threw his ball right in the water, even though he had never done this before. Similarly, when someone suggested, for fun, that he might then try to throw a potato at a turtle that was nearby, he found a potato and tossed it at the turtle. To be certain that Kanzi was not being somehow 'cued' inadvertently by people, he was tested with headphones. In this test he had to listen to a word and point to a picture of the word that he heard. Kanzi did this easily, the first time he took the test.

About this time, Kanzi also began to combine symbols. Unlike other apes, he did not combine symbols ungram-

Kanzi uses his keyboard to say that he intends to drink some of the coke in the picture. Unlike other apes, Kanzi uses symbols to describe his intended actions, such as where is going to go, the games he is going to play, and the food he intends to eat.

Mulika uses the joystick to chase a target on the television set and a chimpanzee version of 'Pacman'. Chimpanzees are very good at such games.

matically to get the experimenter to give something that was purposefully being held back. Kanzi's combinations had a primitive English word order and conveyed novel information. For example, he formed utterances such as 'Ball go group room' to say that he wanted to play with a specific ball – the one he had seen in the group room on the previous day. Because the experimenter was not attempting to get Kanzi to say this, and was indeed far from the group room, such a sentence conveyed something that only Kanzi – not the experimenter – knew before Kanzi spoke.

Thus Kanzi's combinations differed from those of other apes in that they often referred to things or events that were absent and were known only to Kanzi, they contained a

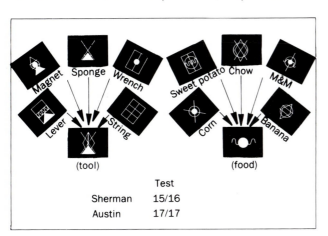

The lexigram-words that Sherman and Austin described as 'Foods' or 'Tools' the first time they were asked to classify them. They looked at each symbol and placed it in the food or the tool category. Because the symbols themselves do not look like foods or tools (nor do they resemble the food or tool words), the only way that Sherman and Austin could have properly categorised these lexigram-words was by understanding what they symbolised.

primitive grammar and were not imitations of the experimenter. Nor did the experimenter ask rhetorical questions such as 'What is this?' to elicit them. Kanzi's combinations include sentences such as 'Tickle bite', 'Keep-way balloon' and 'Coke chase'. As almost nothing is yet known of how pygmy chimpanzees communicate, they could use a form of simple language in the wild. Kanzi understands spoken English words, so the ability that is reflected in language comprehension is probably an older evolutionary adaptation than is the ability to talk.

Studying ape language presents a serious challenge to the long-held view that only humans can talk and think. Certainly, there is now no doubt that apes communicate in much more complex and abstract ways than dogs, cats and other familiar animals. Similarly, apes that have learned some language skills are also able to do some remarkable non-linguistic tasks. For example, they can recognise themselves on television and even determine whether an image is taped or live. They can also play video games, using a joystick to catch and trap a video villain.

Scientists have only just begun to discover ways of tapping the hidden talents for language and communication of our closest relatives. Sharing 98 per cent of their DNA with human beings, it has long been wondered why African apes seem so much like us at a biological level, but so different when it comes to behaviour. Ape-language studies continue to reveal that apes are more like us than we ever imagined.

E.S. Savage-Rumbaugh

See also 'Biological aspects of language' (p. 128) and 'Human speech and language' (p. 134)

Part Four

Primate social organisation

Humans have a complex pattern of social organisation, but so do many non-human primates. However, some other primates do not form social groups: their social behaviour depends on when they are active.

Most primates that feed at night do so alone, although some – for example, the lesser bushbaby (*Galago senegalensis*) – form small sleeping groups at the end of the night. Prosimian primates (lemurs, lorises and tarsiers) are mainly nocturnal, and most are therefore solitary. A few nocturnal lemurs, such as the avahi (*Avahi laniger*), live in monogamous family groups consisting of a mated pair and a small number of offspring, but no nocturnal primates live in social groups larger than this. Solitary species do, of course, interact socially; they are simply not gregarious creatures. Encounters between individuals occur during the night and sleeping groups are also a form of social interaction. Nocturnal primates usually depend more on the sense of smell than do those active by day, so olfactory signals (**4.4**) and vocalisations (**3.4**) are important in their interactions, whereas visual signals (**4.5**) are more so for diurnal species.

Diurnal species usually live in relatively large and reasonably stable groups, ranging in size from the family groups of gibbons to the herds of baboons. All monkeys and apes, with one exception, are diurnal. The exception is the nocturnal owl monkey (*Aotus*), which, like some prosimians, is monogamous. Most diurnal species form sizeable groups, but the orang-utan (*Pongo pygmaeus*) is almost solitary in habits – its average group size is less than two.

Diurnal habits seem to encourage the formation of sizeable groups; thus, diurnal lemurs in Madagascar also live in social groups. These range in size from the family groups of the indri (*Indri indri*) to the troops of up to two dozen formed by the ring-tailed lemur (*Lemur catta*). As diurnal habits probably represent a secondary development in lemurs, social groups probably evolved in parallel in lemurs and simians.

Two main selection pressures may account for the formation of social groups in primates. The first is predation. Primates may gain some protection from predators by living in groups, perhaps simply by increasing the number of pairs of eyes available to spot a threat, or possibly through an increased potential for fighting off the predators. The second possibility is that group life may increase the efficiency with which food sources (especially scattered fruit trees) can be found in tropical forests.

Both pressures may have acted and it is easy to see why nocturnal species are less likely to live in groups. Most are quite small so that stealthy movement may be the best way of avoiding predators. They may depend less

A male silverback gorilla beats his chest during a threat display.

on their eyes for finding food, so there is little benefit to be gained from living in groups. Group life is likely to increase local competition for resources and any benefits of groups must outweigh the costs of such competition. For each species, therefore, a particular balance will exist between the costs and benefits of group life; and this balance differs for nocturnal and diurnal species.

Primates can be classified into four categories on the basis of their social organisation: solitary individuals, pairs, one-male ('harem') groups and multimale groups (**4.2**). One-male groups contain one adult male, two or more adult females and a variable number of immature individuals; multimale groups have at least two adult males. Gorillas usually live in groups containing a single, fully adult (silverback) male, whereas chimpanzee groups contain several fully adult males. This classification to some extent reflects the size of the social group, but medium-sized groups of about a dozen individuals can have either one male or several. In any case, groups of a given size need not have the same internal structure. This applies to dominance hierarchies. For example, in multimale groups of macaques and baboons there is a clear rank order among the adult males, whereas in the multimale groups of spider monkeys and chimpanzees there is not.

For all primate species, the primary social link is the mother—infant bond (**4.2**). In group-living primates, relationships between females and successive generations of their female offspring (matrilines) usually form the core of the group. Primate social groups are stable only in a relative sense, as individuals migrate between them when they become sexually mature (**4.3**). In most, males leave whereas females remain behind. In the exceptional cases where females leave their natal groups, the core of the group is formed by a set of related males. This happens in spider monkeys (*Ateles*), red colobus monkeys (*Colobus badius*) and chimpanzees. This difference between male and female social migration adds a further level of complexity to primate groups.

Patterns of relatedness among mammals living in social groups are, of course, fundamental to theories of the evolution of altruistic behaviour (**4.1**). Paternity and the migration of individuals between groups are both relevant here.

Species-specific patterns are especially clear for primates that live monogamously, such as indris and gibbons. Most species living in larger groups also keep to an identifiable social pattern. Chimpanzees, for example, live in multimale social units with female migration. However, a few species show a range of social groupings. The Hanuman langur of India (*Presbytis entellus*) lives in harem groups in some areas whereas in others it lives in multimale groups. Probably the most extreme variation is seen in humans, as different populations favour monogamy, polygyny (one man with several wives) or polyandry (one woman with several husbands). Here, it is impossible to identify a species-specific pattern. Discussions of the biological origins of human social behaviour are thus fraught with difficulty.

Social behaviour and evolutionary theory

When an animal gives an alarm call, it warns other nearby animals that a predator is in the vicinity. But it also attracts the predator's attention to itself when it might have escaped notice by hiding. In effect, it behaves altruistically by risking its own life for the benefit of others.

In its original form, Darwin's theory of evolution by natural selection has always found it difficult to explain how *altruistic behaviour* could evolve. Any gene that increased the actor's risk of death while other individuals benefited by being able to live longer should soon be eliminated. However, an alternative view of the way in which genes are passed on to future generations allows us to see how altruism could evolve. When an individual behaves altruistically towards a relative, the genes they share will be propagated when that relative reproduces, even if the altruist itself dies. Hence, any gene for altruism would be preserved, providing such behaviour is directed towards close genetic relatives.

This solution to the problem of how altruism could evolve was first recognised by J.B.S. Haldane in 1958 and elaborated by W.D. Hamilton in 1964. Hamilton pointed out that, in social species, conventional measures of genetic fitness (such as the number of offspring that an individual produces) actually consist of two quite distinct components. One is the offspring produced by the individual's own unaided efforts; the other is offspring that the individual produces as a direct result of the help it receives from others.

Hamilton used the term *inclusive fitness*: a given individual's reproductive success stripped of all the components due to help from others, plus the number of extra copies of that gene passed on by that animal's relatives as a direct result of its help (see Box 1). This explanation for the evolution of altruism towards relatives is known as the theory of *kin selection*.

An individual hence has two choices on how to ensure that its genes are represented in future generations. One is by breeding itself; the other is by foregoing reproduction to help a genetic relative to breed. The second option is preferable whenever the relative's chances of reproducing are greater than the prospective altruist's (perhaps because it lacks the resources to breed, or is very young or so inexperienced that it would have difficulty rearing its own young). These two are really the opposite ends of a continuum, but contrasting them in this way reminds us that simple Darwinian processes can often lead to complex and apparently paradoxical outcomes.

Describing behaviour in this way reminds us that evolution operates by the transmission of genes from one generation to the next. This 'gene's-eye view' is neatly described by the idea of the *selfish gene*. Genes do not, of course, themselves have motives. However, viewing them as though they behave selfishly reminds us that we must always ask how a given gene might benefit if its carriers behave in a particular way. It is also important to note that this need not imply that the behaviour itself is under the direct control of genes.

Although sociobiologists tend to phrase their arguments in terms of a gene for a behaviour, this is usually just a convenient shorthand rather than a statement about the underlying biological determinants of behaviour. A learned behaviour can be interpreted sociobiologically just as easily as one that is under direct genetic control.

Altruism in primates

The idea of kin selection was conceived as a solution to the problem of altruism, but it has implications for the opposite form of behaviour – spite. Individuals should be more spiteful or aggressive towards less closely related individuals. There have been several attempts to test these ideas on primates by asking, for example, whether animals groom or attack other individuals in proportion to their relatedness.

A female vervet monkey scans for eagles

A chain of grooming chimpanzees.

Although the results obtained often seem to confirm the predictions of kin selection, the tests themselves may be flawed. For one thing, the assumption that grooming is an altruistic act – that the groomer gains nothing from it – is open to doubt. Social grooming is not always done simply to remove parasites and dirt from the fur; it can play a part in the establishment of alliances. Worse, theoretical analyses suggest that inclusive fitness would benefit by devoting all grooming time to the closest relative and not among one's relatives in proportion to their relatedness. One test, however, does provide some evidence for kin selection. Caged vervet monkeys (*Cercopithecus aethiops*) are more likely to give alarm calls on sighting a predator if they are caged with related rather than with unrelated individuals.

A more convincing case of kin selection comes from looking at how animals support each other when they get involved in fights. Animals that regularly come to each other's aid on such occasions are said to form a *coalition*. In many species, coalitions are most often formed between close genetic relatives, suggesting that kin selection may be important. However, not all coalitions are formed between relatives, and other explanations – such as reciprocal altruism – may also apply.

Animals do not willy-nilly commit themselves to helping an ally. Female rhesus macaques (*Macaca mulatta*), for example, are less likely to support an ally against a very high-ranking opponent, even when the ally is closely related to them (although they are more willing to support a close relative than a partner who is less closely related). This is what we might expect if animals weigh up the costs and benefits of going to another's aid. Supporting an ally that is going to lose the fight anyway because the opponent is powerful is not very likely to help in the propagation of one's genes. Living to fight another day may be more sensible.

Genetic altruism is also found in those species in which older offspring help their parents to raise the next litter rather than themselves breeding. Such behaviour is common among South American marmosets and tamarins, which mate monogamously. An animal that gives up the opportunity to breed for itself in order to contribute to its

parents' rearing success clearly performs an act of genetic altruism. Such helping behaviour is more likely to evolve when the offspring's chances of breeding for itself are poor (as in crowded populations or unpredictable environments). Whether this is true for marmosets or tamarins is not known, but pairs with helpers are more likely to rear their offspring successfully than are those without.

Another way in which kin can co-operate is by related individuals migrating together. Among rhesus macaques, for example, brothers often move from one troop to another as a group. In this way, they provide each other with support during the difficult business of gaining entry to a strange group. Male vervet monkeys, on the other hand, prefer to migrate individually into groups into which older brothers or cousins have already migrated; because relatives are more likely to support each other in conflicts, they may then find it easier to gain entry to such groups.

Kin recognition

Primates have long memories and can remember their relatives and friends even after a lengthy absence. Kin selection

1. GENES AND ALTRUISM

W.D. Hamilton's definition of inclusive fitness leads to his celebrated condition for the spread of an altruistic gene: an altruistic gene that depresses the fitness of its possessor will spread, providing

$$rB > C$$

where B is the number of offspring produced by a relative as a direct result of an individual's help (the Benefit), r is the coefficient of relationship between the donor and the recipient of this help and C is the number of offspring that the altruist loses by helping its relative to breed more

successfully (the Cost).

The coefficient of relationship, r, is the probability that the two individuals both possess the gene in question by inheritance from a common ancestor. In nearly all vertebrates, $r = 0.5$ between parents and their offspring and between full siblings, and $r = 0.25$ between half-siblings and between grandparents and their grandchildren.

Essentially, r decreases by a half for every birth that separates two individuals in their family tree, or pedigree.

Robin Dunbar

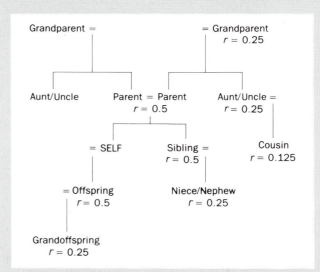

A pedigree showing how a central individual ('SELF') is related to various individuals (e.g. parent, sibling and cousin) with the coefficient of relationship, r, indicated.

might lead to the evolution of other mechanisms of *kin recognition*. These are found in several species, including rhesus macaques. Here, juveniles that are reared apart from birth show a preference for their genetic relatives over unrelated individuals, even though they have never seen any of them before. The mechanism involved is uncertain, but may include similarity of body odours and facial features.

Reciprocal altruism

Another form of altruism, *reciprocal altruism*, may be widespread among primates. There are some interspecific forms of altruism (such as by large fish that refrain from eating the small cleaner fish that clean their teeth) that cannot possibly involve genetic relatedness. Such behaviour could evolve if both parties exchanged mutual benefits on a reciprocated basis. So long as the benefits exchanged are not greater than their costs, the individuals need not be related. Kin selection allows animals to incur a genetic cost if the 'debt' is repaid by an increase in inclusive fitness by helping a relative. Reciprocal altruism allows such a cost to be incurred only if the debt is fully repaid within the benefactor's lifetime. Consequently, although it may be profitable for an animal to sacrifice its life for a relative, it can never afford to do so if the exchange is based simply on reciprocal altruism.

Unrelated male baboons may form coalitions for their mutual protection against more powerful males. In some cases, an animal may help its ally defend an oestrous female against a more dominant male who is trying to take the female for himself. In such cases, the helper does not himself get the chance to mate with the female, but he may be able to count on his ally's support when he is in a similar predicament on a later occasion.

Not all cases of reciprocal altruism need involve an exchange of the same 'commodity': providing the costs and benefits match up, individuals may exchange quite distinct benefits. A male baboon will sometimes form a special relationship with a particular female (see p. 153). Such long-

lasting relationships seem to be based on the fact that the male provides the female and her offspring with protection against higher-ranking members of the group while he benefits from exclusive sexual access to the female. In another example, a low-ranking male chimpanzee supported a second-ranking male against the top-ranking one, so permitting the second-ranking male to become the dominant individual. In return, his low-ranking ally gained access to receptive females that he would not otherwise have enjoyed.

Evolutionarily stable strategies

Sociobiology offers us a great deal more than mere explanations for the evolution of altruistic behaviour. One of its most important concepts is that of an *evolutionarily stable strategy* (ESS). This idea derives from a branch of applied mathematics called *game theory*, and is relevant to the ways in which animals resolve conflicts. It predicts that, in a situation where an animal has a choice of how to behave, then the most profitable option will often depend on what the other individuals in the population are doing.

For example, male gelada baboons (*Theropithecus gelada*) acquire harems of females in two ways. One option is to fight a harem-holder so as to take over his entire harem of five or six females. A second is to join another male's unit as a subordinate *follower* without challenging his ownership; a follower can then build up relationships with one or two peripheral females who make a small harem that eventually separates off from the parent unit. The best strategy is clearly to take over an entire unit, because by so doing a male gains many more breeding females than he can as a follower. However, there are only a limited number of units in the population large enough to be worth fighting for.

Consequently, as an increasing number of males opt to take over a unit, so a male's tenure as harem-holder declines. Reproductive success depends not just on the number of females that a male can mate with on any particular day but also on the time over which he can do so. The initial advantage that a male gains from taking over a large unit is hence soon offset by the fact that he cannot survive for very long as a harem-holder. It then pays some males to become followers.

A balance may be maintained between the two reproductive strategies: if too many males become followers, the pressure on owners of large units is reduced and they hold their harems for longer; this shifts the balance back in their favour, which in turn attracts more males back to the takeover strategy. Natural selection may hence help to account for some of the diversity of behaviour that we see in primate societies.   *Robin Dunbar*

Animals that regularly come to each other's aid when one of them gets involved in a fight are said to form a coalition. Here, two one-male units of gelada baboons confront each other. The holder of the harem and his adult 'follower' male threaten the male of another unit (on the right), while their females line up in their 'attack shadow' behind them (to the left).

See also 'Mating and parental care' (p. 150)

2. PRIMATE AGGRESSION

We often think of aggression in humans as being abnormal, violent behaviour. However, it is a normal, common and adaptive facet of the behaviour of animals and plays a fundamental part in primate social life. It is not related to any predatory bloodthirstiness; the most confirmed vegetarian can be aggressive when necessary.

Violence is just one form of aggressive behaviour in primates. Much aggression is a harmless threat, a mild assertion of ownership of a disputed resource. The threats usually combine visual and vocal displays. A male squirrel monkey (*Saimiri sciureus*), for example, shows off his erect penis and a gorilla beats his chest and hoots. Ring-tailed lemurs (*Lemur catta*) engage in a 'stink-fight', each male smearing a scent on his tail, which he waves conspicuously in the air. Sometimes, the aggression escalates to physical contact, such as hitting and biting and the combatants can suffer serious injury. In many species, adult males have higher mortality rates than females, in part because of fatal injuries incurred in such fights.

Konrad Lorenz's view that animals avoid physical fighting, using displays to settle a dispute, is too simple. Rather, whether animals display or fight depends on the costs and benefits of doing so: on how much the individual values the resource being fought over, how likely he or she is to win and the costs of fighting (such as the risk of being injured). For example, when only one female in the troop is in oestrus, male savanna or yellow baboons (*Papio cynocephalus*) fight more frequently and fiercely than when several females are available.

Dominance—subordinance relationships are a feature of many primate groups. By a

Two older adult female Hanuman langurs charge an adolescent male to retrieve an infant he has snatched and wounded.

show of aggression, high-ranking individuals can displace those of lower rank from food, water, a sleeping site, a social partner and a mate. Sometimes no aggression is involved; a subordinate may move away from a more dominant individual before a threat is necessary. Those with high ranks often benefit from their status. Dominant vervets (*Cercopithecus aethiops*) have priority over preferred food and dominant male Japanese macaques (*Macaca fuscata*) have the first choice of females in oestrus. High rank can thus sometimes lead to improved breeding success. It does not guarantee such benefits; lower-ranking individuals may get what they want in other ways.

Dominance relationships in primates are also complicated by the fact that individuals can form coalitions and can co-operate to defeat a higher-ranking animal (see p. 147). Males sometimes buffer themselves from aggression by carrying an infant, which deflects the attack of another male.

Another way in which aggression can improve reproductive success is through infanticide. Among some primates, including langurs (*Presbytis*), colobus (*Colobus*), guenons (*Cercopithecus*) and howler monkeys (*Alouatta*), males taking over a new troop, or after a change in a dominance hierarchy, may kill young infants already in the group. Once their infants are dead, the females soon come into oestrus again, allowing the new dominant males to sire their own offspring.

The level of aggression between groups of primates is variable, both within and between species. It depends largely on the rewards and difficulties of defending the home range and it generally takes the form of visual and vocal displays rather than physical contact. Vervet monkeys, for

example, crash noisily through the branches of trees and show off their white chests, canine teeth and penises. Many species, particularly territorial ones, have calls used to communicate with other groups, such as the dawn chorusing of mantled howler monkeys (*Alouatta palliata*). Less often, groups come to blows. For example, chimpanzees sometimes chase and kill members of another community.

How aggressive and how dominant a primate is depends on several things. Youngsters become more involved in aggressive encounters as they grow up, as they start to compete for food and social partners and as they join more in the social life of the group. Some of the aggression inflicted upon them by their older relatives may be punishment for unacceptable behaviour.

Gender has an effect, but not a simple one. Male toque macaques (*Macaca sinica*) are more frequently aggressive than females but among rhesus macaques (*M. mulatta*) the reverse is true, while female pigtail macaques (*M. nemestrina*) are involved in more frequent, but less damaging, aggression than males. Female aggression may just be minor squabbles over food whereas males will fight intensely over mates.

Kinship is important; young females often stay in the group with their female relatives while males emigrate, so that females form stronger bonds and come into conflict more often than do males. Within these matrilines, the initial rank of a young female often depends on her mother's rank, the daughter gaining the support of her mother in disputes that she might not win alone. Among baboons and langurs, the daughter eventually comes to outrank her mother, but among macaques the mother continues to dominate her adult

An adult male silverback mountain gorilla hoots during a vigorous threat display.

daughters and the younger daughters rise in rank above their older sisters. Males, on the other hand, form dominance relationships based on their own fighting abilities and their ranks change with time.

Reproductive hormones have only a small effect on the aggressiveness of primates. There are some changes with the oestrous cycle, aggression peaking at ovulation (rhesus macaques) or just before it (ruffed lemurs, *Varecia variegata*), but these may relate to the social contact the females have. Among males, testosterone has a minor role in aggressiveness and

(Right) An adult male baboon injured in a fight.

(Below) Two adult male gelada baboons fighting. As in many other primates, adult males have higher mortality rates than females, in part because of fatal injuries incurred in such fights.

Violent behaviour can easily be triggered when people demonstrate in a crowd.

status. Experience and social factors are far more important in determining the winner of a fight. On the other hand, hormone secretion can be changed by fighting; levels of testosterone in rhesus males rise as they become more dominant and fall when they lose rank. Adrenal hormones are also at low levels in dominant males and young rhesus monkeys with low levels are more likely to win fights than those with high levels.

Contrary to Lorenz's ideas and to popular belief, animals, including primates, do not have an aggressive drive that builds up inside them and that has to be worked off by fighting. Neither is aggression a simple response to pain or frustration. Internal motivation and external cues, such as the desirability of a disputed resource and indicators of the fighting ability of the opponent, regulate when and how much fighting there is. The social environment may also be important: a male may defer to another individual when alone but attack him when he has allies present.

Although there are genetic effects on the levels of aggressive behaviour, in social animals such as primates the environment in which the young animal grows up is likely to be much more important. A young primate may learn what rank to assume from the way other individuals behave towards it. Play fighting also gives clues about the individual's own fighting ability.

There are some similarities between humans and other primates in aspects of aggressive behaviour, such as facial expressions and the ability to form dominance relationships and coalitions. However, primates are very variable in, for example, territorial aggression, and there is no norm to which humans might be expected to conform. As in other primates, biological factors such as levels of hormones, brain activity and physiological arousal have a minor effect on the differences in aggression among people. Gender is also important, with women being less likely than men to come to blows. Genes may also have a small influence, but our childhood environment is far more important. Individuals who are beaten as children tend to use violence themselves as adults, perhaps because they have learnt that this is acceptable.

Humans, however, are very different from other primates in the development of culture and particularly in the use of language to justify, condemn and plan violence. Although our aggressive behaviour may have its roots in our biological past, social, economic and political factors are now far more important than biological ones in controlling human aggression. *A.K. Turner*

See also 'Mating and parental care' (p. 150), 'Home range and territory' (p. 155) and 'Facial patterns as signals and masks' (p. 161)

Mating and parental care

Mating and parental care are the keys to successful reproduction. There is, however, a clear difference in the weight placed on them by the two sexes. Female primates must make a substantial commitment of time and energy to pregnancy and lactation once they have conceived. This investment naturally leads females to emphasise parental care. Males, on the other hand, are not directly constrained by the needs of the developing offspring, and, in principle at least, are free to concentrate entirely on mating. Because one male can fertilise many females, there should be a natural tendency towards *polygyny* (one male mating with several females) whenever other factors do not prevent it.

Whether or not a male can behave promiscuously depends on the ecological and social strategies of the females. The most important factor is the pattern of female distribution, as this determines the extent to which a male can prevent other males from mating with them. Female dispersion is determined by the balance between two counteracting factors – predation and food. Risk of predation may promote the formation of large groups as a form of defence, and the competition over limited food sources that may result from crowding favours the dispersion of animals into smaller groups.

Common types of primate mating systems. **(Top left)** In many of the prosimians (galagos and lemurs), as well as the orang-utan, males and females (accompanied by their dependent young) live solitarily, each in its own territory. Male territories are larger than those of the females, and typically overlap the territories of two to three females, so giving the male sexual access to several females. **(Top centre)** If the male forms a permanent pairbond with a female in this situation, the result is monogamy, as seen in gibbons and some of the smaller South American cebid monkeys. **(Top right)** In the marmosets and tamarins, several males may join a female on her territory, so giving rise to polyandry. **(Lower left)** When females prefer to live in relatively large groups, more males are attracted into the group and this produces the multimale/multifemale groups seen in baboons and macaques. **(Lower centre)** Where females live in smaller groups, a single male may be able to prevent other males from joining the group, as in the one-male groups typical of the langurs and some of the African guenons. **(Lower right)** In the chimpanzee, brothers band together to defend a large joint territory, and this gives them access to more females, each of whom lives in her own separate territory.

Females on their own

When there is little predation, females may space out to minimise feeding competition. If the females' ranges are small enough, a male may be able to defend an area with several females in it, thus achieving a form of polygyny. Such a mating system is typical only of more primitive nocturnal primates, such as mouse lemurs (*Microcebus*) and bushbabies (*Galago*), which are largely solitary.

If, on the other hand, females are very widely dispersed, a male may be unable to defend more than one female at a time and *monogamy* may result. The slow-moving potto (*Perodicticus*), for example, is probably forced into monogamy. Monogamy, however, is relatively rare among primates, as in nearly all mammals. It has been reliably reported only in four groups of non-human primates: in gibbons, in some Old World monkeys, in some South American monkeys and in some Malagasy lemurs. Of these, only gibbons and some lemurs seem to be obligatory monogamists. The South American marmosets and tamarins, for example, may vary from monogamy to polygyny and even *polyandry* (one female with several males) (see Box 1).

Opinions differ as to why primates might mate monogamously. One hypothesis is that males form a monogamous pairbond with a particular female whenever the sizes of the females' territories are so large that the males cannot defend an area large enough to contain the ranges of more than one female. If they could do so, they would and the result would be polygamy, with the male and females living more or less solitary lives even though they occupy the same ranging area, as occurs among galagos and orang-utans.

A second hypothesis argues that, because adequate food is the most important factor determining a female's ability to reproduce successfully, a male may himself be able to reproduce more effectively if he defends a territory, so

Male marmosets and tamarins, like this golden lion tamarin (*Leontopithecus rosalia*), are mainly responsible for carrying and caring for the twin infants.

ensuring that his female has access to an exclusive food supply. A third possibility is that females that give birth to relatively large infants need help from a male to rear them. This is all the more necessary if she normally produces twins (as many small primates do). A final suggestion is that males benefit reproductively if they protect their offspring, either against predators or against other males who might kill them off in order to breed with the female.

Although there is evidence in support of all four theories, the last one seems the most likely. Infanticide has been observed in many primates and it is the only explanation of why the male should stay with the female all the time in large species that are at little risk of being caught by predators. On the other hand, eagles and snakes often prey on small monkeys such as marmosets and tamarins. A female of these species would find it almost impossible to escape from an attack while carrying twin offspring on her back, and it is surely no accident that the male often carries the infants in these species.

Thus, monogamy appears to evolve when the females choose to space out and live singly for ecological reasons. They benefit by having a male around to reduce the risks that their infants run from being killed by predators or by competitors.

A monogamous pair of titi-monkeys (*Callicebus*).

Females in groups

Because most diurnal primates are attacked by predators, females do better by living in groups for protection. Whenever this is the case, males compete for control over the groups of females. If groups are small (less than about 10 females), a dominant male may be able to keep other competitors away and thus monopolise matings with the group. *One-male groups* of this kind are probably the commonest form of primate mating system, as most species live in small groups in forests. However, primates living in more open country, such as baboons (*Papio*) and macaques (*Macaca*), are exposed to much greater risks of predation and tend to live in larger groups. As groups become larger, a male is unable to prevent other males from joining his group and there may be a shift from polygyny with defence of a harem to the defence of individual females as they become receptive to mating in *multimale groups*.

Competition for access to females inevitably means that some males are prevented from mating. In the large multi-male groups of baboons and macaques, males are usually arranged in a *dominance hierarchy* on the basis of fighting ability, and most matings are performed by the one or two top-ranking males. A males's rank tends to rise until he reaches his prime and then decline as old age sets in. Because mating success depends on rank, his reproductive activity also shows a rise and fall. In species that form single-male groups, on the other hand, a male can mate only while he has control over a group of females. In some, like the langurs (*Presbytis*) of Asia, males who have been ousted from their groups in a takeover fight may try to acquire control of another group. In other cases, such as the gelada baboon (*Theropithecus gelada*) of East Africa, a male gets only one opportunity to own a harem during his lifetime.

As males may suffer long periods when they have difficulty in obtaining a mate, alternative ways of gaining access to females have evolved. In the multimale groups typical of baboons, low-ranking males often try to establish special friendships with particular females. These relationships involve intense grooming and persist over many years, in contrast to the normal mating ties of dominant males, which last for a few days at most. The male provides support for his female and for her offspring whenever they are attacked by other members of the group; in return, the male is usually granted privileged access to the female when she comes into oestrus. High-ranking males often try to usurp this privilege, but are seldom successful because the female refuses to co-operate and may move with her preferred partner to the edge of the group where they are less conspicuous.

In species that form single-male groups, the male's access to his harem may be absolute and exclusive, but his ability to capture and retain a group depends on his prowess. Males which, because of their age or size, are unable to win a group of females by fighting must try other methods if they are to breed. A young male gelada baboon, for example, may join another male's unit as a subordinate *follower* without any sexual access to the females. Once accepted within the unit by the owner, the young male gradually builds up a relationship with one or two of the more peripheral females. These may develop into full sexual rela-

1. SOCIAL CHANGES

Most primates live in social groups. The composition of these varies from a single adult male and female with their young, to many males, females and young, making groups of 60 or more. Within each group, social relationships between and within the sexes and between adults and young have long been studied in the field. The scope of this research has now broadened to include the study of how, when and why animals transfer between groups.

Social behaviour and mating patterns vary widely between species and, in some instances, between populations of the same species. Within the social group, males and females interact at different rates, with characteristically different styles of interaction. Finally, individuals of each sex in a group often behave quite differently from one another. In some species, only one or a few individuals mate. The others are excluded from breeding, either through competition with animals of the same sex or because they are too young, too old or too new to the group to be acceptable as mates.

This hierarchy of differentiation between species, populations, sexes and individuals of the same sex has been documented over thousands of hours of observation by many researchers. Three species illustrate the richness and diversity of the information that is emerging from this research: the saddle-back tamarin (*Saguinus fuscicollis*) from South America,

and the common chimpanzee (*Pan troglodytes*) and savanna or yellow baboon (*Papio cynocephalus*) from Africa.

Saddle-back tamarins live in groups containing up to 12 individuals. These groups were once thought to represent a monogamous adult pair with their maturing young, and young transients who move from group to group until they find a mate and a vacant patch of forest. However, it is now known that in many of these groups the relationship betwen males and females is *polyandrous*, not monogamous.

In a polyandrous mating system, two or more males mate with a single female. Saddle-back tamarin males also help the female raise her young. Females typically have twins. From soon after birth, they are carried by the males and are retrieved by the mother only to be nursed. The young leave their parents as they approach adulthood. A co-operative, community breeding system of this kind probably exists in other closely related South American monkeys as well, but it has no known parallels among the Old World primates.

Among chimpanzees, males constitute the core of the group. Often they are brothers, half-brothers, or fathers and sons. Male chimpanzees frequently move, feed and groom together, and jointly defend the boundaries of their range against males in neighbouring groups. Although they can be ranked in a

A group of female common chimpanzees foraging with their young in a mangrove swamp.

tionships and the young follower and his females eventually constitute a 'unit within a unit'. About 2 years after first joining the group, the follower and the females who bear him allegiance may leave to set up an independent unit of their own.

These alternative reproductive modes may be temporary, being pursued only by males at times during their lives when they are unable to follow the species' normal strategy. Male baboons, for example, tend to form special friendships early and late in life, but monopolise oestrous females when they achieve high rank during their physical prime. In other cases, alternative strategies may be equally effective in creating opportunities to reproduce. Male gelada baboons gain more females by taking over an entire unit than by becoming followers, but their very size makes such units susceptible to take-over, so that such males cannot retain control over their harems for as long as followers can. These differences usually cancel out over a reproductive lifetime, so that males do equally well by pursuing either way of acquiring females with whom to breed.

dominance hierarchy based on the direction of aggression between individuals, aggression is in fact quite rare within groups and most interactions seem to reinforce affiliative bonds.

Male chimpanzees share their range with females, but only associate closely with them during periods of female sexual receptivity. Females spend much of their time foraging with their young, without other adult company of either sex, and, unlike males, maturing females usually leave the group in which they were born and join another. Individual females show different mating preferences: some mate repeatedly with just one male, whereas others mate with several males in quick succession.

The social groups of baboons are much more spatially cohesive than those of chimpanzees, and females are at their core. Female social relationships with one another are strongly influenced by their biological relatedness: biologically closely related females, such as mothers and daughters or sisters, tend to forage, rest and groom together, and to support one another against other, less closely related animals.

Adult female baboons can be ranked in a social hierarchy. Usually a female's daughters rank immediately below their mother and above all other females to whom their mother is dominant. Among the sisters, there is often an inverse relationship between rank and birth order, with the eldest sister ranking lowest and the youngest sister ranking highest. If birth rates and survival rates are high, these *matrilineal groups* can be quite large.

In contrast to males, which transfer to another group as they approach maturity, female baboons usually spend their lives in the social group into which they were born. Maturing males may try to join groups into which their brothers, half-brothers or old playmates have already transferred, but as adults they usually have far fewer close kin around them than do females. Rates of aggression are higher between males than between females. Like females, males can be ranked in a dominance hierarchy, but a male's position in that hierarchy seems to be determined by many attributes, including his age, health, fighting ability, confidence, length of residence in the group, and ability to form alliances with other males.

The determinants of mating success of male baboons and of mate choice by females are complex. The early belief that the biggest, fiercest males were the most successful breeders has given way to the recognition that other factors, such as a male's success in forming friendly relations with females, may be important in determining whether he will be acceptable as a mate.

A.F. Richard

Parental care

An infant primate depends on its mother for all its food for 2 to 6 months after birth, depending on its size. Although it then begins to feed for itself, it may continue to take milk for some time. Most primate infants are carried by their mothers for a further 6 to 12 months and will depend on them (and perhaps on other close relatives) for support during fights or for protection against danger for another 3 to 4 years. This imposes a considerable burden on the female. During lactation, in particular, the energetic demands on the female are so high that she is usually unable to begin another pregnancy and does not become fertile until well after the previous infant can look after itself.

A female must maximise her lifetime production of young by finding the right balance between providing each offspring with enough care to reach maturity and giving it so much as to cause undue delay to her next conception. She might even vary her investment in an offspring according to its ability to produce descendants. For example, males often leave their natal groups to reproduce, and, because their success depends on size, a female may be expected to invest quite heavily in her sons to ensure that they are as large as possible when adult. On the other hand, daughters, which often remain with and support their mothers, may be especially valuable to the mother when her dominance rank declines with age. Hence it may sometimes be important for females to invest in daughters rather than sons.

Females of some species such as baboons and rhesus macaques have a longer interbirth interval (and hence invest more time and energy in each infant) after giving birth to a daughter than they do after bearing a son. We cannot yet estimate what the optimum behaviour for a female might be, but it is clear that this will vary with a species' ecological and social strategies.

Although females are largely responsible for parental care, males sometimes play an important part. For example, male marmosets and tamarins normally take on the larger share of the responsibility for carrying and caring for

An adult female savanna baboon (second from right) with an adult male 'friend' (left, behind), her juvenile daughter (right) and newborn infant.

2. HUMAN MATING PATTERNS

Primate reproductive systems are diverse and flexible, so we should not be surprised to find that the same is true of humans. Although we understand little about the evolution of mating systems, they must be related to the particular biological circumstances of each species. For example, the lengthy dependence of human infants imposes severe demands on the mother, who usually requires help to rear her large-brained and slow-growing offspring. Pairbonding and monogamous mating patterns in humans might hence have evolved to provide the female with an assistant. Polygyny could then evolve only where males command sufficient resources to provide for the needs of several females at once.

Some evidence for this idea is that monogamy or *serial polygamy* (having only one partner at a time, even though men and women may have several different partners over their lifetime) is the norm in hunter-gatherer societies that have little surplus wealth, whereas polygyny (one man with several wives) is common in agricultural societies where some males can accumulate wealth.

However, this simple theory has three main drawbacks. First, there is a chicken-and-egg problem: how could we have evolved large-brained, slow-growing infants before males became pairbonded helpers? The second is that there is no good biological reason why a helper should have to be the father; the mother's sister may be just as effective. But perhaps the greatest difficulty is that it runs counter to the behavioural and anatomical evidence suggesting that in recent evolutionary history humans were predominantly polygamous.

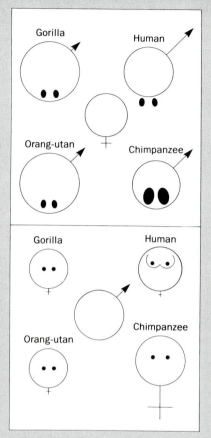

The anatomical evidence includes our striking sexual dimorphism in body size and in characters relating to reproduction and sexual display, such as the distribution and abundance of body hair in males. These are features of species that mate polygamously, not only among primates but also among mammals in general. Human males have relatively small testes, indicating adaptation for one-male groups, such as harems.

The behavioural evidence includes the disparities in the numbers of offspring sired by different males in societies ranging from hunter-gatherers to modern-day Americans. The wealthiest or most powerful men often have the most wives and concubines, and produce the most children. Among the Ache Indians of Paraguay, for example, the women openly court the best hunters as lovers, even though they risk terrible penalties if caught doing so by their husbands.

The final lesson, however, must be that there can be no such thing as a 'biologically' best way of doing things, especially when it comes to reproductive behaviour. Mating systems in all species are a product of negotiation between the sexes. As a result, they can change as circumstances change; and different individuals can pursue different mating patterns within the same social group.

Robin Dunbar

Genital size in relation to body size for great apes and humans. The top four outer circles show the body sizes of males relative to the size of a typical female, as well as the relative sizes of the testes and the erect penis (arrow on circle). The lower four outer circles show the body size of females relative to the size of a typical male, and the relative development of the perineum before the first pregnancy (cross beneath circle) and the mammary glands. Testis size increases as males have to compete more directly with each other for females.

the twin infants; with older young, the female has them only for a few minutes at a time to suckle them.

Even in species that mate polygamously, males may help to rear the young. They may protect them from predation, either by keeping watch or, in rare cases, by driving predators away. Males may also help to protect infants and juveniles from aggression by other members of the group.

This is especially likely in cases where the male has a close social relationship with the mother, as in special friendships between a male and female baboon (see Box 1).

Robin Dunbar

See also 'Social behaviour and evolutionary theory' (p. 145) and 'Home range and territory' (p. 155)

Home range and territory

Primates have a wide variety of ranging behaviours. The areas in which they confine their general day-to-day activities (their *home ranges*) can vary in size, differ in the degree to which they are defended against other members of the same species, and may or may not change during an individual's lifetime. Many of these differences are closely tied to differences in mating patterns, breeding system, body size and diet, both within and between species.

Whether a primate changes its home range during its lifetime varies according to both species and sex. Some primates, such as sportive lemurs (*Lepilemur*), live a solitary existence and others, such as gibbons (*Hylobates*), live in monogamous family units. In these species, movement at maturation by either sex to a new home range is usual. Parents may also help their offspring, particularly their daughters, to gain access to adjacent home ranges.

However, most primate species live in stable groups containing several adult females and one or more adult males. In these cases, females usually remain in their natal group, whereas males disperse at maturity and seek breeding opportunities elsewhere, possibly in a neighbouring troup with an adjacent home range. Macaques (*Macaca*), baboons (*Papio*) and langurs (*Presbytis*) provide familiar examples of such behaviour.

Why males disperse is uncertain, but dispersal may provide mechanisms for avoidance of inbreeding: females may not accept close relatives as mates because their inbred offspring would be unfit. In those species in which males hold harems, such as many langurs, supernumerary adult males that have left their natal group may join together in a bachelor male band while each individual awaits an opportunity to become master of a harem. But in species in which more than one adult male lives with a group of females, such as olive baboons (*Papio anubis*), it is not unusual for dominant males to transfer between breeding groups so that they are present in the one in which most mating opportunities occur at any time.

Defence

Individuals or groups of most primates actively defend part or all of their home range against other members of their own species. Those that defend the whole of their range are referred to as *territorial*. Territories are defended with displays, vocalisations and interactions. For example, adult gibbons defend their territory against incursions by other gibbons, particularly adult members of the same sex. At the other extreme, some species, such as baboons, have an extensive area of overlap between home ranges, within which groups usually avoid each other. An intermediate

situation is provided by some species of langur, in which one of two groups in the area where the home ranges overlap is dominant over the other.

The degree of territoriality may depend on the costs and benefits of defending resources, in each case. For example, defence of parts of their home range by chacma baboons (*Papio ursinus*) is rare, and is usually associated only with the defence of scarce water resources. The costs of territoriality (such as expenditure of time or energy) depend on the predictability and stability of the resource involved in time and space: in general, primates defend their range only if the distribution of food makes such defence feasible. Thus, when food supplies are dense and evenly distributed, individuals may be dispersed singly or in small groups that defend feeding territories. In contrast, species living on locally abundant but short-lived and clumped resources frequently live in large groups that do not defend feeding territories, as feeding interference at a clump is unimportant.

For example, in the tropical forests of southeastern Peru, tamarins (*Saguinus*), which eat a variety of uniformly distributed and predictable fruits, defend territories – presumably to reduce feeding interference by other tamarins. But in the same forests, squirrel monkeys (*Saimiri*), which specialise in eating figs, gather in large numbers on a single tree. This is probably because figs ripen in large, concentrated and unpredictable patches, which are uneconomic

Male gibbons defend the territorial rights of their family group by singing loudly, usually in the dark just before sunrise. A song bout can last from 10 minutes up to 2 hours. Here, a male Kloss's gibbon (*Hylobates klossii*) in the rain forests of Mentawai Islands, western Sumatra, sings on a platform near the edge of his territory, while his mate probes for insects and their offspring collects ants on the back of his hand.

to defend. When conditions change so that food clumps become smaller and feeding interference is more likely, primate groups may temporarily split into smaller feeding units. Spider monkeys (*Ateles*), baboons and chimpanzees (*Pan*) all do this on occasion.

Range size

The area of primate home ranges varies from less than 0.2 hectares (for lesser mouse lemurs, *Microcebus murinus*) up to more than 50 square kilometres (for patas monkeys, *Erythrocebus patas*). Why is there such variation? Perhaps the size of the home range is the minimum needed to provide a group's food. Comparative studies of several primate species have provided tests of the predictions of this dietary hypothesis.

Large species, or those living in large groups, should tend to occupy large home ranges; similarly, species living on rare food should also have large ranges. We would therefore predict that large-bodied consumers of fruit or insects living in large groups (such as chimpanzees, baboons or patas monkeys) will range over large areas, whereas small-bodied leaf-eaters living in small groups (such as sportive lemurs) should occupy the smallest ranges or territories. And, indeed, these crude predictions are true.

However, at a finer level, such predictions are not so well satisfied. As Kleiber's law shows, the energy needs of individual mammals increase with (approximately) the three-quarters power of body weight and, for animals of the same weight, the energy needs of a group increase in direct proportion to group size. In fact, the observed relationship between body size and home range is that the latter increases much more rapidly in larger animals than expected on a simple energetic prediction. This does not mean that the energetic hypothesis is totally wrong; after all, the crude predictions hold up. Perhaps the difference between the observed and expected values arises because large primates living in large groups have to travel between food patches, whereas the smaller primates in smaller groups can spend their lives within a single patch. This means that the ranges occupied by the more energetically needy groups contain disproportionately large sections in which there is little or no food.

Comparisons between species also show that other factors can be important. For a given body weight, terrestrial species have larger home ranges than arboreal species, perhaps because the latter can move in three dimensions and do not need to cover as large an area to gather food. Similarly, diurnal species tend to have larger home ranges than do nocturnal ones, possibly because the difficulties and risks of foraging in an unfamiliar area restrict the home range of species that feed at night.

Although comparisons between species have demonstrated, at least in general terms, some factors that may affect primate ranging behaviour, there is also considerable

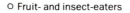
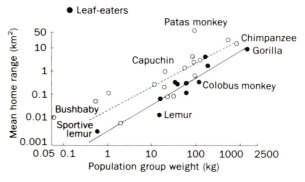

Theory predicts that large-bodied primates that are consumers of fruit or insects and live in large groups (e.g. chimpanzees, baboons and patas monkeys) will range over large areas when feeding, whereas small-bodied leaf-eaters (e.g. sportive lemurs) will occupy the smallest home ranges or territories. This is found to be the case when the average areas of home ranges and the weight of the population living in each home range are compared.

variation in the size of home ranges within species. Such intraspecific variation may be explicable in the same way. The abundance and distribution of food and resources may be particularly important; for example, individuals or groups in areas where there is little food tend to have large home ranges, and home ranges tend to vary in size over the year according to the availability of food.

Type of habitat, predation, access to water, disease and social factors (particularly intraspecific competition and access to mates) also influence ranging behaviour. For example, savanna baboons (*Papio*) forage in small groups during the day, but gather together in groups sometimes containing several hundred individuals each evening at sites that are relatively safe from predators.

Home range and human evolution

A recently recognised correlate of primate ranging behaviour may have particular implications for understanding human evolution. Those primates with relatively large brains have large home ranges, perhaps because species with large home ranges need to remember complex information about food distribution. Perhaps the selective forces that lead to an increased home-range size, such as a shift to a widely distributed, often clumped and variable food source (e.g. ripe fruit), could also select for increased brain size, such as that that occurred in the human lineage. A shift to such a food source might also entail the development of a flexible social system, with individuals frequently ranging widely but also grouping when possible at food sources. Paul Feuerbach's claim that 'you are what you eat' may be very relevant to the origins of modern humans.

Paul H. Harvey
Andrew F. Read

See also 'Body size and energy requirements' (p. 41), 'Mating and parental care' (p. 150) and 'Smell as a signal' (p. 157)

Smell as a signal

Most mammals have a highly developed sense of smell and use olfactory signals in social communication. In primates, communication by smell is most prevalent among prosimians, although it is developed to some extent among New World monkeys. Old World monkeys, apes and humans (catarrhines) have a markedly reduced sense of smell and do not use this mode of communication a great deal, although such signals may be important in some social contexts.

Visual or vocal signals are instantaneous and can change rapidly, but olfactory communication is relatively slow and probably cannot transmit complex information. However, once a chemical signal has been emitted, it can spread in all directions and may persist. The animal leaving the signal may have moved on long before the signal is perceived by another individual, and the intensity of the odour may indicate to the perceiver when the signal was deposited.

Olfactory cues can allow mammals to distinguish species, individual, sex, sexual condition, group or kinship identity, relative dominance and emotional state. Although much work remains to be done on olfactory communication in primates, it seems that scent is most frequently used for interindividual and intergroup spacing, dominance and combative (agonistic) interactions, and as an indicator of sexual state.

Scent dispersion may be an incidental feature of a primate's behaviour, or it may involve a characteristic pattern of scent marking. The scent may be simply released into the air or deposited onto a substrate – voluntarily or involuntarily – by the animal releasing the scent. Olfactory signals typically originate from sources such as the urine, faeces, saliva, and labial (lip) and anogenital glands.

Prosimians, and to a lesser extent New World monkeys, also have specialised skin glands for marking, which are mostly on the neck, upper limbs and chest. Unspecialised skin glands may also be used for marking. In many New World monkeys, scent marking using the neck, chest and anogenital glands or with urine is common. In general, olfactory communication among Old World monkeys and apes is an incidental behaviour that does not involve specialised scent glands.

The forms, functions and social context of olfactory communication in primates can best be illustrated by examples, and these are now available for most major primate groups.

Nocturnal prosimians

Most prosimians spend much of their time scent marking, usually with urine. All members of the loris group regularly mark in this way; some lemurs urine mark regularly but others do so only rarely. Lorises and bushbabies have highly stereotyped patterns of urine marking and use this as a means of social communication. There have been various interpretations of such behaviour, which have included cleaning hands and feet or moistening them for a better grip, spatial orientation and cooling, but these are based largely on observations of captive animals. The most thorough study of urine marking in the wild has been on Allen's bushbaby (*Galago alleni*) in Gabon, West Africa, using a radiotracker to record urination.

In most bushbabies, as well as in many New World monkeys, urine marking is performed by bringing a hind-foot forwards under the penis or clitoris, with the sole turned upwards, urinating on the foot and rubbing this with the hand. Lorises normally deposit urine in droplets on the substrate, either directly or in several jerky movements ('rhythmic micturation').

Female Allen's bushbabies live in groups, which share a common range and sometimes nest together. Different groups of females have separate home ranges with borders that overlap slightly. Females visit overlapping borders at least once a week and mark almost four times more often at the borders of their ranges than in the centre and make a social 'croaking' call eight times more often during border

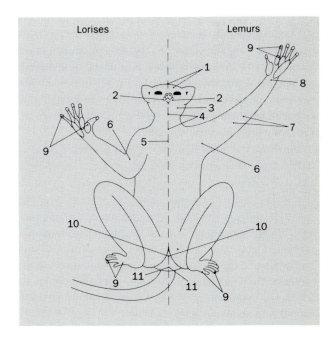

Distribution of the specialised skin (cutaneous) glands used for scent marking by prosimians: 1, unspecialised glands of the crown and forehead; 2, glands of the lips; 3, submaxillary glands; 4, neck glands; 5, chest glands; 6, brachial glands; 7, glands of the elbow region; 8, antebrachial glands; 9, unspecialised glands of the hands and feet; 10, glands of the external genitalia; 11, glands of the anal region.

visits than at other times. This is the only loud vocalisation that is answered in kind by conspecifics.

Male bushbabies have ranges that overlap with those of one or more female groups, but not with those of other adult males. When they are not feeding, males spend most of their time visiting females and looking out for neighbouring males in limited areas. Males urine mark and croak much more frequently in the zones of overlap between their home ranges. Furthermore, males spend most of their time near zones of overlap of female home ranges, where female marking is most frequent and where they have the greatest chance of encountering a female.

Urine marking in nocturnal prosimians may act mainly to maintain distance between males and to maintain social contact between males and females, especially during oestrus. The earlier theories of why these animals use urine marking seem to be wrong.

Diurnal prosimians

Although they have good eyesight, the diurnal prosimians of Madagascar nonetheless have a strong sense of smell, and many of them have a complex repertoire of stereotyped and ritualised scent marking. All diurnal primates (except orang-utans) live in relatively permanent social groups and scent is important in communication between groups and individuals.

Olfactory communication has been studied in detail in two diurnal lemurs – the brown lemur (*Lemur fulvus*) and the ring-tailed lemur (*L. catta*). The brown lemur has many large and specialised scent glands, especially in the scalp, on the scrotum and in the anogenital region. The most conspicuous, stereotyped marking occurs when a male or female sniffs a vertical branch or another member of the species and then turns around, backs up, and rubs its hindquarters on the object. Usually the legs are raised and suspended in mid-air while the lemur grips the support with its hands. Male brown lemurs may also rub their foreheads and hands against such objects.

Wild brown lemurs mark during sexual behaviour, as an alarm response to humans, during intergroup encounters, and spontaneously during undisturbed movement. Olfactory marking and anogenital sniffing of females by males increases during the brief breeding season. These prosimians can identify the identity and sex of a conspecific solely by scent.

Ring-tailed lemurs scent mark with secretions of the forearm and brachial (chest) glands as well as with the anogenital region, and combine scent with visual communication more than any other primate. Brachial marking involves a rhythmic rubbing of the inner surfaces of the forearms on suitable supports. Sometimes the forearm is rubbed against the chest to mix the glandular secretions, or the tail is rubbed between the arms, thus impregnating it with scent. The glandular zone of the male

Brown lemurs and ring-tailed lemurs mark with scent glands in the anogenital region. Here, a ring-tailed lemur marks a branch in a tree. Ring-tailed lemurs often perform elaborate stereotyped behaviours when scent marking and thus combine visual with olfactory communication. Ring-tails normally use anogenital marking during agonistic (e.g. injurious or intimidating) encounters with members of their own or a different social group, and as a displacement activity when an animal is nervous.

forearm bears a hardened spur on its internal border and when a male marks a branch he leaves a scratch mark visible over a distance of several metres as well as his odour. The mark serves as both an olfactory and a visual signal.

Male ring-tailed lemurs mainly brachial mark in areas bordering a neighbouring group and near the centre of the group's home range. Adult males leave the group during its midday siesta for a 'marking period' lasting from 2 to 20 minutes, when they actively mark adjacent branches.

Males also perform stereotyped brachial marking during agonistic encounters. Tail marking is used exclusively in such encounters, usually between males. After the male anoints its tail, it is brought over the head and shaken in the air, perhaps to disperse the odour. The tail wave of a dominant male can send two subordinate adult males running for the bushes. During the breeding season, the frequency of brachial marking in captive males decreases, while that of tail waving reaches a maximum.

Both males and females mark with their anogenital glands, mainly during intergroup or intragroup aggressive encounters and in other tense situations. Females also mark more frequently during oestrus. Marking probably has a sexual significance in ring-tailed lemurs. By contrast, marking during agonistic interactions is a spacing signal and spontaneous marking near group borders probably serves a similar function.

New World monkeys

New World monkeys rely more on olfactory signals than do Old World monkeys and apes, as many species show stereotyped marking behaviours and possess specialised skin glands. Furthermore, unlike Old World monkeys and apes, neotropical primates do not have a large repertoire of facial expressions or visual displays, and they do not show visual signs (such as conspicuous swellings or changes in skin colour) of their reproductive status.

All species of marmosets and tamarins have specialised scent glands in the anogenital area and on the midchest above the sternum (breastbone). The external appearance, internal structure and sexual differentiation of these glands vary among species. Tamarins and marmosets mark with a combination of urine and secretions from glands around the genital organs, but only rarely show sternal marking. The anogenital area is rubbed against a substrate or conspecific. If an animal is highly aroused, it combines anogenital and sternal marking by rubbing its entire ventral surface over the object.

Individuals can identify species, sex, agonistic status and individual from scent marks. Marking often occurs and is easily evoked by a variety of stimuli. Its behavioural functions in marmosets and tamarins, as in other primates, depend on the recipient's experience, the signaler's identity, the social and environmental context, and on other signals.

Marmosets and tamarins have a unique social structure among primates in that one female per group gives birth to young (usually twins) and more than one adult male may remain in the group to help care for them. Females close to giving birth scent mark quite frequently and their mark is very attractive to adult males. This may help strengthen the bonds between group males and the reproductive female, and may also help to raise hormonal levels associated with care in male helpers. In the common marmoset (*Callithrix jacchus*), the level of the hormone prolactin is five times higher in males carrying young than in those without infants (prolactin brings about the full development of the mammary glands and secretion of milk in females). Group cohesion, spacing and territoriality, intergroup and intragroup aggression, parent–infant interactions, sexual arousal, male–female bonding and reproductive synchrony may also be influenced by olfactory messages.

New World monkeys also use olfactory cues in social communication. All species so far studied use olfactory signals, most commonly stereotyped urine marking, which may also involve chest rubbing. Marking in cebids has several functions and similar modes of marking may have different uses in species with different social structures (see Box). For example, in squirrel monkeys (*Saimiri*), females and infants form the centre of the group, whereas males are peripheral; breeding is seasonal and olfactory signals advertise the oestrous condition of females and stimulate appropriate changes in the reproductive physiology and behaviour of males. In contrast, in spider and woolly monkeys males and females do not always forage together and subgroups often form and break up throughout the year; breeding is not seasonal and the sexual condition of females is probably communicated by continuous olfactory signals that alert males to the location of oestrous females.

SOME MARKING BEHAVIOURS OF CEBID MONKEYS

Genus	Mode of scent marking or olfactory communication	Social context or hypothesised function
Callicebus (titi monkeys)	• Genital and nose-to-nose sniffing • Chest marking (sternal gland)	• Initial greeting and precopulatory behaviour • Territorial disputes
Aotus (night or owl monkeys)	• Anogenital and nose-to-nose sniffing • Anogenital rubbing • Urine marking	• Initial encounter, pre-and postcopulatory (sniffing) • Agonistic interactions • Agonistic and tense situations
Saimiri (squirrel monkeys)	• Urine marking • Anogenital rubbing • Chest and sternal gland marking • Genital display	• During breeding season, females mark more, males sniff more; may stimulate synchronisation of breeding • Displacement activity • During agonistic interaction and courtship (genital display)
Cebus (capuchin monkeys)	• Urine marking • Stereotyped anointing of urine of head and shoulders by males • Glands in midline of chest, mainly by males	• Group and self-advertisement by dominant group male • Intergroup spacing • Social interactions between sexes • Agonistic interactions • Advertisements of oestrus and sexual arousal
Alouatta (howler monkeys)	• Urine marking • Stereotyped anointing of urine of head and shoulders by males • Glands in midline of chest, mainly by males	• Intergroup cohesion • Intergroup and intragroup agonistic encounters • Advertisement of oestrus
Ateles (spider monkeys) *Lagothrix* (woolly monkeys)	• Urine marking • Saliva and sternal gland rubbing • Pectoral sniffing	• Intragroup and intergroup agonistic encounters • General arousal • Group cohesion • Advertisement of sexual condition and sexual arousal • Social appeasement
Brachyteles (woolly spider monkey or muriqui)	• Urine marking	• Advertisement of oestrus • Reduce intermale conflict in mating aggregations
Cacajao (uakaris)	• Genital sniffing and licking • Anal rubbing • Urine marking • Sternal rubbing	• Copulation • Greeting • Advertisement of oestrus • Agonistic interactions between males (urine and sternal marking)

We know little about olfactory communication in the other two genera of cebids – the sakis (*Pithecia*) and bearded sakis (*Chiropotes*) – but *Pithecia* has sternal and neck glands.

Old World monkeys, apes and humans

Olfactory communication is probably least developed and utilised in the Old World monkeys, apes and humans although olfaction is quite important in some of them. In most species, there are visible signs of oestrus, or females actively solicit sexual behaviour during this period. However, oestrus is often accompanied by an increase in male sniffing. For example, in the vervet monkey (*Cercopithecus aethiops*), patas monkey (*Erythrocebus patas*), talapoin monkey (*Miopithecus talapoin*) and some macaques (*Macaca*) males often sniff the female's anogenital region and the same is true to a lesser extent in the great apes (chimpanzees, gorillas and orang-utans).

Olfactory cues often indicate female sexual attractiveness to the male: for example, vaginal secretions can stimulate sexual interest in male rhesus macaques (*Macaca mulatta*) and male talapoins become less attracted to females if the olfactory stimulus is removed. Females then compensate by increasing sexual invitations, so that, although smell plays some part as a sexual cue, it is only one of many signals involved.

The importance of olfactory communication in humans is little studied but we may smell more than we think. Humans have scent, or *apocrine*, glands associated with hair follicles primarily in the underarm, anogenital region, around the nipples, and on the skin of the chest and abdomen. In fact, if we compare humans with chimpanzees and gorillas, there is a great deal of similarity, with all three species having relatively well-developed scent-producing organs.

There is considerable uniformity across cultures in the perception of odours. For example, people from different cultures identify odours and perceive them as pleasant or unpleasant in a similar way. Odour associations, however, are learned and there are few, if any, inherited reactions to smells among humans.

Smells may be more important than we think in human communication. Blind people, such as Helen Keller, have claimed to be able to recognise individuals by their scent. In experiments, people can recognise whether a garment has been worn by a male or female and couples can discriminate between their own or a partner's scent and that of a stranger. Furthermore, human mothers and infants can recognise one another's odours (as can close kin) and synchrony of menstrual cycles in humans may be achieved through olfactory cues.

A reminder of the possible importance of smell in our own society is provided by the sale of perfumes, colognes

An adult male chimpanzee 'inspects' a female by touching her vulva and sniffing his finger. Such genital inspections may occur at any time but are commonest when females do not have sexual swellings.

and deodorants, products designed to cover up our natural body odours.

Smell in primate life

Olfaction in primates can signal individual identity, species identity, sex, reproductive condition, social status and emotional condition. It may also have a function in group cohesion, intergroup and intragroup spacing, parent–offspring recognition, sexual arousal and sexual synchronisation and act as a stimulus for various hormonal changes. In many insects, specific chemicals (termed *pheromones*) trigger very specific responses, so that there is a relatively simple relationship between the olfactory signal and the resulting behaviour.

Pheromones, in this sense, are extremely rare in mammals. Instead, there is usually a loose relationship between the complex message contained in any olfactory signal and the multiplicity of possible responses. The interpretation of an olfactory signal depends on the individual who receives it, on past lifetime experience, on experience with the signaller, and on social context. Most social communication in primates involves many senses and olfactory cues are only one of a complex set of social signals.

R.W. Sussman

See also 'Mating and parental care' (p. 150), 'Home range and territory' (p. 155) and 'Facial patterns as signals and masks' (p. 161)

Facial patterns as signals and masks

All primates, including humans, use their facial features and muscles to generate expressions. Our own perception tends to label facial expressions as outward manifestations of an emotive state; a smile shows happiness. Like many kinds of behaviour, facial expressions help to regulate social relationships. At this level, the smile (or its simian equivalent) is a display that disarms aggression and eases social interactions.

Monkeys, apes and humans share a common repertoire of facial expressions that differ mainly in their intensity or frequency. By contrast, the colours and patterns of faces often differ greatly from species to species or even from one subspecies to another. In some primates, colour and pattern make their expressions easier to see and may give extra emphasis to their grimaces. For other species, this is only a weak effect and, for yet others, face patterns are emphatic masks that suppress, obscure or distract from expression.

Many nocturnal primates – such as lemurs, lorises, bushbabies and night monkeys – have dark eye-mask patterns. Although these are striking to the onlooker, their main function is probably to reduce glare around the hypersensitive but largely colour-blind eyes. Because the upper lips of prosimians are narrow, anchored at the front and well endowed with sensory bristles, facial grimaces are ancillary

to overall body postures and resemble the expressions of small carnivores as much as those of simians.

Although diurnal lemurs have colour vision their bold colouring is still an adjunct of scent, the primary channel for communication. For example, the ring-tailed lemur (*Lemur catta*) scents its tail and waves it about as a dispenser. It reinforces the message with bold black and white rings like a barber's pole.

In most lemurs and many New and Old World monkeys, face markings are subsidiary to bold patterns on the body generally. In many of these species, it is not facial expression, but body posture, scent and vocalisation that are the dominant modes of communication. In some, notably the tamarins, marmosets and squirrel monkeys, a small repertoire of facial expressions may be enhanced by a colour frame to the eyes, mouth or ears or by colourful tufts that can be erected or depressed.

As with many other mammals or birds, these markings make a species immediately recognisable. In forests with several related species living side by side, this may help to maintain the identities of species and groups. In some cases, the distinctive geometry of facial patterns is most prominent in, and has probably evolved as part of species-specific displays. Such displays are particularly important during competition over status, territory, food and mates. They almost certainly inhibit hybridisation between species, although this is not their primary function.

Patterns concentrated on the face are most characteristic of forest-dwelling Old World monkeys and it is in this group of primates that the signal functions of face patterns are most clearly linked to behaviour and ecology. Two groups of Old World monkeys, mandrills and guenons, show how patterns evolved to fit the peculiar needs and circumstances of each species. In both cases, the development of patterns can be reconstructed because a shift into a new environment has generated new problems, which have been solved by opening a visual, colour-coded channel of communication to augment sound, touch and scent.

Mandrills

The forest-dwelling mandrill (*Papio (Mandrillus) sphinx*) is the best-known example of spectacular face colouring – blue muzzle, red nose, white whiskers and orange beard surround the male mandrill's mouth. Long, sharp canines in greatly enlarged jaws are the focus of this colourful confection. All baboon-like primates have similar teeth and jaws and all use frequent and exaggerated yawns as part of their social regulatory system, but no baboon species has a colourful face like that of the mandrill. In common with

Coloured tufts of the cotton-top tamarin (*Saguinus oedipus*) serve to enlarge the size and conspicuousness of the head and make expressive movement of the ears, brow and mouth less ambiguous.

The grimace of the mandrill. This common facial expression is augmented by coloured skin and fur and by a complex structure on the muzzle that simulates a snarl. This expression appears to signify the mandrill's principal mode of greeting.

A male savanna baboon displays his weaponry with an exaggerated yawn.

other well-armed mammalian species, such displays of weaponry actually inhibit aggression (possibly by advertising the risks, even to a more powerful aggressor). Paradoxically, they also enhance cohesion within a multimale society.

For savanna baboons (e.g. *Papio cynocephalus*) and geladas (*Theropithecus gelada*), the clear light of their open habitat renders every movement conspicuous. Even from a distance, prominent grey or black muzzles can be seen to open to reveal a flash of white teeth and pink gums. This is impossible for inhabitants of the dark and heavily obstructed forest floor. The male mandrill's facial colour scheme is adaptive, because blue and red wavelengths travel better at low light levels. The colours and their exact distribution and structuring also have a visual logic that is highly specific to the mandrill. Take the use of red. Modern humans exaggerate the natural flesh colour of their lips by painting them red, to enhance their visibility and attractiveness. Mandrills go further – they have evolved intense scarlet skin on their upper and lower lips, all over the nostrils and along a narrow line up the bridge of the nose.

Analysis of these markings as functional designs suggests that there are several visual effects. Red and pink lips (augmented by white whiskers) surround and advertise the teeth when the mouth is open. When it closes, the circular red nose blob remains a marker for the central focus of the male mandrill's face. The red nasal line, which only develops in mature males, is a measure of its length for,

with a muzzle so cluttered with cheeks, tufts and contrasting colours, its length would otherwise be difficult to perceive.

Like their baboon relatives, mandrills periodically aggregate in multimale troops, sometimes of hundreds of individuals. At other times, small family groups disperse widely so that contact is continuously lost and regained, generally within dense vegetation. In these circumstances, baboon males would be obliged to yawn almost continuously. Wild mandrills are not well studied, but it seems from captive individuals that male mandrills conserve energy by merely raising the lips at the corner of the mouth in what looks like a Kabuki actor's snarl. This ritualised gesture exposes the canines without parting the jaws – it is a low-intensity version of the full yawn and seems to have even less overtly aggressive connotations. A human analogy for this gesture and behaviour is the Maori facial expression known as blustering; indeed, the lips form a similar dumb-bell shape in both of these ritualised 'greetings'.

The muscles that pull open the corners of the mouth lie beneath the furry cheeks and do not produce the blue creases that embellish the mandrill's muzzle (in spite of their similarity to the folds on the muzzle of a snarling dog). In fact, these exaggerated structures are fixed and are built from modifications to the skin and subcutaneous tissue and by inflation of the underlying maxillary bone. The half-sized females have a toned-down version of the blue stripes on a shorter, uninflated muzzle.

The conspicuousness of any structure is influenced by the direction and intensity of the light that falls on it. In forest, the light source is always overhead and its intensity is low, so that upper surfaces are always the best lit. In these conditions, the most conspicuous sign of a ritualised snarl are the wrinkles on the upper surfaces of the muzzle.

The male maxillary sinus continues to enlarge with age until the field of vision is substantially reduced. This may be offset by the greater size and accumulated experience of older males, but there must be other advantages for a device that progressively hampers its possessor. What could these be?

The closeness and unexpectedness of mandrill encounters may favour easy recognition of rank as manifest in the sizes of male muzzle inflation. If so, intermale competition would select for signals that allow age and experience to be assessed. Females might also select males by the same criteria. How are these decisions made? Are mandrills primarily responding to well-established and common primate gestures that have been selected for enhanced sensory impact, or are they responding to a new and elaborate demonstration of fitness?

The first explains the evolution of the signal in terms of the receiver's need for an instantaneous response to a potentially ambiguous situation. By amplifying the visual channel of communication the transmitter uses colour and shape to transform gestures into an instantly evocative signal. The development of appropriate responses to such signals probably needs to be learnt. Because colour and shape combinations are unique and have instant impact, both transmissions and reception use little time and energy. The receivers's eye or ear is the primary selector for signal properties that enhance and may effectively transform a pre-existing mode of communication.

The second interpretation of signal selection suggests

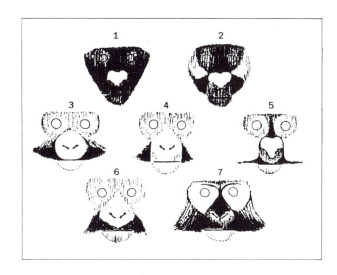

Schematic diagram of the black markings on the faces of seven members of the *Cercopithecus cephus* group. Small alterations in contour can transform the geometry and visual impact of face patterns. 1, *C.(c.) petaurista petaurista*; 2, *C.(c.) petaurista buttikoferi*; 3, *C. (c.) erythrotis*; 4, *C. (c.) sclateri*; 5, *C. (c.) ascanius schmidti*; 6, *C. (c.) cephus*; 7, *C. (c.) ascanius atrinasus*.

that the transmitter advertises an attribute that will impress the viewer with a message of quality. The muzzle is a 'handicap' that flaunts male quality, and the visual medium's power to communicate specific messages is subsidiary to this.

Brighter colouring, 'snarl mimicry' and enlargement of features all elaborate a localised set of cues. Although these have been exaggerated in a specific and idiosyncratic way, they derive from a common primate behavioural sequence that regulates interactions between individuals. In this case, a painted snarl is a more economic and effective message than a monochrome yawn.

The mandrill's ancestral stock and its competitive multimale society originated in the savanna. For such dangerously armed animals, the potential for conflict might have increased in a closed environment. There would have been selection for devices that reduce these dangers and enhance cohesion. The evolution of a permanent blue snarl can be anthropomorphised as the acquisition of a fixed smile in surroundings where the impolite pay a penalty.

Guenons

Another example of brilliant face patterns is found in the African forest guenons belonging to the species group *Cercopithecus cephus*. These small arboreal monkeys are unusual in that each of the five species and many of the 12 subspecies has very different and distinctive face patterns, whereas larger (but close) relatives in the *C. nictitans* group have plain, unadorned faces. All known members of the *C. cephus* group jerk, shake, weave or 'flag' their heads. A comparison between the two groups may help to explain why faces have become flags in one and not the other.

Four frames from a cine film of a bout of head weaving by the moustached monkey (*Cercopithecus cephus*). 'Flagging' patterns are very varied in this species but normally involve momentary yet repeated monitoring of the object of display. In this case, the display has been elicited by a monkey puppet close to the camera lens.

The elaboration of colour and pattern on the face in *C. cephus* correlates with recent evolutionary changes towards small body size, larger group sizes, and the capacity to feed and travel over fine branches and twigs. These monkeys are almost restricted to the main forest blocs and their immediate outliers. By contrast, their larger, heavier relatives of the *C. nictitans* group range through virtually all the diverse and fragmented forests of Africa. They are conservative in having plain agouti coats and a generalised body plan and probably represent the older, longer established branch of a common *cephus–nictitans* lineage.

The two species groups co-exist through many areas of forest in equatorial Africa and feed on similar types of food. The most significant differences between them concerns not food but feeding techniques. The *C. nictitans* species are systematic gleaners following well-established routines within a home range; *C. cephus* species are more opportunistic and look for insects and other ephemeral sources of food.

Greater sensitivity to visual cues probably arose from the evolutionary shift by the *C. cephus* group into more fragile and exposed vegetation, and intensive searching for small and active food items. It may also help reduce the vulnerability of monkeys to eagles. However, the main impetus to develop a channel of visual communication seems to have come from the need to conserve energy while making signals.

Social cohesion in guenons is served by two mechanisms. One is presentation of the genitalia, the other eye-avoidance. Both inhibit aggression and dispersion. In a single-male social system, yawning only occurs during rare pauses in territorial confrontations. 'Presenting' is cumbersome and wasteful of energy on small branches and is little seen in the *C. cephus* group. Eye-avoidance, on the other hand, is exaggerated and ritualised into conspicuous head movements. The resulting signal is easy to transmit, and its reception can be improved by increasing colour and contrast on the facial disc.

Changing the boundaries and tonal intensities of facial markings can generate many alternative designs. Each can

1. HUMAN FACIAL EXPRESSIONS

Facial expressions are an indispensable part of human communication. They display our moods and transmit messages of great subtlety, eloquence and power. Experts in this silent language can, as Jonathan Swift observed,

. . . read a nod, a shrug, a look,
Far better than a printed book;
Convey a libel in a frown,
And wink a reputation down

Our complex facial signals continue an ancient primate tradition, and many of them have a good deal in common with those of monkeys and apes. The human laugh, for example, is similar to the relaxed open-mouth face adopted by apes and monkeys during boisterous play. Opinions differ on the pedigree of the smile, with some tracing it to the monkey grimace — basically a fearful face — and others viewing it as a low-intensity laugh. Human smiles come in so many forms that there may be room for both explanations.

Not all of our facial signals can be found in the faces of non-human primates. Certain familiar expressions — for instance, those signifying disgust and surprise — are human specialities.

The mobility of the face is essential to this system of communication. Over the course of evolution, changes have taken place in the musculature around the mouth, allowing new signals to develop. Alterations to the triangularis muscle, for example, which pulls the corners of the mouth downwards, made possible our repertoire of sad expressions. Changes in another muscle, the zygomaticus major, which moves the corners of the lips

During boisterous play, monkeys and apes, such as these chimpanzees, adopt a distinctive facial expression that is clearly related to the human laugh.

upwards and backwards, created our characteristic smile.

A single region of the face can carry a wealth of information. The eyebrows, for example, can be raised (together or singly), lowered, knit, shrugged or flashed, to create distinctive signals. Lips and tongue supply an equally vivid indication of our changing moods. Additional variety is created by using the same signal to mean different things in different situations: a wink, for instance, can be conspiratorial, erotic or just plain friendly, depending on context.

Facial displays are often accompanied by hand movements, creating a vast array of expressive gestures, which convey complex information economically and in silence.

The way we use our facial expressions and gestures varies greatly from place to place. In northern Italy, 'no' is signalled by

a conventional shake of the head, but in the south the accepted signal is the so-called 'Greek no' — an upwards toss of the head. The dividing line between shake and toss lies between Naples and Rome. In other countries, the tossed head may be interpreted either as a form of affirmation or as a beckoning motion.

However, some facial signals are intelligible in many corners of the globe. The eyebrow flash, a friendly greeting, is a case in point. When giving this signal, people raise their eyebrows for about a sixth of a second, conveying an air of delighted surprise — and often eliciting an equally friendly flash in return. The flash has been observed as far apart as Europe and Samoa, as well as among the San (Bushmen) of southern Africa and the Quechua Indians of South America, prompting some to regard it as a universal signal with roots in our evolutionary past.

When it comes to expressing emotions, members of widely different cultures have much in common. If people from various countries are shown a photograph of a happy, smiling face, for example, they usually agree in their interpretation. They also tend to concur over disgust, surprise, sadness, anger, fear and contempt. Such findings imply that beneath all the cultural complexity of mankind, there is a core of basic emotional expressions that are understood all over the world.

Societies do differ in the rules that govern the display of emotion. For example, Americans express disgust when viewing a disturbing film, regardless of whether they are alone or accompanied, but Japanese do so only when alone. In

Basic emotional expres[s] are understood all over [the] world.

serve as a distinctive flag or signal and *C. cephus* monkeys illustrate well the diversity of shapes that result from small changes in facial markings.

The development of many different and distinctive facial patterns in geographically separated populations of the *C. cephus* group is probably an accident of timing, as the elaboration of colour and contrast in the face seems to have taken place after a population with a rudimentary face pattern had become isolated in fragments of forest during arid periods.

If the ultimate effect of a face pattern is to make a monkey look very different, that difference, although skin-deep, can become a barrier to communication and to mating between different populations. There is remarkably little mixing along the boundaries between the various *C. cephus* group populations. The divergence of patterns in related populations could provide a mechanism for speciation, even if these patterns evolved to provide a population of animals with an exclusive channel on which to broadcast their own messages.

Trends in colour and form

The raw material for change in visual signals is the genetic variation in individual colour and form. However, the trend towards bolder patterns is probably due to the efficiency of colour-coded geometric shapes – which are easy to find, to follow and to remember. In controlled experiments, animals can be conditioned to make immediate responses to simple geometry and strong colours. In natural contexts, such immediacy of response is likely to have been a powerful selective force favouring the evolution of ever bolder colour and geometry in signal patterns. Visual signals are hence partly encoded in the susceptibilities of animal eyes and brains: in one sense, the signal is 'designed' in the eye of the receiver. Here lies a largely unexplored area of evolutionary biology.

Jonathan Kingdon

See also 'Smell as a signal' (p. 157)

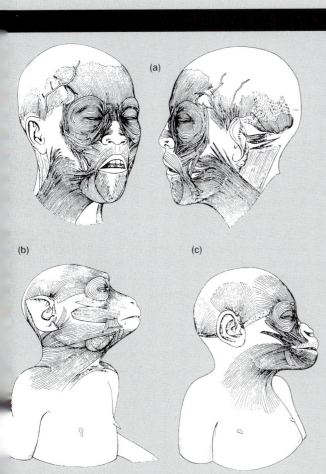

Smiling reinforces the bond between parents and baby.

company, they are more likely to conceal their disgust beneath polite smiles.

Facial expressions are important from birth, forming a channel of communication between parent and child. Babies are born with a complete set of facial muscles, which are immediately set to work in the service of crying. Experiments on babies just 2 hours old have shown that sweet, sour and bitter solutions elicit different facial expressions. This could be of survival value, alerting the mother to the danger of poisoning.

Smiling makes its appearance in the infant's repertoire of faces at 3 to 4 weeks of age. Thereafter, it plays an important part in the developing bond between parents and baby. At first, two dots on a card will produce a smile but, later on, infants become increasingly selective, responding only to faces and keeping the sunniest smiles for loved ones. The laugh develops more slowly, appearing at about 4 months of age.

From the earliest months, infants are adept at distinguishing between various facial expressions worn by adults, such as those conveying happiness, surprise or sadness. Before long, they can discriminate between different degrees of emotion, at least in the cases of happy and fearful faces. Later on, between the ages of 1 and 2 years, they show signs of understanding adult facial signals. As their understanding deepens, they are reassured and encouraged to explore by smiles and deterred by fearful or disapproving looks.

We continue to uncover new subtleties in our facial language. Psychologists now realise, for example, that we express emotion in an asymmetric fashion – with the left side of the face being more expressive than the right – especially if the expressions are posed rather than spontaneous. Another revelation has been the discovery that our facial expressions can affect our moods; smiling, it seems, may make us happy. Our nods, shrugs and looks can still surprise us.

Stephen Young

nobility and the eloquence of the human face (a) depend on a complex work of muscles. The facial muscles of monkeys and apes, represented by the rhesus macaque (b) and a young orang-utan (c), are less entiated.

Part Five

Human evolution in a geological context

Our knowledge of living species allows us, at least partially, to reconstruct the anatomy and behaviour of those species living in the past, and to link living and extinct forms in evolutionary trees. But for a full picture of what happened in the past – and why – we need to know what kinds of habitats were occupied, what ecological relationships there were, where and when new species evolved or went extinct, and how and when they spread from their areas of origin. In this context, useful metaphors, coined by the ecologist Evelyn Hutchinson, are 'the ecological theatre' and the 'evolutionary play'. In Part 5, we are interested in the ecological theatre – the backdrop and context for primate evolution.

Primates evolved about 70 million years ago when global climates were warmer and the continents were in different places; for example, North America was linked to Europe and Asia and the southern continents – South America and Africa – were separated by wide seas from the northern landmass.

Primate evolution took place against a changing climatic and geographic background. Global climates (**5.2**) have changed greatly during the past 60 million years, especially in the past 20 million. Overall, they have become cooler and more seasonal, with less forest, more desert and more ice on earth. The shapes and locations of continents have also changed (**5.1**). Some connections have been severed (for example, North America from Europe in the Eocene epoch) while others have been created (as between Africa and Eurasia in the Miocene and between North and South America in the Pliocene).

Some changes in global climates must be linked to these shifting continental patterns, but others, especially the dramatic cycles of glacials and interglacials that grew increasingly important during the past 2.5 million years, reflect a combination of 'intrinsic' factors, including mountain building and continental movements, and 'extrinsic' agencies, such as changes in the earth's orbit and tilt that affected the distribution of solar energy.

Changes in environments and habitats in various parts of the world are now well established (**5.5**). These shifts have been clarified using a synthesis of a broad range of information from studies of land rocks and deep-sea sediments to plant and animal fossils (**5.4** and **5.5**). Our increasingly thorough understanding of how to date rocks containing

The eruption of Oldoinyo Lengai, Tanzania, in 1966.

167

primates and other fossils on land as well as those in the oceans (**5.3**) means that we can order all this information into a coherent framework.

Periods of environmental stability were interspersed with those of marked change. It seems increasingly probable that more evolutionary change — including an increase in the rate of evolution and the first appearance or the extinction of species — occurs at times of rapid environmental change than during periods of relative stability.

One particularly interesting period of evolutionary change in mammals, especially primates, was around 2.5 million years ago when there was a global shift from warm and wet to cooler and drier conditions. In Africa, Europe, Asia and North America, new species appeared in bursts as the result of evolution and dispersal made possible by new geographic and ecological connections and also disappeared because of a combination of local or total extinctions. All this can clearly be seen by careful sampling of well-dated fossil-bearing sediments.

Africa is a good example of the kind of changes that went on at this time. Open grasslands and woodlands spread at the expense of forests, new species of mammal adapted to the open country (such as grazers and runners) appeared and older species migrated or became extinct. Among these changing species were hominids.

Around 2.5 million years ago, hominids seem to have diversified. This may be in part an artefact of a fossil record that is still far from adequate, but the increase in the number of species is probably real. One new species complex comprised the robust australopithecines, whose anatomy seems to have been adapted to a diet dominated in dry periods by hard fruits and other low-quality plant food. Work on bone assemblages (**5.4**) suggests that they preferred open savanna habitats where such food was most abundant.

After 2.5 million years ago, another new complex appeared. This consisted of species of *Homo* (**6.6**) adapted to a diet with more meat. The earliest forms seem to have preferred more wooded habitats, such as along river banks, and probably obtained most of their meat by scavenging (**5.5**). Later forms of *Homo* may have been more active hunters in open habitats where more game animals were present.

Whether these evolutionary changes resulted directly from a climatic change 2.5 million years ago or whether this shift merely helped in the survival of lineages that had already evolved is unclear. We need to know a great deal more about the primate fossil record before we can provide the answer.

Land movements and species dispersal

The world's land masses have not always been where they are today. During the past 700 million years they have moved, dispersed and joined together. These events have affected the evolution and diversity of plants and animals by causing changes in climate, creating barriers – oceans or mountains – to distribution, or assisting dispersal through the formation of intercontinental land bridges, such as the Panamanian isthmus. Palaeogeography reconstructs the past positions of the lands, seas and oceans to assist our understanding of the evolution of the earth and its inhabitants, among them humans.

Many studies can do little more than suggest the presence of *epicontinental seas* (shallow seas on a continental shelf) that may become land bridges between continents during global falls in sea level or during uplift or depression of the land. To show the existence of ephemeral land bridges by studying sediments or fossils is difficult because suitable terrestrial sediments are rare. For example, there are only six localities of Oligocene age in the whole of Africa that have produced remains of land animals. However, one of these – Fayum in northern Egypt – has produced most of our knowledge of the early evolution of monkeys and apes.

The fossil record is so incomplete that since 1876 (the year Alfred Russel Wallace described the distribution of fossil monkeys) scientists have speculated about how animals – especially primates and their relatives – have come to occupy distant lands.

Continental movement

Palaeogeography involves the mapping of the lands and the seas of the past. The theory of continental displacement is now a major factor in so doing, although it has only recently been generally accepted. Why the earth's crustal plates move, some at the rate of 5 centimetres a year, is still not fully understood. As late as the 1960s, maps were published showing the positions of the earth's landmasses and oceans as unchanged throughout time, although a few scientists had questioned this static view of geography. As long ago as 1620 Francis Bacon noted the similarities of the west African and eastern South American coastlines; in 1859, Antonio Snider-Pellegrini had South America and Africa joined, then ruptured by Noah's flood; in 1910, Frank Taylor had the continents displaced by the moon's tidal forces.

To these catastrophe theories were added Alfred Wegener's studies between 1912 and 1929. He noted that the same Permian plants and reptiles were found both in South America and Africa and that the modern coastlines of those continents could be fitted together to form an ancient landmass. This landmass, joined also with India, Antarctica and Australia, became known as the supercontinent *Gondwana*. To the north of Gondwana lay *Laurasia*, comprising North America and Eurasia. About 200 million years ago, they formed the supercontinent of *Pangaea*. Wegener called the mechanism that broke apart this ancient continent 'horizontal continental displacement' – *continental drift* – but for many years his idea was geological heresy.

To explain the similarities between ancient plants and animals on distant landmasses that had not moved, most palaeobiogeographers were forced to imagine the presence of trans-oceanic land bridges at convenient geological times; Wegener's continental displacement hence seemed unnecessary. One of these bridges was named Lemuria and was thought to have joined India with Madagascar across the Indian Ocean, so that primates – primarily lemurs – could have had easy access to both regions.

How did the idea of continental displacement affect these beliefs and what is their relationship to palaeogeography? Crustal plates – the huge segments into which the earth's surface is divided – are made up of both continental material (the landmasses and the continental shelves) and ocean floor, and not, as was once thought, exclusively of continental material. The plates move in relation to each other and as they jostle for space in the lithosphere their margins undergo structural stresses that may be released as earthquakes or volcanoes.

There are two main types of phenomena at plate margins: 'active' events caused by colliding plates and 'passive' events, where plates are spreading apart. The term 'active' comes from the process that recycles material back into the earth's upper mantle. The crust of oceanic plates is more dense than that of continental plates, so that when the two collide the oceanic plate is forced down and sinks under the continental plate into the upper mantle. This process, called *subduction*, can result in the formation of mountain ranges on the edge of the continental plate. Associated with this are deep-seated earthquakes and intense volcanicity, sometimes with disastrous results.

Palaeogeographers need to identify 'active' and 'passive' plate margins in the geological record so that their past positions can be plotted from the history of ocean-floor spreading. This is done by studying the oceanic crust formed by the hot, upwelling basaltic magma that spills onto the margins of both spreading plates. Magma contains iron (usually titanomagnetite) that lines up with the earth's magnetic field, and when it cools this polarity fossilises. Any reversals of the earth's magnetic field also fossilise. These changes in polarity can be measured and form the basis of an important method for dating fossil localities,

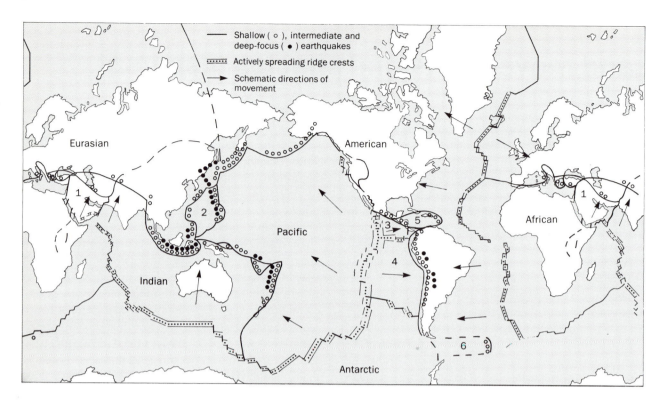

Shallow (o), intermediate and
deep-focus (•) earthquakes

Actively spreading ridge crests

Schematic directions of
movement

The earth's surface is divided into huge segments called crustal plates, which move in relation to one another. The major plates are named on the map; the minor ones are (1) Arabian; (2) Philippine; (3) Cocos; (4) Nazca; (5) Caribbean; and (6) Scotia. At the plate margins, plates either collide ('active' events) or spread apart ('passive' events). An example of 'active' plate movement occurs in the southwestern Pacific where the Nazca plate (made up of oceanic floor material) is butting into the South American plate and building the Andes at the plate margin. 'Passive' plate margins occur in the mid-Atlantic where the South American plate, moving to the west, is spreading away from the African plate. At the spreading margins, new and mainly basaltic oceanic crust forms a ridge, which, when it breaks the surface of the ocean, forms islands such as Ascension and the Azores.

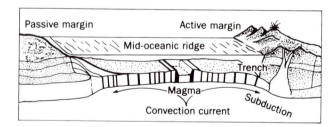

The elements of ocean crust development (not to scale). Hot, upwelling basaltic magma spills onto the margins of both spreading plates. The magma contains iron minerals (usually titanomagnetite) that line up with the earth's magnetic field. Their polarity is fossilised when the magma cools. Similarly, any reversals of the earth's magnetic field will also be fossilised. These events are shown as alternating black and white vertical blocks.

such as Olduvai Gorge in Tanzania – a key site for the study of human evolution.

The other minerals of basalt – potassium and argon – can be used to date the time of its origin. Oceanic basalts of the same age and the same polarity can be identified throughout the world to give a geomagnetic timescale for their deposition onto plate margins. This information,

together with that on the spreading rate of plate margins at the oceanic ridge, can be used to trace the positions of the margins through time by subtracting the spreading rate from the distance the margins have moved since they appeared.

Mapping the ancient world

Various problems arise when the past positions of the crustal plates are plotted in this way. The earth, unlike a map, is not flat. However, there are mathematical methods of overcoming the problem of projecting a sphere onto a flat surface, Mercator's being the best known. Their inherent errors do not matter much for a modern map, but when used for palaeogeography, Mercator's mathematics not only distort the shapes of the continents but also produce seas where none has existed. This problem has been partly solved using a Winkel 'Tripel' projection for palaeogeographic maps.

However, when reconstructing Pangaea at about 180 million years ago, even Winkel's formula produces large areas of sea floor, the so-called Tethys Ocean (which is distinct from the Tethys Sea), for which there is no geological evidence. It has been suggested that the diameter of the earth has increased by a fifth since the late Triassic, because when Pangaea is plotted onto a globe four-fifths of the size of the modern earth, the anomalous ocean of Tethys disappears; it is a geometric artefact of a cartographic formula. This controversial proposal suggests that the earth's expansion has contributed as much to continental displacement as has ocean-floor spreading, although, at present, no mechanism to explain how the earth could have expanded is known.

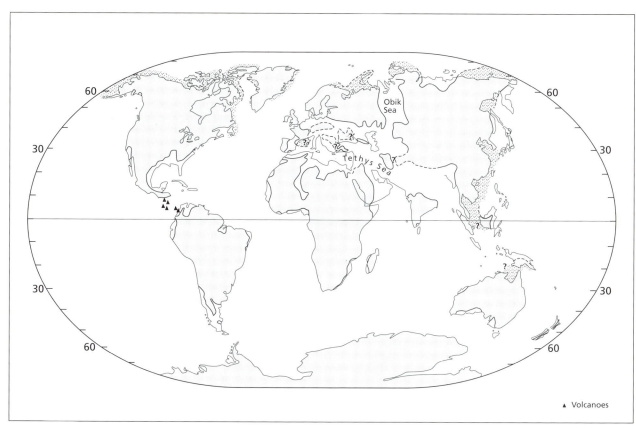

A composite map of the maximum extent of the oceans during the Palaeogene (65 to 23 million years ago). The shorelines indicate the maximum extent of marine deposition during the Palaeocene, Eocene and Oligocene. The shelf areas that were probably mainly land are stippled.

Fossil distribution

What is the relevance of fossil distribution to modern views of palaeogeography? Obviously, disturbances to the pattern of the landmasses create barriers for some organisms and new habitats for others. Palaeobiogeographers have always tried to link the physical activities of the earth's crust with the distribution of plants and animals.

Since the general acceptance of the theory of continental displacement in the late 1960s, there has been a surge of new information about the biogeography of the ancient world. There has also been controversy. One group of workers, 'panbiogeographers', holds that fossils can never contradict the modern distributions and patterns of relationships of living organisms. Another group, 'vicariance biogeographers', believes that if an ancestral biota is divided by the appearance of an ocean or a mountain range, the new barrier can be used to define and hence date new taxa in the separated habitats. Yet another group, 'dispersal biogeographers', claims that speciation occurs only after a population has crossed a barrier into a new habitat so that a barrier usually predates a new taxon.

Fossils are not as important to vicariant approaches to biogeography as they are to dispersal biogeography. Fortunately, palaeontologists are continually finding new fossils from new localities that suggest that some taxa had cosmopolitan distributions before they became extinct in any particular area. All aspects of biogeographical theory can be seen in the conflicting theories for the origins of the platyrrhine monkeys of the New World.

Origins of New World monkeys

The closest living relatives of the South American monkeys are the Old World monkeys of Africa. To explain the geographical separation of these groups, some have postulated an ancestral anthropoid primate whose fossil remains are unknown but which lived both in North America and in Europe, in Africa or in southern Asia. Alternatively, animals may have crossed the Atlantic on rafts of floating vegetation or by 'island hopping': in this case, fossil anthropoids might be found on oceanic islands or in undersea volcanic ridges. Other suggestions include a vicariance event, such as drifting apart of South America and Africa and a dispersal of animals via the Bering Strait land bridge and the Caribbean. However, by the time that the first known fossil platyrrhine had reached South America (at least 27 million years ago) the continents had almost reached their modern positions. Modern palaeogeography thus cannot provide an explanation of platyrrhine origins.

The Arabian connection

Many boreholes have been made into oil-bearing strata in the Middle East, enabling rocks containing the same marine fossils to be correlated over long distances. This is important because the Tethys epicontinental sea probably formed a barrier to the intercontinental 'dispersal' of terrestrial animals between Afroarabia and Eurasia during most of the Mesozoic and nearly all of the Cenozoic eras. Some marine fossils of the Tethys found in the Indo-West Pacific province – around the Indian Ocean – differ substantially from those of the Mediterranean faunal province. It follows that the Tethys must have been divided at some time from the Indian Ocean by a land bridge.

The ancient Afroarabian non-sedimentary, granitic rocks of Nubia began to break up and form an embryonic Red Sea rift during the late Cretaceous. By early Palaeocene times, continental rifting had given way to a shallow marine rift extending about 1200 kilometres south from the modern Mediterranean coast. Arabia itself was moving away from the Horn of Africa – to create the Gulf of Aden rift – but was still connected to Africa in the Afar region of Ethiopia by part of southwestern Yemen.

The geological history of the Arabian plate is relatively well known. Its modern margins roughly follow the coastline of the Arabian peninsula, are slightly to the east of the River Tigris and slightly north of and parallel to the Turkey–Iraq–Syria border near the Gulf of Alexandretta.

On the northern and eastern margins of the Arabian plate, marine deposition of Tethyan sediments seems to have continued throughout most of the Cretaceous (when the Arabian plate collided with southwestern Asia), all of the Palaeocene and most of the Eocene. The northeastern, anticlockwise movement of Arabia away from Africa gradually constricted the Tethys epicontinental sea and prompted the formation of the Zagros Mountains in Iran.

During middle Eocene times, the Tethys seaway still connected the Atlantic with the Indian Ocean through the Arabian Gulf, itself only as wide as it is today. A worldwide fall in sea level at the Eocene/Oligocene boundary may have bridged this last gap. In the early Oligocene, when a diverse population of primates lived in the Fayum area of Egypt, marine fossils show that the Tethys seaway still formed a barrier to their dispersal into Eurasia.

The history of the Tethys Sea in the Middle East during the earliest Miocene (about 23 million years ago) is sketchy as marine sedimentation was discontinuous. A land bridge may sometimes have been present at this time. However, by about 18 million years ago at the latest, the seaway was permanently closed: marine fossils found in the Indian Ocean realm have never been found in Mediterranean rocks of the same age. The land bridge seems to have been present between the head of the modern Arabian Gulf and a structural feature called the Qatar–south Fars (coastal Iran) arch.

Discoveries of middle Miocene terrestrial mammals, 16 to 19 million years old, in eastern Saudi Arabia show an essentially African fauna. For example, rodents, a rhinoceros, a giraffe and a mastodon (a type of elephant) were present. The mastodon – *Gompthotherium cooperi* – is also found in the early Miocene rocks (about 22 million years old) of the Dera Bugti region, Pakistan. Also, the possible descendants of the rodent family found in Saudi Arabia also occur in Pakistan. Consequently, terrestrial animals seem to have used the newly formed bridge between Afroarabia and Asia some 20 million years ago.

In the same way, a new genus of Miocene hominoid – *Heliopithecus leakeyi* – occurs at Ad Dabtiyah in Saudi Arabia. It resembles *Afropithecus turkanensis* from northern Kenya and the two genera are regarded by some as synonymous.

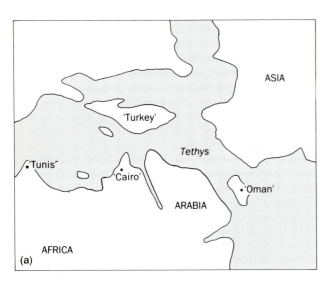

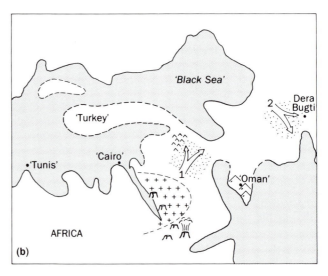

(a) A palaeogeographic cartoon showing the probable position of the Tethys epicontinental seaway in the Middle East during the middle Eocene, about 45 million years ago. At this time, and until (at the earliest) about 30 million years ago, the Tethys was an effective barrier to the dispersal of terrestrial animals between Afroarabia and Eurasia. (b) A palaeogeographic cartoon of earliest Miocene times (about 23 million years ago) showing the probable position of the first land bridge between Afroarabia and Eurasia. The arrows show (1) deposition of sands eroded from the western Arabian highlands. These sands – the Ahwaz sandstone of southern Iraq and Kuwait – are a major source of oil and in eastern Saudi Arabia their equivalents contain fossil rodents and bovids (cattle and their relatives). Other sands (2), eroded from the Himalayas, contain fossil mammals at Dera Bugti, Pakistan.

Undoubtedly, tectonic events and climatic changes in the region during the Miocene affected the habitats of these hominoids and of other mammals. In turn, these changes are reflected in the distribution and diversification of hominoid species as they adapted to or crossed new regional barriers.

Recently, a late Miocene fauna has been found in Abu Dhabi, United Arab Emirates, that includes a canine of an Old World monkey (tribe Papionini). This is only the second Miocene primate fossil known from Arabia. The fauna (including types of elephant, hippopotamus and horse) dates to about 6 million years, just before the earliest record of hominids in Africa. The fossil localities also provide evidence of habitats linked to the drying-up of the Mediterranean – the Messinian Crisis – when lower sea levels not only increased the amount of land available for hominid dispersal but also affected climate. This event was again a long-term effect of the closure of Tethys.

During the early Pliocene (about 5 million years ago), the ancient link between Africa and Arabia – the Ethiopian–Yemen isthmus – was ruptured by the continued movement of the Arabian plate away from Africa. Arabia is now virtually isolated from Africa. New oceanic crust is still being generated in the Red Sea and Gulf of Aden rifts. At some time in the future, the Arabian Gulf will disappear and the Indian Ocean will again be connected to the Mediterranean through the Red Sea. The fauna of Africa will then be again isolated from the rest of the world and the subsequent changes in climate will once again influence the diversity of mammals, especially hominids.

Peter J. Whybrow

See also 'Climatic change in the past' (p. 174), Methods of dating' (p. 179), 'The fossil history of primates' (p. 199), 'Evolution of New World monkeys' (p. 209) and 'Evolution of apes' (p. 223)

Climatic change in the past

In recent geological time the earth has been increasingly restless, not only because of mountain building and other movements of its crust, but also as a result of changes in climate. Climatic oscillations have probably been as violent during the past few million years as they have at any time in earth history, and this has affected primate evolution in many ways. Climatic variability modified such important habitats as river valleys and lake basins, and caused forests, grasslands and deserts to expand and contract across the continents. It also altered the oceans, causing sea levels to rise and fall, which in turn periodically exposed continental shelves as dry land. The climates that provided the backdrop to human evolution were those of the last great Ice Age.

The Alpine Ice Age model

The *Einzeit* or Ice Age theory was first announced in 1837 by Louis Agassiz, a renowned specialist on fossil fishes who was later to found the Harvard Museum of Comparative Zoology. Evidence that glaciers and ice sheets had formerly been more extensive came from the Alps in Agassiz's native Switzerland. Convincing as his case was, we can now see – with hindsight – that these mountains were singularly ill-suited to be a model for studying the history of the last great Ice Age. For a start, the Alps have been uplifted during recent geological times. And as the land has risen, the accumulation of snow and ice has increased, making glaciation more likely regardless of any change in global climate. Equally important, formerly glaciated terrain preserves a very incomplete stratigraphic record of earth history. The ice, as it advanced, scoured and bulldozed its way through earlier sedimentary deposits, eroding and overturning them in the process.

Nonetheless, it was to the Alps and other formerly glaciated lands that most scientific attention was drawn during the later nineteenth century. Albrecht Penck and Eduard Brückner found evidence of more than one past extension of the Alpine ice cap, in the form of a series of fluvioglacial outwash terraces in the valleys draining the German Alps. They recognised four glacial stages within the last Ice Age, and named them after different river valleys: Günz, Mindel, Riss and Würm. This four-stage sequence of cold *glacials* and intervening warmer *interglacials* was to be immensely influential. It provided a template for climatic history not only in other glaciated regions, such as North America and northern Europe, but also in the tropics where four wet phases (or *pluvials* as they were termed) were recognised, matching the four alpine glacial stages. A similar four-stage model for sea-level history was proposed from marine

terraces around the Mediterranean, although this region has been as tectonically unstable as the Alps.

Sea levels fluctuate in concert with climate because when there is ice on the northern continents, water is taken out of the hydrological cycle, and when it melts, water returns to

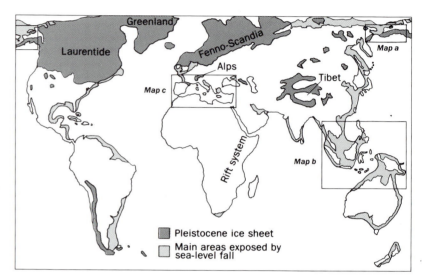

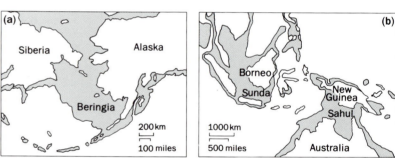

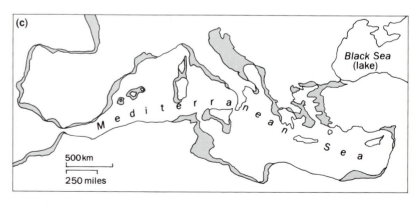

The world during a glacial stage of the last Ice Age. Major ice sheets covered not only Greenland and Antarctica, as they do today, but also North America and northern Eurasia. The ice that was locked up on land caused sea levels to fall by more than 100 metres. Coastlines changed dramatically where there were shallow continental shelves offshore – for example, in the Bering Strait and between Southeast Asia and Australia. Enlargements show the sea-level fall in these two regions and the Mediterranean basin in more detail. While the Mediterranean Sea remained connected to the Atlantic Ocean throughout the Plio-Pleistocene, the Black Sea became isolated as a giant freshwater lake.

Extent of land ice today and at the peak of a Pleistocene glacial cycle. The biggest of these ice sheets were 5 kilometres thick and their weight depressed the earth's crust by more than 1 kilometre

Ice sheet	Area (million square kilometres)	Ice volume (million cubic kilometres)	Sea-level equivalent (metres)
Present day			
Antarctic	12.53	23.45	59
Greenland	1.73	2.60	6
N. America	(negl.)	—	—
Fennoscandia	(negl.)	—	—
Other	0.64	0.20	0.5
Total	14.90	26.25	65
Peak of glacial cycle			
Antarctic	13.81	26.00	66
Greenland	2.30	3.50	11
N. America	15.76	33.01	83
Fennoscandia	6.66	13.32	34
Other	5.20	1.14	3
Total	43.73	76.97	197
Difference	28.83	50.72	132

the oceans. Some of the most detailed records of sea-level history come from corals that grew near to the former ocean surface. While some corals have been drowned and now lie well below the modern sea level, such as off the coast of Barbados, others, such as on the north coast of New Guinea, are now exposed on land.

When growth of the ice sheets was greatest, sea levels dropped by over 100 metres to create land bridges on con-tinental shelves. At these times it was possible to walk from eastern Asia to Alaska across the then dry Bering Strait, or from England to the continent of Europe. This certainly aided the spread of plants and animals, and encouraged the migration of early hominids from Africa to Eurasia and thence (late in the Ice Age) to Australia and the Americas. The inundation that occurred at times of rising sea levels may also have stimulated new human adaptations to coastal environments. Certainly the crossing from Southeast Asia to Australia, about 40000 or possibly 50000 years ago, had to be accomplished by raft or boat, for there has always been a significant water gap between these two continents.

The four-stage alpine model dominated ice-age research through the first half of the twentieth century, and brought with it a series of wider conclusions, few of which are considered valid today. Among these was the idea that the last Ice Age began abruptly during the Pleistocene epoch about 2 million years ago, following a long period of stable and temperate (albeit gradually deteriorating) climate. The fact that only four Pleistocene glaciations were recognised suggested that the warmer interglacials must have lasted longer than the intervening cold stages.

Despite valiant efforts by the Serbian mathematician Milutin Milankovitch, it proved impossible to match the alpine model to any known theories of past climatic change, in this case to astronomical variations in the earth's orbit and axial tilt. Finally, the archaeological discoveries

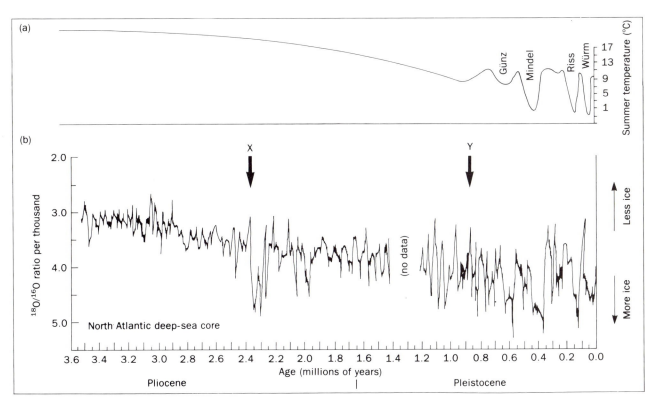

Glacial and interglacial cycles for the Plio-Pleistocene (a) as originally envisaged from the evidence of past glaciation in the Alps and (b) from oxygen-isotope measurements from a North Atlantic deep-sea core. Evidence of glaciation in the Northern Hemisphere goes back much further in time than was once thought (to point X); an important intensification of climatic change occurred about 900000 to 800000 years ago (point Y).

that were made during the late nineteenth and early twentieth centuries were fitted into, and often used to help date and hence to prop up, the alpine model of Ice Age history. Indeed, some archaeologists still discuss the Old Stone Age in Europe and the Mediterranean region with reference to a four-stage model of climatic change.

Modern subdivisions of the Ice Age

A framework that came to replace the alpine model emerged from three independent developments of the late 1940s. The first was the discovery of radiocarbon dating, the earliest of a series of new dating techniques, mostly based on the rate of decay of unstable radioisotopes. The traditional way of dating rocks is through palaeontology (or the study of fossils), but as one moves towards recent geological times this method becomes less and less applicable. Palaeontological dating assumes that the appearance and radiation of new species, and the extinction of old ones, were effectively instantaneous when considered on a geological timescale. While this assumption may be valid for events in the distant past, it is not true for more recent changes, as human evolution itself demonstrates. For this time period a sound chronology was lacking until the advent of radioisotopic methods. One of these new methods (potassium-argon) was to demonstrate the great antiquity of early human evolution in East Africa.

The second of the post-World War II developments was the discovery of *oxygen-isotope analysis*. This technique, based on the ratio between stable rather than unstable isotopes, provided not a dating tool but what was initially thought to be a 'geological thermometer'. Because of the phenomenon known as isotopic fractionation, slightly less of the heavy isotope oxygen-18 (^{18}O) is precipitated at higher temperatures relative to the light isotope oxygen-16 (^{16}O). One of the most important ways that chemical precipitation takes place from sea water is as calcium carbonate in organisms such as corals, molluscs and foraminifera. Further work has shown oxygen isotopes to reflect not only past temperatures but also, and more important, past ice volumes: it gives an index of past glaciations.

The third and final development was the invention of the Kullenberg piston corer for the recovery of deep-sea sediments. From a stratigraphic perspective the deep ocean bed represents the opposite conditions to those of glaciated terrain. Here, sedimentation proceeds slowly and steadily, uninterrupted by erosion. But obtaining intact sediment cores from onboard a ship 4 kilometres or more above the ocean floor is not easy. The Kullenberg corer was the first to recover cores that spanned all of the Pleistocene. Cores covering the whole of the late Cenozoic are now available as a result of the advent in 1979 of a hydraulic piston corer as part of the world Ocean Drilling Programme.

Oxygen-isotope analysis has now been applied to calcareous microfossils, notably foraminifera, from deep-sea sediment cores. This has produced a continuous record of ice volume fluctuations and therefore of glacial–interglacial cycles during the past few million years, and is a record very different from that recognised by Penck and Brückner in the Alps. First, many more than four glaciations are recorded in deep-sea sequences. Eight major climatic (that is, glacial–interglacial) cycles have occurred during the past 0.8 million years alone, with many other, less-intense cycles before this. Warmer interglacials represent only around 10 per cent of this time, and the climate was almost constantly changing between colder and warmer, or between wetter and drier conditions. According to the oxygen-isotope scheme, warm stages (with low ice volume) are given odd numbers working back from the present day, and colder glacial stages have even numbers; thus the present interglacial – or Holocene – is oxygen-isotope stage 1, the last glacial maximum stage 2, and so forth.

Foraminifera in a deep-sea ooze. These are small marine organisms whose shells (or tests) are made of calcium carbonate. The tests are often well preserved in deep-sea sediments and can be analysed for their oxygen-isotope contents, which provide a measure of past glaciation.

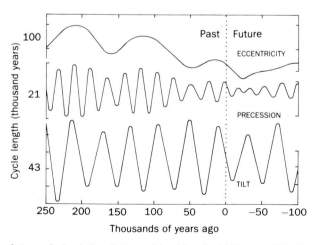

Astronomical variations in the earth's orbit and axial tilt as predicted by Milutin Milankovitch. There are three separate cycles, each with a different wavelength. When superimposed, these cycles match well to the sequence of glacial and interglacial fluctuations reconstructed from deep-sea cores.

This new stratigraphic framework could be tested against theories of climatic change much more rigorously than was previously possible. In the 1970s, the CLIMAP research group compared the oceanic oxygen-isotope record of glaciation and the input of solar radiation predicted by the Milankovitch astronomical theory. The fit was near perfect, giving strong support to the idea that variations in the earth's orbit acted as a pacemaker for Ice Age climate. These variations result from the superimposition of three separate cycles with wavelengths of 100000, 43000 and 21000 years, and it appears that these cycles – and the middle one in particular – operated throughout the late Cenozoic and not just during the Pleistocene.

Climatic change during the Cenozoic

There were important shifts in the tempo of climate, but these did not coincide with the start of the Pleistocene, now estimated at around 1.64 million years ago (but conventionally often put at 1.83 million years). The last two main shifts were at 0.8 and at 2.4 million years ago (see p. 175), the earlier marking the onset of major glaciation in Greenland and other Northern Hemisphere landmasses. By the Pliocene, about 5 million years ago, the Ice Age in the Southern Hemisphere was already well underway, with Antarctica carrying major ice sheets since at least the middle Miocene. Oxygen isotopes show an abrupt climatic change at about 14 million years, and this may mark the establishment of an ice sheet over East Antarctica similar in size to the one existing today. Glaciation around the South Pole certainly occurred before this, however, and the appearance of iceberg-rafted debris in deep-sea sediments is evidence of glaciers calving into the southern oceans from about 26 million years ago.

An ice cap terminating on land seems to have existed in Antarctica even before this. Seismic records of relative sea level show a major withdrawal of the sea from land (a marine regression) during the Oligocene, probably

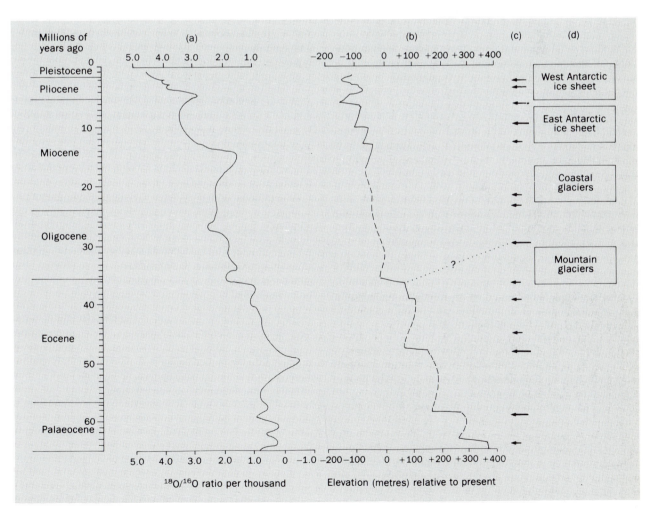

Oxygen-isotope measurements (a) on bottom-dwelling foraminifera in tropical deep-sea cores show a stepped pattern in the build up of land ice during the Cenozoic. Most of this ice accumulated over Antarctica before the Pliocene, initially as mountain glaciers that later expanded to terminate in the sea, and most significantly with the establishment of a true ice sheet over East Antarctica during the middle Miocene (d).

The global sea-level curve (b) reflects a progressive decline of about 400 metres during the Cenozoic as a result of sea-floor spreading, which caused the expansion of ocean basins. Superimposed on this gradual decline are more abrupt falls in sea level (c), caused by glaciation on land. These are indicated in the oxygen-isotope record and in seismic profiles of coastal sediments.

because of the accumulation of land ice, while subglacially extruded volcanic rocks in West Antarctica date back to 27 million years. Oxygen isotopes suggest glaciation even further back in time, to the Eocene–Oligocene boundary at 35 million years ago, if not earlier.

These shifts were the result of longer-term changes than those produced by astronomical fluctuations, and were almost certainly related to plate tectonics. The build-up of ice in the Northern Hemisphere may have resulted from the uplift of the Tibetan and Colorado plateaus disturbing global atmospheric circulation (Tibet has risen by some two vertical kilometres during the Plio-Pleistocene). Glaciation in Antarctica was probably initiated by the final break-up of the great southern continent, Gondwanaland. So long as Antarctica was joined to Australia and South America, cold polar ocean currents were deflected northwards towards the Equator and returned as warmer tropical waters. Once the link was broken, however, a circum-Antarctic current developed around the South Pole, isolating it thermally. The opening of Drake Passage between Tierra del Fuego and the Antarctic peninsula from about 22 million years ago may have been critical.

Tectonic changes were also important in determining regional environmental histories. The compression of the zone between the European and African tectonic plates, for example, led to the temporary closure of the Straits of Gibraltar during the Miocene. As a result, Atlantic waters no longer flowed into the Mediterranean Sea, which progressively dried up to become a series of giant salt lakes – the so-called Messinian salinity crisis. Another region where tectonic and climatic histories were intertwined was East Africa. Here the opening of the Rift System during the later Cenozoic led to a diversification of local climates that encouraged adaptation and speciation among the higher apes.

West of the rifts, rainfall was high enough to support tropical moist forest, but to the east, and in the rifts themselves, the climate became drier and more open, savanna vegetation came to dominate. Whether a move down from the trees encouraged bipedalism and other human adaptive traits is hard to know. However, it may be significant that Plio-Pleistocene hominids and modern chimpanzees and gorillas have disjunct distributions in tropical Africa; the apes are found only in moist forests and adjacent woodlands whereas the hominids lived in the savanna lands within and to the east of the rift system.

To find terrestrial sequences that match the deep-sea record of global climatic change is a major aim of palaeoclimatology. Among the most complete land-based records are those from loess (wind-blown glacial silts), cave deposits, pollen analysis, cores through the ice sheets themselves, and the sedimentary records of long-lived lakes, such as those of the East African rifts. Tropical lake levels, which are a good indicator of wet and dry climatic phases, are now known to have been low at glacial maxima and high during the early part of interglacials (and not the other way round, as the old 'glacial equals pluvial' view envisaged). One of the best-known sequences of lake sediments in East Africa comes from Olduvai Gorge, the source of hominid fossils and stone artefacts that have revolutionised our ideas about human origins. This kind of conjunction has meant that earth scientists and palaeoanthropologists now regularly work together in interdisciplinary teams.

Our understanding of environmental change over the recent geological past is quite different from that which existed a few decades ago. The Pleistocene did not, as was once thought, mark the main break-point in recent earth history. Because the change to a colder and more variable climate began well before this, it is more appropriate to refer to a 'late Cenozoic Ice Age'. Even this label disguises the fact that conditions were not always glacial in character, and that glaciation was just one of a whole series of important changes, such as the expansion and contraction of deserts in low latitudes.

Fluctuations in climate have intensified during the past million years, and have placed increasing pressure on organisms and ecosystems. Adaptability to change has been a key to success for most terrestrial plants and animals during the late Cenozoic. Hominids are no exception. The evolutionary success of our ancestors is testimony to their versatility in the face of a changing environment, first in the savannas of Africa and later in the new and hostile climates encountered in the lands beyond it.

Neil Roberts

See also 'Land movements and species dispersal' (p. 169), 'Methods of dating' (p. 179), 'Fossil deposits and their investigation' (p. 187) and 'Reconstructing past environments' (p. 191)

Methods of dating

The fossil record of primates begins in the latest Cretaceous period, so primate palaeontologists are interested in techniques of dating applicable over the past 70 million years. Fossil bones themselves are rarely datable with any precision, and these are mainly of late Pleistocene or Holocene age. In general, it is the geological materials with which they are found that are dated. For this reason, dating usually begins with an attempt to order past events, and to relate fossils to rock layers that can themselves be dated. Once this is done, the ages of fossils can be estimated by determining the ages of rocks that lie lower and higher in a stratigraphic section.

During the past 50 years, many techniques for measuring the age of rocks and minerals have been established. These fall into three categories:

- Methods that depend on radioactive decay of one element or another – *isotopic methods*; for example, radiocarbon, potassium-argon, fission-track, uranium disequilibrium and thermoluminescence dating
- Methods that depend on slow chemical processes; for example, amino acid racemisation dating
- Methods that require calibration by radioactive or chemical means; for example, palaeomagnetic polarity stratigraphy, tephrochronology and biochronology

Each technique has its own age range, its own restrictions on materials that are suitable and a need for an event to 'set the clock' – and also an inherent uncertainty in the result.

Radiocarbon dating

Radiocarbon or carbon-14 (^{14}C) dating is based on the decay of ^{14}C atoms to nitrogen-14 (^{14}N) by beta-emission. Because the half-life of ^{14}C is only 5730 years, it must be constantly produced or it would no longer be present on earth. This production takes place in the upper atmosphere where ^{14}C is formed from neutron reactions with ^{14}N and other nuclides. Once produced, the ^{14}C is oxidised to carbon dioxide ($^{14}CO_2$), and enters biological systems through various biochemical reactions, and the surface waters of lakes and oceans by diffusion. As a result, living organisms are radioactive, as are the carbonates precipitated from most natural waters. When an organism dies, or when carbonate minerals form, they are removed from this active carbon cycle and the ^{14}C within them begins to decay. By comparing the activity of their ^{14}C with its assumed initial activity, an age can be computed from the ratio of the two numbers.

There are various uncertainties in this estimate, which arise from statistical errors at several stages of the dating process – during the determination of radioactivity, by the contamination of samples by older or younger carbon, and the preferential incorporation by the sample of one isotope over another when carbon is withdrawn from the general environment and enters living material. These sources of error can be dealt with by increasing the period of examination of each sample, dating multiple samples, and measur-

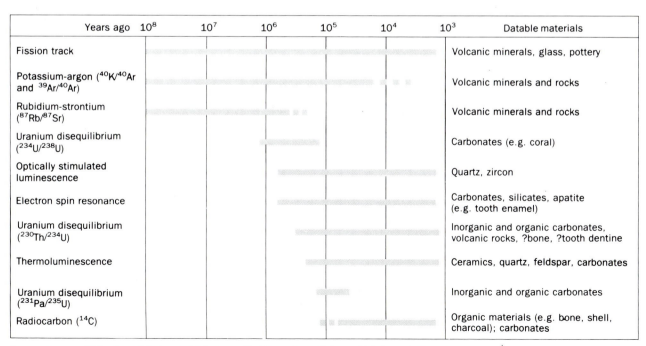

Years ago	10^8	10^7	10^6	10^5	10^4	10^3	Datable materials
Fission track							Volcanic minerals, glass, pottery
Potassium-argon ($^{40}K/^{40}Ar$ and $^{39}Ar/^{40}Ar$)							Volcanic minerals and rocks
Rubidium-strontium ($^{87}Rb/^{87}Sr$)							Volcanic minerals and rocks
Uranium disequilibrium ($^{234}U/^{238}U$)							Carbonates (e.g. coral)
Optically stimulated luminescence							Quartz, zircon
Electron spin resonance							Carbonates, silicates, apatite (e.g. tooth enamel)
Uranium disequilibrium ($^{230}Th/^{234}U$)							Inorganic and organic carbonates, volcanic rocks, ?bone, ?tooth dentine
Thermoluminescence							Ceramics, quartz, feldspar, carbonates
Uranium disequilibrium ($^{231}Pa/^{235}U$)							Inorganic and organic carbonates
Radiocarbon (^{14}C)							Organic materials (e.g. bone, shell, charcoal); carbonates

Age ranges over which selected dating methods are applicable, and materials on which they can be used.

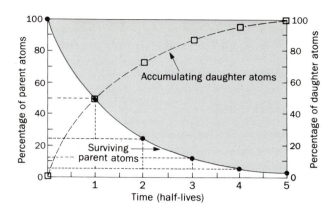

Curves showing the decay of a radioactive parent (P) to a single stable daughter (D). The sum P + D is 100 per cent, whereas the ratio D/P increases from 0 to 1 after one half-life, 3 after two half-lives, and so on.

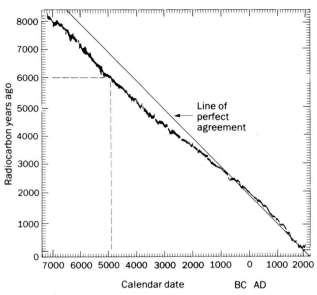

Radiocarbon ages are corrected to calendar ages using a curve established by radiocarbon dating samples of wood that have been given a calendar age by counting tree rings. A radiocarbon age of 6000 years corresponds to a calendar age of 4900 BC.

ing the content of the stable carbon isotope ^{13}C to determine the amount of preferential incorporation. Most radiocarbon dates are accompanied by an estimate of the probable error: the plus/minus term (standard deviation) quoted with the date.

Variations in the rate of production of ^{14}C in the past also affect the age estimate, but any uncertainties can be eliminated by calibrating samples against tree rings of known age. Ages are usually expressed in years before present (with the present taken as AD 1950). With careful work, an accuracy of about 2 per cent can be achieved.

The use of particle accelerators as sensitive mass spectrometers has made it possible to measure the number of ^{14}C atoms in a sample directly, rather than waiting for their decay. This method has now been applied in radiocarbon dating. Only very small samples (1 mg or less) are needed so the technique can be used to age valuable palaeontological and archaeological material that previously could not be dated by the traditional radiocarbon method. A recent example of this was the dating of the Turin Shroud to the fourteenth century AD. Because such small samples are sufficient for the accelerator mass spectroscopy (AMS) method, a tiny piece of charcoal or a single wheat grain can now be radiocarbon dated.

The AMS technique is proving useful in many other ways. For example, it has done much to refute claims for the presence of humans in the New World 50000 or 100000 years ago. Skeletons thought to be very old turn out to date to only a few thousand years ago using this new method.

An application of the radiocarbon method to primate palaeontology has been to date extinct lemurs in Madagascar. Some fossils of extinct species found at Amparihingidro in the north-west of the island are only about 3000 years old, and those at Lake Itampola in the south are only about 1000 years old. These forms have therefore disappeared in recent times – since the colonisation of Madagascar by humans.

Potassium-argon dating

The potassium-argon method is used to date volcanic rocks and minerals and is important in primate palaeontology. It depends on the fact that about one part in 10000 of naturally occurring potassium (^{40}K) is radioactive and decays slowly but steadily to the stable isotopes argon (^{40}Ar) and calcium-40 (^{40}Ca). In natural samples, the fraction of ^{40}K is constant, but the ^{40}Ar content increases with age. By comparing the amounts of ^{40}K and ^{40}Ar, an age can be computed (the half-life of ^{40}K is 1250 million years). The ^{40}Ar in a sample comes mainly from two sources – the radioactive decay of ^{40}K and the atmosphere. As argon makes up about 0.9 per cent of the earth's atmosphere by volume, a correction must be

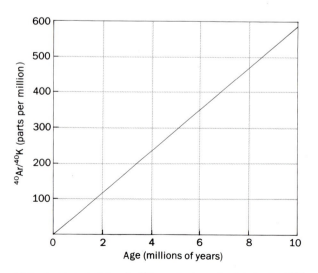

After volcanic material cools, ^{40}Ar accumulates through decay of ^{40}K, changing the $^{40}Ar/^{40}K$ ratio. Over short times, the change in ratio is nearly linear because of the long half-life of ^{40}K (1250 million years).

1. CORRELATING THE EAST AFRICAN HOMINID SITES

Once a hardened volcanic ash layer or *tuff* in one stratigraphic section has been dated by the potassium-argon method, its identification in other sections can date those as well. The technique is known as *tephrochronology*.

Nearly all volcanic ashes (*tephras*) from different eruptions can be distinguished from one another by chemical analysis of their contents (glass and various crystals). This is because each ash is the product of a unique mix of processes before and during an eruption, such as partial melting of the source rocks, storage in a magma chamber and crystallisation.

Some volcanic ash layers extend over several thousand kilometres, allowing strata in different depositional basins to be linked. In East Africa, several tephras first known from the Turkana Basin (Omo, Koobi Fora and West Turkana) have been identified from many other areas, including the Awash Valley, some 1100 kilometres to the north-east, and also the deep sea in the Gulf of Aden and the Somali Basin.

The figure shows some of these correlations, which allow us not only to match these widely separated fossil localities stratigraphically but also to apply palaeoclimatic information from the deep-sea cores to the hominid sites on land.

The Koobi Fora Formation contains 58 distinct tuffs. The dispute over the age of the so-called KBS Tuff was eventually resolved by K-Ar and ^{40}Ar/^{39}Ar dating. It was just below the KBS Tuff that the *Homo habilis* skull KNM-ER 1470 was found. For several years, the tuff was thought to be around 2.6 million years old, on the basis of preliminary K-Ar dates and results from fission-track dating. Later, the date was revised, with all the methods confirming an age of 1.88 + 0.02 million years.

Important evidence for the younger age came from correlation of the KBS Tuff with Tuff H-2 of the Shungura Formation in the Omo Valley, which had been dated at about 1.85 million years old. Correlations of pig fossils in Ethiopia and Kenya (see Box 2) also suggested that the deposits just under the KBS Tuff were close to 2 million years old.

Another, even more important result of recent tephrochronological studies in East Africa has been the discovery that several ash layers of — it now turns out — quite different age had all been mapped (erroneously) as the KBS Tuff.

F.H. Brown

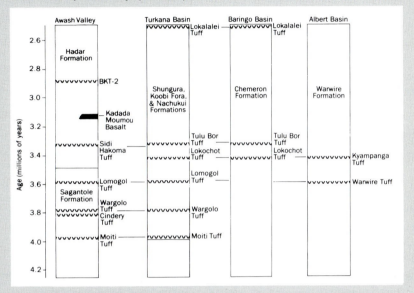

Some volcanic ash layers (tephras) extend over immense areas and connect fossil hominid sites stratigraphically at the localities shown. Many of the hominids known from the Hadar site were found in deposits between the BKT-2 and Sidi Hakoma Tuffs. Their dates were uncertain until these correlations were made. The gracile australopithecine known as 'Lucy' was found above the Kadada Moumou Basalt and below the BKT-2 Tuff.

made for this in order to determine the amount of radiogenic argon in the sample.

Potassium-argon dating is usually applied to minerals separated from hardened volcanic flows (tuffs) because they are often interspersed with fossil-bearing sediments, and are formed quickly at temperatures high enough to remove any argon of radioactive origin that was initially present.

The main uncertainties in potassium-argon ages arise from errors of measurement of potassium and radiogenic argon, by contamination of the sample with older materials, from argon contained within the dated material that is not produced by radioactive decay of potassium (excess argon), and from leakage of argon from the samples. The last problem is serious for lava flows that have been altered by weathering or other geochemical processes.

Potassium-argon dates are normally expressed in millions of years, together with a statement of the probable error. With good material the errors are generally about 1 to 3 per cent of the age. Potassium-argon ages can be used only to date stratigraphic levels between which a fossil lies. They hence provide boundary dates only, and a palaeontologist must assess the timing of events between the dated layers. For example, it may be judged that sedimentation was more or less continuous, or that there is a gap in the section, and so on.

This method has been more important in understanding the primate fossil record than any other dating technique. Its use to establish dates for boundaries between geological periods, and between epochs of the Tertiary period, makes it possible to state the approximate age of many primate fossils by studying the fossil remains with which they are associated. In East Africa and elsewhere, where volcanism and sedimentation happened at the same time, it is possible to establish the age of primate fossils precisely by dating tuffs in the fossil-bearing strata. This has been particularly successful for Pliocene and Pleistocene hominid fossils at sites such as Koobi Fora and West Turkana in Kenya and Omo and Hadar in Ethiopia (see Box 1).

An important variant of the K-Ar method is ^{40}Ar/^{39}Ar dating, in which the sample is irradiated to produce ^{39}Ar from ^{39}K. The argon is then extracted in a series of steps at higher and higher temperatures. This method has the advantages that potassium (computed from the ^{39}Ar content) is measured on the same sample as the ^{40}Ar and that an age can be calculated for each fraction of the gas. It is also possible to detect if excess argon is present.

The most elegant variation of the ^{40}Ar/^{39}Ar dating technique is the single-crystal fusion method, which uses a laser to melt previously irradiated crystal fragments to release the argon. Because the heating is so localised, background argon (of atmospheric origin) is reduced so that precise ages can be measured on individual small crystals. The technique greatly reduces the amount of sample needed for an age determination.

Potassium-argon dates could be cross-checked by rubidium-strontium (Rb-Sr) dating of volcanic rock materials, but this is seldom done.

Fission-track dating

Fission-track dating is based on the spontaneous fission of uranium-238 (^{238}U), during which a trail of damage is created near the site of the uranium atom. Its main use in primate palaeontology lies in its application to volcanic rocks and minerals. When these are formed, they contain no fission tracks. The number of tracks increases with time at a rate that depends on the uranium content. By measuring the uranium content and the density of tracks, an age can be computed.

Zircon is the material most commonly used for fission-track dating. It normally contains more uranium than other volcanic minerals, any tracks formed within it are exceptionally stable, and it is very resistant to weathering. In addition, individual zircon grains can sometimes be dated, and volcanic zircons can be identified by their sharp crystal outlines. Other materials that have been dated in this way

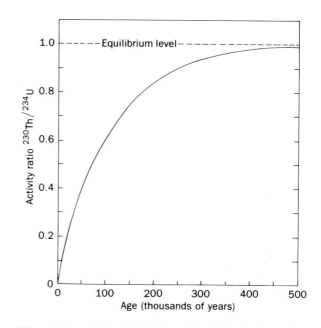

When calcite crystallises it contains uranium but no thorium. As time passes ^{234}U decays to form ^{230}Th, which is itself radioactive. Initially, the activity of ^{230}Th is zero but it increases as ^{230}Th atoms form, until it decays as rapidly as it forms and the activity ratio is 1.00. Although the ^{234}U/^{238}U activity ratio has been set equal to 1.00 to draw this curve, it is usually greater (1.15 in sea water), which alters the shape of the curve. In practice, the shape is corrected by measuring the ^{234}U/^{238}U ratio in the sample.

include apatite, biotite, sphene, and volcanic glasses such as obsidian.

Because fission tracks are only about 10 micrometres long, they must be enlarged so that they can be seen under an optical microscope. An internal surface of the grain to be dated is exposed by grinding and polishing, and the surface is chemically etched. Then the tracks in a fixed area are counted. The concentration of ^{238}U is measured by irradiating the sample with a known number of neutrons, which induce ^{235}U (but not ^{238}U) to undergo fission; the sample is then repolished and re-etched, and the uranium concentration computed from the density of new tracks.

An important application of the fission-track method has been to check potassium-argon dates at East African hominid sites.

Uranium disequilibrium dating

Several different elements are formed as naturally occurring radioactive isotopes of uranium – uranium 235 (^{235}U) and uranium-238 (^{238}U) decay by emission of alpha- and beta-particles to stable isotopes of lead. For example, uranium-234 (^{234}U) is the third daughter isotope and thorium-230 the fourth of the parent isotope ^{238}U, and proctanium-231 (Pa) is the second daughter product of ^{235}U. An uranium-containing mineral will in time contain each one of the elements in the decay series, in a concentration related to each element's half-life. This condition is termed *radioactive equilibrium*.

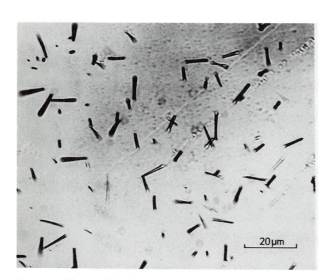

A sample of zircon polished to reveal an internal surface and etched so that the fission tracks can be seen. The number of tracks per unit area increases with the age of the sample at a rate determined by the uranium content.

Measurements being taken in Pontnewydd Cave, North Wales, where a hominid molar of early Neanderthal type and associated Acheulean stone tools were found in 1981. The lowermost archaeological layers were shown by uranium disequilibrium dating of a stalagmite to be at least 220 000 years old. This date was confirmed by thermoluminescence measurements on the same stalagmite and on a burnt flint.

Under radioactive equilibrium, the radioactivities of each of the decay products in the series are equal. However, these decay products may be separated from each other by processes such as weathering, differential adsorption, crystallisation of minerals that incorporate one element but exclude another and various biological events to form a system that is out of equilibrium. How much out of equilibrium is a measure of the time when the series was disrupted.

Uranium-disequilibrium dating systems, especially those that depend on the ratio between ^{234}U and ^{238}U, have been applied to non-marine carbonates, such as calcite in caves. The half-life for this process is 248 000 years so that the method has a range of about 1 million years.

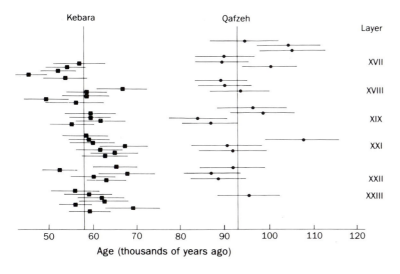

Thermoluminescence ages of burnt flints from Kebara and Qafzeh caves, Israel, for which the external dose was measured by burying dosimeters at the site. Neanderthal fossils were recovered at Kebara (the younger site), whereas early modern human fossils were found at Qafzeh.

The related thorium-230/uranium-234 ($^{230}Th/^{234}U$) method is also used to date inorganic carbonates. Like other uranium-series methods, it depends on the high solubility of uranium in water. Thus, ground and surface water seeping into limestone caves usually contains uranium but not its daughter isotopes, such as ^{230}Th, which are relatively insoluble. Once crystals of calcite precipitate as stalactites and stalagmites on the cave walls and floors, however, ^{230}Th starts accumulating as the result of the decay of ^{234}U and ^{238}U and this continues until equilibrium is reached. The ratio of ^{230}Th to ^{234}U provides a measure of the time that has elapsed since crystal formation.

The $^{230}Th/^{234}U$ method is useful for mineral samples younger than 300 000 years and has been applied to cave sites in Europe that were once occupied by early *Homo sapiens*, where there are no volcanic rocks suitable for dating by the potassium-argon method. These include Bilzingsleben (Germany), Vértesszöllös (Hungary) and Pontnewydd (Wales), which have ages of 500 000 to 200 000 years.

Uranium-series dating of archaeological remains in caves can be prone to error because of possible difficulties in working out the order of calcite deposition, especially where fragments of cave wall have broken off and layers have become mixed up. There is also the possibility that the dated calcite was contaminated by uranium from an external source, such as dust particles, or that some of the uranium leached from the carbonate after precipitation. For these reasons, several layers of deposit usually need to be dated and other techniques used to check the results.

Thermoluminescence, optically stimulated luminescence and electron spin resonance

The basis of these methods is the same: they measure the number of electrons caught up in defects in the lattice structure of crystals. The defects are caused by decay of small amounts of radioactive elements such as potassium, thorium and uranium within the crystal. The number of trapped electrons increases with time through exposure to this radiation so that the crystal acts as a dosimeter. Only when the electrons are released from the traps is the clock reset to zero.

In the thermoluminescence (TL) method, the accumulated dose of radiation in the crystal lattice is measured by heating the sample to a high temperature to excite the trapped electrons. As they escape from the lattice they emit light known as *thermoluminescence*. The intensity of thermoluminescence is proportional to the number of trapped electrons. The age of the material is obtained by dividing the accumulated dose by the annual dose. The latter is determined by measuring the amount of uranium, thorium and potassium within the sample and in the soil or rock surrounding it, or by irradiating the sample artificially and remeasuring its thermoluminescence. A companion

2. FOSSILS AS DATING INDICATORS

Before the days of radiometric dating, the best way of dating a fossil primate site was by comparing fossil mammals from the site with those from a dated sedimentary sequence elsewhere. For some sites without rocks suitable for radiometric dating, such relative dating still provides the main clues to the site's age. Even at those sites that can be radiometrically dated, it is essential to consider evidence from both fossils and rocks before an age is finally accepted.

When fossils are collected from sediments spanning a temporal range whose relative age can be determined because younger rocks lie above older rocks, there are usually changes through time in lineages of both single species and groups of species. For example, the size or complexity of a tooth in a species of pig may increase in successively younger rocks. In such cases, the 'stage of evolution' can be used as a dating tool.

Some sedimentary sequences are rich in fossils throughout and also contain datable volcanic rocks. One such is the Omo Group in Ethiopia and Kenya, which is exposed to the west, north and east of Lake Turkana and ranges from more than 4 million years to under 1 million years old. Many important hominid fossils have come from these rocks. The many animal fossils known from this sequence have been invaluable in clarifying the age of these hominids, particularly those from Koobi Fora, east of Lake Turkana.

When the hominid skull KNM-ER 1470 from the Koobi Fora Formation of the Omo Group was found in 1972, the geology of the sedimentary sequence was not fully worked out. A radiometric determination on a volcanic rock just above the hominid suggested an age of 2.6 million years. However, mammalian faunas associated with the cranium suggested that it was younger, close to 2.0 million years.

The pig genus *Mesochoerus* was particularly helpful here. Pig fossils are well known from a long and well-dated sequence in Omo Group rocks in Ethiopia, only 150 kilometres north of Koobi Fora. In two species, *Mesochoerus limnetes* and *M. olduvaiensis*, there was a steady increase in size of the third molar through time. The relevant *Mesochoerus* sample from Koobi Fora matched that from the 2-million-year levels in the Ethiopian part of the sequence.

Subsequent careful redating of the Kenyan rocks showed that their radiometric age was indeed close to 2.0 million years (1.88 + 0.2 million), not 2.6 million years as had previously been believed.

Caves in South Africa are an important source of fossil hominids, but contain no rocks suitable for radiometric dating. In the past 20 years, analysis of the fossil mammals in the cave sequences, especially the bovids (giraffe, pig and cattle family), has made it possible to compare each site with the calibrated East African sequence.

The Pliocene and early Pleistocene faunas of eastern and southern Africa are as dissimilar as are their counterparts today, so exact matches are difficult. Nevertheless, enough is now known to place the principal South African sites in relative order: they run (from oldest to youngest) Makapansgat, Sterkfontein, Kromdraai and Swartkrans.

Progress is also being made towards giving these sites dates. For example, Makapansgat bovids are similar to those found at several sites in East Africa ranging from 3.7 to 2.5 million years ago. If all the evidence is taken into account, the date for the deposition of the Makapansgat cave sediments is probably around 3 million years ago.

These estimates are not as precise as the age determinations for the East African hominid sites, but they do help to clarify the evolutionary patterns of the southern populations of early hominids.

A third example of the use of fossil faunas in dating comes from the later hominid site of Jebel Qafzeh in Israel. From Qafzeh has come an important series of early modern *Homo sapiens*. On the basis of small mammals such as rodents its age was estimated as close to 90 000 years. But evidence from stone tools and the hominids themselves suggested an age of close to 40 000 years. Recent results from thermoluminescence dating suggest that the most probable age is indeed close to 90 000 years (see p. 183).

This is another demonstration of the importance of considering the faunal evidence as well as other kinds of dating evidence before accepting an age for a hominid site.

David Pilbeam

See also 'Evolution of australopithecines' (p. 231) and 'Evolution of early humans' (p. 241)

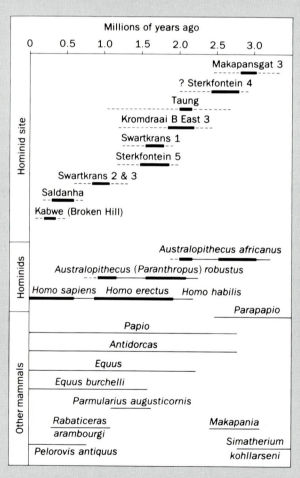

Ages of some southern African hominid sites based on their fossil faunas. Also shown are estimated time ranges of the fossil hominid species known from the sites and of some of the mammalian taxa used to date them. The numbers after the site names are the stratigraphic units (members). *Parapapio* and *Papio* are baboons; *Equus* and *Equus burchelli* are zebras; the remaining species are bovids (buffaloes and antelopes).

technique called optically stimulated or photo-stimulated luminescence uses light instead of heat to evict the electrons from the traps.

In the electron spin resonance (ESR) method, the number of trapped electrons in the sample is determined not by driving them out by heating but by measuring their absorption of microwave radiation. Traps occupied by a single electron act as paramagnetic centres with a static magnetic field. When placed in a microwave-frequency electromagnetic field the electrons in the traps oscillate between orientation with and against the field. Energy is absorbed from the applied field according to the number of traps occupied by single electrons and correlates to the age of the sample. An advantage of ESR over TL is that a sample can be tested repeatedly by ESR whereas TL dating can be done only once.

TL and ESR measure the time elapsed since the last draining of electron traps – when the sample's clock was reset to zero. For burnt flint artefacts this happens when the material is first heated – for example, in a hearth. Exposure to sunlight does this for sediments while they are being transpoprted and deposited. Burnt flints at Palaeolithic sites, deposits of loess, cave sediments, bone and teeth are among the materials that can be dated by these methods. They are less precise than radiocarbon but have a wider age range and can also be used to date inorganic materials. Careful adjustments have to be made for uptake of radioactive elements from the environment.

The TL method has had an important role in the controversy over the relationship between Neanderthals and anatomically modern people. Dates for burnt flints found at the cave sites of Kebara and Qafzeh in Israel support the idea that Neanderthals were not direct ancestors of modern humans, because they arrived in the Middle East several tens of thousands of years after the first anatomically modern people in the area.

Amino acid racemisation

This dating method depends on the slow chemical conversion of left-handed amino acids present in living organisms to their right-handed counterparts. As this is a chemical (rather than nuclear) process, the rate of conversion is very sensitive to the environmental conditions in which it occurs. Not only temperature, but also the composition of the material in contact with the specimen changes the rate of conversion, and this limits the value of the technique.

The best material for this method at present seems to be eggshell of extinct and modern species of ostrich and owl, which is often found at archaeological sites. The technique may be especially useful in Africa at sites with remains of early modern humans that fall between the ranges of the radiocarbon and potassium-argon methods, between about 40000 and 200000 years old. In colder regions, the age range of the method may extend up to a million years.

Palaeomagnetic polarity stratigraphy

This dating method requires prior calibration. The magnetic field of the earth runs from pole to pole. At irregu-

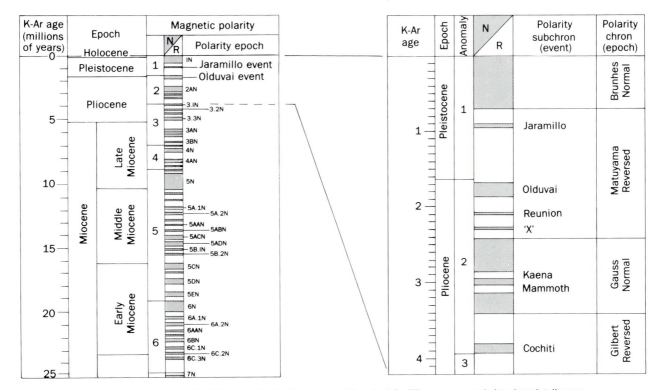

Magnetic polarity intervals for the past 25 million years (left) with the interval from 0–4.2 million years expanded to show details more clearly (right). Normal intervals are shaded; reversed intervals, white.

lar intervals in geological time the polarity of this field has changed so that the modern pattern (positive in the Northern Hemisphere and negative in the Southern Hemisphere) has been reversed. Processes such as cooling of lava, settling of magnetic particles during sediment deposition and growth of iron-rich minerals within sedimentary rocks can preserve a record of the magnetic field when the rocks were formed. The field direction is measured using a magnetometer. Potassium-argon dating of lavas whose polarity has been measured in this way gives a timescale of the change of polarity for about the past 12 million years. This has been extended to the beginning of the Mesozoic era by study of magnetic anomalies on the ocean floor.

The pattern of ancient changes to the earth's polarity in samples through a stratigraphic section is compared with the known pattern of the palaeomagnetic polarity timescale. Most rock strata are not continuous, so that their approximate age must be established by fossils or by isotopic dating before their magnetic signature can be fitted to the correct time period.

This method gives important information on several primate fossil localities where the chronology is already reasonably well known – for example, at the hominid site of Olduvai Gorge in Tanzania. A most significant contribution has been to give age estimates of the Miocene sediments of the Siwalik region of northern Pakistan, where mammalian fossils, including hominoids, have been found. The faunas of the Nagri and Dhok Pathan Formations in this region are now known to be between 6 and 12 million years old. As 13 palaeomagnetic transitions exist in the sequence between 6.5 and 8.6 million years ago, it is possible to establish an accurate chronology for this portion of the sequence.

F.H. Brown

See also 'Climatic change in the past' (p. 174), 'Fossil deposits and their investigation' (p. 187), 'Evolution of australopithecines' (p. 231) and 'Evolution of early humans' (p. 241)

Fossil deposits and their investigation

Understanding fossils as part of a larger geological and biological story rather than as isolated collectors' items has changed the way in which we learn about the past. Instead of having too few fossils and too little information from each one, we now face the challenge of sorting through and integrating vast amounts of diverse information from fossils in their geological setting or *context*. From this we can learn about how our human ancestors lived, died and were preserved.

The value of context is widely recognised, and modern palaeoanthropological expeditions include specialists who study it in the field and in the laboratory. Fossils are now often left where they were found until the site can be described by geologists. Small amounts of matrix may be left on specimens so that there is a record of the type of rock that encased them. This represents a significant change from previous methods of collecting and preparation.

Types of deposits

Fossils of land vertebrates, including hominids and their ancestors, are found in a variety of different deposits, which geologists classify according to the sedimentary environment they represent. This environment determines the nature of the rocks and the preservation of the fossils. Many of the best-preserved fossil hominids have been found in deposits formed at the margin of ancient lakes, but caves, river systems and volcanically active areas are also important. Such deposits contain the fossil record of most Cenozoic land vertebrates. In a few cases, such as the fossil-rich Eocene–Oligocene deposits of the Fayum in Egypt (see p. 205), the primate-bearing river sediments grade into marine beds laid down at the edge of the sea,

when the Mediterranean coast was nearer than it is today. Generally, however, marine deposits do not preserve many fossils of land vertebrates.

Caves

Caves generally form in limestone rocks through dissolution of the limestone ($CaCO_3$) by ground water rich in carbon dioxide. They can also occur in sandstones and as lava tubes in volcanic rocks. Cave deposits are formed by sand, silt and clay brought in by flowing water, by precipitation of $CaCO_3$ as travertine, and by collapse of the cave roof and walls, to give *cave breccia*. The end result is usually a very complex interlayering of irregular units, as is the case with the australopithecine cave deposits at Sterkfontein and similar sites in South Africa.

Most cave deposits represent relatively short periods of deposition (less than 10 000 to 100 000 years) and often involve special circumstances leading to bone concentration, such as the accumulation of carcasses in carnivore lairs (see p. 329). The fossil bones are often well preserved and may be encased in hard travertine. Such deposits are not easy to date because of the absence of volcanic material and because it is difficult to correlate deposits from different caves so as to judge their relative ages.

River systems

Rivers leave behind various types of sediments where they build up (or *aggrade*) their beds rather than erode them. Sands and gravels are found in the deposits left by an active river channel or subchannels (such as *crevasse splay* channels, where a flooded river breaks through its banks and flows onto a floodplain). River banks (or *levees*) consist of alternating beds of sand and silt next to the channel. Floodplains themselves are made up primarily of clays and silts that often reflect periods of soil formation. Some wet and swampy floodplains form carbon-rich deposits called *lignites*. Individual fluvial strata are usually broken into geographically discontinuous units over distances of tens of metres to kilometres, depending on the scale of the river system. There may be long periods when very little sediment is laid down and soil forms, followed by a short period of rapid build-up of sediment during the sporadic floods that characterise most rivers.

Volcanic ash and lava that provide materials for radiometric dating are sometimes incorporated into fluvial deposits, which can also be dated by measuring their palaeomagnetic polarity – the direction of the magnetic field preserved in the rocks at about the time of their deposition. Many important hominoids have been found within fluvial deposits.

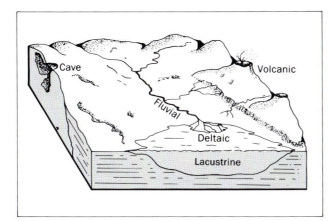

The four major depositional settings that preserve the fossil record of human evolution. There are many subenvironments within each setting, and taphonomic processes that affect skeletal remains differ among these subenvironments.

Lakes and deltas

Lakes are catchments for the water and sediment transported by rivers. They may be fresh if there is an outflow, or alkaline if the drainage is closed. Sediments deposited in the lakes themselves include fine-grained silts and clays, limestones, diatomites and the remains of shelled invertebrates. Alkaline lakes may deposit various kinds of salts such as gypsum and halite, and also more unusual precipi-

(Above) Overview of an excavation in Pleistocene lake-margin deposits north-east of Lake Turkana, northern Kenya, showing trackways of hippopotamus and hominid exposed on a bedding surface. The walls of the excavation reveal fine-grained, thinly layered sediments that are typical of lake-margin settings. (Below) Cross-section of the trench excavated by Kenyan Kimolo Mulwa through one of the hippo prints.

tates such as chert (a hydrated silicate). Their individual sediment beds are usually thin and geographically continuous.

Deposits at lake margins are more complex and may derive from beach barrier bars, lagoons or deltas. The sediments vary from coarse conglomerate to fine silt and clay. Sedimentary structures and spatial relationships between the different units (*facies relationships*) allow each type of environment to be distinguished. Datable volcanic materials can occur within the strata of lakes and deltas, and such strata also retain palaeomagnetism (although this may sometimes be obscured by chemical reactions). The important fossil site of Koobi Fora in Kenya includes good examples of hominid-bearing lake-margin deposits.

Volcanic deposits

Volcanoes may be inhospitable places to live near, but the unique composition of the volcanic sediments can be very favourable for preserving fossils and for correlating beds over wide areas. Volcanic material such as ash and pumice (tephras) may fall over wide areas and be worked into the soil or, if the ash is thick, it may form a distinct, continuous unit that blankets the terrain. Lavas, mudflows and hot, gas-charged ash flows can cover the landscape and follow the courses of rivers, burying the underlying fluvial deposits. Consolidated volcanic strata (tuffs) are generally horizontal, except near the mouth of a volcanic cone or vent. If volcanic outcrops are discontinuous, they can sometimes be correlated with each other (see p. 181).

Animals living near a volcanic eruption are rarely preserved as fossils, but this has happened in East Africa. The ash-falls from some volcanoes included an unusual igneous material called *carbonatite*, which is rich in calcium carbonate. This caused rapid fossilisation not only of bones but also of softer materials such as chitin and wood. This mode of preservation is responsible for most of the Miocene primate record in western Kenya, such as at Fort Ternan, and for the hominid footprints at Laetoli in Tanzania (see p. 325).

Methods of studying fossil-bearing deposits

Study of the geological context of fossil-bearing deposits involves several different approaches.

Lithostratigraphy is the study of different types of sedimentary layers – their distribution in space and succession through time. A stratigrapher is a geologist who specialises in measuring, mapping and ordering sediments. Part of his or her job is to study correlations between strata from different places. This is particularly important because it shows the age relationships – older, younger or contemporaneous – of deposits in different areas. One of the goals of lithostratigraphy is to establish a *relative time* framework, or stratigraphic sequence, for all the other information that can be gathered from the study of rocks and fossils.

This can be done at a wide range of scales, from distances of a few metres in cave deposits to tens of kilometres in deposits from streams, lakes or volcanoes.

There are various approaches to determining the environments in which rocks were deposited. In *lithofacies* analysis, the relationships of rock types, sedimentary structures and unit boundaries are interpreted in terms of ancient environments, often by comparing them with analogous modern sediments. *Microstratigraphy* aims to reconstruct the centimetre-by-centimetre details of particular environments, often at important palaeontological or archaeological sites. *Petrology* is the study of microscopic properties of rocks using thin sections. It may help in correlation and environmental reconstruction. The *geochemistry* of sedimentary rocks can reveal the chemical conditions under which they formed. *Stable-isotope* studies, particularly of oxygen and carbon, are providing important new information on palaeoclimates and lake chemistry. Finally, in *basin analysis*, geologists look at the structure of a sedimentary basin and at the sources of the deposits that filled it.

Chronostratigraphy, the study of the time represented by various sediments, depends on lithostratigraphy, but goes much further in attempting to establish an *absolute time* framework for all the other information derived from the rocks and fossils. This is done using *radiometric dating* and *magnetostratigraphy*. For radiometric methods, such as potassium-argon dating, to be successful, the rock or crystal containing the radioactive elements must be sealed against any escape of the parent isotope and its daughter product, and the time when the radiometric 'clock' starts must be close to the time of deposition. This usually limits the use of this technique to volcanic ashes and flows.

If no radiometrically datable rocks are available, then magnetostratigraphy can be used to calibrate against a global magnetic polarity timescale (GMPTS) that has been established in places where volcanic rocks or other information provide absolute ages. If the general age of a locality is known, and if there are enough sediments to provide a distinctive magnetostratigraphic pattern, then it is often possible to date the locality by correlating it to the GMPTS.

Chronostratigraphy has recently expanded into studies of short intervals of time or *isochrons* that can be traced in sedimentary rocks. This is done by following the magnetic reversals along an outcrop and studying the sediments that occur between them. It is sometimes possible to follow the changes in an ancient environment almost as if one were walking across a buried landscape. This method has great potential for allowing us to look at the fossil faunas and environments in particular time slices from different basins and even from different continents.

TAPHONOMY — THE SCIENCE OF BURIAL

Deciphering how fossil samples are related to the original plant and animal community is part of *taphonomy*, the study of preservation and its effect on the fossil record. Interest in the ecology of fossil hominids has stimulated much recent research in taphonomy. There is now a great deal of information on the bone assemblages associated with hominid fossils, and this tells us much about the ecological communities as well as the feeding and foraging behaviour of early humans.

Information about ancient communities of organisms is transferred into the fossil record through a series of stages. Between each stage, some of the information about such ecological parameters as species diversity and habitat use is lost or altered by the taphonomic processes listed in the lower part of the diagram.

Taphonomic processes that affect organic remains between death and fossilisation are particularly important in biasing the evolutionary record of humans and other organisms. Once a fossil collection is made, the reconstruction of the original community begins.

The fossils themselves give information on the identity of the animals and plants and something about their ecological niches. Contextual studies give information on habitats, age of deposits and palaeoclimate. Taphonomy and palaeoenvironmental studies give information on taphonomic biases that affected the fossil assemblage. Such studies also tell us about the behaviour of predators and scavengers, including hominids. Using all of this information, palaeoecologists seek to understand ancient communities and the ecological forces that helped to shape human evolution. *Anna K. Behrensmeyer*

See also 'Reconstructing past environments' (p. 191) and 'The hominid way of life' (p. 325)

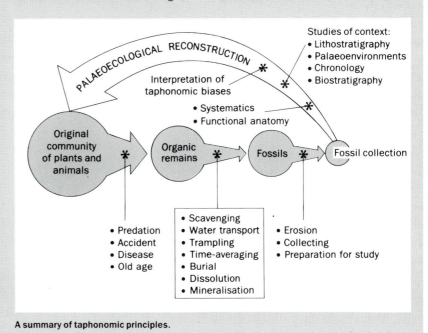

A summary of taphonomic principles.

Biostratigraphy is the study of the vertical succession of fossil animals and plants. Before absolute dating and magnetostratigraphy were developed, fossils gave geologists the only time framework that could show rocks in one area to be older or younger than those in another. Fossils are still used to date important localities such as the South African australopithecine caves, and can sometimes provide more precise chronology than can radiometry.

Reconstructions of ancient ecology depend on the careful study of *biofacies*, the consistent associations of particular fossils in sedimentary rocks. Biofacies analysis goes hand in hand with the study of the sedimentary environments (lithofacies analysis), and both are essential in palaeo-ecology.

The goal of palaeoecology is to determine the features of the original living communities of organisms and their habitats. However, associations of fossils may not accurately represent such communities because of the complexities of burial and preservation, which selectively destroy and mix remains from different sources (see Box 1).

The importance of geological context

Information from studying fossils in context may reveal the ways in which humans and other organisms were inter-related parts of an evolving system. With the new tools of chronostratigraphic correlation, we may find that changes in microfossils in the deep oceans happened at the same time as shifts in the distribution of animals on land. We may then be able to relate both to large-scale climatic events. Through such interdisciplinary research we are beginning

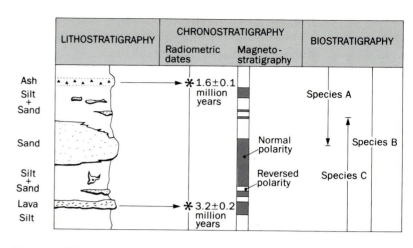

Three essential components of the study of fossils in *context*. The rock record provides information on the succession of sediment types and depositional environments (lithostratigraphy), as well as materials for dating (chronostratigraphy) and documentation of the appearance and disappearance of fossil species (biostratigraphy) through the period spanned by the deposits. Note that an age estimate for a new locality that had species A, B and C together would be more precise – that is, reflect a shorter span of time – than an age estimate based on radiometric dates.

to discover how the course of primate evolution over the past 30 million years has been shaped by global climatic changes, by plate tectonics, and by the evolution of plants and animals.

Anna K. Behrensmeyer

See also 'Climatic change in the past' (p. 174), 'Methods of dating' (p. 179), 'Reconstructing past environments' (p. 191), 'The fossil history of primates' (p. 199), 'Evolution of apes' (p. 223) and 'Evolution of australopithecines' (p. 231)

Reconstructing past environments

The study of the interrelationships between fossil animals and their surroundings – *palaeoecology* – is in many ways the same as the study of living animals, but it uses very different sources of information. The relationships between living animals and their environment can be studied directly, but those of fossil animals must be inferred from indirect evidence. This chapter describes the nature of this evidence and shows how it has been used in the study of the palaeoecology of fossil apes, monkeys and humans in Africa and Asia.

Sources of ecological information

The evidence available to palaeoecologists represents only a few of the many factors that operate in living ecosystems. Climate is perhaps the single most dominant influence on ecological systems, but except in very broad terms it is almost unknown for most palaeoecological reconstructions. Fossil pollens in a continuous core taken from sediments at the bottom of a lake sometimes allow temperatures to be inferred by analogy with the distribution of vegetation today, and variations in rainfall may be inferred from expansion or contraction of rivers and lakes. However, information on ancient climate is usually restricted to analysis on a global or at best a continental scale. A little information may be available on features such as hills and rivers, but this is usually extremely local and provides no general picture of regional topography or of its effects on microclimate.

Vegetation can itself sometimes provide a valuable source of information on palaeoecology either in the form of pollen or remains of fruits and leaves. Because most plants have ecologically limited ranges, the identification of fossil plants and comparison with living species provides some insight into the structure and complexity of their habitats. For instance, the species diversity and probable canopy structure of fossil trees tell us much about the complexity of the forest and its palaeoecology. There are problems in interpreting palaeobotanical evidence, however, mainly because plant remains can be dispersed well away from their original habitat by wind and by water and some parts of plants do not fossilise well.

Fossil animals also provide palaeoecological information, although they are not often found in the same fossil bed as fossil plants. Many taphonomic factors – those associated with the preservation of fossils – may so alter the composition of a fossil animal assemblage that the animals in the death assemblage may not represent the living community; bones may be further modified by scavenging, weathering and wear.

Further changes may occur during fossilisation and even during subsequent excavation, so the species in the excavated assemblage of fossil bones may give a very biased picture of the community in which the animals once lived. However, any palaeoecological study must attempt to reconstruct these past communities and it is the recognition and correction of such biases that makes taphonomy such an important part of the subject.

Extinct faunas also differ from living faunas in that they incorporate a time element. A *chronofauna* is one that has maintained its basic structure over a geologically significant time. Changes in climate or other conditions can lead to faunal changes, which can manifest themselves in changes to particular species, to the community, or to the fauna as a whole. Where the information from fossils is complete enough to record such changes, palaeoecology provides a powerful tool that is not available to those who study the ecology of living communities.

The simplest method of reconstructing the ecology of extinct faunas is to identify the species present, to compare them with their living counterparts, and, by analogy with the ecology of those living species, to infer that of the fossils. This method is open to many sources of error, because animals are ecologically more diverse than are plants, so that even closely related species have very different ecological requirements. In an attempt to overcome this problem, taxonomic comparisons may be combined into a single index based on the inferred ecological affinities of all the animals making up a fossil fauna.

Sometimes the taxonomic aspect of the fossil fauna is simplified by assessing the ecological adaptations of its constituent animals without reference to details of classifica-

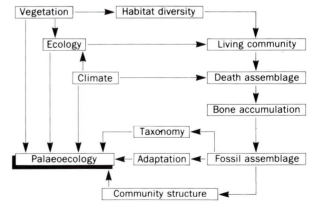

Interrelationships between ecology, palaeoecology and taphonomy, and the factors affecting each. Ecological factors influence the development of living communities of animals; these contribute to fossilised bone assemblages; and the fossils are used to reconstruct the palaeoecology, which is the nearest approximation to the original ecology that can be achieved.

tion. Single characters, or groups of characters, provide evidence on the adaptations of animals; for example, wear patterns on teeth indicate diet, and the shape of limb bones indicates adaptations to running or climbing. Ecological parameters such as size, diet and locomotor adaptations can be combined for a whole fauna, and measures of the ecological diversity of fossil faunas can be compared with those of living faunas to make inferences about palaeoecology.

Diversity within particular taxonomic groups can also be compared with the diversities of their modern relatives. For example, the size distribution of primates or antelopes from different habitats can provide an indication of the habitat in which they lived. Even the number and diversity of species can provide information for a group such as the primates, because more than three or four species are today found together only in tropical rain forests, and the same was probably true in the past.

All these palaeoecological inferences are based only on analogy: the interpretation of palaeoclimatic, geological, palaeobotanical or palaeontological evidence is based on what we understand of what takes place today. The time component in the fossil record also means that there is potential confusion arising from temporal changes in a fos-

sil fauna. Despite all these difficulties, however, some attempt can be made to interpret palaeoecology so long as it is remembered that the evidence can be biased and is entirely inferential. Several such attempts have been made in the study of the evolution of apes and humans.

Hominoid environments in the past

The earliest known higher primates (catarrhines) have been found in Oligocene sediments about 30 to 40 million years old in the Fayum Depression in northern Egypt. Geological evidence shows that it was an area of floodplains, with localised ponds and meandering, slow-moving streams. Conditions were stable enough for soils to develop in these moist, lowland alluvial deposits. The trunks, leaves and fruits of many large trees have been preserved, probably indicating a wet tropical climate. There are mangroves in the deposits, so the sea was close by. The fossil molluscs resemble modern species living in shallow freshwater marshes, and although the vertebrate fauna is unlike any living today, the diversity of the different forms suggest a rich and varied habitat.

The primate fauna is also diverse, with at least nine species. These have a size distribution similar to that of the New World monkeys of the Central and South American tropical forests. As many as four species could have lived in the area at any one time. All this suggests that, by analogy with studies of modern environments, the Fayum had a wet and warm tropical climate, and was a low-lying tropical rain

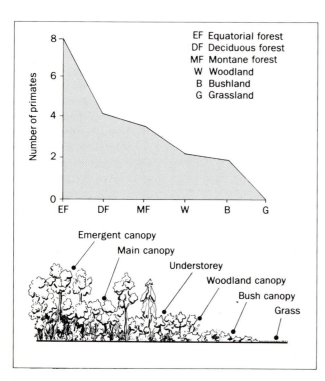

Numbers of simian primate species in tropical African forests expressed in terms of the degree of plant cover. On the left of the scale is equatorial evergreen forest with three tree canopies and two of bush and ground cover; next is semi-deciduous forest with two tree canopies and much more dense bush and layers of ground vegetation; then comes woodland with a single tree canopy and a pronounced bush canopy, and ground cover, which is predominantly grass; this is followed by bushland with only two vegetation layers, one of bush and one of grass; finally, comes grassland with a single layer of grass. The numbers of simian species present in these habitats vary from over eight to none.

EARLY HOMINID ENVIRONMENTS IN AFRICA

Locality (approximate age in millions of years)	Palaeoenvironment
Tabarin, Kenya (5–4)	Lake margin, with locally variable savanna elements
Middle Awash, Ethiopia (4.5–3.9)	Fluvial conditions, with extensive tectonic activity associated with the formation of the East African Rift
Laetoli, Tanzania (3.7–3.2)	Savanna woodland, with well-defined wet and dry seasons
Hadar, Ethiopia (3.6–2.6)	Lake and associated floodplain, with braided streams and rivers
Omo, Ethiopia (Shungura) (3.3–1.4)	After 2.1 million years ago, dry savanna flanking river banks with gallery forest and dry-thorn savanna; before this date, the environment was probably forested
Koobi Fora, Kenya (3.3–1.4)	Before about 1.6 million years ago, a freshwater lake with floodplains, gallery forest and dry-thorn savanna; during later times, the lake fluctuated from fresh to brackish
Olduvai, Tanzania (1.9–<1)	Salt lake with surrounding floodplains with seasonal streams and rivers and dry woodland savanna; tectonic changes after 1.5 million years ago resulted in the drying up of the lake
Transvaal, South Africa (Makapansgat 3, Sterkfontein 4 and 5, Swartkrans 1, Kromdraai and Taung) (3–1.4)	All were mosaic environments, with Makapansgat Member 3 and Sterkfontein Member 4 being less open (more bush/woodland) than Swartkrans Member 1 and Sterkfontein Member 5; this suggests a trend from wetter to drier conditions through time

(Above) The early Miocene site of Mfwangano Island, Lake Victoria, Kenya. Its palaeoecology is analogous to that of present-day tropical rain forests. This conclusion is based on fossilised fruit remains, such as those shown here from *Entandrophragma*, a large forest tree sometimes called African mahogany (Below). The fossil fauna also has the ecological structure of modern forest-adapted faunas.

forest on an alluvial plain interspersed with swamp and open water. In such an environment, early simian primates such as *Aegyptopithecus* and *Propliopithecus* lived.

The palaeoecology of East Africa during Miocene times, some 23 to 5 million years ago, was quite different. Most of the evidence comes from the plateau of equatorial eastern Africa, which is 1000 to 2000 metres high and hundreds of kilometres from the sea. Two parts of the African Miocene will be discussed here: the early Miocene from 20 to 18 million years ago and the middle Miocene from 15 to 14 million years ago. Faunas from both periods include species of fossil ape.

Evidence from the early Miocene of East Africa comes from fossil sites on alluvial plains, such as Rusinga and Mfwangano Islands on Lake Victoria, and also from sites that preserve fossil soils developed on volcanic tuffs, such as Songhor in Kenya and Napak in Tanzania. Plant remains occur in the alluvial deposits, mainly as fruits and seeds of a

mixture of species. These indicate that in places there was wet tropical forest, whereas elsewhere deciduous woodlands were widespread.

Both these types of vegetation occur in eastern Africa today, so that the climate in early Miocene times was not very different from the modern one. Fossils of land snails also suggest the same mixture of habitats, and freshwater molluscs indicate that there were large areas of water. Land snails in the volcanic soils are most similar in type and diversity to those living in tropical rain forest today. The mammalian faunas from the early Miocene are more similar to living faunas than were those of the Oligocene, being barely half their age. Their diversity also supports the view that there was a mixture of tropical rain forest and open woodland in the early Miocene of East Africa.

Hominoid primates lived in both types of ancient habitat, but, like today, there were more species in evergreen forest than in deciduous woodland. More species (at least four or five) of the fossil apes *Proconsul* and *Rangwapithecus* are found associated with typical forest plants and animals than with more open, wooded environments, which have only one or two species. These early hominoids thus seem to have been still primarily adapted to a forest way of life.

In middle Miocene times in East Africa, there was the same mixture of sedimentary conditions as in the early Miocene. There is evidence of floodplains on the Lake Victoria island of Maboko and soils developed on volcanic tuffs are present at Fort Ternan. There are few useful plant and gastropod remains, and most information comes from vertebrate fossils. The taxonomic and ecological diversity of this fauna again suggests a mixed ecology, consisting mainly of forests with more open canopies and more deciduous trees than in the early Miocene. At least three hominoid species were present, together with monkeys at some sites. It is not yet clear which habitat they preferred. There is a new genus of hominoid (*Kenyapithecus*) with thick-enamelled cheek teeth as well as descendants of early Miocene forms.

Later in the Miocene (between 12 and 6 million years ago), the evidence from fossil deposits in Africa is sparse. Hominoids from this period are better known from Europe and Asia, and the radiation of hominoids with thick-enamelled teeth is particularly well represented in Indo-Pakistan. Here, the fossils occur in sediments laid down by shallow, braided river channels that emerged from the developing Himalayas. The vegetation associated with such ephemeral habitats was probably constantly changing. The deposits span a much longer period than of any of the East African sites mentioned so far, and faunal changes can thus be related to changes in palaeoecology.

For instance, the disappearance of hominoids from the Siwalik sequence in northern Pakistan occurs at about the same time as the disappearance of large and small browsing mammals and their replacement with animals with higher-crowned (hypsodont) teeth adapted for grazing. Isotopic

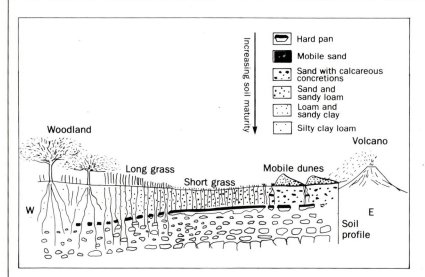

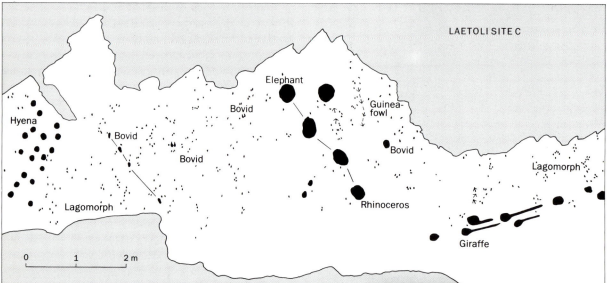

LAETOLI SITE C

Woodland

Long grass

Short grass

Mobile dunes

Volcano

Hard pan
Mobile sand
Sand with calcareous concretions
Sand and sandy loam
Loam and sandy clay
Silty clay loam

Increasing soil maturity

W   E

Soil profile

Elephant

Bovid

Guinea-fowl

Hyena

Bovid

Bovid

Bovid

Lagomorph

Lagomorph

Rhinoceros

Giraffe

0   1   2 m

The Plio-Pleistocene hominid locality at Laetoli (Tanzania) can be reconstructed from the remains of footprints, mammals and sedimentary evidence. Analysis of the ecological diversity of the fauna shows that the site has the closest analogy not with modern grassland faunas but with a mixture of woodland and grassland habitats. In reality, there was probably a mixture of bush, woodland and grassland at the site between 3.8 and 3.5 million years ago, which varied according to local conditions. An example of the type of habitat occupied by early hominids at Laetoli and lower Bed I, Olduvai – *Acacia* woodland around Lake Nakuru, Kenya – is shown on the top right.

The diagrammatic section (top left; not to scale) shows the soil/vegetation association running from east to west across the ecosystem of the Serengeti Plains today. Wind direction is generally from east to west, with calcareous windblown tuffs from the still-active volcano Oldoinyo Lengai being wind-sorted to form mobile sand dunes and progressively more mature soils to the west away from the influence of the volcano. As the soils become more mature, with a greater amount of silt and clay, the vegetation changes also, first to longer grass and finally to woodland. This forms a close parallel to the situation at Laetoli and at Olduvai Gorge (lower Bed I) during the Plio-Pleistocene. Volcanic activity would have produced immature soils, changing soils and a great variety of habitat, leading to rich mammalian faunas and good opportunities for scavenging and plant gathering for the early hominids living there. Footprints of numerous animals, including hominids (see p. 325), have been found on an open area of wind-blown tuffs. Some of the trails at Laetoli site C are shown on the plan (centre). Guinea-fowl and elephant prints (right) are common at all the footprint sites.

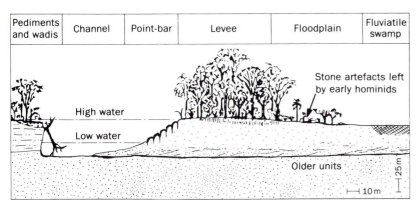

Reconstruction of the habitats and soils in the Plio-Pleistocene Shungura Formation, Omo River (Ethiopia). Raised banks (levees) next to the river had thick vegetation and/or forest, while on the floodplain away from the river the predominant vegetation was grass. Most

hominid activity (in the form of scatters of stone artefacts left by early *Homo*) was concentrated along the edge of the gallery forest next to the more open floodplains. The photograph is an aerial view of such an environment in southwestern Ethiopia today.

analysis of soil carbonates shows a parallel change from woody vegetation to grasses. This local change from woodland to more open grassland meant that the hominoids, as part of the forest fauna, were unable to adapt to the new environment. The ecological diversity of the faunas with which the hominoids are associated in India suggests the presence of subtropical deciduous forest. It also confirms how variable the conditions must have been.

The characteristic hominoids of these late Miocene environments are *Sivapithecus* (including *Ramapithecus*). They had broadly similar dental and facial adaptations as the East African *Kenyapithecus*, and because both forms are associated with tropical to subtropical deciduous forest, the thick-enamelled apes could be adapted to the more open deciduous forest during this period. This happened before the emergence of human ancestors (hominids), and this lessens the ecological division between tree-living apes and terrestrial hominids.

Hominids are well represented in Pliocene and Pleistocene sediments in eastern and southern Africa, and many are associated with relatively open environments. Some of the South African hominid fossils are the bones of prey assembled by large carnivores such as leopards and hyenas (see p. 232), but the East African examples are preserved in terrestrial deposits laid down around lake margins at such sites as Olduvai Gorge, East Turkana (Koobi Fora), Omo and Hadar. Pollen remains at these sites show the presence there of grasses and trees typical of mixed habitats, with grassland, closed woodland and forest on lakesides and riverbanks, and forest on mountain slopes.

The taxonomic composition of antelopes and their relatives (bovids) emphasises the open aspect of the environment at many hominid sites, but the diversity of small mammals (such as rodents) points to some dense local vegetation as well – for example, at Olduvai and Laetoli. This mixture of vegetation types in the fossil record arises from taphonomic bias, with the rodent bones representing animals living and dying near water and the bovid bones a mixture of local animals with those transported in from the

surrounding open grassland. However, it is likely that fossil hominids lived in areas of mixed habitat.

It may be that different species of early hominid lived in differing environments. During the Plio-Pleistocene, 4 to 1 million years ago, early australopithecine hominids were widespread in eastern and southern Africa. Two kinds lived in South Africa, where they are known from caves in wooded to open grassland habitats. In eastern Africa, australopithecines initially lived in well-wooded habitats, as at Laetoli, but in the late Pliocene, most are associated with more open savanna environments.

With the appearance of our own genus, *Homo*, by 2 million years ago, there was an interesting development. Early *Homo* (*H. habilis*) lived at the same time as australopithecines, but where they occur in the same areas the australopithecines are associated with more open habitats whereas *Homo* apparently lived in more wooded habitats, often on the banks of rivers. These early hominids probably depended on animal scavenging and plant food for their subsistence. Areas with more plant cover would offer more varied opportunities for food gathering than open savannas, and also gave greater protection from large carnivores. Later in human evolution, another species of *Homo* (*H. erectus*) lived in more open habitats in Africa. This habitat shift may well reflect increased hunting by these hominids.

Just before 1 million years ago, hominids spread out from Africa for the first time into Europe and Asia, increasing their range of habitats as they extended well into the temperate zone. This spread has continued until today when humans occupy even such inhospitable areas as Antarctica, and it will continue, with increasing exploitation of marine and perhaps even extra-terrestrial environments.

Peter Andrews

See *also* 'Climatic change in the past' (p. 174), 'Fossil deposits and their investigation' (p. 187), 'The fossil history of primates' (p. 199), 'Evolution of apes' (p. 223), 'Evolution of australopithecines' (p. 231) and 'Evolution of early humans' (p. 241)

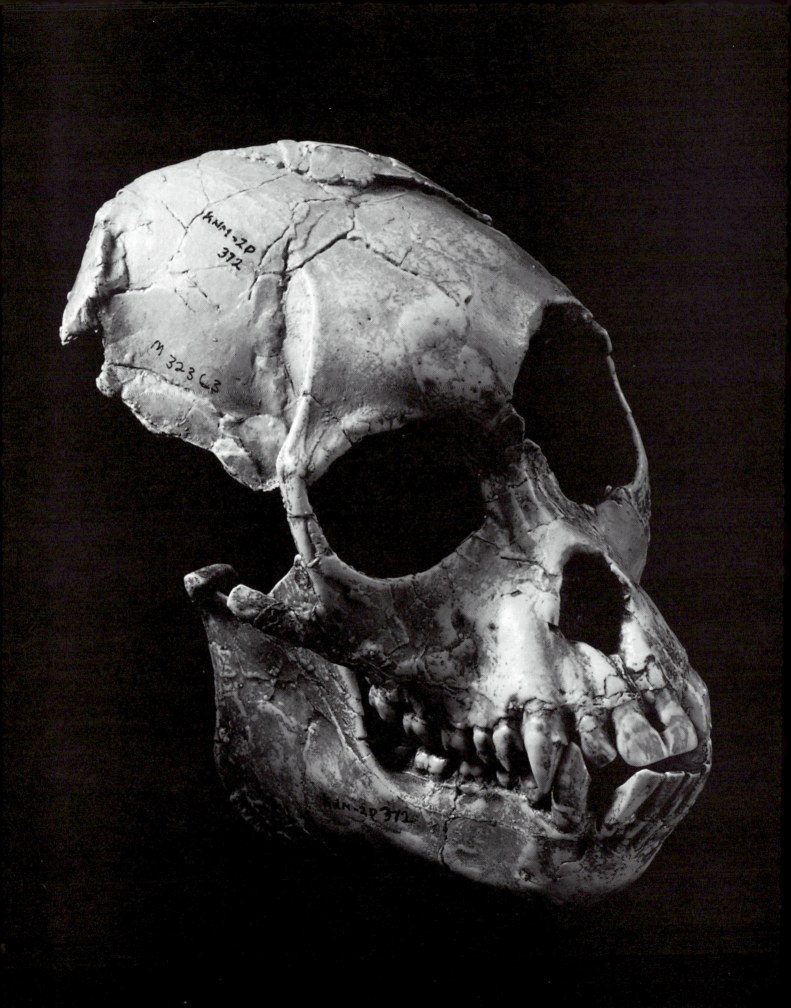

Part Six

The primate fossil record

The fossil record helps in our understanding of the evolutionary history of any plant or animal group and gives essential information about the timing of important evolutionary events, such as the first and last appearances of species. It tells us about animal communities unlike any today. In addition, it provides us with creatures that had combinations of characters that we do not see in living forms.

All fossil records are very incomplete, and that of primates is no exception: far more forms must have lived than those that have been found as fossils. Fossil records are also geographically unbalanced. For example, Africa is poorly sampled before the Oligocene epoch, yet we have good reasons to believe that Africa was a major centre of primate evolution, and that the abundance of primates of modern aspect in the Eocene of North America and Europe reflects their migration there from the south more than evolution *in situ*. Studying primates provides a new perspective on ourselves and helps to reconstruct our ancestry. Five major primate groups are well established by anatomical and behavioural studies of living species (**1.3**): lemurs and lorises; tarsiers; New World monkeys or ceboids; Old World monkeys or cercopithecoids; and the Old World hominoids (apes and humans). The first two are collectively called the prosimians and the last three the anthropoids or simians. Tarsiers are slightly closer to simians than are lemurs and lorises.

Fossil species can be added to this framework, generally as side branches with no living descendants, but sometimes close to or — occasionally — actually on a lineage of living species. For the first 30 or 40 million years of primate evolution, prosimians were very abundant (**6.1**). Today, however, lemurs and lorises are no longer a diverse group and the small, insect-eating tarsiers consist of only one genus with four or five species in Southeast Asia. The larger-brained simians had two parallel radiations, one in South and Central America (**6.2**) and the other in the Old World, initially in Africa (**6.3** to **6.6**).

Most primate fossils are merely fragments of jaw or isolated teeth, and few species are known from large samples. The assignment of specimens to species is based on comparisons with related living species. There are often differences of opinion about how individual fossils should be sorted into species. This means that the schemes presented in the following chapters are not the only plausible versions of the taxonomy of the primate fossil record. The determination of how species are related to each other is the second critical step in using the evolutionary record. Fossils have contributed surprisingly little to our understanding of relationships among living species. Indeed, in a few cases, genetic comparisons suggest

**Skull of *Proconsul africanus*
from Rusinga Island, Kenya.**

197

relationships different from those inferred using morphological information. For example, morphologists used to think that the African apes (the two chimpanzees and the gorilla) and the Asian orang-utan were each other's closest relatives. Genetically, however, the African apes are closer to humans. As genetic studies expand, we can probably expect more surprises.

Taxonomy has a major impact on the determination of relationships. For example, the sample of *Homo habilis* from the late Pliocene and early Pleistocene of Africa (**6.6**) could represent either one or two species. How individual specimens are sorted into species determines the distribution of morphological characters within species, and thereby influences decisions about their relationships.

Reconstruction of past behaviours requires a thorough knowledge and understanding of living species, especially their functional anatomy, development and ecology (see Parts 1 and 2). Behavioural reconstruction is most difficult in those cases where extinct species differ radically from living ones. The fossil colobine monkey *Mesopithecus* (**6.3**) resembles today's langurs (*Presbytis*), so reconstructing the basics of its behaviour is not difficult. By contrast, the extinct hominoid *Sivapithecus* has a unique combination of features, and is unlike any living monkey or ape (**6.4**).

Once the taxonomy, relationships, behavioural reconstruction and dating are established for a fossil group, one can look at evolutionary patterns and how they change through time. Many explanations for change in the primate record invoke biotic factors, such as competition between species or even between groups of species. For example, the archaic primates (plesiadapiforms) of the Palaeocene and Eocene are often said to have been driven to extinction because of the rise of the more competitive rodents (**6.1**). Old World monkeys are sometimes seen as outcompeting and almost replacing apes during the past 20 million years (**6.3** and **6.4**). However, abiotic factors, such as environmental change, are equally likely explanations for these shifts. Whatever has driven primate evolution, we will never understand it without an adequate fossil record.

The fossil history of primates

The order Primates – the 'first ones' – is notable for the extent of its fossil record, which dates from the latest part of the Cretaceous period. The extinct genera recognised by palaeontologists greatly outnumber living ones.

Where and when primates first appeared remains uncertain because fossil evidence of the earliest representatives of the order is lacking. However, it is widely agreed that primates emerged from archaic terrestrial and nocturnal insectivores (shrew-like animals) during late Cretaceous times, becoming a group distinct from other mammals between 90 and 65 million years ago. Tree-shrews (order Scandentia), bats (Chiroptera), flying lemurs (Dermoptera) and rodents (Rodentia) have been variously linked to primates and there is recent evidence of a close relationship between flying lemurs and primates. This chapter summarises the primate fossil record, from the primitive so-called archaic primates of Palaeocene and Eocene times to human ancestors, hominids, of the Plio-Pleistocene.

It has been suggested that Africa was the continent of origin of primates. Unfortunately, African mammals are very rare in the first third of the Tertiary period, immediately following the Cretaceous, whereas Palaeocene and Eocene primates are widespread and abundant in Eurasia and North America.

The story of the order Primates apparently begins with two species of the archaic primate *Purgatorius*, which lived in the late Cretaceous and early Palaeocene of eastern Montana, USA, at least 65 million years ago. The cheek teeth of *Purgatorius* have sharp cusps, which may imply that it ate insects, as do small living insectivorous primates such as mouse lemurs (*Microcebus*) and the dwarf bushbaby (*Galago demidovii*). This first primate was a mouse-sized animal whose skeleton and locomotor adaptations are so far unknown.

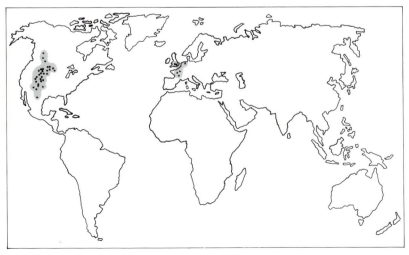

The principal sites of discovery of archaic primates (plesiadapiforms) in the Palaeocene and Eocene.

Archaic primates

The initial radiation of the archaic primates (the plesiadapiforms) occurred in the Northern Hemisphere, suggesting that the group may indeed have originated in this hemisphere. By middle Palaeocene times (around 60 million years ago), archaic primates had diversified into at least four families: the Picrodontidae, Carpolestidae, Plesiadapidae and Paromomyidae. (Some authorities include a fifth family, the Microsyopidae, in this group.) These 'half-lemurs' were mostly the size of rats or mice, although there were a few larger species the size of domestic cats.

The teeth of all archaic primates show an evolutionary trend towards leaf- and fruit-eating specialisations and away from the sharp-cusped, primitive dental patterns of their insect-eating predecessors. The view that the plesiadapiforms should be classified as primates has been challenged because none had all the features that characterise later primates. For example, they lacked a bony strut at the side of the orbit (*postorbital bar*) so that their eyes were not surrounded by a complete bony ring. They also did not have expanded brains nor perhaps opposable thumbs and great (big) toes, and they had few obvious adaptations for life in trees. Most had large, angled incisors, which may have been useful for opening seeds and fruits, and many had low-crowned cheek teeth with flattened and sometimes jagged cusps that resemble miniature versions of the cheek teeth of later folivorous and frugivorous primates.

There is a strong similarity between the teeth of some Palaeocene archaic primates (e.g. *Plesiadapis*) and later forms called adapids from the Eocene (e.g. *Notharctus*). This provides the main basis for the suggestion that the plesiadapiforms, although primitive, are indeed related to the primates of modern aspect from Eocene to recent times, which are collectively called euprimates. There is, however, some intriguing new evidence from the ear region and postcranial skeleton, implying that at least some plesiadapiforms may have been related to flying lemurs. It has even been suggested that plesiadapiforms should be removed from the primate order entirely.

The infraorder Plesiadapiformes takes its name from the common Palaeocene genus *Plesiadapis*, which is the best known and most widely distributed of the group. Large parts of the fossilised skeleton have been found in Colorado and in France, where it occurs in abundance. The name means 'half towards the sacred bull', Apis, and is based on George Cuvier's misnomer for a lemur-like primate from the French Eocene, *Adapis*, which he thought was related to cattle. Named in the 1870s, *Plesiadapis* was

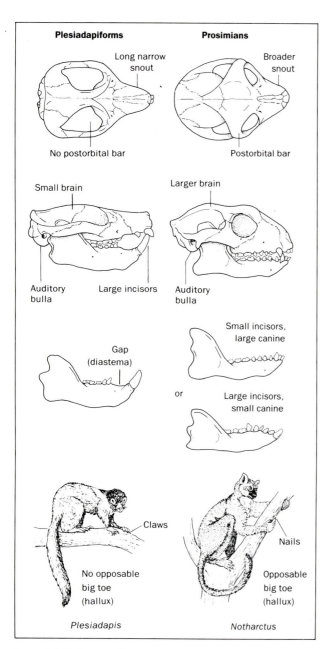

Characteristic features of archaic primates and early modern primates.

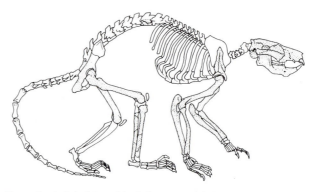

Reconstructed skeleton of the Palaeocene archaic primate *Plesiadapis tricuspidens* based on specimens found at Berru, near Rheims, France. Notice the stocky limbs and rat-like skull. Large claws, deep from top to bottom and compressed from side to side, would have assisted in climbing.

aye-aye (*Daubentonia madagascariensis*), an aberrant Malagasy lemur, are convergent.

The paromomyids are little-known, *Plesiadapis*-like primates, which diversified in the middle Palaeocene. An early member of this radiation, such as *Plesiolestes* from the Palaeocene of Wyoming or *Navajovius* from Montana, may be close to the direct ancestry of the primates of modern aspect that first appear in the earliest Eocene of France and Wyoming, but such a relationship has not been clearly shown.

Another early family of archaic primates, the picrodontids, had teeth resembling those of bats. A fourth family, the carpolestids – known as the 'fruit-stealers' because of their specialised blade-like premolars – are small primates from Palaeocene deposits in western North America. Like *Purgatorius*, these animals are about the same size as the smallest of living primates, such as dwarf bushbabies, mouse lemurs and pygmy marmosets.

Specialisations of teeth are of great interest to palaeontologists because they often reveal the details of evolutionary change in populations from successive time zones. Unfortunately, these microevolutionary transitions are not generally documented for extinct primates because of gaps in the fossil record. Populations of 'fruit-stealers' show gradual enlargement through time of the back lower premolar into a large serrated blade such as that found in *Carpolestes*. This cuts against the upper premolars, which had multiple cusps. This mechanism has a parallel in the teeth of some living Australian marsupials, such as rat kangaroos (*Bettongia*), which use them to cut up vegetation. The subtle but well-established changes in tooth anatomy among carpolestids provide the best example of evolution in progress among primates, even though these plesiadapiforms left no later descendants.

The heyday of plesiadapiforms was in the Palaeocene epoch in North America, Europe, and perhaps Asia. In the early Eocene, around 50 million years ago, the plesiadapiforms began to decline, perhaps because they were outcompeted as arboreal fruit- and leaf-eaters by rodents,

thought to have molars somewhat like those of *Adapis*. Most species of *Plesiadapis* were the size of squirrels, but a few were as large as cats. They had distinctive incisors, with large upper teeth opposing inclined lower teeth, separated by a large gap from the lemur-like cheek teeth.

It has been suggested that the limb bones of *Plesiadapis* show adaptations for arboreal life, but this archaic primate had robust, stocky limbs and also a primitive, small brain. Fingers and toes ended in large, laterally flattened claws, which were probably used in climbing rather than for digging. Because it is so widespread in Europe and North America, *Plesiadapis* must presumably have migrated on the ground between forests. The dental specialisations of all plesiadapids suggest that they were not direct ancestors of later primates; the resemblances in the front teeth to the

EVOLUTION OF PROSIMIANS

The term prosimian, literally 'before ape', covers the grades of primate evolution that preceded higher primates and gave rise to them. Prosimians are distinguished from other primates by what they lack. They do not have the following features characteristic of modern monkeys and apes: large brain, short muzzle, fused frontal bones, formation of a postorbital plate behind the eyes, shovel-shaped (spatulate) incisors, fused joint (symphysis) between the two halves of the lower jaw, large carotid arteries or feet with nails on all toes.

Three groups of prosimians are generally recognised: the archaic primates or proprimates (Plesiadapiformes), the 'tarsier-like primates' (Tarsiiformes) and the 'lemur-like primates' (Lemuriformes).

Archaic primates are characteristic of the Palaeocene epoch (65 to 56 million years ago). As the epoch progressed, they became more specialised. All looked like squirrels in general appearance but there was a wide range of dental types, indicating diverse diets. The group might include tree shrews (Scandentia) and flying lemurs or colugos (Dermoptera) as descendants, but it is otherwise extinct.

Prosimian primates of modern aspect, the tarsiiforms and lemuriforms, first appeared in Eocene times (beginning 56 million years ago). They share various features that indicate a common ancestry. The ancestral form is not present in the fossil record of Europe or North America, so primates of modern appearance probably originated in Africa or possibly South Asia.

There is only one living tarsiiform genus — Tarsius, the tarsier of Southeast Asia. Tarsius obviously cannot represent the full diversity of tarsiiform primates known from the Eocene but it does provide a reasonably good living model for the appearance of some early members of the tarsiiform group.

There are some 20 living genera of lemuriform primates, including all of the lemurs of Madagascar, and the lorises and bushbabies of Asia and Africa. Fossils representing the loris and bushbaby group — the modern family Lorisidae — are first known from the early Miocene of East Africa and the middle to late Miocene of southern Asia.

Malagasy lemurs themselves have a fossil record spanning only the past few thousand years and recently extinct lemurs are hence no more than subfossils. They show that Madagascar once supported many different types of lemur, including some much larger than any known today. Most of these fossils, however, can be allocated to the modern families Lemuridae, Indridae and Daubentoniidae, and contribute little to understanding the evolutionary history of any of the living lemur families.

Fossil prosimians are important intermediates between more generalised mammals and higher primates, and living prosimians may provide an approximate model for the early stages of primate evolution.   *Philip D. Gingerich*

Prosimians

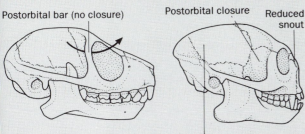

Unfused midline joint in the lower jaw (mandibular symphysis)

Postorbital bar (no closure)

Unfused frontal bones

Grooming claw

Simians

Larger, more forward-facing eyes

Small upper incisors separated by a cleft

Fused mandibular symphysis

Postorbital closure   Reduced snout

Larger, more rounded braincase

Fused frontal bones

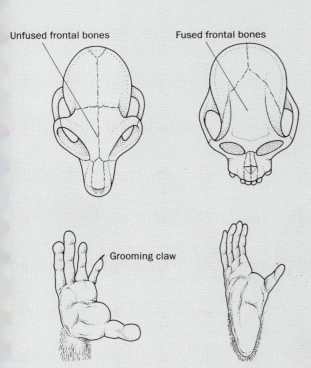

The main distinctions between prosimians and simians (anthropoids).

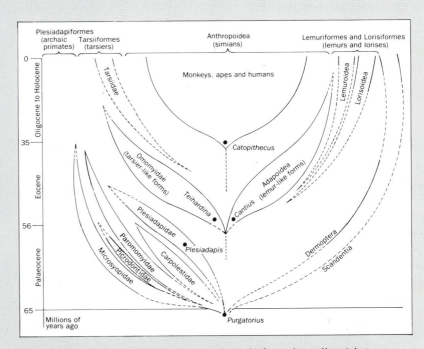

Successive evolutionary radiations of primates during the Cenozoic era. Uncertain phylogenetic relationships are indicated by dotted lines. The families of archaic primates (plesiadapiforms) and the position of some Palaeocene and Eocene genera are shown. The taxonomic status of the plesiadapiform family Microsyopidae is unclear; some classifications include its members in other plesiadapiform families whereas others regard them as primitive insectivores. Tree-shrews (order Scandentia) and flying lemurs (order Dermoptera) may be closely related to primates and are shown as possibly sharing an ancestor with primates in the late Cretaceous.

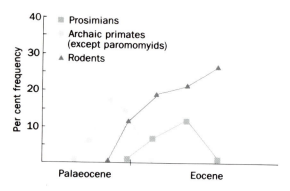

The heyday of the plesiadapiforms was in the Palaeocene in North America, Europe and perhaps Asia. This graph (based on the fossil record in North America) shows that these archaic primates had begun to decline by the early Eocene, perhaps because they were outcompeted as tree-living fruit- and leaf-eaters by early rodents, which increased in numbers dramatically at about this time. As the plesiadapiforms became extinct, early modern-looking primates, the omomyids and adapids, also began increasing in numbers. These primates probably did not cause the extinction of the archaic primates; more likely, they gradually took over some of the ecological niches left vacant as the plesiadapiforms disappeared.

which had an explosive adaptive radiation in the early Eocene. By the end of the Eocene, around 35 million years ago, the plesiadapiforms were gone from Europe and only one species of paromomyid survived in North America. The plesiadapiforms were entirely replaced by rodents, lemurs and primates of modern aspect.

The earliest modern primates

Primates that look more like modern prosimians (lemurs, lorises and tarsiers) – the first euprimates – appear in early Eocene deposits in Belgium, France, England and Wyoming. At this time, some 56 million years ago, the North Atlantic had not yet finally come into being and very early Eocene mammals could move freely between Europe and North America via the Faeroes, Iceland and Greenland. The first two of these early primates of modern aspect are a mouse-sized form, *Teilhardina*, and a larger rat-sized contemporary, *Cantius*, both found in Europe and western North America. Either *Cantius* or *Teilhardina* could be a direct ancestor of all later primates, including humans, but no links connecting either to the earliest Old World anthropoid primates of the Egyptian Oligocene (see p. 205) have yet been found. These two primates gave rise to two highly diversified families, the Omomyidae (*Teilhardina*) and the Adapidae (*Cantius*).

There are about 40 genera of these Eocene prosimians. They share many dental and postcranial features with modern prosimians (see Box). None of these northern Eocene forms has characteristics of the suborder Anthropoidea, which must therefore have arisen in the second half of the Eocene, very likely in Africa. Two fossils, *Altiatlasius* and *Azibius*, from, respectively, the Palaeocene and Eocene of North Africa, may have been euprimates, but the fossil evidence is insufficient for a clear interpretation.

The best-known Eocene prosimians show distinct arboreal adaptations in limbs, hands and feet, and had large brains and eyes that were directed forwards, with fully developed postorbital bars. Many had long hindlimbs with a large opposable great toe and sometimes lengthened ankle bones. These features, together with the cusp patterns on their teeth, show that most Eocene prosimians were agile, tree-dwelling animals, specialised for eating fruit and leaves. They had distinctly larger brains for their size than did most other Eocene mammals.

Primates were once thought to be rare in the past. However, they are now known to have been common wherever there were warm temperate to tropical forests in the early Cenozoic. Among living prosimians, nocturnal species can be distinguished from diurnal ones because of their relatively larger eyes and hence larger orbits. Applying this standard to Eocene prosimians suggests that some were active during the day and some by night.

(Above) Reconstruction of the omomyid *Shoshonius*, from the Eocene of Wyoming, USA. This early primate, which lived about 50 million years ago, was nocturnal and closely resembled modern tarsiers of Southeast Asia in some features of the skull base. (Left) One of the fossilised skulls of *Shoshonius*, dorsal view with the front pointing downwards. It is comparable in size to a tarsier skull (5–6 cm long).

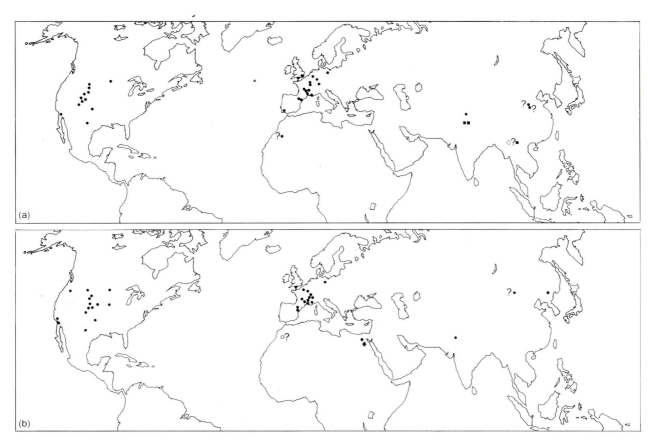

The principal sites (mostly Eocene and Oligocene) of discovery of early true primates: (a) lemur-like forms (family Adapidae) and (b) tarsier-like forms (family Omomyidae). The affinities of some of the Asian and African fossils are unclear. A possible omomyid (*Altiatlasius*) from Morocco (○) could be of late Palaeocene age, which (if correctly assigned) would make it the earliest known true primate; three adapids from India, Pakistan and China (■) are Miocene in age. *Afrotarsius* from the Oligocene of the Fayum region in Egypt (◆) is classified with modern tarsiers in the family Tarsiidae rather than in Omomyidae. Two fossils from the Eocene of Burma (◇), *Pondaungia* and *Amphipithecus*, have a mixture of prosimian (adapid) and simian features. If simian, they may predate the earliest simians from Fayum.

The Eocene primates have been divided into two principal groups – the 'tarsier-like' and 'lemur-like' forms. The tarsier-like primates are commonly allocated to the single family Omomyidae, with three subfamilies: Anaptomorphinae, Omomyinae and Microchoerinae. The microchoerines are known only from Europe and may be more closely allied with the living Southeast Asian tarsiers (family Tarsiidae), which are represented today by only one genus, *Tarsius*. The Eocene lemur-like primates are generally classified in the family Adapidae, with separate subfamilies – Notharctinae and Adapinae – for the mainly North American and the mainly European forms, respectively.

The Adapidae and Omomyidae differ in several respects. The ear bones of adapids were not extended into a tube as is the case in omomyids. Adapids were usually rather larger than omomyids, which were squirrel-sized or smaller. Most notharctines were between a kitten and an adult cat in size, matching the range from the modern gentle lemurs (*Hapalemur*) through the brown lemur (*Lemur* or *Eulemur fulvus*) to the ruffed or variegated lemur (*Varecia variegata*). Both tarsier-like and lemur-like Eocene prosimians were specialised for leaping and jumping. The adapids had some skeletal similarities to leaping indrid lemurs, and omomyids characteristically had an elongated heel and foot, resembling the development taken to an extreme in modern bushbabies and tarsiers.

Tarsier-like primates (omomyids)

Teilhardina, an anaptomorphine, was named in honour of the religious philosopher and palaeontologist Pierre Teilhard de Chardin. Fossil specimens, mainly jaws, occur in the earliest Eocene deposits of Belgium. The teeth had a generalised, tarsier-like pattern and seem to have been adapted for processing insects. *Teilhardina* has also been found in the earliest Eocene deposits in Wyoming. With an age of around 56 million years, it may be near the base of the radiation that produced all the living primates (perhaps with the exclusion of lemurs and lorises). It is thus one of the two oldest, small, generalised euprimates, the other being the earliest species of *Cantius* (a notharctine), which has also been found near London, England, and in the Wyoming Eocene.

If *Teilhardina* is close to the origin of the simian primates (Anthropoidea) and *Cantius* near that of the prosimian primates (lemurs and lorises), then the first main division among surviving primates must have occurred before then, perhaps about 65 to 60 million years ago. *Teilhardina* probably weighed 50 to 80 grams. A gorilla weighing 160 kilograms (350 lb) is about 2600 times heavier, which illustrates the scale of size increase among primates in the past 50 to 60 million years.

Another early North American omomyid with a more advanced dentition, the anaptomorphine *Tetonius*, is known from many jaws and one well-preserved skull. It is also about 56 million years old and is the oldest known primate skull. It had an enlarged brain and small face. The cheek teeth suggest that *Tetonius* was insectivorous, like modern tarsiers, but it was smaller than *Tarsius*, being comparable in size to mouse lemurs or dwarf bushbabies. A somewhat younger omomyine dating back to about 50 million years ago, *Shoshonius*, is now well documented through the discovery of six skulls in Wyoming. *Shoshonius* has some similarities to *Tarsius* that are not found in other omomyids. This may indicate a specific relationship to tarsiers and it certainly shows that tarsier-like primates were very diverse by the end of the early Eocene.

An omomyine from the middle Eocene of North America called *Hemiacodon* is unusual in that many post-cranial remains have been found. These show that its heel was somewhat elongated and was probably adapted for powerful leaping. The metatarsal of the great toe shows that this digit could be opposed to the other digits, as is typical of non-human primates of modern aspect. Another omomyine, *Rooneyia*, is known from a well-preserved skull from the early Oligocene of western Texas. Like the microchoerines of Europe, the skull of this primate had an extended, tubular ectotympanic bone (the external auditory meatus), joining the inner ear to the outside world. The earliest anthropoids, such as the somewhat younger *Aegyptopithecus* from Egypt (see p. 207), lack such a tube, and it was never acquired by the New World monkeys. We can hence be sure that the ancestors of simians (monkeys and apes) did not have this auditory tube.

Necrolemur, from the middle Eocene of south-central France (Quercy), is the best-known microchoerine primate and is relatively well documented. Its skull shows resemblances to that of tarsiers in several features. Like both *Rooneyia* and *Tarsius*, *Necrolemur* had a long external auditory tube. The presence of this feature in both omomyines and microchoerines at such an early date disqualifies them from direct ancestry of monkeys and apes. Moreover, the structure of the auditory bulla (the bony shell forming the underside of the middle-ear cavity) and nearby blood vessels is not at all like that of simians. The bones of the lower limb (tibia and fibula) of *Necrolemur* may have been fused, as in modern tarsiers, an adaptation otherwise unique among primates. *Necrolemur* also had a forward-shifted foramen magnum, large forward-facing orbits, a large brain and a small face – all suggesting that it was a leaping form that held its body erect.

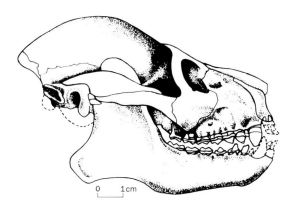

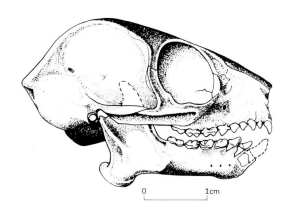

Reconstruction of the skulls of (above) a representative adapid (*Leptadapis magnus*), a lemur-like primate, and (below) an omomyid (*Necrolemur antiquus*), a tarsier-like primate. Both are from the middle Eocene deposits in the Quercy caves, south-central France. Notice the shorter snout, larger central incisors and larger eyes of the omomyid. The ectotympanic bone of omomyids was extended into a tube; adapids lacked a tubular ectotympanic bone, having a free ring within the bulla. The simian primates (monkeys, apes and humans) may be related to one of these groups (adapids, omomyids) or they may have arisen from another African stock. The omomyids gave rise to modern tarsiers.

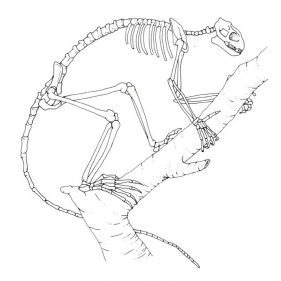

Reconstructed skeleton of the adapid *Smilodectes gracilis* from the middle Eocene of the Bridger Basin, Wyoming, USA. This early modern primate was similar in size to modern lemurs but had shorter limbs. Notice the long tail, the grasping foot and opposable big toe.

Lemur-like primates (adapids)

The omomyids might have been a source for the higher primates but the Eocene adapids have also been proposed as candidates for this. Their smaller, unspecialised incisors, fused jaws and details of the cheek teeth may foreshadow developments in simians better than do the same parts of omomyids.

Adapis was the first fossil primate to be described (by Cuvier in 1821). It is known from several skulls, many mandibles and some limb bones from the Quercy caves in France and from several other sites. Cuvier first regarded this primate as a relative of hoofed mammals. Since the turn of the century, however, the similarities between *Adapis*, a

Reconstruction of a scene from the Oligocene of Egypt (below), based on the fossils recovered from the Fayum Depression (or badlands) south-west of Cairo, and (above) the barren landscape of Fayum today. A wide range of animals lived in the tropical forests and woodlands that covered the area 30–40 million years ago, including several primate species. In the palm on the lower left of the drawing is *Aegyptopithecus*, on the centre right is *Parapithecus* gathering fruit, and on the far right is *Afrotarsius* clinging to a spiral vine. In the foreground of the photograph are the fossilised remains of logs.

related genus (*Leptadapis*) and the modern Malagasy lemurs have been emphasised. The molars of *Adapis*, which show some similarity to deer teeth, also resemble those of sportive lemurs (*Lepilemur*) and gentle lemurs (*Hapalemur*), suggesting that *Adapis* was a leaf-eater. Its skeleton shows that it was a climber with relatively short hindlimbs. In this feature, it resembled lorises and was unlike any modern Malagasy lemur.

Notharctus was the second earliest North American fossil primate to be described (in 1870). Skeletons of this animal and of the closely related *Smilodectes* are the most completely preserved of any primates older than the Pleistocene epoch. They are often compared to modern lemurs, but their feet are less specialised for grasping, clinging and leaping.

It is unclear whether monkeys, apes and humans are derived from adapids, from omomyids or from some as yet unknown African group. Early fossil relatives of apes and humans had unspecialised heels and limbs and lacked elongated auditory tubes. Hence, they probably cannot be derived from an omomyid with specialised foot bones or a tubular ectotympanic bone.

Primates from the Eocene and Oligocene of Africa

Sedimentary deposits in a part of Egypt called the Fayum Depression (or badlands), about 60 kilometres south of the Giza Pyramids near Cairo, contain the earliest-known relatives of tarsiers (*Afrotarsius*) and lorises, an omomyid species and the earliest Old World anthropoids. Fossils of numerous other mammals, birds, reptiles and plants have also been found in these deposits, which are called the Jebel Qatrani Formation. Redating of the deposits shows that they range from at least 31 million to as much as 40 million years old. The geologically oldest Fayum primates are thus late Eocene in age. At this time, Africa was cut off from Eurasia by the Tethys seaway and the Fayum primates lived in tropical forests close to the coastal outlet of a major river system.

Primates were first discovered in this rich fossil-bearing area in 1906. The primate radiation in Africa must have diversified in the late Eocene at the latest – perhaps much earlier – because the dozen or so species from the Fayum Oligocene belong to five different families. Moreover, poorly preserved specimens that may be euprimates have been found in Morocco and Algeria.

Remains of two primate genera and species have recently been recovered from deposits that probably represent the late Eocene in the Fayum. The skull known for one of these forms, *Catopithecus*, already shows distinctive anthropoid features, such as postorbital plates. The earliest Oligocene primate site in the Fayum includes species of two genera: *Oligopithecus* and *Qatrania*. The first of these resembles the later Fayum anthropoids *Aegyptopithecus* and *Propliopithecus* in the structure of its canines and premolars. Similarities to

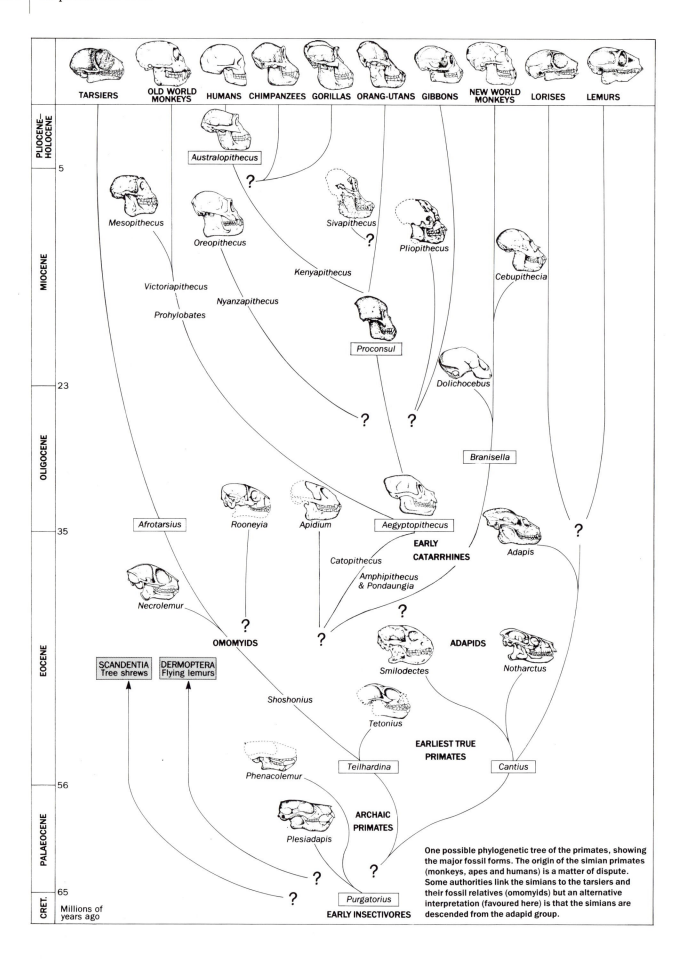

TARSIERS   OLD WORLD MONKEYS   HUMANS   CHIMPANZEES   GORILLAS   ORANG-UTANS   GIBBONS   NEW WORLD MONKEYS   LORISES   LEMURS

PLIOCENE–HOLOCENE

5

MIOCENE

Australopithecus

?

Mesopithecus

Oreopithecus

Sivapithecus

?

Pliopithecus

Kenyapithecus

Victoriapithecus

Cebupithecia

Nyanzapithecus

Prohylobates

Proconsul

23

OLIGOCENE

Dolichocebus

?   ?

Branisella

35

Afrotarsius

Rooneyia

Apidium

Aegyptopithecus

EARLY CATARRHINES

Adapis

?

Catopithecus

Amphipithecus & Pondaungia

Necrolemur

?

OMOMYIDS

?

ADAPIDS

Smilodectes

Notharctus

EOCENE

SCANDENTIA Tree shrews   DERMOPTERA Flying lemurs

Shoshonius

Tetonius

EARLIEST TRUE PRIMATES

Teilhardina

Cantius

56

Phenacolemur

PALAEOCENE

ARCHAIC PRIMATES

Plesiadapis

?   ?

65

CRET.

Millions of years ago

?

Purgatorius

EARLY INSECTIVORES

One possible phylogenetic tree of the primates, showing the major fossil forms. The origin of the simian primates (monkeys, apes and humans) is a matter of dispute. Some authorities link the simians to the tarsiers and their fossil relatives (omomyids) but an alternative interpretation (favoured here) is that the simians are descended from the adapid group.

older but little-known Far Eastern genera (the Eocene *Amphipithecus* and *Pondaungia*) could suggest a possible southern Eurasian origin for the Fayum catarrhines, but an African origin is more likely. Apart from this possible group of early catarrhines represented by *Oligopithecus*, *Catopithecus*, *Propliopithecus* and *Aegyptopithecus*, a separate and distinct family (Parapithecidae) that also belongs in the Anthropoidea is represented in the Fayum by *Qatrania*, *Parapithecus* and *Apidium*.

The teeth and postcranial skeleton of *Apidium* somewhat resemble those of Old World monkeys. The lower molars of *Parapithecus* and of primitive *Apidium* are similar to those of guenons (*Cercopithecus*). *Apidium* had molar teeth with multiple, small cusps, some with a pattern resembling that of Old World monkey molars; some authorities believe that these may be shared derived characters. The postcranial skeleton of *Apidium* suggests that it was an actively jumping and leaping animal of riverine and mangrove forests, a habitat similar to that of titi monkeys (*Callicebus*) today. Its feet were similar to those of some lemurs and some New World monkeys. However, many of the skeletal similarities between *Apidium* and New World monkeys consist only of primitive retentions or convergent adaptations related to leaping.

Aegyptopithecus and *Propliopithecus* from the Fayum resemble apes in dental features and are considered by some to be the earliest members of the Hominoidea, the taxonomic unit containing apes and humans; but others regard them simply as primitive catarrhines. *Aegyptopithecus* is the best-known Oligocene anthropoid. The teeth and skeleton suggest that it or a similar form was a precursor to *Proconsul*, which itself was probably broadly ancestral to modern great apes. These forms seem to represent the mainstream of ape evolution, from which the human lineage emerged in the late Miocene or Pliocene. *Aegyptopithecus* almost certainly lived in the tall trees of a monsoon rain forest where fruits abounded. It was a frugivorous quadruped, with adaptations for climbing and leaping. Differences between the sexes in body, canine and jaw size suggest that *Aegyptopithecus* had a polygynous social system.

Miocene apes of Africa

Proconsul from the early and middle Miocene (23 to 15 million years ago) of eastern Africa is diversified into many species. It is the most completely known extinct simian primate. Fossils have come from Kenya and Uganda and show a range in size equal to that extending from large monkeys, such as *Colobus*, to female gorillas. Another genus, *Afropithecus*, related to *Proconsul* but with distinct links to *Aegyptopithecus*, has recently been described. Smaller eastern African Miocene apes – *Micropithecus*, *Limnopithecus* and *Dendropithecus* – may be direct close relatives of modern lesser apes (gibbons and siamangs) or they may just be primitive catarrhines. These early apes, like those of the Fayum (but

Reconstructed skull of *Aegyptopithecus zeuxis*, an ancestral catarrhine, from the Fayum Oligocene. Notice the centrally fused frontal bones, the postorbital plate (left eye socket) and the large ascending wings of the premaxilla. The cranium was discovered in 1966; the mandible and incisors are restored from other specimens.

unlike modern lesser apes), were also sexually dimorphic.

The skeleton of *Proconsul* shows a blend of primitive, unique and advanced features. The animal was a monkey-like quadruped although it resembled apes in some features of its hands and feet and also lacked a tail. The pelvis had a blend of monkey-like, ape-like and unique features, while the sacrum was flattened and ape-like. There are few skeletons of primates from the middle to late Miocene or the Pliocene and the lineage that led to our own kind has not yet been found.

The Eurasian genus *Sivapithecus*, and perhaps *Gigantopithecus*, are related to the orang-utan (*Pongo*) and not to the radiation of African apes and humans. 'Ramapithecus', now considered by most to be a female *Sivapithecus*, was long thought to be an ancestor of the hominid *Australopithecus* on the basis of shared characters in teeth and jaws, but its similarities to *Australopithecus* are parallelisms or shared primitive features.

The conclusion that the *Sivapithecus* group and other Eurasian apes are not closely related to *Australopithecus* suggests that Africa was the site of the ape/human split. Unfortunately, the African fossil record has a gap between about 13.5 and 5 million years ago. *Kenyapithecus* from Fort Ternan in Kenya, dated to 14 million years ago, was once thought to be an African *Ramapithecus*. The Fort Ternan find has teeth similar to those of *Sivapithecus*. In fact, *Kenyapithecus* almost certainly predates the split between the African great apes and *Australopithecus*.

African Pliocene hominids

Fossils of *Australopithecus* from 5 to 1 million years old have been found in eastern and southern Africa. For the period from 4 to 2.5 million years ago, the anatomy of this hominid is well established from finds made, for example, at Hadar (Ethiopia), Laetoli (Tanzania), eastern and western Lake Turkana (Kenya) and also southern Africa. *Australopithecus* is generally agreed to be the oldest known undoubted hominid. Although it was fully adapted for upright walking, its brain ranged in size from that of a chimpanzee to little more than that of a gorilla, and it is uncertain whether it used tools. *Australopithecus* species had flat faces with flaring nostrils. At least some were markedly sexually dimorphic.

By 2.5 to 2 million years ago, the manufacture of stone tools had begun and some branch of the *Australopithecus* group had given rise to a new species, *Homo habilis*, which first appears at this time in both eastern and southern Africa. From Africa, apparently before 1 million years ago, a larger species, *Homo erectus*, fanned out into Eurasia. Since then, its descendants, our own species *Homo sapiens*, have filled the earth.

Elwyn Simons

See also 'Land movements and species dispersal' (p. 169), 'Reconstructing past environments' (p. 191), 'Evolution of New World monkeys' (p. 209), 'Evolution of Old World monkeys' (p. 217), 'Evolution of apes' (p. 223), 'Evolution of australopithecines' (p. 231) and 'Evolution of early humans' (p. 241)

Evolution of New World monkeys

Present-day New World primates are the South and Central American branch of the simian (anthropoid) stock. They are called monkeys because of their grade position within the order – above the prosimians, below the apes. Generally speaking, they are more or less equivalent to the Old World cercopithecoids, but the term 'monkey' has itself no evolutionary or taxonomic meaning. There is only a limited resemblance between the neotropical New World monkeys (called platyrrhines because of the wide gap between their nostrils) and the Afro-Eurasian cercopithecoid monkeys, such as the macaques and baboons. Platyrrhines have never lived on the ground, despite the wide-spread ancient savannas in South America, whereas the success of cercopithecoids is due to their invasion of grasslands. The most significant ground-use by a platyrrhine is in the deepest, wettest parts of the Amazon basin.

The point is an essential one: the New and Old World monkeys should not be equated, for they are monkeys in name only. In morphology, behaviour and ecology each group has developed its own evolutionary identity since their common stem group began to divide into many descendant lines some 40 million years ago. These separate evolutionary paths have produced far more variety among the forms in the New World than in the Old World.

Although evolutionary histories are often read from the fossil record, to unravel the platyrrhine past we must begin with the present: the fossil record of New World monkeys amounts to only a few hundred fragmentary specimens. With such limited information it is difficult to link fossil to living species, and to cluster the higher taxonomic groups, such as tribes, subfamilies and families. Furthermore, studies based mostly on living species meet with difficulty in distinguishing shared derived features (indicative of a close phylogenetic relationship) and primitive features, which are not reliable phylogenetic markers. The molecular evidence as yet offers only limited help: it confirms the general outlines of the phylogenetic groupings presented here but differs in the placement of certain genera, and it has not resolved the relationships among the higher taxonomic groups.

Classification of living New World monkeys

Estimates of the number of extant platyrrhine species vary greatly, perhaps because of a lack of attention from taxonomists. A rough count of about 50 species for living and extinct genera (Box 1) suggests that New World monkeys are numerically about as diverse as Old World monkeys or the lemurs and lorises (strepsirhine primates). However, numbers alone are misleading, for the Old World forms are spread across three continents and the strepsirhines have been in existence much longer than platyrrhines.

The classification of platyrrhines into families and genera is in a state of flux, but here the debate reflects new ideas rather than neglect. The arrangement outlined here is based on phylogenetic principles and attempts to strike a balance between what we know, what we think we know and what we expect to find as platyrrhine evolution becomes better understood. It differs markedly from traditional classifications, largely because it uses higher categories, such as subfamilies and families, as collective labels for unified phylogenetic groups rather than as expressions of the morphological distinctiveness of groups of genera (see Box 2).

This classification reflects the biological message that platyrrhine phylogeny is closely related to adaptation: the radiation of New World monkeys is linked to feeding. Related animals maintain generally similar ecological niches. Adaptive shifts tend to reflect the expansion of dietary opportunities, often accompanied by changes in size and concomitant locomotor modifications. There are few examples of parallel evolution in different lineages. However, there is some convergent evolution of specific features or functional capacities, such as the semi-prehensile tail of capuchins and the fully prehensile tail of howler and spider monkeys.

Of the five platyrrhine groups that can be recognised, the three fundamental ones are:

- Marmosets and tamarins plus Goeldi's monkey, *Callimico goeldii* (subfamily Callitrichinae in Box 1)
- Sakis and uakaris (tribe Pitheciini in Box 1)
- Spider, woolly and howler monkeys (subfamily Atelinae in Box 1)

Most taxonomists now agree that the members of all three groups each share a common stem, or ancestry. The groups represent an evolutionary arena that includes some very divergent adaptive types. The fourth and fifth groups are:

- Squirrel and capuchin monkeys (subfamily Cebinae in Box 1)
- Titi and owl monkeys (tribe Homunculini in Box 1)

The interrelationships, affinities and taxonomic position of these two groups are more controversial (see Box 2).

Phylogeny, fossils and adaptation

The marmosets and tamarins (tribe Callitrichini) present one of the most fascinating and enduring problems in primate evolution. They are small, have smooth (unconvoluted) brains, simple grasping hands, claws on fingers and toes (apart from the great toe), uncomplicated molar teeth, and a genetically fixed pattern of non-identical twinning; they also rely heavily on the sense of smell. These characteristics are quite different from those of most monkeys, and have been interpreted in very different ways. Some compare marmosets and tamarins with early mammals or their modern analogues (such as tree-shrews), suggesting that marmosets are primitive. Another – and perhaps more likely – view is that some of these features are novelties, secondarily derived from the more typical traits of anthropoid primates.

In this view, the features of marmosets and tamarins result from selection for small size ('dwarfing'), a reversion to an insectivorous diet and high reproductive output. For example, locomotor specialisations make possible their unique ability to range freely through the tropical forest, especially just below the canopy. When searching there for insects and especially when collecting tree saps and gums, their small arms and hands cannot span thick branches or trunks. The slender, clawed hands and feet probably evolved to act like grappling irons. The delivery of twins rather than singletons and the unconvoluted brains may also be an outcome of reduction in body size.

With an insect-based diet, marmosets and tamarins are the masters of the marginal habitat; they colonise the boundaries between different vegetation zones, treefalls and remnant or felled forests. This adaptive pattern may also have evolved through a decrease in size, which is certainly true for the miniature pygmy marmoset (*Cebuella pygmaea*), smallest of the living simian primates. But it is not clear how this idea of an evolutionary reduction in body size can be extended to other small-bodied platyrrhines, such as squirrel monkeys (*Saimiri*), which have different ecologies. The related Goeldi's monkey (*Callimico*) is also small, yet has only a few of the special features of marmosets and tamarins. *Callimico goeldii* has thus puzzled taxonomists; it is a species characterised by traits shared with two different groups of platyrrhines, one primitive, the other derived. For this reason it has been classified in no less than three different families (Cebidae, Callitrichidae and Callimiconidae).

Only two fossil species, *Micodon kiotensis* and *Mohanamico hershkovitzi*, from the middle Miocene site of La Venta in western Colombia, may be related to modern callitrichines. One is known only from three tiny isolated teeth; the other by a nearly complete, beautifully preserved mandible. Apart from these fossils, circumstantial evidence indicates that callitrichines already existed during the Miocene epoch (between 23 and 5 million years ago): various lineages of their nearest living relatives, the cebines, are convincingly represented as fossils during the middle of that period. These include an extinct species of squirrel monkey, *Saimiri* (previously *Neosaimiri*) *fieldsi*, and another *Saimiri*-like species (*Laventiana annectens*) from La Venta, as

well as *Dolichocebus gaimanensis* from a late Oligocene site in Argentina. As the cebines and callitrichines seem to belong to a single evolutionary lineage, their common ancestor must have lived before the time of *Dolichocebus*; callitrichines thus originated long before *Micodon*. However, as we know almost nothing about the anatomy of early callitrichines, their lifestyle remains a matter of speculation.

The cebines are like callitrichines in their reliance on insects, which they extract from piles of dead leaves, from green leaves and from the broken ends of branches. This

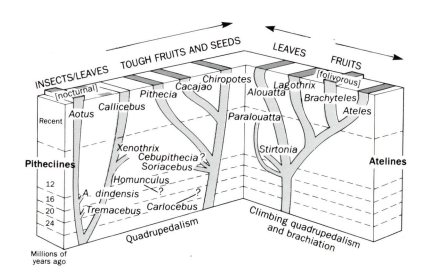

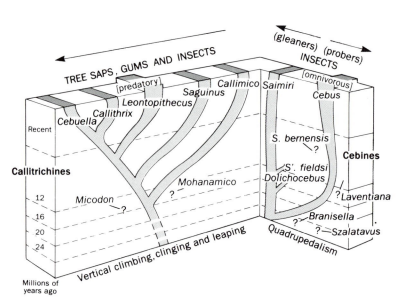

Phylogeny and radiation of New World monkeys. Each panel represents a monophyletic group (subfamily). Panels are paired to represent alternative adaptive strategies within a generalised family-specific adaptive zone. For example, the frugivory–faunivory zone used by cebids is segregated into canopy feeders (cebines) and vertically ranging feeders (callitrichines). Differentiation of the family Atelidae is more complex. A diet of harder fruits and a mix of items (leaves, seeds and insects) provides the protein for the *Callicebus–Aotus* group; seeds for sakis and uakaris; and fruits and leaves for atelines. Food resources and locomotor patterns are shown. Branches linking taxa without fossils do not imply any estimates of their time of origin.

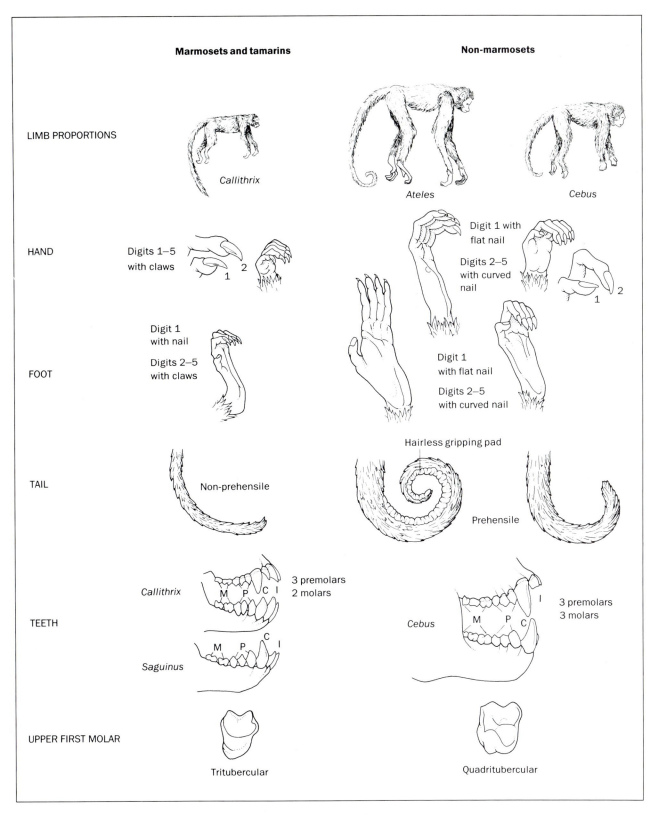

Marmosets and tamarins — **Non-marmosets**

LIMB PROPORTIONS — *Callithrix* — *Ateles* — *Cebus*

HAND — Digits 1–5 with claws — Digit 1 with flat nail / Digits 2–5 with curved nail

FOOT — Digit 1 with nail / Digits 2–5 with claws — Digit 1 with flat nail / Digits 2–5 with curved nail

TAIL — Non-prehensile — Hairless gripping pad / Prehensile

TEETH — *Callithrix* — M P C I — 3 premolars 2 molars — *Cebus* — M P C I — 3 premolars 3 molars — *Saguinus* — M P C I

UPPER FIRST MOLAR — Tritubercular — Quadritubercular

The traditional division of New World monkeys into a 'marmoset' ('callitrichid') and 'non-marmoset' ('cebid') group reflects a presumed shift from a primitive, marmoset pattern to an advanced, non-marmoset pattern, as body size increased and there was less reliance on insects in an arboreal habitat. Many features of 'callitrichids' (referred to here as callitrichines) are, rather, derived. Most 'non-marmoset' traits may hence be primitive, except for the 'prehensile' tail (which is not found in all 'non-marmosets'). According to this view, the claw-bearing marmosets are monophyletic. This means that Goeldi's monkey (*Callimico*), a single species that is sometimes classified in its own family, is a marmoset. In having one offspring per litter and three molars, *Callimico* is simply showing ancestral platyrrhine traits that were transformed in the ancestor of the marmosets and tamarins.

1. A CLASSIFICATION OF LIVING AND FOSSIL NEW WORLD MONKEYS

Superfamily Ateloidea
FAMILY ATELIDAE
Subfamily Atelinae
  Tribe Atelini
    Ateles, Brachyteles, Lagothrix
  Tribe Alouattini
    Alouatta
    †*Stirtonia tatacoensis* (La Venta, Colombia; Miocene)
    †*Stirtonia victoriae* (La Venta, Colombia; Miocene)
    †*Paralouatta varonai* (Cueva de Mono Fosil, Cuba; Quaternary)

Subfamily Pitheciinae
  Tribe Pitheciini
    Pithecia, Chiropotes, Cacajao
    †*Soriacebus ameghinorum* (Pinturas, Argentina; Miocene)
    †*Soriacebus adrianae* (Pinturas, Argentina; Miocene)
    †*Cebupitheca sarmientoi* (La Venta, Colombia; Miocene)

  Tribe Homunculini
    Aotus, Callicebus
    †*Tremacebus harringtoni* (Sacanana, Argentina; Miocene)
    †*Homunculus patagonicus* (Rio Gallegos, Argentina; Miocene)
    †*Aotus dindensis* (La Venta, Colombia; Miocene)
    †*Xenothrix mcgregori* (Long Mile Cave, Jamaica; subrecent, 300 000–10 000 years ago)

  Tribe indeterminate*
    †*Carlocebus ameghinorum* (Pinturas, Argentina; Miocene)
    †*Carlocebus intermedius* (Pinturas Argentina; Miocene)

FAMILY CEBIDAE
Subfamily Cebinae
  Cebus, Saimiri
  †*Dolichocebus gaimanensis* (Gaiman, Argentina; Miocene)
  †*Saimiri fieldsi* (La Venta, Colombia; Miocene)
  †*Laventiana annectens* (La Venta, Colombia; Miocene)
  †*'Saimiri' bernensis* (Cueva de Berna, Dominican Republic; subrecent, 300 000–10 000 years ago)

Subfamily Callitrichinae
  Tribe Callitrichini
    Callithrix, Cebuella, Leontopithecus, Saguinus

  Tribe Callimiconini
    Callimico
    †*Mohanamico hershkovitzi* (La Venta, Colombia; Miocene)

  Tribe indeterminate*
    †*Miocodon kiotensis* (La Venta, Colombia; Miocene)

Subfamily Branisellinae
  †*Branisella boliviana* (Salla, Bolivia; Oligocene)
  †*Szalatavus attricuspis* (Salla, Bolivia; Oligocene)

Fossil forms are denoted by a dagger sign. Important sites are given in parentheses. For 'Saimiri' bernensis, the quotation marks indicate a misclassification; bernensis should be classified in a different genus.
* Indeterminate forms cannot be allocated beyond the level of subfamily.

2. THREE CLASSIFICATIONS OF LIVING NEW WORLD MONKEYS

HERSHKOVITZ (1977)	FORD (1986)	ROSENBERGER (this chapter)
Ceboidea	Ceboidea	Ateloidea (Superfamily)
Cebidae	Cebidae	Atelidae (Family)
Cebinae	*Cebus*	Atelinae (Subfamily)
Cebus	*Saimiri*	Atelini (Tribe)
	Callicebus	*Ateles*
	Aotus	*Brachyteles*
Saimiriinae		*Lagothrix*
Saimiri	Atelidae	
	Atelinae	
	Atelini	Alouattini
	Ateles	*Alouatta*
Aotinae	*Brachyteles*	
Aotus	*Lagothrix*	
	Alouattini	Pitheciinae
Callicebinae	*Alouatta*	Pitheciini
Callicebus		*Pithecia*
	Pitheciinae	*Chiropotes*
Alouattinae	*Pithecia*	*Cacajao*
Alouatta	*Chiropotes*	
	Cacajao	Homunculini
Pitheciinae		*Aotus*
Pithecia	Callitrichidae	*Callicebus*
Chiropotes	Callitrichinae	
Cacajao	*Cebuella*	Cebidae
	Callithrix	Cebinae
Atelinae	*Saguinus*	*Cebus*
Ateles	*Leontopithecus*	*Saimiri*
Brachyteles		
Lagothrix	Callimiconinae	Callitrichinae
	Callimico	Callitrichini
Callimiconidae		*Cebuella*
Callimico		*Callithrix*
		Leontopithecus
		Saguinus
Callitrichidae		
Cebuella		Callimiconini
Callithrix		*Callimico*
Saguinus		
Leontopithecus		

Three groups of New World monkey genera, 11 or 12 of the total of 16, can easily be placed in separate higher taxa. There is less agreement about the other genera, and about the general structure of platyrrhine classification.

The classification of P. Hershkovitz (1977) is a variant of those presented by many authorities during this century, such as W.E. Le Gros Clark, J. R. and P.H. Napier and G.G. Simpson. The arrangement of S. M. Ford (1986) is based on a cladistic system. The third classification – used in this chapter – also emphasises phylogenetic relationships, but incorporates adaptive change and attempts to account for all the known fossils (Box 1).

purposeful foraging behaviour contrasts with the opportunistic insect-eating of the frugivorous titi monkeys (*Callicebus*) and owl monkeys (*Aotus*) – members of the other branch of the platyrrhine radiation and roughly the same size as *Saimiri*.

Although squirrel monkeys and capuchins (*Cebus*) are superficially quite different, in part because of their difference in size, they share many derived features that indicate a common ancestry. Among these are a high ratio of brain to body weight, a foreshortened face, close-set orbits, a rounded braincase, marked sexual dimorphism and a capacity to alter their diet greatly during lean periods. *Cebus* shows other interesting traits that parallel those of early hominids, such as augmented manual dexterity and thick-enamelled molar teeth. The fossil *Dolichocebus*, known from an almost complete skull, suggests that the basic shape of the cebine braincase and some details of *Saimiri* anatomy were established more than 18 million years ago. The nearly complete lower jaw of *Saimiri fieldsi* suggests the presence, 15 million years ago, of an essentially modern version of the squirrel monkey.

A new set of fossils from La Venta – represented by a talus (ankle bone) and a well-preserved lower jaw with nearly all its teeth – is intermediate in morphology between squirrel monkeys and callitrichines. Dentally, *Laventiana* is closest to *Saimiri*, sharing several intricate details of its premolars but not its characteristic molar pattern. The fossil also lacks the thick-enamelled molars of *Cebus* monkeys and thus has a primitive cebine pattern. As this morphology is also like that of callitrichines, it suggests that callitrichines and cebines are closely related and that the La Ventan *Saimiri fieldsi* may be a direct ancestor of modern squirrel monkeys.

The pitheciins – the sakis and uakaris – were until recently the least studied and worst understood of all the platyrrhines. Some are confined to the deepest regions of Amazonia, where they thrive under conditions that thwart other primates. Their habitats are inundated for many months of the year by the Amazon. These incessant cycles of flooding have led to the evolution of new dispersal systems among trees, and a flora based on nutrient-poor soils washed in by the floods from the highlands of Brazil and Guyana. Many plants have fruits and seeds with thick coatings (which may waterproof them) and foliage with toxic secondary compounds that repels browsers. Primate numbers are accordingly low.

Sakis and uakaris are the only frugivorous platyrrhines adapted to cope with these conditions. They have powerful incisors and canines for husking fruit and flat postcanine teeth powered by strong muscles for crushing and grinding seeds. *Cacajao* even forages on the ground for seeds and sprouting seedlings when the floodwaters recede.

We do not yet understand the evolutionary or ecological position of sakis and uakaris. They are not merely an isolated genealogical side branch, as the living titi and owl monkeys (including the fossils *Aotus dindensis* and *Tremacebus harringtoni*) are related to them. Other fossils recovered recently from Argentina, such as *Soriacebus*, are also close relatives. *Cebupithecia sarmientoi*, from La Venta, is in many respects virtually a fully modern saki. From Patagonia, *Homunculus* and *Carlocebus* may be close relatives either of the sakis and uakaris or of the titi and owl monkey group.

The fourth subfamily, the Atelinae, includes the spider, woolly and howler monkeys. They are the largest platyrrhines and are often compared to apes. Climbing quadrupedalism is their typical locomotor style. However, spider monkeys (*Ateles*) and the muriqui or woolly spider monkey (*Brachyteles arachnoides*) are fast and acrobatic suspensory locomotors, and can brachiate like gibbons. All have prehensile tails used in posture, locomotion and grasping. Their shoulders, hindlimbs and feet are also adapted for hanging. By contrast, the tail of *Cebus*, the nearest thing to an ateline in the other wing of platyrrhine radiation, lacks the elongation, flexibility, neural circuitry and gripping pad shared by all atelines. Cebines also lack long limbs and flexible joints connected with climbing. Their semi-prehensile tails evolved convergently.

The howler monkeys (*Alouatta*) are sometimes classified in a subfamily (Alouattinae) of their own, because of their unusual skull and specialised vocal mechanisms. However, there is little doubt that this genus is merely a divergent ateline. All four genera share a complex of anatomical features correlated with the supple prehensile tail.

In their diets, atelines range from leaf-eating (howler monkeys) to fruit-eating (spider monkeys) and in their locomotor habits from sluggish quadrupedal climbing to lithe acrobatics. The woolly monkey (*Lagothrix*) is intermediate in this respect, but the muriqui, despite teeth specialised for eating fruit and foliage, is much more like spider monkeys in anatomy and locomotion.

The fossil record of atelines is provocative. Teeth from two species have been found at La Venta. Both are allocated to the genus *Stirtonia*. They are morphologically and functionally similar to *Alouatta* and some question the need to place them in a separate genus from living howlers. However, a highly distinctive Pleistocene form (*Paralouatta varonai*) has recently been found in Cuba. Its large, uptilted face resembles a howler monkey, but its braincase is more primitive. It recalls other atelines, such as *Lagothrix*, which lacks the relatively small brain that is a correlate of a leaf diet in *Alouatta*. The teeth of *Paralouatta* are also relatively smaller than in living howlers or in *Stirtonia*, so the fossil form could

The distribution of New World monkey fossils in South America and the West Indies.

not have been as extremely adapted for leaf-eating as the modern howler.

The remains of *Paralouatta* are much more primitive than those of *Stirtonia* but are far younger. Even more surprisingly, they were found outside South America. Did howlers originate from a stock that dispersed to Central America only to migrate back to South America before the middle Miocene? That seems unlikely. It is more probable that a proto-howler dispersed from South America earlier in the Miocene, leaving behind an ancestral stock that also gave rise to the *Stirtonia–Alouatta* group. *Paralouatta* may be a recently extinct descendant of the proto-howler group.

Geography of platyrrhine evolution

How did platyrrhines manage to enter South America in the first place? Did they come from Africa, which has a rich fossil record of early anthropoids in the Fayum deposits of Egypt that are well over 31 million years old? Or did they come from North America, where more archaic adapid and omomyid primates – but no recognisable anthropoids – lived from at least 56 million years ago?

Each of these views has its own merits. Both require an unlikely crossing of a sizeable span of sea water (a strait or an ocean), much wider than anything filtering the Central American and Carribean platyrrhines. Continental drift and plate tectonics alone do not provide an adequate explanation. The fossil evidence is still too meagre for anything more than speculation, but the idea of a North American origin does seem preferable.

South America poses other fascinating questions for biogeographers. While primates flourished during the early Cenozoic in the northern landmasses of Laurasia, South America was an island continent, without fossil evidence of any platyrrhines. The formation of the Panamanian land bridge eventually led to a torrent of exchange between North and South America. It was at this later stage that the ancestors of today's Central American monkeys, including tamarins, capuchins, squirrel monkeys, spider and howler monkeys, may have entered from the south, but it is uncertain whether they came all at once as forests linked up, or in a series of intermittent moves. This invasion led to the evolution of several native Central American populations sometimes regarded as distinct species – *Cebus capucinus* (white-faced capuchin), *Saimiri oerstedii* (Costa Rican squirrel monkey), *Ateles geoffroyi* (black-handed spider monkey) and *Alouatta pigra* (Guatemalan howler).

An earlier northwards expansion yielded the Caribbean platyrrhines. Although there are few fossils, these animals – found in pre-Columbian cave deposits in Jamaica and Cuba and in Haiti and the Dominican Republic – do not seem to derive from today's Central American monkeys (except perhaps *Ateles anthropomorphus*, which may be a modern spider monkey). The others have a diverse ancestry: *Xenothrix* may be closely related to South American titi and owl

Two endangered New World monkey species in the Atlantic Coastal Forest, Brazil: (above) the golden lion tamarin (*Leontopithecus rosalia*) and (below) the buffy-headed marmoset (*Callithrix flaviceps*).

monkeys; '*Saimiri*' *bernensis* – which deserves a genus of its own – is possibly an early form of capuchin; and *Paralouatta* a primitive form of howler monkey. Such extensive taxonomic differentiation is not unusual among island mammals.

The third extension of the platyrrhine range from its centre in the continental lowlands of South America involves the unique fauna of the Atlantic Coastal Forest. This forest is now only a patchy mosaic covering less than 1 per cent of its original extent along the eastern seaboard and southeastern uplands of Brazil. It holds two endemic genera, *Leontopithecus* (lion tamarins) and *Brachyteles*

(muriqui), which are among the most endangered primates in the world, together with several other unique species. Their history is a blank. However, the Pleistocene–Recent (Holocene) Lagoa Santa cave deposits from the State of Minas Gerais, which contains several primate species, are not yet well described. The lessons of the Caribbean platyrrhines suggests that an interesting story may be waiting to be discovered among these remains.

The fossils from South America offer only two small clues to platyrrhine origins. The earliest are *Branisella boliviana*, from Salla in Bolivia, and a new genus, *Szalatavus attricuspis*, from the same area. The '*Branisella* Zone' locality has a late

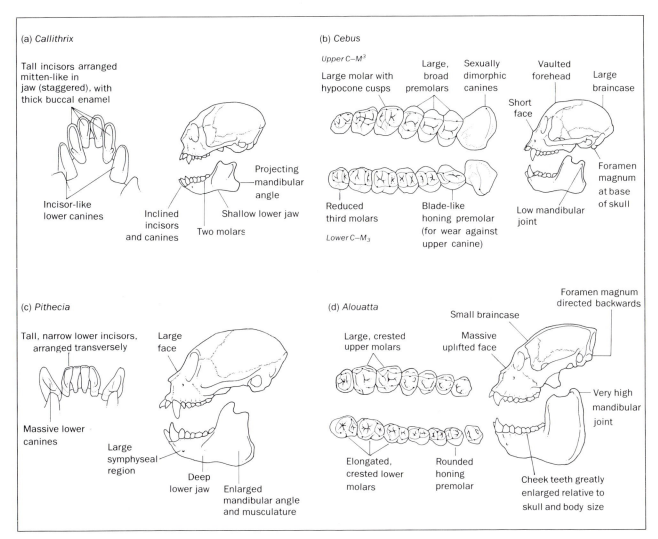

Comparison of the skulls and teeth of members of the four monophyletic subfamilies of New World monkeys recognised here.

(a) **Common marmoset (*Callithrix*).** The shape of the lower incisors and related features are shared with the pygmy marmoset (*Cebuella*), but are lacking in tamarins and Goeldi's monkey. They are adaptations for scraping bark and harvesting gums.

(b) **Capuchin monkey (*Cebus*).** All the features shown here are derived among platyrrhines and are also shared with the squirrel monkey (*Saimiri*). They relate to a seasonally variable and omnivorous diet, which demands manipulative skills. *Cebus* has puffy-cusped molar crowns, which are suited for chewing wood when dislodging insects from their nests, and for feeding on hard fruit. The unusual dental proportions with molars reduced from behind indicate a close relationship with callitrichines.

(c) **Saki monkey (*Pithecia*).** The saki has an enlarged jaw musculature and big face, which reflect a powerful dentition, with massive canines and protruding incisors. The front teeth are used to split and penetrate fruits, such as legumes, that are well protected by woody shells. This lets sakis and other pitheciins eat fruits while other platyrrhines are waiting for them to ripen and soften.

(d) **Howler monkey (*Alouatta*).** The rounded outer surface of the front premolar, which works against the upper canine in occlusion, is the only shared derived feature that occurs in other atelines. Other traits that unite howlers with atelines are evident in the postcranial skeleton, muscles and brain. The unusual skull and lower jaw is associated with the same specialised vocal apparatus, involving an enlarged hyoid bone. The large, crested cheek teeth and small incisors are associated with leaf-eating.

Oligocene age of 27 million years, around 10 million years younger than previously thought. This does not mean that platyrrhines arose significantly later than the appearance of catarrhines – a position embraced by some who favour an African origin for New World monkeys: it only sets the upper limit on the date of their appearance. The recognition of a new genus (*Szalatavus*) in the late Oligocene of Bolivia suggests that more will be discovered as explorations continue in fossil-rich parts of the Andes. Study of platyrrhine origins will make little progress until more South and Central American fossils are discovered.

Evolutionary patterns

Among the three major divisions of the modern primates – platyrrhines, catarrhines and prosimians – platyrrhines are uniquely diverse anatomically and behaviourally, despite being restricted to just one continent and a sliver of another. They have a broader range of feeding and locomotor adaptations and a greater variety of social systems and mating strategies than other primates. Prosimians are as diverse in their adaptations and taxonomic abundance, but they are distributed across three continents and are an older radiation. How, then, can we explain the diversity of the platyrrhines; and how does it relate to the overall pattern of their evolution?

One obvious point is that South America contains the world's last huge tracts of continuous closed tropical forest. Brazil alone had more than 3.5 million hectares (14000 square miles) of such forest in 1984, more than half the total remaining in South America. This vast area, now fast diminishing, contains the full measure of platyrrhine diversity – all of the 16 genera and perhaps as many as 50 species. South American forests comprise 50 to 60 per cent of the world's tropical forests – one and a half times as much as continental Africa and Asia and 60 times as much as Madagascar. Their ecological diversity is increased by their three-dimensional structure with innumerable coexisting species. The spatial scale of the neotropics contributes directly to the richness of its platyrrhine fauna.

Less is known about the the temporal dimension of platyrrhine evolution because the platyrrhine fossil record is so poor. The isolation of the continent, which continued well after platyrrhines first arrived, must have discouraged the immigration of other potential primate competitors that may have lived in Central America. Without such press-

Distribution of adaptive features among the major primate groups. Prosimians and New World monkeys are comparable in their diversity, sharing many convergent adaptations, but only among the New World monkeys are all patterns represented; Old World monkeys have the fewest.

	New World monkeys	Old World monkeys	Apes	Prosimians
Locomotion				
Quadrupedal	■	■	■	■
Clinging and leaping	■			■
Suspension	■		■	■
Diet				
Fruit	■	■	■	■
Leaves	■	■	■	■
Insects/other animals	■			■
Exudates (e.g. gums)	■			■
Mating/social systems				
Solitary			■	■
Monogamy	■	■	■	■
Polyandry	■			
One male	■	■	■	
Multimale	■	■		■
Fission–fusion*	■		■	
Litter size				
Singletons	■	■	■	■
Twins	■			■
Activity rhythms				
Diurnal	■	■	■	■
Nocturnal	■			■

* Some primates, such as spider monkeys and chimpanzees, live in social units that commonly split up into feeding parties of variable composition; these are called fission–fusion societies.

ure for constant adaptive radiations, the various platyrrhine niches may have become entrenched. The longevity of several modern genera, including *Saimiri* and *Aotus*, which have survived since the middle Miocene, may well reflect this. At least three others from the unique La Venta site are only a little more removed from modern genera (*Alouatta*, *Pithecia* and *Callimico*) and represent enduring ecological niches and lineages.

The deeply rooted lineages of some modern platyrrhines contrast with the better-known evolutionary patterns of the Old World catarrhines, which show a chain of successful adaptive radiations. In the New World, the fossils we are sampling may in fact reflect all that there ever was – a single adaptive radiation that has continued without much replacement since its origins.   *A.L. Rosenberger*

See also 'Non-human primates' (p. 24), 'Conservation of primates' (p. 33), 'Diets and guts' (p. 60), 'Primate reproduction' (p. 86), 'Mating and parental care' (p. 150) and 'The fossil history of primates' (p. 199)

Evolution of Old World monkeys

The group of higher primates called the Old World anthropoid primates, or catarrhines, is taxonomically more diverse today but morphologically more homogeneous than its sister taxon, the New World anthropoids or platyrrhines. Modern catarrhines are represented by only two superfamilies – the Cercopithecoidea (Old World monkeys) and Hominoidea (apes and humans). There is still controversy about the classification and evolutionary relationships of these subgroups.

Living Old World monkeys

The living Old World monkeys comprise a single family, Cercopithecidae, with two subfamilies, Cercopithecinae (cheek-pouched monkeys) and Colobinae (leaf monkeys) (see Box). All cercopithecids share several distinctive features that make it likely that they have a common ancestry, and they thus constitute a monophyletic group. As with other catarrhines (hominoids), they have only two premolars in each jaw. The three molars in each quadrant are long and have two crests (lophs) connecting transverse pairs of cusps (bilophodont condition). There is usually considerable sexual dimorphism, especially in the size and shape of the canines and the front lower premolar, and the upper canine has a deep groove that extends onto the root, particularly in males. Old World monkeys are not united by special features of the skull, but the rest of the skeleton does have some unique and diagnostic characters – such as the various structures that aid in rapid quadrupedal locomotion along branches or on the ground.

The two subfamilies also have diagnostic features, especially in diet, which are reflected in their vernacular names. The cercopithecines are cheek-pouched monkeys, and have buccal sacs used for storing food; they will eat almost anything, but often concentrate on fruit. The colobines eat leaves, which they digest in specialised guts convergently similar to those of ruminant artiodactyls such as cattle. Dietary preferences are also reflected in teeth. Cercopithecines retain more 'primitive', rounded bilophodont molars, with rather large incisors, the lower ones having completely lost the enamel on their inner surfaces. By contrast, colobines have relatively smaller incisors and sharper, high-cusped teeth.

Modern cercopithecines include both tree-climbing and terrestrial species, whereas living colobines almost all live, run and leap in trees and have reduced or almost absent thumbs. The skull of colobines has widely spaced orbits, a narrow nasal opening and a short face, whereas that of cercopithecines – especially in the long-snouted baboons – shows the opposite pattern.

A CLASSIFICATION OF LIVING AND FOSSIL OLD WORLD MONKEYS

Superfamily Cercopithecoidea
  Family Cercopithecidae (Old World monkeys)
    Subfamily Cercopithecinae (cheek-pouched monkeys)
      Tribe Cercopithecini
        Subtribe Allenopithecina
          Allenopithecus (Allen's swamp monkey)
        Subtribe Cercopithecina
          Cercopithecus (guenons)
          Miopithecus (talapoin)
          Erythrocebus (patas monkey)
      Tribe Papionini
        Subtribe Papionina
          Papio
            P. (Papio) (baboons)
            P. (Mandrillus) (drill/mandrill)
            †*P. (Dinopithecus)*
          Cercocebus
            C. (Cercocebus) (terrestrial mangabeys)
            C. ('Lophocebus') (arboreal mangabeys)
          †*Parapapio*
          †*Gorgopithecus*
          Theropithecus (gelada baboon)
        Subtribe Macacina
          †*Procynocephalus*
          †*Paradolichopithecus*
    Subfamily Colobinae
      Subtribe Colobina
        Colobus (black colobus monkeys)
        Procolobus
          P. (Procolobus) (olive colobus monkey)
          P. (Piliocolobus) (red colobus monkey)
        †*Libypithecus*
        †*Cercopithecoides*
        †*Paracolobus*
        †*Rhinocolobus*
        †*Microcolobus*
      Subtribe Presbytina
        Presbytis (surelis)
        Semnopithecus
          S. (Semnopithecus) (langurs)
          S. (Trachypithecus) (leaf monkeys)
        Pygathrix
          P. (Pygathrix) (douc langur)
          P. (Rhinopithecus) (snub-nosed langurs)
        Nasalis
          N. (Nasalis) (proboscis monkey)
          N. (Simias) (Pagai Island langur)
    Subfamily Colobinae (uncertain affinities)
      †*Mesopithecus*
      †*Dolichopithecus*
    Subfamily Victoriapithecinae
      †*Prohylobates*
      †*Victoriapithecus*
  Family Oreopithecidae*
      †*Oreopithecus*
      †*Nyanzapithecus*
      †*Rangwapithecus*

Subgenera (shown in parentheses) are called genera in some classifications. Fossil genera and subgenera are denoted by a dagger sign.

* Many authorities classify the oreopithecids among the Hominoidea (or even as a distinct superfamily).

Within the Cercopithecinae, the African guenons and their relatives make up the tribe Cercopithecini, and the baboons, mangabeys and macaques form the Papionini. The latter all have an essentially similar chromosome complement (karyotype) with a diploid number of 42. The Cercopithecini have lost the distal (hindmost) cusp on the third molar, and their diploid chromosome numbers range between 48 and 72, often in groups separated by multiples of 6. This diversity of karyotypes might reflect a pattern of speciation in closely adjacent populations.

Representative living Old World monkeys: a cercopithecine (below), the chacma baboon (*Papio hamadryas ursinus* (or *P. ursinus*)), from the savannas of southern Africa; and a colobine (above), the Asian proboscis monkey (*Nasalis larvatus*), from the mangrove forests of Borneo.

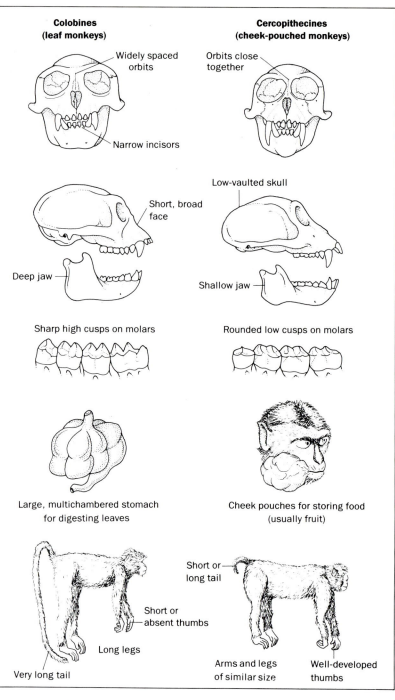

Features characterising the modern subfamilies of Old World monkeys, the Colobinae and Cercopithecinae.

The taxonomy of living colobines fits well with their geographical distribution (see p. 34). However, the differences between African and Asian forms are not as strong as between cercopithecine tribes, with only minor contrasts in teeth and limbs.

Molecular primatologists have concentrated on analysing the relationships among relatively distantly related primates and among hominoids. Little is known of the genetics of cercopithecid genera. The difference between colobines and cercopithecines is comparable in several ways to that between orang-utans and African apes, so that these two phyletic splits may have occurred at about the same time.

Early diversification

The origin of the Old World monkeys is not well reflected in the fossil record. A form called *Propliopithecus*, known from early Oligocene deposits in Egypt around 33 million years old, may have been close to the common ancestry of all modern catarrhines. With the exception of a single upper tooth from Uganda, however, no fossil with clear ties to the cercopithecids is known from Oligocene or early Miocene deposits.

By early middle Miocene times, 17 to 15 million years ago, several varieties of early cercopithecid existed in northeastern Africa. *Prohylobates* is represented by parts of four lower jaws from Egypt and Libya, and *Victoriapithecus* left a few jaws, some limb bones and hundreds of isolated teeth at Maboko, Kenya. Specimens from other sites have

Evolutionary relationships, time ranges and major groupings of Old World monkeys. The genera and subgenera (and species groups for *Theropithecus*) are along the top, together with their classificatory subdivisions. Solid lines represent the time ranges of fossils, dashed lines the estimated ranges, large dots are forms known today or from single sites in the past, and dotted lines indicate hypothesised evolutionary relationships; question marks indicate especially uncertain links. Large circles (marked A, B and C) represent uncertainty of branching sequence among specific groups: A, the original division between colobines and cercopithecines; B, the split between African and Asian colobines; and C, the split among living Asian colobines.

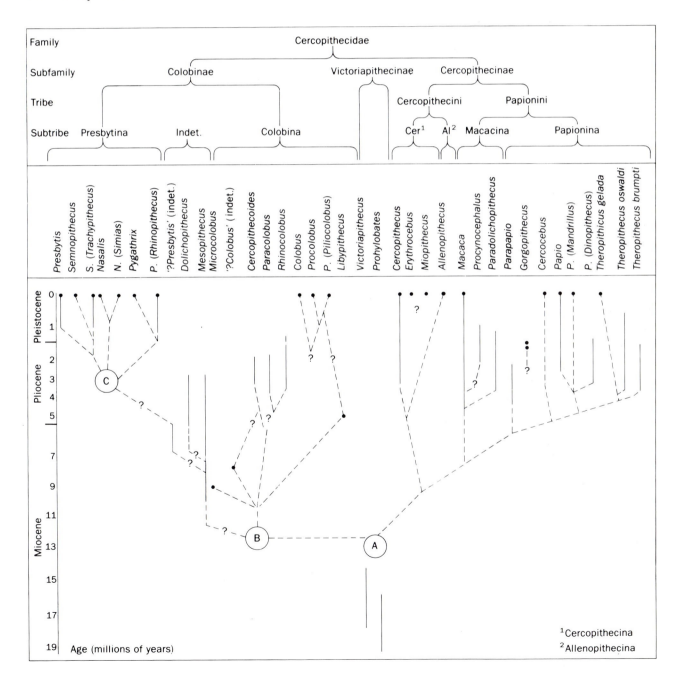

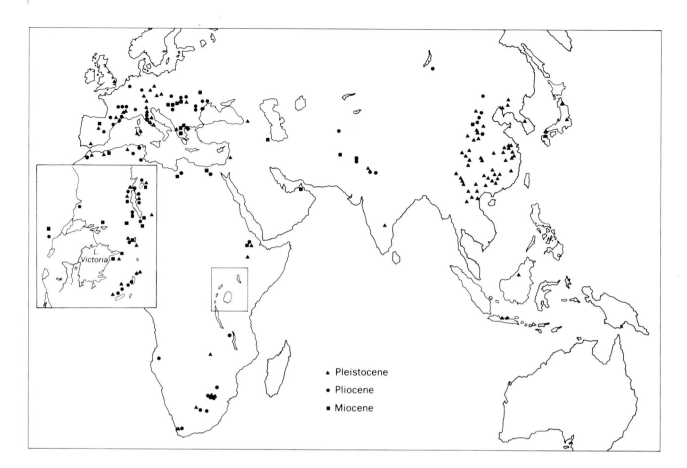

Principal sites of discovery of Old World monkey fossils in the Miocene, Pliocene and Pleistocene.

been assigned to one or the other genus, and it has been suggested that the two may not really be different.

These early cercopithecids, best termed the subfamily Victoriapithecinae, show that monkeys were present in more open habitats than those dominated by hominoids. They moved on the ground to some extent, and ate more leaves than hominoids. Modern species have a similar way of life, and this may have promoted the divergence of the first cercopithecoids from their ancestors.

By the late Miocene (8 to 9 million years ago), cercopithecoids were present across the Old World and had replaced most of the hominoid and early catarrhine lineages that had dominated the earlier Miocene. At least six and perhaps as many as 10 independent lineages developed a strong commitment to life on the ground, and monkeys invaded all types of habitat from the fringes of deserts to snowy forests.

The enigmatic European catarrhine *Oreopithecus bambolii* is known from a crushed skeleton and some jaws and limb bones from 8 to 9 million-year-old sites in Italy (see p. 225). Its teeth are highly distinctive, but some authors see certain dental similarities to cercopithecids, suggesting that the two lineages shared a common ancestor. However, the postcranium is more like that of hominoids. Some African species dating to between 19 and 14 million years old resemble *Oreopithecus* and are placed with it in the family Oreopithecidae. It is unclear whether this unique group should be placed in the Cercopithecoidea, in the Hominoidea or even in its own superfamily.

African monkeys of the Miocene and Plio-Pleistocene

Monkeys from late Miocene times are rare in Africa, but a very small colobine is known from Kenya, and both colobines and macaque-like cercopithecines are present across the continent's northern fringe. It is likely that the Sahara desert had become a barrier to north–south movement of mammals by 7 million years ago, leading to the separation of the Papionini into sub-Saharan baboons and mangabeys on one side of the desert and North African and Eurasian macaques on the other. African and Eurasian colobines may also have been separated at this time. There is no fossil evidence, but the Cercopithecini probably diverged from ancestral cercopithecines even earlier, entering the high canopies of the rain forest perhaps around 10 million years ago.

The African Pliocene was a time of great diversification of Old World monkeys. Wide expanses of plains alternated with forests in the east and south, offering numerous habitats for both colobines and cercopithecines. The radiation of the colobines is perhaps the most impressive, with up to seven species present in late Pliocene times, 2 million years ago, around Lake Turkana in Kenya. *Cercopithecoides* species were terrestrial, medium-sized to large colobine monkeys of Kenya and South Africa; their heavily worn

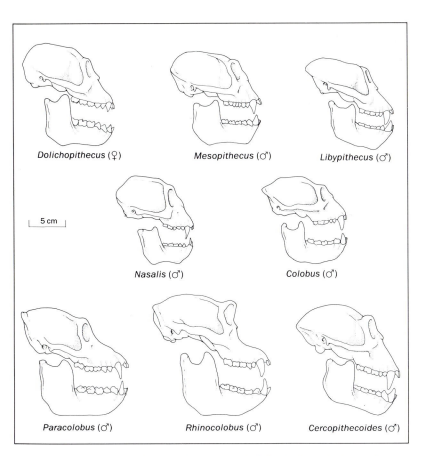

Right side views of reconstructed skulls of extinct colobine monkeys, accompanied (centre) by the skulls of two modern species (*Colobus polykomos* and *Nasalis larvatus*) for comparison (drawn approximately to the same scale). Notice the difference in size between the living and extinct forms.

Although *P. hamadryas* (in its broad sense) is widespread today in Africa, it was not common in Plio-Pleistocene times, except in South Africa between 2 and 1.5 million years ago. Another large form was previously placed in its own genus *Dinopithecus*, but is now assigned to a subgenus of *Papio*; it is known only between 3 and 1.5 million years ago.

The gelada (*Theropithecus gelada*) lives today only in the Ethiopian highlands, but in the past it had a much wider distribution. The living gelada, a specialised ground-dweller, feeds mainly on grass blades and seeds; its incisors are relatively small as it uses its fingers for food preparation. The first specimens showing distinctive gelada-like molars appeared by 4 million years ago, and at least three extinct species are known.

Theropithecus darti is present in eastern and southern sites older than 2.5 million years and has a fully terrestrial skeleton and somewhat reduced incisors. Populations of *T. oswaldi* increase in size after about 2 million years ago, spreading into northwestern Africa and even India. The large, later Pleistocene animals have very small incisors and short, stout canines. In this, they show parallels to hominids. The distinction between *T. oswaldi* and its probable ancestor, *T. darti*, is fairly arbitrary, but the latter has larger front teeth. *Theropithecus brumpti*, which has even larger incisors and a distinctive facial shape, is known only in the Lake Turkana region between 3.3 and 2.3 million years ago.

teeth probably reflect an abundance of grit in their diet, from foraging on the ground where living colobines seldom stay. Even larger were the highly arboreal *Rhinocolobus* and less 'specialised' *Paracolobus* of the Turkana Basin. All three forms were larger than any living colobine, in the range of mid- to large-sized baboons. Fossils of several species of smaller colobines, some probably belonging to the living genera, are also known.

At the same time, papionins were represented by members of several lineages. *Parapapio* from southern and eastern Africa was partly terrestrial and had a little derived skull. It was perhaps close to the common ancestry of later papionins and was somewhat like Eurasian macaques. Fossils of mangabeys and guenons are rare, but the extant baboons *Papio* and *Theropithecus* are well represented in the Pliocene and Pleistocene. All populations of the common savanna baboons living today appear to interbreed and are thus best grouped in a single species, *Papio hamadryas*. This includes not only the maned Hamadryas baboon but also the guinea, olive, yellow and chacma baboons, which previously were regarded as separate species. Fossil populations of this species first appear by about 2.5 million years ago, alongside a smaller species that persisted for 0.5 to 1 million years.

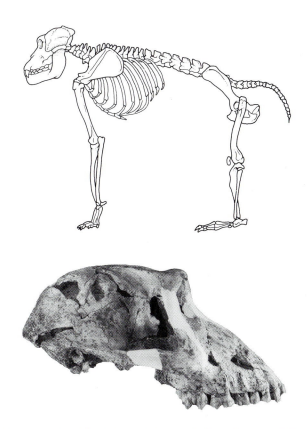

Reconstruction of the skeleton of a large male *Theropithecus oswaldi*, a terrestrial 'giant baboon' of the East African Pleistocene. The separate skull, a female, is from South Africa.

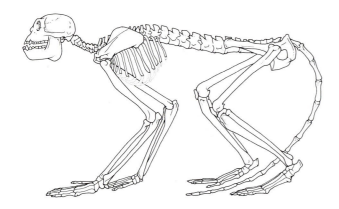

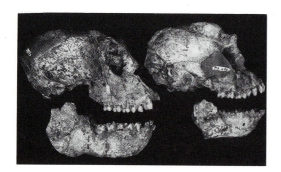

Reconstruction of the skeleton of *Mesopithecus pentelicus*, a semiterrestrial colobine of the late Miocene and Pliocene of Europe. This female specimen (assembled from many unassociated parts) was found in Greece and is about 8 million years old. The separate skulls are male (left) and female (right).

The oldest members of this lineage have skulls and teeth similar to those of *Papio*, suggesting a close phyletic link between these genera, as well as much parallel evolution within *Theropithecus*. The *T. brumpti* lineage probably diverged early from the common ancestor of *T. gelada, T. darti* and *T. oswaldi*.

Eurasian monkeys of the Miocene to Pleistocene

The colobines entered Eurasia long before the cercopithecines, and diverged into European and Asian subgroups. Dozens of skulls and postcranial elements of *Mesopithecus* have been found, especially in the Balkans in deposits dating to between 9 and 8 million years ago. Other populations extended as far east as Afghanistan and perhaps India, and westwards to France and England as recently as 3 million years ago.

Mesopithecus was probably similar to the living Hanuman langur (*Semnopithecus* or *Presbytis entellus*) in its adaptation to life in forests and on the ground; its thumb is less reduced than in any other colobine, but more than in cercopithecines. A possible descendant of *Mesopithecus* is *Dolichopithecus*, a larger, longer-faced and more terrestrial colobine from

deposits in central and southern Europe dating to between 6 and 3 million years ago, and perhaps somewhat later in Mongolia. Other Asian fossil colobines are mainly members of the living genera, whose relationships are still unclear.

The only Eurasian cercopithecines (other than a single *Theropithecus* maxilla) are the macaques and their extinct relatives. There are four main groups of macaque species: the North African (and extinct European) Barbary macaque (*Macaca sylvanus*); the lion-tailed macaque (*M. silenus*) group of India and Southeast Asia; the Toque macaque (*M. sinica*) group of South and East Asia; and the widespread group of crab-eating macaques (*M. fascicularis*).

Both morphology and biochemistry agree in distinguishing these groups, although the details of their relationships are not yet clear. Macaque-like papionins first appear in North Africa in the late Miocene when the Mediterranean Sea dried up, and had entered Europe by the earliest Pliocene, when it had refilled. Many European populations between England and the Caucasus have been named, but none can readily be distinguished from *M. sylvanus*. Macaques persisted in Europe until the last interglacial, about 100000 years ago, after which they were restricted to North Africa.

In Asia, macaques spread to India by around 3 million years ago; two Chinese teeth may be 5 million years old. Crania from the Pleistocene of China probably represent a member of the *sinica* group, and the several living species on Sulawesi are probably derived from a *silenus* group population that crossed from Borneo on a land bridge when sea levels were lower, and then speciated in isolated parts of the island.

Macaques are not particularly specialised for life on the ground. In this, they are comparable to mangabeys and to *Parapapio*. In the late Pliocene and early Pleistocene of Europe, a larger, more terrestrial lineage flourished as the genus *Paradolichopithecus*. Less well-preserved specimens from China and India may represent a second macaque 'experiment', or an extension of the range of *Paradolichopithecus*, which is also known from Central Asia.

The entry of humans into Asia by 1 million years ago may have driven these large monkeys to extinction, perhaps because they, like the large geladas of Africa, were hunted for food.

Eric Delson

See also 'Classification and evolutionary relationships' (p. 17), 'Non-human primates' (p. 24), 'Conservation of primates' (p. 33), 'Jaws and teeth' (p. 56), 'Diets and guts' (p. 60), 'Primate locomotion and posture' (p. 75), 'Land movements and species dispersal' (p. 169), 'Reconstructing past environments' (p. 191), 'The fossil history of primates' (p. 199), 'Evolution of apes' (p. 223) and Part 8 'Genetic clues of relatedness' (pp. 293–321).

Evolution of apes

One of the problems in understanding ape evolution is that there are very few living apes – only four or five genera, depending on whether or not we include the human genus, *Homo*. Only two ape genera, *Pan* (chimpanzees) and *Hylobates* (gibbons), have more than one living species and only *Hylobates* has more than two (around nine altogether). This situation is relatively recent because apes were once much more diverse and widespread.

The inclusion here of humans among the apes emphasises the distinction between a phylogenetic *clade* of relatedness and a *grade* of biological organisation. Humans have as their closest living relatives the other apes, and some apes are more closely related to humans than they are to one another. Therefore, in a phylogenetic sense, humans are apes. We share several features with other apes (such as a broad chest, very mobile arms and the lack of a tail), which indicate that we are derived from a common ancestor not shared with our next closest relatives, the Old World monkeys. In terms of biological organisation, however, humans are fundamentally different from the other apes, which by contrast form a fairly homogeneous group.

With respect to living species, then, the term 'ape' is used here as a grade, and humans are discussed only peripherally. With many fossil species we are confronted with a similar problem: species that appear to be phyletic apes are unlike living apes in many anatomical features. It is not always clear just how behaviourally and ecologically like modern apes many of these animals were. As they may not have achieved a modern grade of organisation, we need to broaden our notions of what an ape is.

Phylogenetic relationships of living apes

The phylogenetic relationships of living apes can be studied using genetics or morphology. All genetic indicators agree in showing that there is more similarity among great apes and humans than between any member of this clade and gibbons. Likewise, within the great ape and human clade, genetic pointers concur in showing the orang-utan (*Pongo*) to be genetically distant from the African apes – the two chimpanzee species and the gorilla – and humans. However, there is less agreement as to the pattern of genetic similarity among chimpanzees, gorillas and humans. There are inconsistencies in the data and in the ways in which the information is analysed. Interpretation is hindered by uncertainties as to whether genetic change occurs at uniform rates in different lineages.

The two branching events that produced the three lineages probably happened at about the same time, so that chimpanzees, gorillas and humans are genetically quite similar. The present consensus is that the gorilla branched first from a chimpanzee/human clade, and that the split between chimpanzees and humans occurred a little later. However, some studies support an initial chimpanzee/gorilla versus human split.

Inferences about relatedness based on comparative morphology attempt to identify shared, derived features, as opposed to retained, primitive features. Genetic phylogenies most often rely on the degree of overall similarity between lineages, although attempts are now being made to identify derived genetic features. The *cladistic* methods used to identify shared derived features suffer from two difficulties. The first is *character polarity*: identifying which of the *states* of a feature are derived, and in what sequence. The second is spotting any convergence and parallelism among apparently shared characters.

These difficulties are illustrated by the different results obtained in recent analyses of great ape and human morphology. Human–African ape, human–orang-utan and African ape–orang-utan clades have all been proposed, each based on a supposedly rigorous application of cladistics. Although the last two clades have few adherents, even the morphological case for a human–African ape clade is still without unequivocal support. Each of the living apes seems to have acquired a few uniquely derived features superimposed on the rather primitive and generalised body plan of their common ancestor, and certain shared features may have resulted from parallel evolution.

The presence of skeletal features related to knuckle-walking in chimpanzees and gorillas, and their absence in modern humans or their fossil antecedents, suggest to many that there was an initial human/African ape split rather than a human and chimpanzee/gorilla split, and that the two African apes are more closely related than either is to humans. However, this conflicts with much genetical evidence that suggests a closer relationship between humans and chimpanzees, which would imply that hominids were once knuckle-walkers.

If humans do not have an ancestral stage when they knuckle-walked, as many morphologists assert, then this very peculiar locomotor behaviour must have been independently derived in the chimpanzee and gorilla lineages. Although morphologists find this also difficult to accept, it is not yet clear whether skeletal features associated with knuckle-walking in chimpanzees and gorillas are indeed homologous or whether they arose by parallel evolution.

Morphology and genetics thus favour a branching sequence gibbons–orang-utan–African apes/humans, but there is still no agreement on the African ape and human branchings.

Fossil apes

The fossil record of ape evolution is confined almost entirely to the Miocene epoch, from 23 to 5 million years ago, which probably covers most of the earlier history of the group. The first evidence for a diversification of the apes is in the early Miocene, and an origin of the group in the latest Oligocene or earliest Miocene seems likely. During the middle and late Miocene, apes underwent an extensive phyletic and geographic radiation, extending their range throughout the equatorial and subequatorial regions of the Old World. This was a brief flowering, and well before the end of the Miocene apes had become extinct over much of the area that they had once occupied.

Ape lineages did persist into the Plio-Pleistocene, although some subsequently became extinct. All these surviving lineages were probably more widespread than they are today. However, their record after about 8 million years ago includes only scanty remains of Pleistocene gibbons and orang-utans, dental remains of a recently extinct Pleistocene giant ape (*Gigantopithecus*) and Pliocene fossils of uncertain affinity, all from southeastern Asia. There is no fossil record of chimpanzees or gorillas at all.

The early Miocene record of Old World higher primates is mostly restricted to a small region centered on the East African Rift Valley. The principal sites are Koru, Songhor, Rusinga, Mfwangano and Kalodirr in Kenya, and Napak in Uganda. These all date to between 20 and 17 million years ago. The diverse array of catarrhine species includes several traditionally considered as the earliest apes and classified within the superfamily Hominoidea. These include members of the genera *Proconsul*, *Rangwapithecus*, *Nyanzapithecus* and *Limnopithecus*. To this group may now be added the newly discovered *Afropithecus* and *Turkanapithecus* from Kalodirr, and *Heliopithecus* (probably the same as *Afropithecus*) from Saudi Arabia. Whether or not any of these are in fact phyletic apes, or hominoids, is discussed below.

Species of the genera *Aegyptopithecus* and *Propliopithecus* from the middle Oligocene Fayum deposits in Egypt were initially considered to be the earliest apes, but they are now widely thought to be primitive catarrhines that predate the split of apes and Old World monkeys.

The early Miocene African genera varied in size from that of a small monkey to perhaps a large chimpanzee. The many species probably occupied forests of varying types, and the teeth suggest that their diet included both fruit and foliage. Most species were probably markedly sexually dimorphic in canine and in body size. But only one fossil collection, that of *Proconsul* from Rusinga, is complete enough to assess body size dimorphism – which may have been substantial. This sample may, however, include two species of different size. If so, dimorphism in individual species may have been no greater than in chimpanzees. The skeleton of *Proconsul* shows none of the specialisations associated with the locomotion and posture of living apes

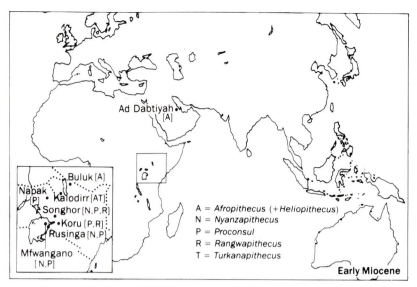

A = *Afropithecus* (+*Heliopithecus*)
N = *Nyanzapithecus*
P = *Proconsul*
R = *Rangwapithecus*
T = *Turkanapithecus*

Early Miocene

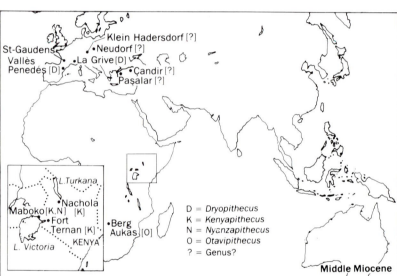

D = *Dryopithecus*
K = *Kenyapithecus*
N = *Nyanzapithecus*
O = *Otavipithecus*
? = Genus?

Middle Miocene

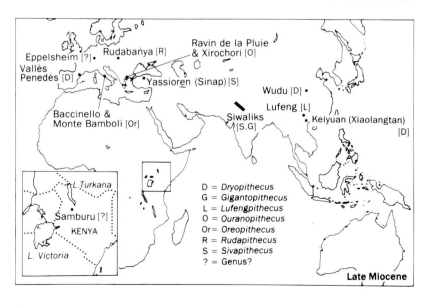

D = *Dryopithecus*
G = *Gigantopithecus*
L = *Lufengpithecus*
O = *Ouranopithecus*
Or = *Oreopithecus*
R = *Rudapithecus*
S = *Sivapithecus*
? = Genus?

Late Miocene

Geographic distributions of fossil hominoids in the early Miocene, 23–16 million years ago, middle Miocene, 16–10 million years ago, and late Miocene, 10–5 million years ago. Only the principal sites are shown.

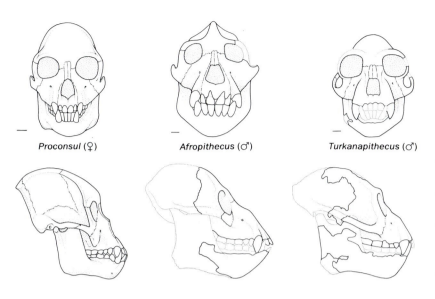

Proconsul (♀)   Afropithecus (♂)   Turkanapithecus (♂)

Representative skulls of late early Miocene apes from Kenya. Notice the width between the orbits and their round to rectangular shape. *Afropithecus* and *Turkanapithecus* have the long snout characteristic of primitive catarrhines from the Oligocene Fayum deposits of Egypt. Males and/or larger specimens of *Proconsul* may have had longer snouts than the female pictured here. Each scale bar = 1 cm.

Oreopithecus

Proconsul

Skeletons and reconstructions of early Miocene *Proconsul* (below) and late Miocene *Oreopithecus* (above). Notice in particular the different proportions of the forelimbs and hindlimbs in the two. *Proconsul* may have been mainly a quadrupedal walker and climber along branches, and done relatively little forelimb suspension. *Oreopithecus* is the only fossil ape whose anatomy suggests the frequent use of suspensory locomotion.

and Old World monkeys. *Proconsul* species probably used quadrupedal walking with some climbing but little suspension from branches.

Species that are certainly phyletic apes are present by the middle Miocene (16–10 million years ago) and are best represented in Africa. By about 15–14 million years ago, apes had migrated into Eurasia. Here they underwent an extensive adaptive radiation, which was probably already underway in Africa before the migrations began. Fragments of small-bodied catarrhines have been found in deposits in China and Pakistan dating to at least 17 million years ago. These may be early members of the gibbon lineage but this cannot be determined without postcranial remains; they might not even be hominoids.

In Africa, *Kenyapithecus* is found at sites that span most of the middle Miocene, such as Maboko, Fort Ternan and Nachola in northern Kenya. *Kenyapithecus* has derived facial and dental features that differ from those of the early Miocene genera and are more like those of modern apes. It has thick layer of enamel on its molar teeth and very robust jaws (which indicate a shift in food preferences and habitat). The diet of *Kenyapithecus* is still uncertain: its teeth and jaws certainly suggest powerful biting and prolonged chewing, perhaps on very hard and tough foods – a diet unlike that of any living primate. The few postcranial remains are still quite primitive and do not suggest much change in behaviour from the early Miocene. There was substantial sexual dimorphism in the canines and probably in body size. The recently discovered *Otavipithecus* from the late middle Miocene of Namibia represents the first record of Miocene apes from southern Africa. It is so far known from one specimen, a lower jaw, that, unlike *Kenyapithecus*, appears to have relatively thin-enamelled teeth.

Remains of middle Miocene apes in Europe and Asia are few and not very revealing. They include species known mainly from their teeth from eastern Europe (Neudorf) and Turkey (Paşalar, Çandir) with teeth generally like that of *Kenyapithecus*. The few postcranial remains suggest that their habitat and activity patterns were probably not too different from those of *Proconsul*. Somewhat later than these earliest Eurasian representatives of apes with thick-enamelled teeth is *Dryopithecus*, sporadically known from western and central Europe. *Dryopithecus* has thin-enamelled teeth and probably had a diet different from that of the apes with thick enamel. It has no obvious antecedents in Africa or elsewhere and its origins are unknown.

The late Miocene witnessed the greatest diversity, and probably the greatest geographic expansion, of apes. Major Eurasian sites include the Vallès Penedès in Spain (*Dryopithecus*), Rudabánya in Hungary (*Rudapithecus*, but possibly assignable to *Dryopithecus*), Baccinello and Monte Bamboli in Italy (*Oreopithecus*), Ravin de la Pluie and Xirochori in Greece (*Ouranopithecus*), Yassioren (Mt Sinap) in Turkey (*Sivapithecus*), the Siwaliks in Indo-Pakistan (*Sivapithecus*) and Lufeng (*Lufengpithecus*), Wudu (*Dryopithecus*) and Keiyuan or

Xiaolangtan (*Dryopithecus*) in China. Unfortunately, the African late Miocene record consists only of a few teeth and fragmentary jaws. The genus '*Ramapithecus*' (which is historically important in the study of human evolution) was once thought to be present at some of these sites as well as at the middle Miocene sites of Fort Ternan, Maboko and Paşalar, but it is now clear that the only distinguishing feature of specimens attributed to this genus was their small size. These are probably females or small species of the genera at these various sites.

Late Miocene genera shared certain similarities. The animal and plant remains with which they are associated suggest that they occupied forests and dense woods. All were moderately large, ranging in size from large monkeys to chimpanzees, with a few very large species – perhaps as large as orang-utans or female gorillas; and all appear to have been moderately or even highly sexually dimorphic. There is no evidence for the presence of more than one ape species living simultaneously at any of these sites.

The elbows of *Rudapithecus* and *Sivapithecus* were almost like those of modern apes, which might suggest that climbing and suspension were important in their behaviour. However, some other features of the forelimbs of *Sivapithecus* are monkey-like, implying quadrupedal walking and

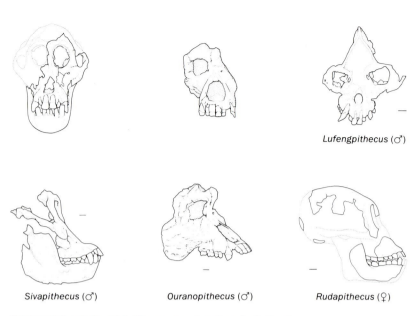

Lufengpithecus (♂)

Sivapithecus (♂)   *Ouranopithecus* (♂)   *Rudapithecus* (♀)

Representative skulls of late Miocene apes from Eurasia. Notice the vertically elongate and close-set orbits, and the long, narrow face of *Sivapithecus* compared with *Ouranopithecus* and *Lufengpithecus* and *Rudapithecus*. Each scale bar = 1 cm.

The Siwalik deposits of northern Pakistan from which have come most of the remains of *Sivapithecus*, a likely member of the orang-utan lineage.

climbing but not suspension. Other parts of the postcranial skeleton of both genera also suggest this type of quadrupedalism, with little of the forelimb-dominated suspensory behaviour thought by most to be the ancestral locomotor pattern of all true apes.

A virtually complete skeleton of *Oreopithecus* has been unearthed. This is similar to modern apes in many features of the trunk and limbs. *Oreopithecus* thus seems to have been more adapted for suspension than was either *Sivapithecus* or *Rudapithecus* (see p. 225).

These three Eurasian lineages hence suggest that there was considerable locomotor diversity among late Miocene apes, and that some were still primitive in features of their postcranial anatomy. Not all of them were as adapted for suspension as are all living apes, including the largely terrestrial gorilla in which vestiges of this heritage are still evident.

All these late Miocene apes were adapted for life in trees, although, given the body sizes of some, they probably came down to the ground occasionally. The disappearance of dense forests and woodlands may have led to their extinction. None shows any sign of the skeletal features associated with the specialised behaviours of living apes. However, none is from Africa, to which the presently more terrestrial chimpanzee and gorilla lines have probably always been confined.

The diets and habitats of late Miocene Eurasian hominoids were probably quite diverse. *Sivapithecus*, *Ouranopithecus* and *Gigantopithecus* had thick-enamelled cheek teeth, and may have had diets similar to that of *Kenyapithecus*, with hard and tough food items. However, they differed in body size and in other features of teeth and jaws, especially in the size and shape of the incisors. *Dryopithecus* species, and probably *Lufengpithecus*, had thinner-enamelled teeth, with *Dryopithecus* also being somewhat smaller. *Oreopithecus* had very unusual teeth and possibly ate leaves more than the others.

By the end of the Miocene, all these Eurasian lineages were extinct in the areas from which they are known as fossils, except in China. Their extinction might have been caused by a cooler, drier and more seasonal world climate, which emerged as the Miocene progressed, and by the resulting decline in evergreen forest and woodland and its partial replacement with deciduous forest, scrub and, perhaps, the first extensive wooded grasslands. Geochemical evidence from fossil soils in the Siwaliks of Pakistan strongly supports this scenario. Soon after the extinction of apes in most of these areas came monkeys that were better adapted to life in more open habitats. The lineages leading to gibbons and the orang-utan persisted, but were confined to the forests of Southeast Asia. The enormous and enigmatic *Gigantopithecus* was probably a ground-dweller in more open habitats before its extinction later in the Pleistocene.

There is no fossil record of gibbons or orang-utans before the Pleistocene, and even these remains tell us only that the Pleistocene species were hardly different from their modern descendants. Although the fossil record of the gorilla and chimpanzees is a complete blank, we can be fairly confident that their ranges did not overlap with those of hominids in East Africa during the past 4 to 5 million years and that they were probably confined to areas west of the Rift Valley.

Phylogenetic relationships of fossil apes

Some argue that the 'apes' of the early Miocene (including *Proconsul*) are primitive catarrhine primates from lineages that branched before the Old World monkey lineage split from the apes, and are therefore neither cercopithecoids nor hominoids in the strict sense. It has been thought that one of the more obvious hallmarks of apes is a shift to a posture and locomotion dominated by the forelimb. The joints of living apes are mobile and the shoulder in particular allows the limb to be extended straight upwards. The humerus is also unlike that of monkeys.

As we have seen, species of *Proconsul* have quite primitive skulls and skeletons. Complete elbow and wrist joints, together with a partial shoulder joint, are known. There is nothing particularly ape-like about the wrist. Both elbow and shoulder have features that are somewhat like those of modern apes, but it is not clear whether these are shared, derived hominoid features. Even if they are, and *Proconsul* is a phyletic ape, what they mean in terms of posture is not clear. Humeral shape is otherwise unlike that of living apes. Other parts of the postcranial skeleton, such as the vertebral column, are also unlike those of living apes and

suggest quadrupedal walking and running, perhaps in the manner of some New World monkeys.

If *Proconsul* and its relatives are indeed apes, then the earliest apes were not much like their living descendants. The situation is no clearer with other, less well-known early Miocene taxa, such as *Rangwapithecus* and *Afropithecus*; they also have primitive postcranial skeletons and skulls.

Middle Miocene genera such as the African *Kenyapithecus* and the lineage present at Neudorf in eastern Europe are only marginally more like modern apes in forelimb morphology. Even the late Miocene *Sivapithecus*, which is unquestionably an ape and which has elbows like those of modern apes, is otherwise quite primitive in humeral morphology, so that suspension and overhand climbing may not in fact be fundamental attributes of the ape lineage. If these locomotor behaviours are not basic characteristics of apes, then a biological, as opposed to a cladistic, definition of 'ape', becomes difficult.

Where these and other middle and late Miocene apes fit within a living ape phylogeny is mostly unclear. The one exception to this is *Sivapithecus*. *Sivapithecus* shares with the orang-utan several features of the skull and face that are almost certainly derived within the Hominoidea, and some of which are uniquely shared to the exclusion of all other simian primates. These include the absence of a bony sinus in the brow area of the skull, a very narrow bony partition between the eyes, vertically elongated orbits and, most important, a set of features in the *subnasal* area that relates to

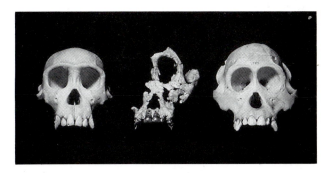

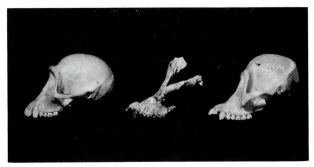

Comparison of a partial 8-million-year-old skull of *Sivapithecus* from the Siwaliks of Pakistan with an orang-utan (right) and chimpanzee (left); front (above) and side (below) views. *Sivapithecus* and the orang-utan share numerous derived facial features relating to the shape and position of the orbits, the morphology of the subnasal area, the embedding of the canine (producing a triangular instead of a squared snout), the profile of the lower face, and the positioning and orientation of the facial skeleton in relation to the braincase.

the way the hard palate joins the premaxillary bone at the base of the nose where the incisors are embedded (the *nasoalveolar clivus*).

The subnasal area is particularly useful because it is often preserved in fossils and consists of several separate characters that associate into three discrete patterns among living apes. Gibbons preserve the primitive simian pattern with a gaping space between the palate and the clivus. In chimpanzees and gorillas, the clivus overlaps the palate to form a large *incisive canal*. The bony opening into this canal is large and there is a precipitous drop from the clivus to the palate. The canal opening in the roof of the mouth is also quite large. In orang-utans, there is also a substantial overlap between the clivus and palate, but in this case the clivus extends well into the nasal cavity. However, both openings

into the canal are narrow slits and the canal itself is greatly compressed. The joining of the clivus and palate within the nasal cavity is smooth, without the abrupt drop characteristic of the African apes. *Sivapithecus* uniquely shares this morphological pattern with the orang-utan, which, together with other facial features, implies that there is a phylogenetic relationship between the two.

In most other respects, however, the cranial anatomy of *Sivapithecus* is unlike that of the orang-utan, as is the postcranial anatomy. Behaviourally and ecologically, *Sivapithecus* was probably not much like an orang-utan, with no evidence of the skeletal adaptations allowing a high degree of limb mobility. Like *Proconsul* and its relatives, these earliest putative members of the orang-utan lineage were not much like their living descendant.

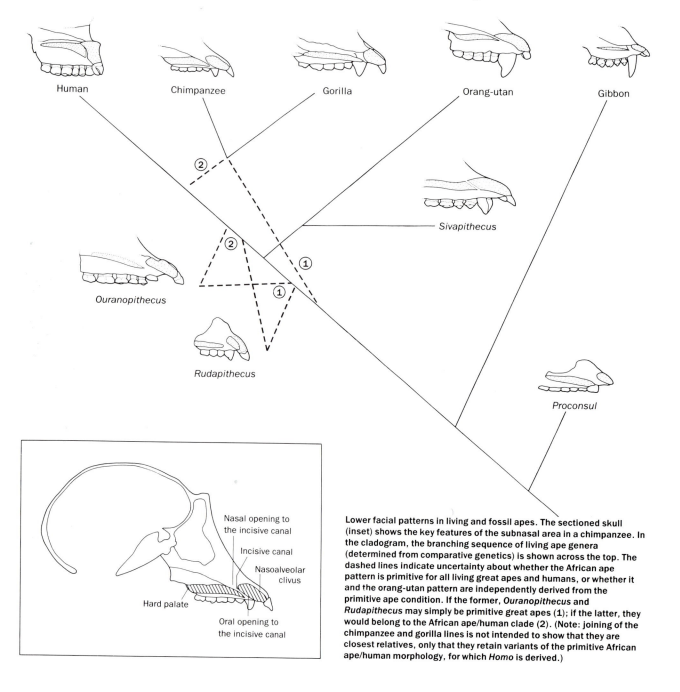

Lower facial patterns in living and fossil apes. The sectioned skull (inset) shows the key features of the subnasal area in a chimpanzee. In the cladogram, the branching sequence of living ape genera (determined from comparative genetics) is shown across the top. The dashed lines indicate uncertainty about whether the African ape pattern is primitive for all living great apes and humans, or whether it and the orang-utan pattern are independently derived from the primitive ape condition. If the former, *Ouranopithecus* and *Rudapithecus* may simply be primitive great apes (1); if the latter, they would belong to the African ape/human clade (2). (Note: joining of the chimpanzee and gorilla lines is not intended to show that they are closest relatives, only that they retain variants of the primitive African ape/human morphology, for which *Homo* is derived.)

The phyletic relationships of other middle and late Miocene genera are more equivocal. The subnasal area of *Rudapithecus* appears to be similar to that in the African apes. *Kenyapithecus* has been claimed to have a primitive lower face but also seems to share some features with the African apes. *Ouranopithecus* and *Lufengpithecus* certainly do not share the orang-utan facial pattern; the former also seems to resemble African apes.

The position of those genera that appear to be related to the African apes depends on the order of evolution of the lower facial patterns. If the orang-utan pattern is derived from that of the African apes, then these extinct genera may simply be primitive great apes not necessarily on the lineage of any living species. If the two lower facial patterns of extant great apes are independently derived from the primitive form, then the possession of either places the fossil on either the orang-utan or African ape lineage. The association of a generally African ape subnasal pattern with mostly primitive postcranial characters in *Kenyapithecus* argues for the first alternative, but the latter cannot be dismissed because the remains are still fragmentary, and there is a possibility of convergence.

The orbits and subnasal region are useful because they are so distinctive in the orang-utan. Because the African apes retain a morphology probably closer to that of primitive great apes, features by which fossils could be linked with their clade are not so obvious. One might be the manner in which the face is joined to the braincase, but this requires relatively complete and undistorted skulls.

Complete but badly crushed skulls are known for *Lufengpithecus*, and less-complete crania for *Ouranopithecus*, *Rudapithecus* and *Kenyapithecus*. The cranium of *Ouranopithecus* (p. 226) shows a few intriguing similarities to that of African apes, or even to hominids, but whether or not these are phylogenetically relevant is not clear. Although *Lufengpithecus* and *Rudapithecus* have none of the key features of the orang-utan clade possessed by *Sivapithecus*, each has other features that may place them as more primitive members of this clade. In most respects, however, all except *Sivapithecus* are variants of a primitive great ape skull. Most may represent lineages that originated before any of the extant great ape branchings. Some fossil apes from the late Miocene of Africa would help clarify the phylogenetic positions of some of these animals.

Tempo of ape evolution

DNA changes at a roughly regular rate within closely related taxa, although there can be considerable differences in rates between more distantly related groups. The genetic distance between lineages can hence be used as a measure of time of divergence. To develop a 'molecular clock' to date divergence times among living animals one must calibrate genetic change with respect to time using the fossil record. It is therefore essential to have a reliable date for the appearance of at least one lineage of living apes. There are two difficulties: recognising early fossil members of a lineage and establishing that there are no earlier members of that lineage. The first issue arises from the problems of fossil phylogeny. The second, which depends to a great extent on an absence of evidence, can be addressed according to the completeness of the appropriate fossil record and the stage of evolution reached by contemporary animals.

The orang-utan lineage has the best potential to calibrate ape evolution. *Sivapithecus* may well be an early member of the orang-utan lineage, despite being very unlike a modern orang-utan in many respects. It has been dated to 12.5 million years ago in the Siwalik sequence of Pakistan. Older sediments give no evidence of *Sivapithecus* or any other large hominoid, and no other Miocene fossil apes can definitely be assigned to the orang-utan lineage. It is unlikely that we would ever find the oldest member of a group, so the date of 12.5 million years ago is a minimum estimate for the origins of the orang-utan lineage.

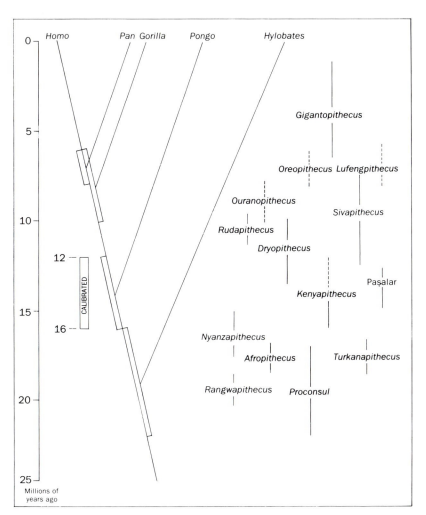

Estimates of the time of branching of living apes, as determined from comparative genetics and based on calibration dates between 12 and 16 million years ago for the origin of the orang-utan lineage. Temporal ranges of fossil ape genera are shown to the right. Solid lines reflect relatively well-known time ranges and dashed lines reflect uncertain temporal positions within a probable interval.

The divergence times of living apes have been calculated assuming both linear and non-linear rates of change, and even decelerating rates in some lineages. A few have used the orang-utan divergence as the calibration point, with a date ranging between 16 and 12 million years ago. The ranges in branching times for the other apes utilising these two dates are: apes–Old World monkeys, 33 to 24 million years ago; gibbons–great apes/humans, 22 to 16 million years; gorilla–chimpanzees/humans, 10 to 6 million years; and chimpanzees–humans, 8 to 6 million years. The Siwalik record of *Sivapithecus* favours the more recent of each range and none of these dates conflicts with the fossil evidence.

Defining apes

It is possible to make some general statements about apes throughout their history. They have mostly been moderately to very large. They have always depended on trees, and have been restricted to dense woods or forests. For much of their history, most were generalised quadrupedal walkers and climbers without any marked locomotor specialisations, and were thus unlike any living primate. The very specialised behaviours of all living apes may be relatively recent. Apes have had varied diets but the diet that characterises many middle and late Miocene lineages with thick tooth enamel and heavily buttressed jaws no longer exists. Each of the living apes is in its own way atypical when seen in the context of ape evolutionary history as a whole.

Apes have usually been sexually dimorphic, sometimes extremely so. This is compatible with social systems based on polygyny. Early and middle Miocene apes of Africa formed communities of a few species, while later Miocene habitats in Eurasia contained only one or two species at most – the pattern seen among apes (but not monkeys) today.

What this tells us about ape biology is unclear. Apes differ from monkeys in life-history profile, with a long gestation period, a long period of maternal care, a long interval between births, late achievement of sexual maturity and a long life. Perhaps it is this extended life-history pattern that is the fundamental ape adaptation. In apes, this strategy is correlated with a relatively large brain. But using measures of relative brain size to infer the life history of fossil apes is fraught with problems. Until we have a way of producing precise estimates of body size for fossils, measures of relative brain size will be ambiguous.

It has often been suggested that apes became extinct because they were competitively inferior to monkeys. The fossil record offers no evidence to support this view. Monkeys arrived in late Miocene Eurasia after the demise of apes, probably because of the spread of more open habitats, and in the middle Miocene of Africa diverse groups of monkeys and apes often coexisted. Today's greatly diminished ape fauna reflects the massive loss of suitable habitat during the past 10 million years as the result of climatic change.

Jay Kelley

See also 'Classification and evolutionary relationships' (p. 17), 'Jaws and teeth' (p. 56), 'Primate locomotion and posture' (p. 75), 'Land movements and species dispersal' (p. 169), 'Reconstructing past environments' (p. 191), 'The fossil history of primates' (p. 199) and Part 8 'Genetic clues of relatedness' (pp. 293–321)

Evolution of australopithecines

Estimates based on comparative biochemistry and the fossil record suggest that the ancestral stock from which modern humans are derived split off from the remainder of the ape family between 8 million years ago (towards the end of the Miocene epoch) and 5 million years ago (during the Pliocene) in Africa. The animals within this segment of the hominoid superfamily are called hominids, a term that covers all primates judged to be more closely related to modern humans than they are to the living African apes – the two species of chimpanzee and the single species of gorilla. There is now strong evidence from investigations of DNA that hominids and chimpanzees form a sister group to the exclusion of the gorilla.

It follows from this that there must exist a fossil record of a lineage, or a series of lineages, of hominids stretching from either 8 or 5 million years ago to the present. The more recent of these fossils pose relatively few problems of identification. Most fossil hominids back to 2 million years ago, and perhaps just beyond, are more closely related to modern humans than they are to chimpanzees and belong to our own genus, Homo. The most recent of these fossil hominids are usually described as archaic variants of our own species, Homo sapiens. The earlier part of the lineage has been allocated to several fossil species, of which Homo erectus and Homo habilis are the two best known.

Compared with the African apes, most of all these forms of Homo have a relatively large brain, relatively reduced chewing (or molar) teeth and limb bones that are, except in points of detail, like those of modern Homo sapiens. However, there are at least four, and perhaps five, species of hominid that lack the expanded brain, the reduced molar teeth and the skeletal features of Homo. They antedate or overlap with the earliest representatives of Homo, and are known collectively as the australopithecines.

Types of australopithecines

Australopithecines are conventionally split into two groups on the basis of their body types – the gracile (more lightly built) and robust (more ruggedly built) forms. Opinions differ about whether the two types should be put in separate genera. If this course is adopted, then the robust australopithecines can be divided into at least two species of the genus Paranthropus: P. robustus from southern Africa and P. boisei from eastern Africa. The name Australopithecus ('southern ape') is then reserved for the two gracile australopithecine taxa: A. africanus from southern Africa and A. afarensis from eastern Africa. Although most scholars use a traditional scheme, with all the australopithecine species classified in one genus (Australopithecus), Paranthropus is here used as a separate genus for the robust australopithecines.

The eastern and southern African versions of robust australopithecine are usually reckoned to be more different from each other than are the regional variants of the gracile forms: indeed, only recently have differences between A. africanus and A. afarensis been widely accepted. Fossil australopithecines are confined to Africa; claims that they have been found in Java, Indonesia, or elsewhere in Asia or Europe are rejected by most workers.

Hominid characteristics

Australopithecines are classed as hominids rather than pongids because, like Homo, they had reduced canine teeth and their limbs were substantially adapted for bipedal walking. However, their brains were relatively small and details of the brain fissures were different from those of later hominids. Moreover, although australopithecine limb bones could resist the loads and stresses of upright stance and locomotion, they did so without having the characteristic shape of the Homo pelvis and thigh bone (femur).

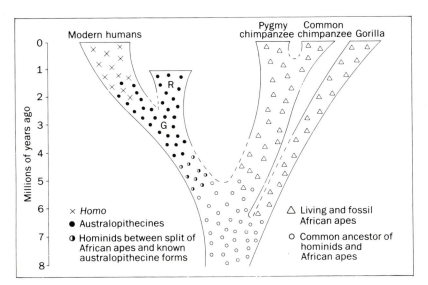

The relationship of hominids to modern humans and African apes. Robust (R) and gracile (G) lineages are indicated.

Two schemes for the nomenclature and taxonomy of australopithecines

	One genus	Two genera
	Australopithecus (Dart)	(1) Australopithecus (Dart)
		(2) Paranthropus (Broom)
■ Gracile forms	A. africanus	A. africanus
	A. afarensis	A. afarensis
■ Robust forms	A. robustus (including A. crassidens)	P. robustus (including P. crassidens)
	A. boisei	P. boisei (including P. aethiopicus)

Furthermore, some of the australopithecines are debarred from inclusion within our direct ancestry because they had their own special adaptations, seen particularly in the shape of the face and in the large premolar and molar teeth of the robust australopithecine subgroup. Some, but certainly not all, of the australopithecines may be ancestral to later *Homo* but it is quite likely that the immediate ancestor of *Homo* has yet to be found.

Australopithecines are often wrongly thought to have had a mosaic of modern human and modern ape features, or, worse, are regarded as a group of 'failed' humans. Australopithecines were neither of these. They were a recognisable, but diverse, group of primates that were no better, nor worse, adapted to the savannas of Plio-Pleistocene Africa than are modern-day chimpanzees and gorillas to their woods and forests. Fossils show that australopithecines lasted for at least 3 million years and perhaps for even longer. They accordingly deserve study in their own right, independent of their connections with modern humans.

History and context of the fossil discoveries

Southern African australopithecines

The first australopithecine fossil was found in southern Africa in 1924 in a cave that was exposed at the Buxton Limeworks, which is close to Taung, near Kimberley. The Taung cave, like those at the other australopithecine sites in southern Africa, was formed as expansions of water channels that ran through the limestone. Once the caves started forming, they developed openings onto the ground surface, through which soil and debris, including bone, were washed in.

It is very likely that australopithecines did not actually occupy the caves. The surface debris became mixed with blocks of limestone that fell from the cave roof, and the mixture was hardened by carbonates leached from the surrounding rock to form a solid filling called a *breccia*. The pure limestone that formed as a skin between the breccia and the surrounding limestone makes these caves particularly good sites for mining and nearly all the early hominid sites in southern Africa have been found in, or near to, limeworkings.

Australopithecine bones were probably introduced into the limestone caves either directly, perhaps by porcupines, or, indirectly, some of them as the food debris of leopards or other large cats feeding in trees growing out of cave openings. These extra uncertainties about how the bones accumulated within the caves make any interpretations of the faunal context of these hominids unusually difficult.

The importance of the Taung find was recognised by Raymond Dart, who published a description of it in 1925. Subsequent explorations in Transvaal Province by Robert Broom resulted in the discovery of further evidence of australopithecines at Sterkfontein and Kromdraai, in 1936 and 1938 respectively, and two further hominid sites,

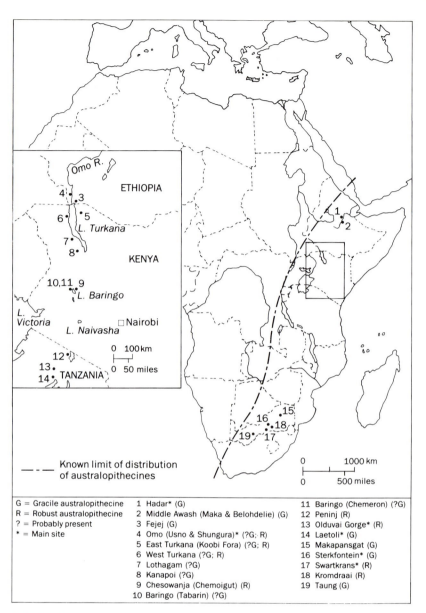

G = Gracile australopithecine	1 Hadar* (G)	11 Baringo (Chemeron) (?G)
R = Robust australopithecine	2 Middle Awash (Maka & Belohdelie) (G)	12 Peninj (R)
? = Probably present	3 Fejej (G)	13 Olduvai Gorge* (R)
* = Main site	4 Omo (Usno & Shungura)* (?G; R)	14 Laetoli* (G)
	5 East Turkana (Koobi Fora) (?G; R)	15 Makapansgat (G)
	6 West Turkana (?G; R)	16 Sterkfontein* (G)
	7 Lothagam (?G)	17 Swartkrans* (R)
	8 Kanapoi (?G)	18 Kromdraai (R)
	9 Chesowanja (Chemoigut) (R)	19 Taung (G)
	10 Baringo (Tabarin) (?G)	

Australopithecine sites in Africa.

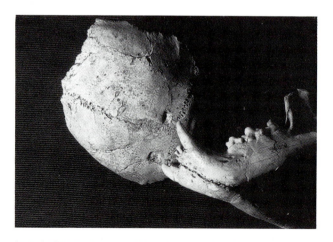

Australopithecine bones could have been introduced into the southern African caves accidentally by leopards and other large cats. There is evidence of this from Swartkrans. The holes in the parietal bones of a juvenile robust australopithecine cranium (SK 54) match the lower canines of a leopard from the same deposit.

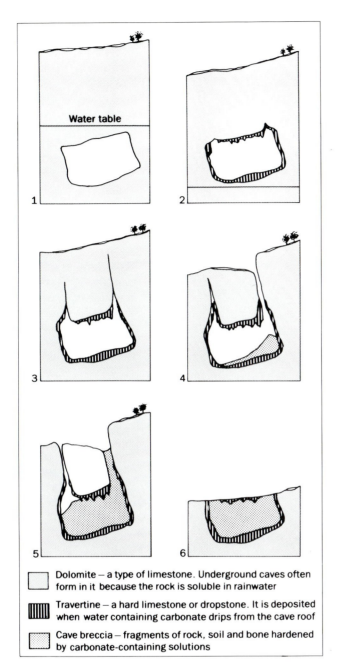

Dolomite – a type of limestone. Underground caves often form in it because the rock is soluble in rainwater

Travertine – a hard limestone or dropstone. It is deposited when water containing carbonate drips from the cave roof

Cave breccia – fragments of rock, soil and bone hardened by carbonate-containing solutions

The southern African limestone cave sites of Kromdraai, Sterkfontein, Swartkrans and Taung, where many early hominid remains have been found, probably formed in the sequence of stages represented here.

Excavations in progress at Swartkrans, South Africa, showing Member 3, which has been dated to around 1.5 million years ago. Remains of robust australopithecines and early *Homo* have been found at the site.

Two australopithecine skulls from southern African cave sites: (right) *Australopithecus africanus* from Sterkfontein ('Mrs Ples', Sts 5) found in 1947 and (left) *Paranthropus robustus* from Swartkrans (SK 48) found in 1950. Seen together, differences between the gracile and robust forms are evident.

Swartkrans and Makapansgat, were found in 1947 and 1948. The Taung skull, from a juvenile hominid, and the collections from Sterkfontein and Makapansgat, may represent the same species of australopithecine, *Australopithecus africanus*. However, the identification of the Taung hominid has recently been challenged by some who suggest that it is actually a robust and not a gracile australopithecine. Other scientists have suggested that the *A. africanus* fossil collection may represent two hominid species, and not just one.

The remains from Kromdraai and Swartkrans are sufficiently different from *A. africanus*, a gracile australopithecine, to be put into a separate robust australopithecine group. The two collections of robust australopithecines from southern African sites are conventionally placed together in a single species, *Paranthropus robustus*, but some researchers have suggested that they should more properly be regarded as two separate species – *P. robustus* from Kromdraai and *P. crassidens* from Swartkrans.

Eastern African australopithecines

Australopithecine fossils from eastern Africa are found in very different geological circumstances. The first fossil was discovered at Garusi in Tanzania, a site that is now included in the Laetoli site complex. More than 40 years elapsed between that first discovery and the re-exploration of the area by Mary Leakey, which resulted in the discovery of fossils that make up part of the collection attributed to *Australopithecus afarensis*, now considered to be a gracile australopithecine species distinct from *A. africanus*. Most of the *A. afarensis* fossils come from Hadar, a region along the Awash River in Ethiopia, where expeditions in the mid-1970s led by Donald Johanson, Yves Coppens and Maurice Taieb unearthed a large collection of hominid remains, including a nearly half-complete skeleton (AL 288-1) nick-named 'Lucy' (see p. 237).

In 1959, at Olduvai Gorge in Tanzania, a cranium that showed clear affinities with the robust australopithecines

The barren Hadar site in the Afar region of Ethiopia, near the Awash River, where many fossils of *Australopithecus afarensis* have been found in Pliocene deposits about 3 million years old. The finds include a nearly half-complete skeleton (AL 288-1 or 'Lucy') and the remains of five to seven individuals, including two infants (AL 333). The photograph shows Donald Johanson's field team combing locality 333, where the australopithecine group was found in 1975. The australopithecines lived beside a freshwater lake fed by rivers from the Ethiopian Escarpment. In contrast to the dry environment today, trees were plentiful on the lakeside and riverbanks, and there was forest on the mountain slopes.

An early form of East African robust australopithecine (*Paranthropus aethiopicus*) from Lomekwi, West Turkana, Kenya (KNM-WT 17000), about 2.5 million years old.

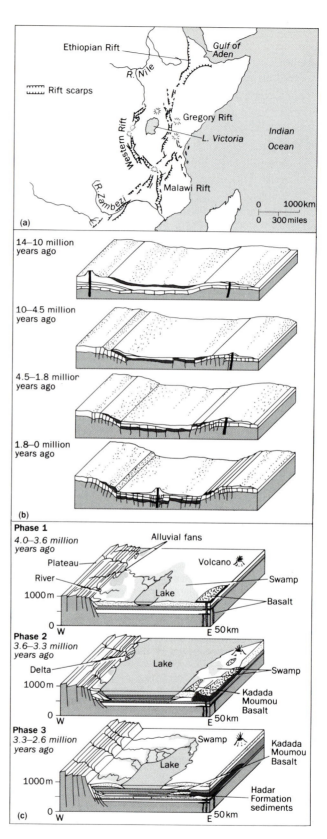

(a)

14–10 million years ago

10–4.5 million years ago

4.5–1.8 million years ago

1.8–0 million years ago

(b)

Phase 1
4.0–3.6 million years ago

Plateau
River
Alluvial fans
Volcano
Swamp
Lake
Basalt
1000 m
0
W   E 50 km

Phase 2
3.6–3.3 million years ago

Delta
Lake
Swamp
Kadada Moumou Basalt
1000 m
0
W   E 50 km

Phase 3
3.3–2.6 million years ago

Swamp
Kadada Moumou Basalt
Lake
Hadar Formation sediments
1000 m
0
W   E 50 km

(c)

Stages in the evolution of the East African Rift in Ethiopia (b) and the australopithecine site of Hadar in the Afar region (c). Hominids lived in the Hadar area and at nearby sites along the Awash River from about 4 million to about 2.5 million years ago. The map (a) shows the rift system today.

already known from southern Africa was discovered by Louis and Mary Leakey. At first, this fossil skull ('Zinj'), labelled Olduvai Hominid (OH) 5, was attributed to a new genus (Zinjanthropus), but it was later included within Paranthropus. Similar finds followed at Peninj in Tanzania, Omo in Ethiopia, and Koobi Fora and Chesowanja in Kenya. All these sites provided evidence of Paranthropus boisei, an eastern African species of robust australopithecine.

By far the largest collection of P. boisei comes from Koobi Fora on the eastern side of Lake Turkana, where expeditions led by Richard Leakey and Glynn Isaac in the 1970s found crania, jaws and teeth of large males and smaller females of this species. The latest East African locality to yield evidence of australopithecines is on the western shoreline of Lake Turkana, where P. aethiopicus (KNM-WT 17000), a primitive-looking P. boisei, was found in 1985. Fragmentary remains that probably belong to a gracile australopithecine have also been found at Omo and Fejej (also in Ethiopia) and at the Kenyan sites of Lothagam, Chemeron and Tabarin and perhaps also at Koobi Fora. Some of these fossils are similar to Australopithecus afarensis and A. africanus, but their affinities remain uncertain; Chemeron may even represent early Homo.

There are parallels between the australopithecines of eastern and southern Africa, for in both areas there are gracile and robust forms. Nonetheless, the fossils are found in very different contexts in the two regions. In eastern Africa, all the sites are related to the Eastern Rift Valley, on, or close

to, the shores of lakes, or on floodplains or sandbars associated with rivers. The australopithecines may indeed have lived in these locations, but it is increasingly clear that many complex influences can determine whether the bones of animals are preserved as fossils at all, and, if so, why they come to rest where they do. It is known, for example, that even at the open-air eastern African sites the numbers and types of fossil animals are unlikely to reflect faithfully the fauna that was contemporary with the hominids. Nevertheless, such sites provide a potentially richer source of evidence on australopithecine habitat and the prevailing climate than can the fossils found in the confines of the more southerly caves.

Dating and habitat

The contrast between the eastern 'open' lake and river-associated sites, and the southern 'closed' cave sites greatly influences the precision with which the fossils can be dated. Evidence for the age of Australopithecus africanus and Paranthropus robustus rests almost entirely on matching their associated fauna with similar but better-dated faunal assemblages from elsewhere in Africa (see p. 184). Australopithecus africanus is known from a span of perhaps a million years, from 3.25 to 2.5 million years ago or less. The younger end of this span is 'fixed' by the age of Taung, which is the least securely dated of all the cave sites. If an older date for Taung is accepted (around 2.5 million years), then there would be

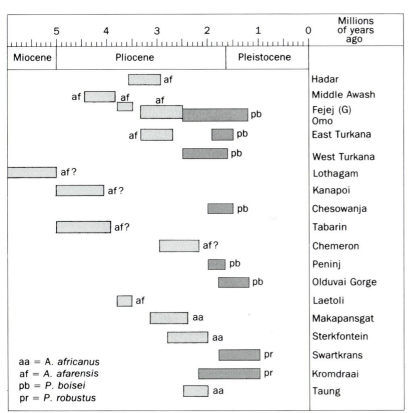

Chronology of the major australopithecine sites in eastern and southern Africa.

View over one of the excavation sites at Koobi Fora, Kenya.

no overlap between *A. africanus* and *P. robustus*, for the latter apparently spans the time range between 2 and 1 million years ago.

Australopithecine sites in eastern Africa can be dated more accurately. The Rift Valley underwent considerable volcanic activity, and ash layers have become interleaved with sands and silts from rivers and streams. The hardened ash layers (tuffs) contain isotopes of elements such as potassium, argon and uranium that can be used to calibrate the time of the eruption, and hence the approximate age of the tuff. Cross-checks on these dates can be made using the record of changes in the direction and polarity of the earth's magnetic field, which is well known for the past 5 million years.

Such techniques have the potential to provide a more precise record of time at eastern African sites. However, the condition of the rocks and experimental difficulties can sometimes result in erroneous dates. For example, 'Lucy' and some of the other Hadar australopithecines are now thought to be closer to 3 million years than 3.5 million years old. However, gracile australopithecines from other sites in eastern Africa, such as Middle Awash, Tabarin and Lothagam, extend the age range of this group of fossils to 4 million years and beyond, perhaps to 5 million years.

The earliest unambiguous evidence of robust australopithecines in eastern Africa is of *Paranthropus boisei* in the Shungura Formation at the Omo River site dated to between 2.75 and 2.5 million years ago, and the most recent evidence consists of several isolated teeth from the Omo that are around 1.5 million years old.

The habitats of the gracile and robust australopithecines were probably different. Several lines of geological evidence indicate a global shift to cooler climates after about 2.5 million years ago. At both the southern and eastern African sites, the associated mammalian fauna shows a shift from a more wooded habitat at the time of the earlier gracile forms to a more open-country and grass-dependent fauna at the time for which there is the best evidence of the later robust australopithecines. The type and diversity of herbivores, especially bovids such as antelopes and pigs, and the changing patterns of small mammals (especially rodents) are useful indicators of changing habitats. There are also differences in plant pollens, which suggest a significant change in the flora and therefore probably in the temperature and rainfall.

Appearance and lifestyle

There is now quite an impressive list of finds of the body parts of australopithecines, yet the known fossil record represents only between 0.02 and 0.00002 per cent of the estimated living population of these hominids. Even the best known of the four taxa has just five or six well-preserved crania, and all but one of these lack anatomically

---

DISTINGUISHING FEATURES OF AUSTRALOPITHECINES

	Australopithecus afarensis	*Australopithecus africanus*	*Paranthropus boisei*	*Paranthropus robustus*
Height (m)	1–1.5	1.1–1.4	1.2–1.4	1.1–1.3
Weight (kg)	30–70	30–60	40–80	40–80
Physique	Light build; some ape-like features (e.g. shape of thorax; long arms relative to legs; curved fingers and toes; marked to moderate sexual dimorphism)	Light build; probably relatively long arms; more 'human' features; probably less sexual dimorphism	Very heavy build; relatively long arms; marked sexual dimorphism	Heavy build; relatively long arms; moderate sexual dimorphism
Brain size (ml)	400–500	400–500	410–530	530
Skull form	Low, flat forehead; projecting face; prominent brow ridges	Higher forehead; shorter face; brow ridges less prominent	Prominent crests on top and back of skull; very long, broad, flattish face; strong facial buttressing	Crest on top of skull; long, broad, flattish face; moderate facial buttressing
Jaws/teeth	Relatively large incisors and canines; gap between upper incisors and canines; moderate-sized molars	Small incisor-like canines; no gap between upper incisors and canines; larger molars	Very thick jaws; small incisors and canines; large, molar-like premolars very large molars	Very thick jaws; small incisors and canines; large, molar-like premolars; very large molars
Distribution	Eastern Africa	Southern Africa	Eastern Africa	Southern Africa
Known date (millions of years ago)	>4–2.5	~3.0–<2.5	2.6–1.2	2–1

important parts of the skull. One of the aims of palaeontologists is to use fossil remains to reconstruct as much as possible of the biology of a fossil species. The reliability of such reconstructions is variable because they depend on analogies, not all of which may be appropriate. Estimates of stature and body weight are relatively precise, but dietary reconstruction is more difficult and any discussion of social behaviour is frankly speculative.

Gracile australopithecines

Estimates of the size and morphology of *Australopithecus africanus* and *A. afarensis* are usually based, respectively, on the skeletons Sts 14 from Sterkfontein and AL 288-1 ('Lucy') from Hadar, together with other, more fragmentary post-cranial remains and evidence from the preserved footprints at Laetoli (see p. 325). Useful information about stature and weight comes from joint surfaces and cross-sections of the shafts of limb bones. Sts 14 and AL 288-1 are both probably female, so that heights and weights derived from them probably underestimate the average body weight for each species. The two fossil species were of similar size. If all the fossils found at Hadar are included in the same taxon (*A. afarensis*), this includes individuals varying in height from 1 m to 1.5 m (3 ft 3 in to 4 ft 11 in), and in weight from 30 kg (66 lb) to as much as 70 kg (154 lb), the average being around 50 kg (110 lb). *Australopithecus africanus* had a similar average weight (45 kg or 100 lb), and was only a little less variable in weight and height than *A. afarensis*.

The skulls of the two varieties of gracile australopithecines differ in detail, but they are of similar overall size. The internal volume of the adult skull (which is usually about 15 per cent less than brain size) ranges from less than 400 to 500 millilitres, so that each form had a similar ratio between brain and body weight. The persistence of good-sized incisors in gracile australopithecines, and the patterns of wear on the teeth, are consistent with at least some fruit-eating.

How *A. afarensis* moved is particularly controversial. Opinions range from those who see these creatures as habitual bipeds, not unlike modern humans, to those who suggest that limb proportions, anatomy and footprints point to an animal that was neither predominantly arboreal nor fully bipedal. Details of the feet and hands suggest that the latter may be a more accurate interpretation. The skeleton of *A. africanus* was probably adapted for bipedal locomotion, but the muscles of the lower limbs may have been arranged in a way unlike those of apes or modern humans. Gracile australopithecines may therefore have fed and moved much like modern baboons, but with more emphasis on bipedalism. Such groups would have spread

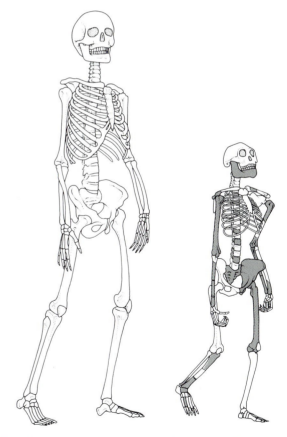

(Right) The skeleton of Lucy reconstructed at Kent State University, Ohio, in dental plaster contrasted with the skeleton of a modern human female of average height in walking position. The original parts of the australopithecine are grey and mirror images of known bones and parts based on other fossils are white. The cranium should also be partly black but has been left white for clarity. Lucy was only about 105 cm (3 ft 5 in) high but other *Australopithecus afarensis* individuals were up to 150 cm (4 ft 11 in) high. Notice Lucy's relatively long arms.

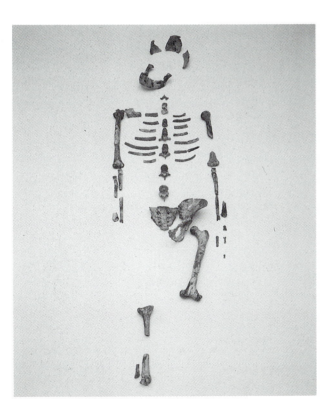

The remarkably complete skeleton of the female gracile australopithecine (*Australopithecus afarensis*) called Lucy (AL 288-1), discovered at Hadar in 1974.

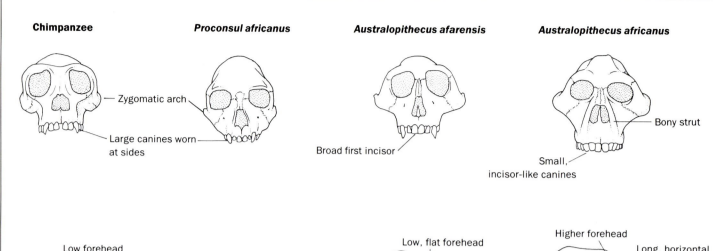

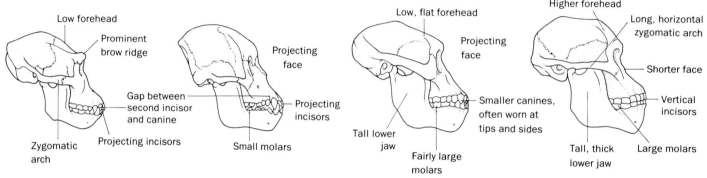

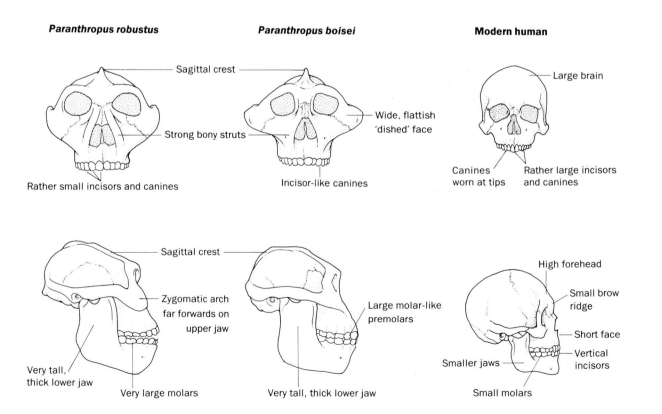

Front and side views of the skulls of the four main types of australopithecine contrasted with the skulls of the early ape *Proconsul*, a chimpanzee and a modern human. The drawings are not to scale.

out to forage on the ground in the day, and then congregated, perhaps in caves or trees, at night.

The population structure and social systems of living monkeys and apes can to some extent be predicted from the average body size, the population range of body size, and habitat. If these living animals are apt analogies, then gracile australopithecines are most likely to have lived in multimale groups, or as single males with a harem. The archaeological record of stone artefacts barely overlaps even the most recent gracile australopithecines and is much later than their first appearance, so the extent to which these hominids fashioned and used tools, if at all, is unknown.

Robust australopithecines

The robust australopithecines from southern Africa (*Paranthropus robustus*) were about 1.2 m (3 ft 11 in) high and weighed between 40 and 80 kg (88–176 lb). The eastern African form (P. *boisei*) was taller (1.3 m, or 4 ft 4 in) but apparently no heavier. The size differences between P. *boisei* mandibles suggest that the differences between the body size of males and females may have been equivalent to those between male and female gorillas, with males up to twice the size of females.

Many of the features of the face, jaws and teeth of the robust australopithecines, especially P. *boisei*, are unique among hominids, although some of these features are shared with other living higher primates. The flat, broad face, the massive, tall mandibles and the large molars all suggest a diet that involved the processing of large amounts of food and the generation of much force between the teeth. The robust australopithecines probably moved in a way similar to the gracile forms. The relatively small head of the femur in the robust forms may be a consequence of the small size of the brain and hence a small birth canal and narrow pelvis, rather than an indication of a radical difference in movement in the two types of australopithecine. Studies of the rate and pattern of formation of the hard outer enamel of teeth suggest that growth and development of the dentition was substantially faster in *Paranthropus* than in modern humans and apes.

The males and females of the eastern African form of robust australopithecine were more different in body size than were the southern variants. The social structure of robust australopithecine groups might also have involved a harem or multimale system. Recent evidence from Swartkrans suggests that bone digging sticks, as well as evidence of burned bone, occurred in the same geological layers that contain the remains of P. *robustus* but the timespan of these layers overlaps the temporal range of *Homo*.

Patterns of australopithecine evolution

We cannot be sure that the first hominids were australopithecines, as recent biochemical and palaeontolo-gical estimates imply that there was a gap of 1.5 or more million years between the earliest known australopithecines and the divergence of hominids from a common ancestor with the African apes. We cannot be sure that australopithecines were the first regularly bipedal apes. We do not even know under what circumstances they (or earlier hominids) might have adopted a predominantly bipedal gait: this might correlate with monogamy, in which males feed females, although the level of australopithecine sexual dimorphism makes this unlikely, or with a shift to feeding on items abundant in the open woodland and savanna fringes. However, the evidence from the postcranial skeleton suggests that the earliest australopithecines may have been as well, if not better, adapted to life in and around trees.

What prompted the australopithecines to make such a shift from the more forested habitat of their ancestors? There is evidence from other fossil groups, especially pigs, that around 5 million years ago there was a climatic shift in central and eastern Africa, which culminated in the establishment of the Sahara as a desert. If such climatic changes triggered the emergence of hominids, what environmental influences led to the emergence of the later robust australopithecines?

The peculiar, if not unique, face and dentition of robust australopithecines have prompted a variety of functional explanations, none of which is consistent with all the evidence, and which range from suggestions that they were seed-eaters to proposals that they were adapted to crush bones. The most plausible hypothesis is that they ate pulpy fruit material, which they had to reach by breaking open a hard outer covering. The advent of the robust australopithecines may have been part of a more widespread evolutionary event, stimulated by interactions between climate and food resources. The period around 2.5 to 2.3 million years ago is marked by many extinctions and first appearances of species in the vertebrate fossil record.

Relationships of the australopithecines

Most of the possible permutations of relationships between the four australopithecine species have had their adherents, but some hypotheses have wider support than others. The two regional forms of robust australopithecine are probably more closely related to each other than either is to gracile australopithecines, or to any other taxon – hence, the readoption here of the genus *Paranthropus*. Thereafter, opinion is divided.

Some interpret A. *africanus* as having affinities with the robust subgroup, with A. *afarensis* as a more primitive ancestral form. Others see A. *africanus* as the more plausible ancestor, and point to purportedly derived features of the skull base as evidence of a link between A. *afarensis* and the two robust taxa. A third arrangement sees A. *afarensis* as primitive, with A. *africanus* as the ancestor of both the robust lineage and the one leading to *Homo*. All these arrangements imply that certain similarities of the cranial base or the face are analagous. The probability that there is significant convergent evolution in the fossil record merely adds to the difficulties of analysing these early hominids.

What is the nature of the group we know as the australopithecines? Are they more closely related to each other than to any other hominid, or do they merely represent a stage, or level, of evolution that may have been achieved by members of more than one hominid lineage? If the former is true, then no known australopithecine can be ancestral to *Homo*. If the latter proves correct, then the australopithecines are a group with a mixed origin. The present evidence is equivocal.

Three views predominate about the relationship between the australopithecines and *Homo*. In the first scheme, *A. afarensis* is the common ancestor of two lineages, one leading to *Homo*, the other leading via *A. africanus* to *P. robustus* and *P. boisei*. The second scheme also sees *A. afarensis* as ancestral to *A. africanus*, but it has the latter as the common ancestor of two lineages, one being *Homo* and the other leading to, and including, the robust australopithecines. A third scheme has fewer supporters, but it may prove to be more durable than the others. In this arrangement, the australopithecines and *Homo* share a common ancestor, which has not yet been found in the fossil record. Two lineages result from such an ancestor. One leads to the robust australopithecines via *A. afarensis*; the other leads, via *A. africanus*, to *Homo*. These and other differences in our perceptions of hominid relationships, however, still owe as much to disagreements about methodology as to differences in interpretations of the fossils themselves.

B.A. Wood

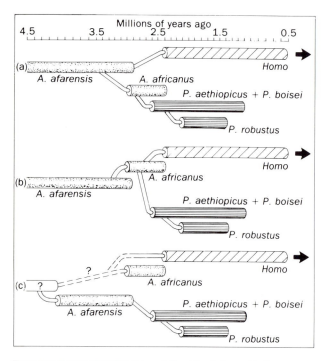

Three hypotheses of evolutionary relationships between the four australopithecine species – *Australopithecus afarensis*, *Australopithecus africanus*, *Paranthropus boisei* (including *P. aethiopicus*) and *Paranthropus robustus* – and the human lineage.

See also 'Jaws and teeth' (p. 56), 'Primate locomotion and posture' (p. 75), 'Human locomotion' (p. 80), 'The human brain' (p. 115), 'Methods of dating' (p. 179), 'Fossil deposits and their investigation' (p. 187), 'Reconstructing past environments' (p. 191), 'Evolution of early humans' (p. 241), 'The hominid way of life' (p. 325), and 'Evolution of human manipulation' (p. 346)

Evolution of early humans

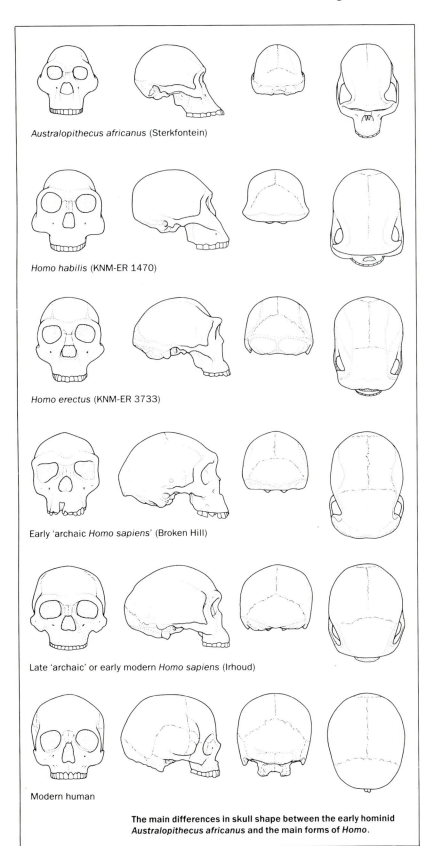

Australopithecus africanus (Sterkfontein)

Homo habilis (KNM-ER 1470)

Homo erectus (KNM-ER 3733)

Early 'archaic *Homo sapiens*' (Broken Hill)

Late 'archaic' or early modern *Homo sapiens* (Irhoud)

Modern human

The main differences in skull shape between the early hominid *Australopithecus africanus* and the main forms of *Homo*.

It is not easy identifying the features that mark the human genus *Homo*, as the group contains not just all living people but our closest fossil relatives as well. Moreover, many features that distinguish humans are behavioural, and leave no fossil evidence. It is very difficult judging whether a particular kind of early human had developed a language, society or art, and other features that can be recognised in fossils are usually used to infer these attributes.

A large brain has usually been the single most important feature, although on its own this may be an unreliable guide to membership of the genus *Homo*. In early fossils, body size must also be taken into account to give an idea of relative brain size; if this were not done, some small-bodied and small-brained early humans might not qualify as human at all. Most members of the genus *Homo* do have a brain volume of more than 700 millilitres (ml), considerably larger than that of the largest robust australopithecine or living ape. To house a brain of such a size, the human cranial vault is large in relation to the face, and the face is tucked under the vault more than is the case in early apes or hominids.

Other diagnostic features of humans include the presence of a prominent nose (as represented by raised bone surfaces around the nasal opening) and a bony spine at the centre of the base of the nasal opening. These characteristics are further reflected in various measurements of the face. The base of the human skull is short and well flexed or folded up. Such distinctive features may be related to the development of language and the remodelling of the throat to give a lower position for the voice box.

The jaws of humans are also notable, because the bone of the lower jaw is rather thin and there may be a vertical front to the jaw or even a bony prominence – a chin. The teeth, and in particular the last of the cheek teeth, are small. Tooth eruption is slow compared with that in apes and early hominids.

Modern humans develop very slowly. They reach sexual maturity late and have a long life. Many people survive past the age of reproduction. We have no idea when this distinctive pattern emerged, and some believe it was already present in early hominids. However, new microscopic techniques for examining fossil bones and teeth suggest that it is a recent evolutionary development, which was linked with the growth demands of a large brain as well as the emergence of culture and language. Complex human abilities require a long learning period and also favour the survival of experienced individuals who can pass on their knowledge.

Our anatomy is different from that of apes and early hominids in other ways. However, there are few fossil remains and we have limited insight into the evolution of the whole skeleton in Homo. All the evidence points to Homo individuals having a modern style of locomotion, whereas, judging from fossils of the hip joint, some earlier hominids did not walk in quite the same way as humans do. Modern humans are characterised by an especially light build, with thin bones and reduced muscles compared with the apes. However, earlier forms of human were much more strongly built, so our rather puny skeletons are not generally typical of the genus Homo.

Homo habilis

By 2.4 million years ago new types of hominid had appeared in the fossil record of eastern and southern Africa. At about the same time, or slightly earlier, the first recognisable stone tools were manufactured, and these evolutionary and behavioural events may have marked the advent of the first true humans known to scientists by the name Homo habilis ('handy man'). This species of the genus Homo was named in 1964 by Louis Leakey, Phillip Tobias and John Napier on the basis of fossils found in Beds I and II at Olduvai Gorge in Tanzania. It was regarded as intermediate between australopithecines and Homo sapiens, and fragments of skull were used to estimate a brain size of about 700 ml, well above the values for australopithecines and those of all except the largest-brained apes. The back teeth, although large, were narrow compared with those of other hominids.

There was immediate controversy about the new human species, H. habilis, because many felt that the fossil material

was not distinct enough to be placed in a new taxon. Some believed that it merely represented an advanced australopithecine, others that the Bed I material, such as Olduvai Hominid (OH) 7, represented an australopithecine, whereas the Bed II material (e.g. OH 13) was an early form of Homo erectus. Even the discovery of further material described as H. habilis from Olduvai (e.g. OH 24, 'Twiggy') did not stop such criticism and it took the discovery of more-complete fossils of similar age from Koobi Fora in northern Kenya to produce a general acceptance of such an early and distinctive species of human.

The material from Koobi Fora was mainly recovered from 1969 to 1976, and includes several partial skulls, mandibles, a hip bone (KNM-ER 3228), partial skeletons (e.g. KNM-ER 1808 and 1500) and various limb bones, in addition to simple stone tools, all dating from the period between about 2.0 and 1.6 million years ago. The specimens are generally known from their National Museums of Kenya catalogue number and the initials of the original site name, East Rudolf.

Perhaps most famous of all these fossils is KNM-ER 1470, found in 1972. This skull has a large brain (volume about 750 ml) and was originally dated to more than 2.6 million years ago. However, this was subsequently revised to about 1.9 million years ago, a date that tallied with the Olduvai record of H. habilis. The braincase has a more human shape than that of the australopithecines, but the face is very long, broad and flat, with prominent australopithecine-like cheekbones. Although no teeth were preserved, the sockets and spaces for them were large by modern human

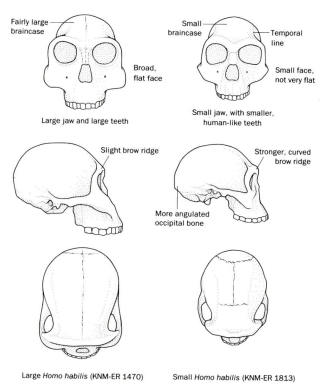

Large Homo habilis (KNM-ER 1470)   Small Homo habilis (KNM-ER 1813)

Reconstructions of the large and small Homo habilis skulls from Koobi Fora, Kenya.

Homo habilis **sites in Africa. Uraha is a new site, perhaps 2.4 million years old, on the northwestern shore of Lake Malawi.**

Two hominid skulls commonly assigned to *Homo habilis*: KNM-ER 1470 (left) and 1813 (right), both from Koobi Fora, Kenya. Hominid 1470 is the more ancient, with a larger brain and larger, flatter face; 1813, although small-brained, is actually more 'human' in several characteristics – for example, its teeth are relatively small.

standards. There are correspondingly large jaws and teeth in other specimens from the same levels at Koobi Fora, and one fragmentary skull probably had an even larger brain than 1470. The bones of the rest of the skeleton suggest that some of these very early humans were large and rather similar to the later species *Homo erectus* in their hip and leg anatomy.

These specimens from Koobi Fora probably represent *H. habilis*, as do the original Bed I finds from Olduvai. However, there are further perplexing finds from Koobi Fora, which complicate the picture of early human evolution. These include specimen KNM-ER 1813, a small-brained (510 ml) skull, which nevertheless looks generally more 'human' than does 1470, and KNM-ER 1805, which has teeth like 1813, a face like 1470, a brain capacity of only about 580 ml, and a braincase with a primitive crest along the midline – a feature otherwise found among hominids only in large robust australopithecines. The meaning of this great variation in morphology is still unclear but it may be that *H. habilis* was not the only human-like inhabitant of eastern Africa between 1.6 and 2.4 million years ago.

Confirmation of this complexity has come from a recent discovery near the base of the Bed I sequence at Olduvai of parts of a skull and a skeleton, which the finders have nicknamed the Dik-dik Hill hominid (OH 62). Features of the fragmentary skull are said to be *Homo*-like, yet the skeletal bones of this small-bodied hominid closely resemble those of the australopithecine 'Lucy' (*Australopithcus afarensis*, AL 288–1) from Hadar in Ethiopia. It is unclear whether this fossil shows that *Homo habilis* was very variable in morphology and body size or that there were two kinds of early *Homo*, one large and the other small.

Homo erectus

About 1.8 million years ago, a new type of early human appeared in the fossil record of eastern Africa, a species that was to persist in Africa for more than a million years, and also become the first human type to spread from that continent to Asia. Most scientists believe that the African and Asian remains represent a single species called *Homo erectus* ('erect man'). The specific name is derived from the name *Pithecanthropus erectus* given to the finds from Indonesia in the nineteenth century, when they were regarded as sufficiently distinct from humans to warrant a separate generic name. A minority of palaeoanthropologists feel that only the Asian finds should be called *H. erectus*, and that the African fossils represent a more primitive species.

If we accept the conventional view, the earliest examples of *H. erectus* are from northern Kenya on the east side (Koobi Fora) and west side (Nariokotome) of Lake Turkana. At the former site, two skulls (KNM-ER 3733 and 3883) and various fragments have been found, while at the latter a nearly complete skeleton of a boy (KNM-WT 15000) was discovered in 1984. These specimens are characterised by brain sizes of about 800 to 900 ml (considerably above those of most *Homo habilis* fossils) and a long and low skull with a broad base. The brow ridges were prominent, but the face is somewhat less projecting than in some *H. habilis* fossils and has a more pronounced nose. The Nariokotome boy's skeleton shows that, although not fully grown, he was already nearly 168 centimetres (5 ft 6 in) tall and heavily built. He had the long-legged build expected of tropical humans, but had some unusual features in his spinal column. Detailed study should produce some firm conclusions about the way his musculature and skeleton differed from our own.

Other examples of early *H. erectus* are known from Olduvai, where a skull dated to about 1.2 million years ago was discovered in 1960. This robust skull (OH 9) had a brain capacity of about 1050 ml, and an enormous brow ridge. Later finds from Olduvai (less than 1 million years old) include jaw fragments, a robustly built hip bone and partial thigh bone, and a small and more lightly built skull, which either represents an extreme variant of the *erectus* type or an entirely separate species. Elsewhere in Africa, fossils attributed to *H. erectus* have been found in adjacent Kenya (Baringo) and further afield in Algeria (Ternifine, now called Tighennif), Morocco (Salé and the Thomas quarries), Ethiopia (Melka Kunturé and Bodo d'Ar) and South Africa (Swartkrans).

By about 1 million years ago, *H. erectus* was also present in Asia, and may have spread to southern Europe. On the basis of a new lower jaw from Dmanisi in the republic of Georgia, it is even possible that *H. erectus* was present in Europe as long ago as 1.5 million years. The Asian populations are best known from the finds of 'Java Man' in the nineteenth century, and 'Peking Man' in the period between World Wars I and II, although several important finds have since been made in Indonesia and China. Indonesian finds are somewhat earlier in date, are more robust and have smaller brains, although there is also an enigmatic sample of skulls,

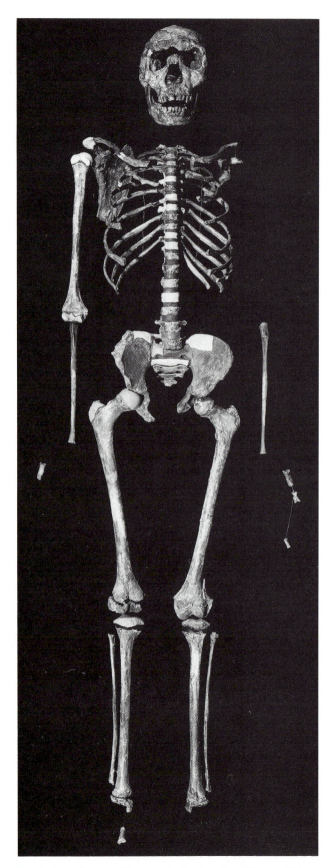

This skeleton of a young *Homo erectus* boy (less than 12 years old) is the most complete specimen of an archaic human ever discovered. The specimen (KNM-WT 15000), found at Nariokotome, Kenya in 1984 and dated to around 1.6 million years ago, shows a tall and well-built physique, even in this young individual.

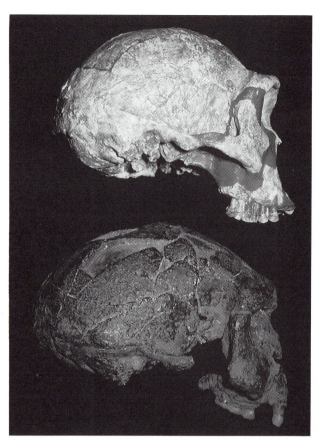

Two human skulls commonly assigned to *Homo erectus*. These specimens illustrate the great variation in *Homo erectus* material from different areas and times. The skull at the top is KNM-ER 3733 from Koobi Fora, Kenya, dated to around 1.6 million years ago. The other skull is Sangiran 17 from Java, Indonesia, which may date from around 700 000 years ago. Some researchers feel that the differences between them are so great that KNM-ER 3733 should not be called *Homo erectus*.

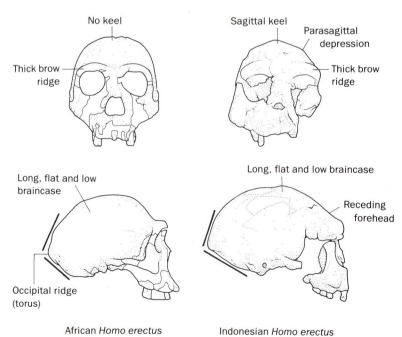

African *Homo erectus*
(KNM-ER 3733)

Indonesian *Homo erectus*
(Sangiran 17)

Early *Homo erectus* from Koobi Fora (KNM-ER 3733) contrasted with a later skull from Sangiran, Java.

all lacking faces, from Ngandong (Solo) in Java, which seem to represent a late-surviving derivative.

The Asian finds show some consistent differences from the African fossils of H. erectus; the skulls are more strongly buttressed with ridges of bone, and the walls of the skull are greatly thickened. The bones of the rest of the skeleton known from Zhoukoudian (the 'Peking Man' cave site) are strongly built, as are their equivalents from Africa. Thigh bones found in the original Javanese excavations look more like modern specimens, and may in fact be geologically younger than the H. erectus skulls.

Information about the way of life of H. erectus has been gathered from caves and open sites. The early African and the Asian representatives used flake tools manufactured from local materials, such as lava, chert and flint, but the later African groups produced larger multipurpose tools, such as handaxes and cleavers. These were also used in Europe during the past 500 000 years.

No doubt H. erectus made tools from wood (and bamboo in parts of Asia), but these implements have rarely been preserved. Unlike later humans, however, they made little use of bone, antler and ivory. The Chinese site of Zhoukoudian suggests that H. erectus used the caves over long periods, although perhaps not continuously – other crea-

tures such as hyenas also lived there. Thick deposits of ash at Zhoukoudian might be hearths built up by generations of use by early humans, but alternatively they might represent natural fires or even simply organic deposits produced by the activities of animals. Nevertheless, open campsites of similar age have been excavated in Europe at, for example, Terra Amata in France, and show that these peoples were nomadic hunters and gatherers, albeit in a way much simpler and more opportunistic than that of any hunter-gatherers alive today. Like the earlier H. habilis, the teeth of H. erectus were rather similar to our own, although larger, and indicate a mixed diet.

'Archaic *Homo sapiens*'

By about 400 000 years ago, there had been enough changes in certain human populations for a new species of early human to be recognised. This may have marked the emergence of our own species, Homo sapiens. The fossil remains concerned are usually known by the rather unsatisfactory term 'archaic Homo sapiens' but it is also possible that they represent a species distinct from Homo erectus and H. sapiens, called Homo heidelbergensis after the Heidelberg jaw, or Homo rhodesiensis after a skull found at Broken Hill (Kabwe) in what was then Northern Rhodesia (now Zambia). This population had a larger brain (around 1100–1300 ml) than H. erectus, with a taller braincase and an expanded parietal region. There were also reductions in the buttressing of the skull and in the projection of the face in front of the braincase, a more prominent face and nose, and changes in the base of the skull that may relate to the presence of a voice box of modern type. Little is known of the rest of the skeleton, but 'archaic H. sapiens' may have been as robust and muscular as H. erectus.

Part of the Zhoukoudian cave complex, Beijing, showing Locality 1 where many *Homo erectus* fossils and stone tools have been found since excavations began there in the 1920s.

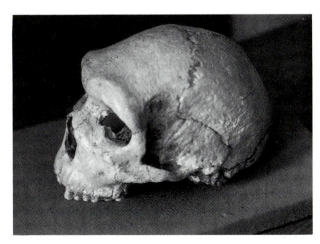

This skull from Petralona, Greece, was found in 1960. Estimates of its age range from more than 700 000 years to less than 200 000 years, but its appearance is most similar to European and African fossils dated to between 200 000 and 400 000 years. It shows a combination of characters found in *Homo erectus* and Neanderthals, as well as others that are present in 'archaic *Homo sapiens*', to which group it is usually assigned.

The principal sites of discovery of *Homo erectus* and 'archaic *Homo sapiens*'. Some of the European fossils may be early Neanderthals.

Which particular fossils from 500 000 to 200 000 years ago actually represent 'archaic *H. sapiens*' is not generally agreed. African fossils such as the skulls from Kabwe (Zambia), Saldanha (South Africa) and Omo 2 (Ethiopia) probably represent this group, but there is less agreement about specimens such as Bodo (Ethiopia), Salé (Morocco) and Ndutu (Tanzania), which some regard as *H. erectus*. Similarly, in Europe there is dispute about whether the fossils from Mauer (Germany), Vértesszöllös (Hungary), Petralona (Greece) and Bilzingsleben (Germany) represent 'advanced' *erectus* or 'archaic' *sapiens*. Throughout this period, it appears that *H. erectus* persisted in the Far East, up to the time of the remains from Hexian in Anhui Province, China (perhaps 250 000 years old) and the Ngandong (Solo)

'Archaic *Homo sapiens*' skull from Dali, China, about 150 000 years old.

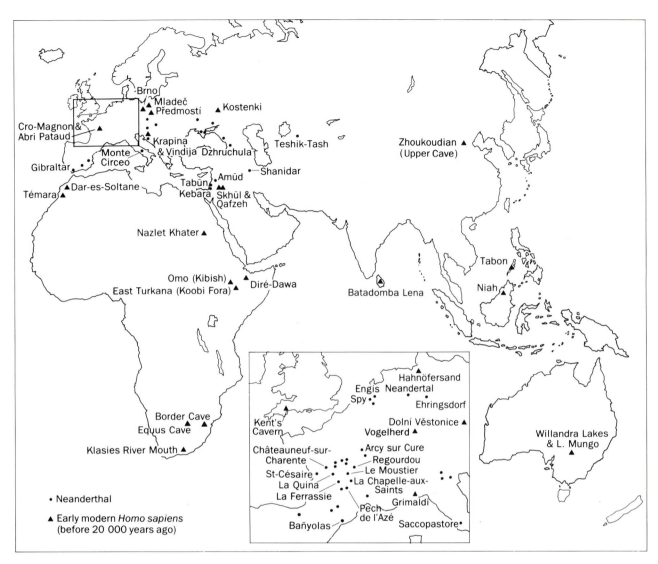

Principal sites of discovery of Neanderthals and early modern humans.

remains from Java (perhaps as young as 100 000 years old). However, in China *Homo erectus* was then succeeded by an enigmatic population assigned to 'archaic *H. sapiens*', which is exemplified by the skull from Dali in Shaanxi Province and the partial skeleton from Jingniushan in Liaoning Province. Possibly earlier examples of this population are the two skulls from Yunxian in Hubei Province.

Neanderthals and modern humans

By about 200 000 years ago further evolutionary changes in European fossils led to the differentiation of a lineage that was ancestral to 'Neanderthal Man' (often regarded as a subspecies of *Homo sapiens*, *H. sapiens neanderthalensis*, but now increasingly treated as a distinct species, *Homo neanderthalensis*). Remains from sites such as Pontnewydd (Wales), Swanscombe (England), Biache (France) and Steinheim (Germany) show specialisations that are particularly common in the later true Neanderthals, who lived from about 120 000 to 30 000 years ago.

These late Neanderthals were highly evolved humans in many respects, but were probably not our direct ancestors. Their brains were large (the volume of 1200–1750 ml was as great or greater than our own), but were more flattened, broader, smaller at the front, and larger at the rear than those of modern humans. The intelligence of the Neanderthals cannot be assessed from their large brains, as they were also large-bodied; males probably weighed about 65

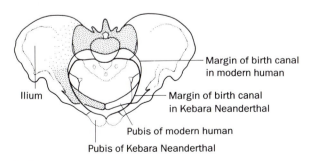

The Kebara Neanderthal pelvis compared to a modern human pelvis. Although the two bones are different in shape, the birth canal in both is the same size. The differences may be related to the way Neanderthals walked.

kg (143 lb), but were less than 170 cm (5 ft 7 in) tall on average. However, we know that they were capable, albeit limited hunters and gatherers, who were able to adapt to the severe conditions of the European Ice Age. Although their stone-tool cultures seem very simple, they were human enough to look after the infirm and the disabled and to bury their dead.

Neanderthals had short, stocky bodies with large heads dominated by an enormous and projecting nose, while the cheekbones were swept back. It seems likely that their large front teeth were used as a clamp for food, toolmaking or skin processing. Above the eyesockets there was a marked brow ridge, very well developed in the centre but reduced at the sides. The cranial vault was long and low, but very broad, and almost round when viewed from behind. The occipital bone (at the rear of the skull) was unusual in several respects, perhaps because of the large rear lobes of the brain. Neanderthals – and even their children – were very muscular. To judge from their body proportions, which in some respects were like those of modern Saami (Lapps) or Inuit (Eskimos), they may have been adapted to life in cold conditions.

One unusual feature of the Neanderthal skeleton is the shape of the front of the hip bone in the pubic area. This was believed to reflect an enlarged birth canal in Neanderthal women, and perhaps a longer gestation period than modern women, but is now thought to be related to differences in the way the hip joints operated.

The most characteristic Neanderthals were European. Related peoples lived in southwestern Asia, at least as far east as Teshik-Tash in Soviet Uzbekistan, and in Iraq (Shanidar) and Israel (Amūd, Kebara and Tabūn). However, there is no firm evidence that Neanderthals ever lived in Africa or the Far East. Some Asian Neanderthals were little different from their European counterparts, but others resemble modern humans more closely, which has led to the proposal that they were ancestors for early modern people. However, new dates suggests that this is unlikely.

Early modern humans

The disappearance of the Neanderthals from Europe and Asia may have had much to do with the appearance of early modern people (*Homo sapiens sapiens* or just *H. sapiens*), who competed with them for resources. These first modern humans were anatomically distinct from Neanderthals with their less-prominent brow ridges, higher, shorter and more rounded skulls, shorter lower jaws with a bony chin (at best only slightly developed in some Neanderthals) and a taller and less-robust skeleton. They also had hips with pubic bones of modern type, suggesting that the hip joints functioned like those of modern people.

The first modern people in Asia, known from the Israeli sites of Qafzeh and Skhūl (see p. 397), had a way of life superficially little different from that of the Neanderthals.

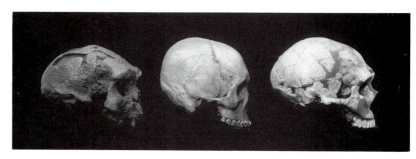

This comparison of skulls of a *Homo erectus* from Java (Sangiran 17, left), a modern *Homo sapiens* (from Indonesia, centre) and a Neanderthal (La Ferrassie from France, right) shows some of the shared or distinctive cranial characteristics of each group. Although the *erectus* and Neanderthal skulls share some features of cranial shape, face size and brow-ridge development, the modern and Neanderthal skulls are more similar in features such as the larger brain and less-projecting face.

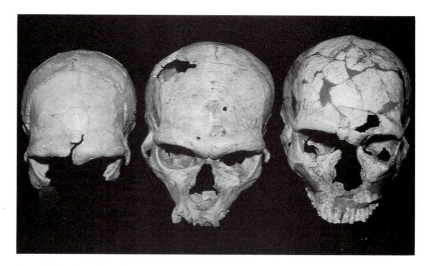

Neanderthal skulls from (left to right) La Quina, La Chapelle-aux-Saints and La Ferrassie show some of the common characters of this group. These include the long, low vault, double-arched brow ridge, long and narrow face, and a large projecting nose.

However. they may have exploited their environment more efficiently. The dating of the early modern fossils from Israel has been problematic. However, recent application of thermoluminescence and electron spin resonance dating to the Skhūl and Qafzeh finds (which include the burial of a child with grave goods) suggests that they are about 100 000 years old, and therefore considerably older than many Neanderthal fossils (see p. 183). If this is so, there must have been a long period of coexistence or alternating occupation of southwestern Asia by the two groups. By 40 000 years ago, however, modern people seem to have been the sole occupants of the region.

The spread of modern people into Europe probably occurred at about this time, and there is some evidence of behavioural differences between Neanderthals and early modern people (sometimes known as the Cro-Magnons after the 1868 discoveries at Cro-Magnon in France). Although most Neanderthal fossils are found with Middle Palaeolithic (Middle Stone Age) or Mousterian tool industries, the Cro-Magnons are invariably associated with

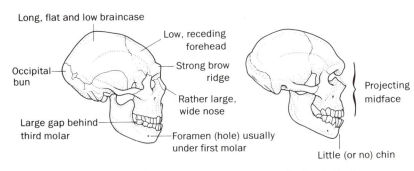

Shanidar 1

- Long, flat and low braincase
- Occipital bun
- Large gap behind third molar
- Low, receding forehead
- Strong brow ridge
- Rather large, wide nose
- Foramen (hole) usually under first molar

La Ferrassie 1

- Projecting midface
- Little (or no) chin

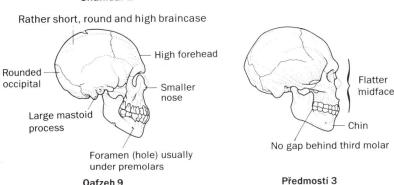

Qafzeh 9

- Rather short, round and high braincase
- Rounded occipital
- Large mastoid process
- High forehead
- Smaller nose
- Foramen (hole) usually under premolars

Předmostí 3

- Flatter midface
- Chin
- No gap behind third molar

Reconstructed skulls of two Neanderthals from Shanidar in Iraq and La Ferrassie in France, showing some of the features that distinguish Neanderthals from early modern *Homo sapiens*, represented here by skulls from Qafzeh in Israel and Předmostí in Czechoslovakia.

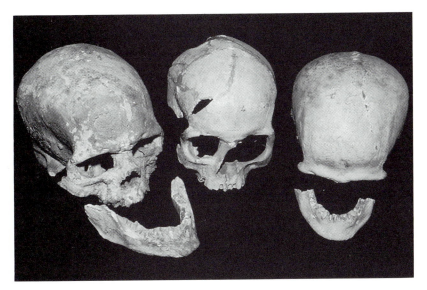

These specimens found in the Cro-Magnon rockshelter in 1868 were the first of the Upper Palaeolithic Cro-Magnons to be published in detail. They show many features of modern Europeans throughout their skeleton, but were quite strongly built, with large heads and brains that were bigger than the modern average, as well as distinctive body proportions, such as long legs.

Upper Palaeolithic industries (the Aurignacian, Périgordian, Gravettian, Solutrean and Magdalenian). These Upper Palaeolithic cultures are much more variable in time and space, and contain many blade tools, some of which were specialised for the working of bone, antler and ivory. These raw materials, although available to the Neanderthals, were hardly used by them. However, some of the last Neanderthals in Europe did briefly develop tool industries with Upper Palaeolithic characteristics, such as the Châtelperronian (in France and Spain) and the Uluzzian (in Italy), which hint at possible contact with the contemporaneous Cro-Magnons.

One of the most remarkable abilities of the Cro-Magnons was in the production of engravings and sculptures. These were part of a whole range of artistic expression that appears after about 35 000 years in Europe, and which reached its heights on the painted walls and ceilings of caves such as Lascaux and Altamira.

If early modern people did not evolve from the Neanderthals of Europe and Asia, where did they originate? Modern people had appeared in China and Australasia by at least 30 000 years ago – they may have arrived in Australia by boat as long ago as 50 000 years. However, there are no fossils that show a local evolution from more archaic predecessors, although this has been claimed by proponents of 'multiregional evolution' for the fossil from Dali in China (p. 246), the Ngandong skulls from Indonesia, and certain robust Australian fossils (p. 401).

It is only in Africa that transitional fossils between premodern and modern types certainly exist and it is here that fossil remains of modern form have been discovered that are as early as, or perhaps even older than, those in Israel. These early modern fossils are at two cave sites in South Africa (Border Cave – see p. 397 – and Klasies River Mouth) and in river and lake deposits in Ethiopia (Omo-Kibish). The South African remains are 100 000 to 70 000 years old and the Omo skeleton could be as old as 130 000 years. They can be classified as modern in anatomy, but these people were not necessarily like modern hunter-gatherers in behavioural sophistication. Equally, some of the fossils show signs of a recent descent from more primitive ancestors, which may be represented by fossils of even greater antiquity from South Africa (Florisbad), East Africa (Ngaloba, Tanzania; Eliye Springs, Kenya; and Omo-Kibish, Ethiopia) and North Africa (Jebel Irhoud, Morocco).

Why the evolution of modern people took place in Africa – why it occurred at all – is still uncertain, but changes in human behaviour as well as geographical isolation may be responsible. Genetic evidence indicates that all living people are closely related and share a recent common ancestor who probably lived in Africa. From that African ancestral group, all the living peoples of the world originated (this idea has been termed the 'Out of Africa' or 'Noah's Ark' model, see p. 392).

The ancestors of Europeans, Asians and the populations of the American and Australian continents probably share common ancestors within the past 60 000 years. The modern people who reached Australia at least 40 000, probably 50 000 years ago must have used boats or rafts, even when sea level was at its lowest because of water locked up in expanded ice caps during the Pleistocene glaciation. To reach the Americas it would have been possible to walk

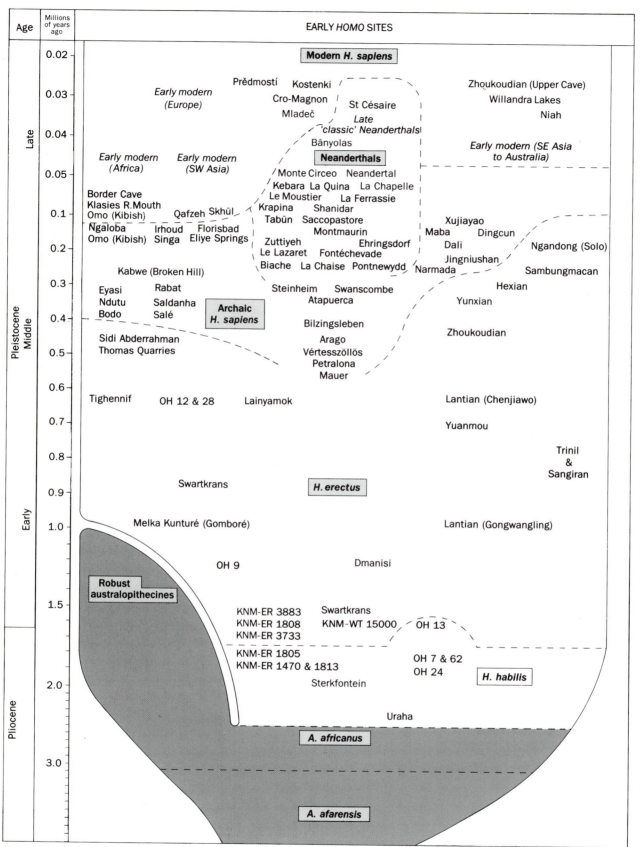

A diagrammatic representation of human evolution during the past 2 million years. Important fossils are placed according to their determined or estimated age and their usual classification.

DISTINGUISHING FEATURES OF EARLY HUMAN SPECIES

	Homo habilis (small)	Homo habilis (large)	Homo erectus	'Archaic Homo sapiens'	Neanderthals	Early modern Homo sapiens
Height (m)	1	c. 1.5	1.3–1.5	?	1.5–1.7	1.6–1.85
Physique	Relatively long arms	Robust but 'human' skeleton	Robust but 'human' skeleton	Robust but 'human' skeleton	As 'archaic H. sapiens', but adapted for cold	Modern skeleton; ?adapted for warmth
Brain size (ml)	500–650	600–800	750–1250	1100–1400	1200–1750	1200–1700
Skull form	Relatively small face; nose developed	Larger, flatter face	Flat, thick skull with large occipital and brow ridge	Higher skull; face less protruding	Reduced brow ridge; thinner skull; large nose; midface projection	Small or no brow ridge; shorter, high skull
Jaws/teeth	Thinner jaw; smaller, narrow molars	Robust jaw; large narrow molars	Robust jaw in larger individuals; smaller teeth than H. habilis	Similar to H. erectus but teeth may be smaller	Similar to 'archaic H. sapiens'; teeth smaller except for incisors; chin development in some	Shorter jaws than Neanderthals; chin developed; teeth may be smaller
Distribution	Eastern (+ southern?) Africa	Eastern Africa	Africa, Asia and Indonesia (+ Europe?)	Africa, Asia and Europe	Europe and western Asia	Africa and western Asia
Known date (years ago)	2–1.6 million	2.4–1.6 million	1.8–0.3 million	400 000–100 000	150 000–30 000	130 000–60 000

from Asia across the Beringia land bridge between Siberia and Alaska, or to travel along a mere southerly coastal route by island hopping. However, it is not certain when this happened. It may have been quite recent (within the past 15 000 years), in which case the arrival of hunters may have been behind the contemporary extinctions of large mammals, such as mastodons, giant ground sloths and sabre-tooth cats. Alternatively, as suggested by discoveries in northern Canada and New Mexico, and studies at the cave of Pedra Furada in Brazil, early modern people may have entered the Americas as early as they arrived in Europe and Australia – that is, before 30 000 years ago. If this is so, they had almost no impact on the American continent for a long period.

What is certain is that the early modern peoples of each part of the world were all similar in basic anatomy and behaviour, but regional differences in physique and culture rapidly developed subsequently. In particular, by 15 000 years ago the Australian continent was peopled by groups who showed a great deal of physical variability. This has led to suggestions that descendants of the primitive Ngandong (Solo) population of Java may have reached Australia and contributed their genes to succeeding generations. Genetic data do not support such a model, because the populations of Australasia seem to be closely related to those of Asia and Europe, as would be expected from a simple spread of people of modern type.

Trends in the evolution of *Homo*

The overall evolution of the genus *Homo* shows certain smooth trends, most notably a steady increase in brain size and a decrease in the size of the teeth. Other changes such as skull shape and thickness, and behaviour as reflected by stone tools, are more episodic.

The fundamental importance of Africa to our evolution is evident from the origin of the genus there, as represented around 2.4 million years ago by H. *habilis*, and the probable origin there of H. *erectus* by about 1.8 million years ago. The places of origin of various behavioural advances – such as the control of fire and the invention of spears, true language and art – are less clear. Neanderthals probably originated outside Africa and can be credited with early burial practices and perhaps also ceremonies. They were also the first humans to adapt to life in cold environments. In spite of these signs of humanity, they were apparently not the ancestors of any living peoples, who instead take their origin from a common ancestral population that lived within the last 150 000 years in Africa.   *C. B. Stringer*

See also 'Jaws and teeth (p. 56), 'The human brain' (p. 115), 'Human speech and language' (p. 134), 'Methods of dating' (p. 179), 'Fossil deposits and their investigation' (p. 187), 'Reconstructing past environments' (p. 191), 'The hominid way of life' (p. 325), 'Early human mental abilities' (p. 341), 'Tools – the Palaeolithic record' (p. 350), 'Ancient art' (p. 361) and 'The dispersion of modern humans' (p. 389)

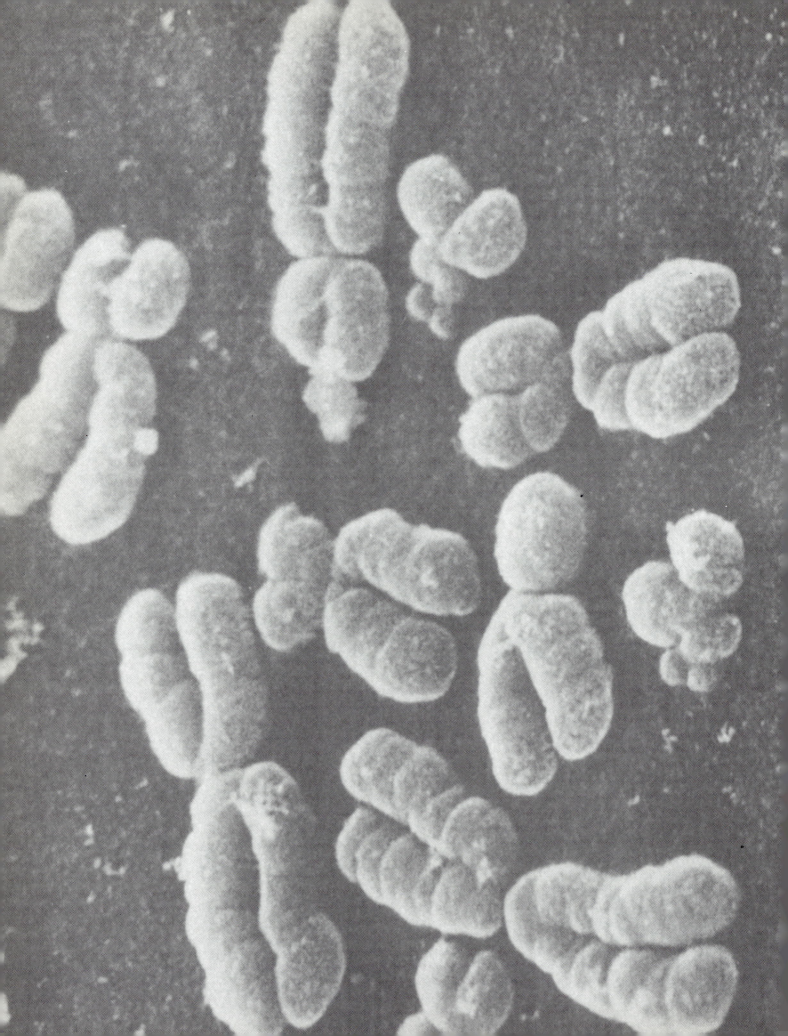

Part Seven

Primate genetics and evolution

The theory of evolution was accepted as fact long before the emergence of genetics. The weakest chapter in *The Origin of Species* is about inheritance: like his predecessors, Darwin was confused about why children often resemble their parents, but sometimes look much more like a distant relative. He inclined to a view of blending inheritance. Sperm and egg picked up 'gemmules' transported by the blood from various organs, and carrying instructions about how to produce similar organs in the next generation.

A child's characteristics are, he thought, a mixture; the average of those of its parents. However, inheritance by blending is fatal to Darwin's theory of natural selection because, if genetics does work this way, then any slight advantage present in one individual and favoured by selection will be diluted out in succeeding generations as its blood mixes with that of others lacking the favoured character. This objection was pointed out by the Scottish engineer Fleeming Jenkin, and greatly worried Darwin. Things were made worse for him when his cousin, Francis Galton, carried out the obvious experiment: transfusing blood between white and black rabbits to see whether this had any effect on the colour of the offspring — which of course it did not. In later editions of *The Origin*, Darwin tried to argue his way out of the problem, but without success.

We now know that he had nothing to worry about. Inheritance is not a process of blending, but involves distinct particles or genes that are transmitted unchanged over generations. Genes can reappear either in children, or in remote descendants; and any gene favoured by natural selection will become more common even if its effects are not manifest in all its carriers. This insight comes from the work of Gregor Mendel, who, with his experiments on peas, founded genetics in the 1860s.

Mendel was extremely fortunate in his choice of organism and in the simple and easily scored characters — pea shape or colour, flower colour and so on — that he chose to study. Genetics before Mendel had failed because the idea of the mixing of bloods was so seductive that biologists concentrated on measuring characters (weight, musicality and so on) which looked as if they might blend. Mendel's breakthrough was to realise the importance of counting things and establishing ratios. Once he had done so clear patterns emerged that seemed to apply to every character he studied. None of this was known to Darwin and Mendel's research was ignored until the beginning of this century. Within five years of its discovery, his laws were applied to human pedigrees and — in spite of a brief period of insane overoptimism when Mendelism was applied blindly in a vain attempt to explain most human attributes — since then our understanding of human inheritance has enormously increased.

Pairs of human chromosomes.

253

Genetics has transformed our understanding of human evolution. In the following chapters, we see that Mendel's laws do indeed apply to humans and to other primates (**7.1**), and that the processes by which new genetic variation appears and the microscopically visible units of inheritance — the chromosomes — are similar in kinds to those in other organisms (**7.3** and **7.4**). Molecular genetics has uncovered hidden genetic diversity in proteins and DNA (**7.2**); and, in combination with medicine and with anthropology, tells us that natural selection is still hard at work in humans (**7.6** and **7.7**). This, in association with random genetic changes in small and isolated populations (**7.5**), leads to biological divergence over time or space: to evolution.

Principles of genetics

Genetics is the study of inherited characters. This simple definition gives no idea of the breadth and complexity of this vast subject: only its basic principles are given here. The essence of genetics lies in its reasoning as much as its methods; between them, these have produced a powerful and unifying theory, which can be applied to most animals, plants and lower organisms.

Biochemists have shown the gene to be a physical entity that can be investigated using sophisticated laboratory procedures. However, until the birth of molecular biology in the 1950s, genetics was unique among the life sciences in that the central area of interest, the gene, was an essentially hypothetical unit devised to explain the way in which inherited characters behave according to a series of rules. Until relatively recently, classical geneticists did not ask how the system works in terms of gene action but strove to understand and interpret patterns of inheritance among the offspring of natural and experimental matings.

Molecular genetics, which combines the theory of classical genetics with biochemical methodology, has enabled scientists to elucidate much about gene organisation and function, and it is also of great practical importance for the development of modern medicine and agriculture. However, the rudiments of genetical understanding are ancient. For instance, early humans must have learnt to identify the key inherited features of the plants and animals that were vital to survival. Long before the advent of science, the awareness that 'like begets like' was entrenched in many cultures. More recently, scientists have exploited this knowledge for many puposes. These have included the improvement of agricultural breeds and the establishment of the sciences of zoological and botanical taxonomy, which eventually led to the Darwinian theory of evolution by the natural selection of inherited differences. However, what was lacking during this pre-genetical age was a knowledge of the mechanisms by which inherited characters are transmitted from one generation to the next.

In sexual reproduction there is fusion of the egg and the sperm to form an *embryo*. The stage at which the union of these *gametes* occurs is known as *fertilisation*. Within the resulting single-celled embryo (*zygote*), a series of complex and delicately controlled events culminates in the birth of a new individual. From a genetical viewpoint, the most striking feature of this process is the fidelity with which physical characteristics are transmitted from parents to offspring. This is the phenomenon of *heredity*. Every type of biological variation, be it visible (such as skin pigmentation or facial features) or invisible (such as variation in the fine structure of protein molecules or even qualities such as intelligence) is influenced by information carried by the genes.

Chromosomes and cell division

The genes of higher organisms, including humans and other primates, are ordered in linear arrays on *chromosomes*. These are visible under the light microscope as intensely stained bodies in cells about to undergo division. Normal primate body or *somatic* cells are said to be *diploid*, or 2n, because they contain in their nuclei two sets of chromosomes, one set inherited from each parent. Chromosomes are most clearly resolved in somatic cells at the stage of cell division called metaphase, and it is at this stage that they are often photographed.

Mitosis

At mitosis (somatic cell division), the nuclear membrane breaks down and the chromosomes, which each consist of two identical *sister chromatids*, arrange themselves along the equator of the dividing cell before being pulled apart at their *centromeres* towards the opposite poles of the cell. One complete set of chromatids moves into each of the two new daughter cells. As soon as the new cells are formed, the nuclear membrane reappears and the chromosomes lose their characteristic appearance and become a diffuse mass called *chromatin*.

Chromatin consists of a highly organised mixture of deoxyribonucleic acid (DNA), which carries the genetic information (genes), and associated proteins. During the next stage of the cell cycle, the DNA copies itself (replicates) so that two sets of chromosomes are available at the next cell division: one for each new daughter cell. Nearly all somatic cells (those that do not lead to the production of gametes) are diploid. Mitosis hence consists of a process of separation at cell division followed by chromosome replication.

Meiosis

Normal human somatic cells contain 46 chromosomes – 23 from the egg and 23 from the sperm. Eggs and sperm (gametes) are formed from germ cells that undergo meiotic cell divisions. In contrast to mitosis, during meiosis the chromosomes undergo two rounds of separation without any replication. Meiosis thus results in cells containing only one member of each chromosome pair. Such cells are referred to as *haploid*.

Before the first meiotic cell division the pairs of equivalent or *homologous* chromosomes line up next to each other. At this stage, the pairs of homologues form *chiasmata*; they become attached at points along the arms. *Cross-overs*, in which homologous parts of the chromosomes *recombine*, occur at these sites, leading to a reassortment of genetic

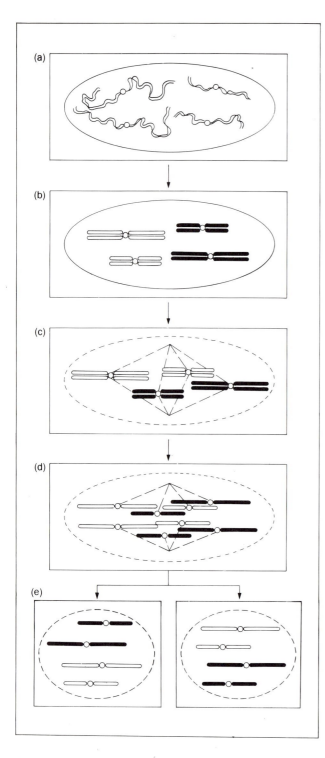

(a)

(b)

(c)

(d)

(e)

Somatic cell division (mitosis). In this stylised version, only eight chromosomes, or four matched or homologous pairs, are shown. (a) In *early prophase*, the chromosomes are thin and filamentous. (b) On entry into *late prophase*, the chromosomes condense and separate into two sister chromatids, which remain attached to each other at the centromere. (c) The nuclear membrane breaks down and the chromosomes align themselves along the equator of the dividing cell on a framework of microtubules called the mitotic spindle (*metaphase*). (d) The sister chromatids move to opposite poles of the cell (*anaphase*). (e) Nuclear membranes form round each new set of chromosomes to give two daughter nuclei (*telophase*), the mitotic spindle disintegrates and the cells separate along the equatorial plane (*cytokinesis*). The chromosomes then decondense into a diffuse mass called chromatin, forming a new *interphase* nucleus. Each new daughter cell contains the full genetic complement of the parent cell.

material between the homologues. After the first meiotic metaphase the chromosomes, which remain attached at the centromere, hence differ in genetical constitution from their parental types. At this stage, each daughter cell contains 23 pairs of sister chromatids.

In the second meiotic division the pairs of chromatids are separated, so that for each primordial germ cell four haploid gametes containing 23 genetically distinct chromosomes are produced.

As genes reside on the chromosomes, the closer together two genes lie on the same chromosome, the less likely it is that they will become separated by crossovers during meiosis. By observing the frequency of recombination between pairs of gene loci it is possible to establish genetic maps giving the order and distance between several genes in a *linkage group*. Comparisons of homologous linkage groups between different mammalian species give information about the evolutionary conservation of segments of chromosomes and sets of genes (see table on p. 258).

All but one of the 23 pairs of human chromosomes are called *autosomes* and are numbered from 1 to 22 in a series of descending size. The remaining two, X and Y, determine the sex of the embryo and are termed *sex chromosomes*. Each of the great apes (our closest primate relatives) has one more pair of chromosomes in its diploid cells, to make a chromosome complement or *karyotype* of 48. Using chromosome banding techniques it has been possible to define the cytological differences and similarities between human and ape species.

Normal females have two X chromosomes and normal males are XY. All eggs, the haploid female gametes, bear an X chromosome, whereas sperm carry either X or Y according to chance. Herein lies the basis of the approximately equal sex ratio at birth; if X- and Y-bearing sperm have an equal chance of fertilising the X-bearing egg, then on average half the offspring will be XX females and half XY males. In humans, the sex ratio at birth is in fact about 1.06 in favour of boys, but the cause of this deviation from unity is not understood.

Mendelian inheritance

Our present-day understanding of genetics is based on the discoveries of Gregor Mendel, an abbot of an Augustinian monastery in Moravia (now in Czechoslovakia). Mendel published his findings on the inheritance of characteristics of plant hybrids in 1866, but the impact of his work remained latent until 1900, when it caused a storm of interest in Europe's scientific community. His new and fundamental approach to investigating heredity was the genetic cross in which parents differing in simple, discrete characters are mated in a controlled fashion and the offspring are categorised according to the parental characters they show (see Box 1).

Patterns of inheritance

Mendel's major findings on the behaviour of genes are well established and can be accurately illustrated with a few well-known examples from human genetics. His first important discoveries of the behaviour of gene pairs are the phenomena of dominance and recessivity. A *dominant* condition exerts its effect on the individual even when the mutant allele is in the heterozygous state. Thus, only one copy of the mutant gene at a locus is required to produce the phenotype, or outward appearance of the individual, and the other allele plays no obvious part. In contrast, a *recessive* condition is manifest only in individuals that have two mutant alleles at the locus; in this case, the heterozygous carriers of the mutant alleles are unaffected.

Huntington's disease (HD) is an example of an autosomal dominant disorder caused by the presence of a single mutant gene. People afflicted with HD suffer a progressive deterioration of the nervous system. The typical signs of a dominant mode of inheritance are found in families with HD: the disease never skips a generation, about half of the children in the sibships are affected and both sexes are able to transmit the disease. On average, half of the gametes produced by an affected parent will carry the HD gene. This accounts for the 50 per cent ratio of affected children.

Huntington's disease is particularly distressing because the symptoms lie dormant for many years, by which time an affected parent has completed having children. Most individuals affected by the Huntington gene are heterozygous. Rare homozygotes are apparently no more severely affected than are the heterozygotes, but this may not be the case for all dominant disorders. Thus, in other cases, homozygotes may be more severely affected or even die before birth. In those instances where the affected phenotype appears in every generation, the identification of a dominant condition is usually fairly simple.

Autosomal recessive disorders are usually more difficult to identify in humans, because the locus needs to be homozygous for the mutant gene before the characteristic phenotype is expressed. Cystic fibrosis (CF) is a well-known serious disease (found mainly in white Caucasians) that is inherited recessively. Many more people carry a mutant CF gene than have the disease. In fact, about 1 in 20

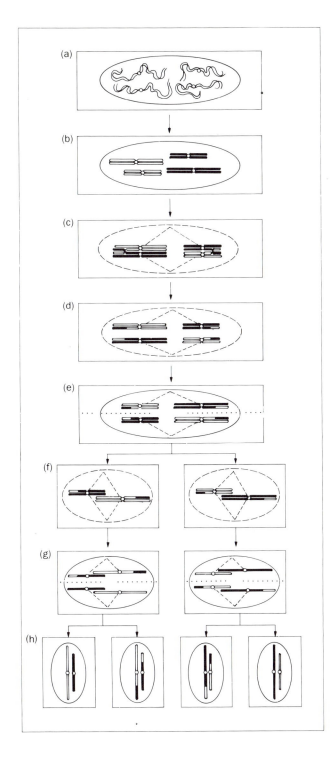

In contrast to mitosis, the cell division leading to the production of sperm and eggs (meiosis) results in cells containing half the normal complement of chromosomes. When the sperm and egg unite, the chromosome number returns to its normal, diploid state. Meiotic cell division consists of two modified mitotic cell divisions in sequence. (a) Early first meiotic prophase. (b) The chromosomes condense so that each cell contains two copies of each pair, as in mitosis but, in contrast to mitosis, they assemble in matched or homologous pairs (one from the maternal, the other from the paternal set). (c) The chromosomes align themselves along the equator . At this stage, the pairs of matched chromosomes form *chiasmata*; they become attached at points along the arms. *Crossing-over*, in which homologous parts of the chromosomes recombine so that there is an exchange of genetic material, occurs at these sites. (d) One chromosome from each pair moves towards each pole of the spindle. (e) The cells divide, each daughter cell receiving half of the normal complement of chromosomes; in humans, this *haploid* set is 23 pairs. Unlike in mitosis, the chromosomes now have a different genetical constitution from their parental types. Up to this point the chromosomes have remained attached at their centromeres. (f) In the second and final meiotic division, the chromosomes once more align along the equator of the dividing cell. This time the centromeres have divided, as in mitosis. (g) The pairs of chromatids separate towards the poles of the spindle and the cell divides. There are now four genetically distinct haploid cells (gametes). In the male, all four daughter cells usually develop into viable sperm, whereas in the female three of the four daughter cells degenerate into small, non-functional *polar bodies*.

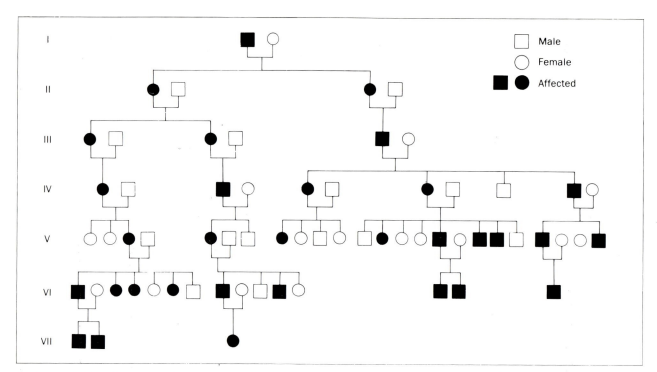

An autosomal dominant pedigree, in this case showing the inheritance of Huntington's disease, which is caused by the presence of a single mutant gene.

Gene loci shared by humans and other primates (on human chromosomes 1–6). The letters are technical terms for various genes, and the numbers those of the appropriate chromosome for each species. Although the actual chromosome involved may change, the grouping of genes is often retained

Autosomal loci	Human	Chimpanzee (Pan troglodytes)	Gorilla (Gorilla gorilla)	Orang-utan (Pongo pygmaeus)	White-cheeked gibbon (Hylobates concolor)	Rhesus macaque (Macaca mulatta)	Baboon (Papio sp.)	Vervet monkey (Cercopithecus aethiops)	Owl monkey (Aotus sp.)
PGD	1	1	1	1	24	1	1	4	12
ENO1	1	1	1	1	24	1	1	4	12
FUCA1	1	1	?	?	3	?	?	4	?
AK2	1	1	?	?	?	1	?	?	12
PGM1	1	1	1	1	5	1	1	4	12
FGR	1	?	?	?	?	?	?	?	12
MYCL	1	?	?	?	?	?	?	?	12
NRAS	1	?	?	?	?	?	?	?	12
TRE	1	1	1	1	?	?	?	?	?
PEPC	1	1	1	1	?	?	1	13	?
FH	1	?	1	1	?	1	?	13	6
GUK1	1	?	?	?	5	1	?	?	?
MDH1	2	13	11	11	?	15	13	?	2
ACP1	2	13	?	11	19	?	?	?	?
IDH1	2	12	12	12	1	9	12	?	16
COL3A1	2	?	?	?	1	?	12	?	?
COL5A2	2	?	?	?	1	?	?	?	?
UGP2	2	?	?	?	?	?	?	?	2
GPX1	3	2	2	?	4	3	?	?	?
ACY1	3	2	?	?	?	?	2	?	?
UMPS	3	2	?	?	?	?	?	?	?
PEPS	4	?	?	?	?	?	5	?	?
PGM2	4	3	3	3	?	6	5	?	14
PPAT	4	3	?	?	?	?	?	?	?
ALB	4	3	3	3	?	?	?	?	1
AFP	4	3	3	3	?	?	?	?	?
GYPA	4	3	3	3	7	?	5	?	?
GYPB	4	3	3	?	?	?	?	?	?
HEXB	5	?	?	4	?	5	?	?	?
MHC	6	5	5	5	1	2	4	21	9
GLO1	6	5	?	?	?	?	4	21	9
SOD2	6	5	5	5	3	2	4	?	9
PGM3	6	5	5	5	17	2	?	?	9
ME1	6	5	5	5	17	?	4	16	9
MYB	6	?	?	?	?	?	?	?	9

1. MENDEL AND THE BEGINNINGS OF GENETICS

Genetics before Mendel got nowhere, as it involved measuring rather than counting. Breeders were interested in things such as milk yield or meat production, and by choosing the best animals as parents succeeded in greatly improving their stocks. However, none of them had much insight into how the characters were passed from generation to generation. Very often they assumed that the parental qualities were blended in some vague way in the offspring. Not until Mendel chose simple characters that could be easily classified and counted as discrete categories was there any progress.

He worked on peas. Pure-breeding stocks were available in which all offspring resembled their parents. Different stocks differed in various distinguishable ways – round or wrinkled pea shape, green or yellow pea colour, tall or short plants, and so on. Peas have the advantage that they carry male and female sexual parts on the same plant, and can be self-fertilised; the male part can cross with the female part of the same individual.

Initially, Mendel studied the various characters, such as pea shape, one at a time. In his first experiment, he crossed a plant with round (R) peas with another with wrinkled (W) peas. He found that all their offspring had round peas. These offspring were self-fertilised, and in the next generation there emerged a ratio of three round peas to one wrinkled. What was going on? This result can be summarised using standard notation:

P_1 round × wrinkled
F_1 all round
F_2 3 round: 1 wrinkled

The P_1 is the first parental generation; the F_1 and F_2 the first and second filial generations. The appearance of the peas – in this case, their shape – is referred to as their *phenotype*.

Mendel's breakthrough was to suggest that underlying the phenotype were some physical particles – now called genes – that were passed on from generation to generation. Each phenotype is controlled by two particles, one from each parent.

Sometimes the visible effects of one particle can mask those of the other, so that individuals might have the same phenotype, but different genetic constitutions or *genotypes*. In the pure lines, all individuals had the same genotype – that is, the round peas were RR and the wrinkled WW. In each of them, the gametes (pollen or egg) carried only one of the particles, and came together in a fertilised egg, the zygote, which again had two. This process can be illustrated with a simple checkerboard.

When the two P_1 pure breeding stocks are crossed together, we get:

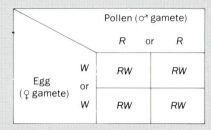

Their offspring, the F_1, are genetically identical to each other; they all have one dose of the R and one of the W particle. The R particle masks the phenotypic effects of the W particle, so that these peas are round.

When the F_1 RW individuals are selfed we get:

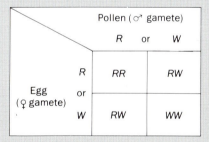

This gives the F_2 generation. The ratio of genotypes is 1 RR : 2 RW : 1 WW. However, as R masks the effect of W, the ratio of phenotypes is 3 round peas to 1 wrinkled.

This led to Mendel's first law: characters are controlled by pairs of determinants that segregate from each other and are restored during the formation of sperm (or pollen) and egg. The emphasis on *segregation* is the essential thing. The R particle can come together in the same F_1 individual with the W particle, but is not contaminated by it – there is no blending.

There are some terms now universally used:

- The alternative states of the particle are *alleles* at one position or *locus*. In the example here, we have the pea-shape locus, with its alleles for round or wrinkled.
- Sperm (or pollen) and eggs carry just one allele at a locus – they are *haploid*. Body cells all carry two alleles – they are *diploid*.
- An individual might have two identical alleles – a *homozygote*; or two different ones – a *heterozygote*.
- If, in a heterozygote, one allele masks the phenotypic effect of the other, that allele is *dominant*. The allele whose phenotype is hidden in a heterozygote is *recessive*.

Mendel went on to consider the inheritance of pairs of different characters at two or more loci simultaneously. He found ratios suggesting that each locus – for example, pea shape and pea colour, or flower colour and plant height – was inherited independently of the others in the same plant, so that there was *independent assortment* of alleles at different loci.

This finding is generally correct, except that we now know that some groups of loci are inherited together to a greater or lesser extent as they occur in close proximity on the same chromosome (the physical unit of inheritance). Such loci are referred to as *linked*.

Mendel's work was the basis of all genetics. It is particularly impressive as he knew nothing about the physical nature of genes, or even where they might be in the organism. With some extensions and modifications, his laws apply to all except the simplest creatures. Humans are no exception.   *Steve Jones*

of white people in Britain are carriers yet only about 1 in 1600 live births are affected by CF.

The rarity of CF relative to the frequency of the CF mutant genes in the population is because the chance of two carriers marrying is only about 1 in 400 and because the two classes of gametes from each parent combine at random. Only about 1 in 4 of the embryos will inherit a mutant gene at the CF locus from both parents. The mating of two heterozygotes carrying mutant alleles, as in CF, gives rise on average to the expected 3:1 ratio of normal progeny to the recessive phenotype. There is a tendency for recessive disorders to occur more frequently among the offspring of consanguineous matings, such as first-cousin marriages. This is because any form of inbreeding will increase the chances of a locus becoming homozygous for the same deleterious allele. The salient features of a recessive mode of inheritance are shown in the pedigree diagram on p. 260.

These cases illustrate the Mendelian law of segregation, which means that a gamete can carry only one gene of any gene pair and that each gene of the pair has an equal chance of being transmitted to the zygote.

A third mode of autosomal inheritance displays a *co-dominant* pattern. In this case, each combination of alleles at an autosomal locus produces a characteristic phenotype.

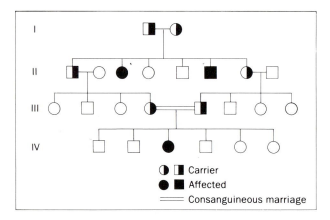

An autosomal recessive pedigree. The heterozygous carrier parents are outwardly normal but they may have one or more affected offspring, on average, and males and females are equally affected. If a carrier or an affected individual marries a normal person, none of their offspring will be affected though half of the heterozygous carrier's children and all of the homozygous-affected person's children will inherit the mutant gene.

Thus, if there are two alleles, *A* and *B*, both classes of homozygotes, AA and BB as well as the *A*B heterozygotes, will be distinguished. Since the introduction of methods for the direct analysis of genetic variation in DNA and proteins, a multitude of examples of co-dominant inheritance have been described.

To define a pattern of inheritance as dominant, recessive or co-dominant is of considerable practical value and implies that in accord with Mendelian principles the phenotype is determined by genes at a single locus. However,

with respect to gene action at the molecular level it is clear that these terms have relatively little meaning. They are also dependent on the level of analysis of the genetic trait.

The haemoglobin disorder sickle-cell anaemia illustrates this point. This autosomal disorder is named after the tendency of red blood cells to compress and become crescent-shaped as the result of abnormal haemoglobin molecules that crystallise abnormally when oxygen levels are reduced. The gene that determines sickle-cell haemoglobin is designated Hb^S (the normal gene is Hb^A). On microscopic investigation, the trait displays a dominant inheritance pattern because the red blood cells of both the heterozygotes ($Hb^S Hb^A$) and the mutant homozygotes ($Hb^S Hb^S$) are seen to sickle. Thus, as expected, three-quarters of the offspring of an $Hb^S Hb^A \times Hb^S Hb^A$ mating will display the sickling phenomenon. However, from a clinical viewpoint the inheritance is autosomal recessive because only the individuals homozygous for the Hb^S gene develop serious symptoms of anaemia. Pedigree analysis indicates that, on average, one in four offspring of carrier parents are affected.

Finally, at the molecular level, where the β-globin gene and the haemoglobin protein products can be assessed directly, the Mendelian pattern is undoubtedly co-

An incomplete pedigree of Queen Victoria and some of her descendants (as published in 1971). Although inbreeding has occurred at various stages (dashed-line connections between the symbols), the transmission of haemophilia is clearly sex-linked. Note that the sisters of haemophiliacs, and their female descendants, are possible carriers. Members of the British royal family are now free of the haemophilia gene.

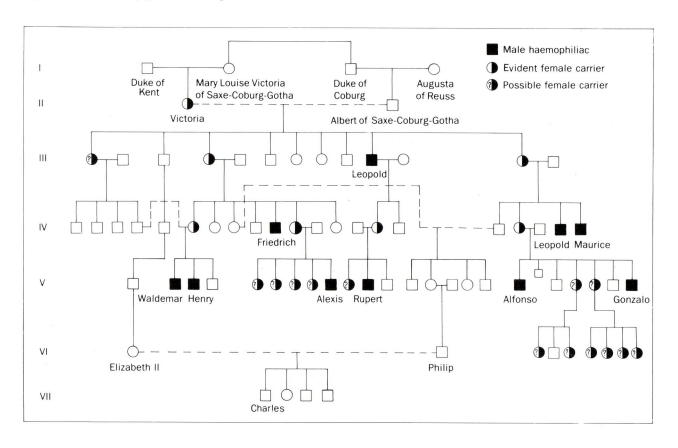

dominant as all three classes of genotype can be distinguished. The detection of heterozygous carriers of genetic disorders such as sickle-cell anaemia is of particular value in genetic counselling.

Sex-linked inheritance

Mendelian logic can also be applied to the special case of sex-linked inheritance. The primate X and Y chromosomes differ considerably in size. The Y has very few genes apart from the male-determining region (see p. 276) whereas the X carries many genes (there is, however, a small region of homology between the two chromosomes). All normal females carry two X chromosomes and thus females that are heterozygous for an X-linked recessive disorder will transmit the disease to half of their sons but to none of their daughters. This is because males, being XY, are effectively homozygous for the genes on the X chromosome and therefore cannot benefit from the protective effect of a normal allele.

Two well-known X-linked genes in humans cause haemophilia (the disorder in which the blood clots very slowly) and Duchenne muscular dystrophy. Apart from very rare cases, these diseases appear only in males and because they are often lethal (although haemophilia can now be controlled by treating the patients with the missing blood-clotting agent), the deleterious gene is carried in the female line. Thus, on average half of the daughters of a carrier mother will in turn become carriers.

Primate model of a human genetic disease

Genetical crossing experiments similar to those of Mendel have now been carried out in many species, such as the fruit fly (*Drosophila*) and the laboratory mouse. However, there are difficulties in analysing genetic segregation in species such as humans and other primates, where controlled matings are unethical or impractical. In these groups, the study of genetics can be a slow process, which relies largely on patterns of inherited variation existing in families. Examples of Mendelian inheritance of visible characters – apart from those known in humans – are relatively uncommon. In non-human primates, most known examples of Mendelian inheritance concern co-dominant alleles detected at the molecular and biochemical levels using techniques such as gel electrophoresis (see p. 265). However, breeding programmes in zoos, where the choice of mates is frequently limited, often create small isolated inbred populations and recessive conditions may then occur with a relatively high frequency (Box 2).

Complexity of genetic variation

The examples so far emphasise the use of Mendelian principles in understanding human and primate pedigrees.

In each case, the relationship between the genotype and the phenotype is established and the phenotype seems to be a relatively clear, well-defined entity. However, in reality it is often difficult to disentangle the relationship between genotype and phenotype. For example, there may be several mutant alleles at a disease locus; a high proportion of cystic fibrosis patients are compound heterozygotes for different mutant CF alleles, rather than homozygotes. Heterozygous combinations of mutant alleles produce a range of phenotypes, leading to mild or severe forms of disease. Sometimes a second gene locus is involved, as in the case of the thalassaemias, a group of related diseases caused by disorders in haemoglobin synthesis. Mutant alleles at the α-globin locus on chromosome 16 give phenotypes quite similar to those at the β-globin locus on chromosome 11.

Phenylketonuria (PKU), an autosomal recessive disorder characterised by the accumulation of the amino acid phenylalanine in the body fluids and severe mental retardation, can result from mutations at two completely separate gene loci. If detected early in life, classical PKU (which is caused by genetic deficiency of the enzyme phenylalanine hydroxylase) can be treated with a phenylalanine-free diet. In contrast, PKU caused by genetic deficiency of the other enzyme, dihydropteridine reductase, cannot be treated with such a diet.

Phenylketonuria also illustrates the effect of the environment, in this case the presence of phenylalanine in food, adding a further layer of complexity to the relationship between genotype and phenotype. In many cases, the extent to which a particular phenotype shows itself is altered by individual genetic peculiarities that are scarcely understood.

A candidate for gene therapy

Several cases of severe combined immunodeficiency (SCID) – a rare syndrome in which the production of white blood cells (lymphocytes) is damaged, leading to a

David, a SCID (severe combined immunodeficiency) patient in 1980, protected from infections by being in a sterile bubble.

2. THE BALD LEMUR — A PRIMATE MODEL FOR A HUMAN GENETIC DISEASE

Mendelian inheritance of a gene with a dramatic effect has been recorded in a family of captive ruffed or variegated lemurs (*Varecia variegata*) at the London Zoo. Here, a ruffed lemur male was introduced from the wild and mated successfully with a wild-caught female, which later died. Their single female offspring was apparently normal. The male then mated with his daughter and produced 13 offspring in 5 litters. Four of the progeny were born naked and the three of these that survived failed to develop any significant body hair.

This pedigree demonstrates that nakedness in these lemurs is inherited in an autosomal recessive manner and must

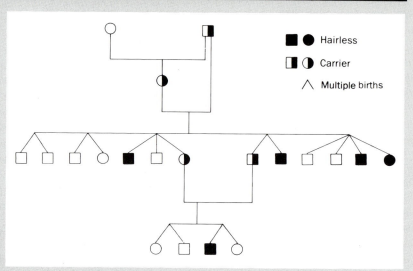

Legend:
■ ● Hairless
◧ ◑ Carrier
∧ Multiple births

Autosomal recessive pedigree, showing the inheritance of hairlessness in the ruffed lemur.

Ruffed lemur mother and two offspring, one with body hair and one bald.

be caused by the presence of a pair of defective genes at a single locus.

The naked animals appear to be as agile and alert as their normal siblings; skin and teeth are also normal. However, the rate of weight gain during infancy is retarded and what hair there is is short and brittle. The abnormal hairs have much lower levels of sulphur than normal, and this suggests that the condition is caused by an alteration in a gene coding for a sulphur-metabolising enzyme.

What could have been regarded simply as a genetic curiosity attracted interest from human geneticists, because the disorder appears to be similar to a genetic

disease in humans called the BIDS syndrome (brittle hair with intellectual impairment, decreased fertility and short stature).

In this disease, which occurs in an isolated religious (Amish) community in the United States, there is an identical disorganised hair structure. The ruffed lemur is therefore potentially useful as an animal model for the BIDS syndrome and futher studies may assist the identification of the primary cause of the disease. Future studies of non-human primates may provide further analogues of inherited abnormalities in humans.

D. Whitehouse

susceptibility to common pathogens – display an autosomal recessive pattern of inheritance. A proportion of such patients lack adenosine deaminase (ADA) activity. This enzyme is determined by a single genetic locus on chromosome 20 and acts to recycle the breakdown products of nucleic acids. The absence of ADA activity leads to the accumulation of metabolites that are toxic to the cellular mechanisms of lymphocyte development.

Although no SCID patients can mount an effective immune response, the severity of the disorder depends largely on environmental factors – namely, the degree of exposure to pathogens. Patients can survive for several years if confined to a germ-free environment. It is possible to treat ADA-deficient patients by bone marrow transplantation, if a suitable donor is available, or by repeated transfusions of red blood cells that supply the missing enzyme activity. More recently, enzyme replacment therapy has involved injections of modified bovine ADA, which also leads to the restoration of the immune system but without

the drawbacks of multiple transfusions. ADA deficiency is also a good candidate for gene therapy because bone marrow cells (which play an important part in the formation of lymphocytes) or lymphocytes themselves are suitable targets for the transfer of functional ADA gene sequences *in vitro*. When returned to the patient, those genetically modified cells express the 'foreign' gene and restore the missing ADA enzyme activity and hence immune function. Clinical trials to assess the effectiveness of gene therapy in the treatment of ADA deficiency are in progress.

Multiple gene inheritance

Most normal human traits that appear to have a genetic base because they 'run in families' cannot be fitted into a simple Mendelian mode of inheritance. For example, body size and shape, skin colour and height display continuous variation and cannot easily be attributed to the action of single loci. Such traits are known as *polygenic* because they are under the control of two or more gene loci, each of which contributes to the final phenotype. In many instances, such as height, it is clear that the environmental factors interact with the polygenes and, in these cases, the pattern of inheritance is said to be *multifactorial*.

In some cases of polygenic inheritance there are clear qualitative distinctions between two classes of phenotype, which nevertheless do not fit a simple Mendelian model. These phenotypes result from the presence of a critical number of mutant genes at the polygenic loci, which give rise to a *threshold effect* below which the phenotype will not be expressed.

Human eye colour is a polygenic trait that displays a threshold effect. It used to be believed that blue is always recessive to brown, but this is not the case. Eye colour varies almost continuously from pale blue to very dark brown, depending on the concentration of various coloured pigments, such as melanin, and probably also on minor structural differences in the iris. Two dark-blue-eyed parents can produce brown-eyed offspring. This is presumably because the child inherits from each parent the appropriate combination of alleles at the polygenic loci, which enables the phenotypic threshold to be crossed.

Mendel's legacy

Mendel's observations, made more than a 100 years ago, relied solely on counting the classes of progeny seeds and plants obtained from his genetic crosses. His paradigm has now been extended and developed and, with the exception of polygenic inheritance, nearly every aspect of genetics from seed colour in peas to the behaviour of chromosomes and differences in the structure of DNA and proteins obeys the laws of Mendelian inheritance. The genetic principles outlined here are true for all but the most simple forms of life. They constitute a vital unifying theme for all biologists at a time when the pace of research and discovery is faster than ever before. One of their most important recent contributions has been to give a new insight into the relationships between humans and their living relatives and to emphasise our position as a primate that obeys the same biological laws as those that apply elsewhere in the living world.

D. Whitehouse

See also 'The nature of evolution' (p. 9), 'Genetic diversity in humans' (p. 264), 'Mutation and human evolution' (p. 269), 'Human chromosomes' (p. 274), 'Distribution of genetic diseases in human populations' (p. 288) and 'Chromosomal evolution in primates' (p. 298)

Genetic diversity in humans

How different from each other are two people – or two chimpanzees? This question is at the heart of our understanding of human evolution. Until recently, we could only guess at its answer: people differ in size and shape, in obvious characters such as skin colour and in more subtle clues such as facial features. But at least to ourselves (if not to the animals themselves) all chimps look much the same.

The revolution in molecular biology has changed all this. We now know more about the diversity of humans than about that of any other creature. As biologists have come closer to understanding the structure and function of genes they have uncovered inherited variation, or *polymorphism*, at almost every level of organisation. Darwin's worry was that there was not enough diversity to allow evolution to take place, and he devoted much of *The Origin* to arguing that there is. Today, if anything, the problem is the opposite. We now know that there is so much polymorphism, particularly in the structure of DNA, that it is hard to see how much of it can play a part in adaptive evolution.

Polymorphism in body structure

No two people look exactly the same. This itself hints at the existence of genetic differences, although it is not easy to measure how many genes are involved. Even identical twins (who share the same genes) differ in appearance to a greater or lesser degree. Some patterns of inheritance are reasonably straightforward. Among Europeans, for example, the gene for fair hair colour is recessive to that for dark; and that for pale-blue eyes is recessive to all other eye colours. Certain facial features – such as the prominent lower lip of the Habsburg dynasty – appear again and again in succeeding generations, suggesting that a dominant allele may be involved. In non-human primates, too, facial features are quite strongly inherited.

Many genes of individually small effect are responsible for most differences in physical appearance. A classic instance of such *polygenic inheritance* is the pattern of finger ridges important in detective work. This polymorphism was discovered by the British scientist Francis Galton more than a century ago, and he was the first to show that chimpanzees have patterns quite similar to those in humans. Fingerprint patterns are largely under genetic control, but characters such as height and body build are also modified by the environment. A whole field of genetics – quantitative genetics – is devoted to disentangling the relative importance of gene and environment in such characters. The *heritability* (loosely speaking, the proportion of total variation in a population caused by genetic variation) of human height, for example, is about 80 per cent.

One of the Habsburg royal dynasty, Ferdinand II (1578–1637), Holy Roman Emperor and King of Bohemia.

We have more subtle genetic differences in our physical make-up. Some people can roll their tongue into a tube; others cannot. About half the European population place their left thumb over the right one when they clasp hands, and about half do the opposite. There are many individual differences in skull form in humans and other primates.

Although the inheritance of such variation is little understood, it reflects underlying genetic diversity. Cryptic variation of this kind also affects our senses. To some people – and some chimpanzees also – the chemical phenylthiourea tastes intensely bitter; but to others it is tasteless. In some cases, variants that are rare in humans are widespread in other primates. For example, red–green colour-blindness, which affects only about one person in 100, is much commoner in squirrel monkeys (*Saimiri*).

Very often, variation in height, weight and characters such as blood pressure and intelligence is continuous: the population cannot be divided into discrete classes but must be measured. This often produces a characteristic pattern; the normal or *Gaussian* distribution, which reflects variation in a large number of polygenes and their interaction with the environment. We do not know how many polygenes are involved in any human character. Variation of this kind is medically important as certain combinations of polygenes may push their carriers over the safe threshold for weight, blood pressure, and so on. It is also important in evolution, which is, after all, largely about changes in shape and appearance. However, we know far less about it than we do about biochemical diversity. In primates other than humans we know nothing about polygenic variation.

Polymorphism on the cell surface

There is extensive variation in the genes that control the chemical cues on the surfaces of cells. These messages are recognised by the immune system – the defence mechanism that reacts to foreign molecules (see p. 304). The ABO blood groups are cues on the surface of red blood cells, the specificity of which depends on the sugar molecule attached to the cell membrane. Only certain combinations of ABO blood can be used for blood transfusion. Nearly 20 other blood-group systems are known. Many, such as Kell, Rhesus and Lutheran, are of anthropological interest and some alter susceptibility to disease. Non-human primates share some of our blood groups. Chimpanzees have O and A blood groups, and the Rhesus system depended for its detection on alleles shared by monkeys and humans. Group O is rare in other primates; gorillas, for example, are all blood group B.

Blood groups are just the tip of the iceberg of cell-surface variation. Early attempts at skin grafting failed because the immune system of the recipient recognised genetic differences in the grafted tissue and rejected it. Work on mice showed that many genes are involved in cell-surface variation; they are nearly all grouped together on a single chromosome, and control a wide range of functions of the immune system. Humans also have a *major histocompatibility system*, the HLA complex, on chromosome 6. Scores of gene loci are involved. The system has an extraordinary level of

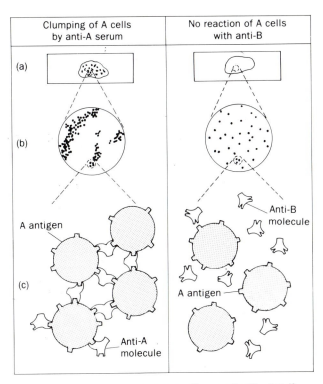

Blood groups: the interactions between antigens and antibodies. If cells of blood group A are mixed with serum containing anti-A antibody, they interact and the cells become linked together into a coagulated mass. If that specific antibody is not present, there is no effect. (a) Seen by the unaided eye: a drop of red blood cells and a drop of serum on a microscope slide. (b) Microscopic view (about ×500). (c) Molecular view: the reaction is a lock-and-key type based on complementary shapes between antigen molecule and antibody molecule (the shapes of the A antigen and of the antibodies, anti-A and anti-B, are conjectural). The size of these molecules is much exaggerated compared to the size of the red blood cell.

polymorphism, so much so that no two individuals (apart from identical twins) have the same antigenic constitution. This extreme diversity may have evolved to avoid infectious diseases, and may also play a part in controlling

1. ELECTROPHORESIS — SEPARATING GIANT MOLECULES

The most widely used technique in molecular biology is also one of the simplest – *electrophoresis*: a means of separating biological molecules by filtering them through a gel with the help of an electrical current. Nearly all the molecules that interest biologists (DNA, amino acids and proteins) are electrically charged. If they are placed in solution in an electrical field, they will move towards the appropriate positive or negative pole at a rate that depends on the charge they carry.

This separation method, first carried out on molecules floating in a liquid, is more effective if the mixture is simultaneously filtered through a gel material. The gel can be an organic material (such as starch or agarose) or a synthetic one (such as polyacrylamide or cellulose acetate).

Different gels have different pore sizes, and sort out molecules according to size

and shape as well as to charge. Sometimes a chemically modified gel to which the molecules being studied become adsorbed is used, and sometimes the gel itself has a gradient in chemical or physical properties that helps to sieve out the molecules.

Various other tricks are also used. For example, when electrophoresing long segments of DNA it helps to put the electrical field through in pulses so that the molecule winds and unwinds as it is forced through the pores of the gel. Another useful technique is to electrophorese proteins on a slab of gel in the usual way, and then to rotate the gel through 90° and to electrophorese it a second time using different conditions. This can separate thousands of different molecules from a single blood sample.

Once molecules have been separated, their position on the gel can be identified in

several ways. DNA can be seen directly by shining ultraviolet light on to it. Sometimes the molecule is radioactively labelled, and its position made visible by placing the gel next to a sensitive film. More often, various stains are used – either generalised stains that identify all DNA or protein bands, or specific ones that use the activity of particular enzymes to break down a substrate whose products are then linked to a dye.

Gel electrophoresis of proteins gave the first hint of the existence of massive human biochemical diversity more than 20 years ago, and is now routinely used to separate DNA and other molecules. It is giving the same kinds of new insight into human medicine and anthropology as the microscope did a century ago, and, like the microscope, will no doubt continue to develop in new and unexpected directions.

Steve Jones

inbreeding. The general structure of this complex is very similar in humans, chimpanzees and rhesus macaques (*Macaca mulatta*), but little is known about the extent of variation in non-human primates.

Genetic variation in chromosome structure

Human chromosomes are small and inconspicuous. Even their number (46 in body cells, 23 in the sperm and egg) was not established until the 1950s. In other animals, there may be variation in the number, arrangement and structure of chromosomes. New staining techniques show that many of these genetic changes were widespread during the evolution of primates. Less is known about polymorphism in human chromosomal structure, although it is clear that most of the major human variants lead to genetic disease. There are some individual differences in the position of the densely staining regions (bands) of the chromosomes, which are an indication of underlying changes in the structure of genes, although the smallest detectable chromosomal change represents thousands of individual genes. At least on the gross level visible down the light microscope, what is most impressive is how stable the amount of chromosomal material has been during the evolution of humans and their relatives.

Polymorphism in gene products

Genes produce proteins – chains of amino acids that make up much of the structure of living tissues. Proteins are charged molecules, and genetic changes in their structure may involve a change in electrical charge, which in turn can alter their shape. One of the most important techniques of molecular biology is *gel electrophoresis*, the separation of molecules in an electrical current that drags them through a sieve made up of a range of materials from polyacrylamide to potato starch (Box 1). Proteins with quite small differences in charge or shape can be separated in this way. The method was first used in a survey of human molecular polymorphism in the 1960s, and the results were unexpected. Instead of most people being alike in most of their genes, as had previously been assumed, about a third of the enzymes surveyed showed differences in electrophoretic mobility between two randomly chosen Englishmen. Diversity was the rule, and not the exception.

We now know that some proteins, such as those that make up the building blocks of the body in, for example, the eye lens and muscle, scarcely vary at all, whereas others have much more variation that can be seen from simple electrophoresis. Protein electrophoresis is still an important tool in the study of genetics and evolution. It gives an insight into polymorphism in animals, such as primates, whose genetics is otherwise hard to study, and provides important clues about patterns of relatedness. Other primates are almost as variable as are humans, and share

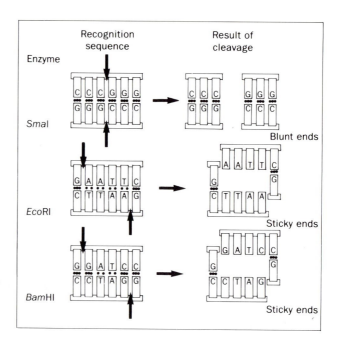

How some restriction enzymes work. These enzymes cut DNA when they encounter a specific sequence of bases (usually four, five or six). They are named after the bacterium from they come: for example, *Eco*RI from *Escherischia coli*, *Bam*HI from *Bacillus amyloliquefaciens* and *Sma*I from *Serratia marcescens*. Some, like *Sma*I, cut the DNA cleanly, leaving blunt ends. Others, like *Eco*RI and *Bam*HI, make offset cuts when they meet their recognition sites. This leaves a 'sticky end', which tends to match up with other DNA sequences. It can be used, for example, to insert human DNA into a bacterial cell as 'recombinant DNA'.

many of their protein polymorphisms with ourselves.

Newer methods of studying proteins allow the actual order of the amino acids involved to be identified. This is much harder work than is simple electrophoresis. Nevertheless, several human proteins (such as haemoglobin) have been *sequenced* in this way. In haemoglobin, sequencing has revealed dozens of hidden variants in addition to those manifest on simple electrophoresis. Some involve changes in single amino acids, or duplication or deficiencies of sections of the protein. Occasionally, different protein chains are fused together, or there may be changes in the time when the protein is produced, which means that a haemoglobin normally found only in embryos appears in the adult.

Polymorphism in the structure of DNA

All inherited differences, whether in height, colour, blood group or proteins, represent changes in the structure of DNA. Molecular biology, using techniques such as restriction enzyme analysis and DNA sequencing, is beginning to give us for the first time an insight into the extent of variation into all our DNA, rather than just in a limited number of gene products. The results are startling. They depend largely on restriction enzymes (or restriction endonucleases as they are sometimes called), which recognise and cut DNA molecules at specific sites defined by the

2. LIFE'S FINGERPRINTS

In the mid-1980s, while surveying DNA variation in the region around the genes coding for β globin (one of the constituents of adult human haemoglobin), the British geneticist Alec Jeffreys made a remarkable discovery: one part of the DNA was uniquely polymorphic. It contained a series of short sequences of bases, repeated a variable number of times – a sort of 'stutter' in the genetic message.

Differences in the number of copies of these short sequences of repetitive DNA (*minisatellite* sequences) led to different patterns of cutting of the DNA by restriction enzymes and hence to unique sets of DNA fragments on an electrophoretic gel (Box 1). A search of the rest of the genome with a copy of the stuttering sequence showed that it was widely scattered over all chromosomes, and could be used to generate a unique and heritable *genetic fingerprint*, which depends on simultaneous variation at many places in our DNA.

Apart from identical twins, no two people have the same genetic fingerprint. This is useful in forensic science, when it is often necessary to try to match a blood or semen stain with a sample from a particular suspect. The value of DNA fingerprinting has been increased by the polymerase chain reaction (Box 3), which means that minute amounts of DNA – for example, that

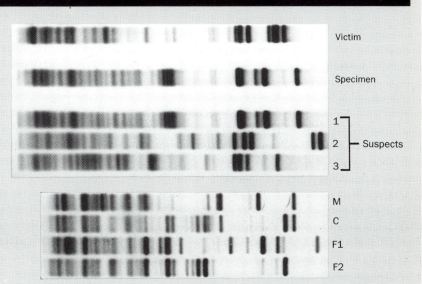

left in a smear of saliva on a cup – can be identified.

Another use is to resolve cases of disputed parenthood: if a child's fingerprint does not match that of its presumed father, then a different man must be involved. This has been useful in immigration cases,

where the authorities claim that an unrelated child is being brought in.

A novel development of fingerprinting is to use only a very short part of the DNA sequence involved. This gives a much simpler and more easily interpreted pattern.   *Steve Jones*

DNA fingerprints: (above) a victim, a specimen and three possible assailants and (below) a mother, child and two possible fathers. Shared bands show that suspect 1 and father 2 are the most likely to be responsible.

---

sequence of bases making up the molecule. Any individual differences in sequence can be picked up in this way.

One part of the genome – the β-globin gene family – has been surveyed in detail for the incidence of such *restriction fragment length polymorphisms*. Many were found. If this part of our DNA is typical of the rest, then there might be as many as 3 million DNA polymorphisms scattered through the human genome. This is a level of variation far larger than anyone had previously imagined. We also have DNA outside the nucleus in the mitochondrion, the main metabolic site of the cell. This is even more variable than is nuclear DNA, and has been much used in studies of human and primate evolution. DNA variation seems to be extensive and universal.

A DNA fingerprint (Box 2) is the result of screening for genetic diversity at many places in the genome at once. Its pattern, although unique, is often complicated and hard to interpret. The method is also technically demanding. Another approach is to look for single, highly variable points in the genome. Several of these so-called single-locus *hypervariable probes* have now been found, and the extent of variation at just one of them is such that nearly all the individuals so far tested have turned out to be unique. The strength of these DNA-based methods of finding genetic polymorphism has recently been increased by new

methods, such as the *polymerase chain reaction* (Box 3) that enable minute amounts of DNA – even the contents of a single cell – to be analysed.

Biochemical technology, from simple electrophoresis of proteins to the most sophisticated analyses of DNA structure, has uncovered more and more human genetic diversity. Its extent is now so great that it is certain that every human being who has lived or ever will live is genetically unique. The same is also likely to be true of our close relatives, the monkeys and apes. How relevant is all this diversity to Darwinian adaptation and the origin of new species such as *Homo sapiens*, which depends on the existence of large amounts of inherited variation?

The right answer to the wrong question?

Darwin would have been astonished by the amount of genetic variability that modern biologists have uncovered. However, he might also have been disturbed: can it really be true that natural selection acts on each of the millions of variable sites in human DNA? There is a real problem here: there are far more genetic differences among individuals than there are differences in biological fitness, as manifest in length of life or number of children. Much of the variation exposed by biological technology may be irrelevant

3. THE POLYMERASE CHAIN REACTION: AMPLIFYING LIFE

Molecular biology has always been led by its techniques, and from x-ray crystallography to Southern blotting (see p. 319) nearly every new method has produced an explosion of information. The latest piece of molecular technology is no exception: it is a simple and cheap way of making millions of copies of a DNA molecule from a single precursor. This means that any amount of very pure DNA can easily be generated from a minute sample — a single human cell, for example — by the *polymerase chain reaction* or PCR.

DNA consists of two complementary strands of bases, the order in one being the mirror image of that in the other. Replication of the strands involves an enzyme, DNA polymerase. This can be made to work in the test-tube and to attach extra bases to one end of a *template*, a short length of unpaired bases that extends from a complete chain.

A template can be generated from a length of natural DNA by heating it, forcing the strands apart. A synthesised short length of DNA of known sequence — a *primer* — will faithfully find its matching length of bases and copy along the template until it runs out of bases to incorporate. By using primers that recognise sequences that bracket a target gene a sequence incorporating the target will be produced.

An ingenious twist to the process is to use a DNA polymerase from a bacterium that lives in hot springs and is therefore stable at the high temperatures used to separate the DNA strands. By repeatedly heating and cooling the mixture, more and more copies of the target are produced: each cycle doubles the number previously present. Thirty cycles produces more than

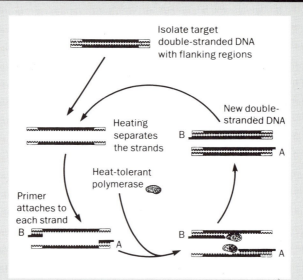

The polymerase chain reaction. This powerful method of copying minute amounts of DNA works rather like an old-fashioned duplicating machine. It depends on a heat-resistant polymerase enzyme that makes a precise copy of a single strand of DNA. Two DNA 'primers' are made that match to a short flanking sequence, one on each side of the gene being studied. The target DNA is heated up to separate the strands, and the primers attach to the appropriate points. The polymerase then quickly makes a copy of each single strand, producing two identical molecules where there was one before. Repeated cycles of heating and cooling can produce thousands of copies of the original in a few hours.

30 billion (3×10^{10}) copies of the target sequence.

This technique produces large amounts of DNA from any gene, and has many uses. It has been useful in looking for mutations in the DNA in the sickle-cell haemoglobin region. In medicine, it can be used to search for low levels of infection with, for example, the human immunodeficiency virus (HIV). It has obvious forensic uses.

With a combination of PCR and DNA fingerprinting the smallest amount of DNA could be a vital clue. PCR has also been used to amplify the DNA from museum specimens and Egyptian mummies (see p. 401).

The potential uses of PCR will, no doubt, be as unpredictable and as varied as those of the many other ingenious tricks of molecular biology. *Steve Jones*

---

to adaptive evolution: it is not acted on by selection, and is sometimes scathingly referred to as 'genetic garbage'. The extent of such variation may then be determined mainly by a balance between its arrival through mutation and random disappearance from a population when, by chance, a carrier of a particular variant fails to reproduce. Much of the work on molecular clocks assumes that molecular change accumulates at a steady rate determined by the balance between these two chance processes.

We may still know rather little about the extent of genetic variation in characters acted on by natural selection, which is, of course, what Darwin was interested in, and what drives the course of human adaptive evolution. Perhaps

molecular biology has given us the right answer to the wrong question. Even so, it has given a wealth of genetic clues about human diversity that allow us to reconstruct patterns of relatedness among the members of a single population, among the peoples of the modern world, and between humans and their primate relatives.   *Steve Jones*

See also 'The nature of evolution' (p. 9), 'Mutation and human evolution' (p. 269), 'Human chromosomes' (p. 274), 'Measuring relatedness' (p. 295), 'Chromosomal evolution in primates' (p. 298), 'Immunological evidence on primates' (p. 303), 'Human evolution: the evidence from DNA sequencing' (p. 316) and 'The dispersion of modern humans' (p. 389)

Mutation and human evolution

Evolution depends on genetic diversity. New species are full of inherited variants not found in their ancestors, and millions of new genes have appeared since the origin of life. All this depends on inherited changes in the structure of DNA (*mutation*). This is often thought of as a harmful process, and it is certainly true that new mutations in humans can produce congenital diseases. However, the process is also central to evolution; many new mutations appear in every generation, even though the rate per gene is usually low. A knowledge of this rate is important, because it may be increased by external agents and because mutations in body cells can lead to cancer.

Measuring the mutation rate

Much research on inherited changes in DNA involves bacteria, which reproduce so quickly that even a rare event like mutation can easily be detected. There are several problems in studying the process in humans. As well as being slow-breeding, humans are diploid – they have two copies of every gene. Recessive mutations in sperm or egg cells are likely to be masked by the normal gene in the other parent. They can be detected, therefore, only when an individual carries two copies of the new gene. Various attempts have been made to get round this problem: for example, new recessive mutations on the X chromosome will show their effects only in males, and this may lead to a change in the sex ratio, which could be used to measure the rate. This method has many errors and we still have no dependable estimates of mutation rates to harmful recessives in humans.

However, some of the commonest genetic abnormalities – such as achondroplastic dwarfism and myotonic dystrophy – are inherited as dominant alleles. If the disease is severe enough to prevent its carriers from surviving or reproducing, then in principle every new patient must represent a new mutation. The mutation rate should hence be the same as the incidence of the disease. This 'direct method' has been much used. However, it has important problems. For example, a new mutation might be recognised by its producing congenital deafness; but as there are many genes involved in normal hearing and a change at any one can lead to its loss, the direct method will overestimate the rate per gene. Infection or accident might lead to deafness and this could also be ascribed to a new mutation. In addition, some children are not the offspring of their presumed father, so that an alleged new mutation may be the result of false paternity.

These problems explain why most estimates of human mutation rates are higher than those in other creatures.

Nevertheless, the direct method has often identified new mutations as they occur. The classic case is the sex-linked recessive mutant for haemophilia in the royal families of Europe. This produces a break in the cascade of reactions that lead to blood clotting. Haemophiliacs bleed extensively after even a minor cut. There was no history of this condition among European royalty before the late nineteenth century, but several of the male descendants of Queen Victoria showed its effects (see p. 260). The genetic accident may have taken place in the august testes of Edward, Duke of Kent – Victoria's father. The best-known sufferer was Tsarevitch Alexis of Russia, Victoria's great grandson. The mutant gene has since disappeared from the present European royal houses.

Modern molecular biology allows a 'blockbuster' approach to estimating human mutation rates. Parents and children are compared for a large number of genes in the hope of identifying any changes. Initially, this method was based on gel electrophoresis of proteins (see p. 265), with a search for mobility differences arising from mutation. This approach detects most, if not all, changes in protein sequence. The largest survey was in Japan, where three new mutations were found among the half a million or so genes tested. This rate is not very different from typical rates in lower organisms, and is much less than that claimed for mutations at loci causing inborn disease. In more recent studies, proteins are electrophoresed on a slab of gel material, which is then turned through 90 degrees and electrophoresed again. After staining, this produces a complicated pattern of dark spots. Gels from parent and offspring are scanned and compared by computer. No new mutations have yet been found among tens of thousands of tests: but the method has real promise for the rapid screening of populations.

Although the rate of mutation per gene is low, there are many new mutations per generation. Much guesswork is involved, but one estimate is about half of all sperms and eggs carry an altered gene not present in the parent: that is, each of us has about a three in four chance of carrying a new mutation in a functional gene. Hence, there are about 3 billion (3×10^9) new mutations in today's human population that were not present in the previous generation.

The nature of mutation

All mutations depend on changes in DNA. There are many ways in which they can arise. Some cause visible changes in chromosome structure (which must reflect an underlying change in the DNA). Others occur at the DNA level, affecting long stretches of the DNA molecule or just a single base.

Mutations can occur either in body cells (*somatic* mutations) or in the cells that lead to the sperm and egg (*germinal* mutations, which are passed to subsequent generations). Cells that descend from a somatic mutation often coexist with normal cells: individuals with more than one genetically distinct lineage of body cells are *mosaics*. Mosaicism is universal; and the ability of the immune system to produce enormous numbers of highly specific antibodies is partially due to somatic mutation.

Chromosomal mutations may arise from *non-disjunction*: the failure of the parental sets of chromosomes to separate correctly during the formation of germ cells. This produces an excess or a deficiency of a chromosome in the offspring. The best-known instances of such mutations include Down's syndrome, which arises from the presence of an extra chromosome 21, and Turner's syndrome, the deficiency of a Y chromosome. Occasionally, the mutation involves the transfer of genetic material to an inappropriate chromosome. Such *translocations* may produce symptoms analagous to those of Down's syndrome without the visible presence of an extra chromosome. *Deletions* arise from the loss of a segment of chromosome and *inversions* arise from the reversal of gene order along a chromosome. Somatic mutations in chromosome structure may be associated with cancer. For example, the Philadelphia (Ph) chromosome rearrangement, which involves a translocation between chromosomes 9 and 22, is an early sign of the development of leukaemia. The study of the mutations that lead to these chromosomal changes is one of the most exciting areas of cancer research.

Most mutations do not lead to a visible change in the structure of chromosomes. There are several types of DNA mutation. Occasionally, one base may be replaced by another: a *base substitition*. This alters the sequence in the codon and may produce an amino acid substitution. For example, one codon for glutamic acid is cytosine–thymine–thymine (CTT). If there is a change of a thymine for an adenosine to give CAT, the amino acid valine is produced instead.

Not all mutations in base order produce a change in an amino acid. For example, if CTT mutates to CTC there is no change in the amino acid. Such *synonymous mutations* are common in the third position of the triplet code. Other types of DNA mutation include *insertion* or *deletion* of a base in the sequence. This can disrupt whole sections of the genetic message, and may lead to synthesis of a particular protein being terminated at the wrong point. Sometimes, mutations involve the insertion of long stretches of DNA into a functional gene. Some of the most important human mutations, such as that for the wasting disease muscular dystrophy, are of this kind.

One of the most startling discoveries of modern molecular biology has been to show that for some mutations (such as that producing Huntington's disease) the inserted DNA segments have a certain autonomy. Some may act independently as viruses and move around the genome. Reshuffling of stretches of DNA in this way means that some parts of the human genome have an extremely high mutation rate. The patterns of the 'genetic fingerprint' used in forensic science (see p. 267) may mutate at a rate of 1 per cent per generation

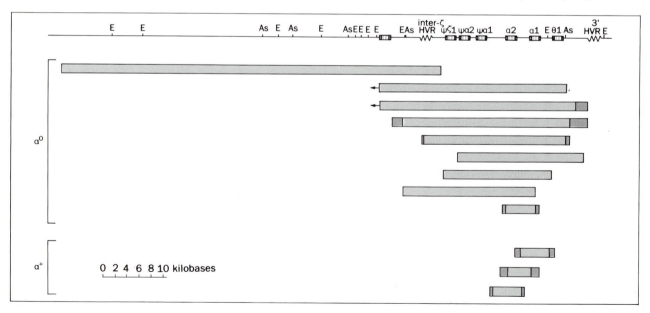

The complexity of mutation, as revealed by molecular biology. The thalassaemias are common in certain parts of the world, where they protect against malaria. It has long been known that the disease results from the loss of part of the α or β haemoglobin molecule. Studies of the loss of DNA sequences show that different individuals with the disease may be carrying very different genetic errors, from the loss of a few bases to the deletion of large sections of the whole globin region. These differences help to explain variation in the severity of the disease. This diagram shows some α-thalassaemia mutations, with the position of the α-globin genes themselves marked as α1 and α2, together with the other members of the gene family, including some pseudogenes. The sections marked HVR (for hypervariable region) are elements of the DNA 'fingerprint'. The solid bars (below) show the sections deleted in different patients, the darker bands indicating where the extent of the deletion is unknown. Such hidden diversity in the course of mutations is widespread.

because of the instability of the repeated DNA segments making up the fingerprint. Mutation may therefore sometimes be a form of 'molecular parasitism' and the distinction between cancer as a disease caused by mutation and one due to viruses becomes blurred.

Artificial mutagenesis

The earliest work on increasing the mutation rate artificially was done on the fruit fly *Drosophila* by the American geneticist H.J. Muller, who won the Nobel Prize in 1946 for his work on the effects of x-rays. He was impressed by the fact that most of the new mutations that he saw were harmful and became concerned that an increase in the human mutation rate might have dire biological consequences. Although his fears are now seen to have been unjustified, his work led to much research into *mutagens* (agents that increase the mutation rate).

Radiation

Visible light is a form of electromagnetic radiation. There are many other kinds of radiation. In general, the shorter the wavelength the more easily the rays pass through living tissue. X-rays can collide with the constituents of cells to produce charged molecules: they are *ionising radiations*. Using an ingenious breeding programme in which irradiated *Drosophila* chromosomes were combined together in a single individual (so that the effects of recessive mutations could be seen) Muller found a strong association between x-ray dose and the induction of mutations. There seemed to be no safe lower limit for radiation: prolonged exposure

to a low dose had the same mutagenic effect as a burst of intense radiation.

Clearly, if this is true for humans there is cause for concern because of the radiation associated with medical x-rays, nuclear power and so on. Fortunately, mammals can repair the effects of low-intensity radiation. If irradiated mice are mated at once, there is a more-or-less direct association between x-ray dose and mutation rate. However, any delay in mating allows the mutations to be repaired. This greatly reduces the effects of chronic low-level radiation. The repair involves a set of specific enzymes; and a congenital absence of these leads to a great increase in mutation rate in some families.

Radiation is sometimes seen as a new biological problem. However, it is important to place artificial radiation into context. The two most important sources of natural radiation are radioactive rocks (which produce radon gas and gamma radiation) and cosmic radiation from space. The amount of these varies greatly from place to place. In Cornwall in southwestern England, where many houses are built on granite, the average radiation exposure is three times that in the rest of Britain; in a few places this dose goes up to 10 times the average, and in some houses in the US built on radioactive waste the figures are twice this. In contrast, the increase in radiation is from 2.5 to 2.9 millisieverts per year for those who are avid consumers of seafood collected near the outfall of Sellafield nuclear power station in Cumbria, northern England – the most polluting in the Western world. This is itself equivalent to the increase in radiation received by those who fly for 100 hours a year. Clearly, radon should be a major public-health concern

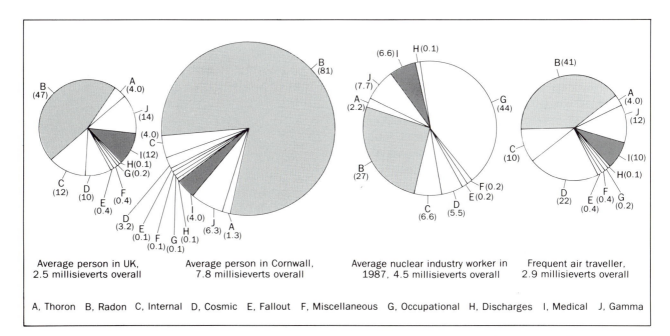

Average person in UK, 2.5 millisieverts overall

Average person in Cornwall, 7.8 millisieverts overall

Average nuclear industry worker in 1987, 4.5 millisieverts overall

Frequent air traveller, 2.9 millisieverts overall

A, Thoron   B, Radon   C, Internal   D, Cosmic   E, Fallout   F, Miscellaneous   G, Occupational   H, Discharges   I, Medical   J, Gamma

Exposure to radiation in different groups in the United Kingdom. For most people, radon gas (B) is by far the most important source of potentially mutagenic radiation; and this is particularly so for those living in places such as Cornwall, where granite is used in buildings. For workers in the nuclear industry, occupational exposure (G) is relatively more important, and for frequent air travellers (five transatlantic trips a year) cosmic radiation (D) begins to play a part. Medical x-rays (I) make up a noticeable part of the annual dose, but fallout from nuclear tests (E) and discharges from nuclear power stations (H) are much less important.

as exposure to this gas might produce 6 per cent of the somatic mutations that lead to lung cancer in the UK.

There is no reason for complacency about the increase in radiation, but no cause for undue alarm either. The immediate effects of atomic explosions or accidents are far more devastating than is their potential for damage to our genetic heritage. This is illustrated by the populations of Hiroshima and Nagasaki in Japan. Soon after the atomic bombings, a survey of genetic damage among the children of survivors began. The bombs themselves killed thousands of people through the acute effects of radiation sickness. However, there is no evidence of genetic damage. Birth defects and chromosomal errors were no more common among children whose parents were close to the bombs than in those whose parents were further away. A massive survey of the genes controlling protein structure uncovered three new mutations out of 700 000 genes in the exposed group, and three out of 500 000 in the children of parents not close to the bomb. These figures are not statistically different from each other.

Chemical mutagenesis

Intense bursts of radiation lead to painful and persistent burns. Certain chemicals produce similar 'radiomimetic' sores. The mutagenic effects of these were studied during World War II. The first found to be mutagens were the war gases such as mustard gas. Since then, hundreds of mutagenic chemicals have been found. Their effects are not as direct as are those of x-rays, and there is no clear relationship between dose and the number of mutations produced.

There has been concern about the possibility that chemicals that are mutagenic in bacteria may be *carcinogenic* in humans. Many cancers arise from an interaction between *oncogenes* – genes involved in cells becoming cancerous – and mutagens. It is not surprising that agents which produce inherited mutations can also to lead to the genetic changes in body cells which lead to cancer. In the 1970s, the American biochemist Bruce Ames tested the relationship between mutagenesis in bacteria and carcinogenesis. Various chemicals (such as those in cigarette smoke) known to be produce cancer in mice turned out to be powerful mutagens in the test bacterium. He went on to examine the effect on these bacteria of other chemicals whose importance in cancer had not then been established. Many were powerful mutagens, and were hence candidates to be human carcinogens.

Some of the chemicals are man-made. Tris-BP was once used as a flame retardant in childrens' clothing. It was a powerful mutagen on the Ames test, and its use has been restricted. Others are chemicals found in food. Many of these are toxic: plants must defend themselves against insects, and have evolved a variety of natural insecticides. Pepper contains a powerful mutagen, as does oil of

bergamot (the flavouring of Earl Grey tea) and saffrole, which is found in natural root beer. Among the most powerful mutagens on the Ames test are aflatoxins, which are found in the fungi growing on badly stored foods; these may be less common today than in earlier times.

Humanity has been exposed since its origin to radiation and to mutagenic chemicals. The advent of civilisation has not greatly increased this exposure.

Age and sex

Mutations arise when DNA is replicated during the formation of sperm and egg. Ageing might be a reflection of the same process in body cells, perhaps because the enzymes that repair mutations cease to work effectively. The rate of mutation is affected by parental age. Down's syndrome (a mutation in chromosome 21) is 20 times more common

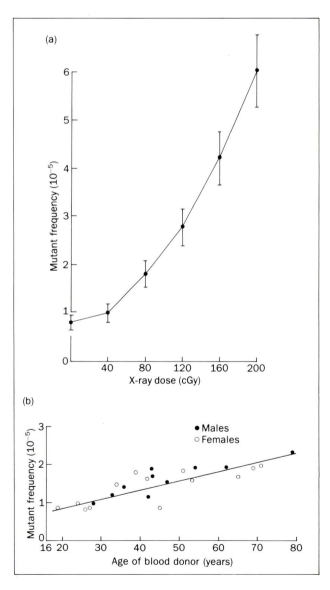

Relationship between the incidence of new mutations removing the activity of an enzyme in white blood cells of blood donors (a) exposed to x-rays during cancer therapy and (b) of increasing age.

in the children of mothers aged 45 compared to the rate in teenage mothers. Paternal age is also important, with certain mutations five times more common among older fathers. A survey of Swedish families transmitting new haemophilia mutations shows a striking increase with the age of the parent: what is more, the rate of mutation among fathers is 10 times that in mothers. It may be more than a coincidence that Edward, Duke of Kent, was aged over 50 when his daughter – who became Queen Victoria and received a haemoglobin gene from him – was born.

Mutation is the source of all the diversity that has led to the evolution of modern humans and to their divergence from other primates. However, mutation is an undirected process: it cannot lead to evolutionary progress unless natural selection is also at work.   *Steve Jones*

See also 'The nature of evolution' (p. 9), 'Genetic diversity in humans' (p. 264), 'Human chromosomes' (p. 274), 'Bottlenecks in human evolution' (p. 281), 'Natural selection in humans' (p. 284), and 'Chromosomal evolution in primates' (p. 298).

Human chromosomes

The 46 chromosomes in the body (somatic) cells of humans can be arranged according to size and position of their centromere. Such an arrangement is known as a *karyotype*. Karyotypes of humans give insights into the genetic changes underlying many diseases and comparison with those of other primates helps to reveal the links between our species and our closest relatives.

Chromosomal abnormalities

Changes in the number of chromosomes

The presence of an extra chromosome 21 (one of the smallest chromosomes) in people with Down's syndrome was the first abnormality to be described. This was important, because Down's syndrome is the commonest cause of severe mental retardation. The extra chromosome arises from a process called *non-disjunction* – the failure of the chromosomes to separate during the meiotic divisions that lead to the formation of sperm or egg. One gamete, usually the egg, then carries two copies of the twenty-first chromosome instead of one; fertilisation by a normal sperm leads to a *trisomic* zygote with three copies. Non-disjunction increases with the age of the mother.

After the discovery of trisomy-21, a few other developmental abnormalities came to be associated with particular trisomies. For example, extra copies of chromosomes 13 and 18 result in severe malformation and a short survival time (Patau's and Edward's syndromes, respectively). Further trisomies have been found, not among newborns but

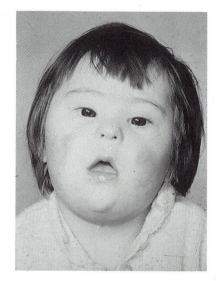

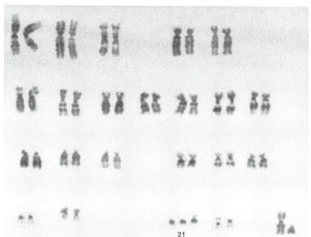

A person with Down's syndrome (above) has three copies, instead of the normal two, of chromosome 21 (below).

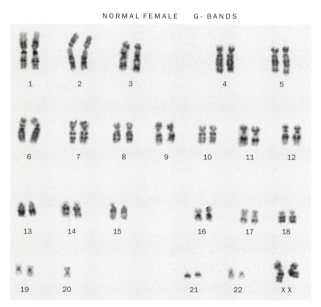

NORMAL FEMALE   G-BANDS

A human female karyotype of 46 chromosomes prepared by the G-banding method (see Box 1) and arranged according to size and position of the centromeres. Notice the two X sex chromosomes.

through chromosome studies on embryos that had spontaneously aborted or miscarried. Examination showed that about half of these embryos had abnormal chromosomes.

Trisomies have now been found for almost all the autosome chromosomes; they account for about half the abnormalities in embryos. The remainder is largely made up of fetuses with two other types of abnormality – triploidy and monosomy. *Triploidy* means the presence in each cell of an extra haploid set of chromosomes, giving 69 chromosomes per cell, usually because two sperm have fertilised one egg. A few rare instances of triploid infants surviving to birth are known, but almost all die before birth. *Monosomy* means a single copy of a particular chromosome instead of the normal two. The monosomic fetuses that commonly miscarry are lacking a sex chromosome, and are described as X_O. Autosomal monosomy appears to be so lethal that the

1. TECHNIQUES FOR STUDYING CHROMOSOMES

Chromosomes are studied at the metaphase stage of mitosis, when body (somatic) cells are undergoing division. It is therefore necessary either to sample rapidly dividing tissue, such as bone marrow, or to induce cells to undergo division by culturing them.

This is most easily done with lymphocytes from a blood sample. These cells are induced to undergo DNA synthesis and subsequent cell division by mitosis by exposure to phytohaemaglutinin (PHA), a protein extracted from kidney beans. PHA was originally used, as its name implies, to agglutinate red cells, and it was only later realised that it acts as an inducer of mitosis in lymphocytes.

The blood sample is cultured for 2 or 3 days in the presence of culture medium; then colchicine (originally obtained from crocuses) is added to prevent the polymerisation of the spindle proteins that is essential for cell division. This holds the cells at metaphase and also aids the spreading of chromosomes in the final preparation. Spreading is also helped by treating the cells with a weak salt solution, so that water enters the cell, causing it to swell and disperse the chromosomes.

After fixation, the cell suspension is dropped onto slides and air-dried. There are then several staining options. Some stains (such as Giemsa) produce uniform

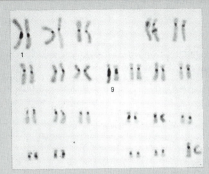

C-banded human female karyotype. Notice the variation in the size of the C band in chromosome pairs 1 and 9.

staining along the chromosome arms so that they can be separated into groups, and distinctive chromosomes can be individually identified.

However, for individual identification of all chromosomes, or regions of chromosomes, a variety of more modern chromosome-banding methods is needed. The most widely used, G-banding, is produced after pretreatment of fixed slides with the enzyme trypsin and/or a warm salt solution, which selectively removes some of the protein component of the chromosome. Subsequent Giemsa staining reveals unique banding patterns on each

chromosome (see the karyotypes on the opposite page).

G-banding does not reveal much normal variation between individuals. For this, Q-banding and C-banding are used. For the former, fluorescent staining, usually quinacrine, without pretreatment is used. This produces banding patterns similar to those shown by G-banding, but, in addition, certain regions fluoresce intensely and these show considerable variation among individuals.

C-banding involves harsh pretreatment of the chromosomes. A large proportion of the non-histone protein and of the DNA itself is removed, so the only areas that then stain are the centromeric regions, particularly of chromosomes 1, 9 and 16, and part of the Y chromosome, which also shows intense fluorescence with quinacrine stain.

The C-band positive regions are sites of concentration of a fraction of repeated sequences of DNA (repetitive DNA) called satellite DNA. These human chromosome *heteromorphisms* are extremely useful in both clinical work and research, as it is usual for no two individuals to exhibit the same pattern if a combination of Q- and C-banding is used. The heteromorphism also acts as a chromosome marker, so that inheritance can be traced.

Joy D.A. Delhanty

---

embryo dies before the stage at which pregnancy can be recognised. The high rates of human miscarriage (15 to 20 per cent of recognised pregnancies, probably at least 40 per cent overall) is thus due mainly to selection against chromosomally abnormal embryos.

Sex-chromosome trisomy

A category that more rarely results in fetal loss is *sex-chromosome trisomy*: in the newborn population it accounts for half

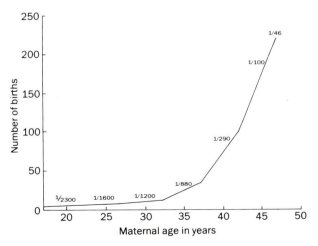

The incidence of Down's syndrome births rises with increasing maternal age.

of those with abnormal chromosomes. Why should an extra sex chromosome be so much less harmful than an extra autosome? First, the human Y chromosome appears to carry relatively little DNA that is transcribed, most of the long arm being composed of highly repetitive satellite DNA, which has no known function. The Y chromosome is, however, strongly masculinising, so that an individual with XXY sex chromosomes (Klinefelter's syndrome) is phenotypically male, although sterile. Males with an extra Y (XYY) are likely to pass undetected in the population, although they are much taller than the average; the increase in height may arise from the extra Y chromosome. Similarly, females with three X chromosomes may pass as normal, but there appears to be an increased risk of mental subnormality.

Unlike the Y chromosome, the X chromosome carries many genes that are actively transcribed. The comparative normality of individuals with extra copies of the X chromosome arises from X-chromosome inactivation (see Box 2), which means that X chromosomes in excess of one per cell are not transcribed. This brings female cells into line with male cells as far as products from genes on a single active X are concerned. A few embryos with X_O sex chromosomes do survive to birth, although many will be 'mosaics' and will also have some cells with two X chromosomes. As adults, such individuals are short in stature, have no secondary sexual characteristics and are sterile (Turner's syndrome). In apparent contradiction to the sex-determining mechanisms, a few males are known with XX sex chromosomes. Recent molecular studies have shown this is caused by a small fragment of the Y chromosome becoming attached to one X chromosome. This fragment presumably contains the recently described testis-determining gene, which is responsible for male development.

Changes in the structure of chromosomes

Shortly after trisomy 21 was found to be associated with Down's syndrome, an individual was discovered with the normal number of 46 chromosomes but with all the other features of Down's syndrome. She had a fusion or *translocation* of the additional chromosome 21 to another chromosome of similar shape (an *acrocentric*, with the centromere close to one end), with the loss of only the short arms of these chromosomes. As the short arms carry few active genes, their loss in a cell is well tolerated. This type of fusion of chromosomes is known as a *Robertsonian* translocation and is important in the evolution of a variety of groups, including primates. The effect is to reduce the chromosome number by one without loss of active genetic material.

Families with more than one member with Down's syn-

drome frequently inherit a Robertsonian translocation from an unaffected 'carrier' parent. The phenotypically normal parent has 45 chromosomes per cell, but a complete complement of active genetic material. However, the presence of the translocated chromosome upsets the normal separation of chromosomes at meiosis, because during the first meiotic division the relevant chromosomes must form a group of three instead of the normal two pairs. This arrangement increases the chance that one of the free chromosomes will pass to the same pole as the translocation. Approximately 5 per cent of those with Down's syndrome have a translocation and carriers of Robertsonian translocations occur in about 1 in 1000 of the newborn population. The great majority of these translocations are between chromosome numbers 13 and 14, so that Down's syndrome is not involved.

A similar number of newborns are carriers of another type of structural rearrangement called *reciprocal translocation*, in which breakage has occurred in two different chromosomes, segments have been exchanged, and the chromosome segments have fused. As with carriers of Robertsonian translocations, the individuals appear normal. However, errors occur during the formation of sperm and egg, as the two translocated chromosomes and the cor-

---

2. THE Y CHROMOSOME

Humans have two copies of each of their 23 chromosomes except for one pair, the sex chromosomes. For this pair, females have two copies of a large functional X chromosome; males have just one X, matched with a smaller Y. This is the basis of the human sex ratio, as half the sperm carry an X and half a Y chromosome.

Sex-linked inheritance arises from the fact that certain gene loci are carried on the X chromosome and therefore always manifest their effects in males, even if they are recessive in females. The mechanism also raises an important question; how can the sexes differ in such large blocks of chromosome material, given that an excess or a deficiency of other chromosomes is usually lethal?

The answer lies in the fact that, in females, about half of the X chromosomes are switched off at any time. Some cells have one of their Xs active, others the alternative. This means that, if a female is heterozygous for a sex-linked locus, then different cells will have different genetic activities. For example, a female heterozygous for sex-linked colour-blindness has half her retinal cells with normal function, and half with an inability to distinguish colours.

The gene responsible for maleness has recently been found. It is the *testis-determining factor* (TDF) gene. The first clue that only a small part of the Y chromosome might be involved came from the very rare cases in which an apparently

normal male turned out to have, not an X and a Y, but two X chromosomes. This was because a tiny piece — presumably that coding for maleness — of his father's Y chromosome had become attached by translocation to the X, and passed on.

The TDF gene is now known to be near the end of the short arm of the Y chromosome. It has been tracked down to within a short sequence of DNA. Surprisingly, its structure has some similarity to that of a gene controlling mating in yeast. Recently, the gene involved has been used to transform the

sex of embryonic mice from female to male.

The Y chromosome is inherited down the male line, and is hence in some ways a complement to mitochondrial DNA (see p. 320). Unfortunately, it seems that the Y chromosome will tell us less about human evolution, as, so far, little variation has been found on it and it has few functional genes. Interactions between the X and the Y chromosomes are important in the genetic barriers between other species, but, for humans, we are still a long way from tracing the origin of Adam.

Steve Jones

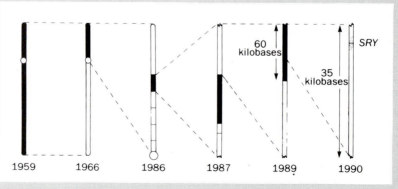

The search for the male-determining gene. Thirty years ago we knew only that it was on the Y chromosome. Since then, studies of chromosome rearrangements and DNA sequence have located it to a short length of DNA. The diagram represents successive magnifications of sections of the Y chromosome. *SRY* is the male-determining region.

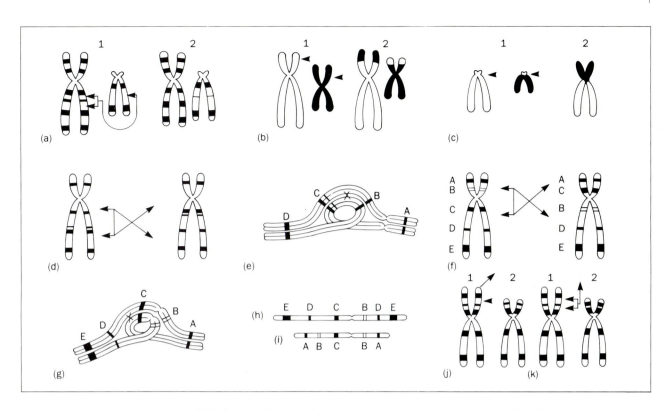

Some chromosomal rearrangements. In all the diagrams, 1 = original chromosomes and 2 = rearranged chromosomes; arrows indicate breakpoints. (a) *Insertion*: both chromosomes change in length. (b) Symmetrical *reciprocal translocation*, resulting in two monocentric chromosomes. (c) *Robertsonian translocation*: chromosome number is reduced by one. (d) and (e) *Paracentric inversion*. (d) The chromosomes before and after paracentric inversion; there is no change in shape of the rearranged chromosomes. (e) Pairing of homologous chromosomes at meiotic prophase; if crossing-over occurs between two non-sister chromatids within the inverted segment, one dicentric and one acentric chromosome result. (f)–(i) *Pericentric inversion*. (f) The chromosomes before and after pericentric inversion, which may produce a change in shape. (g) Pairing of homologue chromosomes at meiotic prophase; crossing-over between two non-sister chromatids within the inverted segment produces two chromatids, each with duplication and deficiency of genetic material (h and i). (j) Terminal deletion. (k) Interstitial deletion.

responding two normal ones must form a group of four. Subsequent separation frequently results in the production of genetically unbalanced gametes, which may result in reduced fertility or malformed offspring.

A much rarer type of structural change involves two breaks in a single chromosome with *inversion* of the free segment and subsequent rejoining. About 1 in 7000 newborns in European populations have a chromosomal inversion. Like the carriers of translocations, such individuals appear quite normal. Effects on gamete formation depend on whether the inversion includes the centromere (*pericentric*) or not (*paracentric*). To pair in meiosis the inverted chromosome and its normal homologue must form a reversed loop. If crossing-over takes place within the loop, the resultant sperm or egg will be duplicated for one region of the chromosome and will be deficient in another. Paracentric inversions may lead to chromosomes with two centromeres or without a centromere at all. These do not usually survive cell division, so that only gametes with no crossing-over within the inverted segment are likely to be viable. Carriers of either type of inversion are likely to have reduced fertility and may have an increased risk of abnormal children. Prenatal diagnosis is now offered to mothers with a high risk of having a chromosomally abnormal child.

A third type of structural change has an immediate effect on the carrier. It is caused by the loss or *deletion* of a segment of the chromosome, usually as a result of two breaks and loss of an intervening segment. As products from both parental copies of active genes are necessary for normal development, loss of one copy by deletion leads to malformation or embryonic death. The best-known example of this in humans is the *cri du chat* syndrome, caused by deletion of the short arm of chromosome 5. The infant's cry resembles that of a cat and there is profound mental retardation.

Chromosomes and cancer

Cancers are derived from a single normal cell that has undergone many sequential genetic changes that result in uncontrolled proliferation, the invasion of surrounding normal tissue and a spread to distant sites (*metastasis*). Early in the history of human cytogenetics it was realised that chromosome abnormality was a feature of malignant cells. The changes appeared to be mostly random until, with the advent of banding techniques (see Box 1), some patterns began to emerge.

In patients with chronic myeloid leukaemia (CML), an

3. PRENATAL SCREENING FOR CHROMOSOMAL ABNORMALITIES

Since 1970 it has been possible to determine the karyotype of a baby before it is born by *amniocentesis*, which involves taking a sample of amniotic fluid from around the fetus. Cells shed from fetal tissues into the fluid are cultured for 10 to 14 days before making chromosome preparations. Prenatal diagnosis is offered to mothers with a relatively high risk of producing a chromosomally abnormal child -- for example, those carrying a translocation or those over the age of 35. A positive finding allows the parents to consider the option of terminating the pregnancy.

The amniotic fluid sample is usually taken in the sixteenth week of pregnancy, so that a result is not obtained until the eighteenth week. Termination at this late stage is distressing, so much research is centred on developing an earlier diagnosis. This has been achieved by taking samples of part of the fetal membranes that are destined to form the placenta (the *chorionic villi*) at 8 to 10 weeks of pregnancy.

Chromosomes are obtained either directly from the chorionic villi or after the tissue has been cultured. The quality of direct preparations may not be good enough to pick up minor alterations. However, culture of chorionic villus tissue introduces the risk of also culturing contaminating maternal cells, which may lead to a false result. Moreover, as the chorionic villi are not part of the developing fetus, there is a risk that the karyotypes of the fetus and the villi have diverged.

For all these reasons, emphasis is now shifting towards trials of early amniocentesis and preliminary screening of maternal serum for biochemical changes that indicate the presence of a chromosomally abnormal fetus.

Joy D.A. Delhanty

apparent loss of material (deletion) from chromosome 22, which created the so-called Philadelphia (Ph) chromosome, turned out to be a reciprocal translocation between chromosomes 9 and 22. Some 90 per cent of CML patients have this rearrangement in their leukaemic cells. Other translocations, such as an exchange between chromosomes 8 and 14 in over 80 per cent of lymphomas of the Burkitt type, were soon found. Unfortunately, solid tumours (such as carcinomas), which are the commonest forms of cancer, are much more difficult to work with. However, it seems that there is much less uniformity of change than with leukaemias and lymphomas. A variety of mechanisms is involved in the loss of genetic material that seems to be necessary in carcinomas.

Chromosomal rearrangements and cancer

The application of molecular biology to cancer research has resulted in tremendous progress. In particular, it has led to a much greater understanding of the role of chromosome rearrangements in the development of malignancy and of the link between some viruses and human cancer. Molecular biologists have identified a group of genes that appears to be instrumental in causing cancer in humans and other mammals. In the cancer-associated or *activated* form, these genes are termed *oncogenes* (cancer genes), but when fulfilling their normal cellular role they are called *proto-oncogenes*.

Oncogenes

More than 20 proto-oncogenes are known and most have been assigned to particular chromosomes. Many oncogenes are highly conserved and are found not only in vertebrates but also in the fruit fly (*Drosophila*) and yeast, indicating that their normal function is essential. Some play a part in the control of cell growth. It appears that proto-oncogenes are instrumental in causing cancer if they are altered in some way or are taken away from their normal controlled environment so that they promote continuous growth.

Proto-oncogenes were first identified as a result of being hijacked by viruses. Certain types of RNA viruses (viruses with RNA instead of DNA as their genetic material) – the acute transforming *retroviruses* – form tumours in animal hosts very rapidly, and transform normal cells to malignant cells in culture. The breakthrough in this research came in the 1980s when it was shown that this type of RNA virus had picked up a cellular proto-oncogene from a previous host, and it was this proto-oncogene, coupled to the viral nucleic acid sequences, that was responsible for the transforming properties of the RNA virus. Examples of some acute transforming retroviruses and their associated cellular proto-oncogenes are given in the table.

There are three main ways in which the normal proto-oncogene can become activated and play a part in malignant transformation. These are: changes in DNA sequence (*point mutation*); changes in position (*transposition*); and an increase in the number of copies (*amplification*).

Transposition and amplification can give rise to visible chromosome changes. In chronic myeloid leukaemia, the 9.22 translocation has the effect of transposing the Abelson proto-oncogene (*c-abl*) from chromosome 9 to a new position on chromosome 22. This leads to the production of a new protein, which may be important for the development of the leukaemia. Similarly, in Burkitt's lymphoma, the *c-myc* proto-oncogene is moved from its normal position on chromosome 8 to a site near one of the active immunoglobin genes (usually on chromosome 14), which greatly affects the level of the *c-myc* gene product. Another common chromosomal anomaly in malignant cells is the presence of *double minutes*, which are very small, paired, spherical pieces of chromosome without centromeres. There can be any number in a cell, from a few to many hun-

Acute transforming retroviruses and associated cellular proto-oncogenes

Virus prototype	Host species	Cellular proto-oncogene
Harvey sarcoma	Rat	H-*ras*
Kirsten sarcoma	Rat	K-*ras*
MC29	Chicken	c-*myc*
Abelson leukaemia	Mouse, cat	c-*abl*

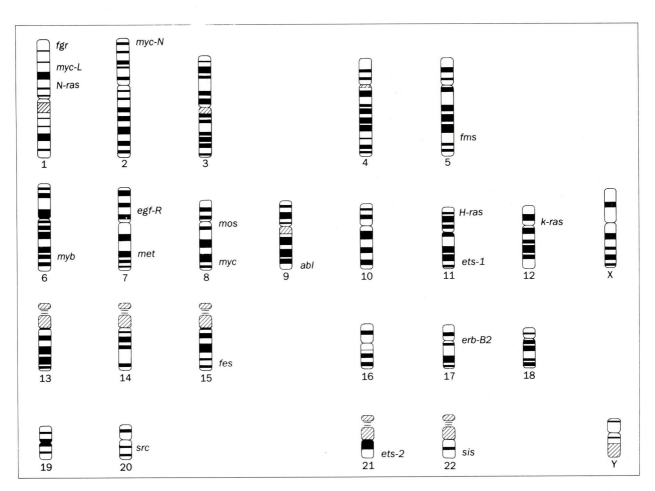

The sites of some proto-oncogenes on human chromosomes. Notice that the proto-oncogenes are distributed among many chromosomes; some are members of related gene families (e.g. *myc* and *ras*). Most of the proto-oncogenes are named after the virus that carries the homologous sequence (e.g. *abl* for Abelson murine leukaemia virus, *mos* for Moloney murine sarcoma virus). The hatched areas of the chromosomes represent polymorphic regions.

dreds. These represent the site of an amplified proto-oncogene. In the childhood tumour neuroblastoma, amplification of a proto-oncogene of the *myc* type is related to the stage of the disease and the chance of survival.

Inheritance of familial cancers

Another type of cancer-related gene is revealed by chromosome abnormalities in a few affected individuals. Retinoblastoma is a rare cancer of the eye in young children. Most cases are sporadic (isolated), but in about 40 per cent the disease is inherited from a parent through a dominant gene. In a few of the sporadic cases, a portion of chromosome 13 is missing in all body cells. This led to experiments that proved that the gene for susceptibility to retinoblastoma is on that chromosome within the deleted region.

Use of polymorphic gene markers from chromosome 13 to study the eye tumours showed that, in about half the cases, gene loci that were heterozygous in normal tissues were homozygous in the tumour. This means that the mutant form of the retinoblastoma gene may itself have become homozygous, and tumour development may have arisen through loss of its normal allele. Various chromosomal mechanisms can give rise to such local homozygosity (see the diagram on the next page).

A mutation in a single copy of a gene appears to be insufficient to lead to malignancy if the normal allele is still present, and further events – leading to homozygosity – are needed to complete the process that occurs in colon and lung cancer as well as retinoblastoma.

Chromosome breakage and cancer

We can now begin to understand the relationship between chromosome breakage and cancer. Irradiation, which causes chromosome damage, also causes cancer, but the mechanism of this was obscure until recently. Chromosome rearrangements involved in oncogene activation and in producing homozygosity for a mutant gene depend on chromosome breakage. One group of genetically determined conditions in humans is known as the *chromosome breakage disorders* (such as Bloom's syndrome and Fanconi's anaemia). These are rare, recessive diseases, which, as well as showing spontaneous chromosome breakage, all have in common the fact that they are cancer-prone.

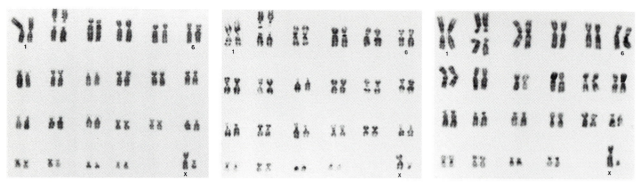

G-banded karyotypes of (left) male orang-utan, (centre) male gorilla and (right) male common chimpanzee, arranged according to their homology with human chromosomes. Some 'highly conserved' chromosomes are marked with the number for the human chromosome equivalent. Chimpanzees have chromosomes that most closely resemble humans. All the great apes have 48 chromosomes; humans have 46 due to fusion of two pairs during evolution.

Evolutionary aspects

If a biochemist received samples of blood from a person and from a chimpanzee for protein analysis, he or she would be unable to determine with any confidence which came from which. However, if a cytogeneticist received the same two samples, it would be immediately obvious which was which as, in common with the other great apes, the chimpanzee (*Pan troglodytes*) has 48 chromosomes in each of its cells and many of its chromosomes show differences from those of humans. In spite of these gross differences, the patterns on the chromosomes of a human being, gorilla, chimpanzee and orang-utan are very similar. Fusion of two pairs of chromosomes accounts for the reduction of the chromosome number from 48 in the great apes to 46 in modern humans and most other chromosomal differences in the four species are inversions and variations in the amount and siting of repetitive DNA, which has no function in the coding of proteins.

The functional identity of human and great ape chromosomes can be seen by gene mapping. For eight autosomes and the X chromosome, there is conservation of the positions and order of genes between the four species. For instance, of the loci assigned to chromosome 1 in humans, eight have also been mapped to chromosome 1 in the great apes. In striking contrast to this similarity of location of transcribed genes is the distribution of repetitive DNA in the different species, and in particular of the very highly repetitive satellite DNA, the location of which is shown by C-banding. Why this should be is not yet clear.

Joy D.A. Delhanty

See also 'Principles of genetics' (p. 255), 'Mutation and human evolution' (p. 269) and 'Chromosomal evolution in primates' (p. 298)

Chromosomal mechanisms of tumour formation

Rb^- — Non-disjunction and loss

Rb^- Rb^- — Non-disjunction and reduplication

Patient with retinoblastoma

Mutant chromosome 13 Normal chromosome 13

Rb^- Rb^+

Rb^- Rb^- Mitotic recombination

Rb^- — Deletion including the *Rb* locus

Rb^- Rb^- Inactivation of *Rb* locus

Rb^- Rb^- Mutation of *Rb* locus

The genetic mechanism of tumour formation in a person who inherits a mutation in one copy of the retinoblastoma gene (Rb^- on the shaded chromosome). The changes lead to loss or inactivation of the normal copy (Rb^+) of the gene. This allows the expression of the mutant gene, which leads to growth of the eye tumour.

Bottlenecks in human evolution

Human populations that are near each other or have recently evolved from a common ancestor usually share the same genes. However, there are some important exceptions to this pattern. Many have arisen by accident; if a population goes through a period of reduced numbers – a *bottleneck* – only the genes of the survivors will persist. Their descendants may then be genetically different from the population before the bottleneck.

The significance of such chance events (*genetic drift*) in evolution is uncertain. Some claim that random change is, on the average, far more important than is natural selection. Whether or not this is true, humans are the best animals for studying the effects of demographic accidents in evolution because our historical records are so good and because we have colonised some parts of the world very recently.

Surnames illustrate the process. They are, in some senses, 'genes'; they pass down the male line in roughly the same way as does the Y chromosome. Names seem to have little effect on the chance of a survival or mating. A particular surname will be lost from a society if, by chance, it is shared by only a few families and none of them has a son. This is more likely to happen if the population is small, or if few children are produced. The number of surnames present can therefore indicate past population size. In remote Italian villages of the Parma Valley with 200 to 300 inhabitants, there are on the average only about 12 surnames per village. Often, more than half the village's population have the same name, and in some places all share a surname found nowhere else in the neighbourhood.

The statistical theory of probability tells us that in a village with 100 males, each with a different surname, it will take 200 generations to lose all names except for one. As this is about 5000 years – far longer than the age of these villages – chance loss of names from a stable population of a hundred or so males is not enough to explain the paucity of surnames in these villages and their divergence from each other. What has probably happened is that in one or a few generations of these isolated communities, only a very small number of men had sons; so that all the other names were lost at a stroke. A single episode of greatly reduced population size has had a disproportionate effect on later generations.

Just how strong this effect can be is seen in migrant populations. The 2.5 million Afrikaners in South Africa share a small number of surnames: Botha, van der Merwe, de Klerk and so on – far fewer than in their ancestral European homeland. This is because they descend from rather few immigrants and hence a limited number of names. Afrikaners illustrate very neatly the parallel between surnames and genes.

The rare disorder porphyria variegata is a genetic defect caused by an autosomal dominant gene. Although under most circumstances it does little damage, its carriers have a severe – and sometime fatal – reaction to barbiturate drugs. All 30 000 Afrikaner carriers of this gene can be traced to a single couple who arrived in South Africa from Holland in the 1690s. The gene is far commoner in South Africa than elsewhere in the world, and the whole of this dramatic shift in genetic constitution can be traced to one random event. This history is an illustration of the *founder principle* in population genetics: the effect on subsequent generations of starting a new population with a few colonisers.

Exactly the same process can be seen in the names and the genes of other isolated human populations – isolated by religious preference (such as in the Amish of North America), by social barriers (as in warring South American tribal groups) or, most dramatically, on oceanic islands (see Box). In these instances, the record of history is confirmed in the genes. What is important to students of human evolution is that the argument can be turned on its head: population history can – in principle at least – be deduced from patterns of gene distribution. This has helped us to understand the origin of the world's peoples, and even gives us a clue as to how the globe was colonised by *Homo sapiens*.

Bottlenecks and population history

Population size can fall drastically in a harsh environment. For example, the population of England was halved by plague only a few hundred years ago, and some villages disappeared altogether. In the same way, many small Pacific islands have archaeological remains that suggest that they were once inhabited, but their original peoples have disappeared through starvation or disease. Col-

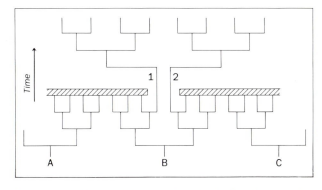

Effects of a population bottleneck on the survival of three lineages (A, B and C). Only two descendants of individual B survive; all their descendants trace their ancestry back to B and hence retain only a sample of the genes originally present in A, B and C.

TRISTAN DA CUNHA — A GENETIC LABORATORY

The remote island of Tristan da Cunha in the south Atlantic was uninhabited until a garrison (nominally to watch over Napoleon in exile on St Helena, thousands of miles away) was placed there in 1817. When this was withdrawn, one William Glass and Thomas Swain decided to stay. They obtained wives by advertising in colonial papers, and a few other immigrants arrived during the next century. By 1960, there were 260 people on the island.

Several bottlenecks after 1817 helped to rearrange the island's genetic structure. For example, in 1885 a boat containing 15 men sank, causing a drastic fall in population. A later bottleneck occurred because of the emigration advised by a pessimistic pastor. In 1885, 60 per cent of the genes in the population could be traced back to two sisters and their husbands. Later bottlenecks changed this figure, but the two sisters were still the top contributors to the genes of 1960. Surnames showed the same pattern with early names at high frequency.

One important effect of the bottleneck was the chance establishment of a rare and harmful gene that was carried in one of the founders. One of the first women on the

Isolated Tristan da Cunha in the Atlantic Ocean.

island must have had the gene for the degenerative eye disease retinitis pigmentosa. Its frequency in most of the world is less than 1 in 4000, but on Tristan in 1961 1 per cent of the population were

carriers. Persistent inbreeding has produced an unusually high frequency of sufferers from this disease on the island – a clear example of the founder effect in action.   *Steve Jones*

onisers of new regions are particularly liable to perish – as we can see from the records of George Anson or James Cook, and from the failed attempts to set up colonies in the New World. In such circumstances, population bottlenecks are likely to occur. A few founders – the survivors of or emigrants from the original population – will establish all subsequent generations. However large the populations may become, all the genes can be traced back to this limited group of ancestors.

The generations immediately following a bottleneck are also likely to consist of just a few people. This means that the only mates available are likely to be relatives, so that inbreeding is inevitable. This leads to further loss of genetic variability and compounds the initial effects of the bottleneck. For example, a population that starts with two individuals – that is, with a severe bottleneck – and doubles in size every generation loses a further 35 per cent or so of its variation by bottlenecking in the first two generations after the founder event. Only 5 per cent more is lost in the next two generations. New mutations will appear in time and population genetics theory makes it possible to infer the size of any past bottleneck by comparing a derived population with its ancestor, taking into account the effects of mutation.

We can hence reconstruct the past history of populations from the present distribution of genes: any reduction in overall variation or simultaneous shift in the frequencies of many genes may reflect a past founder event, which may have happened tens, hundreds or thousands of years ago.

Neutral genes and genetic history

Although this statistical argument is neat, it is bedevilled by the fact that, if the genes being compared in the ancestral and the new population are under selection (perhaps because of an environmental change in the new habitat), the genetic structure of the population will alter even without a bottleneck. This means that we must try and use *neutral* genes – those unaffected by natural selection – when making such calculations. As we can never be certain that any gene really is neutral there is always a weakness in the argument. If one accepts this, however, the calculations suggest that there were some important population bottlenecks in our evolutionary history. Genetic variation in non-coding sections of nuclear DNA, in the mitochondrion and even in blood groups and enzymes (although there is more danger of selection being involved here) have been used as clues about human populations in ancient times.

We can infer that a bottleneck has occurred in the past if we see a locally high frequency of some generally less-common neutral genetic variant. For instance, the blood group O is extremely common among American Indians, and reaches a frequency of 95 per cent among the Indian populations of South America (see p. 393). Perhaps such high frequencies were attained as a result of a bottleneck in the colonisers who reached North America from northeastern Asia perhaps some 20000 or so years ago, from an ancestral Asian population that now has an O frequency of about 55

The distribution of genetic variation in the β-globin region in different parts of the world

Haplotypes	British	Cypriot	Italian	Asian Indian	Thai	Melanesian A	Melanesian B	Polynesian	African A	African B
+ − − − −	16	59	32	58	29	44	73	43	0	3
− + − + +	15	14	15	28	0	10	19	6	2	4
− + + − +	5	8	2	15	2	3	0	0	1	0
+ − − + +	0	0	0	0	0	3	8	0	0	0
− + + − −	1	1	1	3	0	0	0	0	0	0
− + + + +	0	0	0	0	0	0	5	1	0	0
+ + − + +	0	0	0	3	0	0	0	0	0	0
− − − − −	0	0	0	1	0	0	2	1	0	0
+ + + − +	0	0	0	1	0	0	0	0	0	0
− − − + +	0	0	0	1	1	0	0	0	0	0
+ + − − −	0	0	0	1	0	0	0	0	0	0
− + − − −	0	0	0	0	0	0	0	0	1	1
− + − − +	0	0	0	0	0	4	0	4	6	6
− − − − +	0	0	0	0	0	2	0	0	16	21
Totals	37	82	50	111	32	66	107	55	26	35

Five places in the DNA were treated with different restriction enzymes (see p. 266). If the DNA was cut – that is, the appropriate sequence of bases was present – the site is marked with a plus; if not, with a minus. This gives a *haplotype*, a combination of closely associated genetic variants; a 'genetic surname' that might be, for example, + + − − − or + + + − +.

There are four common types in the human population as a whole, with various rarer combinations that may have derived from them more recently. Their distribution divides into an African and a non-African branch. This may reflect an ancient split between the population of Africa and that of the rest of the world – possibly dating to the emergence of modern humans from their native continent a little more than 100 000 years ago. If we assume that each of the four ancestral haplotypes was equally common in ancient Africa, then the shift in frequencies can be used to calculate the size of the bottleneck in the emerging population (see main text). This calculation is full of assumptions, but is at least partly supported by recent information in the geographic patterns of other genes such as those of mitochondria and in haplotypes of other nuclear genes, such as that for human growth hormone.

per cent, helped possibly by a series of bottlenecks as they spread through the American continent.

Genetic variations in modern human populations can hint at bottlenecks that may have occurred even longer ago in our evolutionary history. One indicator of genetic variation in a population is its average *heterozygosity*: the probability that an individual has two different alleles at a locus (such as an enzyme locus) or a series of loci. Australian Aborigines have low heterozygosity. This is probably the result of a bottleneck at the onset of the colonisation of Australia, perhaps 60000 years ago. Some caution is called for here, as Australian Aborigines have always been rare: in 1770, there were probably less than 500000 of them. We cannot be certain that their lack of variation was caused by a bottleneck at the earliest time, but it is very likely to have arisen from a low population size at some time in their history.

A comparison of heterozygosities over the world points to the striking fact that Africa is the most genetically variable continent. This itself implies that Africa is the birthplace of modern *Homo sapiens* – as indeed is suggested by the fossil record – and that there was loss of variation as people migrated from Africa to the rest of the world. If this is true, then there was a bottleneck at the very beginning of the colonisation of Eurasia. There is now some genetic evidence in favour of this view from mitochondria (see p. 320).

Other parts of our genetic heritage also point to Africa as the cradle of modern humankind and provide a chance to calculate the size of the first emigrant population to leave that continent. A survey of the non-coding region of DNA close to the β-globin genes shows that there are four dif-ferent and ancient variants common to most human populations. However, their distribution is not random; three are found at similar frequencies among all non-African population whereas the fourth is found only among Africans. Assuming that the emerging population did indeed lose their African variants in transit, it is possible to estimate the size of the bottleneck that was involved.

This calculation suggests a severe bottleneck: say, six breeding individuals for 70 years (although a less-marked bottleneck for a longer period would also produce the same result). Given that only adult humans are reproductively active, and some may have had more than one mate at a time, this corresponds to an actual population size of around 50 individuals, which is still an astonishingly small number to be the ancestors of all non-African humans. Even alternative estimates of the site of the bottleneck – for example, roughly 500 people for 200 years – are startling enough. It is important to realise that this argument depends on assuming that natural selection does not affect the various types differentially inside and outside Africa. In our present state of ignorance, this assumption seems a reasonable one.

The probability of extinction of any organism increases as population size decreases. Humans may have once been very rare, very close to extinction; perhaps we are lucky to be here at all.

Shahin Rouhani

Steve Jones

See also 'The nature of evolution' (p. 9), 'Evolution of early humans' (p. 241), 'Distribution of genetic diseases in human populations' (p. 288) and 'The dispersion of modern humans' (p. 389)

Natural selection in humans

The origin of life was an improbable event, although once it had arisen it was remarkably tenacious and infinitely adaptable. Life's attributes are due to *natural selection*: to inherited differences in the chances of passing on genes. *Mutation*, the random appearance of new genetic variation, cannot itself lead to progress. For organisms to adapt to a new environment, some mutations must increase the chances of survival and reproduction of their carriers.

Humans are in many ways more adapted to the vicissitudes of their environment than are other primates. As Darwin pointed out, evolutionary progress in humans has, just as in other creatures, taken place through selection. Some of our ancestors carried genes that increased their ability to survive and reproduce. These genes became more common in subsequent generations. Our rapid evolution reflects the action of strong natural selection. Nowadays, we think of ourselves as in control of our own biological future. It does seem as if some of the forces that drive genetic change – such as inherited differences in the ability to avoid predators, disease or starvation – have been held at bay. What sorts of selection have acted on humans? Is there still any opportunity for it to do so?

Selection is most likely to occur if more individuals are born than can be supported by the resources available. This is the situation for much of humanity in the Third World today, and for nearly all of it in the past. The chances of surviving to adulthood often depend on an individual's genetic constitution. Selection can act not only through differences in survival but also because of differences in the ability of survivors to reproduce. Individual reproductive differences of this kind are particularly important agents of selection in animals, like ourselves, who produce relatively few young. Even today, there are great differences in individual fecundity. The number of children per woman varies from none to 10 or more; and differences in mating success among males, although harder to measure, may be even greater. There are also inherited differences in the age of puberty that might affect the rate of reproduction. Longevity also runs in families. Any of these differences in survival or reproduction that are under genetic control give the opportunity for natural selection.

We know less about natural selection upon ourselves than we do about its action on fruit flies. Nevertheless, a great deal of selection of one kind or another has been identified in humans.

Directional selection

The propagation of one genotype at the expense of others leads to evolutionary change. Change is much more inter-esting than is stability, and more is known about directional than about other modes of selection. It may, however, be relatively unusual.

The lineage leading to modern humans has undergone rapid and consistent changes in brain size, leg length and many other characters over the past few tens of thousands of years. The exact nature of the selective agent is not known, but there must have been a considerable advantage to those individuals with relatively large brains, part of which was probably involved with the development of language and of society. Although we can only speculate about the nature of past selection, geographic patterning of the genetic differences among living populations (clines) is much easier to study. They often reflect the action of a selective force. Much of our knowledge of directional selection in humans comes from studies of how gene frequencies vary from place to place.

Climate

There are some striking geographical patterns for genes controlling visible characters. Such trends may be associated with parallel changes in the environment that exert a selective effect. Many involve climate. Most tropical peoples have slim bodies and long limbs, whereas those from colder climates are more compact. Humans lose most of their metabolic heat from the body surface, much of it by sweating. An individual can lose more than 2 litres of water in an hour in this way. The body shape of peoples living in hot and relatively humid places increases the ratio of skin surface to body mass, whereas that of Arctic peoples does the opposite. The skeletal proportions of early *Homo sapiens* resemble those of modern tropical populations, suggesting that the first humans evolved in hot climates and that the squat shape of Inuit (Eskimos) and others have emerged in a few tens of thousands of years of climatic selection. Although it is dangerously easy to produce plausible stories, other geographical changes in body structure might also have a climatic basis. Curly African hair might help to lose heat by evaporation of sweat, while the long, fine Arabic nose could possibly be favoured in dry climates where water loss from the lungs must be reduced.

The most striking geographical variation in human appearance is in skin colour. An explanation based on resistance to heat does not work: black objects heat up more rapidly in the sun than do white, and experiments carried out by the US army show that black soldiers become exhausted on sunny days before whites. Malignant melanoma is a skin cancer whose incidence increases with exposure to sunlight. It is much commoner in whites than in blacks. However, it usually kills after sufferers have

Most tropical peoples, such as the Samburu of northern Kenya (left), have slim bodies and long limbs. A more compact shape characterises those in colder climates, such as the Inuit of Greenland (right).

passed on their genes, so that differential resistance to cancer is not an effective mode of selection on skin-colour genes.

More important is the effect of skin pigment on vitamin balance. We obtain most of our vitamins from food, but vitamin D – whose absence leads to rickets – can be synthesised from the action of ultraviolet light on a derivative of cholesterol. The rate of synthesis depends on the amount of ultraviolet light that passes through the skin, and hence on the intensity of pigmentation. African skin transmits only about a tenth of the ultraviolet light that can pass through the skin of a white person, and a black exposed to ultraviolet light can synthesise much less vitamin D than that produced by a white. Individuals who carried genes for reduced skin pigment may have been favoured as humans spread from the tropics to cool and cloudy parts of the world. It is still unclear why black skins are favoured in hot places. Although excess vitamin D is harmful, it is unlikely that even very pale-skinned people could synthesise enough to cause damage. It may be that dark pigment protects other vitamins from being broken down by ultraviolet rays.

Diet

Diet may also play a part in determining the distribution of genes. In most mammals, and in most peoples of the world, adults cannot digest fresh milk because they lack the milk-

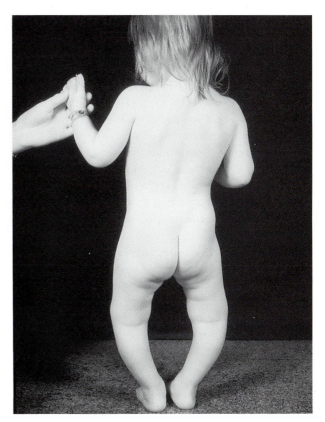

Lack of vitamin D causes rickets in children. The vitamin is synthesised by the action of ultraviolet light on the skin; and hence depends on the intensity of pigmentation.

digesting enzyme lactase. Milk contains a sugar, lactose, which is broken down by infants into glucose and galactose and absorbed. Only in Europe and a few other places does this ability persist into adult life. Elsewhere, the gene for lactase is switched off in late childhood. Persistent lactose absorption is present in cultures that have a history of rearing cattle and hence of drinking milk in adulthood. For example, some of the patches of high frequency of lactose tolerance in West Africa are in populations such as the Fulani, who, unlike their neighbours, keep cattle.

Disease

Disease is an important agent of directional natural selection. There are many cases in which individuals of different genotype are more or less susceptible to infection. Some of these reflect differences in the ability of the pathogens to invade cells with different cell-surface antigens. This can lead to an association between a gene and a disease. The Duffy blood-group locus has two alleles, one of which (Fy⁻) is common only in West Africa. Its distribution is associated with one form of malaria caused by the parasite *Plasmodium*. The parasite recognises the Duffy antigen and uses it as an attachment site before burrowing through the membrane of the red blood cell. It is less able to attach to the Fy⁻ antigen than to the products of other alleles. There are several associations of cell-surface antigens with disease (see table, opposite page); for example, carriers of blood group B may be relatively resistant to plague and this might possibly explain why it is common in areas of past epidemics.

Natural selection of this kind also operates inside the cell. One form of an enzyme involved in energy metabolism, glucose-6-phosphate dehydrogenase⁻ (G6PD⁻), is commonest in malarious areas. Individuals with the normal and the mutant form of this enzyme are resistant to infection, as their red blood cells are unusually sensitive to the malaria parasite's waste products and are rapidly destroyed, killing the *Plasmodium* at the same time. There is a tie with natural selection by diet here, as carriers of this variant cannot metabolise broad beans, and suffer from a condition known as favism should they eat them. When the antimalarial drug primaquine was first used, G6PD⁻ individuals became ill after treatment as the enzyme is also involved in drug breakdown. The various ways in which the red blood pigment haemoglobin evolves in response to selection by malaria are described in Chapter 1.1 (p. 14).

Although selection by climate, by diet and by disease is responsible for many geographical changes in gene frequency, it is important to realise that such patterns can also arise at random. Geographical change is certainly not in itself a proof of the action of natural selection.

Stabilising selection

Life is characterised by stability rather than by change. Many mutations disrupt a well-adapted system and are re-

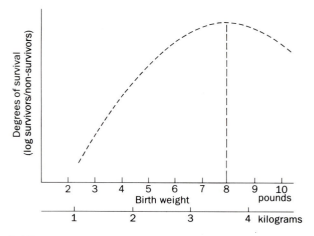

Stabilising selection for birth weight in humans. In this study of several thousand births, about one baby in 20 died in the first month. Those below the optimum birth weight of about 8 pounds (3.6 kilograms) were less likely to survive, as were those who weighed more than the optimum. Most of the mortality is associated with stabilising selection for birth weight. This work was carried out 50 years ago; since then, childhood mortality has been much reduced, and the strength of stabilising selection is far less than it used to be.

moved by selection. *Stabilising selection* retains the existing value of a character. It is the commonest form of selection, but it has not been widely studied.

Most babies weigh about 3.6 kilograms (8 pounds) at birth. Those below this weight survive less well and, more surprisingly, babies heavier than the average also have an increased death rate. Natural selection acts in a stabilising fashion. Much of the mortality in the first year after birth is associated with such selection. Stabilising selection also exists in adults. Individuals well above or below the average for height and intelligence pass on their genes less successfully than those near the mean, perhaps because they find it more difficult to find a mate.

Mutations that deviate from the norm often interfere with biochemical processes and are rigorously removed by selection. Much of the body is made up of the building blocks of cells, which must fit accurately with each other. This is true for the fibrous protein – collagen – that makes up much of our skin, the crystallin proteins in the eye and the cellular factories of metabolism in mitochondria and ribosomes. Any mutation that changes the shape of such molecules will almost always be at a disadvantage as it reduces their ability to interact with each other or with their substrate. Stabilising selection of this kind can be a very conservative force.

Stabilising selection is a powerful agent that leads to genetic homogeneity. To explain how genetic variation is maintained in the face of such widespread censorship by natural selection is one of the main problems of population genetics.

Natural selection for genetic diversity

There are several selective mechanisms that, unlike directional or stabilising selection, maintain genetic polymorphism. One of the most widely discussed is *heterozyote advantage*: the situation in which individuals carrying two different alleles at a locus are more fit than are those who have two copies of the same allele. The classic case of heterozygote advantage is the maintenance of the sickle-cell gene in places where malaria is endemic.

As we have seen, individuals who have the allele for normal haemoglobin and that for sickle-cell are resistant to malaria; the heterozygotes are at an advantage. A more subtle form of the same mechanism may be at work for other recessive genetic diseases. Parents who have had an affected child may show *reproductive compensation*: they have more children subsequently than do other members of the population, thus ensuring that copies of the defective gene are passed on. However, heterozygote advantage has a cost: the appearance, each generation, of individuals who are unfit because they are homozygous – for example, AA and SS children in malarious areas. It is hard to see how humans could afford to maintain many polymorphisms in this way and the idea of strong heterozygote advantage at many variable gene loci, beguiling though it is, has few supporters.

There are less expensive ways in which selection can maintain genetic diversity. One of these is *frequency-dependent selection*. An allele is advantageous as long as it is rare, but loses this advantage as it becomes common. The associations between diseases and histocompatibility types may reflect a history of this kind in our parasites and ourselves.

Cell-surface antigens are part of the body's system of combating invaders. An infectious agent usually carries a cell-surface cue distinct from those of its host, and can hence be identified and attacked by the immune system. A mutation that allows the parasite to copy a host antigen will be at an advantage as it evades this defensive mechanism, and will spread among the parasite population. The disease is then no longer recognised as foreign by individuals carrying certain cell-surface antigens and can infect them. There will then be selection in favour of any mutation in the host's cell-surface antigens that allows the parasite once again to be recognised as foreign. This sets off an evolutionary race between host and parasite, which can lead to 'gene for gene' evolution – every mutation to a successful mimic in the parasite is countered by an equivalent to a new cell-surface type in the host. New mutations are hence profitable when they are rare, but are less so as they become common. Frequency-dependent selection of this kind is a potent means of promoting genetic diversity.

The neutral theory of evolution

Although natural selection can be a powerful force, there is so much variation at the molecular level that it is hard to see how more than a small proportion of our genes could be influenced by it. How could a population afford the constant loss of relatively unfit individuals if selection is simultaneously at work at tens of thousands of variable gene loci? And how could selection influence those thousands of variants in parts of the DNA – such as introns and repeated sequences – that produce no proteins? Most molecular polymorphism (which means most genetic polymorphism) is probably little influenced by selection. Instead, it arises by mutation, and is lost by chance.

At the molecular level, natural selection acts mainly as evolution's policeman, removing mutations that deviate from a functional norm, but ignoring those that do not interfere with the orderly function of a well-adapted system. Only very occasionally is a new mutant accepted as an improvement. Such unusual eposodes of selection lead to adaptive evolution. This so-called *neutral theory of evolution* predicts that evolutionary change at the molecular level proceeds at a steady rate, so that there is a molecular evolutionary clock which allows the dates of divergence of one lineage from another to be inferred by comparing their genes. Like all beautiful theories, it has its critics; it is far too soon to dismiss natural selection at the molecular level.

Natural selection has been displaced from its Darwinian role as the engine of all evolutionary change. Nevertheless, there is much evidence for strong selection acting in modern human populations, and selection has certainly driven most of the changes in form and behaviour that differentiate us from our ancestors and from our relatives.

Steve Jones

Some associations between histocompatibility antigens and disease in European populations. The chances of contracting certain diseases may be more than 50 times greater for those inheriting a particular set of cell-surface antigens

Disease*	Histocompatibility antigen	Percentage with antigen		Relative risk
		Affected	Normal	
Joints				
Ankylosing spondylitis	B27	89	9	69.1
Reiter disease	B27	80	9	37.1
Gastrointestinal tract				
Coeliac disease	B8	68	22	7.6
Skin				
Psoriasis vulgaris	B17	19	7	5.3
	B13	19	5	4.1
	B37	7	2	3.9
Connective tissue				
Juvenile rheumatoid arthritis	B27	25	9	3.9
Rheumatoid arthritis	DR4	68	25	3.8
Systemic lupus erythematosus	B8	40	20	2.7
Endocrine system				
Juvenile diabetes mellitus	DR4	51	25	3.6
	DR3	46	22	3.3
Nervous system				
Myasthenia gravis	B8	44	19	3.3
Multiple sclerosis	DR2	51	27	2.7

* Included are all associations between histocompatibility antigens and diseases in at least 600 patients from a dozen different studies and with a combined relative risk of at least 2.7. Relative risk is the risk of developing the disease when one has the antigen compared with that for individuals without it.

See also 'The nature of evolution' (p. 9), 'Human adaptations to the physical environment' (p. 46), 'Mutation and human evolution' (p. 269) and 'Bottlenecks in human evolution' (p. 281)

Distribution of genetic diseases in human populations

Hereditary diseases occur in human populations for a variety of reasons, some biological and some cultural. Why do some diseases occur in preference to others in some parts of the world? The following factors need to be taken into account:

- the kinds of mutations that lead to the disease;
- their mode of inheritance;
- the mutation rate;
- the strength of selection against the disease; and
- the structure of the population – large, random-mating populations or an isolate (a relatively small population with much inbreeding)

The distribution of genetic diseases in modern human populations can be understood in terms of natural selection acting at the present or in the past, of random (and often unknown) events in our history, and of the interaction of genes with environmental factors that may themselves be difficult to identify.

Mutation rate

Diseases whose incidence depends mainly on mutation rate include those in which the genetic anomaly is manifested in all or nearly all instances, and prevents or greatly restricts the reproduction of its victims. This group includes major chromosomal aberrations, the incidence of which in newborns can be up to about six per thousand. Examples of conditions where there is an extra chromosome include Down's syndrome (trisomy of the small autosome 21), with an incidence of about one or two per thousand, and Klinefelter's syndrome (karyotype 47 with three sex chromosomes, XXY), which has a frequency of a little more than one per thousand.

Structural chromosomal aberrations are much rarer than the numerical ones but there are many more types. They can lead to severe, complex birth defects with mental retardation – for example, the *cri du chat* sydrome caused by a deletion at the short arm of chromosome 5. The chromosomal aberrations observed at birth are a small fraction only of all those present at fertilisation, as most are eliminated during pregnancy. A substantial fraction shows up as 'spontaneous miscarriages'; more than 50 per cent of embryos spontaneously aborted in the first 3 months of pregnancy carry a chromosomal aberration.

The second group of conditions, the incidence of which is determined mainly by mutation rate, are dominant and X-linked recessive diseases that are so severe that they

In the dominantly inherited type of achondroplasia, growth at the ends of the long bones and at the base of the skull is stunted. The result is a type of disproportionate dwarfism characterised by short limbs and a normal-sized head and body. Somerset (aged 11), who has the condition and is the smaller of the two boys here, is 2 years older than his brother Sebastian.

impair reproduction of their carriers. An example of a dominant disease is achondroplasia, a type of dwarfism, in which arms and legs are especially short owing to defective growth of the bones. Another example is neurofibromatosis – a condition in which the body of a patient may be covered by many tumours containing connective as well as neuronal tissue, whereas the skin of others may show only a few so-called *cafe-au-lait* spots.

The best-known X-linked recessive condition of this kind is Duchenne muscular dystrophy, which leads to death around the twentieth year of life. Such patients usually do not reproduce at all. Another example is haemophilia A, which is caused by a mutation within the gene for the clotting factor VIII. Factor VIII therapy has reduced the selective disadvantage of haemophilia A mutations in recent years. This will lead to an increase in the incidence and prevalence of this condition, unless the mutation rate is reduced, or natural selection is replaced by artificial selection through genetic counselling and prenatal diagnosis. The mutant gene, one copy of which was present in Queen Victoria, has, however, disappeared from the European Royal family.

A third X-linked condition with a high mutation rate is the far(X) syndrome, a type of mental retardation, which is even more common among males than Duchenne disease or haemophilia A. There is some evidence that its high prevalence may be caused by a combination of a high mutation rate with a selective advantage of female carriers.

Molecular evidence suggests that Duchenne muscular dystrophy, haemophilia and the far(X) syndrome may have relatively higher mutation rates because of the unusual length and complex structure of the genes producing them. For example, the dystrophin gene, mutations of which lead to Duchenne disease, is about 2000 kilobases (2 million base pairs) long.

Altogether, more than 1000 dominant and about 300 X-linked diseases are known. Their overall incidence at birth, including those leading to disease later in life, is estimated at about 8 to 10 per thousand, so that the continuing input of new mutations is an important source of genetic disease in all human populations.

Random processes

In some of the more common dominant diseases, such as Huntington's chorea, there is little obvious selective disadvantage under present-day conditions and very few, if any, new mutants have been observed. The relatively high prevalence of these diseases in some places (such as South Wales) might be caused, at least in part, by some selective advantage in the past. In addition, random shifts of gene frequencies, such as genetic drift and founder effects, may have played a part.

Past selection and random change have been decisive for the incidence of autosomal recessive diseases, of which more than 600 are known. Most of them are rare; heterozygous unaffected carriers are hence much more common than the clinically affected homozygotes. For example, many more people carry the cystic fibrosis gene than have the disease. Similarly, phenylketonuria (PKU) – where there is a defect of protein metabolism that causes an excess of the amino acid phenylalanine in the blood and severe mental retardation – affects about one in every 10000 newborn Caucasians in Europe and North America. It can be concluded from the Hardy–Weinberg law (Box 1) that, in a randomly mating population, about 1 in 50 individuals is heterozygous for PKU. Hence, heterozygotes are roughly 200 times more common than homozygotes and only about 1 in 100 copies of the PKU allele is found in homozygotes. The disease is therefore subject to strong natural selection. Its frequency may then be determined more by random fluctuations within the mostly small and relatively isolated population groups from which all human populations have originated, although small selective advantages or disadvantages of heterozygotes may also be involved.

The frequencies of such diseases show great variations among populations. This contrasts with the dominant and X-linked conditions mentioned above, which are maintained by an equilibrium between mutation rate and strong selection, and which tend to show similar incidences in different populations.

An unusually high incidence of particular autosomal recessive diseases is conspicuous in population groups that have lived in relative isolation. An example is the Finnish-speaking population of Finland where some recessive diseases commonly observed in most other populations, such as PKU, are virtually absent. However, in this small population, several diseases affecting the skin, teeth, hair, eyes, kidneys and other organs (e.g. cornea plana congenita and congenital chloride diarrhoea) that have almost never been observed anywhere else are relatively common. What seems to have happened is that such genes were present in very small groups that subsequently grew in numbers without much intermingling with other populations; this *founder effect* may lead to appreciable gene frequencies, and to correspondingly high frequencies of homozygotes.

There is one important systematic difference in the incidence of autosomal recessive diseases between industrialised countries and more traditional populations in other parts of the world: in general, in 'modern' populations, recessive diseases are much rarer. This is because the proportion of consanguineous marriages, such as between first cousins, has gone down during the past century from several per cent to a few per thousand. As relatives have a fraction of their genes in common by descent from a common ancestor, there is always a certain probability that a gene will become homozygous in an individual because it is transmitted from a common ancestor through two different paths (see Box 2).

What happens if in a certain population the fraction of consanguineous matings suddenly decreases? This will lead immediately to a decrease of homozygotes and hence of affected individuals. This is what has happened in 'modern' populations within the past 100 years or so. In the long run, however (and assuming that mutation rates remain unchanged), the number of mutant genes and of heterozygotes will increase because a smaller fraction is eliminated in homozygotes. This process is slow, and needs hundreds of generations before a new equilibrium is reached. Most present-day populations originate from a mixture of ancient, relatively isolated subgroups. There is always a chance that in such subgroups a few genes will have become relatively common, and others relatively rare, through genetic drift. These genes will usually differ among subgroups. Once the groups start mixing, frequencies of the rare recessives at each locus will decline.

Modern populations are hence enjoying an unusually low incidence not only of autosomal recessive diseases, but also of other genes that are deleterious in homozygotes.

Balancing selection

In populations of some tropical and subtropical countries, a few hereditary blood diseases are common, even though

1. THE HARDY–WEINBERG RULE: HOW GENES BEHAVE IN POPULATIONS

Imagine a shipwreck – or, to exercise the imagination further, two simultaneous shipwrecks – on a fertile, remote and deserted island. The 60 passengers in the first ship come from a typical English village, the 40 in the second from the Republic of Albinia, where, for no obvious reason, the entire population consists of albinos.

As there are no other distractions, the castaways mate with each other and have children. Their desire to mate is such that the choice of spouse is made without reference to where the partner came from – that is, to whether he or she is albino or has normal skin pigmentation. What will happen to the albino gene in future generations?

It might seem obvious that, because normal pigmentation is dominant to albinism, then somehow the normal allele A is 'stronger' than the recessive a, and will in time spread to replace it. This argument was accepted almost without discussion in the very early days of genetics. However, as the mathematicians G.H. Hardy and W. Weinberg showed, it is wrong.

Normal or AA individuals make up 0.6 (or 60%) of the castaways; 0.4 (or 40%) of them are albinos, aa. We can make a diagram of how their genes will mix in the first generation of mating:

	Sperm		
	AA 0.6	Aa 0	aa 0.4
Egg AA 0.6	0.36	0	0 24
Egg Aa 0	0	0	0
Egg aa 0.4	0.24	0	0.16

The results of these matings are:

♂ ♀	F₁
AA × AA	AA homozygotes
AA × aa	all Aa heterozygotes
aa × aa	all aa homozygotes

Adding up the squares, in the next generation the frequencies of the different genotypes will be:

$$AA = 0.36$$
$$Aa = 0.24 + 0.24 = 0.48$$
$$aa = 0.16$$

The frequencies of the alleles A and a will be:

$$A = 0.36 + \text{half of } 0.48 = 0.6$$
$$a = 0.16 + \text{half of } 0.48 = 0.4$$

In other words, the frequency of the alleles has not changed, but the frequencies of the genotypes has. If we plug the new frequencies of AA, Aa and aa into the same diagram for the next generation of mating, then the frequencies of neither the allele nor the genotype will change; the population is at equilibrium – the Hardy–Weinberg equilibrium.

This sum shows that in the absence of any process such as selection or mutation, allele frequencies do not change: the fact that normal pigmentation is dominant to albino does not mean that it will spread. It has other important implications, and works for any frequencies of two alleles, as can be seen from some simple algebra. Let us say that the frequency of the allele A is p and of allele a is q. If there are only two alleles, then $p + q$ must equal 1, or 100%.

Assuming that individuals mate at random, we can treat the population as a pool of genes combining with each other to produce fertilised eggs in the proportions p and q:

	Sperm	
	A(p)	a(q)
Egg A(p)	AA(p^2)	Aa(pq)
Egg a(q)	Aa(pq)	aa(q^2)

That is, after one generation of random mating, the frequencies of the genotypes will be:

AA	Aa	aa
p^2	$2pq$	q^2

Furthermore, these frequencies will persist in future generations.

This simple equation has some very useful properties. For example, if we have a gene locus with a dominant allele A and a recessive allele a in a population, we can distinguish only two visible phenotypes: recessive homozygotes aa (albinos in our example) and a class of individuals with the phenotype of the dominant allele A (with normal skin pigment), which will be a mixture of AA and Aa.

The ratio of the three genetic classes is particularly important when looking at harmful recessive alleles for human genetic disease (many of which are rare). The Hardy–Weinberg rule allows us to work out how many heterozygotes, or carriers, there are for any recessive gene in comparison to the number of homozygotes – those affected by the recessive condition. The results are sometimes surprising.

Frequency of homozygotes (q^2)	Frequency of heterozygotes ($2pq$)	Ratio
1 in 10	1 in 2.3	4.3 to 1
1 in 100	1 in 5.6	18 to 1
1 in 1000	1 in 16	61 to 1
1 in 10 000	1 in 51	198 to 1
1 in 100 000	1 in 159	630 to 1
1 in 1 000 000	1 in 501	1998 to 1

The table shows that for typical human harmful recessive alleles (with a frequency of 1 in 5000 or lower) there are far more copies of the damaged allele present in carriers – who are unaware of their genotype – than in the homozygotes who suffer from the disease. This means that simplistic eugenic ideas of getting rid of genetic disease by preventing sufferers from reproducing are of no value.

Steve Jones

homozygotes are severely affected by a haemolytic anaemia. For example, in Africa south of the Sahara and north of the Zambezi River, the sickle-cell gene (Hb^s) is so common that, in some ethnic groups of eastern Africa, a notable proportion (up to 5 to 6 per cent) of all newborns are homozygous and suffer from sickle-cell anaemia. The sickle-cell gene also has a relatively high frequency in some Mediterranean populations, in Arabia, and in parts of southern India (see p. 16) All these occurrences probably go back to a single mutation, although some geneticists claim a triple origin in three African countries on the basis of studies of the DNA sequence associated with the Hb^s gene in each population. There are several other Hb variants.

These local incidences of physiologically related blood diseases suggest a common explanation. This explanation is now known: heterozygotes for the sickle-cell gene – and probably also for the other common haemoglobin variants – have an increased resistance to malaria, especially its most dangerous variety caused by *Plasmodium falciparum*. In an environment where several per cent of all children die from malaria, even a slight resistance to this infection in

2. FIRST-COUSIN MARRIAGES

First cousins have one pair of grandparents in common. These grandparents together have four alleles for each gene locus. For each of the alleles, there is a probability of 1 in 64 of being transmitted through both parents to a child from a first-cousin marriage, giving a combined probability of $4 \times 1/64 = 1/16$ for these four alleles together. Hence, there is a 1 in 16 probability that a child from a first-cousin marriage will become homozygous for such an allele; or, to put in a different way, the fraction of its genes that have become homozygous because of their common origin is 1/16.

This fraction is called the inbreeding coefficient, F. With gene frequencies p for the (common, dominant) allele A and q for the (rare, recessive) allele a, the ratio between homozygotes and heterozygotes is $q^2/(2pq)$; among children from consanguineous marriages, it is

$$\frac{q^2 + Fpq}{2(1 - F)pq}$$

The smaller the frequency q, the more this ratio deviates from that expected with random mating; in other words, there are more homozygotes but fewer heterozygotes with first-cousin marriages than with random mating.

This explains why among parents of children with autosomal recessive diseases, consanguineous marriages are more frequent than in the general population. The rarer the recessive gene, the greater will be this difference.

F. Vogel

heterozygotes is bound to create a substantial selective advantage – enough to compensate for the loss of mutant genes due to the severe illness of homozygotes.

Such *balanced polymorphisms* (where the gene loss in homozygotes is compensated for by a selective advantage of heterozygotes) are well known to population geneticists working with other species such as insects. In humans, other instances probably exist. One example, involving variants of the X-linked enzyme glucose-6-phosphate dehydrogenase or G6PD (which give carriers increased resistance to malaria), is described in Chapter 7.6. In contrast to individuals carrying the variant haemoglobins, those carrying G6PD-variants are, as a rule, healthy; they suffer from haemolytic episodes only when exposed to oxidising drugs (such as the antimalarial drug primaquine) or certain foods.

It is possible that similar mechanisms may have operated to increase gene frequencies of other autosomal recessive diseases. In the Ashkenazi Jewish population of eastern Europe, for example, three recessive disorders have attained unusually high incidences: Tay-Sachs, Gaucher's and Niemann-Pick diseases. All three affect the metabolism of lipids in the body because of deficiencies of lysosomal enzymes that normally degrade biological macromolecules, and they lead to progressive deterioration of brain function. The history of isolation and inbreeding among the Ashkenazi Jews offers excellent conditions for genetic

drift and founder effects, but it is a strange coincidence that diseases with similar causes have become common in the same group. For example, many different Gaucher mutations have been identified. For these hereditary conditions, therefore, a common heterozygotic advantage rather than mere chance might be involved.

Environmental influences

Genetic factors are involved in many common anomalies and diseases: congenital malformations, 'constitutional' diseases such as coronary heart disease or diabetes, and mental disorders. The prevalence of such diseases often varies from one population to the next, and even within the same populations at different times. In Western Europe, for example, coronary heart disease and diabetes were rare in the years during and after World War II – probably as a result of food shortages.

Classical epidemiology is mainly concerned with such environmental influences; but interaction of these influences with genetic mechanisms is probably important in deciding whether an individual remains healthy. Evolutionary mechanisms such as those that apply to simple monogenic diseases might therefore operate even in diseases such as these. For example, genotypes leading to diabetes in middle or advanced age in today's living conditions might once have provided a more efficient way of utilising food in periods of scarcity and might therefore have become more common. In European populations, diseases such as dermatitis, asthma and hay fever are common; they have a strong genetic basis. There is now good evidence that such genotypes afford protection against intestinal worm infestation – a common cause of diarrhoea and anaemia in areas with low standards of hygiene, including most European populations up to the end of the last century.

F. Vogel

Scanning electron micrograph of sickled and normal red blood cells.

See also 'The nature of evolution' (p. 9), 'Principles of genetics' (p. 255), 'Mutation and human evolution' (p. 269), 'Human chromosomes' (p. 274), 'Bottlenecks in human evolution' (p. 281), 'Natural selection in humans' (p. 284) and 'The evolutionary future of humankind' (p. 439)

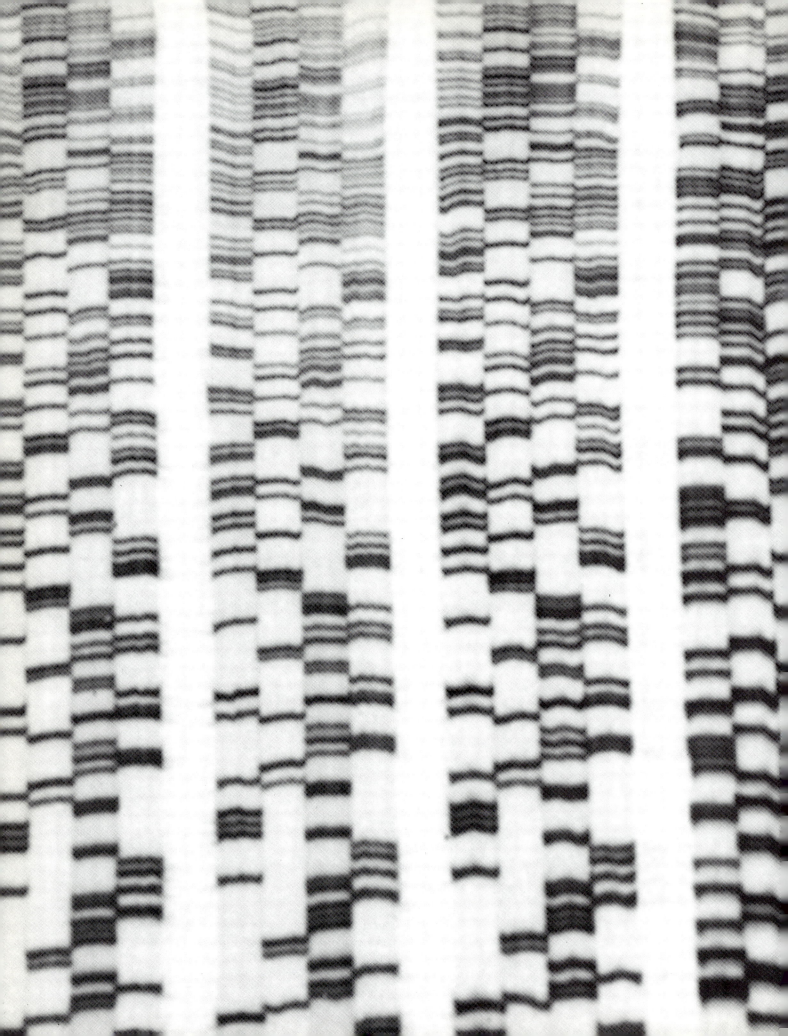

Part Eight

Genetic clues of relatedness

Much of biology involves tracing the patterns of relatedness among living creatures and inferring when they last shared a common ancestor. Long before Darwin, the great systematist Linnaeus had realised that the living world showed signs of order and could be arranged into groups of greater or lesser degrees of affinity. The whole of taxonomy — the classification of plants and animals — depends on this assumption. Taxonomy by itself is little more than stamp-collecting: sorting objects into categories. Darwin's great contribution was to realise that there must be a mechanism for producing regularity in the living world. The mechanism he suggested was evolution — 'descent with modification', to use his own phrase. Much of *The Origin of Species* is devoted to proving that the more similar a pair of species the more recently they must have shared a common ancestor. Structural resemblance, Darwin argued, must prove shared descent.

Although Darwin had no idea of how inherited information was transmitted from generation to generation there are some intriguing genetical hints of shared ancestry in *The Origin*. He mentions, for example, how stripes like those in a zebra may appear in young horses. However, not until the development of genetics was there any real understanding of what this meant, and until very recently we had almost no real idea of the degree to which we share a common heritage with our primate relatives.

The basic anatomical plan of humans and chimpanzees is clearly more similar than is, for example, that of humans and lemurs. However, just what this means is confused by the difficulty of measuring the degree of similarity of a general design and uncertainties about how much it reflects an adjustment to the specialised lifestyle of each creature, rather than a common descent. What we need are cues of affinity unaffected as far as possible by the need to adapt to the environment. Natural selection eliminates history; it can quickly obscure the record of shared ancestry by retaining favourable genes and removing others.

Molecular biology has helped to solve this problem by providing thousands of hints of shared ancestry hidden in our genes. Comparing these in different species gives some idea of how much they share a common evolutionary history. Differences among species arise through the accumulation of different mutations in each evolving lineage; and if — as many claim — this happens at a constant rate, then it gives a 'clock' that can show the sequence in which each species last shared an ancestor with others. In a group whose fossil record is good enough to allow the date of this common ancestor to be measured, the genetic divergence of its descendants can be used to calibrate the molecular clock and date the separation of the other members of the group (**8.1**). Molecular biology has shown us that we are all living fossils; we all contain evidence of our ancestry.

Sequences of bacterial DNA prepared by gel electrophoresis, showing the bands in four tracks.

There are many genetic indicators that can be used in this way. Some — such as the cues of individual identity present on the cells of all animals with an immune system — have been known for many years, but are still giving us valuable information on patterns of relatedness (**8.3**). Others have come to light recently. The physical units of inheritance, the chromosomes, of humans and other primates share much of their structure, but the details of change tell us a great deal about how the various species diverged (**8.2**).

Proteins are the products of genes, and a mass of information is available on their patterns of change in a wide variety of primates (**8.4**). It is now becoming possible to look at evolutionary change in the DNA itself, either by comparing overall levels of structural similarity (**8.5**) or by the painstaking analysis of the sequences of segments of DNA (**8.6**).

As we learn more about divergence at the molecular level the idea of an evolutionary clock that always ticks at the same rate is beginning to look naive; perhaps because natural selection acts on most of the DNA and proteins as well as on body form. However, the most encouraging fact to emerge from molecular evolution is just how well its results fit with what we know from fossils and from comparative anatomy. Although there is still plenty of disagreement about the details of the patterns of change — much of which is manifest in the following chapters — Darwin would have been delighted by their contents.

Measuring relatedness

In Chapter 8.3, Vincent Sarich describes how in 1967, when he and Allan Wilson published a molecular timescale for human evolution, the fossil hominoid *Ramapithecus* (now *Sivapithecus*) was still widely considered a hominid, and therefore a direct ancestor of human beings. Since *Ramapithecus* had been dated at around 14 million years ago, the lineage leading to modern humans must have diverged from that leading to the great apes at least by then.

Such an early divergence provided a respectable span of time for the development of human uniqueness. However, Sarich and Wilson's timescale suggested that a figure of some 5 million years was more appropriate for the separation of the human lineage, and their evolutionary tree implied that the three lineages leading to humans, chimpanzees and gorillas all separated at about that time. Sarich and Wilson's work therefore underlined two important issues in human evolution: the nature of the relationships between humans and the great apes, and the timing of their divergence. Both remain controversial.

Sarich and Wilson used immunological techniques to enable them to compare the molecules of a blood protein, serum albumin, between various hominoid and other primates. The most important feature of their approach is that it was indirect, with similarity between protein molecules assessed via the intermediate means of antibodies to their structure. How well an indirect technique measures similarity is controversial but the immunological approach does enable comparisons among species to be carried out relatively easily.

Sarich and Wilson used only a single protein, and hence compared only a minute proportion of the genetic complement, or genome, of the animals concerned. The most controversial element in their work was the way in which the date of divergence of the human lineage was calculated. Because it was widely believed to be wrong, this relatively recent divergence date (and the associated principle of the 'molecular clock') received intense scrutiny. This is ironic, given that *Ramapithecus* was subsequently removed from its key position as the earliest hominid and that the human divergence date of around 5 million years ago has now become quite acceptable.

The use of the molecular clock in dating times of divergence on an evolutionary tree is illustrated in the Box on p. 296 and described in more detail in Chapter 8.3. This approach assumes some degree of regularity of change over time. If the tree is to be dated in absolute terms, some extrinsic information is also needed.

This extra information is usually a palaeontologically determined date for one or more of the branchpoints of the tree. All the other dates are then worked out in proportion

to the relative lengths of the branches. Clearly, the reliability of the calibration date is crucial. It is also important to emphasise that the empirical support for the idea of the molecular clock is a separate issue from why such a clock might exist. It would be convenient for molecular evolution if clock-like behaviour could be relied on; some studies support the idea whereas others do not. One commentator has suggested that, at best, there are several 'sloppy clocks'.

In addition to the appeal of apparent regularity of change, molecular data have other properties that might help in studying evolutionary relationships. One is the objectivity with which such information can be determined and compared. Even before the advent of DNA sequencing (determining the order of base pairs along a DNA molecule), electrophoresis and immunology had shown that humans, chimpanzees and gorillas were strikingly similar in their molecular make-up. When it became possible to compare proteins from these species in terms of the identity and order of their amino acids and, subsequently, to compare stretches of their DNA, the genetic similarity became still better substantiated and more challenging to explain. How was it that two such anatomically and behaviourally distinct animals as humans and chimpanzees could appear so genetically similar?

Molecular biologists rose to the challenge. Wilson and his colleagues attempted to quantify the anatomical differences between species of frog on the one hand, and between living hominoids on the other. They then compared these values with the scores for molecular differ-

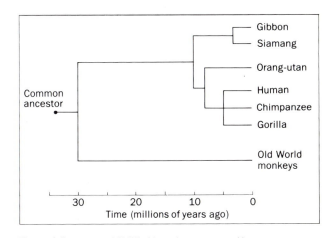

Times of divergence of Old World monkeys, apes and humans as estimated by Vincent Sarich and Allan Wilson in 1967 using an immunological approach. They assumed that Old World monkeys and hominoids separated about 30 million years ago and, presuming approximate constancy of the rate of evolutionary change, this led to an estimated time of divergence of humans, gorillas and chimpanzees of about 5 million years ago.

CALIBRATING THE MOLECULAR CLOCK

The tree shown in the upper diagram on the right marks the numbers of events that happened on each branch. It is constructed so that following any pathway from a given branchpoint to any species at the tips of the tree involves the same number of steps. For example, from the branchpoint marked with an asterisk it is $3 + 5 = 8$ steps to A, the same to B, and also to C. This tree can hence be drawn against a timescale if a single rate of change applies over the whole tree. The number of changes on each branch then reflects the time, in relative units, that has elapsed on that branch.

To convert relative time to absolute time, all we need is the absolute date for just one branchpoint. For example, if we know from fossils that species A and B last shared an ancestor with species C 40 million years ago at the branchpoint marked with the asterisk, then A and B must themselves have diverged $40 \times 5/8 = 25$ million years ago. The root would be $40 \times 10/8 = 50$ million years old and the divergence of species D and E was $40 \times 2/8 = 10$ million years ago.

A uniform rate of change in molecules over time is often referred to as the *molecular clock*. If the assumption of uniform change is justified, then we can use it to calibrate evolutionary trees.

No one expects that change will occur metronomically: evolution is, after all, a probabilistic process. How inaccurate the clock is will determine its credibility in any given case. The second tree illustrates this. It shares with the first tree the feature that the number of steps on its branches is 35. However, the steps are disposed unevenly; from the point marked with the asterisk in the second tree, it is now $3 + 5$

$= 8$ steps to A, $3 + 2 = 5$ steps to B, and 6 steps to C.

How big such discrepancies must be to invalidate the assumption of an idealised, uniform rate everywhere on the tree is still the subject of dispute.

It is important to realise that evolutionary trees are necessarily reconstructions of past events. Different workers may make quite different assumptions about the processes of evolution in reconstructing their trees, even when they are analysing the same information. Some methods of tree reconstruction actually assume the existence of a uniform rate of change and it is, therefore, hardly surprising that the resulting trees can be drawn against a single timescale like that in the first diagram.

Such prior assumption of a 'molecular clock' is often defended on theoretical grounds, but really needs to be justified empirically in each case. Sometimes a rearrangement of the branching pattern of a tree will make the changes look more evenly distributed, but the new pattern of branching may still be quite unacceptable in terms of other biological evidence.

If a good deal of change has occurred between two molecular sequences, a simple inspection will not reveal all changes because later changes may have overwritten or reversed earlier ones. In such a case, the number of observed differences must then be augmented statistically so that the estimated number of changes becomes larger.

Many methods of tree reconstruction inevitably go at least some way to doing this. For data in the form of distances between pairs of species, some sort of

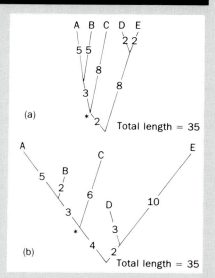

(a) Total length = 35

(b) Total length = 35

Evolutionary trees, (a) assuming a uniform rate of change on all branches and (b) assuming different rates of change on some branches.

logarithmic transformation is usually used; this is defended theoretically on the grounds of simple probability assumptions, based again on idealised behaviour.

Recent progress in reconstructing evolutionary trees from molecular sequence data involves sophisticated procedures to identify local 'zones', each with an internal, uniform rate but differing in that rate from the rates of other zones. These developments represent a departure from the elegant simplicity of the molecular clock but may be more in accord with reality.   *A.E. Friday*

---

ence between the corresponding species. Frogs, although anatomically relatively similar to one another, proved to be different in molecular terms. In contrast, the hominoids were relatively dissimilar anatomically but very close in molecular structure. Could the molecular and anatomical characters have 'uncoupled' during evolution, or were the molecules available for study simply not those involved in coding for the anatomical differences?

Most of the molecules compared were structural components of tissues, rather than those implicated in the control of development. In other words, the basic materials out of which humans and chimpanzees are built are very similar but the precise genetic instructions for how to put them together may be different. As far as 'uncoupling' is concerned, there are many known instances – sickle-cell anaemias being one – of small molecular changes with large effects. Equally, there are some large-scale molecular changes, including those leading to the deletion of whole proteins present in normal individuals, that have an

apparently negligible effect on physiological function and on fitness.

The distinction between structural and control molecules is by no means absolute, but the controversy is another illustration of the way in which molecular studies of relatedness have widened the discussion of cause and effect in evolution.

All the methods for measuring genetic relatedness described in Chapters 8.2 to 8.6 have their advocates. For example, immunological cross-comparisons are an easier way of assessing differences between molecules than is direct sequencing. However, their indirectness has meant that their value has been disputed by some, not least because a third species (the animal used to make the antibodies for testing) is involved.

Another indirect method is DNA–DNA hybridisation. Because single-stranded DNA of one species is allowed to seek out its complement in the single-stranded DNA of another, it has been claimed that problems of determining whether the corresponding pieces of DNA are being compared have been overcome: the DNA itself does the recognising. Certainly, this technique does compare a very large proportion of the total genome and this may increase the reliablity of its estimates of overall relatedness compared to other approaches.

However, our main attention should perhaps be directed not to how *similar* humans, chimpanzees and gorillas are but rather to where and what differences exist in their genomes. Protein or nucleic acid sequencing provides unsurpassable accuracy in comparisons of individual sites in a molecular sequence. Primates, and hominoids in particular, are the mammals best studied in this way. Considerable effort once went into protein sequencing, and this method still provides most of the total sequence evidence on human relationships and evolution.

It is now rather unusual for a protein to be sequenced, because it is easier to determine the base sequence of the DNA coding for it. This provides the protein's amino acid sequence and also determines which codon was actually used in cases where an amino acid can be coded by any one of several codons. DNA sequence information thus allows study of changes at the 'silent' sites at which the substitution of one base for another may not lead to a change in an amino acid. As some organisms preferentially use a particular codon where alternative sequences code for the same amino acid, DNA sequencing also allows patterns of codon usage to be compared.

The precision of direct, complete DNA sequencing is most illuminating in what it reveals about the organisation of the genome. The blocks of coding sequence, the *exons*, involved in the production of a protein, are interspersed with *introns* (intervening sequences). With complete DNA sequences it is possible to compare the blocks of exons and introns, their lengths, and the positions of their boundaries in hominoids and other primates. Such sequences reveal the position and nature of those stretches of DNA that control the expression of clusters of genes. There may be evolutionary information in the disposition of repeated blocks of sequence, many instances of which are found in genomes. Sequencing also allows the identification and location of *pseudogenes*. These resemble functional genes but are not expressed; indeed, they may contain mutations of kinds that ensure that any gene product cannot be made or would be defective.

This new ability to recognise discrete blocks of DNA and to reconstruct their behaviour and movement within the genome on an evolutionary timescale resembles an approach to assessing genetic relatedness at a different level of the genome – that of the chromosomes. Vast lengths of DNA are woven into chromosomes, together with much wrapping and housekeeping material. Events such as inversions of sections of chromosomes certainly move DNA around, but on such a scale that the reorganisation can often be revealed by a light microscope.

Every way of looking at genetic relatedness has its advantages and disadvantages, and the evidence from each must always be evaluated by reference to a body of theory. It is no good finding similarities in genomes and using these to support claims of relationship unless we have an idea about whether, for example, the similarities came about quite independently in the lineages being studied. Evolutionary history makes a lot more sense when the information available can be tested against a theory of how change might occur.

A.E. Friday

See *also* 'The nature of evolution' (p. 9) and the other chapters in this part

Chromosomal evolution in primates

Cytogenetics – the study of chromosomes – may be a valuable method for comparing primate species in the hope of learning more about their phylogeny and evolution. Unlike most genetic comparisons, variation in the chromosomes can be seen directly through the microscope. Chromosomal comparisons also differ from other genetic analyses in that they are generally qualitative, not quantitative; certain key features are present or absent throughout an entire species.

Deviations from the diploid, or 2n, number and karyotype of a species do occur as rare pathological characters, or as polymorphisms – genetic variants detectable with appreciable frequencies in a population. Polymorphisms are rare among primate chromosomes, but some species are more highly polymorphic than others. For example, the savanna or yellow baboon (Papio cynocephalus) is chromosomally almost monomorphic, but local populations of the owl monkey (Aotus) can show several different karyotypes.

Chromosomal comparisons are therefore best done with several representatives of each species, to ensure that any differences are characteristic of the species and not merely of the individual. In cytogenetic analysis the following methods are mainly used: G-banding (which permits the identification of each chromosome and of any structural rearrangements), C-banding (which stains small areas of certain chromosomes and is often variable within and between species) and NOR-banding (which stains only chromosomal features called nucleolar organisers) (see p. 275). The development of these techniques in the 1970s revolutionised cytogenetics. Until then, mammalian chromosomes could be seen only as uniformly stained silhouettes, and it was almost impossible to distinguish one chromosome from another. In certain insects, such as the fruit fly (Drosophila), a complex and intricate series of bands can be observed in the chromosomes of the salivary glands of the larva with minimal preparation. Such fine resolution cannot yet be achieved for mammalian chromosomes, which take on their characteristic forms only during the condensation that occurs just before cell division.

Relation of gene to chromosome

Since the mid-1960s, it has become apparent that the genome of eukaryotes (organisms with a cell nucleus) is a far more complicated terrain than it had once appeared. Classical Drosophila genetics had suggested that chromosomes are simply a linear arrangement of genes, but we now know that most DNA is not genic and probably has no organismal functions: the relation of gene to chromosome is like that of oasis to desert.

This non-genic DNA has properties that are just beginning to be understood. Satellite DNA, which comprises about 4 per cent of the human genome, consists of short, simple DNA sequences repeated millions of times and localised to specific regions on all the chromosomes. Of the four major satellite DNAs in humans, three are also present in the genomes of the great apes; one, human satellite II, seems to have been eliminated from the chromosomes of chimpanzees, but remains in those of gorillas and orang-utans.

Other classes of DNA vary in the extent of their function and in their distribution. Some are localised whereas others (such as Alu repeats, which are more common within G than between G bands and each of which is about 300 nucleotides long) are interspersed with unique-sequence DNA – DNA that consists of sequences present in only one or just a few copies per genome. About half of the genome consists of unique sequences, which include the genes. Yet even within unique-sequence DNA, extensive similarities are often found between bits of DNA that arose as the result of a duplication in the past, and subsequently began to diverge in structure or function. Thus, we find that genes are rare and that they are related in sequence to other DNA segments.

Each gene of the α-haemoglobin gene family, for example, is around 1000 base pairs long, and 423 of these pairs translate into the amino acids of the α-haemoglobin protein. Only three genes in this gene family are known to be the source of a functional protein product; ζ, α2 and α1 (and perhaps θ1 as well). Yet the α-globin gene cluster occupies about 30 000 base pairs – a considerable extravagance for only three or four functioning genes. What is more, this gene family is but a pinprick in a single visible band near the tip of the short arm of chromosome 16. The entire cluster of genes can be missing in one form of a disease known as

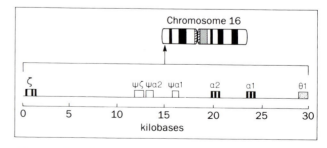

A tiny proportion of the genome codes for proteins. The human α-globin gene cluster contains only three or four genes of known function, yet occupies about 30 000 base pairs of DNA near the tip of the short arm of chromosome 16. The functional genes (ζ, α1 and α2) are shown here with black coding sequences and white non-coding sequences; non-functional pseudogenes are shown as open boxes; the function of θ1 (stippled box) is not yet known. This entire gene cluster can be deleted without anything being noticeably different on the chromosome.

α-thalassaemia, with no observable change in the chromosome's banding pattern.

The gross difference in scale between molecular and cytogenetic analysis makes it difficult to relate genic to chromosomal changes. Genic differences are impossible to detect in the visible chromosome, and chromosomal differences may arise with few or no detectable alterations in the structure and function of genes – only in their general locations.

This has important evolutionary implications. Random breakage of a chromosome is unlikely to affect the structure or function of the genetic material, in that a break is unlikely to occur near anything functional. We should therefore expect that most individuals heterozygous for a chromosomal rearrangement that does not involve the gain or loss of genetic material are clinically normal; as is indeed the case. Changes in the amount of genetic material (as opposed to rearrangements) are invariably manifested as phenotypic pathologies, unless the change occurs in a region that is completely inert genetically, such as the long arm of the Y chromosome. Phenotypic change and variation in chromosome structure are not closely linked and hence need not accompany one another.

Chromosomal change

Evolution proceeds by the differential proliferation of hereditary variants that arise from mutation. These genetic changes fall into two broad classes: genic or DNA mutations, which can be inferred but not observed, and chromosomal mutations, which involve directly visible rearrangements.

Genic mutations result primarily from substitution of one nucleotide for another, an event that recurs with a low but predictable frequency. By contrast, chromosomal changes arise from the breakage of chromosomes in two or more independent locations and their subsequent reunion – events most unlikely to be repeated. Chromosomal mutations also limit the ways in which chromosomes can pair and segregate during meiosis, and are hence very likely to affect reproduction. As the formation of new species involves the erection of reproductive barriers, chromosomes may be involved in this process. It is, however, unlikely that chromosomal rearrangements produce the adaptive anatomical differences often associated with speciation: these are more likely to involve allelic substitutions.

Only a limited number of the mechanisms of chromosomal change have occurred in primate evolution. For example, in plants and in some animals, polyploidy – the accumulation of additional chromosome sets – has been important, but this has not taken place in primates.

The diagram on the right shows the commonest ways in which mammalian karyotypes evolve. An *inversion* is the reversal of a chromosome segment; a *translocation* is the transfer of chromosomal material between two chromosomes; and *fusions* and *fissions* are the joining or splitting of chromosomes, with a consequent change in chromosome number. All these rearrangements are *balanced*; they involve the rearrangement – but not the gain or loss – of chromosomal material. *Amplification* and *reduction* refer to genomic expansions and contractions of DNA, such as that found in heterochromatin (tightly coiled DNA), which is stained by C-banding. All but the last category of changes involve the breakage and reunion of chromosomes.

The carrier of a new chromosomal rearrangement is faced with the difficulty of transmitting it to the next generation. The fate of most rearrangements is not to be passed on, but a very few will be perpetuated. In humans, the commonest spontaneous balanced rearrangements are translocations, but these are not readily transmitted to offspring

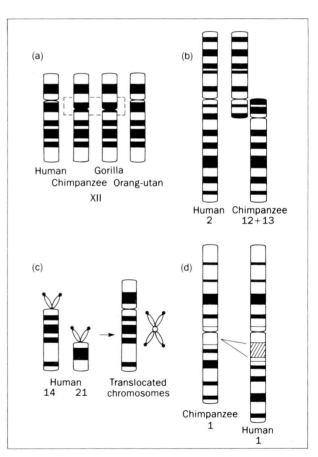

Major avenues of chromosomal change: (a) G-banded chromosome 12 of humans, and its homologues in chimpanzees, gorillas and orang-utans, reveal a small inversion shared by chimpanzees and gorillas. (b) The large human chromosome 2 is the result of a fusion of two smaller chromosomes still possessed by all great apes. The G bands of chimpanzee chromosomes 12 and 13 match up almost perfectly with the short and long arms, respectively, of human 2. The additional material on the short arm of each of the chimpanzee homologues was added subsequent to the fusion in the human line. (c) Translocations are difficult to find among the homologues of the ape and human karyotypes, but are often found as human chromosomal abnormalities. This is a translocation between chromosomes 14 and 21 (which results in a large and a tiny chromosome) – often a cause of Down's syndrome in humans. (d) The amplification of a block of highly repetitive DNA in the human homologue of chromosome 1 results in a large C-band region, not found in any of the apes.

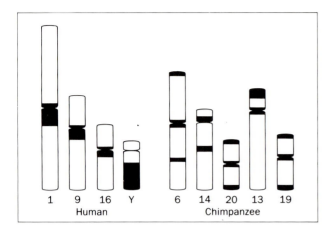

1	9	16	Y	6	14	20	13	19

Human — Chimpanzee

Unique C-band regions usually vary in size within a species, but in location across species. The major regions (apart from centromeres) stained by C-banding in humans are on chromosomes 1, 9, 16 and Y. In chimpanzees, however, these regions are absent. Instead, we find two chromosomes with C bands in the middle of their long arms (chromosomes 6 and 14) and several others with C bands at their tips.

as they are often accompanied by a reduction in fertility. Inversions, which are rarer but more easily passed on, make up most of the observable structural differences among the karyotypes of apes and humans. Over the generations, therefore, a rare structural variant may spread from within a family to characterise a population descended from that family, and ultimately to characterise a species descended from that population. This spread is governed by the microevolutionary action of genetic drift, a process that leads to the divergence of populations through random fluctuations, the effects of which depend on the size and isolation of the populations involved.

The chromosomal processes within species seem to account well for the patterns among them. One major exception to this is the amplification or reduction of repetitive DNA. Here we find that, within species, C bands containing such DNA often vary in size but not in location, whereas related species often have C bands in different places. All the chromosomes of hominoid primates (apes and humans) have small C bands at the centromere. Additional prominent C-banded regions in humans are on chromosomes 1, 9, 16 and Y. Chimpanzees lack those C bands, but have others: in the middle of the long arm of two other chromosomes, as well as at the tips of several chromosomes. Gorillas have terminal bands like those of chimpanzees, and C bands on homologues of chromosomes 16 and Y, as in humans. Orang-utans have C bands only at the centromere.

Rates of chromosomal evolution

Most of the G bands of the human karyotype (2n = 46) are easily matched in the karyotypes of macaques and baboons (2n = 42), in spite of the difference in chromosome number. However, they are much more difficult to match in the karyotype of the white-handed or common gibbon

(*Hylobates lar*) to which humans nevertheless appear to be more closely related on the basis of anatomical and molecular evidence.

In fact, the chromosomes of H. *lar* are virtually unmatchable even with other species of *Hylobates*. *Hylobates lar* (2n = 44) and H. *syndactylus* (the siamang; 2n = 50) are so similar genetically and anatomically that viable hybrid offspring have been raised. Yet these hybrids have two quite different haploid sets of chromosomes mixed in each of their cell nuclei (2n = 47).

Gibbons therefore appear to be evolving very rapidly in their chromosomes, at a pace not at all commensurate with their anatomical or genetical rates of change. Why this is so is unknown, but perhaps the social structure and ecology of gibbons (key features of which are monogamy, territoriality and arboreality) assist the incorporation of chromosomal variants through genetic drift. Support for this idea arises from the extensive chromosomal diversity of *Callicebus* (titi monkeys), a genus that has a marked social and ecological resemblance to the gibbons. Much slower chromosomal change is found among the macaques and baboons (tribe Papionini), which live in fluid groups and have large local populations.

Social structure and ecology may be closely related to rates of chromosomal evolution in primates, but other factors must also be involved. Chromosomal diversity in the genus *Cercopithecus* (which includes the guenons and vervet monkeys), for example, cannot be readily explained in this way. What is clear is that rates of chromosomal evolution vary widely across the primates, and are often correlated with factors tending to promote random divergences between populations.

Phylogeny of hominoids based on chromosomes

Chromosomes should in principle be able to clarify any ambiguities present in genic or morphological phylogenies. They are stably inherited, yet vary across species; and can be subjected to cladistic analysis (the determination of shared ancestral or novel traits among species).

However, this expectation has largely not been met: chromosomal evolution is more complicated and difficult to understand than had been hoped; and it is often hard to measure the chromosomal differentiation of closely related species. For example, although the karyotypes of

Relative rates of chromosomal evolution among monkeys, apes and humans

■ Slow	Papionini (macaques and baboons)
	Callitrichidae (marmosets and tamarins)
■ Medium	Pongidae and Hominidae (great apes and humans)
	Colobinae (leaf-monkeys)
	Most Cebidae (cebid monkeys)
■ Fast	Hylobatidae (gibbons)
	Cercopithecini (guenons and vervet monkeys)
	Aotinae (owl and titi monkeys)

the closely related vervet monkey (*Cercopithecus aethiops*) and the rhesus macaque (*Macaca mulatta*) are clearly different, it is not easy to estimate exactly how different or to tell exactly what the differences are. This is due largely to the technical problems of studying primate chromosomes, but these should be sorted out in time.

Although nearly every species of primate has now been karyotyped, the great apes have been studied in the greatest detail. Each has been given its own karyotype and system of numbering. When we compare the chromosomes of apes and humans, however, it is useful to use the human homologue as a reference, and to designate the chimpanzee, gorilla and orang-utan chromosomes (which appear, for example, to be homologous to human chromosome 14) as XIV, even though the specific chromosome involved is number 15 of the chimpanzee and orang-utan karyotype and is chromosome 18 of the gorilla.

In a phylogenetic reconstruction of the superfamily Hominoidea based only on chromosomes it would be impossible to place the gibbons, because their chromosomes are so highly derived. It is more appropriate to compare the karyotypes of great apes with those of baboons and macaques, which have not changed greatly since Old World monkeys diverged from the hominoids, and in whose karyotypes many of the human chromosomes can be found almost intact.

Nucleolar organisers (NORs) contain many copies of the genes for ribosome structure (the ribosome is the cell organelle on which protein assembly occurs). Baboons and macaques, and most of the gibbons also, have only one pair of metacentric chromosomes bearing NORs (metacentric chromosomes have their centromeres halfway along so that they appear 'two-armed' when segregating during cell division). All the great apes – the two chimpanzees, gorillas and orang-utans – have several pairs of acrocentric chromosomes with NORs (acrocentric chromosomes appear 'one-armed' because their centromeres are located near one end). It thus appears that the radiation of the great apes during the Miocene epoch was accompanied by a 'colonisation' of various chromosomes by NORs. This was accompanied by a fission of three pairs of chromosomes that raised the diploid number from the ancestral 2n = 42 to 2n = 48.

The branching of the orang-utan from the lineage leading to humans, chimpanzees and gorillas was associated with the emergence of chromosomal regions that stain brightly after being treated with quinacrine. These differ from ordinary quinacrine or Q bands (the distribution of which is virtually identical to that of G bands), and the 'Q-brilliant' zones are restricted to the chromosomes of humans, chimpanzees and gorillas. They probably reflect localisations of repetitive DNA. Curiously, the Q-brilliant material differs in its chromosomal localisation in each species. Humans, chimpanzees and gorillas also have fewer NOR-bearing chromosomes than does the orang-utan; a common African ancestor must therefore have lost the nuclear organisers from chromosomes II and IX.

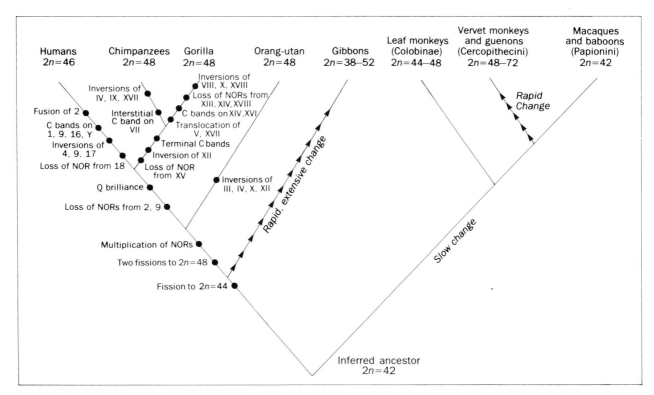

The major chromosomal alterations that have occurred during the evolution of Old World simians. Each dot represents an event inferred from a comparison of the karyotypes of living species. Within any branch, the sequence of dots is arbitrary. Emphasis is given to humans and great apes, whose chromosomes have been more extensively studied than those of other primates. NORs = nucleolar organisers.

Split of humans from chimpanzees and gorillas

Analysis of DNA sequences has proven vexingly ambiguous in attempting to discern the two closest relatives among humans, gorillas and chimpanzees. Most analyses of mitochondrial DNA are so equivocal as to render a clear solution impossible, the preferred phylogeny relying critically on the choice of outgroup and clustering technique. A few regions of nuclear DNA have been analysed and are similarly difficult to interpret. For example, simply in the β-globin gene cluster on chromosome 11, the ψη sequence links humans to chimpanzees, γ¹ links gorillas to chimpanzees, γ² links gorillas to humans, and β-globin itself has linked chimpanzees to gorillas and to humans in different studies.

The immunoglobulin genes provide a similarly cloudy picture: Ig C_{α_1} seems to favour chimpanzees–gorillas, Ig C_{ε_3} to favour chimpanzees–humans and Ig C_{ε_2} humans–gorillas. Similarly, from a stretch of DNA homologous between the X and Y chromosomes, the X chromosome favours chimpanzees–gorillas, and the Y chromosome chimpanzee–humans. An analysis of ribosomal RNA genes seems to link humans to chimpanzees, while the gene for involucrin seems to link gorillas to chimpanzees. Apparently, the divergences were temporally so close, and the population dynamics sufficiently complex, that molecular genetics does not provide a simple solution to this phylogenetic problem.

Cytogenetics seems to offer greater support for a link between chimpanzees and gorillas than alternative arrangements, although, like other genetic data, there is some ambiguity. Here, for example, a possible inversion of chromosome IX at least superficially links humans to chimpanzees, whereas a C band on the Y chromosome superficially seems to link humans to gorillas. Nevertheless, the genetic *divergence* of humans is well marked cytogenetically. The unique features of the human karyotype include a fusion of two chromosome pairs (reducing the diploid number to 2n = 46, and forming human chromosome 2), and the emergence of C-banded regions below the centromeres of chromosomes 1, 9 and 16, and on the long arm of the Y chromosome. The common ancestor of chimpanzees and gorillas passed on unique cytogenetic characters to both its daughter species. Most striking is the set of terminal C bands in chimpanzees and gorillas. (This has also evolved independently in a common ancestor of two gibbon species, *Hylobates concolor* and *H. syndactylus*, probably linking them as one another's closest relatives.) An apparent inversion of chromosome XII also distinguishes chimpanzees and gorillas from humans and orang-utans. Several inversions are unique to the karyotype of each species, but only one translocation is established in this group – an exchange between chromosomes V and XVII in the gorilla. The major unique and shared features of the karyotypes of the Old World anthropoid primates are shown in the diagram on the previous page.

The study of primate chromosomes is still in its infancy. Human chromosomes are extraordinarily similar to those of the great apes, but the significance of the few detectable differences is not yet known.

J. Marks

See also 'Principles of genetics' (p. 255), 'Mutation and human evolution' (p. 269) and 'Human chromosomes' (p. 274)

Immunological evidence on primates

Genetic isolation between two populations sets in motion a process of differentiation between them. The differences between modern species have all developed since they last had a common ancestor, and can be apportioned between two lineages from the ancestor to the living species. The best indicator of differentiation is obtained by counting unit changes. In recent years this has become possible: we simply count the number of positions at which two species have different nucleotides or amino acids in related genes or proteins. This concept is simple, but it is often laborious and expensive to carry out. Much easier techniques are available for estimating the number of sequence differences between species in proteins or DNA. For proteins, we can make use of immunology (see Box on p. 304), which has been used for over 80 years to compare related species. I and my colleague Allan Wilson realised the potential of immunological comparisons of proteins such as albumins for deriving and dating phylogenetic trees of apes and humans in 1967 at the University of California in Berkeley.

Albumins as a measure of relatedness

Serum albumin, a small protein found in blood plasma, is a single polypeptide chain of 584 amino acids coded for at a single gene locus. By the 1960s, it was already known that its rate of amino acid substitutions was appropriate for testing questions of primate evolution. To make comparisons between species, purified human albumin is injected into rabbits, which respond to this challenge by recognising those portions of the surface of the injected human albumin that differ from their own, and produce antibodies that react with each of those different portions. After several injections over 5 to 10 weeks, the rabbit is bled and the serum is separated from the red cells. This serum (*rabbit anti-human albumin*) contains antibody populations in sufficient variety to recognise some 30 to 40 distinct antigenic sites on the surface of the human albumin.

Each antibody molecule has two identical reactive ends, which will recognise only one antigenic site. Each can thus link two molecules of albumin, and each albumin can be linked to several different antibody molecules reacting with different antigenic sites to form a complex network. If human albumin is mixed with the rabbit serum, this complex network will be large enough to precipitate out. The amount of precipitate can be assessed in various ways.

If we now try the same experiment, but substitute, say, baboon (*Papio*) for human albumin, we again get a precipitate, but significantly less of it. Why is this? The immune system is exquisitely sensitive. For example, human anti-A antigen reacts with red blood cells of types A and AB, but

not with those of type B; anti-B antigen reacts with B and AB, but not with A. Yet the A and B antigens differ only in whether there is an amino ($-NH_2$) or hydroxy ($-OH$) group on the terminal sugar of the large molecule that makes up the blood group antigen.

Our immunisation experiments show that the albumin genes of baboons and humans have undergone independent mutational changes, some of which alter the amino acid sequence of the albumins. When the antibody populations in the rabbit anti-human albumin serum are exposed to baboon albumin, three reactions are possible:

- Some antigenic sites on the surface of the baboon albumin will be identical to the corresponding areas on human albumin. Antibodies to those sites will bind just as tightly as they do to human albumin
- Other areas on the baboon albumin will have an amino acid that differs from its human homologue, or a shape that has been slightly altered by nearby substitutions. Antibodies directed to those areas will exhibit a variety of binding strengths
- The baboon albumin area might show two or more amino acid replacements, or a markedly altered conformation, so that antibodies directed against this site will not bind

The reaction between baboon albumin and an anti-human albumin will hence produce a less-tightly bound and smaller albumin–antibody complex, and we will see less precipitate.

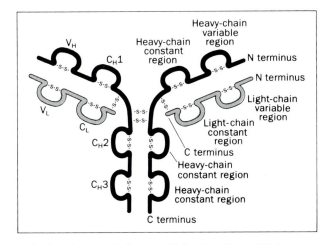

Antibodies – immunogobulins – owe their extraordinary ability to recognise a large variety of foreign antigens to the high mutation rate of their 'variable' regions, which bind to the antigen. Rather like haemoglobin, an immunoglobulin molecule is made up of a pair of two distinct protein chains, the light (L) and the heavy (H) chain. Each has a variable (V) and a constant (C) region, and they are joined to each other by chemical bonds. They form pockets into which antigens can fit (antigen-binding sites).

GENETICS AND THE IMMUNE SYSTEM

The body has a defence mechanism that protects it against invasion. Any invader can be recognised only by comparing it with the native population; and the immune system is a machine for testing cells to see whether or not they belong, whether they are 'self' or 'not self'. The cues of identity used are largely under genetic control. Immunology is hence a way of looking for genetic differences, and was so used in the earliest studies of inherited divergence among people and among species.

The immune system can synthesise millions of different proteins, called *antibodies*, each of which identifies and attacks a specific invader or *antigen*. The antibody is produced in response to the first invasion and the system then 'remembers' the earlier challenge, conferring immunity to subsequent incursions. Antibodies circulate in the blood and attach themselves to their targets.

There is also a system of cellular immunity involving cells that recognise and destroy the invader. There are two main classes of *lymphocyte*, the main cells involved: *B cells*, which make antibodies, and *T cells*, which are the attackers. Other cells help in the process.

Both the cellular and the circulating responses depend on the synthesis of very specific defensive molecules, only one of which is made by any particular T or B cell. Each cell's specialisation is genetic and identical clones of cells are produced when an antigen is encountered. There is a mechanism of tolerance that prevents the body from attacking itself, as it 'learns' its own identity during early life.

Some parts of the amino acid chain of antibody molecules are extremely variable. How all the myriad of distinct antibodies is produced is not clear, but the process probably involves variation in two classes of genes, with some coding for more or less constant regions, and others undergoing rearrangement, reshuffling and mutation during the life of their carrier to generate millions of different specificities.

Many other genes are involved in the immune system. Some control the animal's own cell-surface antigens – the *transplantation antigens*, which cause tissue rejection and make up much of the *major histocompatibility complex* (MHC, which in humans is referred to as the *HLA system*) that covers some four million DNA base pairs on chromosome 6. They are extremely variable – a single gene in the system may exist in scores of different forms. There are vast numbers of alternative types, so that no two people

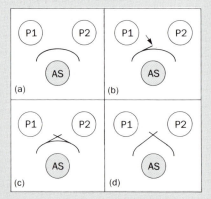

One way of comparing genes using the immune system. An antibody (or, strictly speaking, an antiserum AS) is prepared to the proteins of one species by injecting them into a rabbit. The rabbit antiserum is placed in the central well of a plate of agar gel, through which proteins can diffuse. Two test wells, P1 and P2, are also shown. If (a) the proteins in the two test wells are identical, a continuous line of precipitated protein is formed. If, as in (b), protein P1 has more genetic similarities to the antiserum, a 'spur' of precipitated line is formed. In (c), there is a mixture of shared and unshared genes between species P1 and P2. If P1 and P2 have no common genetic determinants, there is a crossed pattern, as in (d).

share the same set of antigens. This is an extreme example of polymorphism.

The genes controlling this extraordinary system are all related. Cell-surface antigens are proteins quite similar to those making up circulating antibodies, and may have descended in the distant past from a common ancestor, which – just like the globin genes – duplicated and diverged to give functionally different products based on the same underlying structure. The gene family directing the immune system is much more complex and more widely dispersed over the genome than is that of the globins but probably arose in the same way.

The immune system is interesting to evolution for several reasons. First, it is a source of diversity and a target for natural selection. In some mammals, it affects mate choice as females avoid mating with an antigenically similar male (who is likely to be a relative). It also gave one of the earliest insights into inherited diffences among species. By injecting the tissues of any animal – say a chimpanzee – into a rabbit, an antibody specific to that animal's antigens is produced. This can be purified and tested against the antigens of other species – for example, by allowing them to diffuse towards the prepared anti-chimp antibody in a gel, and measuring the intensity of the lines of precipitated protein where they meet.

The closer the genetic relatedness of two species, the more the antigens of one will cross-react with an antibody to the other. This is a simple way of measuring evolutionary affinity, which was first used (on birds) more than 50 years ago. Immunology was hence the precursor of the whole field of comparative genetics, which tells us so much about primate relatedness.   *Steve Jones*

See also 'The nature of evolution' (p. 9) and 'Natural selection in humans' (p. 284)

We can extend this comparison by making antisera against the albumins of various other primates. For example, comparisons can be made with anti-baboon albumin within the Old World monkey group, with anti-*Cebus* (capuchin monkey) albumin within the New World monkeys, anti-*Varecia* (ruffed lemur) albumin within the Malagasy prosimians, and so on.

What advantages do immunological measures have for tracing descent and tracking modification, and how might they be used to do this? All species of interest here have an albumin that will cross-react with antisera made against any other; we can therefore compare any pair of species along the same scale. Second, we know the units of change underlying most of the differences measured – single amino acid substitutions.

Immunology has answered some important questions in primate evolution. First, the albumin differences among the living apes and ourselves are very small. They are quite comparable to those between a horse and donkey or zebra, or sheep and goat, or lion and tiger, or, for that matter, between two subspecies of gophers living on opposite sides of the Colorado River. Second, it is now clear that the albumin picture is representative of the genome as a whole, for no protein or DNA shows significantly larger differences between species than do the albumins.

Implications of the albumin evidence

There are two interpretations of these findings: either the common ancestor of humans and apes lived so recently

The amount of antigen/antibody reaction produced by the indicated albumin and anti-human albumin relative to that given by human albumin and the same antiserum

Species tested	Per cent reaction	Species tested	Per cent reaction
Humans (*Homo*)	100	Baboon (*Papio*)	73
Chimpanzee (*Pan*)	95	Spider monkey (*Ateles*)	60
Gorilla (*Gorilla*)	95	Ruffed lemur (*Varecia*)	35
Orang-utan (*Pongo*)	85	Dog (*Canis*)	25
Gibbon (*Hylobates*)	82	Kangaroo (*Macropus*)	8

that there has not been time for much genetic differentiation, or differentiation has proceeded very slowly along the lineages that link our common ancestor with that of living apes. Until quite recently, most students of human evolution prefered the second interpretation.

Many people do not like the idea that one of our ancestors was similar to a living ape. The more recent our divergence from the common ancestor, the more likely that this is true. This bias was reinforced in the 1960s by the attribution of relatively old fossils to specific existing hominoid lineages that predated the divergence of the lines leading to modern apes. The most famous of those attributions was the placing of *Ramapithecus*, now called *Sivapithecus* or *Kenyapithecus*, (up to 14 million years old) in the hominid line; in addition, *Proconsul major* and *P. nyanzae* (about 20 to 16 million years old in eastern Africa) were held, to be, respectively, proto-gorillas and proto-chimps. Finally, the gibbon line was seen as containing *Pliopithecus* (about 16 to 10 million years old in Europe) and perhaps even *Propliopithecus* (around 35 million years old in the Fayum deposits of Egypt).

Accepting these allocations meant that the gorilla, chimpanzee and human lineages must have been distinct from one another by at least 20 million years ago and from that leading to gibbons by up to 35 million years ago. The immunological similarities among their serum proteins and DNAs then had to be attributed to very slow changes in the amino acid sequences over the past 35 million years. If this is true, and albumin evolution among ourselves and apes has in fact slowed down compared with that in other lineages, then ape and human albumin must have diverged less from the ancestral condition than have albumins of other primates. The ancestral albumins are, of course, not available, but the amount of change from the ancestral to the living form can be measured. Consider, for example, the 40 per cent difference between the reactions given by human and by spider monkey (*Ateles*) albumins (see the table). We can place this into its evolutionary context by using a more distantly related species as our outgroup comparison. The use of the Malagasy lemur *Varecia* as an outgroup allows us to compare change along the albumin lineages of humans and spider monkeys, and to find out that it is essentially the same. Similar tests, using the spider monkey as the outgroup, allow us to compare the albumin changes along the various ape and Old World monkey

lineages; again, we found them not to differ significantly from one another.

To look at the primates as a whole, we used non-primates such as dog, bear and cat as the outgroup, and found that, if anything, the albumins of simian primates have changed slightly more than have those of prosimians such as *Varecia*; that is, they gave slightly lower reactions with antisera to carnivore albumins. Not all comparisons give such a consistent result. For example, the albumin of the New World owl monkey *Aotus* reacts about as well with antisera to human albumin as do the albumins of Old World monkeys, but the *Aotus* albumin also reacts better with antisera to carnivore albumins than does the albumin of simian primates. The *Aotus* albumin reacts strongly with anti-human albumin because its lineage has changed more slowly. But *Aotus* is the exception; the rule is for very similar amounts of change along two lineages from their time of most recent common ancestry to the present. It allows us to date divergence events – in other words, to produce *molecular clocks*.

Calibration of the albumin clock

Any molecular clock must be calibrated. To calibrate the albumin clock we need to know the relationship between the number of amino acid sequence differences and the immunological distance, and the timescale on which we are operating.

Each 1 per cent decrease in precipitate in the albumin tests indicates about two sequence differences. For example, human and baboon albumins differ by 27 per cent in cross-reaction, while those of either and the ruffed lemur differ by 65 per cent. Therefore, we can predict that human and baboon albumins have different amino acids at about 54 out of the 584 positions in the molecule, while ruffed lemur albumin differs from both at about 130 positions.

No primate of modern aspect appears in the fossil record earlier than about 56 million years ago, and no primate at all is present before about 65 million years ago (the African record is, however, largely unsampled). The maximum divergence times among living primates may hence not greatly exceed 60 million years or so. There is about 35 per cent change along the albumin lineages of the simian primates since their separation from those leading to living prosimians, or about 0.6 per cent immunological differentiation for each million years per lineage. Two typical primates whose albumins differ by 12 per cent (6 per cent change along each lineage) will hence have last shared a common ancestor 10 million years ago. By this reasoning, gorillas, chimpanzees and humans, whose albumins differ by about 5 per cent from each other, separated from one another about 4 million years ago. This will, of course, be a minimum estimate if the radiation of primates began more than 60 million years ago.

The absolute number of amino acid differences between any two of these albumins is only about 10, which makes for rather a coarse clock. However, this calculation does rule out any suggestions that *Ramapithecus* (now included in the Eurasian genus *Sivapithecus* or the African genus *Kenyapithecus*) was a hominid, or that humans, gorillas and chimpanzees last shared a common ancestor 20 million years or more ago. This figure of 20 million years is, after all, almost a third of the time for which primates have existed, and so should produce a difference between humans, chimpanzees and gorillas of about one-third of the maximum within-primate albumin difference of about 20 to 25 per cent – yet we found only 5 per cent divergence.

The molecular clock – and in practical terms that means the immunological clock – is most useful when there is a fossil record to integrate into our evolutionary understanding. Its major contribution is its new capacity to derive the branching order of a phylogeny. The fossil record can never represent more than a tiny portion of the evidence for any evolving group of species and hence cannot serve to tie all the information from comparative anatomy and behaviour into a single history.

This can be illustrated by one of the most valuable results to have emerged from comparative studies of molecules – that gorillas and chimpanzees are no more similar to one another genetically than either is to us. The African apes hence would not share any common ancestry after the human lineage branched off. More recent work suggests that chimpanzees and ourselves might share a period of common ancestry after the gorilla line branched off. Thus the latest common ancestor of the African apes is also our own ancestor. This constrains attempts at reconstructing our evolutionary history. Living chimpanzees and gorillas are so similar that some feel that they should be placed in the same genus, *Pan*. All of the extensive anatomy and behaviour common to gorillas and chimpanzees must have characterised their common ancestor, which was, the molecules tell us, also our own ancestor.

I wrote in 1968, largely on the basis of immunological evidence, 'we begin the reconstruction and understanding of our recent history with a form not unlike a small chimpanzee'. I see no reason to amend that judgement. If we could go back to the Africa of 4 to 5 million years ago and observed the last common ancestor of the African apes and ourselves, as well as the immediate ape ancestor of the australopithecines, we would consider them both chimpanzees. We may, with luck, have that prediction tested by future fossil discoveries.

V. Sarich

See *also* 'Evolution of apes' (p. 223), 'Measuring relatedness' (p. 295), Reconstructing human evolution from proteins' (p. 307), 'DNA–DNA hybridisation in the study of primate evolution' (p. 313) and 'Human evolution: the evidence from DNA sequencing' (p. 316)

Reconstructing human evolution from proteins

Only a small proportion of the 3000 million base pairs of DNA in the human genome code for proteins, and these sequences represent the most evolutionarily conservative part of the DNA. The proportion of coding to non-coding DNA is so small that much of the human genome drifts apart from other mammalian genomes at a rate close to the mutation rate. Change of this kind is so fast that mammals in different orders (such as mice and humans) show only slight evidence of evolutionary relatedness when their non-coding DNAs are compared. However, non-coding DNA can be very informative in revealing closer patterns of relatedness such as those between gorillas, chimpanzees and humans. The fraction of DNA that codes for proteins does not accept mutations freely, as they are likely to interfere with function and to encounter adverse selection. Amino acid sequences hence evolve more slowly than non-coding DNA, and are useful in revealing more distant evolutionary relationships.

This chapter looks at the history of primates, particularly humans and apes, as revealed by genealogical reconstructions based on amino acid sequences. Sequence data on proteins that have evolved slowly – for example, calmodulin, which is involved in calcium-binding – allow us to trace the deeper roots of the primates back to the first eukaryotic organisms (those with a distinct nucleus in their cells) about 1500 million years ago. Studies of this kind show that protein evolution accelerated when life radiated into new physical and ecological environments, as advantageous mutations were then selected at new functional sites in proteins. This happened, for example, when tetrapod vertebrates first emerged on land.

Natural selection favoured mutations that adapted the novel functional sites and a multitude of other molecular sites to work more efficiently together and hence protected these improved arrays of molecular sites from further change. A striking example of a speed-up in protein evolution followed by a slow-down occurred in primates when advantageous mutations transformed an embryonic haemoglobin of earlier primates into a fetal haemoglobin that helped extend the period of fetal life (and hence prenatal brain development) in higher primates. Such patterns of change support the Darwinian view that natural selection is a major force behind the evolution of molecules and organisms.

Less than a hundred years after the publication of *The Origin of Species* in 1859, students of phylogeny had largely agreed that the two lineages of Asiatic apes (gibbons and orang-utans), the African apes (chimpanzees and gorillas)

and humans were descended from a common ancestor shared by no other living species. In 1945, the American zoologist George Gaylord Simpson, in the *Principles of Classification and a Classification of Mammals*, placed the four types of living apes and humans in the superfamily Hominoidea. However, there is still no general agreement on the morphological evidence of the branching order within the Hominoidea. Are the African apes most closely allied with humans (a view that Darwin suggested in 1871 in *The Descent of Man*) or are they most closely allied with orang-utans, as depicted by Simpson's subfamily Ponginae, in which chimpanzees (*Pan*) and gorillas (*Gorilla*) are grouped with orang-utans (*Pongo*)?

In contrast to the rather ambiguous morphological picture, all protein and DNA studies agree in grouping African apes and humans into a single group to which no other living species belong. Moreover, new morphological studies largely agree with the molecular work on human origins. Rather than giving humans a unique evolutionary position in the living world, evidence from both morphology and molecular studies places humans with apes within the superfamily Hominoidea.

If the biblical account of creation were true, then independent features of morphology, proteins and DNA sequences would not be expected to be congruent with each other. Chaotic patterns, with different proteins and different DNA sequences failing to indicate any consistent set of species relationships, would contradict the theory of evolution. However, such patterns do not exist: the molecular phylogeny of primates and of all vertebrates is remarkably similar to the picture that emerges from morphology. The classical picture itself led taxonomists to believe in a natural system of classification, a hierarchy that proceeded from the most closely related taxa (those that diverged more recently) to the most distantly related taxa (those that diverged less recently). This argument, first put forward by Darwin, persuaded many taxonomists who had been creationists to become evolutionists, because evolution offered a rational explanation for patterns of diversity.

Phylogenetic evidence from primate proteins

The earliest studies of primate proteins, more than 85 years ago, were based on their immunological properties. They hinted at the close kinship of humans to African apes but did not challenge the traditional taxonomic grouping of African and Asiatic apes in the family Simidae (that is, Pongidae) and the position of humans alone in Hominidae.

By the early 1960s, extensive immunological data on serum proteins from many primates led to the conclusion that *Pan* and *Gorilla* were most closely related to *Homo*. Both immunological and electrophoretic data on proteins showed that the close kinship between the two African ape genera was not necessarily closer than the kinship of each of them to *Homo*. In fact, with the best antisera less antigenic distance was detected between *Pan* and *Homo* than between either *Pan* and *Gorilla* or *Homo* and *Gorilla*.

Immunology also led to the idea that molecular evolution had slowed in the lineage leading to humans. Human serum proteins show only small antigenic differences from orang-utans and gibbons, and tiny differences from gorillas and chimpanzees. Given the extensive morphological evolution involved, the extent of protein evolution between humans and other hominoids is surprisingly small. Alternatively, if the 'molecular clock' is applied to immunological distances and the divergence between hominoids and Old World monkeys arbitrarily set at 30 million years ago, the human–African ape split occurs at 5 million years ago.

Amino acid sequences can support either view of primate history. Protein evolution could have slowed in the descent of hominoids, but this would not rule out a relatively late common ancestry of humans, chimpanzees and gorillas.

Fibrinopeptides

The first methods for amino acid sequencing were developed in the 1950s, and within a few years were being used on fibrinopeptides A and B from various mammals. The two molecules are only 15 to 20 amino acids long – and thus were not too difficult to sequence. By 1972, their sequences were available from more than 40 mammals, including 12 primates.

Fibrinopeptides A and B are portions of fibrinogen, one of the blood plasma proteins. When they are removed from the fibrinogen by the enzyme thrombin, they start forming a mesh of fibrin fibres – a blood clot. As the only function of fibrinopeptides is to shield the polymerisation site of fibrinogen, they do not require a highly conserved amino acid sequence. They have evolved rapidly and the fibrinopeptides of different mammalian orders and even of closely related mammals vary greatly from each other. For example, those of sheep and cattle (in the family Bovidae) differ in 17 of their 40 amino acid positions.

Hominoid fibrinopeptides have evolved even more slowly than those of the bovids. The fibrinopeptide sequences of humans, chimpanzees and gorillas are identical and differ from those of orang-utans in only two of their 30 positions and from those of the siamang and gibbons in one and three further positions, respectively.

An evolutionary tree that requires the fewest sequence changes to account for the descent of hominoid fibrinopeptides can be constructed. An amino acid replacement

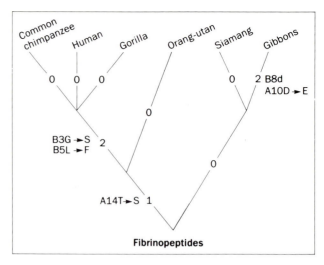

Fibrinopeptides

Evolutionary tree for humans and apes based on fibrinopeptides A and B. This reconstruction by the parsimony criterion of fewest sequence changes was carried out on the two fibrinopeptide A and three fibrinopeptide B positions that show amino acid differences among hominoids. The ancestral amino acid replacements at the hominoid root were established by comparing the sequences for humans and apes with those for the Old World monkey, New World monkey and lemur/loris outgroup. Numbers on the links between adjacent ancestral and descendant branch points are the numbers of sequence changes. The nature of the changes are recorded along the side of the links. For example, Al4T → S, which is placed alongside the link between the hominoid root and the branch point for divergence of the orang-utan from the gorilla/human/common chimpanzee clade, means that at fibrinopeptide A sequence position 14 the ancestral amino acid residue threonine (T) changes to descendant amino acid residue serine (S). There are two ancestral to descendant changes on the link to gibbon, and the small 'd' of the change designated B8d stands for a deletion (i.e. the amino acid residue at fibrinopeptide B sequence position 8 was deleted).

Here and elsewhere in this chapter, amino acid residues are designated by Dayhoff's single-letter code (each of the 20 amino acids is represented by a different letter): A = alanine; R = arginine; D = asparagine; N = aspartic acid; C = cysteine; E = glutamic acid; Q = glutamine; G = glycine; H = histidine; I = isoleucine; L = leucine; K = lysine; M = methionine; F = phenylalanine; P = proline; S = serine; T = threonine; W = tryptophan; Y = tyrosine; V = valine.

is shared by orang-utans, gorillas, humans and chimpanzees, and two further amino acid replacements are shared by gorillas, humans and chimpanzees. A phylogenetic tree for hominoid fibrinopeptides, based on the principle that organisms that diverged more recently will have fewer differences in their DNA sequence than those that diverged longer ago, supports the grouping *Gorilla*, *Pan* and *Homo*, separate from *Pongo*.

Myoglobins and haemoglobins

Most of the amino acid sequences from different animals have come from myoglobins and haemoglobins. The myoglobin of mammals and other vertebrates is a single-chained protein, typically 153 amino acid residues long. It is involved in oxygen storage in muscle. Haemoglobin, the oxygen-transporting protein of red blood cells, is made up of four chains – two identical α chains and two identical β chains (see p. 10). Each α chain is 141 residues long and each β chain has 146 residues.

Sequences of over 400 globin chains of mammals and a wide scatter of other taxa are now available. These give information not only on specific parts of the phylogenetic tree (such as the hominoids) but on the branching pattern of major lineages. The amino acids in the α and β chains of haemoglobin in hominoids vary in seven positions. In the myoglobin sequence, the differences among hominoids show up in four positions.

The seven positions of β- and α-haemoglobin sequences showing amino acid differences among primates

	β80	β87	β104	β125	α12	α23	α113
Human	N	T	R	P	A	E	L
Common chimpanzee	N	T	R	P	A	E	L
Pygmy chimpanzee	N	T	R	P	A	E	L
Gorilla	N	T	K	P	A	D	L
Orang-utan	N	K	R	Q	T	D	L
Gibbon	D	K	R	Q	T	D	H
Old World monkeys	N	Q	K	Q	A	E	L
New World monkeys	N	Q	R	Q	A	D	H
Tarsier	N	K	R	Q	A	D	H
Lorises	N	K	R	Q	A	D	H
Lemurs	N	Q	T	A	T	E	H

Amino acid residues are designated by the Dayhoff single-letter code (see opposite page).

```
                   α–Haemoglobin chain
Chimpanzee         VLSPADKTNVKAAWGKVGAHAGEYGAEALERMFLSFPTTKTYFPHFDLSH
Pygmy chimpanzee   VLSPADKTNVKAAWGKVGAHAGEYGAEALERMFLSFPTTKTYFPHFDLSH
Human              VLSPADKTNVKAAWGKVGAHAGEYGAEALERMFLSFPTTKTYFPHFDLSH
Gorilla            VLSPADKTNVKAAWGKVGAHAGDYGAEALERMFLSFPTTKTYFPHFDLSH
Orang-utan         VLSPADKTNVKTAWGKVGAHAGDYGAEALERMFLSFPTTKTYFPHFDLSH (50)

Chimpanzee         GSAQVKGHGKKVADALTNAVAHVDDMPNALSALSDLHAHKLRVDPVNFKL
Pygmy chimpanzee   GSAQVKGHGKKVADALTNAVAHVDDMPNALSALSDLHAHKLRVDPVNFKL
Human              GSAQVKGHGKKVADALTNAVAHVDDMPNALSALSDLHAHKLRVDPVNFKL
Gorilla            GSAQVKGHGKKVADALTNAVAHVDDMPNALSALSDLHAHKLRVDPVNFKL
Orang-utan         GSAQVKGHGKKVADALTNAVAHVDDMPNALSALSDLHAHKLRVDPVNFKL (100)

Chimpanzee         LSHCLLVTLAAHLPAEFTPAVHASLDKFLASVSTVLTSKYR
Pygmy chimpanzee   LSHCLLVTLAAHLPAEFTPAVHASLDKFLASVSTVLTSKYR
Human              LSHCLLVTLAAHLPAEFTPAVHASLDKFLASVSTVLTSKYR
Gorilla            LSHCLLVTLAAHLPAEFTPAVHASLDKFLASVSTVLTSKYR
Orang-utan         LSHCLLVTLAAHLPAEFTPAVHASLDKFLASVSTVLTSKYR (141)

                   β–Haemoglobin chain
Chimpanzee         VHLTPEEKSAVTALWGKVNVDEVGGEALGRLLVVYPWTQRFFESFGDLST
Pygmy chimpanzee   VHLTPEEKSAVTALWGKVNVDEVGGEALGRLLVVYPWTQRFFESFGDLST
Human              VHLTPEEKSAVTALWGKVNVDEVGGEALGRLLVVYPWTQRFFESFGDLST
Gorilla            VHLTPEEKSAVTALWGKVNVDEVGGEALGRLLVVYPWTQRFFESFGDLST
Orang-utan         VHLTPEEKSAVTALWGKVNVDEVGGEALGRLLVVYPWTQRFFESFGDLST (50)

Chimpanzee         PDAVMGNPKVKAHGKKVLGAFSDGLAHLDNLKGTFATLSELHCDKLHVDP
Pygmy chimpanzee   PDAVMGNPKVKAHGKKVLGAFSDGLAHLDNLKGTFATLSELHCDKLHVDP
Human              PDAVMGNPKVKAHGKKVLGAFSDGLAHLDNLKGTFATLSELHCDKLHVDP
Gorilla            PDAVMGNPKVKAHGKKVLGAFSDGLAHLDNLKGTFATLSELHCDKLHVDP
Orang-utan         PDAVMGNPKVKAHGKKVLGAFSDGLAHLDNLKGTFAKLSELHCDKLHVDP (100)

Chimpanzee         ENFRLLGNVLVCVLAHHFGKEFTPPVQAAYQKVVAGVANALAHKYH
Pygmy chimpanzee   ENFRLLGNVLVCVLAHHFGKEFTPPVQAAYQKVVAGVANALAHKYH
Human              ENFRLLGNVLVCVLAHHFGKEFTPPVQAAYQKVVAGVANALAHKYH
Gorilla            ENFKLLGNVLVCVLAHHFGKEFTPPVQAAYQKVVAGVANALAHKYH
Orang-utan         ENFRLLGNVLVCVLAHHFGKEFTPQVQAAYQKVVAGVANALAHKYH (146)
```

Comparison of the amino acid sequences of α- and β-haemoglobin chains in humans and great apes. Over the 287 amino acid positions of these haemoglobin chains, the two chimpanzees and humans are identical; the gorilla differs by two amino acid residues, and the orang-utan by four. This is an extremely small degree of haemoglobin evolution, considering that orang-utans, African apes and humans last shared a common ancestor in the middle Miocene epoch, more than 10 million years ago.

Three amino acid replacements (at myoglobin position 23 and β-haemoglobin positions 87 and 125) are shared by humans, chimpanzees and gorillas but not by gibbons or orang-utans. In addition, there is an amino acid replacement (at α-haemoglobin position 23) in *Homo* and *Pan* (both pygmy and common chimpanzees) but not in *Gorilla* and the Asian hominoids. These globin amino acid sequences support the grouping of *Homo*, *Pan* and *Gorilla* but do not place *Pongo* and *Hylobates* closest to this group. The most parsimonious myoglobin solution places *Hylobates* closest to *Pan*, *Gorilla* and *Homo* (by a single change at position 110), and the most parsimonious haemoglobin tree places *Pongo* closest to *Hylobates* (by a replacement at α12).

These trees cannot therefore resolve the branching order of the Hominoidea. However, mitochondrial DNA sequences and nuclear DNA–DNA hybridisation all give a confident grouping of *Pongo* closest to *Pan*, *Gorilla* and *Homo*. If we accept that the first split separates gibbons from all other hominoids, the myoglobin and haemoglobin trees now have four amino acid replacements (at myoglobin positions 23 and 110 and β-haemoglobin positions 87 and 125 on the stem to human, chimpanzees and gorillas) and one amino acid replacement (α-haemoglobin position 113) on the stem to *Pongo* and the other large hominoids.

The fetal haemoglobin of higher primates supports an African ape–human grouping. Fetal haemoglobin, like adult haemoglobin, has four chains but has γ chains in place of the adult β chains. The γ chain has the same number of amino acids as does a β chain, but differs in about 20 per cent in sequence. In catarrhine primates, two different genes on the same chromosome code for γ-haemoglobin chains. These arose from duplication of an ancestral γ-haemoglobin gene, and, except for a single glycine–alanine difference at position 136, the two human γ chains have identical amino acid sequences.

The DNA coding for linked γ-haemoglobin genes of humans, chimpanzees, gorillas, orang-utans, gibbons and rhesus monkeys (*Macaca mulatta*), together with those of spider monkeys (*Ateles*), tarsiers (*Tarsius syrichta*), brown lemurs (*Lemur fulvus*), dwarf lemurs (*Cheirogaleus*) and galagos (*Galago*), have all been sequenced and the non-coding regions of these primates support the species relationships that emerge from studies of the coding regions. Human, chimpanzee and gorilla ^Gγ chains, with glycine at position 136, have identical amino acid sequences, and differ from the corresponding orang-utan γ chain by only two amino acid replacements. Human and chimpanzee ^Aγ chains (with alanine at this position) also have identical sequences, but differ from gorilla ^Aγ at two positions.

Support for a late African ape–human split

Fibrinopeptides, myoglobins, adult and fetal haemoglobins, and carbonic anhydrase all provide evidence for an African ape–human group separate from Asian apes.

To break up this group by including orang-utans requires 11 additional amino acid replacements. These proteins also indicate that *Pan* and *Homo* rather than *Pan* and *Gorilla* are closest relatives, as an additional amino acid replacement is required to group *Pan* with *Gorilla* rather than with *Homo*. DNA evidence supports this conclusion also: to break up the human–chimpanzee–gorilla group by adding the orang-utan needs more than 90 additional nucleotide substitutions. The molecular data show that *Homo* and *Pan* are identical in 99.6 per cent of their amino acid sequences and 98.4 per cent of their DNA nucleotide sequences. This genetic correspondence to our closest ape relative could be evidence both for a late common ancestry and for a slow-down in the rate of molecular evolution.

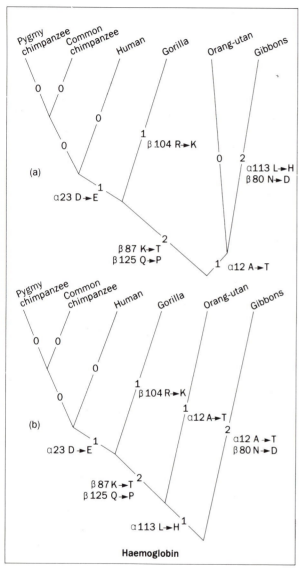

Evolutionary tree for humans and apes based on haemoglobins: (a) lowest number of amino acid replacments needed; (b) amino acid replacements constrained by other evidence. The reconstruction in (a) by the parsimony criterion of fewest sequence changes was carried out on the four β-haemoglobin and three α-haemoglobin positions that show amino acid differences among hominoids. The ancestral amino acid residues at the hominoid root were established by comparing the sequences for humans and apes with those for the Old World monkey, New World monkey, tarsier and lemur/loris outgroup. At α-haemoglobin position 12, ancestral residue alanine (A) changes to threonine (T) in the gibbon and orang-utan but not in the chimpanzee/human/gorilla clade. Thus the most parsimonious solution for haemoglobin sequences requires grouping the gibbon and the orang-utan. However, since the overall molecular evidence places the orang-utan closest to the chimpanzee/human/gorilla clade, the reconstruction constrained by other evidence (b) requires parallel A to T changes at α-haemoglobin position 8 in separate gibbon and orang-utan clades.

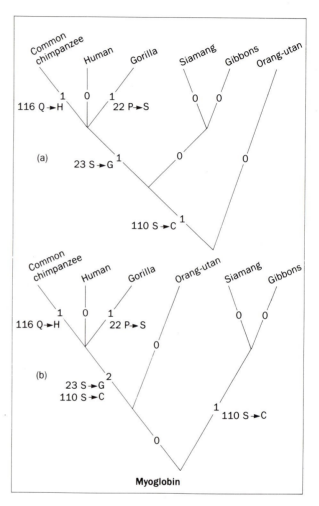

Evolutionary tree for humans and apes based on myoglobins: (a) lowest number of amino acid replacements needed; (b) amino acid replacements constrained by other evidence. The reconstruction in (a) by the parsimony criterion of fewest sequence changes was carried out on the four myoglobin positions that show amino acid differences among hominoids. The ancestral amino acid residues at the hominoid root were established by comparing the sequences for hominoids with those for the Old World monkey, New World monkey and lemur/loris outgroup. At position 110, ancestral residue serine (S) changes to cysteine (C) in the gibbon clade (siamang and gibbon) and in the common chimpanzee/human/gorilla clade but not in the orang-utan. Thus the most parsimonious solution for myoglobin sequences alone requires grouping the gibbon clade with the chimpanzee/human/gorilla clade. However, because the overall molecular evidence (involving not just amino acid sequences but also protein immunology and DNA hybridisation and sequence comparisons) places the orang-utan closest to the common chimpanzee/human/gorilla clade, the reconstruction constrained by other evidence (b) requires parallel S to C changes at position 110 in the gibbon and the common chimpanzee/human/gorilla/orang-utan clades.

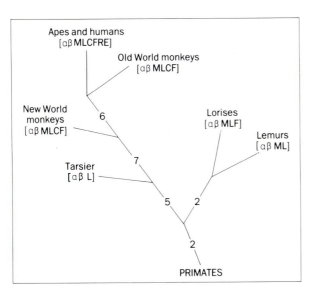

Apes and humans
[αβ MLCFRE]

Old World monkeys
[αβ MLCF]

New World
monkeys
[αβ MLCF]

6

Lorises
[αβ MLF]

Lemurs
[αβ ML]

Tarsier
[αβ L]

7

5   2

2

PRIMATES

Relationships of the main primate groups from combined protein sequences. The numbers on the stems are the minimum number of nucleotide replacements affecting amino acid sequences needed above the shortest tree to break up the relevant group.

Earlier history of the primates

Because natural selection slows the rate of amino acid change, comparative amino acid sequences are useful in studying the earlier evolutionary history of primates. A computer search is carried out for the trees that involve the fewest amino acid changes to generate patterns of relatedness and the best of them is chosen.

More than 500 protein chains of a wide range of vertebrates have been used in this way. The results agree with the classical morphological picture of vertebrate phylogeny, the primates dividing into two major groups: lorisiforms with lemuriforms, and *Tarsius* with the anthropoids (simians). Anthropoids in turn divide into ceboids (New World monkeys) and cercopithecoids (Old World monkeys) plus hominoids. Once again, the molecular evidence on phylogeny agrees with the morphological evidence.

The tempo and mode of protein evolution

Some apparent conflicts between the evolutionary trees for protein sequences and the classical morphological picture of phylogeny emerge if proteins are assumed to evolve at a constant rate, as claimed by proponents of the molecular clock hypothesis.

The trees for homologous protein sequences give molecular clock dates that are in some cases far too ancient and in other cases far too recent when compared with the fossil record. For example, using the calmodulin family of proteins, the clock places the last common ancestor of protozoans, plants and metazoans at over 2000 million years ago and the original calmodulin at a time (12 000 million years ago) long before earth existed. Molecular trees for globins,

cytochromes c, lens crystallins, carbonic anhydrases and fibrinopeptides give the following clock calculations: about 800 million years ago for the most recent common ancestor of vertebrates (several hundred million years too early, according to the fossil record); about 160 to 180 million years ago for the bird–mammal ancestor (over 100 million years too late); and among anthropoid primates some far too recent dates (such as a human–African ape split at only 1 to 2 million years ago).

The discrepancies between these dates and the fossil record suggest that there is no such thing as a universal molecular clock. Rather, molecular evolution – like morphological evolution – varies in rate. Fossil evidence on phylogeny suggests that there must have been a trend over the past 1500 million years towards a slowing in sequence evolution, with episodes of increased speed during major radiations of life (perhaps when selection acted on duplicated genes to generate new protein functions). The rate slowed when natural selection preserved such functional advantages. Calmodulin and globin show how natural selection is both a creative and a conservative force in evolution.

Calmodulin, with its four calcium-binding *domains* (polypeptide regions folded into compact units), is a highly conserved member of a family of eukaryotic proteins that controls levels of calcium within cells. Chicken and human calmodulins have identical amino acid sequences and vary from eel calmodulin by just one amino acid replacement, and from scallop calmodulin by just three.

The root of its phylogenetic tree, 1500 million years ago, marks the origin by gene duplications of the first calmodulin-like protein. Protozoans, plants and multicellular animals diverged about 1000 million years ago. The rate of evolution of the earliest calmodulin was about 40 times faster than that of its evolution from the first eukaryotes to their present-day animal, plant and protozoan descendants.

This evolutionary conservatism is related to calmodulin's range of functions. It must bind calcium, change shape and interact with many other enzymes. All this constrains its structure and conserves the amino acids involved. The versatility of present-day calmodulin was shaped by adaptive amino acid replacements during its early rapid evolution, and those in the earliest calmodulins were mainly at sites that remain unchanged in living organisms.

In branches of the calmodulin family involved in muscle function, evolution was much faster during the emergence of jawed vertebrates and tetrapods than during the descent of birds and mammals. This pattern suggests that selection brought about protein changes that led to improvements in muscle physiology important in the radiation of the tetrapods.

Rates of globin evolution were much faster in the early jawed vertebrates and early tetrapods than in the lineages to mammals and birds. In the early history of haemoglobin,

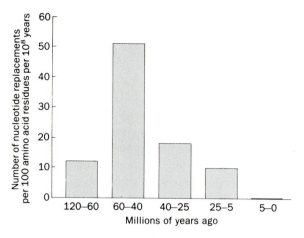

Accelerated and then decelerated rates of sequence change in the evolutionary history of the human $^G\gamma$-haemoglobin chain. Numbers of nucleotide replacements affecting amino acid sequences are from link lengths along the lineage that descended from the ε-γ-η-globin gene of the opossum–placental mammal ancestor to the human $^G\gamma$-**globin** gene in a maximum-parsimony tree constructed for globin genes. The time period of 120 to 60 million years ago is from this ancestor to the primate ancestor; the period 60 to 40 million years ago is from primate to anthropoid ancestor; the period 40 to 25 million years ago is from anthropoid to catarrhine ancestor; the period 25 to 5 million years ago is from catarrhine to *Homo–Pan* ancestor; and the period 5 to 0 million years ago is from *Homo–Pan* ancestor to modern humans.

Accelerated and then decelerated rates in the evolutionary history of the human $^G\gamma$-haemoglobin chain

Evolutionary period	Age (millions of years)	Number of NR*	Rate (NR%)†
Marsupial–placental mammal to primate ancestor	120–60	12	14
Primate to anthropoid ancestor	60–40	13	51
Anthropoid to catarrhine ancestor	40–25	4	18
Catarrhine to *Homo–Pan* ancestor	25–5	3	10
Homo–Pan ancestor to humans	5	0	0

* NR = nucleotide replacements changing the amino acid sequence; numbers of NR are from link lengths along the lineage that descended from the εγη-globin gene of the opossum–placental mammal ancestor to the human $^G\gamma$-globin gene in a maximum-parsimony tree constructed for globin genes.
† NR% = number of NR per 100 amino acid residues per 10^8 years.

there were about 69 nucleotide replacements affecting amino acids per 100 codons per 10^8 years, whereas in later periods from about 300 million years ago to the present day there were only about 16 per 100 codons. Rates of globin evolution were four to five times faster in earlier vertebrates than in the past 300 million years, as the primitive single-chain haemoglobin of the early vertebrates evolved into a tetramer with interacting subunits. The vertebrates were evolving into larger and more active animals and needed a haemoglobin that could deliver oxygen. The transition of monomeric haemoglobin to a tetramer occurred in two stages. In the first, more frequent amino acid replacements took place at prospective contact sites between identical chains. The second stage began with the gene duplication that produced separate α and β genes. This time there was fast evolution in the contact sites between the chains. Natural selection perfected the functional sites and then preserved them. This is evident from the fact that later on –

from the common ancestor of reptiles, birds and mammals to the present day – they were among the slowest evolving positions.

Although there was an acceleration of evolution at less critical surface sites during the emergence of primates, the rates of haemoglobin evolution slowed in the lineage descending to humans. Primate fetal haemoglobin shows this clearly. The fastest rate of amino acid change occurred in the single γ lineage of early primates when the embryonic γ haemoglobin evolved towards the fetal haemoglobin of simian primates, and the slowest occurred in the final 5 million years of human descent. Several of the nucleotide substitutions on the pre-simian γ lineage increased the oxygen-binding affinity of fetal haemoglobin. This ensured a favourable balance in the transport of oxygen from mother to fetus and helped make possible the extended fetal life and prenatal brain development of higher primates, showing, once again, how molecular evolution is closely coupled to the adaptive changes in morphology and behaviour that are the main preoccupation of primatologists.

Morris Goodman

See also 'Classification of primates' (p. 20), 'Measuring relatedness' (p. 295), 'Immunological evidence on primates' (p. 303), 'DNA–DNA hybridisation in the study of primate evolution' (p. 313) and 'Human evolution: the evidence from DNA sequencing' (p. 316)

DNA–DNA hybridisation in the study of primate evolution

The continuity from generation to generation links ancestors and descendants together in a chain of genetic change. If we could compare the DNA sequences of each generation with those of its ancestors we would find that the changes in each generation are small, but that the net change over time is cumulative. Genetic divergence is hence directly related to time. Although we cannot compare the DNAs of members of past generations, we can compare the DNAs of different living organisms that once shared a common ancestor. This allows us to measure the genetic change that has occurred in two lineages since they began to diverge, helps to reconstruct branching patterns of groups of living organisms and, in some cases, to estimate the date when a particular divergence happened. Since the early 1960s, one way of making such comparisons has been DNA–DNA hybridisation.

The DNA–DNA hybridisation technique (see next page) depends on the properties of the DNA molecule, with its sequence of paired bases held together by hydrogen bonds: adenine (A) in one strand pairs with thymine (T) in the other strand, and cytosine (C) pairs with guanine (G). Sequences of bases form genes, most of which are present as a single copy in the genome of each cell. However, between 3 and 5 per cent of genes occur in more than one copy in each genome; there may be thousands or even millions of copies, which can make up to 40 per cent of the total volume of DNA in the cell nucleus.

At least five different branching patterns for the phylogeny of the hominoids have been proposed. There is general agreement that the gibbons (*Hylobates*) are the descendants of the oldest hominoid branch and that the

orang-utan (*Pongo*) lineage is the next-oldest branch. The principal controversies concern the branching pattern of the lineages leading to the African apes – the gorilla (*Gorilla*) and the two chimpanzees (*Pan*) – and humans (*Homo*). Some methods of analysis produce a simultaneous triple branching for gorillas, chimpanzees and humans. This is unlikely and probably indicates only that the methods being used cannot resolve two branches close together in time.

The three more likely branching patterns for the African apes and humans are numbered 1, 2 and 3 on the diagram below left. There is little support for pattern 3, and it may be set aside. Most morphological and some genetic studies favour pattern 2, whereas most molecular comparisons favour pattern 1.

Building trees from DNA–DNA hybridisation

A phylogenetic tree for the five hominoid genera and several cercopithecoids (Old World monkeys) can be based on information from DNA–DNA hybridisation. The average difference in hybridisation (as shown by the ΔT_{50H} values) provides each point of divergence. The most closely related pair of species are joined first; then the next most closely related taxon is joined to the first pair; and so on, until all taxa have been joined in descending order from the top of the tree (see below).

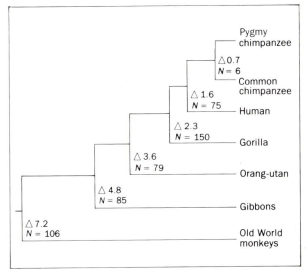

Patterns of relationship among the hominoid primates based on information from DNA–DNA hybridisation, assuming that the DNA evolutionary clock ticked at about the same rate along each branch. The lengths of the branches are therefore taken to be equal.
Δ = the average ΔT_{50H} values for DNA–DNA comparisons;
N = the number of DNA–DNA hybrids that were averaged (see text for explanation).

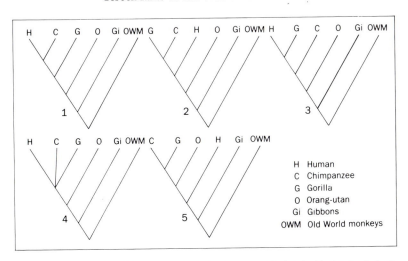

Possible patterns of relationship among the hominoid primates derived from morphological and molecular evidence.

H Human
C Chimpanzee
G Gorilla
O Orang-utan
Gi Gibbons
OWM Old World monkeys

THE DNA HYBRIDISATION TECHNIQUE

When double-stranded DNA in solution is boiled, the hydrogen bonds between the A–T and G–C pairs break or 'melt', and the double-stranded DNA is converted into single strands. The hydrogen bonds between complementary bases are the weakest in DNA, so that the rest of the molecule is not damaged by boiling. As a melted sample of DNA cools, the single strands collide by chance. If two strands with complementary base sequences collide, they reassociate into the double strands because the pairs of A–T and G–C bases 'recognise' one another and re-establish the hydrogen bonds between them.

If the temperature during reassociation is between about 45 and 55 °C, then a *duplex DNA* molecule will form, which may contain many mismatched base pairs. At 60 °C, however, the base-pairing must be at least 80 per cent accurate to form a thermally stable duplex so that the single strands of the DNA of any species will reassociate only with their complementary partners, hence restoring the double-stranded structure to its original state.

When the single-stranded DNAs of two different species are combined and incubated at 60 °C, *hybrid* double-stranded DNA molecules may form between homologous base sequences – those descending from a common ancestor. Only homologous sequences have the 80 per cent *complementarity* needed to form thermally stable duplexes at this temperature. Interspecific DNA–DNA hybrid duplexes will contain mismatched bases because the two lineages have undergone genetic changes since they diverged from their common ancestor.

In a hybrid duplex, an A base may be opposite a C, or a G opposite a T, and no bonds will form between them. Because the melting temperature depends on the number of hydrogen bonds between the two strands, such mismatches will cause the hybrid DNAs to melt at a temperature lower than that required to melt double strands from a single species.

During hybridisation, DNA is extracted from the nuclei of cells and separated from the proteins and other cell components. Its long strands are sheared into fragments of about 500 nucleotides. Most of the repeated sequences are removed from the DNA of the reference species used for comparison with others to give a fraction containing all of the sequences that originally occurred as one copy per genome, plus at least one copy of each different repeated sequence. This *single-*

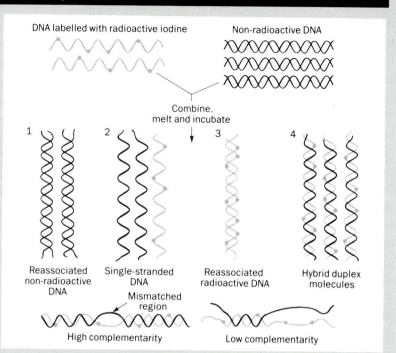

Formation of DNA hybrids. One part of radiolabelled DNA is combined with 1000 parts of non-radioactive DNA, from the same species or from a different species. The DNAs are melted and incubated together for 120 hours at 60 °C. Four combinations will be produced: 1, duplexes of non-radioactive single strands; 2, single strands that do not reassociate; 3, a small number of duplexes in which both strands are labelled; and 4, many hybrid duplexes in which one strand is labelled. The melting temperature of a duplex is determined by the extent of complementarity between base pairs: the greater the mismatch, the lower the melting temperature.

copy DNA is then labelled with an isotope, such as iodine-125, to produce a *tracer*.

Radioactive DNA of the tracer species is combined with a much larger amount of unlabelled DNA (the *driver*) from the same species to form *homoduplex* hybrids. If the same tracer is combined with driver DNAs of different species, *heteroduplex* hybrids form. The homoduplex hybrids are the standard against which the heteroduplexes are compared.

The tracer–driver combinations are boiled for 5 minutes to dissociate the double-stranded molecules into single strands. To enable the single strands of DNA to reassociate into duplexes they are incubated for 120 hours at 60 °C. Each of the tracer–driver combinations is then placed on a column of hydroxyapatite (a form of calcium phosphate) that binds the double-stranded but not the single-stranded DNA. The columns are immersed in a water bath at 55 °C and the temperature of the water is raised in increments of 2.5 degrees to 95 °C.

At each of the 17 temperatures the single-stranded DNA fragments produced by the melting of duplexes are washed from each column into a vial. The radioactivity in each of the 425 vials shows how much each hybrid has melted at each temperature. These values are plotted as *melting curves* of dissociation at different temperatures. The difference in the curves at each temperature between homoduplex and heteroduplex curves is a measure of the difference between the tracer and each driver species.

The difference in melting temperature can be calculated in several ways. It is often calculated as the temperature at which half the single-copy DNA sequences are in the duplex form and half have dissociated into single strands. This is called the T_{50H} (the temperature at 50 per cent hybridisation). The difference in this parameter (the ΔT_{50H}) between the two species is an indicator of how much their sequences have diverged since they shared a common ancestor. *C.G. Sibley*

In such a tree it is assumed that the molecular clock has been synchronous; that is, that the average rate of DNA evolution was the same along each branch. The lengths of the branches are therefore taken to be equal. However, a tree can also be produced by a method that does not assume that this is true (see diagram top right). Such a tree has branches that are nearly equal, except for that of the gibbons, which is shorter than the others. This may be due to experimental error or to a slower average rate of DNA evolution along the gibbon lineage. The branches in this tree are well separated except for those of the gorilla ($\Delta T_{50H} = 2.3$) against chimpanzees and humans

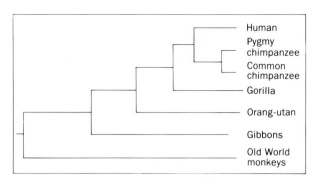

```
                              ┌──────── Human
                         ┌────┤
                    ┌────┤    ├──────── Pygmy chimpanzee
               ┌────┤    └──── Common chimpanzee
          ┌────┤    └────────── Gorilla
     ┌────┤    └───────────────── Orang-utan
─────┤    └──────────────────────── Gibbons
     └──────────────────────────────── Old World monkeys
```

Patterns of relationship among the hominoid primates based on information from DNA–DNA hybridisation, assuming that the DNA evolutionary clock ticked at different rates along the branches. The branch lengths are therefore unequal.

(ΔT_{50H} = 1.6). These differ by only 0.7 ΔT_{50H} units, and estimates of the DNA hybridisation for these two divergence points overlap by 0.6 ΔT_{50H} units. The patterns of separation are not yet clear, and more work using DNA hybridisation and other techniques is called for.

The DNA molecular evolutionary clock seems to be ticking at about the same average rate in all the hominoid lineages. ΔT_{50H} values can hence be used to date divergence points dated from the divergence points that can now be obtained from fossils. The orang-utan branch has been dated as between 13 and 16 million years ago. If the value of 16 million years ago is correct, then 16 can be divided by the average ΔT_{50H} of 3.6 for the orang-utan to obtain a time constant for ΔT_{50H} = 1.0 of 4.4. If 13 million

Dates for the divergence of the hominoid lineages obtained from DNA hybridisation and from fossils

	Millions of years		
Dates from DNA–DNA hybridisation			
Orang-utan branch = 13.0		or	16.0
Common chimpanzee–pygmy chimpanzee	2.5		3.1
Human	5.8		7.1
Gorilla	8.3		10.1
Dates from fossils			
Orang-utan branch = 13.0		or	16.0
Gibbon	17.3		21.1
Old World monkeys	26.0		31.7

years ago is used for the orang-utan lineage then the time constant is 3.6.

When the average ΔT_{50H} values for the other divergence points are multiplied by these constants, dates in good agreement with the fossil record emerge (see table above). However, there are as yet no fossils for some sections of this timespan. Some molecular evidence suggests that the human branch diverged more recently than 5.8 million years ago, but there are on the other hand human-like fossils from around 5 million years ago. To the primatologist, we are all living fossils, and the DNA–DNA hybridisation technique gives a unique insight into our own relationship with our extinct ancestors.

C.G. Sibley

See also 'The nature of evolution' (p. 9), 'Evolution of apes' (p. 223), 'Evolution of australopithecines' (p. 231) and other chapters in this part

Human evolution: the evidence from DNA sequencing

All DNA comes from pre-existing DNA and the order of bases along the DNA molecule – its *sequence* – contains much of the information needed to reconstruct human history. The task of producing the complete human sequence of 3000 million base pairs – the Human Genome Project, as it is known – has only just begun. However, DNA sequencing is already producing intriguing glimpses of our evolutionary history.

In the parts of the molecule that code for proteins, the four nucleotide components or bases – adenosine (A), cytosine (C), guanine (G) and thymine (T) – are read consecutively in triplets (*codons*) by the cellular machinery. Each codon corresponds to a particular amino acid under the rules of the genetic code. Most amino acids can be coded by more than one codon, so even if the order of the amino acids in a protein (its primary structure or sequence) is known, it is impossible to be certain which codon is involved and the precise identity of the bases in the corresponding DNA.

During the past decade, however, molecular geneticists have been able to identify the exact sequence of bases in stretches of DNA by direct methods.

Exons, introns and pseudogenes

The DNA of most organisms is not simply a linear collection of genes, each made up of codons and coding for a different protein. There are some surprises in the way a cell's complement of DNA (the genome) is organised. For example, the DNA that codes for a single protein is usually split into several stretches (*exons*), each separated by non-coding regions (*introns*), which may be of considerable length. The exons and introns related to a particular protein are demarcated by flanking sequences, which are recognised by the enzymes involved in reading and copying the coded message.

There are also regions of DNA, which, if read in codons, might code for recognisable proteins. However, they may have inappropriately placed or missing messages about where the cellular machinery should start and stop reading, and may also have accumulated mutations that, while they do not render the message unrecognisable, are enough to produce a defective protein. Such regions are called *pseudogenes*, because they look like functional genes, yet their message is not used by the cell to make protein. Whether or not they are entirely without function is not certain.

Both pseudogenes and functional genes may be derived from other genes during evolution by *duplication* of long stretches of DNA and the subsequent accumulation of mutations. Much of the genome is therefore organised as a series of *gene families*: collections of genes related in their position, their origins and their functions. The rate of gene duplication is fairly low, and some of the products of past duplications may have been so scrambled that they now defy recognition.

Gene duplication and other complications

An alarming possibility for those attempting to reconstruct evolutionary history from the genomes of living animals is that in some cases of gene duplication the closely related genes in a gene family may continue to exchange DNA sequences, so that the independence of their evolution is thrown into doubt.

For example, there is evidence that some distinctive repeated sequences of DNA, dispersed throughout the genome, may be transposable; that is, mobile within the genome. Also, there appear to be duplicated γ-globin genes in some anthropoid primates. From the way these genes are distributed among animals that diverged tens of millions of years ago, the duplication seems to have been a relatively early event. However, the duplicated γ-globin genes are strikingly similar to each other in humans. One interpretation of this unexpected similarity in the face of

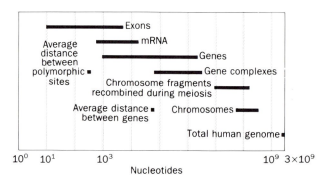

The size of the human genome on a scale from 1000 to 3000 million nucleotides. The figures at the bottom are a logarithmic scale of numbers of bases; the bars show different elements of the genome. Exons are the coding segments of genes. Messenger RNA (mRNA) is longer than most exons as, before editing, it includes segments of non-coding information. Genes vary greatly in size, and may be arranged in gene families that are themselves very different in length. During meiosis (which is involved in the formation of sperm and egg) there may be visible points of breakage and reunion along the chromosomes. The lengths of the chromosomes themselves vary by 10 times or more. Restriction fragment length polymorphisms (see Box 1) turn up every few hundred bases; working genes are separated by around 100 000 apparently functionless DNA bases from each other; and the whole genome consists of around 3000 million base pairs.

ancient divergence is that there has been exchange of DNA between the duplicated genes. Regions of DNA might also be transferred between distantly related organisms by viruses, but the extent of this is not yet known.

Restriction maps

The DNAs of humans and their closest living relatives have been compared using a variety of techniques, each of which is appropriate to a particular level of comparison. For example, *restriction enzymes* can be used to cut a DNA molecule (Box 1). Each enzyme recognises a specific number and order of bases, and, by using a variety of such enzymes, a *restriction map* of the cut points can be built up.

Such restriction maps are a useful first step in the study of evolution at the DNA level, but there is controversy about how they should be analysed. The loss of a particular restriction site seems to be more frequent than is its gain, and this must be taken into account. Differences in sequence between the DNAs of different species can be roughly estimated using restriction site data. However, the restriction map does not contain anything like the information that can be obtained by full sequencing of the DNA.

DNA sequencing

In DNA sequencing, a battery of genetical and biochemical techniques is used to determine the order of bases in a stretch of DNA (see Boxes 1 and 2). Such sequences are so far available for only a few corresponding parts of the genomes of humans and apes, although there is much more information for humans alone. The technique of DNA–DNA hybridisation (which involves a less precise, but much more extensive, comparison of the genetic material of humans and apes) has hence been quite widely used.

DNA sequences from two regions of the primate genome have provided most fuel for speculation about human relationships. The first of these includes the families of globin genes that code for parts of a variety of oxygen-binding molecules, such as haemoglobin (the oxygen-carrying molecule of blood). Sequences for functional globin genes and globin pseudogenes of humans, chimpanzees, gorillas, orang-utans and gibbons (and, indeed, more widely amongst the primates) have now been compared. Previously undiscovered globin genes are still being revealed and sequenced. The genomes of organelles called mitochondria, which are present in the cytoplasm of most eukaryotic cells (those with their genetic material contained within a distinct nucleus), have also been at least partially sequenced for a range of primates.

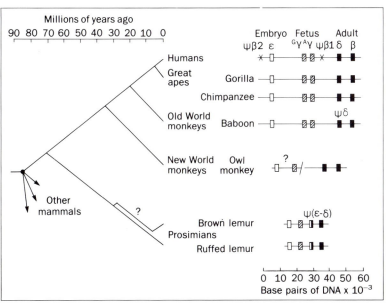

Evolution of the β-globin gene cluster in humans and other primates. β-, γ- and ε-like genes, as determined by DNA sequencing and hybridisation, are represented by filled, hatched and open boxes, respectively. Human globin pseudogenes are indicated by crosses; corresponding pseudogenes probably exist in the β-globin gene cluster of the gorilla, chimpanzee and baboon. Some linkage relationships remain uncertain. The divergence time between the brown and ruffed lemurs (*Lemur fulvus* and *Varecia variegata*) is problematical.

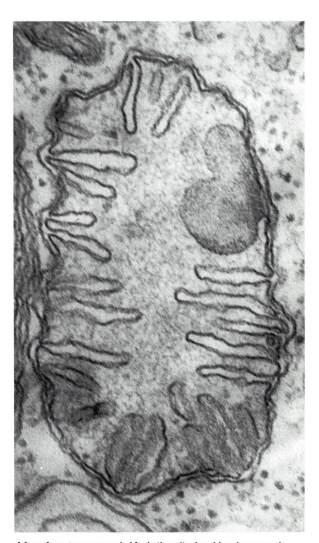

A few of our genes are coded for in the mitochondrion, here seen in section in the cytoplasm of a cell. Mitochondrial DNA can give useful insights into evolution (see p. 319 and Box 3 on p. 320). (×105 000)

1. CUTTING, SPLICING AND SEQUENCING GENES

DNA consists of an extraordinarily long sequence of bases, arranged in strings that may be millions of units long. Very often, these strings must be cut and rejoined. For example, during sexual reproduction there is recombination: offspring have mixtures of the genes of their mother and father, even when those genes are on the same chromosome. Certain viruses can insert themselves into the DNA molecule, and there are protective mechanisms for cutting out these molecular parasites. In the same way, most organisms can cut out and repair damage to the DNA caused by mutations.

All these events involve slicing through the DNA and re-establishing it in a new arrangement. In the past 20 years we have learned a great deal about how this is done, and have been able to modify the natural mechanisms of cutting and splicing DNA to found the new science of *genetic engineering*. Many of its methods are essential to our new understanding of human genetics and evolution.

The whole field turns on the discovery that bacteria have *restriction enzymes* that can cut DNA at very specific sites. Each of the hundred or so now available recognises and cuts a particular four- or six-base sequence of DNA. The more frequent that sequence – for example, GGCC or GAATTC – along the DNA molecule, the smaller the ensuing pieces will be.

Some restriction enzymes recognise common sequences, others rare ones, and by judicious use of the enzymes available it is possible to cut the DNA into pieces of almost any desired length. The cut sections can be separated using electrophoresis, the movement of charged molecules through a filtering medium when placed in an electrical field (see p. 265). For DNA, this usually involves a gel made of agarose. The separated fragments can be seen with dyes or by shining ultraviolet light (which is absorbed by DNA) onto the gel.

As soon as this method was used on human DNA, its importance became apparent: DNA *restriction fragments* from different people are often of different lengths, showing that the relevant cutting sites – and hence DNA sequences – are at different places along the molecule. This gave the first insight into the extraordinary amount of genetic variation or polymorphism at the DNA level in humans.

The method is also important in medical genetics, as *restriction fragment length polymorphisms* (RFLPs) associated with a damaged gene can be traced down the generations in families with genetic diseases, and often give a clue as to who is carrying the defect. This information is essential when giving genetic advice or testing fetuses to see if they are genetically damaged.

It is possible to link the cut pieces of DNA together in novel combinations using other enzymes called ligases. The new arrangement can be inserted into a bacterium, and thousands of identical copies made. In some cases – such as the gene for human growth hormone – the bacterium can even make a very pure human protein. The process is simplified by stitching the new gene into a *cloning vector* derived from a virus, which can itself be inserted into a bacterial chromosome.

Further refinements of the technology allow the DNA sequence of a cell to be established. The DNA is randomly cut into many pieces and each is cloned into a different bacterial culture to give a DNA *library* containing all the genetic information sliced into convenient sections.

There are various ways of reading the sequence in each section. One is to take a radioactively labelled single strand of the DNA and treat it chemically to break it at specific nucleotide sites. Different chemicals break A, G, C or T. Electrophoresis allows fragments differing only in a single nucleotide to be separated. The hundreds of bands that result are stretched in four lanes treated to identify each base along the length of the gel, allowing the order of bases to be read by ticking off the order of the bands.

Modifications of this and other sequencing methods, the use of yeast rather than bacteria to clone genes and the availability of powerful computers to analyse the information that emerges make it possible to sequence genes very quickly. There is now much excitement about the possibility of sequencing the 3 billion (3×10^9) base pairs that make up the human genome. Even before the Human Genome Project has come to fruition the new genetic technology has given us insights into human gene structure unthinkable even a few years ago.

Steve Jones

See also 'Genetic diversity in humans' (p. 264)

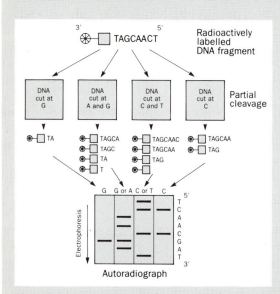

One way of reading the sequence of bases in DNA. In the Maxam–Gilbert method, DNA is cut into fragments with a restriction enzyme. The fragments are separated by electrophoresis and then radioactively labelled at one end. The mixture is then divided into four batches, each of which is treated with a chemical that attacks one (or sometimes two) of the four DNA bases A, G, C and T. This gives a series of short sections of radioactively labelled DNA, the lengths of which are determined by where A, G, C or T are in the molecule. The four batches are electrophoresed on adjacent tracks on the same gel; and the DNA sequence read from the position of the bands on the gel as manifest on x-ray film.

2. HUNTING FOR GENES WITH A SOUTHERN BLOT

One of the most important techniques of molecular biology depends on a simple trick thought up by Edward Southern of the University of Edinburgh. It is a way of looking for a particular sequence along the DNA. Once a gene has been cloned (see Box 1), hundreds of copies of that gene (or of its artificially synthesised messenger RNA) can be made and labelled with a radioactive marker. This *probe* can then be used to search for identical or similar genes elsewhere in the genome or in related species. When it finds the appropriate matching sequence, the probe – and its attached radioactive label – binds to it.

Southern blotting involves cutting the DNA that is to be searched with a restriction enzyme (Box 1) to give a series of fragments. These are then separated by electrophoresis (p. 265), to give lengths of DNA of different size. The fragments are washed through the gel on to a filter material. The probe is then applied to the filter, and binds on to any pieces that contain the appropriate sequence. Autoradiography of the filter detects radiation and hence the presence and location of lengths of DNA similar to those in the probe.

This method has been very useful in comparative studies of different species. For example, a probe for a human globin gene has been used to search for its analogues on other primates, and even in distantly related vertebrates such as fish. Even better, the efficiency of binding of the probe to the target gene is a measure of how similar the two are; the less sequence in common, the weaker the attachment of the probe to the target. This is a crude but effective way of testing how much evolutionary change there has been of a particular gene in two related species.

Steve Jones

Gene mapping with a Southern blot. After the DNA has been cut with a restriction enzyme, the fragments are separated by electrophoresis. The separated lengths of DNA are then 'blotted' onto a filter by placing gel and filter in close contact. A radioactively labelled gene probe containing the DNA target sequence is incubated with the filter, and binds to the appropriate cut length of DNA. The fragment containing the gene of interest hence becomes radioactive, and can be identified using x-ray film.

See also 'Genetic diversity in humans' (p. 264)

Mitochondrial DNA

The inner cavity of the mitochondrion contains enzymes involved in the release of food energy and also some DNA, present in several copies. Mitochondrial genomes are circular and lack the non-coding regions present in nuclear DNA (see Box 3, p. 320). The partial autonomy of mitochondria may reflect their possible origin as organisms in their own right, which were incorporated into cells in the early evolution of eukaryotic organisms.

The human mitochondrial genome was completely sequenced in 1981 in what was then a *tour de force* of molecular biology that involved the sequencing of some 16 000 base pairs. It has also been completely sequenced for mouse, cow, toad and fruit fly. Mitochondrial genes are maternally inherited (via the cytoplasm of the egg), and have a higher average rate of change than nuclear genes. This is an advantage for studying populations within species. However, the unusual mode of inheritance and the ability of the mitochondrial genome to cross boundaries

between some closely related species cause problems of interpretation. There are, for example, mouse populations that have the nuclear genes of one species and the mitochondrial genes of a closely related one. It has been claimed that the relatively recent dates estimated from mitochondrial DNA sequences for the divergence of humans and chimpanzees may reflect a transfer of mitochondrial DNA between them. Recent evidence suggests that paternal inheritance of mitochondrial DNA is possible, but this seems to be very unusual.

The value of mitochondrial DNA is illustrated by a study of human mitochondrial DNA from people from different parts of the world. All the mitochondrial DNAs examined may stem from one woman, postulated to have lived some 200 000 years ago, possibly in Africa. The reconstructed pathways of evolution suggest that each geographic area was colonised repeatedly, but this interpretation has recently been challenged (Box 3).

Comparing ape and human DNA sequences

What do DNA sequence comparisons tell us of the evolutionary history of humans and apes? First, they confirm the observation, originally made on the basis of comparison of proteins, that the genomes of humans, chimpanzees and gorillas are very similar: so similar, in fact, that there has been speculation that the differences in anatomy between humans and chimpanzees might arise not so much in the genes that code for the proteins making up flesh and bones, but from differences in *regulatory genes*. Such genes, in a manner as yet very imperfectly known, affect the details of growth and development: the way in which the otherwise virtually identical building blocks of the body are put together.

Secondly, evolutionary trees estimated from DNA sequences complement other evidence in suggesting that the closest living relatives of humans are chimpanzees and gorillas. It is not yet possible to suggest the precise patterns of relationship among these three, although a statistically vulnerable case might be made for a somewhat more recent evolutionary divergence of humans and chimpanzees than for either of these and the gorilla. There is, however, general agreement from DNA sequence studies that the lineage leading to orang-utans is older, and that the lineage leading to gibbons is older still.

In making comparisons between corresponding sequences of different species, the sequences are lined up and the differences between each pair of sequences are identified. In order to estimate times of evolutionary divergence of species and the patterns of relationship, it is necessary to make assumptions about the processes that lead to the accumulation of these differences during evolution. There is no clear agreement about which assumptions are the most realistic, and different workers can, and do, come to different conclusions using identical data.

One rather controversial assumption is that rates of molecular evolution are approximately constant for a given region of DNA. This enables the calculation of relative times of divergence. Approximate constancy of rate of change (often rather optimistically referred to as the 'molecular clock'; see p. 296) has also been claimed for protein molecules, although others disagree.

A constant rate might best be explained by the speculation that most changes at the molecular level accumulate without any significant involvement of natural selection; the changes are 'neutral' (or very nearly so) in terms of their effects on their carriers. This logic is used to support a comparison only of changes at the third-base position in the codon triplet in related organisms because such changes usually do not change the amino acid sequence (they are hence described as *silent* changes). Others claim that in those cases where molecules have been sufficiently studied some adaptive significance has usually been uncovered. An apparent constancy of rate might then result from an averaging out of the effects of complex selective forces on DNA over long periods. In addition, many biologists feel that there is good evidence that DNA sequences do not evolve at what even the most optimistic could call a constant rate.

There are differences in rates of change for the various gene families, and higher rates of change in introns as compared to the protein-coding exons. Molecular evolution may be slower in hominoids and higher in rodents compared to other mammals, perhaps because of the effects of generation time. Clearly, if there is no consistent time-dependence of molecular evolution any estimation of the pattern and the dating of evolution cannot depend on such an assumption, although moderately different rates of change can be accommodated by this approach.

Another method involves reconstructing past events in molecular evolution by working down a postulated tree from the present-day sequences. It assumes that evolution is basically a divergent process (that is, that animals and

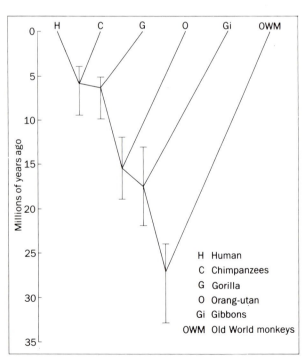

An evolutionary tree for primates based on globin and mitochondrial gene sequences. The pattern represents a consensus of recent studies, but the relationships between humans, chimpanzees and gorillas remain questionable. The bars indicate ranges of estimated times for the branch points.

3. WAS EVE AN AFRICAN?

Nearly all our genes are coded for in the DNA of the nucleus. However, a few are in the cytoplasm, where they are associated with mitochondria, the sites of much of our energy metabolism. In plants, the chloroplasts (which trap the sun's energy) also have their own genome. Both might be a relic of an ancient evolutionary past, when the ancestors of these organelles lived as free-living creatures that were later incorporated into the cells of modern creatures.

Differences in the genetic code of nucleus and mitochondrion are a clue to their independent origin, as is the fact that mitochondrial genes lack the introns and long stretches of functionless DNA found in the nucleus. The small size of mitochondrial DNA (mtDNA) means that its sequence of about 16 500 bases has been completely established in humans.

Mitochondria can give useful insights into evolution. They have some helpful properties. First, they evolve very quickly. Because there are no repair enzymes (such as those found in the nucleus) that can correct mutations, mtDNA accumulates genetic changes at about 10 times the rate of nuclear DNA. Second, mtDNA sometimes behaves oddly, because mitochondrial genes occasionally cross the barriers between species. In addition, mtDNA is mainly maternally inherited: it passes down the female line. This is because sperm provides almost no cytoplasm (and hence no mitochondria) to the fertilised egg.

The egg has thousands of mitochondria and it is these that are passed to the developing embryo. A few male mitochondria may leak through, but mitochondrial inheritance is largely matrilineal.

Mitochondrial DNA hence contains within itself a history of the world's women. Inevitably, this has led to publicity about the search for 'Eve' who had within her cells the mitochondrial genes that are the ancestors of all those existing today. The mitochondrial Eve story, which – like its biblical counterpart – once seemed a clear and convincing tale about where humanity was born, has, however, become an increasingly murky one. The problem turned out to be a failure of understanding and communication between two fields, population genetics and statistics. Geneticists published a tree of relatedness of mitochondrial DNA from different peoples that seemed to show that the African lineage was distinct, with those in the rest of the world forming a relatively homogeneous group that had split off from the African lines of descent. This fitted neatly with what the fossils say about the probable origin of humankind in Africa. Eve was, it seemed, black.

However, a new statistical study of just how this tree was made shows that an African source is no more likely than is an origin of the ancestral mitochondrion in many other parts of the world. Molecular geneticists simply had not realised just what an enormous amount of information is needed to produce a reliable evolutionary tree from DNA sequences. Although there are some intriguing hints, such as the higher level of genetic diversity in Africa, African Eve was, it turned out (to quote T.H. Huxley, Darwin's Victorian protagonist) 'a beautiful theory, killed by an ugly fact'.

Even when an increased understanding of molecular patterns in human population

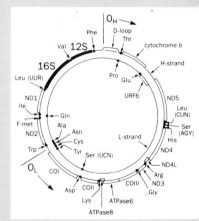

The order of the genes along the mitochondrion. The DNA – unlike that of the nucleus – is arranged as a closed loop. A number of functional genes are coded for in the mitochondrion. These include cytochrome *b* (involved in energy metabolism) and the genes for 16S and 12S ribosomal RNA (which are important in the synthesis of proteins). The D-loop (or displacement loop) contains no functional genes and, as it accumulates mutations particularly quickly, has been much used to study mitochondrial evolution.

their molecules get progressively more unlike one another). The evolutionary tree (or trees – there may be several) whose pattern demands the minimum amount of change is held to be the best estimate. This assumption is not strong enough to provide more than the order of branchings on a tree, and the number of events on each branch, once the position of its root has been determined.

Any assignment of absolute dates to the branching-points of an evolutionary tree must be based on the evidence of the fossil record and of geology. Because evolutionary trees estimated using DNA from sequencing studies can supply only relative times of divergence, at least one independent calibration point is needed to convert these into absolute times. Estimates of times of divergence based on the fossil record are themselves subject to uncertainty, and opinions differ on which particular divergences are best used as benchmarks for calibrating trees based on molecular evidence.

Several recent studies indicate that humans, chimpanzees and gorillas diverged from one another between 4 and 10 million years ago; that the orang-utan lineage diverged from those three between 12 and 19 million years ago; and that the gibbon lineage diverged between 13 and 22 million years ago.

The evolutionary tree here is based on globin and mitochondrial gene sequences. The time ranges for the branching-points reflect both the different relative times obtained and the different calibration points used by different workers. This diagram shows a satisfying general agreement with most of the trees that emerge from independent evidence from the biology of living primates described in earlier chapters. However, it is a statistical estimate of evolutionary history, and is open to re-evaluation in the light of new information.

A challenge has recently come from a study of the skin protein involucrin. The gene for involucrin has a complex pattern of repeats of a sequence of 10 codons throughout most of its length. These repeats seem to have been created by successive additions in one direction. When the pattern of repeats, themselves containing characteristic point mutations, is analysed it is possible to make a strong case for a closer relationship between chimpanzees and gorillas than either have to humans. As always, the case is only as good as the assumptions made about the relative probability of different evolutionary events, such as additions and deletions of blocks of sequence. There may well be further surprises in store concerning the relationships of humans, chimpanzees and gorillas.

A.E. Friday

See also 'The nature of evolution' (p. 9), 'Genetic diversity in humans' (p. 264), 'Measuring relatedness' (p. 295), 'Chromosomal evolution in primates' (p. 298), 'Immunological evidence on primates' (p. 303) and 'DNA–DNA hybridisation in the study of primate evolution' (p. 313)

finally makes it possible to establish where the ancestral mitochondrion actually came from, any Eve can never be much more than a statistical artefact. As each of us has two parents, four grandparents and so on, and

The evolutionary tree that was used to infer that Eve was an African. The tree of relatedness was made by comparing the mitochondrial sequence of 189 people from different continents. There were 135 distinct DNA sequences. When molecular biologists arranged these in order of affinity, it seemed that nearly all the African sequences (no block on the ends of the lines) grouped together, as did the non-African sequence (symbols on the line ends). A more sophisticated statistical study of the differences among the various groups has, however, shown that several other trees, with the root in different parts of the world, explain the results equally well. Eve may have been an African, but that is all we can say from the mitochondrial data. The shape of this tree is a device to save space.

as there were a limited number of people alive at any time, then if one traces any gene back for long enough one will reach a hypothetical common ancestor. For example, everyone with a particular name (at least a name which originated only once) descends from the first male to bear that name. This does not, of course, mean that this individual was the sole man alive at that time. There were thousands of others, many of whom bore names that have since gone extinct.

Exactly the same is true of the mitochondrial 'Eve'. There were large numbers of other women around when she flourished, but, by chance (the accidental loss of genes from women who had only sons, or no children at all), their mitochondrial genotypes have disappeared.

Steve Jones

See also 'Bottlenecks in human evolution' (p. 281)

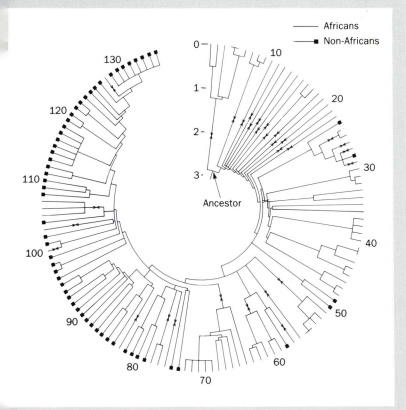

Africans ──
Non-Africans ──■

Ancestor

Part Nine

Early human behaviour and ecology

The behaviour of ancient humans attracts at least as much research interest today as does taxonomy or evolutionary relationships, and has considerably greater general appeal. Reconstructing past behaviours depends on a sound understanding of how the behavioural system functions today, whether it involves social structure, manipulation or stone tools. The general principles that emerge can then be applied to comparable situations in the past. This approach has had considerable success with behaviours that are amenable to relatively straightforward interpretation, such as those associated with diet (**2.7, 9.1, 9.6** and **9.8**), subsistence (**2.7, 9.1, 9.5, 9.7** and **9.9**), manipulation (**9.4**) and locomotion (**2.8, 2.9** and **9.1**). Areas such as intelligence (**9.3**) and social organisation (**9.1, 9.2** and **Part 4**) are more problematic.

Hominids had diverged from apes by the end of the Miocene epoch, some 5 million years ago, but did not evolve anatomically into recognisably modern humans until a little before 100 000 years ago. Modern human behaviours such as decorative and representational art (**9.6**) appeared even later, beginning only after 45 000 years ago.

Early humans undoubtedly lived in small groups, like their ape cousins, until late in the Pleistocene (**10.2**). The current view is that throughout the long australopithecine phase (**6.5**), which lasted until less than 2 million years ago, hominids were basically ape-like in their levels of behavioural complexity and social organisation. They mainly depended, as do all primates including humans, on plants for food, and there is as yet little direct evidence that they ate more meat than do some chimpanzee populations today. However, recent isotopic studies (**9.8**) suggest that australopithecines included more meat in their diet than many of us had suspected.

There is no evidence that australopithecines regularly flaked stones to make tools, but cobbles may have been used as hammers, and bones and sticks as digging implements. The extent to which these early hominids were or were not like humans in critical social and reproductive behavioural patterns has been much debated since their discovery, and this debate continues. Judging from brain size and likely rates of growth and development, however, their capability for complex behaviour was probably ape-like.

Sparks fly as a lump of quartzite is flaked to make a tool.

323

By around 2.5 million years ago some hominids began to flake stone systematically and to use the sharp flakes to cut up animal carcasses (**9.1** and **9.5**). After 2 million years ago, these early species of *Homo* developed larger brains and their postcranial anatomy and limb proportions became more human-like. However, reconstructing the behaviour of such hominids 'in the middle' — between the still basically ape-like australopithecines and the late Pleistocene modern humans — has proved difficult and contentious. It has nonetheless stimulated a great deal of research.

One much-debated issue concerns diet and subsistence. *Homo habilis* and *Homo erectus* ate more animal food than the australopithecines did. But was meat obtained by hunting or scavenging (**2.7**, **9.1** and **9.7**)? Was it eaten daily, monthly or seasonally? Did the hunter share it out? What effect did meat-eating have on social organisation and behaviour? To what extent did these pre-modern *Homo* species behave like fully modern humans? Some argue that the record shows distinctly non-human behaviour until very late in the human story (**9.7**) — although this interpretation is a little difficult to square with, for example, brain size (**3.2**), which had increased to modern dimensions by several hundred thousand years ago.

Several problems remain even after *Homo sapiens* entered the scene. For example, hominids that were ruggedly built but basically modern in their anatomy appeared between 130 000 and 100 000 years ago, but the first clear indication of fully modern behavioural capabilities is not found until much later. Speech and language may, perhaps, have appeared as early as 100 000 years ago (**3.5**).

Even while foraging as hunters and gatherers, people probably began to live, at least seasonally or occasionally, in larger social groups (**9.9** and **10.2**), perhaps as early as 20 000 years ago. Between 12 000 and 9000 years ago, there was a major shift in the subsistence of some groups to a reliance on domesticated plants (**9.9**) and animals (**9.10**). These changes allowed people to give up their nomadic lifestyle and to settle in permanent communities, with a subsequent growth in population size and density. The rest, as they say, is history.

The hominid way of life

Patterns of behaviour related to reproduction, obtaining food and other matters of survival are involved in the descent and divergence of species, so studies of behavioural change are crucial to an understanding of evolution. Much of the uniqueness of the human species lies in the behaviour that distinguishes us from our closest biological relatives. The early hominid way of life may therefore illuminate the processes by which we evolved and the major events that mark the origin of humans.

Two ingredients are needed in order to infer the activities or behaviour patterns of early hominids: evidence from the fossil and archaeological records (such as fossilised bones or stone tools) and a framework for interpreting these that must come from present-day experiments and observation. Two simple examples will illustrate the interaction of evidence and interpretation.

The fossilised footprints at Laetoli (Tanzania) and bones, especially from the pelvis and leg, discovered at Hadar (Ethiopia) both indicate that bipedal walking appeared early in human evolution. The footprints are direct evidence for hominids striding on two legs. The fossil bones themselves provide evidence of muscle attachments and bone morphology, which, according to modern biomechanics, show the usual stresses and muscular forces associated with bipedal locomotion. Subtle clues of bone morphology suggest, however, that the movements of these early hominids were not exactly like those of modern humans, perhaps because of a compromise between time spent in trees and that on the ground.

The interpretation of these fossils is hence based on (and can therefore be tested by) observations of locomotor anatomy and behaviour in humans and other living primates. Biomechanics and functional anatomy allow inferences to be made about patterns of movement from the morphology of fossil bones.

The 3.6-million-year-old footprint trails of three hominid individuals, probably *Australopithecus afarensis*, preserved in fossilised volcanic ash at Laetoli, Tanzania. The tracks were found by members of Mary Leakey's excavation team in 1978 and 1979. Crossing the hominid trails are the prints of an extinct horse called *Hipparion*. The discovery of the footprints confirmed that early hominids walked upright on two legs in a characteristically human fashion and that their footbones were arranged like a modern human's, with no gap between the big toe (toe 1) and the other toes.

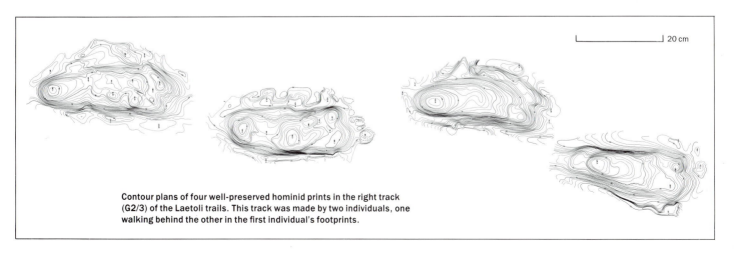

Contour plans of four well-preserved hominid prints in the right track (G2/3) of the Laetoli trails. This track was made by two individuals, one walking behind the other in the first individual's footprints.

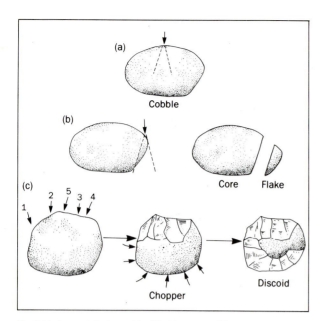

Hominid stone artefacts are identified by repeated fracturing of stone through conchoidal impact, as shown here. (a) At the point of impact (arrowed) of one stone on another, a force is generated in the shape of a cone. (b) If a brittle piece of rock is struck on its edge, the force will detach a thin, sharp sliver of stone, called a flake; the original piece is the core. (c) The earliest groups of stone artefacts (assemblages) have pieces (e.g. choppers and discoids) that are modified repeatedly in this way. Although these artefacts may have been used as tools, it is known that the sharp flakes were also useful in activities that involved cutting.

A second example comes from archaeology. Hominids began manufacturing tools from stone around 2.5 million years ago, an inference based on pieces of chipped stone excavated from sediments of this age and on methods for recognising human instances of stone fracture. The oldest stone artefacts are crude but can be distinguished from naturally broken rocks by regular patterns of scars over a rock from which slivers of stone have been detached by consistent fracture. Often, the modified stones, or *cores*, and the sharp slivers, or *flakes*, are found together. When these occur in a context in which geological movement and collision of stones, such as by stream action, is unlikely, it is reasonable to infer that the stone tools were produced by hominids. In this case, as in most interpretations of archaeological evidence, geological information is essential.

Distinctive features of human behaviour

Human behaviours are often complicated and subtle. They involve an intricate web of features, much more than simple improvements in physical speed, power, size, or rate of reproduction. Several aspects of modern human behaviour and ecology are often considered in accounts of human evolution. These range from patterns of locomotion, through diet and foraging, to a complex of social behaviours, such as sexuality, language and culture.

Observations of living apes and monkeys have helped enormously to refine our ideas about the behavioural traits

that distinguish humans. Such studies have often closed the gap between people and apes, so that the differences in some aspects of behaviour now appear to be matters of degree. For instance, chimpanzees make tools for certain tasks, such as preparing sticks for catching termites (see p. 342). Groups of chimpanzees are also known to accumulate debris (such as nutshells and stone hammers) in a way similar to that found in archaeological sites. Tool use or manufacture alone is hence not unique to human beings; it is the extraordinary degree of dependence on such use that is distinctive of the world's peoples.

Because modern hunter-gatherers are often presumed to provide a reasonable picture of early human foragers, and living apes are closely related to modern humans, studies of these two groups might provide an insight into early hominid life. Such field studies are no doubt significant, but any more specific inferences about the behaviour and ecology of early hominids must rely on material evidence from the geological record. The way of life or the physical characteristics of living apes or humans do not necessarily help us to infer the activities of early hominids. For example, fossilised skeletal remains show that some early Pleistocene hominids had anatomical adaptations, such as large teeth and massive facial skeletons, outside the range of any modern apes and people.

The behaviour and ecology of early hominids should

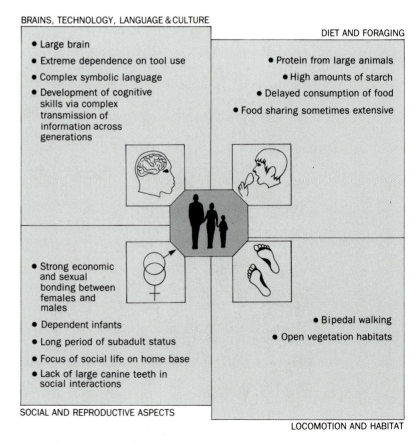

Some of the characteristics that distinguish modern humans from other primates.

thus not be treated as a simple amalgam of modern apes and humans. Evidence from the geological record is crucial: modern primates and human foragers can do little more than provide hypotheses about early hominid behaviour, and certainly cannot produce inferences about the activity patterns of particular hominids or the timing of events in their evolution.

Many characteristics of early human behaviour are, however, difficult to reconstruct, as no appropriate material evidence is available. Mating patterns and language are obvious examples – social life, words and grammar leave no traces in the fossil record. Bones, teeth and stone implements are preserved, so that questions about early locomotion, diet and technology are more tractable. Questions of social life and language may be accessible from studies of ancient environments, or from certain aspects of anatomy and behaviour that leave material evidence. For example, slower maturation rates in infants and increased dispersal of food resources (requiring the exchange of food between males and females) might favour hominid males who contributed resources to the infant–mother unit to a degree greater than that seen in other primates.

The fossil record bears directly on this suggestion. The teeth and crania of immature fossil specimens suggest that developmental rates in hominids earlier than *Homo erectus* (that is, before about 1.7 million years ago) may have been faster than that of modern humans. Second, hominids around 1.6 million years ago in eastern Africa faced a major shift to a drier climate, which was probably accompanied by a decrease in the availability of food. At this time, therefore, both these factors might have favoured an increased involvement of males in families and hence a shift in hominid social arrangements.

Inference often blends into guesswork in such arguments: just how complex social characteristics might be interpreted from such indirect clues is by no means generally agreed. Our ideas about the way of life of human ancestors will no doubt change in response to new fossil evidence, and with improvements in the way we interpret it. At present, three main types of fossil evidence are relevant to early hominid behaviour and ecology: the fossils themselves, archaeological traces, and information on the geological and environmental context in which these hominids lived.

Inferences from fossils

Fossilised bones provide information on the skeleton and on its modification during life by growth, biomechanical stresses, and changes caused by diet and pathology. They can hence provide important behavioural and ecological clues.

Direct measurements of the volume of the braincase can be obtained from complete fossilised crania, although these are rarely found. More often, only fragments of hominid skulls are available, and so estimates of partial cranial capacity have to be used to infer the total volume of the brain. Brain size increased through time and is often viewed as a general monitor of complexity and plasticity of behaviour, or as an indication of sophistication in aspects of behaviour such as toolmaking, foraging, social life and language. Using endocasts – impressions made by the folds of the cortex on the inside of the braincase – some attempts have been made to infer changes in the organisation of the brain, such as expansion of sensory association areas and of areas concerned with motor control or with speech (see p. 116). However, such markings are vague and difficult to relate directly to brain function and behaviour.

In all mammals the brain becomes larger as body size increases. The behavioural significance of increasing brain size hence depends crucially on the extent of any concomitant increase in body size. Unfortunately, the hominid fossil record before 100 000 years ago contains very few associated skulls and postcranial bones from the same individuals, so that the relationship between the brain and body size in early hominids is not yet worked out in detail. Nevertheless, broad inferences on several ecological parameters can be made by examining body-size relationships that apply generally to all mammals or to primates. For instance, an apparent increase in body size in early *Homo erectus* might have led to consequent increases in mobility, size of home range, longevity and developmental time, and improved resistance to predation. Such generalisations represent second-order inferences, being dependent on accurate estimates of body size from fossil bones.

Locomotor and activity patterns might also be inferred from fossils. An example can be drawn from the robustness of the limb bones of 'archaic' *Homo sapiens* and Neanderthals. The skeletons of these hominids were capable of absorbing higher levels of stress from muscular activity than do the bones of modern humans, and this provides us with a general statement about body posture, locomotion and degree of muscular activity, even if it is not useful in making inferences about specific activities.

Microscopic pits and scratches on tooth enamel etched by food particles and associated grit provide potential inferences about diet, especially since the development of scanning electron microscopy. However, it is not yet clear to what extent the type, number and distribution of enamel defects on the surfaces of hominid teeth reflect overall diet during a lifetime, rather than diet for a brief time just before death. Microwear studies suggest that early hominids regularly ate fibrous fruits, but they have yet to be applied widely enough to identify major transitions in hominid diet.

Studies of sex, age, rate of development and pathology from fossil bones can give important insights into hominid behaviour. In primates, as in most mammals, a larger body size in males compared with females reflects the male competition seen in polygynous social systems, in which there is more variation in the mating success of individual males than in monogamous systems. Sexual dimorphism in skeletal size among early hominids might offer one of the few insights into their social life. It was relatively great in some species of Plio-Pleistocene hominids but was reduced in late Pleistocene hominids such as Neanderthals to the level seen in modern humans.

Humans are born in an immature state and undergo a relatively longer maturation period than do apes and other primates. This change in developmental timing during hominid evolution was accompanied by a complex of distinctively human behaviour patterns, such as increased dependence on learning, enhanced parental care and the defence of a home base. Such a shift in developmental timing has usually been assumed to occur very early in hominid evolution, a view originally supported by studies of the eruption pattern of australopithecine teeth. However, recent refinements in analysing tooth development indicate that the dentitions of hominids earlier than *Homo erectus* have developmental rates characteristic of apes rather than humans. An extended period of infant maturation with all its implications for social behaviour may hence have evolved later than was previously believed.

Pathology can also give an insight into ancient patterns of behaviour. For example, dental caries, systemic diseases, and healed and unhealed injuries provide information on diet, mortality, and the capacity for recovering from disease.

Inference from archaeological remains

The archaeological record began when hominids began manufacturing artefacts from hard materials. Stone flakes, cores, and other rocks that could not have been modified or transported by geological processes represent the primary archaeological remains of early hominids. Archaeological traces often include debris associated with artefacts, such as animal bones or plant remains.

Because stone artefacts are more likely to be preserved than bones, the presence and geographical expansions of hominids are best indicated by the distribution of stone tools. One exception is the island of Java, where fossil remains of *Homo erectus* are known from the early and middle Pleistocene but definite stone tools are not known before the late Pleistocene. The presence of stone artefacts may also provide information about small-scale patterns of movement and land use. For instance, at Olduvai Gorge (Tanzania) around 1.8 million years ago hominids travelled at least 18 kilometres to obtain quartzite and other raw materials used for toolmaking. By 100 000 years ago, sources of raw materials were sometimes more than 100 kilometres away from the sites where the tools were dropped. At Olduvai and also at Olorgesailie (Kenya), the association of handaxes with stream channels and of choppers and flake tools with lake margins suggests that early

(Above) One of the archaeological sites (FxJj 3) at Koobi Fora, East Turkana, soon after its discovery by Richard Leakey in 1969. Geologist Bill Bishop looks at the cluster of hippo bones and stone artefacts found weathering out on the surface where the top of the KBS Tuff is seen. The bone and stone cluster is shown in detail on the left.

Pleistocene hominids made and used different tools in different parts of their habitat.

Stone tools also provide some direct evidence on hominid behaviour, as the methods of manufacture may indicate what capacities of hand and brain were available. For example, the presence of cores no larger than a few centimetres in size from Olduvai and Koobi Fora show that a powerful fingertip precision grip was used over 1.5 million years ago. Symmetrically shaped handaxes, such as those made in Europe, Africa and parts of Asia from 1.5 to 0.2 million years ago, show that hominids could produce a specific tool form from rocks of very different original shape (see p. 352).

The working surfaces of stone or bone tools can also show how they were used by comparing them with modern experimental tools of stone or of bone. Such experiments can determine whether a particular edge was used for cutting meat, sawing wood or slicing soft plant matter. Unfortunately, these techniques have been applied to only a few kinds of stone raw material, and in any case traces of use are seldom detectable; tool function has as yet been determined for fewer than a dozen of the tens of thousands of stone artefacts known from a million or more years ago. However, these studies show that early hominids used tools in a variety of tasks related to feeding.

Stone artefacts are usually found in a group, or *assemblage*. Assemblages are the traditional units of archaeological analysis. Different shapes or styles of tool have long been assumed to signify distinctive cultural attributes, and variation in tool assemblages may indicate cultural variation or

Looking south-east across Olduvai Gorge, with the extinct volcano Lemagrut in the distance. The famous hominid site in Tanzania was formed by a stream cutting down through lake sediments during the past 200 000 years. The sequence of lake beds, I to IV (from oldest to youngest), is visible. The sediments of Bed I, which contain the earliest fossil and archaeological remains, accumulated between about 1.85 and 1.70 million years ago.

Sun-bleached bones of large mammals lie outside a maternity den of spotted hyenas (*Crocuta crocuta*) in Amboseli National Park, Kenya. Hyenas collect and chew on bones. Bone concentrations like this mimic those associated with stone artefacts at early archaeological sites. By studying the bones that carnivores collect in modern habitats, archaeologists can learn how to distinguish carnivore from hominid bone-collecting behaviour in the prehistoric record.

diverse traditions, even among the earliest toolmaking hominids. Whatever the merits of this idea, there is no doubt that studies of stone-tool assemblages can provide much information about the behaviour and capacities of early hominids.

Throughout the early Pleistocene, for example, stone tools were homogeneous and change was remarkably slow. By 100 000 years ago there were many more specialised tools, a trend that reached a peak during the Upper Palaeolithic, when there were rapid stylistic changes and considerable geographic variation in tool patterns. This means a shift from the cultural uniformity of archaic hominids, to the innovation and the spatial division of behaviour that characterise modern culture. Tool assemblages may hence reflect an overall complexity of hominid behaviour, which may be related to new ways of transmitting information. For instance, the blossoming of symbolic expression portrayed on cave walls, in rockshelters and by carved figurines starting 30 000 years ago shows that novel modes of information transfer encouraged innovation. Speech and language no doubt played a major part in this.

Animal bones also give clues to hominid behaviour. Bones can be collected and deposited in several ways – by flowing water, by carnivores (e.g. hyenas), by rodents (e.g. porcupines) and by hominids – and the deposition process must be distinguished before such material can be reliably interpreted. Archaeological sites dated to around 1.8 million years at Olduvai illustrate how animal bones can be used to infer the activities of early toolmakers. On the surfaces of some of the Olduvai bones are cut marks made by stone tools, implying that the hominids processed meat, marrow or hide. Other possible causes of damage to bone surfaces by, for example, carnivore teeth, trampling and recovery during excavation, can usually be eliminated by

The middle Pleistocene site of Olorgesailie in Kenya under excavation by Glynn Isaac's team in 1964. Hundreds of handaxes, dating to around 800 000 years ago, have been preserved as an open-air display and can be viewed from the catwalk shown in the photograph.

L_____I 1 cm

A fragment of a fossilised animal bone from the Kenyan site of Olorgesailie, showing deep cut marks thought to have been made by stone tools.

CANNIBALISM OR RITUAL DISMEMBERMENT?

A belief in cannibalism seems to be inherent in the human mind; tales of the practice stretch back at least to the Greek myths, and the subject's popularity remains undiminished. 'Survival cannibalism' can occur in rare and extreme circumstances, such as among survivors of a plane crash in the Andes. But a careful study of historical and ethnographic accounts shows that ritual or habitual cannibalism is rare or non-existent: there are no reliable first-hand witnesses of the practice, and almost all reports are based on hearsay.

Where prehistory is concerned, cannibalism has long been a favourite and dramatic theory, from the Palaeolithic to Minoan Crete and the Anasazi of the American Pueblo culture. All these interpretations depend on indirect clues and on assumptions, as nobody has yet found definite evidence of the practice, such as human remains inside preserved human faeces (coprolites).

What appeared at first sight to be overwhelming evidence for cannibalism was uncovered at the Neolithic cave of Fontbrégoua, southeastern France, where the bones of over a dozen people of the second millennium BC were found in three disposal pits, next to 10 pits containing animal bones. The human bones bore cut marks and breakage patterns identical to those on the animal remains, and were claimed to result from cannibalistic defleshing of fresh bones. However, the mortuary rituals of some Australian Aborigines can produce similar kinds of remains, from bodies left exposed to decompose, then defleshed and broken up for secondary disposal. Several individuals may be deposited together. So the onus of proof is still on those hoping for cannibalism at Fontbrégoua.

As for Neanderthals, scholars in the early part of this century assumed almost routinely that they practised cannibalism, an idea that fitted the prevailing view of Neanderthals as shambling, uncultured brutes. It is now recognised that they were relatively sophisticated, and recent re-evaluation of the evidence for cannibalism in the period demolished the myth.

Two principal sites were heralded as providing evidence of Neanderthal cannibalism: Krapina and Monte Circeo. Krapina, a cave in Yugoslavia, was first dug in 1899 and has yielded over 650 fragments of bones from dozens of individuals, dating to between 100 000 and 50 000 years ago. These were interpreted as a cannibal feast, in which bodies had been smashed open to get at marrow and brains, and flesh cut off.

This gruesome image does not stand up to scrutiny. The bones display no evidence of the impact fractures characteristic of marrow extraction by humans. Instead, the extensive fragmentation can be explained by roof-falls, crushing by sediments, and

the use of dynamite during excavation. There are linear grooves and striations on some bones that seem to be cut marks; but a detailed comparison of these with butchery traces on reindeer bones at the Mousterian (Neanderthal) site of Combe Grenal, France, showed a great difference in the location, orientation and length of the marks.

On the other hand, the Krapina marks resemble in appearance, location and frequency cut marks on human bones from secondary burials in a Michigan ossuary of the Late Woodland period (fourteenth century AD). It is therefore probable that the Krapina bones, like those at Fontbrégoua, were defleshed with stone tools after partial decomposition as a stage in a mortuary practice.

At Monte Circeo, Italy, two Neanderthal bones were found in Guattari Cave in 1939: a skull and a jawbone, probably from the same individual. The context of the find was extraordinary: the skull lay in a 'ring of stones' on the cave floor, the hole at its base was enlarged, and there were fractures around the right temple. Inevitably, it was assumed that the Neanderthal, a man of about 45, had been killed by a blow to the head and his brains extracted through the basal hole for consumption. These factors – together with the position in a stone circle – all pointed to ritual cannibalism. Many popular works on prehistory have accepted this view unquestioningly.

However, more careful analysis suggests that the 'ring of stones' was not artificial but caused by a landslide; and the animal bones lying all over the cave floor, some of them bearing gnaw marks, and the presence of hyena bones and coprolites indicate that Monte Circeo was a hyena den around 50 000 years ago when the bones were deposited there. No cut marks have been seen on bones from the cave, and there are few stone tools on the floor.

The skull itself displays no modification by humans, and it is known that hyenas sometimes carry human skulls into their

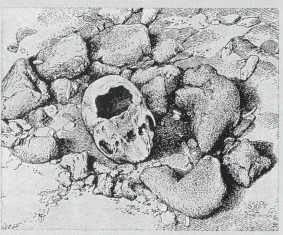
The Monte Circeo Neanderthal skull in the 'ring of stones' — evidence for ritual cannibalism?

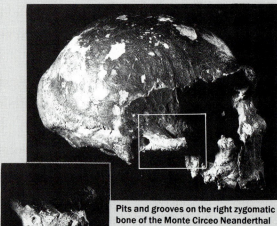
Pits and grooves on the right zygomatic bone of the Monte Circeo Neanderthal skull, one of several pieces of evidence suggesting that hyenas gnawed the head.

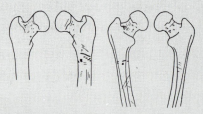
Composite drawings by Mary Russell showing the positions of the linear striations on fragments of femur from the Krapina Neanderthal site (bold lines) and the cutmarks on a comparative sample of human bones from the fourteenth-century AD site of Juntunen, Michigan, where skeletons were defleshed with stone tools before being buried for the second time.

lairs. The fractures on the skull are consistent with hyena tooth marks; the enlarged hole at the fragile base has gnawed edges without a trace of stone tools, and the jawbone was also gnawed by hyenas. Since the cave was used by Neanderthals before hyenas took possession, it is possible that the carnivores took the head from a burial in or near the site, but the skull's preservation suggests that it was never interred.

One cannot deny the possibility that cannibalism occasionally existed in prehistory, but concrete evidence is hard to find. Research is underway into marks on other human bones from early periods, but as yet they can all be interpreted as the result of mortuary practices (as at Krapina) or carnivore activity (as at Monte Circeo). In view of the extreme scarcity of cannibalism in historic times, its very existence in prehistory is becoming hard to swallow.

Paul G. Bahn

microscopy on experimental and ancient bones. However, not all marks on fossilised animal bones can clearly be attributed to a specific agent.

Scratches on and damage to the Olduvai bones indicate that they were modified both by hominids and by carnivores. Studies of modern and ancient bone assemblages formed by carnivores such as hyenas show that the bones that accompany stone tools have different characteristics, which are shown by the sizes of the prey animals, the species and the skeletal parts in the assemblage. The accumulation of stone artefacts and the features of the bone assemblage show that the Olduvai hominids carried tools to the places where parts of animal carcasses were also carried; transport of these two kinds of materials by hominids was more important at these sites than were the actions of carnivores and natural processes.

The Olduvai bones allow further inferences to be made about diet, foraging and the interaction of hominids with other species. For example, the marks of stone tools and patterns of damage indicate that hominids sliced off meat and cracked the bones of large ungulates for marrow – a dietary innovation unknown among earlier hominids or other primates. However, this does not mean that the diet of early *Homo* was mostly of animal origin; the microwear on the teeth of a few specimens of early *Homo* suggests that fruit was significant in the diet. It is difficult to judge how hominids obtained their animal bones. Although hunting has been the conventional interpretation, at Olduvai animal bones appear to have been obtained in part by scavenging of carcasses. However, it is difficult to distinguish bones obtained by hunting from those gained by chasing a predator off a carcass soon after the kill.

Archaeological sites can also provide evidence on more complex aspects of early behaviour. The Plio-Pleistocene sites at Olduvai and elsewhere were once thought to be the campsites, or home bases, of early hominids – safe refuges for sleeping, sharing food and social activities. If this is true then fundamental human behaviours, such as social learning focused around a home base, division of labour, exchange of food, infant care and increased investment by fathers in offspring, were already developed about 2 million years ago.

Detailed study of the Olduvai sites, however, has suggested that these presumed classic cases of early campsites were probably not genuine home bases of the kind used by modern hunter-gatherers, as the attraction of carnivores to such sites of bone accumulation prohibited their use as a focus for social activity. A more plausible view is that the 1.8-million-year-old sites at Olduvai were places where stone-tool materials had been previously left and were revisited when hominids needed to use tools for processing animals and plants. Real home bases and their social correlates probably originated later than was once believed; clear evidence of hearths and constructed shelters do not appear earlier than 500 000 to 300 000 years ago.

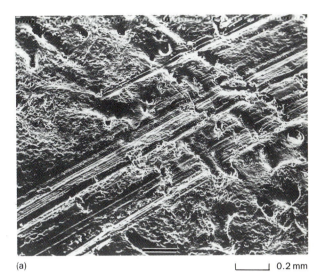

(a) ⌞___⌟ 0.2 mm

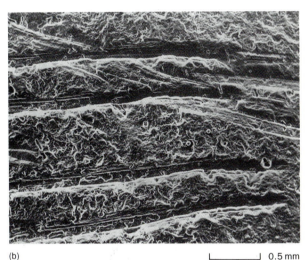

(b) ⌞___⌟ 0.5 mm

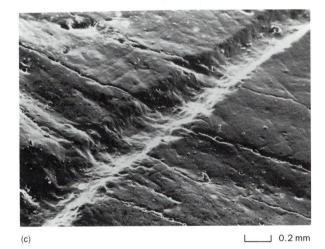

(c) ⌞___⌟ 0.2 mm

Scratches on animal bones found at Olduvai Gorge suggest that they were modified both by hominids and by carnivores. The scanning microscope helps to identify which. (a) A cut mark on a modern bone made experimentally with a stone tool, showing the striations that typically accompany a single mark seen by eye on the bone surface. (b) A series of grooves with the distinctive characteristics of stone-tool cut marks on a fossil bone from one of the 1.8-million-year-old sites at Olduvai. (c) A scratch with the characteristics of a carnivore tooth mark on a fossil bone from another site, also 1.8 million years old, at Olduvai.

INFERENCES ABOUT HOMINID BEHAVIOUR AND ECOLOGY

Hominids and time periods (years ago)	Inference	Nature of the evidence
A. Hominid ancestors *?8–5 million*	• Equatorial African origin	• Humans are genetically closest to African apes, which today are distributed across equatorial Africa; earliest hominid fossils are in eastern Africa
B. Earliest hominids *5–3 million*	• Habitually bipedal on the ground; occasionally arboreal	• Postcranial anatomy of fossils from Hadar in Ethiopia (but disagreements about similarity to modern human bipedalism and degree of arboreality)
	• Inhabited a mosaic of grassland, woodland and thick shrub	• Faunas from Laetoli in Tanzania, Hadar, and Makapansgat in South Africa
3–2 million	• Occupation of open savannas	• Fossil pollen and fauna
	• Emphasis on a fibrous plant diet in robust australopithecines	• Microwear on teeth; large teeth and jaws
	• First known manufacture of stone tools	• Tools from Ethiopia, Kenya, Malawi, Zaire dated between 2.5 and 2.0 million years
C. Plio-Pleistocene hominids *2.0–1.5 million* [Stone technology and changes in diet, brain size, etc. are usually associated with *Homo*]	• Increased commitment to bipedalism on the ground	• Postcranial anatomy associated with archaic *Homo* established
	• Increased dexterity related to tool use and toolmaking, and possibly foraging	• Anatomy of hand bones and characteristics of stone tools and cores
	• Stones and animal bones carried repeatedly to specific sites	• Earliest known complex sites with many stone artefacts and fossils
	• Use of tools to procure and process food	• Bone and stone tools with distinctive traces of use
	• Dietary increase in protein and fat from large animals	• Cut marks made by stone tools on animal bones
	• Scavenging and possible hunting of large animals; processing of animals at specific spots	• Limb bones of animals concentrated at undisturbed archaeological sites
	• Increased cognitive capacities associated with making tools, foraging, social arrangements and/or developing linguistic skills	• Increase in brain size from about a third to a half that of modern humans
	• Changes in maturation rate	• Implied by brain size increase and possible changes in tooth development
	• Increased mobility and predator defence	• Large stature evident in skeletal remains of early *Homo erectus* from West Turkana in Kenya
D. Early Pleistocene hominids *1.5–0.1 million*	• Occupation of new habitats and geographic zones	• Sites occur in previously unoccupied areas of eastern Africa; first appearance of hominids outside Africa
	• Definite preconception of tool form	• Biface handaxes of consistent shape made from rocks of varying original shape
	• Manipulation of fire	• Indications of fire differentially associated with archaeological sites
	• Increased levels of activity and stress on skeletons	• Massive development of postcranial and cranial bones
E. Late Pleistocene hominids *100 000–35 000* [Neanderthals]	• Increased sophistication of toolkit and technology; still slow rate of change to tool assemblage	• Larger number of stone-tool types than before; complex preparation of cores
	• Intentional burial of dead and suggestions of ritual	• Preservation of skeletons, some with objects
	• Maintenance of high activity levels (locomotor endurance; powerful arms) and high levels of skeletal stress (e.g. teeth used as tools)	• Robust skeletons, especially thick leg bones and large areas for muscle attachment on arm bones; prominent wear patterns on incisor teeth
35 000–10 000 [fully modern *Homo sapiens*]	• Decreased levels of activity and stress on skeleton	• Decrease in skeletal robusticity (also seen in early modern humans before 35 000 years ago)
	• Enhanced technological efficiency	• Innovations in stone- and bone-tool production (e.g. blades and bone points)
	• Innovations in hunting and other foraging activities, including systematic exploitation of particular animal species	• Evidence of spearthrower and harpoon, and trapping and netting of animals; animal remains in archaeological middens
	• Colonisation of previously uninhabited zones	• For example, sites in tundra in Europe and Asia; colonisation of the Americas (Australasia was probably first inhabited around 50 000 years ago)
	• Elaboration of artistic symbolic expression and notation	• Engraving, sculpting and painting of walls and figurines; repetitive marks on bones; jewellery
	• Surge of technological and cultural differentiation and change	• Variation in toolkits over space and time
	• Harvesting and first cultivation of grains; first domestication of animals	• Evidence of seeds and fauna from sites dating to the end of the Pleistocene

Human activities, in the past as in the present, are not mainly directed towards the convenience of archaeologists. Instead of confirming a neat segregation of time and place of different activities (which might be reflected in an easily interpreted distribution of artefacts), studies of modern foragers have shown that different activities may be performed at the same place, that specific artefacts and other refuse are not produced in proportion to the frequency of a particular activity, and that refuse is often moved either actively or by geological processes.

The relationship between behaviour and the location of archaeological materials is quite complicated. Although a division of excavations into diverse types such as camp, butchery, quarry and factory sites is still acceptable to many archaeologists, it has proved difficult to ascribe most Pleistocene sites to one of these simple categories. Only the archaeological record of the past 35 000 years or so, starting with the Upper Palaeolithic, shows clear signs of bone middens, hearths and huts, and other features distinctive of the daily organisation of modern foragers. However, even the earliest archaeological records give evidence of the delayed consumption of food and the existence of sites for processing food and flaking stone. Whether this evidence implies that the social and foraging arrangements of hominids earlier than 1.5 million years ago resembled those of modern hunter-gatherers is still not clear.

Inferences from geological context

The geological setting greatly assists the behavioural interpretation of archaeological remains, and can also give an insight into the ecological context in which early hominids lived. Study of sediments allows inferences to be made about the distribution of physical features, such as lakes, streams and floodplains, and geochemical analyses, together with plant and animal fossils, give information about climatic fluctuations, vegetation and the ecological communities in which hominids lived.

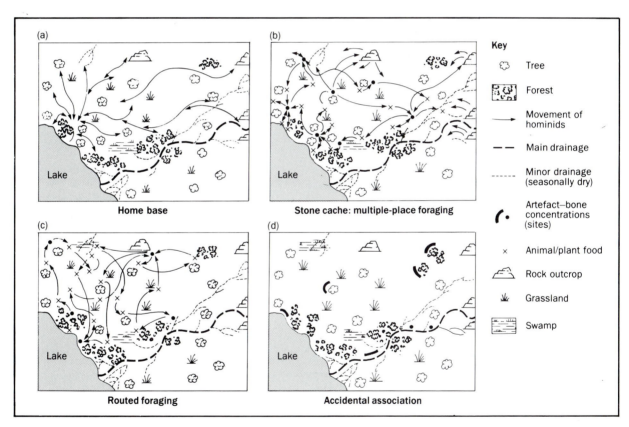

Four rival interpretations of how stone artefacts and animal bones become concentrated in ancient sediments.

(a) In the home-base model, hominids bring stone tools and food, including parts of carcasses, to a social focus on the landscape (central place). Individuals of the social group disperse in their foraging activities and return to this central place where the social group reunites.

(b) Hominids create stone caches while carrying stone tools and raw material to the foraging area from distant sources. When individuals or small groups of hominids find animal and plant foods that require processing with stone tools, they return repeatedly to places nearby where stone was previously left.

(c) Routed foraging refers to sites made when hominids stop on a continuous round of foraging – at rock outcrops, watering holes, sleeping places, or other spots where there are attractive resources. Bones and carried stones are discarded in these repeatedly visited stopping places.

(d) Bone and stone-tool accumulations may become associated accidentally in several ways. For instance, bone-collecting carnivores and tool-using hominids may be attracted to the same places (e.g. shade trees). Some sites may also be produced if water action redeposits stones and bones in the same places along a stream course. These accumulations may be more dispersed than in models (a)–(c), though hominid behaviour could also result in vaguely defined clusters of bones and artefacts over the landscape.

Inferences about the ancient environment must necessarily provide a rather indirect insight into hominid activity. For example, although savannas were once believed to represent a specific, uniform habitat requiring certain specific adaptations by hominids – such as tools for defence and hunting, bipedalism and the expanded brains needed for survival in open grasslands – they actually provide a rich array of habitats and a comparably rich series of behavioural possibilities. Evidence of hominids in savannas thus offers no strict reconstruction of their way of life. Bone anatomy and archaeological relics can give much more direct information.

Geological context may sometimes provide information about intentional burial, a distinctively human practice that originated during the late Pleistocene. Such evidence, especially when found in unequivocal association with a burial trench or with grave goods, usually consists of bones from a single individual. Although several finds of Neanderthals give evidence of intentional burial, later burials associated with modern *Homo sapiens* and with Upper Palaeolithic artefacts are far more elaborate and assorted and involve a variety of body positions and grave goods (see p. 345).

Evolution of human behaviour

We have shown here how a rich array of inferences can be made from the fossil, archaeological and contextual record of hominid evolution. Despite the diversity of these clues, only a tiny part of the pattern of hominid life can yet be reconstructed. Some of the primary inferences about hominids include aspects of their locomotion, activity, diet, tool manufacture, movement, geographic distribution and environmental setting. Secondary inferences can often be made about the general sophistication and elements of social and foraging behaviour. Further ideas about social organisation, mating systems and language are based on information so far removed from the present prehistoric data that they stand largely as untestable speculations.

Some current ideas about aspects of early hominid behaviour and ecology, as inferred from palaeontology and archaeology, are summarised on p. 332. This is a conservative list, and excludes some possibilities for which no clear evidence yet exists. For instance, the use of tools made of wood or other perishable materials by hominids more than 3 million years ago is probable; but this interpretation is not developed here because no evidence of such use remains. This lack of evidence may also mean that some patterns of human behaviour appeared earlier than listed here. For example, although the earliest stone tools currently known are around 2.5 million years old and may have been used to process animal foods, there is no definite indication of such activity for sites older than about 1.8 million years.

Valid historical inferences about hominid behaviour must be based on material evidence that points to a specific set of ideas about the past. Evidence from the prehistoric record, fragmentary though it inevitably is, can be used to eliminate certain possibilities, to estimate the probable accuracy of alternatives, or to show how multiple factors helped to create the prehistoric evidence. Filling in our knowledge of early hominid behaviour and ecology in the future will depend not only on new and refined information about the past but also on experiments and observations that will allow us to improve the way in which we make valid inferences from such findings. *Richard Potts*

See also other chapters in this part and 'Jaws and teeth' (p. 56), 'Primate locomotion and posture' (p. 75), 'The human brain' (p. 115), 'Human speech and language' (p. 134), 'Mating and parental care' (p. 150), 'Fossil deposits and their investigation' (p. 187), 'Reconstructing past environments' (p. 191), 'Evolution of australopithecines' (p. 231), 'Evolution of early humans' (p. 241), 'Reconstructing ancient populations' (p. 402) and 'Human populations before agriculture' (p. 405)

Studying human evolution by analogy

The fossil record is composed of the bones of long-dead animals, and the archaeological record is little more than a collection of the discarded tools and food refuse of pre-historic hominids. That our understanding of the past must come from such a restricted set of materials has always been a problem for prehistorians and palaeontologists. It has resulted in a belief that archaeology and palaeontology can comment on only certain aspects of the past – the physical form of extinct animals, and the technology of past peoples. Ecology and behaviour – vast and critical areas of evolution – are, at this level, invisible to us.

Those interested in early humans have long sought ways of getting around the limited nature of their material. A principal means of doing this has been to use observations on the present to 'flesh out the bones' of the past. Because behaviour does not fossilise, its reconstruction has always depended on the extrapolation of modern patterns into the past, the underlying assumption being that the present can serve as a model for the past and can extend our knowledge beyond the directly observable.

Although such analogues have fleshed out the meagre bones, they have also raised some important questions. How should observations on and knowledge of today's world be used to throw light on the past without simply imposing current perceptions upon history? The danger has always been that the prehistoric world will simply be a reflection of the world in which we ourselves live.

Contemporary peoples

Perhaps the classic analogue model used in studies of human evolution is the *ethnographic parallel*. This consists of seeking out parallels between the archaeological record and that of ethnography – the study of the way of life of contemporary peoples. Inferences might then be made about aspects of prehistory. For example, at Star Carr, a pre-historic site in northern Britain dating to around 9500 years ago, the preparation of animal skins was inferred from the archaeological evidence. A parallel for this activity was found by the excavator, Grahame Clark, among the Caribou Eskimo. In this population the processing of animal skins is carried out by women, and Clark was thus able to infer that women must have been present at Star Carr – from which further deductions about social organisation could in turn be made.

Ethnography has often been used in this way, with the aim of extending the interpretation of archaeological evidence. The underlying assumption has been that an archaeologically observable material culture is correlated with other aspects of social and economic organisation.

This technique has been used to elucidate the function of artefacts, the sexual division of labour, and the kinship organisation of prehistoric peoples.

Although there is no doubt that our knowledge of the contemporary world will always, consciously and uncon-sciously, illuminate the past, various problems arise from an uncritical application of ethnography. Some of these result from an inadequately rigorous methodology, par-ticularly the selective use of ethnographic information; others are more fundamental.

The range of sources for ethnographic material is vast: at least 700 non-industrialised societies are now known. Each society includes within itself many smaller populations and communities, which, if studied in detail, would no doubt show further variability in patterns of human behaviour. Furthermore, ethnographic material comes from a large number of different sources – from early travellers, from professional ethnographers, from missionaries; and prob-ably sometimes from the imagination of the observer! Even when all this is taken into account the ethnographic record may be biased, just like the archaeological record, by pre-servation. The ethnographic record is a sample of human behaviour, not a true representation of its overall pattern of variation.

A classic use of ethnography to reconstruct the past was Richard Lee's study of the diet of hunter-gatherers. Lee showed that hunter-gatherers in the Kalahari Desert, south-

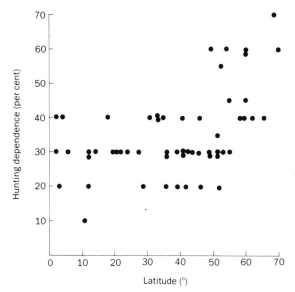

Relationship between latitude and the amount of food obtained from hunting for living hunter-gatherers. This shows that meat becomes increasingly important in the high latitudes. For example, tropical hunter-gatherers such as the Kalahari San subsist on only 20 per cent hunted animal food, whereas the Inuit (Eskimos) obtain the bulk of their diet from meat.

western Africa, subsisted principally off vegetable food and were far from being ferocious hunters; indeed, gatherer-hunters would be a more apposite term for them. He supplemented this observation with a cross-cultural study of contemporary peoples that revealed that hunting animals was only important at high latitudes, as in the Arctic region. From this he inferred that for most hunter-gatherer populations gathering was more significant ecologically and behaviourally than hunting.

This interpretation led to a considerable re-evaluation of many prehistoric and evolutionary issues. However, when the distribution of modern hunter-gatherers in tropical Africa is examined, it can be seen that they occur only in areas of low and high rainfall. These are habitats where mammals are not abundant, in contrast to areas with middling levels of rainfall where game animals are common and edible plants are scarce. In prehistory, these areas, now occupied by pastoralists, were inhabited by hunter-gatherers far more dependent on animal foods than would be expected on the basis of their modern counterparts.

Further difficulties arise if we consider the diversity of modern human behaviour. Examples can usually be found either to 'disprove' or support any archaeological interpretation. For example, pottery is made by women in some societies, by men in others, or by a few specialists in yet others. Any attempt to deduce sex roles from the presence or absence of pottery styles can hence be supported or refuted by reference to the ethnographic record. Strict rules are therefore necessary to ensure that a 'parallel' truly is analogous, that the conditions in the archaeological and the modern contexts are similar, and that the comparison is fair. Needless to say, determining the criteria by which comparability can be established is fraught with difficulties.

Animals

Many of the problems of the ethnographic parallel come from the variety and diversity of human behaviour and

			PREHISTORIC EXTRAPOLATION
Hunter-gatherers principally dependent on plant foods	Hunting more important	Hunter-gatherers principally dependent on plant foods	
Desert hunter-gatherers (Kalahari San)	No living hunter-gatherers	Forest hunter-gatherers (Pygmy, Dorobo, etc.)	ETHNOGRAPHIC RECORD
Large mammals scarce	Very high number of large mammals	Abundance declines in forests	AVAILABILITY OF LARGE MAMMALS
Arid environments (plants with underground storage organs)	Grasses dominant (low availability of plant food)	Woodland and forests (fruits, etc.) abundant	PLANT FOODS AND STRUCTURE

0   Rainfall (mm)   2000
Increasingly arid ◄————— —————► Increasingly wet

Resources available to tropical African hunter-gatherers, such as the San of the Kalahari Desert and the Pygmies of the Central African rain forests. Very dry and wet places are rich in plant foods and poor in animal ones. In intermediate habitats, the reverse is true. In Africa today, living hunter-gatherers are known only from the wettest and driest regions, and are principally dependent on plant foods. The ethnographic record can tell us nothing about the intermediate regions where hunting is likely to have become more significant.

(Above) A Hadza woman digging for a tuber and (left) Hadza men butchering a scavenged giraffe. The Hadza are hunter-gatherers who live in Tanzania. Studies of the foraging behaviour of living peoples provide both information about tools found in the archaeological record and ecological and behavioural information for modelling prehistoric situations.

Chimpanzees from the Taï forest, Ivory Coast, 'sharing' part of a red colobus monkey that was hunted. Information about the way a carcass is consumed may help the interpretation of bones found in archaeological contexts, while chimpanzee behaviour may indicate ancestral hominid behaviour.

culture. Few clear-cut rules or laws emerge from the wealth of ethnographic observations now available, so that it is difficult to infer behaviour from observations of material culture. The inadequacy of the ethnographic parallel is less a shortcoming of archaeology than a general weakness in the human and social sciences – there is considerable controversy as to whether it is possible to establish general and predictive models of behaviour.

This problem should be less severe when dealing with animals, whose behaviour is more limited and predictable, and perhaps more appropriate for extrapolation from the present to the past. On this basis, animals have been used extensively in palaeontology, and have been central to the study of human evolution. The behaviour of modern non-human primates in particular has been used to flesh out the fossils of early hominids, and to provide insight into human social and behavioural evolution.

Fossil hominids from a million years or more ago might be expected to have had patterns of behaviour resembling those of non-human primates more closely than those of modern humans. The behaviour, social organisation and ecology of non-human primates should hence be able to act as a better guide to the adaptations of early hominids, while their anatomy might reflect functional similarities. Some classic studies have been carried out in this field, many of which use aspects of a single non-human primate species as a model for an early hominid species. Among the favourite species are chimpanzees and baboons. Baboons, it has been argued, are an appropriate model because they live in open savanna regions – the habitat of some early hominids. Many baboon adaptations should thus coincide. On this basis, it has been suggested that early hominids lived in large groups as a means of avoiding predators.

Perhaps the best-known analogue model based on

baboons is the seed-eating hypothesis. The baboons in question are a particularly specialised species, the gelada baboon (Theropithecus gelada). These live exclusively in the highlands of Ethiopia, where they are adapted to highly seasonal, open and relatively nutrient-poor environments. They survive by specialised harvesting of grass, the only resource that occurs abundantly.

To this end, gelada baboons have undergone a series of evolutionary modifications. Their hands are particularly dextrous, to enable them to manipulate the fine grass stems. As they spend much of their day feeding, they have also adopted a bottom-shuffling locomotion that enables them to move along while grazing without standing up. To facilitate this movement, geladas, unlike other baboons, have fatty deposits on their buttocks and maintain an erect trunk while in this sitting position. Their teeth also reflect their specialised diet: they have reduced front teeth (incisors and canines) and enlarged back teeth (premolars and molars) because the grass seeds that constitute most of their food are hard and small, requiring little or no preparation with the front teeth but considerable grinding.

These characteristics parallel many found in hominids – a move to erectness, fatty deposits on the buttocks, high manual dexterity, and small front teeth compared with back ones. On the basis of this analogy, early hominids could have gone through a seed-eating phase while they were developing upright stance and bipedal locomotion.

Baboons represented a good analogue for early hominids because of a shared environment. In evolutionary biology, however, an additional and probably more useful basis for comparison is a shared evolutionary history or phylogeny. The more closely any two species are related, the more similar their behaviour might be expected to be.

The closest relative to hominids is the chimpanzee, and both species of chimpanzee have been used as models in human evolution. The common chimpanzee (Pan troglodytes) is extremely flexible in terms of its individual behaviour, is innovative and is capable of complex communication. Recent research has shown that chimpanzees hunt animals and use tools when feeding. Bonds between related individuals, particularly between mother and offspring, are also very strong. As all of these features occur to an even more marked extent in humans, it might be that chimpanzees can provide an excellent model for early hominid behaviours.

Phylogeny and environment can thus provide useful analogies; a combination of the two might strengthen the use of animal models in studies of human evolution. Recent studies on savanna-dwelling chimpanzees in Senegal and Tanzania may be particularly relevant. For example, it is now clear that chimpanzees in more open environments forage more widely than forest-dwellers. This variation also highlights the fact that even for animals behaviour is not necessarily the same throughout the species, varying between populations and environments and according to age and sex. For example, tool use is more common in western than in eastern populations of chimpanzees, and is often more frequent among females than males. Conversely, hunting is more commonly carried out by males than by females.

Although studies of living anthropoid primates have helped to enhance the understanding of human evolution and to make the subject more comprehensible to a wider audience, animal analogues often suffer from the same limitations that have bedevilled ethnographic parallels. No matter how closely the living species is related to the extinct one, nor how similar their environment, we are never likely to observe an exact match. Evolution does not stop, and even conservative animals will undergo evolutionary change after a separation of lineages. Indeed, the presence of a closely related species is itself likely to act as an important selective pressure and to lead to divergence. Chimpanzees are not 'protohominids', as they have had to adapt and survive in a world full of humans.

Species cannot share the whole of their phylogeny and their environment. If they did, they would be the same species, which early humans and apes clearly are not. The analogue approach cannot therefore easily cope with differences between species, although these are likely to be as significant as are similarities.

Species will each respond differently to a new environment because of their different phylogenies. When apes and monkeys colonise terrestrial habitats, pre-existing adaptations are critical in determining the direction of evolutionary change. Monkeys evolved from an evolutionary heritage of quadrupedal running on the tops of branches. Adaptation to the ground would for them be tackled best by continuing this quadrupedal running. For an animal, such as an ape, that is often suspended below branches, movement on the ground may best be dealt with by limited bipedalism.

Choosing the right analogy

How can the potential of analogue models be realised? We need the present to understand the past, but we do not want the past to become the present dimly perceived. Scientists who work with past events – palaeontologists, geologists, archaeologists, astronomers – do not and cannot observe their subject of study directly. The events, and the processes that lead to them, are long gone, and are represented solely by a set of residues (fossils, rocks, tools, and so on). Any observations must therefore be indirect. In contrast, scientists who work in the present are able to study by direct observation the processes in which they are interested – for example, relationships between predator and prey, or the factors affecting the growth of a tree. It is this difference between direct and indirect observation that structures the distinction between studies of the present and of the past.

However, the difference may not be as sharp as appears at first. All scientific knowledge is based on inference – the use of scientific principles to derive information from observations. Present-day ecological patterns are really no more 'directly observable' than are the patterns of the past. Rather, they are inferred from information that is often as remote as fossils are from the mechanisms of evolution or the animals themselves. An ecologist cannot directly observe a predator–prey system, nor a social anthropologist a social system. In each case, there must be inferences from other information – perhaps counts of animal numbers and deaths, or oral reports provided by people in a society. Knowledge therefore rests less on the question of direct versus indirect observation than on the length of the chain of inference from data to the reconstructed patterns of the past. Analogue models are critical to any study of the past, because they provide the basis for the chains of inference essential to knowledge. Studying the past is different only in the length and reliability of the chains of inference used.

The most important element determining the validity of an analogue model is an ancient one – the principle of *uniformitarianism*. This principle was first proposed by the great nineteenth-century geologist, Charles Lyell, and it laid the basis for modern geology as well as paving the way for studying the past. The principle can be reduced to a single element: processes observable today can be used to explain events in the past. It sets the limits of analogies based on the present world in unravelling the past; it is the patterns, processes and principles derived from contemporary studies, not the events themselves, that should be extrapolated back in time. In this way the present can serve as a source of expectations about the past, without acting as a strait-jacket. Modern patterns of variability are hence much more useful than detailed studies of single species in making statements about the past.

The recent growth of behavioural ecology has led to several models that can be used to reconstruct the behaviour of early hominids. These relate the variability in a behavioural or ecological parameter to an environmental or social condition. By examining such patterns of association, it may be possible to make predictions (which can be tested with the fossil or archaeological record) of the behaviour or adaptation of hominids and ancient humans.

This approach has now been used in the study of baboon adaptation, and has suggested implications for early hominids. Baboon behaviour is not now seen simply as invariable and species-specific, but is analysed in its relation to ecological conditions. Feeding behaviour in particular changes with habitat, so that in drier conditions the proportion of grass eaten by gelada baboons increases – in other words, food quality decreases as the habitat becomes more marginal. Contrasting baboon genera (*Papio* and *Theropithecus*) have alternative solutions to food shortage, with *Papio* eating more meat and *Theropithecus* becoming a highly specialised grass feeder. Such models of the relationship between habitat and feeding behaviour for a savanna-dwelling primate can be extrapolated to early hominids.

Sometimes it is possible to quantify these models more formally. For example, there is a relationship between the body size of primates and the area over which they range for food. Larger animals require a greater feeding area, and the increase of home range can be predicted from body size. Using equations derived from this analysis, the area over which early hominids ranged for their food can be estimated from their size.

A direct comparison with living primates suggests that early hominids should have had a home range with a radius of less than a kilometre. However, when this is compared with a direct measure of minimum home range, based on the distance stone tools were discarded from their source of raw material, it is possible to see that even by 2 million years ago some early hominids were ranging much more broadly over the East African savanna than any living non-human primates. For example, at the site of Koobi Fora the radius of the home range was between 1 and 3 kilometres and at Olduvai Gorge it was between 3 and 6 kilometres. In this case, the primate-based analogue model has high-lighted differences between early hominids and the ex-pected pattern, showing that it is possible to use con-temporary models to document differences rather than similarities between the past and present.

Such models can also be used to expand our inferences about the behaviour of early hominids beyond that which is visible in the fossil record. This is particularly important for aspects of social behaviour that were undoubtedly central in human evolution. An analysis of the variability in the size of primate genitalia in relationship to social organisation shows that testis size varies in relation to mating strategy: where animals live in monogamous pairs, testes are small; where males associate with more than one female, there is an increase in size; and when several males compete directly within a group for access to females (a competitive multimale system as opposed to a harem system), testis size is even larger (see p. 154).

As genitalia do not appear in the fossil record, the testis size of modern males can be used to throw light on the reproductive behaviour of early hominids. After allowance is made for body size, human testis size is larger than would be expected for a monogamous species, on the margins between that of a typical harem-holding and a typical multimale group.

This comparative approach can also be applied to ethno-graphic data, when reconstructing prehistoric human behaviour. The technology of modern hunter-gatherers varies in relation to environment, and its complexity is a function of the extent to which a population is time-stressed, or pressured into carrying out subsistence activi-ties quickly. The shorter the time available, the more effort is put into the efficiency of tools, and the more com-plex the technology. This model may allow archaeologists to infer the selective pressures operating on prehistoric populations on the basis of the complexity of their tools.

Testing analogue models

Virtually all the models described could in principle be tested in the fossil and archaeological record. They are not directly observable, but their behavioural and ecological attributes have consequences that may manifest them-

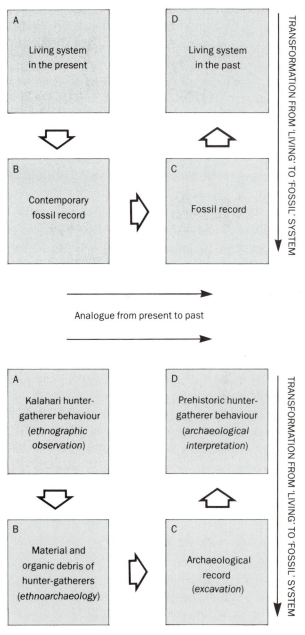

Relationship between the past and the present. The top set of boxes shows the route of inference in using analogue models; the bottom set gives an example. The aim is to know something about life in the past (D), but only fossils are available to us (C). We can use observations on the present (A), but the route of inference must be via B – that is, how the contemporary living system would be transformed into a fossil record. In this way we can compare B and C to assess similarities and differences between A and D. The large open arrows indicate the line of reasoning for the correct use of analogy.

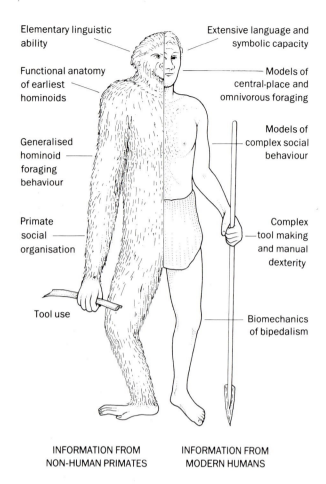

Elementary linguistic ability

Functional anatomy of earliest hominoids

Generalised hominoid foraging behaviour

Primate social organisation

Tool use

Extensive language and symbolic capacity

Models of central-place and omnivorous foraging

Models of complex social behaviour

Complex tool making and manual dexterity

Biomechanics of bipedalism

INFORMATION FROM NON-HUMAN PRIMATES

INFORMATION FROM MODERN HUMANS

Prehistoric hominids were like neither modern hunter-gatherers nor non-human primates, but were unique organisms. Knowledge of each, used correctly, can help us to identify their uniqueness.

selves in the debris of the past. Here lies the ultimate test of an analogue model – that its material consequences can be observed. It is, after all, life in the past that is of interest to us, not simply its fossils. Analogue models can help, because they can show points of comparison between life in the present and life in the past. However, because the past is only accessible through fossils, it is important that analogue models can be directly compared with the fossil record. As the diagram on p. 339 shows, correct use of analogue models must be through an inferential route A→B→C→D. The present can then cast light on the past rather than simply recreating it in its own image.

For the most part both ethnographic and animal analogues have been drawn from information collected for other purposes. However, as archaeologists and palaeontologists have become more aware of the methodological problems involved in interpreting the fossil record they themselves have initiated programmes of research that directly investigate how behaviour of living organisms may be manifested as fossils. Among the most important contributions made by this taphonomical or ethnoarchaeological approach have been studies of how hunting by large carnivores may be distinguished from that of early hominids.

Analogue models can enhance our view of human evolution. Used correctly, they can transform prehistory from a series of mute bones and stones into a dynamic picture of the past. With their aid, ancient hominids need not simply be categorised as either advanced chimpanzees or backward hunter-gatherers, but as unique forms of life.

Robert Foley

See also 'Mating and parental care' (p. 150), 'Home range and territory' (p. 155), 'The hominid way of life' (p. 325), 'Toolmaking by apes' (p. 342), 'Subsistence – a key to the past' (p. 365), 'Reconstructing ancient populations' (p. 402) and 'Tribal peoples in the modern world' (p. 433)

Early human mental abilities

Every day, each of us performs many tasks beyond the abilities of any other animal. To a certain extent we depend on specialised adaptations, particularly bipedal locomotion and the precision grip between thumb and the first two fingers. But even without these, an ape such as a chimpanzee can carry out many straightforward tasks analogous to those performed by humans. The ape's ultimate limitations, which are apparent even after rigorous training, are not so much physical as behavioural and mental, and reflect the fact that human intelligence far exceeds that of our nearest relatives.

The human brain is highly adapted to promoting a cultural way of life, and can be regarded as the most specialised organ of the body. Only humans depend for their success on elaborate systems of culturally transmitted information. There is no doubt that the brain has taken several million years to assume this special complexity.

Fossils allow us to chart an evolutionary sequence of cranial form, from the australopithecines and early Homo through Homo erectus and 'archaic Homo sapiens' to modern people. This physical evidence for an evolutionary development of the brain is itself convincing, but impressions of hominid brains on the inside of skulls (endocasts) give only limited information about internal structure, and hardly any insight into rates of change in behaviour or the evolution of culture. For the past 2 million years, however, at least some hominids have left impressions of their behaviour in the form of stone artefacts and other traces recoverable by archaeology. Much as a footprint conveys information not apparent from a set of bones, modification of the environment gives clues about cognitive abilities, and hence indirectly about the brain.

Any reconstruction of past cognitive developments cannot be entirely balanced because of the differences between humans and our relatives. Human prehistory is marked by a trail of archaeological evidence that goes back to Pliocene times, 2.5 million years ago. There is nothing remotely similar for chimpanzees or gorillas. Although chimpanzees use simple tools, such as termite-fishing sticks and leaf sponges, there is no archaeological record of these; only humans are dependent on tools that can leave a long-term record.

The processes that have 'forced' high intelligence in hominids are not fully understood. One idea is of an autocatalytic feedback model, in which increased intelligence and increased use of technology stimulate each other repeatedly. Social competition may also be invoked. Technology provides the best evidence of intellectual development. Various approaches can be used, including analyses of sequences of past actions (operational chains) and models based on the ideas of psychologists, including Jean Piaget and other researchers.

Tools give information about culture and its transmission. They were made through increasingly complex routines and came to assume very complicated forms. Even in the earliest stone industries raw materials could be transported several kilometres from their place of origin; they act for us as 'visiting cards', signalling the distances travelled by their makers.

From the time that an element of behaviour is manifest in stone-working, early hominids show abilities not found in living apes. Their goals were longer term and were reached by more lengthy 'operational chains'. Stone tools themselves represent only an intermediate means, produced by the steps of transport and manufacture, but aimed at a subsequent end, such as processing animal carcasses or making wooden tools aimed at an even more remote goal.

There are certain behavioural continuities between the abilities of chimpanzees and our own, particularly in the use of tools (see p. 342). The last common ancestor of the hominids and chimpanzees probably lived more than 5 million years ago. We do not know whether that ancestor's tool-using abilities approached those of chimpanzees. Plants are important in tool use by modern apes, so they probably featured in early hominid behaviour long before the first stone tools, even though they left no trace. Bipedalism, which gives the hands more scope for tool use, was fully evolved by about 3.6 million years ago.

Toolmaking

The most basic step in making a stone tool – striking a flake from a cobble – is relatively simple. To strike a sequence of flakes, in such a way that each one helps in the removal of others, demands much more ability, not so much in terms of manual dexterity as in control by the brain. Each step must be evaluated for its own merits, and its consequences for future steps. No ape in captivity has yet been induced to strike more than a single flake from a cobble. Stone-working cannot be operated by an inflexible and mechanical routine, because there are too many possibilities at every strike. Control of the process can be maintained only by constant re-evaluation 'in the mind's eye' – a phrase that suggests the importance of visual imagination.

The modified cobbles (core tools) found on early sites do not represent simple experiments, but pieces flaked using well-tried routines that involved the recurrence of similar forms. An important question about early human abilities is whether the tools are deliberately shaped in a set form, or are simply the end-results of flaking along a path of least

TOOLMAKING BY APES

Many animals use tools. Vultures smash ostrich eggs using stones and Galápagos finches probe into bark for insects with sticks. However, apes, especially chimpanzees, are the pre-eminent users and makers of tools. Many primates in the wild or in captivity can use tools to acquire or process food, for hygiene, and during displays to members of the same species or at predators. This demands dexterity, some cognition – such as understanding the relations between two objects, say food and a twig – and the ability to plan which tool to use. In toolmakers, such cognitive skills, rather than trial and error, come into play.

The making of tools requires choosing an appropriate material from the surrounding environment. A specific tool type may be used for each task. Wild chimpanzees select sticks for probing into a termite mound on the basis of width, strength and length. They modify the stick, stripping the leaves so that it suits its purpose. A leaf used as a sponge for soaking up water from a crevice will first be chewed and crumpled to make it absorbent. It may also be used to clean blood or excrement off the body. Thus the raw material is not seen as a single tool, but can suit a variety of purposes.

In West Africa – in, for example, the Taï Forest, Ivory Coast – chimpanzees use hammer sticks and stones with a wooden anvil to crack open palm nuts. The hammers and anvils are seldom modified, but as they occur mainly where the roots of fallen trees have raised the rocky subsoil, chimpanzees have to carry the food to the sites or the hammers or stones to the fruiting trees. This requires foresight and planning.

Stones and twigs may also be used by chimpanzees to smash bones and extract the marrow from animals such as monkeys, which have been captured during co-operative hunts. A chimpanzee 'toolkit' with successional use has even been described. Researchers have reported seeing a young female using four different types of tools, each with a different function, to get honey from a hive.

Chimpanzees in contact with humans may extend their tool-using and toolmaking capacities to incorporate human materials. They will, for instance, invent new tools to solve the problems of a captive environment, making ladders from branches or poles to climb trees protected by electric fences at their base, or using makeshift rakes to get hold of distant objects. Chimpanzees trained to use symbols will even ask for tools from other chimpanzees. Tool use thus forms part of the social traditions of chimpanzee society, and can be learned during infancy or later in life.

Not all apes use or make tools as well as do chimpanzees. Orang-utans in the wild have yet to be seen to use tools to any great extent, but in captivity they can be competent tool users. One captive orang-utan was taught to break a flint with a hammerstone, producing a sharp cutting edge, to slice a string and so gain access to a food box.

Gorillas do not seem to use or make tools much in the wild or in captivity although they will hurl stones, branches or grass at intruders and, like chimpanzees, build nests for sleeping in. One female gorilla, Koko, trained to use sign language could manipulate a variety of objects as tools.

Perhaps the natural environment of orang-utans and gorillas does not challenge their cognitive capacity enough to stimulate a need for tools. Toolmaking is related to the problem to be solved, to the incentive to solve it (such as access to an especially nutritious food or escape from captivity) and to the time and energy needed to make the tool. The substrate for the tool must be present, as well as sufficient time to risk making a tool that does not work.

All apes probably have the ability to make tools, but only chimpanzees consistently have the need in their natural environment. Among apes, there has been selection for a general ability to solve problems, and making and using tools represents one solution to such problems.

P.C. Lee

See also 'Testing the intelligence of apes' (p. 111)

Learning how to make and use tools is an important part of a chimpanzee's upbringing. (Above) While an adult female in Taï Forest, Ivory Coast, uses an 8-kilogram hammerstone to crack open hard palm nuts, her 3-year-old daughter watches a male using a small stick to extract bits of kernel from a nut opened and partly eaten by the female. (Below) An infant looks on as her mother 'fishes' for ants in Gombe National Park, Tanzania.

resistance: flakes might be produced only by following certain sets of rules that can determine form, without the maker having the intention of creating a special shape. Yet even the second view is sufficent testimony to the abilities of the early stone-workers. They had to execute the routine in a controlled way, to have in mind the different options for working a core, and must hence have assimilated the results of past experience.

The working of a stone to a set form was plainly established by 1.5 million years ago when early humans made large, bifacial cutting tools, or Acheulean handaxes. This tells us a great deal: that an 'arbitrary', preconceived form was held in the mind, and could be impressed on stone. This has been seen as a fundamental hallmark of culture. Such form is shown even in the earliest handaxes, where the ideas of an imposed long axis, bifacial working, and controlled curves are brought together. In even earlier Oldowan stone industries similar ideas may underlie the careful flaking of discoid cores or core tools.

Linguistic abilities may or may not be associated with

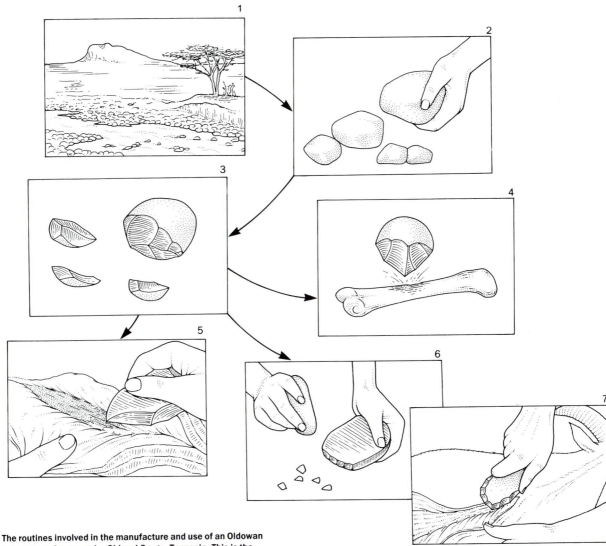

The routines involved in the manufacture and use of an Oldowan industry, at, for example, Olduvai Gorge, Tanzania. This is the minimum number of steps documented at early sites; the complete range of processes did not necessarily occur on a single site.

1. Visit to source of raw materials
2. Selection of suitable pieces
3. Basic flaking, yielding heavy core/core tool and lighter flakes
4. Use of heavy elements to batter (e.g. bones)
5. Use of flakes to cut (may leave cut marks on bone)
6. Retouching of flakes with a hammerstone
7. Use of tool with retouched edge (e.g. on skins); microwear analysis of tools is the only source of knowledge of materials other than bone

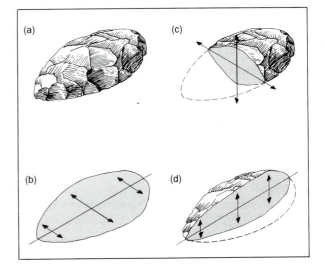

such an imposition of arbitrary form. Language seems to go hand-in-hand with lateralisation of the brain, but chimpanzees may also show signs of lateralisation in the form of handedness. The proportions of flakes struck in particular directions suggest that hominids may have been predominantly right-handed as long ago as 1.9 million years.

Evidence on the transport of raw materials is particularly helpful to the archaeologist: even on the earliest sites, stone tools may be made of materials that must have been carried for several kilometres. The stones were selected, as differing proportions of artefacts were made from particular stones. At Olorgesailie in Kenya, a middle Pleistocene site

Ideas embodied in a bifacial handaxe. Acheulean bifaces were made with varying degrees of symmetry. Most examples have one or more of the following characteristics, and the finest specimens include all. The basic design (a) can incorporate (b) bilateral symmetry of the major plane around a long axis; (c) quadrilateral symmetry in the transverse section; and (d) bilateral symmetry around the long axis in the thickness plane.

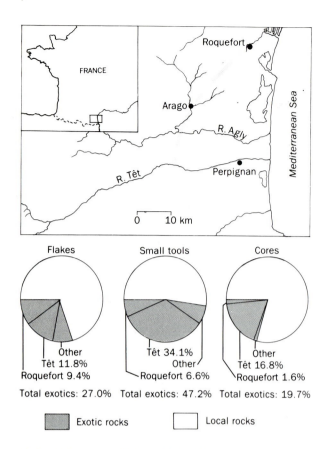

Flakes   Small tools   Cores

Other
Têt 11.8%
Roquefort 9.4%

Têt 34.1%
Other
Roquefort 6.6%

Other
Têt 16.8%
Roquefort 1.6%

Total exotics: 27.0%   Total exotics: 47.2%   Total exotics: 19.7%

Exotic rocks   Local rocks

The hominids occupying the Lower Palaeolithic site of Arago in southwestern France betweeen 400 000 and 300 000 years ago obtained some of the raw materials for their tools from distant sources – for example, good-quality chalcedony and chert from Roquefort-des-Corbières about 30 kilometres to the north-east and quartzite from the River Têt, at least 20 kilometres to the south. The pie diagrams show the percentages of exotic rocks in flakes, small tools and cores found in Layer G at the site.

All peoples of recent times knew how to kindle fire, often by means of a bow drill like these Igwi San of the Kalahari. Fire use may go back much further in time than fire-making.

dating to around 800 000 years ago, finds of manuports (unmodified stones) are of a type of lava available about a kilometre away, but unsuitable for toolmaking. By contrast, lavas suitable for handaxe-making were brought from volcanic mountains several kilometres distant. This shows active discrimination on a rational basis, doubtless reinforced by the hard work involved in carrying stones. At Olduvai in Tanzania, too, some handaxe sites in Bed IV, aged about 700 000 years, are made up of specimens of selected lavas brought from as much as 20 kilometres away. Similar transport distances are known from the French site of Arago (about 300 000 years ago).

In some circumstances, it must have been worthwhile to carry hundreds of kilograms of tools for distances difficult to cover in less than a day's walk. *Homo erectus* was thus able to plan at least a day's activity at a time (or had exchange networks, or both) – and, if the return journey is taken into account, perhaps further ahead. Such carrying must have had a useful economic return, or it could not have persisted for hundreds of thousands of years.

The production of artefacts and the transport of raw materials both give insights into routines that were repeated, with variations in detail, many millions of times through the Stone Ages. Other routines are preserved with far less certainty. The manufacture of wooden tools can be inferred from microwear traces on stone tools, and within the past 300 000 years from preserved wooden tools such as spears. The abilities demanded to work wood were essentially similar to those used in stone-working. Control of fire would have helped, although its early prehistory is controversial.

Coping with the cold

Early sites in Africa have some suggestion of the use of fire, but clear evidence of its controlled creation occurs only in the past 10 000 or 20 000 years. There is good evidence for its use in Europe and Asia within the past 500 000 years, and human colonisation of temperate lands may have been impossible without it. This is not certain, because this occupation took place mainly during periods when the world's climate was warmer than today. It seems likely, however, that the seasonal and diverse northerly climes placed more demands on planning and cultural specialisation than did the tropics and subtropics.

The management of hunting and gathering in such circumstances represents an economy rather than mere opportunistic existence, and selection for advanced cognitive abilities must have increased as the climate worsened. Populations that advanced northwards in the warmth of the interglacials probably had a hard time when colder glacial climates returned. Apparently, such populations were rolled back southwards, as late as the peak of the last glacial period 20 000 to 18 000 years ago, even with the technological improvements in clothing and structures represented in the Upper Palaeolithic sites of the Russian plains and elsewhere. Although these innovations arise from manual skills they depend equally on complex routines controlled by the brain.

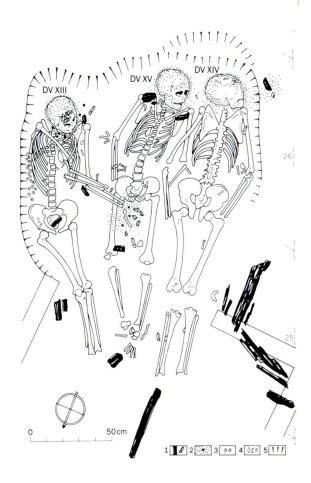

Middle and Upper Palaeolithic burials are known from Europe and Asia. Those of Neanderthals, such as the example here from Kebara Cave in Israel (above), are simpler than later Upper Palaeolithic burials, such as the triple burial from Dolní Věstonice in Czechoslovakia (right), which often include personal decorations. Key to the symbols on the reconstruction by B. Klíma of the Dolní Věstonice burial: 1, charred wood covering the bodies; 2, red pigment; 3, mollusc shells used as decorations and land snails; 4, human teeth, perforated animal teeth used for decoration and pendants of mammoth ivory; 5, grave walls.

Representational art and burial

We gain most insight into such routines where organic preservation is good. This rarely applies beyond the past 10000 years. Nevertheless, a greatly increased variety of skills appears within the past 100000 years, coinciding approximately with the first appearance of modern humans. In the past 40000 years, we see the first shaped bone tools, decoration and representational art, and pointers towards secondary skills – for example, bone needles indicating the existence of thread and sewing. Many archaeologists therefore look on the coming of modern humans and then of the Upper Palaeolithic as the greatest watersheds in human evolution. They may well be right. However, much of the detail of earlier cultures is lost to us and we should not assume that all important changes were concentrated within a short period late in human evolution.

Deliberate burial is one major development that appears before art and the technological advances mentioned above. It is found first around 100000 years ago, and has a geographical distribution over most of Eurasia. Burial suggests an awareness of the possibility of future life and demonstrates the existence of formal ritual. Even so, we should remember that most human remains found in caves

occur in bits and pieces, and that some of them have cut marks (see p. 330): Middle Palaeolithic burial practices do not fit neat preconceptions about 'care' for the dead. The continued, worldwide practice of burial in Upper Palaeolithic times implies a continuity not seen in economic practices or in stone tools.

Technological specialisation often affected the economy. The sophisticated bone and antler tools of the Magdalenian (about 17000 to 12000 years ago), which include spearthrowers and harpoon heads, must have given greater success in hunting, and the chance for more selection of prey species. The earlier Mousterian sites occupied by Neanderthals often contain a mixed bag of remains, but later Upper Palaeolithic sites frequently show a concentration on single species, such as reindeer or horse.

All this reinforces the view that through the past 30000 to 40000 years the brains of modern *Homo sapiens* were similar to our own. Physical and cultural evidence points to lower levels of mental ability and craft skill in earlier periods. Nevertheless, we may have to concede that the foundations of many basic human skills were laid 1 or even 2 million years ago, rather than at the origins of our own species.

J.A.J. Gowlett

See also 'The human brain' (p. 115), 'The hominid way of life' (p. 325), 'Evolution of human manipulation' (p. 346), 'Tools – the Palaeolithic record' (p. 350) and 'Ancient art' (p. 361)

Evolution of human manipulation

Fine manipulative skills and a dependence on tools to exploit resources are hallmarks of the human species. They have enabled living humans to adapt to a greater variety of environments and to maintain higher population densities than any other primate. Until recently, the evolutionary background to this manipulative prowess was poorly known. However, recent discoveries and new analyses of early human arm and hand fossils, and of ancient tools, are giving a new insight into the evolutionary sequence that led to our present dexterity.

Human manipulative skills are in part the products of a series of anatomically based abilities, not all of which leave palaeontological or archaeological traces. The human hand lies at the centre of these skills, and its ability to assume a variety of positions and to resist high levels of mechanical force allows it to perform a great variety of tasks. Its mobility arises from a combination of flexion of the fingers (at the joints between the *phalanges*, or finger bones, and the *metacarpals*, the five bones that connect the wrist to the *carpals*, or wrist bones) and finger rotation (mainly of the thumb and little finger towards the palm at the joints between the carpal and metacarpal bones). It is enhanced by having a thumb sufficently long in relation to the other fingers to allow the fingertips to touch, whether palm to palm or with the thumb on the sides of the other fingers.

These grip positions are enhanced by our ability to rotate the palmar side of the second finger towards the thumb. In addition, the joint at the base of the middle finger, between the carpal and metacarpal bones, is obliquely oriented to resist forces generated by the thumb pressing objects against the other fingers; in apes, it is transverse, because it resists primarily the forces produced during locomotion. Human fingertips, too, are large, so as to resist a force applied to them.

We are also able to position precisely our whole hands through flexion and extension at the wrist, rotation of the forearm, flexion and extension of the elbow, and extensive movement at the open ball-and-socket joint of

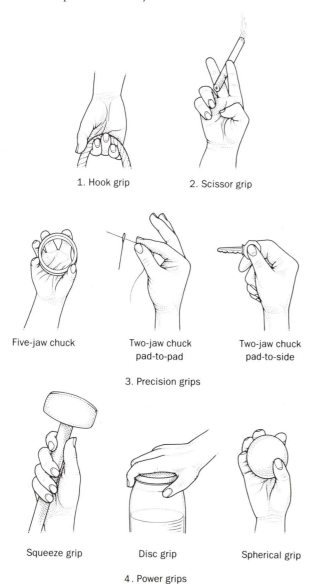

1. Hook grip   2. Scissor grip

Five-jaw chuck   Two-jaw chuck pad-to-pad   Two-jaw chuck pad-to-side

3. Precision grips

Squeeze grip   Disc grip   Spherical grip

4 . Power grips

Human hand grips. The ability of the human hand to rotate the thumb and most of the other fingers permits an infinite range of grips, of which those shown here are the most common. By contrast, the ape hand is largely limited to grip positions in which the fingers flex, or fold, over objects and the thumb grips small objects between its palmar surface and the side of the index finger.

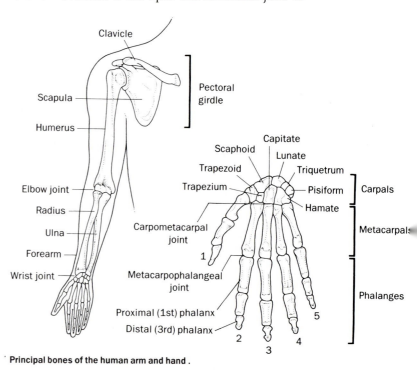

Principal bones of the human arm and hand .

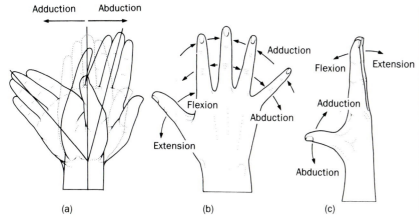

Movements of the wrist, fingers and thumb in humans.

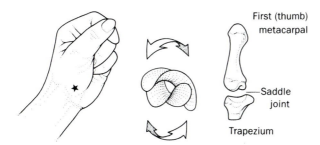

Human hand in the grip position, with the joint between the first (thumb) metacarpal and the trapezium enlarged. Most movements of the thumb take place at this joint. The surfaces of this carpometacarpal (or trapeziometacarpal) joint resemble a saddle. The opposite concave–convex surfaces of the trapezium and the first metacarpal form an interlocking joint mechanism. In chimpanzees, the saddle joint interlocks more, which restricts movement.

the shoulder. These patterns of mobility of the human shoulder and arm are shared with apes and are related to the suspensory locomotion of these primates and of our ancestors; they have been maintained by us for manipulative purposes. However, the degree of mobility of the human hand is far greater than in other primates.

Our arms and hands would be of little use without fine neurological control or hand-to-eye coordination. We have greatly expanded motor and sensory portions of our brains for perception and for control of our hands, and this is reflected in a high density of nerve endings in the muscles, joints and skin of the hand. Aided by the moist, ridged palm we can manipulate extremely small items with precision. Unfortunately, these neurological and dermal structures do not leave fossils, so we must infer their development from underlying skeletal structures and their products – the tools that form the archaeological record.

Australopithecines – pounders and movers

The earliest evidence for human manipulative abilities comes from hand and arm bones of australopithecines, especially the early East African species *Australopithecus afarensis*. The few hand and arm bones known for the early

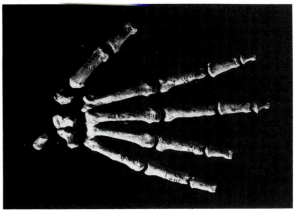

The hand bones of *Australopithecus afarensis* from Hadar, Ethiopia. The bones probably represent more than one individual of about the same size. They show that the relative finger lengths were similar to those of modern humans, but other features, such as the small fingertips and rather curved finger bones, were similar to those of chimpanzees.

South African species *A. africanus* are indistinguishable from those of *A. afarensis*, and from those of the later *A.* (or *Paranthropus*) *boisei* and *robustus*.

These hands have an interesting mixture of human and chimpanzee features. Among the former are the relative finger lengths (they lack either thumb foreshortening or elongation of the other fingers), the orientation of the thumb away from the other fingers (more in *opposition* to them), and the ability to rotate the second finger towards the thumb. Among the ape-like features, however, are the restricted range of rotation of the thumb and little finger, a transversely flat articulation at the base of the middle finger, and small fingertips. In addition, the hand bones of *A. afarensis* had attachments for powerful wrist and finger flexor muscles, similar to those seen in ape hands and used by them in suspensory locomotion, and rather curved finger bones that result from that powerful flexion of the fingers.

The *A. afarensis* hand bones thus show an anatomical pattern primarily adapted for locomotion with only slight modifications for manipulation, probably for pounding with large hammerstones or possibly for throwing. Other aspects of the limbs also indicate that, although bipedal, *A. afarensis* spent much of its time climbing in trees. There is no evidence that this australopithecine made or used tools more than do living chimpanzees.

The first real tool users

The first major changes in human manipulative prowess appear with the emergence of the genus *Homo*, in the species *Homo habilis*. Fossilised hand bones indicate a modern human pattern of joint mobility at the thumb. The powerful finger-flexion musculature was maintained in *H. habilis*, but was associated with fingertips even larger than those of modern humans, and with straight finger bones. *Homo habilis* shows for the first time major expansion and probable reorganisation of the human brain, fully terrestrial bipedalism, and the manufacture and use of stone tools.

Those stone tools, known as the *Oldowan* industry, were extremely simple and represent the outcome of a single basic idea – that one can produce a sharp edge by knocking a flake off a cobble (see pp. 326 and 351). However, that technology was enough to expand significantly the food available to hominids to include portions of carcasses, marrow in long bones and the flesh of hard-shelled fruit, as well as soft fruits and underground roots. This dietary range provided the selective pressure that began the anatomical modification of the human hand, even if, at this stage of human evolution, technology was little more than a means of expanding the availability of resources within the context of an ape-like lifestyle.

Between the appearance of *Homo erectus*, around 1.7 million years ago, and the emergence of archaic members of our species, *Homo sapiens*, around 400 000 years ago, human manipulative skills changed only gradually. Hand and arm fossils indicate a continuation of the robust human-like pattern seen in *H. habilis*. Interestingly, a few neck vertebrae from early *H. erectus* show little of the expansion of the spinal cord, indicative – in modern humans – of greater neurological control of the arm and especially of the hand.

Therefore, despite changes in the patterns of hand movement, with a greater range of grip positions in *H. habilis* and *H. erectus*, the fine control we associate with human manipulation must have come later.

Stone-tool technology remained simple; small flakes struck from cobbles were the commonest tools but these were joined by larger (sometimes very large) tools such as handaxes, usually of coarser stone. One of the major advances of this technological complex (the *Acheulean* industry) over the Oldowan was the manufacture of tools on flakes rather than on cores. This is the first evidence of form being imposed on the raw material available.

Towards the end of this period, two innovations appear: the use of soft hammers of bone or wood to shape stone more precisely and the careful preparation of stone before flake removal in an attempt to control the flake's shape (the prepared-core or *Levallois* technique). Humans spread into seasonal climates such as subtropical Africa and Asia (between 1.5 and 1 million years ago) and subsequently into temperate Eurasia (around 500 000 to 400 000 years ago), by which time fire had also been controlled. These technological changes probaby reflect an increasing human ability to cope with harsher and more seasonal environments. Interestingly, this later geographic expansion was

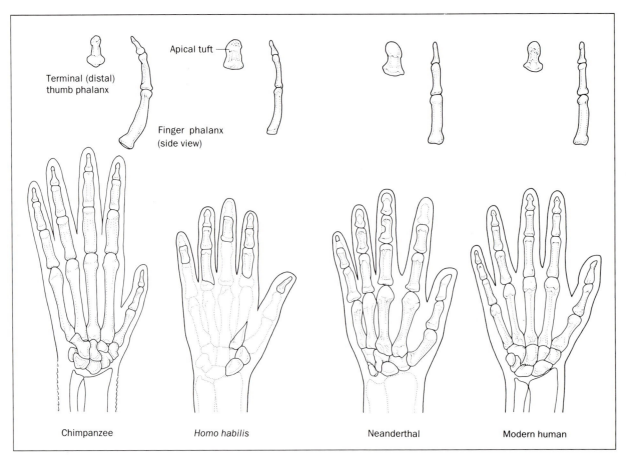

Reconstructed hands of a modern chimpanzee, *Homo habilis* from Olduvai (OH 7), a Neanderthal (Shanidar 4) and a modern human. Missing portions of the *Homo habilis* and Neanderthal hands have been dotted in. Notice the longer fingers on the chimpanzee hand, the large apical tufts on the *Homo habilis* and Neanderthal fingertips, and the generally heavy build of the *Homo habilis* and Neanderthal hand bones.

associated with an increase by a third in the size of the human brain.

The Neanderthal power grip

Abundant fossil and archaeological evidence is available for the Neanderthals of Europe and western Asia, and also for their contemporaries in eastern Asia and Africa, who were the immediate predecessors of modern humans. The technology of these hominids, the *Middle Palaeolithic* industry, shows a continued refinement of the flake-oriented toolkits of their ancestors.

Flaking of prepared cores became common, retouching of flakes with soft hammers to produce evenly curved, notched or sawtoothed-edged implements was frequent, and some of the edges were shaped through pressure (as opposed to percussion) flaking. Most of these tools were still held in the hand, and hafts are extremely rare. There are a few wooden and bone tools, but these are crude, often much more so than the stone implements: they were probably used briefly and then discarded. Middle Palaeolithic assemblages also suggest that technology still lacked the long-term planning and task-specificity we associate with modern toolkits. This lesser degree of organisation is echoed in other aspects of archaeological remains from this period, although those who left them had brains the same size as those of modern humans.

Associated Neanderthal remains fill out this picture. Like their predecessors, Neanderthals had hands and arms with the same overall proportions as those of modern humans. They were nonetheless extremely muscular, as is manifest in enlarged muscle attachments throughout the shoulder, arm and hand. Muscles used in bringing the arm down, as in throwing or striking a blow, and in grasping between the thumb and fingers, were particularly developed. These muscular developments were associated with large joint surfaces and fingertips, which served to resist the forces generated when the hand and arm were in action. In addition, the two finger bones of the Neanderthal thumb were about the same length, rather than the first being longer than the second, as it is in modern humans; this increased the strength of the power grip used to hold objects across the base of the thumb.

The articulations of Neanderthal hands indicate a range of finger movement similar to those of modern humans. However, slight differences in the shape of the shoulder joint and orientation of the joint surface at the elbow suggest that Neanderthals used their arms more frequently in flexed positions than modern humans do and did less throwing. The shapes of the joint surfaces at the base of the index and middle fingers also suggest that they used the oblique grips of modern humans (required, for instance, to hold a hammer in line with the forearm) far less than we do. Nonetheless, Neanderthal neck vertebrae show that they had the enlarged spinal cord and hence fine neurological control of the hand that we have today.

The anatomy of hands and arms, together with the tools they left behind, indicates that Neanderthals used toolkits that were mechanically inefficient compared with those of modern humans. To compensate for the minimal leverage and generalised nature of most of their working edges, Neanderthals (and their ancestors) acquired powerful arms and hands to provide the force required for effective use. In addition, their arms and hands were shaped by the habitual grip positions dictated by their technology, especially by the rarity of hafting, and hence of effective projectiles and hammers, which required tools to be held close to the body.

Modern manipulative skills

With the emergence and spread of anatomically modern humans after 100 000 years ago came the appearance of manipulative skills similar to our own. The hand and arm remains of these early modern people are indistinguishable from those of athletic living people, in terms of articular configurations, proportions of the hand bones and of the upper limbs, and levels of muscularity.

These anatomical changes are associated subsequently with several technological improvements, such as those seen in *Upper Palaeolithic* industries. All served to reduce the load on the human frame and to increase the efficiency of tool use. Although flake and core tools were still used, the toolkit consisted more and more of tools based on long prismatic blades struck off specially prepared stone cores. These blades provided relatively uniform blanks for the manufacture of points, knives and other sharp edges. At the same time, hafts of wood and of polished bone appear. These permitted the development of a simple technology in which tools were fashioned for specific tasks and spare parts were available. They also promoted the frequent manufacture of effective projectiles, hammers and other compound tools. Tools, together with a complex organisation of technology and more sophisticated means of subsistence, allowed early modern humans to exploit a greater variety of resources and to expand rapidly over the remainder of the inhabitable world.

Human manipulative prowess, as reflected in both our anatomy and our technology, emerged slowly during human evolution. However, within the past 40 000 years it has become one of the dominant aspects of our biological and cultural adaptation.   *Erik Trinkaus*

See also 'Primate locomotion and posture' (p. 75), 'Evolution of australopithecines' (p. 231), 'Evolution of early humans' (p. 241), 'The hominid way of life' (p. 325), 'Early human mental abilities' (p. 341) and 'Tools – the Palaeolithic record' (p. 350)

Tools – the Palaeolithic record

Stone tools represent the principal cutting edge of past technology. They are so durable that they provide a framework for mapping out human activities from the distant past to recent times.

Stone tools were apparently not in use during the earliest stages of hominid evolution. There are no signs of flaked tools more than 3 million years old, although, if used, they should probably have been found at the hominid sites of Laetoli and Hadar in eastern Africa. They have, however, been found at some sites older than 2 million years. In these late Pliocene times wooden tools may have been in use, but no traces remain. Such vagaries of preservation must govern our view of the past, but this does not mean that we overrate the role of stone tools. They had real importance to their makers, for processing plants and cutting meat, and for making other tools. They allowed wood to be shaped, hides to be scraped and sinews to be prepared. The cutting edge of a thin flake of flint or obsidian matches that of steel, lacking only its flexibility. Shaped scraper edges are also extremely effective. In recent times, stone arrowheads and axes have often served their purpose so well that they long survived the coming of metal.

The simplest stone tool is just a natural stone – such as a water-worn cobble – selected for use in hammering or battering as sometimes done by chimpanzees. These were among the first tools ever used, since any further step in stone-toolmaking requires a simple hammerstone of this nature. The hammer is used to strike flakes from a core (the conventional name for the struck piece). The alternative – to break up a natural stone by throwing or dropping – can produce pieces with useful sharp edges, but not a sophisticated tool.

Some of the earliest known tools, from the Shungura Formation of the Omo Valley in Ethiopia, are little more than split-up cobbles, but elsewhere, even on the earliest sites, toolmaking always involved controlled flaking. Various fine-grained rocks show *conchoidal fracture*; struck shock waves running through the stone along a curved route detach a curved flake. Such rocks include many lavas, as well as flint and chert, and have been used in toolmaking from early times.

The essential elements of stone-toolmaking are *flakes* and *cores*; flakes are the relatively thin pieces that are detached, and cores are their sources (see p. 326). Hundreds of flakes may be taken from a single core by the *knapper* – as the skilled stone-worker is called.

The earliest stone tools

The oldest known stone tools are dated to more than 2 million years ago, from sites in Ethiopia, Kenya, Zaire and Malawi. Artefacts from the Shungura Formation near the Omo River are dated to 2.0 to 2.2 million years ago; some from levels at Hadar overlying the australopithecine sites may be as old 2.6 million years. Others from eastern Zaire (Senga), Kenya (West Turkana) and Malawi (Mwimbi) may also be of late Pliocene age.

Most of the oldest sites are found along the Rift Valley system of eastern Africa, notably at Olduvai, Chesowanja, East Turkana (Koobi Fora) and Melka Kunturé. Olduvai Gorge in Tanzania (see p. 329) has yielded far more stone tools than any other early site. It consists of a series of separate sites scattered around an ancient lake basin, which has been exposed by the cutting of a gorge through the sediments. The lowest bed at Olduvai, Bed I, is about 1.9 million years old and is the basis for the definition and classification of all early stone *industries*. Tools from Olduvai and other early African sites involve a variety of forms – the *Oldowan* industrial complex.

The Oldowan industry at sites in Olduvai Bed I and lower Bed II consists primarily of simple core forms made from cobbles, and associated flakes. A flake is often modified or *retouched* for use by striking small chips from one or more of

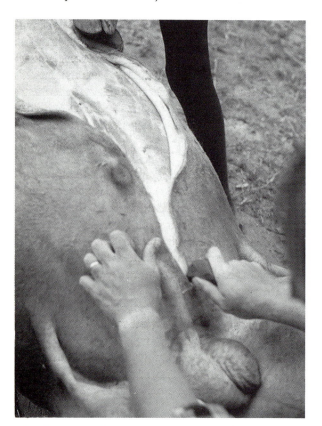

Cutting the hide of a wildebeest with a stone tool. The cutting edge of a thin stone flake matches that of steel.

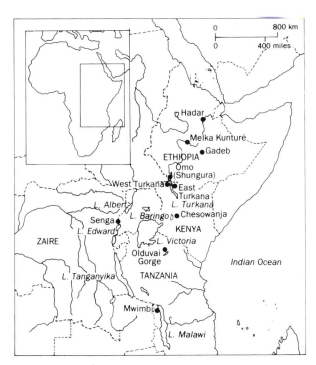

Early archaeological sites in eastern Africa, all older than about 1.4 million years, where Oldowan tools have been found. The oldest known stone artefacts date to more than 2 million years ago, from Hadar (Kada Gona), Senga, Omo and West Turkana.

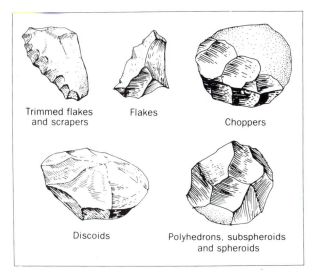

The basic elements of an Oldowan toolkit. Flakes, including those suitable for modification (retouch) into flake scrapers, are produced during the manufacture of choppers, discoids, and all the heavier forms of Oldowan tool. These so-called core forms may have been used as a source of more flakes, or may have been shaped deliberately to be used as heavy-duty tools.

its edges. Similar tools also occur in southern and north-western Africa – for example, Sterkfontein in South Africa and Ain Hanech in Tunisia. These sites are over a million years old, but their exact date is unknown. By about 1.5 million years ago some variants of the Oldowan are more refined, meriting the term *Developed Oldowan*, as at Gadeb in Ethiopia or Karari on the east side of Lake Turkana.

Early signs of human occupation exist in a broad belt stretching across the tropics and subtropics through Arabia and the Indian subcontinent to the east of Asia. In Asia, volcanic rocks that allow potassium-argon dating are rare on archaeological sites, so that there we have a much hazier picture of human evolution. A few possible cores or core tools found in deposits around 2 million years old near Riwat in northern Pakistan may indicate early human activity but the status and dating of these finds remain uncertain. Many early Palaeolithic sites have been found in China, but none is as old as the earliest sites in Africa. Among the oldest are the Lantian sites in Shanxi Province, which have recently been dated to 1.3 million years.

It is often argued that early humans emerged in Africa and spread into Asia, but the hard evidence is still equivocal, particularly since some of the best-known finds of Asian fossil hominids – the *Homo erectus* specimens of Java – are not accompanied by stone tools. Perhaps the local sharp splintered bamboo made stone tools unnecessary, but stone artefacts have been found at some other localities in eastern Asia. In China, the early sites do preserve a few stone tools, as at the Lantian sites and at Xihoudou near Kehe in Shanxi Province.

The best-known early site complex in China is that of Zhoukoudian (formerly Choukoutien), near Beijing, which was occupied for many years from about 500 000 years ago. Here, enormous numbers of stone tools are associated with *Homo erectus* in cave deposits. They are comparable in technology to the Oldowan and Developed Oldowan of Africa, with choppers and core-scrapers, but include many larger flakes. There is good evidence for fire at Zhoukoudian, although shaped hearth arrangements have not been found. Hearths first appear about 300 000 years ago at Terra Amata in southern France.

In parts of eastern Asia, early humans may have used bamboo, not stone, for many of their tools.

The Acheulean tradition

Early in the history of stone-toolmaking, advances were made in the shaping of tools. Even before 1.6 million years ago, a pattern of *bifacial* working appeared in Africa. Flakes were detached from two opposed faces of a stone, leaving an edge. In *choppers*, this edge runs part way around the circumference; in *discoids*, it runs around the entire circumference. It is not certain that these choppers and discoids were all intended to be shaped core tools. Some of them may have been no more than cores, with a form arrived at through a pattern of 'least resistance' when producing successive flakes. Nevertheless, the symmetrical form of some pieces, together with later developments in toolmaking, suggest that many specimens were deliberately shaped. Such bifacial working increases in the later Developed Oldowan assemblages, as at Olduvai Bed II.

The next step came with the imposition of a definite long axis. This appears as a quantum leap in the archaeological record – we suddenly find evolved tools (*handaxes* or *bifaces*)

in which the long axis is linked with a walnut shape, and the edge between the two faces shaped by bifacial working runs around most or all of the margin (see p. 343).

These tools must have been very satisfactory, because they were made for more than a million years. They are found in most of the Old World occupied more than 100 000 years ago. All such handaxe industries are now referred to as the *Acheulean*, derived from the French site of St Acheul. Far older Acheulean sites are found in Africa, where the earliest sites are about 1.5 million years old – as at Olduvai Bed II and Peninj, also in Tanzania. The handaxes recur in eastern Africa at, for example, Kariandusi, Kilombe, Isimila, Olorgesailie (see p. 329) and Kalambo

The extent of the Acheulean handaxe industry, 1.6 to 0.15 million years ago, with some important sites indicated. At some sites in this time range, the older forms of core tools, flakes and scrapers outnumber handaxes (e.g. Isernia) or handaxes were not made at all (e.g. Clacton and Zhoukoudian). Three representative Acheulean tools are shown: a handaxe from St Acheul in France, a cleaver made on a large flake from the Saharan site of Erg de Tihodaine in Algeria and a handaxe from Hunsgi in the state of Karnataka, India.

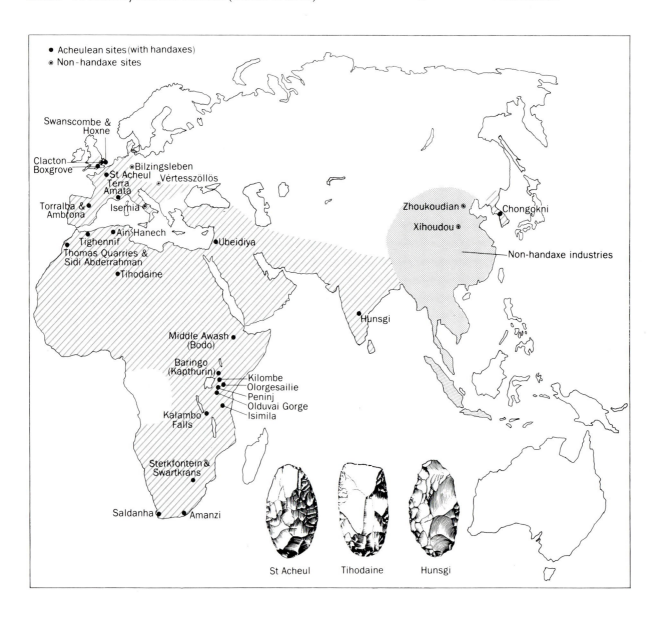

- • Acheulean sites (with handaxes)
- ⊙ Non-handaxe sites

Swanscombe & Hoxne
Clacton
Boxgrove
Bilzingsleben
St Acheul
Terra Amata
Vértesszöllös
Torralba & Ambrona
Isernia
Ain Hanech
Tighennif
Thomas Quarries & Sidi Abderrahman
Tihodaine
Ubeidiya
Zhoukoudian ⊙
Xihoudou ⊙
Chongokni
Non-handaxe industries
Hunsgi
Middle Awash (Bodo)
Baringo (Kapthurin)
Kilombe
Olorgesailie
Peninj
Olduvai Gorge
Isimila
Kalambo Falls
Sterkfontein & Swartkrans
Saldanha
Amanzi

St Acheul   Tihodaine   Hunsgi

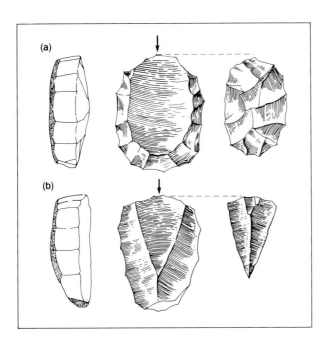

Stages in the manufacture of (a) a Levallois flake and (b) a Levallois point. The technique may have originated in Africa around 300 000 years ago; by 200 000 years ago it was being used around the Mediterranean and in western Europe, wherever there were suitable raw materials. (About a third natural size.)

Falls, which allow us to trace similar ideas through a very long period of time. (From Kalambo Falls in Zambia have come some of the earliest preserved wooden tools, including a possible club; these are probably aged about 200 000 years.)

The stone artefacts at these site complexes vary considerably, even in levels of the same age. At some sites, handaxes or bifaces are associated with many smaller flake tools, others contain mainly choppers or picks, and in some cases there are no handaxes.

The Acheulean was a far more widespread tradition than the Oldowan, occuring throughout Africa, extending into Europe and across Asia. However, the oldest traces of human occupation in Europe do not include Acheulean tools. Early sites, such as Isernia in Italy (about 730 000 years old) and possibly also Vallonnet in southern France (about 900 000 years old), appear to have mainly choppers and flake tools; handaxes appear only later on, as at Ambrona and Torralba in Spain, and Boxgrove and Hoxne in southern England.

Further east, at Bilzingsleben in Germany and Vértessöl-lös in Hungary (important sites also of *Homo erectus*/'archaic *Homo sapiens*' fossils), the industries consist of small artefacts, such as small cores, choppers and associated flake tools. In southeastern England, there is an industry without hand-axes, the *Clactonian*. This consists of chopper-cores and flake tools, and is earlier than most handaxe industries in Britain.

The Acheulean is widespread in the Middle East and common in parts of the Indian subcontinent, Mongolia and South Korea. In contrast, it is almost absent from China.

There was probably considerable cultural variability in the Lower Palaeolithic in all parts of the Old World, with Acheulean handaxes found in most but not all areas. In Asia, there is little evidence of human occupation before 100 000 years ago north of a line from the Caucasus to Mongolia.

About 150 000 years ago the great handaxe tradition began to evaporate, perhaps because of developments in flaking techniques and the specialisation of flake tools, which had begun at least 100 000 years earlier. The principal new feature is the *Levallois technique*, named after a site in France. This involves the careful shaping of a core by the removal of many flakes from one face, all with the aim of producing one special flake, which is detached last. The technique may have originated in Africa, where very large flakes were used for making handaxes. These were struck from large cobbles, and preparatory flaking helped to ensure the right shape.

It is not easy to date the appearance of such artefacts, as they are too late for most potassium-argon dating, and beyond the range of radiocarbon. Nevertheless, the trend is clear: smaller and more refined handaxes; more carefully shaped and retouched flake tools; and a reliance on the Levallois technique in areas with suitable raw materials.

At Kapthurin near Lake Baringo in Kenya, around 200 000 years ago, large handaxes made on Levallois flakes are accompanied by long blade-like flakes (*flake-blades*). At Gademotta in Ethiopia, similar developments are seen at about 160 000 years ago. Elsewhere around the Mediterranean and in western Europe, industries of fine, long flakes occur at about the same time. Baker's Hole in southeastern England and Rocourt in Belgium are two such sites.

The Middle Palaeolithic

These early – and in some ways precocious – developments herald a new phase of flake industries collectively known as the *Middle Palaeolithic* (the Oldowan and Acheulean constituting the Lower Palaeolithic). The Middle Palaeolithic is often conceived of archaeologically as a dull period, lasting with little change until about 40 000 years ago, after which everything altered. This does not do justice to the Middle Palaeolithic: it was in fact full of technical change.

Among the flake industries that came to predominate almost everywhere in Europe, Asia and Africa, the *Mousterian* (named after Le Moustier in France) is commonly regarded as the tool assemblage belonging to Neanderthals in western Europe, North Africa and the Middle East. However, the relationship is not absolute: some Neanderthals may have made other tools, and in the Middle East, early modern humans – for example, those at the sites of Skhūl and Qafzeh – are associated with Mousterian tools.

Most Mousterian industries belong to the last glaciation, from about 100 000 to 40 000 years ago. But the label is deceptively specific. The chief features of the Mousterian

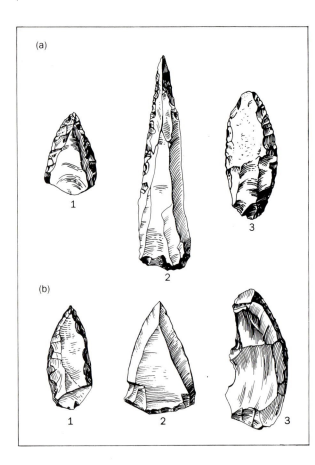

Typical Mousterian assemblages from the Levant and France. (a) Tabūn Cave, Mount Carmel, Israel: 1, Mousterian point; 2, elongated Mousterian point; 3, sidescraper. (b) Combe-Grenal, Dordogne (1 and 3) and Houppeville, Normandy: 1, Mousterian point; 2, Levallois point; 3, sidescraper. (About a half natural size.)

are simple discoid or Levallois flaking, aimed at the production of flakes suitable for conversion into various types of *side-scraper* (with retouch along one or more edges). Scrapers (which were not necessarily used for scraping) had existed from the Oldowan onwards, but they now became the dominant tool forms, and were often carefully retouched. Another characteristic tool, the so-called Mousterian *point*, is much less common, as are the remaining specialised handaxes.

The Middle Stone Age of Africa and Asia

In Africa, and much of Asia, industries equivalent to the Mousterian are embraced within the *Middle Stone Age*. This is a general term for varied styles of toolmaking that occupy the period from about 150 000 years ago to perhaps 20 000 to 10 000 years ago. Most involve flake industries, but they usually lack the emphasis on the side-scrapers of the Mousterian.

Many of the African industries have lightly trimmed flakes, including in the early stages flake-blades – as in the *Preaurignacian* of Haua Fteah (Libya) and along the Orange River (South Africa). There are many regional variants of the

Middle Stone Age. In central and western Africa there are sometimes heavy-duty tools, as in the *Sangoan* at Kalambo Falls. The *Lupemban* of Angola also has long heavy picks. In much of Africa, small, finely shaped bifacial points are found, such as at Stillbay, Pietersburg and Bambata in southern Africa. Along the Nile there is a variety of industries using the Levallois technique even on tiny pebbles, as in the *Halfan*.

In northwestern Africa an industry named the *Aterian* is distinctive for having bifacial points with tangs, some of which suggest that the tools had hafts. Although there is no direct evidence, it does seem likely that many of the small points are projectile tips. Also found in this period are miniature tools (*microliths*) at such sites as Klasies River Mouth on the southern coast of South Africa (see p. 369). Some of these may be more than 60 000 years old.

In general, the Middle Stone Age is much less known in Asia. Mousterian-like toolkits are known from Iraq, Iran and Afghanistan, and as far east as Lake Baikal in Siberia. Further into southern Asia, the industries are sometimes characterised as 'Mousteroid', but are not Mousterian in the classic sense. In peninsular India, there is a widespread industry, dated at around 40 000 to 20 000 years, characterised by *notched scrapers* (flakes retouched with several deep indentations) and *denticulates* (flakes with jagged edges) as well as by side-scrapers. The Levallois technique was used on quartz. In some areas, heavy-duty tools have been found. In southeastern Asia and China, there were flake industries, but few sites have been dated.

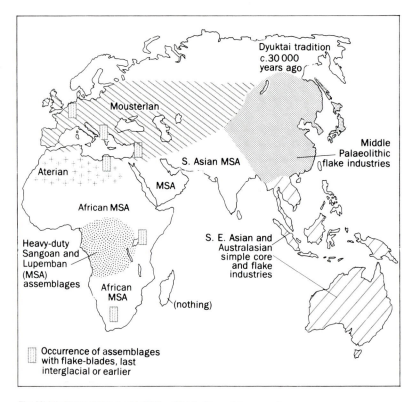

The Middle Palaeolithic world. MSA = Middle Stone Age.

The blade industries of the Upper Palaeolithic

Major technological changes were afoot in the Middle East about 40 000 years ago. In just a few thousand years Middle Palaeolithic flake industries were replaced by the blade industries typical of the Upper Palaeolithic. *Blades* are long and narrow flakes, produced from specialised cores, with a prismatic form. Each successive blade takes its form from the ridges left on the core by the removal of the previous blades.

This technical advance is important, because such relatively uniform blades could easily serve as blanks for the production of a range of standard and more specialised tools. These include various *burins* (engraving tools) and scrapers. Piercing and boring tools also show that more specialised tasks were performed. In the past, archaeologists often linked the origins of the Upper Palaeolithic with the advent of modern humans, but now we know that the two need not concur. Apart from the occurrence of early modern humans with the Mousterian at Skhūl and Qafzeh in Israel, at St Césaire in France a late Neanderthal is associated with an early Upper Palaeolithic industry termed the *Châtelperronian*.

In the Near East, the Upper Palaeolithic evolved between about 50 000 and 40 000 years ago. Its characteristic tech-nology is found at an early date at sites in the Negev Desert and along the North African coast. It appears in Europe a little later, and had reached the north-west by at least 35 000 years ago.

The Upper Palaeolithic was not entirely new. Long, blade-like flakes had appeared more than 100 000 years ago in both Africa and Europe. They also occur in the Mousterian of the Levant, and in Greece. It is quite plain, though, that none of these is as sophisticated as a typical Upper Palaeolithic complex.

We must be careful in dating the Upper Palaeolithic, since it originated at the limits of radiocarbon dating. This is particularly true of the crucial period at about 40 000 years ago, and might lead to a distorted view of the transition between the Upper Palaeolithic and the preceding Mousterian. At Nahal Zin in the Negev, radiocarbon and uranium dates agree on 45 000 years ago for an early Upper Palaeolithic industry: at the Haua Fteah cave, the date of the transition is about 40 000 years ago. One or two dates in southeastern Europe suggest a similar time for the appear-ance of the Upper Palaeolithic, but in parts of western Europe the new techniques may have arrived later.

Upper Palaeolithic blade industries are found in much the same area as the Mousterian, across much of Eurasia. They also extend into southern and eastern Asia and across Siberia. In Africa, they are found only in the very north. Elsewhere, Middle Stone Age industries continued into the last 20 000 years as flake industries were preferred.

In most of Europe, the earliest Upper Palaeolithic belongs to a complex called the *Aurignacian*, which lasted for several thousand years. This is characterised by long retouched blades, short, steep-sided scrapers, and bone

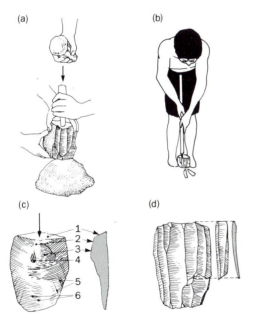

Upper Palaeolithic toolmakers used special techniques to produce blade tools from a carefully prepared core. One way was to hold the core in the hand and strike it with a hammer of stone, wood or bone. Another way was to place the core on a large stone on the ground and then to detach the flake with a hammer and punch (a) – the indirect percussion or punch technique. Blades could also have been detached by exerting pressure on the core with a pointed tool, such as a sharpened piece of antler or bone (b). A detached flake (c) is slightly curved in side view and has some distinctive features on its ventral (release) surface: 1, striking platform; 2, percussion cone; 3, small conchoidal bulb of percussion; 4, splinter; 5, striations; 6, ripples or waves of percussion, the concavity of which is towards the percussion cone. After blades have been struck in sequence from the striking platform, the core can look like a prism (d).

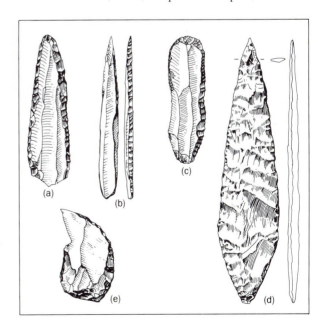

Some representative Upper Palaeolithic tools. (a) Aurignacian blade (Caminade shelter, Dordogne); (b) Gravettian point (Corbiac, Dordogne); (c) Gravettian endscraper (Dolní Věstonice, Czechoslovakia); (d) Solutrean point (Fourneau du Diable, Dordogne); (e) Magdalenian burin (Dordogne). (About a half natural size.)

points. Hitherto, bone tools had been rare, but from now onwards we see them commonly and in ever greater variety, especially in Europe. In glacial Europe, bone and antler were perhaps preferred to wood, which was probably used in other parts of the world. But as wood is so rarely preserved we may get a false impression that bone tools were unduly common in Europe.

The Aurignacian complex extended from Russia in the east to France and Spain in the west. Suddenly, about 27 000 years ago, it was replaced by another tradition – the *Gravettian* (known as the *Périgordian* in France). This was characterised by *backed blades* (blunted down one edge, possibly hafted as projectile points), and by *end-scrapers* (blades retouched round the end). Gravettian ideas endured to about 12 000 years ago across Europe, but local sequences differ in detail and have a variety of names.

The predominant grouping for the period 17 000 to 12 000 years ago is the *Magdalenian*. In parts of France and Spain, this follows a major interruption by another localised tradition, the *Solutrean*, which lasted from about 21 000 to 18 000 years ago. In this, the most characteristic tool form is the long, laurel-leaf bifacial point made on a blade. These were shaped by pressure-flaking, a technique in which many parallel wafer-thin flakes are detached from an edge by pressure rather than by striking a blow. The large

Solutrean points are the most sophisticated of all stone tools, matched only by similar forms found much later in Mexico and Predynastic Egypt.

In later stages (from 13 000 to 11 000 years ago), Magdalenian tools included beautifully worked bone and antler objects, such as *harpoons* and *spearthrowers*. Similarly decorated artefacts might have been used in the rest of the world, but have not survived. The underwater site of Tybrind Vig in Denmark and the cave collection of Nahal Hemar in Israel are exceptionally well-preserved Stone Age sites of the last 10 000 years, which give some small indication of the wealth of wooden and other artefacts that has perished elsewhere.

The microlithic revolution

Throughout the Stone Age, the emphasis was on tools in the range 4 to 6 cm long. Towards the end of the Pleistocene, specialised small tools became more important, with carefully shaped cores geared towards the production of small flakes or blades, and finely retouched end-products. As with other innovations, we cannot pick out a single centre or an unbroken tradition for the introduction of these *microliths*. The earliest sites are in southern Africa, such as Klasies River Mouth in Cape Province and Sehonghong

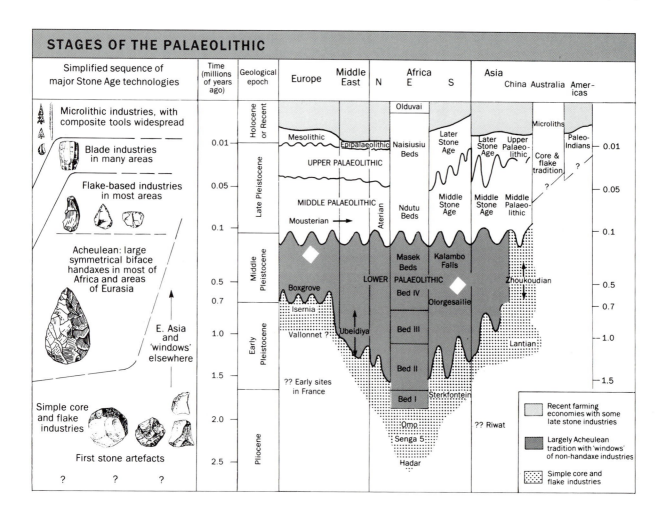

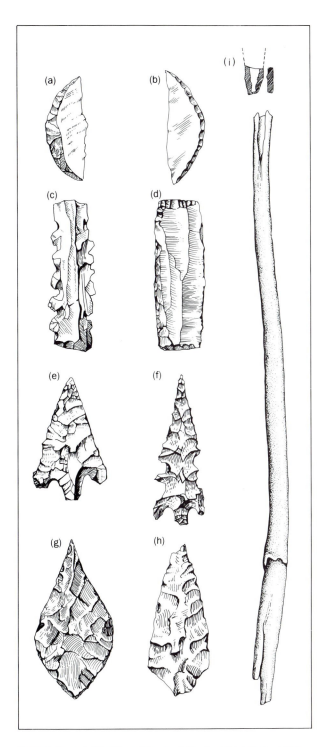

Towards the end of the Stone Age, specialised small artefacts called microliths were added to toolkits throughout Africa, Europe, the Middle East and Asia. They were used not only as projectile points but also in many composite tools. Here is a selection from various sources: (a) crescent (El Wad, Mt Carmel, Israel; Natufian); (b) crescent (Shaheinab, Sudan; Neolithic); (c) denticulate triangle (Abu Ghosh, Israel; Neolithic); (d) rectangle (Périgord, France; Magdalenian); (e) projectile point (Fourneau du Diable, Dordogne, France; Solutrean); (f) arrowhead (Abu Ghosh, Israel; Neolithic); (g) arrowhead (Maiden Castle, England; Neolithic); (h) obsidian projectile point (Zohapilco, Mexico); (i) arrowshaft (Stellmoor, Germany; Mesolithic). (About natural size.)

in Lesotho, dating to 40 000 years ago or more. Microliths occur sporadically in the Upper Palaeolithic. They appear, for example, at around 25 000 years ago in the Gravettian of southern Russia, and again in the Solutrean in France. 'Geometric' forms of microliths (such as triangles, crescents and trapezes) appear at about 20 000 years ago in the Haua Fteah sequence, only to disappear soon afterwards, when small-backed blades again predominate.

It is very tempting to link microliths with the introduction of bows and arrows, but the first certain arrow tips come only in the *Hamburgian* and *Ahrensburgian* phases in northern Germany, 13 000 to 10 000 years ago. Here there is no doubt because the arrows themselves are preserved. Microliths were used not only as projectile points, but in many composite tools. Sometimes they were arranged in series to make up sickle blades, and some weapons had fearsome arrays of small razor-like bladelets. Microliths soon became dominant almost throughout the Old World. Their size and form vary, but the theme is the same throughout Europe, the Middle East, Africa, and all the way across Asia, and represents a real 'microlithic revolution'.

In Europe, microliths are the major artefacts of the *Mesolithic*, lasting from about 10 000 to 5500 years ago, but flaked axes also became important in the postglacial, as did large flakes in some areas. This period started with simple, obliquely blunted forms, but later on geometric forms were much favoured. Many Middle Near Eastern caves have a microlithic component, starting more than 20 000 years ago. Oblique blunted bladelets and triangles formed part of the *Kebaran* industry around Mount Carmel in Israel about 15 000 years ago, and retouched bladelets and crescents are found in the succeeding *Natufian*. There is much regional variety in the microlithic industries of this area, as well as abrupt stylistic changes with time.

Australia and New Guinea, and the New World

Human populations expanded across the landmasses of the Old World through the Pleistocene, until they burst out into the territories of new continents. These areas provide much of the most important Stone Age evidence.

Even at times of low sea level during the Pleistocene, Australia and New Guinea were separated from the mainland of Asia by at least 100 kilometres of open sea. They can hence only have been occupied by people who used boats. The date of the earliest colonisation may never be known, but recent work in the north of Australia suggests that it took place at least 50 000 years ago. The density of sites in the range 20 000 to 30 000 years old in the south of the continent tends to confirm such an estimate.

The oldest stone tools are in the Australian *core-tool and scraper* tradition. The examples found at Lake Mungo (about 30 000 years old) are typical of this. Almost all of the retouched tools are scrapers, either steep-edged forms on cores, or flake scrapers. This tradition endured on mainland Australia until about 6000 years ago, and in Tasmania until recent times. On the mainland, a new complex of point and adze forms, together with backed microliths, appeared after that date.

The simplicity of Australian artefacts does not necessarily imply a primitive level of culture. Some other late tools of the mainland, such as the *Hoabinhian* of Southeast Asia, also appear crude. Although flaked stone tools of the area are simple, *polishing* of stone tools started at an earlier date in New Guinea than anywhere else in the world – outside this area it is not found until the introduction of agriculture in the Neolithic.

The Americas preserve a great wealth and variety of tools. People reached the New World relatively late, from the

THROWING

If we did not throw things, how would society be different? There would be no ball games, little hunting except by snaring, and less fighting, and – perhaps – the world would never have been colonised. The widespread use of missiles, from rocket to beachball, comes from the ability to throw with force and accuracy. This is a skill uniquely developed by humans and is so pervasive that it may have developed in our ancient past. However, the early evidence for it is circumstantial and it is rarely discussed in most accounts of human evolution.

How could an apparently vulnerable naked ape survive and flourish in the African savanna without natural defences, such as large canine teeth or claws? Such viability may reflect a long history of weaponry: a cornered band of early hominids armed with rocks would be formidable opponents. There was a change in the hominid condition between 3 and 2 million years ago, which may result from a new hominid ability to injure other creatures.

Archaeological research during the past 20 years suggests that Pleistocene hominids ate more meat than do modern non-human primates. The first association of stone tools and butchered bones appeared more than 2 million years ago. Much of the meat may have been acquired by scavenging, rather than by hunting – a risky pursuit because of the competition from large carnivores. A band of hominids would be at less risk if armed with rocks. Stone throwing could lead to more effective hunting and hence open up further opportunities. Most early hominid sites are, moreover, near stream channels, where many stones suitable for missiles lie about.

Hand-thrown stones can be lethal. In the early eighteenth century, J. W. Vogel described the Hottentots in southwestern Africa who 'know how to throw very accurately with stones . . . It is also not rare for them to hit a target the size of a coin with a stone at 100 paces.' In 1925, H. Basedow showed how effective this accuracy can be:

The Australian aboriginal makes adequate use of any suitable shaped piece of stone he happens to find while in pursuit of game; both in the Musgrave Ranges and the northern Kimberleys stones are used in their natural shape for hurling into a flying flock of birds, for shying at a

bounding wallaby, for bringing down nuts of the baobab, and for precipitating fledgelings out of a nest.

Early humans may have behaved in the same way, for the ability to grip a stone appropriately dates well back into our prehistory.

Comparisons of the hands of *Australopithecus afarensis* with those of modern humans and non-human primates suggest that 'Lucy' and her contemporaries of around 3 million years ago would have been able to grip and to control their hand movements sufficiently to throw small spherical objects. More manipulative prowess came later with *Homo habilis*.

The archaeological evidence is more tenuous. Within the assemblages of early stone artefacts excavated at Olduvai Gorge in Tanzania are many unmodified stones that appear to have been carried in by the toolmakers – *Homo habilis* – around 1.9 million years ago. Many are of a suitable size and shape for throwing. There are few such stones at archaeological sites of comparable age at Koobi Fora in Kenya, but the hominids

would have had easy access to cobbles and pebbles in the nearby streams. Acheulean sites of a million years in age or younger, such as Olorgesailie in Kenya, have many stones suitable for throwing.

Excavations of Mousterian sites have revealed that by 40 000 to 30 000 years ago, people occasionally stockpiled objects, probably for ammunition. Among the finds were more than 100 stone spheroids at La Quina in France and piles of dried clay balls – some of them small enough to have served as slingshot – at Achenheim in Germany.

The subsequent appearance of spearthrowers (before 12 000 years ago), bows and arrows (about 12 000 years ago) and slings (about 5000 years ago) in archaeological and pictorial records, documents times when these more-advanced ballistic weapons were probably in widespread use.

Barbara Isaac

See *also* 'Evolution of human manipulation' (p. 346)

The massacre of La Pérouse's watering crew in Samoa. The sailors were first assailed by stones and then, when disabled, finished off with clubs. Out of the 61 crew members, 12 were killed and many others wounded. The artist shows slings as well as stone-throwing, although the published account of the ill-fated expedition of 1785–88 gives no evidence for the use of slings.

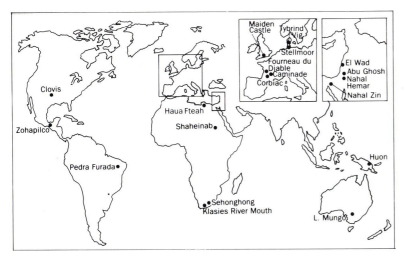

Location of some of the Upper Palaeolithic sites mentioned in this chapter.

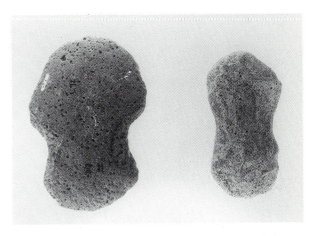

Two grooved 'waisted' axes from Huon Peninsula, Papua New Guinea. The groove suggests hafting at an early date, possibly 40 000 years ago.

north via Beringia, a land bridge between Siberia and Alaska exposed at times of low sea level. The date of the first crossings is controversial, but the recent excavation and dating of the Toca da Boçeirao (Pedra Furada) site in Brazil, if accepted, may indicate that the movements began more than 30 000 years ago. The industry at this site implies an early tradition of straightforward flakes with scrapers and core tools.

The period from 12 000 to 10 000 years ago showed abundant signs of human occupation and a variety of tools. Distinctive bifacially worked projectile points dominate the picture – for example, the fluted *Clovis* points of central North America, and the later *Folsom* varieties. In the Andes, the earliest points seem to be worked mainly on one face, but bifacial types soon follow. Elsewhere, as far apart as Brazil and California, much larger bifaces resembling those of the Acheulean are found, but they do not seem to be more than a few thousand years old. Arrowheads of every form are found in the later cultures, including many similar to Old World types. Grindstones are also common.

The end of the Stone Age

In most of the Old World, the Palaeolithic and Mesolithic of the hunters, gatherers and herd followers were replaced in the past few thousand years by the *Neolithic* industries associated with farming peoples. This was a highly complex process of adaptation, resulting in enormous social changes and technological advances that gave rise to many new styles of artefact. Two widespread changes are the appearance of polished stone tools, such as axes (often with shaft holes), and a reduced emphasis on prismatic blades.

The Stone Age gradually came to an end because of the advent of metal technology. Copper-working spread from a few centres, starting about 8000 years ago. Bronze was uncommon until after 2000 BC. Only in the past few hundred years was the triumph of metal over stone complete.

Mochica hunters of the Classic period of Peruvian prehistory (about AD 0–500) use spearthrowers in this drawing of a hunting scene. The spearthrower effectively lengthens the throwing arm and increases the projectile's speed and range.

In many civilisations, metal-working went on side by side with stone-working. For example, in the Indus Valley around 2000 to 2500 BC, copper and bronze weapons were in common use and were almost invariably used for arrow-heads, but stone implements were still made in great quantity. These included mace heads and celts (axes), and large numbers of narrow bladelets produced from microlithic cores.

In the European Beaker phase of about the same period, people had the use of gold, silver and copper. Copper was used in knives, but finely flaked, bifacial daggers and superbly formed barbed-and-tanged arrowheads were made from flint. At the dawn of the Bronze Age, therefore, we find flint-working at its most sophisticated. Axes were made of stone, and include specimens shaped out in square section, to emulate the metal axes that were coming into use, and which gradually assumed a monopoly. In Europe, stone tools passed out of use after the full onset of the Bronze Age in the second millennium BC.

Iron-working is rare before 1000 BC, and came into use in southern Africa only after AD 1. Stone-toolmaking survived in some areas of Africa and is known today in parts of Ethiopia.

Although there were early centres of metal-working in southern and southeastern Asia, the new skills did not reach all the outlying islands, and in the 1780s Australia and New Guinea still had an entirely Stone Age economy. In the Americas, too, metal-working had been invented but had not completely displaced stone tools before the arrival of Europeans. In Mexico, Cortes's soldiers were amazed to find that fine obsidian blades were used by barbers for shaving. In recent years, the American flint knapper Don Crab-

Clovis tools from southwestern USA. These stone spear points were made by flaking over the whole surface and then removing a flake or 'flute' from the base (usually from both sides), presumably to allow the point to be more firmly fastened to a spear shaft. Clovis points first appeared in North America around 12 000 years ago. The smallest of the three points here (left) from Nogales in Arizona is 6.5 cm long; the largest (right), from Blackwater No. 1 site near Clovis in New Mexico, is 11.7 cm long.

tree has discovered a technique of making obsidian blades suitable for use in surgery – they have an edge far sharper than steel.

J.A.J. Gowlett

See also 'Methods of dating' (p. 179), 'Evolution of early humans' (p. 241), 'The hominid way of life' (p. 325), 'Early human mental abilities' (p. 341) and 'The dispersion of modern humans' (p. 389)

Ancient art

The existence of artistic depictions in the Palaeolithic period was first established through the discovery in France in the 1860s of decorated objects of bone, stone and ivory, in association with tools and fauna of the period; but *parietal art* – images drawn on the walls of caves and rockshelters – was not authenticated until 1902. The first real claim for the existence of Palaeolithic cave art was that made for the Spanish cave of Altamira by a local landowner, Don Marcelino de Sautuola, in 1880. Two decades were to pass before his claims were taken seriously after similar finds in the French caves of La Mouthe, Font de Gaume and Les Combarelles.

Decorated objects (*portable art*) of late Pleistocene age have now been found in other parts of the world: for example, animal figures painted on stones in Apollo 11 cave, Namibia, in levels dating to at least 19 000 years ago; and, in Shikoku, Japan, pebbles from the cave of Kamikuroiwa, dating to 12 165 years ago, have what seem to be breasts and 'skirts' engraved on them. In China, a piece of antler with abstract engraved decoration has been found in the cave of Longgu, Hebei Province, dating to about 13 000 years ago.

Rock art of similar antiquity has also appeared in other continents, such as South America where the rockshelters of Pedra Furada and Perna in the Piauí region of Brazil have red-painted human figures dating to at least 10 000 to 12 000 years ago. Australia also has several caves with ancient finger-markings and deeply engraved circles and grids in them. Some of the finger-markings probably date to between 15 000 and 24 000 years ago (Koonalda Cave, South Australia) and the engravings are at least 13 000 years old (Early Man shelter, northeastern Queensland). Human blood has even been detected in pigments used on Tasmanian cave walls and in some rockshelters in the Northern Territory; radiocarbon dating of this yields dates of around 10 000 and possibly even 20 000 years ago.

However, Europe remains supreme in the quantity and quality of its surviving Palaeolithic art. Portable art is found from Spain to Siberia, with concentrations in southwestern France and in Central and Eastern Europe. Tens of thousands of pieces are known; many sites have produced none or only a few, whereas others – for example, Parpalló in Valencia, eastern Spain, and Enlène in the French Pyrenees – have yielded thousands.

The distribution of decorated caves is very different, although they are most abundant in areas rich in decorated

These human figures found at Perna rockshelter in the Piauí region of Brazil are the oldest dated paintings in the New World. The panel was buried by later occupation layers and the figures (painted in red) survived because of the dryness of the site. Radiocarbon dating of charcoal from the earth that covered them suggests that they were painted at least 10 000 to 12 000 years ago.

1 cm

Early portable art from the Apollo 11 rockshelter, southern Namibia – two fitting fragments of a stone slab with a painting of an animal with feline and bovine features. A pair of human legs has been added, probably at a later date.

Finger-markings at Karlie n' Goinpool, South Australia. Their date is unknown but they are probably as old as the finger-markings at Koonalda Cave (15 000–24 000 years ago).

El Castillo and at Niaux in the French Pyrenees has produced radiocarbon dates of 14 000, 13 000 and 12 890 years ago, respectively. In other cases, stylistic dating has been tried – comparing the parietal figures with dated portable specimens from the same cave or the same region.

However, stylistic dating is full of pitfalls. Proponents of it have tended to oversimplify the development of art, seeing it as a simple progression from archaic to realistic. Pigment analyses and direct dating methods are rapidly replacing stylistic schemes and are revealing that the evolution of art was far more complex than previously thought, with styles co-existing and lasting for long periods.

The earliest Palaeolithic art in Europe dates to around 40 000 years ago (apart from early scattered examples of non-figurative marking) with some of the finest examples being among the most ancient; for example, the ivory human and animal figures from Vogelherd and other German sites, dating to the Aurignacian period, over 30 000 years ago. However, most Palaeolithic art belongs to the latter part of the Ice Age – the Magdalenian period from around 17 000 to 10 000 years ago. Although what has survived must represent only a fraction of Palaeolithic aesthetic activity – we see only non-perishable materials – the art comprises an astonishing variety and mastery of techniques.

The simplest forms of portable art are slightly modified natural objects such as incised, sawn or perforated teeth and shells, used as beads or pendants. The most abundant art object is the engraved stone slab or *plaquette*, hundreds of which have been found in such sites as La Marche in west-

objects: the Périgord, French Pyrenees and Cantabrian Spain. No decorated caves have yet been found in Central Europe, despite its richness in portable art and the existence of suitable caves. One or two painted caves are known in Romania and in the Urals. At present, there are 140 in France, 108 in Spain, 21 in Italy, 2 in Portugal and 1 in Yugoslavia. As with portable art, some sites have only one or two figures, but others, such as the French caves of Lascaux or Trois-Frères, have hundreds.

Portable art is relatively easy to date, since it is usually found with tool assemblages, bones or charcoal; but the dating of parietal art is notoriously difficult. Recent analyses have found organic material in pigments – for example, charcoal – and a radiocarbon date of 14 300 years ago has been obtained from a charcoal dot at Cougnac in France. Charcoal in bison figures at the Spanish sites of Altamira and

A statuette of a mammoth, carved in ivory, from the Vogelherd cave, southern Germany, dating to around 32 000 years ago.

Panel of two stylised horses, numerous dots and several hand stencils in the French cave of Pech Merle, Quercy. The natural rock shape on the right, resembling a horse's head, determined the location of the tiny head of the horse figure facing right. A recent experiment by Michel Lorblanchet to recreate this panel using the pigment-spitting techniques of the Australian aborigines showed that it required a total of 32 hours' work.

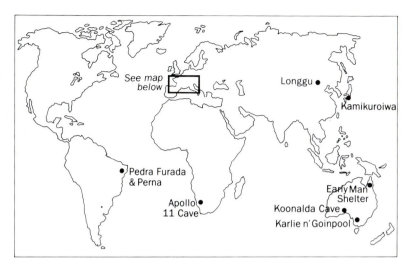

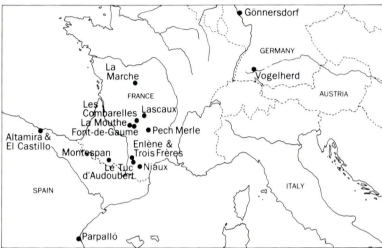

Location of rock art sites mentioned in this chapter.

central France and Gönnersdorf in northwestern Germany. A similar technique involved engraving shoulderblades. Carved antler and bone objects are plentiful in the Magdalenian, including some magnificently sculptured spearthrowers. One remarkable skill was that of engraving around bone shafts and antler batons, so that the animals remained in perfect proportion even though the whole figure could not be seen at once.

Terracotta models were produced in several places, especially in Czech sites around 24 000 years ago, and figurines were carved in soft stones and in ivory, the most famous of these being the 'Venus figurines', which depict females of a wide range of age and physique.

The division between portable and parietal art is one of convenience, since there exist blocks of stone, which, though moveable, could not be carried around. All are from well-lit rockshelters. Some Aurignacian examples bear deep engravings, and others have traces of painted figures.

Like portable art, parietal art made use of natural forms, such as bosses on the ceiling at Altamira used as bulging

bison bodies. There are many examples of wall shapes or stalagmitic formations being used to accentuate or to represent parts of figures.

The simplest form of marking cave walls was to run fingers over them, leaving traces in the soft layer of clay. This technique, perhaps the most ancient of all, spans the whole period. As in portable art, engraving is the most abundant technique on cave walls, ranging from very fine incisions, only visible if lit from the side, to broad deep lines.

Work in clay was limited to the French Pyrenees, and uses a spectrum of techniques from simple fingerholes and tracings to engravings in cave floors, bas-relief, and large three-dimensional figures; for example, the famous bison of Le Tuc d'Audoubert and the headless bear of Montespan. Bas-relief parietal sculpture occurs only in western France where the limestone could be shaped. But whereas clay-work is always found in the dark depths of caves, sculpture occurs only in the well-lit front parts or in rockshelters.

Palaeolithic artists had only four basic colours to work with: red, yellow, brown and black. The main minerals (manganese dioxide for black, iron oxide for the others) were usually available locally. Experiments suggest that water was used for fixing the pigments to the rock surface. They were applied with the finger, brushes, pads or crayons; however, a spraying technique was sometimes used for hand stencils, which are abundant in some caves, notably that of Gargas in the French Pyrenees.

The sophisticated and complex bichrome and polychrome figures of the Magdalenian, characterised by the Altamira bison, are often thought to be typical of Palaeolithic art, but in fact they are rare and appear relatively late. Most of the art – outline drawings or engravings – was undoubtedly done quickly and easily by artists of experience and talent. There is no reason to assume, as most scholars have in the past, that the art was all done for and by men.

Most figures were drawn on surfaces that were easy to reach; but in some cases, ladders or scaffolding must have

Haut-relief in clay – the bison of Le Tuc d'Audoubert cave, Ariège, France, dated about 14 000 years old. The cow (on the right) measures about 61 cm and the bull (left) about 63 cm long.

been used, and in Lascaux the sockets cut into a gallery's walls show how the platform was constructed. Lighting seems to have been no problem, given the abundance of art in the dark depths of caves. However, only 85 stone lamps are known from the 30 000 years of the Upper Palaeolithic, so it is probable that burning torches must usually have been used. The caves are merely the places where parietal art has survived most successfully: there have been recent finds of Palaeolithic-style engravings in the open air in Spain, France and Portugal.

In cave art, figures range from tiny to enormous; there are no groundlines and no landscapes. Most of the animal figures are adults drawn in profile; their sex is rarely depicted. Definite scenes are very rare, and it is often impossible to prove that figures are associated rather than simply juxtaposed. Animal figures are dominated by the horse and bison; deer, mammoth and ibex are fairly abundant but carnivores are rare. Fish, birds and humans are far more plentiful in portable art than in parietal. Insects and plants are limited to portable art, and are extremely rare. Palaeolithic art is not a bestiary nor a random accumulation of pictures: there are repeated patterns and structures here.

Non-figurative markings may have been of equal importance, but are harder to study. They cover a tremendous range, from a single dot or line to complex constructions and jumbles of overlapping lines known as 'macaronis'. The simpler motifs are abundant and widespread, but the complex forms are local, and may be 'ethnic markers'.

There have been many attempts to interpret Palaeolithic art. The first was that of 'art for art's sake', implying that it had no meaning, and was mindless play. This was rapidly replaced by explanations based on the view that the art was all hunting and fertility magic. However, these theories depend on wishful thinking with evidence distorted or ignored in order to uphold the chosen view. In fact, there are very few Palaeolithic figures with supposed 'missiles' on them; the animal bones in most caves bear little relation to the species depicted on the walls; genitalia are rare; and copulation scenes virtually non-existent.

In the 1950s, French scholars led by André Leroi-Gourhan began to see the caves as having been systematically decorated as a composition based on an ideal or 'standard layout'. He discovered repeated 'associations' in the art, and claimed a basic dualism, with horses representing the male and bison the female. This idea was extended to the non-figurative 'signs', which were divided into 'phallic' and 'vulvar'.

Although the details of this work are no longer accepted, recent studies have confirmed the fundamental role and opposition of horse and bison. Some species (such as bison or aurochs) are rarely or never depicted together. Leroi-Gourhan may not have found a universal formula, but he did discover order and repetition. Current research includes attempts to identify the work of individual artists, to see the art as a means of recording and transmitting vital information, and to link Palaeolithic art to shamanism and to hallucinatory images.

No single explanation can suffice for an art spanning 20 000 years and a vast area of the world, in which some figures are on open display, others hidden in inaccessible crannies. The art must contain messages of many kinds, which we can never read. Nevertheless, much can be learned of their content and context, their execution, location and associations; and the study of Palaeolithic art still provides our only direct evidence of the beliefs and preoccupations of Palaeolithic people.

Paul G. Bahn

Subsistence – a key to the past

When biologists begin to investigate the behaviour of a new or poorly known species, perhaps the first question they try to answer is what it eats and how it obtains its food. Subsequent questions involve the relationships between feeding and reproduction and a consideration of behavioural organisation. Anthropologists are equally concerned with how our ancestors made a living, and how their relationships with the environment may have changed with time. Anthropologists also ask how the remarkable variety in lifestyle, technology and social complexity in past and present human societies arose.

Some modern peoples live in small and mobile social units, moving their camps and residences often. Some of these groups obtain their foods by hunting animals and gathering wild plants. Others may be equally mobile but raise domesticated herds of animals and obtain much of their food from managed flocks. Still other groups may cultivate plants that yield the foods on which they depend. Even when people eat similar foods, their societies may vary enormously in the way the labour is organised in the production and distribution of food. We are all aware of the vast differences between an industrial system of production and that of self-sufficient agriculturalists who produce food only for their families and close relatives.

Anthropologists seek to describe and to explain this variety, and, together with archaeologists, to investigate the biological origins of our species and the processes that might explain something of the remarkable diversity of human behaviour. When and why did our hominid ancestors begin to hunt animals and to diverge from our closest biological relatives, who are all essentially plant feeders? When and how did humans first domesticate plants and animals? Why did some groups turn to agriculture and pastoralism, whereas others even today are still hunter-gatherers? In short, determination of the subsistence patterns of different groups of humans and of our ancestors is a basic issue for those who seek to understand our past and present diversity.

How did our ancestors get their food?

Archaeologists are faced with a central challenge: the past is gone, and any statements about the past are inferences justified largely by observations we make in the modern world. We seek to make arguments about what the past was like from what we find and dig up in the present. The challenge of justifying the meanings we give to these observations is extremely important in the study of subsistence, as it is crucial in our attempts to understand the past.

The hunting hypothesis

From the early days of archaeology it was assumed that the association of ancient stone tools and animal bones was proof that early humans were hunters and that dating the shift to predation as a regular subsistence strategy might enlighten us as to the appearance of other distinctively human characteristics. The *hunting hypothesis*, a more recent (mid-1960s) integration of these assumptions, argued that a series of related attributes distinguishes us from other primates, and that these capacities and behaviours are functionally linked and related to the beginnings of hunting by our ancestors. It suggested, for example, that early humans became big-game hunters, and that this activity favoured co-operation among males. The products of hunting were shared with adult females and their young, fostering a new form of social bonding and integration. In turn, this behavioural shift favoured an increase in brain size and in intelligent planning based on economic reciprocity. In short, the basic elements of the modern human family – a sexual division of labour, linked with parental investments by both males and females in rearing offspring – came into being in the context of a shift to big-game hunting.

Subsistence was hence seen as the key to understanding and dating our emergence as modern humans. Even at archaeological sites representing the dawn of hominid tool use, animal bones are associated with stone tools. Because these bones are from relatively large animals, many researchers concluded that we were, perhaps, already big-game hunters – and, by extension, distinctively human – when stone tools first appeared. Hominids of 2 million years ago were inferred to have lived in family groups with regular food-sharing between adult males and females. Females were seen as gathering plants and caring for chil-

Naturally exposed deposits at the middle Pleistocene site of Saldanha (or Elandsfontein), South Africa, dating to approximately 240 000 years ago. Notice the association of bones and stone tools.

dren while males were hunting. There was even speculation about the presence of rudimentary language among our ancient ancestors.

All this reconstruction emerged from an assumption that the association of bones and stone tools means that ancient hominids were big-game hunters. Central to this reconstruction was the logical argument that this particular subsistence behaviour could be linked to other behaviours to describe our evolutionary past.

Reassessment of the evidence

Since the early 1980s, this view has been challenged on a point of archaeological methodology: what meaning can justifiably be assigned to a simple association between animal bones and stone tools? Archaeologists can now begin to distinguish between bones accumulated by hominids on the one hand and by other animals, such as hyenas, leopards, porcupines and wolves, on the other. Many cases of association between bones and tools, previously accepted as evidence for hunting, now seem likely to be much more complex than previously thought, as many sites had been occupied by both hominids and other bone-collecting animals. Moreover, studies of cave and rock-shelter sites in Britain and elsewhere show that many of the bones previously thought to represent hominid meals probably resulted instead from the activities of other animals that used the same caves.

Which, if any, of the animal bones recovered from these deposits can tell us anything about hominid diet? Here we face the basic challenge of archaeology: how do we reliably infer a past from the remains recovered from archaeological sites?

Archaeologists have been hard at work trying to discriminate between animal bones resulting from the activities of hominids and those resulting from the many other agents that might contribute animal bones to a deposit. Many now feel – although others disagree – that even the bones definitely associated with hominid behaviour have properties more in accord with the inference of hominid scavenging than with hunting as the means of obtaining meat. It is even possible to argue that systematic hunting was not practised by early hominids until after the appearance of modern humans, perhaps around 60 000 years ago, instead of in the very ancient past of more than 2 million years ago.

Here we see how important subsistence questions are to our views of the past. If hunting appeared simultaneously with the other distinctive characteristics of the human debut, it is hard to see it as the main cause of those characteristics.

How does our food differ from that of our ancestors?

Systematic hunting may thus have been a behaviour whose appearance roughly coincided with that of our own spe-

cies. Recent reformulations of the hunting hypothesis state that specific behaviours are subject to natural selection: those individuals who are genetically capable of certain kinds of 'non-traditional' behaviour have increased fitness. In the context of our ancient hominid ancestors, for example, selection might tend to 'fix' those behavioural characteristics that foster improved reproductive success, such as hunting and food sharing.

It is clear, however, that in fully modern humans other mechanisms are involved in behaviour. We have a unique ability: we can abstract properties from experience, reintegrate these properties in our minds, and imagine conditions not yet experienced. This process can involve the experiences of many generations, and it makes possible the planning of subsistence activities. The ability to pool information and to generalise from our experiences gives the subsistence practices of modern groups a character very different from that of our earlier ancestors. Learning has enormous advantages over natural selection in terms of the transmission of information; it promotes flexibility, it is rapid, and it is free of the direct genetic cost of selection.

Learning and selection, both of which involve a form of inheritance, sometimes work together, but they may also operate quite independently. Anthropologists refer to this ability to *symbol* – to assign meaning to experience and to respond with an appropriate behaviour – as culture. The human capacity for culture is based on genetic information responsive to natural selection, but the actual form that culture takes and the individual actions of humans are not as clearly tied to genetic change as are, for example, bipedalism or brain size. This new dimension to the study of behaviour plays an important part in archaeological investigations of fully modern humans. We cannot 'see' culture, but we *can* see the consequences of cultural abilities. The investigation of 'how culture works' is hence a major challenge.

Around 40 000 to 35 000 years ago, soon after the appearance of fully modern people, we see remarkable changes in the archaeological record. For the first time, items of personal ornamentation, elaborate burial of the dead, the beginnings of art, and many other results of cultural behaviour become manifest. This evidence is absent from the archaeological record of previous hominid species. There is also a tremendous increase in behavioural variety and an extraordinary expansion of humans into previously uninhabited areas. Culturally organised behaviour has revolutionised our evolution in a way that may have been quite independent of genetic change.

These changes are reflected in many local and seasonal shifts and specialisations in the subsistence practices of human populations. Our behaviour begins to be organised in a way that shows anticipation and an ability to cope with unanticipated conditions that might negate well-laid plans. Culturally organised behaviour can respond to dynamic environments in ways analogous to the response of genetically conditioned behaviour to natural selection, but with much greater speed and flexibility.

Use of aquatic resources

A good example of the problem of understanding how culture works is given by the example of human use of shellfish and other aquatic foods. These remains appear in archaeological sites of pre-modern hominids – in Italy as early as 140 000 years ago and in South Africa, at Klasies River, in association with stone tools and hominid remains dating to more than 90 000 years ago. However, archaeological sites of the ancient periods (before 200 000 years ago) give no convincing evidence that our hominid ancestors exploited these foods.

Do these early examples of hominid use of a new resource foreshadow the systematic harvesting of the sea and land by modern humans? Current arguments illustrate nicely the nature of archaeology: how do we assign meaning to what we recover from the archaeological record, and what behaviour is indicated by what we find? These early uses of aquatic resources are probably only a part of the behavioural diversification seen with the first steps towards hunting before the appearance of fully modern humans. However, they have also been seen as evidence of culturally organised behaviour. This disagreement illustrates the importance of developing reliable methods for inference when we treat archaeological remains in terms of what they can tell us about behaviour.

The use of aquatic resources by modern humans also illustrates the difficulty of determining how culture works. The earliest regular use of aquatic resources shows some interesting patterns. The earliest dates are clustered along the coast of Japan and regularly become more recent as we move south towards the Equator. In the Southern Hemisphere, a similar pattern of more recent dates in equatorial regions characterises materials recovered from the west coast of Africa. Why such regularity, and why such regular shifts in the use of these foods through time and with respect to geography?

In the modern world itself, hunter-gatherers over the past two centuries may show a vestige of this pattern, but it is considerably confused. Some of the most complex social systems of the non-agricultural world are among peoples dependent on aquatic resources in northern temperate environments like the west coast of North America. However, some of the most mobile and least complex cultures are found in analogous environments of South America. Why do subsistence practices, which in one context vary with the environment, seem to be unrelated to social and cultural forms of organisation?

There are many opinions on this issue, from a complete denial of any relationship between forms of cultural organisation and forms of subsistence base to the claim that subsistence is an important but complicated variable that determines the form of culture. Unlike behaviour conditioned only by natural selection, culturally organised behaviours can respond very quickly to changed circumstances. It is therefore certain that the form of a cultural system is conditioned by a very complex set of interrelated factors. Methods for determining the nature of these factors are just beginning to be developed.

Domestication of plants and animals

The origins of agriculture illustrate this methodological difficulty. Early explanations of the development of agriculture saw the problem in very 'human' terms. What might make an astute human realise that if a seed was planted, a plant would grow? There was much early speculation as to the sorts of accidents that might produce this realisation. It

Accumulations of waste products such as shell debris — middens — provide direct clues to human subsistence in the distant and recent past. Deposits containing marine molluscs, bones and Mousterian tools at the Italian coastal site of Grotta dei Moscerini near Sperlonga, Latina, show that Neanderthals exploited aquatic resources around 50 000 years ago. The photograph above shows the cave deposits being excavated in 1949. In Australia, shell middens that were in use until quite recent times, perhaps up until the nineteenth century, can be seen eroding in sand dunes on the northern coast of New South Wales (right).

(Above) Hunter-gatherers with a complex social system and limited residential mobility: the Southern Kwakiutl at Blunden Harbor, British Columbia photographed in 1901. (Right) Highly mobile hunter-gatherers: the Ona (Selk'nam) in their camp, Tierra del Fuego, probably photographed between 1918 and 1924.

was generally assumed that any rational human would recognise agriculture's potential for improving life. Growing one's food would make possible a settled and more secure life; would provide more leisure for investment in 'culture' (such as art and religion) and in the invention of pottery, weaving and the construction of permanent buildings; and would lead to the possibility of a more full intellectual life. Did this indeed happen?

Modern work shows that many of the 'achievements' thought to flow naturally from the invention of agriculture in fact occur first in other contexts. Pottery first appears in Japan among hunting and gathering peoples dependent on the sea, and complex societies are found among other non-agriculturalists along the Northwest Coast of North Amer-

An example of mobile agriculturalists: the Machiguenga of Peru. This temporary residence was built near a residential site that was last used 10 years before. The Machiguenga maintain a primary residence and also build secondary residences near abandoned gardens to take advantage of the fishing, hunting and gathering opportunities offered at these locations where the climax vegetation has been removed.

ica. Many agriculturalists are not sedentary but regularly move from place to place. Many archaeological sequences also show that a knowledge of agriculture and domesticated plants existed long before there was a real shift from hunting and gathering to agriculture.

The simple accumulation of knowledge hence does not explain cultural change and development. Culture appears to respond in regular but complex ways to selective pressures, and it shows regular patterns that change with time. Certain cultural forms may well be associated with forms of subsistence, but there are other, more subtle forces at work that are still not understood.

This chapter began with a statement pointing to the importance of a knowledge of subsistence for a biologist studying a poorly known species. It showed how important this knowledge is for gaining an understanding of our early, precultural hominid ancestors. When the discussion shifted to subsistence and lifeways as documented among fully modern people, however, things became complicated. One of the things that distinguishes humans from other animals is the ability to recognise problems and design strategies for dealing with them. Subsistence is basic and very important, but we are capable of rapid and opportunistic responses to selection resulting in a restructuring of society, of labour and of subsistence practices. Subsistence is therefore an important driving force of cultural evolution, but not the only one. Its properties as a selective agent may be altered by humans themselves: we operate in a far more complex selective context than does any other species.

Lewis R. Binford

See also 'Human diet and subsistence' (p. 69), 'The hominid way of life' (p. 325), 'Studying human evolution by analogy' (p. 335), 'Early human mental abilities' (p. 341), 'Reconstructing prehistoric diet' (p. 369), 'Origins of agriculture' (p. 373) and 'Human populations before agriculture' (p. 405)

Reconstructing prehistoric diet

Palaeonutrition, a useful but awkward term, is the reconstruction of prehistoric diets and their nutritional value from archaeological remains. It asks, 'What did prehistoric humans eat?' and 'How well were they fed?'; in other words, 'How adaptive were the food choices of prehistoric populations in their natural and social en-·vironments?'. Archaeologists now ask such questions frequently, and the emphasis in studies of human evolution has accordingly shifted from a preoccupation with the brain to an equal interest in the stomach.

Palaeonutrition involves many disciplines, but it has two main themes. The first is the reconstruction of diets from archaeological finds of food wastes and of the artefacts used in obtaining and processing foods. The other is the study of human skeletons to assess nutritional well-being and to determine components of diet using chemical analysis. These approaches are complementary, so that the hypotheses about diet arrived at by one can be tested through the other. The conclusions can then be evaluated in the light of our knowledge of human nutrition, and compared with ethnographic models developed from living populations.

Hunting and gathering

Humans have been hunting and gathering for more than 99 per cent of their time on earth and some isolated groups, such as the Mbuti and Efe Pygmies of the Ituri Forest, Zaire (see pp. 403 and 436), still obtain all or most food in this way. Hunter-gatherers acquire an intimate knowledge of edible wild foods and the times of the year at which they are available. It may seem a precarious means of existence, with every day a struggle to extract every available scrap of food from the vicinity. In reality, studies of modern hunter-gatherers show that their lives are not such a brute struggle. A few hours of work per day is often enough to fill the larder and a good deal of free time may be available for more enjoyable activities. Nor do hunter-gatherers eat absolutely everything that comes to hand: human diets are culturally patterned and many items that are known to be edible may not be considered to be food. Even so, hunter-gatherer diets are usually very diverse, which greatly increases their chances of including all the necessities of a balanced diet.

This mode of subsistence was successful enough for hunter-gatherers to penetrate virtually every habitat on earth, from the tropics to the poles. Specialised adaptations were necessary at the extremes of this range. Thus the northern Inuit (Eskimos) depend for more than 90 per cent of their diet on meat and fat, and are genetically adapted to produce glucose from these (instead of from carbohydrates which are the usual energy staples in diets with more vegetable content). Plants make up to 90 per cent of most hunter-gatherer diets, especially in the middle latitudes, with meat or fish providing essential proteins. The plant foods are obtained by gathering, which is primarily the province of women, while hunting and fishing are male activities.

This pattern is of great antiquity and is probably as old as hunting itself. Exceptions to the rule are scarce. In Arctic populations, men hunt and women fish. Animal protein can also be obtained by gathering, as in the collection of shellfish, attested to by ancient shell mounds in all parts of the world where there are intertidal molluscs. On the southern shore of South Africa, there are shell mounds that may be as old as 100 000 years.

Gathering may be the most ancient means of human subsistence, but it leaves the least evidence. Its artefacts include containers for carrying the food (gourds, nets and leather bags) and digging sticks. These rarely survive in archaeological deposits, but are frequently depicted in rock paintings and engravings, especially in Africa. A recurring motif shows women with digging sticks weighted with perforated, round stones; many such stones have been found.

Artefacts associated with hunting are more common in archaeology, and develop in sequence from spears wielded by hand, through improvements like the spearthrowers of the Americas (see p. 359) to the worldwide use of bows and arrows. The stone, bone and later metal points of these projectiles are usually the only surviving evidence, but hunting scenes are a favourite theme in prehistoric art. Although fishing is more rarely depicted, it can also leave evidence in the form of bone fish-hooks, harpoon points and net sinkers. Other artefacts associated with food are those used for processing: knives, upper and lower grindstones, pounders, cooking pots and the like. The only evidence of the importance of manioc (cassava) to early inhabitants of

The early modern people who occupied this cave at Klasies River Mouth on South Africa's southeastern coast relied heavily on shellfish 100 000 to 80 000 years ago.

Hunting and gathering are common themes in prehistoric art. These three rock paintings are from Cape Province, South Africa. (Left) A woman about to dig up a bulbous plant with a weighted digging stick (East Qriqualand). (Centre) Stone Age fishermen spearing fish from small boats or floats, one of which is anchored (Mount Fletcher district). (Right) A wounded and dying eland staggers as it is pursued by spear-carrying men and dogs (Barkly East). Most of the rock paintings in South Africa are attributed to San (Bushmen) painters and are probably only a few centuries old, but paintings as old as 26 000 years have survived in cave deposits (e.g. Apollo 11, Namibia; see p. 361).

Amazonia are the small stone chips, which, when set in resin on a board, served as a tool for grating the tubers. The resulting pulp was baked into cakes on ceramic griddles as a final step in ridding this otherwise toxic food of its cyanide.

Although artefacts can tell us much about culinary techniques, food wastes are better indicators of the species used as food and of their relative amounts. This work involves identifying plant and animal species from fragmentary remains discarded or excreted by their consumers or charred in their cooking fires. The results are inevitably biased in favour of seeded fruits, nuts and grains, and against soft plants such as bananas and tubers. Pollen grains collected in the vicinity may help to fill some of the gaps.

Preservation favours vertebrates over invertebrates (unless the latter have shells). The food wastes of humans, particularly bones, must be distinguished from those of other predators and scavengers, usually by microscopic examination of the marks made by butchering implements or gnawing teeth (see p. 331). While keeping such distortions of the record in mind, archaeologists can calculate the proportions of food represented by these scraps of evidence and can hence produce hypotheses about prehistoric diet.

Food production

During the past 10 000 years, people in several parts of the world domesticated animals and plants. Their neighbours quickly adopted the new food-producing technology, leaving modern hunter-gatherers only in those few parts of the globe that are too inhospitable for herding or agriculture. This change in food procurement is called the 'agricultural revolution', even though it took many centuries to accomplish. Farming reduced the number of plant and animal species in the diet, while artefacts became more specialised (and easier for archaeologists to identify).

Central and North America developed a food pattern of maize, beans and squash, accompanied in the archaeological record by grindstones (*manos* and *metates*) and tortilla griddles. In the Andes, potatoes were also eaten. Wheat and barley became the staples of the Mediterranean and Eurasia, sorghum of Africa, and rice of Southeast Asia. Outside the tropics, where root crops and fruits were important, cereals became the main foods and were supplemented by meat. In contrast to hunting and gathering, agriculture also left scars on the landscape.

For adherents of today's supermarket culture, the shift from collection of food to producing it seems obvious progress. Yet the archaeological evidence suggests that food production developed in response to problems caused by the undue success of hunter-gatherers, whose rate of food extraction came to exceed the carrying capacity of the environment. It also suggests that some people resisted the introduction of agriculture for centuries after first making its acquaintance, and that the change from a diverse diet of wild foods to dependence on a few crops resulted in poorer nutrition.

In modern society, this problem is overcome by using large amounts of energy for the international transport of food. Early agricultural communities could not overcome nutritional imbalances in this way. Instead, they developed techniques such as heating maize with lime before grinding to improve its amino acid balance, and leavening bread by fermentation, a process that changes its trace of zinc

Changing a lethal poison into a staple food. A young Acawai girl in Guyana photographed in 1917 grating manioc tubers on a wooden board set with stone chips.

HOW BONES REVEAL DIET

The strontium content of human bone (usually expressed as the strontium/calcium ratio) is a measure of the relative amounts of plant and animal food in the diet. Strontium content depends on the ground water of a given area, which determines the level of strontium found in local plants. The element is preferentially excreted by animals. Herbivores thus have reduced strontium levels, and carnivores lower levels still. Measuring these values allows us to determine the relative amounts of animal and plant foods from strontium/calcium ratios in human skeletons recovered by excavation.

This analysis has shown that the onset of cereal agriculture in the Middle East was preceded by a period of high intake of plant food — implying intensive collecting of wild cereals — followed by a temporary decline. This presumably resulted from overexploitation of the wild resources, a problem solved by the domestication of cereals. Such successes with strontium analysis are leading to further research into the possible value of other trace elements — for example, barium, zinc and iron — as dietary indicators.

Diet has also been reconstructed by the determination of stable carbon isotope ratios in bone. This method is based on characteristic differences in the ratio of carbon-13 (^{13}C) to carbon-12 (^{12}C) in plants with two different photosynthetic systems. (The ratios are expressed as δ^{13}C values per mil, indicating a deviation from the ^{13}C/^{12}C ratio of an international carbonate standard.)

Trees, shrubs and temperate grasses utilise C_3 photosynthesis, forming three-carbon compounds from carbon dioxide in the air. This discriminates against those carbon dioxide molecules with the heavier ^{13}C isotope. C_3 plants hence have lower ^{13}C/^{12}C ratios than C_4 plants, which do not discriminate as strongly.

The C_4 group comprises grasses from the tropics and subtropics and includes maize, sorghum and sugar cane. When a C_4 plant becomes a new dietary staple in a C_3 plant area, there is a dramatic effect on the carbon isotope ratios of the consumers, as manifest in the introduction of maize agriculture from the tropical to the temperate regions of the Americas.

In the lower Illinois Valley, for example, the proportion of carbon in human bone protein derived from C_4 plants changed from zero to about 75 per cent between AD 800 and 1200. This is not the same as saying that 75 per cent of the population's diet consisted of maize; we do not understand human metabolism well enough to know exactly how different components of the diet translate into different tissues in the body, although the problem is now being investigated with laboratory animals.

The reverse of the Illinois Valley case exists in the Yellow River (Huang He) basin of northern China. Archaeological remains show that cereal agriculture started there some 7000 to 8000 years ago, with rice (a C_3 plant) as the dominant crop in the south and millet (C_4) dominant in the north.

Millet maintained its position in the Yellow River basin for thousands of years, until it was largely replaced by wheat and rice. Human skeletons from the area, ranging in age from about 5000 to 500 BC, have ^{13}C contents that suggest that between 50 and 80 per cent of their carbon was derived from millet. During the Warring States period and the Han Dynasty (fifth century BC to second century AD), the ^{13}C content declined dramatically to a level that suggests there was no millet in the diet at all. In modern inhabitants of the region, about 25 per cent of skeletal carbon is derived from C^4 plants, in this case mostly maize.

Marine organisms also have characteristic carbon isotope ratios. The ^{13}C/^{12}C ratios of inshore marine foods are similar to those of C_4 plants and thus very different from C_3 plants. This contrast has been used to assess the importance of marine foods in the diets of hunter-gatherers in South Africa, Denmark and British Columbia, where most land plants are C_3. Differences between the isotope ratios of nitrogen and strontium in marine and terrestrial foodwebs are also now being investigated.

Carbon isotope analysis must be carried out on bone protein, or collagen, which survives for only tens of thousands of years. Although such carbon isotope ratios are also manifest in bone carbonate (which makes up about 3 per cent of bone mineral), this is subject to *diagenesis* — it is altered by chemicals in the ground. Strontium and other trace elements in the bone are similarly affected. New techniques for eliminating this problem hold out the promise of analysing trace elements and carbon isotopes in much older materials.

Tooth enamel is much less affected by diagenesis than is bone and this has been used to measure the carbon isotope ratios of fossils as old as 200 million years. The ratios in teeth of early southern African hominids are now being investigated and may provide a measure of how much meat they ate.

Most of the animals that lived in the Transvaal during the late Pliocene and early Pleistocene were grazers with an increased proportion of ^{13}C from their C_4 diets. The teeth of *Australopithecus africanus*, *Paranthropus (Australopithecus) robustus* and *Homo habilis* show that they were not grass eaters, so any increase in their ^{13}C contents is therefore probably due to a diet incorporating the meat of grazers. Comparison of the carbon isotope ratios of early hominid species could in this way advance our understanding of the role of diet in human evolution.

N.J. van der Merwe

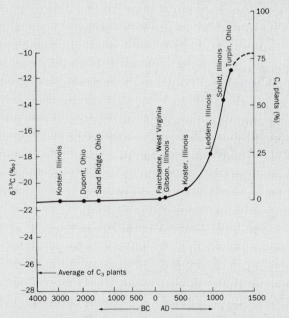

A food-producing revolution among the hunter-gatherer peoples of the North American woodlands happened when maize (a C_4 plant) was introduced about AD 200. The carbon-13 (^{13}C) contents of human skeletons from Illinois, Ohio and West Virginia (as shown on the left vertical axis) indicate the amounts of carbon from C_4 plants in bone protein. This value changed from zero to 75 per cent over a relatively short period.

into a form that can be metabolised. Zinc deficiency stunts growth; leavening of bread counteracts this problem, but lime processing of maize unfortunately makes it worse.

Nutritional stress

The nutritional status of prehistoric communities can be deduced from studies of *palaeopathology*. Various deficiency diseases manifest themselves in the skeleton, causing, for, instance, small overall size, knobbly joints, abcesses and dental caries. Severe undernutrition causes transverse bands of dense calcification (Harris lines) inside long bones, and these are visible on radiographs. One common indicator of nutritional stress is porotic hyperostosis, a result of iron-deficiency anaemia. More red blood cells are produced to compensate, causing the marrow spaces in the skeleton to expand and thinning the outer layer of bone. In the skull, the outer layer may even disappear in places, revealing the porous bone underneath. The condition is most commonly seen on the forehead and the upper surface of the eye sockets. Another useful indicator of malnutrition is the death rate of children of weaning age – that critical period when they have to adapt to foods other than breast milk.

A good case study of nutritional change associated with the introduction of agriculture comes from the archaeology of the lower Illinois Valley, central USA. Here, around AD 600, people of this valley exploited the wild plants and animals of forest and floodplain. They also acquired maize by trading with agriculturalists further afield. Four cen-

turies went by before they themselves began to grow maize, but by AD 1200 their lives had changed to such an extent that they were living in large villages in the uplands beyond the river valley. This change was, however, accompanied by an increase in weaning deaths, a delay in growth of the skeleton to full size until after the age of 25, and a fourfold increase in the occurrence of porotic hyperostosis to a level where it affected more than half the population.

Here, then, food production increased nutritional stress and brought health problems in its wake, even while it allowed a dramatic increase in population. Unlike the world's population explosion of the past 200 years, the population increases associated with early agriculture did not result from an increase in life expectancy. Hunter-gatherers and early agriculturalists both had disease and other problems to contend with besides food, with the result that the proportion of people who survived beyond the age of 30 was not large for either group. This pattern was maintained until well after the industrial revolution. The English astronomer Edmond Halley, who studied not only comets but also populations, described the situation in the first half of the eighteenth century as follows: 'How unjustly we repine at the shortness of our lives, and think ourselves wronged if we attain no old age; whereas it appears that one half of those born are dead in seventeen years' time.'

Bone chemistry

Palaeopathology is a general indicator of nutritional stress, but is not very specific about its cause. Archaeological food waste by itself is also not very accurate in quantifying prehistoric diets. However, because of advances in bone chemistry over the past 15 years, carbon and nitrogen isotopes, and trace elements such as strontium and barium, can now be used as indicators of the prevalence of certain major foods in the diet (see p. 371).

Such methods have been used to track the spread of agricultures, such as maize in the Americas and rice from southern to northern China, and the importance of marine foods in hunter-gatherer diets in Europe, North America and southern Africa. This and other research will shed new light on the diets of early hominids and write a whole new chapter in the study of palaeonutrition.

N.J. van der Merwe

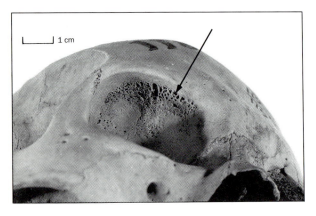

1 cm

A skull of an individual suffering from iron-deficiency anaemia. The general condition is known as porotic hyperostosis, in which the outer layer of bone is thinned to the point of exposing the porous bone underneath. This commonly occurs in the eye sockets, as is the case here, and is known as cribra orbitalia. Such palaeopathologies enable physical anthropologists to study nutritional stress in past populations.

See also 'Human diet and subsistence' (p. 69), 'Selecting and processing food' (p. 65), 'Subsistence – a key to the past' (p. 365), 'Origins of agriculture' (p. 373), 'Reconstructing ancient populations' (p. 402), 'Human populations before agriculture' (p. 405) and 'People and disease' (p. 411)

Origins of agriculture

There are dozens of staple crops grown in temperate and tropical parts of the world as well as uncounted numbers of crops of lesser dietary and economic importance. Many of the latter have a very local distribution. This variety of crops and the environments in which they grow make it impossible to identify a single set of circumstances that led to agriculture everywhere in the world.

Origins are inherently difficult to identify, particularly when, as is the case with agriculture, they occurred over short spans of time rather than as the culmination of a long period of gradual change. Unless plants have hard edible seeds, they are rarely preserved in archaeological sites and it is also difficult distinguishing between plants that were harvested wild and those that were cultivated.

Despite these problems, evidence from botany and archaeology allows us to identify the points of origin of many of today's crops. Botanists have been concerned for many years with the distributions of plant species and with reconstructions of primitive forms through field plantings and genetic studies. Archaeologists have recovered direct evidence of plants through their carbonised, desiccated and waterlogged remains, and through impressions in clay or other materials. Indirect evidence of agriculture also emerges from the implements used to harvest, process, store and cook plants.

Although such studies give a reasonably comprehensive picture, most of the details are dimly perceived and there are still large gaps in our geographical and temporal coverage of crop plant evolution. Research into the origins of agriculture has gained a great deal since the 1960s from the use of flotation, a water separation technique, which has produced large samples of seeds from sites where conventional excavation had failed to reveal traces of food remains. It should profit equally in the future from new analytical methods that will allow better discrimination of wild and domestic forms, or, through the use of carbon and other isotopes, tell us whether people ate imported or local plants and whether meat or vegetables made up the greater part of the diet (see p. 371).

Adaptation to environmental change

Towards the end of the Pleistocene, around 14000 years ago, the retreat of glacial ice led to rapid changes in the climates and environment of the northern temperate zones. In more equatorial regions, environmental changes were less perceptible, except in coastal areas where sea levels rose by some 100 metres as the icecaps melted. Throughout the world, the sea inundated coastal land that had been occupied by hunters and gatherers and perhaps by early cultivators. The changes in weather patterns and rainfall that accompanied the melting of the ice caps led in turn to other profound alterations in landscapes, such as the incursion of forests into grassy steppelands or Arctic tundra. As these forests gradually spread towards higher latitudes, they interrupted previously open stretches of land, changing the habitats of animals, cutting their routes of migration, and providing opportunities for entirely new species. To a large extent the change was a shift of established biotic provinces into the newly warm regions, but the effect was to transform the environments of the major landmasses in the temperate climatic zones.

Humans adapted to these changing circumstances by migrating with the shifting habitats, and by intensifying their hunting efforts within relatively small forest territories. Where archaeological remains exist, there is evidence that people began to make greater use of game, such as deer, and of smaller species, such as rabbits, foxes, birds and snails. From rivers and newly flooded estuaries, early humans harvested clams and mussels, crabs, fish and turtles. They began also to make extensive use of hundreds of potentially edible plant foods, including cereal grains in places where they were now abundant. Human adaptations then became more generalised and people utilised a wider variety of plants and animals.

That late Pleistocene people were highly successful in hunting and in gathering wild foods is manifest in the many campsites found in virtually every environment. Although most of these people continued to migrate to reach seasonally available foods, they enjoyed a healthy diet and suffered little from communicable diseases. Their diversified and specialised technology was also the foundation from which agricultural implements later developed. By

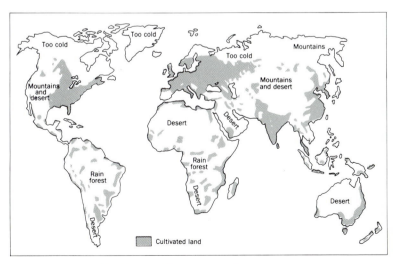

The principal cultivated areas of the world today.

20 000 to 30 000 years ago, people already had knives that could be used for reaping grain and also mortars and grinding stones for crushing paint pigments and smashing nuts that later were adapted to the milling of cereals.

Immediately after the Pleistocene, most humans continued, as some still do today, to hunt and to collect wild foods. But in a few places in each of the major landmasses, between 12 000 and 9000 years ago, people began to cultivate suitable species of cereal grains and root crops. Southwest Asia, equatorial Africa, the Southeast Asian mainland, Central America, and lowland and highland South America were all scenes of early agriculture. From each of these regions, within a few thousand years of its origin, agriculture had spread nearly to its modern geographical limits. At the same time, where suitable animals were available, people began to domesticate livestock, at first for food and later for bearing loads and pulling wagons or ploughs.

All this greatly increased the food supply and usable energy. In turn, human populations began to expand slowly, and, for the first time in history, to have a severe impact on the environment. This was particularly true when colonists from agricultural regions moved out in search of new fields and were forced to create arable lands from forests, and when dry steppe lands bloomed through the introduction of irrigation water.

The intensive use of land that followed these practices soon depleted soils and compelled people to move on again. Much of human agricultural history amounts to a cycle of use, abuse, abandonment and re-use as localities waxed and waned in fertility. Until the use of fallowing, alternate cropping and fertilisers, shifting agriculture was the norm, as it still is in some forested regions today.

Subsistence agriculture

There are two main types of subsistence agriculture – one based on seeds, such as wheat, rice and millet, and the other on tubers, such as potato, taro and cassava. Seed-crop cultivation, which originated in the tropical or subtropical arid parts of the world, usually involves a few highly productive species that grow in nearly pure stands. The hard seeds of the cereal grains, which are high in protein, can be stored for long periods without destroying their food values or their ability to germinate.

The other major type of agriculture, vegeculture (in which cuttings or sets rather than seeds are planted), is based on tubiferous crops native to the humid tropical lowlands of America, Southeast Asia and Africa. These starchy plants require tropical wet conditions for growth, but they tolerate long dry or cold seasons and need an annual dry

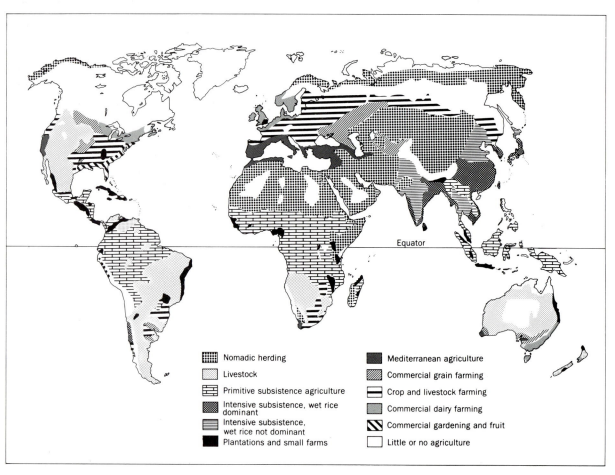

Nomadic herding

Livestock

Primitive subsistence agriculture

Intensive subsistence, wet rice dominant

Intensive subsistence, wet rice not dominant

Plantations and small farms

Mediterranean agriculture

Commercial grain farming

Crop and livestock farming

Commercial dairy farming

Commercial gardening and fruit

Little or no agriculture

Equator

Dominant types of agricultural production.

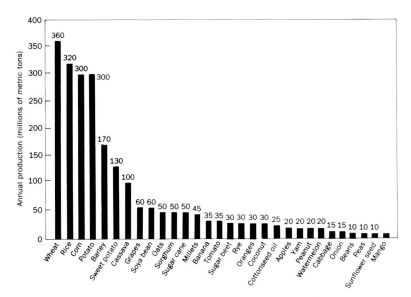

Estimated total production of the world's main food crops.

Among many tropical fruits that could be cultivated more widely are (above) the white sapote (*Casimiroa edulis*) and (below) the winged bean (*Psophocarpus tetragonolobus*). The earliest known archaeological occurrence of the winged bean is in New Guinea. It grows well in tropical climates and has a protein content equivalent to that of the soya bean. The sapote fruit is cultivated in tropical regions of Central America. Black sapote (*Diospyros digyna*) is more often cultivated than white sapote. Both varieties have been found in archaeological sites in southern Mexico dating back 5000 years.

interval of more than 2 months for successful propagation. Most of them can be stored either above or below ground. Cultivation of this kind generally involves many more species than seed-crop agriculture, making vegeculture ecologically more stable. Shifting cultivation, rather than permanently fixed fields, is typical of such regions. Because the major tubiferous crops are starchy, proper human nutrition necessitates protein supplement from meat, fish, cereal grains, legumes or nuts.

Apart from these staples, tree-borne crops such as bananas, coconuts, dates, fruit, olives and various kinds of nuts are also important in some regions. These, and berries, grapes, greens and an assortment of vegetables, may be found either in vegeculture or in seed-cultivation regions and they provide both essential nutrients and tasty variety. Some 3000 species of plants are currently cultivated for food, but only 20 of these provide most of the world's vegetable food. .

The archaeological record for seed-crop cultivation is much better known than that for vegeculture, because seeds are preserved more readily than is the softer flesh of the other crops. The regions of seed cultivation also gave rise to the earliest complex urban civilisations, so they are better known because they have attracted most archaeological attention. In Southwest Asia, domestication began 10 000 years ago in southern Palestine, and there is evidence of agriculture around 8000 years ago in Tehuacán in Mexico and Ayacucho in Peru. Dates for other parts of the world are much less certain, but the best evidence suggests that most of the major plants and livestock were domesticated well before 4000 years ago, by which time the main modern pre-industrial techniques of farming, including the use of ploughs, fertilisers, fallowing and irrigation, had also developed.

Only after the rise of industry and of scientific breeding did agriculture and animal husbandry begin to shift away from labour-intensive and traditional methods and become a specialised, energy-consuming system. Although the major crops have been domesticated for many millennia, there is now renewed interest in lesser-known plants, some of which might transform agriculture and provide hope for billions of the world's people. One such plant is the pejibaye palm fruit (*Guilielma gasipaes*), the most nutritionally balanced food known, at present cultivated only in Central America.

Origins of domesticated plants

The environments involved in early domestication varied from temperate, grassy parkland forests to arid steppe lands and from humid, tropical marshes to rain forests and cold, high mountains. The domestication of plants occurred wherever there were nutritious, edible and productive wild species.

Human selection resulted in plants with more desirable traits, such as larger size, ease of harvesting and threshing, or better flavour. In time, the best of these plants were moved from their natural habitats into fields where suitable conditions could be provided by clearing trees, fertilising soils and irrigation. Further selection for plants that best tolerated these new conditions improved yields to an even greater extent. Few single localities can now be identified as the place where any of the major food crops originated. Rather, we must think of broad geographic regions, within which domestication probably took place.

The Americas provided three types of crops of major importance and a host of lesser known species. Maize (*Zea mays*), now a staple food throughout much of the world, beans (*Phaseolus* spp.), squash (*Cucurbita* spp.) and tomatoes (*Lycopersicon esculentum*) were first domesticated in the Mexican highlands. A second staple food, white potatoes (*Solanum* spp.), originated in the Andean mountains, where other tubers such as oca (*Uxalis tuberosa*) and the cereal grain quinoa (*Chenopodium quinoa*) were also early domesticates. Vegeculture in the lowland, forested Amazon basin contributed manioc (*Manihot esculenta*), sweet potatoes (*Ipomoea batatas*) and yautia (*Xanthosoma*). Compared with other parts of the world, the Americas were deficient in domestic animals. Two camelid species, llamas and alpacas, in the Andes were the only herded livestock on the American continents, but a few smaller species were raised for food – guinea-pigs in the Andes, and dogs and turkeys in Central and North America.

The 'fertile crescent' of the Old World in Southwest Asia is the homeland of wheat (*Triticum*), barley (*Hordeum*), various legumes, grapes, melons, dates, and pistachios and almonds. This area also produced the first domesticated sheep and goats, and, later, pigs, cattle and bees. Olives were domesticated in the northern Mediterranean region and, together with grapes, figs and cereals, formed part of a distinct agriculture. In tropical West Africa, an indigenous vegeculture based on yams (*Dioscorea* spp.) and oil-palm

trees originated, while several millets (*Eleusine* spp.) and sorghum (*Sorghum vulgare*) were domesticated in the temperate eastern sub-Saharan zone. Cattle and asses, and perhaps dromedary camels, were probably domesticated in the Saharan region before the area became too dry after the Pleistocene to support livestock.

Another major centre of vegeculture is Southeast Asia, where taro (*Colocasia esculenta*), yams (*Dioscorea*), breadfruit (*Artocarpus altilis*), sago palm, coconuts (*Cocos nucifera*) and bananas (*Musa* spp.) were domesticated. The history of rice (*Oryza sativa*), the modern Asian staple, is still poorly known. It is generally thought that rice is native to moist, lowland regions of Southeast Asia, but today, as a result of breeding, there are two principal rice varieties, wet and dry. The original variety, wet rice, must be flooded during much of its growing period, whereas dry rice depends, like wheat, only on rainfall. In northern China, crops such as millets (*Panicum* and *Setaria*), soya beans (*Glycine*) and mulberry (*Morus alba*) were indigenous domesticates. Pigs are native to China, chickens to Southeast Asia and humped cattle and water buffalo may originally have been Indian domesticates. The people of central Asia domesticated both horses and Bactrian camels.

Students of agricultural origins have focused on individual species such as maize or rice, and have given relatively little attention to the other plants that may have made up an agricultural and dietary complex. However, the importance of any crop can be measured only in terms of its overall dietary potential. For example, maize alone is a poor food, leading to pelagra unless it is supplemented with a source of protein. Tuberous plants are also low in protein, which is often supplied by fish, pigs or insects. Protein-rich leguminous plants, which also provide necessary amino acids, are grown in association with maize and squash to form the typical triad of indigenous Middle American agriculture. Soya beans occupied the same niche in northern China after the second millennium BC, and legumes were part of the agricultural complex in the Near East at the onset of domestication. These also fix nitrogen in the soil and can be used as a fallow crop to restore the fertility of land. We see, then, that the local mix of plants and animals may be as important to agricultural success as is the presence of any single component of diet.

Other factors more difficult to evaluate include palatability, ease of preparation and storage, and cultural preferences. The importance of such factors in the history of agriculture is manifest in the history of millets. These were harvested in the Middle East and Mesoamerica as early as wheat, barley and maize, but quickly fell from use in these regions in favour of the other three crops. In the same way, some highly nutritious local crops such as grain amaranths, chenopods, marsh elder, sunflower, and many varieties of beans and leguminous shrubs were given up in favour of maize in America. Prestige crops such as maize and wheat have become dominant through much of the world, even

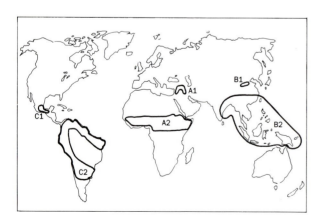

Different regions of the world gave rise to the main food crops: **A1**, Near East (barley, wheat, peas, lentils and chickpeas); **A2**, Africa (millets, sorghum, groundnuts, yams, dates, coffee and melons); **B1**, North China (millets and rice); **B2**, Southeast Asia (rice, bananas, sugar cane, citrus fruits, coconuts, taro and yams); **C1**, Mesoamerica (maize, squash, beans and pumpkins); **C2**, South America (lima beans, potatoes, sweet potatoes, manioc and peanuts).

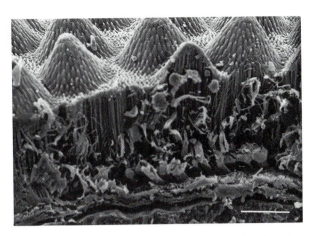

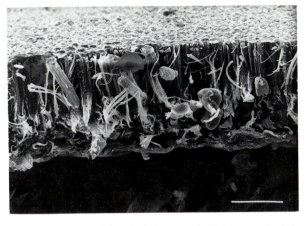

Photomicrographs of the longitudinal surface of the seedcoat (testa) of wild and domesticated varieties of peas. (Left) Purple pea (*Pisum sativum elatius*), the wild progenitor of the cultivated pea, showing the thick, rough testa (scale bar: 100 micrometres). (Right) The cultivated pea (*P. sativum sativum*) showing the thinner, smooth testa (scale bar: 50 micrometres).

though we now realise that they may not be the most nutritionally complete or the most suited to local conditions.

It will be a rare accident if the 'first' instance of cultivation of any species is ever found, because it is probable that most plants were 'domesticated' repeatedly through trial and error and only became widespread as agricultural crops after prolonged experience and in favourable circumstances. Much of the world had little to contribute to domestication, but the species that were tamed spread quickly, so that within a few thousand years domesticated crops or animals were found virtually throughout the world, except on the islands of the Pacific and in Australia. The rapid spread of these new products and techniques was no doubt helped by improved verbal communication, boat travel, and the gradually increasing numbers of people who required living and farming space.

In Europe, where the spread of agriculture has been well studied, we can chart the progress of farmers northwards across the continent as they planted farmland, cut forests, and displaced the hunters who had remained in isolated forest enclaves. At first, these farmers moved into thinly forested regions with light soils, especially along river valleys. Later, as these soils became depleted and populations continued to grow, the farmers cleared forests, creating both farm and growing land. In the process, they caused accelerated leaching of nutrients and soil erosion, which altered vegetation and soils. World-wide, where conditions were suitable, seed cultivation expanded at the expense of vegeculture, even though these crops depleted soils more quickly than the products of vegeculture.

Transformations

The direct manipulation of plants and animals to make them work for human benefit was, after fire, mankind's greatest harnessing of the world's natural energy. Fire enabled humans to move out of warm climates, and perhaps led to dietary innovations through cooking; agri-

culture provided the dependable food base that enabled vastly more people to occupy diverse habitats around the world. The use of stored foods to buffer seasonal shortages, to free labour for artistic endeavours and monumental tasks, and to secure political allegiance, transformed our relations with the other inhabitants of the world and our own species.

The remarkable fact that food production started throughout the world within a relatively short time after around 10 000 years ago remains unexplained. However, at this time the world was undergoing changes in temperature, sea level and the distribution of plants and animals, and these events surely created both problems and opportunities for people as they adjusted to them. One response to the changes was agriculture. This event occupied only a moment in the timespan of human evolution, yet it provided a new evolutionary impetus to a system that had reached the limits of hunting and gathering on a technology based on direct use of naturally occurring raw materials such as flint, bone, hide, wood and fibre.

Before agriculture, there is little evidence that transformation of these raw materials into something other than their natural state had yet been developed. Domestication, in contrast, is a transformation in which individual plants and animals are selected and bred for desirable characteristics, thereby creating new forms of life and useful products. A transformation also took place in the uses of food and of animals. Crops could be used to purchase labour from outside the family, to provide food at festivals and to feed livestock. In return for food and protection, animals furnished meat and milk, hides, wool and other materials. Larger animals could take the place of human labour and could do work for which humans were ill suited. Livestock could also be banked against want, used to purchase services, turned into gifts, and sacrificed to local gods to secure greater fertility.

To early agriculturalists, therefore, crops and livestock came to represent much more than food and it was in part these subsidiary qualities that made agriculture such an attractive alternative to hunting and gathering. With agriculture, for the first time in history, humans could harness labour by using food as a currency and a medium of exchange. This idea, like that of domestication itself, spread very quickly.

Agriculture also had effects on the family. With domestication, children could work in the fields, tend livestock, carry water, fetch firewood and mill grain: all tedious and repetitive tasks. The larger families of agriculturalists increased the potential for extending kinship ties and cementing alliances through marriage. Children can therefore be seen as an important resource that facilitated the shift to food production and later to complex urban societies.

Along with the new treatment of foods, there came an increased dependence on a few species of highly productive plants and animals that lent themselves to manipulation. This simplified human diets in comparison with those of the more eclectic hunters and gatherers and replaced a dependence on animal proteins with year-round ingestion of starches and carbohydrates, largely as milled and cooked cereals or tubers. Some of the most obvious effects of this change in diet were in the teeth where dental caries became a worldwide problem for the first time. With the spread of processed and cooked foods came a reduction in the jaw musculature and the advent of overbite (overlapping of the upper incisor teeth with the lower ones).

With agriculture, human populations became subject to entirely new health problems, such as nutritional diseases and periodic famine and starvation. As societies became more sedentary, there was more potential for intergroup strife, unsanitary conditions, and the spread of parasites and diseases. The growth of populations ultimately led to competition for productive lands and other raw materials. Such competition was accelerated when leaders began to

convert their surplus grains into goods. There were also social and cultural developments associated with the emergence of a privileged élite.

Remember, however, that any sketch of agricultural origins is very much at the mercy of archaeological evidence. Such evidence is more complete in the drier tropical and temperate latitudes and is especially deficient in the wet tropics where much vegeculture originated. In these cases, we must depend on secondary evidence, such as the presence of sedentary villages and of artefacts for processing food. Archaeological finds are largely accidental and accumulate at a slow pace; we can hence now expect only a gradual refinement of our understanding of dates of origins of particular crops, of the importance of local domesticates, and of the nutritional and social consequences of agriculture.

What prompted the shift to agriculture?

The transition to agriculture around 10 000 years ago was a world-wide phenomenon, but seems to have occurred earliest in the wet and dry tropics and to have spread later to the temperate regions. The environmental changes after the Pleistocene altered the abundance and geographic distribution of species, and may have played a part in speciation when new ecological niches emerged. Tropical environments underwent no great changes at that time except for local effects caused by rising sea levels. It is therefore difficult to point to any single environmental cause for the shift to agriculture.

A possible underlying factor is that humans crossed a threshold of knowledge on the nature of plants, on the technology to make use of them, and on methods of storage that permitted a settled way of life and the propagation of plants. Tropical peoples living where many useful species existed, along with abundant fish and mammalian

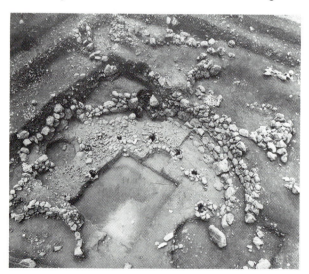

Round houses with stone foundations at the early Natufian village of Ain Mallaha, Israel – early evidence of sedentism in western Asia. The village was occupied between about 12 500 and 10 500 years ago.

Raised garden beds for the cultivation of sweet potato (*Ipomoea batatas*) in the drained floor of the Grand Baliem Valley, Irian Jaya. Cultivation of swamplands in New Guinea began at least 9000 years ago.

The sickle may have been critical in the domestication of wheat and other cereal grains. Peasant farmers still use it for reaping as here, in China. On the near right is a reconstruction of a Neolithic sickle, using 8000-year-old flint blades from Ali Kosh in Iran set into a modern wooden handle, with a modern sickle for comparison.

before there is evidence of domestication, but it appears as a complex only at the time that agriculture is manifest in the seeds themselves.

Impact on the environment

Throughout human history people have had impacts on their local environment through cutting of trees for shelter and fuel, collecting vegetable foods, hunting and the disposal of wastes. These impacts became more severe when hunters discovered the efficacy of fire-drives in hunting, and the burning of vegetation to stimulate the growth of grass and browse to attract game animals. But these activities did little to alter the land itself. Agriculture did this, eventually creating serious and irreversible changes when farmers began to plough the soil, clear forests to create fields, move rivers to irrigate wheat or rice, and burn forests to gain a few extra years of agricultural productivity from nutrient-deficient soils. Erosion and the alteration of the balance of species became inevitable.

With small populations even these effects were minimal. What has made the agricultural era especially powerful in its ability to change the environment is the accumulation of people. Around densely settled pre-industrial communities a wasteland develops where the ground is picked clean of fuel, stripped of vegetation, trampled by innumerable feet, and gouged for building materials. Such conditions may force people to move their villages periodically to fresh landscapes where the process of degradation begins anew. Problems arise when there is no longer fresh land to exploit. Then human populations reach a precarious balance with the ability of the land to support them and leave themselves vulnerable to periodic natural disasters such as droughts, which in turn may lead to malnutrition, disease and starvation.

Modern civilisation is built on agriculture that ultimately depends on a sustainable natural environment. Although agricultural systems have become enormously productive, they have also become highly specialised and, in some instances, the efforts to extend cultivation to new regions have had destructive consequences for fragile ecosystems.

The paradox today is that we cannot exist without specialisation and mechanisation, yet such systems can be sustained only through further alteration of the environment and of the plants themselves. The challenge, as it has been since the beginning, is to sustain productivity, maintain resources, and be prepared to buffer inevitable catastrophic losses that human populations periodically face.
Frank Hole

foods, probably made the transition via garden plots around houses; for example, the gardens in Java or South America where upwards of 50 species could be cultivated in very small spaces. These peoples were reasonably settled even before agriculture, and the conditions around their houses would have been suitable for the accidental propagation of vegetative plants. The hut-building and the clearing of living space might favour this by removing competition. A shift to agriculture would entail only minor changes in lifestyle.

A commitment to agriculture based on hard, dry, cereal grains, on the other hand, involved many more factors. Mere harvesting of these plants and resowing would be unlikely to produce the morphological changes characteristic of domesticated varieties. However, reaping with a sickle might select for non-shattering seed heads and allow such mutant plants to become dominant in sown fields; the sickle may therefore have been critical to the domestication of wheat, barley, some millets and rice.

After harvest, it is necessary to remove the hard, indigestible exosperm of grain and to reduce the seed to groats, or to a flour that can be soaked, boiled or baked. Ceramic vessels or basketry were needed for this. Such seeds also lend themselves to storage, which requires containers of earth, ceramic or basketry. Protection of such stored food and the need for cooking encourages settled habitation. A set of interrelated technologies was hence a precondition for cereal-based agriculture. Some of this was available long

See also 'Selecting and processing food' (p. 65), 'Human diet and subsistence' (p. 69), 'Reconstructing prehistoric diet' (p. 369), 'Domestication of animals' (p. 380), 'Reconstructing ancient populations' (p. 402), 'People and disease' (p. 411) and 'Tribal peoples in the modern world' (p. 433)

Domestication of animals

All animals are dependent on others. Such relationships can be at many levels, from the total dependence of one on another represented by parasitism to the warning calls made by many birds when they see an enemy. Early hominids would have been as subject to these interspecific associations as much as were other primates, but another relationship developed when prey became a large part of the hominid diet and the human species evolved as the master predator. Many of the intricacies of human social behaviour evolved from the need for a communal effort to provide food for the group. It may seem a small step from hunting wild animals to herding them, but there is a large gap between the relationship of a predator with its prey and the relationship of humans with their domesticated animals. What separates them is the concept of ownership, for domestication is a cultural as well as a biological process and hence it could occur only at a relatively late date in human history.

Domestication takes place when populations of animals are incorporated into the social structure of the human group and become objects of ownership, inheritance, purchase and exchange. The morphological changes that occur in domestic animals come second to this integration into a human group.

The process of domestication resembles evolution, in which the parent animals have been reproductively separated from the wild population. They form a founder group, which is changed over successive generations, not only in response to natural selection under the new regime imposed by the human community and its environment but also by artificial selection, which may be for characters favoured for economic, cultural or aesthetic reasons. In nature, the evolution of a subspecies is promoted when a segment of a population becomes reproductively isolated. With domestic animals, this separation leads to the development of different breeds.

There has been much discussion on the similarities and differences between taming, herding and domestication. Some archaeologists argue that they are simply stages in the long process of animal exploitation, whereas others maintain that they are very different in nature. Whatever the merits of these arguments, all have in common the acceptance that such animals are subject to some form of human ownership.

Taming

All mammals can be tamed, as can many reptiles and birds. For an animal to be tamed, rather than merely becoming accustomed to humans, it is usually necessary to remove it from its mother when it is very young and to rear it in close contact with a human. Whether the animal will remain tame as an adult depends to a great extent on its social behaviour patterns. A social carnivore like a wolf is very much easier to tame than a solitary hunter like a leopard. Another characteristic that is genetically determined and affects taming is the natural spacing of individuals in an animal group. Some bovids, such as buffalo, sheep and goats, are highly gregarious in the wild and like being close together, which means that they can be bunched together easily and restrained. Other members of the bovid family, and also most deer, although still herd animals, require more space around them, with the result that they easily panic and do not thrive in confinement. The most difficult of all animals to tame are those that are solitary, need a lot of space between individuals, and are territorial.

Towards the end of the Pleistocene, it is probable that hunter-gatherers often tamed young animals that were caught when their mothers were killed in the hunt. A few of these could have been the precursors of the first domesticated animals, but most probably remained merely ephemeral animal companions.

Herding

There are many social and economic levels at which animals are herded. Pastoralism may develop with animals that are at an early stage of domestication, with fully domesticated livestock, or with animals that are singled out from the wild population but still freely interbreed with it.

The transition from hunting to herding again centres on ownership. Animals that are herded are owned and protected. In an environment where there is a plentiful supply of wild animals that can be killed whenever meat is required, there is little reason for herding. In marginal areas, on the other hand, it is worth the effort to supply livestock with water and to protect them from other predators, especially as they can then be used to supply the extra resource of milk, and sometimes blood.

Animal remains from archaeological sites in western Asia, of around 9000 years ago, show that the earliest Neolithic people still obtained most of their meat from hunted gazelle. These animals can be driven into enclosed areas to be slaughtered. Gazelle are not normally amenable to herding whereas goats and sheep, being more gregarious, will follow a human leader. A few goats and sheep probably browsed and grazed around the earliest Neolithic settlements. These animals would have been led away from their endemic, mountain habitats and were living and breeding under human control. Although they differed

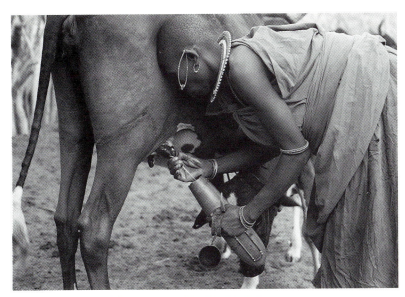

A Maasai woman milking a cow in Kenya.

little in appearance from wild goats and sheep, they were reproductively isolated from them.

By planting cereals and herding their expanding flocks of goats and sheep the Neolithic pastoralists could survive – and indeed increase in numbers – in an environment that was becoming increasingly arid and depleted of wild animals.

The herding of reindeer (*Rangifer tarandus*) in Scandinavia in ancient and modern times is a type of pastoralism that differs from that of the hot regions of the world. It is practised in areas that are outside the climatic limits for agriculture and the reindeer remain within the natural distribution of their wild ancestors. As well as being exploited for meat, milk and hides, reindeer are useful as draught animals, although their breeding is not controlled to the extent found in most domestic animals. The only form of selection is natural selection imposed by the harsh environment in which they live.

Herding intermediate between pastoralism and intensive livestock husbandry is represented by the putting out of pigs to pannage, a prominent feature of the agricultural economy of medieval Europe. The pigs were allowed to roam freely in woods and forests, and although they were fully domesticated they were allowed to interbreed with wild boar whenever possible; this was encouraged because it increased the size of the domestic pigs. The same practice is manifest in animal remains from Neolithic lake villages in Switzerland, where bones of small domestic pigs are mixed with those of very large wild boar; bones of mature individuals intermediate in size between the two have also been found.

Ranching is a form of herding that differs little from hunting. The livestock usually live entirely as wild animals but they are nominally owned, kept within broad boundaries under human control and rounded up once a year or so to be marked or branded. The animals provide the same resources of meat, hides and fat as hunted animals, and they are not milked. Where plenty of land is available (as on the cattle ranches of the Americas or the wildlife ranches of Africa), this is an efficient way of producing meat.

An aspect of herding and ranching that is socially very important is that the greater the number of animals the higher the status of the owner or 'chief'. In this context it is of interest to look at the laws and rituals of hunting in medieval Europe, where the beasts of the chase were treated more like ranched than like wild animals in that they could be hunted only by the élite of society and were protected by royalty.

The spread of domestic and feral animals

It is usual to accuse the human species of desecrating the natural world and of exterminating many other species of animals and plants. It is true, for example, that the aurochs or wild ox (*Bos primigenius*) of Europe and western Asia was hunted to extinction by the seventeenth century AD. Yet European domestic cattle, which are all descendants of the aurochs, must now be counted as one of the most successful of all mammals.

The European rabbit (*Oryctolagus cuniculus*) is a fascinating example of a species that has proliferated as a result of human activity and most probably has been saved from extinction. At the end of the Pleistocene, around 12 000 years ago, the rabbit was restricted in its distribution to Spain and the southern edge of France, and it could have become extinct if the living animals had not been moved around Europe by the Romans. At first, rabbits were carefully protected and bred in warrens but they soon spread to the wild and gradually reached their present enormous numbers and worldwide distribution. All these rabbits are *feral*: they are animals that have returned to the wild, and all have descended from domestic stock many hundreds of years ago.

Several other domesticated animals became feral during prehistory. These include the Soay sheep of the islands of St

Soay sheep were probably taken to the islands of St Kilda, Scotland, in about 1500 BC

Kilda in the Outer Hebrides of Scotland and the wild goats and sheep on several Mediterranean islands, of which the European mouflon (*Ovis musimon*) from Corsica and Sardinia is a notable example. This wild sheep was once thought to be relic of a truly wild European sheep, but, because of the lack of fossil evidence for sheep in the Pleistocene of the Mediterranean, it is now believed that the mouflon is an ancient feral sheep like the Soay.

Another example of a relic domesticate is the dingo or wild dog of Australia. Again, because of the absence of dingo fossils, it is believed that this dog was taken to Australia by aboriginal people at least 3000 years ago. This animal is a valuable representative of the dogs that must have been widespread in Asia in prehistory, and it is very similar to its presumed progenitor, the Indian wolf (*Canis lupus pallipes*).

Although there might appear to be a great variety of domesticated animals, this is not in fact the case. It is puzzling, for example, why the people who arrived in Australia with their dogs did not domesticate kangaroos. And why did the North American Indians not domesticate the bighorn sheep, and why were none of the antelopes in Africa domesticated in ancient times? It can only be surmised that at the time the gathering and hunting way of life provided enough food to make unnecessary the change from predation to protection of animals.

There are some animals whose relationship with humans is better described as commensalism than domestication. The best example of these are the pariah dogs of Asia and Africa. These live by scavenging around human towns, settlements and roads. They are not owned but live as wild or feral animals, which are tolerated because they feed on debris and by so doing are of benefit to the community. Indeed, it may be that it was scavenging in this way that helped forge the first bonds between tamed wolf and human.

Physical changes caused by domestication

A domestic animal is one that has been bred in captivity for purposes of economic profit to a community that maintains a mastery over its breeding, organisation of territory, and food. The domestic animal is reproductively isolated from its wild counterpart and is exposed to both natural and artificial selection, which, over many generations, leads to genetic change. Interbreeding is still possible between the domesticate and its wild progenitor, although the mating pair may look very different from each other.

Domestication can cause a change in the rate of growth of different parts of an animal that may result in changes in its proportions. This might result from stress and hormonal changes caused by the animal's emotional and physical dependance on its human owner. Certain effects of domestication are common to a large number of mammals and can be summarised as follows:

- **Size.** The early stages of domestication always result in a reduction in the overall size of the body, probably caused by inadequate feeding, combined with selection because small animals are more easily handled and housed. For example, skeletal remains of the first dogs and of all the early livestock animals are smaller than those of their wild progenitors.

- **Outward appearance.** Animals that looked different from their wild progenitors may have been selected for because they could be identified and might thus increase the prestige of the owner. A tamed animal that was different in colour, such as a black wolf or a white sheep, would then be especially favoured. Perhaps a wolf with lop ears and a curled tail might be selected and bred from because it would look different and would appear to be submissive. Extra long ears, a curled tail, and variations in the length and colour of the coat are characters that are common to many domestic species. The horns of sheep and cattle may have become variable in size and curvature for the same reason.

- **Internal anatomy.** It is in the skull that changes are most obvious. In nearly all domestic animals the face is shortened and there is compaction of the cheek teeth because teeth usually respond more slowly to selection for smaller size than does bone. Later, the numbers, size and positions of the teeth may become anomalous. The brain is reduced in size relative to the size of the body and the sense organs may become less acute, although the eyes and outer ears may be enlarged. Gestation period and general physiology are not altered, but breeding seasons may become irregular and are often increased in frequency. The size of the litter is increased. Fattiness increases, especially in castrated animals. In wild bovids, fat is stored around the kidneys and under the skin, whereas in domesticated species it is present through the muscle and stored around the tail.

- **Behaviour.** Apart from the cat, all domestic mammals are descended from wild species that are social rather

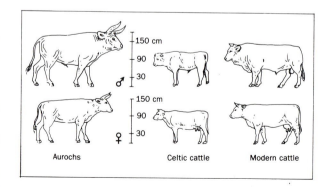

Many domestic animals are smaller than their wild ancestors — for example, cattle are smaller than aurochs and pigs are smaller than wild boar. When people first began domesticating animals, they may have found it easier to manage a large herd of small animals rather than a small herd of a few large ones, and selected for smallness.

By the eighth century BC, Assyrian sheep were fully domesticated with a wool fleece and fat tail, as shown in this stone relief from the Central Palace, Nimrud.

Centres of animal domestication

Many of the common domestic animals of today were first domesticated in western Asia between 10 000 and 6000 years ago (see p. 384). This was correlated with the beginnings of settlement, food storage and the cultivation of cereals.

The progress from hunting and gathering to early agriculture and the keeping of animals can be traced in the remains of animals and plants from the Mesolithic and earliest Neolithic periods in western Asia. On the earliest sites, 11 000 years old, a wide variety of wild mammals as well as fish, molluscs, birds and plants provided food for humans. The mammals included wild cattle, wild boar, gazelle, deer, foxes and rodents. It is likely that at this period and for several thousand years earlier there was a close association between tamed wolves and people, but there is little evidence from the bones to indicate that the dog (*Canis familiaris*) had yet emerged as the first domestic animal. Cultural evidence for this can be seen, however, in the burial of a woman in close proximity with her dog at the Natufian site of Ain Mallaha in northern Israel (see p. 384).

Later in the Neolithic, around 9000 years ago and still before the invention of pottery, there is a great change in the proportions of the animal species found in archaeological sites in western Asia. Cultivated grain is present and remains of goat and sheep outnumber those of all other

than solitary. Patterns of social behaviour are little altered by domestication, so that, for example, although a highly bred dog may look very different from a wild wolf its behaviour is still recognisably wolf-like. Many behavioural changes result from the retention of juvenile characteristics that make the animal more affectionate and submissive. This is obviously advantageous to the owner who wishes to retain dominance over the animal, and it is a basis of artificial selection.

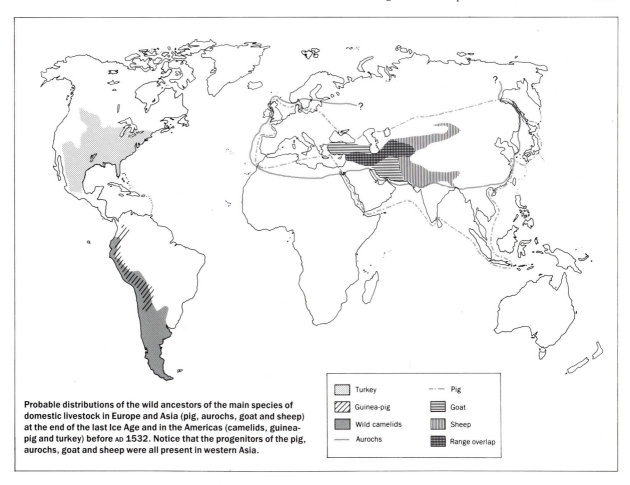

Probable distributions of the wild ancestors of the main species of domestic livestock in Europe and Asia (pig, aurochs, goat and sheep) at the end of the last Ice Age and in the Americas (camelids, guinea-pig and turkey) before AD 1532. Notice that the progenitors of the pig, aurochs, goat and sheep were all present in western Asia.

	Turkey		Pig
Guinea-pig		Goat
Wild camelids		Sheep
Aurochs		Range overlap

The dog was probably the first animal to be domesticated, first by late Ice Age hunters for use as retrievers of wounded animals and later by early farmers for use as herders and guardians of tamed livestock. The earliest evidence for a close relationship between dogs and people comes from the burial of an elderly woman with her dog beneath her left hand at the Natufian site of Ain Mallaha in northern Israel (about 9600 BC).

DATES OF EARLY DOMESTICATION OF ANIMALS

Domesticate	Wild progenitor	Principal region of origin	Date
Dog	Wolf (Canis lupus)	Western Asia	c. 12 000 BP
Goat	Bezoar goat (Capra aegagrus)	Western Asia	c. 9000 BP
Sheep	Asiatic mouflon (Ovis orientalis)	Western Asia	c. 9000 BP
Cattle	Aurochs (Bos primigenius)	Western Asia	c. 8000 BP
Pig	Boar (Sus scrofa)	Western Asia	c. 8000 BP
Reindeer	Reindeer (Rangifer tarandus)	Northern Eurasia	Unknown
Rabbit	Rabbit (Oryctolagus cuniculus)	Iberia	Roman
Horse	Horse (Equus ferus)	Central Asia	c. 6000 BP
Donkey	Ass (Equus africanus)	Arabia, North Africa	c. 6000 BP
Dromedary	Camel (Camelus sp.)	Arabia	c. 5000 BP
Bactrian camel	Camel (Camelus ferus)	Central Asia	c. 5000 BP
Llama	?Guanaco (?Lama guanicoe)	South America	c. 7000 BP
Alpaca	? (? Lama sp.)	South America	?c. 7000 BP
Guinea-pig	Cavy (Cavia sp.)	South America	?c. 3000 BP
Cat	Cat (Felis silvestris)	Western Asia	?c. 5000 BP
Guinea-fowl	Guinea-fowl (Numidia meleagris)	North Africa	c. 2300 BP
Yak	Yak (Bos mutus)	Himalayas	Unknown
Water buffalo	Water buffalo (Bubalus arnee)	Southern Asia	c. 6000 BP
Mithan	Gaur (Bos gaurus)	Southeast Asia	Unknown
Bali cattle	Banteng (Bos javanicus)	Southeast Asia	Unknown
Chicken	Jungle fowl (Gallus gallus)	Southern Asia	c. 4000 BP
Turkey	Turkey (Meleagris gallopavo)	North America	AD 500
Goldfish	Carp (Carassius sp.)	China	AD 960

BP = years before present.

The nomenclature used here and in the main part of the chapter for the domestic species and their wild progenitors follows the Linnean system; for example, *Canis familiaris* for the dog and *Canis lupus* for its wild progenitor, the wolf. Where Linnaeus gave only one name for both the wild and the domestic forms – for example, *Capra hircus* for the goat – this is retained for the domestic form and the next available name is used for the wild species, in this case *Capra aegagrus*.

animals. The small size of the bones indicates that these goats and sheep had lived under human control and had probably been poorly fed.

Goats (*Capra hircus*) and sheep (*Ovis aries*) were domesticated after dogs, and were followed by cattle and pigs, all in western Asia in the early Neolithic. All domestic species are generally considered to be descended from a single wild progenitor. The ancestor of the dog is the wolf (*Canis lupus*), goats are descended from the scimitar-horned species of western Asia (*Capra aegagrus*) and sheep are descended from the Asiatic mouflon (*Ovis orientalis*). All European domestic cattle (*Bos taurus*) are descended from the extinct aurochs, whereas the humped cattle of southern Asia and Africa (*Bos indicus*) may be descended from a somewhat different form of the aurochs, known from fossils in India and named *Bos namadicus*. However, this probably belonged to the same species as the aurochs since modern humped and unhumped cattle will interbreed freely and have fertile offspring.

Domestic pigs are all descended from the wild boar (*Sus scrofa*), which, like the aurochs, was widespread in Europe and Asia. Although evidence for the first domestication of the pig comes from western Asia, it is likely that there were many centres, including southeastern Asia and western Europe, where pigs were bred in the prehistoric period.

Domestication of the horse (*Equus caballus*) took place later than that of other livestock, and the earliest remains have been recovered from the Ukraine, north of the Black Sea. The peoples who first domesticated the horse around 6000 years ago were the ancestors of the Scythians, who were probably the greatest horsemen of the ancient world. The ass (*Equus asinus*) appears to have been domesticated at about this period in western Asia or North Africa, and rapidly spread into the Middle East. Behavioural studies

Herding llamas at 4260 metres in the Peruvian highlands.

and osteological evidence indicate that the onager (*Equus hemionus*) was never domesticated, although wild onagers were interbred with domestic horses and asses to produce hybrids. The breeding of mules (the progeny of a male donkey and a female horse) was particularly favoured by the Romans, who used them as draught animals, but the practice was begun much earlier, probably by the Sumerians and then the Assyrians.

Four members of the camel family have been domesticated. The dromedary (*Camelus dromedarius*) was probably domesticated in Arabia at around the same period as the donkey, and the Bactrian camel (*Camelus bactrianus*) was domesticated further east. The llama (*Lama glama*) and the alpaca (*Lama pacos*) were domesticated in South America, perhaps as early as 7000 years ago, to provide meat, transport and wool. In the Andes, the guinea-pig (*Cavia porcellus*) was also domesticated for its meat.

Although the cat (*Felis catus*) is generally assumed to have been first domesticated by the ancient Egyptians, it is just as likely that this domesticated carnivore was also a product of western Asia, which means that the only domestic animal to have a definite origin in Africa is the guinea-fowl (*Numida meleagris*).

Southern Asia was a centre for domestication for the yak (*Bos grunniens*), the water buffalo (*Bubalus bubalis*) and two less-common species of cattle from southeastern Asia, the mithan and Bali cattle (*Bos frontalis* and *B. javanicus*). Domestic chickens also originated from southern Asia and are descended from the jungle fowl (*Gallus gallus*).

There were two domestic animals in North America before the Spanish conquest, the dog and the turkey (*Meleagris gallopavo*). Remains of dogs have been found on very early sites in both North and South America and maybe their progenitor was the North American wolf. Domesticated turkeys were kept in corrals by the Pueblos of the southwestern states from AD 500 to 700.

The best-known domestic animal to originate from China is the goldfish (*Carassius auratus*), but it is possible that in parts of this vast country many other species of animals

such as dogs, horses and pigs were domesticated in the early prehistoric period.

Domestication and socioeconomic change

The dog, the first animal to be domesticated, remains today the most important animal to be treated as an intimate within human societies. The first tamed wolves may have just been animal companions, but they soon took over the roles of waste-disposer, hunting partner, watch-dog and bed-warmer.

Towards the end of the last Ice Age, the method of hunting in Europe and Asia changed from the short-distance attack using spears and large stone axes to long-distance projectiles, such as arrows armed with small stone flakes called microliths. This change of weapon could have been associated with the worldwide spread of the domestic dog, which meant that wounded animals could be followed and retrieved when they were shot at a distance. Once agriculture and livestock husbandry had become established, dogs were used as herders and guardians and for driving off wild grazing animals from growing crops.

Dogs were also used for traction in North America and the Arctic, and for meat, fat and hides in China and Southeast Asia. In some countries, dogs have been treated with reverence, as in ancient Egypt and China, whereas in others they have long been regarded as untouchable outcasts. In this century, the breeding of dogs has become a profitable business, but through it all the dog continues to fulfil a psychological need for affection and companionship.

The herding of livestock, the keeping of farm animals, and the use of the ox, the ass and the horse for transport have provided the foundations on which civilisations have been built. During the last half of this century, the intensification of farming and the settlement of nomadic pastoralists, with consequent overgrazing, are leading to changes that may be cataclysmic.

Domestication involved an accelerating process of elimination of the great natural diversity of wild animals and plants to replace them with the few species that could be easily managed and manipulated. Within these species, the growth of modern farming has led to a loss of diversity within the breeds themselves because there is no longer a need for adaptation to local environments, and artificial insemination can produce genetic uniformity over whole continents. It is not too late to avoid the danger of this course by conserving the ancient and unimproved breeds of livestock. By encouraging traditional pastoralism and the ranching of wild herbivores for meat in the non-industrialised countries, it may also be possible to avoid the famines and surplus stocks of food that have become a feature of the world today.   Juliet Clutton-Brock

See also 'Origins of agriculture' (p. 373)

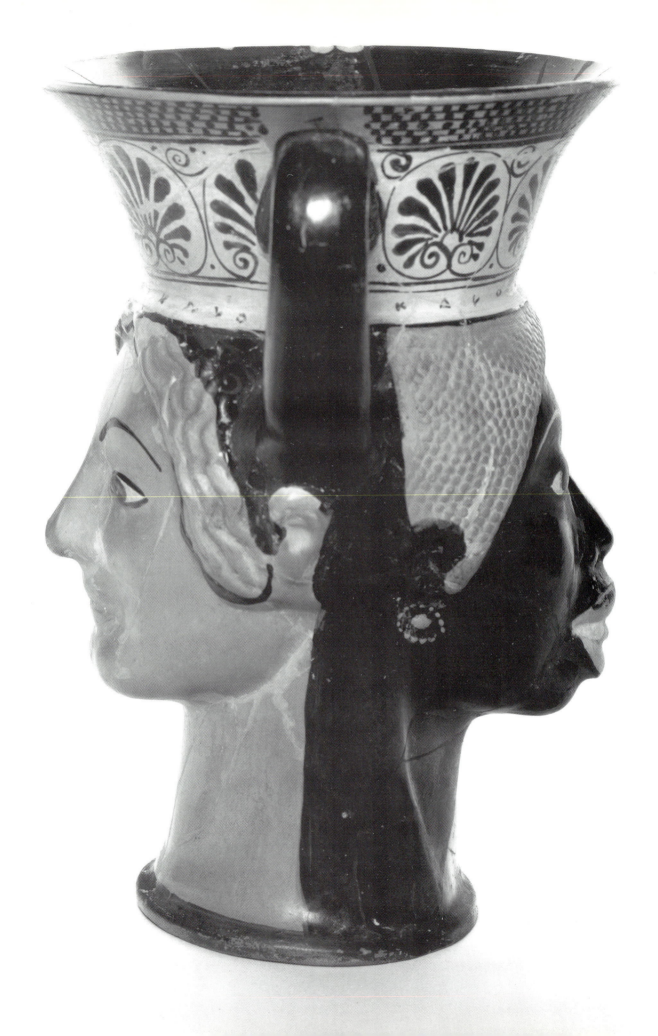

Part Ten

Human populations, past and present

As earlier chapters show, the study of human beings makes sense only when seen in the context of our animal relatives. Anatomy, palaeontology and genetics all combine to show that humans are primates, and primates mammals. We are hence exposed to the same laws of birth and death as are monkeys, apes and mice. Although we can ameliorate the cruelties of nature to some extent, humanity is as subject to the basic rules as is any other species. Nowhere is this more manifest than in the control of human numbers and the growth and spread of population. Thomas Malthus's discussion of the differences in the rate of growth of population and of resources in England is the first statement of modern ecological theory; and the balance between birth and death has ruled humanity in the past as it will in the future.

Even if life in ancient times did not appear brutish and nasty to those who lived it, it was certainly shorter than it is today. Studies of skeletons and other clues show that the age structure of populations thousands of years ago was very different from that of modern societies, with very few people living to a ripe old age. Before the origin of agriculture, *Homo sapiens* was rather a rare creature, living in scattered bands that probably had little contact with each other and that were much less settled than we are today (**10.2** and **10.3**).

A population structure of this kind had many important genetic and ecological consequences. One of the most striking is that the pattern of disease was quite different; many infectious diseases demand a minimum population size to provide the pool of susceptible individuals needed to stop an infection from dying out (**10.4**). A parodoxical result is that as human populations grew and spread over the globe they may have become less healthy than in earlier times. Changes in patterns of contact among peoples can still have a dramatic effect on disease, as is seen in the rapid spread of the human immunodeficiency virus (HIV) over the past three decades.

The introduction of agriculture was perhaps the most important cultural event in human history. Humans had filled most of the world before farmers first appeared (**10.1**), but farming was the spark for the population explosion that has continued, with some interruptions, ever since. Cultivation of plants began around 10 000 years ago, with several independent sites of origin: for example, wheat and barley in Western Asia, rice and millet in China, maize in

Attic vase in the form of two female heads, one white the other black, dated to before 510 BC and probably from Tanagra, Greece.

387

Central America and the northern Andes, with other centres in Southeast Asia, Central Africa and elsewhere (**9.9**).

In each area, the increase in food supply led to rapid population growth, suggesting that for much of human history our numbers were limited by a shortage of food. The increase in numbers led to movement of populations by long-range migration or simply by slow diffusion, either into previously uninhabited regions (such as the remote Pacific islands) or into areas already occupied by hunters and gatherers.

Sometimes the agriculturalists absorbed the genes of the earlier populations, leaving trends still manifest today (**10.1**). Only a few parts of the world retain peoples whose mode of life is similar to that before, or in the early phases of, agriculture. Many of these have already incorporated much of the modern world into their behaviour, and they are unlikely to survive as members of our history for much longer (**10.7**).

Agriculture led to population pressure, and to the expansion of farming peoples. World patterns of language can still be related to these economic events. The ancestor of nearly all European languages may have been brought from its origin in the eastern Mediterranean, and the same is true of the languages of the Pacific Islands, spread as they were by early cultivators from their Asian home (**10.1**).

The figures on human population are startling. Not only are the populations of most countries increasing in number (**10.5**) but in many of them the rate of increase is also growing. This has led to striking changes in age structure, with far more young people than old. Barring catastrophes (such as might strike parts of Africa with the spread of AIDS), this means that further rapid growth in the near future is unavoidable. Much of the developed world has passed through the phase of increase made possible by improvements in public health and have reached a new equilibrium. Contraception has played an important part here, and research on new methods of fertility control gives hope that humans may be more able to control their own demography in future (**10.6**).

The human species is now undergoing a demographic shift as great as that which led to the migration of populations, genes and cultures in early farming times. The United Nations estimates that the world's population is 5.4 billion today and predicts that it will increase to 8.5 billion by the year 2025 and 10.2 billion by 2050, with very different patterns of growth in different parts of the world. Future anthropologists — if such there be — will see evidence of this shift for thousands of years to come.

The dispersion of modern humans

The biological variety of living human populations has from the beginnings of anthropology been approached through the study of race. For almost two centuries following Linnaeus, anthropologists attempted to define discrete units of humanity, and to find criteria for distinguishing among these 'races' as sharply as possible. Individuals best conforming to such criteria were viewed as 'pure'. All this happened before the emergence of genetics.

Any prospect of understanding human variation in these terms has failed. 'Race' certainly exists, in the general sense of local limitations of the global variation in universal human traits. For example, all normal human skin produces melanin, and the amount can be increased by tanning; but the genetic constitution of different populations determines the range of variation in skin colour among individuals of a population. The same is true for hair form, cranial shape, stature, and so on. Such population differences are important in the study of disease incidence and susceptibility, of microevolution and adaptation, and as clues to the development and dispersion of modern people. For disease, certain abnormal types of haemoglobin, such as the sickling trait which is common in equatorial Africa, make red blood cells less susceptible to invasion by malarial organisms. The populations that contain this gene do not coincide with any traditionally recognised 'racial' group. There is little evidence for any association of disease with other traditional racial attributes such as skin colour.

Human populations in different parts of the world have adjusted to the physical environment in various ways, but surprisingly little is known of the adaptive significance of these physical differences. Skin colour is understood best but not completely: as we saw in Chapters 2.2 and 7.6 melanin screens the dermis from the harmful effect of solar ultraviolet light. This may have favoured the intense pigmentation of some Sudanese people and the fair skin of Europeans who need exposure to ultraviolet, to avoid rickets by generating vitamin D. Nose shape is also associated with climate: a narrow nose may better moisten and warm cold air before it reaches the lungs. Body form also obeys certain general rules, like Allen's rule on the relative size of extremities as governing heat loss: Inuit (Eskimos) are short-limbed, and Africans of the sunny tropics are the opposite. Such proportions are under genetic control: transportation to the tropics would not turn an Inuit child into a spindly Sudanese.

Such variation must be an outcome of the evolution of modern *Homo sapiens*, although we have learned little about just how this happened.

Traditional studies of race

There have been several attempts to categorise the variety of present humans. Many of these are unnecessarily procrustean, but have some value in purely descriptive terms. A typical classification based on human visible variation is as follows:

- **Caucasoid**, from northern Europe to northern Africa and India. These are depigmented to a greater or lesser degree. Hair in males is generally well developed on the face and body, and is mostly fine and wavy or straight. A narrow face and prominent narrow nose are both typical.
- **Negroid** (or Congoid), in sub-Saharan Africa. Skin pigment is dense, hair woolly, noses broad, faces generally short, lips thick, and ears are squarish and lobeless. Stature varies greatly, from pygmy to very tall (in the latter the face is long). The most divergent group are the Khoisan (Bushman and Hottentot) peoples of southern Africa.
- **Mongoloid**, found in all Asia except the west and south (India), in the northern and eastern Pacific, and in the Americas. The skin is brown to light, hair coarse, straight to wavy, and sparse on the face and body. The face is broad and tends to flatness. The eyelid is covered by an internal skinfold in the central populations but such folds are less marked or absent elsewhere. The teeth often have crowns more complex than in other peoples, and the inner surfaces of the upper incisors frequently have a shovel appearance.

  The Chinese, Koreans and Japanese are the 'typical' populations and have probably shown considerable expansion in historical times. In central and northeastern Asia and among Inuit the flatness of face and nose is still more marked. In more marginal populations, such as the Ainu of Japan, aboriginal Taiwanese, Philippine Islanders, Indonesians and Southeast Asians these traits are less marked. The same is true of Polynesians and Micronesians. In American Indians, the face is usually broad but nasal bridges are apt to be more prominent relative to the eyes; the teeth are especially complex in pattern and shovelled incisors are particularly prevalent.
- **Australoid**, the aboriginals of Australia and Melanesia. Skin is dark; hair predominantly wavy (Australia) or frizzy (Melanesia), with blondness in children (lost in adulthood) being common throughout. The head is long and narrow, the forehead sloping with prominent brow ridges, and the face has a projecting jaw.

13

12

1

2

3

4

Such descriptions of the distribution of modern human variety have been useful in the study of human evolution only as a source of hypotheses. Until about 1930 not even this was true. Human fossils were still extremely few, and some of them involved mistakes in stratigraphy or even, as in the case of the Piltdown Man (p. 448), outright fraud. Questions were not posed as to origins, which were simply accepted as somehow 'given'. Any apparent blurring of distinctions between 'races', as perceived in variations from the supposed type of a race, was explained as a mixture of some more sharply defined earlier races or types: and this is as far as the quest for an explanation for human geographic differences went, except for claims of hypothetical migrations of primordial peoples.

Now that the Pleistocene setting of human evolution is better understood and far more fossils are available we can pose hypotheses as to the origins of geographical differences in modern humans. These lie between two extremes. The first sees racial differences as already existing at the stage of *Homo erectus*, in populations of different regions. Skeletal distinctions among fossil populations may have persisted to the present although modern populations undoubtedly represent generally similar *Homo sapiens*. While not denying contact and some migration, those who hold this view of human evolution see it as essentially separate in the main areas of the world. This is the *multiregional continuity* or 'Candelabra' hypothesis.

The second position is the *replacement* or 'Out of Africa'

hypothesis. This emphasises the general homogeneity of living humans and sees present populations as primarily descended from one main population, which originated relatively recently in a single region, later migrating outwards. Other populations, possible deriving from *Homo erectus* although they might have contributed to some extent to different living peoples, were in the main replaced by the more modern arrivals from elsewhere. According to proponents of this view, racial differences came later, after the predominance of *Homo erectus*; they see humankind as genetically more homogeneous, most if not all of the earliest populations having disappeared.

It is difficult to distinguish between these views solely on the basis of morphological patterns in living populations or

Representatives of the main regional groups or 'races' of people today:

Africans or Negroids: 1, Maasai; 2, San (Bushman); 3, Ghanaian

Caucasians or Caucasoids: 4, Finn; 5, Palestinian

Mongoloids of Mainland Asia and Polynesians: 6, Mongolian; 7, Tamang, Nepal; 8, Chinese, Hong Kong; 9, Hawaiian Islander

Australo-Melanesians: 10, Australian Aborigine; 11, Dani, New Guinea

American Indians: 12, Quechua, Peru; 13, Dene, Canada

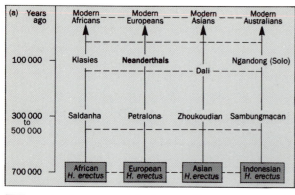

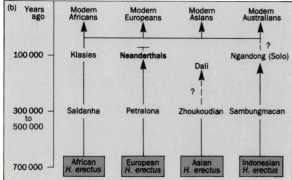

Opposing interpretations of the emergence of present-day regional human populations. Significant fossils in different regions are shown at their approximate levels in time, starting from a base of *Homo erectus*. In (a), the multiregional continuity model, each line evolves locally to present populations; similarity among these is explained by gene exchange at all time levels (implied by the horizontal dashed lines). Local continuity is argued by perceived morphological similarities. In (b), the 'Out of Africa' or replacement model, similarity among modern humans is explained by the late expansion of a single form that evolved in Africa and then replaced the local populations in Asia and Europe. Morphological connections with previous regional forms are doubted.

on a preliminary assessment of distinctions among fossils. Many further kinds of evidence from living humans can now be used.

Molecular patterns of relationships

Genetic analysis became possible with the discovery of systems of blood groups. This work was the first to emphasise the weaknesses of previous racial studies. Vast amounts of data now show population differences in blood-group frequency. As such antigen systems directly express the genotype, which more complex traits like skin colour or body height do not, it was once expected that a coherent genetic classification of the human populations might emerge. This has not been the case.

The ABO blood groups were first described in 1900. They are strongly patterned over the surface of the world. Groups A and B are both at high frequency in Africa and much of Asia, extending into the Pacific through Melanesia. In northwestern Europe, B is lower, O and A higher. In native populations of the Americas, A and B are almost absent, except in western central North America, where A becomes common. In Polynesia, B declines towards the periphery and A and O rise, and in aboriginal Australia again, B is absent and A is high.

Such a distribution is difficult to interpret in purely historical terms. Gene frequencies appear to be relatively stable over moderate amounts of time; for example, gypsies in western Europe preserve frequencies close to those of their original home, India. The worldwide distribution might suggest the operation of selection, but little is known about such selection on the ABO system (although a history

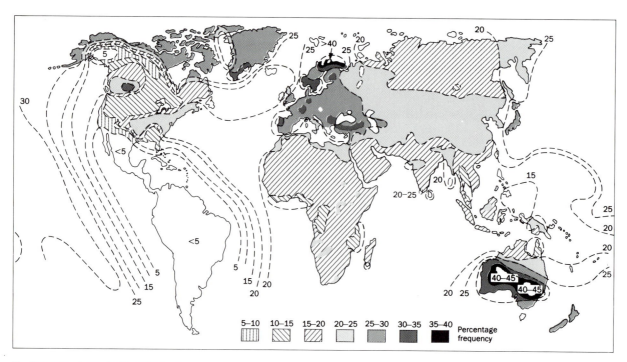

The frequency of gene *A* of the ABO blood-group system.

of differential resistance to disease has been suggested). The founder principle and genetic drift may be more important. For example, the settlement of Polynesia, beginning about 1500 BC, involved a serial colonisation of island groups eastwards (see Box 1). Such a succession of small groups, probably composed of related families, each drawn as a minor part of the last, is the ideal situation for the reduction and loss of a gene by chance in small samples. Similar chance events may have applied in the small tribal popu-

lations of Australia, which probably suffered occasional extinction and repopulation during an occupation of the continent going back to about 50 000 years. For the Americas, movement by immigrants from Asia across the relative cold of the Bering Strait area might have led to a purge of disease organisms, so that both chance and the removal of an agent of selection by disease caused the A and B alleles to decrease.

As natural selection eliminates history, the present dis-

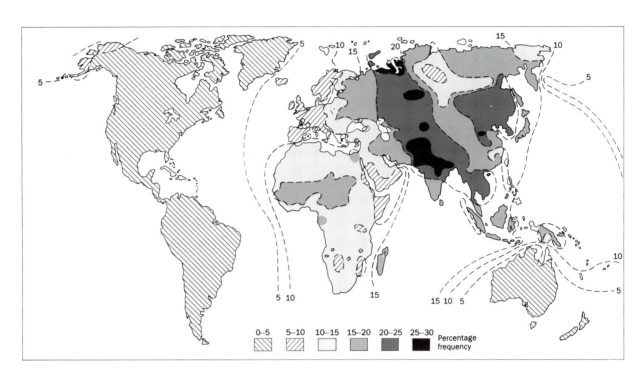

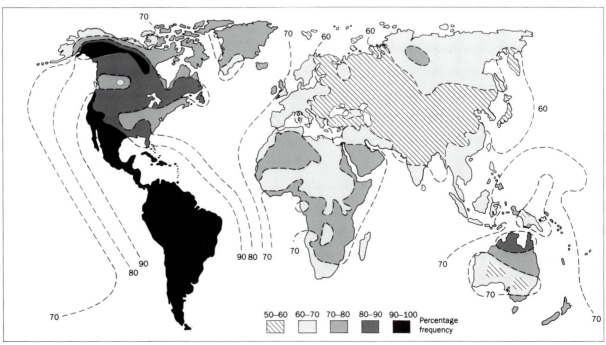

The frequencies of genes *B* (upper map) and *O* (lower map) of the ABO blood-group system.

1. THE PEOPLING OF THE PACIFIC

Thor Heyerdahl's book *Kon-Tiki* has sold 20 million copies, which is probably more than all other anthropology books put together. It is an example of the view that in order to recreate the past it is necessary only to re-live it. Heyerdahl, a Norwegian, was convinced that the culture of Polynesia was close to that of South America. He sailed a raft for 8000 kilometres from Peru to establish that such a journey was possible; and deduced that this must be the probable route of human penetration into the Pacific. This deduction was daring, to say the least; but genetics now gives us the chance to test it. The story of how the Pacific was peopled is perhaps the most satisfying example of how genetics, linguistics, archaeology and palaeontology can combine to sort out patterns of human migration.

The physical ties among the peoples of the Pacific were noted by Captain Cook and his companions on their third voyage round the world. James King, Cook's astronomer and second lieutenant, observed in 1779:

> The inhabitants of the Sandwich [Hawaiian] Islands are undoubtedly of the same race with those of New Zealand, the Society and Friendly [Tonga] Islands, Easter Island, and the Marquesas, . . . From what continent they originally emigrated, and by what steps they have spread through so vast a space, those who are curious in disquisitions of this nature may perhaps not find it very difficult to conjecture. . . they bear strong marks of affinity to some of the Indian tribes. . . and the same affinity may again be traced amongst the Battas [Battaks of northern Sumatra] and the Malays.

The patterns of genes in modern populations confirm some of his views, and add a great deal to our understanding of this area, which includes some of the first and some of the last parts of the world to be occupied by modern humans.

The archaeological and fossil records suggest that we got to some places very early on. Recent finds of stone tools and red ochres in Arnhem Land in northern Australia show that humans were there between 60 000 and 50 000 years ago. They reached Tasmania more than 20 000 years ago, extinguishing many native plants and animals on their way. In Papua New Guinea, too, there has been human habitation for at least 40 000 years.

In contrast, many of the Pacific islands have been settled for less than 5000 years, and islands such as Pitcairn were occupied 1000 years ago with populations that then became extinct.

Language supports this pattern of settlement. In Papua New Guinea, an ancient homeland populated by groups isolated from each other by geography and culture, there are about 700 languages, many of which are very distinct and have only a few speakers. In the highlands, there were ditches for drainage and for growing taro tubers at least 9000 years ago.

The other main centre of languages – and of an expanding agricultural population – in the Far East was in the Yangtze (Chang Jiang) basin in eastern China about 8000 years ago. These rice growers spread southwards and were the source of a vast movement of people, cultures and genes that today covers much of eastern Asia and the Pacific. Their culture and the Austronesian languages associated with it spread to the Philippines by 3000 BC, to central Polynesia by 200 BC; and ultimately to Hawaii (AD 300) and New Zealand (AD 800). The vast area has a common linguistic heritage; the word for 'eye' (*mata*) is the same in the Philippines, Fiji, Samoa and Easter Island.

Many genes – for blood groups, enzymes, mitochondrial DNA and nuclear DNA sequences – have been mapped in the Pacific region. Some clear large-scale patterns emerge. There is a genetic link – as the eighteenth-century voyagers saw – between the modern populations of Southeast Asia and those of the myriad of small islands making up Polynesia. This is clearly seen in the patterns of the maternally inherited mitochondrial genome.

In Japan and East Asia, many people lack a short section of the DNA in the mitochondrion. This deletion does no harm, but is a characteristic of Southeast Asian populations. It is also found throughout Polynesia, and on the coast of Papua New Guinea, bolstering the linguistic ties that show that these peoples originally came from somewhere in that part of Asia. However, the native populations of central New Guinea and of Australia, with their wild diversity of language, do not carry this ancestral cue; they travelled more slowly and for far smaller distances than did the Polynesians.

Populations of the most distant Polynesian islands are genetically rather uniform, suggesting – not surprisingly – that they went through a series of bottlenecks as they spread across the Pacific. In the isolated parts of Papua New Guinea, too, there is a shortage of genetic variation, showing that these mountain valleys are just as isolated.

Micronesians, from the Marina, Caroline and Marshall islands, are also distinct, suggesting that they followed a different path of colonisation. There is some indication of two distinct groups among the Australian Aborigines, perhaps a relic of a second invasion some time after the arrival of the first Australians.

Although much remains to be done, there is a pleasing symmetry between the evidence from genes and that of history. However, there is one finding that will certainly disappoint those millions of people who were introduced to anthropology by Thor Heyerdahl. There is no indication of any genetic link between South America and Polynesia; population genetics has sunk the Kon-Tiki.   *Steve Jones*

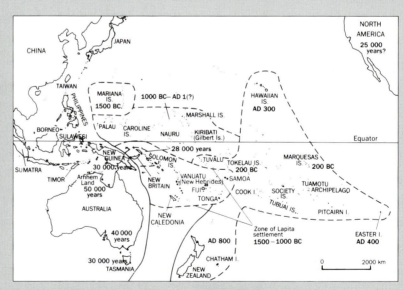

Humans have been in Papua New Guinea and Australia for far longer than in Polynesia. This pattern of settlement is reflected in language, with a group of ancient and highly differentiated languages in New Guinea, and a different and less-diverse language family that spread from southern China in most of the Pacific islands.

tribution of the *ABO* gene frequencies is unlikely to retain much evidence of ancient migrations and population relationships. The same may be true of most other blood-group systems. The MNSs system is complex: the M allele is somewhat more frequent than N in Europe and Africa, M is very high in the Americas, and N very high in Australian aboriginals. The Rhesus (CDE) system is more complex still, with many variants. Again, the adaptive qualities of each in relation to disease is not known, and their distribution might reflect older disease patterns that have changed greatly in recent times.

The MNSs and Rhesus systems have variants peculiar to or especially frequent in Africa, to a degree that might suggest a long isolation of these populations from those of Europe or Asia. Similarly, the Duffy system with two antigens a and b also has a 'silent' allele (Fy¹), which is virtually restricted to Africa and gives some protection against the form of malaria caused by *Plasmodium vivax*. *Plasmodium falciparum*, which causes a more taxing malaria, is resisted by haemoglobin S, the haemoglobin sickling variant.

The Gm trait of blood serum consists of several antigens, which occur as sets of linked loci, inherited as groups or *haplotypes*. It shows sharper differences among major populations than do most red-cell systems, and may hence be more informative about their past distributions. The antigens on white blood cells resemble the Gm system in that they are complex linked blocks of genes, and also promise an insight into the long-term association of such linkage groups with particular populations.

All these systems are useful for microevolutionary studies. Sometimes they even show some correspondence with local linguistic change. For example, on the island of Bougainville in the Solomons, Melanesians speaking Papuan languages have MNS frequencies quite distinct from those of neighbouring tribes speaking Austronesian languages (whose frequencies resemble those of Austronesian speakers elsewhere in the Solomons). However, the same distinctions do not hold for New Guinea.

A further insight into patterns of relatedness emerges when blood systems are combined to give a compound measure of genetic distance. Europeans then appear to be closer to Africans, and Australoids to Mongoloids. However, most of the variation in blood groups is between individuals within populations and between small groups, not between the so-called 'races' of humankind. Such compound measures of affinity are particularly influenced by one or a few highly variable systems (such as Gm), so that newly discovered genes may not provide much new information.

Any attempt at an analysis of long-term population movements needs a starting-point, or root. This is not only hard to define but also presupposes the existence of one original population, and migration outwards from this single source. Evolutionary trees, however extensive the information on which they are based, are hence not in themselves able to distinguish between the two hypotheses for modern origins.

Genetic study at the molecular level is so laborious that it has not yet given much new insight into the differences among human populations. One attempt has been made, using the gene cluster of human β-haemoglobin. Using restriction enzymes to find cleavage sites detects the presence or absence of these sites and produces a series of closely linked genetic differences or haplotypes. Study of individuals from different regions suggest that Africans form one grouping and all non-Africans (including Melanesians, Polynesians and Asians) form another.

One application of molecular techniques may be particularly promising. This uses the DNA of the mitochondria, the sites of energy metabolism in the cytoplasm of cells. This extra-nuclear DNA (*mtDNA*) consists, in humans, of a loop of 16 500 base pairs, far less than the total chromosomal DNA. It is hence much easier to analyse in detail, and the complete sequence of mtDNA is known (see p. 320). This DNA is transmitted only in the maternal line, via the ovum, and is not subject to the shuffling of gene groups – recombination – found in the nucleus. Change takes place only through mutation, which takes place at a much higher rate than in nuclear DNA. Studies of mtDNA determine maternal lineages. These may be very ancient. They differ by virtue of substitutions at various restriction sites. One study based on 12 restriction enzymes revealed 196 polymorphic sites, many of which can distinguish among a number of different female lineages.

The largest number of different lineages occurs in Africa. By this hypothesis Africa seems to be the source of populations elsewhere in the world, with new lineages arising in the emergent population. Thus other regions of the world

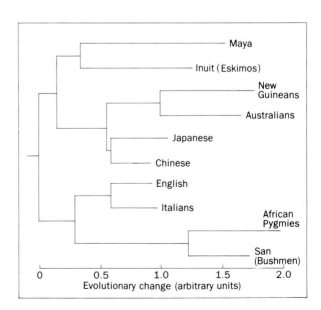

An evolutionary tree based on the frequencies of 58 different blood-group genes. Note the main east–west division among the 10 populations, with Europeans and Africans opposed at the highest level to Asians, Australo-Melanesians and native Americans.

have both 'African' and non-African lineages. Europe was colonised by populations having a large number of female lineages (albeit fewer than Africa), with Asia, Australia and New Guinea founded by successively smaller numbers of lineages. This pattern might arise because population bottlenecking has reduced the number of lineages. The assemblages of lineages in a particular place are not specially related, although one New Guinea cluster seems to have its closest relative in Asia, not Africa. In Asia, a deletion of a short section of the mtDNA is common to Chinese, Japanese and some Pacific peoples. It is also found in South America.

Rates of lineage divergence are about 2 to 4 per cent per million years, using the probable times of human colonisation for America and New Guinea as a reference point. If this clock is accurate, a common ancestor might then have existed in Africa at some time from 290 000 to 140 000 years ago. Humans may have migrated from Africa during this period, and because the oldest population cluster of types outside Africa with no African types is estimated to be 90 000 to 180 000 years old, this sets an approximate minimum age for the emergence of these people from Africa. MtDNA gives some fascinating hints about ancient migrations. However, in other animals, such as mice and fruit flies, patterns of distribution of mtDNA appear to give positively misleading clues about patterns of historical relatedness among populations. The mitochondrial case is as yet far from proven.

However, most molecular patterns do lean towards the hypothesis of dispersal of modern humans from one general area – Africa. They also imply that racial distribution is two-dimensional, with no important contributions to modern populations from ancient peoples, such as local survivors of *Homo erectus*. MtDNA mapping does seem to provide the possibility of long-range probes of the past. None of the lineages yet found is sufficiently divergent from others to suggest that it arose before the appearance of modern *Homo sapiens*.

Morphological patterns of relationship

Other information is also useful in studying historical relationships. Fingerprint and palmprint patterns in Pacific populations show a striking separation: Polynesians, Micronesians (both speakers of Austronesian languages), Melanesian Austronesian speakers and other Melanesians further divided by the Papuan language spoken can all be distinguished. This may reflect a history of subdivision and drift in these island populations. This pattern is much clearer than that which emerges from blood-group studies in the Pacific. The dispersion of these populations may have started 4000 years ago or more. Fingerprint analyses have not yet been carried out on continental populations, but the method might be valuable for studying problems such as the history of migrations among American Indians.

Other useful morphological characters include those of the skeleton. Cranial measurement had its beginning in the first half of the nineteenth century. A large amount of information soon became available, as skulls could be collected while living individuals could not. The only analysis was to use ratios indices to convey shape. The *cranial index* (breadth over length × 100) classed specimens as *dolichocranial* (long, with an index below 75), *mesocranial* and *brachycranial* (short, index over 80). Other ratios also proliferated: relative height of skull, height of face, breadth of nose, and so on. This approach was often used to produce a classification based on combinations of such categories. Populations of skulls were commonly subdivided into 'types', which were supposed to have entered into the population at its origin.

In spite of the vast amounts of information gathered, it soon proved impossible to make effective comparisons.or to produce population histories based on anything more than supposition. The Coefficient of Racial Likeness was an attempt by the English statistician Karl Pearson to compare skull series by combining a number of measurements. This was a first attempt to cumulate the information present into a whole, and it gave impetus to the collecting of sets of skulls. However, the method failed to take account of the

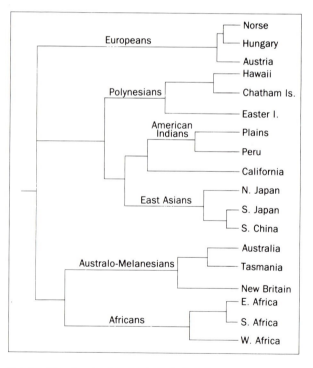

Relationships of modern humans from skull measurements.
A dendrogram (in no sense a 'family tree') computed from generalised distances based on multivariate analysis of 57 measurements on male crania. All 18 populations group themselves into regional 'racial' types. Australo-Melanesians are distantly connected with Africans. Polynesians, American Indians and East Asians form a major Mongoloid population cluster, which is distantly connected to Europeans, who appear quite isolated. When female skulls of the same populations are analysed in the same way, however, Polynesians are grouped primarily with Australo-Melanesians, and Africans are distantly connected with other Mongoloids and Europeans. In such analyses, different methods provide slightly different results.

correlation among measurements, and hence placed too much emphasis on difference in overall size.

Since Pearson's time, this problem has been overcome by computers and the development of *multivariate statistics*. These summarise measurements as a new set of transformed figures between which correlation is removed and which are more specific in meaning and importance ('discriminant functions' or principal components are usual forms). These help to relate populations to each other, and they also reveal a lot about the underlying differences in form.

Such techniques tend to gather populations of skulls into groups corresponding quite well with geography – that is, Africans, Europeans, Australo-Melanesians, Far East Asiatics, Polynesians and American Indians. Discrimination among these is mainly based on distinctions not fully revealed by the traditional measurements or ratios. Breadth of the cranium, particularly at the base, is a major factor, as is relatively anterior or posterior positioning of the face, especially at the sides of the facial mask. Such distinctions are most marked between Inuit or inner Asiatic Mongoloids such as Buriats of the Lake Baikal (Ozero Baykal) region on one hand, and Africans and Australo-Melanesians on the other.

Fine distinctions in the relative projection of the root of the nose and the eye orbit are also important. Mongoloids such as the Buriats have a relatively high face. Inuit of Greenland have very flat faces, with a flat nasal saddle. Polynesians, as exemplified by Hawaiians, have large and quite flat faces; they are distinguished by a particularly prominent upper nasal and facial region. American Indians and Europeans are not far from the global mean in any direction, although the Americans are somewhat closer to Hawaiians than to Europeans. American Indians have a flattish face, but the root of the nose and the space between the eyes is relatively high. Australians and Melanesians have narrow skulls and low faces, with a jutting tooth-bearing part, which, together with a protruding eyebrow ridge, dis-

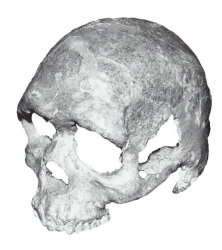

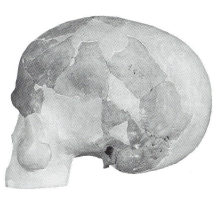

Supporters of the 'Out of Africa' model of human evolution contend that early modern people from the Israeli cave sites of Qafzeh (above) and Skhūl represent a population that spread from Africa around 100 000 years ago. The skull from Border Cave in southeastern South Africa (below), dated to around 80 000–90 000 years ago, might be a southern representative of such an ancestral population of modern *Homo sapiens*.

tinguishes them well from Africans. The African face is short but broadish across the eyes, and the skull is narrow. Though small-skulled, southern African San (Bushmen) share the main African characters. (The portrait photographs on pp. 390–1 and 434–5 show some of these distinguishing features.)

Such cranial analyses can also be used on prehistoric material. An analysis of 'size' and 'shape' distances based on the means of nine measurements on a large number of European skull series from the Mesolithic to Roman times shows a general homogeneity among groups from any given cultural complex, such as the Bell Beaker people in the third millennium BC. It also discerns two major cranial forms – long-skulled/broad-faced in the north and long-skulled/narrow-faced in the south. The latter form (sometimes referred to as Mediterranean) appears to have expanded at the expense of the former (the Cromagnonoid). These real differences in skull form do not coincide at all with the long-accepted typological 'races' in Europe – Nordic, Mediterranean and Alpine. Indeed, the last, traditionally seen as an invading physical group, disappears.

Such multivariate comparisons might also be used to

Early modern people occupied Skhūl Cave on the slopes of Mount Carmel, Israel, as much as 90 000 to 100 000 years ago.

2. GENES AND LANGUAGE

The first evolutionary tree was published 200 years ago by an English judge, William Jones. It was based not on genes, but on language. Using shared words and sentence structure he traced similarities between languages as different as English, Sanskrit and Persian. He inferred that they had diverged from a common ancestor, an extinct 'Indo-European' protolanguage, which contained the word for 'beech tree' but not for 'vine' or 'palm tree', suggesting that it originated in temperate climes.

A century later, Jacob Grimm — of fairy-tale fame — went further; he thought that language changed in a predictable way, with, for example, a tendency in English for hard consonants to become soft: the Latin *pater* has become 'father', and *tres* has changed to 'three'.

The rate of change of different languages may be about the same; comparisons of those whose history is known suggest that on the average two languages have 85 per cent of their features in common after 1000 years of separation, making it possible to work out the date when languages began to diverge by comparing their key features. Language is hence an 'evolutionary clock', which can date past events by comparing living entities. Some optimists believe that this clock can trace the history of human speech for tens of thousands of years.

Genetics is itself a language; a set of instructions passed from one generation to the next. It has a vocabulary, the genes themselves; a grammar, the means of translating genetic information into a coherent message; and a literature, the millions of inherited cues that make up every human being. The history of genes and of language can both be used to trace ancient migrations. There are some remarkable parallels between the two that suggest that they have common patterns of evolution.

Sometimes this pattern confirms what we already know. Pembrokeshire, in southwestern Wales, was settled by a group of English-speaking Flemings in the twelfth century. The boundary between the two peoples can be traced by the sharp switch in placenames from English (Haverfordwest) to Welsh names (Maenclochog). There are differences in the frequency of genes for blood groups between English and Welsh speakers in this region, which reflect their origin. Even without written records we could infer that the two populations must have had a separate history.

On the European scale, too, the mass movements of peoples with different languages are still manifest in their genes. Thousands of Europeans have been scored for blood groups, cell-surface variation and for inherited differences in the structure of proteins.

Superimposed on large-scale trends in

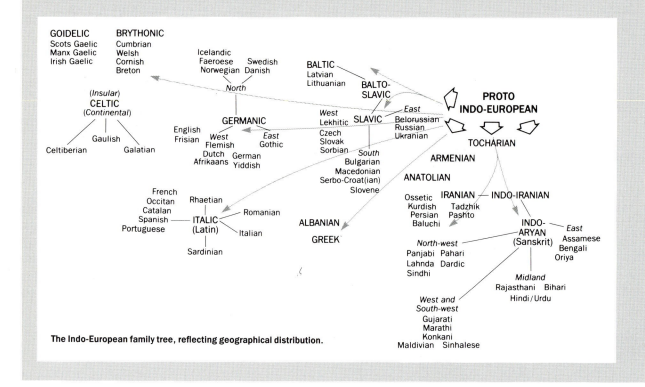

The Indo-European family tree, reflecting geographical distribution.

study much older specimens. Late Pleistocene skulls do in some cases approximate to their regional successors; examples are Mladeč l (for Europeans) and Keilor (for Australians). There are, however, difficulties in applying these techniques, which are only partly due to insufficient material. One is statistical. Another arises from the fact that there are slightly greater differences between ancient and modern peoples than appears to the eye. For example, specimens from Liujiang in southern China or Border Cave in South Africa (p. 397) have a prominent eyebrow ridge in an otherwise modern-appearing skull.

However, some findings do emerge from such comparisons. Although not many specimens are available, skulls that can readily be related to fully modern specimens do not extend far into the past; perhaps around 30 000 years. By contrast, existing populations are surprisingly close to one another. Neanderthal and other archaic specimens are certainly far removed from modern populations. These results appear to negate the explanation of regional continuity and evolutionary divergence. However, they are neutral in the matter of African origins for *Homo sapiens*.

Modern humans appeared in different parts of the world

the frequency of these genes from west to east, there are differences between people speaking different languages. Of the 33 sharp boundaries across Europe that separate genetically distinct peoples, 31 are boundaries between languages or dialects.

The Basques, who speak a distinctive language, are genetically quite different from their neighbours. Basque may even be a relic of the language spoken by the people who lived in Europe before agriculture spread from the eastern Mediterranean, bringing with it the language that developed into the modern Indo-European tongues.

Most of these differences reflect the mass movement of peoples during the early history of Europe. Language has acted as a barrier to mating and the exchange of genes for hundreds of years. In some parts of the world, patterns of genes and language are the only record of such ancient migrations. The peoples of the New World are genetically quite similar to those in the Far East, and probably migrated across the Bering Strait within the past 20 000 or 30 000 years or so.

Some linguists claim that nearly all the 2000 or so languages spoken in the Americas before the arrival of Columbus belong to a single language family, which may itself be traceable to an ancestral Asiatic tongue. In North America, the greatest diversity of language is in those areas that escaped glaciation during the last Ice Age some 15 000 years ago. At the end of this glaciation, the regions once covered with ice were invaded by peoples speaking one of a few languages. In South America, there is still a fit between the geographical patterns of language and those of genes.

Unlike genes, language can be transmitted by learning. 'Horizontal' transmission of this kind can obscure any relation between genetic and linguistic history. In the Pacific, for example, there is a sharp genetic change near Fiji in spite of a smooth gradient in language.

The rapid spread of languages such as English in the last century or so will no doubt destroy many rare and ancient tongues, and further confuse the relation between genes and speech. Remarkably enough, however, there remains a shared worldwide pattern of the two systems of communication.

A worldwide tree of genetic affinity based on blood groups, enzymes and other genes shows that the human species is divided into two main groups, one within Africa and the other filling the rest of the world. Other patterns also emerge, such as the relationship between the peoples of the New World and those of Asia, and the lack of any genetic link between Polynesians and South Americans (see Box 1). Linguists have tried to draw similar trees showing the relationships between the world's languages.

As language changes more rapidly than genes and can spread by learning, this has not been easy and many of the branches on the tree are still controversial. However, there seems to be some fit between the family tree of human languages and that of our genes, which suggest that they share a common history. For example, the ancient genetic split between Africans and non-Africans fits well with the distinctiveness and diversity of sub-Saharan languages, especially those in West Africa.

The similarities between the two trees suggest that they may share a common root, and that the origin of languages might even trace back to the origin of modern humans. Indeed, language may have been the catalyst that led to the rapid spread of modern humans throughout the world. The plight of the deaf and dumb in modern societies shows how difficult it may have been for less-effective Neanderthal speakers — if so they were — to cope with an invasion of a competitor armed with such a potent behavioural weapon as speech.

Steve Jones

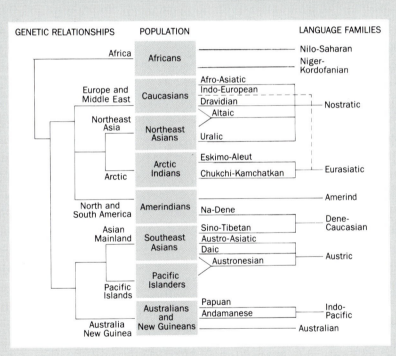

Trees of relatedness for genes and languages. The left portion shows the patterns of genetic relationships among the world's populations; the right, patterns of linguistic similarity. There is a general correspondence between the two trees.

at widely differing times. In Africa and Southwest Asia, they were early. They may have been excluded from Europe, constrained by the presence of Neanderthals, as they appeared there only about 38 000 years ago when they had already reached Australia and a few Melanesian islands. The Far East is difficult to assess. The Liujiang skull, however, is believed to have a date of 67 000 years. The remains from Zhoukoudian (Upper Cave) are 20 000 to 30 000 years old. Although modern, their shape suggests that they are not antecedent to today's Chinese, and their affiliation is not clear.

The New World does not help us with the emergence of modern populations generally, because the first Americans arrived so recently. There is considerable variation in physical and cranial form among the indigenous American populations, which might result from differences among arriving migrant groups. It might also arise from local micro-evolution and the founder effect. On the other hand, some features are shared by all New World populations, which distinguishes them within the general Mongoloid group.

There are two views of the arrival of the first Americans. One, involving linguistic and genetic evidence (Box 2), envisages three main migrations: Paleoindian (the earliest and

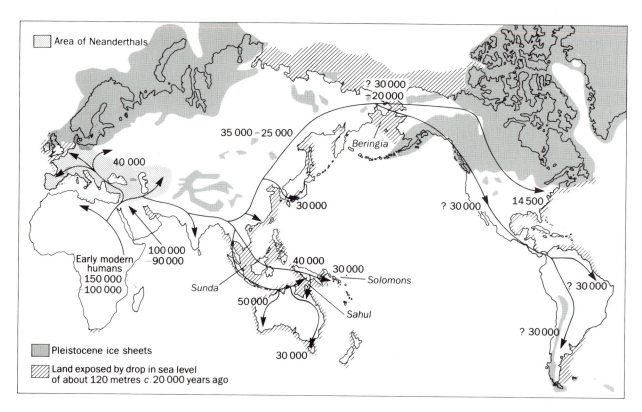

Area of Neanderthals

? 30 000
-20 000

35 000 - 25 000

Beringia

40 000

30 000

100 000
-90 000

? 30 000

14 500

Early modern
humans
150 000
100 000

40 000

30 000

Solomons

Sunda

? 30 000

50 000

Sahul

? 30 000

30 000

Pleistocene ice sheets

Land exposed by drop in sea level
of about 120 metres *c*. 20 000 years ago

Possible dispersal routes of modern *Homo sapiens*, assuming an early appearance of modern humans in Africa 150 000 to 100 000 years ago and a migration out of Africa to the Middle East. Movements into the Far East and the Indonesian areas are suggested, although so far these are speculation. During this dispersal, the northwestern Old World was occupied by Neanderthals, and there were land bridges in Southeast Asia (Sunda), Australasia (Sahul) and the Bering Strait area (Beringia). It is uncertain when the New World was first colonised; it could have been as early as 30 000 years ago – as sites such as Pedra Furada in Brazil and Monte Verde in Chile suggest – or only about 15 000 years ago. The land bridges were not as wide throughout the late Pleistocene as shown here. As the temperature rose and fell, so did the level of the sea. The deepest drop of 120 metres below modern sea levels, exposing the land shown on the map, occurred at the peak of the ice age around 20 000 years ago. At other times, the drop averaged only 40–60 metres.

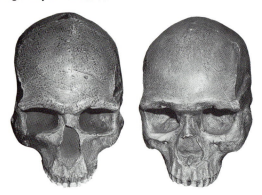

Skulls of early modern *Homo sapiens* from (left) Předmostí, Czechoslovakia, dated to about 26 000 years ago, and (right) the Upper Cave at Zhoukoudian, near Beijing, dated between 20 000 and 30 000 years ago. The Zhoukoudian people could either be descended from Chinese populations of *Homo erectus* (the multiregional continuity model) or they represent the descendants of a population of modern humans who left their ancestral home in Africa within the past 100 000 years or so (the replacement or 'Out of Africa' model). Similarly, the ancestors of modern Europeans (represented by Předmostí) either were Neanderthals (multiregional continuity model) or, more likely, also shared an African ancestor with the Zhoukoudian people.

the one responsible for most of the variation); Na-Dene (now centred on northwestern North America); and Eskimo-Eleut. The migrating populations are supposed to have originated in three areas of northeastern Asia: the north coast, the interior and the Pacific littoral, respectively. The second hypothesis proposes a first movement, at perhaps 20 000 years ago, which penetrated south via a corridor between the existing ice sheets, and a second that was held up until the icecaps melted and which gave rise to northern tribes and Inuit.

A problem in all this is the poverty of archaeological evidence before about 12 000 years ago. A few cave sites in North and South America, such as Pedra Furada in Brazil, are believed by some workers to give such evidence. But not all are persuaded; in spite of much research, there are no signs of widespread occupation of the Americas during the late Pleistocene, or of coherent cultural patterns like those evident in Europe and Australia.

Australasia is another matter. Although there were considerable expanses of water along the migration route, people were occupying Australia and New Guinea (then joined by a land bridge) at least 50 000 years ago. Aboriginal populations of recent times show little variation: North Australians are perhaps closer to Melanesians than are others, and the Tasmanians (now extinct) also differed slightly from other Australian populations. There was greater variation at many times before 6000 years ago, to the extent that the specimens are often divided into 'robust' and 'gracile' groups. To the former belong the more heavily built skulls from Kow Swamp, Lake Nitchie and Willandra Lakes. In the latter group are the less-robust specimens

3. FOSSIL DNA

Fossil bones gave the first direct proof that humans are related to primates; and in the past few years fossil DNA has opened the possibility that we may soon be able to look directly at the genes of our ancestors. A few gene products have already been examined in this way. Egyptian mummies retain blood-group antigens, and this has allowed the relationships of some family groups to be sorted out. Comparisons of different hair forms known to be under genetic control show that a previously unidentified mummy was probably the mother of the heretic pharoah Akhenaton.

In the mid-1980s it transpired that some mummies — dried by wind or sand or frozen, rather than chemically preserved — retain large amounts of DNA. As such mummies are found all over the world, and not just in Egypt, this gives the prospect at least of sorting out patterns of ancient relatedness or even of migrations of long ago. DNA has also been found in human bones from Greenland (although these were only about 500 years old) and, recently, in a 10 000-year old skull from Kow Swamp in Australia.

Most of the fossil DNA found so far consists only of repeated sequences of non-functional DNA (the *Alu* sequences, which make up a large part of all human genomes and are widespread in other primates), so it is not very useful.

However, there has been one remarkable finding of DNA in a series of 8000-year-old brains of North American Indians found in a Florida swamp. Although much of the genetic material has been broken down, it was possible to extract segments of the mitochondrial DNA. This shows similarities to that of modern native Americans and also to that of Asiatics, confirming the generally accepted view that humans entered the New World across the Bering Strait land bridge. The Kow Swamp skull also contains mitochondrial DNA.

Fragments of DNA coding for parts of the immune system have also been found in human remains, opening up the possibility of fusing molecular palaeontology and the evolutionary genetics of antigens and antibodies.   *Steve Jones*

from Lake Mungo and Keilor. Migrations from different regions have been postulated to explain these differences, as has input from a Southeast Asian *Homo erectus* population.

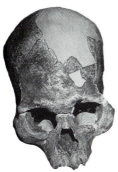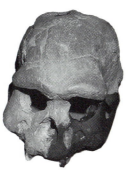

Archaeological dates suggest that Australia was first peopled around 50 000 years ago. The continent thus contains the oldest-known evidence of modern humanity outside Africa and the eastern Mediterranean. But there are arguments about the origin of the fossil humans found there. Proponents of the multiregional continuity model of human evolution argue that the heavily built skull (left) from Kow Swamp (perhaps about 10 000 years old) represents a population that evolved from *Homo erectus* in Java (e.g. Sangiran 17; right). An alternative theory is that the Kow Swamp hominids and more lightly built forms represented by material from Lake Mungo (about 30 000 years old) are a broad grouping of early modern people that derived originally from Africa, with little or no gene flow from Asian *Homo erectus*.

However, the morphological diversity within early Australians was merely variation on only one fundamentally similar form, as Melanesian and Australian populations form a broad grouping, which craniometry distinguishes from those of other Asian regions.

Although the earliest skeletal remains (Lake Mungo) are about 30 000 years old, the continuous archaeological record in Australia may go back at least as far as 50 000 years ago. As there was probably only one general avenue of entry to the continent, and as there are no signs (in spite of the robusticity of such specimens as Kow Swamp) of evolution from *Homo erectus* within it, Australia probably contains the earliest evidence of fully modern humanity outside Africa and the Near East. The implications of this for the theory of the spread of modern humans from Africa to the east remain uncertain.   *W.W. Howells*

See also 'The nature of evolution' (p. 9), 'Human adaptations to the physical environment' (p. 46), 'Evolution of early humans' (p. 241), 'Genetic diversity in humans' (p. 264), 'Bottlenecks in human evolution' (p. 281), 'Natural selection in humans' (p. 284), 'Was Eve an African?' (p. 320) and 'Tools — the Palaeolithic record' (p. 350)

Reconstructing ancient populations

Palaeodemography is concerned with the study of the human population before the opening of recorded history. For most of this Old Stone Age or Palaeolithic period, our ancestors depended on hunting, gathering and, more recently, fishing for survival. Measures of world population size on the eve of the transition to agriculture, some 12 000 to 10 000 years ago, come from estimates of the maximum population density that this way of life could sustain. These generally range from 5 to 10 million people, and the highest figure – calculated on the assumption that the world was 'saturated' with hunter-gatherers – is only 15 million.

All this implies very low rates of population growth – some 0.02 per cent a year, or even less. In the period 8000 BC to AD 1, by contrast, world population probably grew at an annual rate of at least 0.05 per cent, with substantially higher rates in areas of intensive cultivation. The Palaeolithic was thus a time of long-term demographic equilibrium, which gave way to a relatively rapid population expansion with the spread of agriculture. The central goal of palaeodemographic enquiry is to explain this lengthy equlibrium and the subsequent growth.

Palaeodemographers pursue this goal in three main ways: by studying archaelogical remains, by observing present-day hunter-gatherers and by constructing models, which range in complexity from rough ecological or demographic analogies to sophisticated computer simulations. The main archaeological remains left behind by Palaeolithic peoples are those of the people themselves: their skeletons. These can tell us their sex, and, within broad limits, their age. Skeletons may also reveal evidence of diseases such as tuberculosis or syphilis, and of malnutrition. Marks left on the pubic bones by the trauma of childbirth might even allow the estimation of the number of children born to a woman in her lifetime, but this claim is not universally accepted.

It is in theory possible to estimate the patterns of longevity in a population from such samples and several studies have been undertaken. However, they face severe practical difficulties. Samples of remains obtained from funerary sites generally under-represent infants and children, making it difficult to estimate mortality in these groups, and the calculations involve an estimate of the growth of the population concerned and an assumption that there was no migration.

Observations of present-day populations avoid these pitfalls, and groups such as the !Kung San (Bushmen) of the Kalahari Desert in southwestern Africa have been the object of intensive demographic study. But it is hazardous to apply present-day findings to the Palaeolithic. Contemporary hunter-gatherers are all in contact with agricultural, or even industrial, societies, and their very survival as hunters and gatherers in the twentieth century makes them unusual. Furthermore, present-day hunter-gatherers are mostly confined to marginal environments (such as deserts or subarctic tundras) rather than the more hospitable areas, which were home to most of our Palaeolithic ancestors. Both types of information thus have their strengths and weaknesses, and the construction of acceptable models of palaeodemography requires the use of each of them.

Population size

A central question for palaeodemographic research is that of population density and the factors that govern it. The population density of modern hunter-gatherers varies between about 0.1 and one person per square kilometre, with substantially higher levels in some areas of exceptionally rich resources. Factors affecting population density are complex and include both ecological and social variables.

An important consideration is the *resource potential* of the environment. This depends on both the resources available and their distribution pattern. The dense, aggregated and easily available resources that characterise some coasts and river banks, for instance, permit much higher densities

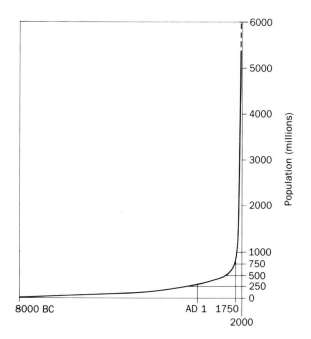

Before the advent of animal and plant domestication, the growth rate of the world's population was only 0.02 per cent a year, or even less. Between 8000 BC and AD 1, however, the rate increased to at least 0.05 per cent. A challenge of palaeodemography is to explain this long period of population stability before the spread of agriculture and the rapid population growth afterwards.

Human populations have been shaped for most of their existence by a hunting and gathering way of life. The Pygmies in the Ituri Forest, northeastern Zaire, still hunt and gather in the equatorial rain forest but also barter for cultivated food from Bantu village agriculturalists. Here, men of the Efe group of Ituri Pygmies eat a honeycomb that they have knocked down from a tree.

than do the sparse and dispersed patterns found in deserts such as the Kalahari. But more subtle factors can also limit population density and the shortage of a single key nutrient, or a high degree of seasonal variation in the availability of resources, may give a false impression of overall abundance.

Factors concerned with the extraction of resources from the environment are also important. These include both the nature of the 'strategies' adopted and their efficiency. Observers of the hunter-gatherer way of life have often been struck by the relatively brief time spent during some seasons in procuring food and the abundance of leisure; but the efficiency of hunting and gathering, in terms of energy expended relative to that obtained, is often low compared with that of cultivation and it may be that their activities are limited by the energy cost of additional food-gathering.

Food is required not only for subsistence but also for feasting and gift exchange, which may play an important part in the social life of hunter-gatherers. This is based around local groups known as *bands* that may have up to 50 members but average around 25. Average band size varies little between hunter-gatherer populations. Differences in population density are reflected more in the numbers of bands occupying a given area. Band size reflects the optimum number for an egalitarian group that is based on face-to-face interaction.

Modern hunter-gatherer bands have considerable fluidity in their composition, and may exchange members or split to form new bands. Local bands form part of larger regional populations whose size is more variable, averaging around 500, and whose members generally come together

for brief periods for hunting or for ritual. Archaeological and indirect evidence both suggest that the exchange of marriage partners between Palaeolithic bands led to the formation of widespread 'mating networks' that linked bands over large areas. Towards the end of the Palaeolithic these appear to have become more restricted, a phenomenon probably linked to the growth of population and to the emergence of local ethnic identity.

Mortality

The disruption of demographic equilibrium at the end of the Palaeolithic evidently came about through an increase in fertility, a decline in mortality, or some combination of the two. Many models of 'progressive' social evolution assume that mortality fell as populations were freed from the constraints of the primitive hunting and gatherering way of life. This interpretation has recently been questioned, and it now seems unlikely that mortality was substantially lower among early agriculturalists than among hunter-gatherers. It may even have been higher.

Estimates of life expectation among modern hunter-gatherers, or inferences from skeletal remains, are uncertain guides to the mortality levels that prevailed in the Palaeolithic. Nonetheless, some useful palaeodemographic information can be gleaned from prehistoric cemeteries. In other circumstances, it can be more fruitful to proceed indirectly and to consider the factors responsible for high mortality during recorded history: infectious disease, famine and warfare.

- *Infectious diseases.* Diseases, the most important mortality factor in history, are unlikely to have been more severe before the transition to agriculture than subsequently, because population densities were too low for the major killing infections to persist. Slow-acting infections (such as tuberculosis) or those capable of remaining indefinitely in the body (such as the chickenpox virus) may, however, have afflicted Palaeolithic peoples. Parasitic diseases such as schistosomiasis (bilharziasis) are also likely to have been important in the tropics, but the overall mortality from infectious dieseases was probably considerably lower among hunter-gatherers than among the more densely settled cultivators.
- *Famine.* Cultivators are also likely to have suffered more from recurrent food shortages. Hunter-gatherers exploit a varied ecosystem, which is naturally buffered against climatic fluctuations or outbreaks of plant disease. They are hence less vulnerable to these factors than agriculturalists who rely on a much smaller number of species maintained at artifically high densities. It is also far easier for hunter-gatherers to move out of an area of local shortage than it is for cultivators who must thereby abandon their rights to the land and its crops.

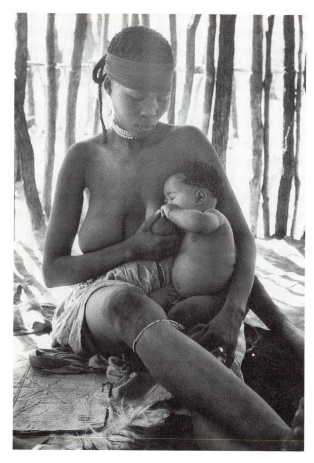

A nursing !Kung San woman. Prolonged breastfeeding helps to reduce the fertility of many traditional populations.

• *Warfare*. Interpersonal violence, together with accidental violent deaths during hunting, may have been more common among hunter-gatherers than among agriculturalists, but the former lack the social and political organisation for sustained, large-scale, hostilities. The high mortality that accompanied historical wars, moreover, arose more from the spread of epidemics and the distruction of crops than from fighting itself, and was probably absent from the Palaeolithic world.

Fertility

If mortality was little higher before the transition to agriculture than subsequently, then it follows that fertility must have been lower to maintain a steady population size. Studies of modern hunter-gatherers have found evidence of low fertility levels. Among the !Kung Bushmen of the Kalahari, for instance, the average interval between successive births is about 4 years, twice that in parts of pre-industrial Europe and substantially longer than those experienced by peasant populations in the contemporary Third World.

The nomadic life of !Kung women makes it difficult for them to afford more frequent births, but the means by which their low fertility is attained are far from clear. One possible explanation relies on nutrition. It has been claimed that a minimal level of body fat is required for successful ovulation and that the balance between energy

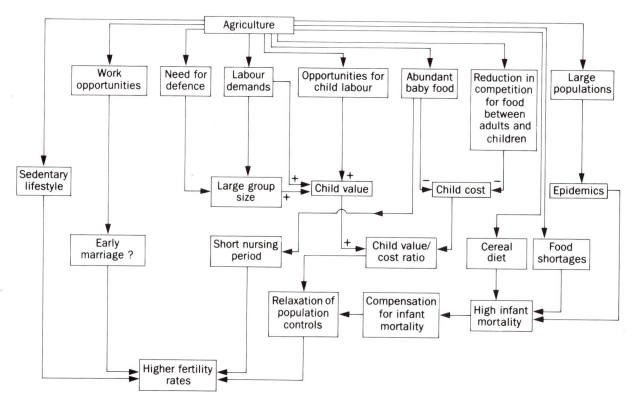

A model of the impact of agriculture on the factors responsible for fertility.

intake and expenditure among hunter-gatherer women is so precarious that a lengthy period must elapse before ovulation is resumed following childbirth and lactation.

Studies of Third World peasant populations, however, have failed to find evidence of a strong link between fatness and fertility. It may be that body fat levels among such women never fall as low as they do among the !Kung, but a more widely favoured explanation is that the latter's prolonged lactation suppresses ovulation for extended periods after birth. An additional possibility is that, despite their own claims to the contrary, the low fertility of the !Kung stems in part from contraception or abortion.

Agriculture and population growth

The close association between population growth and the spread of agriculture leaves little doubt that the two developments were related, but which came first and what initiated the process are controversial.

One appealing explanation invokes the climatic changes and rise in sea levels that accompanied the end of the Pleistocene. These events may have produced coastlines rich in resources, which encouraged hunter-gatherer populations to become sedentary, resulting in increased fertility and population density. Such population pressures may, in turn, have led to the establishment in the hinterland of settlements whose members, too numerous to support themselves by hunting and gathering, were forced to rely on cultivation for their subsistence.

An alternative explanation suggests that the demographic equilibrium of the Palaeolithic was imperfect, so that world population eventually grew beyond the point at which hunting and gathering were viable means of subsistence. This theory, however, has itself been criticised for failing to explain why late Pleistocene hunter-gatherers should have responded to population pressure by taking the arduous course of turning to agriculture rather than by a marginal reduction in fertility.

A contrasting view has it that the reliance on cultivation arose from an increase in the demand for foodstuffs on the emergence of the social hierarchy that resulted from the growth of alliances between local bands and the consequent feasting and ritual exchanges. This explanation has the support of social anthropological theory and of some archaeological evidence. But it is difficult, on this basis, to see why the transition to agriculture should have been so long delayed, and the origin of humanity's first 'population explosion' remains an enigma.   *J. Landers*

See *also* 'Studying human evolution by analogy' (p. 335), 'Reconstructing prehistoric diet' (p. 369), 'Origins of agriculture' (p. 373), 'Human populations before agriculture' (p. 406), 'People and disease' (p. 411) and 'Fertility control: past, present and future' (p. 425)

Human populations before agriculture

Demography is central to an understanding of human evolution, because its most important elements – fertility and mortality – are the fundamental aspects of evolution itself. Individuals do not evolve. Rather, they are born; they may live long enough to reproduce, and their reproductive efforts may exceed or fall short of the species' average. If such variation in mortality and fertility is both heritable and influences fitness, the adaptation of the population will change with time.

A study of human vital history is also important to our understanding of the biology of hunter-gatherer, agricultural and industrialised people. Human populations can be characterised not only by the way they use resources and by their social organisation, but also by their demographic structure. This includes colonisation and migration, growth rates, and the capacity to deal with forces that might cause oscillations in the numbers of births and deaths. Among the greatest threats to modern society is the current population dilemma, which, even with immediate action, will not be solved in all parts of the world for at least another century. It is clear that such control depends on a thorough understanding of the forces of human demographic evolution, especially those that have characterised most of our species' existence. This chapter examines the demographic profiles of humans before the agricultural revolution.

Palaeodemographic information

There is little demographic information for early hominids living in Plio-Pleistocene times. South African australopithecine remains are biased in favour of the very young and the old. This is unlikely to reflect the age structure of the living population unless it is assumed that the primary cause of death during this period of hominid evolution was predation by large carnivores. *Homo erectus* fossils from China and from Java certainly indicate a low life expectancy, although some of the adults may have attained extreme age. Patterns of Neanderthal life expectancy are similar: half died by the age of 20, and very few ever survived into the fourth decade.

These assumptions are based on skeletal remains that probably inadequately represent what were once the living populations. Also, because the rates of bony maturation for these populations are not known, age determinations based on them are very approximate. The mobility and low population densities of Pleistocene hunter-gatherers also mean that there are no cemeteries from which we can estimate early levels of human life expectancy. Two possible exceptions are the cave sites with a date of around 10 000 years ago at Taforalt and Afalou-bou-Rhummel on the north coast of Africa. The best estimates for life expectancy of Pleistocene humans based on this limited skeletal evidence is well under 25 years.

We can also examine living groups that may have a demographic structures analogous to that of early humans. Some caution is, of course, necessary before making this kind of inference. First, modern nomadic societies are represented by relatively small tribes, made up of even smaller basic units – bands or even nuclear families. Attempts can be made to estimate the age-specific life events that have produced a certain population structure, but the small size of the census precludes any hope of actuarial precision. Ethnographers witness few deaths, even though their observations may cover many years.

In such surveys, fertility rates must often be reconstructed from the memories of women who have completed their reproduction. Such women may fail to report the birth of children who died in infancy, they may conceal infanticides, adult ages or even names and kinship, or they may choose not to co-operate altogether. Corroboration from other sources is, by the nature of the societies, limited. Any inaccuracies based on the recall of births and deaths (which may be remembered mainly in relation to important past occurences such as famines, raids, rites of passage or other events) will be magnified in a pre-literate society. Such people seem not to be greatly concerned with counting events or the measurement of long periods of time – or telling the truth to intrusive anthropologists. In addition, many of the few remaining traditional cultures are now

The human species today is unique in having a prolonged old age after parenting has ceased. Although frail and deaf, eighty-year-old Tepaona continued to construct and repair canoes, fish, and serve as an expert in traditional ritual activity on Nukumanu Atoll, Papua New Guinea.

confined to environments that have poor and unpredictable resources, such as the Kalahari Desert of Namibia and Botswana. The value of their demographies in modelling our past is thus diminished by the reduction in population density brought about by such habitats.

Aboriginal demographic patterns have also been altered by contact with modern cultures. European diseases have been introduced and there has been emigration. Even the means of subsistence have been affected. These factors have had a great impact on many hunter-gatherers. For instance, the traditional cultures of Arctic peoples and of societies like the Shoshoni of the arid Great Basin of North America have largely disappeared. Three decades ago, there were only a few hundred Aborigines in the central desert of Australia out of contact with whites; there are none today. Anthropological studies of the San people (Bushmen) in the Kalahari Desert show that there has been considerable interaction with Bantu populations. Furthermore, archaeological evidence shows that San of the Dobe area were in close contact with Iron Age herders for more than a thousand years. Thus, claims that this group is ecologically and demographically close to a stone-age society should be treated with caution.

Several native South American tribes and undisplaced Pygmies of the Congo Basin may still be exceptions to this general tragedy. Medical and anthropological surveys show them to be healthy and resilient to many aspects of outside interference that might affect their demographic rates or population composition. Such stability is ephemeral, as these few remaining cultures of complex ecosystems will soon disappear, along with their climax tropical rain forests. At present, however, studies of modern isolated Amazonian populations that are sedentary and minimally agricultural can still provide indirect demographic data for the hunter-gatherer stage of human evolution. For direct demographic information we must turn to the skeletal remains of pre-agriculturalists. As true nomadic hunter-gatherers left no cemeteries, the closest approximations are provided by the skeletons of semi-sedentary intensive gatherers.

Such palaeodemographic information presents its own problems, as it largely depends on the age distributions of the people buried in the prehistoric cemeteries. These can supply useful estimates of mortality, but only when important assumptions hold: there must have been minimal differential burial and recovery by age or by sex; the intrinsic growth rate of the population using the cemetery was close to zero; and standards for ageing the dead from skeletal development and degeneration are without bias. The first two assumptions are difficult to verify but may be true in many instances. The last one is a subject of debate among anthropologists, some of whom argue that the age of adult skeletons is often underestimated, which produces a downward bias in the estimates of longevity in prehistoric populations.

Hunter-gatherer life expectancy and fertility

Some 10 000 years ago, small, semi-nomadic communities inhabited the northwestern coast of Africa. Anthropologists in the 1950s described them as 'Epipalaeolithic' on the basis of their small, geometric tools. These stone-age North Africans had a hunting, fishing and gathering economy akin to the Mesolithic of Europe. Today, the environments of Morocco and Algeria are largely desiccated, but were rich and varied 10 000 years ago. Shellfish were gathered from tidal flats along the Mediterranean. Rock carvings illustrate a hunting technology and suggest at least a partial reliance on game animals.

What is remarkable about these people is that they returned their dead to specific cave cemeteries. Two such sites have been studied by archaeologists. The Moroccan cave at Taforalt had skeletons of nearly 200 individuals of all ages. Along the coast in Algeria and as old as Taforalt, the cavernous Afalou-bou-Rhummel produced some 50 adult skeletons. First described in 1934, the Afalou assemblage lacks infants and adolescents. The burials at Taforalt, with supplementary information from a smaller cemetery, have produced an estimate of a pre-Neolithic life table. The pattern of life expectancy is termed the *Maghreb* type, after the peninsula in which the cave cemeteries were discovered.

The Carlston-Annis shell midden represents a late Archaic habitation and cemetery in the woodlands of Kentucky, eastern USA. Radiocarbon dates ranging from 4000 to 2500 BC suggest a long period of use. Plant and animal remains indicate that the site was occupied only in late summer and autumn and that the people who camped there ate nuts, acorns, waterfowl, deer and especially shellfish. The deep shell midden produced nearly 400 articulated burials, which were aged on the basis of the pelvic bones, cranial sutures, tooth wear and other bony indicators. The survivorship profile assumes unbiased sampling from a population with constant birth and death dates and no growth or decline in numbers during the period in which the cemetery was in use.

A third population, at Libben on the Portage River in Ohio, dates from about AD 750 to 1000. These people were completely sedentary, yet were clearly hunter-gatherers. The abundant refuse pits reveal an environment that provided a year-round diet rich in animal protein, especially fish, small mammals and migratory birds. The site contains evidence of reliance on a trap and weir economy, perhaps a dozen generations of habitation, and a cemetery of well over a thousand individuals – possibly the largest and best preserved in North America. The village probably comprised fewer than 100 inhabitants at a time. In the same manner as for the Carlston-Annis cemetery, a survivorship profile was produced, using a multifactorial approach to the ageing of the adult skeletons.

The Yanomami Indians of southern Venezuela had experienced very little contact with civilisation when surveyed during the 1960s. Today, they remain hunter-gatherers who rely on minimal horticulture and live in over 150 small semipermanent villages, many of which had still not been contacted at the time of the survey. Few stable villages contain more than 200 inhabitants, and all the villages are well isolated from each other, being separated by about a full day's walk through the jungle. The age-specific mortality rates of the Yanomami are based on a careful census of 29 such villages in the 1960s.

Although the relative contributions of childhood and adult mortality to this pattern differ somewhat across the four populations, they are quite similar in average survivorship. Mean life expectation for each of the three extinct populations was between about 20 and 22 years, a remarkable similiarity for populations so diverse in time and space. Average longevity for the Yanomami is also similar.

On the other hand, these survivorship curves are very different from that of a modern industrialised population with a life expectancy at birth of 70 years. Hunter-gatherer infant mortality was about one in four, which is about the same level as that observed in large industrial cities of the nineteenth century before the advent of water treatment and effective medical intervention for childhood diseases. Although the same is true of Yanomami newborn males, the loss of female infants is more than one in three because of infanticide. By contrast, modern industrialised populations suffer infant mortality rates of less than 1 in 40.

During the next four years of childhood the traditional societies lose at least another 10 per cent of their number, and perhaps much more. In the USA, in 1960, this 4-year child mortality rate was about 1 in 200. Of those who reach 5 years of age in the hunter-gatherer populations, only three-quarters would enter the reproductive period and perhaps a third would complete it.

What are the implications of these levels of mortality in the hunter-gatherer populations, which are much greater than those recorded for any contemporary or historical population? Most important is the extremely 'bottom-heavy' hunter-gatherer age pyramid. Nearly 20 per cent of the Yanomami population is less than 5 years old, and the median age is close to 20. Even modern Third World countries (some of which display extremely squat age pyramids because of large intrinsic growth rates) do not approach these extremes. The palaeodemographic data imply that the villages were rather like modern child day-care centres, and that there was only about one productive adult for each dependant. Expanding populations such as the Yanomami must provide for an even greater proportion of dependants.

By contrast, there are three adults for every two non-producers (under 15 and over 50 years of age) among the !Kung San. This may explain why archaeological remains of hunter-gatherers before European contact are confined to the richest of palaeoenvironments. The relentless forces of mortality at every age assured that only a small proportion

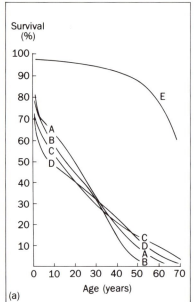

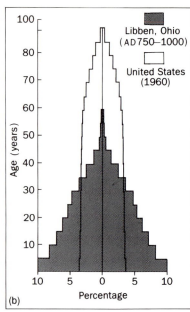

(a) Survival patterns in three extinct and one modern hunter-gatherer populations: A, Carlston-Annis, Kentucky, USA (4000–2500 BC); B, Libben, Ohio, USA (AD 750–1000); C, Yanomami, males only; and D, 'Maghreb' – Afalou-bou-Rhummel and Taforalt, North Africa (10 000 years ago). Curve E shows the survival profile of a modern post-industrial population, the USA in 1960. The average life expectancy of the recent US population of nearly 70 years contrasts sharply with the values for the other populations (A, 22.4 years; B, 19.9 years; C, 21.5 years; D, 21.1 years).

(b) Age-pyramids for a hunter-gatherer population (Libben, AD 750–1000) and a modern industrial population (the US, in 1960). The short and broad Libben pyramid, based on an estimated average census, suggests an age structure, a dependency ratio and a pattern of relationships between the generations quite different from those of today.

of a hunter-gatherer society was 'elderly' in our sense of the word. The Libben and Carlston-Annis profiles of prehistoric North America also imply a system of kinship that effectively extended over only two generations. Any 20-year-old was likely to have only a single surviving parent. Any newborn with two or more surviving grandparents was quite the exception.

Fertility must have been high to balance the annual death toll, and age distributions show that an average of seven children must have been born to each of those few women in the traditional societies who reached the menopause. Indeed, the total fertility rate for the Yanomami is over eight. (These people benefit from somewhat lower adult mortality and are currently increasing at a rate of about 1 per cent a year.) Thus, the vital history of our species is curious: fertility rates have usually been near the biological maximum but longevity rates have not.

Fertility rates even greater than that of such hunter-gatherer groups existed in the populations of French- and English-speaking New World colonials of the eighteenth century, and especially in the twentieth-century Hutterites of northwestern USA and Canada. These are the most fecund people yet observed with completed families total-

A Yanomami family group collects bananas to take back to their village in the Amazon forest.

ling more than 10 children. Hutterite fertility is a product of both unlimited nutrition and a desire for large families, conditions that rarely persisted in primitive societies. Periods of food shortage in poor environments and a regime of natural breastfeeding both supress ovulation, and lactating women return to their normal ovulatory cycles only after many months. This effect is not by itself strong enough to end population growth in a modern developing country, but it may have been sufficient to hold primitive completed fertilities well below that of the Hutterites. Even a total fertility rate equivalent to that of the Yanomami, which might be regarded as 'natural fertility', is probably greater than that typical of most hunter-gatherers.

Uninterrupted reproduction is not at all desirable to nomadic hunter-gatherers. !Kung women, for example, space their births almost 4 years apart, as they find it difficult to care for and carry more than a single young child at one time. Even the sedentary Yanomami limit the sizes of their families, as 5 to 10 per cent of all Yanomami pregnancies are purposely aborted. In addition, perhaps a quarter of all Yanomami live births become victims of infanticide. Since nearly all of these are females – who largely determine the subsequent generation's growth capacity – it is astonishing that the Yanomami population is increasing at all. This is the most important demographic lesson to be learned from modern hunter-gatherers: despite their very high mortality, births can easily outnumber deaths, and there is

always a margin of potential fertility above that required to maintain the size of the population. Net reproductive rates can exceed the replacement level within a generation, permitting a prompt return to previous densities after a population decline or the colonisation of a new area.

Cause of death in ancient populations

Demographic anthropology's most important question is: 'What killed in primitive populations?' Although there are no obvious culprits, infectious disease is the primary suspect. Compared with agricultural populations, hunter-gatherers were more isolated and lived in smaller groups. Infectious diseases that give survivors long-lasting immunity could never have become endemic in such situations. Among the small and dispersed villages of the native cultures of South America, such as the Yanomami, some infectious pathogens cannot survive very long, but must be reintroduced. When antibodies to measles, mumps, rubella, influenza or polio viruses are measured, a high incidence in some villages is found, but only in those older than a certain age. Children born after the epidemic remained free of the rare and transient disease. Ancient populations probably never encountered the acute infections (such as measles) in which the pathogens disappear after the death or recovery of the host, because the necessary urban reservoirs needed to maintain them did not exist. This means that the infectious diseases that accounted for most of the mortality of more densely settled agricultural societies probably had not evolved to their present forms before the Neolithic.

Another class of infections is endemic in isolated Amazonian tribes. These include the Epstein-Barr virus, cytomegalovirus, and varius kinds of herpes and hepatitis. These viruses persist in infected persons indefinitely and are often reactivated. However, since they are endemic, their host populations all have a high level of resistance. This type of host–pathogen relationship has considerable antiquity and was probably prevalent among sparsely settled hunter-gatherers. Since we share staphylococci, streptococci and coliform bacteria with other primates, these were probably present in hominids from their origin, as were the innocuous varieties of bacteria that cause life-threatening diseases today, such as diphtheria, tetanus and botulism. When such bacteria are prevalent though harmless it shows that our species is well adapted to them. Although many common bacterial and viral agents today cause little apparent sickness, they may have played an important part in the high mortality of hunter-gatherer populations, as most resistance to endemic organisms can be depressed by injury, starvation and cold.

Modern human tuberculosis, the treponematoses (such as syphilis and yaws), and a variety of tropical helminth worms and protozoans may be relics of a third class of human diseases, the extent and importance of which in aboriginal times is still unknown. Their peculiar characteristics (the most important of which is their chronic nature) could enable them to remain endemic yet hazardous to small populations with a tenuous network of contagion. Palaeopathologists have suggested a variety of degenerative and inflammatory disorders that may have been important causes of disability and death in the past. However, the non-specific response of bone tissue to infection usually limits the identification of specific disease-causing organisms.

Human diseases that may be endemic in another mammalian host are called *zoonoses*. Modern examples are tularaemia (rabbit fever), tick-borne encephalitis, scrub typhus and other rickettsial diseases, some malarias, trypanosomes, trichinoses, and many others. Some require an insect vector for transfer from mammal to human; others may be contracted directly. This large and variable class of infections has all the attributes of a force of mortality that could be both persistent and deadly in low-density human populations. Some ecosystems contained a large number of animal species with which mobile hunter-gatherers would interact. Cyclical changes may have produced an ever-changing battery of relatively novel pathogens, genetic resistance to which would have accumulated slowly or remained forever out of reach.

The demands of their economy may have compromised the health and safety of hunter-gatherers more than would those facing early agriculturalists. Numerous healed long-bone fractures in the skeletons from Libben and Carlston-Annis, as well as the higher mortality for males at both sites, suggest the perils of a foraging way of life. Anthropologists have become increasingly aware that farmers do work harder. Agriculture permits the generation of excess food through more labour. In producing more food than they can consume, societies came into existence in which some produce for themselves and at the same time are obliged to supply others – the foundation of true, sedentary village life.

Barring conflict, the daily activities of the farmstead had few inherent dangers. Storage of crops eliminated the need for constant toil, at least during part of the year, whereas gathering knew no holidays. The Inuit hunt and the Polynesian fishing voyage were sometimes accompanied by great risks, and a hunter-gatherer would often be forced to forage during poor conditions. The simple impact of

Flint projectile point (arrowed) embeddded near the articulation of two lumbar vertebrae found at Libben site, Ottawa County, Ohio.

exposure to the elements may have been important in the mortality of a foraging population. Older people suffer gradual loss of the ability to buffer temperature extremes, especially cold. Could this help to explain the almost complete loss of very old adults from temperate populations?

Aggression may have also played a part. There is some evidence of violent death at the archaeological sites mentioned here, including a few bone-imbedded flint projectile points at Libben and at Taforalt, but the number of individuals who met premature deaths at the hands of others will never be known. Among historical Algonquin tribes, who were probably related culturally to the people at Libben, the private ownership of hunting and trapping grounds could not be violated on pain of death. Were men killed for the same reasons at Libben? The data are clear for the Yanomami, for which there is evidence of the frequency of violent encounters. This population may well represent an extreme; however, the Yanomami certainly make a case for the existence of personal or group territories – vigorously defended – before the advent of settled agriculture.   *R.S. Meindl*

See also 'Studying human evolution by analogy' (p. 335), 'Reconstructing ancient populations' (p. 402), 'People and disease' (p. 411), 'Demographic analysis' (p. 422) and 'Tribal peoples in the modern world' (p. 433)

People and disease

Many historians and scientists believe that infectious diseases have had a profound influence on human evolution and culture. Here I show the importance of population size in determining whether an agent of infectious disease can become established. The continual expansion of human population since prehistoric times has led to successive invasions of our species by increasing numbers of diseases. This has had a significant effect on the history of population growth.

Agents of infectious disease

Infectious diseases can be divided into those caused by microparasites and by macroparasites, a division based on the epidemiology of the *pathogens* rather than their taxonomy.

Microparasites include most viruses, bacteria and protozoans. They are small and have short generation times, with extremely high rates of direct reproduction within their host and a tendency to induce immunity to reinfection in the hosts that survive the initial onslaught. The duration of infection is short in relation to the lifespan of the host and is usually transient. *Macroparasites* include the parasitic arthropods and worms (the helminths). They have much longer generation times than microparasites and rarely if ever undergo direct multiplication within the same host individual. The immune responses that they elicit depend on the number of parasites present and are of relatively short duration. Infections by macroparasites therefore tend to be persistent, and hosts are continually reinfected.

Both classes of parasite complete their life cycles by passing from one host to the next either directly or via one or more intermediate hosts. Direct transmission may be between hosts (as in venereal diseases) or by transmission stages that may be picked up by inhalation (e.g. influenza), by ingestion (e.g. roundworm) or by penetration through the skin (e.g. hookworm). Indirect transmission can involve biting by vectors (e.g. mosquitoes for malaria), or penetration by free-living stages that are produced by molluscan intermediate hosts (as in schistosomiasis). In other cases (e.g. the tapeworm), the parasite is ingested when an infected intermediate host is eaten uncooked or untreated by smoking or drying.

Epidemiological theory suggests that population size is very important in determining whether a pathogen can become established in a host (see Box 1, p. 412).

Infectious diseases before farming

Ten thousand years ago, the nomadic foraging groups of early humans probably supported a parasite fauna closely resembling that of the higher apes. Parasites with high transmission rates and little or no induced immunity were probably the only ones able to establish themselves in the scattered groups of around 50 or 100 individuals that made up these simple societies. Macroparasites with a direct life cycle (e.g. roundworms, guineaworms, lice and ticks) were fairly common, as were some of the less-pathogenic gut and blood pathogens (e.g. *Salmonella* and hepatitis viruses). This range of diseases is still found in a few tribal peoples in isolated parts of the world. Macroparasites with indirect life cycles (e.g. the pork worm *Trichinella*) would also have been common because of a diet of uncooked meat.

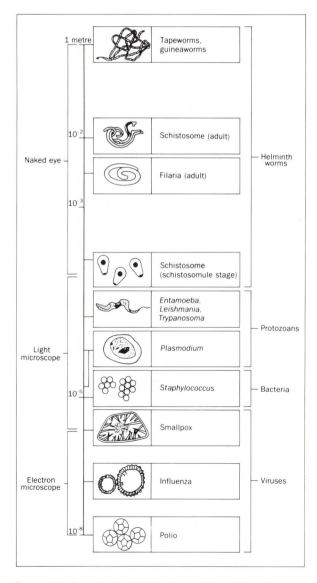

Comparative sizes of various infective agents. Those visible with the naked eye are described as macroparasitic and those smaller than this as microparasitic.

Trypanosomiasis, sleeping sickness, was probably a disease of primitive humans. This protozoan pathogen (*Trypanosoma*) is widespread among the wild animals of the African savannas, where it is transmitted between hosts by tsetse flies. Its relatively benign interaction with its hosts suggests a long evolutionary association. These wild hosts provided a large reservoir of infected animals, which sus-

tained the disease, while occasional infections of humans were usually debilitating or fatal. Baboons are the only primates resistant to the effects of the five different species of African trypanosome, and it seems likely that this pathogen was as endemic to populations of early humans as it is in different parts of Africa today.

The period between 100 000 and 10 000 years ago when

1. EPIDEMIOLOGICAL THEORY

The life cycle of a microparasite with a direct life cycle can be described by a flowchart of the various classes in the host population. Mathematical models of such simple pathogens consist of four differential equations that describe the rates at which individuals are born into the susceptible section of the population and pass through each successive stage of infection before dying or becoming immune:

$$dX/dt = \mu N - \mu X - \beta XY \qquad (1)$$
$$dH/dt = \beta XY - (\mu + \sigma)H \qquad (2)$$
$$dY/dt = \sigma H - (\mu + \gamma)Y \qquad (3)$$
$$dZ/dt = \gamma Y - \mu Z \qquad (4)$$

where X is the susceptible class, H the latent class, Y the infectious class, Z the immune class, N the number of susceptibles, β the transmission rate, $1/\sigma$ the period of time individuals carry latent infections, and $1/\gamma$ the period of time for which infected individuals are infectious. The host population size is assumed to remain constant, so that the birth rate of individuals into the susceptible class equals the net death rate, μ.

Two useful parameters can be derived from these equations. They allow us to compare the epidemiological characteristics of many different pathogens. The first of these is the reproductive rate of the infection, R. This is the average number of secondary infections that a single infected individual produces during his or her encounter with the pathogen. It allows us to measure the rate at which the pathogen grows in a host population. For the microparasite with the direct life cycle described in the diagram,

$$R = \frac{\sigma \beta X}{(\sigma + \mu)(\gamma + \mu)} \qquad (5)$$

The biological basis of R can be understood by noting that secondary infections are produced at a rate βX, throughout the expected duration of infection $1/(\gamma + \mu)$; of these, a fraction $\sigma/(\sigma + \mu)$ survive the latent period to become the second generation of infectious individuals. The disease will only be able to establish itself in a community when R is greater than one; once R falls below one the disease should begin to decline and will eventually go extinct.

As equation (1) includes a measure of the number (N) of susceptibles, we can use it to determine a second key parameter – the density of the host population at which the pathogen is just able to establish itself, N_T. For a microparasite with a direct life cycle

$$N_T = (\gamma + \mu)(\sigma + \mu)/\beta \sigma \qquad (6)$$

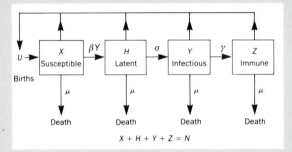

Flow chart of a hypothetical microparasite with a direct life cycle. The four subpopulations represent the susceptible (uninfected), infected but latent, infectious, and recovered and immune sections of the population.

This means that the minimum number of hosts required to allow a pathogen to establish in a population is inversely related to the duration of the latent and infectious periods of the disease: the longer a disease has a hold on an individual, the smaller the host population needed for its establishment. Increases in transmission efficiency decrease the minimum population size at which the disease can become established.

Studies of cities and islands of different sizes suggest that populations of around 400 000 to 500 000 individuals are required to maintain endemic infections of measles. Such concentrations of people have been present for less than 2000 years, suggesting that measles has been a human pathogen for less than 100 generations.

The *intrinsic growth rate* of a disease, R_0, is the value of R, the reproductive rate, in an initially disease-free population. If all individuals are susceptible, then $X = N$ and

$$R_0 = N/N_T \qquad (7)$$

A direct estimate of the intrinsic reproductive rate, R_0, is usually impossible because of the difficulty of estimating the transmission factor, β. However, R_0 may be estimated from the relation

$$R_0 = 1 + L/A \qquad (8)$$

Here, L is human life expectancy ($L = 1/\mu$) and A is the average age at which individuals acquire the infection.

Epidemics spread more rapidly in a population with no prior experience of a disease than in one in which the disease is endemic. This is due mainly to the presence of immune individuals, which reduce the numbers to whom an infection may be transmitted. Epidemiologists use the term

herd immunity to describe the proportion of immune individuals in a population.

Many diseases occur with a regular interval or cycle. This is due to the decline in susceptible individuals during a epidemic and their subsequent increase due to births. The period, T, of these cycles for a directly transmitted microparasite can be obtained from the equations in the flow diagram as

$$T = 2\pi[LD](R_0 - 1)]^{\frac{1}{2}} = 2\pi(AD)^{\frac{1}{2}} \qquad (9)$$

Here, D is the sum of the lengths of the latent and infectious periods, $D = (1/\sigma + 1/\gamma)$, and L and A are life expectancy and average age of the host at infection, respectively. The period of the cycle is thus a function of the transmission rate of the pathogen (which determines age at first infection) and the duration of the latent and infectious periods. Decreases in these periods decrease the period of cycles, while decreases in transmission increase cycle length.

Similar equations may be obtained for macroparasites and for parasites with more complex life cycles involving another species of host. Although the mathematics varies, the equations for thresholds of establishment and intrinsic growth rate of such pathogens are quite similar to those for simple microparasites.

The intrinsic growth rate of a disease usually consists of the product of the transmission rates of the parasite and its life expectancy during the various stages of its life cycle. The threshold for the establishment of a parasite consists of a rearrangement of this expression when $R_0 = 1$. If we can estimate the duration of the various stages of infection of the parasite, we can thus gain some idea of its ability to establish itself in a host population. *A. Dobson*

human populations expanded to occupy most of the world was also one of relatively low incidence of infectious disease. Such a rapid rate of expansion was perhaps made possible in part because of the absence of pathogens in the new habitats. Low population densities and fairly abundant food reduced the chance of more pathogenic diseases becoming established and the impact of those that did. The advent of fire allowed meat to be cooked and reduced the incidence of many parasites with indirect life cycles. The migration from Africa may also have reduced the incidence of diseases that had evolved with humans and were highly adapted to a savanna climate. In particular, human movement into cooler climates would have reduced the incidence of some insect-transmitted diseases.

The more sedentary habits of the early farmers probably increased the incidence of macroparasites with direct life cycles, mainly because of the increased transmission of their long-lived, free-living stages around primitive camps and dwellings. Water probably became contaminated with the amoeba that can cause dysentery. Early 'slash and burn' agriculture increased the habitats available for *Anopheles* mosquitoes, the vector of malaria. The widespread prevalence of the sickle-cell blood trait in Africa (see p. 16) suggests that this is an ancient human disease. As mosquitoes need standing water to reproduce, malaria probably first appeared when humans moved away from the savannas and into moister places.

After the agricultural revolution

Once crops had been successfully domesticated, population density increased enormously, and the land supported 10 to 20 times more people than before. The increasing use of rice as a food lead to the development of primitive irrigation schemes in China perhaps as early as 8500 years ago, Mesopotamia and Egypt about 5000 years ago and, somewhat later, in the Indus Valley and on the Peruvian coast.

The presence of eggs of the blood fluke *Schistosoma* in the kidneys of two Egyptian mummies from the twentieth dynasty (1200 BC), suggests that rice cultivation allowed another major parasite with an indirect life cycle to become established. The disease schistosomiasis (bilharziasis) is caused by the presence of these helminth worms in the blood, liver and spleen of infected individuals. The parasite passes through aquatic snails during successive cycles of its development. Although different schistosome species are specific towards the snails they infect, collectively they infect a wide variety of mammals and were probably present in small mammals before humans appeared on the scene.

Although only a few mammals are needed to sustain an infection of these pathogens, the threshold number of snails needed is quite large. The development of irrigation schemes allowed snail populations to increase, while the presence of many people working in the rice fields enhanced the abilities of the parasite to exploit humans. Much of the power of the Egyptian pharaohs may have rested in the fact that the peasants spent most of the day paddling in schistosome-infected waters and the resultant infections sapped their revolutionary energies.

Irrigation allowed the first cities to grow. Communications between towns began to be established, and human populations became large enough to sustain many microparasites with direct life cycles, such as amoebae, bacteria and viruses. It is in these first cities that the virus diseases of childhood started to appear. Many of the earliest to infect humans were likely to have evolved from diseases of domestic animals. Measles, for example, is closely related to rinderpest (a disease of cattle) and canine distemper. It thus seems unlikely that diseases needing a large host population to sustain themselves could have established themselves much before 3000 BC.

Smallpox (which probably derived from cowpox), rubella, typhoid and dysentery also arose at this period. All these diseases require populations of around 100 000 to 500 000 to be sustained. Many of the plagues of the Old Testament resulted from populations becoming sufficiently numerous to sustain epidemics of new pathogens. As humans had not previously been exposed to these diseases, levels of resistance were low and mortality rates high. After several visitations by a specific pathogen, however, levels of genetic resistance and the proportion of immune individuals in the population start to increase, leading to reduced rates of infection and a more regular pattern of prevalence.

As centres of civilisation expanded, other diseases became important. In the Yellow River (Huang He) basin in China, technological advances in irrigation allowed rice to become a major crop. Although by 202 BC the Han Dynasty had control of the whole basin, it was another thousand years before the adjacent Yangtze River (Chang Jiang) basin was successfully colonised. This may have been due to differences in the climate of the two areas and hence their suitability for the survival of intermediate hosts of parasites such as malaria and schistosomiasis; severe winters in the Yellow River valley kept the numbers of intermediate hosts down. Ancient Chinese histories contain traditional cures for schistosomiasis and malaria. Even today, diseases such as malaria and dengue fever. are more prevalent in the Yangtze River basin than in the Yellow River valley.

In the Mediterranean, people were able to live a relatively disease-free existence. The development of new crops and a switch to grain and olives entailed little exposure to new diseases, although malaria was present. The Greeks and even the Romans were still troubled by intestinal worms, although the development of aquaducts and drainage systems must have done more than traditional cures to reduce this problem.

Hippocrates (460–377 BC) was the first to record diseases with enough precision to allow them to be identified today

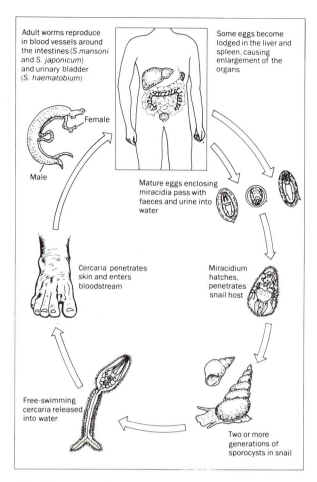

Life cycle of three of the blood flukes that cause schistosomiasis (bilharzia) — *Schistosoma mansoni*, *S. haematobium* and *S. japonicum*. The disease is endemic in tropical areas with poor sanitation. Humans become infected from contaminated water in which there are free-swimming schistosome larvae called cercariae. These penetrate the skin, lose their tails and pass into the blood circulation. Eggs are eventually laid in blood vessels around the intestines (*S. mansoni* and *S. japonicum*) or urinary bladder (*S. haematobium*). Those that do not escape into the urine or faeces become lodged in organs such as the liver and spleen. Snails are an essential link in the chain of infection.

Labels within figure: Adult worms reproduce in blood vessels around the intestines (*S.mansoni* and *S. japonicum*) and urinary bladder (*S. haematobium*); Female; Male; Some eggs become lodged in the liver and spleen, causing enlargement of the organs; Mature eggs enclosing miracidia pass with faeces and urine into water; Cercaria penetrates skin and enters bloodstream; Miracidium hatches, penetrates snail host; Free-swimming cercaria released into water; Two or more generations of sporocysts in snail

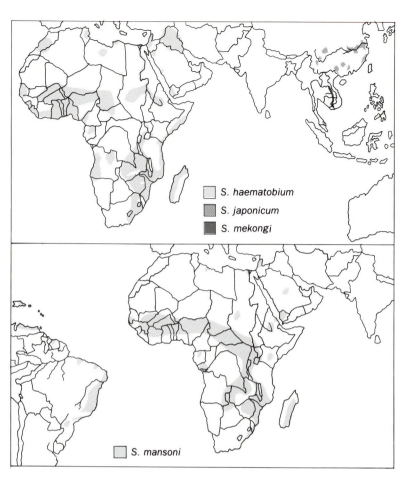

Geographical distribution of four blood flukes that cause schistosomiasis: *Schistosoma haematobium* and *S. mansoni* in Africa, *S. mansoni* in South America, and *S. japonicum* and *S. mekongi* in the Far East.

Map legend: S. haematobium; S. japonicum; S. mekongi; S. mansoni

as malaria, mumps, diphtheria, tuberculosis and perhaps influenza. It is interesting to note that none of his records gives any suggestion that smallpox, measles and bubonic plague were present (but the plague of Athens, 430–429 BC, which killed a quarter of the population, may have been measles). Modern estimates suggest that it requires a city of roughly 500 000 people to produce the 7000 susceptible individuals needed annually to sustain an endemic infection of measles. The population of Athens was then only around 155 000, and this may explain why the disease rapidly died out after the initial pool of susceptible individuals had been exhausted.

By the first century AD, trade links were established between three of the world's four major civilisations. This led to an enormous increase in the size of the host population, and many diseases became established throughout Europe and Asia for the first time. Smallpox is believed to

The entrance to the doctors' quarters in the Roman city of Ephesus in Turkey is marked by a worm coiled around a stick. This traditional and grossly unpleasant means of winding guineaworms (*Dracunculus*) out from the lymph glands is still practised in several regions of the world today.

have been present in India since around 1000 BC. Because of its relatively short incubation period the disease travelled less easily by land than by sea, so it was a long time before it made its way to Europe. However, once established, it remained epidemic throughout much of the world. In a smallpox epidemic in Rome in AD 165–80, a quarter of the populace died, and 5000 a day died in a second epidemic in AD 251–66.

These and other epidemics may have played a significant part in strengthening the position of the Christians. The administration of even small amounts of aid to the infected, particularly the giving of water, can significantly reduce mortality. Perhaps this gave the Christians an advantage in the Roman epidemics and convinced many non-believers to join their ranks!

The Middle Ages and the Black Death

The period between the fifth and eleventh centuries saw an increase in human population that is matched only by that of the present day. The prime reason for this was the reduction in the pathogenicity of microparasites with direct life cycles as human populations evolved resistance to them and levels of immunity built up. Anglo-Saxon records mention 49 outbreaks of epidemics between AD 526 and 1087; these were characterised by a pattern of increasing frequency and declining virulence. This decrease in mortality was accompanied by an increase in food availability as agriculture developed. The invention of the mould-board

plough allowed top soil to be broken up each year, and this reduced the densities of rodents and other small mammals by removing suitable habitat for their burrows. This not only increased the efficiency of crop production in the summer, but reduced rates of loss from stored supplies in the winter.

This upheaval amongst the small-mammal populations may have forced the black rat (*Rattus rattus*) into closer contact with human populations. Although originally of Indian origin, the species had spread throughout Europe by Roman times. The rat lives by scavenging from human refuse; thatched wooden houses and sailing vessels are ideal habitats for it. Ship-borne rats were responsible for the introduction of the plague bacillus (*Pasteurella pestis*) into Europe during the middle of the fourteenth century.

The presence of plague caused spectacular rates of mortality in human populations, with estimates of the total number of deaths varying between 25 and 40 per cent of the population of Europe in the period 1346–50. Its introduction came about through several circumstances, each of which contributed to its successful invasion of Europe. The first of these was a shifting northwards of the traditional caravan routes joining China and India to Persia and Turkey. These now ran through grasslands rather than desert. Horsemen could travel much more rapidly and usually moved around 100 kilometres (62 miles) a day. Plague had already invaded China from its original focus in Burma and this may have led to the 50 per cent drop in the population of China between 1200 and 1400.

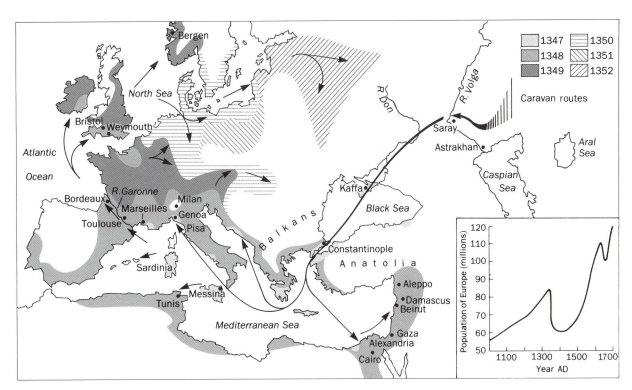

Approximate chronology of the Black Death as it spread across Europe in the middle of the fourteenth century. Inset: The population of Europe for the years AD 1000–1700. The impact of the two major epidemics of plague in the fourteenth century can plainly be seen.

The disease then became endemic in the small-mammal populations of the steppes of Manchuria and Mongolia, which are contiguous with those bordering the new caravan routes of Asia. The bacillus could spread rapidly along these trails in the mammal pests of grain carried by travellers. It reached the Crimea in 1346. Here, plague boarded ships in infected black rats and penetrated the whole of Europe and the Near East.

Plague's extreme pathogenicity led to the epidemic becoming known as the Black Death. The high death rates were probably caused by the interaction between the pathogen and the low nutritional status of the European population. This was mainly the result of crop failures in the 'little ice age' that preceded the plague's arrival.

Plague is epidemiologically fascinating, as it may be transmitted either indirectly by fleas as bubonic plague, or directly as pneumonic plague. This allows it to sustain itself when host population densities are low and to spread rapidly when they are high. The ability of the disease to use both small mammals and humans as hosts also reduces the intensity of selection for reduced pathogenicity between the bacillus and its human host.

Although plague was on the decline for much of the sixteenth century, it reappeared in London as the Great Plague of 1665. This was followed by the Great Fire of London in 1666, after which the replacement of roof thatch with slate tiles considerably reduced the contact between fleas and humans. It also seems likely that throughout this time the black rat was being displaced by the brown rat (*Rattus norvegicus*), which is a less suitable host for the plague bacillus and spends less time in close proximity to humans.

Introduction of diseases to the New World

The discovery of the New World by the explorers of the fifteenth and sixteenth centuries had immense epidemiological effects on the endemic people of the Americas. Successful colonisation probably owes more to the diseases that Europeans brought with them than to any of their more traditional weapons.

The New World populations in the fourteenth century resembled those of the Old World at the birth of Christianity. Intestinal worms and protozoan infections are found in bodies from pre-Columbian burial sites. In much of South America the traditional herd animals were llamas and alpacas. As these beasts live in small groups high in the Andes, there was little contact between humans and populations of smaller hosts within which diseases might become established. One important exception to this was again trypanosomiasis and its close relative, leishmaniasis. The protozoan pathogens that cause these diseases are endemic in many small mammals. For example, *Trypanosoma cruzi*, the causative agent of Chagas' disease, is particularly prevalent in the populations of guinea-pigs that were kept in large numbers by Andean farmers as a source of meat. The pathogen is transmitted indirectly to people by bloodsucking bugs.

Although the population of the New World probably numbered around 100 million before Columbus's arrival, this population had never been exposed to the microparasites with direct life cycles that were by then common amongst the residents of Europe. Introduction of these pathogens to populations with no natural resistance

2. IMMUNISATION AND THE ERADICATION OF DISEASE

The development of vaccines for many of the directly transmitted microparasitic diseases of humans led to the decline in juvenile mortality rates seen in Western countries during the twentieth century. These diseases are still major causes of death in the Third World. Epidemiological theory can help to explain why vaccination has been successful against some pathogens and why it may be less so against others.

A vaccination scheme should be designed to reduce the size of the pool of susceptible individuals to a level below the threshold needed for the pathogen to sustain itself. If R_0 is the basic reproductive rate of the disease (see Box 1), the proportion, p, of the population that must be vaccinated to prevent the pathogen establishing must be greater than

$$1 - (1/R_0)$$

This expression can predict p in terms of L, the average life expectation of individuals in the population ($1/\mu$); A, the average age

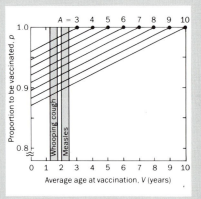

of first infection in the pre-vaccination era; and V, the average age at which individuals are vaccinated. To eradicate the pathogen by vaccination, p must be greater than

$$(1 + V/L)/(1 + A/L)$$

As p cannot exceed 1, eradication is only possible if A is greater than V; that is, the average age of vaccination is earlier than the average age of infection. Thus, although vaccination may be useful against diseases such as rubella in developed countries, it is unlikely to be as powerful a method of control against diseases such as malaria in developing countries, where a large proportion of the infant population is infected by the age of 6 months.   *A. Dobson*

The approximate relationship between the proportion (*p*) of a community that must be immunised (at or near birth) and the average age at vaccination (*V*) to eradicate an infection. The solid lines represent the boundaries between eradication (above the line) and persistence (below the line) for various values of the average age at first infection (*A*) in the population before the introduction of immunisation. The average life expectancy is taken to be 70 years. The shaded vertical bands depict the ranges of values of *V* for immunisation against whooping cough and against measles in England and Wales during the periods 1965–75 and 1968–75, respectively.

or immunity led to enormous mortality. The population of Mexico fell from 20 million to about 3 million in the 50 years from 1518 until 1568 and then to 1.6 million in the next 50 years. Most of these deaths were from successive epidemics of smallpox, measles and typhus. The native Americans who visited the camps of European settlers in eastern North America also picked up a variety of childhood diseases, and these rapidly devastated their numbers.

It seems likely that malaria and yellow fever were also introduced to the Americas in the post-Columbian era. These spread rapidly. The former was very destructive in the absence of sickle-cell haemoglobin, and the latter was a major problem to the garrisons of European soldiers in the Caribbean islands.

Europe and the modern age

It is only from around 1650 that population statistics are reliable enough to produce real estimates of the birth and survival rates of human populations. Many of these records are kept by military sources. They suggest that human survival rates have been improving from around the beginning of the sixteenth century. Most of this improvement occurs well before the full development of preventive medicine, and much may result from developments in the practice of agriculture, which allowed food to become cheaper and more plentiful and hence reduced the impact of disease.

Although diseases of childhood were well established in towns in the seventeenth and eighteenth centuries, they were transmitted only intermittently in the smaller populations of rural areas. Less than 2 per cent of the European population lived in cities of 100 000 or more before 1800. Joining the army or going to school was when many contagious diseases were contracted or passed on.

'The Cow Pock – or – the Wonderful Effects of the New Inoculation!' by the English caricaturist James Gillray (1802), inspired by the publications of the Anti-Vaccine Society.

Lady Mary Wortley Montagu (1689–1762) learned of smallpox inoculation when her husband was British Ambassador to Constantinople. She helped to introduce the technique into England in 1721.

Even by the time of Napoleon it was noted that skinny and ill-fed urban recruits survived much longer than did large, muscular and well-fed recruits from the countryside, who were repeatedly ill. This probably resulted from a reduced exposure to pathogens and hence a lower level of immunity in the smaller populations of isolated towns and villages.

The first influenza epidemic in Europe was from 1556 to 1560, at about the same time as a similar epidemic in Japan (1556). The influenza virus, a directly transmitted microparasite, has a very short latent period and is highly contagious. It therefore needs large populations in order to establish itself. Its first recorded appearance in the human population seems to have caused around 20 per cent mortality. The great influenza pandemic that followed World War I in 1918–19 led to the deaths of 20 million people – more than had died in the war itself. This high mortality may again have been associated with the low levels of nutrition in the human population following wartime rationing.

The impact of medical science since 1700

It was not until the beginning of the eighteenth century that medical science began to take the offensive against infectious disease. The first example of this was the development of crude inoculations against smallpox. It had been noticed in ancient China and India that people who caught the disease and survived never caught it again. This led to experiments in China, before the tenth century AD, on the inoculation of uninfected persons with liquid obtained from a pustule. The disease induced by inoculation was much milder than that obtained from natural infection, and this technique spread along the caravan trails and was practised in many parts of Asia.

Lady Mary Wortley Montagu, wife of the British ambassador to Turkey, brought the technique back to England in 1721, where its use was widely advocated by Sir Hans Sloane, the President of the Royal Society. It became a widespread practice in England throughout the century and in skilful hands the case mortality rate was about 2 per cent. However, inoculated smallpox could still cause outbreaks of severe natural smallpox. Edward Jenner's discovery in 1798 that inoculation with cowpox could produce similar levels of protection at considerably lower levels of risk, was therefore quickly adopted. It was used all over Europe within 2 to 3 years; by 1802 it had been successfully transported to India and by 1804 had reached the Spanish colonies in South America, the Philippines and China.

Industrial development in the nineteenth century saw the development of efficient sewage schemes. These reduced the contact rates between humans and the transmission stages of many gut-dwelling pathogens, and possibly led to the elimination of many macroparasitic worms. In London, in 1840, Edwin Chadwick developed long, narrow, fast-flow sewer pipes to replace the more traditional large-bore sewers. This led to an almost immediate reduction in cholera in Britain as it removed contaminated water from sources of drinking water. Thus, increases in levels of sani-tation and water management, rather than any advances in medical technique, led to reductions in infant mortality in the nineteenth century.

In the 1880s, the microscope helped in the discovery of germs; the first were the bacilli of anthrax (Louis Pasteur, 1877–9) and tuberculosis (Robert Koch, 1882). However, the migration of people away from the land and into the industrial cities throughout the nineteenth century probably served to increase rates of transmission of directly transmitted diseases. The mortality rates caused by these pathogens continued to decline, while the development of large-scale vaccination schemes in the twentieth century finally helped to reduce their incidence. Cities were probably not self-sustaining until around 1900. Before this, they were maintained only by immigration from the surrounding countryside where 80 to 90 per cent of the population still lived.

Diseases in the modern world

Infectious diseases continue to have a major impact on the human population. The epidemiological situation of many developing countries is similar in some ways to that of Europe in the seventeeth and eighteenth centuries. Although smallpox has been eradicated, malaria, measles, rubella and other childhood diseases are still major causes

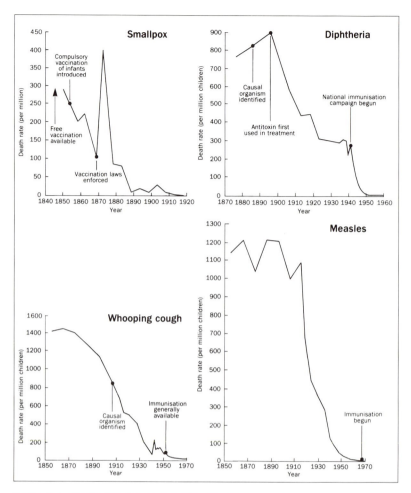

Decline in death rates from four common microparasitic diseases in England and Wales: smallpox, diphtheria, whooping cough and measles. Also shown are the approximate times when the causal organism was identified (for diphtheria and whooping cough) and the dates when vaccines were available.

The numbers of people infected world-wide with the commonest parasitic diseases (World Health Organization estimates, 1989)

Disease	Common name	At risk (millions)	Infected (millions)	Prevalence ranges (%)
Dracunculiasis	Guineaworm	140	10	10–60
Intestinal infections				
Amoebiasis	Amoebic dysentery	4000	400	—
Ancylostomiasis	Hookworm	4000	900	30–90
Ascariasis	Roundworm	4000	1000	20–95
Giardiasis		World-wide	200	
Strongyloidiasis	Threadworm	World-wide	30	
Trichuriasis	Whipworm	World-wide	500	up to 95
Leishmaniasis (visceral and cutaneous)	Kala azar, oriental sore, espundia, chiclero ulcer	370	12	up to 70
Lymphatic filariasis	Elephantiasis	900	90	15
Onchocerciasis	River blindness	80	18	10–40
Schistosomiasis	Bilharziasis	600	200	22–50
Trypanosomiasis (African)	Sleeping sickness	50	0.04	1–5
Trypanosomiasis (American)	Chagas' disease	100	13–15	10–70

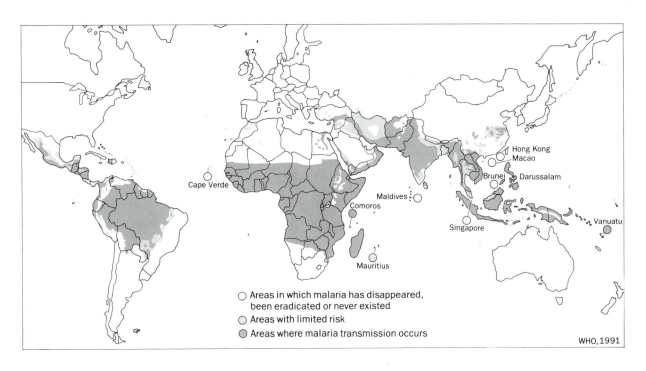

Areas in which malaria has disappeared, been eradicated or never existed
Areas with limited risk
Areas where malaria transmission occurs

WHO, 1991

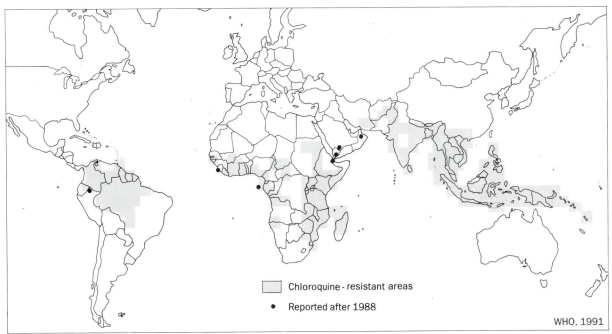

Chloroquine - resistant areas
Reported after 1988

WHO, 1991

of death. Malaria, in particular, is showing a resurgence as the world's number one disease. Following the widespread use of drugs and insecticides against the pathogen and its mosquito vector in the middle years of the twentieth century, genetic resistance has evolved to these compounds, and malaria is rapidly returning to areas once declared free of infection.

Macroparasites such as hookworms, roundworms and schistosomes continue to debilitate millions of people. Each year, schistosomiasis alone kills hundreds of thousands of people and up to as many as 200 million people could be disabled because of the disease.

Malaria is showing a major resurgence as the world's number one disease. It is estimated that 150–200 million people are infected with the malaria parasite (*Plasmodium*) at any one time, with nearly a million children under 5 years dying from it each year. Following the widespread use of drugs and insecticides against the pathogen and its mosquito vector earlier this century, genetic resistance has evolved to these compounds and malaria is returning to areas that had been declared free of the infection (lower map).

The rapidly growing global epidemic of AIDS (acquired immune deficiency syndrome) is causing widespread mortality in Africa and many developed countries. Huge numbers of people are also at risk in Asia. In the Third World, there is increasing evidence of links between poverty and AIDS.

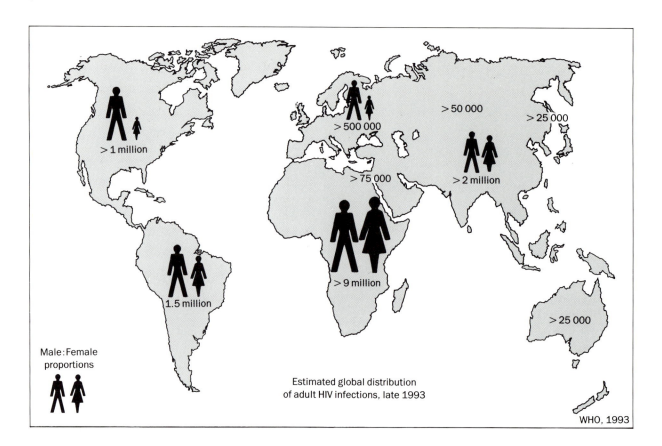

> 1 million
> 500 000
> 50 000
> 25 000
> 75 000
> 2 million
> 9 million
1.5 million
> 25 000

Male:Female
proportions

Estimated global distribution
of adult HIV infections, late 1993

WHO, 1993

The geography of HIV infection (late 1993 figures). Although sub-Saharan Africa still has by far the most infections (9–10 million adults may be harbouring HIV), other regions are catching up fast. By the mid-1990s, the number of people infected in Asia could rise to 3 million, most of them in India and Thailand.

The AIDS epidemic was first identified in the West when a variety of unusual or rare disease syndromes began to occur in male homosexuals and intravenous drug users. Intensive immunological and molecular studies identified two viruses, human immunodeficiency viruses (HIV-1 and HIV-2), as the aetiological agents of the disease. Surveys of an epidemic of 'slimming disease' in Africa revealed that this epidemic was also caused by HIV. By the start of the 1990s, the AIDS epidemic was recorded from all the world's countries. In 1993, it was estimated that more than 2 million adults had the disease, and over 14 million young people and adults were infected with HIV. In sub-Saharan Africa by the mid-1990s the number infected with HIV is expected to reach 10 million, of which a high proportion will be babies born to HIV-positive women. By the year 2000, the World Health Organization has predicted that about 30 million adults and children will be infected with HIV world-wide and there will be 15 million AIDS cases.

Like many of its predecessors, AIDS is a disease that can establish itself only if the numbers of people required to sustain it become large enough. The origin of HIV remains uncertain, but molecular and immunological evidence suggests that there is a link between the two HIV agents and similar viruses in simian primates. Divergence between

HIV-1 and SIV-1 (simian immunodeficiency virus type 1) could have occurred as much as a century ago. The disease may then have maintained itself in small isolated communities in Africa for many years before spreading more widely in Africa and into the Western world.

HIV is primarily transmitted by sexual contact, by the shared use of needles in the case of intravenous drug addicts, and from infected mother to infant. Control of the AIDS epidemic is considerably hampered by the long latent period of the disease (8–9 years on average) and difficulties associated with identifying individuals who are infected with HIV, but have not yet developed the clinical symptoms associated with AIDS. At present, the prospects for a cure look bleak.

Because HIV eventually disables the immune system, a variety of other opportunistic pathogens are increasing in incidence, especially in the developing nations where the effects of disease are made worse by poverty and poor nutrition. The World Health Organization estimates that 50 to 75 per cent of all recorded deaths of infants and young children can be attributed to a combination of malnutrition and infection. Unless more active moves are made to alleviate poverty and to reduce population in the world's developing nations, it seems likely that disease and malnutrition will continue to cause pain and suffering on a vast scale.

A. Dobson

See also 'Origins of agriculture' (p. 373) and 'Reconstructing ancient populations' (p. 402)

Trends in population growth

The population of the world, currently some 5.4 billion, is increasing at an annual rate of a little below 2 per cent. Even if the rate falls to below 1 per cent by the end of this decade, demographers predict that the world's population will reach 8.5 billion by the year 2025 and 10.2 billion by 2050. Population growth on this scale is unprecedented.

World population was some 300 million by the middle of the eighteenth century, corresponding to a long-term annual rate of increase of little more than 0.05 per cent. The present phase of demographic expansion began around 1750 and has continued since then at an increasing rate. In the nineteenth century, world population grew at an estimated 0.5 per cent annually, increasing to about 0.8 per cent in the early twentieth century and 1.8 per cent after World War II. Between 1965 and 1970, the growth rate topped 2.05 per cent so that it is now on the decline.

Populations of European origin grew more rapidly than others before 1900, but in the twentieth century their growth has fallen to very low levels, while that of Third World countries has risen substantially. This presents a major challenge, not simply because production must be expanded to meet demand, but also because rapidly growing populations contain a large proportion of children, who need investment in health and education. The countries of the developed world, where low birth rates have all but brought an end to population growth, face the reverse problem, because a large and growing population of elderly people must be supported by a shrinking labour force.

The need to understand such trends in population growth led, in the 1950s, to the *theory of demographic transition*. This sees population growth as a consequence of the move from a traditional demographic regime, dominated by high rates of mortality and fertility, to one of low mortality and fertility, brought about by social and economic change. In its early form, the theory assumed that all countries followed a similar path of development and differed only in the timing of the changes concerned. The process was thought to have begun in late eighteenth-century England, and subsequently in other European countries, with a substantial reduction in mortality arising from economic growth and social progress.

This removed the social 'need' for high fertility, but the spread of family limitation, and the consequent fall in the birth rate, did not appear until the end of the nineteenth century, because it required a fundamental change in the way people thought about fertility. In particular, the old religious injunctions 'be fruitful' had to be replaced by a new outlook attuned to the economic advantages of small families. The intervening phase was consequently one of rapid population growth.

The developed countries had mostly completed this transition by the second quarter of the twentieth century, but in much of the Third World it seemed only to be getting under way soon after 1945. The decline in mortality, however, was much more rapid in Asia and Latin America than in nineteenth-century Europe, with life expectations increasing by as much as 15 years in two decades. It owed more to imported medical technology than to indigenous

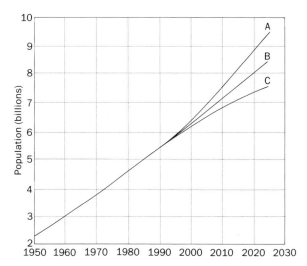

Three projections of the growing human population. If the growth rate were to remain approximately 1.8 per cent a year until the year 2000 and decline thereafter to 0.98 per cent in 2025, the world population would reach almost 8.5 billion in 2025 (B). If the growth rate were to decline at a faster rate and reach 0.59 per cent by 2025, the population in 2025 would be around 7.6 billion (C). If the growth rate were to climb to 1.9 per cent at the end of the century before declining, the population in 2025 would be more than 9.4 billion (A).

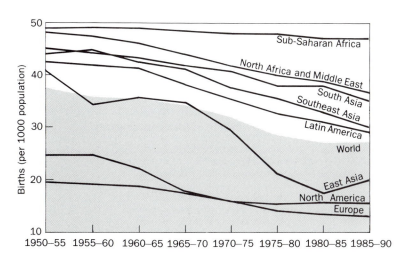

Birth rates have declined since the end of World War II in many countries, but in sub-Saharan Africa they have not.

DEMOGRAPHIC ANALYSIS

The origins of *demography* – the statistical study of populations (particularly human ones) – can be traced back to the 'political arithmetic' of seventeenth-century England. The field was pioneered by the English clergyman and economist Thomas Malthus, whose *Essay on the Principles of Population* was first published in 1798. Charles Darwin acknowledged the work of Malthus as a central influence on his own theories of evolution.

During the twentieth century, the great expansion of demography has mainly reflected the call for accurate population statistics for the planning and provision of services, and for taxation, defence and electoral representation. An increasing need today is for demographic research into the recent expansion of world population.

Many of the techniques of 'formal' demography, or demographic analysis, are aimed at the resolution of practical problems (such as population censuses and surveys) but others seek to illuminate the biology of demographic change – fertility, mortality and population growth. Some of the mathematical techniques used are complicated, but their underlying logical basis is straightforward.

Demographic data

Demographers need two types of information: the census or *stock* data (the size and other characteristics of a population at a given time) and the *vital* data (the 'vital events' of birth, death and marriage).

Censuses. Modern population censuses or surveys (the former covers all members of the population whereas the latter includes only a sample) have developed from the first English census, held in 1801. Such material is available in many European countries from the nineteenth century onwards. However, it is rare before then and in other parts of the world may not exist until 1900. Where there are no censuses available, an historical population study can make use of other materials, such as taxation returns.

The most elementary form of census data is a simple count or *enumeration*. It is better to have some information as well on the structure of the population: in particular, on the *sex ratio* (the relative numbers of males and females) and on the *age structure* (the numbers in the various age groups). Modern censuses provide details on many other variables, such as occupation, marital status or ethnic affiliation.

Births, marriages and deaths. Birth, death and migration are responsible for changes in a population's size and age structure. In modern societies, the vital events of birth and death are usually registered by government agencies. However, in many

countries such civil registration began much later than the introduction of regular censuses – in England not until 1837 – and in much of the Third World there is still no effective system of vital registration. It requires a network of trained officials, which is difficult in countries with a scattered population and poor communications.

In the absence of civil registration, demographers must rely on limited surveys, or estimate the numbers of births and deaths occurring between censuses. In much of Europe before 1900, many of the functions now performed by the state devolved on the churches, and the parish registers of baptisms, burials and marriages have been widely used as sources of vital data.

Such information has varying amounts of detail. The minimum requirements are the totals of births, deaths and marriages, but for most purposes we need information on the people involved. For instance, in the case of births, published tables usually give parental occupation, maternal age and marital status, and location. The registration of deaths generally involves the collection of information on age, occupation and place of residence, as well as on the cause of death.

Mortality

Changes in population size are, in the absence of migration, wholly determined by the balance of births and deaths. Demographers treat these two events as manifestations of the vital processes of fertility and mortality, and try to measure these by disentangling their effects from those of population size and structure. We can illustrate this by looking at analyses of mortality.

The study of mortality statistics is the oldest branch of demography. It is important because, apart from medical applications, it forms the basis of life assurance. The vocabulary of demographic analysis reflects this, as the term used to denote its central concept is *risk*. We can think of a mortality as higher or lower in a population in terms of the chance that any member of the population will die over a given period. This probability is referred to as risk, and the extent of risk in a population indicates the prevailing strength of mortality.

One obvious way of measuring risk in a population is simply to count the numbers of deaths. This method is useful if we want to look at short-term changes in mortality (for instance, to compare the effects of winter and summer), but it breaks down as soon as we want to compare populations of different sizes.

Such comparisons can be undertaken by dividing the number of deaths by the average population size over the period. The result, conventionally multiplied by a thousand, is termed the *crude death rate*

An enumerator takes details for India's 1991 census.

(CDR). National CDRs are now generally below 20 per 1000. The average figure for the industrialised countries is about 9.4 and that for the rest of the world is 12.2. In the past, however, CDRs were much higher. Many European countries had rates in excess of 30 per 1000 before the nineteenth century, with even higher levels elsewhere in the world.

Useful as the CDR is, it has shortcomings as an indicator of differences in mortality levels, because it takes no account of the ages of the people concerned. A population whose members are mainly young men and women will have a much lower CDR than will one with many old people. This problem can be tackled by constructing *age-specific mortality rates* for each of the age groups concerned.

The calculations are the same as those that led to the CDR, but now we restrict our attention to one age group at a time. Age-specific mortality rates are good indicators of the risks of death at any age in a population, and sets of such rates produce *life tables*.

The life table is the workhorse of mortality analysis, and from it we can derive several indicators of mortality, the most familiar being the average *life expectation*. This measure (technically, the 'expectation of life at birth') is the average lifespan of an individual born into a population, calculated on the assumption that mortality levels do not change. This assumption is not always realistic, but life expectation at birth is a useful measure because it provides a basis on which to compare the mortality of populations with different age structures.

Most of the advanced industrial nations now have life expectations around 70 or above, and even some populations in the Third World (particularly in Latin America) have figures in excess of 60. However, many of the world's poorest countries still have life expectations below 50.

When mortality levels are as high as this,

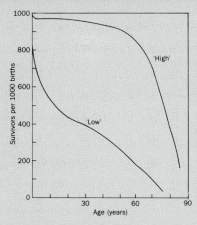

Survival curves for populations with high and low expectation of life.

the average expectation of life is a misleading guide to the actual experience of most people, because a very large proportion of infants and young children die. The average lifespan of those who survive these early years is hence substantially greater than the expectation at birth.

We can see this by looking at the *survival curve*: the number of people, for every thousand live births, who survive to successive ages at a particular set of age-specific mortality rates. The shapes of curves for populations with high and low life expectations are quite different.

The survival curve for the population with a high life expectation is virtually rectangular; the number of survivors falls

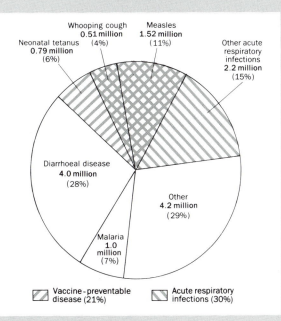

The principal causes of the 14 million child deaths in Third World countries each year. Almost two-thirds of the deaths are accounted for by four specific causes – diarrhoea, respiratory infections, measles and neonatal tetanus.

in the first year of life, but subsequently few lives are lost until late in middle age, beyond which the number of deaths rises steeply into the sixties and seventies. The curve corresponding to a low life expectation shows a rapid fall in the numbers of survivors in the early years of life, with a more gradual reduction beyond adolescence.

When expectation of life is low, the probability of survival from birth to age 15 may be a better indicator of the prevailing risks of mortality than is average life expectation. In many parts of Europe, before the nineteenth century, this probability was as low as 50 per cent, with a quarter or more of all live-born infants dying before their first birthday. The latter proportion, measured by the *infant mortality rate*, is of great interest to demographers as it is often taken as an indicator of public health.

In Britain, as in many industrialised countries, the infant mortality rate is now below 10 per 1000 live-born. This is high relative to mortality at other ages in such countries, but greatly below the levels prevailing in the Third World, where infant mortality is often above 100 per 1000. .

Fertility

In demography, *fertility* refers to actual reproductive behaviour, and *fecundity* to the capacity to reproduce (a measure usually restricted to females). Fertility is more complex than mortality. This is because death is an event that can occur only once to any one, but must eventually befall all of us, whereas a woman may give birth many times or not at all.

Where family size is consciously controlled through contraception or abortion, further complications appear, because the probability of future births depends on the number of children a woman already has. There are many measures of fertility, all of which share an underlying logic, based, as in the case of mortality, on relating the number of vital events to the size of the population at risk.

The *crude birth rate* (CBR), which is analogous to the CDR, is a convenient measure when only total births and overall population size are available. However, like the CDR, it is unsatisfactory, as it includes people who, because of age or sex, are not at risk of childbirth. The *general fertility rate* avoids this pitfall by using only the female population between the ages of 15 and 44. A better solution is to construct separate fertility rates for each female age group.

The resulting *age-specific fertility rates* can then be used to calculate the average number of children a woman is expected to have during her life. This figure (the *total fertility rate*) is a useful for comparing fertility levels of populations with different age structures.

When, as was the case in most parts of

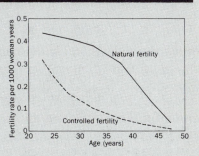

Fertility rates with and without family limitation.

the world until recently, nearly all women are married at puberty no special allowance need be made for variations in the age and incidence of marriage. In much of Europe, however, marriage was once delayed for years after puberty and many women remained celibate. This European marriage pattern has now spread to the Third World, particularly among educated groups in the cities, and under these circumstances it is important to calculate marital fertility rates separately from those of the general female population.

There are considerable differences in fertility levels between countries. In many industrial nations, the total fertility rate is close to, or less than, 2, whereas the average for the Third World is slightly less than 5. Much of this variation springs from the use of contraception and abortion to control family size. The extent of such family limitation can be seen by looking at the pattern of age-specific marital fertility rates in relation to age.

If there is no family limitation – *natural fertility* – fertility rises from adolescence to a peak in the early twenties and then declines, gently at first and then steeply from the mid-thirties. This leads to a convex age curve of fertility, which depends on underlying biological changes in fecundity.

Family limitation leads to a different age pattern, because couples have the desired number of children early in married life and then cease to reproduce. This leads to peak fertility soon after marriage and a subsequent decline. Some women, however, continue childbearing into their late thirties for such reasons as late marriage, desire for a large family or accidental pregnancy. The decline in fertility tends to level off in this age group, producing a curve that is concave in shape rather than convex.

The large-scale use of family limitation in most of Europe and its settlements dates from the late nineteenth century; the main exceptions are parts of France, where it began 100 years earlier, and certain élite groups who practised family limitation as early as the seventeenth century. Since World War II, family limitation has spread to Japan and to several countries in the

Continued

DEMOGRAPHIC ANALYSIS (cont.)

'One-child' family planning poster, China.

Third World, particularly in eastern Asia and Latin America. .

The onset of family limitation has led to a reduction in fertility levels. In England, for instance, the total fertility rate fell from 4.8 in the 1870s to 1.8 by 1940. Several

Latin American countries now have CBRs below 30 per 1000 and China's is below 20. By contrast, most sub-Saharan African countries (where family limitation is still rare) have CBRs above 40 (see p. 421).

It is widely assumed that, without family limitation, fertility will be high and approach the physiological maximum. However, populations in modern Third World countries and in historical Europe — and also some modern hunter-gatherers — have considerable variations in levels of natural fertility.

In many Third World countries, women marrying at puberty expect to have no more than five or six children, whereas the total fertility rate for the Hutterites, a North American Lutheran community who do not practice family limitation, is close to 10. Parish registers from eighteenth-century France, before the spread of family limitation, also show marked regional variations in marital fertility. Total fertility

rates in the north-east of the country were around 8.8 whereas those in the south-west were only 6.5.

Some of this variation in fertility may be due to attempts to space out births, but the most important factor seems to be the duration of breastfeeding, as prolonged lactation can extend the period during which ovulation is suppressed for 2 years, or for as much as 4 years in the !Kung San hunter-gatherer group. Acute famine can have a similar impact (probably for psychological as well as physiological reasons), but moderate chronic malnutrition has little effect on fertility.

J. Landers

See also 'Reconstructing ancient populations' (p. 402), 'Human populations before agriculture' (p. 406) and 'Fertility control: past, present and future' (p. 425)

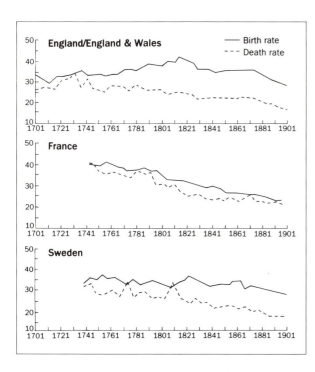

Birth and death rates (per 1000 population) in three European countries during the eighteenth and nineteenth centuries, showing how different populations can have different patterns of growth.

economic or social developments. Hence, it is often argued, government-sponsored birth-control campaigns are needed to produce a rapid reduction in fertility.

Demographic transition theory remains a useful framework for thinking about population change, but newer research throws doubt on the notion that there is a single,

necessary, path of demographic development: different populations have shown very different patterns of growth. In much of Europe, birth rates were kept well below those of pre-transitional Third World populations by the late age of marriage and a high incidence of celibacy. Indeed, in eighteenth-century England, it was the partial relaxation of this system that was chiefly responsible for population growth, as the onset of sustained decline in mortality was delayed until the 1870s. In Sweden, by contrast, eighteenth-century population growth was mainly due to mortality decline, whereas France showed still another pattern in which mortality and fertility declined simultaneously and the rate of population growth remained correspondingly low throughout the nineteenth century.

The impact of medical technology on Third World mortality has also varied considerably, depending on the social patterns and developmental policies of the countries concerned. For instance, Sri Lanka had by the 1970s attained a life expectation of 68 years, close to that of the United States and some 14 years above Syria, despite the latter's substantially larger national income per head of population.

The reasons for the declines in fertility of many countries remain controversial. Changes in economic circumstances may have played a larger part than have changes in mental attitudes or government-promoted family planning campaigns, even where, as in China, these have taken stringent legislative form.

J. Landers

See also 'Reconstructing ancient populations' (p. 402)

Fertility control: past, present and future

The pressure on the world's resources brought about by overpopulation has led to an awareness of the need for contraception to counteract a potential disaster. Most people see contraception as a conscious decision to prevent pregnancy by artificial means or through manipulation of normal reproduction. However, even today, nature's own contraceptive, breastfeeding, still prevents more pregnancies than all other methods combined, especially in Third World countries. The contraceptive effect of breastfeeding requires no conscious involvement of the mother other than to feed her baby.

The decline in the popularity of breastfeeding has increased the need to develop other methods of contraception. Although some countries, notably in eastern Europe, still rely on abortion, the most popular method of contraception remains the steroid-containing pill. This method exploits the effect of *oestrogen* (produced by the developing ovarian follicle) and *progesterone* (secreted by the corpus luteum) to suppress the secretion of two gonadotrophins secreted by the pituitary gland. As a result, ovarian activity is inhibited. Not all modern contraceptive methods are reliable. They may also be unacceptable for health or religious reasons, and there is much research into the development of new contraceptive methods to meet demands for population control in the twenty-first century.

The ovarian follicle containing the unfertilised egg grows under the influence of two gonadotrophins – *follicle-stimulating hormone* (FSH), which is responsible for follicle growth, and *luteinising hormone* (LH), which stimulates the secretion of the steroid hormones androgen and subsequently oestradiol from the developing follicle and of progesterone from the corpus luteum.

As the follicle develops, it secretes more oestradiol, and this in turn triggers a large release of LH – the *preovulatory LH surge*. LH then causes the follicle to release the egg (*ovulation*), and transforms the remains of the follicle into the corpus luteum. Release of LH and FSH is stimulated by secretion of *gonadotrophin-releasing hormone* (GnRH) by the hypothalamus at the base of the brain. GnRH itself is under the control of oestradiol and progesterone secreted by the ovary, thus completing a feedback loop involving the hypothalamus, pituitary and ovary.

Breastfeeding – nature's contraceptive

During pregnancy, steroids secreted by the placenta inhibit the release of GnRH, so that, at delivery, the pituitary gland contains only about 1 per cent of the normal amount of LH. In the virtual absence of LH and FSH, growth of the follicle within the ovary ceases. If a woman does not suckle her baby, normal ovulatory cycles resume some 8 to 12 weeks after delivery – the time taken for the pituitary to regain its normal secretory abilities. However, if a mother breastfeeds, normal ovulatory cycles can be delayed for as

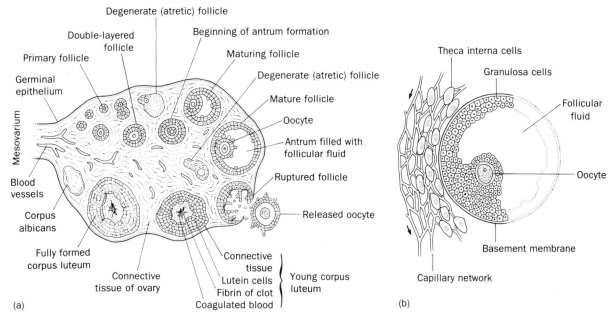

(a)

(b)

Diagrammatic cross-section through a hypothetical human ovary (a) to show all stages of the growth of a follicle and the development and demise of a corpus luteum. The cellular organisation of the follicle (b) is also shown to emphasise that there is no direct blood supply to the granulosa cells or oocyte within the follicle.

long as 3 or 4 years. Growth of the follicles is then usually suppressed but, even if growth occurs, the pre-ovulatory surge of LH is prevented by continued suckling. Hence, there is no ovulation and the mother remains infertile.

The duration of the infertile period after birth varies between women and between societies. Because of this, breastfeeding is often regarded as an unreliable contraceptive. The main reason is that the suppression of ovarian activity (and thus of fertility) depends on the baby's pattern of suckling. When suckling occurs frequently during the day, as in many African, Asian or South American societies, there is a long period of infertility. In industrialised countries, where breastfeeding is much less frequent (typically three to five times a day), the period of infertility is much shorter. If Western women suckle their babies frequently, then the infertility can be as long as their African, Asian or South American counterparts.

The nervous signals in the nipple produced by suckling pass to the brain, where they cause the release of oxytocin to stimulate milk ejection, and of prolactin, which stimulates milk production. The signal also suppresses the normal pattern of GnRH release, leading to a reduction in the amount of LH released from the pituitary and preventing normal follicle growth. For this suppression to continue, suckling must be maintained to an extent that varies between individuals, as the duration, frequency and intensity of suckling depend on interactions between mother and child.

Nutrition can also affect the suckling pattern and hence the duration of infertility. Supplementary feeding can reduce the baby's appetite and hence the length of each suckle, even if there is no change in how often breastfeeding takes place. In women who suckle only three to five times a day, supplementary feeding often leads to the return of fertility. Where mothers suckle their babies more than 10 times a day, the impact of extra feeding is less.

Such a return of fertility, even though the mother is still breastfeeding, accounts for the occurrence of pregnancy in 3 to 20 per cent of lactating mothers in societies without contraception. Such mothers may not experience a menstrual period for several years, as they progress from suppression of menstruation through pregnancy to suppression through breastfeeding and on to the next pregnancy. Suckling will act as a contraceptive in all women, provided it is sufficiently strong.

Natural family planning

The terms 'rhythm' and 'safe period' to designate methods of birth control based on periodic abstinence have been replaced by the term 'natural family planning'. Such methods are based on the recognition of natural signs of ovulation and of the infertile phase of the menstrual cycle, which begins 3 days after ovulation and lasts until menstruation.

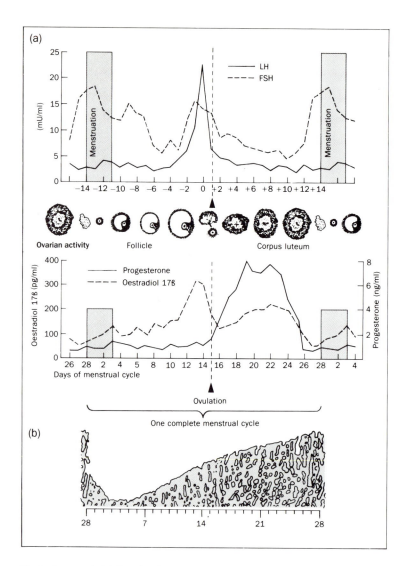

The top two panels (a) show the changes in the pituitary gonadotrophins FSH (follicle-stimulating hormone) and LH (luteinising hormone) during the menstrual cycle. FSH and LH drive the growth of the ovarian follicle, resulting in the secretion of oestradiol from the follicle. This in turn leads to the repair and proliferation of the endometrial lining of the uterus. The preovulatory surge of LH induces ovulation and the follicle transforms into the corpus luteum, which secretes progesterone. The progesterone causes the endometrium to become secretory, which allows implantation of the fertilised egg, should conception occur. If conception does not occur, the corpus luteum regresses and dies. The decline in progesterone causes sloughing of the endometrium – menstruation. The bottom panel (b) shows the regrowth of the endometrial lining after menstruation.

The calendar method relies on ovulation occurring 12 to 14 days before the beginning of the next menstrual period, but it is imprecise and requires very regular menstrual cycles. A more reliable indication of the infertile luteal phase comes from body temperature. Progesterone produced by the corpus luteum raises temperature by 0.2 to 0.4 °C and maintains it until menstruation. However, at least 10 per cent of temperature charts are difficult to interpret, owing to reduced corpus luteum function, especially during breastfeeding. The 'Billings method' relies on changes in the mucus produced by the cervix of the uterus under the influence of oestrogen and progesterone at different times of the menstrual cycle.

None of the natural family planning methods is very reliable on its own and even when all are used in conjunction, pregnancies can occur in up to 20 per cent of women using them a year.

Other methods of contraception

The internal methods available to women are summarised in the diagram below. Pregnancy rates for these, and for barrier methods (condoms and diaphragms), vary from 0.1 per cent for 1 year of use to 25 per cent.

The contraceptive pill. During the normal menstrual cycle, the secretion of LH and FSH is controlled by the ovarian hormones oestradiol and progesterone. They modify the response of the pituitary gland to the stimulatory actions of GnRH and regulate its secretion by the hypothalamus. High levels of oestradiol and progesterone in the luteal phase slow the frequency of release of GnRH pulses, alter the output of both LH and FSH, and hence suppress the development of ovarian follicles.

The pill works in the same way. It contains synthetic forms of oestrogen and progesterone, either in combination or in a progestagen-only pill. The usual cycle consists of 3 weeks of pill-taking followed by 1 week off. During this final week, there is menstrual bleeding because of the with-

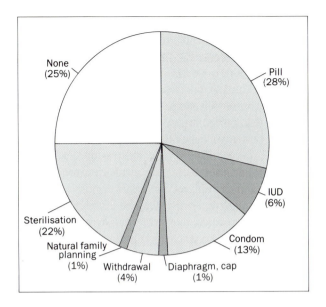

Use of various forms of contraceptive in the UK (**1983 figures**).

drawal of steroids from the uterus. However, women have taken the pill continuously for up to 3 months without problems.

The amount of steroid in a 1-month supply of the combined pill is now less than that in a single pill made up to the original specification. Because of this dramatic reduction in steroid content, the safety of the pill has been greatly increased. A major element in the reduction of the pill's side-effects has been the realisation that it is not safe for all women. Risk factors include high blood pressure, smoking, obesity and a family history of cardiovascular problems. For smokers, risks may be prohibitive at 35 whereas for non-smokers the age limit is 45.

The original pill gave a constant daily dose of oestrogen and progestagen. More recent types attempt to mimic the changes in the relative proportions of the two that occur in the natural cycle. The overall dose of steroids in these triphasic pills, in which the composition varies over the 3-week period, is even less than in the conventional pill. Although control of the cycle is adequate there may be problems if such pills are not taken in order, unlike conventional pills which are all exactly the same.

The progestagen-only pill is not much used, but it has none of the disadvantages or risks of oestrogen, and progestagen itself is much safer in the absence of oestrogen. It is the best pill for insulin-dependent diabetics, for women over 35 and for breastfeeding women as, unlike the combined pill, it has no effect on lactation. The progestagen-only pill alters the cervical mucus, making it sticky and hostile to sperm. It also causes the lining of the uterus to change earlier than in the normal cycle, and reduces the possibility of implantation of the fertilised ovum. In many women, this pill also reduces the secretion of gonadotrophins and prevents the mid-cycle surge of LH, thus stopping ovulation itself. Its major problem is the occa-

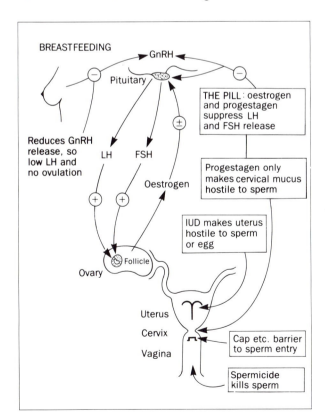

Present methods of contraception in women. GnRH = gonadotrophin-releasing hormone; FSH = follicle-stimulating hormone; LH = luteinising hormone.

sional occurrence of variable periods of menstrual bleeding. New formulations should reduce this.

Long-acting forms of progestagen that can be injected every 2 to 3 months are useful for women who cannot reliably take a daily pill, but problems may still arise with disturbed menstrual bleeding. New systems for delivering progestagens are also being developed. The simplest is a capsule the size of a matchstick, which is inserted beneath the skin under local anaesthetic. The progestagen diffuses out through the capsule wall to provide contraception for up to 5 years. The implants can easily be removed and replaced, a major advantage over injectable forms if problems arise. In many women, they result in long-term suppression of menstruation (amenorrhoea). Although this is sometimes unacceptable it is seen as a positive advantage in some cultures. Normal fertile menstrual cycles resume soon after removal of the implant.

Progestagen has also been used in a vaginal ring, a doughnut-shaped device that is placed at the top of the vagina. It can be left in place for 3 months and can be removed at any time. Progestagen-containing intra-uterine devices containing a reservoir of synthetic progestagen are also effective.

Intra-uterine devices (IUDs). These have been in use for 70 years and are of three basic types: inert, copper and medicated. The exact mechanism of action is still unknown but all cause an inflammatory reaction in the lining of the uterus so that protective white cells engulf the sperm or fertilised ovum. Copper-containing devices alter the levels of enzymes and trace elements in the lining of the uterus, and copper is a spermicide. Progestagen-releasing IUDs suppress normal development of the uterine lining and may inhibit ovulation.

IUDs may increase the amount of blood lost at menstruation, but this side-effect is less of a problem with copper or progestagen devices, and in any case declines with the duration of use. Although the IUD is not suitable for many women, and although users are exposed to an increased risk of pelvic infection, there are few serious side-effects. The device can be left in place for several years with little involvement on the part of the woman herself.

Future methods

Better methods of long-term delivery of steroids and the preparation of steroids with greater specific activity and fewer side-effects may further refine the pill. Some new approaches to contraception are on the horizon.

Analogues of gonadotrophin-releasing hormones. Interference with the action of GnRH inhibits the menstrual cycle by reducing the secretion of LH and FSH. More than 1000 GnRH analogues, both agonists (similar but more potent) and antagonists (GnRH blockers), have been

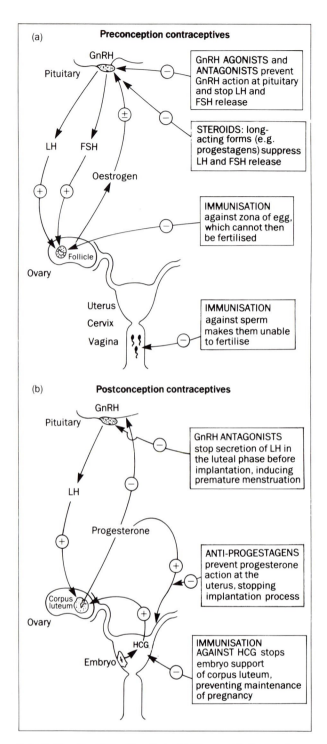

Potential female contraceptives that act (a) by preventing conception and (b) by preventing implantation or embryonic development after conception.

synthesised. These are potential contraceptives without side-effects.

GnRH agonists have been in clinical use since 1977. They were developed to induce ovulation in the treatment of infertile patients who lacked GnRH. But it was soon noticed that, when taken daily, they inhibited ovulation by provoking inappropriate secretion of gonadotrophin. In most women who take a GnRH agonist for contraception, follicles still develop and blood levels of oestradiol fluctuate. When the level falls, vaginal bleeding may occur, giving an unpredictable period of menstruation. In about one-third of women, the agonist suppresses follicular growth and ovulation and blood oestradiol levels remain low, leading to amenorrhoea. Normal menstrual cycles soon resume when the GnRH agonist is no longer taken. Prolonged agonist treatment has been used to suppress gonadal function for treatment of hormone-dependent cancers, and short-term treatment has been used for pathological conditions of the uterus.

GnRH antagonists also suppress gonadal function by blocking GnRH receptors in the pituitary. They can be used intermittently to block specific stages of the menstrual cycle, by preventing secretion of LH and FSH and thus suppressing the growth of follicles or the function of the corpus luteum. They are still in the early stages of development.

The major problem with GnRH analogues is that they are broken down if taken orally. To overcome this, analogues can be delivered by a nasal spray or by implants. Like the progestagen implants, the GnRH analogue is incorporated in a biodegradable polymer, which is implanted beneath the skin to release the drug over a long period.

The main drawback to the use of GnRH analogues as contraceptives is that follicular development, and hence oestradiol production, is often so greatly suppressed that symptoms of oestrogen deficiency such as hot flushes and vaginal dryness may arise. Long-term oestrogen deficiency may also result in the loss of bone mineral, which could lead to osteoporosis in later life. Such side-effects may be overcome by setting the dose of GnRH analogue low enough to avoid complete suppression of ovarian activity. Alternatively, supplementation with very low doses of oestrogen may be used, as is commonly prescribed for women around the menopause.

Short-term use is probably acceptable, and GnRH analogues are particularly suitable during lactation, as any GnRH analogue passing from mother to baby in the milk is not active.

Antiprogesterones. Progesterone is the key to the establishment and maintenance of pregnancy. An antiprogesterone will induce menstruation and prevent implantation in the luteal phase of the cycle and will induce abortion in early pregnancy. New antiprogestagens are potent and highly specific, but there are difficulties in regular use. To be effective the drug must be given after ovulation but before implantation. The length of normal menstrual cycles is so variable that reliance on an antiprogestagen as a contraceptive (or, to be more correct, as an antipregnancy drug) may disrupt cycles because of wrongly timed administration.

Contraceptive vaccines. For long-term contraception, a vaccine has many benefits, as immunisation should be needed only occasionally to maintain infertility. Three targets have been identified. Human *chorionic gonadotrophin* (hCG) is produced by the ovum around the time of implantation to stimulate the maintenance of the corpus luteum, and thus to provide progesterone in the early stages of pregnancy. Immunisation against hCG should prevent this and result in an early abortion, seen as a menstrual period. Trials of this vaccine are under way.

The *zona pellucida*, a shell surrounding the egg within the follicle, binds the sperm during early stages of fertilisation. Active immunisation against the zona produces long-term infertility in monkeys. The antibodies produced act as a barrier and prevent fertilisation. If their levels fall and a sperm does enter an egg, then the resulting pregnancy is normal. This is therefore a true contraceptive vaccine. There has been rapid progress in this field and the important proteins in the human zona pellucida have now been identified and

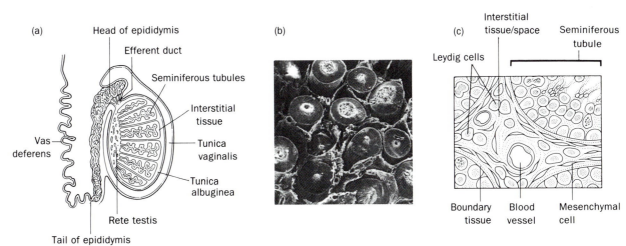

(a) Cross-section through the human testis and epididymis, showing the efferent ducts leading to the vas deferens. (b) Scanning electron micrograph of a cut surface of the testis, showing individual seminiferous tubules embedded in interstitial tissue. (c) Diagrammatic representation of the organisation of the interstitial tissue. Notice that blood capillaries and lymphocyctes are present only in the interstitial space, which also contains the testosterone-secreting Leydig cells. The boundary tissue separates the interstitial space from the seminiferous tubules, which contain the nurse or Sertoli cells and the developing spermatozoa.

DEVELOPMENTS IN FERTILITY TREATMENTS

About 10 per cent of relationships are involuntarily infertile or subfertile. The male partner is the cause in about a third of cases, the female in another third, and a combination of male and female factors accounts for the remainder.

Male infertility arises from the failure of spermatogenesis in the testes or by extratesticular factors that affect the production or function of sperm or its flow from the testes. The main causes of female infertility are failure to ovulate, obstruction of the fallopian tubes, or abnormalities in the vagina, cervix or uterus. Some infertility has no obvious cause and is described as *idiopathic.*

Treatments for male infertility include antibiotics for infection of the genital tract, immunosuppression for the presence of autoantibodies against sperm, surgery for the correction of genital abnormalities and obstructive *azoospermia* (absence of sperm), and hormonal and vitamin treatments. Success is usually measured in terms of improvements in seminal quality. Such improvements are, however, rarely accompanied by improvements in pregnancy rates.

In the female, the appropriate treatment may include stimulants for ovulatory abnormalities, surgery for tubal blockage and hormonal therapy for disorders of the uterus and other pelvic structures.

Pregnancies do occur after treatment of abnormal factors in male, female or both partners but continued infertility occurs in up to 75 per cent of cases where the couple have been trying to have a family for more than 2 years. Assisted conception methods concentrate on the presentation of spermatozoa directly to the oocyte. They were first used in cases of unexplained infertility but are now also used in patients with disorders of ovulation and those with varying degrees of sperm abnormalities. As long as sperm can be collected from the ejaculate and suspended in medium, then assisted conception can be tried.

Artificial insemination. When artificial insemination with husband or partner sperm (AIH) was first introduced, sperm were simply inserted in and around the cervix of the uterus at the time of ovulation. Ovulation can be accurately controlled with drugs. This treatment is helpful in certain situations – for example, where there are coital difficulties or only a small ejaculate is produced – but does not greatly improve pregnancy rates, especially among patients suffering from unexplained infertility.

Intrauterine insemination (IUI) and **intraperitoneal insemination** (IPI) both require that sperm are collected from the partner's semen because other constituents of seminal plasma are toxic to the female reproductive tract. The prepared sperm are introduced into the uterine cavity with a catheter or injected into the peritoneal cavity through the posterior fornix of the vagina. Ovulation is induced whenever possible. Sperm introduced in this way are very close to the oocytes as they rupture from their follicles. It is still difficult to assess the efficacy of this treatment as intrauterine insemination is now performed for all categories of infertile patients.

In vitro *fertilisation* (IVF) and **intravaginal culture** (IVC) provide 'test-tube babies'. The first was born in 1978 and IVF has since become almost routine. It entails bringing sperm and occyte together outside the body. The resulting embryo (2 to 3 days old) is then transferred back into the uterus. The technique was developed to help couples whose infertility resulted from obstructed or damaged fallopian tubes. Its use has been extended to most infertile patients.

IVF succeeds best in patients with obstructed or damaged tubes. The overall success rate is between 10 and 25 per cent at each attempt at treatment. Although failure can occur at any stage,

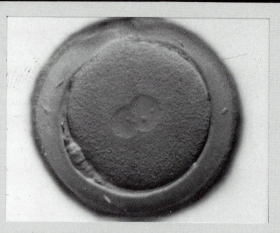

The fusion of male and female human pronuclei after penetration of the outer covering of the egg (zona pellucida) by a single sperm. The pronuclei appear as the two small circles that are merging in the centre of the fertilised egg.

between 60 and 70 per cent of couples treated do produce an embryo. It is at the stage of embryo replacement or transfer back into the womb that most failures occur as the embryos do not implant into the uterine wall.

Before treatment, the woman is given drugs to stimulate the ovaries to produce and grow several follicles, each containing an oocyte. Ultrasound scans are used to watch the growth of these follicles and when they are 'mature' the eggs are collected. With laparoscopy, a fibre-optic telescope is pushed through the abdominal wall and this allows the surgeon to withdraw eggs using a needle inserted into each mature follicle. With ultrasound-guided egg collection, the surgeon uses the picture produced by an ultrasound scan to guide the needle to the ovary.

The eggs and sperm are then mixed

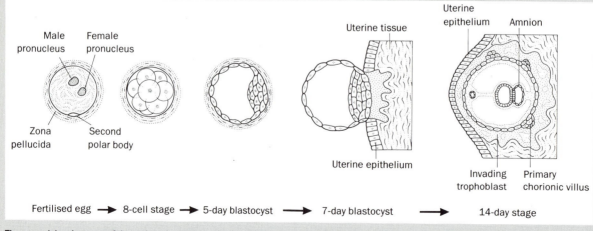

Fertilised egg → 8-cell stage → 5-day blastocyst → 7-day blastocyst → 14-day stage

The normal development of the embryo from the pronuclear stage through the stage of cellular proliferation to implantation of the embryo in the uterine wall.

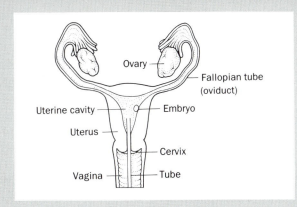

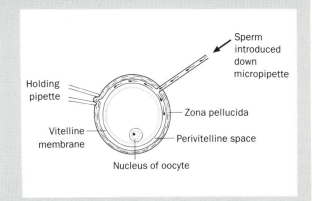

Replacement of the 2- to 3-day-old embryo in the womb after *in vitro* fertilisation. A 78-hour human embryo is shown below.

With micro-insemination sperm transfer (MIST) or subzonal insemination (SUZI; see below), fertilisation is helped by injecting sperm in a micropipette through the zona pellucida into the space between the oocyte and the zona.

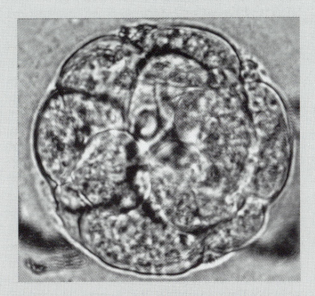

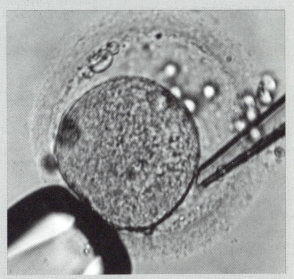

together in a prepared fluid. Once an embryo has started developing, it is placed in the uterine cavity by means of a fine soft tube threaded through the cervical canal. Up to three embryos can be transferred in this way.

Gamete intrafallopian tube transfer (GIFT) is similar to IVF in the way the ovary is stimulated to produced oocytes, which are collected laparoscopically. After egg collection, sperm are added and this mixture is then introduced down the laparoscope and into the fallopian tube where fertilisation can occur.

GIFT has the advantage over IVF in that fertilisation occurs in a natural physiological environment, rather than outside the body. However, it does not allow the success or failure of the process to be observed. The technique cannot be used in cases where there is tubal blockage or damage.

Micro-assisted fertilisation (MAF), **micro-insemination sperm transfer** (MIST) or

subzonal insemination (SUZI) are recent developments. They are used when there is a very low sperm count or where there is poor sperm motility or many abnormal forms, when the sperm may be of insufficient quality to attempt even IVF.

Fertilisation is helped by injecting the sperm in a micropipette through the zona pellucida (the outer covering of the egg) into the space between the oocyte and the zona. Fertilisation rates of 20 to 30 per cent may be achieved. Another technique, 'zona drilling', involves puncturing holes in the zona pellucida so that sperm can enter and fertilise the oocyte.

Donor insemination (DI) is available to couples for whom it is inadvisable or impossible to use the partner's sperm. It is an alternative to adoption when the infertility is on the male side or when there is a chance of producing an abnormal baby. Very careful counselling is required. Donors are screened for infections and for genetic diseases, such as cystic fibrosis.

Whenever possible, couples are prescribed a donor whose blood group and hair and eye colour match theirs.

The treatment is usually via simple vaginal (cervical) insemination at the correct time in the ovulatory cycle. Timing of ovulation, usually by ultrasound scanning and hormonal screening, is the critical factor in achieving good pregnancy rates (50 to 70 per cent overall at the end of 12 cycles of treatment). There are, of course, important ethical questions that must be considered.

Assisted conception has no significant risks other than an increased risk of multiple births and the hazards that occur with such pregnancies. There is no reported increase in fetal abnormalities and, although there is a potential risk of infection when using donor sperm, with careful monitoring of donors and quarantining sperm frozen in liquid nitrogen such risks can be kept to the minimum.   *D.I. Lewis-Jones*

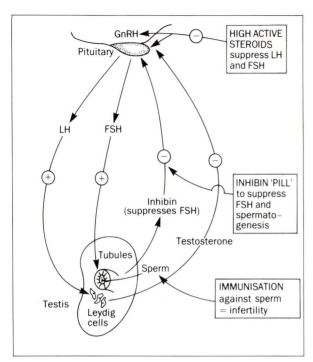

Potential male contraceptives.

sequenced. Using this information, short lengths of the protein (peptides) are being developed for immunisation and the prospects are promising.

A similar situation occurs naturally in up to 5 per cent of infertile couples, where either the man or the woman spontaneously develop antibodies to *sperm antigens*. These make the sperm incapable of fertilisation. Sperm antigens might be suitable for the production of antibodies. However, in contrast to the zona pellucida, there are several hundred of these on the sperm and the most important have not yet been identified. Immunisation (at least against zona and sperm antigens) is potentially free of side-effects and should provide long-term protection. The major difficulty is in producing enough antibody to make a reliable vaccine. Nevertheless, this approach, particularly immunisation against zona proteins, offers an anticonception vaccine that should have a great impact as a safe contraceptive.

The male pill. In adult men, spermatogenesis is principally under the control of *testosterone* secreted by the Leydig cells

in the interstitial space of the testis. The role of FSH is now uncertain. A greater understanding of the control of spermatogenesis may open new avenues for the development of a reliable male contraceptive. Because high levels of testosterone are required in the testis, suppression of LH leads to a reduction in intratesticular testosterone and a reduction or failure of sperm production. A potentially reliable male pill might thus be developed that acts by reducing LH and hence testosterone.

As in women, GnRH analogues can be used to suppress the release of LH and FSH and to reduce the secretion of testosterone. They are used to treat prostate cancer. However, the loss of sex drive that can accompany the withdrawal of testosterone may limit the potential of GnRH analogues as a male contraceptive.

In contrast, treatment of men with testosterone will inhibit the output of LH, resulting in a reduction of testosterone production within the testis to a level below that which will support spermatogenesis. With the development of new, long-acting testosterone derivatives, a practical male contraceptive has now been developed and should soon be generally available. Because these agents are not active if taken orally, the hormone must be administered by intramuscular injection, but this causes minimal discomfort. In addition, because the contraceptive is itself testosterone, there is no loss of sex drive. Clinical trials have shown that this male 'pill' is reliable and acceptable.

The initial optimism about the use of the gonadal hormone inhibin (which specifically suppresses FSH) as a male contraceptive has evaporated. There are problems with the production of inhibin in sufficient quantities. The original premise that suppression of FSH would stop spermatogenesis has been overtaken by the revolution in understanding of the role of LH-driven testosterone in controlling spermatogenesis. FSH thus no longer appears to be a suitable target for a male contraceptive.

In spite of research into the basic physiology of reproduction, which is identifying new and exciting areas of contraception, it is chastening to realise that more births are still prevented by nature's own contraceptive, breastfeeding, than by all the artificial methods combined.

Alan S. McNeilly

Tribal peoples in the modern world

The Dassanetch cattle-herders of southern Ethiopia say that their country is the centre of the earth. From the point of view of modern industrial civilisation, however, their territory is remote and peripheral – as are the Dassanetch themselves and the other peoples like them. Yet such peoples still account for perhaps 4 per cent of the world's population. They are commonly called 'tribal peoples'; a term not wholly satisfactory as the word 'tribal' has too many different meanings, but no adequate alternative exists.

During the expansion of European colonisation in the seventeenth to nineteenth centuries, millions of native peoples were driven from their lands or wiped out; killed or dying of introduced diseases to which they had no immunity. Nevertheless, many survived relatively undisturbed because they lived in, or had retreated to, territories remote from the centres of industrial civilisation. The expansion of population and industry since World War II means that these areas also are being invaded and that the remaining tribal peoples are therefore under pressure as never before.

Tribal peoples, in the sense used here, are organised in small communities, generally based on some form of kinship linkage, and normally taking decisions by consensus; in any case, without a centralised state organisation. Those that farm use extensive rather than intensive farming techniques – such as shifting agriculture ('swidden' or 'slash and burn') or nomadic or semi-nomadic livestock herding. They have low levels of production and low inputs. Some live wholly or partly on wild produce, gathering plants and hunting or fishing. Their economic self-sufficiency distinguishes them from peasants, who live at least partly by the market economy.

Tribal peoples remain separate from urban industrial civilisation, with their own systems of thought and values, among them a profound involvement in the land by which they live, which is often held to be sacred. Such beliefs and values are a continuation of those that were common to all humankind, before part of it developed urban, commercial and state systems, and later industrial civilisation. Nineteenth-century scientists, influenced by the general dominance of evolutionary theory in all fields of thought, classified such peoples as 'survivals', representing earlier stages in the social evolution of mankind.

This way of thinking has been rejected by most anthropologists, who see in the societies they study personal relationships and ways of thought reflecting not an absence of development but development of a different kind from that of industrial civilisation. They also recognise that there is no connection between culture and physical evolution, as modern tribal peoples are drawn from every major ethnic group. However, the idea of tribal peoples as evolutionary throwbacks remains rooted in the public mind.

We may also include as 'tribal' people who, though they have now lost their tribal organisation and economy, practised it until recently and still identify themselves by it, retaining important elements of their traditional culture. If we include such groups, the number of tribal people in the world today is about 200 million.

In many cases – as in the Indians of the Americas or the Australian Aborigines – tribal peoples are the native, or indigenous, peoples of the country in which they live, whose ancestors occupied it before it was colonised. In others, they are groups related to the majority population, who have developed separately or have gone on following a traditional way of life while the rest have become modernised.

In Asia, the tribal peoples are those who have followed a separate development through living in mountains, forests or deserts. In India, the 'scheduled tribes' comprise about 40 million people belonging to around 400 tribal groups. Many still live by shifting cultivation, hunting and gathering. Today, they face increasing alienation of their lands, invasion of their forests by timber and paper companies, and hydroelectric schemes that evict thousands. The tribal peoples of Southeast Asia, too, are shifting cultivators and many are still hunters and gatherers. They include the forest people of Malaysia, whose lands are invaded by logging companies, and the hill tribes of Thailand, Vietnam, Cambodia and Laos, whose societies have been dismembered by war.

An Indian tribal settlement in Araku Valley, Andrah Pradesh.

TRIBAL PEOPLES AND THEIR WAYS OF LIFE

The population figures here must be taken as a very rough guide. An exact enumeration is impossible, because of the difficulty of census-taking in many areas, the problem of defining who is and is not 'tribal', and the fact that available figures have been collected at different dates with different biases

Inuit: 98 500. Hunting, fishing, paid labour, state support

North American Indians: 2.6 million. Farming, hunting, fishing, trapping, paid labour, state support

Central American Indians: 13 million. Farming, paid labour

Arabian Nomads: 5 million. Herding, farming, paid labour

African Nomadic Pastoralists: 14 million. Herding, some farming, paid labour

'Pygmies': 170 000. Gathering, hunting, client labour for farmers

South American Lowland Indians: 1 million. Farming, fishing, hunting; a few nomadic gatherer-hunters; now some paid labour

Andean Indians: 17.5 million. Farming, paid labour

ENDANGERED TRIBES

Peoples who face the worst threats in today's world include:

Yanomami (Brazil): The Yanomami of the Brazilian and Venezuelan rain forest were one of the last major Amazonian peoples to keep their land and way of life intact. But since 1987 their land has become the scene of a gold rush as tens of thousands of prospectors have invaded it. In 1987–89, 1500 of the 9000 or so Yanomami in Brazil died of diseases caught from the miners. In 1991, the Yanomami's land was given legal protection, but this will be difficult to enforce.

Tribes of the Chittagong Hills (Bangladesh): The lands of these 10 tribes – subsistence farmers and Buddhists by religion – have, since the 1970s, been invaded by Bengali Muslim settlers. A movement demanding more local automony for the tribes has led to repression by the Bangladeshi military and the area has been sealed off. There have been reports of the torture and killing of thousands of villagers and the burning of villages.

San ('Bushmen') of the Kalahari (Namibia, South Africa, Botswana and Angola): The group of peoples known as Bushmen, San and other names have been hunted and exploited for centuries by both blacks and whites. Farms, ranches and game parks now occupy most of their former hunting grounds. Today, in spite of romantic images perpetuated by the media, almost none follow the old hunter-gatherer way of life. Most are now farm labourers for little or no pay, or depend on government handouts. Some are attempting to remain independent by taking up subsistence farming and herding.

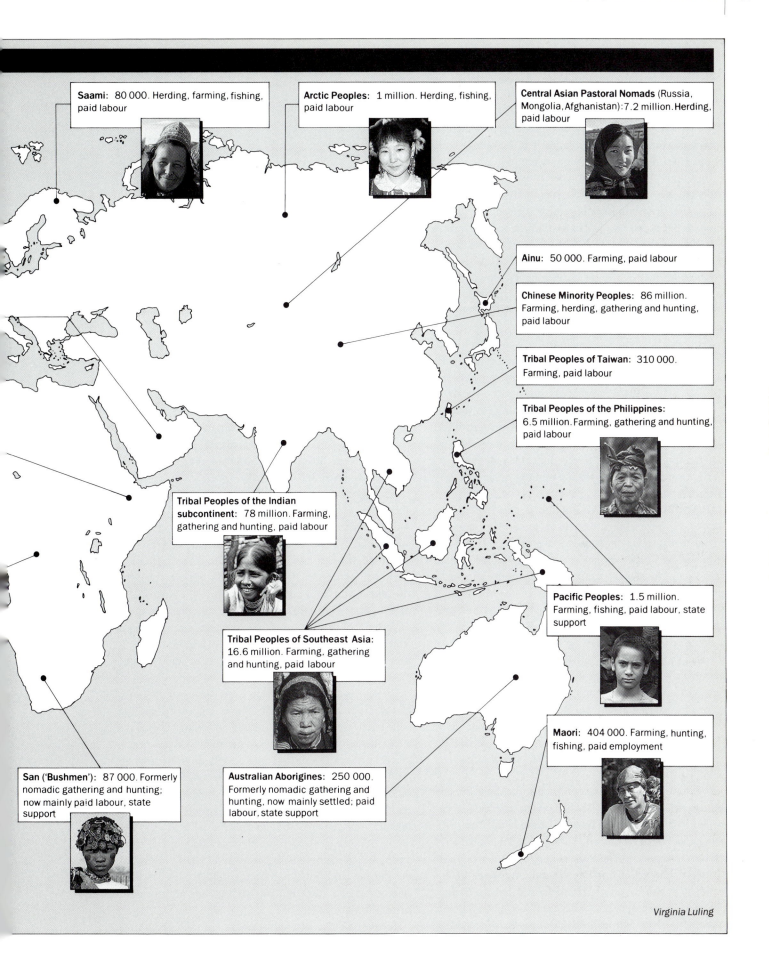

Saami: 80 000. Herding, farming, fishing, paid labour

Arctic Peoples: 1 million. Herding, fishing, paid labour

Central Asian Pastoral Nomads (Russia, Mongolia, Afghanistan): 7.2 million. Herding, paid labour

Ainu: 50 000. Farming, paid labour

Chinese Minority Peoples: 86 million. Farming, herding, gathering and hunting, paid labour

Tribal Peoples of Taiwan: 310 000. Farming, paid labour

Tribal Peoples of the Philippines: 6.5 million. Farming, gathering and hunting, paid labour

Tribal Peoples of the Indian subcontinent: 78 million. Farming, gathering and hunting, paid labour

Pacific Peoples: 1.5 million. Farming, fishing, paid labour, state support

Tribal Peoples of Southeast Asia: 16.6 million. Farming, gathering and hunting, paid labour

Maori: 404 000. Farming, hunting, fishing, paid employment

San ('Bushmen'): 87 000. Formerly nomadic gathering and hunting; now mainly paid labour, state support

Australian Aborigines: 250 000. Formerly nomadic gathering and hunting, now mainly settled; paid labour, state support

Virginia Luling

The 2 million or so tribal people of Indonesia are being overwhelmed by a massive government plan to deal with overpopulation by moving colonists onto their land. In the Philippines, the 6.5 million tribal people live mainly in the mountains; they include settled farmers with superbly constructed systems of hillside terracing. But they are increasingly being turned out of their lands in favour of large-scale commercial agriculture, logging and mining.

In China, about 6 million of the 86-million-strong 'minority peoples' were until recently living by shifting cultivation or by hunting and gathering. Nomadic pastoral peoples of Central Asia live in both China and the former USSR (now the Commonwealth of Independent States, CIS); in the Mongolian Republic, they are the majority. Policies in both the USSR and China in theory allowed much autonomy to minority peoples, but in practice have frequently subjected them to forced assimilation, and colonisation of their lands.

Peoples following a pastoral nomadic way of life – herding cattle or camels together with sheep and goats – exist in North Africa, Arabia and the Middle East, and in the Sahelian belt of Africa. Pastoral nomadism is well adapted for survival in areas too arid for settled farming. However, it has often been seen by those in power as 'primitive' and wasteful, and the nomads themselves as an unreliable and dangerous element in the population. Many governments have pursued policies of settling nomads in one place by persuasion or force.

The value of pastoral techniques is slowly being accepted. However, nomadic peoples are under increasing pressure as their grazing lands are taken over for large-scale irrigation and other agricultural schemes, or for wildlife reserves, and as they compete for the remainder with peasant farmers. In Africa, because of the shortage of pasture, the droughts that ravaged the Sahel in the 1970s and 80s hit the nomads particularly hard.

Some groups in Africa are (or were until recently) hunters and gatherers, combining this with exchange of products or a client relationship with farmers. Among the most famous are the 'Pygmy' peoples of West and Central Africa, some of whom still retain their way of life. The San ('Bushmen') peoples of southern Africa, on the other hand, have almost entirely ceased to be hunters as their last remaining hunting grounds have been taken over for farms, ranches or wildlife parks.

In the Americas, after the conquest and colonisation by Europeans, the surviving 'Indians' were gradually compelled to live on a small fraction of the lands they once inhabited. The degree to which they retain their tribal ways of life varies greatly. The Indians of North America, once farmers or hunters, all now interact to some degree with the national economy, although most still retain distinct cultures. Government policy has been to confine them to tracts of land known in the USA as reservations and as reserves in Canada. The degree to which a tribe has survived

Yali men cooking a pig, Irian Jaya, New Guinea.

and kept its identity depends largely on the adequacy of their remaining land; those without land often drift to the cities. Although a few groups have prospered, most tribes suffer unemployment rates of up to 40 per cent, and incomes on the reserves can be as little as a quarter of the national average. The exploitation of coal, oil and uranium on Indian land, though it may bring in some money, reduces their land base still further.

When Columbus arrived in the 'new world', there were about 50 million indigenous people living in South America. Within a few decades of European contact some 96 per cent of the population was eliminated. Nevertheless, in Central America, and in the highlands of South America, the Indian population is still numerically important (and in Guatemala and Bolivia forms the majority). Traditionally, these people were settled farmers, practising various forms of communal land tenure. Now deprived of most of their land, and with their traditional systems of tenure abolished, they suffer the extreme poverty, oppression and violence that are endemic in the region.

The lowland Indians of South America, including those of the tropical forests, by tradition combined shifting cultivation with hunting, gathering or fishing. They have suffered one of the worst rates of destruction by white colonisers. In Brazil alone, of some 5.7 million Indians when the Portuguese arrived, fewer than 200 000 survive today. Those who survived did so because their territories are remote and hard to reach. But the twentieth century has seen the opening up of the Amazon and other forests. The future of these lowland tribes depends on whether their traditional territories can be protected by law. Threats to the Indians lands include mining, drilling for oil, hydroelectric projects, cattle ranches, and settlement by peasant farmers from outside.

Northern Canada and Alaska are the home of arctic hunting peoples – Indians and Inuit (Eskimo). The latter also live

'Pygmies' preparing poison and arrows for a hunt in the Ituri Forest, Zaire.

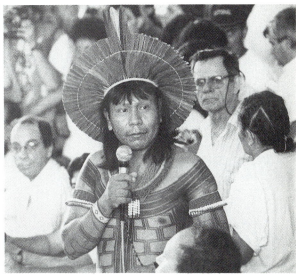

A Kayapo Indian at the historic Altamira meeting in 1989, protesting against the building of a dam in his group's territory in Amazonia, Brazil.

in Greenland and Siberia. Other arctic peoples are the 'small northern peoples' of Siberia, and the Saami (Lapps) of Scandinavia. These peoples are traditionally hunters, trappers and fishers, and, in the case of the Siberian peoples and the Saami, herders of reindeer. In North America and Siberia, oil drilling, mining, and military bases and training grounds occupy land and destroy the hunting way of life. The northern peoples of the CIS are now minorities in their own lands, and uncontrolled industrial development has severely damaged their environment and their health.

The Aboriginal people of Australia used to live by gathering and hunting alone. At the time of British colonisation in 1788, there may have been as many as 700000 of them; by 1900, this number had been reduced to 66000. Until recently, they were allowed no legal claim to any of their former land. Today, there are at least 250000 Australian Aborigines, but none now lives entirely in the old way, and they include many detribalised urban people. The Aborigines are the poorest group in Australia today, and disease, malnutrition and alcoholism are common. There is an ever-growing movement for Aboriginal rights, but their land claims face competition from mining and cattle and sheep farming.

The 42 tribes of the Maori of New Zealand have fared better than most colonised peoples; yet they now own only 5 per cent of the land that was once theirs, and are the poorest section of the New Zealand population. Once farmers, hunters and fishers, nearly four out of five Maori now live in cities, which leads to weakening of tribal ties.

The first problem facing tribal peoples today is how to survive at all, both as individuals and as groups with their own identities; for this, adequate land is indispensible. The second is how to reconcile their identity and culture with the impact of the modern world. Tribal peoples have always fought against those who encroached on their land, and much of modern history is based on their defeat. Today, although groups in a few parts of the world carry on guerilla warfare against colonists, such peoples are increasingly forming intertribal organisations to maintain their rights and identities by non-violent means, using national and international law, and appealing to world opinion.

Virginia Luling

Conclusion

The evolutionary future of humankind

This encyclopedia has mainly been about the past. Sometimes it has tried to reconstruct history from the fragments of information that remain from times long gone. More often, it has inferred past events from studies of the present by, for example, making evolutionary trees of similarity based on the genetics of living creatures. The disagreements between students of the extinct and the extant that appear at several places in this book show how hard it is to reconstruct the processes that gave rise to modern humans.

This problem is much worse when trying to tell the evolutionary future. One of the few predictable things about evolution is its unpredictability: which dinosaur could have guessed that descendants of the shrew-like creatures playing at its feet would soon replace it; and how could it have been predicted only 30 000 years ago that one moderately common primate would be among the most abundant of mammals while its genetically almost indistinguishable relatives were near extinction? The opportunistic nature of evolution – its ability to cope with the unexpected – means that, just as in politics, it is almost impossible to guess what is going to happen next.

There have, of course, been many attempts to do so. Most fictional predictions by authors of greater or lesser literary merit involve a Lamarckian view of evolution: heavily used organs get larger; those no longer needed disappear. Thus there arise creatures as different as the terrestrial masters and the subterranean slaves in H. G. Wells's *The Shape of Things to Come*. Less pretentious utopias have our descendants with x-ray vision or computers as brains. However, if we can be sure about anything it is that humanity will not become superhuman. We will, as always, build on our present weaknesses rather than make a new evolutionary start. The mechanisms of change that shape the future will certainly be those that led to modern humans.

Biologists who try to predict the future always run the dreadful risk of being taken seriously, either by themselves or – even worse – by

An artistic impression – based on a scanning electron micrograph – of a human egg surrounded by vast numbers of sperm.

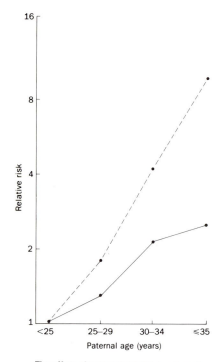

The effect of increasing father's age on the relative rate of mutation to achondropastic dwarfism (broken line) and osteogenesis imperfecta, a skeletal disorder (continuous line); with the rate at age 20 arbitrarily set at 1.00. The incidence of mutation increases greatly with age in both cases.

politicians who cannot believe the depth of our biological ignorance. The early days of human genetics were marred by statements of great (and quite unjustified) confidence about the fate awaiting us unless genetically defective individuals were prevented from reproducing. Ideas derived from the eugenics movement (p. 443) led to the horrors of the Nazi experiment; and, although this is less widely known, to the American immigration laws that prevented eastern Europeans from escaping it. Since then, most geneticists have been more careful about discussing the social implications of their subject and less confident about their ability to do so. There have, nevertheless, been changes in the genetics of human populations that are certain to affect our evolutionary future. We can at least speculate about what that might be.

Evolution involves variation, a struggle for existence, and natural selection. Random events also play an important part, particularly in small populations. What will happen to these processes over the next thousand years?

Variation

Genetic diversity arises from mutation. It can be introduced into populations by immigration, and may be lost by random accident, particularly from small populations.

The human mutation rate can be altered by many things. Some mutagens became more abundant with Western civilisation. There has been an increase of ionising radiation associated with x-rays, nuclear technology and flying; and some of the benefits of civilisation – for example, smoking, hairdyes, food preservatives and pesticides – have increased our exposure to chemical mutagens. However, it is important to see this in context. Humans have always been exposed to mutagenic agents. Many plants have evolved chemical – and mutagenic – defences against pests. One estimate has it that we ingest 10 000 times as much natural as synthetic pesticide. Spices such as black pepper carry a dose of chemicals that cause mutations in bacteria. Some foods produce more mutagens as they become stale, and fungal pests of stored food synthesise aflatoxins, which are among the most potent mutagens known.

Exposure to many of these chemicals has gone down. Increased consumption of fresh fruit and vegetables (some of which contain antimutagens) may also be important in reducing the mutation rate. The most widespread increase in radiation is among people who live in houses built of granite or on granite bedrock, but the use of synthetic materials will reduce this. Although it is hard to make predictions about a rare event such as mutation it seems unlikely that external agents will increase the human mutation rate enough to alter our genetic diversity.

One factor has certainly changed the pattern of human mutation and will probably continue to do so. This is the age of reproduction. The mean age at first reproduction in Western societies is at least 5 years older than in preagricultural peoples. This is complicated by the fact that women cease reproducing at an earlier age in more economically advanced societies. The mutation rate of body cells increases with age, and much of the 'epidemic' of cancer in Western societies results from the increased proportion of old people. The same is true for the cells that produce sperm and eggs, as is manifest in the increased incidence of chromosomal and genetic mutations with age. This will probably lead to a considerable alteration in the human mutation rate – and hence of the new variation on which selection might act – within a century or so.

Increased mobility increases the input of new variation because of immigration from genetically distinct populations. The first of tens of thousands of African slaves reached the United States in the seventeenth century. Nearly all came from West Africa, where the Duffy Fy^- blood group is common. Since then, genetic exchange with whites has introduced the typically European Fy^a variant, and in some American black populations this has reached a frequency of 30 per cent. No doubt other genes from local whites have also entered, so that American blacks – and the adjacent white population – have both gained genetic variation not present in their ancestors. The amount of diversity entering modern populations in this way is much greater than that arising from any increase in the mutation rate.

African slaves chained together in Washington, DC, in 1819.

Natural selection

There is no immediate relationship between the growth of the human population and the 'struggle for existence' or the intensity of natural selection. For 50 000 years the size of the human population scarcely increased at all; and before the appearance of Europeans the population of the Americas had reached only a few million in the 20 000 years or so since humans entered that continent. However, modern tribal populations, sparse though they are, suffer from high childhood mortality and many males fail to find a mate. The struggle to survive and to pass on genes was certainly as great in these early populations as in the cities of today.

Medicine has changed the way in which natural selection works. In the past, disease was an important selective agent, and genetic differences in susceptibility to particular infections affected many human genes. In the West, such diseases are now rare, but they are still common in the Third World, and may become more so as pressure of population pushes people into squalid cities. Such a change in population and way of life may have been what sparked off earlier epidemics.

The spread of epidemics depends crucially on the size and mobility of the population at risk. In the past, disease outbreaks were often very localised: local groups each had a unique history of disease that did not spread beyond their borders. In Amazonian tribal peoples, for example, antibodies show that the incidence of particular infections varies greatly (and apparently at random) from group to group. In adjacent villages, the proportion with antibodies showing an earlier infection with measles varied from 0 to 98 per cent and with influenza from 0 to 89 per cent. Increased mobility means that such epidemics may be able to spread far more quickly than in earlier times. It is far too early to dismiss infectious disease as an agent of natural selection. As disease organisms themselves evolve in unpredictable ways, it is hard to guess just how important selection by disease will be in future generations: the evolution of new diseases such as AIDS, which may provoke a genetic response in its hosts, emphasises this.

Medical care will certainly have an effect on our genetic future. One of the best-known examples of natural selection in humans is the greater death rate of light or heavy babies compared to those near the average weight (see p. 286). Over the past 20 years there has been a worldwide tendency, in developed countries at least, for the intensity of this stabilising selection to decrease so that genes that were until recently under strong selection are, with the benefit of medical care, protected from its action.

Environmental changes of this kind have affected many genes. The effect is sometimes striking. Until recently, children with the inborn error phenylketonuria, who are unable to metabolise the amino acid phenylalanine, nearly always died young. Now they can be diagnosed at birth and given a diet free from this substance. Many survive to adulthood. The action of natural selection has been greatly modified by a simple environmental change. As we understand more and more about the biochemistry of genetic disease, this approach will no doubt be applied to many of them.

EUGENICS

Human genetics has a dark history. Long before Gregor Mendel, philosophers were entranced by parallels between animal breeding and the improvement of the human race and many suggested that the best should be bred from or the worst should be prevented from so doing. The genetic betterment of humankind was strongly advocated by the English scientist Francis Galton.

Galton, a cousin of Charles Darwin, was an inspired dabbler in science. He was the first to suggest the use of fingerprints in detective work, produced the first weather map, and tested the efficacy of prayer by comparing the survival of those much prayed for (such as British monarchs) with those less favoured.

Galton's book *Hereditary Genius* (1869) was the earliest study of human genetics. He looked at patterns of 'eminence' (loosely defined) in the relatives of those known to be eminent, and found a strong tendency for distinction to run in families; genius was, it seemed, determined by genes. From this, it was a short step to recommending that only those genetically favoured should be allowed to reproduce. Galton founded the 'science' of *eugenics* — of being well born.

This idea fitted well with the temper of the times. Its influence increased with the rediscovery of Mendel's laws around 1900. Within 5 years, Mendelism was being applied to human pedigrees. Soon there appeared the first of a series of pedigrees purporting to show the inheritance of behaviours such as criminality, idiocy, and even of sea-going or of pathological running away among slaves.

Predictably enough, such genetical fictions were soon applied to differences between human groups. One particularly notorious work, *Race-crossing in Jamaica*, declared that inter-racial matings were undesirable on the grounds that the offspring might inherit the long legs of the black parent and the short arms of the white, and hence be unable to bend down to pick up things.

It is easy to laugh at such fantasies. However, they had social and political effects that lasted for many years after the ideas themselves had been discredited. The first attempt to limit European immigration into the United States came in the 1920s.

The legislators were much influenced by a committee, the Eugenics Record Office, who claimed that there was a severe danger of the genetic heritage of the USA being damaged by the immigration of genetically inferior peoples, most notably those from eastern Europe. President Calvin Coolidge himself said that 'America must be kept American. Biological laws show that Nordics deteriorate when mixed with other races'.

Quotas were set limiting the entry from each country. These lasted until the 1960s. They meant, for example, that many of those trying to escape the depradations of another monomaniac — Hitler — bent on the biological improvement of the human race were denied entry. Other eugenical laws allowing the sterilisation of mental defectives or habitual criminals remained on the statute books of some US states until equivalently recently. By the mid-1930s, more than 20 000 sterilisations on eugenic grounds had been carried out in the USA.

Remnants of eugenic thought can be seen today among those who claim, for example, that working-class children do badly in school because they have inherited genes for low intelligence. However, perhaps the most encouraging thing about modern human genetics is that as the means of making 'eugenic' decisions have improved, the interest in applying them to the betterment of the human race has almost disappeared. New methods for prenatal diagnosis or for the identification of carriers of inherited disease are applied only to advise the individuals or families involved of the chances of having an affected child and not to some general scheme of social engineering.

As is often the case in science, geneticists have become much more humble about their understanding of their subject as they realise how little they really know. Eugenics was based on ignorance and prejudice rather than on fact; a science with these at its centre was bound to die. *Steve Jones*

There have, of course, been many other changes in our environment and these are are set to continue. Many have genetic implications. For example, genes for certain enzyme variants predispose their carriers to severe breathing difficulties if they smoke: 300 years ago this was a new force of natural selection, whose future now depends on the future of the smoking habit.

Changes in diet may have more dramatic genetic effects. The diet of Western nations now contains much more animal fat than it did in the Middle Ages. This has greatly increased the incidence of death from coronary heart disease; and individuals bearing genes that reduce the ability to break down animal fats are more at risk than others. The intensity of natural selection on these genes depends strongly on future patterns of diet. These are hard to predict, but it does seem likely that much of the developing world will follow the Western course. Any change in our way of life is certain to alter the balance of natural selection – genes once harmful may lose their disadvantage, while others, harmless at present, will pose a threat to their carriers.

Optimists often claim that medical advance and improvements in our environment will greatly increase our length of life; men may become immortals. Without genetic variation, there can be no evolutionary progress. Depressingly enough, it seems that we may already have reached the end of the road of increasing human longevity, in Western societies at least. The great killer of past centuries was infectious disease, and improvements in public health had a dramatic effect on life expectancy. In the United States, mean life expectancy at birth rose from 47 to 75 years during the present century as infectious disease was controlled, leaving cancer and heart disease as the main causes of mortality.

Such diseases are themselves influenced by external agents, such as smoking or diet. However, recent attempts to control these have had little effect; and adult life expectancy has scarcely increased in the past decade. For example, women of 65 had a life expectancy of 18.6 years in 1989 – exactly the same as in 1979. Far more of us now reach the age limit set by the genetically programmed and intrinsic decay of body processes. As selection works less effectively on those who have already reproduced it is unlikely that our life expectancy can continue to increase. Bernard Shaw was wrong; we will not get back to Methuselah.

Population structure

The most important event in recent human evolution was the invention of the bicycle. There has been an extraordinary increase in mobility in the past few hundred years. One effect of this has been greatly to increase the pool from which we can choose our potential partners. The social structure of tribal populations (such as South American Indians) means that each group may consist of only a few tens of sexually mature individuals, and the number of potential partners may be even less as a few males monopolise the females. There is constant warfare between adjacent groups, which reduces the chance of their exchanging mates.

English/Nigerian couple with their baby.

Even in more settled populations, there may be a surprisingly restricted choice of partners. Parish records show that in many rural parts of nineteenth-century Europe, husbands and wives were on the average born less than 10 kilometres apart, so that their marital choice was made from a small group of potential mates. In most of Europe this distance is now ten times as great. The effect is also manifest in the decline in cousin marriages by more than half in the past century. There has hence been a dramatic increase in the size of human breeding populations in only a hundred years, an increase that is likely to continue.

This has important genetic implications. Small and isolated populations soon become inbred: the pool of potential mates is restricted to individuals who are related and have a recent ancestor in common. Mating between relatives leads to an increased chance of any child carrying two copies of a gene that has descended from its parents' common ancestor. The effect of such inbreeding can be striking. Populations on islands or in isolated communities have an increased incidence of genetic disease caused by recessive alleles.

Inbreeding leads to an overall loss of genetic variation as well. A sudden decrease in its extent – which is happening today – means that children are less likely to have two copies of a harmful gene, and may hence be in good genetic health. This may explain some of the recent increase in human height and longevity. However, this phase cannot last: sooner or later the later harmful genes will again reappear in double dose, so that future generations may have to pay the price for our temporary reprieve from the equilibrium between the appearance of harmful genes by mutation and their loss by the death of homozygotes.

Small and isolated populations diverge from each other because of the random loss of particular alleles. This can be seen in South America, where adjacent tribes have unique blood group and enzyme variants or 'private polymorphisms' that have not passed through the impermeable social and geographic barriers that surround them. Even in Italian villages isolation and inbreeding over the past few centuries have led to divergence in the frequencies of ABO blood groups and other genes.

This pattern of small, isolated and partially inbred populations has characterised humanity for most of our evolutionary history. Its effects persist even in the cities of today. The genetics of Hiroshima and Nagasaki has, for good historical reasons, been extensively studied. The genotypes of tens of thousands of the citizens have been tested by gel electrophoresis of polymorphic proteins. Hiroshima and Nagasaki each turn out to possess unique and rare genes not present in the other. These genes are relics of the random differentiation of the small and isolated tribes who coalesced thousands of years ago to found the two cities. The past history of the local tribes is thus preserved in the genetics of the modern population.

As such accidental evolution can happen only in small populations the change in human breeding structure means that the union of once isolated populations will become widespread. No longer will the human species be made up of a network of small and isolated

Change in the distance between birthplaces of marriage partners around villages in Oxfordshire, 1600–1850. The distance was stable at around 8 miles (12 km) for 250 years, but has risen since 1850 – and continues to rise rapidly. The further apart a married couple were born, the less likely they are to share a common ancestor, and the less the chance of inbreeding.

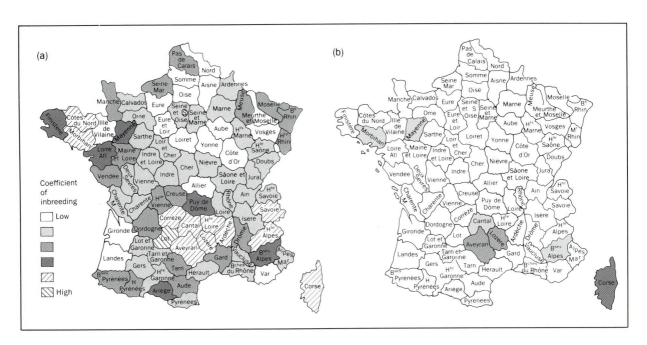

populations, each evolving more or less independently. Instead, future generations of humanity will behave much more as a single genetic unit.

Many geneticists believe that evolution is particularly rapid in groups of small populations that exchange occasional migrants: each group can change independently of the others, so that one or more of them is likely to be able to cope with any new selective challenge that may arise. The rapidity of human evolution may be partly due to our tribal structure, whose genetic effects were increased by the repeated bottlenecks experienced as human populations spread into new parts of the world. Increased mobility means that this phase of history is now at an end and, perhaps, that human evolution is now almost over.

Steve Jones

Changes in inbreeding in France 1920s (a) to 1950s (b). The intensity of shading shows the proportion of marriages which were between relatives. The number of departments with relatively high inbreeding levels has declined greatly, and continues to do so.

See also 'The nature of evolution' (p. 9), 'Genetic diversity in humans' (p. 264), 'Mutation and human evolution' (p. 269), 'Bottlenecks in human evolution' (p. 281), 'Natural selection in humans' (p. 284), 'Distribution of genetic diseases in human populations' (p. 288), 'First-cousin marriages' (p. 291) and 'People and disease' (p. 411)

Appendix I

Who's who of historical figures

Agassiz, Louis (1807–73). Swiss geologist and naturalist. Developed the idea of ice ages, and founded the Museum of Comparative Zoology at Harvard University (1859), to which he gave all his collections. Remembered for his work on fossil fish, but strongly against the theory of evolution because of his belief in an 'ideal' for each species. Believed in repeated creation events after catastrophic extinctions caused by the ice ages.

Arambourg, Camille (1885–1969). French palaeontologist (born Algeria) who led a French mission to survey the lower Omo Valley in southern Ethiopia (1932–3) and returned to the area for two field seasons in 1967–9 as leader of the French contingent of the International Omo Research Expedition. Arambourg was especially interested in the palaeontology and prehistory of North Africa. In 1954, discovered with R. Hoffstetter the middle Pleistocene site of Ternifine (now called Tighennif) in Algeria and named the hominid remains from there *Atlanthropus mauritanicus* (= *Homo erectus*). Also described the hominid jawbone (also now called *Homo erectus*) from Sidi Abderrahman in Morocco. Was professor of palaeontology at the Muséum national d'Histoire naturelle, Paris (1936–56).

Bishop, Walter William (1931–77). British geologist whose studies in the 1960s and 1970s on late Cenozoic mammalian faunas and sedimentary environments of the East African Rift Valley helped to clarify the stratigraphy and dating of many important hominoid sites. Was co-organiser of the East African Geological Research Unit for many years. Hominid sites found by his students include Chemeron and Chesowanja west of Lake Baringo in Kenya. Trained at Birmingham, he worked for the Uganda Geological Survey (1956–9), was director of the Uganda National Museum, Kampala (1962–5) and taught at the University of London from 1965, becoming professor of geology at Queen Mary College in 1974. He died just before taking up the directorship of Yale University's Peabody Museum. Co-edited *Background to Evolution in Africa* (1967) and *Calibration of Hominoid Evolution* (1972) and edited *Geological Background to Fossil Man* (1978).

Black, Davidson (1884–1934). Canadian anatomist who in 1927 named a new hominid *Sinanthropus pekinensis* on the basis of a molar tooth found at the Choukoutien (now Zhoukoudian) Cave complex near Beijing. Raised funds for the early excavations at the site, and was founder and first director of the Cenozoic Research Laboratory (part of the Geological Survey of China) at the Peking Union Medical College, where he was professor of anatomy (1920–35). The tooth and the other hominid fossils from Zhoukoudian, among them an almost complete skull found in 1929, were later included in *Homo erectus*.

Bordes, François (1919–81). Influential French prehistorian, known for his pioneering study of the River Seine's sediments, for his expertise in replicating Palaeolithic flint tools, and especially for his revolutionary classification of the Mousterian (Middle Palaeolithic) stone-tool industries of southwestern France by the *système Bordes*. This involved plotting percentages of 63 tool-types on cumulative graphs, and led him to distinguish four different groupings. He saw these as distinct toolkits representing separate tribes, but other scholars believe that chronology, geography and function are also factors in this patterning. Bordes' major excavations included the multilayered Mousterian sites of Combe-Grenal and Pech de l'Azé (Dordogne).

Boucher de Perthes, Jacques (1788–1868). French amateur prehistorian who proved the existence of 'antediluvian' artefacts (flaked stone tools). He discovered early Palaeolithic handaxes in gravel pits in the valley of the Somme. Although the interpretation of his finds was often problematical, he is considered the founder of prehistory in France. His findings attracted many geologists (including **Charles Lyell**) and led to further discoveries in England and elsewhere.

Boule, Pierre Marcellin (1861–1942). French palaeontologist, one of the founders of Paris's Institut de Paléontologie humaine and of the journal *L'Anthropologie* (1890), which he edited from 1893 to 1940. Best known for his study (1908) of the first complete Neanderthal skeleton, from La Chapelle-aux-Saints (Corrèze, France). The extrapolation of this old man's stooped arthritic posture to all Neanderthalers led to the erroneous view of them as shambling primitives that persisted for decades. Boule was aware of the osteoarthritis in the specimen's spine, but could not conceive that Neanderthals might have walked erect or been ancestral to modern humans. His eminence ensured that nobody bothered to check or expand this analysis until the 1950s. In his book *Les Hommes Fossiles* (1921), he proclaimed the Piltdown skull to be a composite of a chimpanzee jaw and a human skull.

Broca, Pierre Paul (1824–80). French surgeon and founder of physical anthropology in France. Pioneered the study of cranial capacity, and discovered the speech centre in the left frontal region of the human brain (1861) – now known as Broca's area. Founder of the Société d'Anthropologie de Paris (1859) and the journal *Revue d'Anthropologie* (1872).

Pierre Marcellin Boule.

Robert Broom at Sterkfontein cave site, South Africa.

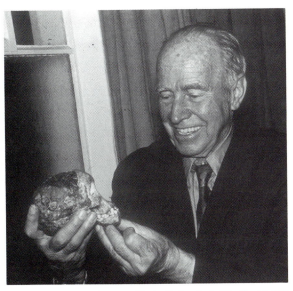

Raymond Dart with the skull of the Taung child, *Australopithecus africanus.*

Broom, Robert (1866–1951). Scots-born South African palaeontologist who, with **Raymond Dart**, changed the study of human evolution by showing that australopithecines were the earliest hominids; also made a major contribution to the study of mammal-like reptiles. After medical training in Scotland and a stint in Australia, he moved to South Africa in 1897 where he combined medicine with studying fossil vertebrates. Was professor at Victoria College, Stellenbosch (1903–10). Gave up medical practice when he became curator of fossil vertebrates, Transvaal Museum (1934–6). Supported Dart's interpretation of the infant skull from Taung and in 1936 began excavations at the Transvaal cave site of Sterkfontein, where he soon found an adult australopithecine, which he at first named *Australopithecus transvaalensis* but renamed *Plesianthropus transvaalensis* in 1937 ('Mrs Ples' = *Australopithecus africanus*). Broom also identified the robust type of australopithecine, *Paranthropus robustus*, at nearby Kromdraai cave in 1938 and found yet more hominid fossils at another Transvaal site, Swartkrans, which he began excavating in 1948. The finds of limb bones at Kromdraai and especially of part of a skeleton at Sterkfontein in 1947 vindicated Dart's claim that australopithecines walked upright and the scientific world at last accepted these fossil forms as human ancestors.

Broom was a non-conformer and a loner; he received many honours but was also criticised for selling vertebrate fossils abroad in the 1920s and, later, for his excavation techniques at hominid sites. Published more than 450 papers and monographs, many of those on the Transvaal australopithecines being co-authored with John T. Robinson, his assistant from 1947 to 1951.

Dart, Raymond Arthur (1893–1988). Australian-born South African anatomist who changed the course of human palaeontology in 1925 when he identified an infant australopithecine skull from Taungs (now Taung) in southern Africa, giving it the name *Australopithecus africanus.* His interpretation of the fossil as a human ancestor was dismissed by establishment figures such as **Arthur Keith** and **Arthur Smith Woodward** in England but it inspired another unconventional palaeontologist in South Africa, **Robert Broom**, to look for more australopithecines in the Transvaal cave sites of Sterkfontein, Kromdraai and Swartkrans. After World War II, Dart supervised excavations at Makapansgat, also in the Transvaal. His interpretation of the broken animal bones in the deposits as australopithecine tools and weapons (their 'osteodontokeratic' – bone, tooth and horn – 'culture') was misguided, although it later encouraged others (notably C.K. Brain) to seek different explanations for the fractured bones and led to interest in the science of burial, or taphonomy.

For several years, Dart's theory that australopithecines were bloodthirsty hunters overshadowed his palaeontological achievements, his studies on the modern peoples of Africa and his interest in brain development. Dart was professor of anatomy at the University of Witwatersrand from 1923 to 1958, and published his autobiography *Adventures with the Missing Link* in 1959. His belief in the australopithecine stage in human evolution was given full recognition in 1985 when the sixtieth anniversary of his announcement of the Taung skull's discovery was celebrated by an international conference in South Africa.

Darwin, Charles Robert (1809–82). The founder of modern evolutionary biology, and indeed of much of modern biology.

Charles Darwin.

Eugène Dubois.

Darwin began as a medical student at the University of Edinburgh, but moved to Cambridge where he became interested in natural history. Between 1831 and 1836 he travelled around the world on HMS *Beagle*, and his observations of fossils and living creatures sparked off the idea that one species might evolve into another. Darwin was greatly influenced by **Charles Lyell's** idea that, in geology, slow processes such as erosion by rivers could have immense effects over long periods of time, and applied this gradualism to changes in living creatures. Sketched out his theory of evolution in 1842, but did not publish it in full until 1859, when *The Origin of Species by Means of Natural Selection* appeared – largely because Darwin learned that **Alfred Russel Wallace** had been working on a theory close to his own. Darwin also published books on barnacles, earthworms, the fertilisation of flowers, orchids, coral reefs and human evolution. Spent 40 years almost as an invalid at Down House in Kent, with a malady that has never convincingly been diagnosed. Buried in Westminster Abbey.

Dawson, Charles (1864–1916). English solicitor and antiquarian, the victim (or perpetrator?) of the celebrated Piltdown Man hoax (see Box) and after whom **Arthur Smith Woodward** named the skull *Eoanthropus dawsoni* (Dawson's Dawn Man). At the dedication of a memorial stone to Dawson in 1938 at the site of the Piltdown gravel pit, **Sir Arthur Keith** likened Dawson's achievement in the history of discovery to that of the French amateur prehistorian **Jacques Boucher de Perthes**.

Dubois, Eugène (1858–1940). Dutch anatomist and palaeontologist, who nursed the ambition of finding the 'missing link' between ancestral apes and modern humans and joined the Medical Corps of the Royal Dutch East Indies Army as a way of getting to the Dutch Indies. Discovered the first *Pithecanthropus erectus* (= *Homo erectus*) fossils at Trinil at Java – in 1890, a tooth and a skull cap, and in 1892 a femur. Claimed that they represented the 'missing link' but others disagreed, believing *Pithecanthropus* to be a precursor of *Homo sapiens*. Dubois returned to the Netherlands in 1895, became increasingly withdrawn and died an embittered man.

Galton, Francis (1822–1911). Charles Darwin's cousin; dilettante, mathematician, traveller, racist and founder of the study of human inheritance. Impressed by the tendency for genius to run in families; published *Hereditary Genius* in 1869. Later became the founder of eugenics, the biological improvement of the human species, a field whose later excesses damaged the development of human genetics. Galton established the scientific study of fingerprints, the idea of 'regression' (which is at the centre of much of statistics), and published the first weather maps in the London *Times*. Other projects included a beauty map of the British Isles, statistical tests of the efficacy of prayer, and the idea of printing photographs together as a composite to gain an idea of the ideal of the

Francis Galton.

THE PILTDOWN FORGERY

The sorry tale of the Piltdown Man hoax affected human evolutionary studies for some 40 years. The fragments of skull found by **Charles Dawson** in a gravel pit at Piltdown in Sussex between 1908 and 1912, plus part of a lower jaw with two molars unearthed by Dawson and **Arthur Smith Woodward**, were accepted by the leading anatomists of the day as the 'missing link' between ancestral apes and modern humans in Darwin's theory of evolution. Scientists wanted a fossil ancestor with a human-sized skull and an ape-like jaw, believing that hominids acquired a large brain before they could walk upright and make tools; and they were given one. Dawson's discovery of other skull fragments in 1915 at a second site 2 miles away from the original finds reinforced their enthusiasm.

These were the first major finds of a fossil hominid since **Eugène Dubois**'s discovery of *Pithecanthropus* in Java in the 1890s. Apart from the Javan material (now called *Homo erectus*), there was little with

which to compare the Piltdown skull: only a jaw from Heidelberg (or Mauer) and the big-boned, 'primitive' Neanderthals.

Not until 1953 was the Piltdown skull formally declared a fake by **Joseph Weiner, Kenneth Oakley** and **Wilfrid Le Gros Clark**, after scientific tests had established that the jawbone had belonged to an ape (later shown to be an orang-utan); that the skullcap was human and older than the jawbone; that the molars were human and modern, and had been filed down; and that all the bones and the mammalian fossils and stone tools with which they were associated had been stained to match the Piltdown deposit and planted in the gravel pit.

Weiner and Oakley suspected Dawson of the fraud and he still remains the frontrunner in a long list of suspects, but others such as Woodward, **Teilhard de Chardin, Grafton Elliot Smith**, the Oxford geologist William Sollas, the Sussex chemist Samuel Woodhead and even the author Arthur Conan Doyle have been

favoured, acting as a co-conspirator with Dawson or independently of him.

Whatever the truth, the Piltdown hoax seriously misled many scientists and delayed the recognition of the australopithecine fossils found by **Raymond Dart** and **Robert Broom** for more than 20 years. The debunking of the skull was the start of a new era in human evolutionary studies.

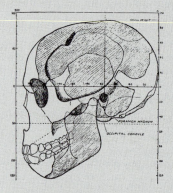

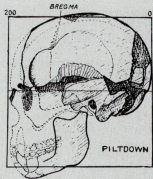

Reconstruction of the Piltdown skull made by (above) Arthur Smith Woodward early in 1913, before the right lower canine was found by Teilhard de Chardin, and (below) Arthur Keith, after the discovery of the ape-like canine. Keith had predicted that the canines would be human, Woodward that they would be ape-like. Notice the larger braincase of Keith's model.

In John Cooke's painting of the main characters in the Piltdown affair, Arthur Keith is in the centre (wearing a laboratory coat), and standing behind him (left to right) are Frank Barlow, Grafton Eliot Smith, Charles Dawson and Arthur Smith Woodward.

criminal or aristocratic face. One of his bequests founded the Laboratory for National Eugenics at University College London (now the Galton Laboratory), the first human genetics department in the world.

Gregory, William King (1876–1970). American palaeontologist with a special interest in fossil vertebrates, especially primates, and mammalian dentition. Worked at the American Museum of Natural History in New York from 1910, becoming curator of comparative anatomy in 1921. Was influential in many ways: argued in his book *Man's Place Among the Anthropoids* (1934) that humans were more closely related to the African great apes than to any other primate group, was a staunch early supporter of **Raymond Dart**'s theory about the Taung skull and was also sympathetic to **G. Edward Lewis**'s ideas about *Ramapithecus*. He followed **Aleš Hrdlička** in questioning (1929) the association of the skullcap and jawbone of the Piltdown skull (see Box).

Haeckel, Ernst (1834–1919). German zoologist, who founded the study of evolution in the German-speaking world. Coined the terms ecology, ontogeny and phylogeny. Convinced that 'ontogeny recapitulates phylogeny': that each creature relives its evolutionary past during its development. Applied the ideas of natural selection and the struggle for existence to human society, with unfortunate political consequences in twentieth-century Germany.

Haldane, John Burdon Sanderson (1892–1964). Evolutionist, physiologist, biochemist and polymath. Of Scottish descent; studied at Oxford and became professor of genetics at University of London (1933–7) and then of biometry at University College London (1937–57). Influential in the mathe-

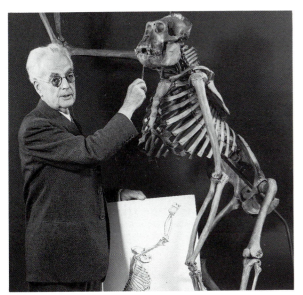

William King Gregory.

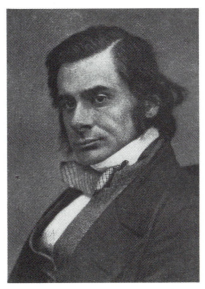

Thomas Henry Huxley.

matical theory of evolution. Established, using mice, the first case of genetic linkage in mammals; suggested that differential susceptibility to disease might have driven much of human evolution, and proposed that closely linked genes might be useful in the diagnosis of genetic disease. Haldane made equally important contributions to the theories of enzyme biochemistry and to the physiology of diving, was a brilliant populariser of science, and was a polemical communist and opponent of the misuse of human genetics for political ends.

Hrdlička, Aleš (1869–1943). American physical anthropologist (born Bohemia) whose research supported the theory that the first American Indians had once lived in Siberia and crossed to to the New World on a land bridge (Beringia) during the late Pleistocene. Was curator of physical anthropology at the National Museum of Natural History (Smithsonian Institution), Washington DC (1910–42). Was one of the few leading palaeontologists to question the association of the human-like cranium and ape-like jaw of the Piltdown skull (see Box) soon after its discovery. Studied the Taung australopithecine skull in South Africa in 1925 but dismissed it as a great ape. Was also highly critical of **G. Edward Lewis**'s claims that *Ramapithecus* was a hominid. Founded the *American Journal of Physical Anthropology* (1918) and the American Association of Physical Anthropologists (1928) and wrote several books, including *Ancient Man in North America* (1907) and *Old Americans* (1925).

Huxley, Thomas Henry (1825–95). 'Darwin's Bulldog', an enthusiastic supporter of evolution by natural selection. English physician and comparative anatomist. Began the comparison of the human brain with that of other primates, and made

important contributions to the study of jellyfish, birds, reptiles and fishes. Famous for his refutation in 1860 of Bishop Samuel Wilberforce and others who attempted to demolish Darwinism on religious grounds; and invented the term 'agnosticism'. An enthusiastic debunker of spiritualism and other woolly ideas. Wrote several books, including *Evidence as to Man's Place in Nature* (1863).

Isaac, Glynn Llywellyn (1937–85). Archaeologist (born South Africa) who specialised in the Early Stone Age of Africa. A major influence on research into the prehistory of human origins since the 1960s through his behavioural intepretations of the Palaeolithic record. Noted for his excavations at Olorgesailie in Kenya (1961–5), Peninj near Lake Natron in Tanzania (1964 and 1982) and at the complex of sites east of Lake Turkana in northern Kenya (1970–9). Professor of anthropology at the University of California, Berkeley, from 1966 to 1983, and joint director with Richard Leakey of the Koobi Fora Research Project at East Turkana. At the time of his early death, he occupied the chair of anthropology at Harvard University. Major publications include *Olorgesailie: Archaeological Studies of a Middle Pleistocene Lake Basin in Kenya* (1977) and *After the Australopithecines* (co-edited with K.W. Butzer, 1975).

Keith, (Sir) Arthur (1866–1955). British anatomist and physical anthropologist who helped 'authenticate' the fraudulent Piltdown skull found by **Charles Dawson** (see Box), and who strongly opposed **Raymond Dart**'s interpretation of the Taung hominid. Not until 1947 did he concede that australopithecines were human ancestors and that hominids walked upright before they acquired large brains. Keith's major position was as conservator of the Hun-

Glynn Isaac at Koobi Fora, Kenya, in 1972.

G. H. R. von **Koenigswald**.

terian Museum, Royal College of Surgeons (1908–33). Wrote several books including *Human Embryology and Morphology* (1902), *The Antiquity of Man* (1915) and *A New Theory of Human Evolution* (1948).

von Koenigswald, Gustav Heinrich Ralph (1902–1982). Palaeontologist (born Berlin with Danish nationality) mostly noted for his field work in Java, where he pioneered the systematic searching for hominid fossils, and for his abundant writings about the *Pithecanthropus* (= *Homo erectus*) fossils that his team found at Ngandong and Sangiran in the 1930s. Also recovered hominoids (*Sivapithecus* and *Ramapithecus*) from Miocene deposits in the Siwalik Hills of Pakistan. Returned to Europe in 1948 and later was the founder, and the curator, of the palaeoanthropology department at the Senckenberg Research Institute in Frankfurt am Main.

Lamarck, Jean-Baptiste (1744–1829). French naturalist, one of the founders of evolutionary biology. Initially a soldier, but became interested in chemistry, meteorology and biology. Pointed out the distinction between vertebrates and invertebrates, and was influential in the taxonomy of insects and molluscs. Noticed that modern species looked rather like those living in ancient times, and suggested that one might have turned into the other. Impressed by evidence of progress from simple to complex in evolution and saw this as a law of life. Also felt that animals can shape the direction of their own evolution by virtue of behaviour, so that a giraffe's stretching of its neck to reach high leaves led to longer necks in future generations. Although his supposed mechanism of inheritance was at fault, so was **Charles Darwin**'s; and Lamarck deserves more than to be remembered only as a failed predecessor of the better known evolutionist. In

France, he retains the recognition he deserves.

Lartet, Edouard (1801–71). French scholar, a founder of palaeontology through his discovery of a jaw of the first-known fossil monkey (*Pliopithecus*) at Sansan in southern France in 1837, a find that made the existence of fossil humans more probable. He helped prove that humans had an ancient past through work at Aurignac (Haute Garonne) in 1860. Proposed a classificatory scheme for the Palaeolithic based entirely on extinct animal bones (aurochs age, reindeer age, etc.). Worked with the wealthy English scholar Henry Christy, excavating many of the best-known rock-shelter occupation sites of the southern French Palaeolithic, such as Le Moustier and La Madeleine. Their discovery of portable Palaeolithic art *in situ* established its existence, as well as the contemporaneity of humans and extinct late Pleistocene animals such as mammoth. Their work was published in *Reliquiae Aquitanicae* (1865–75).

Leakey, Louis Seymour Bazett (1903–72). Pioneer East African prehistorian, anthropologist and palaeontologist (born Kenya), an individualist who was never far from controversy throughout his working life and who with his wife **Mary** (b. 1913) established that East Africa had a key role in human prehistory. Excelled at finding fossil and archaeological sites. Was curator of the Corydon (now the National) Museum, Nairobi (1945–61), and founded the affiliated Centre for Prehistory and Palaeontology. Early work on the prehistory of the East African Rift Valley led him to a search for early Miocene hominoid fossils in western Kenya where, in 1948, Mary found an 18-million-year-old skull of *Proconsul africanus* on Rusinga Island, Lake Victoria. Later, Leakey worked at an important, middle Miocene site (Fort

Jean-Baptiste **Lamarck**.

Louis Leakey with the skull of *Zinjanthropus boisei* (now called *Australopithecus* or *Paranthropus boisei*) **in 1959**.

Ternan), also in western Kenya, and found an upper jaw of *Kenyapithecus wickeri*. In 1959, at Olduvai Gorge in Tanzania, it was again Mary Leakey who discovered the 'Nutcracker Man' skull, which Louis named *Zinjanthropus boisei* (now called either *Australopithecus* or *Paranthropus boisei*). Other important hominid finds followed, notably a smaller form that Leakey, **Philip Tobias** and **John Napier** named *Homo habilis* in 1964. Leakey believed that *Homo habilis* ('Handy Man') was a toolmaker contemporaneous with *Zinjanthropus* around 1.8 million years ago but was, unlike 'Zinj', a direct ancestor of modern humans.

Louis Leakey was also involved in a still-controversial search for early human occupation of North America (at Calico Hills, California), and was instrumental in inducing a succession of women, among them Jane Goodall, Dian Fossey and Birute Galdikas, to study great apes to provide insights into early hominid behaviour. Made no mention of the Taung skull in *Adam's Ancestors* (1934). His other books included *The Stone Age Races of Kenya* (1935), *The Miocene Hominoidea of East Africa* (with W.E. Le Gros Clark, 1951), *Olduvai Gorge Vol. 1* (1967), *Unveiling Man's Origins* (with Vanne Goodall, 1969) and *By the Evidence: Memoirs 1932–1951* (1974).

Mary Leakey continued the work at Olduvai in the 1970s, and at the Pliocene site of Laetoli where 3.5-million-year-old australopithecine footprints were discovered in 1978. A team led by the Leakeys' son **Richard** found more hominid fossils around Lake Turkana in northern Kenya, including *Homo habilis* and *Homo erectus*, in the 1970s and 1980s.

Le Gros Clark, (Sir) Wilfrid Edward (1896–1971) British anatomist who became a leading authority on primate and human evolution and has been dubbed the first primatologist. Served as a medical officer in Borneo, which led to pioneering studies on the anatomy of tree shrews. Professor at Oxford from 1934 to 1961. Played a major part in ensuring the recognition of australopithecines as hominids by speaking out in 1947 in favour of **Raymond Dart**'s assessment of the Taung skull. Like many thinkers and teachers, his contributions to studies of human evolution have not had the full public recognition they deserve as, unlike his contemporary **Louis Leakey**, he never found any hominid fossils. However, his books – *Early Forerunners of Man* (1934), *History of the Primates* (1949), *Antecedents of Man* (1959) and *Man-apes or Ape-men?* (1967) – have had a major scholarly influence on interpretations of primate evolution and human origins. With **Joseph Weiner** and **Kenneth Oakley** he exposed the Piltdown Man remains as a hoax in 1953.

Lewis, G. Edward (1908–). American geologist who while a graduate student at Yale University discovered a hominoid lower jaw in rocks at Haritalyangar in the Siwalik Hills, India, that he described in 1934 as the type specimen of *Ramapithecus* ('Rama's ape'). Believed that *Ramapithecus* was an early hominid, but this view was not widely shared until it was forcefully advocated by Elwyn Simons and others in the 1960s. By the 1980s, however, opinions had reversed; most now believe *Ramapithecus* to be the same as, or closely related to, *Sivapithecus* – a non-hominid Miocene ape.

Libby, Willard Frank (1908–80). American chemist who devised (1946) and developed the fundamentals of the radiocarbon dating method in the early 1950s, for which he received a Nobel prize (1960). The technique had a revolutionary impact on

Carl Linnaeus.

archaeology because organic materials could be given an absolute date through measurement of the proportion of the radioactive isotope carbon-14 remaining in, for example, seeds, wood, charcoal or bone from an archaeological site. The method continues to be refined and remains crucial to dating archaeological material less than 50 000 years old.

Linnaeus, Carolus (Carl von Linné) (1707–78). The founder of biological systematics, or taxonomy. Swedish biologist who developed a system for classifying living things based on their anatomy. Not concerned with evolution, as he saw each species as a fixed and divinely created type. Founded the binomial system, in which each species has a generic and a specific name (e.g. *Homo sapiens* or *Mus musculus*), and named more than 10 000 animals and plants in this way. The tenth and much revised edition of his book *Systema Naturae*, which is now seen to mark the beginning of taxonomy as a science, was published in 1758. Many of his specimens were sold after his death to the Linnean Society of London, where they remain.

Lyell, (Sir) Charles (1797–1875). Scottish geologist; friend and mentor of **Charles Darwin** (who said of Lyell 'I see through his eyes'). Darwin took Lyell's *Principles of Geology* (1830–33) on HMS *Beagle*; and was much impressed by Lyell's argument that gradualism – the slow accumulation of change over immense periods of time – could lead to great alterations in the earth's surface. Lyell pointed out that events in the past were shaped by the same laws as those acting at present; he was a uniformitarian, as was Darwin.

Malthus, Thomas (1766–1834). English clergyman and economist. Pointed out that in all creatures – including humans – the

potential to produce offspring exceeds the growth of the resources needed to support them. In his *Essay on the Principles of Population* (1798), Malthus suggested that numbers of plants and animals increased geometrically (2, 4, 8, 16, etc.), whereas resources could only grow arithmetically (2, 4, 6, 8, 10, etc.). Early in his studies, **Charles Darwin** read this essay, and was greatly struck by it. It helped to lead to the idea of natural selection; that there were inherited differences in the chances of surviving in the struggle between population and resources.

Mendel, Gregor (1822–84). Founder of genetics. Born in what is now Czechoslovakia; entered Augustinian monastery of Brunn (now Brno). Studied science in Vienna, but failed his examinations. Before Mendel, genetics had got nowhere as those involved were interested in characters (height, weight, etc.) that were measured and did not use the sort of inherited variation that allowed the counting of discrete classes in succeeding generations. Mendel used lines of peas that differed from each other in distinct ways – round or wrinkled, green or yellow, and so on. Careful breeding showed that characteristic ratios of the various classes appeared in each generation, and allowed Mendel to work out the laws that now bear his name (see p. 259). There have been various claims that he massaged his results, or that he did not fully understand them; but it is clear that Mendel is the real originator of modern genetics, His results, published in 1865, fell into obscurity for 40 years, but were simultaneously rediscovered by several biologists and their importance quickly realised.

Napier, John Russell (1917–87). British anatomist who began his scientific career as an orthopaedic surgeon and went on to

Sir Charles Lyell.

Gregor Mendel.

make a major contribution to functional anatomy as a discipline linking medicine and primatology. He and colleagues and students developed a distinctive approach to primate evolutionary biology. Fossil forms also figured prominently in his studies, especially *Proconsul africanus* and *Homo habilis* (which Napier, Philip Tobias and **Louis Leakey** named as a new species in 1964). Author of three influential books – *A Handbook of Living Primates* (1967), *The Roots of Mankind* (1971) and *The Natural History of Primates* (1985), the first and last co-authored with his wife Prue Napier. He was the first director of the Primate Biology Program at the Smithsonian Institution, Washington DC.

Oakley, Kenneth Page (1911–81). British geologist and palaeontologist, best known for his work at the British Museum (Natural History) in London on the relative dating of bones through analysis of their fluorine content. With this technique he helped expose the Piltdown fraud in 1953, by revealing that the collection of human and animal bones found by **Charles Dawson** at Piltdown in Sussex between 1912 and 1915 came from a variety of sources and periods (see Box). His books include *Man the Toolmaker* (1949) and *Frameworks for Dating Fossil Man* (1961).

Schultz, Adolph (1891–1976). Swiss primatologist renowned in scholarly circles for his comparative measurements on primates. Was professor of anthropology at Johns Hopkins University, Baltimore, from 1925 to 1951 and then director of the Anthropological Institute in Zurich from 1951 to 1962. Established an important collection of primate skulls and skeletons now housed in Zurich. Played an active part in the foundation of the journal *Folia Primatolo-* *gica* and the morphological handbook *Primatologia*.

Simpson, George Gaylord (1902–84). American vertebrate palaeontologist who made significant contributions to studies of primate and human evolution from a sound background of the origins and evolution of mammals. Explored the implications of the genetic foundation of the evolutionary synthesis for the interpretation of the fossil record. On the staff of the American Museum of Natural History, New York, from 1927 to 1959, with parallel appointments first at Columbia University and then at Harvard. His classification of mammals (1945) is a standard work. Other publications include *Tempo and Mode in Evolution* (1944), *The Meaning of Evolution*(1949), *Major Features of Evolution* (1953) and *Principles of Animal Taxonomy* (1961).

Smith, (Sir) Grafton Elliot (1871–1937). British anatomist and anthropologist (born Australia) who became an authority on primate brains. Believed that the brain led the way in human evolution, a conviction that led him to endorse the fraudulent Piltdown skull, with its human-sized brain but ape-like jaw (see Box). Found the lunate sulcus in the human brain. Supported **Marcellin Boule**'s contention that Neanderthals were not closely related to humans. Was professor of anatomy at Cairo (1900–9), Manchester (1909–19) and, finally, University College London (1919–36). Among his students were **Raymond Dart** and **Davidson Black**. His stay in Egypt led to an interest in mummification methods and to the extreme view that all cultural advances spread from Egypt, a theory that he elaborated in his books *Migrations from Egypt* (1915), *The Evolution of the Dragon* (1919), *The Diffusion of Culture* (1933), etc. At the end of his life, he cautiously supported **Charles Darwin**'s conjecture of an African origin for humans and listed the australopithecines among several groups that were 'relevant' to human origins.

Teilhard de Chardin, Pierre (1881–1955). French Jesuit, palaeontologist and philosopher. Studied palaeontology in Paris with **Marcellin Boule**. While at a seminary in Hastings in Sussex, England, he occasionally joined in **Charles Dawson**'s excavations at Piltdown and found the canine tooth (1913) that supported **Arthur Smith Woodward**'s reconstruction of Piltdown Man (see Box). Has been accused of perpetrating the Piltdown hoax by, for example, Stephen Jay Gould or of conniving in its cover-up. Was a missionary in China between 1923 and 1946, went on palaeontological expeditions in Asia, and became involved in the excavations at Choukoutien (now Zhoukoudian) near Beijing, where fossils of *Sinanthropus pekinensis* (= *Home erectus*) were being found by **Davidson Black** and others. After Black's death, Teilhard de Chardin directed the excavations until **Franz Weidenreich** arrived to take charge. Made some important contributions to Cenozoic geology and palaeontology. Moved to the USA in 1946 and worked at the Wenner-Gren Foundation for Anthropological Research in New York from 1951.

Wallace, Alfred Russel (1823–1913). Co-discoverer of the idea of evolution by natural selection. Born in Wales; naturalist and traveller in South America and Malaysia. Mapped the distribution of species, and noticed a discontinuity in the Malay Archipelago (now known as Wallace's Line), which separated the fauna of Asia from that of Australia. Hit upon the theory of natural selection while in Malaya, after – like **Charles Darwin** – having read **Thomas Malthus**'s essay on population. Wrote to Darwin with his ideas in 1858, and a joint paper was published in the *Proceedings* of the Linnean Society of London in that year. In later life, Wallace became a strong supporter of Darwinism, a socialist and – in stark contrast to his distinguished co-evolutionist **T.H. Huxley** – a strong supporter of spiritualism.

Wegener, Alfred Lothar (1880–1930). German meteorologist and geophysicist who in 1912 proposed the theory of continental drift – that the continents had once been joined together and had wandered apart. His ideas were scorned at first but he was proved correct in the 1960s when the plate tectonics theory was developed and techniques for studying the earth's magnetic field showed that the positions of the continents had changed with respect to the magnetic poles. Wegener's chief work is *Die Entstehung der Kontinente und Ozeane* (1915) translated as the *Origin of Continents and Oceans* (1924).

George Gaylord Simpson.

Alfred Russel Wallace.

Weidenreich, Franz (1873–1948). German anatomist and anthropologist, best known for his detailed descriptions of the *Sinanthropus* fossils found at Zhoukoudian near Beijing. Established the name *Homo erectus* in 1940, the genus that now includes all the *Sinanthropus* and the Javanese *Pithecanthropus* material. Taught in Germany and then succeeded **Davidson Black** as head of the Cenozoic Research Laboratory at the Peking Union Medical College (1935–41), where he collaborated with **Pierre Teilhard de Chardin** on the Zhoukoudian excavations. After the outbreak of World War II, Weidenreich moved to the US to work at the American Museum of Natural History, New York (1941–48), fortunately taking casts, drawings, notes and photographs of the Zhoukoudian fossils with him – the original material mysteriously disappeared in China in 1941. Published a series of monographs about *Sinanthropus* in *Palaeontologia Sinica* between 1936 and 1943 and summarised his view of human evolution in *Apes, Giants and Man* (1946).

Weiner, Joseph Sydney (1915–82). British (born South Africa) environmental physiologist and physical anthropologist, best known for his work in uncovering the Piltdown forgery (see Box). He suspected that the skull was a fake (fabricated by **Charles Dawson**) and enlisted the help of **Wilfrid Le Gros Clark** and **Kenneth Oakley** in proving the fraud. Weiner was also a key figure in developing the concept of human biology

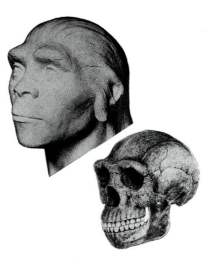

Reconstruction by Franz Weidenreich of the head of a female *Sinanthropus* (= *Homo erectus*) and the skull from which it was made.

as a scientific discipline and in establishing the Society for the Study of Human Biology (1958). After teaching physical anthropology at Oxford (1946–65), he joined the London School of Tropical Medicine and Hygiene as professor and as director of the Medical Research Council Environmental Physiology Unit (1965–80). Supervised the Human Adaptability Project of the International Biological Programme (1964–74). His books include *The Piltdown Forgery* (1955) and *Man's Natural History* (1971), and he was joint author (with G.A. Harrison. J.M. Tanner and N.A. Barnicot) of *Human Biology: An Introduction to Human Evolution, Variation and Growth* (1964).

Wilson, Allan Charles (1934–91). New Zealand molecular evolutionist. At the University of California, Berkeley, his laboratory introduced the techniques of DNA analysis into evolutionary biology. Strongly advocated the concept of the molecular clock. Best known for his work on the inheritance of mitochondrial DNA. Also involved in the first work on fossil DNA, and – before the development of DNA methods – in immunological work on the relationships and probable date of divergence of humans and other primates.

Woodward, (Sir) Arthur Smith (1864–1944). British palaeontologist who became a leading authority on fossil fishes but who is better known for his part in the Piltdown Man affair (see Box). As keeper of geology at the British Museum (Natural History) (1902–24) he was the one to whom **Charles Dawson** gave the Piltdown skullcap in May 1912. The two even looked for and found more fragments of the skull and the all-important lower jaw in the Piltdown gravel pits. Woodward's reconstruction produced a creature with a human skull and an ape jaw. He was convinced that the skullcap and lower jaw were associated and his formal 'authentification' of the skull as a 'missing link' at the Geological Society of London in December 1912 played a large part in the success of the hoax.

Geological timescale

Millions of years	Era	Period	Epoch			MAJOR EVENTS IN PRIMATE EVOLUTION
0		Quaternary	Holocene Pleistocene			
			Pliocene	Late	1.64	First-known humans (*Homo*)
5				Early	5.2	First-known hominids (*Australopithecus*)
10		Neogene		Late		
15			Miocene	Middle		Split between colobine and cercopithecine monkeys
						Spread of African mammals, including hominoids, into Eurasia
20				Early		First-known lorises
						First-known Old World monkeys
						Early apes (*Proconsul*)
					23.3	Primates disappear from N. America
25	Cenozoic		Oligocene	Late		New World monkeys (platyrrhines) appear in S. America
30		Tertiary				
				Early		Primates disappear from Europe
35					35.4	First-known tarsiers
			Eocene	Late		Early Old World simians
40						
45		Palaeogene		Middle		Adapids and omomyids common in N. America, Europe and Asia
50						? First-known simians
55				Early		First-known modern-looking primates (adapids and omomyids)
					56.5	
60			Palaeocene	Late		
				Early		
65					65.0	First-known archaic primates (plesiadapiforms)
	Mesozoic		Cretaceous	Late		

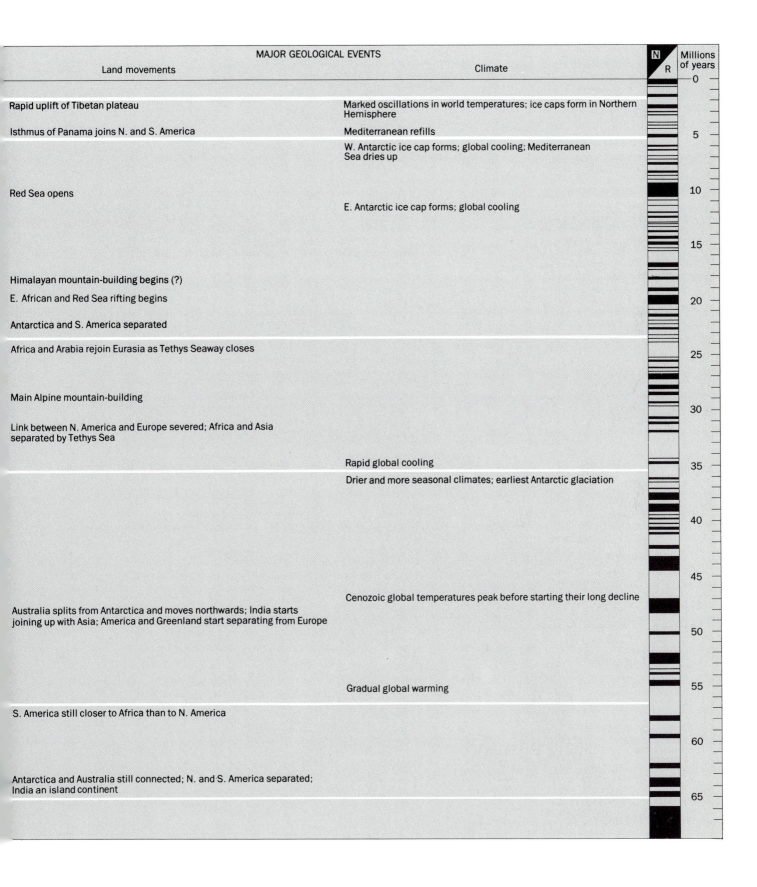

MAJOR GEOLOGICAL EVENTS

Land movements	Climate	N R	Millions of years

Land movements:

Rapid uplift of Tibetan plateau

Isthmus of Panama joins N. and S. America

Red Sea opens

Himalayan mountain-building begins (?)

E. African and Red Sea rifting begins

Antarctica and S. America separated

Africa and Arabia rejoin Eurasia as Tethys Seaway closes

Main Alpine mountain-building

Link between N. America and Europe severed; Africa and Asia separated by Tethys Sea

Australia splits from Antarctica and moves northwards; India starts joining up with Asia; America and Greenland start separating from Europe

S. America still closer to Africa than to N. America

Antarctica and Australia still connected; N. and S. America separated; India an island continent

Climate:

Marked oscillations in world temperatures; ice caps form in Northern Hemisphere

Mediterranean refills

W. Antarctic ice cap forms; global cooling; Mediterranean Sea dries up

E. Antarctic ice cap forms; global cooling

Rapid global cooling

Drier and more seasonal climates; earliest Antarctic glaciation

Cenozoic global temperatures peak before starting their long decline

Gradual global warming

Millions of years scale: 0, 5, 10, 15, 20, 25, 30, 35, 40, 45, 50, 55, 60, 65

World map of sites

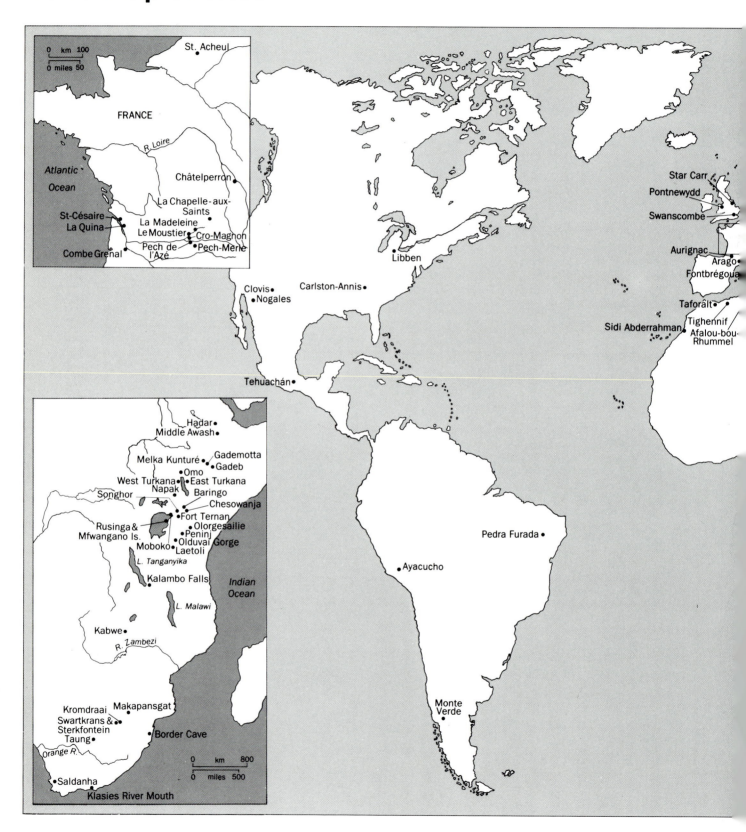

FRANCE

St. Acheul
Châtelperron
La Chapelle-aux-Saints
St-Césaire
La Quina
La Madeleine
Le Moustier
Cro-Magnon
Pech de l'Azé
Pech-Merle
Combe Grenal

Atlantic Ocean
R. Loire

Star Carr
Pontnewydd
Swanscombe
Aurignac
Arago
Fontbrégoua
Taforált
Sidi Abderrahman
Tighennif
Afalou-bou-Rhummel

Libben
Clovis
Nogales
Carlston-Annis
Tehuachán

Hadar
Middle Awash
Gademotta
Melka Kunturé
Gadeb
Omo
West Turkana
East Turkana
Napak
Baringo
Songhor
Chesowanja
Fort Ternan
Rusinga & Mfwangano Is.
Olorgesailie
Peninj
Moboko
Olduvai Gorge
Laetoli
L. Tanganyika
Kalambo Falls
Indian Ocean
L. Malawi
Kabwe
R. Zambezi
Kromdraai
Makapansgat
Swartkrans & Sterkfontein
Taung
Border Cave
Orange R.
Saldanha
Klasies River Mouth

Pedra Furada
Ayacucho
Monte Verde

456

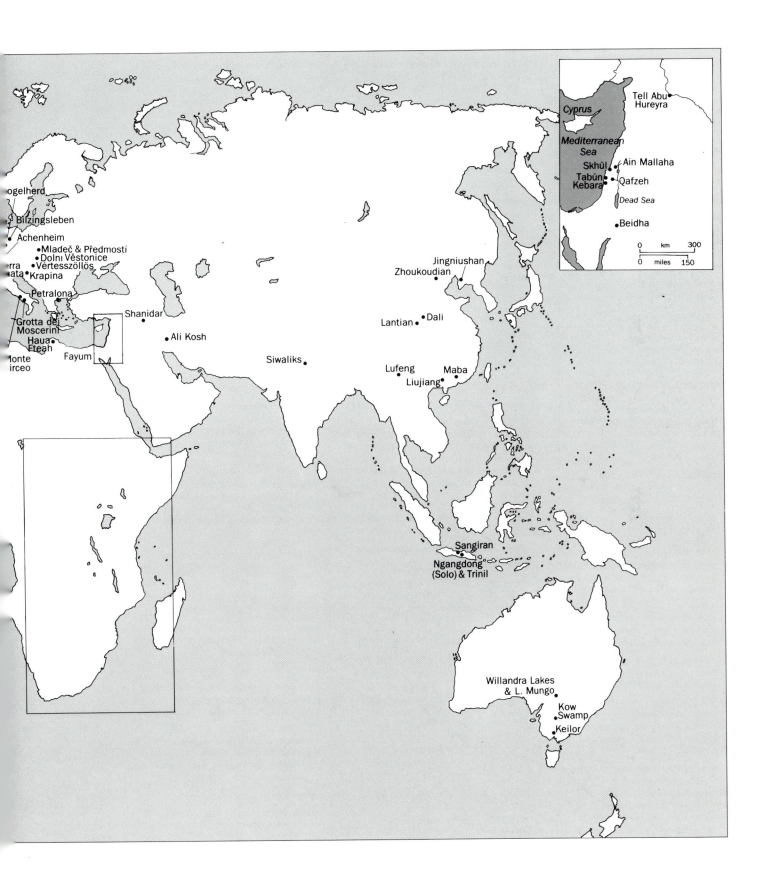

ogelherd
Bilzingsleben
Achenheim
Mladeč & Předmostí
Dolní Věstonice
Vértesszöllös
erra
ata
Krapina
Petralona
Grotta dei
Moscerini
Haua
Fteah
Monte
irceo
Fayum

Shanidar
Ali Kosh
Siwaliks

Jingniushan
Zhoukoudian
Lantian   Dali
Lufeng   Maba
Liujiang

Sangiran
Ngangdong
(Solo) & Trinil

Willandra Lakes
& L. Mungo
Kow
Swamp
Keilor

Tell Abu
Hureyra
Cyprus
Mediterranean
Sea
Skhūl   Ain Mallaha
Tabūn   Qafzeh
Kebara
Dead Sea
Beidha

| 0 | km | 300 |
| 0 | miles | 150 |

Glossary

Abbreviations: adj., adjective; pl., plural. Asterisks before terms denote cross-references to entries that give more information

A

abduction movement away from the body's midline (e.g. extending an arm sideways). The opposite of *adduction

abiotic non-living

aboriginal indigenous; native

absolute (chronometric) date a date in years of a fossil or the rock in which it is found. Methods of absolute dating are based on the decay of radioactive isotopes (e.g. *potassium-argon and *radiocarbon dating)

absorption uptake of fluid or other substances by living cells and tissues; assimilation of nutritive material by living cells; of light, when neither reflected nor transmitted

Acheulean (Acheulian) a *Lower Palaeolithic toolmaking tradition characterised by handaxes and cleavers and named after St Acheul, near Amiens in northern France. It was widespread in Africa, Europe and parts of Asia from around 1.5 million to 150 000 years ago and is associated with *Homo erectus* and 'archaic *Homo sapiens*'. Some say it lasted in Europe (as the *Mousterian of Acheulean tradition) until 60 000 years ago

achondroplasia an inherited human disorder affecting both sexes that results in a form of dwarfism characterised by short arms and legs

adapid a member of the Adapidae, a family of extinct lemur-like primates that mainly lived during the Eocene epoch but did not disappear until the late Miocene. The details of their relationships to modern prosimian and simian primates are uncertain

adaptation an evolutionary process by which an organism becomes adjusted to its environment; a feature fitted through natural selection for some special activity

adaptive radiation diversification of members of an evolving group of related species into different environments or ways of life

adduction movement towards the body's midline (e.g. bringing an outstretched arm to the side of the body). The opposite of *abduction

adrenal gland an organ near the upper end of each kidney in mammals, consisting of an inner medulla that secretes the catecholamines adrenaline and noradrenaline, and an outer cortex stimulated by adrenocorticotropic hormone (ACTH) from the *pituitary to produce specific steroid hormones – **glucocorticosteroids** (e.g. cortisol) and sex steroids (e.g. dehydroepiandrosterone). The adrenal cortex

also secretes **mineralocorticoids** such as aldosterone, which act on the kidney to regulate salt and water balance

afferent conducting towards. Applied to nerves carrying impulses from a sense organ to the brain or spinal cord and to blood vessels or ducts supplying an organ with fluid. The opposite of *efferent

agonistic behaviour any activity related to fighting, whether aggressive or submissive

allele (adj. **allelic**) one of two or more forms of a particular *gene, such as the alleles for *A*, *B* and *O* at the *ABO* blood-group locus

allometry (adj. **allometric**) relative growth relationships between two parts of an organism or between two species

altricial applies to small and poorly developed offspring born after a relatively short *gestation, with little hair, and eyes and ears sealed by membranes. Altricial mammals breed more rapidly than *precocial mammals

altruism (adj. **altruistic**) an act or behaviour that benefits another of the same species at some cost to the donor

alveolus (adj. **alveolar**) cavity; tooth socket; small pit

amino acid a building block of a protein. One of a group of organic compounds in which the molecule contains one or more amino groups and one or more carboxyl groups. Around 20 different amino acids are the basic components of proteins; 10 of these cannot be made by the human body and thus form an essential component of the diet (**essential amino acids**)

amygdala (amygdaloid nucleus) a mass of *grey matter in the tip of each *temporal lobe of the brain that is associated with the control of arousal in, for example, aggressive and sexual behaviours. It is also a centre for eliciting vocalisations in primates

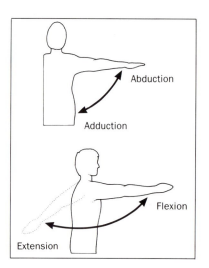

Abduction / Adduction / Flexion / Extension

analogy (adj. **analogous**) resemblance in function but not in structure and origin. An analogous structure or analogue has a similar function to one in a different organism but has a completely different evolutionary and developmental origin (e.g. the wings of a bat and an insect). *See also* homology

androgen the general name for the steroid *hormones (e.g. androstenedione and testosterone) that govern reproductive function and stimulate the development of secondary sexual characteristics in males (e.g. beard growth in humans). They are mainly secreted by the testes (about 95%) but small amounts are produced by the *adrenal cortex, and also by the ovaries in females

aneuploid not having the normal *diploid number of chromosomes

anterior of or towards the front of the body. The opposite of *posterior

anthropoid a member of the primate suborder Anthropoidea (Old and New World monkeys, apes and humans). Alternative informal names are simian or higher primate

antibody a defensive protein produced by the immune system, usually in response to a foreign *antigen. Antibodies are very specific, recognising one particular antigen. The high mutation rate of the genes for the proteins involved is important in this

antigen a cue of identity, recognised by an *antibody. It may be an invader such as a bacterium, but all our cells also carry antigens that are important in recognising 'self' versus 'not-self' (e.g. the histocompatibility antigens and the blood groups). *See also* cell-surface antigen

apes the primate group that includes the gibbons, orang-utans, gorillas and chimpanzees; gibbons are often called the lesser apes and the others great apes

aphasia a disorder caused by brain damage that affects a person's ability to communicate in speech and writing

apical towards the tip; the distal end

arboreal tree-living. Arboreal quadrupedal primates such as lorises and squirrel monkeys use all four limbs in moving about trees

arboreal theory of primate evolution a theory that holds that many features of primates (e.g. large forward-facing eyes) first evolved as adaptations for life in trees

archaic ancient

'archaic *Homo sapiens*' the name given to fossil humans that lived in Africa, Europe and Asia from about 400 000 to 200 000 or 100 000 years ago with features intermediate between *Homo erectus* and modern *Homo sapiens*, and which may represent a separate species. There is disagreement about which fossils belong in this category

archaic primate a member of the suborder Plesiadapiformes, an extinct group of primates that lived from very late *Cretaceous to early *Eocene times, reaching their peak during the *Palaeocene. The relationships of the different groups of archaic primates to one another and to more modern-looking primates (*adapids and *omomyids) are uncertain

arcuate nucleus a small mass of *grey matter at the base of the *hypothalamus, just above the pituitary gland. It regulates the release of pituitary hormones that are involved in the control of reproductive function

arcuate sulcus a cleft in the frontal lobes of the brains of *higher primates that divides the motor areas (behind) from the prefrontal *association areas (ahead)

artefact any object used, modified or made by humans, from a flaked stone tool to a rocket launcher

arthropod a member of the animal phylum Arthropoda (insects, arachnids, millipedes, crustaceans, etc.)

assemblage a group of objects found together in an archaeological setting

association area one of several parts of the *cerebral cortex that seem to perform complex sensory or motor analyses or may integrate information from more than one sense

auditory bulla a bony structure under the *middle-ear cavity, formed by the petrosal bone in primates (the petrosal is fused into the *temporal bone in humans)

auditory meatus (external auditory tube) the external opening of the ear canal

Aurignacian the first major *Upper Palaeolithic tool complex in Europe, named after Aurignac rockshelter in the French Pyrenees first dug by Edouard Lartet in 1860, and characterised by long, *retouched *blades, short, steep-sided scrapers and bone points with split bases. It began about 40 000 years ago in some parts of Europe and lasted for several thousand years

australopithecine the common name (derived from *Australopithecus* = 'southern ape') for a member of the early *hominid group that lived in southern and eastern Africa between about 4 (perhaps 5) and 1 million years ago, or a feature typical of these forms. The australopithecines *Australopithecus afarensis* and *Australopithecus africanus* are usually described as **gracile** (lightly built) and *Paranthropus* (or *Australopithecus*) *robustus* and *Paranthropus boisei* as **robust** (more ruggedly built)

autosome (adj. **autosomal**) any *chromosome that is not a sex chromosome

axon (nerve fibre) the unbranched cytoplasmic process up to several metres long that transmits impulses away from the cell body of a nerve cell (neurone)

B

basal ganglion (pl. **ganglia**) one of several large, interconnected masses of *grey matter deep in the *white matter of the forebrain, including the caudate and lenticular nuclei (together known as the **corpus striatum**) and substantia nigra. They are a major target for outputs from the *cerebral cortex and are especially important in the initiation of action, including movement and posture

basal metabolic rate (BMR) the rate at which the total energy obtained from food is used by an animal in its thermoneutral zone (where it does not need to use extra energy either for warming or for cooling itself) to maintain body processes (e.g. heart beat, breathing and protein synthesis)

basalt fine-grained igneous rock formed by the consolidation of lava flows

base in biochemistry, the nitrogenous components of the *nucleotide unit in a nucleic acid such as *DNA

base pair a matching pair of *nucleotides in the *DNA or *RNA molecule. In DNA, the match is usually of adenine (A) with guanine (G) and cytosine (C) with thymine (T). This mirror-imaging means that one DNA strand can be synthesised from the information contained in the other

Beringia the name given to the *land bridge across the Bering Strait that periodically linked Siberia and Alaska during the *Pleistocene epoch, when the sea level was sometimes as much as 200 metres lower than at present. During the last *glacial period (ice age) it allowed people to cross from Asia to the New World at least 15 000 and perhaps as early as 30 000 years ago

biface see handaxe

bilophodonty the pattern of two transverse ridges on the *molar teeth of Old World monkeys

binomial nomenclature the Linnean system of giving every organism two Latin names, usually printed in italic (sloping) type, indicating the genus and species to which it belongs. The generic name always starts with an uppercase letter and the specific name with a lowercase letter (as in *Homo sapiens*, the **binomen** for modern humans)

biogeography the geographic distribution of plants and animals and its study

biota (adj. **biotic**) all plants and animals of a given region or time

bipedal locomotion (bipedalism) walking on the hindlimbs, especially in the upright, human way

blade a long, narrow *flake, at least twice as long as broad, with a prismatic shape, struck from a specially prepared stone (core) and used as a tool or as a blank from which another type of tool, such as a burin (for engraving) can be made. Industries with a high proportion of blades were prominent at the start of the *Upper Palaeolithic, 40 000–30 000 years ago

blood group an inherited cue of identity on the surface of blood cells. Blood groups are

*antigens that may be recognised as foreign by *antibodies and lead to the clumping (agglutination) of blood cells when transfusions are made between people with incompatible blood groups. Blood-group systems include the ABO, Rhesus, Duffy, Lutheran and Kell, and more than a dozen minor ones

BMR see basal metabolic rate

bottleneck a brief reduction in population numbers, followed by an expansion. Population bottlenecks may happen after a famine or natural disaster, but are more likely when a small group of emigrants found a new colony. Bottlenecks (including the *founder effect) are important genetically as only a small sample of the initial population passes on its genes

bovid a member of the family Bovidae (antelope, cattle, sheep, etc.) in the mammalian order Artiodactyla (even-toed ungulates)

brachiation movement through trees by hanging from branches and swinging alternate arms from branch to branch. Gibbons use this style of locomotion. True brachiation includes a free flight phase

brainstem the stem-like part of the brain connecting the *cerebral hemispheres with the spinal cord and including the *midbrain, pons and medulla oblongata

breccia a rock made of coarse angular fragments in a lime (calcium carbonate) matrix. It is common in *hominid cave sites in southern Africa (e.g. Sterkfontein)

Broca's area the region of the human brain involved in speech production, lying in the lower back part of the frontal cortex of the left *cerebral hemisphere and named after the French surgeon Pierre Paul Broca (1824–80)

brow ridge (supraorbital torus) ridge of bone above the eye sockets

buccal relating to the cheek or mouth; the cheek side of a tooth

bulb of percussion the swelling on the fracture surface of a stone *flake directly below the place where the hammer struck

bulla a rounded prominence, such as the bony floor of the middle ear (auditory bulla) in many mammals

C

caecum blind-ended pouch (diverticulum) from the gut, branching off, in mammals, at the junction of the small intestine and *colon. Some leaf-eaters have a long, wide caecum in which cellulose is broken down by bacteria (**caecal fermentation**), as in sportive lemurs, *Lepilemur*. In meat-eaters, the caecum is either absent or small

calcareous composed of, or containing lime (calcium carbonate)

calibration in geology, the assignment of an *absolute age to at least one point on a relative chronological framework. Many *radiocarbon dates need calibration — adjustment according to an independent timeframe, as given by tree-ring dating

calorie a unit of energy equal to the amount of heat needed to raise the temperature of 1 gram of water from 14.5 to 15.5 °C; 1000 calories = 1 kilocalorie (kcal) or 1 Calorie. Although the *joule is now the preferred energy unit in scientific work (1 calorie = 4.1868 joules), kilocalories are still widely used to indicate the energy content of foods and a person's daily energy needs

canine one of the pointed teeth at the corners of the mouth. In mammals, there is usually one on each side of the upper and lower jaws, between the incisors and premolars. They are larger in males of monkey and ape species that compete to mate with females

capillary one of the very narrow, thin-walled blood vessels that form an interconnecting network in most tissues between small branches of arteries (arterioles) and those of veins (venules)

carbon-14 dating see radiocarbon dating

carnivore a member of the mammalian order Carnivora (hyenas, dogs, lions, etc.); also used for other flesh-eaters although the term **faunivore** is preferred to avoid confusion

catarrhine a member of the primate infraorder Catarrhini (Old World monkeys, apes and humans)

Caucasoid (caucasian) relating to, or a member of the modern human populations indigenous to Europe, North Africa, Southwest Asia and the Indian subcontinent, and their descendants elsewhere

ceboid a member of the primate superfamily Ceboidea (New World monkeys)

cell mosaics genetically different cells within the same organism. These may arise naturally through mutation — giving rise, for example, to individuals with one blue eye and one brown — or can be produced experimentally in mice and other creatures by fusing embryos

cell-surface antigen an inherited cue of identity on the surfaces of cells (e.g. *blood groups and histocompatibility antigens). Many are controlled by a group of closely linked gene *loci, the **major histocompatibility complex**. As there is much variation in this system, every individual — except for identical twins — is unique

Cenozoic the era from 65 million years ago to the present, also called the Age of Mammals. It is divided into the *Tertiary and *Quaternary periods

centromere a constricted part of a *chromosome that is important during cell division because the spindle fibres are attached to it. Chromosomes can be classified according to the position of the centromere as **metacentric** (centromere near the middle), **acrocentric** (centromere near one end) and **telocentric** (centromere very near one end)

cercopithecoid a member of the primate superfamily Cercopithecoidea (Old World monkeys)

cerebellum the largest part of the *hindbrain, comprising a pair of rounded,

fissured masses that bulge back behind the pons and medulla oblongata, usually overhung by the occipital lobes of the *cerebral hemispheres. Three broad bands of nerve fibres (peduncles) connect it to the brainstem. Like the cerebral hemispheres, the cerebellum has an outer cortex of *grey matter and a core of *white matter. It is concerned with the co-ordination of movements

cerebral cortex the outer layer of *grey matter of the *cerebral hemispheres, comprising layers of nerve cells and their interconnections. In most modern primates, especially apes and humans, it is thrown into a series of folds (gyri) separated by troughs (sulci) that provide a large surface area. The **Sylvian fissure** (in monkeys, apes and humans) separates the temporal lobe from the frontal and parietal lobes, the **central sulcus** separates the frontal and parietal lobes, and the **parieto-occipital sulcus** separates the parietal and occipital lobes. The cortex is the part of the brain most directly responsible for higher mental functions, such as learning, memory and consciousness, for the analysis and interpretation of sensory information and general movement, and for the association and integration of these functions. Different functions are localised to different regions called the *motor cortex, sensory cortex, *association areas, etc.

cerebral hemispheres (cerebrum) paired enlargements of the forebrain behind and above the olfactory lobes. In primates, especially apes and humans, they are very large and the mass of convoluted tissue extends back to cover most of the *midbrain and *hindbrain. The hemispheres are separated by a deep fissure but connected by a band of nerve fibres, the **corpus callosum**. Each has an outer layer of *grey matter, the *cerebral cortex, below which lies the *white matter, and each has four lobes, which are named according to the skull bones that they are next to (**frontal, parietal, temporal and occipital**). In modern primates, the frontal lobes overlap the olfactory bulbs and the occipital lobes the cerebellum. Functionally, the two hemispheres are not equal; for example, in humans the left is usually dominant for speech

character a morphological feature or trait

character state any of the range of values or expressions of a particular character; assessment of a character as either primitive or an evolutionary later state (derived)

Châtelperronian the earliest *Upper Palaeolithic or final *Middle Palaeolithic industry of central and southwestern France, dated to 36 000–32 000 years ago and showing features of both the *Aurignacian and *Mousterian technologies, named after the cave site of Châtelperron in Allier, central France. At St-Césaire in Charente-Maritime, it is associated with a late *Neanderthal

cheek teeth *premolars and *molars (postcanine teeth)

chromatid one of the two copies of a duplicated *chromosome produced during the later stages of cell division. Chromatids

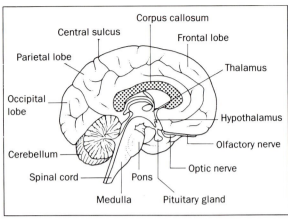

Human brain in section.

are joined at the *centromere but later separate and pass to the daughter cells

chromosome the physical unit of heredity, on which most genes are carried, comprising a complex of *DNA and proteins that becomes microscopically visible at cell division as a thread-like structure. Genes on the same chromosome are said to be linked. By suitable staining, chromosomes show **bands** that allow each one to be identified

clade a complete group of organisms derived from a common ancestor; the basic unit of cladistics

cladistic analysis the grouping of species or other taxa by their shared possession of similar novel (derived) characters that were not present in the remote common ancestor, the aim being to distinguish closely related taxa from those only remotely related

classification allocating species and other taxa to a hierarchy of categories based on observed similarities and differences and giving them individually distinctive names

cleaver a large, bifacially flaked stone tool with a transverse or oblique cutting edge much like an axe, usually found with *handaxes at *Acheulean sites but also present in some *Mousterian industries

clone a group of organisms or cells derived from one parent and therefore genetically identical

cloning the production of new individuals by asexual means, so that they are identical copies of their progenitor. Bacteria often reproduce clonally, and many copies of individual human genes inserted into them can be produced in this way

coalition an association between individuals (usually of the same sex) in a primate social group characterised by mutual support in aggressive encounters

cochlea the spirally coiled bony tube in the *inner ear containing the sensory receptors by which sounds are perceived. The sensory cells respond to vibrations of fluid inside the cochlea caused by the transmission of sound waves from the outer ear via the eardrum (tympanic membrane) and the ear ossicles in the *middle ear

cognition the mental act or process by which knowledge is acquired, including perception, intuition and reasoning

colon the part of the large intestine between the *caecum and the rectum

connective tissue the tissue that binds together and is the support of more specialised internal tissues and organs. Broadly, it includes bone, cartilage and ligaments, as well as adipose (fatty) and elastic tissues

conspecific belonging to the same species

contagious disease in the narrow sense, a disease transmitted only by direct physical contact but often more generally any disease transmitted from one person to another

context the conditions or setting, as in the geological context of a fossil

continental drift the slow movement of the continents and their crustal plates over the earth's surface. See also plate tectonics

convergence; in biology, the parallel development of the same feature in unrelated organisms (**convergent evolution**) either by chance or because of adaptation to meet similar functional requirements (the resemblances are therefore *analogous rather than *homologous); in neurology, the merging into one pathway of nerve fibres from different parts of the brain

core (nucleus) a lump of stone, such as a cobble, worked to produce *flakes or *blades. The core itself may be shaped to serve as a **core tool** (e.g. a *handaxe)

core industry a set of stone artefacts mainly consisting of *core tools

corpus luteum the glandular mass of yellow tissue that forms at the site of a ruptured follicle after the release of a ripe egg (ovulation) and which secretes the hormone progesterone to maintain the early stages of pregnancy. It becomes inactive and degenerates if no fertilised egg embeds (implants) in the lining of the uterus

cortex see cerebral cortex

cranium the braincase, including the upper facial bones. It and the lower jaw (mandible) make up the **skull**. The bones that form the sides and top of the cranium are the frontal, parietals (2), occipital and temporals (2); two other bones, the sphenoid and ethmoid, lie beneath the brain, and several others, including the upper jaw (maxilla), comprise the facial skeleton

creationism the belief that life was created by some supernatural being and not by organic evolution

Cretaceous the last geological period of the Mesozoic era, about 145 to 65 million years ago. Primates evolved from small insectivorous mammals in the latter part of the Cretaceous

crossing-over the physical exchange of genetic material between *homologous chromosomes, that gives rise to the genetical process of **recombination**. It always occurs during the formation of sperm or egg cells (*meiosis), and may also take place during the cell divisions that produce body cells (*mitosis)

cusp a pointed or rounded projection on the

biting surface of a cheek (premolar or molar) tooth

cut mark any mark on a bone made by a tool of stone, metal or other material

cytoplasm the living contents of a cell inside the cell membrane, except for the nucleus

D

Darwinian theory of evolution The theory proposed by Charles Darwin in *The Origin of Species, or the Preservation of Favoured Races in the Struggle of Life* (1859). There is inherited variation (*polymorphism) in populations of animals and plants, more creatures are born than can survive (a struggle for existence), and individuals carrying certain favourable variants are more likely to survive and pass them on than are others (*natural selection). Over long periods, natural selection gives rise to new forms of life (the origin of species)

Darwinism evolution through *natural selection. Neo-Darwinism is a fusion of the arguments put forward in *The Origin* with the mechanisms of hereditary discovered by Gregor Mendel (1822–84). Non-Darwinian evolution is a misleading term that is sometimes used to describe models of variation that place more weight on *genetic drift than on natural selection

death rate see mortality rate

degenerate to become less specialised or functionally useless

deletion a mutation involving the loss of part of a *chromosome, or *bases in a DNA sequence

demography the statistical study of populations

dendrite one of many short, branching cytoplasmic processes on the cell body of a nerve cell (neurone) that receive electrical impulses from other neurones

dental formula the shorthand notation for the number of teeth on each side of the upper and lower jaws, using the abbreviations I for incisors, C for canines, P for premolars and M for molars. For the permanent teeth of humans it is I2/2; C1/1; P2/2; M3/3 (the number before the slash gives the number for the upper jaw, that after the slash the number for the lower jaw)

dentine the substance composed of collagen and hydroxyapatite that comprises the root and interior of the crown of a tooth

deoxyribonucleic acid see DNA

derived character a new (novel) feature developed in a more recent common ancestor and retained by its descendants but absent in any earlier ancestral stock

digit a toe or finger

dimorphism two distinctive forms; for example, differences in size or shape between male and female of a species (**sexual dimorphism**)

diploid having two sets of genetic material, one from each parent. Sperm and egg cells are each haploid, with one copy of the

chromosome complement, and fuse to form a diploid cell, the zygote. All mammals are diploid but simple organisms such as some *protozoans are haploid, and some plants have multiple sets of chromosomes (polyploidy). The number of chromosomes in a diploid set, the **diploid number**, is designated $2n$; in humans, $2n = 46$

distal away from the trunk or towards the end of a limb; the side of a tooth towards the back of the mouth.

diurnal active in the day-time; occurring every day

divergence; divergent evolution the evolution of closely related species in different directions

DNA deoxyribonucleic acid, the self-replicating genetic material in all living cells – two chains of *nucleotides containing phosphate and the sugar deoxyribose twisted around each other into a double helix and linked by hydrogen bonds between the complementary bases of the nucleotides (adenine with thymine or guanine with cytosine)

DNA sequence the order of bases along the DNA that carries the information needed to

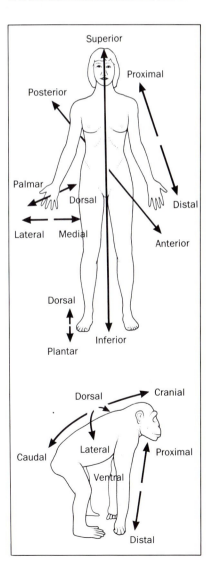

code for proteins. There are 3000 million *base pairs in the human DNA sequence (genome)

dominance hierarchy a rank relationship between two or more individuals based on some criterion such as aggressive interaction or priority of access to food

dominant in genetics, an allele that when present in the *heterozygous state with a recessive allele at the same position (locus) on the chromosome masks its effects. Thus, an individual with one copy of the recessive allele for albinism (absence of pigmentation) and one for the dominant allele for normal skin coloration has normal skin

dorsal relating to, or near the back or upper surface of the body. The opposite of *ventral

Down's syndrome a form of mental subnormality named after the London physician John L.H. Down (1828–96), caused by a chromosome defect (there are three copies of chromosome 21 instead of the usual two). It is characterised by a slight slant to the eyes (hence the former name of the condition, mongolism), a small round head, short stature, broad hands and feet, and a varying degree of mental handicap. The condition, which is commoner in children born to older women, can be diagnosed by prenatal screening

Duchenne muscular dystrophy a sex-linked inherited disease nearly always restricted to males, leading to weakness and wasting of the muscles and eventual death. It is associated with a lack of dystrophin, a protein in muscle fibres

E

earth's magnetic field *see* magnetic field

ecology the interrelationships between organisms and their environment, and their study

ecosystem a system of ecological interrelationships within a physically defined area (tropical forest, savanna grassland, etc.)

efferent conducting outwards. Aplied to motor nerves carrying impulses from the brain or spinal cord and to vessels or ducts draining fluid from an organ. The opposite of *afferent

electrophoresis the separation of molecules on the basis of electrical charge in an electric field. **Gel electrophoresis** involves placing the molecules on a gel of starch, acrylamide or other materials so that separation also depends on the shape and size of the molecule

enamel the hard, white material containing over 96 per cent apatitic calcium phosphate that covers the outer surface of crowns of teeth – the hardest biological substance known

encephalisation the evolutionary trend towards an increase in brain size beyond that expected by an increase in body size, as happened in human evolution. The **encephalisation quotient** (EQ), a number reflecting this increase, is obtained by comparing the estimated brain weight of, for

example, an early hominid, with that of a hypothetical 'average mammal' of equal body weight

endangered species a species in danger of extinction

endemic applied to species restricted to a certain region or part of a region; in epidemiology, applied to diseases that are constantly present at relatively low levels among a particular population

endocast a naturally occurring (fossilised) or artificially made cast of the brain

endocrine gland a ductless gland secreting *hormones directly into the bloodstream (e.g. the *pituitary and *adrenal glands, and the *placenta)

environment the complex of external conditions, abiotic (e.g. temperature) and biotic (e.g. food supply) affecting organisms

enzyme (adj. **enzymatic**) a biochemical catalyst based on specialised protein molecules that speeds up biochemical processes. For example, lactase acts on lactose (milk sugar) to produce glucose and galactose during digestion

Eocene the second epoch in the Tertiary period, about 56.5 to 35.4 million years ago

epicontinental sea a sea covering part of a continental landmass. Its floor may be exposed when sea levels fall during *glacial periods, and a land bridge results

epidemic the sudden outbreak of infectious disease that spreads rapidly through a population, affecting many people

epidemiology the study of the incidence, transmission and distribution of diseases, and their control or prevention

epididymis the long, coiled tube leading from each testis to its vas deferens

epithelium (adj. **epithelial**) a tissue consisting of one or more layers of tightly bound cells that covers the external and internal surfaces of the body. It lines the gut, glands, etc.

epoch a subdivision of a geological period (e.g. the Miocene epoch in the Tertiary period)

era the largest division of geological time, including one or more periods (e.g. Cenozoic)

esophagus *see* oesophagus

estrogen *see* oestrogen

estrous cycle *see* oestrous cycle

ethnoarchaeology the study of contemporary crafts with a view to understanding ancient technologies

eugenics the 'science' of improving the human race by selectively breeding from those alleged to have a favourable genetic endowment, or preventing those claimed to carry harmful genes from having children. Founded by Sir Francis Galton (1822–1911), and once widely promoted, eugenics is now a discredited field

eukaryote (adj. **eukaryotic**) an organism whose cells contain a distinct nucleus in

which the *DNA is organised into *chromosomes, and *mitochondria. Fungi, protozoans, plants and animals are eukaryotes; bacteria are prokaryotes (their cells lack a membrane-enclosed nucleus and other cellular organelles)

evolution the genetic changes in populations that over generations lead to new types of organisms

evolutionary (phylogenetic) tree the graphic representation of evolutionary relationships among organisms

exon that part of the *DNA message whose information is expressed as a protein. *See also* intron

extension the action that increases or straightens the angle between two bones in a joint. The opposite of *flexion.

extensor any muscle that extends or straightens a limb or other part. The opposite of *flexor

extinction the disappearance of a species or other group of organisms from part or all of its geographical range

F

Fallopian tube (oviduct) one of a pair of slender ducts that lead from the ovary to the uterus, into which egg cells are released on ovulation and in which fertilisation normally takes place

family the major division of an *order, containing a set of closely related *genera. In animals, the ending is 'idae' (as in Hominidae, the human family)

fault a fracture of the earth's crust, across which there has been observable displacement

fauna the animals of a region, country, special environment or period

faunivore (adj. **faunivorous**) a meat-eater; preferred to carnivore, which is best restricted to mammals in the order Carnivora

femur (adj. **femoral**) the thigh bone, the large bone in the upper part of the hindlimb

fertilisation the union of sperm and egg cells (gametes) to form a zygote

fertility the reproductive performance of an individual or population, measured as the number of viable offspring produced over a period

fibula the long bone, which, with the tibia, forms the lower part of the hindlimb (the outer and thinner shin bone in humans)

fitness a measure of the reproductive success (which includes the ability to survive until reproduction) of one *genotype in a population relative to others

flake a piece struck from a larger stone (the core) by percussion or pressure, which leaves characteristic marks on the core. Flakes serve as blanks from which more complex artefacts, **flake tools**, can be made. *See also* bulb of percussion

flake-blade a long, *blade-like flake made in Africa, Europe and the Middle East from about 200 000 to 150 000 years ago and a forerunner of *Middle Palaeolithic and *Middle Stone Age industries

flexion the action that decreases or makes more acute the angle between two bones in a joint. The opposite of *extension

flexor any muscle that bends a limb or other part by its contraction

flora the plants of a region, country, special environment or period

fluvial relating to or occurring in a river

folivore (adj. **folivorous**) a leaf-eater

follicle-stimulating hormone (FSH) a protein *hormone secreted by the *pituitary gland, which stimulates the growth of follicles in the ovaries and the formation of sperm in the testes

forager one who collects wild plant and animal food

foramen magnum the large opening in the back of the skull through which the spinal cord passes to join the brainstem

forebrain the furthest forward part of the brain, consisting of a few important masses of *grey matter – the two *cerebral hemispheres, the *basal ganglia, the diencephalon (*thalamus and *hypothalamus) – and associated *white matter

forest canopy the dense upper layer of vegetation formed by the widest upper branches of trees

formant frequencies the peaks of acoustic energy passing through the *supralaryngeal (vocal) tract and determined by its length and shape, distinctive for all vowels and consonants. They are numbered from lowest to highest – the first formant ($F1$), the second ($F2$), etc.

formation in geology, a fundamental unit of stratigraphic classification, used for subdividing rock strata on the basis of their general characteristics. Formations are often given geographic names (e.g. the Koobi Fora Formation and Hadar Formation in the East African Rift System), and may be combined into groups or subdivided into members

fossil any preserved remains or traces of past life, more than about 10 000 years old, embedded in rock either as mineralised remains or as impressions, casts or tracks

fossiliferous containing fossils

fossilisation the burial of a dead plant or animal in sediment and the eventual mineralisation of all or part of it

founder effect the genetical consequences of founding a new population with a few individuals. If, for example, only 10 people start a new colony, there can be only 20 copies of any *gene in subsequent generations. If one of these copies is a rare harmful *recessive, its frequency will immediately jump to 5 per cent from its initially very low level in the ancestral population

frontal bone the bone forming the forehead and the upper parts of the eye cavities (orbits) in a mammal

frontal lobe the front part of the *cerebral hemispheres of the mammalian brain, in front of a cleft, the central sulcus. In primates, it is separated from the temporal lobe by the Sylvian fissure

frugivore (adj. **frugivorous**) a fruit-eater

FSH see follicle-stimulating hormone

G

gallery forest a stretch of forest along the sides of a river in an area of open country

gamete (germ cell) *haploid reproductive cell, that fuses with another gamete of the opposite sex to produce a *diploid cell, the zygote, in a process called fertilisation; sperm or egg cell

gastrocnemius the large calf muscle. It flexes the knee and the ankle joint

gene the unit of heredity, comprising a length of *DNA (*RNA in some viruses) that influences an organism's form and function. In all cells, genes are borne in linear order on *chromosomes. The position a gene occupies on a chromosome is called its **locus** (pl. loci), and different forms of a gene occupying the same locus are **alleles**

gene family a group of closely linked gene loci with related functions, such as the globin gene family that contains several genes concerned with oxygen transport in blood and muscle. They usually arise by the duplication of a single gene followed by divergence in function

gene flow the exchange of genes among populations, either directly by migration or indirectly by the diffusion of genes over many generations

gene frequency the proportion of the various alleles at a locus within a population

genetic distance the overall genetic difference among populations or species, averaged over as many genes as possible

genetic drift the random change of gene frequences over time. It can take place rapidly in small populations, such as those on isolated islands, but happens in all populations, regardless of size

genome the complete set of genetic information in a living organism. The human genome, for example, consists of 3000 million *base pairs

genotype the set of *alleles at a particular *locus. It is also sometimes used to refer to the complete allelic constitution over all loci. See also homozygous; heterozygous

genus (pl. **genera**) a group of closely related *species. In *binomial nomenclature, the genus is the first of two words in naming a species (e.g. Homo = genus and sapiens = species). A group of closely related genera is a *family

gestation the period from fertilisation to birth in placental mammals. In humans, it lasts about 266 days (or about 280 days counting from the first day of the last menstrual period)

glacial maximum the peak of a *glacial period when glaciers and ice caps are at their greatest extent. The last one was about 18 000–20 000 years ago

glacial period (glaciation) an ice age, when glaciers and ice caps were much more extensive than they are today, the world's climate was colder and drier, and sea levels were sometimes up to 200 metres lower. The last ice age began around 75 000 years ago and lasted until 15 000–13 000 years ago. The *land bridges (*Beringia, *Sahul and *Sunda) that formed when sea levels fell played a large part in the spread of ancient humans across the world

globin one of the group of proteins involved with the transfer of oxygen in the blood and other tissues

gluteus maximus the largest muscle of the buttock, it helps to extend the thigh at the hip joint. In humans, it acts not during normal walking but when more power is needed, as in running or rising from a chair. It also helps to balance the trunk during activities involving the arms (carrying, throwing, etc.)

gonad a reproductive organ (testis in males, ovary in females) that produces *gametes and various hormones

gonadotrop(h)in one of the group of hormones that act on the gonads (ovaries and testes), such as *follicle-stimulating hormone and *luteinising hormone produced by the *pituitary gland, and chorionic gonadotrophin produced by the *placenta

gracile slender or light in build, often used to categorise the *australopithecine species Australopithecus afarensis and A. africanus

grade a level of organisation in evolution, defined from individual features (e.g. brain size). Evolutionary (traditional) *classifications use the concept for distinguishing between groups. The distinction between lower and higher primates (Prosimii and Anthropoidea) is a grade division

great apes chimpanzees and gorillas (in Africa) and orang-utans (in Asia)

grey matter concentrations of nerve connections (*axons)

grooming cleansing of the fur by a mammal using the hands or teeth, either itself or another member of its social group. In primates especially, grooming between individuals (allogrooming) reinforces social bonds and can last for hours, with several individuals involved

growth hormone (somatotrop(h)in) the protein hormone secreted by the *pituitary gland that stimulates growth of bones and muscles and increases protein synthesis

H

habitat the natural home or environment of a plant or animal

h(a)emoglobin the oxygen-carrying protein of the blood, consisting of two α- and two β-globin chains, plus haem (which contains iron)

h(a)emophilia an inherited error of blood clotting. The commonest form involves problems with one clotting factor – factor VIII – and is *sex-linked

hafting providing an axe or spearpoint with a handle

half-life the time required for the decay of half of the initial number of atoms in a radioactive isotope, so a period of one half-life halves the isotope amount and one of two half-lives leaves a quarter, etc. Each radioactive isotope has a distinctive half-life, which remains constant. For radiocarbon (carbon-14), it is 5730 years

handaxe (biface) stone *core tool with a long, triangular or oval axis and two worked faces – the characteristic tool of the long-lived *Acheulean tradition of the *Lower Palaeolithic

handedness using one hand in preference to the other for a particular task, such as writing or carying a baby. About 90 per cent of people are right-handed. This bias to the right is connected to the functioning of the left and right *cerebral hemispheres. Some primates also prefer to use one hand for certain tasks but the human species seems to be unique in having a marked preference for the right hand.

haploid having only one set of the genetic material. Simple organisms such as some *protozoans are haploid, as are sperm and egg cells, which fuse to form a *diploid cell, the zygote. The number of chromosomes in a haploid set, the **haploid number**, is designated n (in humans, n = 23)

haplorhine a member of the group containing tarsiers and anthropoid primates (monkeys, apes and humans), classified as the suborder Haplorhini in some schemes. The nostrils of haplorhines are surrounded by hairy skin whereas those of lemurs and lorises (strepsirhines) are surrounded by an area of moist naked skin, the rhinarium

hemoglobin see haemoglobin

hemophilia see haemophilia

herbivore (adj. **herbivorous**) a plant-eater

heterozygote (adj. **heterozygous**) a *diploid organism with two different alleles at a *locus. For example, somebody of blood group AB is a heterozygote for the A and B alleles in the ABO blood-group system

higher primates simians (monkeys, apes and humans), in the suborder Anthropoidea

hindbrain the part of the brain comprising the *cerebellum, pons and medulla oblongata

hindgut the colon, at the end of the digestive tract

hippocampus a mass of *grey matter in the

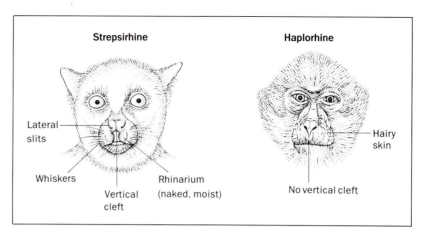

Strepsirhine — Lateral slits, Whiskers, Vertical cleft, Rhinarium (naked, moist)

Haplorhine — Hairy skin, No vertical cleft

*cerebral cortex on the inner rim of the temporal lobe, formed by a sort of rolling up of the edge of the cortex. It has been implicated in memory and arousal functions

histocompatibility antigen see cell-surface antigen

histone a group of small proteins that often bind to *DNA

Holocene the second epoch of the Quaternary period, from about 10 000 years ago to the present. This name is preferred to the alternative Recent

home range an area in which an animal or group of animals seeks food

hominid conventionally, any member of the human family Hominidae (all species of *Australopithecus* and *Homo*)

hominoid a member of the primate superfamily Hominoidea – gibbons (Hylobatidae), great apes (Pongidae), *hominids (Hominidae) and several extinct families

Homo the genus to which humans belong. The number of extinct species is uncertain but at least five forms are usually recognised: *Homo habilis* (small and large forms, probably two species), *Homo erectus*, 'archaic *Homo sapiens*' and modern *Homo sapiens*. *Neanderthals are sometimes given their own name, *Homo neanderthalensis*

homologous chromosomes a pair of chromosomes in a *diploid cell, one received from each parent

homology (adj. **homologous**) resemblance in structure and origin. A homologous feature or homologue has the same evolutionary origin and basic form to one in a different organism but may not have the same final form and function (e.g. the skeletons of a bat wing and a human arm). *See also* analogy

homozygote (adj. **homozygous**) a *diploid organism with identical alleles at a *locus. For example, somebody of blood group AA is homozygous for the A allele in the ABO blood-group system

horizon in geology, a thin layer of rock in a stratified sequence with some characteristic feature, such as particular fossils

hormone a chemical substance produced in one part of the body by ductless glands of the endocrine system, which is carried in the bloodstream to another organ or tissue where it induces a specific physiological response. Examples of hormones are corticosteroids from the *adrenal cortex, *growth hormone from the *pituitary gland and *androgens from the testes

humerus the bone of the upper part of the forelimb (the arm in humans)

hunter-gatherer one who lives by hunting and scavenging wild animals, gathering plants and, in some places, collecting shellfish and fishing, often moving in small groups (bands) from place to place. Before 10 000–12 000 years ago, all humans subsisted in this way but today this lifestyle is followed for all or most of the time by only a few populations (e.g. the Mbuti Pygmies of the Ituri forest, Zaire)

hyoid bone a small, isolated, U-shaped bone in the neck just above the *larynx and below the tongue and linked by a ligament to the styloid process of the *temporal bone. It provides attachment for the tongue and neck muscles

hypothalamus a region of the forebrain below the *thalamus and forming part of the floor of the brain. It is linked to the *pituitary gland and besides controlling the secretion of pituitary hormones it is involved in body functions such as temperature control, eating, water balance and sex

I

ice age see glacial period

immunoglobulin one of the serum proteins involved in *antibody defence

incisor one of the front teeth of mammals. In monkeys, apes and humans, which have two incisors on each side of the upper and lower jaws, they are cutting teeth – hence the name

industry a set of tools made of one material (e.g. stone) with the same types repeated consistently within a limited geographic area or timespan, suggesting that it is the product of one group of people. Similar industries are usually grouped into an **industrial tradition** (e.g. *Oldowan and *Acheulean)

infanticide the killing of infants by humans or non-human primates. In male Hanuman langurs (*Presbytis entellus*), for example, it is thought to be an indirect form of male–male competition; a band of males may attack a troop of females with its single adult male, drive out the resident male and kill dependent infants

infectious disease (communicable disease) any disease that can be transmitted from one person to another

inferior towards the tail or, in humans, the feet (or below)

inner ear the innermost part of the ear within a cavity formed by the petrosal bone (the petrous part of the *temporal bone in humans), containing a spirally coiled bony tube (*cochlea), which is concerned with hearing, and three semicircular canals and two other chambers (utricle and saccule), which are concerned with balance and sensing movement

insectivore (adj. **insectivorous**) an insect-eater; also a member of the mammalian order Insectivora (shrews, moles, etc.)

insula an area of the *cerebral cortex that is covered over and hidden from view by the sides of the deep lateral cleft (Sylvian fissure) in each hemisphere

insulin a protein hormone involved in the regulation of blood sugar that is produced in the pancreas

interglacial between two *glacial periods (ice ages). The world is in an interglacial at present

interspecific between different species

intraspecific between individuals of the same species

intron a length of *DNA within a functional gene that produces an *RNA transcript, but whose contribution is edited out before the functional *messenger RNA is made

invertebrate a multicellular animal without a backbone

isotope a chemical element with the same atomic number and identical chemical properties as another but with a different atomic weight

J

joule the SI unit of energy, equal to the work done when the point of application of a force of 1 newton is displaced through a distance of 1 metre in the direction of the force. 1 joule = 0.2388 *calories

K

K-Ar dating see potassium-argon dating

karyotype the *chromosome complement of a body cell, individual or species, and its representation by a photograph or drawing, with the chromosomes visible at cell division (mitosis) arranged in pairs in order of size. The human karyotype is 46 (23 pairs of chromosomes)

kilocalories unit of 1000 *calories; 1 kilocalorie = 4186.8 *joules.

Kleiber's law an empirical relationship for the *allometric scaling of *basal metabolic rate to body weight raised to the three-quarters power in mammals

knapper see stone-knapper

knuckle-walking a type of four-legged (quadrupedal) locomotion practised by chimpanzees and gorillas, which support their body on the backs of the knuckles rather than on the palms or fingers

L

lactation secretion of milk in mammary glands, a characteristic of mammals; a

period when milk is produced for nursing offspring

lacustrine relating to or of a lake

land bridge a floor of an *epicontinental sea that emerges as dry land when sea levels fall during glacial periods. By linking landmasses it is a dispersal route for land plants and animals, as were *Beringia, *Sahul and *Sunda for ancient humans

larynx the valve-like structure in the front of the neck that guards the opening into the trachea (windpipe). It is responsible for the production of vocal sounds, for controlling the flow of air to and from the lungs and it also prevents food and other substances from entering the lungs. It is made up of a framework of cartilages bound together by *ligaments and membranes, within which are housed the *vocal folds (or vocal cords)

lateral away from the body's midline, at the side

lateralisation the transfer of a function to one side of a bilaterally symmetrical body. For example, most people are right-handed; the speech functions of the brain are largely determined by its left side

Laurasia one of the two supercontinents (the other being Gondwanaland) formed from the break-up of Pangaea around 200 million years ago, comprising what is now North America, Greenland, Europe and parts of Asia

lesser apes gibbons and the siamang in the primate family Hylobatidae

leuk(a)emia any of a group of malignant disorders in which the bone marrow and other blood-forming tissues produce too many immature or abnormal forms of white

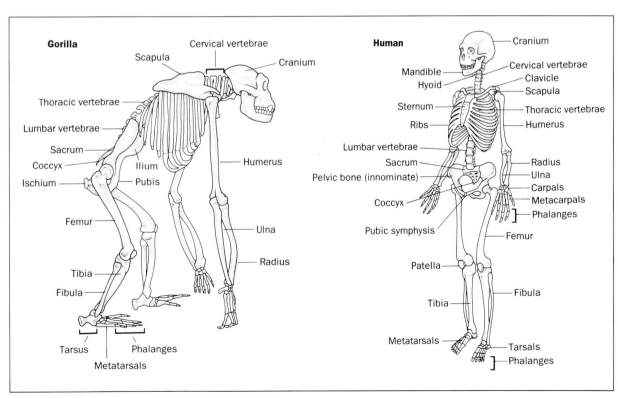

Gorilla
Cervical vertebrae
Scapula
Cranium
Thoracic vertebrae
Lumbar vertebrae
Sacrum
Coccyx
Ilium
Humerus
Ischium
Pubis
Femur
Ulna
Tibia
Fibula
Radius
Tarsus
Phalanges
Metatarsals

Human
Cranium
Mandible
Cervical vertebrae
Hyoid
Clavicle
Scapula
Sternum
Thoracic vertebrae
Ribs
Humerus
Lumbar vertebrae
Sacrum
Radius
Pelvic bone (innominate)
Ulna
Carpals
Coccyx
Metacarpals
Phalanges
Pubic symphysis
Femur
Patella
Fibula
Tibia
Metatarsals
Tarsals
Phalanges

blood cell (leucocytes) that suppress the production of normal blood cells

lexigram a geometric symbol, much like a Japanese or Chinese graphic sign. Lexigram symbols can be used in place of spoken words by chimpanzees. They do not draw them but point to specific ones to convey their intent

LH *see* luteinising hormone

life cycle the various stages in a species between fertilisation of the germ cells (gametes) to produce a zygote in one generation and fertilisation in the next

life expectancy the average period an individual can expect to live after a specific age, assuming that mortality levels of the population do not change

life history the various stages an individual passes through from birth to death

life table a set of mortality rates for different age classes in a population

ligament a strong band of white, fibrous, *connective tissue linking two bones or cartilages at a joint. It strengthens the joint and restricts its movement to certain directions

limbic system a complex system of nerve pathways and networks within the temporal lobes of the *cerebral hemispheres, involving several different brain structures (e.g. *amygdala and *hippocampus) and associated with emotion, arousal and memory

lineage a line of common descent

lingual relating to or close to the tongue; the inside or tongue side of a tooth

linkage in genetics, the tendency for particular groups of *loci to be inherited together, because they are carried on the same *chromosome

living floor a level in an archaeological site that was once at the surface, with stone tools, bones and other remains lying where they were placed or dropped by hominids

locus (pl. **loci**) the site (nucleotide sequence) on a *chromosome occupied by a particular gene

loess a deposit of wind-blown silt

longevity the lifespan of individuals in a population

Lower Pal(a)eolithic the earliest part of the Old Stone Age, beginning with the *Oldowan tradition of toolmaking around 2.6 million years ago and including the Karari and *Acheulean traditions. It ended 200 000–150 000 years ago with the development of *flake tools

lower primates prosimians (lemurs, lorises and tarsiers), members of the suborder Prosimii

luteinising hormone (LH) a gonadotrophin, a protein hormone secreted by the *pituitary gland that stimulates *ovulation, formation of the *corpus luteum and *progesterone synthesis by the ovaries, and *androgen synthesis by the interstitial cells in the testes

lymph the clear fluid, containing water, salts, protein, etc. and some white blood cells (mostly lymphocytes), that derives from tissue fluids and is transported by vessels of the **lymphatic system** back into the bloodstream

lymph node one of several small swellings at intervals along the lymphatic vessels that filter lymph, preventing foreign particles such as bacteria from entering the bloodstream, and produce *lymphocytes

lymphocyte one of several classes of white blood cell involved in the immune response

lymphoma a cancer of the *lymph nodes, excluding Hodgkin's disease

M

magma (adj. **magmatic**) a hot molten rock material formed within the earth's crust from which igneous rock results after cooling and crystallisation

Magdalenian the principal *Upper Palaeolithic tradition of western Europe, named after the rockshelter of La Madeleine (dug by Edouard Lartet in the 1860s) in the Dordogne, southwestern France, and dating from about 17 000 to 12 000 years ago. Fine bone and antler tools are characteristic of the later stages. Many decorated caves and art objects date to this time

magnetic field the force field surrounding a magnet. The earth has a magnetic field approximately aligned with its spin axis. The field has changed direction several times

magnetic reversals repeated, but irregular, changes in the direction of the earth's magnetic field, from north-pointing (**normal polarity**) to south-pointing (**reversed polarity**), and back. *See also* palaeomagnetism

mandible (adj. **mandibular**) the lower jaw, consisting (in monkeys, apes and humans) of a single, fused bone

matriline (adj. **matrilineal**) the female line of descent

maxilla (adj. **maxillary**) one of two bones forming the upper jaw, the other being the premaxilla. The premaxilla bears the incisors. In humans, the maxilla covers the premaxilla

medial (mesial) in anatomy, towards or near the body's midline

member in geology, a subdivision of a rock *formation

meiosis (adj. **meiotic**) the cell division involved in the production of *haploid germ (sperm and egg) cells from their *diploid progenitors

melanin any of a range of black or brown pigments in hair, the skin and eyes. In the skin, production of melanin is increased by the action of sunlight, and this protects the underlying tissue from the sun's rays

mesial *see* medial

Mesolithic the stone age epoch that followed the *Palaeolithic and preceded the *Neolithic in Europe. It lasted for a few thousand years from about 12 000–10 000

years ago, and is characterised by the use of small stone tools (*microliths) and by a broad-based hunting and gathering economy after the last ice age

messenger RNA (mRNA) a segment of the *DNA message transcribed into *RNA. It carries the information needed for protein synthesis from DNA to the *ribosomes

Messinian crisis the drying up of the Mediterranean Sea during the Miocene epoch, about 6 million years ago

metatarsal one of five parallel bones of the middle region of the foot, between the ankle (tarsus) and toes (phalanges)

metazoan a multicellular animal

microlith a small stone tool, usually under 3 centimetres long and of various shapes, used in composite tools and as projectile points (e.g. barbs and tips for spears and arrows). Microliths are especially characteristic of the *Mesolithic in Europe, but the tradition first appeared in Africa, 40 000 or more years ago, and was present in Europe and the Middle East at least 20 000 years ago. *See also* Natufian

microwear microscopic patterns of wear or damage on the edge of a stone tool that provide clues to the way in which the tool was used. The wear often appears as a kind of 'polish'

midbrain the part of the brainstem, excluding the pons and medulla oblongata, between the *forebrain and the *hindbrain

midden the accumulation of refuse, often shell debris, resulting from human use

middle ear the part of the ear containing the ear ossicles (malleus, incus and stapes), which transmit sound vibrations from the outer ear to the inner ear. It is usually protected on the undersurface by a sheet of bone, the *auditory bulla. The major primate groups are characterised by specific spatial relationships between the bony ring that supports the ear drum (tympanic membrane) and the auditory bulla

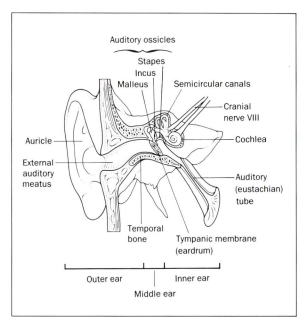

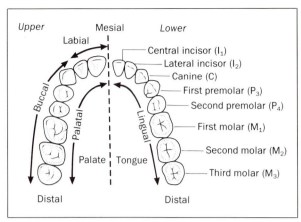

Human tooth rows.

Middle Pal(a)eolithic the stone age epoch between the *Lower Palaeolithic and the *Upper Palaeolithic in Europe and the Middle East, from about 200 000–150 000 to 50 000–40 000 years ago, characterised by flake tools (e.g. *Mousterian industries)

Middle Stone Age the rough equivalent in sub-Saharan Africa and in southern and eastern Asia of the Middle Palaeolithic, from about 150 000 to perhaps 30 000 years ago. There are many regional variants but all include flake industries

Miocene the fourth epoch of the Tertiary period, about 23.3 to 5.2 million years ago

mitochondrion a cellular organelle involved in energy metabolism. Each has its own small circular genome, the **mitochondrial DNA (mtDNA)**

mitosis (adj. **mitotic**) the division of body (somatic) cells, which produces two *diploid cells from a diploid progenitor

molar a broad, often squarish cheek tooth that has no precursor in the milk dentition. In simian primates (monkeys, apes and humans), which have three permanent molars on each side of the upper and lower jaws (as is typical for placental mammals), the teeth are adapted for crushing and grinding. The third and last molar in humans is also called the wisdom tooth. Milk premolars are often termed milk molars in dentistry, but this conflicts with the standard terminology for mammals

molecular clock a concept based on the assumption (often a daring one) that mutations accumulate at a steady rate, used to estimate the time at which two evolving lineages diverged

Mongoloid relating to or a member of the modern human populations indigenous to eastern Asia (China, Korea and Japan) and northeastern Asia, and their descendants elsewhere. The native peoples of the Americas are sometimes so called

monogamy (adj. **monogamous**) the social system in which males and females live in exclusive pair relationships, sometimes for the whole of their lives

monophyletic group a complete set of organisms derived from one ancestral stock

monozygotic twins 'identical' twins formed by the splitting of a fertilised egg. Apart from mutations that may arise during development, they carry the same genes

morphology (adj. **morphological**) the form and structure of an organism, and their study

mortality (death) rate the ratio of deaths in an area or group to the population of that area or group

mosaics see cell mosaics

motor control area the part of the *cerebral cortex in the frontal lobe involved in controlling voluntary movements of the body and limbs

Mousterian a stone *flake industrial tradition, named after the French site of Le Moustier in the Dordogne, associated – typically but not exclusively – with *Neanderthals and characterised by small *handaxes, side-scrapers and triangular points

mRNA see messenger RNA

mtDNA see mitochondrial DNA

multimale group a stable social group containing several adult females and more than one sexually mature male

muscular dystrophy one of a group of inherited diseases marked by weakness and wasting of the muscles such as those of the back, shoulders and hip region. See also Duchenne muscular dystrophy

mutagen an agent, such as x-rays or certain chemicals, capable of producing *mutations

mutation an alteration in an individual's genetic constitution

N

nasal of or relating to the nose

Natufian a *Mesolithic culture of the eastern Mediterranean (Levant), dated to about 12 800–10 500 years ago and named after Wadi en-Natuf in Palestine. Natufians hunted and gathered but some lived in seasonal or permanent settlements. They harvested wild cereals extensively and used sickles and pounding tools

natural selection the differential survival and reproduction of individuals of different *genotype within a population

Neanderthal a lineage of ancient humans that lived in Europe and Western Asia as far east as Iraq and Uzbekistan between about 120 000 and 30 000 years ago, although there were possible forerunners of Neanderthals in Europe up to 300 000 years ago. Those with characteristic ('classic') Neanderthal features – stocky build, large heads, large brains and large, projecting noses – are known from Western Europe after 90 000 years ago. There is uncertainty about the affinities of Neanderthals, and there is no consensus about the scientific name these hominids should have. Some call them a subspecies of modern humans (*Homo sapiens neanderthalensis*) but others, who believe that they are not directly ancestral to modern humans, see them as a distinct species, *Homo neanderthalensis*

Neogene a sub-period (or period in some geological timescales) of the Cenozoic era, divided into the *Miocene and *Pliocene epochs

Neolithic the New Stone Age, usually associated with the beginnings of agriculture, pottery and sedentism in the Old World. In parts of western Asia, farming began as early as 10 000 years ago (although without pottery). It took several thousands of years for agriculture to reach northern Europe

neonate newly born mammal

neoteny the persistence of a juvenile character in adulthood

neotropical occurring in the tropical regions of the New World (South and Central Americas)

nerve fibre see axon

neural of or relating to a nerve or the nervous system

neuroblastoma a malignant tumour originating from immature nerve cells that mostly affects infants and children up to 10 years old

neurone a nerve cell, the basic unit of the nervous system specialised for conducting electrical impulses. It usually consists of a cell body, which contains the nucleus and from which cytoplasmic processes called dendrites project, and the axon, which relays impulses from the cell body over long distances

neutral mutation a mutation that has no discernable effect on the *phenotype of the individual carrying it and that is hence not acted on by *natural selection. Many alleged neutral mutations may not be so, but most models of *molecular clocks assume that the majority of changes in protein or DNA structure are neutral

New World monkeys South and Central American monkeys, in the superfamily Ceboidea

niche the place of an organism in its *ecosystem, including the resources it exploits and its association with other organisms and the environment

nocturnal active at night

nomad (adj. **nomadic**) one who continually moves from place to place to find food

normal polarity epoch a period of earth history when the earth's *magnetic field was north-pointing, as it is today

nucleic acid a chain of *nucleotides in association with sugar and phosphate molecules, including DNA (deoxyribose nucleic acid) and RNA (ribose nucleic acid)

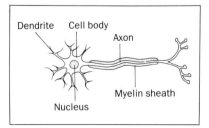

A neurone (nerve cell).

nucleotide a unit of a nucleic acid, consisting of a sugar, a base (usually adenine, thymine, guanine and cytosine in DNA) and a phosphate group

nucleus the part of the cell, held within a membrane in higher organisms (*eukaryotes), which contains the *chromosomes; an anatomically and functionally distinct group of nerve cells within the brain or spinal cord

O

occipital bone the fused composite bone that forms the back part of the base of the braincase (cranium). On it are two rounded projections, the **occipital condyles**, that articulate with the first (atlas) vertebra of the backbone. Between the condyles is the foramen magnum, the opening through which the spinal cord passes

occipital lobe the back part of the *cerebral hemispheres

occlusion the position of the teeth when the jaws are closed and their biting surfaces touch or occlude

(o)esophagus the part of the digestive tract between the pharynx and stomach

(o)estradiol one of the major *(o)estrogens

(o)estrogen the general name for the steroid hormones (e.g. oestradiol and oestrone) that control female reproductive function. They are mainly secreted by the ovaries, but small amounts are produced by the *adrenal cortex and the *placenta, and by the testes in males

(o)estrous cycle reproductive cycle in female mammals comprising growth of the ovarian follicles and secretion of *oestrogen, *ovulation accompanied by the urge for mating (**oestrus** or 'heat'), formation of the *corpus luteum in the ovary and secretion of the hormone *progesterone. The stages occur at regular intervals in the absence of pregnancy, but if an egg is fertilised the corpus luteum enlarges with further production of hormones. In simian primates (monkeys, apes and humans), the lining of the womb is periodically discharged after the progesterone stage (**menstruation**). The term oestrus is not strictly applicable to simians, and the term **menstrual cycle** is hence more appropriate for them

(o)estrus (adj. **(o)estrous**) the period when female mammals, including prosimians, are sexually receptive. Regulated by hormones it usually coincides with ovulation. Simian primates do not generally have a typical mammalian oestrus

Old World monkeys monkeys in all geographical areas except South and Central America, in the superfamily Cercopithecoidea

Oldowan the oldest-known tradition of toolmaking named after Olduvai Gorge in Tanzania, where some of the largest and best-described sets of Oldowan tools have been found. They appear at sites in Africa dating between about 2.6 and 1 million years ago, many of them in the East African Rift System. They typically include core forms made from cobbles from which flakes were struck, modified (retouched) cores (choppers, etc.), retouched flakes (scrapers, etc.) and hammerstones. A variant of the tradition, **Developed Oldowan**, appeared around 1.4 million years ago. An Oldowan-like technology is known from Asia; the Chinese sites may be more than a million years old

olfaction (adj. **olfactory**) the sense of smell; the smelling process

olfactory lobe the front lower part of the *cerebral hemispheres where the olfactory nerves terminate. It is concerned with the sense of smell

Oligocene the third epoch of the Tertiary period, about 35.4 to 23.3 million years ago

omnivore (adj. **omnivorous**) a regular eater of both animal and plant food

omomyid a member of the Omomyidae, a family of extinct tarsier-like primates mainly of the Eocene epoch. The last known omomyids are Oligocene in age. The details of their relationship to modern primates are uncertain

oncogene a gene involved in tumour formation. In its unmutated form (a **proto-oncogene**), it may have important functions in normal cells

ontogeny (adj. **ontogenetic**) the development of an individual from egg to adult

oocyte developing egg cell that divides twice by *meiosis to form an ovum (**oogenesis**). Up to the first meiotic division, which occurs in the ovary, the egg cell is termed a **primary oocyte**; after ovulation, it is a **secondary oocyte**. The second meiotic division is only activated by fertilisation on penetration of the outer membrane of the egg cell by a sperm. Each meiotic division is unequal; accompanying the large egg cell is a much smaller, non-functional cell called a **polar body**

opposable thumb a thumb that can rotate along its long axis so that its fleshy tip can touch other fingertips, found only in Old World simians. It allows the precision grip of humans

oral relating to or of the mouth

orbit the bony socket for the eye

orbital convergence the realignment of the visual axis of the orbits during primate evolution from sideways-facing to front-facing lines of sight

order a major taxonomic division of a class (e.g. order Primates in the class Mammalia)

organelle a functional membrane-enclosed body inside cells (e.g. a nucleus and a *mitochondrion)

outgroup comparison the comparison of the features of a particular group with those of another to determine evolutionary relationships

ovary (pl. **ovaries**) the main female reproductive organ, which produces egg cells (oocytes) and steroid hormones in a regular cycle in response to hormones (gonadotrophins) from the *pituitary gland. There are two ovaries, one on each side of the body

ovum (pl. **ova**) a mature egg cell, produced by the second *meiotic division of an *oocyte

ovulation the release of an egg from the ovary at the start of its passage through the Fallopian tubes (oviducts) to the uterus

oxygen-isotope ratio the ratio of stable isotopes of oxygen (oxygen-18 and oxygen-16) measured in fossils of calcareous organisms (e.g. foraminifera and mollusc shells). It gives information about past temperatures and the extent of ice cover during glacial periods and interglacials

P

pair-bonding the development of a social bond between the male and female of a *monogamous pair

pal(a)eo- prefix derived from the Greek *palaios*, meaning old, ancient

pal(a)eoanthropology the study of the human fossil record and archaeology

Pal(a)eocene the first epoch of the Tertiary period, about 65 to 56.5 million years ago

Pal(a)eogene a sub-period (or a period in some geological timescales) of the Cenozoic era, divided into the *Palaeocene, *Eocene and *Oligocene epochs

Pal(a)eolithic the Old Stone Age, the first and longest part of the stone age that began some 2.6 million years ago in Africa with the first recognisable stone tools belonging to the *Oldowan industrial tradition and ended some 12 000–10 000 years ago with the *Mesolithic. In Europe, it is usually divided into the *Lower, *Middle and *Upper Palaeolithic. Rough equivalents of the Middle and Upper Palaeolithic in Africa and Asia are the *Middle and *Later Stone Ages. Throughout the Palaeolithic agriculture was unknown

pal(a)eomagnetism the earth's *magnetic field preserved in rocks when they formed, and its study. The field direction gives information about the past positions of land masses relative to the magnetic poles and can be used to describe the movement of continents relative to one another. Lavas whose polarity has been measured in this way can be dated by the *potassium-argon method, which gives a timescale of the changes of polarity for about the past 20 million years. The method is useful for the relative dating of extinct primates as the polarity 'signature' of rock samples from the fossil sites can be compared with the pattern of the established polarity sequence

palate (adj. **palatal**) the bony roof of the mouth

pancreas a gland behind the stomach that supplies the duodenum with digestive enzymes and secretes the hormones *insulin and glucagon into the blood

pandemic an epidemic so widely spread that vast numbers of people are affected world-wide. A classic example is the Black Death, the virulent plague that swept through Europe from Asia in the fourteenth century

parasite an organism that for some or all of its life lives on or in the body or cell of another organism (host), deriving its food from the host. The host does not benefit from the association and is often harmed by it Human parasites include viruses, bacteria, protozoans and worms

parasite load the number and types of parasites carried by an organism

parietal bone a paired bone that forms part of the side walls and most of the roof of the mammalian braincase (cranium)

parietal lobe the region of the *cerebral cortex beneath the *parietal bone, lying behind the central sulcus partly between the frontal and occipital lobes and above the temporal lobes

parsimony principle the notion that evolution has followed the most economical route, involving the assumption that closely related species (those that diverged more recently) will consistently have fewer differences than species that diverged longer ago

pastoralist one whose way of life is based on the herding of domesticated animals (e.g. cattle, sheep, goats or llamas)

pathogen any disease-producing microorganism (e.g. a bacterium)

pathogenicity the ability to cause disease

pathology the characteristic symptoms and signs of disease or dysfunction, and the study of their nature and causes

pedigree a reconstruction of past matings in a family, much used in the study of inherited diseases

pelvic (hip) girdle the skeletal structure supporting the legs in humans and corresponding parts in other vertebrates; it consists of the right and left hip bones, which articulate with the *sacrum and with each other at the pubic symphysis

pelvic inlet the brim of the pelvic cavity. In human females, it is usually wider and has a larger absolute circumference than the heart-shaped inlet of males

period a unit of geological time, a division of an era (e.g. the Quaternary and Tertiary periods in the Cenozoic era)

periodontal relating to the tissues surrounding the teeth

phalange (phalanx) (pl. **phalanges**) finger or toe bone

pharynx (adj. **pharyngeal**) a long, muscular tube leading from the cavity of the *larynx upwards to the back parts of the mouth and nose. It acts as a passageway for food to the oesophagus, as an air passage from the nose and mouth to the larynx, and also as a resonating chamber for the sounds produced in the larynx

phenotype (adj. **phenotypic**) the observable and measurable characteristics of an organism, a result of the interaction of *genotype and environment

phonation the production of vocal sounds, especially speech, through the use of the *vocal folds (or vocal cords)

phoneme any of the set of speech sounds in a language that distinguish one word from another (e.g. [b], [g] and [p] in 'bet' 'get' and 'pet')

phonetics the study of speech sounds, especially of their production, transmission and perception

photosynthesis (adj. **photosynthetic**) the synthesis of carbohydrates by plants from simple precursors using solar energy and chlorophyll

phyletic applies to a group of species with a common ancestor; a line of direct descent

phylogenetic (evolutionary) tree a schematic diagram of the evolutionary or genealogical relationships among a group of species

phylogeny (adj. **phylogenetic**) the evolutionary history or genealogy of a species or group of species

pituitary gland the major *endocrine gland, a small body attached by a short stalk to the underside of the brain below the *hypothalamus that secretes important hormones (e.g. adrenocorticotrophin, *gonadotrophins, *growth hormone, *prolactin and thyroid-stimulating hormone), under the control of the hypothalamus

placenta in placental mammals, an organ between mother and fetus that develops on the internal wall of the *uterus and passes oxygen, nutrients and other substances to the fetus and receives waste material from it. It also secretes various hormones (e.g. progesterone and oestrogen) that help maintain pregnancy

plasticity an adaptability to environmental change

plate tectonics the theory that the earth's crust is divided into fragments (plates) that move relative to each other and are responsible for continental drift and for crustal features (e.g. mountain ranges) when they collide

platyrrhine member of the primate infraorder Platyrrhini (New World monkeys)

Pleistocene the first epoch of the Quaternary period, now internationally agreed to date from about 1.64 million to 10 000 years ago. Some geological timescales still put the Pliocene/Pleistocene boundary at about 1.8 million years ago. The Pleistocene is characterised by a series of *glacial periods and *interglacials

Pliocene the final epoch of the Tertiary period, about 5.2 to 1.64 million years ago

polar body a small cell produced with the much larger egg cell when an *oocyte undergoes the first and second meiotic divisions. Polar bodies have no known function

polygamy a relationship involving several mature members of one sex and one or more mature members of the other

polygenic inheritance the inheritance of characters (e.g. height, weight and behaviour) that depends on the simultaneous action of many genes of small effect (**polygenes**) in consort with the environment

polygyny a relationship involving one sexually mature male and at least two sexually mature females

polymorphism (adj. **polymorphic**) the existence of alternative allelic forms at a *locus within a population. Thus, in humans, there is a polymorphism for the ABO blood groups

polyphyletic group a set of organisms derived from at least two distinct ancestral stocks

polyploid having more than two *haploid chromosome sets, as commonly in plants. In humans, this is always lethal

postcranium the vertebrate skeleton excluding the skull (cranium and lower jaw). In quadrupeds, it is behind the cranium (hence the name). The complete human postcranial skeleton has 177 separate bones

postglacial in archaeology, refers to the period since the end of the last *glacial period or ice age – the past 10 000 years

postorbital bar bony strut at the side of the orbits in living primates and many other mammals, ensuring that the eye is surrounded by a complete bony ring

postorbital constriction narrowing of the skull behind the orbits

potassium-argon (K-Ar) dating a radiometric method for dating volcanic rocks based on the rate of decay of the isotopes potassium-40 to argon-40

precocial applies to larger and well-developed offspring born after a relatively long *gestation with a good coat of hair and eyes and ears open by birth or soon afterwards. Precocial mammals breed more slowly than *altricial mammals

prehension the act of grasping

prehensile tail a tail adapted for grasping, especially for wrapping around a support, confined to the larger New World monkeys among primates

premolar a tooth between the *canines and *molars in mammals and intermediate in form. Apes and humans have two permanent premolars on each side of the upper and lower jaws

presenting typically a female pattern of behaviour in which a part of the body (e.g. swelling around the genitals) is displayed to the male to indicate receptivity

primitive character a character present in the basic common ancestor of a group of species

progestagen one of a group of steroid compounds that, like progesterone, help to maintain pregnancy as their main function. Because they prevent the release of mature eggs from the ovaries (ovulation), progestagens are a major constituent of oral contraceptives

progesterone a steroid hormone secreted by the *corpus luteum in the ovaries, by the *placenta and in small amounts by the *adrenal cortex and testes. It prepares the uterus to receive the fertilised egg, maintains the uterus during pregnancy, and prevents the further release of mature eggs from the ovaries. It is the precursor of several other hormones

prolactin a hormone secreted by the *pituitary gland with complex functions that include the initiation of milk production after childbirth and the production of *progesterone by the corpus luteum in the ovaries. Excess secretion of prolactin (hyperprolactinaemia) is associated with the stopping of menstrual periods (amenorrhoea), and also infertility in women and impotence in men

pronuclei the *haploid nucleus of either the mature ovum or sperm after fertilisation but before fusion of the nuclear material

prosimian any primate in the suborder Prosimii (lemurs, lorises and tarsiers)

prostate a gland in the male that surrounds the neck of the bladder and the *urethra and secretes a liquid constituent of semen

protein a molecule made up of chains of amino acids – the foundation of most of the body's structures

protozoan one of a group of simple, single-celled organisms with a nucleus, such as the malaria parasite (*Plasmodium*), trypanosomes and foraminifera

pseudogene a *gene whose DNA sequence is close to that of a functioning gene but which has accumulated so many mutations that it no longer functions: the 'rusting hulk' of a gene

Q

quadrupedal locomotion walking on four legs

Quaternary the period of the Cenozoic era that began about 1.64 million years ago (or about 1.8 million years ago in some geological timescales)

R

radiation *see* adaptive radiation

radioactivity (adj. **radioactive**) the emission of ionising radiation from an unstable chemical isotope

radiocarbon dating a radiometric method for dating organic material such as wood, charcoal and bone based on the rate of decay of the isotope carbon-14 to nitrogen-14. It is effective for the past 50 000 years and potentially for 80 000 years with the accelerator mass spectrometry (AMS) technique

radiogenic being radioactive, producing decay elements useful for dating

radiometric dating absolute dating methods based on the measurement of radioactive decay, such as *potassium-argon and *radiocarbon

recessive an *allele whose *phenotypic effects are more or less masked by its dominant alternative when it is present in a *heterozygote

recombinant DNA a *DNA molecule made up from the joining of two distinct DNA

molecules. Human genes inserted into bacteria are an example of recombinant DNA, but so are sperm and eggs, all of which possess new combinations of a DNA sequence not found in either parent

relict organ an organ that is no longer functional

restriction enzyme an enzyme that cuts *DNA whenever it encounters a specific sequence of bases – often four or six bases long

restriction site a particular set of *DNA bases recognised by a *restriction enzyme. Differences in the position of such sites give rise to **restriction fragment length polymorphisms**

retina (adj. **retinal**) the inner, light-sensitive layer of the eye

retouch the secondary flaking of a stone core or flake to shape a tool

reversed polarity epoch a period when the earth's *magnetic field was south-pointing; the opposite of the orientation today

Rhesus (Rh) a blood-group system first discovered in the rhesus macaque, *Macaca mulatta*. Those *homozygous for the Rhesus-negative allele lack the Rhesus *cell-surface antigen, whereas those with one or two copies of the Rhesus-positive allele produce it

ribonucleic acid *see* RNA

ribosome a cellular organelle made up of **ribosomal RNA (rRNA)** and protein, which is the site of protein synthesis

rift valley long narrow trough bounded by faults, formed by the fracturing of the earth's crust and the subsidence of blocks of crust, and often marked by chains of volcanoes. Many primate and hominid fossils have been found at sites in the East African Rift System, a discontinuous series of rift valleys that runs for 3 000 kilometres from the Afar region of Ethiopia to southern Malawi

RNA ribonucleic acid, a nucleic acid made up of a series of four bases (adenine, guanine, thymine and uracil), a ribose sugar and a phosphate group. Not itself the carrier of the genetic information in higher organisms (although it may be so in viruses), but an important intermediary – in one of several forms – in translating the genetic message

robust ruggedly built, especially the face and jaws. Often used to categorise the australopithecine species *Paranthropus* (or *Australopithecus*) *robustus* and *Paranthropus* (or *Australopithecus*) *boisei*

ruminant herbivorous mammals such as cows and sheep that chew the cud and have

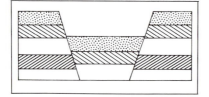

Formation of a rift valley.

complex stomachs containing bacteria for digesting cellulose

S

sacrum the bone that forms the end of the backbone, usually composed of several fused vertebrae (five in humans) to give strength and stability to the lower back. It articulates with the last lumbar vertebra above, the coccyx below and the pelvic (hip) bones at the side

Sahul the name given to the land area periodically exposed between New Guinea and Australia during the Pleistocene, when the sea level was as much as 200 metres lower than at present (the average drop during the past 100 000 years was, however, closer to 40–60 metres). The landbridge would have helped people to colonise Australia for the first time, probably 60 000 to 50 000 years ago, but their supposed journey from mainland Asia via Indonesia would still have involved some sea crossings of considerable distance

satellite DNA a portion of the DNA that forms a distinct band when it is separated on the basis of molecular weight by centrifugation. It consists of many repeats of the same short set of sequences

savanna (savannah) subtropical or tropical grassland with scattered shrubs and trees and a pronounced dry season, typical of eastern Africa

scala naturae a ladder of increasing complexity, also called the phylogenetic scale. In the past, living primates were arranged on such a scale that led from lemurs to monkeys to apes and on to humans

scaling adjustment of individual characters to match differing body size

sedentary applied to people who settle permanently in one place, and base their agricultural and/or hunting and gathering economy there. The opposite of *nomadic

sedimentary rock a rock formed by the accumulation and hardening of rock particles (**sediments**) derived from existing rocks and/or organic debris and deposited by agents such as wind, water and ice at the earth's surface. The source of fossils

'selfish DNA' a metaphor for *DNA sequences that appear to act in their own interests rather than those of their carriers. Some apparently functionless sequences that are repeated thousands of times in the *genome may have invaded by virtue of their 'selfish' behaviour

seminal vesicle one of the pair of glands in the male that open into the vas deferens before it joins the *urethra and secretes most of the fluid constituents of semen

sex chromosome a *chromosome involved in the determination of sex (the X and Y chromosomes in humans)

sex hormone chiefly, an *androgen, *gonadotrophin or *oestrogen

sex linkage a *locus carried on the *X or *Y chromosome is said to be sex-linked. Most are on the X, and give rise to a characteristic pattern of inheritance in which males always show the effects of a gene that acts as a *recessive in females. Sex-linked characters include genes responsible for conditions such as *haemophilia and *Duchenne muscular dystrophy

sex ratio the ratio of males to females in a population

sexual dimorphism the differences in shape, size, colour, etc. between males and females of a species

shared derived character a feature shared by descendants from an ancestral stock that was not present in the remote common ancestor

sibling the offspring of the same parents

sickle-cell an(a)emia an abnormal form of *haemoglobin caused by a single amino-acid mutution in β-globin. Those *heterozygous for the sickle-cell allele are protected against malaria, and show few signs of the disease. Those with two copies of the allele are much more severely affected

simian any member of the primate suborder Anthropoidea (monkeys, apes and humans); a higher primate

sister group the next most closely related group (e.g. New World monkeys are the sister group of Old World monkeys)

soleus in humans, a broad flat muscle in the calf of the leg that flexes the foot so that the toes point downwards

spearthrower a device, made of bone, antler or wood and often decorated, introduced in *Magdalenian times for improving the force behind a thrown spear. About the length of a human forearm, with a finger grip at one end and at the other a hook or knob that engages with the spear, it gives the thrower's arm the equivalent of an extra segment

speciation the development of new *species, usually by divergence between subpopulations of an original species after geographical separation

species the basic units of biological classification, defined by the American zoologist Ernst Mayr (b. 1904) as 'groups of actually or potentially interbreeding natural populations, which are reproductively isolated from other such groups'

sternum the breastbone

stone-knapper a person who works stone tools

stratigraphy in geology, the study of sequences of rocks, their characteristics and relative positions, and the correlation of rocks of the same age in different places; also applied to layered deposits at archaeological sites

strepsirhine a member of the group containing lemurs and lorises, classified as the suborder Strepsirhini in some schemes. The nostrils of strepsirhines are surrounded by an area of moist, naked skin (the **rhinarium**) whereas those of tarsiers and simians (haplorhines) are surrounded by hairy skin

stria terminalis a tract of nerve fibres in the brain that links the *amygdala to the *hypothalamus

subcutaneous under the skin

sulcus (pl. **sulci**) one of the many infoldings of the surface of the brain. The ridge on each side of a sulcus is termed a **gyrus**. See also cerebral cortex

Sunda the name given to the land area periodically exposed between mainland Southeast Asia and the western Indonesian islands during the Pleistocene, when the sea level was as much as 200 metres lower than at present (the average drop during the past 100 000 years was, however, closer to 40–60 metres). The land bridge could have been a route from mainland Asia for migrating ancient humans – Homo erectus and, later, early Homo sapiens

superior higher in relation to another structure (towards the head in humans)

supralaryngeal (vocal) tract the airway above the larynx – the cavities of the mouth and nose, and the pharynx

survivorship curve a graphic representation of the number of living individuals in each age class in a population

suture in anatomy, the line or junction of two parts immovably connected, as between the bones of the adult skull in humans

Sylvian fissure the cleft demarcating the temporal lobe from the frontal and parietal lobes of the *cerebral hemispheres in all living primates

symbol a feature of a language or behaviour that conveys a meaning

symphysis (adj. **symphyseal**) the line marking the fusion of two bones that were separate at an earlier stage of development, such as the symphysis of the right and left halves of the lower jaw (the mandibular symphysis). It also refers to a joint where two bones are separated by a tough kind of cartilage (fibrocartilage) that minimises movement, an example being the joint between the pubic bones of the *pelvic, or hip, girdle (pubic symphysis)

syntax the way words are arranged or modified to show relationships of meaning within sentences

taphonomy (adj. **taphonomic**) the processes or events affecting the preservation of animal remains as fossils

taxon (pl. **taxa**) any defined unit (e.g. species, genus, family and order) in the classification of organisms

taxonomy (adj. **taxonomic**) the rules, principles and procedures used in classifying organisms

tectonic activity the building of mountains, the formation of *rift valleys and continental drift. See also plate tectonics

temporal bone one of a pair of bones that form part of the side wall and base of the human braincase (cranium) and cover the auditory ossicles in the *middle ear. In mammals generally, separate squamosal and petrosal bones form this part of the cranium; these are fused in humans

temporal lobe the side parts of each *cerebral hemisphere, separated from the frontal lobe by a cleft, the Sylvian fissure, in primates

tendon a tough, inelastic cord of white fibrous connective tissue joining a muscle to a bone

terrestrial ground-living

Tertiary the first period (or sub-era in some geological timescales) of the Cenozoic era, from 65 to 1.64 million years ago. When called a sub-era, the Tertiary is divided into the **Neogene** and **Pal(a)eogene** periods

testis (pl. **testes**) one of the pair of male reproductive organs that produce spermatozoa and secrete male steroid hormones (*androgens)

testosterone the principal steroid hormone in males. See androgen

Tethys Sea the ancient seaway that separated Eurasia from Africa and Arabia

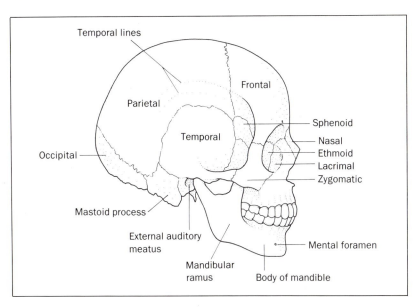

during most of the Mesozoic era; the remains of it today form the Mediterranean Sea

tetrapod a four-footed animal, one of the land vertebrates (amphibians, reptiles, birds and mammals)

thalamus a large mass of *grey matter deep in the *cerebral hemispheres in the middle of the forebrain. All information entering the *cerebral cortex is first relayed through the thalamus

thalass(a)emia a group of hereditary blood diseases, widespread in Mediterranean countries, Asia and Africa, in which there are various abnormalities in the haemoglobin molecule caused by defective globin genes. The red cells cannot function properly, leading to anaemia and enlargement of the spleen. α-thalassaemia is characterised by non-production of functional α-globin, β-thalassaemia by the non-production of functional β-globin. Individuals inheriting the disease from both parents are severely affected but those inheriting it from only one have a mild or symptomless condition

thorax (adj. **thoracic**) the chest, the part of the body between neck and abdomen, enclosing the lungs, heart, oesophagus and associated structures. In mammals, the diaphragm separates it from the abdomen

thyroid gland an *endocrine gland in the neck. It secretes the iodine-containing hormones thyroxine and tri-iodothyronine that regulate the metabolic rate, and calcitonin (in mammals) that lowers the level of calcium in the blood by causing the deposition of calcium phosphate in bones

tibia (adj. **tibial**) the long bone, which with the fibula, forms the lower part of the hindlimb (the inner and larger shin bone in humans)

transcription the copying of the genetic information in *DNA into an *RNA molecule – the first step in protein synthesis

transfer RNA a short *RNA molecule that binds on to particular amino acids, and lines them up by attaching itself to the appropriate set of three bases in a *messenger RNA molecule

translation the mechanism used by *ribosomes to decipher the information coded in *messenger RNA to synthesise proteins

translocation the movement of part of one *chromosome to join an inappropriate (non-homologous) chromosome, one of the main

mechanisms of evolutionary change in chromosomes. It can also produce inborn disease, and is frequently seen in cancer cells

trisomy the presence of an extra copy of a particular chromosome. For example, trisomy-21 – the presence of an extra chromosome 21 – leads to the inborn error *Down's syndrome

tuff a rock composed of consolidated volcanic ash and rock fragments, important in radiometric dating

U

ungulate a hoofed mammal (horses, pigs, deer etc.)

Upper Pal(a)eolithic the epoch that followed the *Middle Palaeolithic in Europe, North Africa and parts of Asia about 40 000 to 12 000–10 000 years ago, characterised by *blade industries (e.g. *Aurignacian). The Later Stone Age in sub-Saharan Africa is a rough equivalent

urethra the tube that conveys urine from the bladder out of the body and, in males, also semen

uterus (adj. **uterine**) the part of the female reproductive tract in placental mammals in which the developing embryo and fetus are nourished before birth. On each side of the body, the upper part is connected to a Fallopian tube (**oviduct**) and the lower part joins the vagina at the **cervix**

V

vasoconstriction a decrease in diameter of blood vessels, especially arteries, by contraction of smooth muscles in their walls. It increases blood pressure

vasodilation an increase in diameter of blood vessels, especially arteries, by relaxation of smooth muscles in their walls. It reduces blood pressure

ventral relating to or nearer the belly or underside (the front of the body in humans). The opposite of *dorsal

ventricle one of the cavities in the brain filled with cerebrospinal fluid, including the two lateral, the third and the fourth ventricles; one of the pair of lower chambers in the heart

vertebral column the backbone; the series of bony or cartilagenous segments (**vertebrae**) running from head to tail along the back of a

vertebrate, enclosing and protecting the spinal cord. Humans normally have 33 vertebrae – 7 neck (**cervical**), 12 chest (**thoracic**), 5 lower back (**lumbar**), 5 hip (**sacral**) and 4 tail (**caudal** or **coccygeal**) – and their sacral and coccygeal vertebrae eventually become fused into two composite bones, the sacrum and the coccyx

vertebrate an animal with a backbone or *vertebral column (fish, amphibians, reptiles, birds and mammals)

vestigial existing only in rudimentary form, applied to organs whose structure and function have diminished during evolution

vital statistics in demography, quantitative data on life events (e.g. birth, death and marriage)

vocal folds (vocal cords) the two muscular folds of tissue projecting from the sides of the *larynx that form a narrow slit (**glottis**) across the air passage. They vibrate as expired air is forced between them and this produces speech and other vocal sounds

W

Wernicke's area the region of the human brain involved in the comprehension of speech, lying in the upper part of the temporal cortex and extending into the parietal cortex in the left *cerebral hemisphere, and named after the German neurologist Carl Wernicke (1848–1905).

white matter concentrations of cell bodies of *neurones

X

X chromosome one of the sex *chromosomes. In all mammals, including humans, XX individuals are female, XY male

Y

Y chromosome one of the sex chromosomes. In humans, any individual with a Y is more or less male; XY is a normal male but XXY is a male with Klinefelter's syndrome. The male sex-determining *locus (the 'testis-determining factor') is on the Y

Z

zona pellucida the thick outer covering of the egg cell that a sperm must penetrate to achieve fertilisation. After union of the gametes, other sperm are prevented from penetrating by changes in the zona

zygote the cell formed from the union of male and female gametes; the fertilised egg

secondary compounds. *American Naturalist* 108: 269–89 (1974).

Glander, K.E. Feeding patterns in mantled howling monkeys. In *Foraging Behavior: Ecological, Ethological, and Psychological Approaches* (eds A. Kamil and T.D. Sargent), pp. 231–59. New York: Garland, 1981.

Glander, K.E. The impact of secondary compounds on primate feeding behavior. *Yearbook of Physical Anthropology* 25: 1–18 (1982).

Huffman, M.A. and Seifu, M. Observations on the illness and consumption of a possibly medicinal plant *Vernonia amygdalina* (Del.), by a wild chimpanzee in the Mahale Mountains National Park, Tanzania. *Primates* 30: 51-63 (1989).

Leopold, A.C. and Ardrey, R. Toxic substances in plants and the food habits of early man. *Science* 176: 512–13 (1972).

McKey, D. *et al.* Phenolic content of vegetation in two African rain forests: ecological implications. *Science* 202: 61–4 (1978).

Milton, K. Factors influencing leaf choice by howler monkeys: a test of some hypotheses of food selection by generalist herbivores. *American Naturalist* 114: 362–78 (1984).

Milton, K. The role of food-processing factors in primate food choice. In *Adaptations for Foraging in Nonhuman Primates* (eds P.S. Rodman and J.G.H. Cant), pp.249–79. New York: Columbia University Press, 1984.

Sears, C. The chimpanzee's medicine chest. *New Scientist* 4 August: 42–4 (1990).

Skinner, M. Bee brood consumption: an alternative explanation for hypervitaminosis A in KNM-ER 1808 (*Homo erectus*) from Koobi Fora, Kenya. *Journal of Human Evolution* 20: 493–503 (1991).

Walker, A. *et al.* A possible case of hypervitaminosis A in *Homo erectus*. *Nature* 296: 248–50 (1982).

Whiten, A. and Widdowson, E.M. (eds). *Foraging Strategies and Natural Diet of Monkeys, Apes and Humans*. Oxford: Clarendon Press, 1992. (Also published in *Philosophical Transactions of the Royal Society* Series B, Vol. 334 (1991).)

Wrangham, R.W. and Waterman, P.G. Feeding behavior of vervet monkeys on *Acacia totilis* and *Acacia xanthophloea*: with special reference to reproductive strategies and tannin production. *Journal of Animal Ecology* 50: 715–31 (1981).

Human diet and subsistence (pp. 69–74)

Cohen, M.N. and Armelagos, G.J. (eds). *Paleopathology and the Origins of Agriculture*. Orlando, FL: Academic Press, 1984.

Harris, D.R. Alternative pathways toward agriculture. In *Origins of Agriculture* (ed. C.A. Reed), pp. 179–243. The Hague: Mouton, 1977.

Harris, D.R. The prehistory of human subsistence: a speculative outline. In *Food, Nutrition and Evolution* (eds D.N. Walcher and N. Kretchmer), pp. 15–35. New York: Masson, 1981.

Harris, D.R. Ethnohistorical evidence for the exploitation of wild grasses and forbs: its scope and archaeological implications. In *Plants and Ancient Man: Studies in Palaeoethnobotany* (eds W. van Zeist and W.A. Casparie), pp. 63–9. Rotterdam: Balkema, 1984.

Harris, D.R. and Hillman, G.C. (eds). *Foraging and Farming: the Evolution of Plant Exploitation*. London: Unwin Hyman, 1989.

Harris, M. and Ross, E. (eds). *Food and Evolution: Toward a Theory of Human Food Habits*. Philadelphia: Temple University Press, 1986.

Harding, R.S.O. and Teleki, G. (eds). *Omnivorous Primates: Gathering and Hunting in Human Evolution*. New York: Columbia University Press, 1981.

Hawkes, J.G. *The Diversity of Crop Plants*. Cambridge, MA: Harvard University Press, 1983.

Hillman, G.C. and Davies, M.S. Domestication rates in wild-type wheats and barley under primitive cultivation. *Biological Journal of the Linnean Society* 39: 39–78 (1990).

Isaac, G.Ll. The food-sharing behavior of protohuman hominids. *Scientific American* 238 (April): 90–108 (1978).

Lee, R.B. and DeVore, I. (eds). *Man the Hunter*. Chicago: Aldine, 1968.

Simoons, F.J. *Eat Not This Flesh*. Madison: University of Wisconsin Press, 1961.

Stahl, A.B. Hominid dietary selection before fire. *Current Anthropology* 25: 151–68 (1984).

Ucko, P.J. and Dimbleby, G.W. (eds). *The Domestication and Exploitation of Plants and Animals*. London: Duckworth, 1969.

Whiten, A. and Widdowson, E.M. (eds). *Foraging Strategies and Natural Diet of Monkeys, Apes and Humans*. Oxford: Clarendon Press, 1992. (Also published in *Philosophical Transactions of the Royal Society* Series B, Vol. 334 (1991).)

Wing, E.S. and Brown, A.B. *Paleonutrition: Methods and Theory in Prehistoric Foodways*. New York: Academic Press, 1979.

Primate locomotion and posture (pp. 75–9)

Fleagle, J.G. *Primate Adaptation & Evolution*. San Diego: Academic Press, 1988.

Fleagle, J.G. and Mittermeier, R.A. Locomotor behavior, body size, and comparative anatomy of seven Surinam monkeys. *American Journal of Physical Anthropology* 52: 301–14 (1980).

Isaac, G.Ll. Aspects of human evolution. In *Evolution from Molecules to Men* (ed. D.S. Bendall), pp. 509–44. Cambridge: Cambridge University Press, 1983.

Jenkins, F.A. Jr. *Primate Locomotion*. New York: Academic Press, 1974.

Jungers, W.L. (ed.). *Size and Scaling in Primate Biology*. New York: Plenum Press, 1985.

Lovejoy, C.O. The origin of man. *Science* 211: 341–50 (1981).

Morbeck, M.E. *et al. Environment, Behavior, and Morphology: Dynamic Interactions in Primates*. New York: Gustav Fischer Verlag, 1979.

Oxnard, C.E. *The Order of Man: A Biomathematical Anatomy of the Primates*. New Haven, CT: Yale University Press, 1984.

Rodman, P. and Cant, J.G.H. *Adaptations for Foraging in Nonhuman Primates*. New York: Colombia University Press, 1984.

Stern, J.T. and Oxnard, C.E. Primate locomotion: some links with evolution and morphology. *Primatologia* 4, Part 11. Basel: Karger, 1973.

Susman, R. L. *et al.* Arboriality and bipedality in the Hadar hominids. *Folia Primatologia* 43: 113–56 (1984).

Human locomotion (pp. 80–5)

Alexander, R.McN. Walking and running. *American Scientist* 72: 348–54 (1984).

Alexander, R.McN. *The Human Machine*. London: Natural History Museum Publications, 1992.

Alexander, R.McN. Characteristics and advantages of human bipedalism. In *Biomechanics in Evolution* (eds J.M.V. Rayner and R. Wootton), pp. 255–66. Cambridge: Cambridge University Press, 1991.

Basmajian, J.V. and DeLuca, C.J. *Muscles Alive*, 5th edn. Baltimore: Williams & Wilkins, 1985.

Carlsoo, S. *How Man Moves*. London: Heinemann, 1972.

Jouffroy, F.K. *et al.* (eds). *Gravity, Posture and Locomotion in Primates*. Florence: Il Sedicesimo, 1990.

Margaria, R. *Biomechanics and Energetics of Muscular Exercise*. Oxford: Clarendon Press, 1976.

McMahon, T.A. *Muscles, Reflexes and Locomotion*. Princeton: Princeton University Press, 1984.

Nordin, M. and Frankel, V.H. *Basic Biomechanics of the Musculoskeletal system*. Philadelphia: Lea & Febiger, 1989.

Primate reproduction (pp. 86–90)

Conaway, C.H. Ecological adaptation and mammalian reproduction. *Biology of Reproduction* 4: 239–47 (1971).

Dukelow, W.R. and Erwin, J. (eds). *Comparative Primate Biology*, Vol. 3: *Reproduction and Development*. New York: Alan R. Liss, 1986.

Hafez, E.S.E. (ed.). *Comparative Reproduction of Nonhuman Primates*. Springfield, IL: Charles C. Thomas, 1971.

Hill, J.P. The developmental history of the primates. *Philosophical Transactions of the Royal Society* Series B 221: 45–178 (1932).

Leutenegger, W. Maternal–fetal weight relationships in primates. *Folia Primatologica* 20: 280–93 (1973).

Luckett, W.P. (ed.). *Reproductive Biology of the Primates* (Contribution to Primatology No. 3). Basel: Karger, 1974

Luckett, W.P. and Szalay, F.S. *Phylogeny of the Primates*. New York: Plenum Press, 1975. (See, in particular, chapters by W.P. Luckett (pp. 157–82) and R.D. Martin (pp. 265–97).)

Martin, R.D. *Primate Origins and Evolution: A Phylogenetic Reconstruction*. London: Chapman and Hall; Princeton: Princeton University Press, 1990.

Steven, D.H. (ed.). *Comparative Placentation: Essays in Structure and Function*. London: Academic Press, 1975.

Posture and childbirth (p. 88)

Berge, C. *et al.* Obstetrical interpretations of the australopithecine pelvic cavity. *Journal of Human Evolution* 13: 573–87 (1984).

Conroy, G.C. *Primate Evolution*, pp. 337–46. New York: W.W. Norton, 1990.

Lovejoy, C.O. Evolution of human walking. *Scientific American* 259 (November): 82–9 (1988).

Hormones and sexual behaviour (pp. 91–4)

Bancroft, J. *Human Sexuality and its Problems*, 2nd edn. Edinburgh: Churchill Livingstone, 1989.

Dixson, A.F. The hormonal control of sexual behaviour in primates. In *Oxford Reviews of Reproductive Biology* (ed. C.A. Finn), Vol. 5, pp. 131–219. Oxford: Oxford University Press, 1983.

Johnson, M. and Everitt, B. *Essential Reproduction*, 3rd edn. Oxford: Blackwell Scientific, 1989.

Money, J. and Ehrhardt, A.A. *Man and Woman, Boy and Girl*. Baltimore: Johns Hopkins University Press, 1972.

Smuts, B.B. *et al.* (eds). *Primate Societies*. Chicago and London: University of Chicago Press, 1986.

Life-history patterns (pp. 95–7)

Harvey, P.H. *et al.* Life histories in comparative perspective. In *Primate Societies* (eds B.B. Smuts *et al.*), pp. 181–96. Chicago and London: University of Chicago Press, 1986.

Jungers, W.L. (ed.). *Size and Scaling in Primate Biology*. New York: Plenum Press, 1985.

Martin, R.D. *Human Brain Evolution in an Ecological Context* (52nd James Arthur Lecture on the Evolution of the Human Brain). New York: American Museum of Natural History, 1983.

Martin, R.D. and MacLarnon, A.M. Gestation period, neonatal size and maternal investment in placental mammals. *Nature* 313: 220–3 (1985).

Rates of breeding (p. 96)

Calder, W.A. *Size, Function, and Life History*. Cambridge, MA: Harvard University Press, 1984.

Fenchel, T. Intrinsic rate of natural increase: the relationship with body size. *Oecologia* 14: 317–26 (1974).

MacArthur, R.H. and Wilson, E.O. *The Theory of Island Biogeography*. Princeton: Princeton University Press, 1967.

Ross, C. The intrinsic rate of natural increase and reproductive effort in primates. *Journal of Zoology, London* 214: 199–219 (1988).

Schaffer, W.M. Optimal reproductive effort in fluctuating environments. *American Naturalist* 108: 783–98 (1974).

Human growth and development (pp. 98–105)

Brundtland G.H. *et al.* Height, weight and menarcheal age of Oslo schoolchildren during the last 60 years. *Annals of Human Biology* 7: 307–22 (1980).

Eveleth, P.B. and Tanner, J.M. *Worldwide Variation in Human Growth*, 2nd edn. Cambridge: Cambridge University Press, 1990.

Falkner, F. and Tanner, J.M. (eds). *Human Growth*, 2nd edn, Vols 1 and 2. New York: Plenum Press, 1985–6. (See, in particular, chapters by R.J. Goss (modes of growth and regeneration); W.A. Marshall and J.M. Tanner (puberty); J.M. Tanner (growth as a target-seeking function); E. Watts (evolution of the human growth curve); and M.E. Wierman and W.F. Crowley, Jr (control of the onset of puberty).)

Fogel, R.W. and Engerman, S.L. (eds). Trends in nutrition, labor welfare and labor productivity: the uses of data on height. *Social Science History* 6: 395–581 (1982).

Greene, L.A. and Johnston, F.E. (eds). *Social and Biological Predictors of Nutritional Status, Physical Growth and Neurological Development*. New York and London: Academic Press, 1980.

Lindgren, G. Height, weight and menarche in Swedish urban school children in relation to socio-economic and regional factors. *Annals of Human Biology* 3: 501–28 (1976).

Stein, Z. *et al. Famine and Human Development*. Oxford: Oxford University Press, 1975.

Tanner, J.M. *Growth at Adolescence*, 2nd edn. Oxford: Blackwell Scientific, 1962.

Tanner, J.M. *Foetus into Man: Physical Growth from Conception to Maturity*, 2nd edn. London: Open Books; Cambridge, MA: Harvard University Press, 1978.

Tanner, J.M. *A History of the Study of Human Growth*. Cambridge: Cambridge University Press, 1981.

Tanner, J.M. Analysis and classification of physique. In *Human Biology*, 3rd edn (by G.A. Harrison *et al.*), pp. 404–23. Oxford: Oxford University Press, 1988.

Tanner, J.M. and Whitehouse, R.H. *Atlas of Children's Growth: Normal Variation and Growth Disorders*. London: Academic Press, 1982.

Tanner, J.M. *et al.* Radiographically determined widths of bone, muscle and fat in the upper arm and calf from age 3–18 years. *Annals of Human Biology* 8: 495–518 (1982).

Evolution of the human growth curve (p. 100)

Tanner, J.M. *et al.* Pubertal growth in the female Rhesus monkey. *American Journal of Human Biology* 2: 101–6 (1990).

Neoteny (p. 104)

Alberch, P. *et al.* Size and shape in ontogeny and phylogeny. *Paleobiology* 5: 296–317 (1979).

Gould, S.J. *Ontogeny and Phylogeny*. Cambridge, MA: Harvard University Press, 1977.

McKinney, M.L. (ed.). *Heterochrony in Evolution: A Multidisciplinary Perspective*. New York: Plenum Press, 1988.

Raff, R.A. and Kaufman, T.C. *Embryos, Genes and Evolution*. New York: Macmillan, 1983.

Shea, B.T. Heterochrony in human evolution: the case for neoteny reconsidered. *Yearbook of Physical Anthropology* 32: 69–101 (1989).

The brain and language

Primate brains and senses (pp. 109–14)

Armstrong, E. and Falk, D. (eds). *Primate Brain Evolution: Methods and Concepts*. New York: Plenum Press, 1982.

Noback, C.R. and Montagna, W. (eds). *The Primate Brain: Advances in Primatology*. New York: Appleton-Century-Crofts, 1970.

Passingham, R. *The Human Primate*. Oxford and San Francisco: W.H. Freeman, 1982.

Testing the intelligence of apes (p. 111)

Essock-Vitale, S. and Seyfarth, R.M. Intelligence and social recognition. In *Primate Societies* (eds B.B. Smuts *et al.*), pp. 452–61. Chicago: University of Chicago Press, 1986.

Gallup. G.G. Self-awareness and the emergence of mind in primates. *American Journal of Primatology* 2: 237–48 (1982).

Goodall, J. *The Chimpanzees of Gombe: Patterns of Behaviour*. Cambridge, MA: Harvard/Belknap, 1986.

Heltne, P.G. and Marquardt, L.A. *Understanding Chimpanzees*. Cambridge, MA: Harvard University Press, 1989.

Menzel, E.W. *Precultural Primate Behaviour*. Basel: Karger, 1973.

Sleep and dreaming (p. 113)

Empson, J. *Sleep and Dreaming*. London: Faber and Faber, 1989.

Hobson, J.A. *The Dreaming Brain*. London: Penguin Books, 1990.

Horne, J. *Why We Sleep*. Oxford: Oxford University Press, 1988.

Winson, J. The meaning of dreams. *Scientific American* 263 (November): 42–8 (1990).

The human brain (pp. 115–23)

Caplan, D. *Neurolinguistics and Linguistic Aphasiology*. Cambridge: Cambridge University Press, 1987.

Jerison, H.J. *Evolution of the Brain and Intelligence*. New York: Academic Press, 1973.

Jerison, H.J. and Jerison, I. (eds). *Intelligence and Evolutionary Biology*. Berlin: Springer-Verlag, 1988.

Kolb, B. and Whishaw, I. *Fundamentals of Human Neuropsychology*, 3rd edn. San Francisco: W.H. Freeman, 1990.

Lecours, A.-R. *et al. Aphasiology*. London: Baillière Tindall, 1983.

MacPhail, E. *Brain Size and Intelligence in Vertebrates*. Oxford: Clarendon Press, 1982.

Steklis, D. and Raliegh, M. *The Neurobiology of Social Communication in Primates*. New York: Academic Press, 1979.

Impressions of ancestral brains (pp. 116–17)

Armstrong, E. and Falk, D. (eds). *Primate Brain Evolution: Methods and Concepts*. New York: Plenum Press, 1982.

Falk, D. Hominid brain evolution: the approach from paleoneurology. *Yearbook of Physical Anthropology* 23: 93–107 (1980).

Falk, D. Cerebral cortices of East African early hominids. *Science* 221: 1072–4 (1983).

Falk, D. Ape-like endocast of 'ape-man' Taung. *American Journal of Physical Anthropology* 80: 335–9 (1989).

Holloway, R.L. The casts of fossil hominid brains. *Scientific American* 231 (July): 106–15 (1974).

Holloway, R.L. The past, present, and future significance of the lunate sulcus in early hominid evolution. In *Hominid Evolution: Past, Present and Future* (ed. P.V. Tobias), pp.47–62. New York: Alan. R. Liss, 1985.

Holloway, R.L. Some additional morphological and metrical observations on *Pan* brain casts and their relevance to the Taung endocast. *American Journal of Physical Anthropology* 77: 27–33 (1988).

The brain and left-handedness (p. 122)

Annett, M. *Left, Right, Hand and Brain: The Right Shift Theory*. London: Lawrence Erlbaum Associates. 1985.

Annett, M. Annotation: laterality and cerebral dominance. *Journal of Child Psychology and Psychiatry* 32: 219–32 (1991).

Bradshaw, J. L. *Hemisphere Specialization*. Chichester: John Wiley, 1989.

Byrne, R.W. and Byrne, J.M. Hand preferences in the skilled gathering tasks of mountain gorillas (*Gorilla g. beringei*). *Cortex* 27: 521–46 (1991).

Fagot, J. and Vauclair, J. Manual laterality in nonhuman primates: a distinction between handedness and manual specialization. *Psychological Bulletin* 109: 76–89 (1991).

Vocal communication by non-human primates (pp. 124–7)

Aich, H. et al. Vocalizations of adult gelada baboons (Theropithecus gelada). Folia Primatologica 55: 109–32 (1990).

Binz, H. et al. Neuronal substrates involved in processing of communicative signals in tree shrews. Neuroscience Letters 112: 25–30 (1990).

Goedeking, P. et al. Primate Vocal Communication. Berlin: Springer-Verlag, 1988.

Masataka, N. and Fujita, K. Vocal learning of Japanese and rhesus monkeys. Behaviour 109: 191–9.

Ploog, D.W. Neurobiology of primate audio-vocal behavior. Brain Research Reviews 3: 35–61 (1982).

Smuts, B.B. et al. (eds). Primate Societies. Chicago: University of Chicago Press, 1986.

Snowdon, C.T. et al. Primate Communication. Cambridge: Cambridge University Press, 1983.

Zimmermann, E. Differentiation of vocalizations in bushbabies (Galaginae) and the significance for assessing phylogenetic relationships. Zeitschrift für Zoologische Systematik und Evolutionsforschung 28: 217–39 (1990).

Zimmermann, E. Ontogeny of acoustic communication in prosimian primates. In Primatology Today (eds A. Ehara et al.), pp. 337–40. Amsterdam: Elsevier Science, 1991.

Zimmermann, E. et al. Variations in vocal patterns of Senegal and South African lesser bushbabies and their implications for taxonomic relationships. Folia Primatologica 51: 87–105 (1988).

Biological aspects of language (pp. 128–33)

Bickerton, D. Language and Species. Chicago: University of Chicago Press, 1990.

Cheney, D. and Seyfarth, R. How Monkeys See the World. Chicago: University of Chicago Press, 1990.

Chomsky, N. Knowledge of Language: Its Nature, Origin, and Use. New York: Praeger, 1986.

Crystal, D. The Cambridge Encyclopedia of Language. Cambridge: Cambridge University Press, 1987.

Darwin, C. The Expression of Emotions in Man and Animals. London: John Murray, 1872.

Harnad, S. et al. (eds). The Origins and Evolution of Language and Speech. New York: New York Academy of Science, 1976.

Hawkins, J. and Gel-Mann, M. (eds). The Evolution of Human Language. New York: Addison-Wesley, 1992.

Lieberman, P. Uniquely Human: The Evolution of Speech, Thought, and Selfless Behavior. Cambridge, MA: Harvard University Press, 1991.

MacWhinney, B. Mechanisms of Language Acquisition. Fairlawn, NJ: Lawrence Erlbaum, 1987.

Wanner, E. and Gleitman, L.R. (eds). Language Acquisition: The State of the Art. Cambridge: Cambridge University Press, 1982.

Brain maturation and language acquisition (p. 131)

Lecours. A.-R., Lhermitte, F. and Bryans, B. Aphasiology. London: Baillière Tindall, 1983.

Yakovlev, P. and Lecours, A.-R. The myelogenetic cycles of regional maturation of the brain. In Regional Development of the Brain in Early Life (ed. A. Minkowski), pp. 3–70 Oxford: Blackwell, 1967.

Human speech and language (pp. 134–7)

Crystal, D. The Cambridge Encyclopedia of Language. Cambridge: Cambridge University Press, 1987.

Gardner, R.A. and Gardner, B.T. A vocabulary test for chimpanzees (Pan troqlodytes). Journal of Comparative Psychology 4: 381–404 (1984).

Gardner, R.A. et al. (eds). Teaching Sign Language to Chimpanzees. Albany: State University of New York, 1989.

Kimura, D. Neuromotor mechanisms in the evolution of human communication. In Neurobiology of Social Communication in Primates (eds H.D. Steklis and M.J. Raleigh), pp. 197–214. New York: Academic Press, 1979.

Lieberman, P. Primate vocalizations and human linguistic ability. Journal of the Acoustical Society of America 44: 1157–64 (1968).

Lieberman, P. The Biology and Evolution of Language. Cambridge, MA: Harvard University Press, 1984.

Lieberman, P. Uniquely Human: The Evolution of Speech, Thought and Selfless Behavior. Cambridge, MA: Harvard University Press, 1991.

Lieberman, P. and Blumstein, S.E. Speech Physiology, Speech Perception, and Acoustic Phonetics. Cambridge: Cambridge University Press, 1988.

MacNeilage, P.F. et al. Primate handedness reconsidered. Behavioral and Brain Sciences 10: 247–303 (1987).

Piattelii-Palmarini, M. (ed.). Language and Learning: The Debate between Jean Piaget and Noam Chomsky. Cambridge, MA: Harvard University Press, 1980.

Evolution of the speech apparatus (p. 136)

Laitman, J.T. and Heimbuch, R.C. The basicranium of Plio-Pleistocene hominids as an indicator of their upper respiratory systems. American Journal of Physical Anthropology 59: 323–44 (1982).

Laitman, J.T. et al. The basicranium of fossil hominids as an indicator of their upper respiratory systems. American Journal of Physical Anthropology 51: 15–34 (1979).

Language training of apes (pp. 138–41)

Hayes, G. The Ape in Our House. New York: Harper, 1951.

Premack, D. Language and Intelligence in Ape and Man. Hillsdale, NJ: Lawrence Erlbaum Associates, 1976.

Patterson, R. and Linden, E. The Education of Koko. New York: Holt, Rinehart and Winston, 1981.

Rumbaugh, D.M. Language Learning by a Chimpanzee: The Lana Project. New York: Academic Press, 1977.

Savage-Rumbaugh, E.S. Ape Language: From Conditioned Response to Symbol. New York: Columbia University Press, 1986.

Primate social organisation

Social behaviour and evolutionary theory (pp. 145–7)

Cheney, D.L. and Seyfarth, R.M. Nonrandom dispersal in free-ranging vervet monkeys: social and genetic consequences. American Naturalist 122: 392–412 (1983).

Daly, M. and Wilson, M. Sex, Evolution and Behavior, 2nd edn. Boston: Willard Grant Press, 1983.

Dawkins, R. The Selfish Gene, 2nd edn. Oxford: Oxford University Press, 1989.

Dunbar, R. and Sharman, M. Is social grooming altruistic? Zeitschrift für Tierpsychologie 64: 163–73 (1984)

Grafen, A. Natural selection, kin selection and group selection. In Behavioural Ecology, 2nd edn (eds J.R. Krebs and N.B. Davies), pp. 62–84. Oxford: Blackwell Scientific, 1984.

Maynard Smith, J. and Price, G. The logic of animal conflict. Nature 246: 15–18 (1973).

McGrew, W.C. and McLuckie, E.C. Philopatry and dispersion in the cotton-top tamarin, Saguinus (o.) oedipus: an attempted laboratory simulation. International Journal of Primatology 7: 401–22 (1986).

Seyfarth, R.M. and Cheney, D. Grooming, alliances and reciprocal altruism in vervet monkeys. Nature 308: 541–3 (1984).

Trivers, R.L. The evolution of reciprocal altruism. Quarterly Review of Biology 46: 35–57 (1971).

Primate aggression (pp. 148–9)

Brain, P.F. and Benton, D. The Biology of Aggression. Alphen aan den Rhijn, The Netherlands: Sijthoff & Noordhoff, 1981.

Dunbar, R.I.M. Primate Social Systems. London: Croom Helm, 1988.

Huntingford, F.A. and Turner, A.K. Animal Conflict. London: Chapman and Hall, 1987.

Smuts, B.B. et al. (eds). Primate Societies. Chicago: University of Chicago Press, 1986.

de Waal, F.B.M. Chimpanzee Politics. London: Jonathan Cape; New York: Harper & Row, 1982. (Reissued in paperback by Johns Hopkins University Press, 1989.)

Mating and parental care (pp. 150–4)

Andelman, S. Ecological and social determinants of cercopithecine mating patterns. In Ecological Aspects of Social Evolution (eds D.I. Rubenstein and R.W. Wrangham), pp. 201–16. Princeton: Princeton University Press, 1986.

Dunbar, R. Reproductive Decisions: An Economic Analysis of Gelada Baboon Social Strategies. Princeton: Princeton University Press, 1984.

Dunbar, R. Primate Social Systems. London: Chapman and Hall, 1988.

Emlen, S. and Oring, L. Ecology, sexual selection and the evolution of mating systems. Science 197: 215–23 (1977).

Kleiman, D.G. Monogamy in mammals. Quarterly Review of Biology 52: 39–69 (1977).

Rasa, A. et al. (eds). Sociobiology of Sexual and Reproductive Strategies. London: Chapman and Hall, 1989.

Smuts, B.B. Sex and Friendship in Baboons. Hawthorne, NY: Aldine, 1985.

van Schaik, C.P. and Dunbar, R. Evolution of monogamy in large primates: a new hypothesis and some critical tests. Behaviour 115: 30–62 (1990).

Wright, P.C. Ecological correlates of monogamy in Aotus and Callicebus. In Primate Ecology and Conservation (eds J.G. Else and P.C. Lee), pp. 159–67. Cambridge: Cambridge University Press, 1986.

Human mating patterns (p. 154)

Betzig, L. et al. (eds). Human Reproductive

Behaviour. Cambridge: Cambridge University Press, 1988.

Home range and territory (pp. 155–6)

Clutton-Brock, T.H. and Harvey, P.H. Primate ecology and social organisation. *Journal of Zoology* 183: 1–39 (1977).

Harvey, P.H. and Clutton-Brock, T.H. Primate home-range size and metabolic needs. *Behavioral Ecology and Sociobiology* 8: 151–5 (1981).

Martin, R.D. Field studies of primate behaviour. *Symposia of the Zoological Society of London* 46: 287–336 (1981).

Mitani, J.C. and Rodman, P.S. Territoriality: the relation of ranging pattern and home range size to defendability, with an analysis of territoriality among primate species. *Behavioral Ecology and Sociobiology* 5: 241–51 (1979).

Smell as a signal (pp. 157–60)

Beauchamp, G.K. *et al.* The pheromone concept in mammalian chemical communication. In *Mammalian Olfaction, Reproductive Processes, and Behavior* (ed. Doty, R.L.), pp. 143–60. New York: Academic Press, 1976.

Charles-Dominique, P. Urine marking and territoriality in *Galago alleni* (Waterhouse, 1837 – Lorisoidea, Primates) – a field study by radio-telemetry. *Zeitschrift für Tierpsychologie* 43: 113–38 (1977).

Duvall, D. *et al.* (eds). *Chemical Signals in Vertebrates*, Vol. 4: *Ecology, Evolution, and Comparative Biology*. New York: Plenum Press, 1986.

Epple, G. Olfactory communication in South American primates. *Annals of the New York Academy of Sciences* 237: 261–78 (1974).

Epple, G. Communication by chemical signals. In *Comparative Primate Biology*, Vol. 2, Part A: *Behavior, Conservation, and Ecology* (eds G. Mitchel and J. Erwin), pp. 531–80. New York: Alan R. Liss, 1986

Halpin, Z.T. Individual odors among mammals: origins and functions. *Advances in the Study of Behaviour* 16: 39–70 (1986).

Harrington, J. Olfactory communication in *Lemur fulvus*. In *Prosimian Biology* (eds R.D. Martin *et al.*), pp. 331–46. London: Duckworth, 1974.

McClintock, M.K. Social control of the ovarian cycle and the function of estrous synchrony. *American Zoology* 21: 243–56 (1981).

Milton, K. Urine washing behavior in the woolly spider monkey (*Brachyteles arachnoides*). *Zeitschrift für Tierpsychologie* 67: 154–60 (1985).

Russell, M.J. Human olfactory communications. In *Chemical Signals in Vertebrates* (eds D. Muller-Schwarze and R.M. Silverstein), pp. 259–73. New York: Plenum Press, 1983.

Schilling, A. Olfactory communication in prosimians. In *The Study of Prosimian Behavior* (eds G.A. Doyle and R.D. Martin), pp. 461–542. New York: Academic Press, 1979.

Snowdon, C.T. *et al.* (eds). *Primate Communication*. Cambridge: Cambridge University Press, 1983. (See, in particular, articles by D.A. Goldfoot and by E.B. Keverne.)

Stoddart, D.M. *The Scented Ape: The Biology and Culture of Human Odour*. Cambridge: Cambridge University Press, 1990.

Van Toller, S. and Dodd, S.H. (eds). *Perfumery:*

The Psychology and Biology of Fragrance. London: Chapman and Hall, 1988.

Facial patterns as signals and masks (pp. 161–5)

Andrew, R.J. The origin and evolution of the calls and facial expressions of the primates. *Behaviour* 20: 1–109 (1963).

Chance. M.R.A. An interpretation of some agonistic postures: the role of 'cut-off' acts and postures. *Symposia of the Zoological Society of London* 8: 71–99 (1962).

Dawkins, R. and Krebs, J.R. Animal signals: information or manipulation? In *Behavioural Ecology: An Evolutionary Approach* (eds J.R. Krebs and N.B. Davies), pp.282–309. Oxford: Blackwell Scientific, 1978.

Gautier, J.-P. and Gautier-Hion, A. Communication in Old World monkeys. In *How Animals Communicate* (ed. T.A. Sebeock), pp. 890–964. Bloomington: Indiana University Press, 1977.

Guilford, T.C. The evolution of conspicuous coloration. *American Naturalist* 131: 7–21 (1988)

Hailman, J.P. *Optical Signals*. Bloomington: Indiana University Press, 1977.

Kingdon, J.S. The role of visual signals and face patterns in African forest monkeys (guenons) of the genus *Cercopithecus*. *Transactions of the Zoological Society of London* 35: 431–75 (1980).

Kingdon, J. What are face patterns and do they contribute to reproductive isolation in guenons? In *A Primate Radiation: Evolutionary Biology of the African Guenons* (eds A. Gautier-Hion *et al.*), pp. 227–45. Cambridge: Cambridge University Press, 1988.

Maynard Smith, J. Sexual selection and the Handicap Principle. *Journal of Theoretical Biology* 157: 239–42 (1976).

Mollon, J. After-effects and the brain. *New Scientist* 61: 886 (1974).

Struhsaker, T.T. and Leland, L. Socioecology of five sympatric monkey species in the Kibale Forest, Uganda. In *Advances in the Study of Behavior*, Vol. 9 (eds J.S. Rosenblatt *et al.*), pp. 159–228. New York: Academic Press, 1979.

Tinbergen, N. 'Derived' activities: their causation, biological significance, origin and emancipation during evolution. *Quarterly Review of Biology* 27: 1–32 (1952).

Vine, L. Communication by facial signals. In *Social Behaviour of Birds and Mammals* (ed. H.J. Crook), pp. 279–354. New York: Academic Press, 1970.

Wickler, W. Socio-sexual signals and their intraspecific imitation among primates. In *Primate Ethology* (ed. D. Morris), pp. 69–147. London: Weidenfeld and Nicolson, 1967.

Zahavi, A. Mate selection: a selection for a handicap. *Journal of Theoretical Biology* 53: 205–14 (1975).

Human facial expressions (pp. 164–5)

Ekman, P. (ed.). *Darwin and Facial Expression*. New York and London: Academic Press, 1973.

Ekman, P.(ed.). *Emotion in the Human Face*. Cambridge: Cambridge University Press, 1983.

Morris, D. *et al. Gestures, their Origins and Distribution*. London: Jonathan Cape, 1979.

Morris, D. *Bodywatching*. London: Jonathan Cape; New York: Crown, 1985.

Nelson, C.A. The recognition of facial

expressions in the first two years of life: mechanisms of development. *Child Development* 58: 889–909 (1987).

Human evolution in a geological context

Land movements and species dispersal (pp. 169–73)

Adams, C.G. An outline of Tertiary palaeogeography. In *The Evolving Earth* (ed. L.R.M. Cocks), pp. 221–35. London: British Museum (Natural History); Cambridge; Cambridge University Press, 1981.

Adams, C.G. *et al.* Dating the terminal Tethyan event. *Utrecht Micropalaeontological Bulletin* 30: 273–98 (1983).

Ciochon, R.L. and Fleagle, J.G. (eds). *Primate Evolution and Human Origins*. Menlo Park, CA: Benjamin/Cummings, 1985.

Falcon, N.L. *et al.* (eds). A discussion on the structure and evolution of the Red Sea and the nature of the Red Sea, Gulf of Aden and Ethiopia Rift Junction. *Philosophical Transactions of the Royal Society* Series A 267: 1–417 (1970).

Howarth, M.K. Palaeogeography of the Mesozoic. In *The Evolving Earth* (ed. L.R.M. Cocks), pp. 197–220. London: British Museum (Natural History); Cambridge: Cambridge University Press, 1981.

Humphries, C.J. and Parenti, L.R. *Cladistic Biogeography* (Oxford Monographs on Biogeography No. 2). Oxford: Oxford University Press, 1986.

Owen, H.G. *Atlas of Continental Displacement, 200 Million Years to the Present*. Cambridge: Cambridge University Press, 1983.

Patterson, C. Methods in palaeobiogeography. In *Vicariance Biogeography: A Critique* (eds G. Nelson and D.E. Rosen), pp. 446–500 (1981).

Simons, E.L. The fossil record of primate phylogeny. In *Molecular Anthropology* (eds M. Goodman and R.E. Tashian), pp. 35–62. New York: Plenum Press, 1976.

Thomas, H. The Early and Middle Miocene land connection of the Afro-Arabian plate and Asia: a major event for hominoid dispersal? In *Ancestors: The Hard Evidence* (ed. E. Delson), pp. 42–50. New York: Alan R. Liss, 1985.

Whybrow, P.J. Geological and faunal evidence from Arabia for mammal 'migrations' between Asia and Africa during the Miocene. *Courier Forschungsinstitut Senckenberg* 69: 189–98 (1984).

Whybrow, P.J. The Arabian Miocene: rocks, fossils, primates and problems. *Proceedings of the Tenth Congress of the International Primatological Society*, Nairobi 1: 85–9 (1986).

Whybrow, P.J. (ed.) Miocene geology and palaeontology of Ad Dabtiyah, Saudi Arabia. *Bulletin of the British Museum (Natural History) Geology* 41(4): 365–457 (1987).

Whybrow, P.J. *et al.* Late Miocene primate fauna, flora and initial palaeomagnetic data from the Emirate of Abu Dhabi, United Arab Emirates. *Journal of Human Evolution* 19: 583–88 (1990).

Climatic change in the past (pp. 174–8)

Hays, J.D. *et al.* Variations in the Earth's orbit: pacemaker of the ice ages. *Science* 194: 1121–32 (1976).

Imbrie, J. and Imbrie, K.P. *Ice Ages: Solving the Mystery*. London: Macmillan, 1979.

Kennett, J.P. Cenozoic evolution of circumantarctic palaeoceanography. In *Antarctic Glacial History and World Palaeoenvironments* (ed. E.M. van Zinderen Bakker), pp.41–56. Rotterdam: Balkema, 1978.

Roberts, N. Pleistocene environments in time and space. In *Hominid Evolution and Community Ecology* (ed. R. Foley), pp.25–53. London: Academic Press, 1984.

Roberts, N. *The Holocene: An Environmental History*. Oxford: Blackwell, 1989.

Robin, G. de Q. The Antarctic ice sheet; its history and response to sea level and climatic changes over the past 100 million years. *Palaeogeography, Palaeoclimatology, Palaeoecology* 67: 31–50 (1988).

Ruddiman, W.F. and Kutzbach, J.E. Forcing of Late Cenozoic Northern Hemisphere glaciation by plateau uplift in Asia and America. *Transactions of the Royal Society of Edinburgh (Earth Sciences)* 81: 301–14 (1991).

Shackleton, N.J. *et al.* (eds) The past three million years: evolution of climatic variability in the North Atlantic region. *Philosophical Transactions of the Royal Society of London Series B* 318: 1–278 (1988).

Street-Perrott, F.A. and Roberts, N. Fluctuations in closed basin lakes as an indicator of past atmospheric circulation patterns. In *Variations in the Global Water Budget* (eds F.A. Street-Perrott *et al.*), pp.331–45. Dordrecht: Reidel, 1983.

Sugden, D. The polar and glacial world. In *Horizons in Physical Geography* (eds M.J. Clark *et al.*), pp. 214–31. London: Macmillan, 1987.

Van Andel, T.H. Late Quaternary sea level and archaeology. *Antiquity* 63: 733–45 (1989).

Vita-Finzi, C. *Recent Earth History*. London: Macmillan, 1973.

Methods of dating (pp. 179–86)

Aitken, M.J. *Science-based Dating in Archaeology*. Harlow, Essex: Longman, 1990.

Aitken, M. J. *et al.* (eds). *The Origin of Modern Humans and the Impact of Chronometric Dating*. Princeton: Princeton University Press, 1993.

Bowman, S. *Radiocarbon Dating*. London: British Museum Publications, 1990.

Brooks, A.S. *et al.* Dating Pleistocene archeological sites by protein diagenesis in ostrich eggshell. *Science* 248: 60–4 (1990).

Dalrymple, G.B. and Lanphere, M.A. *Potassium-argon Dating: Principles, Techniques and Applications to Geochronology*. San Francisco: W.H. Freeman, 1969.

Faure, G. *Principles of Isotope Geology*, 2nd edn. New York: John Wiley, 1986.

Harland, W.B. *et al.* *A Geologic Time Scale 1989*. Cambridge: Cambridge University Press, 1990.

Mankinen, E.A. and Dalrymple, G.B. Revised geomagnetic polarity time scale for the interval 0–5 m.y. B.P. *Journal of Geophysical Research* 84: 615–26 (1979).

McDougall, I. The present status of the geomagnetic polarity time scale. In *The Earth: Its Origin, Structure, and Evolution* (ed. M.W. McElhinny), pp. 543–66. New York: Academic Press, 1979.

McDougall, I. and Harrison, T.M. *Geochronology and Thermochronology by the ^{40}Ar/^{39}Ar Method* (Oxford Monographs on Geology and Geophysics No. 9). Oxford: Oxford University Press, 1988.

McKeever, S.W.S. *Thermoluminescence of Solids*. Cambridge: Cambridge University Press, 1985.

Parkes, P.A. *Current Scientific Techniques in Archaeology*. London: Croom Helm; New York: St Martins Press, 1986.

Pearson, G.W. *et al.* High precision ^{14}C measurement of Irish oaks to show the natural ^{14}C variations from AD 1840–5210 BC. *Radiocarbon* 28: 911–34 (1986).

Roth, F. and Poty, B. (eds). *Nuclear Methods of Dating* (Solid Earth Library Vol. 5). Dordrecht: Kluwer Academic, 1989.

Stuiver, M. and Kra, R. (eds). Proceedings of the 12th International Radiocarbon Conference, June 24–28, 1985, Trondheim, Norway. *Radiocarbon* 28 (2B, calibration issue) (1986).

Taylor, R.E. *Radiocarbon Dating: An Archeological Perspective*. New York: Harcourt Brace Jovanovich, 1987.

Correlating the East African hominid sites (p. 181)

Feibel, C.S. *et al.* Stratigraphic context of fossil hominids from the Omo Group deposits: northern Turkana Basin, Kenya and Ethiopia. *American Journal of Physical Anthropology* 78: 595–622 (1989).

Haileab, B. and Brown, F. H. Turkana Basin-Middle Awash Valley correlations and the age of the Sagantole and Hadar Formations. *Journal of Human Evolution* 22: 453–68 (1992).

Sarna-Wojcicki, A.M. *et al.* Ages of tuff beds at East African early hominid sites and sediments in the Gulf of Aden. *Nature* 313: 306–8 (1985).

Fossils as dating indicators (p. 184)

Cooke, H.B.S. and Maglio, V.J. Plio-Pleistocene stratigraphy in East Africa in relation to proboscidean and suid evidence. In *Calibration of Hominoid Evolution* (eds W.W. Bishop and J.A. Miller), pp. 303–29. Edinburgh: Scottish Academic Press, 1972.

Valladas, M. *et al.* Thermoluminescence dating of Mousterian 'Proto-Cro-Magnon' remains from Israel and the origin of modern man. *Nature* 331: 614–16 (1988).

Vrba, E.S. Early hominids in southern Africa: updated observations on chronological and ecological background. In *Hominid Evolution: Past, Present and Future* (ed. P.V. Tobias), pp. 195–200. New York: Alan R. Liss, 1985.

Fossil deposits and their investigation (pp. 187–90)

Behrensmeyer, A.K. Transport/hydrodynamics of bones. In *Palaeobiology: A Synthesis* (eds D.E.G. Briggs and P.R. Crowther), pp. 232–5. Oxford: Blackwell Scientific, 1990.

Behrensmeyer, A.K. Terrestrial vertebrate accumulations. In *Taphonomy: Releasing the Data Locked in the Fossil Record* (eds P. Allison and D. Briggs), pp. 291–335. New York: Plenum Press, 1991.

Behrensmeyer, A.K. and Hill, A.P. *Fossils in the Making: Vertebrate Taphonomy and Paleoecology*. Chicago: University of Chicago Press, 1980.

Behrensmeyer, A.K. and Hook, R.W. Paleoenvironmental contexts and taphonomic modes in the terrestrial fossil record. Chapter 2 in *The Evolutionary Paleoecology of Terrestrial Ecosystems* (by the ETE Consortium). Chicago: University of Chicago Press, 1992.

Bishop W. W. (ed.). *Geological Background to Fossil Man*. Edinburgh: Scottish Academic Press, 1978.

Brain C.K. *The Hunters or the Hunted?: An Introduction to African Cave Taphonomy*. Chicago: University of Chicago Press, 1981.

Coppens, Y. *et al.* *Earliest Man and Environments in the Lake Rudolf Basin: Stratigraphy, Paleoecology, and Evolution*. Chicago: University of Chicago Press, 1976.

Leakey, M.D. and Harris, J.M. (eds). *Laetoli: A Pliocene Site in Northern Tanzania*. Oxford: Clarendon Press, 1987.

Leakey, M.G. and Leakey, R.E. (eds). *Koobi Fora Research Project*, Vol. 1: *The Fossil Hominids and an Introduction to their Context, 1968–1974*. Oxford: Clarendon Press, 1978.

Reconstructing past environments (pp. 191–5)

Andrews. P. *Owls, Caves and Fossils*. London: The Natural History Museum, 1990.

Andrews, P. *et al.* Patterns of ecological diversity in fossil and modern mammalian faunas. *Biological Journal of the Linnean Society* 11: 177–205 (1979).

Badgley, C. The paleoenvironment of South Asian Miocene hominoids. In *The Evolution of East Asian Environments* (ed. O. White), pp. 796–811. Hongkong: Center of Asian Studies, 1984.

Behrensmeyer, A.K. Taphonomy and palaeoecology in the hominid fossil record. *Yearbook of Physical Anthropology* 19: 36–50 (1975).

Bonnefille, R. Cenozoic vegetation and environments of early hominids in East Africa. In *The Evolution of East Asian Environments* (ed. R. O. White), pp. 580–612. Hongkong: Center of Asian Studies, 1984.

Bown, T.M. *et al.* The Fayum forest revisited. *Journal of Human Evolution* 11: 603–32 (1982).

Evans, E.M. *et al.* Palaeoecology of Miocene sites in western Kenya. *Journal of Human Evolution* 10: 35–48 (1981).

Fleagle, J.G. Size distributions of living and fossil primate faunas. *Paleobiology* 4: 67–76 (1978).

Janis, C.M. Prediction of primate diets from molar wear patterns. In *Food Acquisition and Processing in Primates* (eds D.J. Chivers *et al.*), pp. 331–40. New York: Plenum Press, 1984.

Nitecki, M.H. and Nitecki, D.V. *The Evolution of Human Hunting*. New York: Plenum Press, 1987.

Shipman, P. *Life History of a Fossil: An Introduction to Taphonomy and Paleoecology*. Cambridge, MA: Harvard University Press, 1981.

Shipman, P. *et al.* The Fort Ternan hominoid site, Kenya: geology, age, taphonomy and palaeoecology. *Journal of Human Evolution* 10: 49–72 (1981).

Shotwell, J.A. An approach to the paleoecology of mammals. *Ecology* 36: 327–37 (1955).

Weigelt, J. *Vertebrate Carcases and their Paleobiological Implications*. Chicago: University of Chicago Press, 1989.

The primate fossil record

The fossil history of primates (pp. 199–208)

Beard, K.C. *et al.* First skulls of the Early

Eocene primate *Shoshonius cooperi* and the anthropoid-tarsier dichotomy. *Nature* 349: 64–7 (1991).

Conroy, G.C. *Primate Evolution*. New York: W.W. Norton, 1990.

Fleagle, J.G. *Primate Adaptation & Evolution*. San Diego: Academic Press, 1988.

Gingerich, P.D. Cranial anatomy and evolution of early Tertiary Plesiadapidae (Mammalia, Primates). *Contributions of the Museum of Paleontology, University of Michigan* 15: 1–140 (1976).

Gingerich, P.D. New species of Eocene primates and the phylogeny of European Adapidae. *Folia Primatologica* 28: 60–80 (1977).

Gingerich, P.D. Primate evolution: evidence from the fossil record, comparative morphology, and molecular biology. *Yearbook of Physical Anthropology* 27: 57–72 (1984).

Gingerich, P.D. *Plesiadapis* and the delineation of the order Primates. In *Major Topics in Primate and Human Evolution* (eds B. Wood *et al.*), pp. 32–46. Cambridge: Cambridge University Press, 1986.

Gingerich, P.D. and Simons, E.L. Systematics, phylogeny, and evolution of early Eocene Adapidae (Mammalia, Primates) in North America. *Contributions of the Museum of Paleontology, University of Michigan* 24: 245–79 (1977).

Martin, R.D. *Primate Origins and Evolution: A Phylogenetic Reconstruction*. London: Chapman and Hall; Princeton: Princeton University Press, 1990.

Simons, E.L. *Primate Evolution: An Introduction to Man's Place in Nature*. New York: Macmillan, 1972.

Simons. E.L. New faces of *Aegyptopithecus* from the Oligocene of Egypt. *Journal of Human Evolution* 16: 273–89 (1987).

Simons, E.L. Discovery of the oldest known anthropoidean skull from the Paleogene of Egypt. *Science* 247: 1567–9 (1990).

Szalay, F.S. and Delson, E. *Evolutionary History of the Primates*. New York: Academic Press, 1979.

Evolution of New World monkeys
(pp. 209–16)

Ciochon, R.L. and Chiarelli, A.B. (eds). *Evolutionary Biology of the New World Monkeys and Continental Drift*. New York: Plenum Press, 1980.

Coimbra-Filho, A.F. and Mittermeier, R.A. *Ecology and Behavior of Neotropical Primates*, Vol. 1. Rio de Janeiro: Academia Brasiliera de Ciencias, 1981.

Delson, E. and Rosenberger, A.L. Are there any anthropoid primate 'living fossils'? In *Casebook on Living Fossils* (eds N. Eldredge and S. Stanley), pp. 50–61. New York: Gustav Fischer, 1984.

Fleagle, J.G. and Rosenberger, A.L. (eds). The platyrrhine fossil record. *Journal of Human Evolution* (special issue) 19(1/2): 1–254 (1990).

Ford, S.M. Callitrichids as phyletic dwarfs, and the place of the Callitrichidae in the Platyrrhini. *Primates* 21:31–43 (1984).

Ford, S.M. Systematics of the New World monkeys. In *Comparative Primate Biology, Vol.1: Systematics, Evolution and Anatomy* (eds D.R. Swindler and J. Erwin), pp. 73–135. New York: Alan R. Liss, 1986.

Hershkovitz, P. *Living New World Monkeys (Platyrrhini), with an Introduction to the Primates*, Vol. 1. Chicago: University of Chicago Press, 1977.

Mittermeier, R.A. *et al. Ecology and Behavior of Neotropical Primates*, Vol. 2. Washington, DC: World Wildlife Fund, 1988.

Rosenberger, A.L. Fossil New World monkeys dispute the molecular clock. *Journal of Human Evolution* 13: 737–42 (1984).

Rosenberger, A.L. Platyrrhines, catarrhines and the anthropoid transition. In *Major Topics in Primate and Human Evolution* (eds B. Wood *et al.*), pp. 66–88. Cambridge: Cambridge University Press, 1986.

Rosenberger, A.L. and Coimbra-Filho, A.F. Morphology, taxonomic status and affinites of the lion tamarins, *Leontopithecus* (Callitrichinae, Cebidae). *Folia Primatologica* 42:149–79 (1984).

Rosenberger, A.L. and Fleagle, J.G. (eds). New World Monkeys. *Journal of Human Evolution* (special issue) 18(7): 595–750 (1989).

Setoguchi, T. and Rosenberger, A.L. Miocene marmosets; first fossil evidence. *International Journal of Primatology* 6: 615–25 (1985).

Setoguchi, T. and Rosenberger, A.L. A fossil owl monkey from La Venta, Colombia. *Nature* 326: 692–4 (1987).

Terborgh, J. *Five New World Primates*. Princeton: Princeton University Press, 1983.

Evolution of Old World monkeys
(pp. 217–22)

Davies, G. and Oates, J.F. (eds). *The Evolutionary Ecology of Colobine Monkeys*. Cambridge: Cambridge University Press, in press.

Fleagle, J.G. *Primate Adaptation & Evolution*. San Diego: Academic Press, 1988.

Gautier-Hion, A. *et al.* (eds). *A Primate Radiation: Evolutionary Biology of the African Guenons*. Cambridge: Cambridge University Press, 1988.

Jablonski, N. G. (ed.). *Theropithecus: The Rise and Fall of a Primate Genus*. Cambridge: Cambridge University Press, 1993.

Lindburg, D.E. (ed.). *The Macaques: Studies in Ecology, Behavior and Evolution*. New York: Van Nostrand, 1980.

Macdonald, D. (ed.). *The Encyclopedia of Mammals*, Vol. 1. London: Allen & Unwin, 1984; New York: Facts On File, 1985.

Strasser, E. and Delson, E. Cladistic analysis of cercopithecid relationships. *Journal of Human Evolution* 16: 81–99 (1987).

Szalay, F. and Delson, E. *Evolutionary History of the Primates*. New York: Academic Press, 1979.

Tattersall, I. *et al.* (eds). *Encyclopedia of Human Evolution and Prehistory*. New York: Garland, 1988.

Evolution of apes (pp. 223–30)

Andrews, P. Aspects of hominoid phylogeny. In *Molecules and Morphology in Evolution: Conflict or Compromise?* (ed. C. Patterson), pp. 23–53. Cambridge: Cambridge University Press, 1987.

Andrews, P. Evolution and environment in the Hominoidea. *Nature* 360: 641–6 (1992).

Beynon, A.D. *et al.* On thick and thin enamel in hominids. *American Journal of Physical Anthropology* 86: 295–309 (1991).

Cacone, A. and Powell, J.R. DNA divergence among hominoids. *Evolution* 43: 925–42 (1989).

Goodman, M. *et al.* Molecular phylogeny of the family of apes and humans. *Genome* 31: 316–35 (1989).

Groves, C.P. Systematics of the great apes. In *Comparative Primate Biology*, Vol. 1 (eds D.R. Swindler and J. Irwin), pp. 187–217. New York: Alan R. Liss, 1986.

Harrison, T. A reassesment of the phylogenetic relationships of *Oreopithecus bambolii* Gervais. *Journal of Human Evolution* 15: 541–83 (1986).

Kelley, J. and Pilbeam, D. The dryopithecines: taxonomy, anatomy, and phylogeny of Miocene large hominoids. In *Comparative Primate Biology*, Vol. 1 (eds D.R. Swindler and J. Irwin), pp. 361–411. New York: Alan R. Liss, 1986.

Martin, L. Relationships among extant and extinct great apes and humans. In *Major Topics in Primate and Human Evolution* (eds B. Wood *et al.*), pp. 161–87. Cambridge: Cambridge University Press, 1986.

Pilbeam, D. Distinguished lecture: hominoid evolution and hominid origins. *American Anthropologist* 88: 295–312 (1986).

Pilbeam, D. *et al.* New *Sivapithecus* humeri from Pakistan and the relationship of *Sivapithecus* and *Pongo*. *Nature* 348: 237–9 (1990).

Rose, M.D. Miocene hominoid postcranial morphology: monkey-like, ape-like, neither, or both? In *New Interpretations of Ape and Human Ancestry* (eds R.L. Ciochon and R.S. Corruccini), pp. 405–17. New York: Plenum Press, 1983.

Walker, A.C. and Pickford, M. New postcranial fossils of *Proconsul africanus* and *Proconsul nyanzae*. In *New Interpretations of Ape and Human Ancestry* (eds R.L. Ciochon and R.S. Corruccini), pp. 325–51. New York: Plenum Press, 1983.

Ward, S.C. and Brown, B. The facial skeleton of *Sivapithecus indicus*. In *Comparative Primate Biology* (eds D.R. Swindler and J. Erwin), pp. 413–52. New York: Alan R. Liss, 1986.

Ward, S.C. and Pilbeam, D. Maxillofacial morphology of Miocene hominoids from Africa and Indo-Pakistan. In *New Interpretations of Ape and Human Ancestry* (eds R.L. Ciochon and R.S. Corruccini), pp. 211–38. New York: Plenum Press, 1983.

Evolution of the australopithecines
(pp. 231–40)

Chamberlain, A.T. and Wood, B.A. Early hominid phylogeny. *Journal of Human Evolution* 16: 116–33 (1987).

Grine, F.E. Trophic differences between 'gracile' and 'robust' australopothecines: a scanning electron microscope analysis of occlusal events. *South African Journal of Science* 77: 203–30 (1981).

Howell, F.C. Hominidae. In *Evolution of African Mammals* (eds V.J. Maglio and H.B.S. Cooke), pp. 154–248. Cambridge, MA: Harvard University Press, 1978.

Johanson, D.C. and White, T.D. A systematic assessment of early African hominids. *Science* 202: 321–30 (1979).

Kimbel, W.H. *et al.* Cranial morphology of *Australopithecus afarensis*: a comparative study based on a composite reconstruction of the adult skull. *American Journal of Physical Anthropology* 64: 337–88 (1984).

Klein, R.G. *The Human Career: Human Biological and Cultural Origins*. Chicago: Chicago University Press, 1989.

Lewin, R. *Bones of Contention: Controversies in the Search for Human Origins*. New York:

Simon and Schuster, 1987; London: Penguin Books, 1991.

Rak, Y. *The Australopithecine Face.* Academic Press: New York and London, 1983.

Rak, Y. Lucy's pelvic anatomy: its role in bipedal gait. *Journal of Human Evolution* 20: 283–90 (1991).

Reader, J. *Missing Links: The Hunt for Earliest Man,* 2nd edn. London: Penguin Books, 1988.

Skelton, R.R. *et al.* Phylogenetic analysis of early hominids. *Current Anthropology* 27: 21–43 (1986).

Smith, B.H. Dental development in *Australopithecus* and early *Homo. Nature* 323: 327–30 (1986).

Tobias, P.V. *Olduvai Gorge,* Vol. 2: *The cranium and maxillary dentition of Australopithecus (Zinjanthropus) boisei.* Cambridge: Cambridge University Press, 1967.

Tobias, P.V. A survey and synthesis of the African hominids of the late Tertiary and early Quaternary periods. In *Current Argument on Early Man* (ed. L.-K. Königsson), pp. 86–113. Oxford: Pergamon Press, 1980.

Walker, A. *et al.* 2.5-Myr *Australopithecus boisei* from west of Lake Turkana, Kenya. *Nature* 322: 517–22 (1986).

White, T.D. *et al. Australopithecus africanus:* its phyletic position reconsidered. *South African Journal of Science* 77: 445–70 (1981).

Wood, B.A. and Chamberlain, A.T. *Australopithecus:* grade or clade? In *Major Topics in Primate and Human Evolution* (eds B. Wood *et al.*), pp. 220–48. Cambridge: Cambridge University Press, 1986.

Evolution of early humans (pp. 241–50)

Andrews, P. and Franzen, J.L. (eds). The early evolution of man, with special emphasis on Southeast Asia and Africa.*Courier Forschungsinstitut Senckenberg* 69: 1–277 (1984).

Andrews, P. and Stringer, C.B. *Human Evolution: An Illustrated Guide.* London: British Museum (Natural History), 1989.

Bräuer, G. and Smith, F.H. *Replacement or Continuity? Controversies in the Evolution of Homo sapiens.* Rotterdam: Balkema, 1990.

Day, M.H. *Guide to Fossil Man,* 4th edn. London: Cassell, 1986.

Delson, E. (ed.). *Ancestors: The Hard Evidence.* New York: Alan R. Liss, 1985.

Klein, R.G. *The Human Career: Human Biological and Cultural Origins.* Chicago: University of Chicago Press, 1989.

Mellars, P. and Stringer, C.B. (eds). *The Human Revolution: Behavioural and Biological Perspectives on the Origins of Modern Humans.* Edinburgh: Edinburgh University Press, 1989; Princeton: Princeton University Press, 1990.

Putman, J.J. The search for modern humans. *National Geographic* 174: 438–77 (1988).

Rightmire, G.P. *The Evolution of Homo erectus: Comparative Anatomical Studies of an Extinct Human Species.* Cambridge: Cambridge University Press, 1990.

Smith, F.H. and Spencer, F. (eds). *The Origins of Modern Humans: A World Survey of the Fossil Evidence.* New York: Alan R. Liss, 1984.

Smith, F. H. *et al.* Modern human origins. *Yearbook of Physical Anthropology* 32: 35–68 (1989).

Stringer, C. and Gamble, C. *In Search of Neanderthals: Solving the Puzzle of Human Origins.* London: Thames and Hudson, 1993.

Tattersall, I. Evolution comes to life. *Scientific American* 267 (August): 62–9 (1992).

Trinkaus, E. (ed.). *The Emergence of Modern Humans: Biocultural Adaptations in the Later Pleistocene.* Cambridge: Cambridge University Press, 1989.

Wood, B. *et al.* (eds). *Major Topics in Human Evolution.* Cambridge: Cambridge University Press, 1986.

Primate genetics and evolution

Principles of genetics (pp. 169–73)

British Medical Association. *Our Genetic Future: The Science and Ethics of Genetic Technology.* Oxford: Oxford University Press, 1992.

Gelehrter, T.D. and Collins, F.S. *Principles of Medical Genetics.* Baltimore, MA: Williams & Wilkins, 1990.

Maxson, L.R. and Daugherty, C. H. *Genetics: A Human Perspective,* 3rd edn. Dubuque, IA: Wm C. Brown, 1992.

Miller, A. D. Human gene therapy comes of age *Nature* 357: 455–60 (1992).

Vogel, F. and Motulsky, A.G. *Human Genetics: Problems and Approaches,* 2nd edn. Berlin: Springer-Verlag, 1986.

Weatherall, D.J. *The New Genetics and Clinical Practice,* 3rd edn. Oxford: Oxford University Press, 1991.

Genetic diversity in humans (pp. 264–8)

Balazs, I. *et al.* Human population genetic studies of five hypervariable DNA loci. *American Journal of Human Genetics* 44: 182–90 (1989).

Bodmer, W.F. and Cavalli-Sforza, L.L. *Genetics, Evolution and Man.* San Francisco: W.H. Freeman, 1976.

Emery, A. E. H. and Mueller, R. F. *Elements of Medical Genetics,* 8th edn. Edinburgh: Churchill Livingstone, 1992.

Hartl, D.L. *Our Uncertain Future: Genetics and Human Diversity,* 3rd edn. New York: Harper and Row, 1990.

Horai, S. and Hayasaka, K. Intraspecific nucleotide sequences in the major non-coding regions of human mitochondrial DNA. *American Journal of Human Genetics* 48: 828–42 (1990).

Jeffreys, A.J. *et al.* Individual-specific 'fingerprints' of human DNA. *Nature* 316: 76–9 (1985).

Lewontin, R.C. *Human Diversity.* New York: Scientific American Library, 1982.

Mollon, J. Worlds of difference. *Nature* 356: 378–9. (1992).

Stephens, J.C. *et al.* Mapping the human genome: current status. *Science* 250: 237-44 (1990).

Vogel, F. and Motulsky, A.G. *Human Genetics: Problems and Approaches,* 2nd edn. Berlin: Springer-Verlag, 1986.

Watson, J.D. *et al. Molecular Biology of the Gene,* 4th edn. Menlo Park, CA: Benjamin/Cummings, 1987.

Mutation and human evolution (pp. 269–73)

Ames, B. N. *et al.* Ranking possible carcinogenic hazards. *Science* 236: 271–80 (1987).

Clarke, R.H. and Southwood, T.R.E. Risks from ionizing radiation. *Nature* 338: 197–8 (1989).

Davies, K.E. and Read, A.P. *Molecular Basis of Inherited Disease.* Oxford: IRL Press, 1988.

Evans, H.J. Mutation as a cause of genetic disease. *Philosophical Transactions of the Royal Society of London* Series B 319: 325–40 (1988).

Koeberl, D.D. *et al.* Mutations causing haemophilia B: direct estimates of the underlying rates of spontaneous germ-line mutations in a human gene. *American Journal of Human Genetics* 47: 202–17 (1990).

Neel, J.V. *et al.* Search for mutations affecting protein charge and/or function in children of atomic bomb survivors: final report. *American Journal of Human Genetics* 42: 663–76 (1988).

Vogel, F. Risk calculations for hereditary effects of ionizing radiation in humans. *Human Genetics* 89: 127–46 (1992).

Weatherall, D.J. *The New Genetics and Clinical Practice,* 3rd edn. Oxford: Oxford University Press, 1991.

Human chromosomes (pp. 274–80)

Emery, A.E.H. and Mueller, R.F. *Elements of Medical Genetics,* 8th edn. Edinburgh: Churchill Livingstone, 1992.

Heim, S. and Mitelman, F. *Cancer Cytogenetics.* New York: Alan R. Liss, 1987.

Weatherall, D.J. *The New Genetics and Clinical Practice,* 3rd edn. Oxford: Oxford University Press, 1991.

The Y chromosome (p. 276)

McLaren, A. The making of male mice. *Nature* 351: 96 (1990).

Mittwoch, U. One gene may not make a man. *New Scientist* 10 November: 40–2 (1990).

Bottlenecks in human evolution (pp. 281–3)

Dean, G. *The Porphyrias.* London: Pitman, 1972.

Diamond, J.M. and Rotter, J.I. Observing founder effect in human evolution. *Nature* 329: 105–6 (1987).

Harrison, G.A. and Boyce, A.J. *The Genetic Structure of Human Populations.* Oxford: Clarendon Press, 1972.

Rouhani, S. Molecular genetics and the pattern of human evolution: plausible and implausible models. In *The Human Revolution: Behavioural and Biological Perspectives on the Origins of Modern Humans* (eds P. Mellars and C. Stringer), pp. 47–61. Edinburgh: Edinburgh University Press, 1989; Princeton: Princeton University Press, 1990.

Smith, J.M. The Y of human relationships. *Nature* 344: 591–2 (1990).

Stoneking, M. and Cann, R.L. African origin of human mitochondrial DNA. In *The Human Revolution* (eds P. Mellars and C. Stringer), pp. 17–30. Edinburgh: Edinburgh University Press, 1989; Princeton: Princeton University Press, 1990.

Wainscoat, J.S.*et al.* Geographic distribution of alpha- and beta-globin gene cluster polymorphisms. In *The Human Revolution* (eds P. Mellars and C. Stringer), pp. 31–8. Edinburgh: Edinburgh University Press, 1989; Princeton: Princeton University Press, 1990.

Natural selection in humans (pp. 284–287)

Bajema, C.J. *Natural Selection in Human Populations.* New York: John Wiley, 1971.

Bodmer, W.F. and Cavalli-Sforza, L.L. *Genetics, Evolution and Man.* San Francisco: W.H. Freeman, 1976.

Guglielmino-Matessi, G.G. *et al.* Climate and the evolution of skullmetrics in man. *American Journal of Physical Anthropology* 50: 494–564 (1979).

Howard, J.C. Disease and evolution. *Nature* 352: 565–7 (1991).

Johnson, R.C. *et al.* Genetic interpretation of racial/ethnic differences in lactose absorption and tolerance: a review. *Human Biology* 53: 1–14 (1987).

Loomis, W.F. Skin-pigment regulation of vitamin D biosynthesis in man. *Science* 157: 501–6 (1967).

Distribution of genetic diseases in human populations (pp. 288–91)

Cavalli-Sforza, L.L. and Bodmer, W.F. *The Genetics of Human Populations.* San Francisco: W.H. Freeman, 1971.

Emery, A.E.H. and Rimoin, D.L. *The Principles and Practice of Medical Genetics*, 2nd edn. Edinburgh: Churchill Livingstone, 1990.

McKusick, V.A. *Mendelian Inheritance in Man*, 9th edn. Baltimore, MD: Johns Hopkins University Press, 1990.

Vogel, F. and Motulksy, A.G. *Human Genetics: Problems and Approaches*, 2nd edn. Berlin: Springer-Verlag, 1986.

Genetic clues of relatedness

Measuring relatedness (pp. 295–7)

Hillis, D.M. and Moritz, C. *Molecular Systematics.* Sunderland, MA: Sinauer Associates, 1990.

John, B. and Miklos, G. *The Eukaryote Genome in Development and Evolution.* London: Allen & Unwin, 1988.

Lewin, R. Molecular clocks run out of time. *New Scientist* 10 February: 38–41 (1990).

Nei, M. *Molecular Evolutionary Genetics.* New York: Columbia University Press, 1987.

Wilson, A.C. The molecular basis of evolution. In *The Molecules of Life* (Readings from *Scientific American*), pp. 120–9. New York: W.H. Freeman, 1985.

Chromosomal evolution in primates (pp. 298–302)

Arnason, U. The role of chromosomal rearrangement in mammalian speciation with special reference to Cetacea and Pinnipedia. *Hereditas* 70:113–18 (1972).

Bianchi, N.O. *et al.* The pattern of restriction enzyme-induced banding in the chromosomes of chimpanzee, gorilla, and orangutan and its evolutionary sgnificance. *Journal of Molecular Evolution* 22: 323–3 (1985).

Bickmore, W.A. and Sumner, A.T. Mammalian chromsome banding – an expression of genome organization. *Trends in Genetics* 5: 144–8 (1989).

de Grouchy, J. *et al.* Chromosomal phylogeny of the primates. *Annual Review of Genetics* 12:289–328 (1978).

Dutrillaux, B. Chromosomal evolution in primates: tentative phylogeny from *Microcebus murinus* (prosimian) to man. *Human Genetics* 48:251–314 (1979).

Kao, F.-T. Human genome structure. *International Review of Cytology* 96: 51–201 (1985).

Marks, J. Hominoid cytogenetics and evolution. *Yearbook of Physical Anthropology* 25:125–53 (1983).

Marks, J. What's old and new in molecular phylogenetics. *American Journal of Physical Anthropology* 85: 207–20 (1991).

Miller, D. A. Evolution of primate chromosomes. *Science* 198: 1116–24 (1977).

Myers, R. and Shafer, D. Hybrid ape offspring of a mating of gibbon and siamang. *Science* 205: 308–10 (1978).

Seuanez, H.N. *The Phylogeny of Human Chromosomes.* Springer: New York, 1979.

Stanyon, R. and Chiarelli, B. Phylogeny of the Hominoidea: the chromosome evidence. *Journal of Human Evolution* 11:493–504 (1982).

Swanson, C. *et al.* Cytogenetics: the Chromosome in Division, Inheritance and Evolution, 2nd edn. Englewood Cliffs, NJ; Prentice-Hall, 1981.

Tantravahi, R. *et al.* Detection of nucleolus organizer regions in chromosomes of human, chimpanzee, gorilla, orangutan and gibbon. *Chromosoma* 56: 15–27 (1976).

Weinberg. J. *et al.* Molecular cytotaxonomy of primates by chromosomal *in situ* suppression hybridization. *Genomics* 8: 47–50 (1990).

White, M. J. D. *Animal Cytology and Evolution*, 3rd edn. London: Cambridge University Press, 1973.

Immunological evidence on primates (pp. 303–6)

Sarich, V. and Wilson, A. Immunological timescale for hominid evolution. *Science* 158: 1200–3 (1967).

Reconstructing human evolution from proteins (pp. 307–12)

Andrews, P.J. Aspects of hominoid phylogeny. In *Molecules and Morphology in Evolution: Conflict or Compromise?* (ed. C. Patterson), pp. 23–53. Cambridge: Cambridge University Press, 1987.

Czelusniak, J. *et al.* Perspectives from amino acid and nucleotide sequences on cladistic relationships among higher taxa of Eutheria. In *Current Mammalogy*, Vol. 2 (ed. H.H. Genoways), pp. 545–72. New York: Plenum Press, 1990.

Fitch, D.H.A. *et al.* Molecular history of gene conversions in the primate fetal gamma-globin genes: nucleotide sequences from the common gibbon, *Hylobates lar. Journal of Biological Chemistry* 265: 781–93 (1990).

Goodman, M. Toward a genealogical description of the primates. In *Molecular Anthropology* (eds M. Goodman and R.E. Tashian), pp. 321–53. New York: Plenum Press, 1976.

Goodman, M. Decoding the pattern of protein evolution. *Progress in Biophysics and Molecular Biology* 37: 105–64 (1981).

Goodman, M. Update to 'Evolution of the immunologic species specificity of human serum proteins'. *Human Biology* 61: 925–34 (1989).

Goodman, M. *et al.* Globins: a case study in molecular phylogeny. *Cold Spring Harbor Symposia on Quantitative Biology* 52: 875–90 (1987).

Goodman, M. *et al.* Pattern and process in vertebrate phylogeny revealed by coevolution

of molecules and morphology. In *Molecules and Morphology in Evolution: Conflict or Compromise?* (ed. C. Patterson), pp. 141–76. Cambridge University Press: Cambridge, 1987.

Koop, B.F. *et al.* A molecular view of primate phylogeny and important systematic and evolutionary questions. *Molecular Biology and Evolution* 6: 580–612 (1989).

Miyamoto, M.M. *et al.* Phylogenetic relations of humans and African apes as ascertained from DNA sequences (7.1 kilobases pairs) of the psi-eta-globin region. *Science* 238: 369–73 (1987).

Sibley, C.G. and Ahlquist, J.E. DNA hybridisation evidence of hominoid phylogeny. *Journal of Molecular Evolution* 26: 99–121 (1987).

Slightom, J.L. *et al.* Orang-utan fetal globin genes. *Journal of Biological Chemistry* 262: 7472–83 (1987).

Tashian, R.E. *et al.* On the evolution and genetics of carbonic anhydrases I, II, and III. In *Isozymes* (eds M.L. Rattozzi *et al.*), pp. 79–100. New York: Alan R. Liss, 1983.

DNA-DNA hybridisation in the study of primate evolution (pp. 313–15)

Caccone, A. and Powell, J.R. DNA divergence among hominoids. *Evolution* 43: 925–42 (1989).

Goodman, M. *et al.* Molecular phylogeny of the family of apes and humans. *Genome* 31: 316–35 (1989).

Sibley, C.G. and Ahlquist, J.E. Reconstructing bird phylogeny by comparing DNAs. *Scientific American* 254 (February): 82–92 (1986).

Sibley, C.G. and Ahlquist, J.E. *Phylogeny and Classification of Birds: A Study in Molecular Evolution.* New Haven, CT: Yale University Press, 1990.

Sibley, C.G. *et al.* DNA hybridization evidence of hominoid phylogeny: a re-analysis of the data. *Journal of Molecular Evolution* 30: 202–36 (1990).

Human evolution: the evidence from DNA sequencing (pp. 316–21)

Brown, W.M. *et al.* Mitochondrial DNA sequences of primates: tempo and mode of evolution. *Journal of Molecular Evolution* 18: 255–39 (1982).

Di Rienzo, A. and Wilson, A.C. Branching pattern in the evolutionary tree for human mitochondrial DNA. *Proceedings of the National Academy of Sciences, USA* 88: 1597–1601 (1991).

Djian, P. and Green, H. Vectorial expansion of the involucrin gene and the relatedness of the hominoids. *Proceedings of the National Academy of Sciences, USA* 86: 8447–51 (1989).

Felsenstein, J. Phylogenies from molecular sequences; inference and reliability. *Annual Review of Genetics* 22: 521–65 (1988).

Hasegawa, M. and Kishino, H. DNA sequence analysis and evolution of Hominoidea. In *New Aspects of the Genetics of Molecular Evidence* (eds M. Kimura and T. Takahata), pp. 303–17. Tokyo: Scientific Societies Press; Berlin: Springer-Verlag, 1991.

Holmes, E.C. Stochastic models of molecular evolution and the estimation of phylogeny and rates of nucleotide substitution in the hominoid primates. *Journal of Human Evolution* 18: 775–94 (1989).

Holmquist, R. *et al.* Higher-primate phylogeny

—why can't we decide? *Molecular Biology and Evolution* 5: 201–16 (1988).

Jeffreys, A.J. *et al.* Evolution of gene families: the globin genes. In *Evolution from Molecules to Men* (ed. D.S. Bendall), pp. 175–95. Cambridge: Cambridge University Press, 1983.

Koop, B. *et al.* Primate eta-globin DNA sequences and man's place among the great apes. *Nature* 319: 234–8 (1986).

Li, W.-H. and Tanimura, M. The molecular clock runs more slowly in man than in apes and monkeys. *Nature* 326: 93–6 (1987).

Maeda, N. *et al.* Molecular evolution of intergenic DNA in higher primates: pattern of DNA changes, molecular clock, and evolution of repetitive sequences. *Molecular Biology and Evolution* 5: 1–20 (1988).

Miyamoto, M.M. *et al.* Phylogenetic relationships of humans and African apes as ascertained from DNA sequences (7.1 kilobase pairs) of the psi-eta-globin region. *Science* 238: 369–73 (1987).

Patterson, C. (ed.). *Molecules and Morphology in Evolution: Conflict or Compromise.* Cambridge: Cambridge University Press, 1987.

Was Eve an African? (p. 320–1)

Gee, H. Statistical cloud over African Eve. *Nature* 355: 583 (1992).

Vigilant, L. *et al.* African populations and the evolution of human mitochondrial DNA. *Science* 253: 1503–7 (1991). (Replies by A.R. Templeton and S.B. Hedges *et al. Science* 255: 737–9 (1991).)

Early human behaviour and ecology

The hominid way of life (pp. 325–34)

Behrensmeyer, A.K. and Hill, A.P (eds). *Fossils in the Making: Vertebrate Taphonomy and Paleoecology.* Chicago: University of Chicago Press, 1980.

Brain, C.K. *The Hunters or the Hunted?: An Introduction to African Cave Taphonomy.* Chicago: University of Chicago Press, 1981.

Bromage, T.G. and Dean, M.C. Re-evaluation of the age at death of immature fossil hominids. *Nature* 317: 525–7 (1985).

Delson, E. (ed.). *Ancestors: The Hard Evidence.* New York: Alan R. Liss, 1985.

Foley, R. (ed.) *Hominid Evolution and Community Ecology.* London: Academic Press, 1984.

Foley, R. *Another Unique Species: Patterns in Human Evolutionary Ecology.* Harlow, Essex: Longman Scientific & Technical; New York: John Wiley, 1987.

Isaac, G.Ll. The archaeology of human origins. *Advances in World Archaeology* 3: 1–87 (1984).

Keeley, L. *Experimental Determination of Stone Tool Uses.* Chicago: University of Chicago Press, 1980.

Kinzey, W.G. (ed.) *The Evolution of Human Behavior: Primate Models.* Albany: State University of New York Press, 1987.

Klein, R.G. *The Human Career: Human Biological and Cultural Origins.* Chicago: University of Chicago Press, 1989.

Potts, R. Home bases and early hominids. *American Scientist* 72: 338–47 (1984).

Potts, R. *Early Hominid Activities at Olduvai.* Hawthorne, NY: Aldine de Gruyter, 1988.

Renfrew, C. and Bahn, P. *Archaeology: Theories, Methods and Practice.* London: Thames and Hudson, 1991.

Smith, B.H. Dental Developments in *Australopithecus* and *Homo. Nature* 323: 327–30 (1986).

Toth, N. and Schick, K. The first million years: the archaeology of protohuman culture. *Journal of Archaeological Method and Theory* 9: 1–96 (1986).

Cannibalism or ritual dismemberment? (p. 330)

Arens, W. *The Man-eating Myth.* Oxford: Oxford University Press, 1979.

Bahn, P. Is cannabalism too much to swallow? *New Scientist* 27 April: 38–40 (1991).

Russell, M.D. Bone breakage in the Krapina hominid collection. *American Journal of Physical Anthropology* 72: 373–9 (1987).

Russell, M.D. Mortuary practices at the Krapina Neandertal site. *American Journal of Physical Anthropology* 72: 381–97 (1987).

Trinkaus, E. Cannibalism and burial at Krapina. *Journal of Human Evolution* 14: 203–16 (1985).

White, T.D. *Prehistoric Cannibalism at Mancos 5MTUMR-2346.* Princeton: Princeton University Press, 1992.

White, T.D. and Toth, N. The question of ritual cannibalism at Grotta Guattari. *Current Anthropology* 32: 103–38 (1991).

Studying human evolution by analogy (pp. 335–40)

Behrensmeyer, A.K. and A.P. Hill (eds). *Fossils in the Making: Vertebrate Taphonomy and Paleoecology.* Chicago: University of Chicago Press, 1981.

Binford, L.R. *Bones: Modern Myths and Ancient Men.* London: Academic Press, 1981.

Blumenschine, R. *Early Hominid Scavenging Opportunities.* Oxford: British Archaeological Reports (International Series No. 283), 1986.

Dunbar, R.I.M. Theropithecines and hominids: contrasting solutions to the same ecological problems. *Journal of Human Evolution* 12: 647–58 (1983).

Foley, R. *Another Unique Species: Patterns in Human Evolutionary Ecology.* Harlow, Essex: Longman Scientific & Technical, 1987.

Foley, R. and Lee, P.C. Finite social space, evolutionary pathways and reconstructing hominid behavior. *Science* 243: 901–6 (1989).

Gould, R. *Living Archaeology.* Cambridge: Cambridge University Press, 1980.

Hodder, I. *The Present Past: An Introduction to Anthropology for Archaeologists.* London: Batsford, 1982.

Kinzey, W.G. (ed.). *The Evolution of Human Behavior: Primate Models.* Albany: State University of New York Press, 1987.

Potts, R. *Early Hominid Activities at Olduvai.* Hawthorne, NY: Aldine de Gruyter, 1988.

Shipman, P. *Life History of a Fossil: An Introduction to Taphonomy and Paleoecology.* Cambridge, MA: Harvard Univerity Press, 1983.

Yellen, J. *Archaeological Approaches to the Present: Models for Reconstructing the Past.* New York: Academic Press, 1977.

Early human mental abilities (pp. 341–5)

Alexander, R.D. Evolution of the human psyche. In *The Human Revolution: Behavioural and Biological Perspectives on*

the Origins of Modern Humans (eds P. Mellars and C. Stringer), pp. 455–513. Edinburgh: Edinburgh University Press, 1989; Princeton: Princeton University Press, 1990.

Gowlett, J.A.J. Mental abilities of early man: a look at some hard evidence. In *Hominid Evolution and Community Ecology* (ed. R.A. Foley), pp. 167–92. London: Academic Press, 1984.

Gowlett, J.A.J. Culture and conceptualisation: the Oldowan–Acheulean gradient. In *Stone Age Prehistory: Studies in Memory of Charles McBurney* (eds G.N. Bailey and P. Callow), pp. 243–60. Cambridge: Cambridge University Press, 1986.

Holloway, R.L. Culture: a human domain. *Current Anthropology* 10: 395–412 (1969).

Isaac, G. Ll. Foundation stones: early artefacts as indicators of activities and abilities. In *Stone Age Prehistory: Studies in Memory of Charles McBurney* (eds G.N. Bailey and P. Callow), pp. 221–41. Cambridge: Cambridge University Press, 1986.

McGrew, W.C. Evolutionary implications of sex differences in chimpanzee predation and tool-use. In *The Great Apes* (eds D.A. Hamburg and E.R. McCown), pp. 441–63. Menlo Park, CA: W. Benjamin, 1979.

Tobias, P.V. The emergence of man in Africa and beyond. *Philosophical Transactions of the Royal Society of London* Series B 292: 43–56 (1981).

Toth, N. The Oldowan reassessed: a close look at early stone artifacts. *Journal of Archaeological Science* 12: 101–20 (1985).

Wynn, T. The intelligence of later Acheulean hominids. *Man* 14: 371–91 (1979).

Wynn, T. The intelligence of Oldowan hominids. *Journal of Human Evolution* 10: 529–41 (1981).

Wynn, T. *The Evolution of Spatial Competence* (Illinois Studies in Anthropology). Champaign: University of Illinois Press, 1989.

Toolmaking by apes (p. 342)

Boesch, C. First hunters of the forest. *New Scientist* 19 May: 38–41 (1990).

Brewer, S.M. and McGrew, W.C. Chimpanzee use of a tool-set to get honey. *Folia Primatologica* 54: 100–4 (1990).

Goodall, J. *The Chimpanzees of Gombe.* Cambridge, MA: Harvard/Belknap, 1986.

McGrew, W.C. Why is ape tool use so confusing? In *Comparative Socioecology: the Behavioural Ecology of Humans and Other Mammals* (eds V. Standen and R.A. Foley), pp. 457–72. Oxford: Blackwell Scientific, 1989.

McGrew, W.C. and Marchant, L.F. Chimpanzees, tools, and termites: hand preferences or handedness? *Current Anthropology* 33: 114–19 (1992).

Evolution of human manipulation (pp. 346–9)

Day, M. H. Hominid postcranial material from Bed I, Olduvai Gorge. In *Human Origins* (eds G. Ll. Isaac and E. R. McCown), pp. 363–74. Menlo Park, CA: W. Benjamin, 1976.

Klein, R.G. *The Human Career: Human Biological and Cultural Origins.* Chicago: Chicago University Press, 1989.

Leakey, M.D. *Olduvai Gorge,* Vol. 3: *Excavation in Beds I and II, 1960–1963.* Cambridge: Cambridge University Press, 1971.

Marzke, M.W. Joint function and grips of the *Australopithecus afarensis* hand, with special reference to the region of the capitate. *Journal of Human Evolution* 12: 197–211 (1983).

Napier, J.R. *Hands*. London: Allen & Unwin, 1980.

Sampson, C.G. *The Stone Age Archaeology of Southern Africa*. New York: Academic Press, 1974.

Susman, R.L. *et al*. Arboreality and bipedality in the Hadar hominids. *Folia Primatologica* 43: 113–56 (1984).

Toth, N. The Oldowan reassessed: a closer look at early stone artifacts. *Journal of Archaeological Science* 12: 101–20 (1985).

Trinkaus, E. *The Shanidar Neandertals*. New York: Academic Press, 1983.

Trinkaus, E. The Neandertals and modern human origins. *Annual Review of Anthropology* 15: 193–218 (1986).

Wymer, J. *The Palaeolithic Age*. London: Croom Helm; New York: St Martin's Press, 1982.

Tools – the Palaeolithic record
(pp. 350–60)

Bailey. G.N. and Callow, P. (eds). *Stone Age Prehistory: Studies in Memory of Charles McBurney*. Cambridge: Cambridge University Press, 1986.

Bar-Yosef, O. Prehistory of the Levant. *Annual Reviews of Anthropology* 9: 101–33 (1980).

Bordes, F. *Typologie du Paléolithique ancien at moyen*, 3rd edn. Bordeaux: Editions du CNRS, 1979.

Bordes, F. and de Sonneville-Bordes, D. The significance of variability in Palaeolithic assemblages. *World Archaeology* 2: 61–73 (1970).

Clark, J.D. (ed.). *The Cambridge History of Africa*, Vol. 1: *From the Earliest Times to c. 500 BC*. Cambridge: Cambridge University Press, 1982.

Gamble, C. *The Palaeolithic Settlement of Europe*. Cambridge: Cambridge University Press, 1986.

Jennings, J.D. *Ancient North Americans*. San Francisco: W.H. Freeman, 1983.

Jennings, J.D. *Ancient South Americans*. San Francisco: W.H. Freeman, 1983.

Leakey. M.D. *Olduvai Gorge*, Vol. 3: *Excavations in Beds I and II, 1960–1963*. Cambridge: Cambridge University Press, 1971.

Marks, A.E. *Prehistory and Environments in the Central Negev, Israel*, Vol. 2. Dallas: Southern Methodist University Press, 1977.

Mellars, P. and Stringer, C. (eds). *The Human Revolution: Behavioural and Biological Perspectives on the Origins of Modern Humans*. Edinburgh: Edinburgh University Press, 1989; Princeton: Princeton University Press, 1990.

Sampson, C.G. *The Stone Age Archaeology of Southern Africa*. New York: Academic Press, 1974.

Soffer, O. *The Upper Palaeolithic of the Central Russian Plain*. Orlando, FL: Academic Press, 1985.

White, P.J. and Connell, J.F. *A Prehistory of Australia, New Guinea and Sahul*. New York: Academic Press, 1982.

Wu Rukang and Olsen, J.W. (eds). *Palaeoanthropology and Palaeolithic Archaeology in the People's Republic of China*. Orlando, FL: Academic Press, 1985.

Throwing (p. 358)

Isaac, B. Thowing and human evolution. *The African Archaeological Review* 5: 3–17 (1987).

Marzke, M.W. and Shackley, M.S. Hand use by early hominids: evidence from experimental archaeology and comparative morphology. *Journal of Human Evolution* 15: 439–60 (1987).

Ancient art (pp. 361–4)

Bahn, P.G. and Vertut, J. *Images of the Ice Age*. Leicester: Windward; New York: Facts On File, 1988.

Leroi-Gourhan, A. *The Art of Prehistoric Man in Western Europe*. London: Thames and Hudson, 1968. Published in US as *Treasures of Prehistoric Art*. New York: Abrams, 1967.

Leroi-Gourhan, A. *The Dawn of European Art: An Introduction to Palaeolithic Cave Painting*. Cambridge: Cambridge University Press, 1982.

Sieveking, A. *The Cave Artists*. London: Thames and Hudson, 1979.

Ucko, P.J. and Rosenfeld, A. *Palaeolithic Cave Art*. London: World University Library, 1967.

Subsistence – a key to the past
(pp. 365–8)

Binford, L.R. *In Pursuit of the Past: Decoding the Archaeological Record*. London: Thames and Hudson, 1983.

Binford, L.R. The hunting hypothesis, archaeological methods, and the past. *Yearbook of Physical Anthropology* 30: 1–9 (1988). (Reprinted in Binford, L.R. *Debating Archaeology*, pp. 282–90. New York: Academic Press, 1990.)

Binford, L.R. Mobility, housing, and environment: a comparative study. *Journal of Archaeological Research* 46: 119–52 (1990).

Dahlberg, F. (ed.). *Woman the Gatherer*. New Haven, CT: Yale University Press, 1981.

Harris, D.R. and Hillman, G.C. (eds). *Foraging and Farming: The Evolution of Plant Exploitation*. London: Unwin Hyman, 1989.

Isaac, G.Ll. The food-sharing behavior of protohuman hominids. *Scientific American* 238 (April): 90–106 (1978).

Lee, R.B. and DeVore, I. (eds). *Man the Hunter*. Chicago: Aldine, 1968.

Nitecki, M.H. and Nitecki, D.V. *The Evolution of Human Hunting*. New York: Plenum Press, 1987.

Tooby, J. and DeVore, I. The reconstruction of hominid behavioral evolution through strategic modeling. In *The Evolution of Human Behavior: Primate Models* (ed. W.G. Kinzey), pp. 183–237. Albany: State University of New York Press, 1987.

Trinkaus, E. (ed.). *The Emergence of Modern Humans: Biocultural Adaptations in the Later Pleistocene*. Cambridge: Cambridge University Press, 1989.

Reconstructing prehistoric diet
(pp. 369–72)

Brothwell, D.R. and Higgs, E. (eds). *Science in Archaeology*. London: Thames and Hudson; New York: Basic Books, 1969.

Huss-Ashmore, R. *et al*. Nutritional inference from paleopathology. In *Advances in Archaeological Method and Theory*, Vol. 5 (ed. M. Shiffer), pp. 395–473. New York: Academic Press, 1982.

Lee, R.B. What hunters do for a living, or, how to make out on scarce resources. In *Man the Hunter* (eds R.B. Lee and I. DeVore), pp.30–48. Chicago: Aldine, 1968.

Lee-Thorp, J.A. *et al*. Isotopic evidence for dietary differences between two extinct

baboon species from Swartkrans. *Journal of Human Evolution* 18: 183–90 (1989).

Schoeninger, M.J. and De Niro, M.J. Nitrogen and carbon isotopic composition of bone collagen from marine and terrestrial animals. *Geochimica et Cosmochimica Acta* 48:625–39 (1984).

Sealy, J.C. and van der Merwe, N.J. Isotope assessment and the seasonal-mobility hypothesis in the southwestern Cape of South Africa. *Current Anthropology* 27:135–50 (1986).

Sillen, A.G. and Kavanagh, M. Strontium and paleodietary research: a review. *Yearbook of Physical Anthropology* 15: 67–90 (1982).

van der Merwe, N.J. Carbon isotopes, photosynthesis, and archaeology. *American Scientist* 70: 596–606 (1982).

Wing, E.S. and Brown, A.G. *Paleonutrition: Method and Theory in Prehistoric Foodways*. New York: Academic Press, 1978.

Origins of agriculture (pp. 373–9)

Cohen, M.N. *The Food Crisis in Prehistory: Overpopulation and the Origins of Agriculture*. New Haven, CT: Yale University Press, 1977.

Flannery, K.V. The origins of agriculture. *Annual Review of Anthropology* 2: 271–310 (1973).

Gebauer, A.B. and Douglas Price, T. (eds). *Transitions to Agriculture in Prehistory* (Monographs in World Archaeology No. 4). Madison, WI: Prehistory Press, 1972.

Grigg, D.B. *The Agricultural Systems of the World: An Evolutionary Approach*. Cambridge: Cambridge University Press, 1974.

Harlan, J.R. *Crops and Man*. Madison, WI: American Society of Agronomy/Crop Science Society of America, 1975.

Harlan, J.R. *et al*. (eds). *Origins of African Plant Domestication*. The Hague: Mouton, 1976.

Harris, D.R. and Hillman, G.C. (eds). *Foraging and Farming: The Evolution of Plant Exploitation*. London: Unwin Hyman, 1989.

Heiser, C.B. Jr. *Seed to Civilization: The Story of Food*, 2nd edn. San Francisco: W.H. Freeman, 1981.

McCorriston, J. and Hole, F. The ecology and seasonal stress and the origins of agriculture in the Near East. *American Anthropologist* 93: 46–69 (1991).

Rambo, A.T. and Sajise, P.E. (eds). *An Introduction to Human Ecology Research on Agricultural Systems in Southwest Asia*. Los Banos: University of the Philippines, 1984.

Reed, C.A. (ed.). *Origins of Agriculture*. The Hague: Mouton, 1977.

Rindos, D. *The Origins of Agriculture: An Evolutionary Perspective*. New York: Academic Press, 1984.

Simmonds, N.W. *Evolution of Crop Plants*. London: Longman, 1976.

Smith, B.D. Origins of agriculture in eastern North America. *Science* 246: 1566–71 (1989).

Ucko, P.J. and Dimbleby, G.W. (eds). *The Domestication and Exploitation of Plants and Animals*. London: Duckworth, 1969.

Vietmeyer, N. Lesser-known plants of potential use in agriculture and forestry. *Science* 232: 1379–84 (1986).

Zohary, D. and Hopf, M. *Domestication of Plants in the Old World*, 2nd edn. Oxford: Clarendon Press, 1993.

Domestication of animals (pp. 380-385)

Bökönyi, S. *History of Domestic Mammals in*

Central and Eastern Europe. Budapest: Akadémiai Kiadó, 1974.

Clark, J.D. and Brandt, S.A. (eds). *From Hunters to Farmers: The Causes and Consequences of Food Production in Africa*. Berkeley: University of California Press, 1984.

Clutton-Brock, J. *A Natural History of Domesticated Mammals*. London: British Museum (Natural History)/ Cambridge: Cambridge University Press, 1987.

Clutton-Brock, J. *The British Museum Book of Cats Ancient and Modern*. London: British Museum Publications, 1988.

Clutton-Brock, J. (ed.). *The Walking Larder: Patterns of Domestication, Pastoralism, and Predation*. London: Unwin Hyman, 1989.

Clutton-Brock, J. and Grigson, C. (eds). *Animals and Archaeology: 3. Early Herders and Their Flocks*. Oxford: British Archaeological Reports (International Series No. 202), 1984.

Davis, S.J.M. *The Archaeology of Animals*. London: Batsford, 1987.

Harris, D.R. (ed.). *Human Ecology in Savanna Environments*. London: Academic Press, 1980.

Hemmer, H. *Domestication: the Decline of Environmental Appreciation*. Cambridge: Cambridge University Press, 1990.

Ingold, T. *Hunters, Pastoralists and Ranchers*. Cambridge: Cambridge University Press, 1980.

Khazanov, A.M. *Nomads and the Outside World*. Cambridge: Cambridge University Press, 1983.

Mason, I.L. (ed.). *Evolution of Domesticated Animals*. Harlow, Essex: Longman, 1984.

Ucko, P.J. and Dimbleby, G.W. (eds). *The Domestication and Exploitation of Plants and Animals*. London: Duckworth, 1969.

Zeuner, F.E. *A History of Domesticated Animals*. London: Hutchinson, 1963.

Human populations, past and present

The dispersion of modern humans
(pp. 389–401)

Bowles, G.T. *The People of Asia*. London: Weidenfeld and Nicolson, 1977.

Coon, C.S. *The Origin of Races*. New York: Knopf, 1962.

Coon, C.S. *Racial Adaptations: A Study of the Origins, Nature and Significance of Racial Variations in Humans*. Chicago: Nelson Hall, 1982.

Delson, E. (ed.). *Ancestors: The Hard Evidence*. New York: Alan R. Liss, 1985.

Hiernaux, J. *The People of Africa*. London: Weidenfeld and Nicolson, 1974.

Howells, W. *The Pacific Islanders*. London: Weidenfeld and Nicolson, 1973.

Kirk, R. and Szathmary, E. (eds). *Out of Asia: Peopling the Americas and the Pacific*. Canberra: Australian National University, 1985.

Mellars, P. and Stringer, C. (eds). *The Human Revolution: Behavioural and Biological Perspectives on the Origins of Modern Humans*. Edinburgh: Edinburgh University Press, 1989; Princeton: Princeton University Press, 1990.

Mourant, A.E. *Blood Relations: Blood Groups*

and Anthropology. Oxford: Oxford University Press, 1983.

Smith, F.H. and Spencer, F. (eds). *The Origins of Modern Humans: A World Survey of the Fossil Evidence*. New York: Alan R. Liss, 1984.

Stewart, T.D. *The People of America*. London: Weidenfeld and Nicolson, 1972.

Stringer, C. The Asian connection. *New Scientist* 17 November: 33–7 (1990).

Stringer, C. The emergence of modern humans. *Scientific American* 263 (December): 68–74 (1990).

Thorne, A.G. and Wolpoff, M.H. The multiregional evolution of humans. *Scientific American* 266 (April): 28–33 (1992).

Tobias, P.V. (ed.). *Hominid Evolution: Past, Present and Future*. New York: Alan R. Liss, 1985.

Trinkaus, E. (ed.). *The Emergence of Modern Humans: Biocultural Adaptations in the Later Pleistocene*. Cambridge: Cambridge University Press, 1989.

Wilson, A.C. and Cann, R.L. Th recent African genesis of humans. *Scientific American* 266 (April): 22–7 (1992).

The peopling of the Pacific (p. 394)
Bellwood, P. The Austronesian dispersal and the origin of languages. *Scientific American* 265 (July): 70–5 (1991).

Hill, A.V.S. and Serjeantson, S.W. (eds). *The Colonisation of the Pacific: A Genetic Trail*. Oxford: Clarendon Press, 1989.

Genes and language (pp. 398–9)
Cavalli-Sforza, L.L. Genes, peoples and language. *Scientific American* 265 (November): 72–8 (1991).

Lewin, R. Ancestral voices at war. *New Scientist* 16 June: 42–5 (1990).

Ross, P.E. Hard words. *Scientific American* 264 (April): 71–9 (1991)

Fossil DNA (p. 401)
Cherfas, J. Ancient DNA: still busy after death. *Science* 253: 1354–6 (1991)

Ross, P.E. Trends in molecular archaeology: eloquent remains. *Scientific American* 266 (May): 72–81 (1992).

Pääbo, S. Ancient DNA. *Scientific American* 269 (November): 60–6 (1993).

Reconstructing ancient populations
(pp. 402–5)

Bender, B. From gatherer-hunter to farmer: a social perspective. *World Archaeology* 10: 204–22 (1978).

Binford, L.R. Post-Pleistocene adaptations. In *New Perspectives in Archaeology* (eds S.R. Binford and L.R. Binford), pp. 313–41. Chicago: Aldine, 1968.

Cohen, M. *The Food Crisis in Pre-history: Overpopulation and the Origins of Agriculture*. New Haven, CT: Yale University Press, 1977.

Hassan, F.A. *Demographic Archaeology*. London: Academic Press, 1981.

Howell, N. Feedbacks and buffers in relation to scarcity and abundance: studies of hunter-gatherer populations. In *The State of Population Theory* (eds D. Coleman and R. Schofield), pp. 154–87. Oxford: Basil Blackwell, 1986.

Menken, J. *et al*. The nutrition-fertility link: an evaluation of the evidence. *Journal of Inter-Disciplinary History* 16: 425–42 (1981).

Wobst, H.M. Locational relationships in Palaeolithic society. In *The Demographic*

Evolution of Human Populations (eds R.H. Ward and K.M. Weiss), pp. 49–58. London: Academic Press, 1976.

Human populations before agriculture
(pp. 406–10)

Acsadi, G. and Nemeskeri, J. *History of Human Life Span and Mortality*. Budapest: Akadémiai Kiadó, 1970.

Black, F.L. Infectious disease in primitive societies. *Science* 187: 515–18 (1975).

Clark, J.D. *The Prehistory of Africa*. London: Thames and Hudson; New York: Praeger, 1970.

Dumond, D.E. The limitation of human population: a natural history. *Science* 187: 713–20 (1975).

Lee, R.B. and DeVore, I. (eds). *Man the Hunter*. Chicago: Aldine, 1968.

Lovejoy, C.O. *et al*. Paleodemography of the Libben site, Ottawa County, Ohio. *Science* 198: 291–3 (1977).

Neel, J.V. and Chagnon, N.A. The demography of two tribes of primitive, relatively unacculturated American Indians. *Proceedings of the National Academy of Sciences, USA* 59: 680–9 (1968).

Ward, R.H. and Weiss, K.M. *The Demographic Evolution of Human Populations*. London: Academic Press, 1976.

People and disease (pp. 411–20)

Anderson, R.M. and May, R.M. *Infectious Diseases of Humans: Dynamics and Control*. Oxford: Oxford University Press, 1991.

Anderson, R.M. and May, R.M. Understanding the AIDS pandemic. *Scientific American* 266 (May): 20–6 (1992).

Black, F.L. Infectious diseases in primitive societies. *Science* 187: 515–18 (1975).

Brookmeyer, R. Reconstruction and future trends of the AIDS epidemic in the United States. *Science* 253: 37–42 (1991).

Burnet, M. and White, D.O. *Natural History of Infectious Disease*. Cambridge: Cambridge University Press, 1972.

Fenner, F. Biological control, as exemplified by smallpox eradication and myxomatosis. *Proceedings of the Royal Society of London Series B* 218: 259–85 (1983).

Gottfried, R.S. *The Black Death*. London: Macmillan, 1984.

Hopkins, D.R. *Princes and Peasants: Smallpox in History*. Chicago: University of Chicago Press, 1983.

Lambrecht, F. Trypanosomes and hominid evolution. *Bioscience* 35: 640–6 (1985).

Latham, M.C. Nutrition and infection in national development. *Science* 188: 561–5 (1975).

McEvedy, C. The bubonic plague. *Scientific American* 258 (February): 74–9 (1988).

McNeill, W.H. *Plagues and People*. New York: Anchor Press/Doubleday, 1976.

Zinsser, H. *Rats, Lice and History*. Boston: Little, Brown, 1935.

Trends in population growth (pp. 421–4)

Arriaga, E.E. Changing trends in mortality decline during the last decades. In *Differential Mortality* (eds L.Ruzicka *et al*.), pp. 105–30. Oxford: Oxford University Press, 1989.

Bongaarts, J. and Potter, R.G. *Fertility, Biology and Behavior: An Analysis of the Proximate Determinants*. London: Academic Press, 1983.

Caldwell, J.C. Routes to low mortality in poor countries. *Population and Development Review* 12: 171–220 (1986).

Caldwell, J.C. and Caldwell, P. High fertility in sub-Saharan Africa. *Scientific American* 262 (May): 82–9 (1990).

Coleman, D.C. and Schofield, R.S. *The State of Population Theory*. Oxford: Basil Blackwell, 1986.

Cox, P.R. *Demography*, 5th edn. Cambridge: Cambridge University Press, 1976.

Durand, J.D. Historical estimates of world population: an evaluation. *Population and Development Review* 3: 253–96 (1977).

Keyfitz, N. The growing human population. *Scientific American* 261 (September): 70–77A (1989).

Landers, J. and Reynolds, V. *Fertility and Resources*. Cambridge: Cambridge University Press, 1990.

McNicoll, G. Consequences of rapid population growth: an overview and assessment. *Population and Development Review* 10: 177–240 (1984).

Riley, J.C. *Sickness, Recovery and Death*. London: Macmillan, 1989.

Scientific American. *The Human Population*. San Francisco: W.H. Freeman, 1984.

Fertility control: past, present and future
(pp. 425–32)

Aitken, J. and Paterson, M. New horizons in contraception. *Nature* 335: 492–3 (1988).

Baird, D.T. The use of antigestagens in fertility regulation. *British Journal of Family Planning* 13: 11–13 (1988).

Fraser, H.M. *et al.* LHRH analogues for female contraception. In *LHRH and its Analogues in Gynaecological Practise* (eds R.W. Shaw and J.C. Marshall), pp. 214–32. London: Butterworths, 1989.

Loudon, N. *Handbook of Family Planning*. Edinburgh: Churchill Livingstone, 1990.

McLaren, A. *A History of Contraception: From Antiquity to the Present Day*. Oxford: Basil Blackwell, 1990.

Potts, M. and Diggory, P. *Textbook of Contraceptive Practice*, 2nd edn. Cambridge: Cambridge University Press, 1983.

World Health Organization Task Force for the Regulation of Male Fertility. Contraceptive efficacy of testosterone-induced azoospermia in normal men. *Lancet* 336: 955–9 (1990).

Wu, F.C.W. Male contraception: current status and future prospects. *Clinical Endocrinology* 29: 443–65 (1988).

Developments in fertility treatments
(pp. 430–1)

Edwards, R.G. *Life Before Birth: Reflections on the Embryo Debate*. London: Hutchinson, 1989.

Edwards, R.G. Assisted human conception. *British Medical Bulletin* 46: 1–864 (1990).

Fredericks, C.M. *et al. Foundations of In Vitro Fertilization: Reproduction Health Technology*. Washington, DC: Hemisphere, 1987.

Hargreave, T.B. *Male Infertility*. Berlin: Springer-Verlag, 1983.

Matson, P.L. and Lieberman, B.A. *Current Views in Assisted Reproduction: Clinical IVF Forum*. Manchester: Manchester University Press, 1990.

Tribal peoples in the modern world
(pp. 433–7)

Bodley, J. *Victims of Progress*, 2nd edn. Menlo Park, CA: Benjamin Cummings, 1982.

Burger, J. *Report from the Frontier: the State of the World's Indigenous Peoples*. London: Zed Press, 1988.

Burger, J. *The Gaia Atlas of First Peoples: A Future for the Indigenous World*. London: Gaia Books/Robertson McCarta, 1990.

Denselow, J.S. and Padoch, C. (eds). *Peoples of the Tropical Rainforest*. Berkeley and Los Angeles: University of California Press, 1987.

Moody, R. (ed.). *The Indigenous Voice: Visions and Realities* (2 vols). London: Zed Press, 1988.

Reader, J. *Man on Earth*. London: Collins, 1988 (published in paperback by Penguin Books, 1990).

Three organisations that publish on tribal peoples:

- The International Workgroup on Indigenous Affairs (IWGIA) (Copenhagen).
- Survival International (London).
- Cultural Survival (Cambridge, Massachusetts).

Appendix I: Who's who of historical figures (pp. 446–53)

Short biographies are included in R. Milner, *The Encyclopedia of Evolution: Humanity's Search for its Origins* (New York: Facts On File, 1990). See also:

Cole, S. *Leakey's Luck: The Life of Louis Seymour Bazett Leakey, 1903–1972*. London: Collins, 1975.

Dart, R.A. *Adventures with the Missing Link*. London: Hamish Hamilton, 1959.

Desmond, A. and Moore, J. *Darwin*. London: Michael Joseph, 1991; New York: Warner Books, 1992.

Findlay, G. *Dr Robert Broom, F.R.S.: Palaeontologist and Physician, 1866–1951*. Cape Town: Balkema, 1972.

Leakey, R.E. *One Life: An Autobiography*. London: Michael Joseph, 1983.

Lewin, R. *Bones of Contention: Controversies in the Search for Human Origins*. New York: Simon and Schuster, 1987; London: Penguin Books, 1991.

Sigmon, B.A. and Cybulski, J.S. (eds). *Homo erectus: Papers in Honor of Davidson Black*. Toronto: University of Toronto Press, 1981.

Spencer, F. (ed.). *A History of American Physical Anthropology, 1930–1980*. New York: Academic Press, 1982.

Spencer, F. *Piltdown: A Scientific Forgery*. London and Oxford: Natural History Museum Publications/Oxford University Press, 1990.

Theunissen, B. *Eugène Dubois and the Ape-Man from Java: the History of the First 'Missing Link' and Its Discoverer*. Dordrecht: Kluwer, 1989.

Tobias, P.V. Piltdown: an appraisal of the case against Sir Arthur Keith. *Current Anthropology* 33: 243–93 (1992).

Trinkaus, E. and Shipman, P. *The Neandertals: Changing the Image of Mankind*. London: Cape, 1993.

Index

Page numbers followed by 'g' refer to definitions in the Glossary; page numbers in italics refer to information given only in an illustration or caption.

M

Acknowledgements

The editors and publishers gratefully acknowledge the help of many individuals and organisations in the preparation of this volume. They include John Barry; Simon Bearder; Elaine Bimpson; Jon C. Caldwell; Cambridge University Library; The Museum of Mankind, London; Jane M. Renfrew; Mary D. Russell; Survival International; Jeremy and Marcia Weston; and the World Health Organization. The executive editor especially thanks Peter Toye and John Bunney for technical support, and Rose Stafford-Fraser for assistance with the artwork acknowledgements.

Bold type indicates page numbers and positions of illustrations.

Original illustrations by: Priscilla Barrett, **25**; Jo Cameron, **24**, **26**, **56**, **57**, **58**, **59**, **78**, **86**, **87**, **88**, **89**, **104**, **109**, **110**, **115**, **117*bl***, **118*b***, **119**, **121**, **123**, **129**, **132**, **134**, **135**, **225**, **226**, **228**, **236**, **237**, **238**, **241**, **242*br***, **244**, **247*br***, **249**, **251**, **340**, **343*t***, **346**, **347**, **348**, **425**, **429**, **430**, **431**, **458**, **460**, **461**, **464**, **465**, **466**, **467**, **470**, **471**; Alison Marshall, **76**, **77**, **78**, **80**, **81**, **95*tr***, **129**, **132**, **200**, **201*l***, **204*b***, **211**, **215**, **218**, **221**, **222**; Anne-Elise Martin, **18**, **42**. Maps and other artwork by Swanston Graphics.

Every effort has been made to obtain permission to use the copyright material listed below; the publishers apologise for any errors or omissions and would welcome these being brought to their attention.

Photographs: **i**, reproduced by courtesy of *Punch*; **ii**, Nancy Burson; **xiv**, **196**, **226**, **362*bl***, **397*b***, © Richard Leakey/photo by Peter Kain; **6**, M.F. Perutz, MRC Laboratory of Molecular Biology; **9**, **448*t***, The Library, University College London; **14*l***, Martin Dohrn/Science Photo Library; **14*r***, CNRI/Science Photo Library; **27*tl***, Konrad Wothe/Bruce Coleman Ltd; **27*tr***, **63**, David Curl/Oxford Scientific Films; **27*bl***, Liz Bomford/Ardea, London; **27*br***, Alan Root/Survival Anglia; **28*l***, **32*l***, **218*b***, **351**, **390**(***no. 2***), 391(***nos. 7***, ***11***), **435**(***San***), Gerald Cubitt; **28*r***, Tony Beamish/Ardea, London; **29*r***, David Chivers/Anthro-Photo File; **29*l***, **30*bl***, Rod Williams/Bruce Coleman Ltd; **30*tl***, Ranka Sekulic/Anthro-Photo File; **30*r***, Francois Gohier/Ardea, London; **31**, © Orion Press/Natural History Photographic Agency; **32*r***, **152**, Mike Birkhead/Oxford Scientific Films; **34*t***, Andrew Young; **34*b***, **35*t***, **214*t***, Russell A. Mittermeier; **35*b***, Chris Terrill/BBC; **37**, **151*t***, photo by Philip Coffey/Jersey Wildlife Preservation Trust; **38**, James Moore/Anthro-Photo File; **43*t***, Gerald Cubitt/Bruce Coleman, Ltd; **43*bl***, © Mantis Wildlife Films/Oxford Scientific Films; **43*bc***, **151*b***, Jim Clare/© Partridge Films Ltd/Oxford Scientific Films; **43*br***, Guy Yeoman/Biofotos; **50**, **285*tr***, **390**(***no. 13***), **391**(***no. 8***), **435**(***Saami***), **436**, © Bryan & Cherry Alexander; **51**, © Ole Bernt Frøshaug Samfoto/Link Picture Library; **52*l***, S.D. Halperin/Animals Animals/Oxford Scientific Films; **52*r***, © Jean-Paul Ferrero/Ardea, London; **59**, Christopher Dean; **62**, J.O. Caldecott; **66**, Joanna Van Gruisen/Ardea, London; **67*l***, **67*r***, Kenneth E. Glander; **68**, **146**, Richard Wrangham/Anthro-Photo File; **70*l***, Borys Malkin/Anthro-Photo File; **70*r***, Hanbury-Tenison/Robert Harding Picture Library; **71**, **72**, **73*t***, D.R. Harris; **73*b***, Katherine Wright; **74**, Iraq Museum, Baghdad; **82**, **83**, reproduced with permission from R. McNeill Alexander, *Animal Movement*, Carolina Biology Reader Series, No. 164. Copyright 1985, Carolina Biological Supply Co., Burlington, North Carolina; **93**, courtesy of John Vince and R. Dryden, photo by R. Dryden; **97**, Ron Giling/Panos Pictures; **103**, J.M. Tanner; **106**, **233*b***, **235**, **237**, **325**, **329*tl***, ***endpapers***, John Reader/Science Photo Library; **113**, John Henry Fuseli, *The Nightmare*, Freien Deutschen Hochstift-Frankfurter Goethe-Museum, photo by Ursula Edelmann; **120**, courtesy of Brigham & Women's Hospital, Boston, Mass.; **122**, **362*br***, **363**, Jean Vertut; **139**, **140**, **141**, Language Project, Emory University; **142**, **148*b***, A.H. Harcourt/Anthro-Photo File; **147**, **149*c***, **153**, Robin Dunbar; **148*t***, Sarah Blaffer Hrdy/Anthro-Photo File; **149*t***, **162*r***, **164*l***, **344**, **391**(***no. 10***), **403**, Irven DeVore/Anthro-Photo File; **149*b***, Paul Mattsson/Impact Photos; **158**, © R.W. Sussman; **160**, courtesy of Toshikazu Hasegawa; **161**, © Stephen Dalton/Natural History Photographic Agency; **162*l***, Erwin & Peggy Bauer/Bruce Coleman Ltd; **164*tr***, C. Hughes/Hutchison Library; **164*br***, Ian Hepburn; **165**, Nigel Luckhurst; **166**, Ian Gibson/Robert Harding Picture Library; **176**, Peter Parks/Oxford Scientific Films; **182**, courtesy of Tony Hurford, The London Fission Track Research Group; **183**, National Museum of Wales; **188*t***, **188*b***, **449*br***, A.K. Behrensmeyer; **193**, **194*t***, P. Andrews; **194*c***, Robin Buxton/Animals Animals/Oxford Scientific Films; **194*b***, Robin Buxton/Oxford Scientific Films; **195**, Ardea, London; **202*t***, All rights reserved, Photo Archives, Denver Museum of Natural History; **202*b***, The Carnegie Museum of Natural History; **205*t***, J.G. Fleagle; **207**, Lee Boltin; **214*b***, © Stephen F. Ferrari/Anthro-Photo File; **218*t***, © Partridge Productions Ltd/Oxford Scientific Films; **221**, **222**, Eric Delson; **227**, © David Pilbeam; **232**, **446*r***, © Transvaal Museum, photo by J.F. Thackeray; **233*t***, © Transvaal Museum, photo by C.K. Brain; **234*t***, Institute of Human Origins, photo by Donald C. Johanson; **234*b***, **244*l***, © National Museums of Kenya, photo by Alan Walker; **243**, **248*t***, © Natural History Museum, London; **244*r***, **245*r***, **400**, **401**, © Chris Stringer; **245*l***, J.D. Clark; **246**, courtesy of Wu Xinzhi; **248*b***, **249**, © Chris Stringer/Musée de l'Homme, Paris; **252**, **285*b***, Biophoto Associates/Science Photo Library; **261**, courtesy of Texas Children's Hospital, Baylor College of Medicine; **262**, David Whitehouse; **264**, **441**, **449*t***, **450*b***, **451*t***, **451*bl***, **452*r***, Mary Evans Picture Library; **267**, courtesy of Cellmark Diagnostics, Blacklands Way, Abingdon Business Park, Abingdon, Oxon; **274**, **275**, **280**, Joy D.A. Delhanty; **282**, Frances Furlong/Survival Anglia Photo Library; **285*l***, **322**, John Reader; **288**, courtesy of Douglas Oram; **291**, Jackie Lewin, Royal Free Hospital/Science Photo Library; **292**, courtesy of Pharmacia Biosystems Ltd; **317**, Biophoto Associates; **328**, **329*bl***, **336*r***, © Glynn Isaac; **329*tr***, Andrew Hill; **329*br***, **331**, Richard Potts; **330*t***, **361*r***, **362*t***, Paul Bahn; **330*b***, photo: T. White, *Current Anthropology* 32 (1991), University of Chicago Press; **336*l***, © photo by James O'Connell; **337**, **342*t***, Ch. Boesch; **342*b***, James Moore/Anthro-Photo File; **345**, courtesy of Bar-Yosef/Expedition Archives; **347**, Institute of Human Origins; **350**, © N. Toth & K. Schick; **358**, from *A Voyage Round the World 1785–8*, vol. 3, 2nd edn (1799), by permission of the Syndics of the Cambridge University Library; **359**, courtesy of J.D. Muke; **360**, **383**, **417*b***, reproduced by permission of the Trustees of the British Museum; **361*l***, W.E. Wendt; **365**, L.R. Binford; **367*l***, courtesy of Istituto Italiano di Paleontologia Umana/photo by A. Guebhard; **367*r***, courtesy of Geoff Bailey; **368*tl***, courtesy of Museum of Anthropology, University of British Columbia; **368*tr***, courtesy of Museo Territorial de Ushuaia, Argentina; **368*b***, Hillard Kaplan; **369**, H.J. Deacon; **370**, courtesy of the Museum of the American Indian; **372**, courtesy of the Dept of Biological Anthropology, University of Cambridge/photo: Gwil Owen; **375**, A-Z Botanical Collection; **377**, Ann Butler; **378*l***, courtesy of the Centre de Recherche Français de Jerusalem (CNRS); **378*r***, courtesy of Jack Golson/photo: C.H.L. Ballard; **379*t***, © Okapia/Oxford Scientific Films; **379*b***, photo: Frank Hole; **381*t***, © Edwin Sadd/Oxford Scientific Films; **381*b***, Eric & David Hosking; **384**, courtesy Simon Davis/*Nature*; **385**, Tony Morrison/South American Pictures; **386**, H.L. Pierce Fund, courtesy, Museum of Fine Arts, Boston; **390**(***no. 1***), **424**, Sean Sprague/Panos Pictures; **390**(***no. 3***), Juliet Highet/Hutchison Library; **390**(***no. 4***), Bernard Gerard; **390**(***no. 5***), Christopher Tordai/Hutchison Library; **390**(***no. 6***), Brian Mozer/Hutchison Library; **390**(***no. 12***), Julio Etchart/Panos Pictures; **391**(***no. 9***), © Steve Benbow/Impact Photos; **397*t***, Chris Stringer/Institut de Paléontologie Humaine, Paris; **397*c***, courtesy of Professor P.V. Tobias/photo by P.M. Fauqust; **404**, Melvin T. Konner/Anthro-Photo File; **406**, R. Feinberg; **409**, Peter Frey/Survival International; **410**, R.S. Meindl; **414**, courtesy of A. Dobson; **417*t***, courtesy of the Boston Athenaeum; **422**, Jyoti M. Banerjee/Fotomedia; **424**, Sean Sprague 1986/Panos Pictures; **430**, Petit Format/CSI/Science Photo Library; **431*l***,***r***, © Dr Simon Fishel, NURTURE (Nottingham University Research and Treatment Unit in Reproduction), Department of Obstetrics & Gynaecology, Nottingham NG7 2UH; **433**, R. Berriedale-Johnson/Panos Pictures; **434**(***S.A. Indian***), Barys Malkin/Anthro-Photo File; **434**(***Pygmies***), © Nick Robinson/Panos Pictures; **434**(***N.A. Indian***), © Luke Holland/Survival International; **434**(***African nomad***), Jeremy Hartley/Panos Pictures; **435**(***Maori***), Annie Price/Survival Anglia; **435**(***Pacific***), Nigel Smith/Hutchison Library; **435**(***Asian nomad***), B. Moser/Granada TV/Hutchison Library; **435**(***Arctic***), Masahiro Iijima/Ardea, London; **435**(***Philippines***), Ron Giling/Panos Pictures; **435**(***India***), Survival International; **437*l***, Phil Ward/Frank Lane Picture Agency; **437*r***, Susan Cunningham/Panos Pictures; **438**, Francis Leroy, Biocosmos/Science Photo Library; **444**, Juliet Highet/Life File; **446*l***, © Musée de l'Homme, Paris; **447*tl***, courtesy of the Bernard Price Institute for Palaeontological Research, University of the Witwatersrand; **447*tr***, © National Museum of the Natural History, Leiden, The Netherlands; **447*b***, National Portrait Gallery, London; **448*b***, Natural History Museum, London; **449*bl***, neg. no. 123929 & **452*l***, neg. no. 334101, courtesy Department of Library Services, American Museum of Natural History; **450*tl***, courtesy of Natur-Museum, Forschungsinstitut Senckenberg; **450*tr***, courtesy of *New Scientist*/© News Chronicle; **451*br***, Science Photo Library; **453*A***, from F. Weidenreich, 'The Skull of *Sinanthropus pekinensis*' in Palaeontologica Sinica, Series D, no. 10, 1943, fig. 19.

Artwork: **10**, courtesy of I. Geis; **11*c***, ***r***, from 'Mapping Our Genes' (US Congress, © Office of Technology Assessment), figs 2.1, 2.2; 13, *ibid.*, fig. 2.3; 16, from M.W. Strickberger, *Evolution* (Jones & Bartlett, 1990), figs 21–3; **24**, after M. Cartmill, in *Primate Locomotion*, ed. F.A. Jenkins Jr (Academic Press, 1974), pp. 45–84, fig. 1; **26*br***, from R.D. Martin, *Primate Origins and Evolution* (Chapman & Hall, 1990), fig. 6.16a; **34*tr***, after J.G. Fleagle, *Primate Adaptation and Evolution* (Academic Press, 1988), fig. 4.1; ***cr***, *ibid.*, figs 5.2, 6.2; ***br***, *ibid.*, fig. 7.1; **41**, K. Schmidt-Nielsen, *Scaling: Why is Animal Size so Important?* (CUP, 1984), fig. 6.1; **45*tl***, from J. Garrow and S. Blaza, in *Human Nutrition*, ed. A. Neuberger & T.H. Jukes (MTP, 1982), pp. 1–22, table 2; ***tr***, from M.A. Holliday, in *Human Growth*, ed. F. Falkner & J.M. Tanner (Plenum Press, 1986), pp. 101–18, fig. 8 [after Holliday, 1971]; ***bl***, after D.R. Wilkie, in *Scale Effects in Animal Locomotion*, ed. T.J. Pedley (Academic Press, 1977), pp. 233–6, fig. 5; **47*t***, from D.F. Roberts, in *American Journal of Physical Anthropology* (1953) 11: 533–8, fig. 2; ***c***, from G.A. Harrison *et al.*, *Human Biology*, 3rd edn (OUP, 1988), fig. 22.5 [after Robinson *et al.*, in Belding, 1943]; **48**, after G.E. Folk, *Textbook of Environmental Physiology*, 2nd edn (Lea & Febiger, 1974), fig. 6.15; **49**, from Harrison *et al.* (1988), fig. 21.6 [after Baker & Daniels, 1956]; **50**, *ibid.*, fig. 21.9; **53**, after M. Pickford, in *Human Evolution* (1986) 1:77–90, fig. 4; **54**, from P.H. Harvey and P.M. Bennett, *Human Sexual Dimorphism*, ed. J. Ghesquiere *et al.*, (Taylor & Francis, 1985), pp. 43–59, fig. 7; **57*l***, after J.W. Osborn (ed.), *Dental Anatomy and Embryology* (Blackwell, 1981), p. 372; **58**, from L. Aiello & C. Dean, *An Introduction to Human Evolutionary Anatomy* (Academic Press, 1990), fig. 5.9; from P. Andrews & C. Stringer, *Human Evolution* (BM(NH), 1989), p. 10; after Aiello & Dean (1990), fig. 5.5; after G.C. Conroy, *Primate Evolution* (Norton, 1990), pp. 306, 307; after R.G. Klein, *The Human Career* (U. Chicago Press, 1989), fig. 3.24; after A. Walker & P. Andrews, in *Nature* (1973) 244: 313–4, figs 2, 4; **62**, D. Chivers; **69**, from C.B. Heiser, *Seed to Civilization*, 2nd edn (W.H. Freeman, 1981), fig. 3.2; **71**, from D.L. Hardesty, *Ecological Anthropology* (J. Wiley, 1977), fig. 3.1; **75**, from Martin (1990), fig. 10.1 [artist: A.-E. Martin]; **76**, after Conroy (1990), fig. 2.15; after Fleagle (1988), fig. 8.14; **77**, *ibid.*, fig. 3.8; **78**, from Aiello & Dean (1990), figs 12.4, 15.1; from Conroy (1990), fig. 6.32; from Klein (1989), fig. 3.3; from Martin (1990), fig. 10.21c, d; after B.A. Wood, *The Evolution of Modern Man* (Peter Lowe, 1976), p. 39; **79**, from Fleagle (1988), fig. 15.12 [artist: J. Sept]; **84*cl***, after R. Margaria, *Biomechanics and Energetics of Muscular Exercise* (OUP, 1976), fig. 3.7; data adapted from D.F. Hoyt & C.R. Taylor, in *Nature* (1981) 292: 239–40, fig. 2; ***tr***, data adapted from C.R. Taylor *et al.*, in *Journal of Experimental Biology* (1982) 97: 1–21; **86**, from Martin (1990), fig. 9.12; **87**, J.R. Napier & P.H. Napier, *The Natural History of the Primates* (BM(NH) & CUP, 1985), fig. 3.37; **88*c***, from Aiello & Dean (1990), fig. 20.15; ***tr***, *ibid.*, figs 20.18, 20.27 [after R.G. Tague and O. Lovejoy, in *Journal of Human Evolution* (1986) 15: 237–55, figs 1–3]; **89*tl***, from Martin (1990), fig. 9.5, with the permission of the Zoological Society of London and Academic Press; ***tc-r***, from Martin (1990), fig. 9.6; ***bl-r***, *ibid.*, fig. 9.7; **91**, A.F. Dixson; **92**, from

D.C. Turner, *General Endocrinology* (W.B. Saunders, 1960), fig. 1–2; **95*tr***, after P.H. Harvey *et al.*, in *Primate Societies*, ed. B. Smuts *et al.* (U. Chicago Press, 1987), pp. 181–96, fig. 16.1; ***bl***, courtesy of R.D. Martin; **98**, from J.M. Tanner, *Growth at Adolescence*, 2nd edn (Blackwell Scientific Publications, 1962), fig. 1 [R.E. Scammon, 1927]; **99**, *ibid.*, fig. 4 [R.E. Scammon, 1930a]; **100**, *ibid.*, fig. 49 [after E.C. MacDowell *et al.*, 1927; after L. Butler & J.D. Metrakos, 1950; after E.T. Engle & J. Rosasco, 1927], fig. 53 [after M. Robinow, 1942a; after K. Simmons & T.W. Todd, 1938; after K. Simons, 1944], fig. 54 [after W.F. Grether & R.M. Yerkes, 1940; after W.C. Young & R.M. Yerkes, 1943; after J.A. Gavan, 1953], fig. 55 [from G. Wageren & M.E. Simpson, 1954]; **101*bl***, from Harrison *et al.* (1988), fig. 14.8 [after Praeder *et al.*, 1963]; ***br***, from J.M. Tanner *et al.*, in *Archives of Disease in Childhood* (1966) 41: 454–71, 613–35, fig. 8; **102**, from W.A. Marshall & J.M. Tanner, *ibid.* (1970) 45: 13–23, fig. 8; **105**, from W.A. Marshall & J.M. Tanner, in *Human Growth*, vol. 2, 2nd edn, ed. F. Falkner & J.M. Tanner (Plenum Press, 1986), pp. 171–210, fig. 12; **111*bl***, from Martin (1990), fig. 8.6; **113*tr***, *cr*, from J. Horne, *Why We Sleep* (OUP, 1988), figs 1.1, 1.2; **122**, from M. Annett, in *Annals of Human Biology* (1976) 3: 317–28, fig. 4; **124**, after H. Binz & E. Zimmermann, in *Behaviour* (1989) 109: 142–62, fig. 1; **125**, from H. Aich *et al.*, in *Folia Primatologica* (S. Karger, 1990) 55: 109–32, fig. 19; **126**, after E. Zimmermann, in *Zeikschrift für Zoologische Systematik und Evolutionsforschung* (1990) 28: 217–19, fig. 9; **127**, after E. Zimmermann, in *Proceedings of the XIIIth Congress of the International Primatological Society*, ed. T. Kimura (1990), figs 1, 2; **130**, from D. Cheney & R. Seyfarth, *How Monkeys See the World* (U. Chicago Press, 1990), fig. 4.4; P. Marler, in *Darwin's Biological Work*, ed. P.R. Bell, (CUP, 1959), pp. 150–206, figs 16, 17; **131**, after A.-R. Lecours *et al.*, *Aphasiology* (Baillière-Tindall, 1983), fig. 18.7; after P. Yakovlev & A.-R. Lecours, in *Regional Development of the Brain in Early Life*, ed. A. Minkowski (Blackwell, 1967), pp. 3–70, fig. 1; **132*tl***, from P. Fletcher, *A Child's Learning of English* (Blackwell, 1985), pp. 64, 91; **134**, P. Lieberman & S. Blumstein, *Speech Physiology, Speech Perception, and Acoustic Phonetics* (CUP, 1988), fig. 2.1; **135**, after J.T. Laitman & R.C. Heimbuch, in *American Journal of Physical Anthropology* (1982) 59: 323–44, fig. 6; after P. Lieberman, *The Biology and Evolution of Language* (Harvard U. Press, 1984), fig. 11.5; **137**, Lieberman & Blumstein (1988), fig. 7.4; **150**, after Fleagle (1988), fig. 3.9; **154**, repr. by permission, R. Martin & R. May, in *Nature*, 293: 7–9, 7, Copyright © 1981 Macmillan Magazines Ltd; **155**, from D. Macdonald, ed., *Encyclopaedia of Mammals*, vol. 1 (Allen & Unwin, 1984), p. 421 [artist: P. Barrett]; **156**, after T.H. Clutton-Brock & P.H. Harvey, in *Journal of Zoology* (1977) 183: 1–39, fig. 1; **157**, from A. Schilling, in *The Study of Prosimian Behavior*, ed. G.A. Doyle & R.D. Martin (Academic Press, 1979), pp. 461–542, fig. 3; **163*tr***, from J.S. Kingdon, in *Transactions of the Zoological Society of London* (1980) 35: 431–75, fig. 16; ***bl***, J.S. Kingdon; **165**, from E. Hüber, in *Quarterly Review of Biology* (1931) 5: 389–437, figs 32a, 36a, 46a, b; **170*t***, L.R.M. Cocks, ed., *The Evolving Earth* (CUP, 1981), fig. 11.2; *bl*, H. Owen, *Atlas of Continental Displacement: 200 Million Years to the Present* (CUP, 1983), fig. 2; **171**, Cocks (1981), fig. 14.2; **180*tr***, based on G.W. Pearson, in *Antiquity* (1987) 61: 98–103, fig. 1; **182**, from M.J. Aitken, *Science-Based Dating in Archaeology* (Longman, 1990), fig. 5.3; **183**, after H. Valladas *et al.*, in *Nature*, 330: 159–60, Copyright © 1987 Macmillan Magazines Ltd; after H. Valladas *et al.*, in *Nature*, 331: 614–16, Copyright © 1988 Macmillan Magazines Ltd; **184**, from Klein (1989), fig. 3.5; **185**, W.B. Harland *et al.*, *A Geologic Time Scale 1989* (CUP, 1990), figs 7.3, 3.17; **192(table)**, after R. Foley, *Another Unique Species: Patterns in Human Evolutionary Ecology* (Longman, 1987), table 8.1; **194**, from M.D. Leakey & J.M. Harris, eds, *Laetoli: a Pliocene Site in Northern Tanzania* (OUP, 1987), fig. 12.6; **195**, from F.C. Howell *et al.*, in *Journal of Human Evolution* (1987) 16: 665–700, fig. 3; **200*l***, from Fleagle (1988), fig. 11.2; after Fleagle (1988), fig. 10.2; **201*l***, from Conroy (1990), fig. 4.4 [after Rosenberger, 1986; after C. Jolly & F. Plog, *Physical Anthropology and Archaeology* (McGraw-Hill, 1986); after P. Hershkovitz, 1977; after D. Swindler & C. Wood, 1973]; after Fleagle (1988), fig. 2.22; ***br***, P.D. Gingerich, in *Major Topics in Primate and Human Evolution*, ed. B.A. Wood *et al.* (CUP, 1986), pp. 32–46, fig. 5; after R.D.E. MacPhee *et al.*, in *Nature* (1983) 301: 509–11, fig. 3; **202**, after Fleagle (1988), fig. 16.10; **204*br***, from Martin (1990), fig. 2.10(a) [artist: A.-E. Martin]; **205**, from Fleagle (1988), fig. 12.5 [artist: S. Nash]; **206**, after P.D. Gingerich, in *Yearbook of Physical Anthropology* (1984) 27: 57–72, fig. 2; **218**, after Fleagle (1988), fig. 6.3; **221*tl***, *ibid.*, figs 6.4, 14.8; after F.S. Szalay & E. Delson, *Evolutionary History of the Primates* (Academic Press, 1979), figs 194, 196, 205; after I. Tattersall *et al.*, *Encyclopedia of Human Evolution and Prehistory* (Garland, 1988), p. 143; ***bl***, from Fleagle (1988), fig. 14.5; 222, from Martin (1990), fig. 2.20; **225*tl***, after Fleagle (1988), figs 13.5, 13.6; bl, from Fleagle (1988), figs 13.7, 13.8; after Fleagle (1988), fig. 13.15; after A. Walker & M. Teaford, in *Scientific American* (Jan 1989) p. 62; **226**, after L. de Bonis *et al.*, in *Nature* (1990) 345: 712–14, fig. 1; after L. Kordos, in *Annales Historico-Naturales Musei Nationalis Hungarica* (1987) 79: 77–88, fig. 3; after J.H. Schwartz, in *Journal of Human Evolution* (1990) 19: 591–605, fig. 1; after S.C. Ward & B. Brown, in *Comparative Primate Biology*, ed. D.R. Swindler & J. Erwin (Alan R. Liss, 1986), pp. 413–52, figs 9, 17; **233**, from C.K. Brain, *The Hunters or the Hunted?* (U. Chicago Press, 1981), fig. 1; **234**, after R.B. McConnell, in *Geodynamic Evolution of the Afro-Arabian Rift System* (Accademia Nazionale dei Lincei; atti dei convegni lincei 47, 1980), pp. 35–43 fig. 1; after V. Kazmin *et al.*, *ibid*, pp. 275–92, fig. 4; after M. Taieb and J.-J. Tiercelin, in *Bulletin Société Géologique de France* (1979), (7), vol. 21(3): 243–53, fig. 4; **237(*Lucy* reconstruction)**, courtesy Dr Owen Lovejoy, Kent State University; **238**, from Conroy (1990), fig. 6.13; **241**, after Conroy (1990), fig. 6.13; after F.C. Howell, in *Evolution of African Mammals*, ed. V.J. Maglio (Harvard U. Press, 1978), pp. 154–248, figs 10.6, 10.9, 10.10, 10.11, 10.12; after W.H. Kimbel *et al.*, in *American Journal of Physical Anthropology* (1984) 64: 337–388, figs 12, 13; **242*br***, after Howell (1978), fig. 10.9; **244**, G.P. Rightmire, *The Evolution of Homo erectus* (CUP, 1990), figs 6, 20; **247*br***, from Y. Rak & B. Arensburg, in *American Journal of Physical Anthropology* 73: 227–231, fig. 3, Copyright © 1987, reprinted by permission of Wiley-Liss, a division of John Wiley and Sons, Inc.; **249**, from E. Trinkaus & W.W. Howells, in *Scientific American* (Dec 1979) pp. 94–105, 98 [artist: W. Powell]; **251**, after Conroy (1990), fig. 6.24 *r*, *l*; after M.H. Day, *Guide to Fossil Man*, 4th edn (Cassell, 1986), figs 12, 13; after Klein (1989), figs 3.29 *r-l*, 4.3, 5.5; after Trinkaus & Howells (1979), p. 98; **256**, after Martin (1990), fig. 11.1; **257**, *ibid.*, fig. 11.2; **258*t***, from F. Vogel & A.G. Motulsky, *Human Genetics*, 2nd edn (Springer, 1986), fig. 3.24; *b*, from D.A. Lalley *et al.*, in *Cytogenetics and Cell Genetics* (S. Karger, 1989) 51: 503–32, 507; **260*b***, from M.W. Strickberger, *Genetics*, 2nd edn (Macmillan, 1976), fig. 12.7 [from *Textbook of Human Genetics* by Max Levitan & Ashley Montagu, Copyright © 1971, 1977, 1978 by OUP Inc., reprinted by permission]; **265**, from A.P. Mange & E.J. Mange, *Genetics: Human Aspects* (Sinauer Associates, 1990), fig. 3; **266**, from D.J. Weatherall, *The New Genetics and Clinical Practice*, 3rd edn, OUP (1991), fig. 22; **268**, *ibid.*, fig. 30; **270**, from Weatherall (1991), fig. 56; **271**, repr. by permission from R.H. Clarke & T.R.E. Southwood, in *Nature*, 338: 197–198, Copyright © 1989 Macmillan Magazines Ltd.; **272**, from H.J. Evans, *Philosophical Transactions of the Royal Society, Series B* (1988) 319: 325–40, figs 3, 4; **275**, after L.S. Penrose & G.F. Smith, Down's *Anomaly* (J. & A. Churchill, 1966), fig. 75; **276**, repr. by permission from A. McLaren, in *Nature*, 351: 96, Copyright © 1991 Macmillan Magazines Ltd.; **283**, repr. by permission from J.S. Wainscott *et al.*, in *Nature*, 319: 491–3, table 1, Copyright © 1986 Macmillan Magazines Ltd.; **286**, from Strickberger (1990), *Evolution*, fig. 21–7; **287**, from Mange & Mange (1990), table 2; **295**, after V. Sarich & A. Wilson, in *Science* (1967) 158: 1200–3, fig. 1; **303**, from Weatherall (1991), fig. 12; **304**, from Martin (1990), fig. 11.20; **314**, adapted from 'Reconstructing Bird Phylogeny of Comparing DNA's' by C.G. Sibley & J.E. Ahlquist, Copyright © (1986) *Scientific American, Inc.*, all rights reserved; **316**, after Weatherall (1991), fig. 43; **317**, A.J. Jeffreys *et al.*, in *Evolution from Molecules to Man*, ed. D.S. Bendall (CUP, 1983), fig. 9.3; **318**, from Weatherall (1991), fig. 29; **319**, *ibid.*, fig. 23; **320**, from J.D. Watson *et al.*, *Molecular Biology of the Gene*, vol. 1, 4th edn (Benjamin/Cummings, 1987) fig. 15.17 [courtesy of G. Attardi]; **321**, from L. Vigilant *et al.*, in *Science* (1991) 253: 1503–7, fig. 3, © 1991 by AAAS; **325**, from Leakey & Harris (1987), fig. D.3 (part); **330*cb***, from M. Russell, in *American Journal of Physical Anthropology* 72: 381–97, fig. 6, Copyright © 1987, reprinted by permission of Wiley-Liss, a division of John Wiley and Sons, Inc.; **344*tl***, after L. Wilson, in World Archaeology (1988) 19: 376–87, fig. 1; **345**, from B. Klima, in *Journal of Human Evolution* (1988) 16: 831–5, fig. 1; **346*l***, after Aiello & Dean (1990), fig. 18.1; ***br***, *ibid.*, figs 16.1, 16.3; **347*tl***, *ibid.*, figs 16.8, 18.6; after W.P. Cooney *et al.*, in *Journal of Bone and Joint Surgery* (1981) 63A: 1371–81, fig. 1; **348**, after Klein (1988), fig. 6.13(1); after A. Zihlman, *The Human Evolution Coloring Book* (Harper & Row, 1982) pl. 102; **351*tr***, after J.A.J. Gowlett, *Ascent to Civilization* (Collins, 1984), pp. 66–7; **352(*handaxes*)**, from F. Bordes, *Typologie du Paleolithique Ancien et Moyen*, CNRS (1981), pls. 65(2), 78(2); from K. Paddaya, 'The Acheulian culture of the Hunsgi Valley' (Deccan College Postgraduate & Research Institute, 1982), fig. 17(1); **353**, from F. Bordes, *The Old Stone Age* (McGraw-Hill, 1968), figs 3, 4; **354*tl***, from Bordes (1968), fig. 33; from D.A.E. Garrod & D.M.A. Bate, *The Stone Age of Mount Carmel* (OUP, 1937), pl. xxxiv, figs 3,4,7; **355*bl***, from Bordes (1968), figs 6, 8(1); ***br***, *ibid.*, figs 54(6), 56(4), 57(9), 58(17), 62(4); **357(*a*)**, from Garrod & Bate, pl. ix, fig. 23; (***b***), from A.J. Arkell, *Shaheinab* (OUP, 1953), fig. 6(95); (***c***), (***f***), from M. Lechevallier, *Abou Gosh et Beisamoun* (CNRS, 1987), figs 13(3), 15(5); (***d***), from H. Laville *et al.*, *Rock Shelters of the Périgord* (Academic Press, 1980), pl. iv, fig. n; (***e***), from Bordes (1968); (***g***), from R.E.M. Wheeler, *Maiden Castle*, Dorset (OUP, 1943), fig. 42(45); (***h***), from C. Niederberger, *Zohapilco* (Instituto Nacional de Antropologia e Historia, 1976), pl. xxi, fig. 14; (***i***), from J.G.D. Clark, *The Earlier Stone Age Settlement of Scandinavia* (CUP, 1975), fig. 5(2); **359*b***, reproduced with permission, from Christopher B. Donnan, *Moche Art and Iconography* (Los Angeles: UCLA Latin American Center Publications, University of California, 1976), p. 135; **370*tl***, from P. Vinnicombe, *People of the Eland* (U. Natal Press, 1976), fig. 188; ***tc***, *ibid.*, fig. 65; ***tr***, J.D. Lewis-Williams, *The Rock Art of Southern Africa* (CUP, 1983), fig. 17; **371**, from N.J. van der Merwe, in *American Scientist* (1982) 70: 596–606, fig. 6; **373**, from Heiser (1981), fig. 13.3; **374**, D.B. Grigg, *The Agricultural Systems of the World* (CUP, 1974), fig. 1; **375**, from N.D. Vietmeyer, in *Science* (1986) 232: 1379–84, fig. 1, © 1986 by AAAS; **376**, from J.R. Harlan, in *Science* (1971) 174: 468–74, fig. 6, © 1971 by AAAS; **382**, from S.J.M. Davis, *The Archaeology of Animals* (Batsford, 1987), fig. 6.7 [artist: J. Boessneck]; **383**, after J. Clutton-Brock, *Domesticated Animals from Early Times* (Heinemann, 1981), fig. 1.4; after R.D. Crawford, in *Evolution of Domesticated Animals*, ed. I.L. Mason (Longman, 1984), pp. 325–33, fig. 47.1; after B. Mller-Haye, *ibid.*, pp. 252–7, fig. 32.1; after C. Novoa & J.C. Wheeler, *ibid.*, pp. 116–127, figs 14.1, 14.2, 14.3, 14.4; **392*tl***, after C.B. Stringer, in *New Scientist* (Nov 1990) 33–37, 34; after C.B. Stringer, in *Scientific American* (Dec 1990) 68–74, 70; ***b***, from Harrison *et al.* (1988), fig. 11.5 [redrawn from A.E. Mourant *et al.*, *The Distribution of the Human Blood Groups*, 2nd edn (OUP)]; **393*c***, *ibid.*, fig. 11.4; b, *ibid.*, fig. 11.3; **394**, P.S. Bellwood, in *The Colonization of the Pacific* ed. A.V.S. Hill & S.W. Serjeantson (Clarendon Press, 1989), pp. 1–59, fig. 1.12; **395**, adapted from 'The Genetics of Human Populations' by L.L. Cavalli-Sforza, © (1974) in *Scientific American Inc.*, all rights reserved; **398**, D. Crystal, *The Cambridge Encyclopedia of Language* (CUP, 1987), p. 298; **399**, from P.E. Ross, in *Scientific American* (Apr 1991), p. 77 [courtesy of L.L. Cavalli-Sforza]; **400**, after N. Roberts, *Hominid Evolution and Community Ecology*, ed. R. Foley (Academic Press, 1984), pp. 25–54, fig. 2.1; **402**, from J. Durand, *Proceedings of the American Philosophical Society* (1967) 111: 136–145, fig. 1; **404**, from F.A. Hassan, *Demographic Archaeology* (Academic Press, 1981), fig. 13.6; **411**, after I.M. Roitt *et al.*, *Immunology* (Gower Publications, 1985), fig. 17.2; **414*tl***, *ibid.*, fig. 10–3; *tr*, J. Farley, *Bilharzia* (CUP, 1991), fig. 1.1; **415*b***, adapted from 'The Bubonic Plague' by C. McEvedy, Copyright © (1988) *Scientific American* Inc. all rights reserved; *insert*, adapted from 'The Black Death' by W. Langer, Copyright © (1964) *Scientific American Inc.*, all rights reserved; **416**, from R. Anderson & R. May, in *Science* (1982) 215: 1053–60, © 1982 by AAAS; **418*tr***, T. McKeown, *The Role of Medicine: Dream, Mirage or Nemesis?* (Princeton U. Press, 1979), figs 8.8, 8.9, 8.12, 8.14; ***br***, with permission of the World Health Organization, from *Bi-Annual Report of the Director-General, 1988–9*, table 14.1; **419*t***, with permission of the World Health Organization, from 'World malaria situation in 1989', parts I and II. *Weekly Epidemiological Record* 66(22/23) 157–163/167–170 (1991), Map 1 (90981); ***b***, *ibid.*, Map 2 (91363); **420**, courtesy of the World Health Organization; **421*bl***, adapted from 'High Fertility in Sub-Saharan Africa' by J.C. Caldwell & P. Caldwell, Copyright © (1990) *Scientific American Inc.*; data adapted from 'UN World Population Prospects 1990' and 'UN Demographic Chart' (1990), courtesy J.C. Caldwell; ***br***, adapted from 'The Growing Human Population' by N. Keyfitz, Copyright © (1989) *Scientific American Inc.*, all rights reserved; **423*tl***, after C. Clark, *Population Growth and Land Use* (Macmillan, 1967), figs 2a, b; ***bl***, *The State of the World's Children*, Unicef Report (OUP, 1990), fig. 4; **424**, from M. Anderson, *Population Change in Northwestern Europe 1750–1850* (Macmillan, 1988), fig. 2; **427*bl***, data from *General Household Survey 1983* (HMSO, 1985); **430**, after M. Johnson, in *New Scientist* (Dec 1989) p. 40 [artist: P. Gardiner]; **440**, from Evans (1988), fig. 1; **444**, from Harrison *et al.* (1988), fig. 9.1b; **445**, from Vogel & Motulsky (1986), figs 6.43, 6.44; **458**, from Aiello & Dean (1990), fig. 16.6; **460**, *ibid.*, fig. 10.16; **461**, *ibid.*, fig. 2.1; **464**, from Conroy (1990), fig. 3.18a; after Napier & Napier (1985), fig. 3.17; **466**, after Fleagle (1988), fig. 2.14; **467*tl***, from Aiello & Dean (1990), fig. 8.2; ***br***, *ibid.*, fig. 10.1.